Bill James presents . . .

STATS™ 1993 Major League Handbook

STATS, Inc. • Bill James

STATS
PUBLISHING

Published by STATS Publishing
A division of Sports Team Analysis & Tracking Systems, Inc.
Dr. Richard Cramer, Chairman • John Dewan, President

Cover by John Grimwade, New York, NY

Photo by Tony Inzerillo, Bensenville, IL

First Edition: November, 1992

Printed in the United States of America

ISBN 0-9625581-6-8

This book is dedicated to

John Doucette, Ken Kozyra, Steve Lysogorski, Bob Marszewski, Ray Pinter, Greg Porzucek, Dave Schultz and Ken Zakel.

MVR's (Most Valuable Reporters) in 1992.

Acknowledgments

Welcome to the fourth annual edition of the **STATS Major League Handbook**. As has been true in the last three years, the office is buzzing with activity to get this book to the presses one week after the end of the regular season. To accomplish this, many had to forego their lounge chair and TV during the playoffs only to replace them with computer screens and piles of numbers. You may recognize many of the names acknowledged from previous years. Among those you'll find some new names too. Without each of these people this book would not be in your hands now.

Dr. Richard Cramer, Chairman of STATS, is the creator of the baseball system which gives us the ability to look at statistics in a million different ways. Dick began working with the design of this system about 14 years ago. The rest of us are mere rookies compared to Dick, considering the amount of time and energy he has put into the design and improvements of the System. This year Dick gave us the capability to highlight the major league leaders for all categories and seasons listed in the Career Section.

John Dewan, President and CEO, continues to direct STATS Inc. as we grow in size each year, and he has once again been the catalyst in producing this book and all its improvements. This year he focused his attention on developing the new sections in this book including Park Factors and Pitcher Projections.

For the second year in a row, Steve Moyer has done a great job coordinating the pieces of the book, insuring that they all fit together. He is also in charge of the Reporter Network and is one of the key players in assuring the timeliness and accuracy of our numbers here at STATS.

Bob Mecca has been a pillar of STATS, Inc. since 1988. He is responsible for the accuracy of all the baseball data in our computer, which in turn, produces the statistics in this book. Once again, he swings his bat thru the statistics and comes up with the Leaders Boards.

Michael Canter dove into STATS' computer with the pitcher projection formula and came out with the new Pitcher Projections section.

Rob McQuown, one of STATS' rookies, worked on generating and formatting the new pitcher hitting and fielding data. He also worked on the Player Profiles, assisted in generating the Park Factors Section and was a key person, working with Bob Mecca, to assure the accuracy of the statistics in our computer system.

Ross Schaufelberger deserves special recognition as a key person in many of the projects here at STATS. With the increased size of STATS, Ross has taken on the management of many of the new staff members. With his enthusiasm and direction, he has become the driving force in many projects. Ross is responsible for the advertising of this book.

Chuck Miller applied his talents to the advertising and artwork coordination. He also worked especially hard perfecting the park diagrams which complement the park factors data.

Throughout the season we check, double check and recheck all the statistics of every game. The final level of triple checking every stat of every 1992 game, down to the most minute level including individual pitches and hit direction, distance and velocity, is an overwhelming project. Thanks to the staff who worked diligently on this colossal project, completing it in time for this book.

Many others in the office worked less directly on this book, but were none the less important in getting this book done while not neglecting STATS' other commitments:

Art Ashley, Vice President, wears many hats here at STATS for long hours each day. He manages our programming staff and also utilizes his own computer expertise to keep our System up to snuff.

Jim Musso works at keeping our fantasy baseball and football operations running smoothly.

Marge Morra and Suzette Neily continue to keep the administrative side of the office in top condition with the help of two new team members Alissa Hudson and Deb Pokres. We're glad to have you aboard.

Jules Aquino, Michael Coulter and Allan Spear are also new names at STATS this year. Besides adding their baseball insights to the STATS operation, they have been working diligently on establishing STATS' niche in the football world under Ross' guidance.

David Pinto brings STATS' information into your living room thru his daily support of the ESPN broadcasts. Don Zminda's handiwork can be seen in other upcoming publications: **The Scouting Report: 1993** and **STATS Baseball Scoreboard: 1993**. Craig Wright continues to oversee our Major League Operations.

Thanks for the expert help with our baseball operation provided by Matt Greenberger, Tom Hilgendorf and Pat Quinn. Finally, the staff assistants play an important role working with our staff members in a variety of different projects. They are: Mike Hammer, Daryl Morey, Jon Passman, Kenn Ruby and Noel Rappin. Noel has played a particularly important role in expanding the depth of our football information.

Thanks to the staff at Howe Sportsdata International who provided the minor league statistics. If you enjoy this part of the book, check out **STATS 1993 Minor League Handbook**.

Last year we dedicated the book to eight of STATS' top reporters of 1991. STATS is lucky to have such a fine group of reporters, so we decided to continue the tradition this year. They are the eyes and ears of STATS at the games. The eight reporters in the dedication are some of the best and they embody what we think are characteristics of our Reporter Team as a whole. Unfortunately we can't list everyone, but our thanks goes out to every member of the Reporter Team.

Thanks again to Rob Neyer for his help throughout the year.

Finally, thanks to Bill James. Four years ago he developed the concept and design for this book; his continual assistance is invaluable.

— Sue Dewan, Vice-President

Table of Contents

Introduction

1) Who is the most feared hitter in the American League?

2) What did Cleveland accomplish by moving their fences in before the start of the 1992 season?

3) Who's the worst hitting pitcher in baseball?

4) Is Jim Abbott really a 7 and 15 pitcher?

Answers:

1) The most feared hitter according to American League managers is clearly Wade Boggs. He's led the American League in intentional walks for **six straight years.**

2) In 1991, it was harder to hit a home run in Cleveland Stadium than in any other park in baseball. Cleveland was out-homered at home that year by 19. They brought the fences in dramatically in 1992; the left and right field fences are now 25-36 feet closer. This change made Cleveland one of the **easiest** home run parks in baseball during the 1992 season. Did it help? You make the call — Cleveland was out-homered at home by 32 in 1992.

3) In 55 at-bats in 1992, John Burkett of the San Francisco Giants managed only **one base hit!** That's a .018 batting average. His career average now stands at .052 (9 for 174), the worst in baseball (100 at-bat minimum).

4) California Angels' left-hander Jim Abbott's nine "tough losses" in 1992 was the second highest total in the majors. (Melido Perez was first with 13.) We expect Abbott to bounce back as we project his 7-15 record to improve to 13-12 in 1993.

This is a sample of the new features we've added to this year's edition of the *Major League Handbook*. There are four major additions this year. One, every category in which a player led the league is now shown in the career section by **highlighting** the stat. This has been done before in other publications, but never to this extent. New category leaders, like the intentional walk example above, are now given the light of day.

Two, we've added a section on park statistics. This allows for a thorough analysis of how each park affects the hitting and pitching statistics of those who play in it. In addition, we're showing field diagrams giving the dimensions of every major league park.

Three, we have a new section giving some additional statistics on pitchers. It has hitting statistics for pitchers giving both 1992 and career statistics. Plus, it has statistics on pitcher fielding and holding runners for 1992.

Finally, we're taking an experimental crack at projecting pitcher performance. We've always felt that it was nearly impossible to predict pitching statistics because pitchers, as a whole, are wildly inconsistent. However, we have discovered a few trends that give us a start in this area. We thought we would share our preliminary work with you.

We hope you enjoy this year's edition!

What's Official and What's Not

The statistics in this book are technically unofficial. The Official Major League Baseball Averages are not released until December. But as usual, we (and our readers) can't wait that long. We've found in the past that if you compare these stats with the official version that comes out in December, you'll find no major differences. We take extraordinary efforts to insure accuracy.

This year, after very thorough year-end research and comparison to statistics printed at year end by the MLB-IBM system, we expect that there will be no differences between our batting and pitching statistics and the official ones that come out in December. On fielding stats, fantasy players who have those rules that allow a player to play the entire next season at a position if he appeared there the year before might be intrigued by Brian Downing's game at second base in the fielding section. On the last day of the year, he was listed in the visiting starting lineup at second, got a hit in the top of the first, and was pulled for Jeff Frye. The official call was a game played, but at no position. We list him for a game played at second base, but no innings played, because he was listed there on the lineup card. We may, however, eventually change our stats, in this case, to conform with the official ones. If Downing decides to postpone his retirement again, you league presidents can do what you choose!

—John Dewan

Career Stats

Another year and more improvements. One of the first things you might notice in this year's edition is the **bold** type highlighting yearly American and National League leaders for every category. We also added career records for a few players who saw no action in 1992. They normally wouldn't show up, but we thought they might resurface in 1993. In other words, you won't have to scramble for your 1992 Handbook to remember what Bo Jackson was like when he used to play baseball.

As always:

- **Age** is seasonal age based on July 1, 1993. This means our age is the player's age as of July 1. By choosing this particular date, almost exactly mid-season, we get the age at which each player will play most during the 1993 season.

- **Hm** and **Rd** in the batters' tables stand for home runs hit at home and home runs hit on the road, respectively.

- **TBB** and **IBB** are Total Bases on Balls and Intentional Bases on Balls.

- **SB%** is Stolen Base Percentage (stolen bases divided by attempts). **OBP** and **SLG** are On-Base Percentage and Slugging Percentage.

- **BFP**, **Bk**, and **ShO** are Batters Faced Pitcher, Balks, and Shutouts.

- For pitchers, thirds of an inning were not officially kept prior to 1982. Therefore, there are no thirds of an inning for 1981 and before for older pitchers.

- For players who played for more than one major league team in a season, stats for each team are shown just above the bottom line career totals.

Jim Abbott

Pitches: Left **Bats:** Left **Pos:** SP   **Ht:** 6' 3" **Wt:** 210 **Born:** 09/19/67 **Age:** 25

			HOW MUCH HE PITCHED						WHAT HE GAVE UP												THE RESULTS					
Year	Team	Lg	G	GS	CG	GF	IP	BFP	H	R	ER	HR	SH	SF	HB	TBB	IBB	SO	WP	Bk	W	L	Pct.	ShO	Sv	ERA
1989	California	AL	29	29	4	0	181.1	788	190	95	79	13	11	5	4	74	3	115	8	2	12	12	.500	1	0	3.92
1990	California	AL	33	33	4	0	211.2	925	246	116	106	16	9	6	5	72	6	105	4	3	10	14	.417	1	0	4.51
1991	California	AL	34	34	5	0	243	1002	222	85	78	14	7	7	5	73	6	158	1	4	18	11	.621	1	0	2.89
1992	California	AL	29	29	7	0	211	874	208	73	65	12	8	4	4	68	3	130	2	0	7	15	.318	0	0	2.77
	4 ML YEARS		125	125	20	0	847	3589	866	369	328	55	35	22	18	287	18	508	15	9	47	52	.475	4	0	3.49

Kyle Abbott

Pitches: Left **Bats:** Left **Pos:** SP/RP   **Ht:** 6' 4" **Wt:** 195 **Born:** 02/18/68 **Age:** 25

			HOW MUCH HE PITCHED						WHAT HE GAVE UP												THE RESULTS					
Year	Team	Lg	G	GS	CG	GF	IP	BFP	H	R	ER	HR	SH	SF	HB	TBB	IBB	SO	WP	Bk	W	L	Pct.	ShO	Sv	ERA
1989	Quad City	A	13	12	0	1	73.2	303	55	26	21	5	0	0	4	30	0	95	3	5	5	4	.556	0	0	2.57
1990	Midland	AA	24	24	2	0	128.1	565	124	75	59	8	4	4	8	73	0	91	6	3	6	9	.400	0	0	4.14
	Edmonton	AAA	3	3	0	0	10.1	61	26	18	17	4	0	1	0	4	0	14	4	0	1	0	1.000	0	0	14.81
1991	Edmonton	AAA	27	27	4	0	180.1	732	173	84	80	22	7	6	1	46	1	120	7	0	14	10	.583	2	0	3.99
1992	Scranton/wb	AAA	5	5	1	0	35	136	20	6	6	0	2	0	0	16	0	34	2	0	4	1	.800	1	0	1.54
1991	California	AL	5	3	0	0	19.2	90	22	11	10	2	3	0	1	13	0	12	1	1	1	2	.333	0	0	4.58
1992	Philadelphia	NL	31	19	0	0	133.1	577	147	80	76	20	6	5	1	45	0	88	9	1	1	14	.067	0	0	5.13
	2 ML YEARS		36	22	0	0	153	667	169	91	86	22	9	5	2	58	0	100	10	2	2	16	.111	0	0	5.06

Paul Abbott

Pitches: Right **Bats:** Right **Pos:** RP   **Ht:** 6' 3" **Wt:** 194 **Born:** 09/15/67 **Age:** 25

			HOW MUCH HE PITCHED						WHAT HE GAVE UP												THE RESULTS					
Year	Team	Lg	G	GS	CG	GF	IP	BFP	H	R	ER	HR	SH	SF	HB	TBB	IBB	SO	WP	Bk	W	L	Pct.	ShO	Sv	ERA
1990	Minnesota	AL	7	7	0	0	34.2	162	37	24	23	0	1	1	1	28	0	25	1	0	0	5	.000	0	0	5.97
1991	Minnesota	AL	15	3	0	1	47.1	210	38	27	25	5	7	3	0	36	1	43	5	0	3	1	.750	0	0	4.75
1992	Minnesota	AL	6	0	0	5	11	50	12	4	4	1	0	1	1	5	0	13	1	0	0	0	.000	0	0	3.27
	3 ML YEARS		28	10	0	6	93	422	87	55	52	6	8	5	2	69	1	81	7	0	3	6	.333	0	0	5.03

Shawn Abner

Bats: Right **Throws:** Right **Pos:** RF/LF/CF   **Ht:** 6' 1" **Wt:** 194 **Born:** 06/17/66 **Age:** 27

			BATTING																		BASERUNNING				PERCENTAGES		
Year	Team	Lg	G	AB	H	2B	3B	HR	(Hm	Rd)	TB	R	RBI	TBB	IBB	SO	HBP	SH	SF		SB	CS	SB%	GDP	Avg	OBP	SLG
1987	San Diego	NL	16	47	13	3	1	2	(1	1)	24	5	7	2	0	8	0	0	0		1	0	1.00	0	.277	.306	.511
1988	San Diego	NL	37	83	15	3	0	2	(2	0)	24	6	5	4	1	19	1	0	1		0	1	.00	1	.181	.225	.289
1989	San Diego	NL	57	102	18	4	0	1	(1	0)	28	13	14	5	2	20	0	0	1		1	0	1.00	1	.176	.213	.275
1990	San Diego	NL	91	184	45	9	0	1	(1	0)	57	17	15	9	1	28	2	2	1		2	3	.40	3	.245	.286	.310
1991	2 ML Teams		94	216	42	10	2	3	(2	1)	65	27	14	11	4	43	1	1	1		1	2	.33	6	.194	.236	.301
1992	Chicago	AL	97	208	58	10	1	1	(0	1)	73	21	16	12	2	35	3	2	3		2	3	.33	3	.279	.323	.351
1991	San Diego	NL	53	115	19	4	1	1	(1	0)	28	15	5	7	4	25	1	1	1		0	0	.00	3	.165	.218	.243
	California	AL	41	101	23	6	1	2	(1	1)	37	12	9	4	0	18	0	0	0		1	2	.33	3	.228	.257	.366
	6 ML YEARS		392	840	191	39	4	11	(7	4)	271	89	71	43	10	153	7	5	7		6	8	.43	14	.227	.269	.323

Jim Acker

Pitches: Right **Bats:** Right **Pos:** RP   **Ht:** 6' 2" **Wt:** 215 **Born:** 09/24/58 **Age:** 34

			HOW MUCH HE PITCHED						WHAT HE GAVE UP												THE RESULTS					
Year	Team	Lg	G	GS	CG	GF	IP	BFP	H	R	ER	HR	SH	SF	HB	TBB	IBB	SO	WP	Bk	W	L	Pct.	ShO	Sv	ERA
1983	Toronto	AL	38	5	0	8	97.2	426	103	52	47	7	1	2	8	38	1	44	1	0	5	1	.833	0	1	4.33
1984	Toronto	AL	32	3	0	9	72	312	79	39	35	3	4	1	6	25	3	33	5	0	3	5	.375	0	1	4.38
1985	Toronto	AL	61	0	0	26	86.1	370	86	35	31	7	1	2	3	43	1	42	2	0	7	2	.778	0	10	3.23
1986	2 ML Teams		44	19	0	9	155	661	163	81	69	13	12	9	3	48	6	69	5	1	5	12	.294	0	0	4.01
1987	Atlanta	NL	68	0	0	41	114.2	491	109	57	53	11	3	3	4	51	4	68	1	0	4	9	.308	0	14	4.16
1988	Atlanta	NL	21	1	0	7	42	184	45	26	22	6	5	3	1	14	3	25	2	0	0	4	.000	0	0	4.71
1989	2 ML Teams		73	0	0	26	126	499	108	36	34	6	6	3	2	32	11	92	3	0	2	7	.222	0	2	2.43
1990	Toronto	AL	59	0	0	19	91.2	403	103	49	39	9	3	1	3	30	5	54	4	1	4	4	.500	0	1	3.83
1991	Toronto	AL	54	4	0	11	88.1	374	77	53	51	16	7	5	2	36	5	44	7	0	3	5	.375	0	1	5.20
1992	Seattle	AL	17	0	0	3	30.2	148	45	19	18	4	1	2	0	12	1	11	1	0	0	0	.000	0	0	5.28
1986	Toronto	AL	23	5	0	6	60	259	63	34	29	6	6	5	2	22	3	32	3	1	2	4	.333	0	0	4.35
	Atlanta	NL	21	14	0	3	95	402	100	47	40	7	6	4	1	26	3	37	2	0	3	8	.273	0	0	3.79
1989	Atlanta	NL	59	0	0	23	97.2	383	84	29	29	5	5	3	1	20	8	68	2	0	0	6	.000	0	2	2.67
	Toronto	AL	14	0	0	3	28.1	116	24	7	5	1	1	0	1	12	3	24	1	0	2	1	.667	0	0	1.59
	10 ML YEARS		467	32	0	159	904.1	3868	918	447	399	82	43	31	32	329	40	482	31	2	33	49	.402	0	30	3.97

Troy Afenir

Bats: Right **Throws:** Right **Pos:** C **Ht:** 6' 4" **Wt:** 210 **Born:** 09/21/63 **Age:** 29

Year Team	Lg	G	AB	H	2B	3B	HR	(Hm	Rd)	TB	R	RBI	TBB	IBB	SO	HBP	SH	SF	SB	CS	SB%	GDP	Avg	OBP	SLG
1984 Asheville	A	115	358	69	16	0	16	--	--	133	44	69	39	1	125	2	4	6	1	2	.33	9	.193	.272	.372
1985 Osceola	A	99	323	80	19	1	6	--	--	119	38	41	20	1	86	0	2	2	3	1	.75	4	.248	.290	.368
1986 Columbus	AA	91	313	68	15	3	14	--	--	131	50	45	22	0	90	3	4	3	0	5	.00	6	.217	.273	.419
1987 Columbus	AA	31	99	20	8	0	2	--	--	34	15	11	6	0	20	0	2	0	0	0	.00	6	.202	.248	.343
Osceola	A	79	294	81	20	1	14	--	--	145	60	68	33	1	75	2	0	8	1	0	1.00	5	.276	.344	.493
1988 Columbus	AA	137	494	122	21	5	16	--	--	201	61	66	45	0	131	5	0	5	11	6	.65	6	.247	.313	.407
1989 Huntsville	AA	65	225	57	15	1	13	--	--	113	31	45	28	0	63	1	0	4	1	3	.25	3	.253	.333	.502
1990 Tacoma	AAA	88	289	72	14	2	15	--	--	135	44	47	30	0	81	1	4	1	1	1	.50	5	.249	.321	.467
1991 Tacoma	AAA	80	262	64	12	3	10	--	--	112	35	38	22	1	59	3	3	6	0	0	.00	5	.244	.304	.427
1992 Nashville	AAA	42	130	33	6	1	6	--	--	59	15	24	11	1	22	0	1	1	5	0	1.00	2	.254	.310	.454
1987 Houston	NL	10	20	6	1	0	0	(0	0)	7	1	1	0	0	12	0	0	0	0	0	.00	0	.300	.300	.350
1990 Oakland	AL	14	14	2	0	0	0	(0	0)	2	0	2	0	0	6	0	0	1	0	0	.00	0	.143	.133	.143
1991 Oakland	AL	5	11	1	0	0	0	(0	0)	1	0	0	0	0	2	0	0	0	0	0	.00	1	.091	.091	.091
1992 Cincinnati	NL	16	34	6	1	2	0	(0	0)	11	3	4	5	0	12	0	1	0	0	0	.00	0	.176	.282	.324
4 ML YEARS		45	79	15	2	2	0	(0	0)	21	4	7	5	0	32	0	1	1	0	0	.00	1	.190	.235	.266

Juan Agosto

Pitches: Left **Bats:** Left **Pos:** RP **Ht:** 6' 2" **Wt:** 190 **Born:** 02/23/58 **Age:** 35

Year Team	Lg	G	GS	CG	GF	IP	BFP	H	R	ER	HR	SH	SF	HB	TBB	IBB	SO	WP	Bk	W	L	Pct.	ShO	Sv	ERA
1981 Chicago	AL	2	0	0	1	6	22	5	3	3	1	0	0	1	0	0	3	0	0	0	0	.000	0	0	4.50
1982 Chicago	AL	1	0	0	1	2	13	7	4	4	0	0	0	0	0	0	1	0	0	0	0	.000	0	0	18.00
1983 Chicago	AL	39	0	0	13	41.2	166	41	20	19	2	5	4	1	11	1	29	2	0	2	2	.500	0	7	4.10
1984 Chicago	AL	49	0	0	18	55.1	243	54	20	19	2	5	1	3	34	7	26	1	0	2	1	.667	0	7	3.09
1985 Chicago	AL	54	0	0	21	60.1	246	45	27	24	3	3	3	3	23	1	39	0	0	4	3	.571	0	1	3.58
1986 2 ML Teams		26	1	0	4	25	139	49	30	24	1	2	0	2	18	0	12	1	0	1	4	.200	0	1	8.64
1987 Houston	NL	27	0	0	13	27.1	118	26	12	8	1	3	0	0	10	1	6	1	0	1	1	.500	0	2	2.63
1988 Houston	NL	75	0	0	33	91.2	371	74	27	23	6	9	5	0	30	13	33	3	5	10	2	.833	0	4	2.26
1989 Houston	NL	71	0	0	28	83	361	81	32	27	3	5	6	2	32	10	46	4	1	4	5	.444	0	1	2.93
1990 Houston	NL	82	0	0	29	92.1	404	91	46	44	4	7	2	7	39	8	50	1	0	9	8	.529	0	4	4.29
1991 St. Louis	NL	72	0	0	22	86	377	92	52	46	4	11	3	8	39	4	34	6	0	5	3	.625	0	2	4.81
1992 2 ML Teams		39	1	0	12	50	227	66	36	34	2	5	4	3	12	2	25	2	0	2	4	.333	0	0	6.12
1986 Chicago	AL	9	0	0	1	4.2	24	6	5	4	0	0	0	0	4	0	3	0	0	0	2	.000	0	1	7.71
Minnesota		17	1	0	3	20.1	115	43	25	20	1	2	0	2	14	0	9	1	0	1	2	.333	0	0	8.85
1992 St. Louis	NL	22	0	0	10	31.2	143	39	24	22	2	3	3	3	9	2	13	2	0	2	4	.333	0	0	6.25
Seattle	AL	17	1	0	2	18.1	84	27	12	12	0	2	1	0	3	0	12	0	0	0	0	.000	0	0	5.89
12 ML YEARS		537	2	0	195	620.2	2687	631	309	275	29	55	28	30	248	47	304	21	6	40	33	.548	0	29	3.99

Rick Aguilera

Pitches: Right **Bats:** Right **Pos:** RP **Ht:** 6' 5" **Wt:** 203 **Born:** 12/31/61 **Age:** 31

Year Team	Lg	G	GS	CG	GF	IP	BFP	H	R	ER	HR	SH	SF	HB	TBB	IBB	SO	WP	Bk	W	L	Pct.	ShO	Sv	ERA
1985 New York	NL	21	19	2	1	122.1	507	118	49	44	8	7	4	2	37	2	74	5	2	10	7	.588	0	0	3.24
1986 New York	NL	28	20	2	2	141.2	605	145	70	61	15	6	5	7	36	1	104	5	3	10	7	.588	0	0	3.88
1987 New York	NL	18	17	1	0	115	494	124	53	46	12	7	2	3	33	2	77	9	0	11	3	.786	0	0	3.60
1988 New York	NL	11	3	0	2	24.2	111	29	20	19	2	2	0	1	10	2	16	1	1	0	4	.000	0	0	6.93
1989 2 ML Teams		47	11	3	19	145	594	130	51	45	8	7	1	3	38	4	137	4	3	9	11	.450	0	7	2.79
1990 Minnesota	AL	56	0	0	54	65.1	268	55	27	20	5	0	0	4	19	6	61	3	0	5	3	.625	0	32	2.76
1991 Minnesota	AL	63	0	0	60	69	275	44	20	18	3	1	3	1	30	6	61	3	0	4	5	.444	0	42	2.35
1992 Minnesota	AL	64	0	0	61	66.2	273	60	28	21	7	1	2	1	17	4	52	5	0	2	6	.250	0	41	2.84
1989 New York	NL	36	0	0	19	69.1	284	59	19	18	3	5	1	2	21	3	80	3	3	6	6	.500	0	7	2.34
Minnesota	AL	11	11	3	0	75.2	310	71	32	27	5	2	0	1	17	1	57	1	0	3	5	.375	0	0	3.21
8 ML YEARS		308	70	8	199	749.2	3127	705	318	274	60	31	17	22	220	27	582	35	9	51	46	.526	0	122	3.29

Scott Aldred

Pitches: Left **Bats:** Left **Pos:** SP **Ht:** 6' 4" **Wt:** 215 **Born:** 06/12/68 **Age:** 25

Year Team	Lg	G	GS	CG	GF	IP	BFP	H	R	ER	HR	SH	SF	HB	TBB	IBB	SO	WP	Bk	W	L	Pct.	ShO	Sv	ERA
1990 Detroit	AL	4	3	0	0	14.1	63	13	6	6	0	2	1	0	10	1	7	0	0	1	2	.333	0	0	3.77
1991 Detroit	AL	11	11	1	0	57.1	253	58	37	33	9	3	2	0	30	2	35	3	1	2	4	.333	0	0	5.18
1992 Detroit	AL	16	13	0	0	65	304	80	51	49	12	4	3	3	33	4	34	1	0	3	8	.273	0	0	6.78
3 ML YEARS		31	27	1	0	136.2	620	151	94	88	21	9	6	4	73	7	76	4	1	6	14	.300	0	0	5.80

Gerald Alexander

Pitches: Right **Bats:** Right **Pos:** RP **Ht:** 5'11" **Wt:** 200 **Born:** 03/26/68 **Age:** 25

Year Team	Lg	G	GS	CG	GF	IP	BFP	H	R	ER	HR	SH	SF	HB	TBB	IBB	SO	WP	Bk	W	L	Pct.	ShO	Sv	ERA
1990 Texas	AL	3	2	0	1	7	39	14	6	6	0	0	1	1	5	0	8	0	0	0	0	.000	0	0	7.71
1991 Texas	AL	30	9	0	4	89.1	402	93	56	52	11	6	3	3	48	7	50	3	1	5	3	.625	0	0	5.24
1992 Texas	AL	3	0	0	1	1.2	12	5	5	5	1	0	1	0	1	0	1	0	0	1	0	1.000	0	0	27.00
3 ML YEARS		36	11	0	6	98	453	112	67	63	12	6	5	4	54	7	59	3	1	6	3	.667	0	0	5.79

Manny Alexander

Bats: Right **Throws:** Right **Pos:** SS **Ht:** 5'10" **Wt:** 150 **Born:** 03/20/71 **Age:** 22

Year Team	Lg	G	AB	H	2B	3B	HR	(Hm	Rd)	TB	R	RBI	TBB	IBB	SO	HBP	SH	SF	SB	CS	SB%	GDP	Avg	OBP	SLG
1989 Bluefield	R	65	274	85	13	2	2	--	--	108	49	34	20	1	49	3	0	2	19	8	.70	2	.310	.361	.394
1990 Wausau	A	44	152	27	3	1	0	--	--	32	16	11	12	1	41	1	1	3	8	3	.73	2	.178	.238	.211
1991 Frederick	A	134	548	143	17	3	3	--	--	175	81	42	44	0	68	2	3	1	47	14	.77	4	.261	.318	.319
Hagerstown	AA	3	9	3	1	0	0	--	--	4	3	2	1	0	3	0	1	0	0	0	.00	0	.333	.417	.444
1992 Hagerstown	AA	127	499	129	23	8	2	--	--	174	70	41	25	0	64	6	4	4	43	12	.78	10	.259	.300	.349
Rochester	AAA	6	24	7	1	0	0	--	--	8	3	3	1	0	3	0	1	0	2	2	.50	0	.292	.320	.333
1992 Baltimore	AL	4	5	1	0	0	0	(0	0)	1	1	0	0	0	3	0	0	0	0	0	.00	0	.200	.200	.200

Luis Alicea

Bats: Both **Throws:** Right **Pos:** 2B **Ht:** 5'9" **Wt:** 165 **Born:** 07/29/65 **Age:** 27

Year Team	Lg	G	AB	H	2B	3B	HR	(Hm	Rd)	TB	R	RBI	TBB	IBB	SO	HBP	SH	SF	SB	CS	SB%	GDP	Avg	OBP	SLG
1988 St. Louis	NL	93	293	63	10	4	1	(1	0)	84	20	24	25	4	32	2	4	2	1	1	.50	12	.212	.276	.283
1991 St. Louis	NL	56	68	13	3	0	0	(0	0)	16	5	0	8	0	19	0	0	0	1	0	1.00	0	.191	.276	.235
1992 St. Louis	NL	85	265	65	9	11	2	(2	0)	102	26	32	27	1	40	4	2	4	2	5	.29	5	.245	.320	.385
3 ML YEARS		234	630	141	22	15	3	(3	0)	202	51	56	60	5	91	6	6	6	3	7	.30	17	.224	.295	.321

Andy Allanson

Bats: Right **Throws:** Right **Pos:** C **Ht:** 6'5" **Wt:** 225 **Born:** 12/22/61 **Age:** 31

Year Team	Lg	G	AB	H	2B	3B	HR	(Hm	Rd)	TB	R	RBI	TBB	IBB	SO	HBP	SH	SF	SB	CS	SB%	GDP	Avg	OBP	SLG
1986 Cleveland	AL	101	293	66	7	3	1	(0	1)	82	30	29	14	0	36	1	11	4	10	1	.91	7	.225	.260	.280
1987 Cleveland	AL	50	154	41	6	0	3	(2	1)	56	17	16	9	0	30	0	4	5	1	1	.50	2	.266	.298	.364
1988 Cleveland	AL	133	434	114	11	0	5	(4	1)	140	44	50	25	2	63	3	8	4	5	9	.36	6	.263	.305	.323
1989 Cleveland	AL	111	323	75	9	1	3	(1	2)	95	30	17	23	2	47	4	6	3	4	4	.50	7	.232	.289	.294
1991 Detroit	AL	60	151	35	10	0	1	(0	1)	48	10	16	7	0	31	0	2	0	0	1	.00	3	.232	.266	.318
1992 Milwaukee	AL	9	25	8	1	0	0	(0	0)	9	6	0	1	0	2	0	2	0	3	1	.75	1	.320	.346	.360
6 ML YEARS		464	1380	339	44	4	13	(7	6)	430	137	128	79	4	209	8	33	16	23	17	.58	26	.246	.287	.312

Roberto Alomar

Bats: Both **Throws:** Right **Pos:** 2B **Ht:** 6'0" **Wt:** 185 **Born:** 02/05/68 **Age:** 25

Year Team	Lg	G	AB	H	2B	3B	HR	(Hm	Rd)	TB	R	RBI	TBB	IBB	SO	HBP	SH	SF	SB	CS	SB%	GDP	Avg	OBP	SLG
1988 San Diego	NL	143	545	145	24	6	9	(5	4)	208	84	41	47	5	83	3	16	4	24	6	.80	15	.266	.328	.382
1989 San Diego	NL	158	623	184	27	1	7	(3	4)	234	82	56	53	4	76	1	17	8	42	17	.71	10	.295	.347	.376
1990 San Diego	NL	147	586	168	27	5	6	(4	2)	223	80	60	48	1	72	2	5	5	24	7	.77	16	.287	.340	.381
1991 Toronto	AL	161	637	188	41	11	9	(6	3)	278	88	69	57	3	86	4	16	5	53	11	.83	5	.295	.354	.436
1992 Toronto	AL	152	571	177	27	8	8	(5	3)	244	105	76	87	5	52	5	6	2	49	9	.84	8	.310	.405	.427
5 ML YEARS		761	2962	862	146	31	39	(23	16)	1187	439	302	292	18	369	15	60	20	192	50	.79	54	.291	.355	.401

Sandy Alomar Jr

Bats: Right **Throws:** Right **Pos:** C **Ht:** 6'5" **Wt:** 215 **Born:** 06/18/66 **Age:** 27

Year Team	Lg	G	AB	H	2B	3B	HR	(Hm	Rd)	TB	R	RBI	TBB	IBB	SO	HBP	SH	SF	SB	CS	SB%	GDP	Avg	OBP	SLG
1988 San Diego	NL	1	1	0	0	0	0	(0	0)	0	0	0	0	0	0	0	0	0	0	0	.00	0	.000	.000	.000
1989 San Diego	NL	7	19	4	1	0	0	(1	0)	8	1	6	3	1	3	0	0	0	0	0	.00	1	.211	.318	.421
1990 Cleveland	AL	132	445	129	26	2	9	(5	4)	186	60	66	25	2	46	2	5	6	4	1	.80	10	.290	.326	.418
1991 Cleveland	AL	51	184	40	9	0	0	(0	0)	49	10	7	8	1	24	4	2	1	0	4	.00	4	.217	.264	.266
1992 Cleveland	AL	89	299	75	16	0	2	(1	1)	97	22	26	13	3	32	5	3	0	3	3	.50	7	.251	.293	.324
5 ML YEARS		280	948	248	52	2	12	(7	5)	340	93	105	49	7	106	11	10	7	7	8	.47	22	.262	.303	.359

Moises Alou

Bats: Right **Throws:** Right **Pos:** LF/CF/RF   **Ht:** 6' 3" **Wt:** 190 **Born:** 07/03/66 **Age:** 26

								BATTING												BASERUNNING				PERCENTAGES		
Year Team	Lg	G	AB	H	2B	3B	HR	(Hm	Rd)	TB	R	RBI	TBB	IBB	SO	HBP	SH	SF	SB	CS	SB%	GDP	Avg	OBP	SLG
1986 Watertown	A	69	254	60	9	8	6	--	--	103	30	35	22	1	72	1	0	0	14	8	.64	5	.236	.300	.406
1987 Macon	A	4	8	1	0	0	0	--	--	1	1	0	2	0	4	0	0	0	0	0	.00	0	.125	.300	.125
Watertown	A	39	117	25	6	2	4	--	--	47	20	18	16	0	36	4	0	2	6	3	.67	0	.214	.324	.402
1988 Augusta	A	105	358	112	23	5	7	--	--	166	58	62	51	4	84	5	0	7	24	12	.67	5	.313	.399	.464
1989 Salem	A	86	321	97	29	2	14	--	--	172	50	53	35	2	69	3	0	2	12	5	.71	6	.302	.374	.536
Harrisburg	AA	54	205	60	5	2	3	--	--	78	36	19	17	1	38	0	0	2	8	4	.67	1	.293	.344	.380
1990 Harrisburg	AA	36	132	39	12	2	3	--	--	64	19	22	16	3	21	1	0	1	7	4	.64	5	.295	.373	.485
Buffalo	AAA	75	271	74	4	6	5	--	--	105	38	31	30	0	43	2	2	4	9	4	.69	8	.273	.345	.387
Indianapols	AAA	15	55	12	1	0	0	--	--	13	6	6	3	0	7	0	0	1	4	3	.57	0	.218	.254	.236
1990 2 ML Teams		16	20	4	0	1	0	(0	0)	6	4	0	0	0	3	0	1	0	0	0	.00	1	.200	.200	.300
1992 Montreal	NL	115	341	96	28	2	9	(6	3)	155	53	56	25	0	46	1	5	5	16	2	.89	6	.282	.328	.455
1990 Pittsburgh	NL	2	5	1	0	0	0	(0	0)	1	0	0	0	0	0	0	0	0	0	0	.00	0	.200	.200	.200
Montreal	NL	14	15	3	0	1	0	(0	0)	5	4	0	0	0	3	0	1	0	0	0	.00	1	.200	.200	.333
2 ML YEARS		131	361	100	28	3	9	(6	3)	161	57	56	25	0	49	1	6	5	16	2	.89	6	.277	.321	.446

Wilson Alvarez

Pitches: Left **Bats:** Left **Pos:** RP/SP   **Ht:** 6' 1" **Wt:** 175 **Born:** 03/24/70 **Age:** 23

		HOW MUCH HE PITCHED						WHAT HE GAVE UP												THE RESULTS					
Year Team	Lg	G	GS	CG	GF	IP	BFP	H	R	ER	HR	SH	SF	HB	TBB	IBB	SO	WP	Bk	W	L	Pct.	ShO	Sv	ERA
1989 Texas	AL	1	1	0	0	0	5	3	3	3	2	0	0	0	2	0	0	0	0	0	1	.000	0	0	0.00
1991 Chicago	AL	10	9	2	0	56.1	237	47	26	22	9	3	1	0	29	0	32	2	0	3	2	.600	1	0	3.51
1992 Chicago	AL	34	9	0	4	100.1	455	103	64	58	12	3	4	4	65	2	66	2	0	5	3	.625	0	1	5.20
3 ML YEARS		45	19	2	4	156.2	697	153	93	83	23	6	5	4	96	2	98	4	0	8	6	.571	1	1	4.77

Rich Amaral

Bats: Right **Throws:** Right **Pos:** 3B/SS   **Ht:** 6' 0" **Wt:** 175 **Born:** 04/01/62 **Age:** 31

								BATTING												BASERUNNING				PERCENTAGES		
Year Team	Lg	G	AB	H	2B	3B	HR	(Hm	Rd)	TB	R	RBI	TBB	IBB	SO	HBP	SH	SF	SB	CS	SB%	GDP	Avg	OBP	SLG
1984 Quad City	A	34	119	25	1	0	0	--	--	26	21	7	24	0	29	0	1	0	12	0	1.00	6	.210	.343	.218
1985 Winston-Sal	A	124	428	116	15	5	3	--	--	150	62	36	59	1	68	2	5	1	26	7	.79	11	.271	.361	.350
1986 Pittsfield	AA	114	355	89	12	0	0	--	--	101	43	24	39	1	65	4	5	2	25	8	.76	5	.251	.330	.285
1987 Pittsfield	AA	104	315	80	8	5	0	--	--	98	45	28	43	2	50	3	6	1	28	6	.82	1	.254	.348	.311
1988 Pittsfield	AA	122	422	117	15	4	4	--	--	152	66	47	56	1	53	1	5	5	54	5	.92	2	.277	.360	.360
1989 Birmingham	AA	122	432	123	15	6	4	--	--	162	90	48	88	2	66	2	7	4	57	14	.80	6	.285	.405	.375
1990 Vancouver	AAA	130	462	139	39	5	4	--	--	200	87	56	88	3	68	4	9	4	20	14	.59	4	.301	.414	.433
1991 Calgary	AAA	86	347	120	26	2	3	--	--	159	79	36	53	0	37	3	3	3	30	8	.79	6	.346	.433	.458
1992 Calgary	AAA	106	403	128	21	8	0	--	--	165	79	21	67	1	69	1	2	1	53	16	.77	7	.318	.414	.409
1991 Seattle	AL	14	16	1	0	0	0	(0	0)	1	2	0	1	0	5	1	0	0	0	0	.00	1	.063	.167	.063
1992 Seattle	AL	35	100	24	3	0	1	(0	1)	30	9	7	5	0	16	0	4	0	4	2	.67	4	.240	.276	.300
2 ML YEARS		49	116	25	3	0	1	(0	1)	31	11	7	6	0	21	1	4	0	4	2	.67	5	.216	.260	.267

Ruben Amaro

Bats: Both **Throws:** Right **Pos:** RF/LF/CF   **Ht:** 5'10" **Wt:** 170 **Born:** 02/12/65 **Age:** 28

								BATTING												BASERUNNING				PERCENTAGES		
Year Team	Lg	G	AB	H	2B	3B	HR	(Hm	Rd)	TB	R	RBI	TBB	IBB	SO	HBP	SH	SF	SB	CS	SB%	GDP	Avg	OBP	SLG
1987 Salem	A	71	241	68	7	3	3	--	--	90	51	31	49	5	28	7	3	6	27	11	.71	5	.282	.409	.373
1988 Midland	AA	13	31	4	1	0	0	--	--	5	5	2	4	0	5	1	0	0	4	0	1.00	1	.129	.250	.161
Palm Sprngs	A	115	417	111	13	3	4	--	--	142	96	50	105	2	61	8	5	2	44	20	.69	13	.266	.421	.341
1989 Quad City	A	59	200	72	9	4	3	--	--	98	50	27	42	4	25	7	0	1	20	8	.71	5	.360	.484	.490
Midland	AA	29	110	42	9	2	3	--	--	64	28	9	10	1	19	1	2	2	7	1	.88	0	.382	.431	.582
1990 Midland	AA	57	224	80	15	6	4	--	--	119	50	38	29	1	23	9	2	2	8	8	.50	4	.357	.447	.531
Edmonton	AAA	82	318	92	15	4	3	--	--	124	53	32	40	2	43	7	5	3	32	14	.70	2	.289	.378	.390
1991 Edmonton	AAA	121	472	154	42	6	3	--	--	217	95	42	63	2	50	6	9	2	36	18	.67	6	.326	.411	.460
1992 Scranton/wb	AAA	18	68	20	4	1	1	--	--	29	8	10	9	3	6	0	0	0	2	2	.50	0	.294	.377	.426
1991 California	AL	10	23	5	1	0	0	(0	0)	6	0	2	3	1	3	0	0	0	0	0	.00	1	.217	.308	.261
1992 Philadelphia	NL	126	374	82	15	6	7	(5	2)	130	43	34	37	1	54	9	4	2	11	5	.69	11	.219	.303	.348
2 ML YEARS		136	397	87	16	6	7	(5	2)	136	43	36	40	2	57	9	4	2	11	5	.69	12	.219	.304	.343

Larry Andersen

Pitches: Right **Bats:** Right **Pos:** RP   **Ht:** 6' 3" **Wt:** 205 **Born:** 05/06/53 **Age:** 40

		HOW MUCH HE PITCHED						WHAT HE GAVE UP												THE RESULTS					
Year Team	Lg	G	GS	CG	GF	IP	BFP	H	R	ER	HR	SH	SF	HB	TBB	IBB	SO	WP	Bk	W	L	Pct.	ShO	Sv	ERA
1975 Cleveland	AL	3	0	0	1	6	23	4	3	3	0	0	1	0	2	0	4	2	0	0	0	.000	0	0	4.50
1977 Cleveland	AL	11	0	0	7	14	62	10	7	5	1	3	0	0	9	3	8	1	0	0	1	.000	0	0	3.21

7

Year Team	Lg	G	GS	CG	GF	IP	BFP	H	R	ER	HR	SH	SF	HB	TBB	IBB	SO	WP	Bk	W	L	Pct.	ShO	Sv	ERA
1979 Cleveland	AL	8	0	0	4	17	77	25	14	14	3	1	2	0	4	0	7	0	0	0	0	.000	0	0	7.41
1981 Seattle	AL	41	0	0	23	68	273	57	27	20	4	0	3	2	18	2	40	0	0	3	3	.500	0	5	2.65
1982 Seattle	AL	40	1	0	14	79.2	354	100	56	53	16	2	3	4	23	1	32	2	0	0	0	.000	0	1	5.99
1983 Philadelphia	NL	17	0	0	4	26.1	106	19	7	7	0	1	1	0	9	1	14	1	1	1	0	1.000	0	0	2.39
1984 Philadelphia	NL	64	0	0	25	90.2	376	85	32	24	5	4	4	0	25	6	54	2	1	3	7	.300	0	4	2.38
1985 Philadelphia	NL	57	0	0	19	73	318	78	41	35	5	3	1	3	26	4	50	1	1	3	3	.500	0	3	4.32
1986 2 ML Teams		48	0	0	8	77.1	323	83	30	26	2	10	5	1	26	10	42	1	0	3	3	.500	0	3	3.03
1987 Houston	NL	67	0	0	31	101.2	440	95	46	39	7	7	4	2	41	10	94	1	0	9	5	.643	0	5	3.45
1988 Houston	NL	53	0	0	25	82.2	350	82	29	27	3	3	3	1	20	8	66	1	2	2	4	.333	0	5	2.94
1989 Houston	NL	60	0	0	21	87.2	351	63	19	15	2	4	5	0	24	4	85	2	1	4	4	.500	0	3	1.54
1990 2 ML Teams		65	0	0	24	95.2	387	79	22	19	2	5	5	2	27	5	93	4	0	5	2	.714	0	7	1.79
1991 San Diego	NL	38	0	0	24	47	188	39	13	12	0	4	2	0	13	3	40	1	0	3	4	.429	0	13	2.30
1992 San Diego	NL	34	0	0	13	35	140	26	14	13	2	1	1	1	8	2	35	0	0	1	1	.500	0	2	3.34
1986 Philadelphia	NL	10	0	0	1	12.2	55	19	8	6	0	2	1	0	3	0	9	0	0	0	0	.000	0	0	4.26
Houston	NL	38	0	0	7	64.2	268	64	22	20	2	8	4	1	23	10	33	0	0	3	3	.500	0	3	2.78
1990 Houston	NL	50	0	0	20	73.2	301	61	19	16	2	5	5	1	24	5	68	2	0	5	2	.714	0	1	1.95
Boston	AL	15	0	0	4	22	86	18	3	3	0	0	0	1	3	0	25	2	0	0	0	.000	0	6	1.23
15 ML YEARS		606	1	0	243	901.2	3768	845	360	312	52	48	40	16	275	59	664	19	6	36	35	.507	0	49	3.11

Brady Anderson

Bats: Left   **Throws:** Left   **Pos:** LF   **Ht:** 6' 1" **Wt:** 185 **Born:** 01/18/64 **Age:** 29

Year Team	Lg	G	AB	H	2B	3B	HR	(Hm	Rd)	TB	R	RBI	TBB	IBB	SO	HBP	SH	SF	SB	CS	SB%	GDP	Avg	OBP	SLG
1988 2 ML Teams		94	325	69	13	4	1	(1	0)	93	31	21	23	0	75	4	11	1	10	6	.63	3	.212	.272	.286
1989 Baltimore	AL	94	266	55	12	2	4	(2	2)	83	44	16	43	6	45	3	5	0	16	4	.80	4	.207	.324	.312
1990 Baltimore	AL	89	234	54	5	2	3	(1	2)	72	24	24	31	2	46	4	4	5	15	2	.88	4	.231	.327	.308
1991 Baltimore	AL	113	256	59	12	3	2	(1	1)	83	40	27	38	0	44	5	11	3	12	5	.71	1	.230	.338	.324
1992 Baltimore	AL	159	623	169	28	10	21	(15	6)	280	100	80	98	14	98	9	10	9	53	16	.77	2	.271	.373	.449
1988 Boston	AL	41	148	34	5	3	0	(0	0)	45	14	12	15	0	35	4	4	1	4	2	.67	2	.230	.315	.304
Baltimore	AL	53	177	35	8	1	1	(1	0)	48	17	9	8	0	40	0	7	0	6	4	.60	1	.198	.232	.271
5 ML YEARS		549	1704	406	70	21	31	(20	11)	611	239	168	233	22	308	26	41	18	106	33	.76	14	.238	.336	.359

Dave Anderson

Bats: Right   **Throws:** Right   **Pos:** 3B   **Ht:** 6' 2" **Wt:** 184 **Born:** 08/01/60 **Age:** 32

Year Team	Lg	G	AB	H	2B	3B	HR	(Hm	Rd)	TB	R	RBI	TBB	IBB	SO	HBP	SH	SF	SB	CS	SB%	GDP	Avg	OBP	SLG
1983 Los Angeles	NL	61	115	19	4	2	1	(1	0)	30	12	2	12	1	15	0	4	0	6	3	.67	1	.165	.244	.261
1984 Los Angeles	NL	121	374	94	16	2	3	(2	1)	123	51	34	45	4	55	2	7	5	15	5	.75	8	.251	.331	.329
1985 Los Angeles	NL	77	221	44	6	0	4	(1	3)	62	24	18	35	3	42	1	4	1	5	4	.56	4	.199	.310	.281
1986 Los Angeles	NL	92	216	53	9	0	1	(0	1)	65	31	15	22	1	39	0	2	1	5	1	.83	11	.245	.314	.301
1987 Los Angeles	NL	108	265	62	12	3	1	(0	1)	83	32	13	24	1	43	1	6	1	9	5	.64	2	.234	.299	.313
1988 Los Angeles	NL	116	285	71	10	2	2	(1	1)	91	31	20	32	4	45	1	5	2	4	2	.67	9	.249	.325	.319
1989 Los Angeles	NL	87	140	32	2	0	1	(1	0)	37	15	14	17	1	26	0	5	1	2	0	1.00	1	.229	.310	.264
1990 San Francisco	NL	60	100	35	5	1	1	(1	0)	45	14	6	3	0	20	0	1	0	1	2	.33	2	.350	.369	.450
1991 San Francisco	NL	100	226	56	5	2	2	(1	1)	71	24	13	12	2	35	0	2	0	2	4	.33	8	.248	.286	.314
1992 Los Angeles	NL	51	84	24	4	0	3	(0	3)	37	10	8	4	0	11	0	1	2	0	4	.00	3	.286	.311	.440
10 ML YEARS		873	2026	490	73	12	19	(8	11)	644	244	143	206	17	331	5	37	13	49	30	.62	49	.242	.312	.318

Eric Anthony

Bats: Left   **Throws:** Left   **Pos:** RF   **Ht:** 6' 2" **Wt:** 195 **Born:** 11/08/67 **Age:** 25

Year Team	Lg	G	AB	H	2B	3B	HR	(Hm	Rd)	TB	R	RBI	TBB	IBB	SO	HBP	SH	SF	SB	CS	SB%	GDP	Avg	OBP	SLG
1989 Houston	NL	25	61	11	2	0	4	(2	2)	25	7	7	9	2	16	0	0		0	0	.00	1	.180	.286	.410
1990 Houston	NL	84	239	46	8	0	10	(5	5)	84	26	29	29	3	78	2	1	6	5	0	1.00	2	.192	.279	.351
1991 Houston	NL	39	118	18	6	0	1	(0	1)	27	11	7	12	1	41	0	0	2	1	0	1.00	2	.153	.227	.229
1992 Houston	NL	137	440	105	15	1	19	(9	10)	179	45	80	38	5	98	1	0	4	5	4	.56	7	.239	.298	.407
4 ML YEARS		285	858	180	31	1	34	(16	18)	315	89	123	88	11	233	3	1	12	11	4	.73	14	.210	.282	.367

Kevin Appier

Pitches: Right   **Bats:** Right   **Pos:** SP   **Ht:** 6' 2" **Wt:** 200 **Born:** 12/06/67 **Age:** 25

Year Team	Lg	G	GS	CG	GF	IP	BFP	H	R	ER	HR	SH	SF	HB	TBB	IBB	SO	WP	Bk	W	L	Pct.	ShO	Sv	ERA
1989 Kansas City	AL	6	5	0	0	21.2	106	34	22	22	3	0	3	0	12	1	10	0	0	1	4	.200	0	0	9.14
1990 Kansas City	AL	32	24	3	1	185.2	784	179	67	57	13	5	9	6	54	2	127	6	1	12	8	.600	1	0	2.76
1991 Kansas City	AL	34	31	6	1	207.2	881	205	97	79	13	8	6	6	61	3	158	7	1	13	10	.565	2	0	3.42
1992 Kansas City	AL	30	30	3	0	208.1	852	167	59	57	10	8	3	2	68	5	150	4	0	15	8	.652	3	0	2.46
4 ML YEARS		102	90	12	2	623.1	2623	585	245	215	39	21	21	10	195	11	445	17	2	41	30	.577	6	0	3.10

Luis Aquino

Pitches: Right **Bats:** Right **Pos:** SP   **Ht:** 6' 1" **Wt:** 195 **Born:** 05/19/65 **Age:** 28

		HOW MUCH HE PITCHED						WHAT HE GAVE UP												THE RESULTS					
Year Team	Lg	G	GS	CG	GF	IP	BFP	H	R	ER	HR	SH	SF	HB	TBB	IBB	SO	WP	Bk	W	L	Pct.	ShO	Sv	ERA
1986 Toronto	AL	7	0	0	3	11.1	50	14	8	8	2	0	1	0	3	1	5	1	0	1	1	.500	0	0	6.35
1988 Kansas City	AL	7	5	1	0	29	136	33	15	9	1	0	1	1	17	0	11	1	1	1	0	1.000	1	0	2.79
1989 Kansas City	AL	34	16	2	7	141.1	591	148	62	55	6	2	4	4	35	4	68	4	0	6	8	.429	1	0	3.50
1990 Kansas City	AL	20	3	1	3	68.1	287	59	25	24	6	5	2	4	27	6	28	3	1	4	1	.800	0	0	3.16
1991 Kansas City	AL	38	18	1	9	157	661	152	67	60	10	2	7	4	47	5	80	1	0	8	4	.667	1	3	3.44
1992 Kansas City	AL	15	13	0	1	67.2	293	81	35	34	5	2	3	1	20	1	11	1	1	3	6	.333	0	0	4.52
6 ML YEARS		121	55	5	23	474.2	2018	487	212	190	30	11	18	14	149	17	203	11	3	23	20	.535	3	3	3.60

Alex Arias

Bats: Right **Throws:** Right **Pos:** SS   **Ht:** 6' 3" **Wt:** 185 **Born:** 11/20/67 **Age:** 25

		BATTING																BASERUNNING				PERCENTAGES		
Year Team	Lg	G	AB	H	2B	3B	HR	(Hm Rd)	TB	R	RBI	TBB	IBB	SO	HBP	SH	SF	SB	CS	SB%	GDP	Avg	OBP	SLG
1987 Wytheville	R	61	233	69	7	0	0	-- --	76	41	24	27	0	29	1	0	1	16	6	.73	2	.296	.370	.326
1988 Chston-Wv	A	127	472	122	12	1	0	-- --	136	57	33	54	3	44	3	10	3	41	12	.77	9	.258	.336	.288
1989 Peoria	A	136	506	140	10	11	2	-- --	178	74	64	49	3	67	7	9	2	31	6	.84	11	.277	.348	.352
1990 Charlotte	AA	119	419	103	16	3	4	-- --	137	55	38	42	0	52	2	9	3	11	5	.69	11	.246	.315	.327
1991 Charlotte	AA	134	488	134	26	0	4	-- --	172	69	47	47	2	41	3	3	3	22	9	.71	9	.275	.340	.352
1992 Iowa	AAA	106	409	114	23	3	5	-- --	158	52	40	44	1	27	6	7	0	14	3	.82	4	.279	.357	.386
1992 Chicago	NL	32	99	29	6	0	0	(0 0)	35	14	7	11	0	13	2	1	0	0	0	.00	4	.293	.375	.354

Jack Armstrong

Pitches: Right **Bats:** Right **Pos:** SP/RP   **Ht:** 6' 5" **Wt:** 215 **Born:** 03/07/65 **Age:** 28

		HOW MUCH HE PITCHED						WHAT HE GAVE UP												THE RESULTS					
Year Team	Lg	G	GS	CG	GF	IP	BFP	H	R	ER	HR	SH	SF	HB	TBB	IBB	SO	WP	Bk	W	L	Pct.	ShO	Sv	ERA
1988 Cincinnati	NL	14	13	0	0	65.1	293	63	44	42	8	4	5	0	38	2	45	3	2	4	7	.364	0	0	5.79
1989 Cincinnati	NL	9	8	0	1	42.2	187	40	24	22	5	2	1	0	21	4	23	0	0	2	3	.400	0	0	4.64
1990 Cincinnati	NL	29	27	2	0	166	704	151	72	63	9	8	5	6	59	7	110	7	5	12	9	.571	1	0	3.42
1991 Cincinnati	NL	27	24	1	1	139.2	611	158	90	85	25	6	9	2	54	2	93	2	1	7	13	.350	0	0	5.48
1992 Cleveland	AL	35	23	1	5	166.2	735	176	100	86	23	6	5	3	67	0	114	6	3	6	15	.286	0	0	4.64
5 ML YEARS		114	95	4	8	580.1	2530	588	330	298	70	26	25	11	239	15	385	18	11	31	47	.397	1	0	4.62

Brad Arnsberg

Pitches: Right **Bats:** Right **Pos:** RP   **Ht:** 6' 4" **Wt:** 210 **Born:** 08/20/63 **Age:** 29

		HOW MUCH HE PITCHED						WHAT HE GAVE UP												THE RESULTS					
Year Team	Lg	G	GS	CG	GF	IP	BFP	H	R	ER	HR	SH	SF	HB	TBB	IBB	SO	WP	Bk	W	L	Pct.	ShO	Sv	ERA
1986 New York	AL	2	1	0	1	8	39	13	3	3	1	0	0	0	1	0	3	0	0	0	0	.000	0	0	3.38
1987 New York	AL	6	2	0	2	19.1	91	22	12	12	5	0	2	0	13	3	14	1	0	1	3	.250	0	0	5.59
1989 Texas	AL	16	1	0	3	48	209	45	27	22	6	1	1	3	22	0	26	6	2	2	1	.667	0	1	4.13
1990 Texas	AL	53	0	0	20	62.2	277	56	20	15	4	2	2	2	33	1	44	8	0	6	1	.857	0	5	2.15
1991 Texas	AL	9	0	0	2	9.2	44	10	9	9	5	0	0	0	5	0	8	1	1	0	1	.000	0	0	8.38
1992 Cleveland	AL	8	0	0	1	10.2	54	13	14	14	6	0	0	2	11	0	5	2	0	0	0	.000	0	0	11.81
6 ML YEARS		94	4	0	29	158.1	714	159	85	75	27	3	5	7	85	4	100	18	3	9	6	.600	0	6	4.26

Andy Ashby

Pitches: Right **Bats:** Right **Pos:** SP   **Ht:** 6' 5" **Wt:** 180 **Born:** 07/11/67 **Age:** 25

		HOW MUCH HE PITCHED						WHAT HE GAVE UP												THE RESULTS					
Year Team	Lg	G	GS	CG	GF	IP	BFP	H	R	ER	HR	SH	SF	HB	TBB	IBB	SO	WP	Bk	W	L	Pct.	ShO	Sv	ERA
1986 Bend	A	16	6	0	4	60		56	40	33	3	0	0	2	34	1	45	3	1	1	2	.333	0	2	4.95
1987 Spartanburg	A	13	13	1	0	64.1	301	73	45	40	8	3	1	2	38	2	52	9	1	4	6	.400	0	0	5.60
Utica	A	13	13	0	0	60	264	56	38	27	3	2	1	1	36	3	51	7	0	3	7	.300	0	0	4.05
1988 Batavia	A	6	6	2	0	44.2	174	25	11	8	3	2	0	1	16	0	32	0	2	3	1	.750	1	0	1.61
Spartanburg	A	3	3	0	0	16.2	68	13	7	5	0	0	0	0	7	0	16	2	3	1	1	.500	0	0	2.70
1989 Spartanburg	A	17	17	3	0	106.2	463	95	48	34	8	3	0	5	49	0	100	8	0	5	9	.357	1	0	2.87
Clearwater	A	6	6	2	0	43.2	173	28	9	6	0	1	0	0	21	0	44	4	1	1	4	.200	1	0	1.24
1990 Reading	AA	23	23	4	0	139.2	591	134	65	53	8	3	5	4	48	0	94	10	2	11	11	.500	3	0	3.42
1991 Scranton-Wb	AAA	26	26	6	0	161.1	691	144	78	62	12	3	4	9	60	2	113	6	0	11	11	.500	3	0	3.46
1992 Scranton/wb	AAA	7	7	0	0	33	133	23	13	11	4	1	1	3	14	0	18	4	0	0	3	.000	0	0	3.00
1991 Philadelphia	NL	8	8	0	0	42	186	41	28	28	5	1	3	3	19	0	26	6	0	1	5	.167	0	0	6.00
1992 Philadelphia	NL	10	8	0	0	37	171	42	31	31	6	2	2	1	21	0	24	2	0	1	3	.250	0	0	7.54
2 ML YEARS		18	16	0	0	79	357	83	59	59	11	3	5	4	40	0	50	8	0	2	8	.200	0	0	6.72

9

Billy Ashley

Bats: Right **Throws:** Right **Pos:** RF **Ht:** 6' 7" **Wt:** 220 **Born:** 07/11/70 **Age:** 22

Year Team	Lg	G	AB	H	2B	3B	HR	(Hm	Rd)	TB	R	RBI	TBB	IBB	SO	HBP	SH	SF	SB	CS	SB%	GDP	Avg	OBP	SLG
1988 Dodgers	R	9	26	4	0	0	0	--	--	4	3	0	1	0	9	0	0	0	1	0	1.00	0	.154	.185	.154
1989 Dodgers	R	48	160	38	6	2	1	--	--	51	23	19	19	1	42	0	0	0	1	0	1.00	0	.238	.321	.319
1990 Bakersfield	A	99	331	72	13	1	9	--	--	114	48	40	25	1	135	3	3	1	17	3	.85	4	.218	.278	.344
1991 Vero Beach	A	60	206	52	11	2	7	--	--	88	18	42	7	0	69	0	0	1	9	2	.82	4	.252	.276	.427
1992 Albuquerque	AAA	25	95	20	7	0	2	--	--	33	11	10	6	0	42	0	0	0	1	0	1.00	2	.211	.257	.347
San Antonio	AA	101	380	106	23	1	24	--	--	203	60	66	16	2	110	6	0	2	13	7	.65	9	.279	.317	.534
1992 Los Angeles	NL	29	95	21	5	0	2	(2	0)	32	6	6	5	0	34	0	0	0	0	0	.00	2	.221	.260	.337

Paul Assenmacher

Pitches: Left **Bats:** Left **Pos:** RP **Ht:** 6' 3" **Wt:** 200 **Born:** 12/10/60 **Age:** 32

Year Team	Lg	G	GS	CG	GF	IP	BFP	H	R	ER	HR	SH	SF	HB	TBB	IBB	SO	WP	Bk	W	L	Pct.	ShO	Sv	ERA
1986 Atlanta	NL	61	0	0	27	68.1	287	61	23	19	5	7	1	0	26	4	56	2	3	7	3	.700	0	7	2.50
1987 Atlanta	NL	52	0	0	10	54.2	251	58	41	31	8	2	1	1	24	4	39	0	0	1	1	.500	0	2	5.10
1988 Atlanta	NL	64	0	0	32	79.1	329	72	28	27	4	8	1	1	32	11	71	7	0	8	7	.533	0	5	3.06
1989 2 ML Teams		63	0	0	17	76.2	331	74	37	34	3	9	3	1	28	8	79	3	1	3	4	.429	0	4	3.99
1990 Chicago	NL	74	1	0	21	103	426	90	33	32	10	10	3	1	36	8	95	2	0	7	2	.778	0	10	2.80
1991 Chicago	NL	75	0	0	31	102.2	427	85	41	37	10	8	4	3	31	6	117	4	0	7	8	.467	0	15	3.24
1992 Chicago	NL	70	0	0	23	68	298	72	32	31	6	1	2	3	26	5	67	4	0	4	4	.500	0	8	4.10
1989 Atlanta	NL	49	0	0	14	57.2	247	55	26	23	2	7	2	1	16	7	64	3	1	1	3	.250	0	3	3.59
Chicago	NL	14	0	0	3	19	84	19	11	11	1	2	1	0	12	1	15	0	0	2	1	.667	0	1	5.21
7 ML YEARS		459	1	0	161	552.2	2349	512	235	211	46	45	15	10	203	46	524	22	4	37	29	.561	0	47	3.44

Pedro Astacio

Pitches: Right **Bats:** Right **Pos:** SP **Ht:** 6' 2" **Wt:** 174 **Born:** 11/28/69 **Age:** 23

Year Team	Lg	G	GS	CG	GF	IP	BFP	H	R	ER	HR	SH	SF	HB	TBB	IBB	SO	WP	Bk	W	L	Pct.	ShO	Sv	ERA
1989 Dodgers	R	12	12	1	0	76.2	321	77	30	27	3	4	2	4	12	0	52	4	2	7	3	.700	1	0	3.17
1990 Vero Beach	A	8	8	1	0	47	215	54	39	33	3	1	1	1	23	0	41	4	5	1	5	.167	0	0	6.32
Yakima	A	3	3	0	0	20.2	79	9	8	4	0	0	0	2	4	0	22	3	0	2	0	1.000	0	0	1.74
Bakersfield	A	10	7	1	0	52	213	46	22	16	3	1	1	3	15	1	34	2	1	5	2	.714	0	0	2.77
1991 Vero Beach	A	9	9	3	0	59.1	223	44	19	11	0	2	1	1	8	0	45	2	0	5	3	.625	1	0	1.67
San Antonio	AA	19	19	2	0	113	497	142	67	60	9	5	3	3	39	3	62	4	2	4	11	.267	1	0	4.78
1992 Albuquerque	AAA	24	15	1	4	98.2	442	115	68	60	8	3	1	2	44	1	66	6	1	6	6	.500	1	0	5.47
1992 Los Angeles	NL	11	11	4	0	82	341	80	23	18	1	3	2	2	20	4	43	1	0	5	5	.500	4	0	1.98

Jim Austin

Pitches: Right **Bats:** Right **Pos:** RP **Ht:** 6' 2" **Wt:** 200 **Born:** 12/07/63 **Age:** 29

Year Team	Lg	G	GS	CG	GF	IP	BFP	H	R	ER	HR	SH	SF	HB	TBB	IBB	SO	WP	Bk	W	L	Pct.	ShO	Sv	ERA
1986 Spokane	A	28	0	0	19	59.2	0	53	24	15	1	0	0	1	22	2	74	7	0	5	4	.556	0	5	2.26
1987 Chston-Sc	A	31	21	3	2	152	642	138	89	71	10	4	1	1	56	2	123	20	1	7	10	.412	1	0	4.20
1988 Riverside	A	12	12	2	0	80	333	65	31	24	5	2	3	0	35	0	73	2	0	6	2	.750	1	0	2.70
Wichita	AA	12	12	4	0	73	313	76	46	39	9	2	3	0	23	0	52	10	0	5	6	.455	0	0	4.81
1989 Stockton	A	7	7	0	0	48.1	204	51	19	14	3	2	1	0	14	0	44	2	0	3	3	.500	0	0	2.61
El Paso	AA	22	13	2	5	85	406	121	60	55	6	2	3	4	34	4	69	4	0	3	10	.231	0	1	5.82
1990 El Paso	AA	38	3	0	24	92.1	384	91	36	25	5	2	3	4	26	4	77	8	0	11	3	.786	0	6	2.44
1991 Denver	AAA	20	3	0	10	44	184	35	12	12	4	2	0	2	24	3	37	1	0	6	3	.667	0	3	2.45
1991 Milwaukee	AL	5	0	0	1	8.2	46	8	8	8	1	2	1	3	11	1	3	1	0	0	0	.000	0	0	8.31
1992 Milwaukee	AL	47	0	0	12	58.1	235	38	13	12	2	1	1	2	32	6	30	1	0	5	2	.714	0	0	1.85
2 ML YEARS		52	0	0	13	67	281	46	21	20	3	3	2	5	43	7	33	2	0	5	2	.714	0	0	2.69

Steve Avery

Pitches: Left **Bats:** Left **Pos:** SP **Ht:** 6' 4" **Wt:** 180 **Born:** 04/14/70 **Age:** 23

Year Team	Lg	G	GS	CG	GF	IP	BFP	H	R	ER	HR	SH	SF	HB	TBB	IBB	SO	WP	Bk	W	L	Pct.	ShO	Sv	ERA
1990 Atlanta	NL	21	20	1	1	99	466	121	79	62	7	14	4	2	45	2	75	5	1	3	11	.214	1	0	5.64
1991 Atlanta	NL	35	35	3	0	210.1	868	189	89	79	21	8	4	3	65	2	137	4	1	18	8	.692	1	0	3.38
1992 Atlanta	NL	35	35	2	0	233.2	969	216	95	83	14	12	8	0	71	3	129	7	3	11	11	.500	2	0	3.20
3 ML YEARS		91	90	6	1	543	2303	526	263	224	42	34	16	5	181	5	341	16	5	32	30	.516	4	0	3.71

Bobby Ayala

Pitches: Right **Bats:** Right **Pos:** SP **Ht:** 6' 2" **Wt:** 190 **Born:** 07/08/69 **Age:** 23

		HOW MUCH HE PITCHED						WHAT HE GAVE UP										THE RESULTS					
Year Team	Lg	G	GS	CG	GF	IP	BFP	H	R	ER	HR	SH	SF	HB	TBB	IBB	SO	WP	Bk	W	L	Pct.	ShO	Sv	ERA
1988 Reds	R	20	0	0	15	33	153	34	23	14	0	3	3	3	12	0	24	1	0	0	4	.000	0	3	3.82
1989 Greensboro	A	22	19	1	1	105.1	467	97	73	48	7	2	3	4	50	0	70	10	2	5	8	.385	0	4	4.10
1990 Cedar Rapds	A	18	7	3	3	53.1	215	40	24	20	6	2	1	4	18	0	59	6	0	3	2	.600	1	1	3.38
Chston-Wv	A	21	4	2	8	74	287	48	23	20	2	2	1	3	21	1	73	0	0	6	1	.857	1	2	2.43
1991 Chattanooga	AA	39	8	1	16	90.2	404	79	52	47	10	4	3	4	58	4	92	10	1	3	1	.750	0	4	4.67
1992 Chattanooga	AA	27	27	3	0	162.2	690	152	75	64	14	8	2	11	58	0	154	9	0	12	6	.667	3	0	3.54
1992 Cincinnati	NL	5	5	0	0	29	127	33	15	14	1	2	0	1	13	2	23	0	0	2	1	.667	0	0	4.34

Bob Ayrault

Pitches: Right **Bats:** Right **Pos:** RP **Ht:** 6' 4" **Wt:** 230 **Born:** 04/27/66 **Age:** 27

		HOW MUCH HE PITCHED						WHAT HE GAVE UP										THE RESULTS					
Year Team	Lg	G	GS	CG	GF	IP	BFP	H	R	ER	HR	SH	SF	HB	TBB	IBB	SO	WP	Bk	W	L	Pct.	ShO	Sv	ERA
1989 Reno	A	24	14	3	5	109.2	478	104	56	46	7	3	4	11	57	3	91	3	3	7	4	.636	1	0	3.78
Batavia	A	4	3	2	1	26	93	13	5	4	2	1	0	2	7	0	20	0	0	2	1	.667	1	0	1.38
Reading	AA	2	1	0	0	8.2	33	3	1	1	0	0	0	0	4	0	8	0	0	0	0	.000	0	0	1.04
1990 Reading	AA	44	9	0	29	109.1	432	77	33	28	4	3	5	2	34	1	84	2	2	4	6	.400	0	10	2.30
1991 Scranton-Wb	AAA	68	0	0	21	98.2	433	91	58	53	11	6	5	5	47	4	103	4	1	8	5	.615	0	3	4.83
1992 Scranton/wb	AAA	20	0	0	14	25.1	110	19	15	14	4	3	2	1	15	3	30	0	0	5	1	.833	0	6	4.97
1992 Philadelphia	NL	30	0	0	7	43.1	178	32	16	15	0	4	3	1	17	1	27	0	0	2	2	.500	0	1	3.12

Oscar Azocar

Bats: Left **Throws:** Left **Pos:** LF **Ht:** 6' 1" **Wt:** 195 **Born:** 02/21/65 **Age:** 28

		BATTING																	BASERUNNING				PERCENTAGES		
Year Team	Lg	G	AB	H	2B	3B	HR	(Hm	Rd)	TB	R	RBI	TBB	IBB	SO	HBP	SH	SF	SB	CS	SB%	GDP	Avg	OBP	SLG
1990 New York	AL	65	214	53	8	0	5	(3	2)	76	18	19	2	0	15	1	0	1	7	0	1.00	1	.248	.257	.355
1991 San Diego	NL	38	57	14	2	0	0	(0	0)	16	5	9	1	1	9	1	0	1	2	0	1.00	1	.246	.267	.281
1992 San Diego	NL	99	168	32	6	0	0	(0	0)	38	15	8	9	1	12	0	4	1	1	0	1.00	3	.190	.230	.226
3 ML YEARS		202	439	99	16	0	5	(3	2)	130	38	36	12	2	36	2	4	3	10	0	1.00	5	.226	.248	.296

Wally Backman

Bats: Left **Throws:** Right **Pos:** 2B **Ht:** 5' 9" **Wt:** 168 **Born:** 09/22/59 **Age:** 33

		BATTING																	BASERUNNING				PERCENTAGES		
Year Team	Lg	G	AB	H	2B	3B	HR	(Hm	Rd)	TB	R	RBI	TBB	IBB	SO	HBP	SH	SF	SB	CS	SB%	GDP	Avg	OBP	SLG
1980 New York	NL	27	93	30	1	1	0	(0	0)	33	12	9	11	1	14	1	4	1	2	3	.40	1	.323	.396	.355
1981 New York	NL	26	36	10	2	0	0	(0	0)	12	5	0	4	0	7	0	2	0	1	0	1.00	0	.278	.350	.333
1982 New York	NL	96	261	71	13	2	3	(1	2)	97	37	22	49	1	47	0	2	0	8	7	.53	6	.272	.387	.372
1983 New York	NL	26	42	7	0	1	0	(0	0)	9	6	3	2	0	8	0	1	0	0	0	.00	2	.167	.205	.214
1984 New York	NL	128	436	122	19	2	1	(0	1)	148	68	26	56	2	63	0	5	2	32	9	.78	13	.280	.360	.339
1985 New York	NL	145	520	142	24	5	1	(0	1)	179	77	38	36	1	72	1	14	3	30	12	.71	3	.273	.320	.344
1986 New York	NL	124	387	124	18	2	1	(1	0)	149	67	27	36	1	32	0	14	3	13	7	.65	3	.320	.376	.385
1987 New York	NL	94	300	75	6	1	1	(0	0)	86	43	23	25	0	43	0	9	1	11	3	.79	5	.250	.307	.287
1988 New York	NL	99	294	89	12	0	0	(0	0)	101	44	17	41	1	49	1	9	2	9	5	.64	4	.303	.388	.344
1989 Minnesota	AL	87	299	69	9	2	1	(0	1)	85	33	26	32	0	45	1	4	1	1	1	.50	4	.231	.306	.284
1990 Pittsburgh	NL	104	315	92	21	3	2	(0	2)	125	62	28	42	1	53	1	0	3	6	3	.67	5	.292	.374	.397
1991 Philadelphia	NL	94	185	45	12	0	0	(0	0)	57	20	15	30	0	30	0	2	3	3	2	.60	2	.243	.344	.308
1992 Philadelphia	NL	42	48	13	1	0	0	(0	0)	14	6	6	6	1	9	0	1	0	1	0	1.00	3	.271	.352	.292
13 ML YEARS		1092	3216	889	138	19	10	(2	8)	1095	480	240	370	9	472	5	67	19	117	52	.69	55	.276	.350	.340

Carlos Baerga

Bats: Both **Throws:** Right **Pos:** 2B **Ht:** 5'11" **Wt:** 185 **Born:** 11/04/68 **Age:** 24

		BATTING																	BASERUNNING				PERCENTAGES		
Year Team	Lg	G	AB	H	2B	3B	HR	(Hm	Rd)	TB	R	RBI	TBB	IBB	SO	HBP	SH	SF	SB	CS	SB%	GDP	Avg	OBP	SLG
1990 Cleveland	AL	108	312	81	17	2	7	(3	4)	123	46	47	16	2	57	4	1	5	0	2	.00	4	.260	.300	.394
1991 Cleveland	AL	158	593	171	28	2	11	(2	9)	236	80	69	48	5	74	6	4	3	3	2	.60	12	.288	.346	.398
1992 Cleveland	AL	161	657	205	32	1	20	(9	11)	299	92	105	35	10	76	13	2	9	10	2	.83	15	.312	.354	.455
3 ML YEARS		427	1562	457	77	5	38	(14	24)	658	218	221	99	17	207	23	7	17	13	6	.68	31	.293	.340	.421

Kevin Baez

Bats: Right **Throws:** Right **Pos:** SS **Ht:** 6' 0" **Wt:** 170 **Born:** 01/10/67 **Age:** 26

Year	Team	Lg	G	AB	H	2B	3B	HR	(Hm	Rd)	TB	R	RBI	TBB	IBB	SO	HBP	SH	SF	SB	CS	SB%	GDP	Avg	OBP	SLG
1988	Little Fls	A	70	218	58	7	1	1	--	--	70	23	19	32	1	30	2	2	3	7	3	.70	3	.266	.361	.321
1989	Columbia	A	123	426	108	25	1	5	--	--	150	59	44	58	3	53	6	9	3	11	9	.55	5	.254	.349	.352
1990	Jackson	AA	106	327	76	11	0	2	--	--	93	29	29	37	4	44	2	11	2	3	4	.43	7	.232	.313	.284
1991	Tidewater	AAA	65	210	36	8	0	0	--	--	44	18	13	12	1	32	4	5	4	1	1	.00	5	.171	.226	.210
1992	Tidewater	AAA	109	352	83	16	1	2	--	--	107	30	33	13	1	57	4	4	5	1	1	.50	9	.236	.267	.304
1990	New York	NL	5	12	2	1	0	0	(0	0)	3	0	0	0	0	0	0	0	0	0	0	.00	1	.167	.167	.250
1992	New York	NL	6	13	2	0	0	0	(0	0)	2	0	0	0	0	0	0	0	0	0	0	.00	1	.154	.154	.154
	2 ML YEARS		11	25	4	1	0	0	(0	0)	5	0	0	0	0	0	0	0	0	0	0	.00	3	.160	.160	.200

Jeff Bagwell

Bats: Right **Throws:** Right **Pos:** 1B **Ht:** 6' 0" **Wt:** 195 **Born:** 05/27/68 **Age:** 25

Year	Team	Lg	G	AB	H	2B	3B	HR	(Hm	Rd)	TB	R	RBI	TBB	IBB	SO	HBP	SH	SF	SB	CS	SB%	GDP	Avg	OBP	SLG
1989	Red Sox	R	5	19	6	1	0	0	--	--	7	3	3	3	0	0	0	0	0	0	0	.00	1	.316	.409	.368
	Winter Havn	A	64	210	65	13	2	2	--	--	88	27	19	23	0	25	3	3	1	1	1	.50	7	.310	.384	.419
1990	New Britain	AA	136	481	160	34	7	4	--	--	220	63	61	72	12	57	7	3	6	5	7	.42	15	.333	.422	.457
1991	Houston	NL	156	554	163	26	4	15	(6	9)	242	79	82	75	5	116	13	1	7	7	4	.64	12	.294	.387	.437
1992	Houston	NL	162	586	160	34	6	18	(8	10)	260	87	96	84	13	97	12	2	13	10	6	.63	17	.273	.368	.444
	2 ML YEARS		318	1140	323	60	10	33	(14	19)	502	166	178	159	18	213	25	3	20	17	10	.63	29	.283	.377	.440

Scott Bailes

Pitches: Left **Bats:** Left **Pos:** RP **Ht:** 6' 2" **Wt:** 171 **Born:** 12/18/62 **Age:** 30

Year	Team	Lg	G	GS	CG	GF	IP	BFP	H	R	ER	HR	SH	SF	HB	TBB	IBB	SO	WP	Bk	W	L	Pct.	ShO	Sv	ERA
1986	Cleveland	AL	62	10	0	22	112.2	500	123	70	62	12	7	4	1	43	5	60	4	2	10	10	.500	0	7	4.95
1987	Cleveland	AL	39	17	0	15	120.1	551	145	75	62	21	4	6	4	47	1	65	3	0	7	8	.467	0	6	4.64
1988	Cleveland	AL	37	21	5	7	145	617	149	89	79	22	5	4	2	46	0	53	2	3	9	14	.391	2	0	4.90
1989	Cleveland	AL	34	11	0	9	113.2	473	116	57	54	7	5	5	3	29	4	47	3	0	5	9	.357	0	0	4.28
1990	California	AL	27	0	0	9	35.1	173	46	30	25	8	1	5	1	20	0	16	0	0	2	0	1.000	0	0	6.37
1991	California	AL	42	0	0	14	51.2	219	41	26	24	5	3	2	4	22	5	41	2	0	1	2	.333	0	0	4.18
1992	California	AL	32	0	0	10	38.2	200	59	34	32	7	1	2	1	28	4	25	2	1	3	1	.750	0	0	7.45
	7 ML YEARS		273	59	5	83	617.1	2733	679	381	338	82	26	28	16	235	19	307	16	6	37	44	.457	2	13	4.93

Mark Bailey

Bats: Both **Throws:** Right **Pos:** C **Ht:** 6' 5" **Wt:** 200 **Born:** 11/04/61 **Age:** 31

Year	Team	Lg	G	AB	H	2B	3B	HR	(Hm	Rd)	TB	R	RBI	TBB	IBB	SO	HBP	SH	SF	SB	CS	SB%	GDP	Avg	OBP	SLG
1984	Houston	NL	108	344	73	16	1	9	(7	2)	118	38	34	53	4	71	2	1	3	0	1	.00	7	.212	.318	.343
1985	Houston	NL	114	332	88	14	0	10	(4	6)	132	47	45	67	13	70	1	1	1	0	2	.00	16	.265	.389	.398
1986	Houston	NL	57	153	27	5	0	4	(1	3)	44	9	15	28	6	45	0	0	1	1	1	.50	7	.176	.302	.288
1987	Houston	NL	35	64	13	1	0	0	(0	0)	14	5	3	10	0	21	0	1	0	1	0	1.00	3	.203	.311	.219
1988	Houston	NL	8	23	3	0	0	0	(0	0)	3	1	0	5	0	6	0	0	0	1	0	.00	1	.130	.286	.130
1990	San Francisco	NL	5	7	1	0	0	1	(0	1)	4	1	3	0	0	2	0	0	0	0	0	.00	0	.143	.143	.571
1992	San Francisco	NL	13	26	4	1	0	0	(0	0)	5	0	1	3	0	7	0	0	0	0	0	.00	0	.154	.241	.192
	7 ML YEARS		340	949	209	37	1	24	(12	12)	320	101	101	166	23	222	3	3	5	2	5	.29	34	.220	.337	.337

Harold Baines

Bats: Left **Throws:** Left **Pos:** DH/RF **Ht:** 6' 2" **Wt:** 195 **Born:** 03/15/59 **Age:** 34

Year	Team	Lg	G	AB	H	2B	3B	HR	(Hm	Rd)	TB	R	RBI	TBB	IBB	SO	HBP	SH	SF	SB	CS	SB%	GDP	Avg	OBP	SLG
1980	Chicago	AL	141	491	125	23	6	13	(3	10)	199	55	49	19	7	65	1	2	5	2	4	.33	15	.255	.281	.405
1981	Chicago	AL	82	280	80	11	7	10	(3	7)	135	42	41	12	4	41	2	0	2	6	2	.75	6	.286	.318	.482
1982	Chicago	AL	161	608	165	29	8	25	(11	14)	285	89	105	49	10	95	0	2	9	10	3	.77	12	.271	.321	.469
1983	Chicago	AL	156	596	167	33	2	20	(12	8)	264	76	99	49	13	85	1	3	6	7	5	.58	15	.280	.333	.443
1984	Chicago	AL	147	569	173	28	10	29	(16	13)	308	72	94	54	9	75	0	1	5	1	2	.33	12	.304	.361	.541
1985	Chicago	AL	160	640	198	29	3	22	(13	9)	299	86	113	42	8	89	1	0	10	1	1	.50	23	.309	.348	.467
1986	Chicago	AL	145	570	169	29	2	21	(8	13)	265	72	88	38	9	89	2	0	8	2	1	.67	14	.296	.338	.465
1987	Chicago	AL	132	505	148	26	4	20	(12	8)	242	59	93	46	2	82	1	0	2	0	0	.00	12	.293	.352	.479
1988	Chicago	AL	158	599	166	39	1	13	(5	8)	246	55	81	67	14	109	1	0	7	0	0	.00	21	.277	.347	.411
1989	2 ML Teams		146	505	156	29	1	16	(5	11)	235	73	72	73	13	79	1	0	4	0	3	.00	15	.309	.395	.465
1990	2 ML Teams		135	415	118	15	1	16	(9	7)	183	52	65	67	10	80	0	0	7	0	3	.00	17	.284	.378	.441
1991	Oakland	AL	141	488	144	25	1	20	(11	9)	231	76	90	72	22	67	1	0	5	0	1	.00	12	.295	.383	.473
1992	Oakland	AL	140	478	121	18	0	16	(10	6)	187	58	76	59	6	61	0	0	6	1	3	.25	11	.253	.331	.391

12

Year	Team	Lg	G	AB	H	2B	3B	HR			TB	R	RBI	BB	IBB	SO										
1989	Chicago	AL	96	333	107	20	1	13	(4	9)	168	55	56	60	13	52	1	0	3	0	1	.00	11	.321	.423	.505
	Texas	AL	50	172	49	9	0	3	(1	2)	67	18	16	13	0	27	0	0	1	0	2	.00	4	.285	.333	.390
1990	Texas	AL	103	321	93	10	1	13	(6	7)	144	41	44	47	9	63	0	0	3	0	1	.00	13	.290	.377	.449
	Oakland	AL	32	94	25	5	0	3	(3	0)	39	11	21	20	1	17	0	0	4	0	2	.00	4	.266	.381	.415
	13 ML YEARS		1844	6744	1930	334	46	241	(118	123)	3079	865	1066	647	127	1017	11	8	76	30	28	.52	185	.286	.346	.457

Jay Baller

Pitches: Right **Bats:** Right **Pos:** RP   **Ht:** 6' 7" **Wt:** 225 **Born:** 10/06/60 **Age:** 32

			HOW MUCH HE PITCHED					WHAT HE GAVE UP												THE RESULTS					
Year	Team	Lg	G	GS	CG	GF	IP	BFP	H	R	ER	HR	SH	SF	HB	TBB	IBB	SO	WP	Bk	W	L	Pct.	ShO	Sv	ERA
1982	Philadelphia	NL	4	1	0	1	8	35	7	4	3	1	1	0	1	2	0	7	0	1	0	0	.000	0	0	3.38
1985	Chicago	NL	20	4	0	4	52	223	52	21	20	8	4	1	1	17	7	31	2	0	2	3	.400	0	1	3.46
1986	Chicago	NL	36	0	0	16	53.2	248	58	37	32	7	4	3	2	28	4	42	2	4	2	4	.333	0	5	5.37
1987	Chicago	NL	23	0	0	9	29.1	139	38	22	22	4	2	0	0	20	2	27	5	2	0	1	.000	0	0	6.75
1990	Kansas City	AL	3	0	0	2	2.1	14	4	4	4	1	0	0	1	2	1	1	1	0	0	1	.000	0	0	15.43
1992	Philadelphia	NL	8	0	0	4	11	51	10	10	10	5	0	1	0	10	0	9	1	0	0	0	.000	0	0	8.18
	6 ML YEARS		94	5	0	36	156.1	710	169	98	91	26	11	5	5	79	14	117	11	7	4	9	.308	0	6	5.24

Scott Bankhead

Pitches: Right **Bats:** Right **Pos:** RP   **Ht:** 5'10" **Wt:** 185 **Born:** 07/31/63 **Age:** 29

			HOW MUCH HE PITCHED					WHAT HE GAVE UP												THE RESULTS					
Year	Team	Lg	G	GS	CG	GF	IP	BFP	H	R	ER	HR	SH	SF	HB	TBB	IBB	SO	WP	Bk	W	L	Pct.	ShO	Sv	ERA
1986	Kansas City	AL	24	17	0	2	121	517	121	66	62	14	5	5	3	37	7	94	1	0	8	9	.471	0	0	4.61
1987	Seattle	AL	27	25	2	1	149.1	642	168	96	90	35	3	6	3	37	0	95	2	2	9	8	.529	0	0	5.42
1988	Seattle	AL	21	21	2	0	135	557	115	53	46	8	3	1	1	38	5	102	3	1	7	9	.438	1	0	3.07
1989	Seattle	AL	33	33	3	0	210.1	862	187	84	78	19	4	8	3	63	1	140	2	0	14	6	.700	2	0	3.34
1990	Seattle	AL	4	4	0	0	13	63	18	16	16	2	0	2	0	7	0	10	1	0	0	2	.000	0	0	11.08
1991	Seattle	AL	17	9	0	2	60.2	271	73	35	33	8	0	2	2	21	2	28	0	0	3	6	.333	0	0	4.90
1992	Cincinnati	NL	54	0	0	10	70.2	299	57	26	23	4	3	3	3	29	5	53	6	0	10	4	.714	0	1	2.93
	7 ML YEARS		180	109	7	15	760	3211	739	376	348	90	18	27	15	232	20	522	15	3	51	44	.537	3	1	4.12

Willie Banks

Pitches: Right **Bats:** Right **Pos:** SP   **Ht:** 6' 1" **Wt:** 195 **Born:** 02/27/69 **Age:** 24

			HOW MUCH HE PITCHED					WHAT HE GAVE UP												THE RESULTS					
Year	Team	Lg	G	GS	CG	GF	IP	BFP	H	R	ER	HR	SH	SF	HB	TBB	IBB	SO	WP	Bk	W	L	Pct.	ShO	Sv	ERA
1987	Elizabethtn	R	13	13	0	0	65.2	332	73	71	51	3	3	4	3	62	0	71	28	3	1	8	.111	0	0	6.99
1988	Kenosha	A	24	24	0	0	125.2	580	109	73	52	3	2	5	4	107	2	113	14	2	10	10	.500	0	0	3.72
1989	Visalia	A	27	27	7	0	174	723	122	70	50	5	2	7	10	85	0	173	22	1	12	9	.571	4	0	2.59
	Orlando	AA	1	1	0	0	7	30	10	4	4	0	0	0	0	0	0	9	2	0	1	0	1.000	0	0	5.14
1990	Orlando	AA	28	28	1	0	162.2	737	161	93	71	15	1	8	7	98	0	114	6	1	7	9	.438	0	0	3.93
1991	Portland	AAA	25	24	1	1	146.1	653	156	81	74	6	2	4	6	76	1	63	14	1	9	8	.529	1	0	4.55
1992	Portland	AAA	11	11	2	0	75	310	62	20	16	2	2	1	0	34	0	41	5	2	6	1	.857	0	0	1.92
1991	Minnesota	AL	5	3	0	2	17.1	85	21	15	11	1	0	0	0	12	0	16	3	0	1	1	.500	0	0	5.71
1992	Minnesota	AL	16	12	0	2	71	324	80	46	45	6	2	5	2	37	0	37	5	1	4	4	.500	0	0	5.70
	2 ML YEARS		21	15	0	4	88.1	409	101	61	56	7	2	5	2	49	0	53	8	1	5	5	.500	0	0	5.71

Floyd Bannister

Pitches: Left **Bats:** Left **Pos:** RP   **Ht:** 6' 1" **Wt:** 190 **Born:** 06/10/55 **Age:** 38

			HOW MUCH HE PITCHED					WHAT HE GAVE UP												THE RESULTS					
Year	Team	Lg	G	GS	CG	GF	IP	BFP	H	R	ER	HR	SH	SF	HB	TBB	IBB	SO	WP	Bk	W	L	Pct.	ShO	Sv	ERA
1977	Houston	NL	24	23	4	0	143	622	138	70	64	11	2	4	4	68	1	112	6	2	8	9	.471	1	0	4.03
1978	Houston	NL	28	16	2	3	110	502	120	59	59	13	7	3	1	63	4	94	7	2	3	9	.250	2	0	4.83
1979	Seattle	AL	30	30	6	0	182	792	185	92	82	25	5	3	4	68	6	155	1	0	10	15	.400	2	0	4.05
1980	Seattle	AL	32	32	8	0	218	918	200	96	84	24	8	5	2	66	4	155	7	0	9	13	.409	2	0	3.47
1981	Seattle	AL	21	20	5	0	121	522	128	62	60	14	2	0	3	39	0	85	7	1	9	9	.500	2	0	4.46
1982	Seattle	AL	35	35	5	0	247	1022	225	112	94	32	10	5	3	77	0	209	6	0	12	13	.480	3	0	3.43
1983	Chicago	AL	34	34	5	0	217.1	902	191	88	81	19	4	4	2	71	3	193	8	1	16	10	.615	2	0	3.35
1984	Chicago	AL	34	33	4	0	218	936	211	127	117	30	3	10	6	80	2	152	10	0	14	11	.560	0	0	4.83
1985	Chicago	AL	34	34	4	0	210.2	928	211	121	114	30	9	8	4	100	5	198	11	0	10	14	.417	1	0	4.87
1986	Chicago	AL	28	27	6	0	165.1	688	162	81	65	17	7	5	2	48	0	92	5	0	10	14	.417	1	0	3.54
1987	Chicago	AL	34	34	11	0	228.2	939	216	100	91	38	9	3	0	49	0	124	5	1	16	11	.593	2	0	3.58
1988	Kansas City	AL	31	31	2	0	189.1	816	182	102	91	22	8	2	5	68	6	113	6	2	12	13	.480	0	0	4.33
1989	Kansas City	AL	14	14	0	0	75.1	323	87	40	39	8	2	1	1	18	1	35	1	0	4	1	.800	0	0	4.66
1991	California	AL	16	0	0	2	25	104	25	12	11	5	0	0	1	10	1	16	1	0	0	0	.000	0	0	3.96
1992	Texas	AL	36	0	0	8	37	173	39	27	26	3	3	7	3	21	6	30	3	0	1	1	.500	0	0	6.32
	15 ML YEARS		431	363	62	13	2387.2	10187	2320	1189	1078	291	79	61	40	846	39	1723	84	9	134	143	.484	16	0	4.06

Bret Barberie

Bats: Both **Throws:** Right **Pos:** 3B/2B **Ht:** 5'11" **Wt:** 180 **Born:** 08/16/67 **Age:** 25

						BATTING												BASERUNNING				PERCENTAGES		
Year	Team	Lg	G	AB	H	2B	3B	HR	(Hm | Rd)	TB	R	RBI	TBB	IBB	SO	HBP	SH	SF	SB	CS	SB%	GDP	Avg	OBP	SLG
1989	Wst Plm Bch	A	124	457	122	16	4	4	--	--	158	63	34	64	7	39	10	5	4	10	4	.71	9	.267	.366	.346
1990	Jacksnville	AA	133	431	112	18	3	7	--	--	157	71	56	87	6	64	11	3	5	20	7	.74	3	.260	.393	.364
1991	Indianapols	AAA	71	218	68	10	4	10	--	--	116	45	29	47	2	47	3	1	2	10	5	.67	4	.312	.461	.532
1992	Indianapols	AAA	10	43	17	3	0	3	--	--	29	4	8	1	0	9	0	0	0	0	1	.00	1	.395	.409	.674
1991	Montreal	NL	57	136	48	12	2	2	(2 | 0)	70	16	18	20	2	22	2	1	3	0	0	.00	4	.353	.435	.515
1992	Montreal	NL	111	285	66	11	0	1	(0 | 1)	80	26	24	47	3	62	8	1	2	9	5	.64	4	.232	.354	.281
	2 ML YEARS		168	421	114	23	2	3	(2 | 1)	150	42	42	67	5	84	10	2	5	9	5	.64	8	.271	.380	.356

Jesse Barfield

Bats: Right **Throws:** Right **Pos:** RF **Ht:** 6' 1" **Wt:** 201 **Born:** 10/29/59 **Age:** 33

						BATTING												BASERUNNING				PERCENTAGES		
Year	Team	Lg	G	AB	H	2B	3B	HR	(Hm	Rd)	TB	R	RBI	TBB	IBB	SO	HBP	SH	SF	SB	CS	SB%	GDP	Avg	OBP	SLG
1981	Toronto	AL	25	95	22	3	2	2	(1	1)	35	7	9	4	0	19	1	0	0	4	3	.57	4	.232	.270	.368
1982	Toronto	AL	139	394	97	13	2	18	(11	7)	168	54	58	42	3	79	3	6	1	1	4	.20	7	.246	.323	.426
1983	Toronto	AL	128	388	98	13	4	27	(22	5)	198	58	68	22	0	110	4	1	5	2	5	.29	8	.253	.296	.510
1984	Toronto	AL	110	320	91	14	1	14	(10	4)	149	51	49	35	5	81	2	1	5	8	2	.80	5	.284	.357	.466
1985	Toronto	AL	155	539	156	34	9	27	(15	12)	289	94	84	66	5	143	4	0	3	22	8	.73	14	.289	.369	.536
1986	Toronto	AL	158	589	170	35	2	40	(16	24)	329	107	108	69	5	146	8	0	5	8	8	.50	9	.289	.368	.559
1987	Toronto	AL	159	590	155	25	3	28	(11	17)	270	89	84	58	7	141	3	1	2	3	5	.38	13	.263	.331	.458
1988	Toronto	AL	137	468	114	21	5	18	(12	6)	199	62	56	41	6	108	1	4	6	7	3	.70	10	.244	.302	.425
1989	2 ML Teams		150	521	122	23	1	23	(7	16)	216	79	67	87	6	150	3	1	3	5	5	.50	8	.234	.345	.415
1990	New York	AL	153	476	117	21	2	25	(12	13)	217	69	78	82	4	150	5	2	5	4	3	.57	6	.246	.359	.456
1991	New York	AL	84	284	64	12	0	17	(11	6)	127	37	48	36	6	80	0	0	1	1	0	1.00	11	.225	.312	.447
1992	New York	AL	30	95	13	2	0	2	(2	0)	21	8	7	9	2	27	0	0	1	1	1	.50	5	.137	.210	.221
1989	Toronto	AL	21	80	16	4	0	5	(1	4)	35	8	11	5	0	28	1	0	0	0	2	.00	1	.200	.256	.438
	New York	AL	129	441	106	19	1	18	(6	12)	181	71	56	82	6	122	2	1	3	5	3	.63	8	.240	.360	.410
	12 ML YEARS		1428	4759	1219	216	30	241	(130	111)	2218	715	716	551	49	1234	34	16	34	66	47	.58	100	.256	.335	.466

Brian Barnes

Pitches: Left **Bats:** Left **Pos:** SP **Ht:** 5' 9" **Wt:** 170 **Born:** 03/25/67 **Age:** 26

			HOW MUCH HE PITCHED						WHAT HE GAVE UP										THE RESULTS					
Year	Team	Lg	G	GS	CG	GF	IP	BFP	H	R	ER	HR	SH	SF	HB	TBB	IBB	SO	WP	Bk	W	L	Pct.	ShO	Sv	ERA
1990	Montreal	NL	4	4	1	0	28	115	25	10	9	2	2	0	0	7	0	23	2	0	1	1	.500	0	0	2.89
1991	Montreal	NL	28	27	1	0	160	684	135	82	75	16	9	5	6	84	2	117	5	1	5	8	.385	0	0	4.22
1992	Montreal	NL	21	17	0	2	100	417	77	34	33	9	5	1	3	46	1	65	1	2	6	6	.500	0	0	2.97
	3 ML YEARS		53	48	2	2	288	1216	237	126	117	27	16	6	9	137	3	205	8	3	12	15	.444	0	0	3.66

Skeeter Barnes

Bats: Right **Throws:** Right **Pos:** 3B/1B **Ht:** 5'11" **Wt:** 180 **Born:** 03/07/57 **Age:** 36

						BATTING												BASERUNNING				PERCENTAGES		
Year	Team	Lg	G	AB	H	2B	3B	HR	(Hm	Rd)	TB	R	RBI	TBB	IBB	SO	HBP	SH	SF	SB	CS	SB%	GDP	Avg	OBP	SLG
1983	Cincinnati	NL	15	34	7	0	0	1	(1	0)	10	5	4	7	0	3	2	0	0	2	2	.50	0	.206	.372	.294
1984	Cincinnati	NL	32	42	5	0	0	1	(1	0)	8	5	3	4	1	6	0	0	0	0	0	.00	1	.119	.196	.190
1985	Montreal	NL	19	26	4	1	0	0	(0	0)	5	0	0	0	0	2	0	0	0	0	1	.00	1	.154	.154	.192
1987	St. Louis	NL	4	4	1	0	0	1	(0	1)	4	1	3	0	0	0	0	0	0	0	0	.00	0	.250	.250	1.000
1989	Cincinnati	NL	5	3	0	0	0	0	(0	0)	0	1	0	0	0	0	0	0	0	0	1	.00	0	.000	.000	.000
1991	Detroit	AL	75	159	46	13	2	5	(1	4)	78	28	17	9	1	24	0	2	1	10	7	.59	1	.289	.325	.491
1992	Detroit	AL	95	165	45	8	1	3	(3	0)	64	27	25	10	1	18	2	2	2	3	1	.75	4	.273	.318	.388
	7 ML YEARS		245	433	108	22	3	11	(6	5)	169	67	52	30	3	53	4	4	3	15	12	.56	7	.249	.302	.390

Tom Barrett

Bats: Both **Throws:** Right **Pos:** 2B **Ht:** 5'10" **Wt:** 170 **Born:** 04/02/60 **Age:** 33

						BATTING												BASERUNNING				PERCENTAGES		
Year	Team	Lg	G	AB	H	2B	3B	HR	(Hm	Rd)	TB	R	RBI	TBB	IBB	SO	HBP	SH	SF	SB	CS	SB%	GDP	Avg	OBP	SLG
1981	Columbus	AAA	55	169	44	11	1	1	--	--	60	27	21	17	0	18	0	4	0	14	4	.78	4	.260	.328	.355
1982	Paintsville	R	61	231	84	5	2	0	--	--	93	59	21	42	0	17	0	0	0	20	0	1.00	0	.364	.462	.403
1983	Ft.Laudrdle	A	103	397	130	21	1	0	--	--	153	80	32	46	0	16	0	0	0	55	0	1.00	0	.327	.397	.385
1984	Nashville	AA	135	510	157	22	6	0	--	--	191	82	44	86	3	41	5	6	6	53	21	.72	8	.308	.409	.375
	Columbus	AAA	5	21	8	1	0	0	--	--	9	3	0	2	0	3	0	0	0	0	1	.00	0	.381	.435	.429
1985	Albany	AA	57	233	61	8	3	1	--	--	78	40	18	25	1	19	2	1	1	23	9	.72	3	.262	.337	.335
	Columbus	AAA	55	169	44	11	1	1	--	--	60	27	11	17	0	18	0	4	0	14	4	.78	4	.260	.328	.355
1986	Albany	AA	132	498	133	20	2	3	--	--	166	75	45	48	0	43	1	11	7	34	21	.62	5	.267	.329	.333
	Columbus	AAA	2	9	3	0	0	0	--	--	3	0	1	0	0	3	0	0	0	0	0	.00	0	.333	.333	.333

Year	Team	Lg	G	AB	H	2B	3B	HR	(Hm	Rd)	TB	R	RBI	TBB	IBB	SO	HBP	SH	SF	SB	CS	SB%	GDP	Avg	OBP	SLG
1987	Reading	AA	136	485	162	20	9	1	--	--	203	107	55	95	5	45	6	12	5	30	17	.64	5	.334	.445	.419
1988	Maine	AAA	114	390	111	16	4	1	--	--	138	69	33	62	3	49	6	9	8	21	7	.75	1	.285	.384	.354
1989	Scr Wil-Bar	AAA	120	443	123	14	6	0	--	--	149	65	25	51	4	47	3	10	3	44	13	.77	5	.278	.354	.336
1991	Pawtucket	AAA	102	331	89	15	1	0	--	--	106	42	27	54	3	39	1	5	8	8	10	.44	5	.269	.365	.320
1992	Pawtucket	AAA	91	323	82	18	4	1	--	--	111	55	21	52	1	31	3	6	2	13	9	.59	5	.254	.361	.344
1988	Philadelphia	NL	36	54	11	1	0	0	(0	0)	12	5	3	7	0	8	1	1	0	0	0	.00	1	.204	.306	.222
1989	Philadelphia	NL	14	27	6	0	0	0	(0	0)	6	3	1	1	0	7	0	3	0	0	0	.00	0	.222	.250	.222
1992	Boston	AL	4	3	0	0	0	0	(0	0)	0	1	0	2	0	1	0	1	0	0	0	.00	0	.000	.400	.000
	3 ML YEARS		54	84	17	1	0	0	(0	0)	18	9	4	10	0	15	1	5	0	0	0	.00	1	.202	.295	.214

Shawn Barton

Pitches: Left **Bats:** Right **Pos:** RP   **Ht:** 6' 3" **Wt:** 190 **Born:** 05/14/63 **Age:** 30

			HOW MUCH HE PITCHED						WHAT HE GAVE UP										THE RESULTS					
Year	Team	Lg	G	GS	CG	GF	IP	BFP	H	R	ER	HR	SH	SF	HB	TBB	IBB	SO	WP	Bk	W	L	Pct.	ShO	Sv	ERA
1984	Bend	A	13	8	1	1	58.1	0	46	28	14	3	0	0	4	24	0	47	2	1	4	5	.444	0	0	2.16
1985	Peninsula	A	22	22	7	0	140.2	555	108	45	36	5	5	4	1	43	1	82	4	2	12	4	.750	5	0	2.30
1986	Reading	AA	17	17	3	0	92.2	404	92	53	39	10	5	2	2	41	2	62	2	1	8	7	.533	1	0	3.79
1987	Maine	AAA	7	4	0	3	26.2	119	25	14	13	2	2	1	0	15	1	19	3	2	1	1	.500	0	1	4.39
	Reading	AA	32	12	3	9	82.1	367	108	50	45	8	1	2	1	31	2	53	5	1	6	5	.545	0	3	4.92
1988	Jackson	AA	22	8	0	8	71.2	305	74	33	26	5	2	1	1	26	3	58	3	3	2	4	.333	0	1	3.27
	Tidewater	AAA	19	2	0	5	32.1	140	34	13	11	1	1	1	0	11	0	27	2	2	2	2	.500	0	0	3.06
1989	Tidewater	AAA	38	0	0	20	33.2	152	41	22	16	3	4	1	3	9	2	27	1	1	0	3	.000	0	5	4.28
1990	Tidewater	AAA	16	0	0	4	21.2	103	27	17	14	1	0	1	1	10	0	23	1	0	0	0	.000	0	1	5.82
	Greenville	AA	15	0	0	11	16.2	79	24	15	15	2	1	0	1	9	1	8	0	0	0	1	.000	0	1	8.10
1991	Jacksnville	AA	14	4	1	3	34.2	143	36	16	12	0	2	0	1	8	0	24	0	1	3	3	.500	1	0	3.12
	Calgary	AAA	17	0	0	6	31	127	25	11	9	3	1	0	0	8	0	22	1	0	2	0	1.000	0	1	2.61
1992	Calgary	AAA	30	0	0	17	53	231	57	31	25	4	3	1	2	24	4	31	1	1	3	5	.375	0	4	4.25
1992	Seattle	AL	14	0	0	2	12.1	50	10	5	4	1	1	0	0	7	2	4	2	0	0	1	.000	0	0	2.92

Kevin Bass

Bats: Both **Throws:** Right **Pos:** LF/RF   **Ht:** 6' 0" **Wt:** 180 **Born:** 05/12/59 **Age:** 34

			BATTING																BASERUNNING				PERCENTAGES		
Year	Team	Lg	G	AB	H	2B	3B	HR	(Hm	Rd)	TB	R	RBI	TBB	IBB	SO	HBP	SH	SF	SB	CS	SB%	GDP	Avg	OBP	SLG
1982	2 ML Teams		30	33	1	0	0	0	(0	0)	1	6	1	1	0	9	0	1	0	0	0	.00	0	.030	.059	.030
1983	Houston	NL	88	195	46	7	3	2	(2	0)	65	25	18	6	1	27	0	4	1	2	2	.50	2	.236	.257	.333
1984	Houston	NL	121	331	86	17	5	2	(1	1)	119	33	29	6	1	57	3	2	0	5	5	.50	2	.260	.279	.360
1985	Houston	NL	150	539	145	27	5	16	(9	7)	230	72	68	31	1	63	6	4	2	19	8	.70	10	.269	.315	.427
1986	Houston	NL	157	591	184	33	5	20	(5	15)	287	83	79	38	11	72	6	1	4	22	13	.63	15	.311	.357	.486
1987	Houston	NL	157	592	168	31	5	19	(10	9)	266	83	85	53	13	77	4	0	5	21	8	.72	15	.284	.344	.449
1988	Houston	NL	157	541	138	27	2	14	(5	9)	211	57	72	42	10	65	6	3	3	31	6	.84	16	.255	.314	.390
1989	Houston	NL	87	313	94	19	4	5	(2	3)	136	42	44	29	3	44	1	1	4	11	4	.73	2	.300	.357	.435
1990	San Francisco	NL	61	214	54	9	1	7	(3	4)	86	25	32	14	3	26	2	2	1	2	2	.50	5	.252	.303	.402
1991	San Francisco	NL	124	361	84	10	4	10	(5	5)	132	43	40	36	8	56	4	2	3	7	4	.64	12	.233	.307	.366
1992	2 ML Teams		135	402	108	23	5	9	(7	2)	168	40	39	23	3	70	1	1	3	14	9	.61	8	.269	.308	.418
1982	Milwaukee	AL	18	9	0	0	0	0	(0	0)	0	4	0	1	0	1	0	1	0	0	0	.00	0	.000	.100	.000
	Houston	NL	12	24	1	0	0	0	(0	0)	1	2	1	0	0	8	0	0	0	0	0	.00	0	.042	.042	.042
1992	San Francisco	NL	89	265	71	11	3	7	(5	2)	109	25	30	16	1	53	1	1	2	7	7	.50	6	.268	.310	.411
	New York	NL	46	137	37	12	2	2	(2	0)	59	15	9	7	2	17	0	0	1	7	2	.78	2	.270	.303	.431
	11 ML YEARS		1267	4112	1108	203	39	104	(49	55)	1701	509	507	279	54	566	33	21	26	134	61	.69	88	.269	.319	.414

Miguel Batista

Pitches: Right **Bats:** Right **Pos:** RP   **Ht:** 6' 0" **Wt:** 160 **Born:** 02/19/71 **Age:** 22

			HOW MUCH HE PITCHED						WHAT HE GAVE UP										THE RESULTS					
Year	Team	Lg	G	GS	CG	GF	IP	BFP	H	R	ER	HR	SH	SF	HB	TBB	IBB	SO	WP	Bk	W	L	Pct.	ShO	Sv	ERA
1990	Expos	R	9	6	0	1	40.1	167	31	16	9	0	1	2	1	19	0	22	1	1	4	3	.571	0	0	2.01
	Rockford	A	3	2	0	0	12.1	63	16	13	12	2	0	1	4	5	0	7	3	0	0	1	.000	0	0	8.76
1991	Rockford	A	23	23	2	0	133.2	592	126	74	60	1	6	8	6	57	0	90	12	2	11	5	.688	1	0	4.04
1992	Wst Plm Bch	A	24	24	1	0	135.1	585	130	69	57	3	4	4	6	54	1	92	9	4	7	7	.500	0	0	3.79
1992	Pittsburgh	NL	1	0	0	1	2	13	4	2	2	1	0	0	0	3	0	1	0	0	0	0	.000	0	0	9.00

Kim Batiste

Bats: Right **Throws:** Right **Pos:** SS   **Ht:** 6' 0" **Wt:** 175 **Born:** 03/15/68 **Age:** 25

			BATTING																BASERUNNING				PERCENTAGES		
Year	Team	Lg	G	AB	H	2B	3B	HR	(Hm	Rd)	TB	R	RBI	TBB	IBB	SO	HBP	SH	SF	SB	CS	SB%	GDP	Avg	OBP	SLG
1987	Utica	A	46	150	26	8	1	2	--	--	42	15	10	7	3	65	0	0	0	4	0	1.00	3	.173	.210	.280
1988	Spartanburg	A	122	430	107	19	6	6	--	--	156	51	52	14	1	101	1	5	1	16	9	.64	13	.249	.274	.363
1989	Clearwater	A	114	385	90	12	4	3	--	--	119	36	33	17	1	67	4	11	1	13	7	.65	7	.234	.273	.309

Year	Team	Lg	G	AB	H	2B	3B	HR	(Hm	Rd)	TB	R	RBI	TBB	IBB	SO	HBP	SH	SF	SB	CS	SB%	GDP	Avg	OBP	SLG
1990	Reading	AA	125	486	134	14	4	6	--	--	174	57	33	13	1	73	2	5	2	28	14	.67	11	.276	.296	.358
1991	Scranton-Wb	AAA	122	462	135	25	6	1	--	--	175	54	41	11	0	72	4	10	4	18	12	.60	5	.292	.312	.379
1992	Scranton/wb	AAA	71	269	70	12	6	2	--	--	100	30	29	7	1	42	1	2	0	6	5	.55	8	.260	.282	.372
1991	Philadelphia	NL	10	27	6	0	0	0	(0	0)	6	2	1	1	1	8	0	0	0	0	1	.00	0	.222	.250	.222
1992	Philadelphia	NL	44	136	28	4	0	1	(0	1)	35	9	10	4	1	18	0	2	3	0	0	.00	7	.206	.224	.257
	2 ML YEARS		54	163	34	4	0	1	(0	1)	41	11	11	5	2	26	0	2	3	0	1	.00	7	.209	.228	.252

Rod Beck

Pitches: Right **Bats:** Right **Pos:** RP   **Ht:** 6' 1" **Wt:** 215 **Born:** 08/03/68 **Age:** 24

			HOW MUCH HE PITCHED						WHAT HE GAVE UP												THE RESULTS					
Year	Team	Lg	G	GS	CG	GF	IP	BFP	H	R	ER	HR	SH	SF	HB	TBB	IBB	SO	WP	Bk	W	L	Pct.	ShO	Sv	ERA
1986	Medford	A	13	6	0	5	32.2	0	47	25	19	4	0	0	1	11	1	21	4	0	1	3	.250	0	1	5.23
1987	Medford	A	17	12	2	1	92	431	106	74	53	5	4	4	4	26	0	69	12	1	5	8	.385	0	0	5.18
1988	Clinton	A	28	23	5	1	177	706	177	68	59	11	4	1	0	27	2	123	3	5	12	7	.632	1	0	3.00
1989	San Jose	A	13	13	4	0	97.1	402	91	29	26	5	1	3	1	26	0	88	2	1	11	2	.846	0	0	2.40
	Shreveport	AA	16	14	4	0	99	416	108	45	39	6	2	2	3	16	3	74	3	2	7	3	.700	1	0	3.55
1990	Phoenix	AAA	12	12	2	0	76.2	345	100	51	42	8	2	4	2	18	1	43	6	0	4	7	.364	0	0	4.93
	Shreveport	AA	14	14	2	0	93	366	85	26	23	4	4	1	1	17	1	71	7	0	10	3	.769	1	0	2.23
1991	Phoenix	AAA	23	5	3	14	71.1	280	56	18	16	3	2	4	2	13	2	35	2	0	4	3	.571	0	6	2.02
1991	San Francisco	NL	31	0	0	10	52.1	214	53	22	22	4	4	2	1	13	2	38	0	0	1	1	.500	0	1	3.78
1992	San Francisco	NL	65	0	0	42	92	352	62	20	18	4	6	2	2	15	2	87	5	2	3	3	.500	0	17	1.76
	2 ML YEARS		96	0	0	52	144.1	566	115	42	40	8	10	4	3	28	4	125	5	2	4	4	.500	0	18	2.49

Tim Belcher

Pitches: Right **Bats:** Right **Pos:** SP   **Ht:** 6' 3" **Wt:** 220 **Born:** 10/19/61 **Age:** 31

			HOW MUCH HE PITCHED						WHAT HE GAVE UP												THE RESULTS					
Year	Team	Lg	G	GS	CG	GF	IP	BFP	H	R	ER	HR	SH	SF	HB	TBB	IBB	SO	WP	Bk	W	L	Pct.	ShO	Sv	ERA
1987	Los Angeles	NL	6	5	0	1	34	135	30	11	9	2	2	1	0	7	0	23	0	1	4	2	.667	0	0	2.38
1988	Los Angeles	NL	36	27	4	5	179.2	719	143	65	58	8	6	1	2	51	7	152	4	0	12	6	.667	1	4	2.91
1989	Los Angeles	NL	39	30	10	6	230	937	182	81	72	20	6	6	7	80	5	200	7	2	15	12	.556	8	1	2.82
1990	Los Angeles	NL	24	24	5	0	153	627	136	76	68	17	5	6	2	48	0	102	6	1	9	9	.500	2	0	4.00
1991	Los Angeles	NL	33	33	2	0	209.1	880	189	76	61	10	11	3	2	75	3	156	7	0	10	9	.526	1	0	2.62
1992	Cincinnati	NL	35	34	2	1	227.2	949	201	104	99	17	12	11	3	80	2	149	3	1	15	14	.517	1	0	3.91
	6 ML YEARS		173	153	23	13	1033.2	4247	881	413	367	74	42	28	16	341	17	782	27	5	65	52	.556	13	5	3.20

Stan Belinda

Pitches: Right **Bats:** Right **Pos:** RP   **Ht:** 6' 3" **Wt:** 187 **Born:** 08/06/66 **Age:** 26

			HOW MUCH HE PITCHED						WHAT HE GAVE UP												THE RESULTS					
Year	Team	Lg	G	GS	CG	GF	IP	BFP	H	R	ER	HR	SH	SF	HB	TBB	IBB	SO	WP	Bk	W	L	Pct.	ShO	Sv	ERA
1989	Pittsburgh	NL	8	0	0	2	10.1	46	13	8	7	0	0	0	0	2	0	10	1	0	0	1	.000	0	0	6.10
1990	Pittsburgh	NL	55	0	0	17	58.1	245	48	23	23	4	2	2	1	29	3	55	1	0	3	4	.429	0	8	3.55
1991	Pittsburgh	NL	60	0	0	37	78.1	318	50	30	30	10	4	3	4	35	4	71	2	0	7	5	.583	0	16	3.45
1992	Pittsburgh	NL	59	0	0	42	71.1	299	58	26	25	8	4	6	0	29	5	57	1	0	6	4	.600	0	18	3.15
	4 ML YEARS		182	0	0	98	218.1	908	169	87	85	22	10	11	5	95	12	193	5	0	16	14	.533	0	42	3.50

Derek Bell

Bats: Right **Throws:** Right **Pos:** LF/CF/RF   **Ht:** 6' 2" **Wt:** 200 **Born:** 12/11/68 **Age:** 24

			BATTING																	BASERUNNING				PERCENTAGES		
Year	Team	Lg	G	AB	H	2B	3B	HR	(Hm	Rd)	TB	R	RBI	TBB	IBB	SO	HBP	SH	SF	SB	CS	SB%	GDP	Avg	OBP	SLG
1987	St.Cathrnes	A	74	273	72	11	3	10	--	--	119	46	42	18	1	60	6	2	3	12	4	.75	5	.264	.320	.436
1988	Myrtle Bch	A	91	352	121	29	5	12	--	--	196	55	60	15	3	67	6	0	4	18	6	.75	9	.344	.377	.557
	Knoxville	AA	14	52	13	3	1	0	--	--	18	5	4	1	0	14	0	0	0	2	1	.67	1	.250	.264	.346
1989	Knoxville	AA	136	513	124	22	6	16	--	--	206	72	75	26	4	92	6	0	4	15	7	.68	6	.242	.284	.402
1990	Syracuse	AAA	109	402	105	13	5	7	--	--	149	57	56	23	0	75	3	0	6	21	7	.75	8	.261	.302	.371
1991	Syracuse	AAA	119	457	158	22	12	13	--	--	243	89	93	57	7	69	9	0	5	27	11	.71	16	.346	.424	.532
1992	Dunedin	A	7	25	6	2	0	0	--	--	8	7	4	4	0	4	0	0	1	3	0	1.00	1	.240	.333	.320
1991	Toronto	AL	18	28	4	0	0	0	(0	0)	4	5	1	6	0	5	1	0	0	3	2	.60	0	.143	.314	.143
1992	Toronto	AL	61	161	39	6	3	2	(2	0)	57	23	15	15	1	34	5	2	1	7	2	.78	6	.242	.324	.354
	2 ML YEARS		79	189	43	6	3	2	(2	0)	61	28	16	21	1	39	6	2	1	10	4	.71	6	.228	.323	.323

Eric Bell

Pitches: Left **Bats:** Left **Pos:** RP   **Ht:** 6' 0" **Wt:** 165 **Born:** 10/27/63 **Age:** 29

			HOW MUCH HE PITCHED						WHAT HE GAVE UP												THE RESULTS					
Year	Team	Lg	G	GS	CG	GF	IP	BFP	H	R	ER	HR	SH	SF	HB	TBB	IBB	SO	WP	Bk	W	L	Pct.	ShO	Sv	ERA
1985	Baltimore	AL	4	0	0	3	5.2	24	4	3	3	1	0	0	0	4	0	4	0	0	0	0	.000	0	0	4.76
1986	Baltimore	AL	4	4	0	0	23.1	105	23	14	13	4	1	1	0	14	0	18	0	0	1	2	.333	0	0	5.01

Year	Team	Lg	G	AB	H		IP			R	ER					BB		SO			W	L	Pct			ERA
1987	Baltimore	AL	33	29	2	1	165	729	174	113	100	32	4	2	2	78	0	111	11	1	10	13	.435	0	0	5.45
1991	Cleveland	AL	10	0	0	3	18	61	5	2	1	0	0	0	1	5	0	7	0	0	4	0	1.000	0	0	0.50
1992	Cleveland	AL	7	1	0	2	15.1	75	22	13	13	1	1	1	1	9	0	10	1	0	0	2	.000	0	0	7.63
	5 ML YEARS		58	34	2	9	227.1	994	228	145	130	38	6	4	4	110	0	150	12	1	15	17	.469	0	0	5.15

George Bell

Bats: Right **Throws:** Right **Pos:** DH/LF **Ht:** 6' 1" **Wt:** 202 **Born:** 10/21/59 **Age:** 33

						BATTING															BASERUNNING				PERCENTAGES		
Year	Team	Lg	G	AB	H	2B	3B	HR	(Hm	Rd)	TB	R	RBI	TBB	IBB	SO	HBP	SH	SF	SB	CS	SB%	GDP	Avg	OBP	SLG
1981	Toronto	AL	60	163	38	2	1	5	(3	2)	57	19	12	5	1	27	0	0	0	3	2	.60	1	.233	.256	.350
1983	Toronto	AL	39	112	30	5	4	2	(1	1)	49	5	17	4	1	17	2	0	0	1	1	.50	4	.268	.305	.438
1984	Toronto	AL	159	606	177	39	4	26	(12	14)	302	85	87	24	2	86	8	0	3	11	2	.85	14	.292	.326	.498
1985	Toronto	AL	157	607	167	28	6	28	(10	18)	291	87	95	43	6	90	8	0	8	21	6	.78	8	.275	.327	.479
1986	Toronto	AL	159	641	198	38	6	31	(15	16)	341	101	108	41	3	62	2	0	6	7	8	.47	15	.309	.349	.532
1987	Toronto	AL	156	610	188	32	4	47	(19	28)	369	111	134	39	9	75	7	0	9	5	1	.83	17	.308	.352	.605
1988	Toronto	AL	156	614	165	27	5	24	(9	15)	274	78	97	34	5	66	1	0	8	4	2	.67	21	.269	.304	.446
1989	Toronto	AL	153	613	182	41	2	18	(8	10)	281	88	104	33	3	60	4	0	14	4	3	.57	18	.297	.330	.458
1990	Toronto	AL	142	562	149	25	0	21	(11	10)	237	67	86	32	7	80	3	0	11	3	2	.60	14	.265	.303	.422
1991	Chicago	NL	149	558	159	27	0	25	(9	16)	261	63	86	32	6	62	4	0	9	2	6	.25	10	.285	.323	.468
1992	Chicago	AL	155	627	160	27	0	25	(16	9)	262	74	112	31	8	97	6	0	6	5	2	.71	29	.255	.294	.418
	11 ML YEARS		1485	5713	1613	291	32	252	(113	139)	2724	778	938	318	51	722	45	0	74	66	35	.65	151	.282	.321	.477

Jay Bell

Bats: Right **Throws:** Right **Pos:** SS **Ht:** 6' 0" **Wt:** 185 **Born:** 12/11/65 **Age:** 27

						BATTING															BASERUNNING				PERCENTAGES		
Year	Team	Lg	G	AB	H	2B	3B	HR	(Hm	Rd)	TB	R	RBI	TBB	IBB	SO	HBP	SH	SF	SB	CS	SB%	GDP	Avg	OBP	SLG
1986	Cleveland	AL	5	14	5	2	0	1	(0	1)	10	3	4	2	0	3	0	0	0	0	0	.00	0	.357	.438	.714
1987	Cleveland	AL	38	125	27	9	1	2	(1	1)	44	14	13	8	0	31	1	3	0	2	0	1.00	0	.216	.269	.352
1988	Cleveland	AL	73	211	46	5	1	2	(2	0)	59	23	21	21	0	53	1	1	2	4	2	.67	3	.218	.289	.280
1989	Pittsburgh	NL	78	271	70	13	3	2	(1	1)	95	33	27	19	0	47	1	10	2	5	3	.63	9	.258	.307	.351
1990	Pittsburgh	NL	159	583	148	28	7	7	(1	6)	211	93	52	65	0	109	3	39	6	10	6	.63	14	.254	.329	.362
1991	Pittsburgh	NL	157	608	164	32	8	16	(7	9)	260	96	67	52	1	99	4	30	3	10	6	.63	15	.270	.330	.428
1992	Pittsburgh	NL	159	632	167	36	6	9	(5	4)	242	87	55	55	0	103	4	19	2	7	5	.58	12	.264	.326	.383
	7 ML YEARS		669	2444	627	125	26	39	(17	22)	921	349	239	222	1	445	14	102	15	38	22	.63	53	.257	.320	.377

Juan Bell

Bats: Both **Throws:** Right **Pos:** SS **Ht:** 5'11" **Wt:** 176 **Born:** 03/29/68 **Age:** 25

						BATTING															BASERUNNING				PERCENTAGES		
Year	Team	Lg	G	AB	H	2B	3B	HR	(Hm	Rd)	TB	R	RBI	TBB	IBB	SO	HBP	SH	SF	SB	CS	SB%	GDP	Avg	OBP	SLG
1989	Baltimore	AL	8	4	0	0	0	0	(0	0)	0	2	0	0	0	1	0	0	0	1	0	1.00	0	.000	.000	.000
1990	Baltimore	AL	5	2	0	0	0	0	(0	0)	0	1	0	0	0	0	0	0	0	0	0	.00	0	.000	.000	.000
1991	Baltimore	AL	100	209	36	9	2	1	(0	1)	52	26	15	8	0	51	0	4	2	0	0	.00	1	.172	.201	.249
1992	Philadelphia	NL	46	147	30	3	1	1	(1	0)	38	12	8	18	5	29	1	0	2	5	0	1.00	1	.204	.292	.259
	4 ML YEARS		159	362	66	12	3	2	(1	1)	90	41	23	26	5	82	1	4	4	6	0	1.00	2	.182	.237	.249

Albert Belle

Bats: Right **Throws:** Right **Pos:** DH/LF **Ht:** 6' 2" **Wt:** 200 **Born:** 08/25/66 **Age:** 26

						BATTING															BASERUNNING				PERCENTAGES		
Year	Team	Lg	G	AB	H	2B	3B	HR	(Hm	Rd)	TB	R	RBI	TBB	IBB	SO	HBP	SH	SF	SB	CS	SB%	GDP	Avg	OBP	SLG
1989	Cleveland	AL	62	218	49	8	4	7	(3	4)	86	22	37	12	0	55	2	0	2	2	2	.50	4	.225	.269	.394
1990	Cleveland	AL	9	23	4	0	0	1	(1	0)	7	1	3	1	0	6	0	1	0	0	0	.00	1	.174	.208	.304
1991	Cleveland	AL	123	461	130	31	2	28	(8	20)	249	60	95	25	2	99	5	0	5	3	1	.75	24	.282	.323	.540
1992	Cleveland	AL	153	585	152	23	1	34	(15	19)	279	81	112	52	5	128	4	1	8	8	2	.80	18	.260	.320	.477
	4 ML YEARS		347	1287	335	62	7	70	(27	43)	621	164	247	90	7	288	11	2	15	13	5	.72	47	.260	.311	.483

Rafael Belliard

Bats: Right **Throws:** Right **Pos:** SS **Ht:** 5' 6" **Wt:** 160 **Born:** 10/24/61 **Age:** 31

						BATTING															BASERUNNING				PERCENTAGES		
Year	Team	Lg	G	AB	H	2B	3B	HR	(Hm	Rd)	TB	R	RBI	TBB	IBB	SO	HBP	SH	SF	SB	CS	SB%	GDP	Avg	OBP	SLG
1982	Pittsburgh	NL	9	2	1	0	0	0	(0	0)	1	3	0	0	0	0	0	0	0	1	0	1.00	0	.500	.500	.500
1983	Pittsburgh	NL	4	1	0	0	0	0	(0	0)	0	1	0	0	1	0	0	0	0	0	0	.00	0	.000	.000	.000
1984	Pittsburgh	NL	20	22	5	0	0	0	(0	0)	5	3	0	0	1	0	0	0	0	4	1	.80	0	.227	.227	.227
1985	Pittsburgh	NL	17	20	4	0	0	0	(0	0)	4	1	1	0	5	0	0	0	0	0	0	.00	0	.200	.200	.200
1986	Pittsburgh	NL	117	309	72	5	2	0	(0	0)	81	33	31	26	6	54	3	11	1	12	2	.86	8	.233	.298	.262
1987	Pittsburgh	NL	81	203	42	4	3	1	(0	1)	55	26	15	20	6	25	3	2	1	5	1	.83	4	.207	.286	.271
1988	Pittsburgh	NL	122	286	61	0	4	0	(0	0)	69	28	11	26	3	47	4	5	0	7	1	.88	10	.213	.288	.241

Year	Team	Lg	G	AB	H	2B	3B	HR	(Hm	Rd)	TB	R	RBI	TBB	IBB	SO	HBP	SH	SF	SB	CS	SB%	GDP	Avg	OBP	SLG
1989	Pittsburgh	NL	67	154	33	4	0	0	(0	0)	37	10	8	8	2	22	0	3	0	5	2	.71	1	.214	.253	.240
1990	Pittsburgh	NL	47	54	11	3	0	0	(0	0)	14	10	6	5	0	13	1	1	0	1	2	.33	2	.204	.283	.259
1991	Atlanta	NL	149	353	88	9	2	0	(0	0)	101	36	27	22	2	63	2	7	1	3	1	.75	4	.249	.296	.286
1992	Atlanta	NL	144	285	60	6	1	0	(0	0)	68	20	14	14	4	43	3	13	0	0	1	.00	6	.211	.255	.239
	11 ML YEARS		777	1689	377	31	12	1	(0	1)	435	171	113	121	23	274	16	42	3	38	11	.78	35	.223	.281	.258

Esteban Beltre

Bats: Right **Throws:** Right **Pos:** SS **Ht:** 5'10" **Wt:** 155 **Born:** 12/26/67 **Age:** 25

							BATTING												BASERUNNING				PERCENTAGES		
Year	Team	Lg	G	AB	H	2B	3B	HR	(Hm | Rd)	TB	R	RBI	TBB	IBB	SO	HBP	SH	SF	SB	CS	SB%	GDP	Avg	OBP	SLG
1984	Calgary	R	18	20	4	0	0	0	--	--	4	1	2	2	0	8	0	0	0	1	0	1.00	1	.200	.273	.200
1985	Utica	A	72	241	48	6	2	0	--	--	58	19	22	18	0	58	3	8	1	8	7	.53	4	.199	.262	.241
1986	Wst Plm Bch	A	97	285	69	11	1	1	--	--	85	24	20	16	2	59	0	4	1	4	2	.67	9	.242	.281	.298
1987	Jacksnville	AA	142	491	104	15	4	4	--	--	139	55	34	40	0	98	3	10	0	9	8	.53	7	.212	.275	.283
1988	Jacksnville	AA	35	113	17	2	0	0	--	--	19	5	6	3	0	28	0	0	0	1	0	1.00	7	.150	.172	.168
	Wst Plm Bch	A	69	226	63	5	6	0	--	--	80	23	15	11	0	38	1	11	1	4	0	1.00	4	.279	.314	.354
1989	Rockford	A	104	375	80	15	3	2	--	--	107	42	33	33	1	83	0	5	1	9	3	.75	8	.213	.276	.285
1990	Indianapols	AAA	133	407	92	11	2	1	--	--	110	33	37	32	1	77	2	5	4	8	2	.80	9	.226	.283	.270
1991	Denver	AAA	27	78	14	1	3	0	--	--	21	11	9	9	0	16	0	0	0	3	2	.60	5	.179	.264	.269
	Vancouver	AAA	88	347	94	11	3	0	--	--	111	48	30	23	0	61	0	7	1	8	7	.53	4	.271	.315	.320
1992	Vancouver	AAA	40	161	43	5	2	0	--	--	52	17	16	8	1	27	1	5	1	4	4	.50	3	.267	.304	.323
1991	Chicago	AL	8	6	1	0	0	0	(0 | 0)	1	0	0	1	0	1	0	0	0	1	0	1.00	0	.167	.286	.167
1992	Chicago	AL	49	110	21	2	0	1	(1 | 0)	26	21	10	3	0	18	0	2	1	1	0	1.00	3	.191	.211	.236
	2 ML YEARS		57	116	22	2	0	1	(1 | 0)	27	21	10	4	0	19	0	2	1	2	0	1.00	3	.190	.215	.233

Freddie Benavides

Bats: Right **Throws:** Right **Pos:** 2B/SS **Ht:** 6'2" **Wt:** 185 **Born:** 04/07/66 **Age:** 27

							BATTING												BASERUNNING				PERCENTAGES		
Year	Team	Lg	G	AB	H	2B	3B	HR	(Hm | Rd)	TB	R	RBI	TBB	IBB	SO	HBP	SH	SF	SB	CS	SB%	GDP	Avg	OBP	SLG
1987	Cedar Rapds	A	5	15	2	1	0	0	--	--	3	2	0	0	0	7	0	0	0	0	1	.00	1	.133	.133	.200
1988	Cedar Rapds	A	88	314	70	9	2	1	--	--	86	38	32	35	3	75	2	4	4	18	7	.72	7	.223	.301	.274
1989	Chattanooga	AA	88	284	71	14	3	0	--	--	91	25	27	22	0	46	2	2	3	1	4	.20	2	.250	.305	.320
	Nashville	AAA	31	94	16	4	0	1	--	--	23	9	12	6	0	24	0	1	0	0	0	.00	1	.170	.220	.245
1990	Chattanooga	AA	55	197	51	10	1	1	--	--	66	20	28	11	0	25	2	3	2	4	2	.67	4	.259	.302	.335
	Nashville	AAA	77	266	56	7	3	2	--	--	75	30	20	12	3	50	3	4	1	3	1	.75	4	.211	.252	.282
1991	Nashville	AAA	94	331	80	8	0	0	--	--	88	24	21	16	3	55	0	3	0	7	7	.50	10	.242	.277	.266
1991	Cincinnati	NL	24	63	18	1	0	0	(0 | 0)	19	11	3	1	1	15	1	1	1	1	0	1.00	1	.286	.303	.302
1992	Cincinnati	NL	74	173	40	10	1	1	(1 | 0)	55	14	17	10	4	34	1	2	0	0	1	.00	3	.231	.277	.318
	2 ML YEARS		98	236	58	11	1	1	(1 | 0)	74	25	20	11	5	49	2	3	1	1	1	.50	4	.246	.284	.314

Andy Benes

Pitches: Right **Bats:** Right **Pos:** SP **Ht:** 6'6" **Wt:** 240 **Born:** 08/20/67 **Age:** 25

							HOW MUCH HE PITCHED				WHAT HE GAVE UP									THE RESULTS					
Year	Team	Lg	G	GS	CG	GF	IP	BFP	H	R	ER	HR	SH	SF	HB	TBB	IBB	SO	WP	Bk	W	L	Pct.	ShO	Sv	ERA
1989	San Diego	NL	10	10	0	0	66.2	280	51	28	26	7	6	2	1	31	0	66	0	3	6	3	.667	0	0	3.51
1990	San Diego	NL	32	31	2	1	192.1	811	177	87	77	18	5	6	1	69	5	140	2	5	10	11	.476	2	0	3.60
1991	San Diego	NL	33	33	4	0	223	908	194	76	75	23	5	4	4	59	7	167	3	4	15	11	.577	1	0	3.03
1992	San Diego	NL	34	34	2	0	231.1	961	230	90	86	14	19	6	5	61	6	169	1	1	13	14	.481	2	0	3.35
	4 ML YEARS		109	108	8	1	713.1	2960	652	281	264	62	35	18	11	220	18	542	6	13	44	39	.530	3	0	3.33

Mike Benjamin

Bats: Right **Throws:** Right **Pos:** SS **Ht:** 6'2" **Wt:** 175 **Born:** 11/22/65 **Age:** 27

							BATTING												BASERUNNING				PERCENTAGES		
Year	Team	Lg	G	AB	H	2B	3B	HR	(Hm | Rd)	TB	R	RBI	TBB	IBB	SO	HBP	SH	SF	SB	CS	SB%	GDP	Avg	OBP	SLG
1989	San Francisco	NL	14	6	1	0	0	0	(0 | 0)	1	6	0	0	0	1	0	0	0	0	0	.00	0	.167	.167	.167
1990	San Francisco	NL	22	56	12	3	1	2	(2 | 0)	23	7	3	3	1	10	0	0	0	1	0	1.00	2	.214	.254	.411
1991	San Francisco	NL	54	106	13	3	0	2	(0 | 2)	22	12	8	7	2	26	2	3	2	3	0	1.00	1	.123	.188	.208
1992	San Francisco	NL	40	75	13	2	1	1	(0 | 1)	20	4	3	4	1	15	0	3	0	1	0	1.00	1	.173	.215	.267
	4 ML YEARS		130	243	39	8	2	5	(2 | 3)	66	29	14	14	4	52	2	6	2	5	0	1.00	4	.160	.211	.272

Todd Benzinger

Bats: Both **Throws:** Right **Pos:** 1B/LF/RF **Ht:** 6'1" **Wt:** 195 **Born:** 02/11/63 **Age:** 30

							BATTING												BASERUNNING				PERCENTAGES		
Year	Team	Lg	G	AB	H	2B	3B	HR	(Hm | Rd)	TB	R	RBI	TBB	IBB	SO	HBP	SH	SF	SB	CS	SB%	GDP	Avg	OBP	SLG
1987	Boston	AL	73	223	62	11	1	8	(5 | 3)	99	36	43	22	3	41	2	3	3	5	4	.56	5	.278	.344	.444
1988	Boston	AL	120	405	103	28	1	13	(6 | 7)	172	47	70	22	4	80	1	6	2	2	3	.40	8	.254	.293	.425

18

Year	Team	Lg	G	AB	H	2B	3B	HR	(Hm	Rd)	TB	R	RBI	TBB	IBB	SO	HBP	SH	SF	SB	CS	SB%	GDP	Avg	OBP	SLG
1989	Cincinnati	NL	161	**628**	154	28	3	17	(6	11)	239	79	76	44	13	120	2	4	8	3	7	.30	5	.245	.293	.381
1990	Cincinnati	NL	118	376	95	14	2	5	(4	1)	128	35	46	19	4	69	4	2	7	3	4	.43	3	.253	.291	.340
1991	2 ML Teams		129	416	109	18	5	3	(2	1)	146	36	51	27	4	66	3	2	3	4	6	.40	7	.262	.310	.351
1992	Los Angeles	NL	121	293	70	16	2	4	(1	3)	102	24	31	15	1	54	0	0	5	2	4	.33	6	.239	.272	.348
1991	Cincinnati	NL	51	123	23	3	2	1	(1	0)	33	7	11	10	2	20	0	1	2	2	0	1.00	2	.187	.244	.268
	Kansas City	AL	78	293	86	15	3	2	(1	1)	113	29	40	17	2	46	3	1	1	2	6	.25	5	.294	.338	.386
	6 ML YEARS		722	2341	593	115	14	50	(24	26)	886	257	317	149	29	430	12	17	28	19	28	.40	34	.253	.298	.378

Juan Berenguer

Pitches: Right **Bats:** Right **Pos:** RP **Ht:** 5'11" **Wt:** 233 **Born:** 11/30/54 **Age:** 38

| | | | HOW MUCH HE PITCHED | | | | | | WHAT HE GAVE UP | | | | | | | | | | | THE RESULTS | | | | | |
Year	Team	Lg	G	GS	CG	GF	IP	BFP	H	R	ER	HR	SH	SF	HB	TBB	IBB	SO	WP	Bk	W	L	Pct.	ShO	Sv	ERA
1978	New York	NL	5	3	0	1	13	65	17	12	12	1	0	1	1	11	0	8	0	0	0	2	.000	0	0	8.31
1979	New York	NL	5	5	0	0	31	126	28	13	10	2	1	1	1	12	0	25	0	2	1	1	.500	0	0	2.90
1980	New York	NL	6	0	0	4	9	46	9	9	6	1	0	0	0	10	2	7	0	0	0	1	.000	0	0	6.00
1981	2 ML Teams		20	14	1	4	91	405	84	62	53	11	2	7	5	51	1	49	2	0	2	13	.133	0	0	5.24
1982	Detroit	AL	2	1	0	0	6.2	34	5	5	5	0	0	0	0	9	1	8	0	0	0	0	.000	0	0	6.75
1983	Detroit	AL	37	19	2	7	157.2	650	110	58	55	19	1	2	6	71	3	129	3	1	9	5	.643	1	1	3.14
1984	Detroit	AL	31	27	2	0	168.1	720	146	75	65	14	2	6	5	79	2	118	7	2	11	10	.524	1	0	3.48
1985	Detroit	AL	31	13	0	9	95	424	96	67	59	12	1	4	1	48	3	82	4	1	5	6	.455	0	0	5.59
1986	San Francisco	NL	46	4	0	17	73.1	314	64	23	22	4	2	1	2	44	3	72	4	2	2	3	.400	0	4	2.70
1987	Minnesota	AL	47	6	0	13	112	473	100	51	49	10	2	4	0	47	7	110	6	0	8	1	.889	0	4	3.94
1988	Minnesota	AL	57	1	0	27	100	428	74	44	44	7	5	4	1	61	7	99	3	5	8	4	.667	0	2	3.96
1989	Minnesota	AL	56	0	0	17	106	452	96	44	41	11	7	5	2	47	0	93	5	3	9	3	.750	0	3	3.48
1990	Minnesota	AL	51	0	0	13	100.1	434	85	43	38	9	5	2	2	58	4	77	5	0	8	5	.615	0	0	3.41
1991	Atlanta	NL	49	0	0	35	64.1	255	43	18	16	5	2	2	3	20	2	53	0	0	0	3	.000	0	17	2.24
1992	2 ML Teams		47	2	0	10	78	343	77	52	47	10	2	3	2	36	7	45	4	3	4	5	.444	0	1	5.42
1981	Kansas City	AL	8	3	0	4	20	97	22	21	19	4	0	3	2	16	0	20	1	0	0	4	.000	0	0	8.55
	Toronto	AL	12	11	1	0	71	308	62	41	34	7	2	4	3	35	1	29	1	0	2	9	.182	0	0	4.31
1992	Atlanta	NL	28	0	0	8	33.1	148	35	22	19	7	1	0	1	16	4	19	2	0	3	1	.750	0	1	5.13
	Kansas City	AL	19	2	0	2	44.2	195	42	30	28	3	1	3	1	20	3	26	2	1	1	4	.200	0	0	5.64
	15 ML YEARS		490	95	5	157	1205.2	5169	1034	576	522	116	32	42	31	604	42	975	43	19	67	62	.519	2	32	3.90

Dave Bergman

Bats: Left **Throws:** Left **Pos:** 1B/DH **Ht:** 6' 2" **Wt:** 195 **Born:** 06/06/53 **Age:** 40

| | | | BATTING | | | | | | | | | | | | | | | | | BASERUNNING | | | | PERCENTAGES | | |
Year	Team	Lg	G	AB	H	2B	3B	HR	(Hm	Rd)	TB	R	RBI	TBB	IBB	SO	HBP	SH	SF	SB	CS	SB%	GDP	Avg	OBP	SLG
1975	New York	AL	7	17	0	0	0	0	(0	0)	0	0	0	2	0	4	0	0	0	0	0	.00	0	.000	.105	.000
1977	New York	NL	5	4	1	0	0	0	(0	0)	1	1	1	0	0	0	0	0	1	0	0	.00	0	.250	.200	.250
1978	Houston	NL	104	186	43	5	1	0	(0	0)	50	15	12	39	9	32	0	1	2	2	0	1.00	5	.231	.361	.269
1979	Houston	NL	13	15	6	0	0	1	(0	1)	9	4	2	0	0	3	0	0	0	0	0	.00	0	.400	.400	.600
1980	Houston	NL	90	78	20	6	1	0	(0	0)	28	12	3	10	2	10	0	3	0	1	0	1.00	1	.256	.341	.359
1981	2 ML Teams		69	151	38	9	0	4	(1	3)	59	17	14	19	3	18	0	2	1	2	0	1.00	4	.252	.333	.391
1982	San Francisco	NL	100	121	33	3	1	4	(2	2)	50	22	14	18	3	11	0	0	1	3	0	1.00	1	.273	.364	.413
1983	San Francisco	NL	90	140	40	4	1	6	(3	3)	64	16	24	24	2	21	1	2	0	2	1	.67	5	.286	.394	.457
1984	Detroit	AL	120	271	74	8	5	7	(4	3)	113	42	44	33	2	40	3	3	6	3	4	.43	4	.273	.351	.417
1985	Detroit	AL	69	140	25	2	0	3	(2	1)	36	8	7	14	0	15	0	1	2	0	0	.00	6	.179	.250	.257
1986	Detroit	AL	65	130	30	6	1	1	(0	1)	41	14	9	21	0	16	0	0	0	0	0	.00	3	.231	.338	.315
1987	Detroit	AL	91	172	47	7	3	6	(4	2)	78	25	22	30	4	23	1	1	3	0	1	.00	1	.273	.379	.453
1988	Detroit	AL	116	289	85	14	0	5	(4	1)	114	37	35	38	2	34	0	2	4	2	0	.00	7	.294	.372	.394
1989	Detroit	AL	137	385	103	13	1	7	(6	1)	139	38	37	44	3	44	2	4	1	1	3	.25	3	.268	.345	.361
1990	Detroit	AL	100	205	57	10	1	2	(1	1)	75	21	26	33	3	17	0	1	2	3	2	.60	7	.278	.375	.366
1991	Detroit	AL	86	194	46	10	1	7	(2	5)	79	23	29	35	2	40	0	0	2	1	1	.50	2	.237	.351	.407
1992	Detroit	AL	87	181	42	3	0	1	(1	0)	48	17	10	20	1	19	0	1	2	1	0	1.00	4	.232	.305	.265
1981	Houston	NL	6	6	1	0	0	1	(0	1)	4	1	1	0	0	0	0	0	0	0	0	.00	0	.167	.167	.667
	San Francisco	NL	63	145	37	9	0	3	(1	2)	55	16	13	19	3	18	0	2	1	2	0	1.00	4	.255	.339	.379
	17 ML YEARS		1349	2679	690	100	16	54	(30	24)	984	312	289	380	36	347	7	21	27	19	14	.58	55	.258	.348	.367

Geronimo Berroa

Bats: Right **Throws:** Right **Pos:** LF **Ht:** 6' 0" **Wt:** 165 **Born:** 03/18/65 **Age:** 28

| | | | BATTING | | | | | | | | | | | | | | | | | BASERUNNING | | | | PERCENTAGES | | |
Year	Team	Lg	G	AB	H	2B	3B	HR	(Hm	Rd)	TB	R	RBI	TBB	IBB	SO	HBP	SH	SF	SB	CS	SB%	GDP	Avg	OBP	SLG
1989	Atlanta	NL	81	136	36	4	0	2	(1	1)	46	7	9	7	1	32	0	0	0	0	1	.00	2	.265	.301	.338
1990	Atlanta	NL	7	4	0	0	0	0	(0	0)	0	0	0	1	1	1	0	0	0	0	0	.00	0	.000	.200	.000
1992	Cincinnati	NL	13	15	4	1	0	0	(0	0)	5	2	0	2	0	1	1	0	0	0	1	.00	0	.267	.389	.333
	3 ML YEARS		101	155	40	5	0	2	(1	1)	51	9	9	10	2	34	1	0	0	0	2	.00	3	.258	.307	.329

Sean Berry

Bats: Right **Throws:** Right **Pos:** 3B **Ht:** 5'11" **Wt:** 210 **Born:** 03/22/66 **Age:** 27

Year	Team	Lg	G	AB	H	2B	3B	HR	(Hm	Rd)	TB	R	RBI	TBB	IBB	SO	HBP	SH	SF	SB	CS	SB%	GDP	Avg	OBP	SLG
1986	Eugene	A	65	238	76	20	2	5	--	--	115	53	44	44	0	73	5	1	2	10	1	.91	2	.319	.433	.483
1987	Ft. Myers	A	66	205	52	7	2	2	--	--	69	26	30	43	2	65	3	1	1	4	4	.50	1	.254	.389	.337
1988	Baseball Cy	A	94	304	71	6	4	4	--	--	97	34	30	31	1	62	2	3	3	24	11	.69	3	.234	.306	.319
1989	Baseball Cy	A	116	399	106	19	7	4	--	--	151	67	44	44	1	68	6	5	5	37	11	.77	6	.266	.344	.378
1990	Memphis	AA	135	487	142	25	4	14	--	--	217	73	77	44	1	89	5	7	5	18	9	.67	10	.292	.353	.446
1991	Omaha	AAA	103	368	97	21	9	11	--	--	169	62	54	48	2	70	3	0	5	8	6	.57	8	.264	.349	.459
1992	Omaha	AAA	122	439	126	22	2	21	--	--	215	61	77	39	1	87	7	2	6	6	8	.43	8	.287	.350	.490
1990	Kansas City	AL	8	23	5	1	1	0	(0	0)	8	2	4	2	0	5	0	0	0	0	0	.00	0	.217	.280	.348
1991	Kansas City	AL	31	60	8	3	0	0	(0	0)	11	5	1	5	0	23	1	0	0	0	0	.00	1	.133	.212	.183
1992	Montreal	NL	24	57	19	1	0	1	(0	1)	23	5	4	1	0	11	0	0	0	2	1	.67	1	.333	.345	.404
	3 ML YEARS		63	140	32	5	1	1	(0	1)	42	12	9	8	0	39	1	0	0	2	1	.67	2	.229	.275	.300

Damon Berryhill

Bats: Both **Throws:** Right **Pos:** C **Ht:** 6'0" **Wt:** 205 **Born:** 12/03/63 **Age:** 29

Year	Team	Lg	G	AB	H	2B	3B	HR	(Hm	Rd)	TB	R	RBI	TBB	IBB	SO	HBP	SH	SF	SB	CS	SB%	GDP	Avg	OBP	SLG
1987	Chicago	NL	12	28	5	1	0	0	(0	0)	6	2	1	3	0	5	0	0	0	0	1	.00	1	.179	.258	.214
1988	Chicago	NL	95	309	80	19	1	7	(5	2)	122	19	38	17	5	56	0	3	3	1	0	1.00	11	.259	.295	.395
1989	Chicago	NL	91	334	86	13	0	5	(2	3)	114	37	41	16	4	54	2	4	5	1	0	1.00	13	.257	.291	.341
1990	Chicago	NL	17	53	10	4	0	1	(0	1)	17	6	9	5	1	14	0	0	1	0	0	.00	3	.189	.254	.321
1991	2 ML Teams		63	160	30	7	0	5	(3	2)	52	13	14	11	1	42	1	0	1	1	2	.33	2	.188	.243	.325
1992	Atlanta	NL	101	307	70	16	1	10	(6	4)	118	21	43	17	4	67	1	0	3	0	2	.00	4	.228	.268	.384
1991	Chicago	NL	62	159	30	7	0	5	(3	2)	52	13	14	11	1	41	1	0	1	1	2	.33	2	.189	.244	.327
	Atlanta	NL	1	1	0	0	0	0	(0	0)	0	0	0	0	0	1	0	0	0	0	0	.00	0	.000	.000	.000
	6 ML YEARS		379	1191	281	60	2	28	(17	11)	429	98	146	69	15	238	4	7	13	3	5	.38	34	.236	.277	.360

Dante Bichette

Bats: Right **Throws:** Right **Pos:** RF **Ht:** 6'3" **Wt:** 225 **Born:** 11/18/63 **Age:** 29

Year	Team	Lg	G	AB	H	2B	3B	HR	(Hm	Rd)	TB	R	RBI	TBB	IBB	SO	HBP	SH	SF	SB	CS	SB%	GDP	Avg	OBP	SLG
1988	California	AL	21	46	12	2	0	0	(0	0)	14	1	8	0	0	7	0	0	4	0	0	.00	0	.261	.240	.304
1989	California	AL	48	138	29	7	0	3	(2	1)	45	13	15	6	0	24	0	0	2	3	0	1.00	3	.210	.240	.326
1990	California	AL	109	349	89	15	1	15	(8	7)	151	40	53	16	1	79	3	1	2	5	2	.71	9	.255	.292	.433
1991	Milwaukee	AL	134	445	106	18	3	15	(6	9)	175	53	59	22	4	107	1	1	6	14	8	.64	9	.238	.272	.393
1992	Milwaukee	AL	112	387	111	27	2	5	(3	2)	157	37	41	16	3	74	3	2	3	18	7	.72	13	.287	.318	.406
	5 ML YEARS		424	1365	347	69	6	38	(19	19)	542	144	176	60	8	291	7	4	17	40	17	.70	34	.254	.286	.397

Mike Bielecki

Pitches: Right **Bats:** Right **Pos:** SP/RP **Ht:** 6'3" **Wt:** 195 **Born:** 07/31/59 **Age:** 33

Year	Team	Lg	G	GS	CG	GF	IP	BFP	H	R	ER	HR	SH	SF	HB	TBB	IBB	SO	WP	Bk	W	L	Pct.	ShO	Sv	ERA
1984	Pittsburgh	NL	4	0	0	0	4.1	17	4	0	0	0	1	0	0	0	0	1	0	0	0	0	.000	0	0	0.00
1985	Pittsburgh	NL	12	7	0	1	45.2	211	45	26	23	5	4	0	1	31	1	22	1	1	2	3	.400	0	0	4.53
1986	Pittsburgh	NL	31	27	0	0	148.2	667	149	87	77	10	7	6	2	83	3	83	7	5	6	11	.353	0	0	4.66
1987	Pittsburgh	NL	8	8	2	0	45.2	192	43	25	24	6	5	2	1	12	0	25	3	0	2	3	.400	0	0	4.73
1988	Chicago	NL	19	5	0	7	48.1	215	55	22	18	4	1	4	0	16	1	33	3	3	2	2	.500	0	0	3.35
1989	Chicago	NL	33	33	4	0	212.1	882	187	82	74	16	9	3	0	81	8	147	9	4	18	7	.720	3	0	3.14
1990	Chicago	NL	36	29	0	6	168	749	188	101	92	13	16	4	5	70	11	103	11	0	8	11	.421	0	1	4.93
1991	2 ML Teams		41	25	0	9	173.2	727	171	91	86	18	10	6	2	56	6	75	6	0	13	11	.542	0	0	4.46
1992	Atlanta	NL	19	14	1	0	80.2	336	77	27	23	2	3	2	1	27	1	62	4	0	2	4	.333	1	0	2.57
1991	Chicago	NL	39	25	0	8	172	718	169	91	86	18	10	6	2	54	6	72	6	0	13	11	.542	0	0	4.50
	Atlanta	NL	2	0	0	1	1.2	9	2	0	0	0	0	0	0	2	0	3	0	0	0	0	.000	0	0	0.00
	9 ML YEARS		203	148	7	24	927.1	3996	919	461	417	74	56	27	12	376	31	551	44	14	53	52	.505	4	1	4.05

Craig Biggio

Bats: Right **Throws:** Right **Pos:** 2B **Ht:** 5'11" **Wt:** 180 **Born:** 12/14/65 **Age:** 27

Year	Team	Lg	G	AB	H	2B	3B	HR	(Hm	Rd)	TB	R	RBI	TBB	IBB	SO	HBP	SH	SF	SB	CS	SB%	GDP	Avg	OBP	SLG
1988	Houston	NL	50	123	26	6	1	3	(1	2)	43	14	5	7	2	29	0	1	0	6	1	.86	1	.211	.254	.350
1989	Houston	NL	134	443	114	21	2	13	(6	7)	178	64	60	49	8	64	6	6	5	21	3	.88	7	.257	.336	.402
1990	Houston	NL	150	555	153	24	2	4	(2	2)	193	53	42	53	1	79	3	9	1	25	11	.69	11	.276	.342	.348
1991	Houston	NL	149	546	161	23	4	4	(0	4)	204	79	46	53	3	71	2	5	3	19	6	.76	2	.295	.358	.374
1992	Houston	NL	162	613	170	32	3	6	(3	3)	226	96	39	94	9	95	7	5	2	38	15	.72	5	.277	.378	.369
	5 ML YEARS		645	2280	624	106	12	30	(12	18)	844	306	192	256	23	338	18	26	11	109	36	.75	26	.274	.350	.370

Dann Bilardello

Bats: Right **Throws:** Right **Pos:** C   **Ht:** 6' 0" **Wt:** 190 **Born:** 05/26/59 **Age:** 34

								BATTING											BASERUNNING				PERCENTAGES		
Year Team	Lg	G	AB	H	2B	3B	HR	(Hm Rd)	TB	R	RBI	TBB	IBB	SO	HBP	SH	SF	SB	CS	SB%	GDP	Avg	OBP	SLG
1983 Cincinnati	NL	109	298	71	18	0	9	(7 2)	116	27	38	15	3	49	1	2	4	2	1	.67	9	.238	.274	.389
1984 Cincinnati	NL	68	182	38	7	0	2	(2 0)	51	16	10	19	3	34	1	4	0	1	0	.00	6	.209	.287	.280
1985 Cincinnati	NL	42	102	17	0	0	1	(1 0)	20	6	9	4	1	15	1	1	0	0	0	.00	5	.167	.206	.196
1986 Montreal	NL	79	191	37	5	0	4	(1 3)	54	12	17	14	3	32	0	7	0	1	0	1.00	5	.194	.249	.283
1989 Pittsburgh	NL	33	80	18	6	0	2	(1 1)	30	11	8	2	0	18	0	1	0	1	2	.33	1	.225	.244	.375
1990 Pittsburgh	NL	19	37	2	0	0	0	(0 0)	2	1	3	4	1	10	0	2	0	0	0	.00	0	.054	.146	.054
1991 San Diego	NL	15	26	7	2	1	0	(0 0)	11	4	5	3	0	4	0	0	0	0	0	.00	0	.269	.345	.423
1992 San Diego	NL	17	33	4	1	0	0	(0 0)	5	2	1	4	1	8	0	3	0	0	0	.00	0	.121	.216	.152
8 ML YEARS		382	949	194	39	1	18	(12 6)	289	79	91	65	12	170	3	20	4	4		.50	27	.204	.257	.305

Mike Birkbeck

Pitches: Right **Bats:** Right **Pos:** SP   **Ht:** 6' 2" **Wt:** 190 **Born:** 03/10/61 **Age:** 32

		HOW MUCH HE PITCHED						WHAT HE GAVE UP												THE RESULTS					
Year Team	Lg	G	GS	CG	GF	IP	BFP	H	R	ER	HR	SH	SF	HB	TBB	IBB	SO	WP	Bk	W	L	Pct.	ShO	Sv	ERA
1986 Milwaukee	AL	7	4	0	2	22	97	24	12	11	0	0	0	0	12	0	13	1	0	1	1	.500	0	0	4.50
1987 Milwaukee	AL	10	10	1	0	45	210	63	33	31	8	1	2	0	19	0	25	2	0	1	4	.200	0	0	6.20
1988 Milwaukee	AL	23	23	0	0	124	538	141	69	65	10	4	2	1	37	1	64	0	11	10	8	.556	0	0	4.72
1989 Milwaukee	AL	9	9	1	0	44.2	214	57	32	27	4	2	3	3	22	2	31	1	0	0	4	.000	0	0	5.44
1992 New York	NL	1	1	0	0	7	33	12	7	7	3	1	0	0	1	1	2	1	0	0	1	.000	0	0	9.00
5 ML YEARS		50	47	2	2	242.2	1092	297	153	141	25	8	7	4	91	4	135	5	11	12	18	.400	0	0	5.23

Bud Black

Pitches: Left **Bats:** Left **Pos:** SP   **Ht:** 6' 2" **Wt:** 185 **Born:** 06/30/57 **Age:** 36

		HOW MUCH HE PITCHED						WHAT HE GAVE UP												THE RESULTS					
Year Team	Lg	G	GS	CG	GF	IP	BFP	H	R	ER	HR	SH	SF	HB	TBB	IBB	SO	WP	Bk	W	L	Pct.	ShO	Sv	ERA
1981 Seattle	AL	2	0	0	0	1	7	2	0	0	0	0	0	0	3	1	0	1	0	0	0	.000	0	0	0.00
1982 Kansas City	AL	22	14	0	2	88.1	386	92	48	45	10	4	3	3	34	6	40	4	7	4	6	.400	0	0	4.58
1983 Kansas City	AL	24	24	3	0	161.1	672	159	75	68	19	4	5	2	43	1	58	4	0	10	7	.588	0	0	3.79
1984 Kansas City	AL	35	35	8	0	257	1045	226	99	89	22	6	1	4	64	2	140	2	2	17	12	.586	1	0	3.12
1985 Kansas City	AL	33	33	5	0	205.2	885	216	111	99	17	8	4	8	59	4	122	9	1	10	15	.400	2	0	4.33
1986 Kansas City	AL	56	4	0	26	121	503	100	49	43	14	4	4	7	43	5	68	2	2	5	10	.333	0	9	3.20
1987 Kansas City	AL	29	18	0	4	122.1	520	126	63	49	16	1	3	5	35	2	61	6	0	8	6	.571	0	1	3.60
1988 2 ML Teams	AL	33	7	0	9	81	358	82	47	45	8	6	3	4	34	3	63	5	6	4	4	.500	0	1	5.00
1989 Cleveland	AL	33	32	6	0	222.1	912	213	95	83	14	9	5	1	52	0	88	13	5	12	11	.522	3	0	3.36
1990 2 ML Teams	AL	32	31	5	1	206.2	857	181	86	82	19	6	7	5	61	1	106	6	1	13	11	.542	2	0	3.57
1991 San Francisco	NL	34	34	3	0	214.1	893	201	104	95	25	11	7	4	71	8	104	6	6	12	16	.429	3	0	3.99
1992 San Francisco	NL	28	28	2	0	177	749	178	88	78	23	8	4	1	59	11	82	3	7	10	12	.455	1	0	3.97
1988 Kansas City	AL	17	0	0	5	22	98	23	12	12	2	1	0	0	11	2	19	0	2	2	1	.667	0	0	4.91
Cleveland	AL	16	7	0	4	59	260	59	35	33	6	5	3	4	23	1	44	5	4	2	3	.400	0	1	5.03
1990 Cleveland	AL	29	29	5	0	191	796	171	79	75	17	4	5	4	58	1	103	6	1	11	10	.524	2	0	3.53
Toronto	AL	3	2	0	1	15.2	61	10	7	7	2	2	2	1	3	0	3	0	0	2	1	.667	0	0	4.02
12 ML YEARS		361	260	32	42	1858	7787	1776	865	776	187	67	46	44	558	44	932	61	37	105	110	.488	12	11	3.76

Willie Blair

Pitches: Right **Bats:** Right **Pos:** RP/SP   **Ht:** 6' 1" **Wt:** 185 **Born:** 12/18/65 **Age:** 27

		HOW MUCH HE PITCHED						WHAT HE GAVE UP												THE RESULTS					
Year Team	Lg	G	GS	CG	GF	IP	BFP	H	R	ER	HR	SH	SF	HB	TBB	IBB	SO	WP	Bk	W	L	Pct.	ShO	Sv	ERA
1990 Toronto	AL	27	6	0	8	68.2	297	66	33	31	4	0	4	1	28	4	43	3	0	3	5	.375	0	0	4.06
1991 Cleveland	AL	11	5	0	1	36	168	58	27	27	7	1	2	1	10	0	13	1	0	2	3	.400	0	0	6.75
1992 Houston	NL	29	8	0	1	78.2	331	74	47	35	5	4	3	2	25	2	48	2	0	5	7	.417	0	0	4.00
3 ML YEARS		67	19	0	10	183.1	796	198	107	93	16	5	9	4	63	6	104	6	0	10	15	.400	0	0	4.57

Lance Blankenship

Bats: Right **Throws:** Right **Pos:** 2B/LF/CF/RF   **Ht:** 6' 0" **Wt:** 185 **Born:** 12/06/63 **Age:** 29

								BATTING											BASERUNNING				PERCENTAGES		
Year Team	Lg	G	AB	H	2B	3B	HR	(Hm Rd)	TB	R	RBI	TBB	IBB	SO	HBP	SH	SF	SB	CS	SB%	GDP	Avg	OBP	SLG
1988 Oakland	AL	10	3	0	0	0	0	(0 0)	0	1	0	0	0	1	0	0	0	0	0	.00	0	.000	.000	.000
1989 Oakland	AL	58	125	29	5	1	1	(1 0)	39	22	4	8	0	31	0	3	1	5	1	.83	0	.232	.276	.312
1990 Oakland	AL	86	136	26	3	0	0	(0 0)	29	18	10	20	0	23	0	6	0	3	1	.75	6	.191	.295	.213
1991 Oakland	AL	90	185	46	8	0	3	(0 3)	63	33	21	23	0	42	3	2	3	12	3	.80	2	.249	.336	.341
1992 Oakland	AL	123	349	84	24	1	3	(1 2)	119	59	34	82	2	57	6	8	1	21	7	.75	10	.241	.393	.341
5 ML YEARS		367	798	185	40	2	7	(2 5)	250	133	69	133	2	154	9	19	5	41	13	.76	18	.232	.346	.313

21

Jeff Blauser

Bats: Right **Throws:** Right **Pos:** SS/2B   **Ht:** 6' 1" **Wt:** 180 **Born:** 11/08/65 **Age:** 27

						BATTING													BASERUNNING				PERCENTAGES		
Year	Team	Lg	G	AB	H	2B	3B	HR	(Hm	Rd)	TB	R	RBI	TBB	IBB	SO	HBP	SH	SF	SB	CS	SB%	GDP	Avg	OBP	SLG
1987	Atlanta	NL	51	165	40	6	3	2	(1	1)	58	11	15	18	1	34	3	1	0	7	3	.70	4	.242	.328	.352
1988	Atlanta	NL	18	67	16	3	1	2	(2	0)	27	7	7	2	0	11	1	3	1	0	1	.00	1	.239	.268	.403
1989	Atlanta	NL	142	456	123	24	2	12	(5	7)	187	63	46	38	2	101	1	8	4	5	2	.71	7	.270	.325	.410
1990	Atlanta	NL	115	386	104	24	3	8	(3	5)	158	46	39	35	1	70	5	3	0	3	5	.38	4	.269	.338	.409
1991	Atlanta	NL	129	352	91	14	3	11	(7	4)	144	49	54	54	4	59	2	4	3	5	6	.45	4	.259	.358	.409
1992	Atlanta	NL	123	343	90	19	3	14	(5	9)	157	61	46	46	2	82	4	7	3	5	5	.50	2	.262	.354	.458
6 ML YEARS			578	1769	464	90	15	49	(23	26)	731	237	207	193	10	357	16	26	11	25	22	.53	22	.262	.338	.413

Mike Blowers

Bats: Right **Throws:** Right **Pos:** 3B   **Ht:** 6' 2" **Wt:** 210 **Born:** 04/24/65 **Age:** 28

						BATTING													BASERUNNING				PERCENTAGES		
Year	Team	Lg	G	AB	H	2B	3B	HR	(Hm	Rd)	TB	R	RBI	TBB	IBB	SO	HBP	SH	SF	SB	CS	SB%	GDP	Avg	OBP	SLG
1989	New York	AL	13	38	10	0	0	0	(0	0)	10	2	3	3	0	13	0	0	0	0	0	.00	1	.263	.317	.263
1990	New York	AL	48	144	27	4	0	5	(1	4)	46	16	21	12	1	50	1	0	0	1	0	1.00	3	.188	.255	.319
1991	New York	AL	15	35	7	0	0	1	(0	1)	10	3	1	4	0	3	0	1	0	0	0	.00	1	.200	.282	.286
1992	Seattle	AL	31	73	14	3	0	1	(0	1)	20	7	2	6	0	20	0	1	0	0	0	.00	3	.192	.253	.274
4 ML YEARS			107	290	58	7	0	7	(1	6)	86	28	27	25	1	86	1	2	0	1	0	1.00	8	.200	.266	.297

Bert Blyleven

Pitches: Right **Bats:** Right **Pos:** SP   **Ht:** 6' 3" **Wt:** 220 **Born:** 04/06/51 **Age:** 42

			HOW MUCH HE PITCHED					WHAT HE GAVE UP										THE RESULTS					
Year	Team	Lg	G	GS	CG	GF	IP	BFP	H	R	ER	HR	SH	SF	HB	TBB	IBB	SO	WP	Bk	W	L	Pct.	ShO	Sv	ERA
1970	Minnesota	AL	27	25	5	1	164	675	143	66	58	17	8	2	2	47	6	135	2	3	10	9	.526	1	0	3.18
1971	Minnesota	AL	38	38	17	0	278	1126	267	95	87	21	12	3	5	59	1	224	5	1	16	15	.516	5	0	2.82
1972	Minnesota	AL	39	38	11	1	287	1158	247	93	87	22	14	6	10	69	7	228	7	1	17	17	.500	3	0	2.73
1973	Minnesota	AL	40	40	25	0	325	1321	296	109	91	16	11	13	9	67	4	258	7	2	20	17	.541	9	0	2.52
1974	Minnesota	AL	37	37	19	0	281	1149	244	99	83	14	13	5	9	77	3	249	3	0	17	17	.500	3	0	2.66
1975	Minnesota	AL	35	35	20	0	276	1104	219	104	92	24	10	8	4	84	2	233	2	0	15	10	.600	3	0	3.00
1976	2 ML Teams		36	36	18	0	297	1225	283	106	95	14	18	6	12	81	6	219	7	2	13	16	.448	6	0	2.88
1977	Texas	AL	30	30	15	0	235	935	181	81	71	20	10	5	7	69	1	182	8	0	14	12	.538	5	0	2.72
1978	Pittsburgh	NL	34	34	11	0	244	1011	217	94	82	17	13	2	6	66	5	182	6	2	14	10	.583	4	0	3.02
1979	Pittsburgh	NL	37	37	4	0	237	1018	238	102	95	21	14	9	6	92	8	172	9	0	12	5	.706	0	0	3.61
1980	Pittsburgh	NL	34	32	5	1	217	907	219	102	92	20	10	2	0	59	5	168	2	1	8	13	.381	2	0	3.82
1981	Cleveland	AL	20	20	9	0	159	644	145	52	51	9	3	3	5	40	1	107	3	1	11	7	.611	1	0	2.89
1982	Cleveland	AL	4	4	0	0	20.1	89	16	14	11	2	0	2	0	11	0	19	0	0	2	2	.500	0	0	4.87
1983	Cleveland	AL	24	24	5	0	156.1	660	160	74	68	8	2	5	10	44	4	123	5	1	7	10	.412	0	0	3.91
1984	Cleveland	AL	33	32	12	0	245	1004	204	86	78	19	6	8	6	74	4	170	6	0	19	7	.731	4	0	2.87
1985	2 ML Teams		37	37	24	0	293.2	1203	264	121	103	23	5	8	9	75	1	206	4	1	17	16	.515	5	0	3.16
1986	Minnesota	AL	36	36	16	0	271.2	1126	262	134	121	50	5	4	10	58	4	215	4	0	17	14	.548	3	0	4.01
1987	Minnesota	AL	37	37	8	0	267	1122	249	132	119	46	4	6	9	101	4	196	13	0	15	12	.556	1	0	4.01
1988	Minnesota	AL	33	33	7	0	207.1	895	240	128	125	21	6	6	16	51	1	145	5	3	10	17	.370	0	0	5.43
1989	California	AL	33	33	8	0	241	973	225	76	73	14	7	7	8	44	2	131	2	0	17	5	.773	5	0	2.73
1990	California	AL	23	23	2	0	134	578	163	85	78	15	2	6	7	25	0	69	6	0	8	7	.533	0	0	5.24
1992	California	AL	25	24	1	0	133	568	150	76	70	17	3	5	5	29	2	70	3	1	8	12	.400	0	0	4.74
1976	Minnesota	AL	12	12	4	0	95	406	101	39	33	3	7	3	4	35	5	75	0	2	4	5	.444	0	0	3.13
	Texas		24	24	14	0	202	819	182	67	62	11	11	3	8	46	1	144	7	0	9	11	.450	6	0	2.76
1985	Cleveland	AL	23	23	15	0	179.2	743	163	76	65	16	4	4	7	49	1	129	1	1	9	11	.450	4	0	3.26
	Minnesota	AL	14	14	9	0	114	460	101	45	38	9	1	4	2	26	0	77	3	0	8	5	.615	1	0	3.00
22 ML YEARS			692	685	242	3	4969.1	20491	4632	2029	1830	430	176	121	155	1322	71	3701	114	19	287	250	.534	60	0	3.31

Mike Boddicker

Pitches: Right **Bats:** Right **Pos:** RP/SP   **Ht:** 5'11" **Wt:** 185 **Born:** 08/23/57 **Age:** 35

			HOW MUCH HE PITCHED					WHAT HE GAVE UP										THE RESULTS					
Year	Team	Lg	G	GS	CG	GF	IP	BFP	H	R	ER	HR	SH	SF	HB	TBB	IBB	SO	WP	Bk	W	L	Pct.	ShO	Sv	ERA
1980	Baltimore	AL	1	1	0	0	7.1	34	6	6	5	1	0	0	0	5	0	4	0	0	0	1	.000	0	0	6.14
1981	Baltimore	AL	2	0	0	1	5.2	25	6	4	3	1	0	0	0	2	0	2	2	0	0	0	.000	0	0	4.76
1982	Baltimore	AL	7	0	0	4	25.2	110	25	10	10	2	1	0	0	12	2	20	0	0	1	0	1.000	0	0	3.51
1983	Baltimore	AL	27	26	10	1	179	711	141	65	55	13	4	3	0	52	1	120	5	0	16	8	.667	5	0	2.77
1984	Baltimore	AL	34	34	16	0	261.1	1051	218	95	81	23	2	7	5	81	1	128	6	1	20	11	.645	4	0	2.79
1985	Baltimore	AL	32	32	9	0	203.1	899	227	104	92	13	9	2	5	89	7	135	5	0	12	17	.414	2	0	4.07
1986	Baltimore	AL	33	33	7	0	218.1	934	214	125	114	30	3	6	11	74	4	175	7	0	14	12	.538	0	0	4.70

Year Team	Lg	G	GS	CG	GF	IP	BFP	H	R	ER	HR	SH	SF	HB	TBB	IBB	SO	WP	Bk	W	L	Pct.	ShO	Sv	ERA
1987 Baltimore	AL	33	33	7	0	226	950	212	114	105	29	7	4	7	78	4	152	10	0	10	12	.455	2	0	4.18
1988 2 ML Teams		36	35	5	0	236	1001	234	102	89	17	4	12	14	77	6	156	6	4	13	15	.464	1	0	3.39
1989 Boston	AL	34	34	3	0	211.2	912	217	101	94	19	8	10	10	71	4	145	4	1	15	11	.577	2	0	4.00
1990 Boston	AL	34	34	4	0	228	956	225	92	85	16	3	1	10	69	6	143	10	0	17	8	.680	0	0	3.36
1991 Kansas City	AL	30	29	1	1	180.2	775	188	89	82	13	10	1	13	59	0	79	3	2	12	12	.500	0	0	4.08
1992 Kansas City	AL	29	8	0	8	86.2	392	92	50	48	5	2	3	8	37	3	47	2	0	1	4	.200	0	3	4.98
1988 Baltimore	AL	21	21	4	0	147	636	149	72	63	14	3	8	11	51	5	100	3	4	6	12	.333	0	0	3.86
Boston		15	14	1	0	89	365	85	30	26	3	1	4	3	26	1	56	3	0	7	3	.700	1	0	2.63
13 ML YEARS		332	299	62	15	2069.2	8750	2005	957	863	182	53	49	83	706	38	1306	60	8	131	111	.541	16	3	3.75

Joe Boever

Pitches: Right **Bats:** Right **Pos:** RP   **Ht:** 6' 1" **Wt:** 200 **Born:** 10/04/60 **Age:** 32

		HOW MUCH HE PITCHED						WHAT HE GAVE UP												THE RESULTS					
Year Team	Lg	G	GS	CG	GF	IP	BFP	H	R	ER	HR	SH	SF	HB	TBB	IBB	SO	WP	Bk	W	L	Pct.	ShO	Sv	ERA
1985 St. Louis	NL	13	0	0	5	16.1	69	17	8	8	3	1	1	0	4	1	20	1	0	0	0	.000	0	0	4.41
1986 St. Louis	NL	11	0	0	4	21.2	93	19	5	4	2	0	0	0	11	0	8	1	0	0	1	.000	0	0	1.66
1987 Atlanta	NL	14	0	0	10	18.1	93	29	15	15	4	1	1	0	12	1	18	1	0	1	0	1.000	0	0	7.36
1988 Atlanta	NL	16	0	0	13	20.1	70	12	4	4	1	2	0	1	1	0	7	0	0	0	2	.000	0	1	1.77
1989 Atlanta	NL	66	0	0	53	82.1	349	78	37	36	6	5	0	1	34	5	68	5	0	4	11	.267	0	21	3.94
1990 2 ML Teams		67	0	0	34	88.1	388	77	35	33	6	4	2	0	51	12	75	3	2	3	6	.333	0	14	3.36
1991 Philadelphia	NL	68	0	0	27	98.1	431	90	45	42	10	3	6	0	54	11	89	6	1	3	5	.375	0	0	3.84
1992 Houston	NL	81	0	0	26	111.1	479	103	38	31	3	10	4	4	45	9	67	4	0	3	6	.333	0	2	2.51
1990 Atlanta	NL	33	0	0	21	42.1	198	40	23	22	6	2	2	0	35	10	35	2	0	1	3	.250	0	8	4.68
Philadelphia	NL	34	0	0	13	46	190	37	12	11	0	2	0	0	16	2	40	1	2	2	3	.400	0	6	2.15
8 ML YEARS		336	0	0	172	457	1972	425	187	173	35	26	14	6	212	39	352	21	3	14	31	.311	0	38	3.41

Wade Boggs

Bats: Left **Throws:** Right **Pos:** 3B/DH   **Ht:** 6' 2" **Wt:** 197 **Born:** 06/15/58 **Age:** 35

		BATTING															BASERUNNING			PERCENTAGES		
Year Team	Lg	G	AB	H	2B	3B	HR	(Hm | Rd)	TB	R	RBI	TBB	IBB	SO	HBP	SH	SF	SB	CS	SB%	GDP	Avg	OBP	SLG
1982 Boston	AL	104	338	118	14	1	5	(4 | 1)	149	51	44	35	4	21	0	4	4	1	0	1.00	9	.349	.406	.441
1983 Boston	AL	153	582	210	44	7	5	(2 | 3)	283	100	74	92	2	36	1	3	7	3	3	.50	15	.361	.444	.486
1984 Boston	AL	158	625	203	31	4	6	(5 | 1)	260	109	55	89	6	44	0	8	4	3	2	.60	13	.325	.407	.416
1985 Boston	AL	161	653	240	42	3	8	(6 | 2)	312	107	78	96	5	61	4	3	2	2	1	.67	20	.368	.450	.478
1986 Boston	AL	149	580	207	47	2	8	(3 | 5)	282	107	71	105	14	44	0	4	4	0	4	.00	11	.357	.453	.486
1987 Boston	AL	147	551	200	40	6	24	(10 | 14)	324	108	89	105	19	48	2	1	8	1	3	.25	13	.363	.461	.588
1988 Boston	AL	155	584	214	45	6	5	(4 | 1)	286	128	58	125	18	34	3	0	7	2	3	.40	23	.366	.476	.490
1989 Boston	AL	156	621	205	51	7	3	(2 | 1)	279	113	54	107	19	51	7	0	7	2	6	.25	19	.330	.430	.449
1990 Boston	AL	155	619	187	44	5	6	(3 | 3)	259	89	63	87	19	68	1	0	6	0	0	.00	14	.302	.386	.418
1991 Boston	AL	144	546	181	42	2	8	(6 | 2)	251	93	51	89	25	32	0	0	6	1	2	.33	16	.332	.421	.460
1992 Boston	AL	143	514	133	22	4	7	(4 | 3)	184	62	50	74	19	31	4	0	6	1	3	.25	10	.259	.353	.358
11 ML YEARS		1625	6213	2098	422	47	85	(49 | 36)	2869	1067	687	1004	150	470	22	23	61	16	27	.37	163	.338	.428	.462

Brian Bohanon

Pitches: Left **Bats:** Left **Pos:** RP/SP   **Ht:** 6' 2" **Wt:** 220 **Born:** 08/01/68 **Age:** 24

		HOW MUCH HE PITCHED						WHAT HE GAVE UP												THE RESULTS					
Year Team	Lg	G	GS	CG	GF	IP	BFP	H	R	ER	HR	SH	SF	HB	TBB	IBB	SO	WP	Bk	W	L	Pct.	ShO	Sv	ERA
1990 Texas	AL	11	6	0	1	34	158	40	30	25	6	0	3	2	18	0	15	1	0	0	3	.000	0	0	6.62
1991 Texas	AL	11	11	1	0	61.1	273	66	35	33	4	2	5	2	23	0	34	3	1	4	3	.571	0	0	4.84
1992 Texas	AL	18	7	0	3	45.2	220	57	38	32	7	0	2	1	25	0	29	2	0	1	1	.500	0	0	6.31
3 ML YEARS		40	24	1	4	141	651	163	103	90	17	2	10	5	66	0	78	6	1	5	7	.417	0	0	5.74

Tom Bolton

Pitches: Left **Bats:** Left **Pos:** RP/SP   **Ht:** 6' 3" **Wt:** 185 **Born:** 05/06/62 **Age:** 31

		HOW MUCH HE PITCHED						WHAT HE GAVE UP												THE RESULTS					
Year Team	Lg	G	GS	CG	GF	IP	BFP	H	R	ER	HR	SH	SF	HB	TBB	IBB	SO	WP	Bk	W	L	Pct.	ShO	Sv	ERA
1987 Boston	AL	29	0	0	5	61.2	287	83	33	30	5	3	3	2	27	2	49	3	0	1	0	1.000	0	0	4.38
1988 Boston	AL	28	0	0	8	30.1	140	35	17	16	1	2	1	0	14	1	21	2	1	1	3	.250	0	1	4.75
1989 Boston	AL	4	4	0	0	17.1	83	21	18	16	1	0	1	0	10	1	9	1	0	0	4	.000	0	0	8.31
1990 Boston	AL	21	16	3	2	119.2	501	111	46	45	6	3	5	3	47	3	65	1	1	10	5	.667	0	0	3.38
1991 Boston	AL	25	19	0	4	110	499	136	72	64	16	2	4	1	51	2	64	3	0	8	9	.471	0	0	5.24
1992 2 ML Teams		37	9	0	9	75.1	345	86	39	38	9	1	1	4	37	3	50	5	2	4	5	.444	0	0	4.54
1992 Boston	AL	21	1	0	6	29	135	34	11	11	0	0	0	2	14	1	23	2	1	1	2	.333	0	0	3.41
Cincinnati	NL	16	8	0	3	46.1	210	52	28	27	9	1	1	2	23	2	27	3	1	3	3	.500	0	0	5.24
6 ML YEARS		144	48	3	28	414.1	1855	472	225	209	38	11	15	10	186	12	258	15	4	24	26	.480	0	1	4.54

Barry Bonds

Bats: Left **Throws:** Left **Pos:** LF **Ht:** 6' 1" **Wt:** 187 **Born:** 07/24/64 **Age:** 28

									BATTING											BASERUNNING				PERCENTAGES		
Year	Team	Lg	G	AB	H	2B	3B	HR	(Hm	Rd)	TB	R	RBI	TBB	IBB	SO	HBP	SH	SF	SB	CS	SB%	GDP	Avg	OBP	SLG
1986	Pittsburgh	NL	113	413	92	26	3	16	(9	7)	172	72	48	65	2	102	2	2	2	36	7	.84	4	.223	.330	.416
1987	Pittsburgh	NL	150	551	144	34	9	25	(12	13)	271	99	59	54	3	88	3	0	3	32	10	.76	4	.261	.329	.492
1988	Pittsburgh	NL	144	538	152	30	5	24	(14	10)	264	97	58	72	14	82	2	0	2	17	11	.61	3	.283	.368	.491
1989	Pittsburgh	NL	159	580	144	34	6	19	(7	12)	247	96	58	93	22	93	1	1	4	32	10	.76	9	.248	.351	.426
1990	Pittsburgh	NL	151	519	156	32	3	33	(14	19)	293	104	114	93	15	83	3	0	6	52	13	.80	8	.301	.406	**.565**
1991	Pittsburgh	NL	153	510	149	28	5	25	(12	13)	262	95	116	107	25	73	4	0	13	43	13	.77	8	.292	**.410**	.514
1992	Pittsburgh	NL	140	473	147	36	5	34	(15	19)	295	109	103	127	32	69	5	0	7	39	8	.83	9	.311	**.456**	**.624**
	7 ML YEARS		1010	3584	984	220	36	176	(83	93)	1804	672	556	611	113	590	20	3	37	251	72	.78	45	.275	.380	.503

Ricky Bones

Pitches: Right **Bats:** Right **Pos:** SP **Ht:** 6' 0" **Wt:** 190 **Born:** 04/07/69 **Age:** 24

				HOW	MUCH	HE	PITCHED			WHAT	HE	GAVE	UP									THE	RESULTS			
Year	Team	Lg	G	GS	CG	GF	IP	BFP	H	R	ER	HR	SH	SF	HB	TBB	IBB	SO	WP	Bk	W	L	Pct.	ShO	Sv	ERA
1986	Spokane	A	18	9	0	4	58.	0	63	44	36	3	0	0	1	29	1	46	7	2	1	3	.250	0	0	5.59
1987	Chston-Sc	A	26	26	4	0	170.1	729	183	81	69	9	4	1	6	45	4	130	5	2	12	5	.706	1	0	3.65
1988	Riverside	A	25	25	5	0	175.1	742	162	80	71	11	2	2	4	64	3	129	14	5	10	4	.714	2	0	3.64
1989	Wichita	AA	24	24	2	0	136.1	611	162	103	87	22	4	3	2	47	5	88	7	3	10	9	.526	0	0	5.74
1990	Wichita	AA	21	21	2	0	137	591	138	66	53	15	7	5	5	45	0	96	6	4	6	4	.600	1	0	3.48
	Las Vegas	AAA	5	5	0	0	36.1	158	45	17	14	2	0	3	1	10	0	25	1	0	2	1	.667	0	0	3.47
1991	Las Vegas	AAA	23	23	1	0	136.1	611	155	90	64	10	2	4	4	43	3	95	6	3	8	6	.571	0	0	4.22
1991	San Diego	NL	11	11	0	0	54	234	57	33	29	3	0	4	0	18	0	31	4	0	4	6	.400	0	0	4.83
1992	Milwaukee	AL	31	28	0	0	163.1	705	169	90	83	27	2	5	9	48	0	65	3	2	9	10	.474	0	0	4.57
	2 ML YEARS		42	39	0	0	217.1	939	226	123	112	30	2	9	9	66	0	96	7	2	13	16	.448	0	0	4.64

Bobby Bonilla

Bats: Both **Throws:** Right **Pos:** RF **Ht:** 6' 3" **Wt:** 240 **Born:** 02/23/63 **Age:** 30

									BATTING											BASERUNNING				PERCENTAGES		
Year	Team	Lg	G	AB	H	2B	3B	HR	(Hm	Rd)	TB	R	RBI	TBB	IBB	SO	HBP	SH	SF	SB	CS	SB%	GDP	Avg	OBP	SLG
1986	2 ML Teams		138	426	109	16	4	3	(2	1)	142	55	43	62	3	88	2	5	1	8	5	.62	9	.256	.352	.333
1987	Pittsburgh	NL	141	466	140	33	3	15	(7	8)	224	58	77	39	4	64	2	0	8	3	5	.38	8	.300	.351	.481
1988	Pittsburgh	NL	159	584	160	32	7	24	(9	15)	278	87	100	85	19	82	4	0	8	3	5	.38	4	.274	.366	.476
1989	Pittsburgh	NL	163	616	173	37	10	24	(13	11)	302	96	86	76	20	93	1	0	5	8	8	.50	10	.281	.358	.490
1990	Pittsburgh	NL	160	625	175	39	7	32	(13	19)	324	112	120	45	9	103	1	0	15	4	3	.57	11	.280	.322	.518
1991	Pittsburgh	NL	157	577	174	**44**	6	18	(9	9)	284	102	100	90	8	67	2	0	11	2	4	.33	14	.302	.391	.492
1992	New York	NL	128	438	109	23	0	19	(5	14)	189	62	70	66	10	73	1	0	1	4	3	.57	11	.249	.348	.432
1986	Chicago	AL	75	234	63	10	2	2	(2	0)	83	27	26	33	2	49	1	2	1	4	1	.80	4	.269	.361	.355
	Pittsburgh	NL	63	192	46	6	2	1	(0	1)	59	28	17	29	1	39	1	3	0	4	4	.50	5	.240	.342	.307
	7 ML YEARS		1046	3732	1040	224	37	135	(58	77)	1743	572	596	463	73	570	13	5	49	32	33	.49	67	.279	.356	.467

Bret Boone

Bats: Right **Throws:** Right **Pos:** 2B **Ht:** 5'10" **Wt:** 175 **Born:** 04/06/69 **Age:** 24

									BATTING											BASERUNNING				PERCENTAGES		
Year	Team	Lg	G	AB	H	2B	3B	HR	(Hm	Rd)	TB	R	RBI	TBB	IBB	SO	HBP	SH	SF	SB	CS	SB%	GDP	Avg	OBP	SLG
1990	Peninsula	A	74	255	68	13	2	8	--	--	109	42	38	47	0	57	1	0	0	5	2	.71	1	.267	.383	.427
1991	Jacksnville	AA	139	475	121	18	1	19	--	--	198	64	75	72	2	123	5	1	3	9	9	.50	21	.255	.357	.417
1992	Calgary	AAA	118	439	138	26	5	13	--	--	213	73	73	60	7	88	5	1	6	17	12	.59	12	.314	.398	.485
1992	Seattle	AL	33	129	25	4	0	4	(2	2)	41	15	15	4	0	34	1	1	0	1	1	.50	4	.194	.224	.318

Pedro Borbon

Pitches: Left **Bats:** Left **Pos:** RP **Ht:** 6' 1" **Wt:** 205 **Born:** 11/15/67 **Age:** 25

				HOW	MUCH	HE	PITCHED			WHAT	HE	GAVE	UP									THE	RESULTS			
Year	Team	Lg	G	GS	CG	GF	IP	BFP	H	R	ER	HR	SH	SF	HB	TBB	IBB	SO	WP	Bk	W	L	Pct.	ShO	Sv	ERA
1988	White Sox	R	16	11	1	2	74.2	299	52	28	20	1	3	3	2	17	0	67	5	14	5	3	.625	1	1	2.41
1990	Burlington	A	14	14	6	0	97.2	381	73	25	16	3	0	0	3	23	0	76	4	1	11	3	.786	2	0	1.47
	Durham	A	11	11	0	0	61.1	266	73	40	37	8	2	2	2	16	0	37	2	1	4	5	.444	0	0	5.43
1991	Durham	A	37	6	1	21	90.2	388	85	40	23	2	5	4	2	35	2	79	4	2	4	3	.571	0	5	2.28
	Greenville	AA	4	4	0	0	29	120	23	12	9	1	1	0	3	10	0	22	2	0	0	1	.000	0	0	2.79
1992	Greenville	AA	39	10	0	14	94	384	73	36	32	6	1	3	3	42	1	79	2	0	8	2	.800	0	3	3.06
1992	Atlanta	NL	2	0	0	2	1.1	7	2	1	1	0	0	0	0	1	1	0	0	0	1	.000	0	0	6.75

Pat Borders

Bats: Right **Throws:** Right **Pos:** C **Ht:** 6' 2" **Wt:** 200 **Born:** 05/14/63 **Age:** 30

Year Team	Lg	G	AB	H	2B	3B	HR	(Hm	Rd)	TB	R	RBI	TBB	IBB	SO	HBP	SH	SF	SB	CS	SB%	GDP	Avg	OBP	SLG
1988 Toronto	AL	56	154	42	6	3	5	(2	3)	69	15	21	3	0	24	0	2	1	0	0	.00	5	.273	.285	.448
1989 Toronto	AL	94	241	62	11	1	3	(1	2)	84	22	29	11	2	45	1	1	2	2	1	.67	7	.257	.290	.349
1990 Toronto	AL	125	346	99	24	2	15	(10	5)	172	36	49	18	2	57	0	1	3	0	1	.00	17	.286	.319	.497
1991 Toronto	AL	105	291	71	17	0	5	(2	3)	103	22	36	11	1	45	1	6	3	0	0	.00	8	.244	.271	.354
1992 Toronto	AL	138	480	116	26	2	13	(7	6)	185	47	53	33	3	75	2	1	5	1	1	.50	11	.242	.290	.385
5 ML YEARS		518	1512	390	84	8	41	(22	19)	613	142	188	76	8	246	4	11	14	3	3	.50	48	.258	.293	.405

Mike Bordick

Bats: Right **Throws:** Right **Pos:** 2B/SS **Ht:** 5'11" **Wt:** 175 **Born:** 07/21/65 **Age:** 27

Year Team	Lg	G	AB	H	2B	3B	HR	(Hm	Rd)	TB	R	RBI	TBB	IBB	SO	HBP	SH	SF	SB	CS	SB%	GDP	Avg	OBP	SLG
1990 Oakland	AL	25	14	1	0	0	0	(0	0)	1	0	0	1	0	4	0	0	0	0	0	.00	0	.071	.133	.071
1991 Oakland	AL	90	235	56	5	1	0	(0	0)	63	21	21	14	0	37	1	3	1	3	4	.43	3	.238	.289	.268
1992 Oakland	AL	154	504	151	19	4	3	(3	0)	187	62	48	40	2	59	9	14	5	12	6	.67	10	.300	.358	.371
3 ML YEARS		269	753	208	24	5	3	(3	0)	251	83	69	55	2	100	12	26	6	15	10	.60	13	.276	.333	.333

Chris Bosio

Pitches: Right **Bats:** Right **Pos:** SP **Ht:** 6' 3" **Wt:** 225 **Born:** 04/03/63 **Age:** 30

Year Team	Lg	G	GS	CG	GF	IP	BFP	H	R	ER	HR	SH	SF	HB	TBB	IBB	SO	WP	Bk	W	L	Pct.	ShO	Sv	ERA
1986 Milwaukee	AL	10	4	0	3	34.2	154	41	27	27	9	1	0	0	13	0	29	2	1	0	4	.000	0	0	7.01
1987 Milwaukee	AL	46	19	2	8	170	734	187	102	99	18	3	3	1	50	3	150	14	2	11	8	.579	1	2	5.24
1988 Milwaukee	AL	38	22	9	15	182	766	190	80	68	13	7	9	2	38	6	84	1	2	7	15	.318	1	6	3.36
1989 Milwaukee	AL	33	33	8	0	234.2	969	225	90	77	16	5	5	6	48	1	173	4	2	15	10	.600	2	0	2.95
1990 Milwaukee	AL	20	20	4	0	132.2	557	131	67	59	15	4	4	3	38	1	76	7	0	4	9	.308	1	0	4.00
1991 Milwaukee	AL	32	32	5	0	204.2	840	187	80	74	15	2	6	8	58	0	117	5	0	14	10	.583	1	0	3.25
1992 Milwaukee	AL	33	33	4	0	231.1	937	223	100	93	21	6	5	4	44	1	120	8	2	16	6	.727	2	0	3.62
7 ML YEARS		212	163	32	26	1190	4957	1184	546	497	107	28	32	24	289	12	749	41	9	67	62	.519	8	8	3.76

Shawn Boskie

Pitches: Right **Bats:** Right **Pos:** SP/RP **Ht:** 6' 3" **Wt:** 205 **Born:** 03/28/67 **Age:** 26

Year Team	Lg	G	GS	CG	GF	IP	BFP	H	R	ER	HR	SH	SF	HB	TBB	IBB	SO	WP	Bk	W	L	Pct.	ShO	Sv	ERA
1990 Chicago	NL	15	15	1	0	97.2	415	99	42	40	8	8	2	1	31	3	49	3	2	5	6	.455	0	0	3.69
1991 Chicago	NL	28	20	0	2	129	582	150	78	75	14	8	6	5	52	4	62	1	4	4	9	.308	0	0	5.23
1992 Chicago	NL	23	18	0	2	91.2	393	96	55	51	14	9	6	4	36	3	39	5	1	5	11	.313	0	0	5.01
3 ML YEARS		66	53	1	4	318.1	1390	345	175	166	36	25	14	10	119	10	150	9	4	14	26	.350	0	0	4.69

Daryl Boston

Bats: Left **Throws:** Left **Pos:** LF/CF/RF **Ht:** 6' 3" **Wt:** 210 **Born:** 01/04/63 **Age:** 30

Year Team	Lg	G	AB	H	2B	3B	HR	(Hm	Rd)	TB	R	RBI	TBB	IBB	SO	HBP	SH	SF	SB	CS	SB%	GDP	Avg	OBP	SLG
1984 Chicago	AL	35	83	14	3	1	0	(0	0)	19	8	3	4	0	20	0	0	0	6	0	1.00	0	.169	.207	.229
1985 Chicago	AL	95	232	53	13	1	3	(1	2)	77	20	15	14	1	44	0	1	1	8	6	.57	3	.228	.271	.332
1986 Chicago	AL	56	199	53	11	3	5	(1	4)	85	29	22	21	3	33	0	3	1	9	5	.64	4	.266	.335	.427
1987 Chicago	AL	103	337	87	21	2	10	(5	5)	142	51	29	25	2	68	0	4	3	12	6	.67	5	.258	.307	.421
1988 Chicago	AL	105	281	61	12	2	15	(6	9)	122	37	31	21	5	44	0	2	1	9	3	.75	5	.217	.271	.434
1989 Chicago	AL	101	218	55	3	4	5	(3	2)	81	34	23	24	3	31	0	4	1	7	2	.78	1	.252	.325	.372
1990 2 ML Teams		120	367	100	21	2	12	(4	8)	161	65	45	28	2	50	2	0	0	19	7	.73	7	.272	.327	.439
1991 New York	NL	137	255	70	16	4	4	(2	2)	106	40	21	30	0	42	0	0	1	15	8	.65	2	.275	.350	.416
1992 New York	NL	130	289	72	14	2	11	(5	6)	123	37	35	38	6	60	3	0	4	12	6	.67	7	.249	.338	.426
1990 Chicago	AL	5	1	0	0	0	0	(0	0)	0	0	0	0	0	0	0	0	0	1	0	1.00	0	.000	.000	.000
New York	NL	115	366	100	21	2	12	(4	8)	161	65	45	28	2	50	2	0	0	18	7	.72	7	.273	.328	.440
9 ML YEARS		882	2261	565	114	21	65	(27	38)	916	321	224	205	22	392	5	14	12	97	43	.69	32	.250	.312	.405

Kent Bottenfield

Pitches: Right **Bats:** Both **Pos:** RP/SP **Ht:** 6' 3" **Wt:** 225 **Born:** 11/14/68 **Age:** 24

Year Team	Lg	G	GS	CG	GF	IP	BFP	H	R	ER	HR	SH	SF	HB	TBB	IBB	SO	WP	Bk	W	L	Pct.	ShO	Sv	ERA
1986 Expos	R	13	13	2	0	74.1	323	73	42	27	2	2	6	3	30	0	41	0	1	5	6	.455	0	0	3.27
1987 Burlington	A	27	27	6	0	161	706	175	98	81	12	3	3	2	42	0	103	9	2	9	13	.409	3	0	4.53
1988 Wst Plm Bch	A	27	27	9	0	181	745	165	80	67	10	3	5	5	47	0	120	4	3	10	8	.556	4	0	3.33
1989 Jacksnville	AA	25	25	1	0	138.2	625	137	101	81	13	6	9	9	73	2	91	6	2	3	17	.150	0	0	5.26

1990	Jacksnville	AA	29	28	2	0	169	718	158	72	64	14	7	4	11	67	1	121	9	2	12	10	.545	1	0	3.41
1991	Indianapols	AAA	29	27	5	0	166.1	712	155	97	75	15	11	5	4	61	7	108	5	1	8	15	.348	2	0	4.06
1992	Indianapols	AAA	25	23	3	1	152.1	629	139	64	58	12	6	4	2	58	1	111	2	0	12	8	.600	1	0	3.43
1992	Montreal	NL	10	4	0	2	32.1	135	26	9	8	1	1	2	1	11	1	14	0	0	1	2	.333	0	1	2.23

Denis Boucher

Pitches: Left **Bats:** Right **Pos:** SP   **Ht:** 6' 1" **Wt:** 195 **Born:** 03/07/68 **Age:** 25

			HOW MUCH HE PITCHED					WHAT HE GAVE UP												THE RESULTS					
Year	Team	Lg	G	GS	CG	GF	IP	BFP	H	R	ER	HR	SH	SF	HB	TBB	IBB	SO	WP	Bk	W	L	Pct.	ShO	Sv	ERA
1988	Myrtle Bch	A	33	32	1	0	196.2	809	161	81	62	11	7	6	8	63	1	169	15	21	13	12	.520	0	0	2.84
1989	Dunedin	A	33	28	1	1	164.2	675	142	80	56	6	3	8	6	58	2	117	13	8	10	10	.500	1	0	3.06
1990	Dunedin	A	9	9	2	0	60	226	45	8	5	1	0	0	2	8	0	62	4	0	7	0	1.000	2	0	0.75
	Syracuse	AAA	17	17	2	0	107.2	449	100	51	46	7	4	4	2	37	2	80	6	0	8	5	.615	1	0	3.85
1991	Syracuse	AAA	8	8	1	0	56.2	241	57	24	20	5	4	1	3	19	1	28	2	0	2	1	.667	0	0	3.18
	Colo Sprngs	AAA	3	3	0	0	14.1	59	14	8	8	1	0	1	0	2	0	9	0	0	1	0	1.000	0	0	5.02
1992	Colo Sprngs	AAA	20	18	6	1	124	497	119	50	48	4	3	4	2	30	1	40	7	2	11	4	.733	0	0	3.48
1991	2 ML Teams		12	12	0	0	58	270	74	41	39	12	3	1	2	24	1	29	1	4	1	7	.125	0	0	6.05
1992	Cleveland	AL	8	7	0	0	41	184	48	29	29	9	1	3	1	20	0	17	1	0	2	2	.500	0	0	6.37
1991	Toronto	AL	7	7	0	0	35.1	162	39	20	18	6	3	1	2	16	1	16	0	4	0	3	.000	0	0	4.58
	Cleveland	AL	5	5	0	0	22.2	108	35	21	21	6	0	0	0	8	0	13	1	0	1	4	.200	0	0	8.34
	2 ML YEARS		20	19	0	0	99	454	122	70	68	21	4	4	3	44	1	46	2	4	3	9	.250	0	0	6.18

Rafael Bournigal

Bats: Right **Throws:** Right **Pos:** SS   **Ht:** 5'11" **Wt:** 160 **Born:** 05/12/66 **Age:** 27

			BATTING																BASERUNNING				PERCENTAGES		
Year	Team	Lg	G	AB	H	2B	3B	HR	(Hm	Rd)	TB	R	RBI	TBB	IBB	SO	HBP	SH	SF	SB	CS	SB%	GDP	Avg	OBP	SLG
1987	Great Falls	R	30	82	12	4	0	0	--	--	16	5	4	3	0	7	1	1	0	0	1	.00	1	.146	.186	.195
1988	Salem	A	70	275	86	10	1	0	--	--	98	54	25	38	0	32	0	6	2	11	6	.65	5	.313	.394	.356
1989	Vero Beach	A	132	484	128	11	1	1	--	--	144	74	37	33	0	21	3	5	3	18	13	.58	19	.264	.314	.298
1990	San Antonio	AA	69	194	41	4	2	0	--	--	49	20	14	8	0	24	0	7	2	2	1	.67	9	.211	.240	.253
1991	Vero Beach	A	20	66	16	2	0	0	--	--	18	6	3	1	0	3	0	1	1	2	1	.67	1	.242	.250	.273
	San Antonio	AA	16	65	21	2	0	0	--	--	23	6	9	2	0	7	0	1	1	2	3	.40	2	.323	.338	.354
	Albuquerque	AAA	66	215	63	5	5	0	--	--	78	34	29	14	1	13	0	8	4	4	1	.80	3	.293	.330	.363
1992	Albuquerque	AAA	122	395	128	18	1	0	--	--	148	47	34	22	5	7	5	10	4	5	3	.63	17	.324	.364	.375
1992	Los Angeles	NL	10	20	3	1	0	0	(0	0)	4	1	0	1	0	2	1	0	0	0	0	.00	0	.150	.227	.200

Ryan Bowen

Pitches: Right **Bats:** Right **Pos:** SP   **Ht:** 6' 0" **Wt:** 185 **Born:** 02/10/68 **Age:** 25

			HOW MUCH HE PITCHED					WHAT HE GAVE UP												THE RESULTS					
Year	Team	Lg	G	GS	CG	GF	IP	BFP	H	R	ER	HR	SH	SF	HB	TBB	IBB	SO	WP	Bk	W	L	Pct.	ShO	Sv	ERA
1987	Asheville	A	26	26	6	0	160.1	704	143	86	72	12	7	4	5	78	1	126	8	2	12	5	.706	2	0	4.04
1988	Osceola	A	4	4	0	0	13.2	65	12	8	6	0	1	0	1	10	0	12	2	0	1	0	1.000	0	0	3.95
1989	Columbus	AA	27	27	1	0	139.2	655	123	83	66	11	7	4	8	116	0	136	12	0	8	6	.571	1	0	4.25
1990	Tucson	AAA	10	7	0	0	34.2	177	41	36	36	5	2	0	0	38	1	29	0	0	1	3	.250	0	0	9.35
	Columbus	AA	18	18	2	0	113	491	103	59	47	7	4	6	0	49	0	109	5	1	8	4	.667	2	0	3.74
1991	Tucson	AAA	18	18	2	0	98.2	450	114	56	48	3	3	0	3	56	2	78	9	0	5	5	.500	2	0	4.38
1992	Tucson	AAA	21	20	1	0	122.1	555	128	68	56	7	6	2	5	64	1	94	7	0	7	6	.538	1	0	4.12
1991	Houston	NL	14	13	0	0	71.2	319	73	43	41	4	2	6	3	36	1	49	8	1	6	4	.600	0	0	5.15
1992	Houston	NL	11	9	0	2	33.2	179	48	43	41	8	3	0	2	30	3	22	5	0	0	7	.000	0	0	10.96
	2 ML YEARS		25	22	0	2	105.1	498	121	86	82	12	5	6	5	66	4	71	13	1	6	11	.353	0	0	7.01

Scott Bradley

Bats: Left **Throws:** Right **Pos:** C   **Ht:** 5'11" **Wt:** 185 **Born:** 03/22/60 **Age:** 33

			BATTING																BASERUNNING				PERCENTAGES		
Year	Team	Lg	G	AB	H	2B	3B	HR	(Hm	Rd)	TB	R	RBI	TBB	IBB	SO	HBP	SH	SF	SB	CS	SB%	GDP	Avg	OBP	SLG
1984	New York	AL	9	21	6	1	0	0	(0	0)	7	3	2	1	0	1	0	0	0	0	0	.00	0	.286	.318	.333
1985	New York	AL	19	49	8	2	1	0	(0	0)	12	4	1	1	0	5	1	0	0	0	0	.00	2	.163	.196	.245
1986	2 ML Teams		77	220	66	8	3	5	(4	1)	95	20	28	13	4	7	4	2	2	1	2	.33	13	.300	.347	.432
1987	Seattle	AL	102	342	95	15	1	5	(5	0)	127	34	43	15	1	18	3	2	4	0	1	.00	13	.278	.310	.371
1988	Seattle	AL	103	335	86	17	1	4	(3	1)	117	45	33	17	1	16	2	3	2	1	1	.50	11	.257	.295	.349
1989	Seattle	AL	103	270	74	16	0	3	(1	2)	99	21	37	21	4	23	1	1	6	1	1	.50	5	.274	.322	.367
1990	Seattle	AL	101	233	52	9	0	1	(1	0)	64	11	28	15	2	20	0	3	6	0	1	.00	6	.223	.264	.275
1991	Seattle	AL	83	172	35	7	0	0	(0	0)	42	10	11	19	2	19	0	5	2	0	0	.00	0	.203	.280	.244
1992	2 ML Teams		7	6	2	0	0	0	(0	0)	2	1	0	1	0	1	0	0	0	0	0	.00	0	.333	.500	.333
1986	Chicago	AL	9	21	6	0	0	0	(0	0)	6	3	0	1	0	0	2	0	0	0	2	.00	1	.286	.375	.286
	Seattle	AL	68	199	60	8	3	5	(4	1)	89	17	28	12	4	7	2	2	2	1	0	1.00	12	.302	.344	.447
1992	Seattle	AL	2	1	0	0	0	0	(0	0)	0	0	0	1	0	1	0	0	0	0	0	.00	0	.000	.500	.000

Cincinnati	NL	5	5	2	0	0	0	(0	0)	2	1	1	1	0	0	0	0	0	0	0	.00	0	.400	.500	.400
9 ML YEARS		604	1648	424	75	6	18	(14	4)	565	149	184	104	14	110	11	16	22	3	6	.33	52	.257	.302	.343

Glenn Braggs

Bats: Right **Throws:** Right **Pos:** LF/RF **Ht:** 6' 4" **Wt:** 220 **Born:** 10/17/62 **Age:** 30

						BATTING													BASERUNNING				PERCENTAGES		
Year Team	Lg	G	AB	H	2B	3B	HR	(Hm	Rd)	TB	R	RBI	TBB	IBB	SO	HBP	SH	SF	SB	CS	SB%	GDP	Avg	OBP	SLG
1986 Milwaukee	AL	58	215	51	8	2	4	(2	2)	75	19	18	11	0	47	1	2	3	1	1	.50	6	.237	.274	.349
1987 Milwaukee	AL	132	505	136	28	7	13	(4	9)	217	67	77	47	7	96	4	2	7	12	5	.71	20	.269	.332	.430
1988 Milwaukee	AL	72	272	71	14	0	10	(6	4)	115	30	42	14	0	60	5	1	2	6	4	.60	6	.261	.307	.423
1989 Milwaukee	AL	144	514	127	12	3	15	(8	7)	190	77	66	42	4	111	4	3	7	17	5	.77	13	.247	.305	.370
1990 2 ML Teams		109	314	88	14	1	9	(5	4)	131	39	41	38	3	64	6	0	4	8	7	.53	4	.280	.365	.417
1991 Cincinnati	NL	85	250	65	10	0	11	(8	3)	108	36	39	23	3	46	2	0	4	11	3	.79	4	.260	.323	.432
1992 Cincinnati	NL	92	266	63	16	3	8	(4	4)	109	40	38	36	5	48	2	1	2	3	1	.75	10	.237	.330	.410
1990 Milwaukee	AL	37	113	28	5	0	3	(1	2)	42	17	13	12	2	21	3	0	3	5	3	.63	1	.248	.328	.372
Cincinnati	NL	72	201	60	9	1	6	(4	2)	89	22	28	26	1	43	3	0	1	3	4	.43	3	.299	.385	.443
7 ML YEARS		692	2336	601	102	16	70	(37	33)	945	308	321	211	22	472	24	9	29	58	26	.69	63	.257	.322	.405

Jeff Branson

Bats: Left **Throws:** Right **Pos:** 2B **Ht:** 6' 0" **Wt:** 180 **Born:** 01/26/67 **Age:** 26

						BATTING													BASERUNNING				PERCENTAGES		
Year Team	Lg	G	AB	H	2B	3B	HR	(Hm	Rd)	TB	R	RBI	TBB	IBB	SO	HBP	SH	SF	SB	CS	SB%	GDP	Avg	OBP	SLG
1989 Cedar Rapids	A	127	469	132	28	1	10	--	--	192	70	68	41	3	90	2	4	4	5	6	.45	10	.281	.339	.409
1990 Chattanooga	AA	63	233	49	9	1	2	--	--	66	19	29	13	2	48	0	1	2	3	1	.75	4	.210	.250	.283
Cedar Rapids	A	62	239	60	13	4	6	--	--	99	37	24	24	3	45	0	0	2	11	3	.79	6	.251	.317	.414
1991 Chattanooga	AA	88	304	80	13	3	2	--	--	105	35	28	31	2	51	1	2	5	3	7	.30	4	.263	.328	.345
Nashville	AAA	43	145	35	4	1	0	--	--	41	10	11	8	2	31	0	1	0	5	4	.56	1	.241	.281	.283
1992 Nashville	AAA	36	123	40	6	3	4	--	--	64	18	12	9	1	19	0	1	0	0	3	.00	1	.325	.371	.520
1992 Cincinnati	NL	72	115	34	7	1	0	(0	0)	43	12	15	5	2	16	0	2	1	0	1	.00	4	.296	.322	.374

Cliff Brantley

Pitches: Right **Bats:** Right **Pos:** RP/SP **Ht:** 6' 1" **Wt:** 190 **Born:** 04/12/68 **Age:** 25

		HOW MUCH HE PITCHED						WHAT HE GAVE UP									THE RESULTS					
Year Team	Lg	G	GS	CG	GF	IP	BFP	H	R	ER	HR	SH	SF	HB	TBB	IBB	SO	WP	Bk	W	L	Pct.	ShO	Sv	ERA
1986 Utica	A	11	11	0	0	60.2	280	68	37	29	5	2	4	4	25	1	42	5	1	3	5	.375	0	0	4.30
1987 Spartanburg	A	20	20	3	0	110.1	494	114	69	59	2	2	2	9	58	2	86	10	3	3	10	.231	0	0	4.81
1988 Clearwater	A	24	24	6	0	166.2	689	126	55	48	2	4	6	5	74	6	124	20	9	8	11	.421	1	0	2.59
Reading	AA	1	1	0	0	6	26	5	4	4	1	0	1	1	2	0	5	0	0	1	0	1.000	0	0	6.00
1989 Reading	AA	11	9	0	1	49	227	49	29	18	1	1	2	2	28	0	35	2	1	3	4	.429	0	1	3.31
Clearwater	A	8	8	1	0	49.2	228	60	31	24	3	1	3	0	19	1	33	6	2	0	5	.000	0	0	4.35
1990 Clearwater	A	8	8	2	0	49	201	44	20	16	3	4	0	1	17	0	37	5	0	1	4	.200	0	0	2.94
Reading	AA	17	17	0	0	87	386	93	51	44	4	3	3	3	39	0	69	4	1	4	9	.308	0	0	4.55
1991 Reading	AA	11	11	2	0	69.2	279	50	17	15	3	8	0	4	25	1	51	2	1	4	3	.571	1	0	1.94
Scranton-Wb	AAA	8	8	0	0	47.1	206	44	26	20	2	1	0	2	25	0	28	0	2	2	4	.333	0	0	3.80
1992 Scranton/wb	AAA	5	5	0	0	30.2	122	19	7	6	1	1	0	2	14	0	26	2	0	3	1	.750	0	0	1.76
1991 Philadelphia	NL	6	5	0	0	31.2	140	26	12	12	0	2	3	2	19	0	25	2	0	2	2	.500	0	0	3.41
1992 Philadelphia	NL	28	9	0	6	76.1	353	71	45	39	6	5	3	4	58	4	32	4	1	2	6	.250	0	0	4.60
2 ML YEARS		34	14	0	6	108	493	97	57	51	6	7	6	6	77	4	57	6	1	4	8	.333	0	0	4.25

Jeff Brantley

Pitches: Right **Bats:** Right **Pos:** RP/SP **Ht:** 5'11" **Wt:** 180 **Born:** 09/05/63 **Age:** 29

		HOW MUCH HE PITCHED						WHAT HE GAVE UP									THE RESULTS					
Year Team	Lg	G	GS	CG	GF	IP	BFP	H	R	ER	HR	SH	SF	HB	TBB	IBB	SO	WP	Bk	W	L	Pct.	ShO	Sv	ERA
1988 San Francisco	NL	9	1	0	2	20.2	88	22	13	13	2	1	0	1	6	1	11	0	1	0	1	.000	0	1	5.66
1989 San Francisco	NL	59	0	0	15	97.1	422	101	50	44	10	7	3	2	37	8	69	3	2	7	1	.875	0	0	4.07
1990 San Francisco	NL	55	0	0	32	86.2	361	77	18	15	3	2	2	3	33	6	61	0	3	5	3	.625	0	19	1.56
1991 San Francisco	NL	67	0	0	39	95.1	411	78	27	26	8	4	4	5	52	10	81	6	0	5	2	.714	0	15	2.45
1992 San Francisco	NL	56	4	0	32	91.2	381	67	32	30	8	7	3	3	45	5	86	3	1	7	7	.500	0	7	2.95
5 ML YEARS		246	6	0	120	391.2	1663	345	140	128	31	21	12	14	173	30	308	12	7	24	14	.632	0	42	2.94

Sid Bream

Bats: Left **Throws:** Left **Pos:** 1B **Ht:** 6' 4" **Wt:** 220 **Born:** 08/03/60 **Age:** 32

						BATTING													BASERUNNING				PERCENTAGES		
Year Team	Lg	G	AB	H	2B	3B	HR	(Hm	Rd)	TB	R	RBI	TBB	IBB	SO	HBP	SH	SF	SB	CS	SB%	GDP	Avg	OBP	SLG
1983 Los Angeles	NL	15	11	2	0	0	0	(0	0)	2	0	2	2	0	2	0	0	0	0	0	.00	1	.182	.308	.182
1984 Los Angeles	NL	27	49	9	3	0	0	(0	0)	12	2	6	6	2	9	0	1	2	1	0	1.00	1	.184	.263	.245

27

Year	Team	Lg	G	AB	H	2B	3B	HR	(Hm	Rd)	TB	R	RBI	TBB	IBB	SO	HBP	SH	SF	SB	CS	SB%	GDP	Avg	OBP	SLG
1985	2 ML Teams		50	148	34	7	0	6	(2	4)	59	18	21	18	5	24	0	3	2	0	2	.00	4	.230	.310	.399
1986	Pittsburgh	NL	154	522	140	37	5	16	(5	11)	235	73	77	60	5	73	1	1	7	13	7	.65	14	.268	.341	.450
1987	Pittsburgh	NL	149	516	142	25	3	13	(10	3)	212	64	65	49	11	69	0	3	4	9	8	.53	19	.275	.336	.411
1988	Pittsburgh	NL	148	462	122	37	0	10	(6	4)	189	50	65	47	6	64	1	4	8	9	9	.50	11	.264	.328	.409
1989	Pittsburgh	NL	19	36	8	3	0	0	(0	0)	11	3	4	12	0	10	0	2	0	0	4	.00	0	.222	.417	.306
1990	Pittsburgh	NL	147	389	105	23	2	15	(8	7)	177	39	67	48	5	65	2	4	5	8	4	.67	6	.270	.349	.455
1991	Atlanta	NL	91	265	67	12	0	11	(3	8)	112	32	45	25	5	31	0	4	4	0	3	.00	8	.253	.313	.423
1992	Atlanta	NL	125	372	97	25	1	10	(4	6)	154	30	61	46	2	51	1	3	4	6	0	1.00	3	.261	.340	.414
1985	Los Angeles	NL	24	53	7	0	0	3	(2	1)	16	4	6	7	3	10	0	2	1	0	0	.00	0	.132	.230	.302
	Pittsburgh	NL	26	95	27	7	0	3	(0	3)	43	14	15	11	2	14	0	1	1	0	2	.00	4	.284	.355	.453
10 ML YEARS			925	2770	726	172	11	81	(38	43)	1163	311	413	313	41	398	5	25	36	46	37	.55	67	.262	.334	.420

George Brett

Bats: Left **Throws:** Right **Pos:** DH/1B   **Ht:** 6' 0" **Wt:** 205 **Born:** 05/15/53 **Age:** 40

						BATTING														**BASERUNNING**				**PERCENTAGES**		
Year	Team	Lg	G	AB	H	2B	3B	HR	(Hm	Rd)	TB	R	RBI	TBB	IBB	SO	HBP	SH	SF	SB	CS	SB%	GDP	Avg	OBP	SLG
1973	Kansas City	AL	13	40	5	2	0	0	(0	0)	7	2	0	0	0	5	0	1	0	0	0	.00	0	.125	.125	.175
1974	Kansas City	AL	133	457	129	21	5	2	(0	2)	166	49	47	21	3	38	0	6	2	8	5	.62	9	.282	.313	.363
1975	Kansas City	AL	159	634	195	35	13	11	(2	9)	289	84	89	46	6	49	2	9	6	13	10	.57	8	.308	.353	.456
1976	Kansas City	AL	159	645	215	34	14	7	(6	1)	298	94	67	49	4	36	1	2	8	21	11	.66	8	.333	.377	.462
1977	Kansas City	AL	139	564	176	32	13	22	(9	13)	300	105	88	55	9	24	2	3	3	14	12	.54	12	.312	.373	.532
1978	Kansas City	AL	128	510	150	45	8	9	(4	5)	238	79	62	39	6	35	1	3	5	23	7	.77	6	.294	.342	.467
1979	Kansas City	AL	154	645	212	42	20	23	(11	12)	363	119	107	51	14	36	0	1	4	17	10	.63	8	.329	.376	.563
1980	Kansas City	AL	117	449	175	33	9	24	(13	11)	298	87	118	58	16	22	1	0	7	15	6	.71	11	.390	.454	.664
1981	Kansas City	AL	89	347	109	27	7	6	(2	4)	168	42	43	27	7	23	1	0	4	14	6	.70	7	.314	.361	.484
1982	Kansas City	AL	144	552	166	32	9	21	(9	12)	279	101	82	71	14	51	1	0	5	6	1	.86	12	.301	.378	.505
1983	Kansas City	AL	123	464	144	38	2	25	(7	18)	261	90	93	57	13	39	1	0	3	0	1	.00	9	.310	.385	.563
1984	Kansas City	AL	104	377	107	21	3	13	(6	7)	173	42	69	38	6	37	0	0	7	0	2	.00	11	.284	.344	.459
1985	Kansas City	AL	155	550	184	38	5	30	(15	15)	322	108	112	103	31	49	3	0	9	9	1	.90	12	.335	.436	.585
1986	Kansas City	AL	124	441	128	28	4	16	(8	8)	212	70	73	80	18	45	4	0	4	1	2	.33	6	.290	.401	.481
1987	Kansas City	AL	115	427	124	18	2	22	(14	8)	212	71	78	72	14	47	1	0	8	6	3	.67	10	.290	.388	.496
1988	Kansas City	AL	157	589	180	42	3	24	(13	11)	300	90	103	82	15	51	3	0	7	14	3	.82	15	.306	.389	.509
1989	Kansas City	AL	124	457	129	26	3	12	(3	9)	197	67	80	59	14	47	3	0	9	14	4	.78	18	.282	.362	.431
1990	Kansas City	AL	142	544	179	45	7	14	(3	11)	280	82	87	56	14	63	0	0	7	9	2	.82	18	.329	.387	.515
1991	Kansas City	AL	131	505	129	40	2	10	(3	7)	203	77	61	58	10	75	0	1	8	2	0	1.00	20	.255	.327	.402
1992	Kansas City	AL	152	592	169	35	5	7	(1	6)	235	55	61	35	6	69	6	0	4	8	6	.57	15	.285	.330	.397
20 ML YEARS			2562	9789	3005	634	134	298	(129	169)	4801	1514	1520	1057	220	841	30	26	110	194	92	.68	215	.307	.372	.490

Rod Brewer

Bats: Left **Throws:** Left **Pos:** 1B   **Ht:** 6' 3" **Wt:** 208 **Born:** 02/24/66 **Age:** 27

						BATTING														**BASERUNNING**				**PERCENTAGES**		
Year	Team	Lg	G	AB	H	2B	3B	HR	(Hm	Rd)	TB	R	RBI	TBB	IBB	SO	HBP	SH	SF	SB	CS	SB%	GDP	Avg	OBP	SLG
1987	Johnson Cty	R	67	238	60	11	2	10	--	--	105	33	42	36	5	40	3	0	2	2	2	.50	4	.252	.355	.441
1988	Springfield	A	133	457	136	25	2	8	--	--	189	57	64	63	7	52	5	1	4	6	4	.60	22	.298	.386	.414
1989	Arkansas	AA	128	470	130	25	2	10	--	--	189	71	93	46	3	46	7	0	3	2	3	.40	8	.277	.348	.402
1990	Louisville	AAA	144	514	129	15	5	12	--	--	190	60	83	54	7	62	9	0	6	0	2	.00	9	.251	.329	.370
1991	Louisville	AAA	104	382	86	21	1	8	--	--	133	39	52	35	1	57	6	0	1	4	0	1.00	10	.225	.300	.348
1992	Louisville	AAA	120	423	122	20	2	18	--	--	200	57	86	49	6	60	5	0	1	0	3	.00	8	.288	.368	.473
1990	St. Louis	NL	14	25	6	1	0	0	(0	0)	7	4	2	0	0	4	0	0	0	0	0	.00	1	.240	.240	.280
1991	St. Louis	NL	19	13	1	0	0	0	(0	0)	1	0	1	0	0	5	0	0	0	0	0	.00	0	.077	.077	.077
1992	St. Louis	NL	29	103	31	6	0	0	(0	0)	37	11	10	8	0	12	1	0	1	0	1	.00	1	.301	.354	.359
3 ML YEARS			62	141	38	7	0	0	(0	0)	45	15	13	8	0	21	1	0	1	0	1	.00	2	.270	.311	.319

Greg Briley

Bats: Left **Throws:** Right **Pos:** LF/CF/DH   **Ht:** 5' 9" **Wt:** 170 **Born:** 05/24/65 **Age:** 28

						BATTING														**BASERUNNING**				**PERCENTAGES**		
Year	Team	Lg	G	AB	H	2B	3B	HR	(Hm	Rd)	TB	R	RBI	TBB	IBB	SO	HBP	SH	SF	SB	CS	SB%	GDP	Avg	OBP	SLG
1988	Seattle	AL	13	36	9	2	0	1	(0	1)	14	6	4	5	1	6	0	0	1	0	1	.00	0	.250	.333	.389
1989	Seattle	AL	115	394	105	22	4	13	(5	8)	174	52	52	39	1	82	5	1	5	11	5	.69	9	.266	.336	.442
1990	Seattle	AL	125	337	83	18	2	5	(4	1)	120	40	29	37	0	48	1	1	4	16	4	.80	6	.246	.319	.356
1991	Seattle	AL	139	381	99	17	3	2	(2	0)	128	39	26	27	0	51	0	1	3	23	11	.68	7	.260	.307	.336
1992	Seattle	AL	86	200	55	10	0	5	(1	4)	80	18	12	4	0	31	1	0	2	9	2	.82	4	.275	.290	.400
5 ML YEARS			478	1348	351	69	9	26	(12	14)	516	155	123	112	2	218	7	3	15	59	23	.72	26	.260	.317	.383

28

Brad Brink

Pitches: Right **Bats:** Right **Pos:** SP   **Ht:** 6' 2" **Wt:** 195 **Born:** 01/20/65 **Age:** 28

				HOW MUCH HE PITCHED					WHAT HE GAVE UP													THE RESULTS					
Year Team	Lg	G	GS	CG	GF	IP	BFP	H	R	ER	HR	SH	SF	HB	TBB	IBB	SO	WP	Bk	W	L	Pct.	ShO	Sv	ERA
1986 Reading	AA	5	4	0	0	23.2	107	22	12	10	2	3	1	1	20	2	8	0	0	0	4	.000	0	0	3.80
1987 Clearwater	A	17	17	2	0	94.1	418	99	50	40	5	4	5	2	39	0	64	1	0	4	7	.364	1	0	3.82
Reading	AA	12	11	1	0	72	308	76	42	40	7	2	4	5	23	2	50	3	2	3	2	.600	1	0	5.00
1988 Maine	AAA	17	17	3	0	86	375	100	43	41	8	2	3	4	21	0	58	4	2	5	5	.500	1	0	4.29
1989 Scr Wil-Bar	AAA	3	3	0	0	11	49	11	7	5	0	1	1	0	6	0	3	0	0	0	1	.000	0	0	4.09
1991 Spartanburg	A	3	3	1	0	16.1	68	15	3	3	1	0	0	0	5	0	16	1	1	2	1	.667	0	0	1.65
Clearwater	A	2	2	0	0	13	46	6	1	1	1	1	0	0	3	0	10	0	1	2	0	1.000	0	0	0.69
Reading	AA	5	5	0	0	34	138	32	14	14	3	2	2	1	6	0	27	1	0	2	2	.500	0	0	3.71
1992 Reading	AA	3	3	0	0	13.2	59	14	6	5	0	1	0	0	3	0	12	0	0	1	1	.500	0	0	3.29
Scranton/wb	AAA	17	17	5	0	111.1	454	100	47	43	15	0	1	2	34	0	92	3	0	8	2	.800	2	0	3.48
1992 Philadelphia	NL	8	7	0	0	41.1	187	53	27	19	2	1	0	1	13	2	16	0	0	0	4	.000	0	0	4.14

John Briscoe

Pitches: Right **Bats:** Right **Pos:** SP   **Ht:** 6' 3" **Wt:** 185 **Born:** 09/22/67 **Age:** 25

				HOW MUCH HE PITCHED					WHAT HE GAVE UP													THE RESULTS					
Year Team	Lg	G	GS	CG	GF	IP	BFP	H	R	ER	HR	SH	SF	HB	TBB	IBB	SO	WP	Bk	W	L	Pct.	ShO	Sv	ERA
1988 Athletics	R	7	6	0	0	25.2	105	26	14	10	1	0	1	1	6	0	23	3	3	1	1	.500	0	0	3.51
1989 Madison	A	21	20	1	1	117.2	524	121	66	55	7	10	9	9	57	0	69	11	1	7	5	.583	0	0	4.21
1990 Modesto	A	29	12	1	12	86.1	373	72	50	44	12	4	1	2	52	0	66	6	0	3	6	.333	0	0	4.59
Huntsville	AA	3	0	0	0	4.2	30	9	7	7	1	0	0	0	7	0	7	1	0	0	0	.000	0	0	13.50
1991 Huntsville	AA	2	0	0	2	4.1	19	1	2	0	0	0	0	0	2	0	6	0	0	2	0	1.000	0	0	0.00
Tacoma	AAA	22	9	0	6	76.1	342	73	35	31	7	2	2	5	44	1	66	3	0	3	5	.375	0	1	3.66
1992 Tacoma	AAA	33	6	0	11	78	368	78	62	51	7	5	2	1	68	5	66	6	0	2	5	.286	0	0	5.88
1991 Oakland	AL	11	0	0	9	14	62	12	11	11	3	0	1	0	10	0	9	3	0	0	0	.000	0	0	7.07
1992 Oakland	AL	2	2	0	0	7	40	12	6	5	0	1	0	0	9	0	4	2	0	0	1	.000	0	0	6.43
2 ML YEARS		13	2	0	9	21	102	24	17	16	3	1	1	0	19	0	13	5	0	0	1	.000	0	0	6.86

Bernardo Brito

Bats: Right **Throws:** Right **Pos:** LF   **Ht:** 6' 1" **Wt:** 190 **Born:** 12/04/63 **Age:** 29

								BATTING												BASERUNNING				PERCENTAGES		
Year Team	Lg	G	AB	H	2B	3B	HR	(Hm	Rd)	TB	R	RBI	TBB	IBB	SO	HBP	SH	SF	SB	CS	SB%	GDP	Avg	OBP	SLG
1984 Batavia	A	76	297	89	19	3	19	--	--	171	41	57	14	1	67	1	2	0	3	4	.43	7	.300	.333	.576
1985 Waterloo	A	135	498	128	27	1	29	--	--	244	66	78	24	1	133	4	0	3	1	4	.20	15	.257	.295	.490
1986 Waterbury	AA	129	479	118	17	1	18	--	--	191	61	75	22	0	127	3	3	3	0	1	.00	10	.246	.282	.399
1987 Williamsprt	AA	124	452	125	20	4	24	--	--	225	64	79	24	2	121	5	0	6	2	6	.25	15	.277	.316	.498
1988 Orlando	AA	135	508	122	20	4	24	--	--	222	55	76	20	2	138	1	0	9	2	2	.50	12	.240	.266	.437
1989 Portland	AAA	111	355	90	12	7	22	--	--	182	51	74	31	4	111	4	2	2	1	3	.25	7	.254	.319	.513
1990 Portland	AAA	113	376	106	26	3	25	--	--	213	48	79	27	3	102	2	2	4	1	4	.20	13	.282	.330	.566
1991 Portland	AAA	115	428	111	17	2	27	--	--	213	65	83	28	2	110	7	0	7	1	0	1.00	9	.259	.311	.498
1992 Portland	AAA	140	564	152	27	7	26	--	--	271	80	96	32	6	124	6	0	5	0	1	.00	18	.270	.313	.480
1992 Minnesota	AL	8	14	2	1	0	0	(0	0)	3	1	2	0	0	4	0	0	1	0	1	.00	0	.143	.133	.214

Doug Brocail

Pitches: Right **Bats:** Left **Pos:** SP   **Ht:** 6' 5" **Wt:** 190 **Born:** 05/16/67 **Age:** 26

				HOW MUCH HE PITCHED					WHAT HE GAVE UP													THE RESULTS					
Year Team	Lg	G	GS	CG	GF	IP	BFP	H	R	ER	HR	SH	SF	HB	TBB	IBB	SO	WP	Bk	W	L	Pct.	ShO	Sv	ERA
1986 Spokane	A	16	15	0	1	85	0	85	52	36	4	0	0	6	53	1	77	10	1	5	4	.556	0	0	3.81
1987 Chston-Sc	A	19	18	0	0	92.1	393	94	51	42	6	3	3	1	28	0	68	4	0	2	6	.250	0	0	4.09
1988 Chston-Sc	A	22	13	5	7	107	447	107	40	32	3	4	2	0	25	0	107	4	3	8	6	.571	0	2	2.69
1989 Wichita	AA	23	22	1	0	134.2	603	158	88	78	11	5	5	1	50	4	95	9	4	5	9	.357	1	0	5.21
1990 Wichita	AA	12	9	0	1	52	227	53	30	25	7	1	0	2	24	0	27	4	0	2	2	.500	0	0	4.33
1991 Wichita	AA	34	16	3	11	146.1	625	147	77	63	15	7	3	4	43	3	108	13	0	10	7	.588	3	6	3.87
1992 Las Vegas	AAA	29	25	4	2	172.1	733	187	82	76	7	6	1	6	63	5	103	6	0	10	10	.500	0	0	3.97
1992 San Diego	NL	3	3	0	0	14	64	17	10	10	2	2	0	0	5	0	15	0	0	0	0	.000	0	0	6.43

Rico Brogna

Bats: Left **Throws:** Left **Pos:** 1B   **Ht:** 6' 2" **Wt:** 202 **Born:** 04/18/70 **Age:** 23

								BATTING												BASERUNNING				PERCENTAGES		
Year Team	Lg	G	AB	H	2B	3B	HR	(Hm	Rd)	TB	R	RBI	TBB	IBB	SO	HBP	SH	SF	SB	CS	SB%	GDP	Avg	OBP	SLG
1988 Bristol	R	60	209	53	11	2	7	--	--	89	37	33	25	2	42	2	2	1	3	4	.43	3	.254	.338	.426
1989 Lakeland	A	128	459	108	20	7	5	--	--	157	47	51	38	6	82	2	3	3	2	4	.33	10	.235	.295	.342
1990 London	AA	137	488	128	21	3	21	--	--	218	70	77	50	8	100	3	3	5	1	2	.33	13	.262	.332	.447
1991 London	AA	77	293	80	13	1	13	--	--	134	40	51	25	2	59	0	3	5	0	1	.00	7	.273	.325	.457

Toledo	AAA	41	132	29	5	1	2	--	--	42	13	13	4	2	26	1	1	0	2	0	1.00	9	.220	.248	.318
1992 Toledo	AAA	121	387	101	19	4	10	--	--	158	45	58	31	2	85	1	4	5	1	1	.50	7	.261	.314	.408
1992 Detroit	AL	9	26	5	1	0	1	(1	0)	9	3	3	3	0	5	0	0	0	0	0	.00	0	.192	.276	.346

Hubie Brooks

Bats: Right **Throws:** Right **Pos:** DH   **Ht:** 6' 0" **Wt:** 205 **Born:** 09/24/56 **Age:** 36

							BATTING												BASERUNNING				PERCENTAGES		
Year Team	Lg	G	AB	H	2B	3B	HR	(Hm	Rd)	TB	R	RBI	TBB	IBB	SO	HBP	SH	SF	SB	CS	SB%	GDP	Avg	OBP	SLG
1980 New York	NL	24	81	25	2	1	1	(0	1)	32	8	10	5	0	9	2	1	0	1	1	.50	1	.309	.364	.395
1981 New York	NL	98	358	110	21	2	4	(2	2)	147	34	38	23	2	65	1	1	6	9	5	.64	9	.307	.345	.411
1982 New York	NL	126	457	114	21	2	2	(1	1)	145	40	40	28	5	76	5	3	5	6	3	.67	11	.249	.297	.317
1983 New York	NL	150	586	147	18	4	5	(4	1)	188	53	58	24	2	96	4	7	3	6	4	.60	14	.251	.284	.321
1984 New York	NL	153	561	159	23	2	16	(12	4)	234	61	73	48	15	79	2	0	2	6	5	.55	17	.283	.341	.417
1985 Montreal	NL	156	605	163	34	7	13	(4	9)	250	67	100	34	6	79	5	0	8	6	9	.40	20	.269	.310	.413
1986 Montreal	NL	80	306	104	18	5	14	(3	11)	174	50	58	25	3	60	2	0	5	4	2	.67	11	.340	.388	.569
1987 Montreal	NL	112	430	113	22	3	14	(9	5)	183	57	72	24	2	72	1	0	4	4	3	.57	7	.263	.301	.426
1988 Montreal	NL	151	588	164	35	2	20	(9	11)	263	61	90	35	3	108	1	0	4	7	3	.70	21	.279	.318	.447
1989 Montreal	NL	148	542	145	30	1	14	(7	7)	219	56	70	39	2	108	4	0	8	6	11	.35	15	.268	.317	.404
1990 Los Angeles	NL	153	568	151	28	1	20	(9	11)	241	74	91	33	10	108	6	0	11	2	5	.29	13	.266	.307	.424
1991 New York	NL	103	357	85	11	1	16	(4	12)	146	48	50	44	8	62	3	0	3	3	1	.75	7	.238	.324	.409
1992 California	AL	82	306	66	13	0	8	(2	6)	103	28	36	12	3	46	1	0	1	3	3	.50	10	.216	.247	.337
13 ML YEARS		1536	5745	1546	276	31	147	(66	81)	2325	637	786	374	61	968	37	12	60	63	55	.53	156	.269	.315	.405

Scott Brosius

Bats: Right **Throws:** Right **Pos:** RF/3B   **Ht:** 6' 1" **Wt:** 185 **Born:** 08/15/66 **Age:** 26

							BATTING												BASERUNNING				PERCENTAGES		
Year Team	Lg	G	AB	H	2B	3B	HR	(Hm	Rd)	TB	R	RBI	TBB	IBB	SO	HBP	SH	SF	SB	CS	SB%	GDP	Avg	OBP	SLG
1987 Medford	A	65	255	73	18	1	3	--	--	102	34	49	26	0	36	0	1	7	5	2	.71	7	.286	.344	.400
1988 Madison	A	132	504	153	28	2	9	--	--	212	82	58	56	1	67	3	4	4	13	12	.52	7	.304	.374	.421
1989 Huntsville	AA	128	461	125	22	2	7	--	--	172	68	60	58	3	62	5	6	6	4	6	.40	11	.271	.355	.373
1990 Huntsville	AA	142	547	162	39	2	23	--	--	274	94	88	81	2	81	1	7	9	12	3	.80	8	.296	.382	.501
Tacoma	AAA	3	7	1	0	1	0	--	--	3	2	0	1	0	3	0	0	0	0	0	.00	0	.143	.250	.429
1991 Tacoma	AAA	65	245	70	16	3	8	--	--	116	28	31	18	0	29	2	1	2	4	2	.67	7	.286	.337	.473
1992 Tacoma	AAA	63	236	56	13	0	9	--	--	96	29	31	23	3	44	1	0	4	8	5	.62	5	.237	.303	.407
1991 Oakland	AL	36	68	16	5	0	2	(1	1)	27	9	4	3	0	11	0	1	0	3	1	.75	2	.235	.268	.397
1992 Oakland	AL	38	87	19	2	0	4	(1	3)	33	13	13	3	1	13	2	0	1	3	0	1.00	0	.218	.258	.379
2 ML YEARS		74	155	35	7	0	6	(2	4)	60	22	17	6	1	24	2	1	1	6	1	.86	2	.226	.262	.387

Jarvis Brown

Bats: Right **Throws:** Right **Pos:** RF   **Ht:** 5' 7" **Wt:** 170 **Born:** 03/26/67 **Age:** 26

							BATTING												BASERUNNING				PERCENTAGES		
Year Team	Lg	G	AB	H	2B	3B	HR	(Hm	Rd)	TB	R	RBI	TBB	IBB	SO	HBP	SH	SF	SB	CS	SB%	GDP	Avg	OBP	SLG
1986 Elizabethtn	R	49	180	41	4	0	3	--	--	54	28	23	18	0	41	4	5	1	15	3	.83	3	.228	.310	.300
1987 Elizabethtn	R	67	258	63	9	1	1	--	--	77	52	15	48	1	50	5	3	0	30	2	.94	3	.244	.373	.298
Kenosha	A	43	117	22	4	1	3	--	--	37	17	16	19	0	24	2	1	2	6	2	.75	2	.188	.307	.316
1988 Kenosha	A	138	531	156	25	7	7	--	--	216	108	46	71	0	89	10	7	5	72	15	.83	10	.294	.384	.407
1989 Visalia	A	141	545	131	21	6	4	--	--	176	95	46	73	0	112	13	4	4	49	13	.79	12	.240	.342	.323
1990 Orlando	AA	135	527	137	22	7	14	--	--	215	104	57	80	1	79	9	5	2	33	19	.63	13	.260	.366	.408
1991 Portland	AAA	108	436	126	5	8	3	--	--	156	62	37	36	1	66	6	3	1	26	12	.68	6	.289	.351	.358
1992 Portland	AAA	62	224	56	8	2	2	--	--	74	25	16	20	0	37	5	1	1	17	1	.94	2	.250	.324	.330
1991 Minnesota	AL	38	37	8	0	0	0	(0	0)	8	10	0	2	0	8	0	1	0	7	1	.88	0	.216	.256	.216
1992 Minnesota	AL	35	15	1	0	0	0	(0	0)	1	8	0	2	0	4	1	0	0	2	2	.50	0	.067	.222	.067
2 ML YEARS		73	52	9	0	0	0	(0	0)	9	18	0	4	0	12	1	1	0	9	3	.75	0	.173	.246	.173

Keith Brown

Pitches: Right **Bats:** Both **Pos:** SP   **Ht:** 6' 4" **Wt:** 215 **Born:** 02/14/64 **Age:** 29

					HOW MUCH HE PITCHED					WHAT HE GAVE UP									THE RESULTS					
Year Team	Lg	G	GS	CG	GF	IP	BFP	H	R	ER	HR	SH	SF	HB	TBB	IBB	SO	WP	Bk	W	L	Pct.	ShO	Sv	ERA
1988 Cincinnati	NL	4	3	0	1	16.1	63	14	5	5	1	0	0	0	4	0	6	1	0	2	1	.667	0	0	2.76
1990 Cincinnati	NL	8	0	0	2	11.1	46	12	6	6	2	1	0	0	3	0	8	0	0	0	0	.000	0	0	4.76
1991 Cincinnati	NL	11	0	0	3	12	56	15	4	3	0	1	0	0	6	1	4	1	0	0	0	.000	0	0	2.25
1992 Cincinnati	NL	2	2	0	0	8	37	10	5	4	2	0	0	0	5	0	5	0	0	0	1	.000	0	0	4.50
4 ML YEARS		25	5	0	6	47.2	202	51	20	18	5	2	0	0	18	1	23	2	0	2	2	.500	0	0	3.40

Kevin Brown

Pitches: Right **Bats:** Right **Pos:** SP   **Ht:** 6' 4" **Wt:** 195 **Born:** 03/14/65 **Age:** 28

			HOW MUCH HE PITCHED						WHAT HE GAVE UP												THE RESULTS					
Year Team	Lg	G	GS	CG	GF	IP	BFP	H	R	ER	HR	SH	SF	HB	TBB	IBB	SO	WP	Bk	W	L	Pct.	ShO	Sv	ERA
1986 Texas	AL	1	1	0	0	5	19	6	2	2	0	0	0	0	0	0	4	0	0	1	0	1.000	0	0	3.60
1988 Texas	AL	4	4	1	0	23.1	110	33	15	11	2	1	0	1	8	1	12	1	0	1	1	.500	0	0	4.24
1989 Texas	AL	28	28	7	0	191	798	167	81	71	10	3	6	4	70	2	104	7	2	12	9	.571	0	0	3.35
1990 Texas	AL	26	26	6	0	180	757	175	84	72	13	2	7	3	60	3	88	9	2	12	10	.545	2	0	3.60
1991 Texas	AL	33	33	0	0	210.2	934	233	116	103	17	6	4	13	90	5	96	12	3	9	12	.429	0	0	4.40
1992 Texas	AL	35	35	11	0	265.2	1108	262	117	98	11	7	8	10	76	2	173	8	2	21	11	.656	1	0	3.32
6 ML YEARS		127	127	25	0	875.2	3726	876	415	357	53	19	25	31	304	12	477	37	9	56	43	.566	3	0	3.67

Kevin D. Brown

Pitches: Left **Bats:** Left **Pos:** RP   **Ht:** 6' 1" **Wt:** 185 **Born:** 03/05/66 **Age:** 27

			HOW MUCH HE PITCHED						WHAT HE GAVE UP												THE RESULTS					
Year Team	Lg	G	GS	CG	GF	IP	BFP	H	R	ER	HR	SH	SF	HB	TBB	IBB	SO	WP	Bk	W	L	Pct.	ShO	Sv	ERA
1990 2 ML Teams		7	3	0	2	23	96	16	7	6	1	1	1	1	8	1	12	2	0	1	1	.500	0	0	2.35
1991 Milwaukee	AL	15	10	0	0	63.2	285	66	39	39	6	5	1	1	34	2	30	6	0	2	4	.333	0	0	5.51
1992 Seattle	AL	2	0	0	0	3	15	4	3	3	1	0	0	0	3	0	2	0	0	0	0	.000	0	0	9.00
1990 New York	NL	2	0	0	1	2	9	2	0	0	0	0	0	0	1	0	0	0	0	0	0	.000	0	0	0.00
Milwaukee	AL	5	3	0	1	21	87	14	7	6	1	1	1	1	7	1	12	2	0	1	1	.500	0	0	2.57
3 ML YEARS		24	13	0	2	89.2	396	86	49	48	8	6	2	2	45	3	44	8	0	3	5	.375	0	0	4.82

Jerry Browne

Bats: Both **Throws:** Right **Pos:** 3B/2B/LF/CF   **Ht:** 5'10" **Wt:** 170 **Born:** 02/13/66 **Age:** 27

								BATTING											BASERUNNING				PERCENTAGES		
Year Team	Lg	G	AB	H	2B	3B	HR	(Hm	Rd)	TB	R	RBI	TBB	IBB	SO	HBP	SH	SF	SB	CS	SB%	GDP	Avg	OBP	SLG
1986 Texas	AL	12	24	10	2	0	0	(0	0)	12	6	3	1	0	4	0	0	0	0	2	.00	0	.417	.440	.500
1987 Texas	AL	132	454	123	16	6	1	(1	0)	154	63	38	61	0	50	2	7	2	27	17	.61	6	.271	.358	.339
1988 Texas	AL	73	214	49	9	2	1	(1	0)	65	26	17	25	0	32	0	3	1	7	5	.58	5	.229	.308	.304
1989 Cleveland	AL	153	598	179	31	4	5	(1	4)	233	83	45	68	10	64	1	14	4	14	6	.70	9	.299	.370	.390
1990 Cleveland	AL	140	513	137	26	5	6	(2	4)	191	92	50	72	1	46	2	12	11	12	7	.63	12	.267	.353	.372
1991 Cleveland	AL	107	290	66	5	2	1	(1	0)	78	28	29	27	0	29	1	12	4	2	4	.33	5	.228	.292	.269
1992 Oakland	AL	111	324	93	12	2	3	(1	2)	118	43	40	40	0	40	4	16	6	3	3	.50	7	.287	.366	.364
7 ML YEARS		728	2417	657	101	21	17	(7	10)	851	341	222	294	11	265	10	64	28	65	44	.60	44	.272	.350	.352

Tom Browning

Pitches: Left **Bats:** Left **Pos:** SP   **Ht:** 6' 1" **Wt:** 195 **Born:** 04/28/60 **Age:** 33

			HOW MUCH HE PITCHED						WHAT HE GAVE UP												THE RESULTS					
Year Team	Lg	G	GS	CG	GF	IP	BFP	H	R	ER	HR	SH	SF	HB	TBB	IBB	SO	WP	Bk	W	L	Pct.	ShO	Sv	ERA
1984 Cincinnati	NL	3	3	0	0	23.1	95	27	4	4	0	1	0	0	5	0	14	1	0	1	0	1.000	0	0	1.54
1985 Cincinnati	NL	38	38	6	0	261.1	1083	242	111	103	29	13	7	3	73	8	155	2	0	20	9	.690	4	0	3.55
1986 Cincinnati	NL	39	39	4	0	243.1	1016	225	123	103	26	14	12	1	70	6	147	3	0	14	13	.519	2	0	3.81
1987 Cincinnati	NL	32	31	2	1	183	791	201	107	102	27	10	7	5	61	7	117	2	4	10	13	.435	0	0	5.02
1988 Cincinnati	NL	36	36	5	0	250.2	1001	205	98	95	26	6	8	7	64	2	124	2	4	18	5	.783	2	0	3.41
1989 Cincinnati	NL	37	37	9	0	249.2	1031	241	109	94	31	12	6	3	64	10	118	2	1	15	12	.556	2	0	3.39
1990 Cincinnati	NL	35	35	2	0	227.2	957	235	98	96	24	13	5	5	52	13	99	5	1	15	9	.625	1	0	3.80
1991 Cincinnati	NL	36	36	1	0	230.1	983	241	124	107	32	8	9	4	56	4	115	3	1	14	14	.500	0	0	4.18
1992 Cincinnati	NL	16	16	0	0	87	386	108	49	49	6	5	4	2	28	7	33	3	1	6	5	.545	0	0	5.07
9 ML YEARS		272	271	29	1	1756.1	7343	1725	823	753	211	82	58	30	473	58	922	23	12	113	80	.585	11	0	3.86

J.T. Bruett

Bats: Left **Throws:** Left **Pos:** RF/CF   **Ht:** 5'11" **Wt:** 175 **Born:** 10/08/67 **Age:** 25

								BATTING											BASERUNNING				PERCENTAGES		
Year Team	Lg	G	AB	H	2B	3B	HR	(Hm	Rd)	TB	R	RBI	TBB	IBB	SO	HBP	SH	SF	SB	CS	SB%	GDP	Avg	OBP	SLG
1988 Elizabethtn	R	28	91	27	3	0	0	--	--	30	23	3	19	0	15	0	0	0	17	4	.81	3	.297	.418	.330
Kenosha	A	3	10	2	0	0	0	--	--	2	2	0	3	0	0	0	0	0	1	1	.50	0	.200	.385	.200
1989 Kenosha	A	120	445	119	9	1	3	--	--	139	82	29	89	2	64	0	0	2	61	27	.69	6	.267	.389	.312
1990 Portland	AAA	10	34	8	2	0	0	--	--	10	8	3	11	0	4	0	0	1	2	1	.67	0	.235	.413	.294
Visalia	A	123	437	134	15	3	1	--	--	158	86	33	101	4	60	4	8	3	50	21	.70	8	.307	.439	.362
1991 Portland	AAA	99	345	98	6	3	0	--	--	110	51	35	40	1	41	3	9	0	21	9	.70	10	.284	.363	.319
1992 Portland	AAA	77	280	70	10	3	0	--	--	86	41	17	60	3	27	1	3	3	29	12	.71	5	.250	.381	.307
1992 Minnesota	AL	56	76	19	4	0	0	(0	0)	23	7	2	6	1	12	1	1	0	6	3	.67	0	.250	.313	.303

Jacob Brumfield

Bats: Right **Throws:** Right **Pos:** CF **Ht:** 6' 0" **Wt:** 170 **Born:** 05/27/65 **Age:** 28

Year	Team	Lg	G	AB	H	2B	3B	HR	(Hm	Rd)	TB	R	RBI	TBB	IBB	SO	HBP	SH	SF	SB	CS	SB%	GDP	Avg	OBP	SLG
1986	Ft. Myers	A	12	41	13	3	1	1	--	--	21	3	5	2	0	11	0	0	0	0	1	.00	0	.317	.349	.512
1987	Memphis	AA	9	39	13	3	2	1	--	--	23	7	6	3	0	8	0	1	0	2	1	.67	0	.333	.381	.590
	Ft. Myers	A	114	379	93	14	10	6	--	--	145	56	34	45	2	78	0	1	0	43	14	.75	12	.245	.325	.383
1988	Memphis	AA	128	433	98	15	5	6	--	--	141	70	28	52	0	104	1	8	5	47	7	.87	2	.226	.308	.326
1989	Memphis	AA	104	346	79	14	2	1	--	--	100	43	25	53	0	74	3	5	0	28	12	.70	1	.228	.336	.289
1990	Baseball Cy	A	109	372	125	24	3	0	--	--	155	66	40	60	6	44	2	2	2	47	10	.82	7	.336	.429	.417
	Omaha	AAA	24	77	25	6	1	2	--	--	39	10	11	7	0	14	0	1	2	10	3	.77	2	.325	.372	.506
1991	Omaha	AAA	111	397	106	14	7	3	--	--	143	62	43	33	0	64	1	2	3	36	17	.68	9	.267	.323	.360
1992	Nashville	AAA	56	208	59	10	3	5	--	--	90	32	19	26	0	35	2	3	0	22	11	.67	1	.284	.369	.433
1992	Cincinnati	NL	24	30	4	0	0	0	(0	0)	4	6	2	2	1	4	1	0	0	6	0	1.00	0	.133	.212	.133

Mike Brumley

Bats: Both **Throws:** Right **Pos:** PH **Ht:** 5'10" **Wt:** 175 **Born:** 04/09/63 **Age:** 30

Year	Team	Lg	G	AB	H	2B	3B	HR	(Hm	Rd)	TB	R	RBI	TBB	IBB	SO	HBP	SH	SF	SB	CS	SB%	GDP	Avg	OBP	SLG
1987	Chicago	NL	39	104	21	2	2	1	(0	1)	30	8	9	10	1	30	1	1	1	7	1	.88	2	.202	.276	.288
1989	Detroit	AL	92	212	42	5	2	1	(1	0)	54	33	11	14	0	45	1	3	0	8	4	.67	4	.198	.251	.255
1990	Seattle	AL	62	147	33	5	4	0	(0	0)	46	19	7	10	0	22	0	4	1	2	0	1.00	5	.224	.272	.313
1991	Boston	AL	63	118	25	5	0	0	(0	0)	30	16	5	10	0	22	0	4	0	2	0	1.00	1	.212	.273	.254
1992	Boston	AL	2	1	0	0	0	0	(0	0)	0	0	0	0	0	0	0	0	0	0	0	.00	0	.000	.000	.000
	5 ML YEARS		258	582	121	17	8	2	(1	1)	160	76	32	44	1	119	2	12	2	19	5	.79	11	.208	.265	.275

Tom Brunansky

Bats: Right **Throws:** Right **Pos:** RF/1B/DH **Ht:** 6' 4" **Wt:** 220 **Born:** 08/20/60 **Age:** 32

Year	Team	Lg	G	AB	H	2B	3B	HR	(Hm	Rd)	TB	R	RBI	TBB	IBB	SO	HBP	SH	SF	SB	CS	SB%	GDP	Avg	OBP	SLG
1981	California	AL	11	33	5	0	0	3	(1	2)	14	7	6	8	0	10	0	0	0	1	0	1.00	6	.152	.317	.424
1982	Minnesota	AL	127	463	126	30	1	20	(10	10)	218	77	46	71	0	101	8	1	2	1	3	.33	12	.272	.377	.471
1983	Minnesota	AL	151	542	123	24	5	28	(8	20)	241	70	82	61	4	95	4	1	3	2	5	.29	13	.227	.308	.445
1984	Minnesota	AL	155	567	144	21	0	32	(14	18)	261	75	85	57	2	94	0	0	4	4	5	.44	15	.254	.320	.460
1985	Minnesota	AL	157	567	137	28	4	27	(12	15)	254	71	90	71	7	86	0	0	13	5	3	.63	12	.242	.320	.448
1986	Minnesota	AL	157	593	152	28	1	23	(15	8)	251	69	75	53	4	98	1	1	7	12	4	.75	15	.256	.315	.423
1987	Minnesota	AL	155	532	138	22	2	32	(19	13)	260	83	85	74	5	104	4	0	4	11	11	.50	12	.259	.352	.489
1988	2 ML Teams		157	572	137	23	4	23	(7	16)	237	74	85	86	6	93	4	1	6	17	8	.68	17	.240	.340	.414
1989	St. Louis	NL	158	556	133	29	3	20	(4	16)	228	67	85	59	3	107	2	0	5	5	9	.36	10	.239	.312	.410
1990	2 ML Teams		148	518	132	27	5	16	(13	3)	217	66	73	66	7	115	4	0	5	5	10	.33	13	.255	.338	.419
1991	Boston	AL	142	459	105	24	1	16	(10	6)	179	54	70	49	2	72	3	0	8	1	2	.33	8	.229	.303	.390
1992	Boston	AL	138	458	122	31	3	15	(10	5)	204	47	74	66	2	96	0	2	7	2	5	.29	11	.266	.354	.445
1988	Minnesota	AL	14	49	9	1	0	1	(0	1)	13	5	6	7	0	11	0	0	0	1	2	.33	0	.184	.286	.265
	St. Louis	NL	143	523	128	22	4	22	(7	15)	224	69	79	79	6	82	4	1	6	16	6	.73	17	.245	.345	.428
1990	St. Louis	NL	19	57	9	3	0	1	(0	1)	15	5	2	12	0	10	1	0	1	0	0	.00	1	.158	.310	.263
	Boston	AL	129	461	123	24	5	15	(13	2)	202	61	71	54	7	105	3	0	8	5	10	.33	12	.267	.342	.438
	12 ML YEARS		1656	5860	1454	287	29	255	(123	132)	2564	760	856	721	42	1071	30	6	68	66	64	.51	138	.248	.330	.438

Steve Buechele

Bats: Right **Throws:** Right **Pos:** 3B **Ht:** 6' 2" **Wt:** 200 **Born:** 09/26/61 **Age:** 31

Year	Team	Lg	G	AB	H	2B	3B	HR	(Hm	Rd)	TB	R	RBI	TBB	IBB	SO	HBP	SH	SF	SB	CS	SB%	GDP	Avg	OBP	SLG
1985	Texas	AL	69	219	48	6	3	6	(5	1)	78	22	21	14	2	38	2	0	1	3	2	.60	11	.219	.271	.356
1986	Texas	AL	153	461	112	19	2	18	(6	12)	189	54	54	35	1	98	5	9	3	5	8	.38	10	.243	.302	.410
1987	Texas	AL	136	363	86	20	0	13	(6	7)	145	45	50	28	3	66	1	4	4	2	2	.50	7	.237	.290	.399
1988	Texas	AL	155	503	126	21	4	16	(8	8)	203	68	58	65	6	79	5	6	0	2	4	.33	8	.250	.342	.404
1989	Texas	AL	155	486	114	22	2	16	(7	9)	188	60	59	36	0	107	5	2	1	1	3	.25	21	.235	.294	.387
1990	Texas	AL	91	251	54	10	0	7	(5	2)	85	30	30	27	1	63	2	7	2	1	0	1.00	5	.215	.294	.339
1991	2 ML Teams		152	530	139	22	3	22	(9	13)	233	74	85	49	4	97	7	11	3	0	5	.00	14	.262	.331	.440
1992	2 ML Teams		145	524	137	23	4	9	(4	5)	195	52	64	52	6	105	7	4	3	1	3	.25	10	.261	.334	.372
1991	Texas	AL	121	416	111	17	2	18	(7	11)	186	58	66	39	4	69	5	10	2	0	4	.00	11	.267	.335	.447
	Pittsburgh	NL	31	114	28	5	1	4	(2	2)	47	16	19	10	0	28	2	1	1	0	1	.00	3	.246	.315	.412
1992	Pittsburgh	NL	80	285	71	14	1	8	(3	5)	111	27	43	34	4	61	2	2	2	0	2	.00	5	.249	.331	.389
	Chicago	NL	65	239	66	9	3	1	(1	0)	84	25	21	18	2	44	5	2	1	1		.50	5	.276	.338	.351
	8 ML YEARS		1056	3337	816	143	18	107	(50	57)	1316	405	421	306	23	653	34	43	17	15	27	.36	86	.245	.313	.394

Jay Buhner

Bats: Right **Throws:** Right **Pos:** RF   **Ht:** 6' 3" **Wt:** 205 **Born:** 08/13/64 **Age:** 28

								BATTING												BASERUNNING				PERCENTAGES		
Year Team	Lg	G	AB	H	2B	3B	HR	(Hm	Rd)	TB	R	RBI	TBB	IBB	SO	HBP	SH	SF	SB	CS	SB%	GDP	Avg	OBP	SLG
1987 New York	AL	7	22	5	2	0	0	(0	0)	7	0	1	1	0	6	0	0	0	0	0	.00	1	.227	.261	.318
1988 2 ML Teams		85	261	56	13	1	13	(8	5)	110	36	38	28	1	93	6	1	3	1	1	.50	5	.215	.302	.421
1989 Seattle	AL	58	204	56	15	1	9	(7	2)	100	27	33	19	0	55	2	0	1	1	4	.20	0	.275	.341	.490
1990 Seattle	AL	51	163	45	12	0	7	(2	5)	78	16	33	17	1	50	4	0	1	2	2	.50	6	.276	.357	.479
1991 Seattle	AL	137	406	99	14	4	27	(14	13)	202	64	77	53	5	117	6	2	4	0	1	.00	10	.244	.333	.498
1992 Seattle	AL	152	543	132	16	3	25	(9	16)	229	69	79	71	2	146	8	1	8	0	6	.00	12	.243	.333	.422
1988 New York	AL	25	69	13	0	0	3	(1	2)	22	8	13	3	0	25	3	0	1	0	0	.00	1	.188	.250	.319
Seattle	AL	60	192	43	13	1	10	(7	3)	88	28	25	25	1	68	3	1	2	1	1	.50	4	.224	.320	.458
6 ML YEARS		490	1599	393	72	9	81	(40	41)	726	212	261	189	9	467	24	4	17	4	14	22	34	.246	.331	.454

Jim Bullinger

Pitches: Right **Bats:** Right **Pos:** RP/SP   **Ht:** 6' 2" **Wt:** 185 **Born:** 08/21/65 **Age:** 27

			HOW MUCH HE PITCHED					WHAT HE GAVE UP											THE RESULTS					
Year Team	Lg	G	GS	CG	GF	IP	BFP	H	R	ER	HR	SH	SF	HB	TBB	IBB	SO	WP	Bk	W	L	Pct.	ShO	Sv	ERA
1989 Charlotte	AA	2	0	0	2	3	14	2	0	0	0	0	0	0	3	0	5	1	0	0	0	.000	0	0	0.00
1990 Winston-Sal	A	14	13	3	0	90	392	81	43	37	5	3	2	7	46	0	85	6	1	7	6	.538	0	0	3.70
Charlotte	AA	9	9	0	0	44	194	42	30	25	7	1	1	3	18	0	33	3	1	3	4	.429	0	0	5.11
1991 Charlotte	AA	20	20	8	0	142.2	595	132	62	56	5	5	1	6	61	2	128	5	3	9	9	.500	0	0	3.53
Iowa	AAA	8	8	0	0	46.2	203	47	32	28	6	1	1	0	23	0	30	7	0	3	4	.429	0	0	5.40
1992 Iowa	AAA	20	0	0	20	22	91	17	6	6	1	1	0		12	3	15	2	1	1	2	.333	0	14	2.45
1992 Chicago	NL	39	9	1	15	85	380	72	49	44	9	9	4	4	54	6	36	4	0	2	8	.200	0	7	4.66

Eric Bullock

Bats: Left **Throws:** Left **Pos:** PH   **Ht:** 5'11" **Wt:** 185 **Born:** 02/16/60 **Age:** 33

								BATTING												BASERUNNING				PERCENTAGES		
Year Team	Lg	G	AB	H	2B	3B	HR	(Hm	Rd)	TB	R	RBI	TBB	IBB	SO	HBP	SH	SF	SB	CS	SB%	GDP	Avg	OBP	SLG
1985 Houston	NL	18	25	7	2	0	0	(0	0)	9	3	2	1	0	3	0	0	0	0	1	.00	0	.280	.308	.360
1986 Houston	NL	6	21	1	0	0	0	(0	0)	1	0	1	0	0	3	0	0	0	2	0	1.00	0	.048	.048	.048
1988 Minnesota	AL	16	17	5	0	0	0	(0	0)	5	3	3	3	0	1	0	0	0	1	0	1.00	0	.294	.400	.294
1989 Philadelphia	NL	6	4	0	0	0	0	(0	0)	0	1	0	0	0	2	0	0	0	0	0	.00	0	.000	.000	.000
1990 Montreal	NL	4	2	1	0	0	0	(0	0)	1	0	0	0	0	0	0	0	0	0	0	.00	0	.500	.500	.500
1991 Montreal	NL	73	72	16	4	0	1	(1	0)	23	6	6	9	0	13	0	0	1	6	1	.86	3	.222	.305	.319
1992 Montreal	NL	8	5	0	0	0	0	(0	0)	0	0	0	0	0	1	0	0	0	0	0	.00	0	.000	.000	.000
7 ML YEARS		131	146	30	6	0	1	(1	0)	39	13	12	13	0	23	0	0	1	9	2	.82	3	.205	.269	.267

Dave Burba

Pitches: Right **Bats:** Right **Pos:** RP/SP   **Ht:** 6' 4" **Wt:** 220 **Born:** 07/07/66 **Age:** 26

			HOW MUCH HE PITCHED					WHAT HE GAVE UP											THE RESULTS					
Year Team	Lg	G	GS	CG	GF	IP	BFP	H	R	ER	HR	SH	SF	HB	TBB	IBB	SO	WP	Bk	W	L	Pct.	ShO	Sv	ERA
1990 Seattle	AL	6	0	0	2	8	35	8	6	4	0	2	0	1	2	0	4	0	0	0	0	.000	0	0	4.50
1991 Seattle	AL	22	2	0	11	36.2	153	34	16	15	6	0	0	0	14	3	16	1	0	2	2	.500	0	1	3.68
1992 San Francisco	NL	23	11	0	4	70.2	318	80	43	39	4	2	4	2	31	2	47	1	1	2	7	.222	0	0	4.97
3 ML YEARS		51	13	0	17	115.1	506	122	65	58	10	4	4	3	47	5	67	2	1	4	9	.308	0	1	4.53

Tim Burke

Pitches: Right **Bats:** Right **Pos:** RP   **Ht:** 6' 3" **Wt:** 205 **Born:** 02/19/59 **Age:** 34

			HOW MUCH HE PITCHED					WHAT HE GAVE UP											THE RESULTS					
Year Team	Lg	G	GS	CG	GF	IP	BFP	H	R	ER	HR	SH	SF	HB	TBB	IBB	SO	WP	Bk	W	L	Pct.	ShO	Sv	ERA
1985 Montreal	NL	78	0	0	31	120.1	483	86	32	32	9	8	3	7	44	14	87	7	0	9	4	.692	0	8	2.39
1986 Montreal	NL	68	2	0	25	101.1	451	103	37	33	7	6	2	4	46	13	82	4	0	9	7	.563	0	4	2.93
1987 Montreal	NL	55	0	0	30	91	354	64	18	12	3	8	2	2	17	6	58	2	0	7	0	1.000	0	18	1.19
1988 Montreal	NL	61	0	0	39	82	350	84	36	31	7	8	5	3	25	13	42	3	1	3	5	.375	0	18	3.40
1989 Montreal	NL	68	0	0	52	84.2	333	68	24	24	6	4	5	0	22	7	54	1	0	9	3	.750	0	28	2.55
1990 Montreal	NL	58	0	0	35	75	316	71	29	21	6	3	3	2	21	6	47	1	1	3	3	.500	0	20	2.52
1991 2 ML Teams		72	0	0	31	101.2	421	96	46	38	8	3	3	4	26	8	59	3	0	6	7	.462	0	6	3.36
1992 2 ML Teams		38	0	0	19	43.1	198	52	29	20	3	3	1	1	18	4	15	4	0	3	4	.429	0	0	4.15
1991 Montreal	NL	37	0	0	16	46	190	41	24	21	3	2	1	4	14	6	25	1	0	3	4	.429	0	5	4.11
New York	NL	35	0	0	15	55.2	231	55	22	17	5	1	2	0	12	2	34	2	0	3	3	.500	0	1	2.75
1992 New York	NL	15	0	0	9	15.2	76	26	15	10	1	1	0	0	3	2	7	2	0	1	2	.333	0	0	5.74
New York	AL	23	0	0	10	27.2	122	26	14	10	2	2	0	1	15	4	8	2	0	2	2	.500	0	0	3.25
8 ML YEARS		498	2	0	262	699.1	2906	624	251	211	49	43	24	21	219	71	444	25	2	49	33	.598	0	102	2.72

John Burkett

Pitches: Right Bats: Right Pos: SP Ht: 6' 2" Wt: 210 Born: 11/28/64 Age: 28

Year	Team	Lg	G	GS	CG	GF	IP	BFP	H	R	ER	HR	SH	SF	HB	TBB	IBB	SO	WP	Bk	W	L	Pct.	ShO	Sv	ERA
1987	San Francisco	NL	3	0	0	1	6	28	7	4	3	2	1	0	1	3	0	5	0	0	0	0	.000	0	0	4.50
1990	San Francisco	NL	33	32	2	1	204	857	201	92	86	18	6	5	4	61	7	118	3	3	14	7	.667	0	1	3.79
1991	San Francisco	NL	36	34	3	0	206.2	890	223	103	96	19	8	8	10	60	2	131	5	0	12	11	.522	1	0	4.18
1992	San Francisco	NL	32	32	3	0	189.2	799	194	96	81	13	11	4	4	45	6	107	0	0	13	9	.591	1	0	3.84
	4 ML YEARS		104	98	8	2	606.1	2574	625	295	266	52	26	17	19	169	15	361	8	3	39	27	.591	2	1	3.95

Ellis Burks

Bats: Right Throws: Right Pos: CF Ht: 6' 2" Wt: 205 Born: 09/11/64 Age: 28

Year	Team	Lg	G	AB	H	2B	3B	HR	(Hm	Rd)	TB	R	RBI	TBB	IBB	SO	HBP	SH	SF	SB	CS	SB%	GDP	Avg	OBP	SLG
1987	Boston	AL	133	558	152	30	2	20	(11	9)	246	94	59	41	0	98	2	4	1	27	6	.82	1	.272	.324	.441
1988	Boston	AL	144	540	159	37	5	18	(8	10)	260	93	92	62	1	89	3	4	6	25	9	.74	8	.294	.367	.481
1989	Boston	AL	97	399	121	19	6	12	(6	6)	188	73	61	36	2	52	5	2	4	21	5	.81	8	.303	.365	.471
1990	Boston	AL	152	588	174	33	8	21	(10	11)	286	89	89	48	4	82	1	2	2	9	11	.45	18	.296	.349	.486
1991	Boston	AL	130	474	119	33	3	14	(8	6)	200	56	56	39	2	81	6	2	3	6	11	.35	7	.251	.314	.422
1992	Boston	AL	66	235	60	8	3	8	(4	4)	98	35	30	25	2	48	1	0	2	5	2	.71	5	.255	.327	.417
	6 ML YEARS		722	2794	785	160	27	93	(47	46)	1278	440	387	251	11	450	18	14	18	93	44	.68	47	.281	.342	.457

Todd Burns

Pitches: Right Bats: Right Pos: RP/SP Ht: 6' 2" Wt: 195 Born: 07/06/63 Age: 29

Year	Team	Lg	G	GS	CG	GF	IP	BFP	H	R	ER	HR	SH	SF	HB	TBB	IBB	SO	WP	Bk	W	L	Pct.	ShO	Sv	ERA
1988	Oakland	AL	17	14	2	3	102.2	425	93	38	36	8	2	2	1	34	1	57	3	6	8	2	.800	0	1	3.16
1989	Oakland	AL	50	2	0	22	96.1	374	66	27	24	3	7	1	1	28	5	49	4	0	6	5	.545	0	8	2.24
1990	Oakland	AL	43	2	0	9	78.2	337	78	28	26	8	5	3	0	32	4	43	5	0	3	3	.500	0	3	2.97
1991	Oakland	AL	9	0	0	5	13.1	57	10	5	5	2	1	2	0	8	1	3	1	0	1	0	1.000	0	0	3.38
1992	Texas	AL	35	10	0	9	103	433	97	54	44	8	2	4	4	32	1	55	5	0	3	5	.375	0	1	3.84
	5 ML YEARS		154	28	2	48	394	1626	344	152	135	29	17	12	6	134	12	207	18	6	21	15	.583	0	13	3.08

Randy Bush

Bats: Left Throws: Left Pos: DH/RF Ht: 6' 1" Wt: 190 Born: 10/05/58 Age: 34

Year	Team	Lg	G	AB	H	2B	3B	HR	(Hm	Rd)	TB	R	RBI	TBB	IBB	SO	HBP	SH	SF	SB	CS	SB%	GDP	Avg	OBP	SLG
1982	Minnesota	AL	55	119	29	6	1	4	(2	2)	49	13	13	8	0	28	3	0	1	0	0	.00	1	.244	.305	.412
1983	Minnesota	AL	124	373	93	24	3	11	(4	7)	156	43	56	34	8	51	7	0	1	0	1	.00	7	.249	.323	.418
1984	Minnesota	AL	113	311	69	17	1	11	(8	3)	121	46	43	31	6	60	4	0	10	1	2	.33	1	.222	.292	.389
1985	Minnesota	AL	97	234	56	13	3	10	(5	5)	105	26	35	24	1	30	5	0	2	3	0	1.00	3	.239	.321	.449
1986	Minnesota	AL	130	357	96	19	7	7	(6	1)	150	50	45	39	2	63	4	1	1	5	3	.63	7	.269	.347	.420
1987	Minnesota	AL	122	293	74	10	2	11	(3	8)	121	46	46	43	5	49	3	5	5	10	3	.77	6	.253	.349	.413
1988	Minnesota	AL	136	394	103	20	3	14	(10	4)	171	51	51	58	14	49	9	0	5	8	6	.57	8	.261	.365	.434
1989	Minnesota	AL	141	391	103	17	4	14	(6	8)	170	60	54	48	6	73	3	0	2	5	8	.38	16	.263	.347	.435
1990	Minnesota	AL	73	181	44	8	0	6	(4	2)	70	17	18	21	2	27	6	0	2	0	3	.00	2	.243	.338	.387
1991	Minnesota	AL	93	165	50	10	1	6	(2	4)	80	21	23	24	3	25	3	0	0	0	2	.00	5	.303	.401	.485
1992	Minnesota	AL	100	182	39	8	1	2	(0	2)	55	14	22	11	3	37	2	0	3	1	1	.50	5	.214	.263	.302
	11 ML YEARS		1184	3000	756	152	26	96	(50	46)	1248	387	406	341	50	492	49	6	32	33	29	.53	61	.252	.335	.416

Mike Butcher

Pitches: Right Bats: Right Pos: RP Ht: 6' 1" Wt: 200 Born: 05/10/65 Age: 28

Year	Team	Lg	G	GS	CG	GF	IP	BFP	H	R	ER	HR	SH	SF	HB	TBB	IBB	SO	WP	Bk	W	L	Pct.	ShO	Sv	ERA
1986	Eugene	A	14	14	1	0	72.1		51	39	31	2	0	0	7	49	0	68	5	1	5	4	.556	0	0	3.86
1987	Ft. Myers	A	5	5	1	0	31.1	133	33	20	19	3	0	0	1	8	0	17	0	0	2	2	.500	0	0	5.46
	Appleton	A	20	19	3	0	121.1	525	101	50	36	4	5	5	5	56	5	89	9	2	10	4	.714	1	0	2.67
1988	Baseball Cy	A	6	6	0	0	32.2	143	32	19	14	2	1	4	2	10	1	20	1	0	1	4	.200	0	0	3.86
	Appleton	A	4	4	0	0	18	73	17	7	6	0	1	1	2	5	0	7	3	0	0	1	.000	0	0	3.00
	Quad City	A	3	0	0	0	6	28	6	3	3	0	1	0	2	4	0	7	1	0	0	0	.000	0	0	4.50
	Palm Sprngs	A	7	7	0	0	42.2	199	57	33	27	3	0	1	4	19	0	37	6	0	3	2	.600	0	0	5.70
1989	Midland	AA	15	15	0	0	68.2	331	92	54	50	6	2	4	3	41	1	49	7	2	2	6	.250	0	0	6.55
1990	Midland	AA	35	6	0	8	87	413	106	68	60	8	6	9	3	55	2	84	3	1	3	7	.300	0	0	6.21
1991	Midland	AA	41	6	0	13	88	394	93	54	51	6	2	7	8	46	0	70	3	0	9	6	.600	0	3	5.22
1992	Edmonton	AAA	26	0	0	16	29.1	130	24	12	10	2	5	1	2	18	2	32	1	0	5	2	.714	0	4	3.07
1992	California	AL	19	0	0	6	27.2	125	29	11	10	3	0	0	2	13	1	24	0	0	2	2	.500	0	0	3.25

Brett Butler

Bats: Left **Throws:** Left **Pos:** CF **Ht:** 5'10" **Wt:** 160 **Born:** 06/15/57 **Age:** 36

							BATTING											BASERUNNING				PERCENTAGES		
Year	Team	Lg	G	AB	H	2B	3B	HR	(Hm | Rd)	TB	R	RBI	TBB	IBB	SO	HBP	SH	SF	SB	CS	SB%	GDP	Avg	OBP	SLG
1981	Atlanta	NL	40	126	32	2	3	0	(0 | 0)	40	17	4	19	0	17	0	0	0	9	1	.90	0	.254	.352	.317
1982	Atlanta	NL	89	240	52	2	0	0	(0 | 0)	54	35	7	25	0	35	0	3	0	21	8	.72	1	.217	.291	.225
1983	Atlanta	NL	151	549	154	21	13	5	(4 | 1)	216	84	37	54	3	56	2	3	5	39	23	.63	5	.281	.344	.393
1984	Cleveland	AL	159	602	162	25	9	3	(1 | 2)	214	108	49	86	1	62	4	11	6	52	22	.70	6	.269	.361	.355
1985	Cleveland	AL	152	591	184	28	14	5	(1 | 4)	255	106	50	63	2	42	1	8	3	47	20	.70	8	.311	.377	.431
1986	Cleveland	AL	161	587	163	17	14	4	(0 | 4)	220	92	51	70	1	65	4	17	5	32	15	.68	8	.278	.356	.375
1987	Cleveland	AL	137	522	154	25	8	9	(4 | 5)	222	91	41	91	0	55	1	2	2	33	16	.67	3	.295	.399	.425
1988	San Francisco	NL	157	568	163	27	9	6	(1 | 5)	226	109	43	97	4	64	4	8	2	43	20	.68	2	.287	.393	.398
1989	San Francisco	NL	154	594	168	22	4	4	(2 | 2)	210	100	36	59	2	69	3	13	3	31	16	.66	4	.283	.349	.354
1990	San Francisco	NL	160	622	192	20	9	3	(3 | 0)	239	108	44	90	1	62	6	7	7	51	19	.73	3	.309	.397	.384
1991	Los Angeles	NL	161	615	182	13	5	2	(2 | 0)	211	112	38	108	4	79	1	4	2	38	28	.58	3	.296	.401	.343
1992	Los Angeles	NL	157	553	171	14	11	3	(1 | 2)	216	86	39	95	2	67	3	24	1	41	21	.66	4	.309	.413	.391
	12 ML YEARS		1678	6169	1777	216	99	44	(19 | 25)	2323	1048	439	857	20	673	29	100	36	437	209	.68	47	.288	.376	.377

Francisco Cabrera

Bats: Right **Throws:** Right **Pos:** C **Ht:** 6'4" **Wt:** 195 **Born:** 10/10/66 **Age:** 26

							BATTING											BASERUNNING				PERCENTAGES		
Year	Team	Lg	G	AB	H	2B	3B	HR	(Hm | Rd)	TB	R	RBI	TBB	IBB	SO	HBP	SH	SF	SB	CS	SB%	GDP	Avg	OBP	SLG
1989	2 ML Teams		7	26	5	3	0	0	(0 | 0)	8	1	0	1	0	6	0	0	0	0	0	.00	0	.192	.222	.308
1990	Atlanta	NL	63	137	38	5	1	7	(4 | 3)	66	14	25	5	0	21	0	0	1	1	0	1.00	4	.277	.301	.482
1991	Atlanta	NL	44	95	23	6	0	4	(2 | 2)	41	7	23	6	0	20	0	0	1	1	1	.50	5	.242	.284	.432
1992	Atlanta	NL	12	10	3	0	0	2	(0 | 2)	9	2	3	1	0	1	0	0	0	0	0	.00	0	.300	.364	.900
1989	Toronto	AL	3	12	2	1	0	0	(0 | 0)	3	1	0	1	0	3	0	0	0	0	0	.00	0	.167	.231	.250
	Atlanta	NL	4	14	3	2	0	0	(0 | 0)	5	0	0	0	0	3	0	0	0	0	0	.00	0	.214	.214	.357
	4 ML YEARS		126	268	69	14	1	13	(6 | 7)	124	24	51	13	0	48	0	0	2	2	1	.67	9	.257	.290	.463

Greg Cadaret

Pitches: Left **Bats:** Left **Pos:** RP/SP **Ht:** 6'3" **Wt:** 215 **Born:** 02/27/62 **Age:** 31

			HOW MUCH HE PITCHED					WHAT HE GAVE UP										THE RESULTS					
Year	Team	Lg	G	GS	CG	GF	IP	BFP	H	R	ER	HR	SH	SF	HB	TBB	IBB	SO	WP	Bk	W	L	Pct.	ShO	Sv	ERA
1987	Oakland	AL	29	0	0	7	39.2	176	37	22	20	6	2	2	1	24	1	30	1	0	6	2	.750	0	0	4.54
1988	Oakland	AL	58	0	0	16	71.2	311	60	26	23	2	5	3	1	36	1	64	5	3	5	2	.714	0	3	2.89
1989	2 ML Teams		46	13	3	7	120	531	130	62	54	7	3	5	2	57	4	80	6	2	5	5	.500	1	0	4.05
1990	New York	AL	54	6	0	9	121.1	525	120	62	56	8	9	4	1	64	5	80	14	0	5	4	.556	0	3	4.15
1991	New York	AL	68	5	0	17	121.2	517	110	52	49	8	6	3	2	59	6	105	3	1	8	6	.571	0	3	3.62
1992	New York	AL	46	11	0	9	103.2	471	104	53	49	12	3	3	2	74	7	73	5	1	4	8	.333	1	1	4.25
1989	Oakland	AL	26	0	0	6	27.2	119	21	9	7	0	0	2	0	19	3	14	0	0	0	0	.000	0	0	2.28
	New York	AL	20	13	3	1	92.1	412	109	53	47	7	3	3	2	38	1	66	6	2	5	5	.500	1	0	4.58
	6 ML YEARS		301	35	4	65	578	2531	561	277	251	43	28	20	9	314	24	432	34	7	33	27	.550	2	10	3.91

Ivan Calderon

Bats: Right **Throws:** Right **Pos:** LF **Ht:** 6'1" **Wt:** 221 **Born:** 03/19/62 **Age:** 31

							BATTING											BASERUNNING				PERCENTAGES		
Year	Team	Lg	G	AB	H	2B	3B	HR	(Hm | Rd)	TB	R	RBI	TBB	IBB	SO	HBP	SH	SF	SB	CS	SB%	GDP	Avg	OBP	SLG
1984	Seattle	AL	11	24	5	1	0	1	(0 | 1)	9	2	1	2	0	5	0	0	0	1	0	1.00	3	.208	.269	.375
1985	Seattle	AL	67	210	60	16	4	8	(6 | 2)	108	37	28	19	1	45	2	1	1	4	2	.67	10	.286	.349	.514
1986	2 ML Teams		50	164	41	7	1	2	(1 | 1)	56	16	15	9	1	39	1	0	0	3	1	.75	1	.250	.293	.341
1987	Chicago	AL	144	542	159	38	2	28	(15 | 13)	285	93	83	60	6	109	1	0	4	10	5	.67	13	.293	.362	.526
1988	Chicago	AL	73	264	56	14	0	14	(6 | 8)	112	40	35	34	2	66	0	0	3	4	4	.50	6	.212	.299	.424
1989	Chicago	AL	157	622	178	34	9	14	(2 | 12)	272	83	87	43	7	94	3	2	6	7	1	.88	20	.286	.332	.437
1990	Chicago	AL	158	607	166	44	2	14	(6 | 8)	256	85	74	51	7	79	1	0	8	32	16	.67	26	.273	.327	.422
1991	Montreal	NL	134	470	141	22	3	19	(7 | 12)	226	69	75	53	4	64	3	1	10	31	16	.66	7	.300	.368	.481
1992	Montreal	NL	48	170	45	14	2	3	(1 | 2)	72	19	24	14	1	22	0	0	2	1	2	.33	4	.265	.323	.424
1986	Seattle	AL	37	131	31	5	0	2	(1 | 1)	42	13	13	6	0	33	1	0	0	3	1	.75	1	.237	.275	.321
	Chicago	AL	13	33	10	2	1	0	(0 | 0)	14	3	2	3	1	6	0	0	0	0	0	.00	0	.303	.361	.424
	9 ML YEARS		842	3073	851	190	23	103	(45 | 58)	1396	444	422	285	29	523	12	4	33	93	47	.66	90	.277	.337	.454

Ken Caminiti

Bats: Both **Throws:** Right **Pos:** 3B **Ht:** 6'0" **Wt:** 200 **Born:** 04/21/63 **Age:** 30

							BATTING											BASERUNNING				PERCENTAGES		
Year	Team	Lg	G	AB	H	2B	3B	HR	(Hm | Rd)	TB	R	RBI	TBB	IBB	SO	HBP	SH	SF	SB	CS	SB%	GDP	Avg	OBP	SLG
1987	Houston	NL	63	203	50	7	1	3	(2 | 1)	68	10	23	12	1	44	0	2	1	0	0	.00	6	.246	.287	.335

35

Year	Team	Lg	G	AB	H	2B	3B	HR	(Hm	Rd)	TB	R	RBI	TBB	IBB	SO	HBP	SH	SF	SB	CS	SB%	GDP	Avg	OBP	SLG
1988	Houston	NL	30	83	15	2	0	1	(0	1)	20	5	7	5	0	18	0	0	1	0	0	.00	3	.181	.225	.241
1989	Houston	NL	161	585	149	31	3	10	(3	7)	216	71	72	51	9	93	3	3	4	4	1	.80	8	.255	.316	.369
1990	Houston	NL	153	541	131	20	2	4	(2	2)	167	52	51	48	7	97	0	3	4	9	4	.69	15	.242	.302	.309
1991	Houston	NL	152	574	145	30	3	13	(9	4)	220	65	80	46	7	85	5	3	4	4	5	.44	18	.253	.312	.383
1992	Houston	NL	135	506	149	31	2	13	(7	6)	223	68	62	44	13	68	1	2	4	10	4	.71	14	.294	.350	.441
6 ML YEARS			694	2492	639	121	11	44	(23	21)	914	271	295	206	37	405	9	13	18	27	14	.66	64	.256	.313	.367

Kevin Campbell

Pitches: Right Bats: Right Pos: RP/SP **Ht: 6' 2" Wt: 225 Born: 12/06/64 Age: 28**

			HOW MUCH HE PITCHED						WHAT HE GAVE UP											THE RESULTS					
Year	Team	Lg	G	GS	CG	GF	IP	BFP	H	R	ER	HR	SH	SF	HB	TBB	IBB	SO	WP	Bk	W	L	Pct.	ShO	Sv	ERA
1986	Great Falls	R	15	15	3	0	85	0	99	62	44	5	0	0	3	32	0	66	6	0	5	6	.455	0	0	4.66
1987	Vero Beach	A	28	28	5	0	184	807	200	100	80	11	6	6	9	64	4	112	11	4	7	14	.333	1	0	3.91
1988	Vero Beach	A	26	26	5	0	163.2	677	166	67	50	6	10	4	3	49	2	115	6	1	8	12	.400	1	0	2.75
1989	Bakersfield	A	31	0	0	17	60.1	255	43	23	17	0	2	5	1	28	1	63	3	0	5	3	.625	0	6	2.54
	San Antonio	AA	17	0	0	7	27	127	29	22	20	3	2	2	0	16	1	28	1	0	1	5	.167	0	0	6.67
1990	San Antonio	AA	49	0	0	29	81	329	67	29	21	1	3	3	1	25	6	84	5	1	2	6	.250	0	8	2.33
1991	Tacoma	AAA	35	0	0	12	75	304	53	18	15	1	3	1	3	35	1	56	5	0	9	2	.818	0	2	1.80
1992	Tacoma	AAA	10	0	0	3	13.1	63	16	6	6	2	0	0	0	8	2	14	3	0	2	2	.500	0	0	4.05
1991	Oakland	AL	14	0	0	2	23	94	13	7	7	4	1	0	1	14	0	16	0	0	1	0	1.000	0	0	2.74
1992	Oakland	AL	32	5	0	6	65	297	66	39	37	4	3	2	0	45	3	38	2	0	2	3	.400	0	1	5.12
2 ML YEARS			46	5	0	8	88	391	79	46	44	8	4	2	1	59	3	54	2	0	3	3	.500	0	1	4.50

Mike Campbell

Pitches: Right Bats: Right Pos: RP **Ht: 6' 3" Wt: 210 Born: 02/17/64 Age: 29**

			HOW MUCH HE PITCHED						WHAT HE GAVE UP											THE RESULTS					
Year	Team	Lg	G	GS	CG	GF	IP	BFP	H	R	ER	HR	SH	SF	HB	TBB	IBB	SO	WP	Bk	W	L	Pct.	ShO	Sv	ERA
1987	Seattle	AL	9	9	1	0	49.1	215	41	29	26	9	2	3	2	25	2	35	1	1	1	4	.200	0	0	4.74
1988	Seattle	AL	20	20	2	0	114.2	507	128	81	75	18	2	5	0	43	1	63	4	4	6	10	.375	0	0	5.89
1989	Seattle	AL	5	5	0	0	21	103	28	22	17	4	0	0	0	10	0	6	0	0	1	2	.333	0	0	7.29
1992	Texas	AL	1	0	0	0	3.2	15	3	4	4	1	0	0	0	2	0	2	0	0	0	1	.000	0	0	9.82
4 ML YEARS			35	34	3	0	188.2	840	200	136	122	32	4	8	2	80	3	106	5	5	8	17	.320	0	0	5.82

Casey Candaele

Bats: Both Throws: Right Pos: SS/3B/LF **Ht: 5' 9" Wt: 165 Born: 01/12/61 Age: 32**

			BATTING																BASERUNNING				PERCENTAGES		
Year	Team	Lg	G	AB	H	2B	3B	HR	(Hm	Rd)	TB	R	RBI	TBB	IBB	SO	HBP	SH	SF	SB	CS	SB%	GDP	Avg	OBP	SLG
1986	Montreal	NL	30	104	24	4	1	0	(0	0)	30	9	6	5	0	15	0	0	1	3	5	.38	3	.231	.264	.288
1987	Montreal	NL	138	449	122	23	4	1	(1	0)	156	62	23	38	3	28	2	4	2	7	10	.41	5	.272	.330	.347
1988	2 ML Teams		57	147	25	8	1	0	(0	0)	35	11	5	11	1	17	0	3	0	1	1	.50	7	.170	.228	.238
1990	Houston	NL	130	262	75	8	6	3	(1	2)	104	30	22	31	5	42	1	4	0	7	5	.58	4	.286	.364	.397
1991	Houston	NL	151	461	121	20	7	4	(1	3)	167	44	50	40	7	49	0	1	3	9	3	.75	5	.262	.319	.362
1992	Houston	NL	135	320	68	12	1	1	(1	0)	85	19	18	24	3	36	3	7	6	7	1	.88	5	.213	.269	.266
1988	Montreal	NL	36	116	20	5	1	0	(0	0)	27	9	4	10	1	11	0	2	0	1	0	1.00	7	.172	.238	.233
	Houston	NL	21	31	5	3	0	0	(0	0)	8	2	1	1	0	6	0	1	0	0	1	.00	0	.161	.188	.258
6 ML YEARS			641	1743	435	75	20	9	(4	5)	577	175	124	149	19	187	6	19	12	34	25	.58	29	.250	.309	.331

John Candelaria

Pitches: Left Bats: Right Pos: RP **Ht: 6' 6" Wt: 225 Born: 11/06/53 Age: 39**

			HOW MUCH HE PITCHED						WHAT HE GAVE UP											THE RESULTS					
Year	Team	Lg	G	GS	CG	GF	IP	BFP	H	R	ER	HR	SH	SF	HB	TBB	IBB	SO	WP	Bk	W	L	Pct.	ShO	Sv	ERA
1975	Pittsburgh	NL	18	18	4	0	121	497	95	47	37	8	6	4	2	36	9	95	1	0	8	6	.571	1	0	2.75
1976	Pittsburgh	NL	32	31	11	1	220	881	173	87	77	22	13	6	2	60	5	138	0	0	16	7	.696	4	1	3.15
1977	Pittsburgh	NL	33	33	6	0	231	917	197	64	60	29	9	6	2	50	2	133	1	2	20	5	.800	1	0	2.34
1978	Pittsburgh	NL	30	29	3	1	189	796	191	73	68	15	8	2	5	49	6	94	3	3	12	11	.522	1	1	3.24
1979	Pittsburgh	NL	33	30	8	2	207	850	201	83	74	25	4	7	3	41	6	101	2	0	14	9	.609	0	0	3.22
1980	Pittsburgh	NL	35	34	7	1	233	969	246	114	104	14	14	12	3	50	4	97	0	2	11	14	.440	0	1	4.02
1981	Pittsburgh	NL	6	6	0	0	41	168	42	17	16	3	1	1	0	11	1	14	0	0	2	2	.500	0	0	3.51
1982	Pittsburgh	NL	31	30	1	1	174.2	704	166	62	57	13	5	6	4	37	3	133	1	0	12	7	.632	1	1	2.94
1983	Pittsburgh	NL	33	32	2	0	197.2	797	191	73	71	15	4	4	2	45	3	157	3	2	15	8	.652	0	0	3.23
1984	Pittsburgh	NL	33	28	3	4	185.1	751	179	69	56	19	10	6	1	34	3	133	1	1	12	11	.522	0	2	2.72
1985	2 ML Teams		50	13	1	26	125.1	530	127	56	52	14	7	7	4	38	3	100	2	0	9	7	.563	1	9	3.73
1986	California	AL	16	16	1	0	91.2	365	68	30	26	4	3	3	3	26	2	81	2	1	10	2	.833	1	0	2.55
1987	2 ML Teams		23	23	0	0	129	544	144	78	69	18	8	6	1	23	0	84	0	1	8	6	.571	0	0	4.81
1988	New York	AL	25	24	6	1	157	640	150	69	59	18	4	6	2	23	2	121	2	12	13	7	.650	2	1	3.38
1989	2 ML Teams		22	6	1	3	65.1	274	66	36	34	11	3	5	0	16	3	51	2	1	3	5	.375	0	0	4.68

Year Team	Lg	G	GS	CG	GF	IP	BFP	H	R	ER	HR	SH	SF	HB	TBB	IBB	SO	WP	Bk	W	L	Pct.	ShO	Sv	ERA
1990 2 ML Teams		47	3	0	15	79.2	345	87	36	35	11	2	6	2	20	5	63	5	0	7	6	.538	0	5	3.95
1991 Los Angeles	NL	59	0	0	10	33.2	138	31	16	14	3	1	3	0	11	2	38	1	1	1	1	.500	0	2	3.74
1992 Los Angeles	NL	50	0	0	11	25.1	108	20	9	8	1	2	2	0	13	3	23	1	0	2	5	.286	0	5	2.84
1985 Pittsburgh	NL	37	0	0	26	54.1	229	57	23	22	7	3	4	1	14	2	47	0	0	2	4	.333	0	9	3.64
California	AL	13	13	1	0	71	301	70	33	30	7	4	3	3	24	1	53	2	0	7	3	.700	1	0	3.80
1987 California	AL	20	20	0	0	116.2	487	127	70	61	17	6	5	1	20	0	74	0	0	8	6	.571	0	0	4.71
New York	NL	3	3	0	0	12.1	57	17	8	8	1	2	1	0	3	0	10	0	1	2	0	1.000	0	0	5.84
1989 New York	AL	10	6	1	1	49	206	49	28	28	8	2	2	0	12	1	37	2	1	3	3	.500	0	0	5.14
Montreal	NL	12	0	0	2	16.1	68	17	8	6	3	1	3	0	4	2	14	0	0	0	2	.000	0	0	3.31
1990 Minnesota	AL	34	1	0	10	58.1	239	55	23	22	9	2	3	0	9	2	44	3	0	7	3	.700	0	3	3.39
Toronto	AL	13	2	0	5	21.1	106	32	13	13	2	0	3	2	11	3	19	2	0	0	3	.000	0	1	5.48
18 ML YEARS		576	356	54	76	2506.2	10274	2374	1019	917	243	104	92	36	583	62	1656	27	26	177	119	.598	13	28	3.29

Tom Candiotti

Pitches: Right **Bats:** Right **Pos:** SP   **Ht:** 6' 2" **Wt:** 200 **Born:** 08/31/57 **Age:** 35

		HOW MUCH HE PITCHED						WHAT HE GAVE UP												THE RESULTS					
Year Team	Lg	G	GS	CG	GF	IP	BFP	H	R	ER	HR	SH	SF	HB	TBB	IBB	SO	WP	Bk	W	L	Pct.	ShO	Sv	ERA
1983 Milwaukee	AL	10	8	2	1	55.2	233	62	21	20	4	0	2	2	16	0	21	0	0	4	4	.500	1	0	3.23
1984 Milwaukee	AL	8	6	0	0	32.1	147	38	21	19	5	0	0	0	10	0	23	1	0	2	2	.500	0	0	5.29
1986 Cleveland	AL	36	34	17	1	252.1	1078	234	112	100	18	3	9	8	106	0	167	12	4	16	12	.571	3	0	3.57
1987 Cleveland	AL	32	32	7	0	201.2	888	193	132	107	28	8	10	4	93	2	111	13	2	7	18	.280	2	0	4.78
1988 Cleveland	AL	31	31	11	0	216.2	903	225	86	79	15	12	5	6	53	3	137	5	7	14	8	.636	1	0	3.28
1989 Cleveland	AL	31	31	4	0	206	847	188	80	71	10	6	4	4	55	5	124	4	8	13	10	.565	0	0	3.10
1990 Cleveland	AL	31	29	3	1	202	856	207	92	82	23	4	3	6	55	1	128	9	3	15	11	.577	1	0	3.65
1991 2 ML Teams		34	34	6	0	238	981	202	82	70	12	4	11	6	73	1	167	11	0	13	13	.500	0	0	2.65
1992 Los Angeles	NL	32	30	6	1	203.2	839	177	78	68	13	20	6	3	63	5	152	9	2	11	15	.423	2	0	3.00
1991 Cleveland	AL	15	15	3	0	108.1	442	88	35	27	6	1	7	2	28	0	86	6	0	7	6	.538	0	0	2.24
Toronto	AL	19	19	3	0	129.2	539	114	47	43	6	3	4	4	45	1	81	5	0	6	7	.462	0	0	2.98
9 ML YEARS		245	235	56	4	1608.1	6772	1526	704	616	128	57	50	39	524	17	1030	64	26	95	93	.505	10	0	3.45

John Cangelosi

Bats: Both **Throws:** Left **Pos:** LF/CF   **Ht:** 5' 8" **Wt:** 160 **Born:** 03/10/63 **Age:** 30

		BATTING															BASERUNNING				PERCENTAGES		
Year Team	Lg	G	AB	H	2B	3B	HR	(Hm | Rd)	TB	R	RBI	TBB	IBB	SO	HBP	SH	SF	SB	CS	SB%	GDP	Avg	OBP	SLG
1985 Chicago	AL	5	2	0	0	0	0	(0 | 0)	0	2	0	0	0	1	1	1	0	0	0	.00	0	.000	.333	.000
1986 Chicago	AL	137	438	103	16	3	2	(1 | 1)	131	65	32	71	0	61	7	6	3	50	17	.75	5	.235	.349	.299
1987 Pittsburgh	NL	104	182	50	8	3	4	(2 | 2)	76	44	18	46	1	33	3	1	1	21	6	.78	3	.275	.427	.418
1988 Pittsburgh	NL	75	118	30	4	1	0	(0 | 0)	36	18	8	17	0	16	1	3	0	9	4	.69	0	.254	.353	.305
1989 Pittsburgh	NL	112	160	35	4	2	0	(0 | 0)	43	18	9	35	2	20	3	1	2	11	8	.58	1	.219	.365	.269
1990 Pittsburgh	NL	58	76	15	2	0	0	(0 | 0)	17	13	1	11	0	12	1	2	0	7	2	.78	2	.197	.307	.224
1992 Texas	AL	73	85	16	2	0	1	(0 | 1)	21	12	6	18	0	16	0	3	0	6	5	.55	0	.188	.330	.247
7 ML YEARS		564	1061	249	36	9	7	(3 | 4)	324	172	74	198	3	159	16	17	6	104	42	.71	11	.235	.361	.305

Jose Canseco

Bats: Right **Throws:** Right **Pos:** RF/DH   **Ht:** 6' 4" **Wt:** 240 **Born:** 07/02/64 **Age:** 28

		BATTING															BASERUNNING				PERCENTAGES		
Year Team	Lg	G	AB	H	2B	3B	HR	(Hm | Rd)	TB	R	RBI	TBB	IBB	SO	HBP	SH	SF	SB	CS	SB%	GDP	Avg	OBP	SLG
1985 Oakland	AL	29	96	29	3	0	5	(4 | 1)	47	16	13	4	0	31	0	0	1	1	1	.50	1	.302	.330	.490
1986 Oakland	AL	157	600	144	29	1	33	(14 | 19)	274	85	117	65	1	175	8	0	9	15	7	.68	12	.240	.318	.457
1987 Oakland	AL	159	630	162	35	3	31	(16 | 15)	296	81	113	50	2	157	2	0	9	15	3	.83	16	.257	.310	.470
1988 Oakland	AL	158	610	187	34	0	42	(16 | 26)	347	120	124	78	10	128	10	1	6	40	16	.71	15	.307	.391	.569
1989 Oakland	AL	65	227	61	9	1	17	(8 | 9)	123	40	57	23	4	69	2	0	6	6	3	.67	4	.269	.333	.542
1990 Oakland	AL	131	481	132	14	2	37	(18 | 19)	261	83	101	72	8	158	5	0	5	19	10	.66	9	.274	.371	.543
1991 Oakland	AL	154	572	152	32	1	44	(16 | 28)	318	115	122	78	8	152	9	0	6	26	6	.81	16	.266	.359	.556
1992 2 ML Teams		119	439	107	15	0	26	(15 | 11)	200	74	87	63	2	128	6	0	4	6	7	.46	16	.244	.344	.456
1992 Oakland	AL	97	366	90	11	0	22	(12 | 10)	167	66	72	48	1	104	3	0	4	5	7	.42	15	.246	.335	.456
Texas	AL	22	73	17	4	0	4	(3 | 1)	33	8	15	15	1	24	3	0	0	1	0	1.00	1	.233	.385	.452
8 ML YEARS		972	3655	974	171	8	235	(107 | 128)	1866	614	734	433	35	998	42	1	45	128	53	.71	89	.266	.347	.511

Ozzie Canseco

Bats: Right **Throws:** Right **Pos:** LF   **Ht:** 6' 3" **Wt:** 220 **Born:** 07/02/64 **Age:** 28

		BATTING															BASERUNNING				PERCENTAGES		
Year Team	Lg	G	AB	H	2B	3B	HR	(Hm | Rd)	TB	R	RBI	TBB	IBB	SO	HBP	SH	SF	SB	CS	SB%	GDP	Avg	OBP	SLG
1984 Greensboro	A	8	1	0	0	0	0	--	--	0	1	0	0	0	0	0	0	0	0	0	.00	0	.000	.000	.000
1985 Yankees	R	20	39	7	0	1	1	--	--	12	2	5	2	0	18	0	0	0	0	0	.00	0	.179	.220	.308
1986 Yankees	R	7	15	2	1	0	1	--	--	6	3	3	5	0	9	0	0	0	0	0	.00	0	.133	.350	.400
Madison	A	42	128	20	1	1	3	--	--	32	17	17	22	0	47	0	0	3	1	1	.50	2	.156	.275	.250
1987 Madison	A	92	309	82	12	4	11	--	--	135	64	54	67	3	104	1	0	6	7	.46	2	.265	.397	.437

1988	Madison	A	99	359	98	17	7	12	--	--	165	63	68	49	3	84	3	1	7	15	8	.65	8	.273	.359	.460
	Huntsville	AA	27	99	22	7	0	3	--	--	38	6	12	6	1	31	0	0	0	3	0	1.00	1	.222	.267	.384
1989	Huntsville	AA	91	317	74	17	2	12	--	--	131	52	52	51	0	88	5	2	4	1	2	.33	1	.233	.345	.413
1990	Huntsville	AA	97	325	73	21	0	20	--	--	154	50	67	47	2	103	7	2	2	2	2	.50	5	.225	.333	.474
1992	Louisville	AAA	98	308	82	19	1	22	--	--	169	53	57	43	0	96	2	1	2	1	1	.50	3	.266	.358	.549
1990	Oakland	AL	9	19	2	1	0	0	(0	0)	3	1	1	1	0	10	0	0	0	0	0	.00	0	.105	.150	.158
1992	St. Louis	NL	9	29	8	5	0	0	(0	0)	13	7	3	7	0	4	0	0	0	0	0	.00	1	.276	.417	.448
	2 ML YEARS		18	48	10	6	0	0	(0	0)	16	8	4	8	0	14	0	0	0	0	0	.00	1	.208	.321	.333

Don Carman

Pitches: Left   Bats: Left   Pos: RP   Ht: 6' 3"   Wt: 201   Born: 08/14/59   Age: 33

			HOW MUCH HE PITCHED						WHAT HE GAVE UP										THE RESULTS					
Year	Team	Lg	G	GS	CG	GF	IP	BFP	H	R	ER	HR	SH	SF	HB	TBB	IBB	SO	WP	Bk	W	L	Pct.	ShO	Sv	ERA
1983	Philadelphia	NL	1	0	0	1	1	3	0	0	0	0	0	0	0	0	0	0	0	0	0	0	.000	0	0	0.00
1984	Philadelphia	NL	11	0	0	9	13.1	61	14	9	8	2	0	0	0	6	4	16	3	0	0	1	.000	0	0	5.40
1985	Philadelphia	NL	71	0	0	33	86.1	342	52	25	20	6	5	5	2	38	3	87	1	0	9	4	.692	0	7	2.08
1986	Philadelphia	NL	50	14	2	13	134.1	545	113	50	48	11	5	3	3	52	11	98	6	2	10	5	.667	1	1	3.22
1987	Philadelphia	NL	35	35	3	0	211	886	194	110	99	34	11	5	5	69	7	125	3	1	13	11	.542	2	0	4.22
1988	Philadelphia	NL	36	32	2	0	201.1	873	211	101	96	20	9	8	4	70	6	116	8	3	10	14	.417	0	0	4.29
1989	Philadelphia	NL	49	20	0	5	149.1	683	152	98	87	21	5	5	3	86	6	81	7	3	5	15	.250	0	0	5.24
1990	Philadelphia	NL	59	1	0	11	86.2	368	69	43	40	13	6	4	4	38	7	58	6	1	6	2	.750	0	1	4.15
1991	Cincinnati	NL	28	0	0	10	36	164	40	23	21	8	3	1	1	19	1	15	2	0	0	2	.000	0	1	5.25
1992	Texas	AL	2	0	0	1	2.1	11	4	3	2	0	0	0	0	0	0	2	0	0	0	0	.000	0	0	7.71
	10 ML YEARS		342	102	7	83	921.2	3936	849	462	421	115	44	31	22	378	45	598	36	10	53	54	.495	3	11	4.11

Cris Carpenter

Pitches: Right   Bats: Right   Pos: RP   Ht: 6' 1"   Wt: 185   Born: 04/05/65   Age: 28

			HOW MUCH HE PITCHED						WHAT HE GAVE UP										THE RESULTS					
Year	Team	Lg	G	GS	CG	GF	IP	BFP	H	R	ER	HR	SH	SF	HB	TBB	IBB	SO	WP	Bk	W	L	Pct.	ShO	Sv	ERA
1988	St. Louis	NL	8	8	1	0	47.2	203	56	27	25	3	1	4	1	9	2	24	1	0	2	3	.400	0	0	4.72
1989	St. Louis	NL	36	5	0	10	68	303	70	30	24	4	4	4	2	26	9	35	1	0	4	4	.500	0	0	3.18
1990	St. Louis	NL	4	0	0	1	8	32	5	4	4	2	0	0	0	2	1	6	0	0	0	0	.000	0	0	4.50
1991	St. Louis	NL	59	0	0	19	66	266	53	31	31	6	3	2	0	20	9	47	1	0	10	4	.714	0	0	4.23
1992	St. Louis	NL	73	0	0	21	88	355	69	29	29	10	8	3	4	27	8	46	5	0	5	4	.556	0	1	2.97
	5 ML YEARS		180	13	1	51	277.2	1159	253	121	113	25	16	13	7	84	29	158	8	0	21	15	.583	0	1	3.66

Chuck Carr

Bats: Both   Throws: Right   Pos: CF   Ht: 5'10"   Wt: 165   Born: 08/10/68   Age: 24

						BATTING												BASERUNNING				PERCENTAGES		
Year	Team	Lg	G	AB	H	2B	3B	HR	(Hm | Rd)	TB	R	RBI	TBB	IBB	SO	HBP	SH	SF	SB	CS	SB%	GDP	Avg	OBP	SLG
1986	Reds	R	44	123	21	5	0	0	--	--	26	13	10	27	0	27	0	5	2	9	1	.90	2	.171	.230	.211
1987	Bellingham	A	44	165	40	1	1	1	--	--	46	31	11	12	0	38	1	3	0	20	1	.95	2	.242	.298	.279
1988	Wausau	A	82	304	91	14	2	6	--	--	127	58	30	14	0	49	1	3	5	41	11	.79	3	.299	.327	.418
	Vermont	AA	41	159	39	4	2	1	--	--	50	26	13	8	0	33	0	3	1	21	9	.70	0	.245	.280	.314
1989	Jackson	AA	116	444	107	13	1	0	--	--	122	45	22	27	2	66	1	7	2	47	20	.70	3	.241	.285	.275
1990	Tidewater	AAA	20	81	21	5	1	0	--	--	28	13	8	4	0	12	0	1	2	6	4	.60	2	.259	.287	.346
	Jackson	AA	93	360	93	20	9	3	--	--	140	60	24	44	2	77	2	3	2	47	15	.76	2	.258	.341	.389
1991	Tidewater	AAA	64	246	48	6	1	1	--	--	59	34	11	18	0	37	1	1	0	27	8	.77	3	.195	.253	.240
1992	Arkansas	AA	28	111	29	5	1	1	--	--	39	17	6	8	1	23	0	0	0	8	2	.80	2	.261	.311	.351
	Louisville	AAA	96	377	116	11	9	3	--	--	154	68	28	31	0	60	3	0	0	53	10	.84	4	.308	.365	.408
1990	New York	NL	4	2	0	0	0	0	(0 | 0)	0	0	0	0	0	2	0	0	0	1	0	1.00	0	.000	.000	.000
1991	New York	NL	12	11	2	0	0	0	(0 | 0)	2	1	1	0	0	2	0	0	0	1	0	1.00	0	.182	.182	.182
1992	St. Louis	NL	22	64	14	3	0	0	(0 | 0)	17	8	3	9	0	6	0	0	0	10	1	.83	0	.219	.315	.266
	3 ML YEARS		38	77	16	3	0	0	(0 | 0)	19	9	4	9	0	10	0	0	0	12	2	.86	0	.208	.291	.247

Mark Carreon

Bats: Right   Throws: Left   Pos: LF/RF/DH   Ht: 6' 0"   Wt: 195   Born: 07/09/63   Age: 29

						BATTING												BASERUNNING				PERCENTAGES		
Year	Team	Lg	G	AB	H	2B	3B	HR	(Hm	Rd)	TB	R	RBI	TBB	IBB	SO	HBP	SH	SF	SB	CS	SB%	GDP	Avg	OBP	SLG
1987	New York	NL	9	12	3	0	0	0	(0	0)	3	0	1	1	0	1	0	0	0	0	1	.00	0	.250	.308	.250
1988	New York	NL	7	9	5	2	0	1	(0	1)	10	5	1	2	0	1	0	0	0	0	0	.00	0	.556	.636	1.111
1989	New York	NL	68	133	41	6	0	6	(4	2)	65	20	16	12	0	17	1	0	0	2	3	.40	1	.308	.370	.489
1990	New York	NL	82	188	47	12	0	10	(1	9)	89	30	26	15	0	29	2	0	0	1	0	1.00	1	.250	.312	.473
1991	New York	NL	106	254	66	6	0	4	(3	1)	84	18	21	12	2	26	2	1	1	2	1	.67	13	.260	.297	.331
1992	Detroit	AL	101	336	78	11	1	10	(5	5)	121	34	41	22	2	57	1	1	4	3	1	.75	12	.232	.278	.360
	6 ML YEARS		373	932	240	37	1	31	(13	18)	372	107	106	64	4	131	6	2	5	8	6	.57	27	.258	.308	.399

Gary Carter

Bats: Right **Throws:** Right **Pos:** C   **Ht:** 6' 2" **Wt:** 214 **Born:** 04/08/54 **Age:** 39

Year Team	Lg	G	AB	H	2B	3B	HR	(Hm	Rd)	TB	R	RBI	TBB	IBB	SO	HBP	SH	SF	SB	CS	SB%	GDP	Avg	OBP	SLG
1974 Montreal	NL	9	27	11	0	1	1	(1	0)	16	5	6	1	0	2	0	0	1	2	0	1.00	0	.407	.414	.593
1975 Montreal	NL	144	503	136	20	1	17	(9	8)	209	58	68	72	8	83	1	10	4	5	2	.71	7	.270	.360	.416
1976 Montreal	NL	91	311	68	8	1	6	(5	1)	96	31	38	30	2	43	1	2	3	0	2	.00	7	.219	.287	.309
1977 Montreal	NL	154	522	148	29	2	31	(22	9)	274	86	84	58	5	103	5	3	7	5	5	.50	9	.284	.356	.525
1978 Montreal	NL	157	533	136	27	1	20	(7	13)	225	76	72	62	11	70	5	2	5	10	6	.63	10	.255	.336	.422
1979 Montreal	NL	141	505	143	26	5	22	(12	10)	245	74	75	40	3	62	5	2	7	3	2	.60	11	.283	.338	.485
1980 Montreal	NL	154	549	145	25	5	29	(12	17)	267	76	101	58	11	78	1	1	8	3	2	.60	9	.264	.331	.486
1981 Montreal	NL	100	374	94	20	2	16	(7	9)	166	48	68	35	4	35	1	3	6	1	5	.17	6	.251	.313	.444
1982 Montreal	NL	154	557	163	32	1	29	(16	13)	284	91	97	78	11	64	6	4	8	2	5	.29	16	.293	.381	.510
1983 Montreal	NL	145	541	146	37	3	17	(6	11)	240	63	79	51	7	57	7	2	8	1	1	.50	14	.270	.336	.444
1984 Montreal	NL	159	596	175	32	1	27	(14	13)	290	75	106	64	9	57	6	0	3	2	2	.50	8	.294	.366	.487
1985 New York	NL	149	555	156	17	1	32	(12	20)	271	83	100	69	16	46	6	0	3	1	1	.50	18	.281	.365	.488
1986 New York	NL	132	490	125	14	2	24	(13	11)	215	81	105	62	9	63	6	0	15	1	0	1.00	21	.255	.337	.439
1987 New York	NL	139	523	123	18	2	20	(9	11)	205	55	83	42	1	73	1	1	6	0	0	.00	14	.235	.290	.392
1988 New York	NL	130	455	110	16	2	11	(5	6)	163	39	46	34	1	52	7	1	6	0	2	.00	14	.242	.301	.358
1989 New York	NL	50	153	28	8	0	2	(1	1)	42	14	15	12	0	15	0	0	1	0	0	.00	5	.183	.241	.275
1990 San Francisco	NL	92	244	62	10	0	9	(6	3)	99	24	27	25	3	31	1	0	2	1	1	.50	2	.254	.324	.406
1991 Los Angeles	NL	101	248	61	14	0	6	(3	3)	93	22	26	22	1	26	7	1	2	2	2	.50	11	.246	.323	.375
1992 Montreal	NL	95	285	62	18	1	5	(2	3)	97	24	29	33	4	37	2	1	4	0	4	.00	4	.218	.299	.340
19 ML YEARS		2296	7971	2092	371	31	324	(162	162)	3497	1025	1225	848	106	997	68	33	99	39	42	.48	180	.262	.335	.439

Joe Carter

Bats: Right **Throws:** Right **Pos:** RF/DH   **Ht:** 6' 3" **Wt:** 225 **Born:** 03/07/60 **Age:** 33

Year Team	Lg	G	AB	H	2B	3B	HR	(Hm	Rd)	TB	R	RBI	TBB	IBB	SO	HBP	SH	SF	SB	CS	SB%	GDP	Avg	OBP	SLG
1983 Chicago	NL	23	51	9	1	1	0	(0	0)	12	6	1	0	0	21	0	1	0	1	0	1.00	1	.176	.176	.235
1984 Cleveland	AL	66	244	67	6	1	13	(9	4)	114	32	41	11	0	48	1	0	1	2	4	.33	2	.275	.307	.467
1985 Cleveland	AL	143	489	128	27	0	15	(5	10)	200	64	59	25	2	74	2	3	4	24	6	.80	9	.262	.298	.409
1986 Cleveland	AL	162	663	200	36	9	29	(14	15)	341	108	121	32	3	95	5	1	8	29	7	.81	9	.302	.335	.514
1987 Cleveland	AL	149	588	155	27	2	32	(9	23)	282	83	106	27	6	105	9	1	4	31	6	.84	8	.264	.304	.480
1988 Cleveland	AL	157	621	168	36	6	27	(16	11)	297	85	98	35	6	82	7	1	6	27	5	.84	6	.271	.314	.478
1989 Cleveland	AL	162	651	158	32	4	35	(16	19)	303	84	105	39	8	112	8	2	5	13	5	.72	6	.243	.292	.465
1990 San Diego	NL	162	634	147	27	1	24	(12	12)	248	79	115	48	18	93	7	0	8	22	6	.79	12	.232	.290	.391
1991 Toronto	AL	162	638	174	42	3	33	(23	10)	321	89	108	49	12	112	10	0	9	20	9	.69	6	.273	.330	.503
1992 Toronto	AL	158	622	164	30	7	34	(21	13)	310	97	119	36	4	109	11	1	13	12	5	.71	14	.264	.309	.498
10 ML YEARS		1344	5201	1370	264	34	242	(125	117)	2428	727	873	302	59	851	60	10	58	181	53	.77	72	.263	.308	.467

Larry Carter

Pitches: Right **Bats:** Right **Pos:** SP   **Ht:** 6' 5" **Wt:** 195 **Born:** 05/22/65 **Age:** 28

Year Team	Lg	G	GS	CG	GF	IP	BFP	H	R	ER	HR	SH	SF	HB	TBB	IBB	SO	WP	Bk	W	L	Pct.	ShO	Sv	ERA
1986 Johnson Cty	R	8	8	0	0	36.1	161	30	22	15	4	0	0	1	18	0	35	1	0	1	5	.167	0	0	3.72
1988 Everett	A	4	4	0	0	21	94	17	14	13	0	0	0	2	14	0	27	4	0	1	3	.250	0	0	5.57
Clinton	A	12	7	0	2	49.1	205	48	20	17	3	1	4	3	14	1	32	6	1	2	4	.333	0	0	3.10
1989 Salinas	A	9	9	1	0	63	250	32	22	14	2	1	2	4	27	2	56	2	0	6	2	.750	0	0	2.00
Shreveport	AA	14	13	1	0	67.1	288	67	39	36	6	2	4	4	21	0	52	2	1	5	4	.556	0	0	4.81
1990 Shreveport	AA	5	4	0	0	18	75	15	7	7	3	0	1	1	4	0	12	1	0	1	0	1.000	0	0	3.50
1991 Shreveport	AA	24	24	1	0	149.1	623	124	61	49	8	7	6	3	51	2	133	3	0	9	8	.529	1	0	2.95
1992 Phoenix	AAA	28	28	2	0	185.1	791	188	95	90	17	6	12	3	62	3	126	8	0	11	6	.647	0	0	4.37
1992 San Francisco	NL	6	6	0	0	33	147	34	17	17	6	2	1	0	18	0	21	2	0	1	5	.167	0	0	4.64

Larry Casian

Pitches: Left **Bats:** Right **Pos:** RP   **Ht:** 6' 0" **Wt:** 170 **Born:** 10/28/65 **Age:** 27

Year Team	Lg	G	GS	CG	GF	IP	BFP	H	R	ER	HR	SH	SF	HB	TBB	IBB	SO	WP	Bk	W	L	Pct.	ShO	Sv	ERA
1990 Minnesota	AL	5	3	0	1	22.1	90	26	9	8	2	0	1	0	4	0	11	0	0	2	1	.667	0	0	3.22
1991 Minnesota	AL	15	0	0	4	18.1	87	28	16	15	4	0	0	1	7	2	6	2	0	0	0	.000	0	0	7.36
1992 Minnesota	AL	6	0	0	1	6.2	28	7	2	2	0	0	0	0	1	0	2	0	0	1	0	1.000	0	0	2.70
3 ML YEARS		26	3	0	6	47.1	205	61	27	25	6	0	1	1	12	2	19	2	0	3	1	.750	0	0	4.75

Vinny Castilla

Bats: Right **Throws:** Right **Pos:** 3B **Ht:** 6' 1" **Wt:** 175 **Born:** 07/04/67 **Age:** 25

Year	Team	Lg	G	AB	H	2B	3B	HR	(Hm	Rd)	TB	R	RBI	TBB	IBB	SO	HBP	SH	SF	SB	CS	SB%	GDP	Avg	OBP	SLG
1990	Sumter	A	93	339	91	15	2	9	--	--	137	47	53	28	1	54	8	1	5	2	5	.29	8	.268	.334	.404
	Greenville	AA	46	170	40	5	1	4	--	--	59	20	16	13	3	23	2	0	1	4	4	.50	7	.235	.296	.347
1991	Greenville	AA	66	259	70	17	3	7	--	--	114	34	44	9	1	35	2	2	4	0	1	.00	4	.270	.296	.440
	Richmond	AAA	67	240	54	7	4	7	--	--	90	25	36	14	2	31	3	0	5	1	1	.50	4	.225	.271	.375
1992	Richmond	AAA	127	449	113	29	1	7	--	--	165	49	44	21	1	68	4	3	6	1	2	.33	19	.252	.288	.367
1991	Atlanta	NL	12	5	1	0	0	0	(0	0)	1	1	0	0	0	2	0	1	0	0	0	.00	0	.200	.200	.200
1992	Atlanta	NL	9	16	4	1	0	0	(0	0)	5	1	1	1	1	4	1	0	0	0	0	.00	0	.250	.333	.313
	2 ML YEARS		21	21	5	1	0	0	(0	0)	6	2	1	1	1	6	1	1	0	0	0	.00	0	.238	.304	.286

Braulio Castillo

Bats: Right **Throws:** Right **Pos:** RF **Ht:** 6' 0" **Wt:** 160 **Born:** 05/13/68 **Age:** 25

Year	Team	Lg	G	AB	H	2B	3B	HR	(Hm	Rd)	TB	R	RBI	TBB	IBB	SO	HBP	SH	SF	SB	CS	SB%	GDP	Avg	OBP	SLG
1990	San Antonio	AA	75	241	55	11	3	3	--	--	81	34	24	14	2	72	2	0	1	11	6	.65	5	.228	.275	.336
1991	San Antonio	AA	87	297	89	19	3	8	--	--	138	49	48	32	2	73	6	1	3	22	10	.69	7	.300	.376	.465
	Scranton-Wb	AAA	16	60	21	9	1	0	--	--	32	14	15	6	0	7	0	0	1	2	1	.67	0	.350	.403	.533
1992	Scranton/wb	AAA	105	386	95	21	5	13	--	--	165	59	47	40	1	96	4	2	4	8	4	.67	9	.246	.320	.427
1991	Philadelphia	NL	28	52	9	3	0	0	(0	0)	12	3	2	1	0	15	0	0	0	1	1	.50	1	.173	.189	.231
1992	Philadelphia	NL	28	76	15	3	1	2	(1	1)	26	12	7	4	0	15	1	0	0	1	0	1.00	1	.197	.238	.342
	2 ML YEARS		56	128	24	6	1	2	(1	1)	38	15	9	5	0	30	1	0	0	2	1	.67	2	.188	.218	.297

Frank Castillo

Pitches: Right **Bats:** Right **Pos:** SP **Ht:** 6' 1" **Wt:** 180 **Born:** 04/01/69 **Age:** 24

Year	Team	Lg	G	GS	CG	GF	IP	BFP	H	R	ER	HR	SH	SF	HB	TBB	IBB	SO	WP	Bk	W	L	Pct.	ShO	Sv	ERA
1987	Wytheville	R	12	12	5	0	90.1	372	86	31	23	4	3	2	5	21	0	83	2	1	10	1	.909	0	0	2.29
	Geneva	A	1	1	0	0	6	23	3	1	0	0	0	0	0	1	0	6	0	0	1	0	1.000	0	0	0.00
1988	Peoria	A	9	8	2	0	51	186	25	5	4	1	0	0	1	10	0	58	0	0	6	1	.857	2	0	0.71
1989	Winston-Sal	A	18	18	8	0	129.1	521	118	42	36	5	2	1	3	24	1	114	1	1	9	6	.600	1	0	2.51
	Charlotte	AA	10	10	4	0	68	283	73	35	29	7	4	2	1	12	3	43	1	0	3	4	.429	0	0	3.84
1990	Charlotte	AA	18	18	4	0	111.1	471	113	54	48	8	6	3	8	27	4	112	5	1	6	6	.500	1	0	3.88
1991	Iowa	AAA	4	4	1	0	25	98	20	7	7	0	0	1	1	7	0	20	2	0	3	1	.750	1	0	2.52
1991	Chicago	NL	18	18	4	0	111.2	467	107	56	54	5	6	3	0	33	2	73	5	1	6	7	.462	0	0	4.35
1992	Chicago	NL	33	33	0	0	205.1	856	179	91	79	19	11	5	6	63	6	135	11	0	10	11	.476	0	0	3.46
	2 ML YEARS		51	51	4	0	317	1323	286	147	133	24	17	8	6	96	8	208	16	1	16	18	.471	0	0	3.78

Andujar Cedeno

Bats: Right **Throws:** Right **Pos:** SS **Ht:** 6' 1" **Wt:** 168 **Born:** 08/21/69 **Age:** 23

Year	Team	Lg	G	AB	H	2B	3B	HR	(Hm	Rd)	TB	R	RBI	TBB	IBB	SO	HBP	SH	SF	SB	CS	SB%	GDP	Avg	OBP	SLG
1990	Houston	NL	7	8	0	0	0	0	(0	0)	0	0	0	0	0	5	0	0	0	0	0	.00	0	.000	.000	.000
1991	Houston	NL	67	251	61	13	2	9	(4	5)	105	27	36	9	1	74	1	1	2	4	3	.57	3	.243	.270	.418
1992	Houston	NL	71	220	38	13	2	2	(2	0)	61	15	13	14	2	71	3	0	0	2	0	1.00	1	.173	.232	.277
	3 ML YEARS		145	479	99	26	4	11	(6	5)	166	42	49	23	3	150	4	1	2	6	3	.67	4	.207	.248	.347

Rick Cerone

Bats: Right **Throws:** Right **Pos:** C **Ht:** 5'11" **Wt:** 195 **Born:** 05/19/54 **Age:** 39

Year	Team	Lg	G	AB	H	2B	3B	HR	(Hm	Rd)	TB	R	RBI	TBB	IBB	SO	HBP	SH	SF	SB	CS	SB%	GDP	Avg	OBP	SLG
1975	Cleveland	AL	7	12	3	1	0	0	(0	0)	4	1	0	1	0	0	0	1	0	0	0	.00	0	.250	.308	.333
1976	Cleveland	AL	7	16	2	0	0	0	(0	0)	2	1	1	0	0	2	0	0	0	0	0	.00	0	.125	.125	.125
1977	Toronto	AL	31	100	20	4	0	1	(0	1)	27	7	10	6	0	12	0	1	0	0	0	.00	3	.200	.245	.270
1978	Toronto	AL	88	282	63	8	2	3	(2	1)	84	25	20	23	0	32	1	4	0	0	3	.00	7	.223	.284	.298
1979	Toronto	AL	136	469	112	27	4	7	(3	4)	168	47	61	37	1	40	1	3	4	1	4	.20	5	.239	.294	.358
1980	New York	AL	147	519	144	30	4	14	(7	7)	224	70	85	32	2	56	6	8	10	1	3	.25	14	.277	.321	.432
1981	New York	AL	71	234	57	13	2	2	(2	0)	80	23	21	12	0	24	0	4	4	0	2	.00	10	.244	.276	.342
1982	New York	AL	89	300	68	10	0	5	(1	4)	93	29	28	19	1	27	1	4	5	0	2	.00	12	.227	.271	.310
1983	New York	AL	80	246	54	7	0	2	(0	2)	67	14	22	15	1	29	1	4	0	0	0	.00	5	.220	.267	.272
1984	New York	AL	38	120	25	3	0	2	(0	2)	34	8	13	9	0	15	1	2	0	1	0	1.00	5	.208	.269	.283
1985	Atlanta	NL	96	282	61	9	0	3	(3	0)	79	15	25	29	1	25	1	0	4	0	0	.00	15	.216	.288	.280
1986	Milwaukee	AL	68	216	56	14	0	4	(3	1)	82	22	18	15	0	28	1	5	5	0	1	.50	5	.259	.304	.380
1987	New York	AL	113	284	69	12	1	4	(1	3)	95	28	23	30	0	46	4	5	4	0	1	.00	8	.243	.320	.335
1988	Boston	AL	84	264	71	13	1	3	(3	0)	95	31	27	20	0	32	3	1	1	0	0	.00	6	.269	.326	.360
1989	Boston	AL	102	296	72	16	1	4	(2	2)	102	28	48	34	1	40	2	4	5	0	0	.00	10	.243	.320	.345

Year	Team	Lg	G	AB	H	2B	3B	HR	(Hm	Rd)	TB	R	RBI	TBB	IBB	SO	HBP	SH	SF	SB	CS	SB%	GDP	Avg	OBP	SLG
1990	New York	AL	49	139	42	6	0	2	(1	1)	54	12	11	5	0	13	0	1	1	0	0	.00	4	.302	.324	.388
1991	New York	NL	90	227	62	13	0	2	(1	1)	81	18	16	30	2	24	1	0	0	1	1	.50	9	.273	.360	.357
1992	Montreal	NL	33	63	17	4	0	1	(1	0)	24	10	7	3	0	5	1	1	0	1	2	.33	0	.270	.313	.381
	18 ML YEARS		1329	4069	998	190	15	59	(30	29)	1395	393	436	320	9	450	24	48	43	6	22	.21	118	.245	.301	.343

Wes Chamberlain

Bats: Right **Throws:** Right **Pos:** RF/LF   **Ht:** 6' 2" **Wt:** 210 **Born:** 04/13/66 **Age:** 27

			BATTING																	BASERUNNING				PERCENTAGES		
Year	Team	Lg	G	AB	H	2B	3B	HR	(Hm	Rd)	TB	R	RBI	TBB	IBB	SO	HBP	SH	SF	SB	CS	SB%	GDP	Avg	OBP	SLG
1990	Philadelphia	NL	18	46	13	3	0	2	(0	2)	22	9	4	1	0	9	0	0	0	4	0	1.00	0	.283	.298	.478
1991	Philadelphia	NL	101	383	92	16	3	13	(9	4)	153	51	50	31	0	73	2	1	0	9	4	.69	8	.240	.300	.399
1992	Philadelphia	NL	76	275	71	18	0	9	(3	6)	116	26	41	10	2	55	1	1	2	4	0	1.00	7	.258	.285	.422
	3 ML YEARS		195	704	176	37	3	24	(12	12)	291	86	95	42	2	137	3	2	2	17	4	.81	15	.250	.294	.413

Darrin Chapin

Pitches: Right **Bats:** Right **Pos:** RP   **Ht:** 6' 0" **Wt:** 170 **Born:** 02/01/66 **Age:** 27

			HOW MUCH HE PITCHED					WHAT HE GAVE UP									THE RESULTS					
Year	Team	Lg	G	GS	CG	GF	IP	BFP	H	R	ER	HR	SH	SF	HB	TBB	IBB	SO	WP	Bk	W	L	Pct.	ShO	Sv	ERA
1986	Yankees	R	13	13	2	0	83.1	341	71	42	30	2	3	3	2	27	1	67	10	1	4	3	.571	2	0	3.24
1987	Oneonta	A	25	0	0	21	40	170	31	8	3	1	2	1	0	17	5	26	6	0	1	1	.500	0	12	0.68
1988	Albany	AA	3	0	0	3	4	26	11	7	5	0	0	0	1	2	0	4	0	0	0	0	.000	0	0	11.25
	Ft.Laudrdle	A	38	0	0	33	63	234	39	8	6	1	4	1	0	19	5	57	3	1	6	4	.600	0	15	0.86
1989	Albany	AA	7	0	0	7	8.2	32	5	0	0	0	0	0	0	1	1	16	2	0	1	0	1.000	0	3	0.00
	Columbus	AAA	27	0	0	21	40	167	33	15	13	3	3	1	1	15	4	38	3	1	2	4	.333	0	5	2.93
1990	Columbus	AAA	6	0	0	5	8.2	41	10	8	7	0	0	0	0	6	0	8	1	0	0	1	.000	0	2	7.27
	Albany	AA	43	0	0	40	52.2	223	43	20	16	2	1	4	1	21	1	61	4	0	3	2	.600	0	21	2.73
1991	Columbus	AAA	55	0	0	28	78.1	328	54	23	17	5	5	3	1	40	3	69	5	1	10	3	.769	0	12	1.95
1992	Scranton/wb	AAA	40	0	0	16	61.2	291	72	39	35	5	2	3	0	33	5	67	7	0	5	4	.556	0	4	5.11
1991	New York	AL	3	0	0	2	5.1	25	3	3	3	0	0	0	0	6	0	5	2	0	0	1	.000	0	0	5.06
1992	Philadelphia	NL	1	0	0	0	2	8	2	2	2	1	0	0	0	0	0	1	1	0	0	0	.000	0	0	9.00
	2 ML YEARS		4	0	0	2	7.1	33	5	5	5	1	0	0	0	6	0	6	3	0	0	1	.000	0	0	6.14

Norm Charlton

Pitches: Left **Bats:** Both **Pos:** RP   **Ht:** 6' 3" **Wt:** 205 **Born:** 01/06/63 **Age:** 30

			HOW MUCH HE PITCHED					WHAT HE GAVE UP									THE RESULTS					
Year	Team	Lg	G	GS	CG	GF	IP	BFP	H	R	ER	HR	SH	SF	HB	TBB	IBB	SO	WP	Bk	W	L	Pct.	ShO	Sv	ERA
1988	Cincinnati	NL	10	10	0	0	61.1	259	60	27	27	6	4	2	2	20	2	39	3	2	4	5	.444	0	0	3.96
1989	Cincinnati	NL	69	0	0	27	95.1	393	67	38	31	5	9	2	2	40	7	98	2	4	8	3	.727	0	0	2.93
1990	Cincinnati	NL	56	16	1	13	154.1	650	131	53	47	10	7	2	4	70	4	117	9	1	12	9	.571	1	2	2.74
1991	Cincinnati	NL	39	11	0	10	108.1	438	92	37	35	6	7	1	6	34	4	77	11	0	3	5	.375	0	1	2.91
1992	Cincinnati	NL	64	0	0	46	81.1	341	79	39	27	7	7	3	3	26	4	90	8	0	4	2	.667	0	26	2.99
	5 ML YEARS		238	37	1	96	500.2	2081	429	194	167	34	31	10	17	190	21	421	33	7	31	24	.564	1	29	3.00

Scott Chiamparino

Pitches: Right **Bats:** Left **Pos:** SP   **Ht:** 6' 2" **Wt:** 205 **Born:** 08/22/66 **Age:** 26

			HOW MUCH HE PITCHED					WHAT HE GAVE UP									THE RESULTS					
Year	Team	Lg	G	GS	CG	GF	IP	BFP	H	R	ER	HR	SH	SF	HB	TBB	IBB	SO	WP	Bk	W	L	Pct.	ShO	Sv	ERA
1990	Texas	AL	6	6	0	0	37.2	160	36	14	11	1	1	1	2	12	0	19	5	0	1	2	.333	0	0	2.63
1991	Texas	AL	5	5	0	0	22.1	101	26	11	10	1	1	0	0	12	0	8	0	0	1	0	1.000	0	0	4.03
1992	Texas	AL	4	4	0	0	25.1	102	25	11	10	2	0	1	0	5	0	13	1	0	0	4	.000	0	0	3.55
	3 ML YEARS		15	15	0	0	85.1	363	87	36	31	4	2	2	2	29	0	40	6	0	2	6	.250	0	0	3.27

Mike Christopher

Pitches: Right **Bats:** Right **Pos:** RP   **Ht:** 6' 5" **Wt:** 205 **Born:** 11/03/63 **Age:** 29

			HOW MUCH HE PITCHED					WHAT HE GAVE UP									THE RESULTS					
Year	Team	Lg	G	GS	CG	GF	IP	BFP	H	R	ER	HR	SH	SF	HB	TBB	IBB	SO	WP	Bk	W	L	Pct.	ShO	Sv	ERA
1985	Oneonta	A	15	9	2	3	80.1	317	58	21	13	2	1	2	3	22	0	84	3	0	8	1	.889	2	0	1.46
1986	Albany	AA	11	11	2	0	60.2	273	75	48	34	6	2	4	3	12	1	34	0	0	3	5	.375	0	0	5.04
	Ft.Laudrdle	A	15	14	3	0	102.2	421	92	37	30	2	4	2	1	36	0	56	1	1	7	3	.700	1	0	2.63
1987	Ft.Laudrdle	A	24	24	9	0	169.1	694	183	53	46	5	6	4	0	28	1	81	4	0	13	8	.619	4	0	2.44
1988	Albany	AA	24	24	5	0	152.2	648	166	75	65	7	4	5	6	44	3	67	2	4	13	7	.650	1	0	3.83
1989	Columbus	AAA	13	11	1	0	73	331	95	45	39	6	6	5	3	21	3	42	1	0	5	6	.455	0	0	4.81
	Albany	AA	8	8	3	0	53.2	213	48	17	15	1	0	1	1	7	0	33	0	0	6	1	.857	0	0	2.52
1990	Albuquerque	AAA	54	0	0	25	68.2	287	62	20	15	3	5	4	2	23	3	47	0	0	6	1	.857	0	8	1.97
1991	Albuquerque	AAA	63	0	0	34	77.1	334	73	25	21	2	4	1	3	30	5	67	7	1	7	2	.778	0	16	2.44
1992	Colo Spngs	AAA	49	0	0	45	58.2	240	59	21	19	2	5	4	0	13	6	39	3	0	4	4	.500	0	26	2.91
1991	Los Angeles	NL	3	0	0	2	4	15	2	0	0	0	0	0	0	3	0	2	1	0	0	0	.000	0	0	0.00

1992 Cleveland	AL	10	0	0	4	18	79	17	8	6	2	1	1	0	10	1	13	2	0	0	0	.000	0	0	3.00
2 ML YEARS		13	0	0	6	22	94	19	8	6	2	1	1	0	13	1	15	2	0	0	0	.000	0	0	2.45

Archi Cianfrocco

Bats: Right **Throws:** Right **Pos:** 1B/3B   **Ht:** 6' 5" **Wt:** 200 **Born:** 10/06/66 **Age:** 26

							BATTING												BASERUNNING				PERCENTAGES		
Year Team	Lg	G	AB	H	2B	3B	HR	(Hm	Rd)	TB	R	RBI	TBB	IBB	SO	HBP	SH	SF	SB	CS	SB%	GDP	Avg	OBP	SLG
1987 Jamestown	A	70	251	62	8	4	2	--	--	84	28	27	9	2	59	1	4	4	2	0	1.00	2	.247	.272	.335
1988 Rockford	A	126	455	115	34	0	15	--	--	194	54	65	26	0	99	6	2	5	6	1	.86	8	.253	.299	.426
1989 Jacksnville	AA	132	429	105	22	7	7	--	--	162	46	50	37	1	126	1	0	5	3	7	.30	8	.245	.303	.378
1990 Jacksnville	AA	62	196	43	10	0	5	--	--	68	18	29	12	1	45	2	0	3	2	0	1.00	4	.219	.268	.347
1991 Harrisburg	AA	124	456	144	21	10	9	--	--	212	71	77	38	2	112	9	2	2	11	3	.79	11	.316	.378	.465
1992 Indianapols	AAA	15	59	18	3	0	4	--	--	33	12	16	5	0	15	2	0	1	1	0	1.00	0	.305	.373	.559
1992 Montreal	NL	86	232	56	5	2	6	(3	3)	83	25	30	11	0	66	1	1	2	3	0	1.00	2	.241	.276	.358

Dave Clark

Bats: Left **Throws:** Right **Pos:** RF   **Ht:** 6' 2" **Wt:** 210 **Born:** 09/03/62 **Age:** 30

							BATTING												BASERUNNING				PERCENTAGES		
Year Team	Lg	G	AB	H	2B	3B	HR	(Hm	Rd)	TB	R	RBI	TBB	IBB	SO	HBP	SH	SF	SB	CS	SB%	GDP	Avg	OBP	SLG
1986 Cleveland	AL	18	58	16	1	0	3	(1	2)	26	10	9	7	0	11	0	2	1	1	0	1.00	1	.276	.348	.448
1987 Cleveland	AL	29	87	18	5	0	3	(1	2)	32	11	12	2	0	24	0	0	0	1	0	1.00	4	.207	.225	.368
1988 Cleveland	AL	63	156	41	4	1	3	(2	1)	56	11	18	17	2	28	0	0	1	0	2	.00	8	.263	.333	.359
1989 Cleveland	AL	102	253	60	12	0	8	(4	4)	96	21	29	30	5	63	0	1	1	0	2	.00	7	.237	.317	.379
1990 Chicago	NL	84	171	47	4	2	5	(3	2)	70	22	20	8	1	40	0	0	2	7	1	.88	4	.275	.304	.409
1991 Kansas City	AL	11	10	2	0	0	0	(0	0)	2	1	1	1	0	1	0	0	0	0	0	.00	0	.200	.273	.200
1992 Pittsburgh	NL	23	33	7	0	0	2	(2	0)	13	3	7	6	0	8	0	0	1	0	0	.00	0	.212	.325	.394
7 ML YEARS		330	768	191	26	3	24	(13	11)	295	79	96	71	8	175	0	3	6	9	5	.64	24	.249	.310	.384

Jack Clark

Bats: Right **Throws:** Right **Pos:** DH/1B   **Ht:** 6' 3" **Wt:** 210 **Born:** 11/10/55 **Age:** 37

							BATTING												BASERUNNING				PERCENTAGES		
Year Team	Lg	G	AB	H	2B	3B	HR	(Hm	Rd)	TB	R	RBI	TBB	IBB	SO	HBP	SH	SF	SB	CS	SB%	GDP	Avg	OBP	SLG
1975 San Francisco	NL	8	17	4	0	0	0	(0	0)	4	3	2	1	0	2	0	0	1	1	0	1.00	0	.235	.263	.235
1976 San Francisco	NL	26	102	23	6	2	2	(2	0)	39	14	10	8	0	18	0	3	2	6	2	.75	0	.225	.277	.382
1977 San Francisco	NL	136	413	104	17	4	13	(7	6)	168	64	51	49	2	73	2	1	3	12	4	.75	7	.252	.332	.407
1978 San Francisco	NL	156	592	181	46	8	25	(10	15)	318	90	98	50	8	72	3	3	9	15	11	.58	15	.306	.358	.537
1979 San Francisco	NL	143	527	144	25	2	26	(10	16)	251	84	86	63	6	95	1	1	6	11	8	.58	9	.273	.348	.476
1980 San Francisco	NL	127	437	124	20	8	22	(8	14)	226	77	82	74	13	52	2	1	10	2	5	.29	12	.284	.382	.517
1981 San Francisco	NL	99	385	103	19	2	17	(7	10)	177	60	53	45	6	45	1	0	6	1	1	.50	12	.268	.341	.460
1982 San Francisco	NL	157	563	154	30	3	27	(9	18)	271	90	103	90	7	91	1	0	5	6	9	.40	20	.274	.372	.481
1983 San Francisco	NL	135	492	132	25	0	20	(11	9)	217	82	66	74	6	79	1	0	7	5	3	.63	14	.268	.361	.441
1984 San Francisco	NL	57	203	65	9	1	11	(2	9)	109	33	44	43	7	29	0	0	3	1	1	.50	9	.320	.434	.537
1985 St. Louis	NL	126	442	124	26	3	22	(8	14)	222	71	87	83	14	88	2	0	5	1	4	.20	10	.281	.393	.502
1986 St. Louis	NL	65	232	55	12	2	9	(4	5)	98	34	23	45	4	61	1	0	1	1	1	.50	4	.237	.362	.422
1987 St. Louis	NL	131	419	120	23	1	35	(17	18)	250	93	106	**136**	13	139	0	0	3	1	2	.33	5	.286	**.459**	**.597**
1988 New York	AL	150	496	120	14	0	27	(13	14)	215	81	93	113	6	141	2	0	5	0	3	.00	5	.242	.381	.433
1989 San Diego	NL	142	455	110	19	1	26	(11	15)	209	76	94	**132**	18	145	1	0	5	6	2	.75	10	.242	.410	.459
1990 San Diego	NL	115	334	89	12	1	25	(16	9)	178	59	62	**104**	11	91	2	0	2	4	3	.57	12	.266	.441	.533
1991 Boston	AL	140	481	120	18	1	28	(18	10)	224	75	87	96	3	133	3	0	5	0	2	.00	17	.249	.374	.466
1992 Boston	AL	81	257	54	11	0	5	(0	5)	80	32	33	56	3	87	2	0	5	1	1	.50	4	.210	.350	.311
18 ML YEARS		1994	6847	1826	332	39	340	(155	185)	3256	1118	1180	1262	127	1441	24	9	83	77	61	.56	174	.267	.379	.476

Jerald Clark

Bats: Right **Throws:** Right **Pos:** LF/1B/RF   **Ht:** 6' 4" **Wt:** 205 **Born:** 08/10/63 **Age:** 29

							BATTING												BASERUNNING				PERCENTAGES		
Year Team	Lg	G	AB	H	2B	3B	HR	(Hm	Rd)	TB	R	RBI	TBB	IBB	SO	HBP	SH	SF	SB	CS	SB%	GDP	Avg	OBP	SLG
1988 San Diego	NL	6	15	3	1	0	0	(0	0)	4	0	3	0	0	4	0	0	0	0	0	.00	0	.200	.200	.267
1989 San Diego	NL	17	41	8	2	0	1	(1	0)	13	5	7	3	0	9	0	0	0	0	1	.00	0	.195	.250	.317
1990 San Diego	NL	52	101	27	4	1	5	(2	3)	48	12	11	5	0	24	0	0	1	0	0	.00	3	.267	.299	.475
1991 San Diego	NL	118	369	84	16	6	10	(8	2)	130	26	47	31	2	90	6	1	4	2	1	.67	10	.228	.295	.352
1992 San Diego	NL	146	496	120	22	6	12	(9	3)	190	45	58	22	3	97	4	1	3	3	0	1.00	7	.242	.278	.383
5 ML YEARS		339	1022	242	45	7	28	(20	8)	385	88	126	61	5	224	10	2	8	5	2	.71	20	.237	.284	.377

Mark Clark

Pitches: Right **Bats:** Right **Pos:** SP **Ht:** 6' 5" **Wt:** 225 **Born:** 05/12/68 **Age:** 25

		HOW MUCH HE PITCHED							WHAT HE GAVE UP										THE RESULTS					
Year Team	Lg	G	GS	CG	GF	IP	BFP	H	R	ER	HR	SH	SF	HB	TBB	IBB	SO	WP	Bk	W	L	Pct.	ShO	Sv	ERA
1988 Hamilton	A	15	15	2	0	94.1	385	88	39	32	10	4	3	0	32	2	60	2	1	6	7	.462	0	0	3.05
1989 Savannah	A	27	27	4	0	173.2	712	143	61	47	8	4	4	1	52	0	132	11	3	14	9	.609	2	0	2.44
1990 St. Pete	A	10	10	1	0	62	254	63	33	21	3	2	2	1	14	0	58	3	1	3	2	.600	1	0	3.05
Arkansas	AA	19	19	5	0	115.1	479	111	56	49	11	6	4	0	37	2	87	6	1	5	11	.313	0	0	3.82
1991 Arkansas	AA	15	15	4	0	92.1	398	99	50	41	2	3	2	2	30	4	76	0	0	5	5	.500	1	0	4.00
Louisville	AAA	7	6	1	0	45.1	189	43	17	15	4	1	3	0	15	0	29	2	0	3	2	.600	1	0	2.98
1992 Louisville	AAA	9	9	4	0	61	250	56	20	19	4	4	0	1	15	0	38	2	0	4	4	.500	3	0	2.80
1991 St. Louis	NL	7	2	0	1	22.1	93	17	10	10	3	0	3	0	11	0	13	2	0	1	1	.500	0	0	4.03
1992 St. Louis	NL	20	20	1	0	113.1	488	117	59	56	12	7	4	0	36	2	44	4	0	3	10	.231	1	0	4.45
2 ML YEARS		27	22	1	1	135.2	581	134	69	66	15	7	7	0	47	2	57	6	0	4	11	.267	1	0	4.38

Phil Clark

Bats: Right **Throws:** Right **Pos:** RF **Ht:** 6' 0" **Wt:** 180 **Born:** 05/06/68 **Age:** 25

		BATTING																		BASERUNNING				PERCENTAGES		
Year Team	Lg	G	AB	H	2B	3B	HR	(Hm	Rd)	TB	R	RBI	TBB	IBB	SO	HBP	SH	SF	SB	CS	SB%	GDP	Avg	OBP	SLG
1986 Bristol	R	66	247	82	4	2	4	--	--	102	40	36	19	2	42	6	1	4	12	1	.92	3	.332	.388	.413
1987 Fayetteville	A	135	542	160	26	9	8	--	--	228	83	79	25	0	43	6	1	6	25	9	.74	16	.295	.329	.421
1988 Lakeland	A	109	403	120	17	4	9	--	--	172	60	66	15	2	43	10	2	7	16	7	.70	9	.298	.333	.427
1989 London	AA	104	373	108	15	4	8	--	--	155	43	42	31	1	49	8	2	1	2	2	.50	16	.290	.356	.416
1990 Toledo	AAA	75	207	47	14	1	2	--	--	69	15	22	14	0	35	4	6	2	1	1	.50	6	.227	.286	.333
1991 Toledo	AAA	110	362	92	13	4	4	--	--	125	47	45	21	0	49	5	3	2	6	6	.50	10	.254	.303	.345
1992 Toledo	AAA	79	271	76	20	0	10	--	--	126	29	39	16	0	35	2	1	2	4	2	.67	8	.280	.323	.465
1992 Detroit	AL	23	54	22	4	0	1	(0	1)	29	3	5	6	1	9	0	1	0	1	0	1.00	2	.407	.467	.537

Will Clark

Bats: Left **Throws:** Left **Pos:** 1B **Ht:** 6' 1" **Wt:** 190 **Born:** 03/13/64 **Age:** 29

		BATTING																		BASERUNNING				PERCENTAGES		
Year Team	Lg	G	AB	H	2B	3B	HR	(Hm	Rd)	TB	R	RBI	TBB	IBB	SO	HBP	SH	SF	SB	CS	SB%	GDP	Avg	OBP	SLG
1986 San Francisco	NL	111	408	117	27	2	11	(7	4)	181	66	41	34	10	76	3	9	4	4	7	.36	3	.287	.343	.444
1987 San Francisco	NL	150	529	163	29	5	35	(22	13)	307	89	91	49	11	98	5	3	2	5	17	.23	2	.308	.371	.580
1988 San Francisco	NL	162	575	162	31	6	29	(14	15)	292	102	109	100	27	129	4	0	10	9	1	.90	9	.282	.386	.508
1989 San Francisco	NL	159	588	196	38	9	23	(9	14)	321	104	111	74	14	103	5	0	8	8	3	.73	6	.333	.407	.546
1990 San Francisco	NL	154	600	177	25	5	19	(8	11)	269	91	95	62	9	97	3	0	13	8	2	.80	7	.295	.357	.448
1991 San Francisco	NL	148	565	170	32	7	29	(17	12)	303	84	116	51	12	91	2	0	4	4	2	.67	5	.301	.359	.536
1992 San Francisco	NL	144	513	154	40	1	16	(11	5)	244	69	73	73	23	82	4	0	11	12	7	.63	5	.300	.384	.476
7 ML YEARS		1028	3778	1139	222	35	162	(88	74)	1917	605	636	443	106	676	26	12	52	50	39	.56	37	.301	.374	.507

Royce Clayton

Bats: Right **Throws:** Right **Pos:** SS **Ht:** 6' 0" **Wt:** 175 **Born:** 01/02/70 **Age:** 23

		BATTING																		BASERUNNING				PERCENTAGES		
Year Team	Lg	G	AB	H	2B	3B	HR	(Hm	Rd)	TB	R	RBI	TBB	IBB	SO	HBP	SH	SF	SB	CS	SB%	GDP	Avg	OBP	SLG
1988 Everett	A	60	212	55	4	0	3	--	--	68	35	29	27	0	54	3	1	2	10	4	.71	3	.259	.348	.321
1989 Clinton	A	104	385	91	13	3	0	--	--	110	39	24	39	0	101	4	4	5	28	16	.64	6	.236	.309	.286
San Jose	A	28	92	11	2	0	0	--	--	13	5	4	13	0	27	1	0	0	10	1	.91	5	.120	.236	.141
1990 San Jose	A	123	460	123	15	10	7	--	--	179	80	71	68	3	98	4	0	4	33	15	.69	13	.267	.364	.389
1991 Shreveport	AA	126	485	136	22	8	5	--	--	189	84	68	61	7	102	3	3	5	36	10	.78	7	.280	.361	.390
1992 Phoenix	AAA	48	192	46	6	2	3	--	--	65	30	18	17	0	25	0	0	2	15	6	.71	8	.240	.300	.339
1991 San Francisco	NL	9	26	3	1	0	0	(0	0)	4	0	2	1	0	6	0	0	0	0	0	.00	1	.115	.148	.154
1992 San Francisco	NL	98	321	72	7	4	4	(3	1)	99	31	24	26	3	63	0	3	2	8	4	.67	11	.224	.281	.308
2 ML YEARS		107	347	75	8	4	4	(3	1)	103	31	26	27	3	69	0	3	2	8	4	.67	12	.216	.271	.297

Roger Clemens

Pitches: Right **Bats:** Right **Pos:** SP **Ht:** 6' 4" **Wt:** 220 **Born:** 08/04/62 **Age:** 30

		HOW MUCH HE PITCHED							WHAT HE GAVE UP										THE RESULTS					
Year Team	Lg	G	GS	CG	GF	IP	BFP	H	R	ER	HR	SH	SF	HB	TBB	IBB	SO	WP	Bk	W	L	Pct.	ShO	Sv	ERA
1984 Boston	AL	21	20	5	0	133.1	575	146	67	64	13	2	3	2	29	3	126	4	1	9	4	.692	1	0	4.32
1985 Boston	AL	15	15	3	0	98.1	407	83	38	36	5	1	2	3	37	0	74	1	3	7	5	.583	1	0	3.29
1986 Boston	AL	33	33	10	0	254	997	179	77	70	21	4	6	4	67	0	238	11	3	24	4	.857	1	0	2.48
1987 Boston	AL	36	36	18	0	281.2	1157	248	100	93	19	6	4	9	83	4	256	4	3	20	9	.690	7	0	2.97
1988 Boston	AL	35	35	14	0	264	1063	217	93	86	17	6	3	6	62	4	291	4	7	18	12	.600	8	0	2.93
1989 Boston	AL	35	35	8	0	253.1	1044	215	101	88	20	9	5	8	93	5	230	7	0	17	11	.607	3	0	3.13
1990 Boston	AL	31	31	7	0	228.1	920	193	59	49	7	7	5	7	54	3	209	8	0	21	6	.778	4	0	1.93

			G	GS	CG	GF	IP	BFP	H	R	ER	HR	SH	SF	HB	TBB	IBB	SO	WP	Bk	W	L	Pct.	ShO	Sv	ERA
1991	Boston	AL	35	35	13	0	271.1	1077	219	93	79	15	6	8	5	65	12	241	6	0	18	10	.643	4	0	2.62
1992	Boston	AL	32	32	11	0	246.2	989	203	80	66	11	5	5	9	62	5	208	3	0	18	11	.621	5	0	2.41
	9 ML YEARS		273	272	89	0	2031	8229	1703	708	631	128	46	41	53	552	36	1873	48	16	152	72	.679	34	0	2.80

Pat Clements

Pitches: Left **Bats:** Right **Pos:** RP **Ht:** 6' 0" **Wt:** 180 **Born:** 02/02/62 **Age:** 31

			HOW MUCH HE PITCHED						WHAT HE GAVE UP													THE RESULTS				
Year	Team	Lg	G	GS	CG	GF	IP	BFP	H	R	ER	HR	SH	SF	HB	TBB	IBB	SO	WP	Bk	W	L	Pct.	ShO	Sv	ERA
1985	2 ML Teams		68	0	0	19	96.1	400	86	37	37	6	6	1	2	40	5	36	3	0	5	2	.714	0	3	3.46
1986	Pittsburgh	NL	65	0	0	19	61	256	53	20	19	1	7	4	2	32	6	31	2	0	0	4	.000	0	2	2.80
1987	New York	AL	55	0	0	20	80	347	91	45	44	4	6	4	3	30	2	36	8	2	3	3	.500	0	7	4.95
1988	New York	AL	6	1	0	1	8.1	41	12	8	6	1	0	2	0	4	0	3	1	0	0	0	.000	0	0	6.48
1989	San Diego	NL	23	1	0	8	39	167	39	17	17	4	5	1	0	15	5	18	1	0	4	1	.800	0	0	3.92
1990	San Diego	NL	9	0	0	3	13	63	20	9	6	1	0	0	0	7	1	6	1	0	0	0	.000	0	0	4.15
1991	San Diego	NL	12	0	0	4	14.1	63	13	8	6	0	0	3	0	9	4	8	0	0	1	0	1.000	0	0	3.77
1992	2 ML Teams		50	0	0	11	48.1	210	48	19	16	0	4	1	4	23	4	20	1	0	4	1	.800	0	0	2.98
1985	California	AL	41	0	0	12	62	247	47	23	23	4	4	0	2	25	2	19	1	0	5	0	1.000	0	1	3.34
	Pittsburgh	NL	27	0	0	7	34.1	153	39	14	14	2	2	1	0	15	3	17	2	0	0	2	.000	0	2	3.67
1992	San Diego	NL	27	0	0	7	23.2	105	25	9	7	0	2	0	2	12	4	11	0	0	2	1	.667	0	0	2.66
	Baltimore	AL	23	0	0	4	24.2	105	23	10	9	0	2	1	2	11	0	9	1	0	2	0	1.000	0	0	3.28
	8 ML YEARS		288	2	0	85	360.1	1547	362	163	151	17	28	16	11	160	27	158	17	2	17	11	.607	0	12	3.77

Dave Cochrane

Bats: Both **Throws:** Right **Pos:** C/LF **Ht:** 6' 2" **Wt:** 180 **Born:** 01/31/63 **Age:** 30

			BATTING																BASERUNNING				PERCENTAGES		
Year	Team	Lg	G	AB	H	2B	3B	HR	(Hm | Rd)	TB	R	RBI	TBB	IBB	SO	HBP	SH	SF	SB	CS	SB%	GDP	Avg	OBP	SLG
1986	Chicago	AL	19	62	12	2	0	1	(1 | 0)	17	4	2	5	1	22	0	1	0	0	0	.00	2	.194	.254	.274
1989	Seattle	AL	54	102	24	4	1	3	(3 | 0)	39	13	7	14	0	27	1	0	0	0	2	.00	2	.235	.333	.382
1990	Seattle	AL	15	20	3	0	0	0	(0 | 0)	3	0	0	0	0	8	0	0	0	0	0	.00	0	.150	.150	.150
1991	Seattle	AL	65	178	44	13	0	2	(1 | 1)	63	16	22	9	0	38	1	1	1	0	1	.00	3	.247	.286	.354
1992	Seattle	AL	65	152	38	5	0	2	(0 | 2)	49	10	12	12	0	34	1	2	0	1	0	1.00	3	.250	.309	.322
	5 ML YEARS		218	514	121	24	1	8	(5 | 3)	171	43	43	40	1	129	3	4	1	3	3	.25	10	.235	.294	.333

Craig Colbert

Bats: Right **Throws:** Right **Pos:** C **Ht:** 6' 0" **Wt:** 190 **Born:** 02/13/65 **Age:** 28

			BATTING																BASERUNNING				PERCENTAGES		
Year	Team	Lg	G	AB	H	2B	3B	HR	(Hm | Rd)	TB	R	RBI	TBB	IBB	SO	HBP	SH	SF	SB	CS	SB%	GDP	Avg	OBP	SLG
1986	Clinton	A	72	263	60	12	0	1	--	--	75	26	17	23	1	53	3	0	1	4	1	.80	7	.228	.297	.285
1987	Fresno	A	115	388	95	12	4	6	--	--	133	41	51	22	2	89	4	3	5	5	5	.50	11	.245	.289	.343
1988	Clinton	A	124	455	106	19	2	11	--	--	162	56	64	41	0	100	1	2	2	8	9	.47	4	.233	.297	.356
1989	Shreveport	AA	106	363	94	19	3	7	--	--	140	47	34	23	5	67	0	2	2	3	7	.30	11	.259	.302	.386
1990	Phoenix	AAA	111	400	112	22	2	8	--	--	162	41	47	31	3	80	3	1	2	4	5	.44	8	.280	.335	.405
1991	Phoenix	AAA	42	142	35	6	2	2	--	--	51	9	13	11	2	38	0	0	1	0	1	.00	7	.246	.299	.359
1992	Phoenix	AAA	36	140	45	8	1	1	--	--	58	16	12	3	0	16	1	2	2	0	1	.00	4	.321	.336	.414
1992	San Francisco	NL	49	126	29	5	2	1	(0 | 1)	41	10	16	9	0	22	0	2	2	1	0	1.00	8	.230	.277	.325

Greg Colbrunn

Bats: Right **Throws:** Right **Pos:** 1B **Ht:** 6' 0" **Wt:** 190 **Born:** 07/26/69 **Age:** 23

			BATTING																BASERUNNING				PERCENTAGES		
Year	Team	Lg	G	AB	H	2B	3B	HR	(Hm | Rd)	TB	R	RBI	TBB	IBB	SO	HBP	SH	SF	SB	CS	SB%	GDP	Avg	OBP	SLG
1988	Rockford	A	115	417	111	18	2	7	--	--	154	55	46	22	2	60	11	2	3	5	3	.63	5	.266	.297	.369
1989	Wst Plm Bch	A	59	228	54	8	0	0	--	--	62	20	25	6	1	29	2	0	2	3	1	.75	5	.237	.261	.272
	Jacksnville	AA	55	178	49	11	1	3	--	--	71	21	18	13	0	33	2	0	1	0	1	.00	9	.275	.330	.399
1990	Jacksnville	AA	125	458	138	29	1	13	--	--	208	57	76	38	4	78	6	3	6	1	2	.33	8	.301	.358	.454
1992	Indianapols	AAA	57	216	66	19	1	11	--	--	120	32	48	7	2	41	3	0	2	1	0	1.00	7	.306	.333	.556
1992	Montreal	NL	52	168	45	8	0	2	(1 | 1)	59	12	18	6	1	34	2	0	4	3	2	.60	1	.268	.294	.351

Alex Cole

Bats: Left **Throws:** Left **Pos:** RF/LF **Ht:** 6' 0" **Wt:** 170 **Born:** 08/17/65 **Age:** 27

			BATTING																BASERUNNING				PERCENTAGES		
Year	Team	Lg	G	AB	H	2B	3B	HR	(Hm | Rd)	TB	R	RBI	TBB	IBB	SO	HBP	SH	SF	SB	CS	SB%	GDP	Avg	OBP	SLG
1990	Cleveland	AL	63	227	68	5	4	0	(0 | 0)	81	43	13	28	0	38	1	0	0	40	9	.82	2	.300	.379	.357
1991	Cleveland	AL	122	387	114	17	3	0	(0 | 0)	137	58	21	58	2	47	1	4	2	27	17	.61	8	.295	.386	.354
1992	2 ML Teams		105	302	77	4	7	0	(0 | 0)	95	44	15	28	1	67	1	1	2	16	6	.73	4	.255	.318	.315
1992	Cleveland	AL	41	97	20	1	0	0	(0 | 0)	21	11	5	10	0	21	1	0	1	9	2	.82	2	.206	.284	.216
	Pittsburgh	NL	64	205	57	3	7	0	(0 | 0)	74	33	10	18	1	46	0	1	1	7	4	.64	2	.278	.335	.361
	3 ML YEARS		290	916	259	26	14	0	(0 | 0)	313	145	49	114	3	152	3	5	4	83	32	.72	14	.283	.363	.342

Victor Cole

Pitches: Right **Bats:** Both **Pos:** SP   **Ht:** 5'10" **Wt:** 160 **Born:** 01/23/68 **Age:** 25

		HOW MUCH HE PITCHED						WHAT HE GAVE UP									THE RESULTS					
Year Team	Lg	G	GS	CG	GF	IP	BFP	H	R	ER	HR	SH	SF	HB	TBB	IBB	SO	WP	Bk	W	L	Pct.	ShO	Sv	ERA
1988 Eugene	A	15	0	0	13	23.2	94	16	6	4	0	0	0	2	8	0	39	3	0	1	0	1.000	0	9	1.52
Baseball Cy	A	10	5	0	2	35	149	27	9	8	0	1	1	1	21	0	29	2	0	5	0	1.000	0	1	2.06
1989 Memphis	AA	13	13	0	0	63.2	303	67	53	45	4	4	1	5	51	1	52	4	1	1	9	.100	0	6	6.36
Baseball Cy	A	9	9	0	0	42	186	43	23	18	2	1	1	1	22	0	30	2	1	3	1	.750	0	0	3.86
1990 Memphis	AA	46	6	0	15	107.2	479	91	61	52	6	4	1	3	70	2	102	2	2	3	8	.273	0	4	4.35
1991 Omaha	AAA	6	0	0	1	13	54	9	6	6	1	0	0	0	9	1	12	0	0	1	1	.500	0	0	4.15
Carolina	AA	20	0	0	17	28.1	116	13	8	6	1	0	1	2	19	1	32	3	2	0	2	.000	0	12	1.91
Buffalo	AAA	19	1	0	9	24	115	23	11	10	2	0	1	1	20	0	23	3	0	1	2	.333	0	0	3.75
1992 Buffalo	AAA	19	19	3	0	115.2	498	102	46	40	8	3	3	4	61	0	69	8	0	11	6	.647	1	0	3.11
1992 Pittsburgh	NL	8	4	0	2	23	104	23	14	14	1	1	1	0	14	0	12	1	0	0	2	.000	0	0	5.48

Vince Coleman

Bats: Both **Throws:** Right **Pos:** LF/CF   **Ht:** 6'1" **Wt:** 185 **Born:** 09/22/61 **Age:** 31

		BATTING																	BASERUNNING				PERCENTAGES		
Year Team	Lg	G	AB	H	2B	3B	HR	(Hm	Rd)	TB	R	RBI	TBB	IBB	SO	HBP	SH	SF	SB	CS	SB%	GDP	Avg	OBP	SLG
1985 St. Louis	NL	151	636	170	20	10	1	(1	0)	213	107	40	50	1	115	0	5	1	110	25	.81	3	.267	.320	.335
1986 St. Louis	NL	154	600	139	13	8	0	(0	0)	168	94	29	60	0	98	2	3	5	107	14	.88	4	.232	.301	.280
1987 St. Louis	NL	151	623	180	14	10	3	(3	0)	223	121	43	70	0	126	3	5	1	109	22	.83	7	.289	.363	.358
1988 St. Louis	NL	153	616	160	20	10	3	(2	1)	209	77	38	49	4	111	1	8	5	81	27	.75	4	.260	.313	.339
1989 St. Louis	NL	145	563	143	21	9	2	(1	1)	188	94	28	50	0	90	2	7	2	65	10	.87	4	.254	.316	.334
1990 St. Louis	NL	124	497	145	18	9	6	(5	1)	199	73	39	35	1	88	2	4	1	77	17	.82	6	.292	.340	.400
1991 New York	NL	72	278	71	7	5	1	(0	1)	91	45	17	39	0	47	0	1	0	37	14	.73	3	.255	.347	.327
1992 New York	NL	71	229	63	11	1	2	(2	0)	82	37	21	27	3	41	2	2	1	24	9	.73	1	.275	.355	.358
8 ML YEARS		1021	4042	1071	124	62	18	(14	4)	1373	648	255	380	9	716	12	35	16	610	138	.82	32	.265	.329	.340

Darnell Coles

Bats: Right **Throws:** Right **Pos:** 3B/1B   **Ht:** 6'1" **Wt:** 185 **Born:** 06/02/62 **Age:** 31

		BATTING																	BASERUNNING				PERCENTAGES		
Year Team	Lg	G	AB	H	2B	3B	HR	(Hm	Rd)	TB	R	RBI	TBB	IBB	SO	HBP	SH	SF	SB	CS	SB%	GDP	Avg	OBP	SLG
1983 Seattle	AL	27	92	26	7	0	1	(0	1)	36	9	6	7	0	12	0	1	0	0	3	.00	8	.283	.333	.391
1984 Seattle	AL	48	143	23	3	1	0	(0	0)	28	15	6	17	0	26	2	3	0	2	1	.67	5	.161	.259	.196
1985 Seattle	AL	27	59	14	4	0	1	(0	1)	21	8	5	9	0	17	1	0	2	0	1	.00	0	.237	.338	.356
1986 Detroit	AL	142	521	142	30	2	20	(12	8)	236	67	86	45	3	84	6	7	8	6	2	.75	8	.273	.333	.453
1987 2 ML Teams		93	268	54	13	1	10	(8	2)	99	34	39	34	3	43	3	5	3	1	4	.20	4	.201	.295	.369
1988 2 ML Teams		123	406	106	23	2	15	(10	5)	178	52	70	37	1	67	7	2	10	4	3	.57	8	.261	.326	.438
1989 Seattle	AL	146	535	135	21	3	10	(4	6)	192	54	59	27	1	61	6	2	3	5	4	.56	13	.252	.294	.359
1990 2 ML Teams		89	215	45	7	1	3	(3	0)	63	22	20	16	2	38	1	1	2	4	0	.00	4	.209	.265	.293
1991 San Francisco	NL	11	14	3	0	0	0	(0	0)	3	1	0	0	0	2	0	0	0	0	0	.00	1	.214	.214	.214
1992 Cincinnati	NL	55	141	44	11	2	3	(1	2)	68	16	18	3	0	15	0	3	2	1	0	1.00	1	.312	.322	.482
1987 Detroit	AL	53	149	27	5	1	4	(3	1)	46	14	15	15	1	23	2	2	1	0	1	.00	1	.181	.263	.309
Pittsburgh	NL	40	119	27	8	0	6	(5	1)	53	20	24	19	2	20	1	3	2	1	3	.25	3	.227	.333	.445
1988 Pittsburgh	NL	68	211	49	13	1	5	(1	4)	79	20	36	20	1	41	3	0	7	1	1	.50	3	.232	.299	.374
Seattle	AL	55	195	57	10	1	10	(9	1)	99	32	34	17	0	26	4	2	3	3	2	.60	5	.292	.356	.508
1990 Seattle	AL	37	107	23	5	1	2	(2	0)	36	9	16	4	1	17	1	0	1	0	0	.00	3	.215	.248	.336
Detroit	AL	52	108	22	2	0	1	(1	0)	27	13	4	12	1	21	0	1	1	0	4	.00	3	.204	.281	.250
10 ML YEARS		761	2394	592	119	12	63	(38	25)	924	278	309	195	10	365	26	24	30	19	22	.46	52	.247	.307	.386

Cris Colon

Bats: Both **Throws:** Right **Pos:** SS   **Ht:** 6'2" **Wt:** 180 **Born:** 01/03/69 **Age:** 24

		BATTING																	BASERUNNING				PERCENTAGES		
Year Team	Lg	G	AB	H	2B	3B	HR	(Hm	Rd)	TB	R	RBI	TBB	IBB	SO	HBP	SH	SF	SB	CS	SB%	GDP	Avg	OBP	SLG
1987 Rangers	R	46	136	35	3	0	0	--	--	38	12	9	3	0	17	0	2	1	2	0	1.00	5	.257	.271	.279
1988 Gastonia	A	75	232	46	12	0	1	--	--	61	23	11	12	0	46	0	4	0	6	2	.75	5	.198	.238	.263
Butte	R	49	190	37	3	4	1	--	--	51	21	19	3	0	34	0	1	1	3	0	1.00	3	.195	.206	.268
1989 Gastonia	A	125	473	107	9	8	3	--	--	141	58	49	10	0	95	2	11	4	8	5	.62	6	.226	.243	.298
1990 Gastonia	A	38	140	45	2	4	4	--	--	67	23	16	4	1	24	1	4	0	7	1	.88	2	.321	.345	.479
Tulsa	AA	65	234	57	9	1	3	--	--	77	24	29	5	1	37	1	3	2	5	4	.56	6	.244	.260	.329
1991 Charlotte	A	66	249	78	9	5	3	--	--	106	33	27	9	2	44	3	5	0	4	5	.44	7	.313	.345	.426
Tulsa	AA	26	102	40	6	2	3	--	--	59	20	28	4	0	11	0	1	3	1	0	.00	4	.392	.404	.578
1992 Tulsa	AA	120	415	109	16	3	1	--	--	134	35	44	16	2	72	0	3	5	7	4	.64	4	.263	.287	.323
1992 Texas	AL	14	36	6	0	0	0	(0	0)	6	1	1	1	0	8	0	1	0	0	0	.00	2	.167	.189	.167

Pat Combs

Pitches: Left Bats: Left Pos: SP   Ht: 6' 4" Wt: 200 Born: 10/29/66 Age: 26

Year Team	Lg	G	GS	CG	GF	IP	BFP	H	R	ER	HR	SH	SF	HB	TBB	IBB	SO	WP	Bk	W	L	Pct.	ShO	Sv	ERA
1989 Philadelphia	NL	6	6	1	0	38.2	153	36	10	9	2	2	0	0	6	1	30	5	0	4	0	1.000	1	0	2.09
1990 Philadelphia	NL	32	31	3	0	183.1	800	179	90	83	12	7	7	4	86	7	108	9	1	10	10	.500	2	0	4.07
1991 Philadelphia	NL	14	13	1	0	64.1	300	64	41	35	7	1	2	2	43	1	41	7	0	2	6	.250	0	0	4.90
1992 Philadelphia	NL	4	4	0	0	18.2	88	20	16	16	0	3	1	0	12	0	11	1	0	1	1	.500	0	0	7.71
4 ML YEARS		56	54	5	0	305	1341	299	157	143	21	13	10	6	147	9	190	22	1	17	17	.500	3	0	4.22

David Cone

Pitches: Right Bats: Left Pos: SP   Ht: 6' 1" Wt: 190 Born: 01/02/63 Age: 30

Year Team	Lg	G	GS	CG	GF	IP	BFP	H	R	ER	HR	SH	SF	HB	TBB	IBB	SO	WP	Bk	W	L	Pct.	ShO	Sv	ERA
1986 Kansas City	AL	11	0	0	5	22.2	108	29	14	14	2	0	0	1	13	1	21	3	0	0	0	.000	0	0	5.56
1987 New York	NL	21	13	1	3	99.1	420	87	46	41	11	4	3	5	44	1	68	2	4	5	6	.455	0	1	3.71
1988 New York	NL	35	28	8	0	231.1	936	178	67	57	10	11	5	4	80	7	213	10	10	20	3	.870	4	0	2.22
1989 New York	NL	34	33	7	0	219.2	910	183	92	86	20	6	4	4	74	6	190	14	4	14	8	.636	2	0	3.52
1990 New York	NL	31	30	6	1	211.2	860	177	84	76	21	4	6	1	65	1	233	10	4	14	10	.583	2	0	3.23
1991 New York	NL	34	34	5	0	232.2	966	204	95	85	13	13	7	5	73	2	241	17	1	14	14	.500	2	0	3.29
1992 2 ML Teams		35	34	7	0	249.2	1055	201	91	78	15	6	9	12	111	7	261	12	1	17	10	.630	5	0	2.81
1992 New York	NL	27	27	7	0	196.2	831	162	75	63	12	6	6	9	82	5	214	9	1	13	7	.650	5	0	2.88
Toronto	AL	8	7	0	0	53	224	39	16	15	3	0	3	3	29	2	47	3	0	4	3	.571	0	0	2.55
7 ML YEARS		201	172	34	9	1267	5255	1059	489	437	92	44	34	32	460	25	1227	68	24	84	51	.622	15	1	3.10

Jeff Conine

Bats: Right Throws: Right Pos: LF   Ht: 6' 1" Wt: 220 Born: 06/27/66 Age: 27

Year Team	Lg	G	AB	H	2B	3B	HR	(Hm	Rd)	TB	R	RBI	TBB	IBB	SO	HBP	SH	SF	SB	CS	SB%	GDP	Avg	OBP	SLG
1988 Baseball Cy	A	118	415	113	23	9	10	--	--	184	63	59	46	1	77	0	5	4	26	12	.68	6	.272	.342	.443
1989 Baseball Cy	A	113	425	116	12	7	14	--	--	184	68	60	40	2	91	3	0	3	32	13	.71	14	.273	.338	.433
1990 Memphis	AA	137	487	156	37	8	15	--	--	254	89	95	94	6	88	1	0	8	21	6	.78	10	.320	.425	.522
1991 Omaha	AAA	51	171	44	9	1	3	--	--	64	23	15	26	2	39	1	0	0	0	6	.00	3	.257	.359	.374
1992 Omaha	AAA	110	397	120	24	5	20	--	--	214	69	72	54	5	67	2	2	6	4	5	.44	6	.302	.383	.539
1990 Kansas City	AL	9	20	5	2	0	0	(0	0)	7	3	2	2	0	5	0	0	0	0	0	.00	1	.250	.318	.350
1992 Kansas City	AL	28	91	23	5	2	0	(0	0)	32	10	9	8	1	23	0	0	0	0	0	.00	1	.253	.313	.352
2 ML YEARS		37	111	28	7	2	0	(0	0)	39	13	11	10	1	28	0	0	0	0	0	.00	2	.252	.314	.351

Dennis Cook

Pitches: Left Bats: Left Pos: SP/RP   Ht: 6' 3" Wt: 185 Born: 10/04/62 Age: 30

Year Team	Lg	G	GS	CG	GF	IP	BFP	H	R	ER	HR	SH	SF	HB	TBB	IBB	SO	WP	Bk	W	L	Pct.	ShO	Sv	ERA
1988 San Francisco	NL	4	4	1	0	22	86	9	8	7	1	0	3	0	11	1	13	1	0	2	1	.667	1	0	2.86
1989 2 ML Teams		23	18	2	1	121	499	110	59	50	18	5	2	2	38	6	67	4	2	7	8	.467	1	0	3.72
1990 2 ML Teams		47	16	2	4	156	663	155	74	68	20	7	7	2	56	9	64	6	3	9	4	.692	1	0	3.92
1991 Los Angeles	NL	20	1	0	5	17.2	69	12	3	1	0	1	2	0	7	1	8	0	0	1	0	1.000	0	0	0.51
1992 Cleveland	AL	32	25	1	1	158	669	156	79	67	29	3	3	2	50	2	96	4	5	5	7	.417	0	0	3.82
1989 San Francisco	NL	2	2	1	0	15	58	13	3	3	1	0	0	0	5	0	9	1	0	1	0	1.000	1	0	1.80
Philadelphia	NL	21	16	1	1	106	441	97	56	47	17	5	2	2	33	6	58	3	2	6	8	.429	1	0	3.99
1990 Philadelphia	NL	42	13	2	4	141.2	594	132	61	56	13	5	5	2	54	9	58	6	3	8	3	.727	1	1	3.56
Los Angeles	NL	5	3	0	0	14.1	69	23	13	12	7	2	2	0	2	0	6	0	0	1	1	.500	0	0	7.53
5 ML YEARS		126	64	6	11	474.2	1986	442	223	193	68	16	17	6	162	19	248	15	10	24	20	.545	3	1	3.66

Steve Cooke

Pitches: Left Bats: Right Pos: RP   Ht: 6' 6" Wt: 220 Born: 01/14/70 Age: 23

Year Team	Lg	G	GS	CG	GF	IP	BFP	H	R	ER	HR	SH	SF	HB	TBB	IBB	SO	WP	Bk	W	L	Pct.	ShO	Sv	ERA
1990 Welland	A	11	11	0	0	46	188	36	21	18	2	1	1	2	17	0	43	6	1	2	3	.400	0	0	3.52
1991 Augusta	A	11	11	1	0	60.2	269	50	28	19	0	3	1	5	35	1	52	3	0	5	4	.556	0	0	2.82
Salem	A	2	2	0	0	13	57	14	8	7	0	0	0	0	2	0	5	4	1	1	0	1.000	0	0	4.85
Carolina	AA	9	9	1	0	55.2	223	39	21	14	2	1	1	4	19	0	46	5	0	3	3	.500	1	0	2.26
1992 Carolina	AA	6	6	0	0	36	144	31	13	12	1	0	1	3	12	1	38	1	0	2	2	.500	0	0	3.00
Buffalo	AAA	13	13	0	0	74.1	325	71	35	31	2	5	3	4	36	2	52	5	1	6	3	.667	0	0	3.75
1992 Pittsburgh	NL	11	0	0	8	23	91	22	9	9	2	0	0	1	4	1	10	0	0	2	0	1.000	0	1	3.52

Scott Cooper

Bats: Left   **Throws:** Right   **Pos:** 1B/3B   **Ht:** 6' 3"   **Wt:** 205   **Born:** 10/13/67   **Age:** 25

Year	Team	Lg	G	AB	H	2B	3B	HR	(Hm	Rd)	TB	R	RBI	TBB	IBB	SO	HBP	SH	SF	SB	CS	SB%	GDP	Avg	OBP	SLG
1986	Elmira	A	51	191	55	9	0	9	--	--	91	23	43	19	2	32	0	1	4	1	4	.20	6	.288	.346	.476
1987	Greensboro	A	119	370	93	21	2	15	--	--	163	52	63	58	7	69	2	0	6	1	0	1.00	5	.251	.351	.441
1988	Lynchburg	A	130	497	148	45	7	9	--	--	234	90	73	58	0	74	2	2	4	0	0	.00	11	.298	.371	.471
1989	New Britain	AA	124	421	104	24	2	7	--	--	153	50	39	55	2	84	6	5	5	1	1	.50	5	.247	.339	.363
1990	Pawtucket	AAA	124	433	115	17	1	12	--	--	170	56	44	39	3	75	7	4	3	2	0	1.00	9	.266	.334	.393
1991	Pawtucket	AAA	137	483	134	21	2	15	--	--	204	55	72	50	11	58	7	4	6	3	4	.43	13	.277	.350	.422
1990	Boston	AL	2	1	0	0	0	0	(0	0)	0	0	0	0	0	1	0	0	0	0	0	.00	0	.000	.000	.000
1991	Boston	AL	14	35	16	4	2	0	(0	0)	24	6	7	2	0	2	0	0	0	0	0	.00	0	.457	.486	.686
1992	Boston	AL	123	337	93	21	0	5	(2	3)	129	34	33	37	0	33	0	2	2	1	1	.50	5	.276	.346	.383
	3 ML YEARS		139	373	109	25	2	5	(2	3)	153	40	40	39	0	36	0	2	2	1	1	.50	5	.292	.357	.410

Joey Cora

Bats: Both   **Throws:** Right   **Pos:** 2B/DH   **Ht:** 5' 8"   **Wt:** 152   **Born:** 05/14/65   **Age:** 28

Year	Team	Lg	G	AB	H	2B	3B	HR	(Hm	Rd)	TB	R	RBI	TBB	IBB	SO	HBP	SH	SF	SB	CS	SB%	GDP	Avg	OBP	SLG
1987	San Diego	NL	77	241	57	7	2	0	(0	0)	68	23	13	28	1	26	1	5	1	15	11	.58	4	.237	.322	.282
1989	San Diego	NL	12	19	6	1	0	0	(0	0)	7	5	1	1	0	0	0	0	0	1	0	1.00	0	.316	.350	.368
1990	San Diego	NL	51	100	27	3	0	0	(0	0)	30	12	2	6	1	9	0	0	0	8	3	.73	1	.270	.311	.300
1991	Chicago	AL	100	228	55	2	3	0	(0	0)	63	37	18	20	0	21	5	8	3	11	6	.65	1	.241	.313	.276
1992	Chicago	AL	68	122	30	7	1	0	(0	0)	39	27	9	22	1	13	4	2	3	10	3	.77	2	.246	.371	.320
	5 ML YEARS		308	710	175	20	6	0	(0	0)	207	104	43	77	3	69	10	15	7	45	23	.66	8	.246	.326	.292

Wil Cordero

Bats: Right   **Throws:** Right   **Pos:** SS   **Ht:** 6' 2"   **Wt:** 185   **Born:** 10/03/71   **Age:** 21

Year	Team	Lg	G	AB	H	2B	3B	HR	(Hm	Rd)	TB	R	RBI	TBB	IBB	SO	HBP	SH	SF	SB	CS	SB%	GDP	Avg	OBP	SLG
1988	Jamestown	A	52	190	49	3	0	2	--	--	58	18	22	15	0	44	4	0	2	3	3	.50	2	.258	.322	.305
1989	Wst Plm Bch	A	78	289	80	12	2	6	--	--	114	37	29	33	2	58	3	1	2	2	5	.29	6	.277	.355	.394
	Jacksnville	AA	39	121	26	6	1	3	--	--	43	9	17	12	0	33	0	3	1	1	2	.33	3	.215	.284	.355
1990	Jacksnville	AA	131	444	104	18	4	7	--	--	151	63	40	56	0	122	5	3	1	9	4	.69	5	.234	.326	.340
1991	Indianapols	AAA	98	360	94	16	4	11	--	--	151	48	52	26	2	89	3	0	2	8	3	.73	4	.261	.315	.419
1992	Indianapols	AAA	52	204	64	11	1	6	--	--	95	32	27	24	2	54	0	1	1	6	7	.46	7	.314	.384	.466
1992	Montreal	NL	45	126	38	4	1	2	(1	1)	50	17	8	9	0	31	1	1	0	0	0	.00	3	.302	.353	.397

Rheal Cormier

Pitches: Left   **Bats:** Left   **Pos:** SP   **Ht:** 5'10"   **Wt:** 185   **Born:** 04/23/67   **Age:** 26

Year	Team	Lg	G	GS	CG	GF	IP	BFP	H	R	ER	HR	SH	SF	HB	TBB	IBB	SO	WP	Bk	W	L	Pct.	ShO	Sv	ERA
1989	St.Pete	A	26	26	4	0	169.2	669	141	63	42	9	6	3	0	33	2	122	4	7	12	7	.632	2	0	2.23
1990	Arkansas	AA	22	21	3	1	121.1	530	133	81	68	9	6	2	5	30	2	102	5	1	5	12	.294	1	0	5.04
	Louisville	AAA	4	4	0	0	24	92	18	8	6	1	0	0	0	3	0	9	4	0	1	1	.500	0	0	2.25
1991	Louisville	AAA	21	21	3	0	127.2	543	140	64	60	5	10	6	6	31	1	74	6	1	7	9	.438	3	0	4.23
1992	Louisville	AAA	1	1	0	0	4	20	8	4	3	0	0	0	1	0	0	1	0	0	0	0	.000	0	0	6.75
1991	St.Louis	NL	11	10	2	1	67.2	281	74	35	31	5	1	3	2	8	1	38	2	1	4	5	.444	0	0	4.12
1992	St.Louis	NL	31	30	3	1	186	772	194	83	76	15	11	3	5	33	2	117	4	2	10	10	.500	0	0	3.68
	2 ML YEARS		42	40	5	2	253.2	1053	268	118	107	20	12	6	7	41	3	155	6	3	14	15	.483	0	0	3.80

Jim Corsi

Pitches: Right   **Bats:** Right   **Pos:** RP   **Ht:** 6' 1"   **Wt:** 220   **Born:** 09/09/61   **Age:** 31

Year	Team	Lg	G	GS	CG	GF	IP	BFP	H	R	ER	HR	SH	SF	HB	TBB	IBB	SO	WP	Bk	W	L	Pct.	ShO	Sv	ERA
1988	Oakland	AL	11	1	0	7	21.1	89	20	10	9	1	3	3	0	6	1	10	1	1	0	1	.000	0	0	3.80
1989	Oakland	AL	22	0	0	14	38.1	149	26	8	8	2	2	2	1	10	0	21	0	0	1	2	.333	0	0	1.88
1991	Houston	NL	47	0	0	15	77.2	322	76	37	32	6	3	2	0	23	5	53	1	0	0	5	.000	0	0	3.71
1992	Oakland	AL	32	0	0	16	44	185	44	12	7	2	4	2	0	18	2	19	0	0	4	2	.667	0	0	1.43
	4 ML YEARS		112	1	0	52	181.1	745	166	67	56	11	12	9	1	57	8	103	2	2	5	10	.333	0	0	2.78

Tim Costo

Bats: Right   **Throws:** Right   **Pos:** 1B   **Ht:** 6' 5"   **Wt:** 220   **Born:** 02/16/69   **Age:** 24

Year	Team	Lg	G	AB	H	2B	3B	HR	(Hm	Rd)	TB	R	RBI	TBB	IBB	SO	HBP	SH	SF	SB	CS	SB%	GDP	Avg	OBP	SLG
1990	Kinston	A	56	206	65	13	1	4	--	--	92	34	42	23	0	47	6	0	8	2	0	1.00	5	.316	.387	.447
1991	Canton-Akrn	AA	52	192	52	10	3	1	--	--	71	28	24	15	0	44	1	0	6	2	1	.67	10	.271	.315	.370

Year Team	Lg	G	AB	H	2B	3B	HR	(Hm	Rd)	TB	R	RBI	TBB	IBB	SO	HBP	SH	SF	SB	CS	SB%	GDP	Avg	OBP	SLG
Chattanooga	AA	85	293	82	19	3	5	--	--	122	31	29	20	0	65	4	0	2	11	4	.73	5	.280	.332	.416
1992 Chattanooga	AA	121	424	102	18	3	28	--	--	208	63	71	48	2	128	11	1	2	4	5	.44	10	.241	.332	.491
1992 Cincinnati	NL	12	36	8	2	0	0	(0	0)	10	3	2	5	0	6	0	0	1	0	0	.00	4	.222	.310	.278

Henry Cotto

Bats: Right **Throws:** Right **Pos:** LF/CF   **Ht:** 6' 2" **Wt:** 178 **Born:** 01/05/61 **Age:** 32

								BATTING											BASERUNNING				PERCENTAGES		
Year Team	Lg	G	AB	H	2B	3B	HR	(Hm	Rd)	TB	R	RBI	TBB	IBB	SO	HBP	SH	SF	SB	CS	SB%	GDP	Avg	OBP	SLG
1984 Chicago	NL	105	146	40	5	0	0	(0	0)	45	24	8	10	2	23	1	3	0	9	3	.75	1	.274	.325	.308
1985 New York	AL	34	56	17	1	0	1	(0	1)	21	4	6	3	0	12	0	1	0	1	1	.50	1	.304	.339	.375
1986 New York	AL	35	80	17	3	0	1	(0	1)	23	11	6	2	0	17	0	0	1	3	0	1.00	1	.213	.229	.288
1987 New York	AL	68	149	35	10	0	5	(5	0)	60	21	20	6	0	35	1	0	0	4	2	.67	3	.235	.269	.403
1988 Seattle	AL	133	386	100	18	1	8	(5	3)	144	50	33	23	0	53	2	4	3	27	3	.90	8	.259	.302	.373
1989 Seattle	AL	100	295	78	11	2	9	(5	4)	120	44	33	12	3	44	3	0	0	10	4	.71	4	.264	.300	.407
1990 Seattle	AL	127	355	92	14	3	4	(2	2)	124	40	33	22	2	52	4	6	3	21	3	**.88**	13	.259	.307	.349
1991 Seattle	AL	66	177	54	6	2	6	(2	4)	82	35	23	10	0	27	2	2	1	16	3	.84	7	.305	.347	.463
1992 Seattle	AL	108	294	76	11	1	5	(2	3)	104	42	27	14	3	49	1	3	1	23	2	**.92**	2	.259	.294	.354
9 ML YEARS		776	1938	509	79	9	39	(21	18)	723	271	189	102	10	312	14	19	9	114	21	.84	46	.263	.303	.373

Danny Cox

Pitches: Right **Bats:** Right **Pos:** RP/SP   **Ht:** 6' 4" **Wt:** 225 **Born:** 09/21/59 **Age:** 33

			HOW MUCH HE PITCHED					WHAT HE GAVE UP								THE RESULTS					
Year Team	Lg	G	GS	CG	GF	IP	BFP	H	R	ER	HR	SH	SF	HB	TBB	IBB	SO	WP	Bk	W	L	Pct.	ShO	Sv	ERA
1983 St. Louis	NL	12	12	0	0	83	352	92	38	30	6	6	1	0	23	2	36	2	0	3	6	.333	0	0	3.25
1984 St. Louis	NL	29	27	1	0	156.1	668	171	81	70	9	10	5	7	54	6	70	2	4	9	11	.450	1	0	4.03
1985 St. Louis	NL	35	35	10	0	241	989	226	91	77	19	12	9	3	64	5	131	3	1	18	9	.667	4	0	2.88
1986 St. Louis	NL	32	32	8	0	220	881	189	85	71	14	8	3	2	60	6	108	3	4	12	13	.480	0	0	2.90
1987 St. Louis	NL	31	31	2	0	199.1	864	224	99	86	17	14	4	3	71	6	101	5	1	11	9	.550	0	0	3.88
1988 St. Louis	NL	13	13	0	0	86	361	89	40	38	6	5	3	1	25	7	47	4	3	3	8	.273	0	0	3.98
1991 Philadelphia	NL	23	17	0	2	102.1	433	98	57	52	14	6	7	1	39	2	46	7	1	4	6	.400	0	0	4.57
1992 2 ML Teams		25	7	0	8	62.2	278	66	37	32	5	5	3	0	27	2	48	1	0	5	3	.625	0	3	4.60
1992 Philadelphia	NL	9	7	0	0	38.1	178	46	28	23	3	3	2	0	19	1	30	0	0	2	2	.500	0	0	5.40
Pittsburgh	NL	16	0	0	8	24.1	100	20	9	9	2	2	1	0	8	1	18	1	0	3	1	.750	0	3	3.33
8 ML YEARS		200	174	21	10	1150.2	4826	1155	528	456	90	66	35	17	363	36	587	27	14	65	65	.500	5	3	3.57

Tim Crews

Pitches: Right **Bats:** Right **Pos:** RP   **Ht:** 6' 0" **Wt:** 195 **Born:** 04/03/61 **Age:** 32

			HOW MUCH HE PITCHED					WHAT HE GAVE UP								THE RESULTS					
Year Team	Lg	G	GS	CG	GF	IP	BFP	H	R	ER	HR	SH	SF	HB	TBB	IBB	SO	WP	Bk	W	L	Pct.	ShO	Sv	ERA
1987 Los Angeles	NL	20	0	0	7	29	124	39	9	8	2	1	1	2	8	1	20	0	0	1	1	.500	0	3	2.48
1988 Los Angeles	NL	42	0	0	12	71.2	301	77	29	25	3	3	5	0	16	7	45	1	0	4	0	1.000	0	0	3.14
1989 Los Angeles	NL	44	0	0	16	61.2	275	69	27	22	7	7	0	2	23	9	56	1	0	0	1	.000	0	0	3.21
1990 Los Angeles	NL	66	2	0	18	107.1	440	98	40	33	9	1	3	1	24	6	76	2	0	4	5	.444	0	5	2.77
1991 Los Angeles	NL	60	0	0	17	76	318	75	30	29	7	4	2	0	19	11	53	3	1	2	3	.400	0	6	3.43
1992 Los Angeles	NL	49	2	0	13	78	339	95	46	45	6	6	5	2	20	9	43	1	0	0	3	.000	0	1	5.19
6 ML YEARS		281	4	0	83	423.2	1797	444	181	162	34	22	16	7	110	43	293	10	1	11	13	.458	0	15	3.44

Chuck Crim

Pitches: Right **Bats:** Right **Pos:** RP   **Ht:** 6' 0" **Wt:** 185 **Born:** 07/23/61 **Age:** 31

			HOW MUCH HE PITCHED					WHAT HE GAVE UP								THE RESULTS					
Year Team	Lg	G	GS	CG	GF	IP	BFP	H	R	ER	HR	SH	SF	HB	TBB	IBB	SO	WP	Bk	W	L	Pct.	ShO	Sv	ERA
1987 Milwaukee	AL	53	5	0	18	130	549	133	60	53	15	6	1	3	39	5	56	2	1	6	8	.429	0	12	3.67
1988 Milwaukee	AL	70	0	0	25	105	425	95	38	34	11	5	6	2	28	3	58	9	2	7	6	.538	0	9	2.91
1989 Milwaukee	AL	76	0	0	31	117.2	487	114	42	37	7	3	6	2	36	9	59	5	0	9	7	.563	0	7	2.83
1990 Milwaukee	AL	67	0	0	25	85.2	367	88	39	33	7	1	4	2	23	4	39	0	1	3	5	.375	0	3	3.47
1991 Milwaukee	AL	66	0	0	29	91.1	408	115	52	47	9	3	1	2	25	9	39	3	3	8	5	.615	0	3	4.63
1992 California	AL	57	0	0	16	87	383	100	56	50	11	3	4	6	29	6	30	4	0	7	6	.538	0	1	5.17
6 ML YEARS		389	5	0	144	616.2	2619	645	287	254	60	21	22	17	180	36	281	23	7	40	37	.519	0	43	3.71

Chris Cron

Bats: Right **Throws:** Right **Pos:** 1B   **Ht:** 6' 2" **Wt:** 200 **Born:** 03/31/64 **Age:** 29

								BATTING											BASERUNNING				PERCENTAGES		
Year Team	Lg	G	AB	H	2B	3B	HR	(Hm	Rd)	TB	R	RBI	TBB	IBB	SO	HBP	SH	SF	SB	CS	SB%	GDP	Avg	OBP	SLG
1984 Pulaski	R	32	114	42	8	0	7	--	--	71	22	37	17	1	20	6	0	2	2	0	1.00	2	.368	.468	.623
1985 Sumter	A	119	425	102	20	0	7	--	--	143	53	59	51	2	98	18	0	1	5	2	.71	8	.240	.345	.336
1986 Durham	A	90	265	55	10	0	7	--	--	86	26	34	29	0	60	6	2	2	0	2	.00	2	.208	.298	.325

Year	Team	Lg	G	AB	H	2B	3B	HR	(Hm	Rd)	TB	R	RBI	TBB	IBB	SO	HBP	SH	SF	SB	CS	SB%	GDP	Avg	OBP	SLG
1987	Quad City	A	111	398	110	20	1	11	--	--	165	53	62	44	2	88	17	0	1	1	3	.25	5	.276	.372	.415
	Palm Sprngs	A	26	92	25	3	0	2	--	--	34	6	9	9	0	27	2	1	2	2	2	.50	3	.272	.343	.370
1988	Palm Sprngs	A	127	467	117	28	3	14	--	--	193	71	84	68	1	147	27	2	6	4	3	.57	10	.251	.373	.413
1989	Midland	AA	128	491	148	33	3	22	--	--	253	80	103	39	5	126	14	1	6	0	1	.00	10	.301	.365	.515
1990	Edmonton	AAA	104	401	115	31	0	17	--	--	197	54	75	28	1	92	5	1	5	7	5	.58	9	.287	.337	.491
1991	Edmonton	AAA	123	461	134	21	1	22	--	--	223	74	91	47	3	103	10	2	11	6	5	.55	12	.291	.361	.484
1992	Vancouver	AAA	141	500	139	29	0	16	--	--	216	76	81	94	12	111	17	2	3	12	4	.75	8	.278	.407	.432
1991	California	AL	6	15	2	0	0	0	(0	0)	2	0	0	2	0	5	0	0	0	0	0	.00	0	.133	.235	.133
1992	Chicago	AL	6	10	0	0	0	0			0	0	0	0	0	4	0	0	0	0	0	.00	0	.000	.000	.000
	2 ML YEARS		12	25	2	0	0	0	(0	0)	2	0	0	2	0	9	0	0	0	0	0	.00	0	.080	.148	.080

Chad Curtis

Bats: Right **Throws:** Right **Pos:** RF/LF/CF **Ht:** 5'10" **Wt:** 180 **Born:** 11/06/68 **Age:** 24

						BATTING														BASERUNNING				PERCENTAGES		
Year	Team	Lg	G	AB	H	2B	3B	HR	(Hm	Rd)	TB	R	RBI	TBB	IBB	SO	HBP	SH	SF	SB	CS	SB%	GDP	Avg	OBP	SLG
1989	Angels	R	32	122	37	4	4	3	--	--	58	30	20	14	2	20	2	1	2	17	2	.89	3	.303	.379	.475
	Quad City	A	23	78	19	3	0	2	--	--	28	7	11	6	0	17	0	1	1	7	5	.58	1	.244	.294	.359
1990	Quad City	A	135	492	151	28	1	14	--	--	223	87	65	57	3	76	12	4	3	63	21	.75	8	.307	.390	.453
1991	Edmonton	AAA	115	431	136	28	7	9	--	--	205	81	61	51	1	58	3	4	4	46	11	.81	10	.316	.389	.476
1992	California	AL	139	441	114	16	2	10	(5	5)	164	59	46	51	2	71	6	5	4	43	18	.70	10	.259	.341	.372

Milt Cuyler

Bats: Both **Throws:** Right **Pos:** CF **Ht:** 5'10" **Wt:** 185 **Born:** 10/07/68 **Age:** 24

						BATTING														BASERUNNING				PERCENTAGES		
Year	Team	Lg	G	AB	H	2B	3B	HR	(Hm	Rd)	TB	R	RBI	TBB	IBB	SO	HBP	SH	SF	SB	CS	SB%	GDP	Avg	OBP	SLG
1990	Detroit	AL	19	51	13	3	1	0	(0	0)	18	8	8	5	0	10	0	2	1	1	2	.33	1	.255	.316	.353
1991	Detroit	AL	154	475	122	15	7	3	(1	2)	160	77	33	52	0	92	5	12	2	41	10	.80	4	.257	.335	.337
1992	Detroit	AL	89	291	70	11	1	3	(1	2)	92	39	28	10	0	62	4	8	0	8	5	.62	4	.241	.275	.316
	3 ML YEARS		262	817	205	29	9	6	(2	4)	270	124	69	67	0	164	9	22	3	50	17	.75	9	.251	.314	.330

Kal Daniels

Bats: Left **Throws:** Right **Pos:** LF **Ht:** 5'11" **Wt:** 205 **Born:** 08/20/63 **Age:** 29

						BATTING														BASERUNNING				PERCENTAGES		
Year	Team	Lg	G	AB	H	2B	3B	HR	(Hm	Rd)	TB	R	RBI	TBB	IBB	SO	HBP	SH	SF	SB	CS	SB%	GDP	Avg	OBP	SLG
1986	Cincinnati	NL	74	181	58	10	4	6	(3	3)	94	34	23	22	1	30	2	1	1	15	2	.88	4	.320	.398	.519
1987	Cincinnati	NL	108	368	123	24	1	26	(13	13)	227	73	64	60	11	62	1	1	0	26	8	.76	6	.334	.429	.617
1988	Cincinnati	NL	140	495	144	29	1	18	(12	6)	229	95	64	87	10	94	3	0	4	27	6	.82	11	.291	.397	.463
1989	2 ML Teams		55	171	42	13	0	4	(2	2)	67	33	17	43	1	33	2	0	2	9	4	.69	2	.246	.399	.392
1990	Los Angeles	NL	130	450	133	23	1	27	(12	15)	239	81	94	68	1	104	3	2	3	4	3	.57	9	.296	.389	.531
1991	Los Angeles	NL	137	461	115	15	1	17	(12	5)	183	54	73	63	4	116	1	0	6	6	1	.86	9	.249	.337	.397
1992	2 ML Teams		83	212	51	11	0	6	(3	3)	80	21	25	22	0	54	2	0	2	0	2	.00	10	.241	.315	.377
1989	Cincinnati	NL	44	133	29	11	0	2	(1	1)	46	26	9	36	1	28	2	0	1	6	4	.60	1	.218	.390	.346
	Los Angeles	NL	11	38	13	2	0	2	(1	1)	21	7	8	7	0	5	0	0	1	3	0	1.00	1	.342	.435	.553
1992	Los Angeles	NL	35	104	24	5	0	2	(1	1)	35	9	8	10	0	30	1	0	1	0	0	.00	7	.231	.302	.337
	Chicago	NL	48	108	27	6	0	4	(2	2)	45	12	17	12	0	24	1	0	1	0	2	.00	3	.250	.328	.417
	7 ML YEARS		727	2338	666	125	8	104	(57	47)	1119	391	360	365	28	493	14	4	18	87	26	.77	51	.285	.382	.479

Ron Darling

Pitches: Right **Bats:** Right **Pos:** SP **Ht:** 6'3" **Wt:** 195 **Born:** 08/19/60 **Age:** 32

			HOW MUCH HE PITCHED						WHAT HE GAVE UP										THE RESULTS					
Year	Team	Lg	G	GS	CG	GF	IP	BFP	H	R	ER	HR	SH	SF	HB	TBB	IBB	SO	WP	Bk	W	L	Pct.	ShO	Sv	ERA
1983	New York	NL	5	5	1	0	35.1	148	31	11	11	0	3	0	3	17	1	23	3	2	1	3	.250	0	0	2.80
1984	New York	NL	33	33	2	0	205.2	884	179	97	87	17	7	6	5	104	2	136	7	1	12	9	.571	2	0	3.81
1985	New York	NL	36	35	4	1	248	1043	214	93	80	21	13	4	3	114	1	167	7	1	16	6	.727	2	0	2.90
1986	New York	NL	34	34	4	0	237	967	203	84	74	21	10	6	3	81	2	184	7	3	15	6	.714	2	0	2.81
1987	New York	NL	32	32	2	0	207.2	891	183	111	99	24	5	3	3	96	3	167	6	3	12	8	.600	0	0	4.29
1988	New York	NL	34	34	7	0	240.2	971	218	97	87	24	10	8	5	60	2	161	7	2	17	9	.654	4	0	3.25
1989	New York	NL	33	33	4	0	217.1	922	214	100	85	19	7	13	3	70	7	153	12	4	14	14	.500	0	0	3.52
1990	New York	NL	33	18	1	3	126	554	135	73	63	20	7	3	5	44	4	99	5	1	7	9	.438	0	0	4.50
1991	3 ML Teams		32	32	0	0	194.1	827	185	100	92	22	12	8	9	71	3	129	16	5	8	15	.348	0	0	4.26
1992	Oakland	AL	33	33	4	0	206.1	866	198	98	84	15	4	3	4	72	5	99	13	0	15	10	.600	3	0	3.66
1991	New York	NL	17	17	0	0	102.1	427	96	50	44	9	7	4	6	28	1	58	9	4	5	6	.455	0	0	3.87
	Montreal	NL	3	3	0	0	17	81	25	16	14	6	0	0	1	5	0	11	4	0	0	2	.000	0	0	7.41
	Oakland	AL	12	12	0	0	75	319	64	34	34	7	5	4	2	38	2	60	3	1	3	7	.300	0	0	4.08
	10 ML YEARS		305	289	29	4	1918.1	8073	1760	864	762	183	78	54	43	729	30	1318	83	22	117	89	.568	13	0	3.57

Danny Darwin

Pitches: Right **Bats:** Right **Pos:** RP/SP **Ht:** 6' 3" **Wt:** 195 **Born:** 10/25/55 **Age:** 37

Year Team	Lg	G	GS	CG	GF	IP	BFP	H	R	ER	HR	SH	SF	HB	TBB	IBB	SO	WP	Bk	W	L	Pct.	ShO	Sv	ERA
1978 Texas	AL	3	1	0	2	9	36	11	4	4	0	0	1	0	1	0	8	0	0	1	0	1.000	0	0	4.00
1979 Texas	AL	20	6	1	4	78	313	50	36	35	5	3	6	5	30	2	58	0	1	4	4	.500	0	0	4.04
1980 Texas	AL	53	2	0	35	110	468	98	37	32	4	5	7	2	50	7	104	3	0	13	4	.765	0	8	2.62
1981 Texas	AL	22	22	6	0	146	601	115	67	59	12	8	3	6	57	5	98	1	0	9	9	.500	2	0	3.64
1982 Texas	AL	56	1	0	41	89	394	95	38	34	6	10	5	2	37	8	61	2	1	10	8	.556	0	7	3.44
1983 Texas	AL	28	26	9	0	183	780	175	86	71	9	7	7	3	62	3	92	2	0	8	13	.381	2	0	3.49
1984 Texas	AL	35	32	5	2	223.2	955	249	110	98	19	3	3	4	54	2	123	3	0	8	12	.400	1	0	3.94
1985 Milwaukee	AL	39	29	11	8	217.2	919	212	112	92	34	7	9	4	65	4	125	6	0	8	18	.308	1	2	3.80
1986 2 ML Teams		39	22	6	6	184.2	759	170	81	65	16	6	9	3	44	1	120	7	1	11	10	.524	1	0	3.17
1987 Houston	NL	33	30	3	0	195.2	833	184	87	78	17	8	3	5	69	12	134	3	1	9	10	.474	1	0	3.59
1988 Houston	NL	44	20	3	9	192	804	189	86	82	20	10	9	7	48	9	129	1	2	8	13	.381	0	3	3.84
1989 Houston	NL	68	0	0	26	122	482	92	34	32	8	8	5	2	33	9	104	2	3	11	4	.733	0	7	2.36
1990 Houston	NL	48	17	3	14	162.2	646	136	42	40	11	4	2	4	31	4	109	0	2	11	4	.733	0	2	**2.21**
1991 Boston	AL	12	12	0	0	68	292	71	39	39	15	1	2	4	15	1	42	2	0	3	6	.333	0	0	5.16
1992 Boston	AL	51	15	2	21	161.1	688	159	76	71	11	7	5	5	53	9	124	5	0	9	9	.500	0	3	3.96
1986 Milwaukee	AL	27	14	5	4	130.1	537	120	62	51	13	5	6	3	35	1	80	5	0	6	8	.429	1	0	3.52
Houston	NL	12	8	1	2	54.1	222	50	19	14	3	1	3	0	9	0	40	2	1	5	2	.714	0	0	2.32
15 ML YEARS		551	235	49	168	2142.2	8970	2006	935	832	187	87	76	56	649	76	1431	37	11	123	124	.498	8	32	3.49

Doug Dascenzo

Bats: Both **Throws:** Left **Pos:** CF/LF/RF **Ht:** 5' 8" **Wt:** 160 **Born:** 06/30/64 **Age:** 29

Year Team	Lg	G	AB	H	2B	3B	HR	(Hm	Rd)	TB	R	RBI	TBB	IBB	SO	HBP	SH	SF	SB	CS	SB%	GDP	Avg	OBP	SLG
1988 Chicago	NL	26	75	16	3	0	0	(0	0)	19	9	4	9	1	4	0	1	0	6	1	.86	2	.213	.298	.253
1989 Chicago	NL	47	139	23	1	0	1	(0	1)	27	20	12	13	0	13	0	3	2	6	3	.67	2	.165	.234	.194
1990 Chicago	NL	113	241	61	9	5	1	(1	0)	83	27	26	21	2	18	1	5	3	15	6	.71	3	.253	.312	.344
1991 Chicago	NL	118	239	61	11	0	1	(0	1)	75	40	18	24	2	26	2	6	1	14	7	.67	3	.255	.327	.314
1992 Chicago	NL	139	376	96	13	4	0	(0	0)	117	37	20	27	2	32	0	4	2	6	8	.43	3	.255	.304	.311
5 ML YEARS		443	1070	257	37	9	3	(1	2)	321	133	80	94	7	93	3	19	8	47	25	.65	13	.240	.301	.300

Jack Daugherty

Bats: Both **Throws:** Left **Pos:** LF/RF/DH **Ht:** 6' 0" **Wt:** 190 **Born:** 07/03/60 **Age:** 32

Year Team	Lg	G	AB	H	2B	3B	HR	(Hm	Rd)	TB	R	RBI	TBB	IBB	SO	HBP	SH	SF	SB	CS	SB%	GDP	Avg	OBP	SLG
1987 Montreal	NL	11	10	1	1	0	0	(0	0)	2	1	1	0	0	3	0	2	0	0	0	.00	0	.100	.100	.200
1989 Texas	AL	52	106	32	4	2	1	(0	1)	43	15	10	11	0	21	1	0	3	2	1	.67	1	.302	.364	.406
1990 Texas	AL	125	310	93	20	2	6	(5	1)	135	36	47	22	0	49	2	2	3	0	0	.00	4	.300	.347	.435
1991 Texas	AL	58	144	28	3	2	1	(0	1)	38	8	11	16	1	23	0	4	3	1	0	1.00	1	.194	.270	.264
1992 Texas	AL	59	127	26	9	0	0	(0	0)	35	13	9	16	1	21	1	0	2	2	1	.67	3	.205	.295	.276
5 ML YEARS		305	697	180	37	6	8	(6	2)	253	73	78	65	2	117	4	8	11	5	2	.71	10	.258	.320	.363

Darren Daulton

Bats: Left **Throws:** Right **Pos:** C **Ht:** 6' 2" **Wt:** 195 **Born:** 01/03/62 **Age:** 31

Year Team	Lg	G	AB	H	2B	3B	HR	(Hm	Rd)	TB	R	RBI	TBB	IBB	SO	HBP	SH	SF	SB	CS	SB%	GDP	Avg	OBP	SLG
1983 Philadelphia	NL	2	3	0	0	0	0	(0	0)	1	1	0	1	0	1	0	0	0	0	0	.00	0	.333	.500	.333
1985 Philadelphia	NL	36	103	21	3	1	4	(0	4)	38	14	11	16	0	37	0	0	0	3	0	1.00	1	.204	.311	.369
1986 Philadelphia	NL	49	138	31	4	0	8	(4	4)	59	18	21	38	3	41	1	2	2	2	3	.40	1	.225	.391	.428
1987 Philadelphia	NL	53	129	25	6	0	3	(1	2)	40	10	13	16	1	37	0	4	1	0	0	.00	0	.194	.281	.310
1988 Philadelphia	NL	58	144	30	6	0	1	(0	1)	39	13	12	17	1	26	0	0	2	2	1	.67	2	.208	.288	.271
1989 Philadelphia	NL	131	368	74	12	2	8	(2	6)	114	29	44	52	8	58	2	1	1	2	1	.67	4	.201	.303	.310
1990 Philadelphia	NL	143	459	123	30	1	12	(5	7)	191	62	57	72	9	72	2	3	4	7	1	.88	6	.268	.367	.416
1991 Philadelphia	NL	89	285	56	12	0	12	(8	4)	104	36	42	41	4	66	2	2	5	5	0	1.00	4	.196	.297	.365
1992 Philadelphia	NL	145	485	131	32	5	27	(17	10)	254	80	109	88	11	103	6	0	6	11	2	.85	3	.270	.385	.524
9 ML YEARS		706	2114	492	105	9	75	(37	38)	840	263	309	341	37	441	13	12	21	32	8	.80	21	.233	.340	.397

Alvin Davis

Bats: Left **Throws:** Right **Pos:** 1B **Ht:** 6' 1" **Wt:** 190 **Born:** 09/09/60 **Age:** 32

Year Team	Lg	G	AB	H	2B	3B	HR	(Hm	Rd)	TB	R	RBI	TBB	IBB	SO	HBP	SH	SF	SB	CS	SB%	GDP	Avg	OBP	SLG
1984 Seattle	AL	152	567	161	34	3	27	(15	12)	282	80	116	97	16	78	7	0	7	5	4	.56	7	.284	.391	.497
1985 Seattle	AL	155	578	166	33	1	18	(11	7)	255	78	78	90	7	71	2	0	7	1	2	.33	14	.287	.381	.441
1986 Seattle	AL	135	479	130	18	1	18	(14	4)	204	66	72	76	10	68	3	2	2	0	3	.00	11	.271	.373	.426
1987 Seattle	AL	157	580	171	37	2	29	(18	11)	299	86	100	72	6	84	2	0	8	0	0	.00	17	.295	.370	.516

Year Team	Lg	G	AB	H	2B	3B	HR	(Hm	Rd)	TB	R	RBI	TBB	IBB	SO	HBP	SH	SF	SB	CS	SB%	GDP	Avg	OBP	SLG
1988 Seattle	AL	140	478	141	24	1	18	(12	6)	221	67	69	95	13	53	4	0	5	1	1	.50	14	.295	.412	.462
1989 Seattle	AL	142	498	152	30	1	21	(13	8)	247	84	95	101	15	49	6	0	6	0	1	.00	15	.305	.424	.496
1990 Seattle	AL	140	494	140	21	0	17	(12	5)	212	63	68	85	10	68	4	0	9	0	2	.00	9	.283	.387	.429
1991 Seattle	AL	145	462	102	15	1	12	(6	6)	155	39	69	56	9	78	0	0	10	0	3	.00	8	.221	.299	.335
1992 California	AL	40	104	26	8	0	0	(0	0)	34	5	16	13	2	9	0	0	1	0	0	.00	2	.250	.331	.327
9 ML YEARS		1206	4240	1189	220	10	160	(101	59)	1909	568	683	685	88	558	28	2	55	7	16	.30	97	.280	.380	.450

Chili Davis

Bats: Both Throws: Right Pos: DH Ht: 6' 3" Wt: 217 Born: 01/17/60 Age: 33

							BATTING												BASERUNNING				PERCENTAGES		
Year Team	Lg	G	AB	H	2B	3B	HR	(Hm	Rd)	TB	R	RBI	TBB	IBB	SO	HBP	SH	SF	SB	CS	SB%	GDP	Avg	OBP	SLG
1981 San Francisco	NL	8	15	2	0	0	0	(0	0)	2	1	0	1	0	2	0	0	0	2	0	1.00	1	.133	.188	.133
1982 San Francisco	NL	154	641	167	27	6	19	(6	13)	263	86	76	45	2	115	2	7	6	24	13	.65	13	.261	.308	.410
1983 San Francisco	NL	137	486	113	21	2	11	(7	4)	171	54	59	55	6	108	0	3	9	10	12	.45	9	.233	.305	.352
1984 San Francisco	NL	137	499	157	21	6	21	(7	14)	253	87	81	42	6	74	1	2	2	12	8	.60	13	.315	.368	.507
1985 San Francisco	NL	136	481	130	25	2	13	(7	6)	198	53	56	62	12	74	0	1	7	15	7	.68	16	.270	.349	.412
1986 San Francisco	NL	153	526	146	28	3	13	(7	6)	219	71	70	84	23	96	1	2	5	16	13	.55	11	.278	.375	.416
1987 San Francisco	NL	149	500	125	22	1	24	(9	15)	221	80	76	72	15	109	2	0	4	16	9	.64	8	.250	.344	.442
1988 California	AL	158	600	161	29	3	21	(11	10)	259	81	93	56	14	118	0	1	10	9	10	.47	13	.268	.326	.432
1989 California	AL	154	560	152	24	1	22	(6	16)	244	81	90	61	12	109	0	3	6	3	0	1.00	21	.271	.340	.436
1990 California	AL	113	412	109	17	1	12	(10	2)	164	58	58	61	4	89	0	0	3	1	2	.33	14	.265	.357	.398
1991 Minnesota	AL	153	534	148	34	1	29	(14	15)	271	84	93	95	13	117	1	0	4	5	6	.45	9	.277	.385	.507
1992 Minnesota	AL	138	444	128	27	2	12	(6	6)	195	63	66	73	11	76	3	0	9	4	5	.44	11	.288	.386	.439
12 ML YEARS		1590	5698	1538	275	28	197	(90	107)	2460	799	818	707	118	1087	10	19	65	117	85	.58	139	.270	.348	.432

Doug Davis

Bats: Right Throws: Right Pos: C Ht: 6' 0" Wt: 180 Born: 09/24/62 Age: 30

							BATTING												BASERUNNING				PERCENTAGES		
Year Team	Lg	G	AB	H	2B	3B	HR	(Hm	Rd)	TB	R	RBI	TBB	IBB	SO	HBP	SH	SF	SB	CS	SB%	GDP	Avg	OBP	SLG
1984 Peoria	A	43	127	28	2	0	2	--	--	36	15	14	18	0	41	4	5	2	1	3	.25	3	.220	.331	.283
1985 Midland	AA	79	252	65	11	0	6	--	--	94	26	29	20	2	48	2	7	1	2	1	.67	6	.258	.316	.373
1986 Midland	AA	48	138	31	5	0	4	--	--	48	24	16	18	0	32	0	0	0	1	0	1.00	2	.225	.314	.348
Palm Sprngs	A	31	100	29	3	0	3	--	--	41	20	20	22	0	26	0	5	2	0	0	.00	3	.290	.411	.410
1987 Midland	AA	63	187	43	5	1	7	--	--	71	28	26	24	0	44	2	5	5	2	4	.33	5	.230	.317	.380
1988 Edmonton	AAA	79	245	63	10	0	1	--	--	76	28	29	28	0	48	1	5	1	2	2	.50	7	.257	.335	.310
1989 Edmonton	AAA	54	147	39	6	1	3	--	--	56	17	22	18	0	40	2	3	0	0	0	.00	6	.265	.353	.381
1990 Midland	AA	42	148	45	8	5	3	--	--	72	22	18	9	0	32	2	0	1	1	1	.50	2	.304	.350	.486
Edmonton	AAA	53	162	40	12	0	2	--	--	58	18	23	25	1	31	1	2	0	0	4	.00	1	.247	.351	.358
1991 Edmonton	AAA	33	113	31	4	0	3	--	--	44	12	18	11	1	23	1	3	1	1	3	.25	3	.274	.341	.389
Memphis	AA	31	89	15	3	0	0	--	--	18	9	4	11	0	20	3	0	0	0	5	.00	2	.169	.282	.202
1992 Tulsa	AA	14	39	8	2	0	0	--	--	10	3	1	3	0	6	0	0	0	0	0	.00	0	.205	.262	.256
Okla City	AAA	61	194	36	10	0	4	--	--	58	20	25	22	0	35	3	4	2	0	5	.00	7	.186	.276	.299
1988 California	AL	6	12	0	0	0	0	(0	0)	0	1	0	0	0	3	1	0	0	0	0	.00	0	.000	.000	.000
1992 Texas	AL	1	1	1	0	0	0	(0	0)	1	0	0	0	0	0	0	0	0	0	0	.00	0	1.000	1.000	1.000
2 ML YEARS		7	13	1	0	0	0	(0	0)	1	1	0	0	0	3	1	0	0	0	0	.00	0	.077	.143	.077

Eric Davis

Bats: Right Throws: Right Pos: LF Ht: 6' 3" Wt: 185 Born: 05/29/62 Age: 31

							BATTING												BASERUNNING				PERCENTAGES		
Year Team	Lg	G	AB	H	2B	3B	HR	(Hm	Rd)	TB	R	RBI	TBB	IBB	SO	HBP	SH	SF	SB	CS	SB%	GDP	Avg	OBP	SLG
1984 Cincinnati	NL	57	174	39	10	1	10	(3	7)	81	33	30	24	0	48	1	0	1	10	2	.83	1	.224	.320	.466
1985 Cincinnati	NL	56	122	30	3	3	8	(1	7)	63	26	18	7	0	39	0	2	0	16	3	.84	1	.246	.287	.516
1986 Cincinnati	NL	132	415	115	15	3	27	(12	15)	217	97	71	68	5	100	1	0	3	80	11	.88	6	.277	.378	.523
1987 Cincinnati	NL	129	474	139	23	4	37	(17	20)	281	120	100	84	8	134	1	0	3	50	6	.89	6	.293	.399	.593
1988 Cincinnati	NL	135	472	129	18	3	26	(14	12)	231	81	93	65	10	124	3	0	3	35	3	.92	11	.273	.363	.489
1989 Cincinnati	NL	131	462	130	14	2	34	(15	19)	250	74	101	68	12	116	1	0	11	21	7	.75	16	.281	.367	.541
1990 Cincinnati	NL	127	453	118	26	2	24	(13	11)	220	84	86	60	6	100	2	0	3	21	3	.88	7	.260	.347	.486
1991 Cincinnati	NL	89	285	67	10	0	11	(5	6)	110	39	33	48	5	92	5	0	2	14	2	.88	4	.235	.353	.386
1992 Los Angeles	NL	76	267	61	8	1	5	(1	4)	86	21	32	36	2	71	3	0	2	19	1	.95	9	.228	.325	.322
9 ML YEARS		932	3124	828	127	19	182	(81	101)	1539	575	564	460	48	824	17	2	28	266	38	.88	61	.265	.360	.493

Glenn Davis

Bats: Right Throws: Right Pos: DH Ht: 6' 3" Wt: 211 Born: 03/28/61 Age: 32

							BATTING												BASERUNNING				PERCENTAGES		
Year Team	Lg	G	AB	H	2B	3B	HR	(Hm	Rd)	TB	R	RBI	TBB	IBB	SO	HBP	SH	SF	SB	CS	SB%	GDP	Avg	OBP	SLG
1984 Houston	NL	18	61	13	5	0	2	(1	1)	24	6	8	4	0	12	0	2	1	0	0	.00	0	.213	.258	.393

Year	Team	Lg	G	AB	H	2B	3B	HR	(Hm	Rd)	TB	R	RBI	TBB	IBB	SO	HBP	SH	SF	SB	CS	SB%	GDP	Avg	OBP	SLG
1985	Houston	NL	100	350	95	11	0	20	(8	12)	166	51	64	27	6	68	7	2	4	0	0	.00	12	.271	.332	.474
1986	Houston	NL	158	574	152	32	3	31	(17	14)	283	91	101	64	6	72	9	0	7	3	1	.75	11	.265	.344	.493
1987	Houston	NL	151	578	145	35	2	27	(12	15)	265	70	93	47	10	84	5	0	5	4	1	.80	16	.251	.310	.458
1988	Houston	NL	152	561	152	26	0	30	(15	15)	268	78	99	53	20	77	11	0	9	4	3	.57	11	.271	.341	.478
1989	Houston	NL	158	581	156	26	1	34	(15	19)	286	87	89	69	17	123	7	0	6	4	2	.67	9	.269	.350	.492
1990	Houston	NL	93	327	82	15	4	22	(4	18)	171	44	64	46	17	54	8	0	0	8	3	.73	5	.251	.357	.523
1991	Baltimore	AL	49	176	40	9	1	10	(3	7)	81	29	28	16	0	29	5	0	2	4	0	1.00	2	.227	.307	.460
1992	Baltimore	AL	106	398	110	15	2	13	(5	8)	168	46	48	37	2	65	2	1	4	1	0	1.00	12	.276	.338	.422
9 ML YEARS			985	3606	945	174	13	189	(80	109)	1712	502	594	363	78	584	54	5	38	28	10	.74	78	.262	.335	.475

Mark Davis

Pitches: Left **Bats:** Left **Pos:** RP/SP **Ht:** 6' 4" **Wt:** 210 **Born:** 10/19/60 **Age:** 32

			HOW MUCH HE PITCHED						WHAT HE GAVE UP												THE RESULTS					
Year	Team	Lg	G	GS	CG	GF	IP	BFP	H	R	ER	HR	SH	SF	HB	TBB	IBB	SO	WP	Bk	W	L	Pct.	ShO	Sv	ERA
1980	Philadelphia	NL	2	1	0	0	7	30	4	2	2	0	0	0	0	5	0	5	0	0	0	0	.000	0	0	2.57
1981	Philadelphia	NL	9	9	0	0	43	194	49	37	37	7	2	4	0	24	0	29	1	1	1	4	.200	0	0	7.74
1983	San Francisco	NL	20	20	2	0	111	469	93	51	43	14	2	4	3	50	4	83	8	1	6	4	.600	2	0	3.49
1984	San Francisco	NL	46	27	1	6	174.2	766	201	113	104	25	10	10	5	54	12	124	8	4	5	17	.227	0	0	5.36
1985	San Francisco	NL	77	1	0	38	114.1	465	89	49	45	13	13	1	3	41	7	131	6	1	5	12	.294	0	7	3.54
1986	San Francisco	NL	67	2	0	20	84.1	342	63	33	28	6	5	5	1	34	7	90	3	0	5	7	.417	0	4	2.99
1987	2 ML Teams		63	11	1	18	133	566	123	64	59	14	7	2	6	59	8	98	6	2	9	8	.529	0	2	3.99
1988	San Diego	NL	62	0	0	52	98.1	402	70	24	22	2	7	1	0	42	11	102	9	1	5	10	.333	0	28	2.01
1989	San Diego	NL	70	0	0	65	92.2	370	66	21	19	6	3	4	2	31	1	92	8	0	4	3	.571	0	44	1.85
1990	Kansas City	AL	53	3	0	28	68.2	334	71	43	39	9	2	2	4	52	3	73	6	0	2	7	.222	0	6	5.11
1991	Kansas City	AL	29	5	0	8	62.2	276	55	36	31	6	2	5	1	39	0	47	1	0	6	3	.667	0	1	4.45
1992	2 ML Teams		27	6	0	1	53	261	64	44	42	9	1	5	1	41	2	34	5	1	2	3	.400	0	0	7.13
1987	San Francisco	NL	20	11	1	1	70.2	301	72	38	37	9	3	2	4	28	1	51	4	2	4	5	.444	0	0	4.71
	San Diego	NL	43	0	0	17	62.1	265	51	26	22	5	4	0	2	31	7	47	2	0	5	3	.625	0	2	3.18
1992	Kansas City	AL	13	6	0	4	36.1	176	42	31	29	6	1	4	0	28	0	19	1	0	1	3	.250	0	0	7.18
	Atlanta	NL	14	0	0	7	16.2	85	22	13	13	3	0	1	1	13	2	15	4	1	1	0	1.000	0	0	7.02
12 ML YEARS			525	85	4	246	1042.2	4475	948	517	471	111	54	43	26	472	55	908	61	11	50	78	.391	2	92	4.07

Storm Davis

Pitches: Right **Bats:** Right **Pos:** RP **Ht:** 6' 4" **Wt:** 225 **Born:** 12/26/61 **Age:** 31

			HOW MUCH HE PITCHED						WHAT HE GAVE UP												THE RESULTS					
Year	Team	Lg	G	GS	CG	GF	IP	BFP	H	R	ER	HR	SH	SF	HB	TBB	IBB	SO	WP	Bk	W	L	Pct.	ShO	Sv	ERA
1982	Baltimore	AL	29	8	1	9	100.2	412	96	40	39	8	4	6	0	28	4	67	2	1	8	4	.667	0	0	3.49
1983	Baltimore	AL	34	29	6	0	200.1	831	180	90	80	14	5	4	2	64	4	125	7	2	13	7	.650	1	0	3.59
1984	Baltimore	AL	35	31	10	3	225	923	205	86	78	7	7	9	5	71	6	105	6	1	14	9	.609	2	1	3.12
1985	Baltimore	AL	31	28	8	0	175	750	172	92	88	11	3	3	1	70	5	93	2	1	10	8	.556	1	0	4.53
1986	Baltimore	AL	25	25	2	0	154	657	166	70	62	16	3	2	0	49	2	96	5	0	9	12	.429	0	0	3.62
1987	2 ML Teams		26	15	0	5	93	420	98	61	54	8	2	3	2	47	6	65	9	1	3	8	.273	0	0	5.23
1988	Oakland	AL	33	33	1	0	201.2	872	211	86	83	16	3	8	1	91	2	127	16	2	16	7	.696	0	0	3.70
1989	Oakland	AL	31	31	1	0	169.1	733	187	91	82	19	5	7	3	68	1	91	8	1	19	7	.731	0	0	4.36
1990	Kansas City	AL	21	20	0	0	112	498	129	66	59	9	1	3	0	35	1	62	8	1	7	10	.412	0	0	4.74
1991	Kansas City	AL	51	9	0	22	114.1	515	140	69	63	11	6	4	1	46	9	53	1	0	3	9	.250	0	2	4.96
1992	Baltimore	AL	48	2	0	24	89.1	372	79	35	34	5	6	4	2	36	6	53	4	0	7	3	.700	0	4	3.43
1987	San Diego	NL	21	10	0	5	62.2	292	70	48	43	5	2	2	2	36	6	37	7	1	2	7	.222	0	0	6.18
	Oakland	AL	5	5	0	0	30.1	128	28	13	11	3	0	1	0	11	0	28	2	0	1	1	.500	0	0	3.26
11 ML YEARS			364	231	30	63	1634.2	6983	1663	786	722	124	45	53	17	605	46	937	68	10	109	84	.565	5	7	3.98

Andre Dawson

Bats: Right **Throws:** Right **Pos:** RF **Ht:** 6' 3" **Wt:** 197 **Born:** 07/10/54 **Age:** 38

			BATTING														BASERUNNING				PERCENTAGES		
Year	Team	Lg	G	AB	H	2B	3B	HR	(Hm | Rd)	TB	R	RBI	TBB	IBB	SO	HBP	SH	SF	SB	CS	SB%	GDP	Avg	OBP	SLG
1976	Montreal	NL	24	85	20	4	1	0	(0 | 0)	26	9	7	5	1	13	0	2	0	1	2	.33	0	.235	.278	.306
1977	Montreal	NL	139	525	148	26	9	19	(7 | 12)	249	64	65	34	4	93	2	1	4	21	7	.75	5	.282	.326	.474
1978	Montreal	NL	157	609	154	24	8	25	(12 | 13)	269	84	72	30	3	128	12	4	5	28	11	.72	7	.253	.299	.442
1979	Montreal	NL	155	639	176	24	12	25	(13 | 12)	299	90	92	27	5	115	6	8	4	35	10	.78	10	.275	.309	.468
1980	Montreal	NL	151	577	178	41	7	17	(7 | 10)	284	96	87	44	7	69	6	1	10	34	9	.79	9	.308	.358	.492
1981	Montreal	NL	103	394	119	21	3	24	(9 | 15)	218	71	64	35	14	50	7	0	5	26	4	.87	6	.302	.365	.553
1982	Montreal	NL	148	608	183	37	7	23	(9 | 14)	303	107	83	34	4	96	8	4	6	39	10	.80	8	.301	.343	.498
1983	Montreal	NL	159	633	189	36	10	32	(10 | 22)	341	104	113	38	12	81	9	0	18	25	11	.69	14	.299	.338	.539
1984	Montreal	NL	138	533	132	23	6	17	(6 | 11)	218	73	86	41	2	80	2	1	6	13	5	.72	12	.248	.301	.409
1985	Montreal	NL	139	529	135	27	2	23	(11 | 12)	235	65	91	29	8	92	4	1	7	13	4	.76	12	.255	.295	.444
1986	Montreal	NL	130	496	141	32	2	20	(11 | 9)	237	65	78	37	11	79	6	1	6	18	12	.60	13	.284	.338	.478
1987	Chicago	NL	153	621	178	24	2	49	(27 | 22)	353	90	137	32	7	103	7	0	2	11	3	.79	15	.287	.328	.568

Year	Team	Lg	G	AB	H	2B	3B	HR	(Hm	Rd)	TB	R	RBI	TBB	IBB	SO	HBP	SH	SF	SB	CS	SB%	GDP	Avg	OBP	SLG
1988	Chicago	NL	157	591	179	31	8	24	(12	12)	298	78	79	37	12	73	4	1	7	12	4	.75	13	.303	.344	.504
1989	Chicago	NL	118	416	105	18	6	21	(6	15)	198	62	77	35	13	62	1	0	7	8	5	.62	16	.252	.307	.476
1990	Chicago	NL	147	529	164	28	5	27	(14	13)	283	72	100	42	**21**	65	2	0	8	16	2	.89	12	.310	.358	.535
1991	Chicago	NL	149	563	153	21	4	31	(**22**	9)	275	69	104	22	3	80	5	0	6	4	5	.44	10	.272	.302	.488
1992	Chicago	NL	143	542	150	27	2	22	(13	9)	247	60	90	30	8	70	4	0	6	2	2	.75	13	.277	.316	.456
	17 ML YEARS		2310	8890	2504	444	94	399	(189	210)	4333	1259	1425	552	135	1349	85	24	107	310	106	.75	176	.282	.326	.487

Steve Decker

Bats: Right **Throws:** Right **Pos:** C   **Ht:** 6' 3" **Wt:** 205 **Born:** 10/25/65 **Age:** 27

									BATTING											BASERUNNING				PERCENTAGES		
Year	Team	Lg	G	AB	H	2B	3B	HR	(Hm	Rd)	TB	R	RBI	TBB	IBB	SO	HBP	SH	SF	SB	CS	SB%	GDP	Avg	OBP	SLG
1990	San Francisco	NL	15	54	16	2	0	3	(1	2)	27	5	8	1	0	10	0	1	0	0	0	.00	1	.296	.309	.500
1991	San Francisco	NL	79	233	48	7	1	5	(4	1)	72	11	24	16	1	44	3	2	4	0	1	.00	7	.206	.262	.309
1992	San Francisco	NL	15	43	7	1	0	0	(0	0)	8	3	1	6	0	7	1	0	0	0	0	.00	0	.163	.280	.186
	3 ML YEARS		109	330	71	10	1	8	(5	3)	107	19	33	23	1	61	4	3	4	0	1	.00	8	.215	.271	.324

Rob Deer

Bats: Right **Throws:** Right **Pos:** RF   **Ht:** 6' 3" **Wt:** 225 **Born:** 09/29/60 **Age:** 32

									BATTING											BASERUNNING				PERCENTAGES		
Year	Team	Lg	G	AB	H	2B	3B	HR	(Hm	Rd)	TB	R	RBI	TBB	IBB	SO	HBP	SH	SF	SB	CS	SB%	GDP	Avg	OBP	SLG
1984	San Francisco	NL	13	24	4	0	0	3	(2	1)	13	5	3	7	0	10	1	0	0	1	1	.50	0	.167	.375	.542
1985	San Francisco	NL	78	162	30	5	1	8	(5	3)	61	22	20	23	0	71	0	0	2	0	1	.00	0	.185	.283	.377
1986	Milwaukee	AL	134	466	108	17	3	33	(**19**	14)	230	75	86	72	3	179	3	2	3	5	2	.71	4	.232	.336	.494
1987	Milwaukee	AL	134	474	113	15	2	28	(11	17)	216	71	80	86	6	**186**	5	0	1	12	4	.75	4	.238	.360	.456
1988	Milwaukee	AL	135	492	124	24	0	23	(12	11)	217	71	85	51	4	**153**	7	0	5	9	5	.64	4	.252	.328	.441
1989	Milwaukee	AL	130	466	98	18	2	26	(15	11)	198	72	65	60	5	158	4	0	2	4	8	.33	8	.210	.305	.425
1990	Milwaukee	AL	134	440	92	15	1	27	(11	16)	190	57	69	64	4	147	4	0	3	2	3	.40	0	.209	.313	.432
1991	Detroit	AL	134	448	80	14	2	25	(12	13)	173	64	64	89	1	**175**	0	0	2	1	3	.25	3	.179	.314	.386
1992	Detroit	AL	110	393	97	20	1	32	(13	19)	215	66	64	51	1	131	3	0	1	4	2	.67	8	.247	.337	.547
	9 ML YEARS		1002	3365	746	128	12	205	(100	105)	1513	503	536	503	26	1210	27	2	19	38	29	.57	31	.222	.326	.450

Jose DeJesus

Pitches: Right **Bats:** Right **Pos:** SP   **Ht:** 6' 5" **Wt:** 195 **Born:** 01/06/65 **Age:** 28

			HOW MUCH HE PITCHED						WHAT HE GAVE UP										THE RESULTS				
Year	Team	Lg	G	GS	CG	GF	IP	BFP	H	R	ER	HR	SH	SF	HB	TBB	IBB	SO	WP	Bk	W	L	Pct.	ShO	Sv	ERA
1988	Kansas City	AL	2	1	0	0	2.2	19	6	10	8	0	0	0	0	5	1	2	0	0	0	1	.000	0	0	27.00
1989	Kansas City	AL	3	1	0	1	8	37	7	4	4	1	0	0	0	8	0	2	0	0	0	0	.000	0	0	4.50
1990	Philadelphia	NL	22	22	3	0	130	544	97	63	54	10	8	0	2	73	3	87	4	0	7	8	.467	1	0	3.74
1991	Philadelphia	NL	31	29	3	1	181.2	801	147	74	69	7	11	3	4	**128**	4	118	10	0	10	9	.526	0	1	3.42
	4 ML YEARS		58	53	6	2	322.1	1401	257	151	135	18	19	3	6	214	8	209	14	0	17	18	.486	1	1	3.77

Jose DeLeon

Pitches: Right **Bats:** Right **Pos:** SP/RP   **Ht:** 6' 3" **Wt:** 226 **Born:** 12/20/60 **Age:** 32

			HOW MUCH HE PITCHED						WHAT HE GAVE UP										THE RESULTS				
Year	Team	Lg	G	GS	CG	GF	IP	BFP	H	R	ER	HR	SH	SF	HB	TBB	IBB	SO	WP	Bk	W	L	Pct.	ShO	Sv	ERA
1983	Pittsburgh	NL	15	15	3	0	108	438	75	36	34	5	4	3	1	47	2	118	5	2	7	3	.700	2	0	2.83
1984	Pittsburgh	NL	30	28	5	0	192.1	795	147	86	80	10	7	7	3	92	5	153	6	2	7	13	.350	1	0	3.74
1985	Pittsburgh	NL	31	25	1	5	162.2	700	138	93	85	15	7	4	3	89	3	149	7	1	2	**19**	.095	0	3	4.70
1986	2 ML Teams		22	14	1	5	95.1	408	66	46	41	9	5	1	5	59	3	79	7	0	5	8	.385	0	1	3.87
1987	Chicago	AL	33	31	2	0	206	889	177	106	92	24	6	6	10	97	4	153	6	1	11	12	.478	0	0	4.02
1988	St. Louis	NL	34	34	3	0	225.1	940	198	95	92	13	10	7	2	86	7	208	10	0	13	10	.565	1	0	3.67
1989	St. Louis	NL	36	36	5	0	244.2	972	173	96	83	16	5	3	6	80	5	**201**	2	0	16	12	.571	3	0	3.05
1990	St. Louis	NL	32	32	0	0	182.2	793	168	96	90	15	11	8	5	86	9	164	5	0	7	**19**	.269	0	0	4.43
1991	St. Louis	NL	28	28	1	0	162.2	679	144	57	49	15	5	4	6	61	1	118	1	1	5	9	.357	0	0	2.71
1992	2 ML Teams		32	18	0	3	117.1	506	111	63	57	7	6	6	2	48	1	79	3	0	2	8	.200	0	0	4.37
1986	Pittsburgh	NL	9	1	0	5	16.1	83	17	16	15	2	1	0	1	17	3	11	1	0	1	3	.250	0	1	8.27
	Chicago	AL	13	13	1	0	79	325	49	30	26	7	4	1	4	42	0	68	6	0	4	5	.444	0	0	2.96
1992	St. Louis	NL	29	15	0	3	102.1	443	95	56	52	7	5	6	2	43	1	72	3	0	2	7	.222	0	0	4.57
	Philadelphia	NL	3	3	0	0	15	63	16	7	5	0	1	0	0	5	0	7	0	0	0	1	.000	0	0	3.00
	10 ML YEARS		293	261	21	13	1697	7120	1397	774	703	129	66	49	43	745	40	1422	52	7	75	113	.399	7	4	3.73

Rich DeLucia

Pitches: Right **Bats:** Right **Pos:** RP/SP   **Ht:** 6' 0" **Wt:** 180 **Born:** 10/07/64 **Age:** 28

			HOW MUCH HE PITCHED						WHAT HE GAVE UP										THE RESULTS				
Year	Team	Lg	G	GS	CG	GF	IP	BFP	H	R	ER	HR	SH	SF	HB	TBB	IBB	SO	WP	Bk	W	L	Pct.	ShO	Sv	ERA
1990	Seattle	AL	5	5	1	0	36	144	30	9	8	2	2	0	0	9	0	20	0	0	1	2	.333	0	0	2.00
1991	Seattle	AL	32	31	0	0	182	779	176	107	103	**31**	5	14	4	78	4	98	10	0	12	13	.480	0	0	5.09

1992 Seattle	AL	30	11	0	6	83.2	382	100	55	51	13	2	2	2	35	1	66	1	0	3	6	.333	0	1	5.49
3 ML YEARS		67	47	1	6	301.2	1305	306	171	162	46	9	16	6	122	5	184	11	0	16	21	.432	0	1	4.83

Rick Dempsey

Bats: Right **Throws:** Right **Pos:** C **Ht:** 6' 0" **Wt:** 195 **Born:** 09/13/49 **Age:** 43

								BATTING											BASERUNNING				PERCENTAGES		
Year Team	Lg	G	AB	H	2B	3B	HR	(Hm	Rd)	TB	R	RBI	TBB	IBB	SO	HBP	SH	SF	SB	CS	SB%	GDP	Avg	OBP	SLG
1969 Minnesota	AL	5	6	3	1	0	0	(0	0)	4	1	0	1	0	0	0	0	0	0	0	.00	0	.500	.571	.667
1970 Minnesota	AL	5	7	0	0	0	0	(0	0)	0	1	0	1	0	1	0	0	0	0	0	.00	1	.000	.125	.000
1971 Minnesota	AL	6	13	4	1	0	0	(0	0)	5	2	0	1	0	1	0	0	0	0	0	.00	1	.308	.357	.385
1972 Minnesota	AL	25	40	8	1	0	0	(0	0)	9	0	0	6	0	8	0	1	0	0	0	.00	2	.200	.304	.225
1973 New York	AL	6	11	2	0	0	0	(0	0)	2	0	0	1	0	3	0	1	0	0	0	.00	1	.182	.250	.182
1974 New York	AL	43	109	26	3	0	2	(1	1)	35	12	12	8	0	7	0	1	1	1	0	1.00	5	.239	.288	.321
1975 New York	AL	71	145	38	8	0	1	(0	1)	49	18	11	21	1	15	0	3	1	0	0	.00	5	.262	.353	.338
1976 2 ML Teams		80	216	42	2	0	0	(0	0)	44	12	12	18	0	21	2	4	0	1	1	.50	2	.194	.263	.204
1977 Baltimore	AL	91	270	61	7	4	3	(1	2)	85	27	34	34	1	34	2	5	3	2	3	.40	9	.226	.314	.315
1978 Baltimore	AL	136	441	114	25	0	6	(4	2)	157	41	32	48	2	54	0	3	6	7	3	.70	11	.259	.327	.356
1979 Baltimore	AL	124	368	88	23	0	6	(1	5)	129	48	41	38	1	37	0	3	4	0	1	.00	12	.239	.307	.351
1980 Baltimore	AL	119	362	95	26	3	9	(5	4)	154	51	40	36	1	45	3	4	1	3	1	.75	11	.262	.333	.425
1981 Baltimore	AL	92	251	54	10	1	6	(4	2)	84	24	15	32	1	36	1	3	0	0	1	.00	5	.215	.306	.335
1982 Baltimore	AL	125	344	88	15	1	5	(2	3)	120	35	36	46	1	37	0	7	5	0	3	.00	10	.256	.339	.349
1983 Baltimore	AL	128	347	80	16	2	4	(3	1)	112	33	32	40	1	54	3	5	5	1	1	.50	9	.231	.311	.323
1984 Baltimore	AL	109	330	76	11	0	11	(6	5)	120	37	34	40	0	58	1	5	4	1	2	.33	11	.230	.312	.364
1985 Baltimore	AL	132	362	92	19	0	12	(4	8)	147	54	52	50	0	87	1	5	2	0	1	.00	2	.254	.345	.406
1986 Baltimore	AL	122	327	68	15	1	13	(7	6)	124	42	29	45	0	78	3	7	0	1	0	1.00	5	.208	.309	.379
1987 Cleveland	AL	60	141	25	10	0	1	(1	0)	38	16	9	23	0	29	1	4	1	0	0	.00	4	.177	.295	.270
1988 Los Angeles	NL	77	167	42	13	0	7	(3	4)	76	25	30	25	0	44	0	0	6	1	0	1.00	5	.251	.338	.455
1989 Los Angeles	NL	79	151	27	7	0	4	(2	2)	46	16	16	30	3	37	1	1	0	1	0	1.00	5	.179	.319	.305
1990 Los Angeles	NL	62	128	25	5	0	2	(2	0)	36	13	15	23	0	29	0	0	0	1	0	1.00	8	.195	.318	.281
1991 Milwaukee	AL	61	147	34	5	0	4	(2	2)	51	15	21	23	1	20	0	1	3	0	2	.00	7	.231	.329	.347
1992 Baltimore		8	9	1	0	0	0	(0	0)	1	2	0	2	0	1	0	0	0	0	0	.00	1	.111	.273	.111
1976 New York	AL	21	42	5	0	0	0	(0	0)	5	1	2	5	0	4	0	1	0	0	0	.00	0	.119	.213	.119
Baltimore		59	174	37	2	0	0	(0	0)	39	11	10	13	0	17	2	3	0	1	1	.50	2	.213	.275	.224
24 ML YEARS		1766	4692	1093	223	12	96	(48	48)	1628	525	471	592	13	736	18	63	42	20	19	.51	131	.233	.319	.347

Jim Deshaies

Pitches: Left **Bats:** Left **Pos:** SP **Ht:** 6' 4" **Wt:** 220 **Born:** 06/23/60 **Age:** 33

		HOW MUCH HE PITCHED						WHAT HE GAVE UP									THE RESULTS					
Year Team	Lg	G	GS	CG	GF	IP	BFP	H	R	ER	HR	SH	SF	HB	TBB	IBB	SO	WP	Bk	W	L	Pct.	ShO	Sv	ERA
1984 New York	AL	2	2	0	0	7	40	14	9	9	1	0	1	0	7	0	5	0	0	0	1	.000	0	0	11.57
1985 Houston	NL	2	0	0	0	3	10	1	0	0	0	0	0	0	0	0	2	0	0	0	0	.000	0	0	0.00
1986 Houston	NL	26	26	1	0	144	599	124	58	52	16	4	3	2	59	2	128	0	7	12	5	.706	1	0	3.25
1987 Houston	NL	26	25	1	0	152	648	149	81	78	22	9	3	0	57	7	104	4	5	11	6	.647	0	0	4.62
1988 Houston	NL	31	31	3	0	207	847	164	77	69	20	8	13	2	72	5	127	1	6	11	14	.440	2	0	3.00
1989 Houston	NL	34	34	6	0	225.2	928	180	80	73	15	11	5	4	79	8	153	8	1	15	10	.600	3	0	2.91
1990 Houston	NL	34	34	2	0	209.1	881	186	93	88	21	17	12	8	84	9	119	3	3	7	12	.368	0	0	3.78
1991 Houston	NL	28	28	1	0	161	686	156	90	89	19	4	7	1	72	5	98	0	5	5	12	.294	0	0	4.98
1992 San Diego	NL	15	15	0	0	96	395	92	40	35	6	3	2	1	33	2	46	1	2	4	7	.364	0	0	3.28
9 ML YEARS		198	195	14	0	1205	5034	1066	528	493	120	56	46	18	463	38	782	17	29	65	67	.492	6	0	3.68

Delino DeShields

Bats: Left **Throws:** Right **Pos:** 2B **Ht:** 6' 1" **Wt:** 170 **Born:** 01/15/69 **Age:** 24

								BATTING											BASERUNNING				PERCENTAGES		
Year Team	Lg	G	AB	H	2B	3B	HR	(Hm	Rd)	TB	R	RBI	TBB	IBB	SO	HBP	SH	SF	SB	CS	SB%	GDP	Avg	OBP	SLG
1990 Montreal	NL	129	499	144	28	6	4	(3	1)	196	69	45	66	3	96	4	1	2	42	22	.66	10	.289	.375	.393
1991 Montreal	NL	151	563	134	15	4	10	(3	7)	187	83	51	95	2	151	2	8	5	56	23	.71	6	.238	.347	.332
1992 Montreal	NL	135	530	155	19	8	7	(1	6)	211	82	56	54	4	108	3	9	3	46	15	.75	10	.292	.359	.398
3 ML YEARS		415	1592	433	62	18	21	(7	14)	594	234	152	215	9	355	9	18	10	144	60	.71	26	.272	.360	.373

Mike Devereaux

Bats: Right **Throws:** Right **Pos:** CF **Ht:** 6' 0" **Wt:** 195 **Born:** 04/10/63 **Age:** 30

								BATTING											BASERUNNING				PERCENTAGES		
Year Team	Lg	G	AB	H	2B	3B	HR	(Hm	Rd)	TB	R	RBI	TBB	IBB	SO	HBP	SH	SF	SB	CS	SB%	GDP	Avg	OBP	SLG
1987 Los Angeles	NL	19	54	12	3	0	0	(0	0)	15	7	4	3	0	10	0	1	0	3	1	.75	0	.222	.263	.278
1988 Los Angeles	NL	30	43	5	1	0	0	(0	0)	6	4	2	2	0	10	0	0	0	0	1	.00	0	.116	.156	.140
1989 Baltimore	AL	122	391	104	14	3	8	(4	4)	148	55	46	36	0	60	2	2	3	22	11	.67	7	.266	.329	.379
1990 Baltimore	AL	108	367	88	18	1	12	(6	6)	144	48	49	28	0	48	0	4	4	13	12	.52	10	.240	.291	.392

54

1991	Baltimore	AL	149	608	158	27	10	19	(10	9)	262	82	59	47	2	115	2	7	4	16	9	.64	13	.260	.313	.431
1992	Baltimore	AL	156	653	180	29	11	24	(14	10)	303	76	107	44	1	94	4	0	9	10	8	.56	14	.276	.321	.464
	6 ML YEARS		584	2116	547	92	25	63	(34	29)	878	272	267	160	3	337	8	14	20	64	42	.60	44	.259	.310	.415

Mark Dewey

Pitches: Right **Bats:** Right **Pos:** RP   **Ht:** 6' 0" **Wt:** 207 **Born:** 01/03/65 **Age:** 28

| | | | HOW MUCH HE PITCHED | | | | | | WHAT HE GAVE UP | | | | | | | | | THE RESULTS | | | | | |
Year	Team	Lg	G	GS	CG	GF	IP	BFP	H	R	ER	HR	SH	SF	HB	TBB	IBB	SO	WP	Bk	W	L	Pct.	ShO	Sv	ERA
1987	Everett	A	19	10	1	5	84.2	365	88	39	31	2	2	6	2	26	1	67	1	2	7	3	.700	0	1	3.30
1988	Clinton	A	37	7	1	11	119.1	474	95	36	19	5	2	1	8	14	0	76	1	5	10	4	.714	0	7	1.43
1989	San Jose	A	59	0	0	57	68.2	301	62	35	24	2	5	1	7	23	5	60	3	0	1	6	.143	0	30	3.15
1990	Shreveport	AA	33	0	0	32	38.1	157	37	11	8	1	3	0	1	10	2	23	1	0	1	5	.167	0	13	1.88
	Phoenix	AAA	19	0	0	17	30.1	130	26	14	9	2	2	1	2	10	2	27	1	0	2	3	.400	0	8	2.67
1991	Phoenix	AAA	10	0	0	10	11.1	59	16	7	5	0	2	1	1	7	5	4	0	0	1	2	.333	0	4	3.97
	Tidewater	AAA	48	0	0	32	64.2	286	61	30	24	2	5	2	0	36	6	38	4	1	12	3	.800	0	9	3.34
1992	Tidewater	AAA	43	0	0	32	54.1	238	61	29	26	5	6	0	0	18	6	55	5	0	5	7	.417	0	9	4.31
1990	San Francisco	NL	14	0	0	5	22.2	92	22	7	7	1	2	0	0	5	1	11	0	1	1	1	.500	0	0	2.78
1992	New York	NL	20	0	0	6	33.1	143	37	16	16	2	1	0	0	10	2	24	0	1	1	0	1.000	0	0	4.32
	2 ML YEARS		34	0	0	11	56	235	59	23	23	3	3	0	0	15	3	35	0	2	2	1	.667	0	0	3.70

Alex Diaz

Bats: Both **Throws:** Right **Pos:** CF   **Ht:** 5'11" **Wt:** 175 **Born:** 10/05/68 **Age:** 24

| | | | BATTING | | | | | | | | | | | | | | | | | BASERUNNING | | | | PERCENTAGES | | |
Year	Team	Lg	G	AB	H	2B	3B	HR	(Hm	Rd)	TB	R	RBI	TBB	IBB	SO	HBP	SH	SF	SB	CS	SB%	GDP	Avg	OBP	SLG
1987	Kingsport	R	54	212	56	1	0	0	--	--	67	29	13	16	0	31	1	4	1	34	9	.79	4	.264	.317	.316
	Little Fls	A	12	47	16	4	1	0	--	--	22	7	8	2	0	3	0	0	0	2	2	.50	1	.340	.367	.468
1988	Columbia	A	123	481	126	14	11	0	--	--	162	82	37	21	3	49	2	9	2	28	8	.78	4	.262	.294	.337
	St. Lucie	A	3	6	0	0	0	0	--	--	0	2	1	0	0	4	2	0	0	0	0	.00	1	.000	.250	.000
1989	St.Lucie	A	102	416	106	11	10	1	--	--	140	54	33	20	3	38	3	5	3	43	16	.73	8	.255	.292	.337
	Jackson	AA	23	95	26	5	1	2	--	--	39	11	9	3	0	11	0	0	0	3	4	.43	1	.274	.296	.411
1990	Tidewater	AAA	124	437	112	15	2	1	--	--	134	55	36	30	4	39	1	7	4	23	13	.64	7	.256	.303	.307
1991	Indianapolis	AAA	108	370	90	14	4	1	--	--	115	48	21	27	2	46	1	3	2	16	3	.84	6	.243	.295	.311
1992	Denver	AAA	106	455	122	17	4	1	--	--	150	67	41	24	0	36	5	5	5	42	11	.79	12	.268	.309	.330
1992	Milwaukee	AL	22	9	1	0	0	0	(0	0)	1	5	1	0	0	0	0	0	0	3	2	.60	0	.111	.111	.111

Mario Diaz

Bats: Right **Throws:** Right **Pos:** SS   **Ht:** 5'10" **Wt:** 160 **Born:** 01/10/62 **Age:** 31

| | | | BATTING | | | | | | | | | | | | | | | | | BASERUNNING | | | | PERCENTAGES | | |
Year	Team	Lg	G	AB	H	2B	3B	HR	(Hm	Rd)	TB	R	RBI	TBB	IBB	SO	HBP	SH	SF	SB	CS	SB%	GDP	Avg	OBP	SLG
1987	Seattle	AL	11	23	7	0	1	0	(0	0)	9	4	3	0	0	4	0	0	0	0	0	.00	0	.304	.304	.391
1988	Seattle	AL	28	72	22	5	0	0	(0	0)	27	6	9	3	0	5	0	1	0	0	0	.00	3	.306	.329	.375
1989	Seattle	AL	52	74	10	0	0	1	(0	1)	13	9	7	7	0	7	0	5	0	0	0	.00	2	.135	.210	.176
1990	New York	NL	16	22	3	1	0	0	(0	0)	4	0	1	0	0	3	0	0	1	0	0	.00	0	.136	.130	.182
1991	Texas	AL	96	182	48	7	0	1	(1	0)	58	24	22	15	0	18	0	4	1	0	1	.00	5	.264	.318	.319
1992	Texas	AL	19	31	7	1	0	0	(0	0)	8	2	1	1	1	2	0	1	0	0	0	.00	2	.226	.250	.258
	6 ML YEARS		222	404	97	14	1	2	(1	1)	119	45	43	26	1	39	0	10	3	0	2	.00	12	.240	.284	.295

Rob Dibble

Pitches: Right **Bats:** Left **Pos:** RP   **Ht:** 6' 4" **Wt:** 230 **Born:** 01/24/64 **Age:** 29

| | | | HOW MUCH HE PITCHED | | | | | | WHAT HE GAVE UP | | | | | | | | | THE RESULTS | | | | | |
Year	Team	Lg	G	GS	CG	GF	IP	BFP	H	R	ER	HR	SH	SF	HB	TBB	IBB	SO	WP	Bk	W	L	Pct.	ShO	Sv	ERA
1988	Cincinnati	NL	37	0	0	6	59.1	235	43	12	12	2	3	2	3	21	5	59	3	2	1	1	.500	0	0	1.82
1989	Cincinnati	NL	74	0	0	18	99	401	62	23	23	4	3	4	3	39	11	141	7	0	10	5	.667	0	2	2.09
1990	Cincinnati	NL	68	0	0	29	98	384	62	22	19	3	4	6	1	34	3	136	3	1	8	3	.727	0	11	1.74
1991	Cincinnati	NL	67	0	0	57	82.1	334	67	32	29	5	5	3	0	25	2	124	5	0	3	5	.375	0	31	3.17
1992	Cincinnati	NL	63	0	0	49	70.1	286	48	26	24	3	2	2	2	31	2	110	6	0	3	5	.375	0	25	3.07
	5 ML YEARS		309	0	0	159	409	1640	282	115	107	17	16	18	7	150	23	570	24	3	25	19	.568	0	69	2.35

Frank DiPino

Pitches: Left **Bats:** Left **Pos:** RP   **Ht:** 6' 0" **Wt:** 180 **Born:** 10/22/56 **Age:** 36

| | | | HOW MUCH HE PITCHED | | | | | | WHAT HE GAVE UP | | | | | | | | | THE RESULTS | | | | | |
Year	Team	Lg	G	GS	CG	GF	IP	BFP	H	R	ER	HR	SH	SF	HB	TBB	IBB	SO	WP	Bk	W	L	Pct.	ShO	Sv	ERA
1981	Milwaukee	AL	2	0	0	2	2	10	0	0	0	0	0	0	0	3	0	3	0	0	0	0	.000	0	0	0.00
1982	Houston	NL	6	6	0	0	28.1	122	32	20	19	1	3	2	0	11	1	25	0	0	2	2	.500	0	0	6.04
1983	Houston	NL	53	0	0	32	71.1	279	52	21	21	2	1	3	1	20	5	67	3	0	3	4	.429	0	20	2.65
1984	Houston	NL	57	0	0	44	75.1	329	74	32	28	3	5	2	1	36	11	65	3	1	4	9	.308	0	14	3.35

Year Team	Lg	G	GS	CG	GF	IP	BFP	H	R	ER	HR	SH	SF	HB	TBB	IBB	SO	WP	Bk	W	L	Pct.	ShO	Sv	ERA
1985 Houston	NL	54	0	0	29	76	329	69	44	34	7	3	3	2	43	6	49	4	1	3	7	.300	0	6	4.03
1986 2 ML Teams		61	0	0	26	80.1	345	74	45	39	11	9	3	2	30	6	70	3	0	3	7	.300	0	3	4.37
1987 Chicago	NL	69	0	0	20	80	343	75	31	28	7	6	4	1	34	2	61	5	0	3	3	.500	0	4	3.15
1988 Chicago	NL	63	0	0	23	90.1	398	102	54	50	6	2	6	0	32	7	69	6	1	2	3	.400	0	4	4.98
1989 St. Louis	NL	67	0	0	8	88.1	347	73	26	24	6	1	5	0	20	7	44	2	0	9	0	1.000	0	0	2.45
1990 St. Louis	NL	62	0	0	24	81	360	92	45	41	8	8	7	1	31	12	49	2	1	5	2	.714	0	3	4.56
1992 St. Louis	NL	9	0	0	3	11	45	9	2	2	0	1	0	0	2	0	8	0	0	0	0	.000	0	0	1.64
1986 Houston	NL	31	0	0	14	40.1	167	27	18	16	5	5	1	2	16	1	27	0	0	1	3	.250	0	3	3.57
Chicago	NL	30	0	0	12	40	178	47	27	23	6	4	2	0	14	5	43	3	0	2	4	.333	0	5	5.18
11 ML YEARS		503	6	0	211	684	2907	652	320	286	51	39	35	8	263	57	510	28	4	34	37	.479	0	56	3.76

Gary DiSarcina

Bats: Right **Throws:** Right **Pos:** SS **Ht:** 6' 1" **Wt:** 178 **Born:** 11/19/67 **Age:** 25

Year Team	Lg	G	AB	H	2B	3B	HR	(Hm	Rd)	TB	R	RBI	TBB	IBB	SO	HBP	SH	SF	SB	CS	SB%	GDP	Avg	OBP	SLG
1988 Bend	A	71	295	90	11	5	2	--	--	117	40	39	27	1	34	2	4	4	7	4	.64	6	.305	.363	.397
1989 Midland	AA	126	441	126	18	7	4	--	--	170	65	54	24	3	54	4	7	5	11	6	.65	17	.286	.325	.385
1990 Edmonton	AAA	97	330	70	12	2	4	--	--	98	46	37	25	0	46	4	5	2	5	3	.63	6	.212	.274	.297
1991 Edmonton	AAA	119	390	121	21	4	4	--	--	162	61	56	29	1	32	9	4	3	16	5	.76	12	.310	.369	.415
1989 California	AL	2	0	0	0	0	0	(0	0)	0	0	0	0	0	0	0	0	0	0	0	.00	0	.000	.000	.000
1990 California	AL	18	57	8	1	1	0	(0	0)	11	8	0	3	0	10	0	1	0	1	0	1.00	3	.140	.183	.193
1991 California	AL	18	57	12	2	0	0	(0	0)	14	5	3	3	0	4	2	2	0	0	0	.00	0	.211	.274	.246
1992 California	AL	157	518	128	19	0	3	(2	1)	156	48	42	20	0	50	7	5	3	9	7	.56	15	.247	.283	.301
4 ML YEARS		195	632	148	22	1	3	(2	1)	181	61	45	26	0	64	9	8	3	10	7	.59	18	.234	.273	.286

Benny Distefano

Bats: Left **Throws:** Left **Pos:** LF **Ht:** 6' 1" **Wt:** 195 **Born:** 01/23/62 **Age:** 31

Year Team	Lg	G	AB	H	2B	3B	HR	(Hm	Rd)	TB	R	RBI	TBB	IBB	SO	HBP	SH	SF	SB	CS	SB%	GDP	Avg	OBP	SLG
1984 Pittsburgh	NL	45	78	13	1	2	3	(0	3)	25	10	9	5	1	13	1	2	0	0	1	.00	3	.167	.226	.346
1986 Pittsburgh	NL	31	39	7	1	0	1	(0	1)	11	3	5	1	0	5	0	0	2	0	0	.00	0	.179	.190	.282
1988 Pittsburgh	NL	16	29	10	3	1	1	(0	1)	18	6	6	3	1	4	0	0	1	0	0	.00	1	.345	.394	.621
1989 Pittsburgh	NL	96	154	38	8	0	2	(2	0)	52	12	15	17	3	30	3	2	0	1	0	1.00	6	.247	.333	.338
1992 Houston	NL	52	60	14	0	2	0	(0	0)	18	4	7	5	1	14	1	0	0	0	0	.00	1	.233	.303	.300
5 ML YEARS		240	360	82	13	5	7	(2	5)	126	35	42	31	6	66	5	4	3	1	1	.50	11	.228	.296	.350

John Doherty

Pitches: Right **Bats:** Right **Pos:** RP/SP **Ht:** 6' 4" **Wt:** 200 **Born:** 06/11/67 **Age:** 26

Year Team	Lg	G	GS	CG	GF	IP	BFP	H	R	ER	HR	SH	SF	HB	TBB	IBB	SO	WP	Bk	W	L	Pct.	ShO	Sv	ERA
1989 Niagara Fls	A	26	1	0	25	47.1	177	30	7	5	1	1	0	3	6	2	45	2	2	1	1	.500	0	14	0.95
1990 Fayettevlle	A	7	0	0	3	9.1	50	17	12	6	0	1	0	1	1	0	6	1	2	1	0	1.000	0	1	5.79
Lakeland	A	30	0	0	20	41	153	33	7	5	1	2	1	1	5	2	23	0	4	5	1	.833	0	10	1.10
1991 London	AA	53	0	0	44	65	281	62	29	16	2	2	2	2	21	0	42	1	1	3	3	.500	0	15	2.22
1992 Detroit	AL	47	11	0	9	116	491	131	61	50	7	5	5	4	25	5	37	5	0	7	4	.636	0	3	3.88

Chris Donnels

Bats: Left **Throws:** Right **Pos:** 3B/2B **Ht:** 6' 0" **Wt:** 185 **Born:** 04/21/66 **Age:** 27

Year Team	Lg	G	AB	H	2B	3B	HR	(Hm	Rd)	TB	R	RBI	TBB	IBB	SO	HBP	SH	SF	SB	CS	SB%	GDP	Avg	OBP	SLG
1987 Kingsport	R	26	86	26	4	0	3	--	--	39	18	16	17	1	17	1	0	2	4	1	.80	1	.302	.415	.453
Columbia	A	41	136	35	7	0	2	--	--	48	20	17	24	1	27	1	0	1	3	1	.75	1	.257	.370	.353
1988 St. Lucie	A	65	198	43	14	2	3	--	--	70	25	22	32	1	53	2	2	1	4	3	.57	4	.217	.330	.354
Columbia	A	42	133	32	6	0	2	--	--	44	19	13	30	2	25	1	2	1	5	0	1.00	3	.241	.382	.331
1989 St.Lucie	A	117	386	121	23	1	17	--	--	197	70	78	83	15	65	6	2	3	18	4	.82	5	.313	.439	.510
1990 Jackson	AA	130	419	114	24	0	12	--	--	174	66	63	111	5	81	1	5	7	11	8	.58	12	.272	.420	.415
1991 Tidewater	AAA	84	287	87	18	2	8	--	--	133	45	56	62	3	55	1	0	3	1	4	.20	13	.303	.425	.463
1992 Tidewater	AAA	81	279	84	15	3	5	--	--	120	35	32	58	1	45	0	3	2	12	0	1.00	8	.301	.419	.430
1991 New York	NL	37	89	20	2	0	0	(0	0)	22	7	5	14	1	19	0	1	0	1	1	.50	0	.225	.330	.247
1992 New York	NL	45	121	21	4	0	0	(0	0)	25	8	6	17	0	25	0	1	0	1	0	1.00	1	.174	.275	.207
2 ML YEARS		82	210	41	6	0	0	(0	0)	47	15	11	31	1	44	0	2	0	2	1	.67	1	.195	.299	.224

John Dopson

Pitches: Right **Bats:** Left **Pos:** SP **Ht:** 6' 4" **Wt:** 235 **Born:** 07/14/63 **Age:** 29

Year Team	Lg	G	GS	CG	GF	IP	BFP	H	R	ER	HR	SH	SF	HB	TBB	IBB	SO	WP	Bk	W	L	Pct.	ShO	Sv	ERA
1985 Montreal	NL	4	3	0	0	13	70	25	17	16	4	0	0	0	4	0	4	2	0	0	2	.000	0	0	11.08

Year	Team	Lg	G	GS	CG	GF	IP	BFP	H	R	ER	HR	SH	SF	HB	TBB	IBB	SO	WP	Bk	W	L	Pct.	ShO	Sv	ERA
1988	Montreal	NL	26	26	1	0	168.2	704	150	69	57	15	5	2	1	58	3	101	3	1	3	11	.214	0	0	3.04
1989	Boston	AL	29	28	2	0	169.1	727	166	84	75	14	5	4	2	69	0	95	7	15	12	8	.600	0	0	3.99
1990	Boston	AL	4	4	0	0	17.2	75	13	7	4	2	0	1	0	9	0	9	0	0	0	0	.000	0	0	2.04
1991	Boston	AL	1	0	0	1	1	6	2	2	2	0	0	1	0	1	0	0	0	0	0	0	.000	0	0	18.00
1992	Boston	AL	25	25	0	0	141.1	598	159	78	64	17	2	2	2	38	2	55	3	3	7	11	.389	0	0	4.08
6 ML YEARS			89	86	3	1	511	2180	515	257	218	52	12	10	5	179	5	264	15	19	22	32	.407	0	0	3.84

Billy Doran

Bats: Both **Throws:** Right **Pos:** 2B/1B **Ht:** 6' 0" **Wt:** 180 **Born:** 05/28/58 **Age:** 35

								BATTING											BASERUNNING				PERCENTAGES		
Year	Team	Lg	G	AB	H	2B	3B	HR	(Hm | Rd)	TB	R	RBI	TBB	IBB	SO	HBP	SH	SF	SB	CS	SB%	GDP	Avg	OBP	SLG
1982	Houston	NL	26	97	27	3	0	0	(0 | 0)	30	11	6	4	0	11	0	0	1	5	0	1.00	6	.278	.304	.309
1983	Houston	NL	154	535	145	12	7	8	(1 | 7)	195	70	39	86	11	67	0	7	1	12	12	.50	6	.271	.371	.364
1984	Houston	NL	147	548	143	18	11	4	(2 | 2)	195	92	41	66	7	69	2	7	3	21	12	.64	6	.261	.341	.356
1985	Houston	NL	148	578	166	31	6	14	(5 | 9)	251	84	59	71	6	69	0	3	5	23	15	.61	10	.287	.362	.434
1986	Houston	NL	145	550	152	29	3	6	(3 | 3)	205	92	37	81	7	57	2	4	5	42	19	.69	10	.276	.368	.373
1987	Houston	NL	162	625	177	23	3	16	(7 | 9)	254	82	79	82	3	64	3	2	7	31	11	.74	11	.283	.365	.406
1988	Houston	NL	132	480	119	18	1	7	(2 | 5)	160	66	53	65	3	60	1	4	2	17	4	.81	7	.248	.338	.333
1989	Houston	NL	142	507	111	25	2	8	(3 | 5)	164	65	58	59	2	63	2	3	3	22	3	.88	8	.219	.301	.323
1990	2 ML Teams		126	403	121	29	2	7	(4 | 3)	175	59	37	79	2	58	0	1	5	23	9	.72	3	.300	.411	.434
1991	Cincinnati	NL	111	361	101	12	2	6	(3 | 3)	135	51	35	46	1	39	0	0	3	5	4	.56	4	.280	.359	.374
1992	Cincinnati	NL	132	387	91	16	2	8	(6 | 2)	135	48	47	64	9	40	0	3	2	7	4	.64	11	.235	.342	.349
1990	Cincinnati	NL	109	344	99	21	2	6	(3 | 3)	142	49	32	71	1	53	0	1	5	18	9	.67	2	.288	.405	.413
	Cincinnati		17	59	22	8	0	1	(1 | 0)	33	10	5	8	1	5	0	0	0	5	0	1.00	1	.373	.448	.559
11 ML YEARS			1425	5071	1353	216	39	84	(36 | 48)	1899	720	491	703	51	597	10	34	37	208	93	.69	76	.267	.355	.374

Brian Downing

Bats: Right **Throws:** Right **Pos:** DH **Ht:** 5'10" **Wt:** 205 **Born:** 10/09/50 **Age:** 42

								BATTING											BASERUNNING				PERCENTAGES		
Year	Team	Lg	G	AB	H	2B	3B	HR	(Hm | Rd)	TB	R	RBI	TBB	IBB	SO	HBP	SH	SF	SB	CS	SB%	GDP	Avg	OBP	SLG
1973	Chicago	AL	34	73	13	1	0	2	(1 | 1)	20	5	4	10	1	17	0	2	0	0	0	.00	3	.178	.277	.274
1974	Chicago	AL	108	293	66	12	1	10	(6 | 4)	110	41	39	51	3	72	2	4	0	0	1	.00	11	.225	.344	.375
1975	Chicago	AL	138	420	101	12	1	7	(5 | 2)	136	58	41	76	5	75	3	11	6	13	4	.76	12	.240	.356	.324
1976	Chicago	AL	104	317	81	14	0	3	(0 | 3)	104	38	30	40	0	55	1	4	3	7	3	.70	2	.256	.338	.328
1977	Chicago	AL	69	169	48	4	2	4	(1 | 3)	68	28	25	34	0	21	2	5	4	1	2	.33	3	.284	.402	.402
1978	California	AL	133	412	105	15	0	7	(2 | 5)	141	42	46	52	2	47	6	4	2	3	2	.60	14	.255	.345	.342
1979	California	AL	148	509	166	27	3	12	(3 | 9)	235	87	75	77	4	57	5	3	2	3	3	.50	17	.326	.418	.462
1980	California	AL	30	93	27	6	0	2	(2 | 0)	39	5	25	12	1	12	0	1	2	0	2	.00	5	.290	.364	.419
1981	California	AL	93	317	79	14	0	9	(6 | 3)	120	47	41	46	1	35	4	3	0	1	1	.50	11	.249	.351	.379
1982	California	AL	158	623	175	37	2	28	(15 | 13)	300	109	84	86	1	58	5	3	8	2	1	.67	14	.281	.368	.482
1983	California	AL	113	403	99	15	1	19	(10 | 9)	173	68	53	62	4	59	5	1	2	1	2	.33	8	.246	.352	.429
1984	California	AL	156	539	148	28	2	23	(9 | 14)	249	65	91	70	3	66	7	3	9	0	4	.00	18	.275	.360	.462
1985	California	AL	150	520	137	23	1	20	(10 | 10)	222	80	85	78	3	61	13	5	4	5	3	.63	12	.263	.371	.452
1986	California	AL	152	513	137	27	4	20	(13 | 7)	232	90	95	90	2	84	17	3	8	4	4	.50	14	.267	.389	.452
1987	California	AL	155	567	154	29	3	29	(11 | 18)	276	110	77	106	6	85	17	2	3	5	5	.50	10	.272	.400	.487
1988	California	AL	135	484	117	18	2	25	(11 | 14)	214	80	64	81	5	63	14	5	6	3	4	.43	12	.242	.362	.442
1989	California	AL	142	544	154	25	2	14	(10 | 4)	225	59	59	56	3	87	6	0	4	0	2	.00	6	.283	.354	.414
1990	California	AL	96	330	90	18	2	14	(11 | 3)	154	47	51	50	2	45	6	0	4	0	0	.00	11	.273	.374	.467
1991	Texas	AL	123	407	113	17	2	17	(8 | 9)	185	76	49	58	7	70	8	1	2	1	0	.50	7	.278	.377	.455
1992	Texas	AL	107	320	89	18	0	10	(4 | 6)	137	53	39	62	2	58	8	0	1	1	0	1.00	7	.278	.407	.428
20 ML YEARS			2344	7853	2099	360	28	275	(138 | 137)	3340	1188	1073	1197	55	1127	129	60	70	50	44	.53	197	.267	.370	.425

Kelly Downs

Pitches: Right **Bats:** Right **Pos:** SP/RP **Ht:** 6' 4" **Wt:** 200 **Born:** 10/25/60 **Age:** 32

								HOW MUCH HE PITCHED		WHAT HE GAVE UP											THE RESULTS				
Year	Team	Lg	G	GS	CG	GF	IP	BFP	H	R	ER	HR	SH	SF	HB	TBB	IBB	SO	WP	Bk	W	L	Pct.	ShO	Sv	ERA
1986	San Francisco	NL	14	14	1	0	88.1	372	78	29	27	5	4	4	3	30	7	64	3	2	4	4	.500	0	0	2.75
1987	San Francisco	NL	41	28	4	4	186	797	185	83	75	14	7	1	4	67	11	137	12	4	12	9	.571	3	1	3.63
1988	San Francisco	NL	27	26	6	0	168	685	140	67	62	11	4	9	3	47	8	118	7	4	13	9	.591	3	0	3.32
1989	San Francisco	NL	18	15	0	1	82.2	349	82	47	44	7	4	4	1	26	4	49	3	3	4	8	.333	0	0	4.79
1990	San Francisco	NL	13	9	0	1	63	265	56	26	24	2	2	1	2	20	4	31	2	1	3	2	.600	0	0	3.43
1991	San Francisco	NL	45	11	0	4	111.2	479	99	59	52	12	4	4	3	53	9	62	4	1	10	4	.714	0	0	4.19
1992	2 ML Teams		37	20	0	7	144.1	636	137	63	54	8	13	6	7	70	3	71	7	1	6	7	.462	0	0	3.37
1992	San Francisco	NL	19	7	0	5	62.1	272	65	27	24	4	7	2	3	24	0	33	4	0	1	2	.333	0	0	3.47
	Oakland	AL	18	13	0	2	82	364	72	36	30	4	6	4	4	46	3	38	3	1	5	5	.500	0	0	3.29
7 ML YEARS			195	123	11	17	844	3583	777	374	338	59	38	29	23	313	46	532	38	16	52	43	.547	6	1	3.60

D.J. Dozier

Bats: Right **Throws:** Right **Pos:** LF **Ht:** 6' 1" **Wt:** 204 **Born:** 09/21/65 **Age:** 27

Year Team	Lg	G	AB	H	2B	3B	HR	(Hm	Rd)	TB	R	RBI	TBB	IBB	SO	HBP	SH	SF	SB	CS	SB%	GDP	Avg	OBP	SLG
1990 St. Lucie	A	93	317	94	11	3	13	--	--	150	56	57	45	0	76	1	0	3	33	5	.87	5	.297	.383	.473
Jackson	AA	29	102	33	5	7	2	--	--	58	20	23	16	0	28	0	0	6	3	1	.75	5	.324	.395	.569
1991 Williamsprt	AA	74	259	72	11	6	8	--	--	119	49	30	39	2	88	1	0	1	25	6	.81	3	.278	.373	.459
Tidewater	AAA	43	171	46	7	5	1	--	--	66	19	22	13	0	41	4	2	2	8	6	.57	3	.269	.332	.386
1992 Tidewater	AAA	64	197	46	8	3	7	--	--	81	32	25	37	3	55	2	1	2	6	3	.67	3	.234	.357	.411
1992 New York	NL	25	47	9	2	0	0	(0	0)	11	4	2	4	0	19	1	1	1	4	0	1.00	0	.191	.264	.234

Doug Drabek

Pitches: Right **Bats:** Right **Pos:** SP **Ht:** 6' 1" **Wt:** 185 **Born:** 07/25/62 **Age:** 30

Year Team	Lg	G	GS	CG	GF	IP	BFP	H	R	ER	HR	SH	SF	HB	TBB	IBB	SO	WP	Bk	W	L	Pct.	ShO	Sv	ERA
1986 New York	AL	27	21	0	2	131.2	561	126	64	60	13	5	2	3	50	1	76	2	0	7	8	.467	0	0	4.10
1987 Pittsburgh	NL	29	28	1	0	176.1	721	165	86	76	22	3	4	0	46	2	120	5	1	11	12	.478	1	0	3.88
1988 Pittsburgh	NL	33	32	3	0	219.1	880	194	83	75	21	7	5	6	50	4	127	4	1	15	7	.682	1	0	3.08
1989 Pittsburgh	NL	35	34	8	1	244.1	994	215	83	76	21	13	7	3	69	3	123	3	0	14	12	.538	5	0	2.80
1990 Pittsburgh	NL	33	33	9	0	231.1	918	190	78	71	15	10	3	3	56	2	131	6	0	**22**	6	**.786**	3	0	2.76
1991 Pittsburgh	NL	35	35	5	0	234.2	977	245	92	80	16	12	6	3	62	6	142	5	0	15	14	.517	2	0	3.07
1992 Pittsburgh	NL	34	34	10	0	256.2	1021	218	84	79	17	8	8	6	54	8	177	11	1	15	11	.577	4	0	2.77
7 ML YEARS		226	217	36	3	1494.1	6072	1353	570	517	125	58	35	24	387	26	896	36	3	99	70	.586	16	0	3.11

Brian Drahman

Pitches: Right **Bats:** Right **Pos:** RP **Ht:** 6' 3" **Wt:** 205 **Born:** 11/07/66 **Age:** 26

Year Team	Lg	G	GS	CG	GF	IP	BFP	H	R	ER	HR	SH	SF	HB	TBB	IBB	SO	WP	Bk	W	L	Pct.	ShO	Sv	ERA
1986 Helena	R	18	10	0	5	65.1	0	79	49	43	4	0	4	0	33	1	40	4	0	4	6	.400	0	2	5.92
1987 Beloit	A	46	0	0	41	79	318	63	28	19	2	4	2	3	22	3	60	5	1	6	5	.545	0	18	2.16
1988 Stockton	A	44	0	0	40	62.1	266	57	17	14	2	1	0	1	27	3	50	3	0	4	5	.444	0	14	2.02
1989 El Paso	AA	19	0	0	8	31	151	52	31	25	3	3	0	1	11	1	23	3	0	3	4	.429	0	2	7.26
Stockton	A	12	0	0	10	27.2	112	22	11	10	0	1	0	2	9	0	30	2	0	3	2	.600	0	4	3.25
Sarasota	A	7	2	0	3	16.2	73	18	9	6	1	1	0	1	5	1	9	1	0	0	1	.000	0	1	3.24
1990 Birmingham	AA	50	1	0	31	90.1	383	90	50	41	6	9	4	3	24	2	72	12	1	6	4	.600	0	17	4.08
1991 Vancouver	AAA	22	0	0	21	24.1	106	21	12	12	2	4	0	0	13	1	17	1	1	2	3	.400	0	12	4.44
1992 Vancouver	AAA	48	0	0	44	58.1	242	44	16	13	5	3	2	0	31	1	34	2	0	2	4	.333	0	30	2.01
1991 Chicago	AL	28	0	0	8	30.2	125	21	12	11	4	2	1	0	13	1	18	0	0	3	2	.600	0	0	3.23
1992 Chicago	AL	5	0	0	2	7	29	6	3	2	0	0	0	0	2	0	1	1	0	0	0	.000	0	0	2.57
2 ML YEARS		33	0	0	10	37.2	154	27	15	13	4	2	1	0	15	1	19	1	0	3	2	.600	0	0	3.11

Rob Ducey

Bats: Left **Throws:** Right **Pos:** LF **Ht:** 6' 2" **Wt:** 180 **Born:** 05/24/65 **Age:** 28

Year Team	Lg	G	AB	H	2B	3B	HR	(Hm	Rd)	TB	R	RBI	TBB	IBB	SO	HBP	SH	SF	SB	CS	SB%	GDP	Avg	OBP	SLG
1987 Toronto	AL	34	48	9	1	0	1	(1	0)	13	12	6	8	0	10	0	0	1	2	0	1.00	0	.188	.298	.271
1988 Toronto	AL	27	54	17	4	1	0	(0	0)	23	15	6	5	0	7	0	2	2	1	0	1.00	1	.315	.361	.426
1989 Toronto	AL	41	76	16	4	0	0	(0	0)	20	5	7	9	1	25	0	1	0	1	1	.67	2	.211	.294	.263
1990 Toronto	AL	19	53	16	5	0	0	(0	0)	21	7	7	7	0	15	1	0	1	1	1	.50	0	.302	.387	.396
1991 Toronto	AL	39	68	16	2	2	1	(0	1)	25	8	4	6	0	26	0	1	0	2	0	1.00	1	.235	.297	.368
1992 2 ML Teams		54	80	15	4	0	0	(0	0)	19	7	2	5	0	22	0	0	1	2	4	.33	1	.188	.233	.238
1992 Toronto	AL	23	21	1	1	0	0	(0	0)	2	3	0	0	0	10	0	0	0	0	1	.00	0	.048	.048	.095
California	AL	31	59	14	3	0	0	(0	0)	17	4	2	5	0	12	0	0	1	2	3	.40	1	.237	.292	.288
6 ML YEARS		214	379	89	20	3	2	(1	1)	121	54	32	40	1	105	1	4	5	10	6	.63	5	.235	.306	.319

Mariano Duncan

Bats: Right **Throws:** Right **Pos:** LF/2B/SS **Ht:** 6' 0" **Wt:** 185 **Born:** 03/13/63 **Age:** 30

Year Team	Lg	G	AB	H	2B	3B	HR	(Hm	Rd)	TB	R	RBI	TBB	IBB	SO	HBP	SH	SF	SB	CS	SB%	GDP	Avg	OBP	SLG
1985 Los Angeles	NL	142	562	137	24	6	6	(1	5)	191	74	39	38	4	113	3	13	4	38	8	.83	9	.244	.293	.340
1986 Los Angeles	NL	109	407	93	7	0	8	(2	6)	124	47	30	30	1	78	2	5	1	48	13	.79	6	.229	.284	.305
1987 Los Angeles	NL	76	261	56	8	1	6	(3	3)	84	31	18	17	1	62	2	6	1	11	1	.92	4	.215	.267	.322
1989 2 ML Teams		94	258	64	15	2	3	(2	1)	92	32	21	8	0	51	5	2	0	9	5	.64	3	.248	.284	.357
1990 Cincinnati	NL	125	435	133	22	**11**	10	(5	5)	207	67	55	24	4	67	4	4	4	13	7	.65	10	.306	.345	.476
1991 Cincinnati	NL	100	333	86	7	4	12	(10	2)	137	46	40	12	0	57	3	5	3	5	4	.56	0	.258	.288	.411
1992 Philadelphia	NL	142	574	153	40	3	8	(3	5)	223	71	50	17	0	108	5	5	4	23	3	.88	15	.267	.292	.389

Year	Team	Lg	G	GS	CG	GF	IP	BFP	H	R	ER	HR	SH	SF	HB	TBB	IBB	SO	WP	Bk	W	L	Pct.	ShO	Sv	ERA
1989	Los Angeles	NL	49	84	21	5	1	0	(0 | 0)	28	9	8	0	0	15	2	1	0	3	3	.50	1		.250	.267	.333
	Cincinnati	NL	45	174	43	10	1	3	(2 | 1)	64	23	13	8	0	36	3	1	0	6	2	.75	2		.247	.292	.368
	7 ML YEARS		788	2830	722	123	27	53	(26 | 27)	1058	368	253	146	10	536	24	40	17	147	41	.78	47		.255	.296	.374

Mike Dunne

Pitches: Right Bats: Left Pos: RP   **Ht: 6' 4" Wt: 221 Born: 10/27/62 Age: 30**

			HOW MUCH HE PITCHED						WHAT HE GAVE UP											THE RESULTS					
Year	Team	Lg	G	GS	CG	GF	IP	BFP	H	R	ER	HR	SH	SF	HB	TBB	IBB	SO	WP	Bk	W	L	Pct.	ShO	Sv	ERA
1987	Pittsburgh	NL	23	23	5	0	163.1	680	143	66	55	10	11	4	1	68	8	72	6	4	13	6	.684	1	0	3.03
1988	Pittsburgh	NL	30	28	1	1	170	752	163	88	74	15	11	8	5	88	3	70	12	7	7	11	.389	0	0	3.92
1989	2 ML Teams		18	18	1	0	99.2	461	125	73	62	8	4	5	3	46	2	42	8	1	3	10	.231	0	0	5.60
1990	San Diego	NL	10	6	0	0	28.2	134	28	21	18	4	1	0	0	17	0	15	4	1	0	3	.000	0	0	5.65
1992	Chicago	AL	4	1	0	0	12.2	54	12	7	6	0	0	0	1	6	1	6	0	0	2	0	1.000	0	0	4.26
1989	Pittsburgh	NL	3	3	0	0	14.1	75	21	12	12	1	1	0	1	9	1	4	1	0	1	1	.500	0	0	7.53
	Seattle	AL	15	15	1	0	85.1	386	104	61	50	7	3	5	2	37	1	38	7	1	2	9	.182	0	0	5.27
	5 ML YEARS		85	76	7	1	474.1	2081	471	255	215	37	27	17	10	225	14	205	30	13	25	30	.455	1	0	4.08

Shawon Dunston

Bats: Right Throws: Right Pos: SS   **Ht: 6' 1" Wt: 175 Born: 03/21/63 Age: 30**

			BATTING															BASERUNNING				PERCENTAGES		
Year	Team	Lg	G	AB	H	2B	3B	HR	(Hm	Rd)	TB	R	RBI	TBB	IBB	SO	HBP	SH	SF	SB	CS	SB%	GDP	Avg	OBP	SLG
1985	Chicago	NL	74	250	65	12	4	4	(3	1)	97	40	18	19	3	42	0	1	2	11	3	.79	3	.260	.310	.388
1986	Chicago	NL	150	581	145	37	3	17	(10	7)	239	66	68	21	5	114	3	4	2	13	11	.54	5	.250	.278	.411
1987	Chicago	NL	95	346	85	18	3	5	(3	2)	124	40	22	10	1	68	1	0	2	12	3	.80	6	.246	.267	.358
1988	Chicago	NL	155	575	143	23	6	9	(5	4)	205	69	56	16	8	108	2	4	2	30	9	.77	6	.249	.271	.357
1989	Chicago	NL	138	471	131	20	6	9	(3	6)	190	52	60	30	15	86	1	6	4	19	11	.63	7	.278	.320	.403
1990	Chicago	NL	146	545	143	22	8	17	(7	10)	232	73	66	15	1	87	3	4	6	25	5	.83	9	.262	.283	.426
1991	Chicago	NL	142	492	128	22	7	12	(7	5)	200	59	50	23	5	64	4	4	11	21	6	.78	8	.260	.292	.407
1992	Chicago	NL	18	73	23	3	1	0	(0	0)	28	8	2	3	0	13	0	0	0	2	3	.40	1	.315	.342	.384
	8 ML YEARS		918	3333	863	157	38	73	(38	35)	1315	407	342	137	38	582	14	23	29	133	51	.72	45	.259	.289	.395

Lenny Dykstra

Bats: Left Throws: Left Pos: CF   **Ht: 5'10" Wt: 180 Born: 02/10/63 Age: 30**

			BATTING															BASERUNNING				PERCENTAGES		
Year	Team	Lg	G	AB	H	2B	3B	HR	(Hm	Rd)	TB	R	RBI	TBB	IBB	SO	HBP	SH	SF	SB	CS	SB%	GDP	Avg	OBP	SLG
1985	New York	NL	83	236	60	9	3	1	(0	1)	78	40	19	30	0	24	1	4	2	15	2	.88	4	.254	.338	.331
1986	New York	NL	147	431	127	27	7	8	(4	4)	192	77	45	58	1	55	0	7	2	31	7	.82	4	.295	.377	.445
1987	New York	NL	132	431	123	37	3	10	(7	3)	196	86	43	40	3	67	4	4	0	27	7	.79	1	.285	.352	.455
1988	New York	NL	126	429	116	19	3	8	(3	5)	165	57	33	30	2	43	3	2	2	30	8	.79	3	.270	.321	.385
1989	2 ML Teams		146	511	121	32	4	7	(5	2)	182	66	32	60	1	53	3	5	5	30	12	.71	7	.237	.318	.356
1990	Philadelphia	NL	149	590	192	35	3	9	(6	3)	260	106	60	89	14	48	7	2	3	33	5	.87	5	.325	.418	.441
1991	Philadelphia	NL	63	246	73	13	5	3	(3	0)	105	48	12	37	1	20	1	0	0	24	4	.86	1	.297	.391	.427
1992	Philadelphia	NL	85	345	104	18	0	6	(5	1)	140	53	39	40	4	32	3	0	4	30	5	.86	1	.301	.375	.406
1989	New York	NL	56	159	43	12	1	3	(2	1)	66	27	13	23	0	15	2	4	4	13	1	.93	2	.270	.362	.415
	Philadelphia	NL	90	352	78	20	3	4	(3	1)	116	39	19	37	1	38	1	1	1	17	11	.61	5	.222	.297	.330
	8 ML YEARS		931	3219	916	190	28	52	(33	19)	1318	533	283	384	26	342	22	24	18	220	50	.81	26	.285	.363	.409

Damion Easley

Bats: Right Throws: Right Pos: 3B   **Ht: 5'11" Wt: 155 Born: 11/11/69 Age: 23**

			BATTING															BASERUNNING				PERCENTAGES		
Year	Team	Lg	G	AB	H	2B	3B	HR	(Hm	Rd)	TB	R	RBI	TBB	IBB	SO	HBP	SH	SF	SB	CS	SB%	GDP	Avg	OBP	SLG
1989	Bend	A	36	131	39	5	1	4	--	--	58	34	21	25	0	21	4	0	0	9	4	.69	1	.298	.425	.443
1990	Quad City	A	103	365	100	19	3	10	--	--	155	59	56	41	0	60	8	1	2	24	8	.75	8	.274	.358	.425
1991	Midland	AA	127	452	115	24	4	6	--	--	165	73	57	58	2	67	7	6	2	22	9	.71	12	.254	.347	.365
1992	Edmonton	AAA	108	429	124	18	3	3	--	--	157	61	44	31	0	44	5	3	6	26	10	.72	13	.289	.340	.366
1992	California	AL	47	151	39	5	0	1	(1	0)	47	14	12	8	0	26	3	2	1	9	5	.64	2	.258	.307	.311

Dennis Eckersley

Pitches: Right Bats: Right Pos: RP   **Ht: 6' 2" Wt: 195 Born: 10/03/54 Age: 38**

			HOW MUCH HE PITCHED						WHAT HE GAVE UP											THE RESULTS					
Year	Team	Lg	G	GS	CG	GF	IP	BFP	H	R	ER	HR	SH	SF	HB	TBB	IBB	SO	WP	Bk	W	L	Pct.	ShO	Sv	ERA
1975	Cleveland	AL	34	24	6	5	187	794	147	64	54	16	6	7	7	90	8	152	4	2	13	7	.650	2	2	2.60
1976	Cleveland	AL	36	30	9	3	199	821	155	82	76	13	10	4	5	78	2	200	6	1	13	12	.520	3	1	3.44
1977	Cleveland	AL	33	33	12	0	247	1006	214	100	97	31	11	6	7	54	11	191	3	0	14	13	.519	3	0	3.53
1978	Boston	AL	35	35	16	0	268	1121	258	99	89	30	7	8	7	71	8	162	3	0	20	8	.714	3	0	2.99
1979	Boston	AL	33	33	17	0	247	1018	234	89	82	29	10	6	6	59	4	150	1	1	17	10	.630	2	0	2.99
1980	Boston	AL	30	30	8	0	198	818	188	101	94	25	7	8	2	44	7	121	0	0	12	14	.462	0	0	4.27

Year	Team	Lg	G	GS	CG	GF	IP	BFP	H	R	ER	HR	SH	SF	HB	TBB	IBB	SO	WP	Bk	W	L	Pct.	ShO	Sv	ERA
1981	Boston	AL	23	23	8	0	154	649	160	82	73	9	6	5	3	35	2	79	0	0	9	8	.529	2	0	4.27
1982	Boston	AL	33	33	11	0	224.1	926	228	101	93	31	4	4	2	43	3	127	1	0	13	13	.500	3	0	3.73
1983	Boston	AL	28	28	2	0	176.1	787	223	119	110	27	1	5	6	39	4	77	1	0	9	13	.409	0	0	5.61
1984	2 ML Teams		33	33	4	0	225	932	223	97	90	21	11	9	5	49	9	114	3	2	14	12	.538	0	0	3.60
1985	Chicago	NL	25	25	6	0	169.1	664	145	61	58	15	6	2	3	19	4	117	0	3	11	7	.611	2	0	3.08
1986	Chicago	NL	33	32	1	0	201	862	226	109	102	21	13	10	3	43	3	137	2	5	6	11	.353	0	0	4.57
1987	Oakland	AL	54	2	0	33	115.2	460	99	41	39	11	3	3	3	17	3	113	1	0	6	8	.429	0	16	3.03
1988	Oakland	AL	60	0	0	53	72.2	279	52	20	19	5	1	3	1	11	2	70	0	2	4	2	.667	0	45	2.35
1989	Oakland	AL	51	0	0	46	57.2	206	32	10	10	5	0	4	1	3	0	55	0	0	4	0	1.000	0	33	1.56
1990	Oakland	AL	63	0	0	61	73.1	262	41	9	5	2	0	1	0	4	1	73	0	0	4	2	.667	0	48	0.61
1991	Oakland	AL	67	0	0	59	76	299	60	26	25	11	1	0	1	9	3	87	1	0	5	4	.556	0	43	2.96
1992	Oakland	AL	69	0	0	65	80	309	62	17	17	5	3	0	1	11	6	93	0	0	7	1	.875	0	51	1.91
1984	Boston	AL	9	9	2	0	64.2	270	71	38	36	10	3	3	1	13	2	33	2	0	4	4	.500	0	0	5.01
	Chicago	NL	24	24	2	0	160.1	662	152	59	54	11	8	6	4	36	7	81	1	2	10	8	.556	0	0	3.03
18 ML YEARS			740	361	100	325	2971.1	12213	2747	1224	1133	307	100	85	63	679	80	2118	26	16	181	145	.555	20	239	3.43

Tom Edens

Pitches: Right **Bats:** Right **Pos:** RP **Ht:** 6' 2" **Wt:** 188 **Born:** 06/09/61 **Age:** 32

			HOW MUCH HE PITCHED						WHAT HE GAVE UP												THE RESULTS					
Year	Team	Lg	G	GS	CG	GF	IP	BFP	H	R	ER	HR	SH	SF	HB	TBB	IBB	SO	WP	Bk	W	L	Pct.	ShO	Sv	ERA
1987	New York	NL	2	2	0	0	8	42	15	6	6	2	2	0	0	4	0	4	2	0	0	0	.000	0	0	6.75
1990	Milwaukee	AL	35	6	0	9	89	387	89	52	44	8	6	4	4	33	3	40	1	0	4	5	.444	0	2	4.45
1991	Minnesota	AL	8	6	0	0	33	143	34	15	15	2	0	0	0	10	1	19	1	0	2	2	.500	0	0	4.09
1992	Minnesota	AL	52	0	0	14	76.1	317	65	26	24	1	4	0	2	36	3	57	5	0	6	3	.667	0	3	2.83
4 ML YEARS			97	14	0	23	206.1	889	203	99	89	13	12	4	6	83	7	120	9	0	12	10	.545	0	5	3.88

Mark Eichhorn

Pitches: Right **Bats:** Right **Pos:** RP **Ht:** 6' 3" **Wt:** 210 **Born:** 11/21/60 **Age:** 32

			HOW MUCH HE PITCHED						WHAT HE GAVE UP												THE RESULTS					
Year	Team	Lg	G	GS	CG	GF	IP	BFP	H	R	ER	HR	SH	SF	HB	TBB	IBB	SO	WP	Bk	W	L	Pct.	ShO	Sv	ERA
1982	Toronto	AL	7	7	0	0	38	171	40	28	23	4	1	2	0	14	1	16	3	0	0	3	.000	0	0	5.45
1986	Toronto	AL	69	0	0	38	157	612	105	32	30	8	9	2	7	45	14	166	2	1	14	6	.700	0	10	1.72
1987	Toronto	AL	89	0	0	27	127.2	540	110	47	45	14	7	4	6	52	13	96	3	1	10	6	.625	0	4	3.17
1988	Toronto	AL	37	0	0	17	66.2	302	79	32	31	3	8	1	6	27	4	28	3	6	0	3	.000	0	1	4.18
1989	Atlanta	NL	45	0	0	13	68.1	286	70	36	33	6	7	4	1	19	8	49	0	1	5	5	.500	0	0	4.35
1990	California	AL	60	0	0	40	84.2	374	98	36	29	2	2	4	6	23	0	69	0	0	2	5	.286	0	13	3.08
1991	California	AL	70	0	0	23	81.2	311	63	21	18	2	5	3	2	13	1	49	0	0	3	3	.500	0	1	1.98
1992	2 ML Teams		65	0	0	26	87.2	372	86	34	30	3	3	5	2	25	8	61	9	1	4	4	.500	0	2	3.08
1992	California	AL	42	0	0	19	56.2	237	51	19	15	2	2	3	0	18	8	42	3	1	2	4	.333	0	2	2.38
	Toronto	AL	23	0	0	7	31	135	35	15	15	1	1	2	2	7	0	19	6	0	2	0	1.000	0	0	4.35
8 ML YEARS			442	7	0	184	711.2	2968	651	266	239	42	42	25	30	218	49	534	22	10	38	35	.521	0	31	3.02

Dave Eiland

Pitches: Right **Bats:** Right **Pos:** SP **Ht:** 6' 3" **Wt:** 210 **Born:** 07/05/66 **Age:** 26

			HOW MUCH HE PITCHED						WHAT HE GAVE UP												THE RESULTS					
Year	Team	Lg	G	GS	CG	GF	IP	BFP	H	R	ER	HR	SH	SF	HB	TBB	IBB	SO	WP	Bk	W	L	Pct.	ShO	Sv	ERA
1988	New York	AL	3	3	0	0	12.2	57	15	9	9	6	0	0	2	4	0	7	0	0	0	0	.000	0	0	6.39
1989	New York	AL	6	6	0	0	34.1	152	44	25	22	5	1	2	2	13	3	11	0	0	1	3	.250	0	0	5.77
1990	New York	AL	5	5	0	0	30.1	127	31	14	12	2	0	0	2	5	0	16	0	0	2	1	.667	0	0	3.56
1991	New York	AL	18	13	0	4	72.2	317	87	51	43	10	0	3	3	23	1	18	0	0	2	5	.286	0	0	5.33
1992	San Diego	NL	7	7	0	0	27	120	33	21	17	1	0	0	0	5	0	10	0	1	0	2	.000	0	0	5.67
5 ML YEARS			39	34	0	4	177	773	210	120	103	24	1	5	7	50	4	62	0	1	5	11	.313	0	0	5.24

Jim Eisenreich

Bats: Left **Throws:** Left **Pos:** RF/LF **Ht:** 5'11" **Wt:** 200 **Born:** 04/18/59 **Age:** 34

			BATTING																	BASERUNNING				PERCENTAGES		
Year	Team	Lg	G	AB	H	2B	3B	HR	(Hm	Rd)	TB	R	RBI	TBB	IBB	SO	HBP	SH	SF	SB	CS	SB%	GDP	Avg	OBP	SLG
1982	Minnesota	AL	34	99	30	6	0	2	(1	1)	42	10	9	11	0	13	1	0	0	0	0	.00	1	.303	.378	.424
1983	Minnesota	AL	2	7	2	1	0	0	(0	0)	3	1	0	1	0	1	0	0	0	0	0	.00	0	.286	.375	.429
1984	Minnesota	AL	12	32	7	1	0	0	(0	0)	8	1	3	2	1	4	0	0	2	2	0	1.00	1	.219	.250	.250
1987	Kansas City	AL	44	105	25	8	2	4	(3	1)	49	10	21	7	2	13	0	0	3	1	1	.50	2	.238	.278	.467
1988	Kansas City	AL	82	202	44	8	1	1	(0	1)	57	26	19	6	1	31	0	2	4	9	3	.75	2	.218	.236	.282
1989	Kansas City	AL	134	475	139	33	7	9	(4	5)	213	64	59	37	9	44	0	3	4	27	8	.77	8	.293	.341	.448
1990	Kansas City	AL	142	496	139	29	7	5	(2	3)	197	61	51	42	2	51	1	2	4	12	14	.46	7	.280	.335	.397
1991	Kansas City	AL	135	375	113	22	3	2	(2	0)	147	47	47	20	1	35	1	3	6	5	3	.63	10	.301	.333	.392
1992	Kansas City	AL	113	353	95	13	3	2	(1	1)	120	31	28	24	4	36	0	0	3	11	6	.65	6	.269	.313	.340
9 ML YEARS			698	2144	594	121	23	25	(13	12)	836	251	237	150	20	228	3	10	26	67	35	.66	37	.277	.322	.390

Cal Eldred

Pitches: Right Bats: Right Pos: SP Ht: 6' 4" Wt: 215 Born: 11/24/67 Age: 25

		HOW MUCH HE PITCHED							WHAT HE GAVE UP									THE RESULTS					
Year Team	Lg	G	GS	CG	GF	IP	BFP	H	R	ER	HR	SH	SF	HB	TBB	IBB	SO	WP	Bk	W	L	Pct.	ShO	Sv	ERA
1989 Beloit	A	5	5	0	0	31.1	127	23	10	8	0	1	0	1	11	1	32	2	2	2	1	.667	0	0	2.30
1990 Stockton	A	7	7	3	0	50	197	31	12	9	2	0	0	3	19	0	75	2	1	4	2	.667	1	0	1.62
El Paso	AA	19	19	0	0	110.1	485	126	61	55	9	3	3	2	47	0	93	4	1	5	4	.556	0	0	4.49
1991 Denver	AAA	29	29	3	0	185	784	161	82	77	13	4	8	12	84	2	168	8	2	13	9	.591	1	0	3.75
1992 Denver	AAA	19	19	4	0	141	570	122	49	47	9	3	6	4	42	0	99	3	0	10	6	.625	1	0	3.00
1991 Milwaukee	AL	3	3	0	0	16	73	20	9	8	2	0	0	0	6	0	10	0	0	2	0	1.000	0	0	4.50
1992 Milwaukee	AL	14	14	2	0	100.1	394	76	21	20	4	1	0	2	23	0	62	3	0	11	2	.846	1	0	1.79
2 ML YEARS		17	17	2	0	116.1	467	96	30	28	6	1	0	2	29	0	72	3	0	13	2	.867	1	0	2.17

Kevin Elster

Bats: Right Throws: Right Pos: SS Ht: 6' 2" Wt: 200 Born: 08/03/64 Age: 28

		BATTING																	BASERUNNING				PERCENTAGES		
Year Team	Lg	G	AB	H	2B	3B	HR	(Hm	Rd)	TB	R	RBI	TBB	IBB	SO	HBP	SH	SF	SB	CS	SB%	GDP	Avg	OBP	SLG
1986 New York	NL	19	30	5	1	0	0	(0	0)	6	3	0	3	1	8	0	0	0	0	0	.00	0	.167	.242	.200
1987 New York	NL	5	10	4	2	0	0	(0	0)	6	1	1	0	0	1	0	0	0	0	0	.00	1	.400	.400	.600
1988 New York	NL	149	406	87	11	1	9	(6	3)	127	41	37	35	12	47	3	6	0	2	0	1.00	5	.214	.282	.313
1989 New York	NL	151	458	106	25	2	10	(5	5)	165	52	55	34	11	77	2	6	8	4	3	.57	13	.231	.283	.360
1990 New York	NL	92	314	65	20	1	9	(2	7)	114	36	45	30	2	54	1	1	6	2	0	1.00	4	.207	.274	.363
1991 New York	NL	115	348	84	16	2	6	(3	3)	122	33	36	40	6	53	1	1	4	2	3	.40	4	.241	.318	.351
1992 New York	NL	6	18	4	0	0	0	(0	0)	4	0	0	0	0	2	0	0	0	0	0	.00	1	.222	.222	.222
7 ML YEARS		537	1584	355	75	6	34	(16	18)	544	166	174	142	32	242	7	14	18	10	6	.63	28	.224	.288	.343

Alan Embree

Pitches: Left Bats: Left Pos: SP Ht: 6' 3" Wt: 185 Born: 01/23/70 Age: 23

		HOW MUCH HE PITCHED							WHAT HE GAVE UP									THE RESULTS					
Year Team	Lg	G	GS	CG	GF	IP	BFP	H	R	ER	HR	SH	SF	HB	TBB	IBB	SO	WP	Bk	W	L	Pct.	ShO	Sv	ERA
1990 Burlington	R	15	15	0	0	81.2	351	87	36	24	3	1	3	0	30	0	58	5	4	4	4	.500	0	0	2.64
1991 Columbus	A	27	26	3	0	155.1	651	125	80	62	4	5	3	4	77	1	137	7	0	10	8	.556	1	0	3.59
1992 Kinston	A	15	15	1	0	101	418	89	48	37	10	3	1	2	32	0	115	6	3	10	5	.667	0	0	3.30
Canton-Akrn	AA	12	12	0	0	79	317	61	24	20	2	3	1	2	28	1	56	2	1	7	2	.778	0	0	2.28
1992 Cleveland	AL	4	4	0	0	18	81	19	14	14	3	0	2	1	8	0	12	1	1	0	2	.000	0	0	7.00

Scott Erickson

Pitches: Right Bats: Right Pos: SP Ht: 6' 4" Wt: 224 Born: 02/02/68 Age: 25

		HOW MUCH HE PITCHED							WHAT HE GAVE UP									THE RESULTS					
Year Team	Lg	G	GS	CG	GF	IP	BFP	H	R	ER	HR	SH	SF	HB	TBB	IBB	SO	WP	Bk	W	L	Pct.	ShO	Sv	ERA
1990 Minnesota	AL	19	17	1	1	113	485	108	49	36	9	5	2	5	51	4	53	3	0	8	4	.667	0	0	2.87
1991 Minnesota	AL	32	32	5	0	204	851	189	80	72	13	5	7	6	71	3	108	4	0	20	8	.714	3	0	3.18
1992 Minnesota	AL	32	32	5	0	212	888	197	86	80	18	9	7	8	83	3	101	6	1	13	12	.520	3	0	3.40
3 ML YEARS		83	81	11	1	529	2224	494	215	188	40	19	16	19	205	10	262	13	1	41	24	.631	6	0	3.20

Cecil Espy

Bats: Both Throws: Right Pos: RF/LF/CF Ht: 6' 3" Wt: 195 Born: 01/20/63 Age: 30

		BATTING																	BASERUNNING				PERCENTAGES		
Year Team	Lg	G	AB	H	2B	3B	HR	(Hm	Rd)	TB	R	RBI	TBB	IBB	SO	HBP	SH	SF	SB	CS	SB%	GDP	Avg	OBP	SLG
1983 Los Angeles	NL	20	11	3	1	0	0	(0	0)	4	4	1	1	0	2	0	0	0	0	0	.00	0	.273	.333	.364
1987 Texas	AL	14	8	0	0	0	0	(0	0)	0	1	0	1	0	3	0	0	0	2	0	1.00	1	.000	.111	.000
1988 Texas	AL	123	347	86	17	6	2	(2	0)	121	46	39	20	1	83	1	5	3	33	10	.77	2	.248	.288	.349
1989 Texas	AL	142	475	122	12	7	3	(2	1)	157	65	31	38	2	99	2	10	2	45	20	.69	2	.257	.313	.331
1990 Texas	AL	52	71	9	0	0	0	(0	0)	9	10	1	10	0	20	0	1	0	11	5	.69	1	.127	.235	.127
1991 Pittsburgh	NL	43	82	20	4	0	1	(1	0)	27	7	11	5	0	17	0	3	2	4	0	1.00	0	.244	.281	.329
1992 Pittsburgh	NL	112	194	50	7	3	1	(0	1)	66	21	20	15	2	40	0	1	1	6	3	.67	3	.258	.310	.340
7 ML YEARS		506	1188	290	41	16	7	(5	2)	384	154	103	90	5	264	3	20	8	101	38	.73	9	.244	.297	.323

Paul Faries

Bats: Right Throws: Right Pos: 2B Ht: 5'10" Wt: 170 Born: 02/20/65 Age: 28

		BATTING																	BASERUNNING				PERCENTAGES		
Year Team	Lg	G	AB	H	2B	3B	HR	(Hm	Rd)	TB	R	RBI	TBB	IBB	SO	HBP	SH	SF	SB	CS	SB%	GDP	Avg	OBP	SLG
1990 San Diego	NL	14	37	7	1	0	0	(0	0)	8	4	2	4	0	7	1	2	1	0	1	.00	0	.189	.279	.216
1991 San Diego	NL	57	130	23	3	1	0	(0	0)	28	13	7	14	0	21	1	4	0	3	1	.75	5	.177	.262	.215
1992 San Diego	NL	10	11	5	1	0	0	(0	0)	6	3	1	1	0	2	0	0	0	0	0	.00	0	.455	.500	.545
3 ML YEARS		81	178	35	5	1	0	(0	0)	42	20	10	19	0	30	2	6	1	3	2	.60	5	.197	.280	.236

Monty Fariss

Bats: Right **Throws:** Right **Pos:** LF/2B/RF   **Ht:** 6' 4" **Wt:** 205 **Born:** 10/13/67 **Age:** 25

Year	Team	Lg	G	AB	H	2B	3B	HR	(Hm	Rd)	TB	R	RBI	TBB	IBB	SO	HBP	SH	SF	SB	CS	SB%	GDP	Avg	OBP	SLG
1988	Butte	R	17	53	21	1	0	4	--	--	34	16	22	20	2	7	2	0	2	2	0	1.00	1	.396	.558	.642
	Tulsa	AA	49	165	37	6	6	3	--	--	64	21	31	22	0	39	0	1	1	2	0	1.00	2	.224	.314	.388
1989	Tulsa	AA	132	497	135	27	2	5	--	--	181	72	52	64	0	112	0	8	6	12	6	.67	13	.272	.351	.364
1990	Tulsa	AA	71	244	73	15	6	7	--	--	121	45	34	36	0	60	1	1	0	8	5	.62	9	.299	.391	.496
	Okla City	AAA	62	225	68	12	3	4	--	--	98	30	31	34	0	48	0	0	2	1	1	.50	7	.302	.391	.436
1991	Okla City	AAA	137	494	134	31	9	13	--	--	222	84	73	91	1	143	0	3	2	4	7	.36	11	.271	.383	.449
1992	Okla City	AAA	49	187	56	13	3	9	--	--	102	28	38	31	1	42	0	0	1	5	4	.56	5	.299	.397	.545
1991	Texas	AL	19	31	8	1	0	1	(1	0)	12	6	6	7	0	11	0	0	0	0	0	.00	1	.258	.395	.387
1992	Texas	AL	67	166	36	7	1	3	(0	3)	54	13	21	17	0	51	2	2	0	0	2	.00	3	.217	.297	.325
	2 ML YEARS		86	197	44	8	1	4	(1	3)	66	19	27	24	0	62	2	2	0	0	2	.00	3	.223	.314	.335

Steve Farr

Pitches: Right **Bats:** Right **Pos:** RP   **Ht:** 5'11" **Wt:** 206 **Born:** 12/12/56 **Age:** 36

Year	Team	Lg	G	GS	CG	GF	IP	BFP	H	R	ER	HR	SH	SF	HB	TBB	IBB	SO	WP	Bk	W	L	Pct.	ShO	Sv	ERA
1984	Cleveland	AL	31	16	0	4	116	488	106	61	59	14	2	3	5	46	3	83	2	2	3	11	.214	0	1	4.58
1985	Kansas City	AL	16	3	0	5	37.2	164	34	15	13	2	1	2	2	20	4	36	3	0	2	1	.667	0	1	3.11
1986	Kansas City	AL	56	0	0	33	109.1	443	90	39	38	10	3	2	4	39	8	83	4	1	8	4	.667	0	8	3.13
1987	Kansas City	AL	47	0	0	19	91	408	97	47	42	9	0	3	2	44	4	88	2	0	4	3	.571	0	1	4.15
1988	Kansas City	AL	62	1	0	49	82.2	344	74	25	23	5	1	3	2	30	6	72	4	2	5	4	.556	0	20	2.50
1989	Kansas City	AL	51	2	0	40	63.1	279	75	35	29	5	0	3	1	22	5	56	2	0	2	5	.286	0	18	4.12
1990	Kansas City	AL	57	6	1	20	127	515	99	32	28	6	10	1	5	48	9	94	2	0	13	7	.650	1	1	1.98
1991	New York	AL	60	0	0	48	70	285	57	19	17	4	0	0	5	20	3	60	2	0	5	5	.500	0	23	2.19
1992	New York	AL	50	0	0	42	52	207	34	10	9	2	1	2	2	19	0	37	0	0	2	2	.500	0	30	1.56
	9 ML YEARS		430	28	1	260	749	3133	666	283	258	57	18	19	28	288	42	609	21	5	44	42	.512	1	103	3.10

Jeff Fassero

Pitches: Left **Bats:** Left **Pos:** RP   **Ht:** 6' 1" **Wt:** 195 **Born:** 01/05/63 **Age:** 30

Year	Team	Lg	G	GS	CG	GF	IP	BFP	H	R	ER	HR	SH	SF	HB	TBB	IBB	SO	WP	Bk	W	L	Pct.	ShO	Sv	ERA
1984	Johnson Cty	R	13	11	2	2	66.2	292	65	42	34	2	0	4	0	39	0	59	1	1	4	7	.364	0	1	4.59
1985	Springfield	A	29	15	1	2	119	533	125	78	53	11	4	3	3	45	3	65	4	3	4	8	.333	0	1	4.01
1986	St. Pete	A	26	26	6	0	176	720	156	63	48	5	7	3	0	56	4	112	5	3	13	7	.650	1	0	2.45
1987	Arkansas	AA	28	27	2	0	151.1	674	168	90	69	16	10	2	1	67	7	118	7	1	10	7	.588	0	0	4.10
1988	Arkansas	AA	70	1	0	36	78	375	97	48	31	1	7	2	3	41	13	72	5	2	5	5	.500	0	17	3.58
1989	Arkansas	AA	6	6	2	0	44	174	32	11	8	1	1	0	1	12	0	38	1	1	4	1	.800	1	0	1.64
	Louisville	AAA	22	19	0	0	112	511	136	79	65	13	8	3	2	47	1	73	8	4	3	10	.231	0	0	5.22
1990	Canton-Akrn	AA	61	0	0	30	64.1	281	66	24	20	5	5	0	1	24	6	61	2	0	5	4	.556	0	6	2.80
1991	Indianapols	AAA	18	0	0	11	18.1	71	11	3	3	1	0	0	1	7	3	12	1	0	3	0	1.000	0	4	1.47
1991	Montreal	NL	51	0	0	30	55.1	223	39	17	15	1	6	0	1	17	1	42	4	0	2	5	.286	0	8	2.44
1992	Montreal	NL	70	0	0	22	85.2	368	81	35	27	1	5	2	2	34	6	63	7	1	8	7	.533	0	1	2.84
	2 ML YEARS		121	0	0	52	141	591	120	52	42	2	11	2	3	51	7	105	11	1	10	12	.455	0	9	2.68

Mike Felder

Bats: Both **Throws:** Right **Pos:** CF/LF/RF   **Ht:** 5' 8" **Wt:** 160 **Born:** 11/18/62 **Age:** 30

Year	Team	Lg	G	AB	H	2B	3B	HR	(Hm	Rd)	TB	R	RBI	TBB	IBB	SO	HBP	SH	SF	SB	CS	SB%	GDP	Avg	OBP	SLG
1985	Milwaukee	AL	15	56	11	1	0	0	(0	0)	12	8	0	5	0	6	0	1	0	4	1	.80	2	.196	.262	.214
1986	Milwaukee	AL	44	155	37	2	4	1	(1	0)	50	24	13	13	1	16	0	1	5	16	2	.89	2	.239	.289	.323
1987	Milwaukee	AL	108	289	77	5	7	2	(1	1)	102	48	31	28	0	23	0	9	3	34	8	.81	3	.266	.329	.353
1988	Milwaukee	AL	50	81	14	1	0	0	(0	0)	15	14	5	0	0	11	1	3	0	8	2	.80	1	.173	.183	.185
1989	Milwaukee	AL	117	315	76	11	3	3	(1	2)	102	50	23	23	2	38	0	7	0	26	5	.84	4	.241	.293	.324
1990	Milwaukee	AL	121	237	65	7	2	3	(1	2)	85	38	27	22	0	17	0	8	5	20	9	.69	0	.274	.340	.359
1991	San Francisco	NL	132	348	92	10	6	0	(0	0)	114	51	18	30	2	31	1	4	0	21	6	.78	1	.264	.325	.328
1992	San Francisco	NL	145	322	92	13	3	3	(1	3)	123	44	23	21	1	29	2	3	3	14	4	.78	3	.286	.330	.382
	8 ML YEARS		732	1803	464	50	25	13	(5	8)	603	277	140	142	6	171	4	36	15	143	37	.79	16	.257	.311	.334

Junior Felix

Bats: Both **Throws:** Right **Pos:** CF   **Ht:** 5'11" **Wt:** 165 **Born:** 10/03/67 **Age:** 25

Year	Team	Lg	G	AB	H	2B	3B	HR	(Hm	Rd)	TB	R	RBI	TBB	IBB	SO	HBP	SH	SF	SB	CS	SB%	GDP	Avg	OBP	SLG
1989	Toronto	AL	110	415	107	14	8	9	(4	5)	164	62	46	33	2	101	3	0	3	18	12	.60	5	.258	.315	.395
1990	Toronto	AL	127	463	122	23	7	15	(7	8)	204	73	65	45	0	99	2	2	5	13	8	.62	4	.263	.328	.441

Year	Team	Lg	G	AB	H	2B	3B	HR	(Hm	Rd)	TB	R	RBI	TBB	IBB	SO	HBP	SH	SF	SB	CS	SB%	GDP	Avg	OBP	SLG
1991	California	AL	66	230	65	10	2	2	(2	0)	85	32	26	11	0	55	3	0	2	7	5	.58	5	.283	.321	.370
1992	California	AL	139	509	125	22	5	9	(5	4)	184	63	72	33	5	128	2	5	9	8	8	.50	9	.246	.289	.361
	4 ML YEARS		442	1617	419	69	22	35	(18	17)	637	230	209	122	7	383	10	7	19	46	33	.58	23	.259	.312	.394

Felix Fermin

Bats: Right **Throws:** Right **Pos:** SS/3B **Ht:** 5'11" **Wt:** 170 **Born:** 10/09/63 **Age:** 29

									BATTING												BASERUNNING			PERCENTAGES		
Year	Team	Lg	G	AB	H	2B	3B	HR	(Hm	Rd)	TB	R	RBI	TBB	IBB	SO	HBP	SH	SF	SB	CS	SB%	GDP	Avg	OBP	SLG
1987	Pittsburgh	NL	23	68	17	0	0	0	(0	0)	17	6	4	4	1	9	1	2	0	0	0	.00	3	.250	.301	.250
1988	Pittsburgh	NL	43	87	24	0	2	0	(0	0)	28	9	2	8	1	10	3	1	1	3	1	.75	3	.276	.354	.322
1989	Cleveland	AL	156	484	115	9	1	0	(0	0)	126	50	21	41	0	27	4	32	1	6	4	.60	15	.238	.302	.260
1990	Cleveland	AL	148	414	106	13	2	1	(1	0)	126	47	40	26	0	22	0	13	5	3	3	.50	13	.256	.297	.304
1991	Cleveland	AL	129	424	111	13	2	0	(0	0)	128	30	31	26	0	27	3	13	3	5	4	.56	17	.262	.307	.302
1992	Cleveland	AL	79	215	58	7	2	0	(0	0)	69	27	13	18	1	10	1	9	2	0	0	.00	7	.270	.326	.321
	6 ML YEARS		578	1692	431	42	9	1	(1	0)	494	169	111	123	3	105	12	70	12	17	12	.59	58	.255	.308	.292

Alex Fernandez

Pitches: Right **Bats:** Right **Pos:** SP **Ht:** 6'1" **Wt:** 205 **Born:** 08/13/69 **Age:** 23

					HOW MUCH HE PITCHED					WHAT HE GAVE UP								THE RESULTS				
Year	Team	Lg	G	GS	CG	GF	IP	BFP	H	R	ER	HR	SH	SF	HB	TBB	IBB	SO	WP	Bk	W	L	Pct.	ShO	Sv	ERA
1990	Chicago	AL	13	13	3	0	87.2	378	89	40	37	6	5	0	3	34	0	61	1	0	5	5	.500	0	0	3.80
1991	Chicago	AL	34	32	2	1	191.2	827	186	100	96	16	7	11	2	88	2	145	4	1	9	13	.409	0	0	4.51
1992	Chicago	AL	29	29	4	0	187.2	804	199	100	89	21	6	4	8	50	3	95	3	0	8	11	.421	2	0	4.27
	3 ML YEARS		76	74	9	1	467	2009	474	240	222	43	18	15	13	172	5	301	8	1	22	29	.431	2	0	4.28

Sid Fernandez

Pitches: Left **Bats:** Left **Pos:** SP **Ht:** 6'1" **Wt:** 215 **Born:** 10/12/62 **Age:** 30

					HOW MUCH HE PITCHED					WHAT HE GAVE UP								THE RESULTS				
Year	Team	Lg	G	GS	CG	GF	IP	BFP	H	R	ER	HR	SH	SF	HB	TBB	IBB	SO	WP	Bk	W	L	Pct.	ShO	Sv	ERA
1983	Los Angeles	NL	2	1	0	0	6	33	7	4	4	0	0	0	1	7	0	9	0	0	0	1	.000	0	0	6.00
1984	New York	NL	15	15	0	0	90	371	74	40	35	8	5	5	0	34	3	62	1	4	6	6	.500	0	0	3.50
1985	New York	NL	26	26	3	0	170.1	685	108	56	53	14	4	3	2	80	3	180	3	2	9	9	.500	0	0	2.80
1986	New York	NL	32	31	2	1	204.1	855	161	82	80	13	9	7	2	91	1	200	6	0	16	6	.727	1	1	3.52
1987	New York	NL	28	27	3	0	156	665	130	75	66	16	3	6	8	67	8	134	2	0	12	8	.600	1	0	3.81
1988	New York	NL	31	31	1	0	187	751	127	69	63	15	2	7	6	70	1	189	4	9	12	10	.545	1	0	3.03
1989	New York	NL	35	32	6	0	219.1	883	157	73	69	21	4	4	6	75	3	198	1	3	14	5	.737	2	0	2.83
1990	New York	NL	30	30	2	0	179.1	735	130	79	69	18	7	6	5	67	4	181	1	0	9	14	.391	1	0	3.46
1991	New York	NL	8	8	0	0	44	177	36	18	14	4	5	1	0	9	0	31	0	0	1	3	.250	0	0	2.86
1992	New York	NL	32	32	5	0	214.2	865	162	67	65	12	12	11	4	67	4	193	0	0	14	11	.560	2	0	2.73
	10 ML YEARS		239	233	22	1	1471	6020	1092	563	518	121	51	50	34	567	27	1377	18	18	93	73	.560	8	1	3.17

Tony Fernandez

Bats: Both **Throws:** Right **Pos:** SS **Ht:** 6'2" **Wt:** 175 **Born:** 06/30/62 **Age:** 31

									BATTING												BASERUNNING			PERCENTAGES		
Year	Team	Lg	G	AB	H	2B	3B	HR	(Hm	Rd)	TB	R	RBI	TBB	IBB	SO	HBP	SH	SF	SB	CS	SB%	GDP	Avg	OBP	SLG
1983	Toronto	AL	15	34	9	1	1	0	(0	0)	12	5	2	2	0	2	1	1	0	0	1	.00	1	.265	.324	.353
1984	Toronto	AL	88	233	63	5	3	3	(1	2)	83	29	19	17	0	15	0	2	2	5	7	.42	3	.270	.317	.356
1985	Toronto	AL	161	564	163	31	10	2	(1	1)	220	71	51	43	2	41	2	7	2	13	6	.68	12	.289	.340	.390
1986	Toronto	AL	163	687	213	33	9	10	(4	6)	294	91	65	27	0	52	4	5	4	25	12	.68	8	.310	.338	.428
1987	Toronto	AL	146	578	186	29	8	5	(1	4)	246	90	67	51	3	48	5	4	4	32	12	.73	14	.322	.379	.426
1988	Toronto	AL	154	648	186	41	4	5	(3	2)	250	76	70	45	3	65	4	3	4	15	5	.75	9	.287	.335	.386
1989	Toronto	AL	140	573	147	25	9	11	(2	9)	223	64	64	29	1	51	3	2	10	22	6	.79	9	.257	.291	.389
1990	Toronto	AL	161	635	175	27	17	4	(2	2)	248	84	66	71	4	70	7	2	6	26	13	.67	17	.276	.352	.391
1991	San Diego	NL	145	558	152	27	5	4	(3	1)	201	81	38	55	0	74	0	7	1	23	9	.72	12	.272	.337	.360
1992	San Diego	NL	155	622	171	32	4	4	(3	1)	223	84	37	56	4	62	4	9	3	20	20	.50	6	.275	.337	.359
	10 ML YEARS		1328	5132	1465	251	70	48	(18	30)	2000	675	479	396	17	480	30	42	36	181	91	.67	91	.285	.338	.390

Mike Fetters

Pitches: Right **Bats:** Right **Pos:** RP **Ht:** 6'4" **Wt:** 212 **Born:** 12/19/64 **Age:** 28

					HOW MUCH HE PITCHED					WHAT HE GAVE UP								THE RESULTS				
Year	Team	Lg	G	GS	CG	GF	IP	BFP	H	R	ER	HR	SH	SF	HB	TBB	IBB	SO	WP	Bk	W	L	Pct.	ShO	Sv	ERA
1989	California	AL	1	0	0	0	3.1	16	5	4	3	1	0	0	0	1	0	4	2	0	0	0	.000	0	0	8.10
1990	California	AL	26	2	0	10	67.2	291	77	33	31	9	1	0	2	20	0	35	3	0	1	1	.500	0	1	4.12
1991	California	AL	19	4	0	8	44.2	206	53	29	24	4	1	0	3	28	2	24	4	0	2	5	.286	0	0	4.84
1992	Milwaukee	AL	50	0	0	11	62.2	243	38	15	13	3	5	2	7	24	2	43	4	1	5	1	.833	0	2	1.87
	4 ML YEARS		96	6	0	29	178.1	756	173	81	71	17	7	2	12	73	4	106	13	1	8	7	.533	0	3	3.58

Cecil Fielder

Bats: Right **Throws:** Right **Pos:** 1B/DH | **Ht:** 6' 3" **Wt:** 250 **Born:** 09/21/63 **Age:** 29

Year Team	Lg	G	AB	H	2B	3B	HR	(Hm	Rd)	TB	R	RBI	TBB	IBB	SO	HBP	SH	SF	SB	CS	SB%	GDP	Avg	OBP	SLG
1985 Toronto	AL	30	74	23	4	0	4	(2	2)	39	6	16	6	0	16	0	0	1	0	0	.00	2	.311	.358	.527
1986 Toronto	AL	34	83	13	2	0	4	(0	4)	27	7	13	6	0	27	1	0	0	0	0	.00	3	.157	.222	.325
1987 Toronto	AL	82	175	47	7	1	14	(10	4)	98	30	32	20	2	48	1	0	1	0	0	.00	6	.269	.345	.560
1988 Toronto	AL	74	174	40	6	1	9	(6	3)	75	24	23	14	0	53	1	0	1	0	1	.00	6	.230	.289	.431
1990 Detroit	AL	159	573	159	25	1	51	(25	26)	339	104	132	90	11	182	5	0	5	0	1	.00	15	.277	.377	.592
1991 Detroit	AL	162	624	163	25	0	44	(27	17)	320	102	133	78	12	151	6	0	4	0	0	.00	17	.261	.347	.513
1992 Detroit	AL	155	594	145	22	0	35	(18	17)	272	80	124	73	8	151	2	0	7	0	0	.00	14	.244	.325	.458
7 ML YEARS		696	2297	590	91	3	161	(88	73)	1170	353	473	287	33	628	16	0	19	0	3	.00	63	.257	.341	.509

Bien Figueroa

Bats: Right **Throws:** Right **Pos:** SS | **Ht:** 5'10" **Wt:** 167 **Born:** 02/07/64 **Age:** 29

Year Team	Lg	G	AB	H	2B	3B	HR	(Hm	Rd)	TB	R	RBI	TBB	IBB	SO	HBP	SH	SF	SB	CS	SB%	GDP	Avg	OBP	SLG
1986 Erie	A	73	249	59	4	0	0	--	--	63	31	30	32	1	26	1	1	3	13	4	.76	9	.237	.323	.253
1987 Springfield	A	134	489	136	13	3	2	--	--	161	52	83	34	2	46	4	12	7	7	7	.50	16	.278	.326	.329
1988 Arkansas	AA	126	407	113	17	2	0	--	--	134	48	32	22	1	49	3	7	1	2	6	.25	16	.278	.319	.329
1989 Louisville	AAA	74	221	48	3	0	0	--	--	51	18	14	12	0	22	0	5	1	0	1	.00	7	.217	.256	.231
1990 Louisville	AAA	128	396	95	19	2	0	--	--	118	41	39	24	2	37	3	7	2	5	1	.83	15	.240	.287	.298
1991 Louisville	AAA	97	269	55	8	2	0	--	--	67	18	14	20	2	27	2	5	0	1	4	.20	10	.204	.265	.249
1992 Louisville	AAA	94	319	91	11	1	1	--	--	107	44	23	33	0	32	2	6	3	2	0	1.00	8	.285	.353	.335
1992 St. Louis	NL	12	11	2	1	0	0	(0	0)	3	1	4	1	0	2	0	0	0	0	0	.00	0	.182	.250	.273

Tom Filer

Pitches: Right **Bats:** Right **Pos:** RP | **Ht:** 6' 1" **Wt:** 198 **Born:** 12/01/56 **Age:** 36

		HOW MUCH HE PITCHED						WHAT HE GAVE UP										THE RESULTS					
Year Team	Lg	G	GS	CG	GF	IP	BFP	H	R	ER	HR	SH	SF	HB	TBB	IBB	SO	WP	Bk	W	L	Pct.	ShO	Sv	ERA
1982 Chicago	NL	8	8	0	0	40.2	187	50	25	25	5	3	0	0	18	2	15	2	0	1	2	.333	0	0	5.53
1985 Toronto	AL	11	9	0	0	48.2	192	38	21	21	6	2	1	0	18	0	24	0	1	7	0	1.000	0	0	3.88
1988 Milwaukee	AL	19	16	2	0	101.2	431	108	54	50	8	5	7	1	33	4	39	5	0	5	8	.385	1	0	4.43
1989 Milwaukee	AL	13	13	0	0	72.1	302	74	30	29	6	2	0	4	23	1	20	1	0	7	3	.700	0	0	3.61
1990 Milwaukee	AL	7	4	0	1	22	99	26	17	15	2	0	0	0	9	0	8	2	0	2	3	.400	0	0	6.14
1992 New York	NL	9	1	0	1	22	88	18	8	5	2	1	0	0	6	2	9	1	0	0	1	.000	0	0	2.05
6 ML YEARS		67	51	2	2	307.1	1299	314	155	145	29	13	8	5	107	9	115	11	1	22	17	.564	1	0	4.25

Chuck Finley

Pitches: Left **Bats:** Left **Pos:** SP | **Ht:** 6' 6" **Wt:** 214 **Born:** 11/26/62 **Age:** 30

		HOW MUCH HE PITCHED						WHAT HE GAVE UP										THE RESULTS					
Year Team	Lg	G	GS	CG	GF	IP	BFP	H	R	ER	HR	SH	SF	HB	TBB	IBB	SO	WP	Bk	W	L	Pct.	ShO	Sv	ERA
1986 California	AL	25	0	0	7	46.1	198	40	17	17	2	4	0	1	23	1	37	2	0	3	1	.750	0	0	3.30
1987 California	AL	35	3	0	17	90.2	405	102	54	47	7	2	2	3	43	3	63	4	3	2	7	.222	0	0	4.67
1988 California	AL	31	31	2	0	194.1	831	191	95	90	15	7	10	6	82	7	111	5	8	9	15	.375	0	0	4.17
1989 California	AL	29	29	9	0	199.2	827	171	64	57	13	7	3	2	82	0	156	4	2	16	9	.640	1	0	2.57
1990 California	AL	32	32	7	0	236	962	210	77	63	17	12	3	2	81	3	177	9	0	18	9	.667	2	0	2.40
1991 California	AL	34	34	4	0	227.1	955	205	102	96	23	4	3	6	101	1	171	6	3	18	9	.667	2	0	3.80
1992 California	AL	31	31	4	0	204.1	885	212	99	90	24	10	10	3	98	2	124	6	0	7	12	.368	2	0	3.96
7 ML YEARS		217	160	26	24	1198.2	5063	1131	508	460	101	46	31	25	510	17	839	36	16	73	62	.541	6	0	3.45

Steve Finley

Bats: Left **Throws:** Left **Pos:** CF | **Ht:** 6' 2" **Wt:** 180 **Born:** 03/12/65 **Age:** 28

Year Team	Lg	G	AB	H	2B	3B	HR	(Hm	Rd)	TB	R	RBI	TBB	IBB	SO	HBP	SH	SF	SB	CS	SB%	GDP	Avg	OBP	SLG
1989 Baltimore	AL	81	217	54	5	2	2	(0	2)	69	35	25	15	1	30	1	6	2	17	3	.85	3	.249	.298	.318
1990 Baltimore	AL	142	464	119	16	4	3	(1	2)	152	46	37	32	3	53	2	10	5	22	9	.71	8	.256	.304	.328
1991 Houston	NL	159	596	170	28	10	8	(0	8)	242	84	54	42	5	65	2	10	8	34	18	.65	8	.285	.331	.406
1992 Houston	NL	162	607	177	29	13	5	(5	0)	247	84	55	58	6	63	3	16	2	44	9	.83	10	.292	.355	.407
4 ML YEARS		544	1884	520	78	29	18	(6	12)	710	249	171	147	15	211	8	42	15	117	39	.75	29	.276	.329	.377

Steve Fireovid

Pitches: Right Bats: Both Pos: RP Ht: 6' 2" Wt: 210 Born: 06/06/58 Age: 35

			HOW MUCH HE PITCHED						WHAT HE GAVE UP											THE RESULTS					
Year Team	Lg	G	GS	CG	GF	IP	BFP	H	R	ER	HR	SH	SF	HB	TBB	IBB	SO	WP	Bk	W	L	Pct.	ShO	Sv	ERA
1981 San Diego	NL	5	4	0	0	26	110	30	8	8	2	0	1	0	7	0	11	0	1	0	1	.000	0	0	2.77
1983 San Diego	NL	3	0	0	1	5	20	4	2	1	0	1	0	0	2	0	1	1	0	0	0	.000	0	0	1.80
1984 Philadelphia	NL	6	0	0	5	5.2	20	4	1	1	0	0	0	0	0	0	3	0	0	0	0	.000	0	0	1.59
1985 Chicago	AL	4	0	0	2	7	38	17	4	4	0	0	0	0	2	0	2	0	0	0	0	.000	0	0	5.14
1986 Seattle	AL	10	1	0	2	21	89	28	11	10	1	0	0	1	4	0	10	1	0	2	0	1.000	0	0	4.29
1992 Texas	AL	3	0	0	0	6.2	31	10	5	3	0	0	0	0	4	2	0	0	0	1	0	1.000	0	0	4.05
6 ML YEARS		31	5	0	10	71.1	308	93	31	27	3	1	1	1	19	2	27	2	1	3	1	.750	0	0	3.41

Brian Fisher

Pitches: Right Bats: Right Pos: SP/RP Ht: 6' 4" Wt: 210 Born: 03/18/62 Age: 31

			HOW MUCH HE PITCHED						WHAT HE GAVE UP											THE RESULTS					
Year Team	Lg	G	GS	CG	GF	IP	BFP	H	R	ER	HR	SH	SF	HB	TBB	IBB	SO	WP	Bk	W	L	Pct.	ShO	Sv	ERA
1985 New York	AL	55	0	0	23	98.1	391	77	32	26	4	3	2	0	29	3	85	3	0	4	4	.500	0	14	2.38
1986 New York	AL	62	0	0	26	96.2	424	105	61	53	14	5	2	1	72	2	67	2	0	9	5	.643	0	6	4.93
1987 Pittsburgh	NL	37	26	6	1	185.1	792	185	99	93	27	6	5	4	72	7	117	3	3	11	9	.550	3	0	4.52
1988 Pittsburgh	NL	33	22	1	3	146.1	645	157	78	75	13	10	6	5	57	4	66	0	4	8	10	.444	1	1	4.61
1989 Pittsburgh	NL	9	3	0	3	17	88	25	17	15	2	1	1	0	10	3	8	1	0	0	3	.000	0	1	7.94
1990 Houston	NL	4	0	0	3	5	24	9	5	4	1	0	2	0	0	0	1	0	0	0	0	.000	0	0	7.20
1992 Seattle	AL	22	14	0	2	91.1	394	80	49	46	9	1	3	1	47	2	26	3	1	4	3	.571	0	1	4.53
7 ML YEARS		222	65	7	61	640	2758	638	341	312	70	26	21	11	252	21	370	12	8	36	34	.514	4	23	4.39

Carlton Fisk

Bats: Right Throws: Right Pos: C Ht: 6' 2" Wt: 223 Born: 12/26/47 Age: 45

								BATTING												BASERUNNING				PERCENTAGES		
Year Team	Lg	G	AB	H	2B	3B	HR	(Hm	Rd)	TB	R	RBI	TBB	IBB	SO	HBP	SH	SF	SB	CS	SB%	GDP	Avg	OBP	SLG
1969 Boston	AL	2	5	0	0	0	0	(0	0)	0	0	0	0	0	2	0	0	0	0	0	.00	0	.000	.000	.000
1971 Boston	AL	14	48	15	2	1	2	(0	2)	25	7	6	1	0	10	0	0	0	0	0	.00	1	.313	.327	.521
1972 Boston	AL	131	457	134	28	9	22	(13	9)	246	74	61	52	6	83	4	1	0	5	2	.71	11	.293	.370	.538
1973 Boston	AL	135	508	125	21	0	26	(16	10)	224	65	71	37	2	99	10	1	2	7	2	.78	11	.246	.309	.441
1974 Boston	AL	52	187	56	12	1	11	(5	6)	103	36	26	24	2	23	2	2	1	5	1	.83	5	.299	.383	.551
1975 Boston	AL	79	263	87	14	4	10	(6	4)	139	47	52	27	4	32	2	0	2	4	3	.57	7	.331	.395	.529
1976 Boston	AL	134	487	124	17	5	17	(10	7)	202	76	58	56	3	71	6	3	5	12	5	.71	11	.255	.336	.415
1977 Boston	AL	152	536	169	26	3	26	(15	11)	279	106	102	75	3	85	9	2	10	7	6	.54	9	.315	.402	.521
1978 Boston	AL	157	571	162	39	5	20	(8	12)	271	94	88	71	6	83	7	3	6	7	2	.78	10	.284	.366	.475
1979 Boston	AL	91	320	87	23	2	10	(5	5)	144	49	42	10	0	38	6	1	3	3	0	1.00	9	.272	.304	.450
1980 Boston	AL	131	478	138	25	3	18	(12	6)	223	73	62	36	6	62	13	0	3	11	5	.69	12	.289	.353	.467
1981 Chicago	AL	96	338	89	12	0	7	(4	3)	122	44	45	38	3	37	12	1	5	3	2	.60	9	.263	.354	.361
1982 Chicago	AL	135	476	127	17	3	14	(7	7)	192	66	65	46	7	60	6	4	4	17	2	.89	12	.267	.336	.403
1983 Chicago	AL	138	488	141	26	4	26	(17	9)	253	85	86	46	3	88	6	2	3	9	6	.60	8	.289	.355	.518
1984 Chicago	AL	102	359	83	20	1	21	(11	10)	168	54	43	26	4	60	5	1	4	6	0	1.00	7	.231	.289	.468
1985 Chicago	AL	153	543	129	23	1	37	(20	17)	265	85	107	52	12	81	17	2	6	17	9	.65	9	.238	.320	.488
1986 Chicago	AL	125	457	101	11	0	14	(5	9)	154	42	63	22	2	92	6	0	4	2	4	.33	10	.221	.263	.337
1987 Chicago	AL	135	454	116	22	1	23	(5	18)	209	68	71	39	8	72	8	1	6	1	4	.20	9	.256	.321	.460
1988 Chicago	AL	76	253	70	8	1	19	(9	10)	137	37	50	37	9	40	5	1	2	0	0	.00	6	.277	.377	.542
1989 Chicago	AL	103	375	110	25	2	13	(4	9)	178	47	68	36	8	60	3	0	5	1	1	1.00	15	.293	.356	.475
1990 Chicago	AL	137	452	129	21	0	18	(5	13)	204	65	65	61	8	73	7	0	1	7	2	.78	12	.285	.378	.451
1991 Chicago	AL	134	460	111	25	0	18	(9	9)	190	42	74	32	4	86	7	0	2	1	2	.33	19	.241	.299	.413
1992 Chicago	AL	62	188	43	4	1	3	(2	1)	58	12	21	23	5	38	1	0	2	3	0	1.00	2	.229	.313	.309
23 ML YEARS		2474	8703	2346	421	47	375	(188	187)	3986	1274	1326	847	105	1375	142	25	78	128	57	.69	204	.270	.341	.458

Mike Fitzgerald

Bats: Right Throws: Right Pos: C Ht: 5'11" Wt: 190 Born: 07/13/60 Age: 32

								BATTING												BASERUNNING				PERCENTAGES		
Year Team	Lg	G	AB	H	2B	3B	HR	(Hm	Rd)	TB	R	RBI	TBB	IBB	SO	HBP	SH	SF	SB	CS	SB%	GDP	Avg	OBP	SLG
1983 New York	NL	8	20	2	0	0	1	(0	1)	5	1	2	3	1	6	0	0	0	0	0	.00	0	.100	.217	.250
1984 New York	NL	112	360	87	15	1	2	(2	0)	110	20	33	24	7	71	1	5	4	1	0	1.00	17	.242	.288	.306
1985 Montreal	NL	108	295	61	7	1	5	(3	2)	85	25	34	38	12	55	2	1	5	5	3	.63	8	.207	.297	.288
1986 Montreal	NL	73	209	59	13	1	6	(1	5)	92	20	37	27	6	34	1	4	2	3	2	.60	9	.282	.364	.440
1987 Montreal	NL	107	287	69	11	0	3	(1	2)	89	32	36	42	7	54	1	3	1	3	4	.43	10	.240	.338	.310
1988 Montreal	NL	63	155	42	6	1	5	(3	2)	65	17	23	19	0	22	0	4	2	2	2	.50	4	.271	.347	.419
1989 Montreal	NL	100	290	69	18	2	7	(3	4)	112	33	42	35	3	61	2	2	2	3	4	.43	8	.238	.322	.386

Year	Team	Lg	G	AB	H	2B	3B	HR	(Hm	Rd)	TB	R	RBI	TBB	IBB	SO	HBP	SH	SF	SB	CS	SB%	GDP	Avg	OBP	SLG
1990	Montreal	NL	111	313	76	18	1	9	(2	7)	123	36	41	60	2	60	2	5	3	8	1	.89	5	.243	.365	.393
1991	Montreal	NL	71	198	40	5	2	4	(1	3)	61	17	28	22	4	35	0	1	3	4	2	.67	5	.202	.278	.308
1992	California	AL	95	189	40	2	0	6	(3	3)	60	19	17	22	0	34	0	3	0	2	2	.50	4	.212	.294	.317
10 ML YEARS			848	2316	545	95	9	48	(19	29)	802	220	293	292	42	432	9	28	22	31	20	.61	65	.235	.321	.346

John Flaherty

Bats: Right **Throws:** Right **Pos:** C   **Ht:** 6' 1" **Wt:** 195 **Born:** 10/21/67 **Age:** 25

								BATTING												BASERUNNING				PERCENTAGES		
Year	Team	Lg	G	AB	H	2B	3B	HR	(Hm	Rd)	TB	R	RBI	TBB	IBB	SO	HBP	SH	SF	SB	CS	SB%	GDP	Avg	OBP	SLG
1988	Elmira	A	46	162	38	3	0	3	--	--	50	17	16	12	0	23	2	3	1	2	1	.67	5	.235	.294	.309
1989	Winter Havn	A	95	334	87	14	2	4	--	--	117	31	28	20	1	44	3	2	2	1	0	1.00	19	.260	.306	.350
1990	Lynchburg	A	1	4	0	0	0	0	--	--	0	0	1	0	0	1	0	0	1	0	0	.00	0	.000	.000	.000
	Pawtucket	AAA	99	317	72	18	0	4	--	--	102	35	32	24	0	43	2	2	2	1	1	.50	11	.227	.284	.322
1991	Pawtucket	AAA	45	156	29	7	0	3	--	--	45	18	13	15	0	14	0	4	0	0	1	.00	1	.186	.257	.288
	New Britain	AA	67	225	65	9	0	3	--	--	83	27	18	31	1	22	1	0	2	0	2	.00	5	.289	.375	.369
1992	Pawtucket	AAA	31	104	26	3	0	0	--	--	29	11	7	5	0	8	1	1	0	0	0	.00	6	.250	.291	.279
1992	Boston	AL	35	66	13	2	0	0	(0	0)	15	3	2	3	0	7	0	1	1	0	0	.00	0	.197	.229	.227

Mike Flanagan

Pitches: Left **Bats:** Left **Pos:** RP   **Ht:** 6' 0" **Wt:** 199 **Born:** 12/16/51 **Age:** 41

			HOW MUCH HE PITCHED						WHAT HE GAVE UP										THE RESULTS					
Year	Team	Lg	G	GS	CG	GF	IP	BFP	H	R	ER	HR	SH	SF	HB	TBB	IBB	SO	WP	Bk	W	L	Pct.	ShO	Sv	ERA
1975	Baltimore	AL	2	1	0	0	10	42	9	4	3	0	0	0	0	6	1	7	0	0	0	1	.000	0	0	2.70
1976	Baltimore	AL	20	10	4	7	85	358	83	41	39	7	2	4	0	33	0	56	2	1	3	5	.375	0	0	4.13
1977	Baltimore	AL	36	33	15	2	235	974	235	100	95	17	10	7	2	70	5	149	5	0	15	10	.600	2	1	3.64
1978	Baltimore	AL	40	40	17	0	281	1160	271	128	126	22	10	5	3	87	2	167	8	1	19	15	.559	2	0	4.04
1979	Baltimore	AL	39	38	16	0	266	1085	245	107	91	23	9	4	3	70	1	190	6	0	23	9	.719	5	0	3.08
1980	Baltimore	AL	37	37	12	0	251	1065	278	121	115	27	10	12	2	71	3	128	12	1	16	13	.552	2	0	4.12
1981	Baltimore	AL	20	20	3	0	116	482	108	55	54	11	0	0	2	37	1	72	6	0	9	6	.600	2	0	4.19
1982	Baltimore	AL	36	35	11	1	236	991	233	110	104	24	5	6	4	76	5	103	9	2	15	11	.577	1	0	3.97
1983	Baltimore	AL	20	20	3	0	125.1	528	135	53	46	10	4	6	2	31	2	50	1	0	12	4	.750	1	0	3.30
1984	Baltimore	AL	34	34	10	0	226.2	947	213	103	89	24	8	6	1	81	5	115	8	0	13	13	.500	2	0	3.53
1985	Baltimore	AL	15	15	1	0	86	379	101	49	49	14	7	2	2	28	0	42	3	0	4	5	.444	0	0	5.13
1986	Baltimore	AL	29	28	2	0	172	747	179	95	81	15	10	6	1	66	4	96	8	1	7	11	.389	0	0	4.24
1987	2 ML Teams		23	23	4	0	144	619	148	72	65	12	6	1	0	51	4	93	3	0	6	8	.429	0	0	4.06
1988	Toronto	AL	34	34	2	0	211	916	220	106	98	23	14	4	6	80	1	99	3	4	13	13	.500	1	0	4.18
1989	Toronto	AL	30	30	1	0	171.2	726	186	82	75	10	8	8	5	47	0	47	4	0	8	10	.444	1	0	3.93
1990	Toronto	AL	5	5	0	0	20.1	94	28	14	12	3	1	0	0	8	0	5	0	0	2	2	.500	0	0	5.31
1991	Baltimore	AL	64	1	0	24	98.1	391	84	27	26	6	4	3	3	25	6	55	2	2	2	7	.222	0	3	2.38
1992	Baltimore	AL	42	0	0	15	34.2	180	50	34	31	3	2	2	5	23	1	17	4	0	0	0	.000	0	0	8.05
1987	Baltimore	AL	16	16	4	0	94.2	410	102	57	52	9	6	1	0	36	1	50	1	0	3	6	.333	0	0	4.94
	Toronto	AL	7	7	0	0	49.1	209	46	15	13	3	0	0	0	15	3	43	2	0	3	2	.600	0	0	2.37
18 ML YEARS			526	404	101	49	2770	11684	2806	1301	1199	251	110	76	41	890	41	1491	84	12	167	143	.539	19	4	3.90

Dave Fleming

Pitches: Left **Bats:** Left **Pos:** SP   **Ht:** 6' 3" **Wt:** 200 **Born:** 11/07/69 **Age:** 23

			HOW MUCH HE PITCHED						WHAT HE GAVE UP										THE RESULTS					
Year	Team	Lg	G	GS	CG	GF	IP	BFP	H	R	ER	HR	SH	SF	HB	TBB	IBB	SO	WP	Bk	W	L	Pct.	ShO	Sv	ERA
1990	San Berndno	A	12	12	4	0	79.2	328	64	29	23	0	1	1	1	30	1	77	1	5	7	3	.700	0	0	2.60
1991	Jacksonville	AA	21	20	6	0	140	567	129	50	42	7	5	2	2	25	2	109	6	0	10	6	.625	1	0	2.70
	Calgary	AAA	3	1	0	0	16	60	10	2	2	1	0	1	0	3	0	16	0	0	2	0	1.000	0	0	1.13
1991	Seattle	AL	9	3	0	3	17.2	73	19	13	13	3	0	0	3	3	0	11	1	0	1	0	1.000	0	0	6.62
1992	Seattle	AL	33	33	7	0	228.1	946	225	95	86	13	3	2	4	60	3	112	8	1	17	10	.630	4	0	3.39
2 ML YEARS			42	36	7	3	246	1019	244	108	99	16	3	2	7	63	3	123	9	1	18	10	.643	4	0	3.62

Darrin Fletcher

Bats: Left **Throws:** Right **Pos:** C   **Ht:** 6' 1" **Wt:** 199 **Born:** 10/03/66 **Age:** 26

								BATTING												BASERUNNING				PERCENTAGES		
Year	Team	Lg	G	AB	H	2B	3B	HR	(Hm	Rd)	TB	R	RBI	TBB	IBB	SO	HBP	SH	SF	SB	CS	SB%	GDP	Avg	OBP	SLG
1989	Los Angeles	NL	5	8	4	0	0	1	(1	0)	7	1	2	1	0	0	0	0	0	0	0	.00	0	.500	.556	.875
1990	2 ML Teams		11	23	3	1	0	0	(0	0)	4	3	1	1	0	6	0	0	0	0	0	.00	0	.130	.167	.174
1991	Philadelphia	NL	46	136	31	8	0	1	(1	0)	42	5	12	5	0	15	0	1	0	1	0	.00	2	.228	.255	.309
1992	Montreal	NL	83	222	54	10	2	2	(0	2)	74	13	26	14	3	28	2	2	4	0	2	.00	8	.243	.289	.333
1990	Los Angeles	NL	2	1	0	0	0	0	(0	0)	0	0	0	0	0	1	0	0	0	0	0	.00	0	.000	.000	.000
	Philadelphia	NL	9	22	3	1	0	0	(0	0)	4	3	1	1	0	5	0	0	0	0	0	.00	0	.136	.174	.182
4 ML YEARS			145	389	92	19	2	4	(2	2)	127	22	41	21	3	49	2	3	4	0	3	.00	10	.237	.276	.326

Scott Fletcher

Bats: Right   **Throws:** Right   **Pos:** 2B/SS   **Ht:** 5'11"   **Wt:** 173   **Born:** 07/30/58   **Age:** 34

					BATTING														BASERUNNING				PERCENTAGES		
Year Team	Lg	G	AB	H	2B	3B	HR	(Hm	Rd)	TB	R	RBI	TBB	IBB	SO	HBP	SH	SF	SB	CS	SB%	GDP	Avg	OBP	SLG
1981 Chicago	NL	19	46	10	4	0	0	(0	0)	14	6	1	2	0	4	0	0	0	0	0	.00	0	.217	.250	.304
1982 Chicago	NL	11	24	4	0	0	0	(0	0)	4	4	1	4	0	5	0	0	0	1	0	1.00	0	.167	.286	.167
1983 Chicago	AL	114	262	62	16	5	3	(1	2)	97	42	31	29	0	22	2	7	2	5	1	.83	8	.237	.315	.370
1984 Chicago	AL	149	456	114	13	3	3	(2	1)	142	46	35	46	2	46	8	9	2	10	4	.71	5	.250	.328	.311
1985 Chicago	AL	119	301	77	8	1	2	(0	2)	93	38	31	35	0	47	0	11	1	5	5	.50	9	.256	.332	.309
1986 Texas	AL	147	530	159	34	5	3	(2	1)	212	82	50	47	0	59	4	10	3	12	11	.52	10	.300	.360	.400
1987 Texas	AL	156	588	169	28	4	5	(4	1)	220	82	63	61	3	66	5	12	2	13	12	.52	14	.287	.358	.374
1988 Texas	AL	140	515	142	19	4	0	(0	0)	169	59	47	62	1	34	12	15	5	8	5	.62	13	.276	.364	.328
1989 2 ML Teams		142	546	138	25	2	1	(0	1)	170	77	43	64	1	60	3	11	5	2	1	.67	12	.253	.332	.311
1990 Chicago	AL	151	509	123	18	3	4	(1	3)	159	54	56	45	3	63	3	11	5	1	3	.25	10	.242	.304	.312
1991 Chicago	AL	90	248	51	10	1	1	(0	1)	66	14	28	17	0	26	3	6	3	0	2	.00	3	.206	.262	.266
1992 Milwaukee	AL	123	386	106	18	3	3	(2	1)	139	53	51	30	1	33	7	6	4	17	10	.63	4	.275	.335	.360
1989 Texas	AL	83	314	75	14	1	0	(0	0)	91	47	22	38	1	41	2	2	2	1	0	1.00	8	.239	.323	.290
Chicago	AL	59	232	63	11	1	1	(0	1)	79	30	21	26	0	19	1	9	3	1	1	.50	4	.272	.344	.341
12 ML YEARS		1361	4411	1155	193	31	25	(12	13)	1485	557	437	442	11	465	47	98	32	74	54	.58	88	.262	.333	.337

Tom Foley

Bats: Left   **Throws:** Right   **Pos:** SS/1B/2B   **Ht:** 6' 1"   **Wt:** 175   **Born:** 09/09/59   **Age:** 33

					BATTING														BASERUNNING				PERCENTAGES		
Year Team	Lg	G	AB	H	2B	3B	HR	(Hm	Rd)	TB	R	RBI	TBB	IBB	SO	HBP	SH	SF	SB	CS	SB%	GDP	Avg	OBP	SLG
1983 Cincinnati	NL	68	98	20	4	1	0	(0	0)	26	7	9	13	2	17	0	2	0	1	0	1.00	1	.204	.297	.265
1984 Cincinnati	NL	106	277	70	8	3	5	(3	2)	99	26	27	24	7	36	0	1	0	3	2	.60	2	.253	.310	.357
1985 2 ML Teams		89	250	60	13	1	3	(2	1)	84	24	23	19	8	34	0	0	0	2	3	.40	2	.240	.294	.336
1986 2 ML Teams		103	263	70	15	3	1	(1	0)	94	26	23	30	6	37	0	2	4	10	3	.77	4	.266	.337	.357
1987 Montreal	NL	106	280	82	18	3	5	(3	2)	121	35	28	11	0	40	1	1	0	6	10	.38	6	.293	.322	.432
1988 Montreal	NL	127	377	100	21	3	5	(3	2)	142	33	43	30	10	49	1	0	3	2	7	.22	11	.265	.319	.377
1989 Montreal	NL	122	375	86	19	2	7	(4	3)	130	34	39	45	4	53	3	4	4	2	3	.40	2	.229	.314	.347
1990 Montreal	NL	73	164	35	2	1	0	(0	0)	39	11	12	12	2	22	0	1	1	0	1	.00	4	.213	.266	.238
1991 Montreal	NL	86	168	35	11	1	0	(0	0)	48	12	15	14	4	30	1	1	1	2	0	1.00	2	.208	.269	.286
1992 Montreal	NL	72	115	20	3	1	0	(0	0)	25	7	7	5	2	21	1	3	2	3	0	1.00	6	.174	.230	.217
1985 Cincinnati	NL	43	92	18	5	1	0	(0	0)	25	7	6	6	1	16	0	0	0	1	0	1.00	1	.196	.245	.272
Philadelphia	NL	46	158	42	8	0	3	(2	1)	59	17	17	13	7	18	0	0	0	1	3	.25	1	.266	.322	.373
1986 Philadelphia	NL	39	61	18	2	1	0	(0	0)	22	8	5	10	1	11	0	0	1	2	0	1.00	1	.295	.389	.361
Montreal	NL	64	202	52	13	2	1	(1	0)	72	18	18	20	5	26	0	2	3	8	3	.73	3	.257	.320	.356
10 ML YEARS		952	2367	578	114	19	26	(15	11)	808	215	224	224	45	339	7	15	19	31	29	.52	42	.244	.304	.341

Tim Fortugno

Pitches: Left   **Bats:** Left   **Pos:** RP/SP   **Ht:** 6' 0"   **Wt:** 185   **Born:** 04/11/62   **Age:** 31

		HOW MUCH HE PITCHED						WHAT HE GAVE UP										THE RESULTS					
Year Team	Lg	G	GS	CG	GF	IP	BFP	H	R	ER	HR	SH	SF	HB	TBB	IBB	SO	WP	Bk	W	L	Pct.	ShO	Sv	ERA
1986 Bellingham	A	6	0	0	4	8	0	2	2	1	0	0	0	1	12	1	11	1	0	0	0	.000	0	1	1.13
Wausau	A	19	0	0	13	31	139	18	17	9	0	2	2	0	26	0	38	6	1	1	1	.500	0	3	2.61
1987 Salinas	A	46	4	1	17	93.1	409	43	36	29	1	3	3	3	84	1	141	19	3	8	2	.800	1	6	2.80
1988 Reading	AA	29	4	0	11	50.2	229	42	29	25	5	1	4	1	36	0	48	5	6	1	5	.167	0	0	4.44
Clearwater	A	9	3	0	2	26	109	17	10	7	1	1	1	0	15	0	28	2	3	1	3	.250	0	0	2.42
1989 Reno	A	5	5	1	0	35.2	161	28	20	10	2	2	0	3	20	2	38	2	2	2	3	.400	0	0	2.52
El Paso	AA	10	4	0	2	26	126	29	24	23	3	1	1	1	21	2	22	4	0	0	3	.000	0	0	7.96
Stockton	A	13	2	0	3	33	134	9	6	5	0	1	0	4	20	1	52	2	1	2	1	.667	0	1	1.36
1990 Beloit	A	31	0	0	29	63.1	263	38	16	11	1	3	0	0	38	3	106	4	0	8	4	.667	0	7	1.56
El Paso	AA	12	2	0	4	28.2	133	23	12	10	0	2	3	1	22	2	24	4	0	2	3	.400	0	2	3.14
1991 El Paso	AA	20	3	0	13	54.1	227	40	14	12	1	0	2	0	25	1	73	3	1	5	1	.833	0	1	1.99
Denver	AAA	26	0	0	10	35.1	152	30	15	14	1	3	2	3	20	2	39	4	0	0	1	.000	0	2	3.57
1992 Edmonton	AAA	26	7	0	4	73.1	318	69	36	29	5	0	1	2	33	0	82	3	1	6	4	.600	0	0	3.56
1992 California	AL	14	5	1	5	41.2	177	37	24	24	5	0	1	0	19	0	31	2	1	1	1	.500	1	1	5.18

Tony Fossas

Pitches: Left   **Bats:** Left   **Pos:** RP   **Ht:** 6' 0"   **Wt:** 187   **Born:** 09/23/57   **Age:** 35

		HOW MUCH HE PITCHED						WHAT HE GAVE UP										THE RESULTS					
Year Team	Lg	G	GS	CG	GF	IP	BFP	H	R	ER	HR	SH	SF	HB	TBB	IBB	SO	WP	Bk	W	L	Pct.	ShO	Sv	ERA
1988 Texas	AL	5	0	0	1	5.2	28	11	3	3	0	0	0	0	2	0	0	1	0	0	0	.000	0	0	4.76
1989 Milwaukee	AL	51	0	0	16	61	256	57	27	24	3	7	3	1	22	7	42	1	3	2	2	.500	0	1	3.54
1990 Milwaukee	AL	32	0	0	9	29.1	146	44	23	21	5	2	1	0	10	2	24	0	0	2	3	.400	0	0	6.44
1991 Boston	AL	64	0	0	18	57	244	49	27	22	3	5	0	3	28	9	29	2	0	3	2	.600	0	1	3.47

| 1992 Boston | AL | 60 | 0 | 0 | 17 | 29.2 | 129 | 31 | 9 | 8 | 1 | 3 | 0 | 1 | 14 | 3 | 19 | 0 | 0 | 1 | 2 | .333 | 0 | 2 | 2.43 |
| 5 ML YEARS | | 212 | 0 | 0 | 61 | 182.2 | 803 | 192 | 89 | 78 | 12 | 17 | 4 | 5 | 76 | 21 | 114 | 4 | 3 | 8 | 9 | .471 | 0 | 4 | 3.84 |

Steve Foster

Pitches: Right **Bats:** Right **Pos:** RP   **Ht:** 6' 0" **Wt:** 180 **Born:** 08/16/66 **Age:** 26

		HOW MUCH HE PITCHED						WHAT HE GAVE UP												THE RESULTS					
Year Team	Lg	G	GS	CG	GF	IP	BFP	H	R	ER	HR	SH	SF	HB	TBB	IBB	SO	WP	Bk	W	L	Pct.	ShO	Sv	ERA
1988 Billings	R	18	0	0	14	30.1	114	15	5	4	0	3	2	3	7	1	27	1	7	2	3	.400	0	7	1.19
1989 Cedar Rapids	A	51	0	0	47	59	245	46	16	14	2	2	1	5	19	6	55	5	5	0	3	.000	0	23	2.14
1990 Chattanooga	AA	50	0	0	42	59.1	277	69	38	35	6	3	8	4	33	4	51	2	2	5	10	.333	0	20	5.31
1991 Chattanooga	AA	17	0	0	16	15.2	64	10	4	2	0	1	0	3	4	0	18	2	1	0	2	.000	0	10	1.15
Nashville	AAA	41	0	0	25	54.2	237	46	17	13	4	2	3	1	29	5	52	0	0	2	3	.400	0	12	2.14
1992 Nashville	AAA	17	7	0	6	50.1	212	53	20	15	3	4	0	1	22	0	28	1	1	5	3	.625	0	1	2.68
1991 Cincinnati	NL	11	0	0	5	14	53	7	5	3	1	0	0	0	4	0	11	0	0	0	0	.000	0	0	1.93
1992 Cincinnati	NL	31	1	0	7	50	209	52	16	16	4	5	2	0	13	1	34	1	0	1	1	.500	0	2	2.88
2 ML YEARS		42	1	0	12	64	262	59	21	19	5	5	2	0	17	1	45	1	0	1	1	.500	0	2	2.67

Eric Fox

Bats: Both **Throws:** Left **Pos:** LF/CF/RF   **Ht:** 5'10" **Wt:** 180 **Born:** 08/15/63 **Age:** 29

		BATTING																	BASERUNNING				PERCENTAGES		
Year Team	Lg	G	AB	H	2B	3B	HR	(Hm	Rd)	TB	R	RBI	TBB	IBB	SO	HBP	SH	SF	SB	CS	SB%	GDP	Avg	OBP	SLG
1986 Salinas	A	133	526	137	17	3	5	--	--	175	80	42	69	7	78	1	9	4	41	27	.60	1	.260	.345	.333
1987 Chattanooga	AA	134	523	139	28	10	8	--	--	211	76	54	40	5	93	2	4	5	22	10	.69	2	.266	.318	.403
1988 Vermont	AA	129	478	120	20	6	3	--	--	161	55	39	39	3	69	2	7	4	33	12	.73	1	.251	.308	.337
1989 Huntsville	AA	139	498	125	10	5	15	--	--	190	84	51	72	1	85	0	11	2	49	15	.77	3	.251	.344	.382
1990 Tacoma	AAA	62	221	61	9	2	4	--	--	86	37	34	20	0	34	0	5	2	8	8	.50	2	.276	.333	.389
1991 Tacoma	AAA	127	522	141	24	8	4	--	--	193	85	52	57	4	82	2	9	4	17	11	.61	6	.270	.342	.370
1992 Huntsville	AA	59	240	65	16	2	5	--	--	100	42	14	27	4	43	0	0	3	16	5	.76	2	.271	.341	.417
Tacoma	AAA	37	121	24	3	1	1	--	--	32	16	7	16	1	25	0	2	2	5	0	1.00	2	.198	.288	.264
1992 Oakland	AL	51	143	34	5	2	3	(0	3)	52	24	13	13	0	29	0	6	1	3	4	.43	1	.238	.299	.364

John Franco

Pitches: Left **Bats:** Left **Pos:** RP   **Ht:** 5'10" **Wt:** 185 **Born:** 09/17/60 **Age:** 32

		HOW MUCH HE PITCHED						WHAT HE GAVE UP												THE RESULTS					
Year Team	Lg	G	GS	CG	GF	IP	BFP	H	R	ER	HR	SH	SF	HB	TBB	IBB	SO	WP	Bk	W	L	Pct.	ShO	Sv	ERA
1984 Cincinnati	NL	54	0	0	30	79.1	335	74	28	23	3	4	4	2	36	4	55	2	0	6	2	.750	0	4	2.61
1985 Cincinnati	NL	67	0	0	33	99	407	83	27	24	5	11	1	1	40	8	61	4	0	12	3	.800	0	12	2.18
1986 Cincinnati	NL	74	0	0	52	101	429	90	40	33	7	8	3	2	44	12	84	4	2	6	6	.500	0	29	2.94
1987 Cincinnati	NL	68	0	0	60	82	344	76	26	23	6	5	2	0	27	6	61	1	0	8	5	.615	0	32	2.52
1988 Cincinnati	NL	70	0	0	61	86	336	60	18	15	3	5	1	0	27	3	46	1	2	6	6	.500	0	39	1.57
1989 Cincinnati	NL	60	0	0	50	80.2	345	77	35	28	3	7	3	0	36	8	60	3	2	4	8	.333	0	32	3.12
1990 New York	NL	55	0	0	48	67.2	287	66	22	19	4	3	1	0	21	2	56	7	2	5	3	.625	0	33	2.53
1991 New York	NL	52	0	0	48	55.1	247	61	27	18	2	3	0	1	18	4	45	6	0	5	9	.357	0	30	2.93
1992 New York	NL	31	0	0	30	33	128	24	6	6	1	0	2	0	11	2	20	0	0	6	2	.750	0	15	1.64
9 ML YEARS		531	0	0	412	684	2858	611	229	189	34	46	17	6	260	49	488	28	8	58	44	.569	0	226	2.49

Julio Franco

Bats: Right **Throws:** Right **Pos:** DH   **Ht:** 6' 1" **Wt:** 190 **Born:** 08/23/61 **Age:** 31

		BATTING																	BASERUNNING				PERCENTAGES		
Year Team	Lg	G	AB	H	2B	3B	HR	(Hm	Rd)	TB	R	RBI	TBB	IBB	SO	HBP	SH	SF	SB	CS	SB%	GDP	Avg	OBP	SLG
1982 Philadelphia	NL	16	29	8	1	0	0	(0	0)	9	3	3	2	1	4	0	1	0	0	2	.00	1	.276	.323	.310
1983 Cleveland	AL	149	560	153	24	8	8	(6	2)	217	68	80	27	1	50	2	3	6	32	12	.73	21	.273	.306	.388
1984 Cleveland	AL	160	658	188	22	5	3	(1	2)	229	82	79	43	1	68	6	1	10	19	10	.66	23	.286	.331	.348
1985 Cleveland	AL	160	636	183	33	4	6	(3	3)	242	97	90	54	2	74	4	0	5	13	9	.59	26	.288	.343	.381
1986 Cleveland	AL	149	599	183	30	5	10	(4	6)	253	80	74	32	1	66	0	0	5	10	7	.59	28	.306	.338	.422
1987 Cleveland	AL	128	495	158	24	3	8	(5	3)	212	86	52	57	2	56	3	0	5	32	9	.78	23	.319	.389	.428
1988 Cleveland	AL	152	613	186	23	6	10	(4	6)	251	88	54	56	4	72	2	1	4	25	11	.69	17	.303	.361	.409
1989 Texas	AL	150	548	173	31	5	13	(9	4)	253	80	92	66	11	69	1	0	6	21	3	.88	27	.316	.386	.462
1990 Texas	AL	157	582	172	27	1	11	(4	7)	234	96	69	82	3	83	2	2	2	31	10	.76	12	.296	.383	.402
1991 Texas	AL	146	589	201	27	3	15	(7	8)	279	108	78	65	8	78	3	0	2	36	9	.80	13	.341	.408	.474
1992 Texas	AL	35	107	25	7	0	2	(2	0)	38	19	8	15	2	17	0	1	0	1	1	.50	3	.234	.328	.355
11 ML YEARS		1402	5416	1630	249	40	86	(44	42)	2217	807	679	499	36	637	23	9	49	220	83	.73	194	.301	.359	.409

Marvin Freeman

Pitches: Right Bats: Right Pos: RP Ht: 6' 7" Wt: 222 Born: 04/10/63 Age: 30

		HOW MUCH HE PITCHED						WHAT HE GAVE UP												THE RESULTS					
Year Team	Lg	G	GS	CG	GF	IP	BFP	H	R	ER	HR	SH	SF	HB	TBB	IBB	SO	WP	Bk	W	L	Pct.	ShO	Sv	ERA
1986 Philadelphia	NL	3	3	0	0	16	61	6	4	4	0	0	1	0	10	0	8	1	0	2	0	1.000	0	0	2.25
1988 Philadelphia	NL	11	11	0	0	51.2	249	55	36	35	2	5	1	1	43	2	37	3	1	2	3	.400	0	0	6.10
1989 Philadelphia	NL	1	1	0	0	3	16	2	2	2	0	0	0	0	5	0	0	0	1	0	0	.000	0	0	6.00
1990 2 ML Teams		25	3	0	5	48	207	41	24	23	5	2	0	5	17	2	38	4	0	1	2	.333	0	1	4.31
1991 Atlanta	NL	34	0	0	6	48	190	37	19	16	2	1	1	2	13	1	34	4	0	1	0	1.000	0	1	3.00
1992 Atlanta	NL	58	0	0	15	64.1	276	61	26	23	7	2	1	1	29	7	41	4	0	7	5	.583	0	3	3.22
1990 Philadelphia	NL	16	3	0	4	32.1	147	34	21	20	5	1	0	3	14	2	26	4	0	0	2	.000	0	1	5.57
Atlanta	NL	9	0	0	1	15.2	60	7	3	3	0	1	0	2	3	0	12	0	0	1	0	1.000	0	0	1.72
6 ML YEARS		132	18	0	26	231	999	202	111	103	16	10	4	9	117	12	158	16	2	13	10	.565	0	5	4.01

Steve Frey

Pitches: Left Bats: Right Pos: RP Ht: 5' 9" Wt: 170 Born: 07/29/63 Age: 29

		HOW MUCH HE PITCHED						WHAT HE GAVE UP												THE RESULTS					
Year Team	Lg	G	GS	CG	GF	IP	BFP	H	R	ER	HR	SH	SF	HB	TBB	IBB	SO	WP	Bk	W	L	Pct.	ShO	Sv	ERA
1989 Montreal	NL	20	0	0	11	21.1	103	29	15	13	4	0	2	1	11	1	15	1	1	3	2	.600	0	0	5.48
1990 Montreal	NL	51	0	0	21	55.2	236	44	15	13	4	3	2	1	29	6	29	0	0	8	2	.800	0	9	2.10
1991 Montreal	NL	31	0	0	5	39.2	182	43	31	22	3	3	2	1	23	4	21	3	1	0	1	.000	0	1	4.99
1992 California	AL	51	0	0	20	45.1	193	39	18	18	6	2	3	2	22	3	24	1	0	4	2	.667	0	4	3.57
4 ML YEARS		153	0	0	57	162	714	155	79	66	17	8	9	5	85	14	89	5	2	15	7	.682	0	14	3.67

Todd Frohwirth

Pitches: Right Bats: Right Pos: RP Ht: 6' 4" Wt: 205 Born: 09/28/62 Age: 30

		HOW MUCH HE PITCHED						WHAT HE GAVE UP												THE RESULTS					
Year Team	Lg	G	GS	CG	GF	IP	BFP	H	R	ER	HR	SH	SF	HB	TBB	IBB	SO	WP	Bk	W	L	Pct.	ShO	Sv	ERA
1987 Philadelphia	NL	10	0	0	2	11	43	12	0	0	0	0	0	0	2	0	9	0	0	1	0	1.000	0	0	0.00
1988 Philadelphia	NL	12	0	0	6	12	62	16	11	11	2	1	1	0	11	6	11	1	0	1	2	.333	0	0	8.25
1989 Philadelphia	NL	45	0	0	11	62.2	258	56	26	25	4	3	1	3	18	0	39	1	1	1	0	1.000	0	0	3.59
1990 Philadelphia	NL	5	0	0	1	1	12	3	2	2	0	0	0	0	6	2	1	0	0	0	0	.000	0	0	18.00
1991 Baltimore	AL	51	0	0	10	96.1	372	64	24	20	2	4	1	1	29	3	77	0	0	7	3	.700	0	3	1.87
1992 Baltimore	AL	65	0	0	23	106	444	97	33	29	4	7	1	3	41	4	58	1	0	4	3	.571	0	4	2.46
6 ML YEARS		188	0	0	52	289	1191	248	96	87	12	15	4	7	107	15	195	4	1	14	9	.609	0	7	2.71

Jeff Frye

Bats: Right Throws: Right Pos: 2B Ht: 5' 9" Wt: 165 Born: 08/31/66 Age: 26

		BATTING																BASERUNNING				PERCENTAGES		
Year Team	Lg	G	AB	H	2B	3B	HR	(Hm	Rd)	TB	R	RBI	TBB	IBB	SO	HBP	SH	SF	SB	CS	SB%	GDP	Avg	OBP	SLG
1988 Butte	R	55	185	53	7	1	0	--	--	62	47	14	35	0	24	1	1	1	16	1	.94	2	.286	.401	.335
1989 Gastonia	A	125	464	145	26	3	1	--	--	180	85	40	72	5	53	1	5	1	33	13	.72	4	.313	.405	.388
1990 Charlotte	A	131	503	137	16	7	0	--	--	167	77	50	80	5	66	2	7	4	28	6	.82	5	.272	.372	.332
1991 Tulsa	AA	131	503	152	32	11	4	--	--	218	92	41	71	0	60	1	5	3	15	8	.65	8	.302	.388	.433
1992 Okla City	AAA	87	337	101	26	2	2	--	--	137	64	28	51	0	39	11	8	0	11	9	.55	9	.300	.409	.407
1992 Texas	AL	67	199	51	9	1	1	(0	1)	65	24	12	16	0	27	3	11	1	1	3	.25	2	.256	.320	.327

Travis Fryman

Bats: Right Throws: Right Pos: SS/3B Ht: 6' 1" Wt: 194 Born: 03/25/69 Age: 24

		BATTING																BASERUNNING				PERCENTAGES		
Year Team	Lg	G	AB	H	2B	3B	HR	(Hm	Rd)	TB	R	RBI	TBB	IBB	SO	HBP	SH	SF	SB	CS	SB%	GDP	Avg	OBP	SLG
1990 Detroit	AL	66	232	69	11	1	9	(5	4)	109	32	27	17	0	51	1	1	0	3	3	.50	3	.297	.348	.470
1991 Detroit	AL	149	557	144	36	3	21	(8	13)	249	65	91	40	0	149	3	6	6	12	5	.71	13	.259	.309	.447
1992 Detroit	AL	161	659	175	31	4	20	(9	11)	274	87	96	45	1	144	6	5	6	8	4	.67	13	.266	.316	.416
3 ML YEARS		376	1448	388	78	8	50	(22	28)	632	184	214	102	1	344	10	12	12	23	12	.66	29	.268	.318	.436

Gary Gaetti

Bats: Right Throws: Right Pos: 3B/1B/DH Ht: 6' 0" Wt: 200 Born: 08/19/58 Age: 34

		BATTING																BASERUNNING				PERCENTAGES		
Year Team	Lg	G	AB	H	2B	3B	HR	(Hm	Rd)	TB	R	RBI	TBB	IBB	SO	HBP	SH	SF	SB	CS	SB%	GDP	Avg	OBP	SLG
1981 Minnesota	AL	9	26	5	0	0	2	(1	1)	11	4	3	0	0	6	0	0	0	0	0	.00	1	.192	.192	.423
1982 Minnesota	AL	145	508	117	25	4	25	(15	10)	225	59	84	37	2	107	3	4	13	0	4	.00	16	.230	.280	.443
1983 Minnesota	AL	157	584	143	30	3	21	(7	14)	242	81	78	54	2	121	4	0	8	7	1	.88	18	.245	.309	.414
1984 Minnesota	AL	162	588	154	29	4	5	(2	3)	206	55	65	44	1	81	4	3	5	11	5	.69	9	.262	.315	.350
1985 Minnesota	AL	160	560	138	31	0	20	(10	10)	229	71	63	37	3	89	7	3	1	13	5	.72	15	.246	.301	.409
1986 Minnesota	AL	157	596	171	34	1	34	(16	18)	309	91	108	52	4	108	6	1	6	14	15	.48	18	.287	.347	.518

Year	Team	Lg	G	AB	H	2B	3B	HR	(Hm	Rd)	TB	R	RBI	TBB	IBB	SO	HBP	SH	SF	SB	CS	SB%	GDP	Avg	OBP	SLG
1987	Minnesota	AL	154	584	150	36	2	31	(18	13)	283	95	109	37	7	92	3	1	3	10	7	.59	25	.257	.303	.485
1988	Minnesota	AL	133	468	141	29	2	28	(9	19)	258	66	88	36	5	85	5	1	6	7	4	.64	10	.301	.353	.551
1989	Minnesota	AL	130	498	125	11	4	19	(10	9)	201	63	75	25	5	87	3	1	9	6	2	.75	12	.251	.286	.404
1990	Minnesota	AL	154	577	132	27	5	16	(7	9)	217	61	85	36	1	101	3	1	8	6	1	.86	22	.229	.274	.376
1991	California	AL	152	586	144	22	1	18	(12	6)	222	58	66	33	3	104	8	2	5	5	5	.50	13	.246	.293	.379
1992	California	AL	130	456	103	13	2	12	(8	4)	156	41	48	21	4	79	6	0	3	3	1	.75	5	.226	.267	.342
12 ML YEARS			1643	6031	1523	287	28	231	(115	116)	2559	745	872	412	37	1060	52	17	67	82	50	.62	168	.253	.303	.424

Greg Gagne

Bats: Right **Throws:** Right **Pos:** SS   **Ht:** 5'11" **Wt:** 173 **Born:** 11/12/61 **Age:** 31

Year	Team	Lg	G	AB	H	2B	3B	HR	(Hm	Rd)	TB	R	RBI	TBB	IBB	SO	HBP	SH	SF	SB	CS	SB%	GDP	Avg	OBP	SLG
1983	Minnesota	AL	10	27	3	1	0	0	(0	0)	4	2	3	0	0	6	0	0	2	0	0	.00	0	.111	.103	.148
1984	Minnesota	AL	2	1	0	0	0	0	(0	0)	0	0	0	0	0	0	0	0	0	0	0	.00	0	.000	.000	.000
1985	Minnesota	AL	114	293	66	15	3	2	(0	2)	93	37	23	20	0	57	3	3	3	10	4	.71	5	.225	.279	.317
1986	Minnesota	AL	156	472	118	22	6	12	(10	2)	188	63	54	30	0	108	6	13	3	12	10	.55	4	.250	.301	.398
1987	Minnesota	AL	137	437	116	28	7	10	(7	3)	188	68	40	25	0	84	4	10	2	6	6	.50	3	.265	.310	.430
1988	Minnesota	AL	149	461	109	20	6	14	(5	9)	183	70	48	27	2	110	7	11	5	15	7	.68	13	.236	.288	.397
1989	Minnesota	AL	149	460	125	29	7	9	(5	4)	195	69	48	17	0	80	2	7	5	11	4	.73	10	.272	.298	.424
1990	Minnesota	AL	138	388	91	22	3	7	(3	4)	140	38	38	24	0	76	1	8	2	8	8	.50	5	.235	.280	.361
1991	Minnesota	AL	139	408	108	23	3	8	(3	5)	161	52	42	26	0	72	3	5	5	11	9	.55	15	.265	.310	.395
1992	Minnesota	AL	146	439	108	23	0	7	(1	6)	152	53	39	19	0	83	2	12	1	6	7	.46	11	.246	.280	.346
10 ML YEARS			1140	3386	844	183	35	69	(34	35)	1304	452	335	188	2	676	28	69	24	79	55	.59	66	.249	.292	.385

Andres Galarraga

Bats: Right **Throws:** Right **Pos:** 1B   **Ht:** 6'3" **Wt:** 235 **Born:** 06/18/61 **Age:** 32

Year	Team	Lg	G	AB	H	2B	3B	HR	(Hm	Rd)	TB	R	RBI	TBB	IBB	SO	HBP	SH	SF	SB	CS	SB%	GDP	Avg	OBP	SLG
1985	Montreal	NL	24	75	14	1	0	2	(0	2)	21	9	4	3	0	18	1	0	0	1	2	.33	0	.187	.228	.280
1986	Montreal	NL	105	321	87	13	0	10	(4	6)	130	39	42	30	5	79	3	1	1	6	5	.55	8	.271	.338	.405
1987	Montreal	NL	147	551	168	40	3	13	(7	6)	253	72	90	41	13	127	10	0	4	7	10	.41	11	.305	.361	.459
1988	Montreal	NL	157	609	184	42	8	29	(14	15)	329	99	92	39	9	153	10	0	3	13	4	.76	12	.302	.352	.540
1989	Montreal	NL	152	572	147	30	1	23	(13	10)	248	76	85	48	10	158	13	0	3	12	5	.71	12	.257	.327	.434
1990	Montreal	NL	155	579	148	29	0	20	(6	14)	237	65	87	40	8	169	4	0	5	10	1	.91	14	.256	.306	.409
1991	Montreal	NL	107	375	82	13	2	9	(3	6)	126	34	33	23	5	86	2	0	0	5	6	.45	6	.219	.268	.336
1992	St. Louis	NL	95	325	79	14	2	10	(4	6)	127	38	39	11	0	69	8	0	3	5	4	.56	8	.243	.282	.391
8 ML YEARS			942	3407	909	182	16	116	(51	65)	1471	432	472	235	50	859	51	1	19	59	37	.61	71	.267	.322	.432

Dave Gallagher

Bats: Right **Throws:** Right **Pos:** RF/LF/CF   **Ht:** 6'0" **Wt:** 184 **Born:** 09/20/60 **Age:** 32

Year	Team	Lg	G	AB	H	2B	3B	HR	(Hm	Rd)	TB	R	RBI	TBB	IBB	SO	HBP	SH	SF	SB	CS	SB%	GDP	Avg	OBP	SLG
1987	Cleveland	AL	15	36	4	1	1	0	(0	0)	7	2	1	2	0	5	0	1	0	2	0	1.00	1	.111	.158	.194
1988	Chicago	AL	101	347	105	15	3	5	(1	4)	141	59	31	29	3	40	0	6	2	5	4	.56	8	.303	.354	.406
1989	Chicago	AL	161	601	160	22	2	1	(1	0)	189	74	46	46	1	79	2	16	2	5	6	.45	9	.266	.320	.314
1990	2 ML Teams		68	126	32	4	1	0	(0	0)	38	12	7	7	0	12	1	7	1	1	2	.33	3	.254	.296	.302
1991	California	AL	90	270	79	17	0	1	(0	1)	99	32	30	24	0	43	2	10	0	2	4	.33	6	.293	.355	.367
1992	New York	NL	98	175	42	11	1	1	(1	0)	58	20	21	19	0	16	1	3	3	4	5	.44	7	.240	.307	.331
1990	Chicago	AL	45	75	21	3	1	0	(0	0)	26	5	5	3	0	9	1	5	0	0	1	.00	1	.280	.316	.347
	Baltimore	AL	23	51	11	1	0	0	(0	0)	12	7	2	4	0	3	0	2	1	1	1	.50	0	.216	.268	.235
6 ML YEARS			533	1555	422	70	8	8	(3	5)	532	199	136	127	4	195	6	43	12	19	21	.48	34	.271	.326	.342

Mike Gallego

Bats: Right **Throws:** Right **Pos:** 2B/SS   **Ht:** 5'8" **Wt:** 160 **Born:** 10/31/60 **Age:** 32

Year	Team	Lg	G	AB	H	2B	3B	HR	(Hm	Rd)	TB	R	RBI	TBB	IBB	SO	HBP	SH	SF	SB	CS	SB%	GDP	Avg	OBP	SLG
1985	Oakland	AL	76	77	16	1	1	1	(0	1)	26	13	9	12	0	14	1	2	1	1	1	.50	2	.208	.319	.338
1986	Oakland	AL	20	37	10	2	0	0	(0	0)	12	2	4	1	0	6	0	2	0	0	2	.00	0	.270	.289	.324
1987	Oakland	AL	72	124	31	6	0	2	(0	2)	43	18	14	12	0	21	1	5	1	0	1	.00	5	.250	.319	.347
1988	Oakland	AL	129	277	58	8	0	2	(0	2)	72	38	20	34	0	53	1	8	0	2	3	.40	6	.209	.298	.260
1989	Oakland	AL	133	357	90	14	2	3	(2	1)	117	45	30	35	0	43	6	8	3	7	5	.58	10	.252	.327	.328
1990	Oakland	AL	140	389	80	13	2	3	(1	2)	106	36	34	35	0	50	4	17	2	5	5	.50	13	.206	.277	.272
1991	Oakland	AL	159	482	119	15	4	12	(6	6)	178	67	49	67	3	84	5	10	3	6	9	.40	8	.247	.343	.369
1992	New York	AL	53	173	44	7	1	3	(1	2)	62	24	14	20	0	22	4	3	1	0	1	.00	5	.254	.343	.358
8 ML YEARS			782	1916	448	70	10	26	(12	14)	616	243	174	216	3	293	22	55	11	21	27	.44	49	.234	.317	.322

70

Ron Gant

Bats: Right **Throws:** Right **Pos:** LF/CF   **Ht:** 6' 0" **Wt:** 175 **Born:** 03/02/65 **Age:** 28

Year	Team	Lg	G	AB	H	2B	3B	HR	(Hm	Rd)	TB	R	RBI	TBB	IBB	SO	HBP	SH	SF	SB	CS	SB%	GDP	Avg	OBP	SLG
1987	Atlanta	NL	21	83	22	4	0	2	(1	1)	32	9	9	1	0	11	0	1	1	4	2	.67	3	.265	.271	.386
1988	Atlanta	NL	146	563	146	28	8	19	(7	12)	247	85	60	46	4	118	3	2	4	19	10	.66	7	.259	.317	.439
1989	Atlanta	NL	75	260	46	8	3	9	(5	4)	87	26	25	20	0	63	1	2	2	9	6	.60	0	.177	.237	.335
1990	Atlanta	NL	152	575	174	34	3	32	(18	14)	310	107	84	50	0	86	1	1	4	33	16	.67	8	.303	.357	.539
1991	Atlanta	NL	154	561	141	35	3	32	(18	14)	278	101	105	71	8	104	5	0	5	34	15	.69	6	.251	.338	.496
1992	Atlanta	NL	153	544	141	22	6	17	(10	7)	226	74	80	45	5	101	7	0	6	32	10	.76	10	.259	.321	.415
	6 ML YEARS		701	2586	670	131	23	111	(59	52)	1180	402	363	233	17	483	17	6	22	131	59	.69	34	.259	.322	.456

Jim Gantner

Bats: Left **Throws:** Right **Pos:** 2B/3B   **Ht:** 5'11" **Wt:** 175 **Born:** 01/05/54 **Age:** 39

Year	Team	Lg	G	AB	H	2B	3B	HR	(Hm	Rd)	TB	R	RBI	TBB	IBB	SO	HBP	SH	SF	SB	CS	SB%	GDP	Avg	OBP	SLG
1976	Milwaukee	AL	26	69	17	1	0	0	(0	0)	18	6	7	6	0	11	1	3	0	1	0	1.00	1	.246	.307	.261
1977	Milwaukee	AL	14	47	14	1	0	1	(0	1)	18	4	2	2	0	5	0	0	0	2	1	.67	1	.298	.327	.383
1978	Milwaukee	AL	43	97	21	1	0	1	(0	1)	25	14	8	5	0	10	2	1	0	2	0	1.00	0	.216	.269	.258
1979	Milwaukee	AL	70	208	59	10	3	2	(0	2)	81	29	22	16	1	17	2	5	3	3	5	.38	3	.284	.336	.389
1980	Milwaukee	AL	132	415	117	21	3	4	(1	3)	156	47	40	30	5	29	1	8	3	11	10	.52	8	.282	.330	.376
1981	Milwaukee	AL	107	352	94	14	1	2	(0	2)	116	35	33	29	5	29	3	9	4	3	6	.33	6	.267	.325	.330
1982	Milwaukee	AL	132	447	132	17	2	4	(2	2)	165	48	43	26	3	36	2	7	3	6	3	.67	6	.295	.335	.369
1983	Milwaukee	AL	161	603	170	23	8	11	(5	6)	242	85	74	38	5	46	6	11	4	5	6	.45	10	.282	.329	.401
1984	Milwaukee	AL	153	613	173	27	1	3	(0	3)	211	61	56	30	0	51	3	2	10	6	5	.55	16	.282	.314	.344
1985	Milwaukee	AL	143	523	133	15	4	5	(4	1)	171	63	44	33	7	42	3	10	4	11	8	.58	13	.254	.300	.327
1986	Milwaukee	AL	139	497	136	25	1	7	(4	3)	184	58	38	26	2	50	6	6	7	13	7	.65	13	.274	.313	.370
1987	Milwaukee	AL	81	265	72	14	0	4	(0	4)	98	37	30	19	2	22	5	4	1	6	2	.75	7	.272	.331	.370
1988	Milwaukee	AL	155	539	149	28	2	0	(0	0)	181	67	47	34	1	50	3	18	2	20	6	.77	10	.276	.322	.336
1989	Milwaukee	AL	116	409	112	18	3	0	(0	0)	136	51	34	21	2	33	10	8	5	20	6	.77	10	.274	.321	.333
1990	Milwaukee	AL	88	323	85	8	5	0	(0	0)	103	36	25	29	0	19	2	4	0	18	3	.86	10	.263	.328	.319
1991	Milwaukee	AL	140	526	149	27	4	2	(1	1)	190	63	47	27	5	34	3	7	4	4	6	.40	13	.283	.320	.361
1992	Milwaukee	AL	101	256	63	12	1	1	(1	0)	80	22	18	12	2	17	0	3	2	6	2	.75	9	.246	.278	.313
	17 ML YEARS		1801	6189	1696	262	38	47	(18	29)	2175	726	568	383	40	501	52	106	52	137	78	.64	135	.274	.319	.351

Carlos Garcia

Bats: Right **Throws:** Right **Pos:** 2B   **Ht:** 6' 1" **Wt:** 185 **Born:** 10/15/67 **Age:** 25

Year	Team	Lg	G	AB	H	2B	3B	HR	(Hm	Rd)	TB	R	RBI	TBB	IBB	SO	HBP	SH	SF	SB	CS	SB%	GDP	Avg	OBP	SLG
1987	Macon	A	110	373	95	14	3	3	--	--	124	44	38	23	2	80	6	2	2	20	10	.67	6	.255	.307	.332
1988	Augusta	A	73	269	78	13	2	1	--	--	98	32	45	22	0	46	1	2	1	11	6	.65	1	.290	.345	.364
	Salem	A	62	236	65	9	3	1	--	--	83	21	28	10	0	32	1	0	3	8	2	.80	9	.275	.304	.352
1989	Salem	A	81	304	86	12	4	7	--	--	127	45	49	18	0	51	4	1	5	19	6	.76	3	.283	.326	.418
	Harrisburg	AA	54	188	53	5	5	3	--	--	77	28	25	8	0	36	0	0	1	6	4	.60	4	.282	.310	.410
1990	Harrisburg	AA	65	242	67	11	2	5	--	--	97	36	25	16	0	36	3	1	1	12	1	.92	6	.277	.328	.401
	Buffalo	AAA	63	197	52	10	0	5	--	--	77	23	18	16	2	40	2	1	2	7	4	.64	5	.264	.323	.391
1991	Buffalo	AAA	127	463	123	21	6	7	--	--	177	62	60	33	5	78	7	6	3	30	7	.81	6	.266	.322	.382
1992	Buffalo	AAA	113	426	129	28	9	13	--	--	214	73	70	24	2	64	4	4	5	21	7	.75	7	.303	.342	.502
1990	Pittsburgh	NL	4	4	2	0	0	0	(0	0)	2	1	0	0	0	2	0	0	0	0	0	.00	0	.500	.500	.500
1991	Pittsburgh	NL	12	24	6	0	2	0	(0	0)	10	2	1	1	0	8	0	0	0	0	0	.00	1	.250	.280	.417
1992	Pittsburgh	NL	22	39	8	1	0	0	(0	0)	9	4	4	0	0	9	0	1	0	0	0	.00	1	.205	.195	.231
	3 ML YEARS		38	67	16	1	2	0	(0	0)	21	7	5	1	0	19	0	1	0	0	0	.00	2	.239	.243	.313

Mike Gardiner

Pitches: Right **Bats:** Right **Pos:** SP/RP   **Ht:** 6' 0" **Wt:** 200 **Born:** 10/19/65 **Age:** 27

Year	Team	Lg	G	GS	CG	GF	IP	BFP	H	R	ER	HR	SH	SF	HB	TBB	IBB	SO	WP	Bk	W	L	Pct.	ShO	Sv	ERA
1990	Seattle	AL	5	3	0	1	12.2	66	22	17	15	1	0	1	2	5	0	6	0	0	0	2	.000	0	0	10.66
1991	Boston	AL	22	22	0	0	130	562	140	79	70	18	1	3	0	47	2	91	1	0	9	10	.474	0	0	4.85
1992	Boston	AL	28	18	0	3	130.2	566	126	78	69	12	3	5	2	58	2	79	8	0	4	10	.286	0	0	4.75
	3 ML YEARS		55	43	0	4	273.1	1194	288	174	154	31	4	9	4	110	4	176	9	0	13	22	.371	0	0	5.07

Jeff Gardner

Bats: Left **Throws:** Right **Pos:** 2B **Ht:** 5'11" **Wt:** 165 **Born:** 02/04/64 **Age:** 29

Year Team	Lg	G	AB	H	2B	3B	HR	(Hm	Rd)	TB	R	RBI	TBB	IBB	SO	HBP	SH	SF	SB	CS	SB%	GDP	Avg	OBP	SLG
1985 Columbia	A	123	401	118	9	1	0	--	--	129	80	50	142	1	40	5	10	1	31	5	.86	9	.294	.483	.322
1986 Lynchburg	A	111	334	91	11	2	1	--	--	109	59	39	81	3	33	4	8	3	6	4	.60	10	.272	.417	.326
1987 Jackson	AA	119	399	109	10	3	0	--	--	125	55	30	58	1	55	3	5	2	1	5	.17	7	.273	.368	.313
1988 Jackson	AA	134	432	109	15	2	0	--	--	128	46	33	69	7	52	1	14	1	13	8	.62	6	.252	.356	.296
Tidewater	AAA	2	8	3	1	1	0	--	--	6	3	2	1	0	1	0	0	0	0	0	.00	0	.375	.444	.750
1989 Tidewater	AAA	101	269	75	11	0	0	--	--	86	28	24	25	1	27	0	4	3	0	0	.00	7	.279	.337	.320
1990 Tidewater	AAA	138	463	125	11	1	0	--	--	138	55	33	84	3	33	1	4	1	3	3	.50	12	.270	.383	.298
1991 Tidewater	AAA	136	504	147	23	4	1	--	--	181	73	56	84	4	48	3	7	5	6	5	.55	8	.292	.393	.359
1992 Las Vegas	AAA	120	439	147	30	5	1	--	--	190	82	51	67	6	48	2	7	2	7	2	.78	9	.335	.424	.433
1991 New York	NL	13	37	6	0	0	0	(0	0)	6	3	1	4	0	6	0	0	1	0	0	.00	0	.162	.238	.162
1992 San Diego	NL	15	19	2	0	0	0	(0	0)	2	0	0	1	0	8	0	0	0	0	0	.00	0	.105	.150	.105
2 ML YEARS		28	56	8	0	0	0	(0	0)	8	3	1	5	0	14	0	0	1	0	0	.00	0	.143	.210	.143

Mark Gardner

Pitches: Right **Bats:** Right **Pos:** SP **Ht:** 6'1" **Wt:** 200 **Born:** 03/01/62 **Age:** 31

Year Team	Lg	G	GS	CG	GF	IP	BFP	H	R	ER	HR	SH	SF	HB	TBB	IBB	SO	WP	Bk	W	L	Pct.	ShO	Sv	ERA
1989 Montreal	NL	7	4	0	1	26.1	117	26	16	15	2	0	0	2	11	1	21	0	0	0	3	.000	0	0	5.13
1990 Montreal	NL	27	26	3	1	152.2	642	129	62	58	13	4	7	9	61	5	135	2	4	7	9	.438	3	0	3.42
1991 Montreal	NL	27	27	0	0	168.1	692	139	78	72	17	7	2	4	75	1	107	2	1	9	11	.450	0	0	3.85
1992 Montreal	NL	33	30	0	1	179.2	778	179	91	87	15	12	7	9	60	2	132	2	0	12	10	.545	0	0	4.36
4 ML YEARS		94	87	3	3	527	2229	473	247	232	47	23	16	24	207	9	395	6	5	28	33	.459	3	0	3.96

Rich Gedman

Bats: Left **Throws:** Right **Pos:** C **Ht:** 6'0" **Wt:** 211 **Born:** 09/26/59 **Age:** 33

Year Team	Lg	G	AB	H	2B	3B	HR	(Hm	Rd)	TB	R	RBI	TBB	IBB	SO	HBP	SH	SF	SB	CS	SB%	GDP	Avg	OBP	SLG
1980 Boston	AL	9	24	5	0	0	0	(0	0)	5	2	1	0	0	5	0	0	0	0	0	.00	1	.208	.208	.208
1981 Boston	AL	62	205	59	15	0	5	(3	2)	89	22	26	9	1	31	1	1	3	0	0	.00	9	.288	.317	.434
1982 Boston	AL	92	289	72	17	2	4	(1	3)	105	30	26	10	2	37	2	4	0	0	1	.00	13	.249	.279	.363
1983 Boston	AL	81	204	60	16	1	2	(0	2)	84	21	18	15	6	37	1	3	0	0	1	.00	4	.294	.345	.412
1984 Boston	AL	133	449	121	26	4	24	(16	8)	227	54	72	29	8	72	1	2	5	0	0	.00	5	.269	.312	.506
1985 Boston	AL	144	498	147	30	5	18	(9	9)	241	66	80	50	11	79	3	3	2	2	0	1.00	12	.295	.362	.484
1986 Boston	AL	135	462	119	29	0	16	(2	14)	196	49	65	37	13	61	4	1	5	1	0	1.00	15	.258	.315	.424
1987 Boston	AL	52	151	31	8	0	1	(1	0)	42	11	13	10	2	24	0	1	3	0	0	.00	2	.205	.250	.278
1988 Boston	AL	95	299	69	14	0	9	(5	4)	110	33	39	18	2	49	3	9	3	0	0	.00	6	.231	.279	.368
1989 Boston	AL	93	260	55	9	0	4	(2	2)	76	24	16	23	1	47	0	3	3	0	1	.00	8	.212	.273	.292
1990 2 ML Teams		50	119	24	7	0	1	(0	1)	34	7	10	20	6	30	1	2	1	0	0	.00	3	.202	.319	.286
1991 St. Louis	NL	46	94	10	1	0	3	(1	2)	20	7	8	4	0	15	0	0	2	0	1	.00	2	.106	.140	.213
1992 St. Louis	NL	41	105	23	4	0	0	(1	0)	30	5	8	11	1	22	0	0	2	0	0	.00	2	.219	.291	.286
1990 Boston	AL	10	15	3	0	0	0	(0	0)	3	3	0	5	0	6	1	0	0	0	0	.00	1	.200	.429	.200
Houston	NL	40	104	21	7	0	1	(0	1)	31	4	10	15	6	24	0	2	1	0	0	.00	2	.202	.300	.298
13 ML YEARS		1033	3159	795	176	12	88	(41	47)	1259	331	382	236	53	509	16	29	28	3	4	.43	80	.252	.304	.399

Kirk Gibson

Bats: Left **Throws:** Left **Pos:** RF **Ht:** 6'3" **Wt:** 225 **Born:** 05/28/57 **Age:** 36

Year Team	Lg	G	AB	H	2B	3B	HR	(Hm	Rd)	TB	R	RBI	TBB	IBB	SO	HBP	SH	SF	SB	CS	SB%	GDP	Avg	OBP	SLG
1979 Detroit	AL	12	38	9	3	0	1	(0	1)	15	3	4	1	0	3	0	0	0	3	3	.50	0	.237	.256	.395
1980 Detroit	AL	51	175	46	2	1	9	(3	6)	77	23	16	10	0	45	1	1	2	4	7	.36	0	.263	.303	.440
1981 Detroit	AL	83	290	95	11	3	9	(4	5)	139	41	40	18	1	64	2	1	2	17	5	.77	9	.328	.369	.479
1982 Detroit	AL	69	266	74	16	2	8	(4	4)	118	34	35	25	2	41	1	1	1	9	7	.56	2	.278	.341	.444
1983 Detroit	AL	128	401	91	12	9	15	(5	10)	166	60	51	53	3	96	4	5	4	14	3	.82	2	.227	.320	.414
1984 Detroit	AL	149	531	150	23	10	27	(11	16)	274	92	91	63	6	103	8	3	6	29	9	.76	4	.282	.363	.516
1985 Detroit	AL	154	581	167	37	5	29	(18	11)	301	96	97	71	16	137	5	3	10	30	4	.88	5	.287	.364	.518
1986 Detroit	AL	119	441	118	11	2	28	(15	13)	217	84	86	68	4	107	7	1	4	34	6	.85	4	.268	.371	.492
1987 Detroit	AL	128	487	135	25	3	24	(14	10)	238	95	79	71	8	117	5	1	4	26	7	.79	5	.277	.372	.489
1988 Los Angeles	NL	150	542	157	28	1	25	(14	11)	262	106	76	73	14	120	7	3	7	31	6	.84	8	.290	.377	.483
1989 Los Angeles	NL	71	253	54	8	2	9	(4	5)	93	35	28	35	5	38	2	0	2	12	3	.80	5	.213	.312	.368
1990 Los Angeles	NL	89	315	82	20	0	8	(2	6)	126	59	38	39	0	65	3	0	2	26	2	.93	4	.260	.345	.400
1991 Kansas City	AL	132	462	109	17	6	16	(4	12)	186	81	55	69	3	103	6	1	2	18	4	.82	9	.236	.341	.403
1992 Pittsburgh	NL	16	56	11	0	0	2	(0	2)	17	6	5	3	0	12	0	1	0	3	1	.75	1	.196	.237	.304
14 ML YEARS		1351	4838	1298	213	44	210	(98	112)	2229	815	701	599	62	1068	51	21	46	256	65	.80	62	.268	.352	.461

Paul Gibson

Pitches: Left   **Bats:** Right   **Pos:** RP   **Ht:** 6' 1"   **Wt:** 185   **Born:** 01/04/60   **Age:** 33

		HOW MUCH HE PITCHED						WHAT HE GAVE UP												THE RESULTS					
Year Team	Lg	G	GS	CG	GF	IP	BFP	H	R	ER	HR	SH	SF	HB	TBB	IBB	SO	WP	Bk	W	L	Pct.	ShO	Sv	ERA
1988 Detroit	AL	40	1	0	18	92	390	83	33	30	6	3	5	2	34	8	50	3	1	4	2	.667	0	0	2.93
1989 Detroit	AL	45	13	0	16	132	573	129	71	68	11	7	5	6	57	12	77	4	1	4	8	.333	0	0	4.64
1990 Detroit	AL	61	0	0	17	97.1	422	99	36	33	10	4	5	1	44	12	56	1	1	5	4	.556	0	3	3.05
1991 Detroit	AL	68	0	0	28	96	432	112	51	49	10	2	2	3	48	8	52	4	0	5	7	.417	0	8	4.59
1992 New York	NL	43	1	0	12	62	273	70	37	36	7	3	1	0	25	0	49	1	0	0	1	.000	0	0	5.23
5 ML YEARS		257	15	0	91	479.1	2090	493	228	216	44	19	18	12	208	40	284	13	3	18	22	.450	0	11	4.06

Bernard Gilkey

Bats: Right   **Throws:** Right   **Pos:** LF   **Ht:** 6' 0"   **Wt:** 190   **Born:** 09/24/66   **Age:** 26

		BATTING																BASERUNNING				PERCENTAGES		
Year Team	Lg	G	AB	H	2B	3B	HR	(Hm	Rd)	TB	R	RBI	TBB	IBB	SO	HBP	SH	SF	SB	CS	SB%	GDP	Avg	OBP	SLG
1990 St. Louis	NL	18	64	19	5	2	1	(0	1)	31	11	3	8	0	5	0	0	0	6	1	.86	1	.297	.375	.484
1991 St. Louis	NL	81	268	58	7	2	5	(2	3)	84	28	20	39	0	33	1	1	2	14	8	.64	14	.216	.316	.313
1992 St. Louis	NL	131	384	116	19	4	7	(3	4)	164	56	43	39	1	52	1	3	4	18	12	.60	5	.302	.364	.427
3 ML YEARS		230	716	193	31	8	13	(5	8)	279	95	66	86	1	90	2	4	6	38	21	.64	20	.270	.347	.390

Joe Girardi

Bats: Right   **Throws:** Right   **Pos:** C   **Ht:** 5'11"   **Wt:** 195   **Born:** 10/14/64   **Age:** 28

		BATTING																BASERUNNING				PERCENTAGES		
Year Team	Lg	G	AB	H	2B	3B	HR	(Hm	Rd)	TB	R	RBI	TBB	IBB	SO	HBP	SH	SF	SB	CS	SB%	GDP	Avg	OBP	SLG
1989 Chicago	NL	59	157	39	10	0	1	(0	1)	52	15	14	11	5	26	2	1	1	2	1	.67	4	.248	.304	.331
1990 Chicago	NL	133	419	113	24	2	1	(0	1)	144	36	38	17	11	50	3	4	4	8	3	.73	13	.270	.300	.344
1991 Chicago	NL	21	47	9	2	0	0	(0	0)	11	3	6	6	1	6	0	1	0	0	0	.00	0	.191	.283	.234
1992 Chicago	NL	91	270	73	3	1	1	(1	0)	81	19	12	19	3	38	1	0	1	0	2	.00	8	.270	.320	.300
4 ML YEARS		304	893	234	39	3	3	(2	1)	288	73	70	53	20	120	6	6	6	10	6	.63	25	.262	.306	.323

Dan Gladden

Bats: Right   **Throws:** Right   **Pos:** LF/CF   **Ht:** 5'11"   **Wt:** 184   **Born:** 07/07/57   **Age:** 35

		BATTING																BASERUNNING				PERCENTAGES		
Year Team	Lg	G	AB	H	2B	3B	HR	(Hm	Rd)	TB	R	RBI	TBB	IBB	SO	HBP	SH	SF	SB	CS	SB%	GDP	Avg	OBP	SLG
1983 San Francisco	NL	18	63	14	2	0	1	(1	0)	19	6	9	5	0	11	0	3	1	4	3	.57	3	.222	.275	.302
1984 San Francisco	NL	86	342	120	17	2	4	(4	0)	153	71	31	33	2	37	2	6	1	31	16	.66	3	.351	.410	.447
1985 San Francisco	NL	142	502	122	15	8	7	(6	1)	174	64	41	40	1	78	7	10	2	32	15	.68	10	.243	.307	.347
1986 San Francisco	NL	102	351	97	16	1	4	(1	3)	127	55	29	39	3	59	5	7	0	27	10	.73	5	.276	.357	.362
1987 Minnesota	AL	121	438	109	21	2	8	(4	4)	158	69	38	38	2	72	3	1	2	25	9	.74	8	.249	.312	.361
1988 Minnesota	AL	141	576	155	32	6	11	(8	3)	232	91	62	46	4	74	4	2	5	28	8	.78	9	.269	.325	.403
1989 Minnesota	AL	121	461	136	23	3	8	(1	7)	189	69	46	23	3	53	5	5	7	23	7	.77	6	.295	.331	.410
1990 Minnesota	AL	136	534	147	27	6	5	(2	3)	201	64	40	26	2	67	6	1	4	25	9	.74	17	.275	.314	.376
1991 Minnesota	AL	126	461	114	14	9	6	(3	3)	164	65	52	36	1	60	5	5	4	15	9	.63	13	.247	.306	.356
1992 Detroit	AL	113	417	106	20	1	7	(3	4)	149	57	42	30	0	64	2	5	5	4	2	.67	10	.254	.304	.357
10 ML YEARS		1106	4145	1120	187	38	61	(33	28)	1566	611	390	316	18	575	39	45	31	214	88	.71	84	.270	.326	.378

Tom Glavine

Pitches: Left   **Bats:** Left   **Pos:** SP   **Ht:** 6' 1"   **Wt:** 190   **Born:** 03/25/66   **Age:** 27

		HOW MUCH HE PITCHED						WHAT HE GAVE UP												THE RESULTS					
Year Team	Lg	G	GS	CG	GF	IP	BFP	H	R	ER	HR	SH	SF	HB	TBB	IBB	SO	WP	Bk	W	L	Pct.	ShO	Sv	ERA
1987 Atlanta	NL	9	9	0	0	50.1	238	55	34	31	5	2	3	3	33	4	20	1	1	2	4	.333	0	0	5.54
1988 Atlanta	NL	34	34	1	0	195.1	844	201	111	99	12	17	11	8	63	7	84	2	2	7	17	.292	0	0	4.56
1989 Atlanta	NL	29	29	6	0	186	766	172	88	76	20	11	4	2	40	3	90	2	0	14	8	.636	4	0	3.68
1990 Atlanta	NL	33	33	1	0	214.1	929	232	111	102	18	21	2	1	78	10	129	8	1	10	12	.455	0	0	4.28
1991 Atlanta	NL	34	34	9	0	246.1	989	201	83	70	17	7	6	2	69	6	192	10	2	20	11	.645	1	0	2.56
1992 Atlanta	NL	33	33	7	0	225	919	197	81	69	6	2	6	2	70	7	129	5	0	20	8	.714	5	0	2.76
6 ML YEARS		172	172	24	0	1117.1	4685	1058	508	447	78	60	32	18	353	37	644	28	6	73	60	.549	10	0	3.60

Jerry Don Gleaton

Pitches: Left   **Bats:** Left   **Pos:** RP   **Ht:** 6' 3"   **Wt:** 210   **Born:** 09/14/57   **Age:** 35

		HOW MUCH HE PITCHED						WHAT HE GAVE UP												THE RESULTS					
Year Team	Lg	G	GS	CG	GF	IP	BFP	H	R	ER	HR	SH	SF	HB	TBB	IBB	SO	WP	Bk	W	L	Pct.	ShO	Sv	ERA
1979 Texas	AL	5	2	0	1	10	45	15	7	7	0	1	1	1	2	0	2	1	0	0	1	.000	0	0	6.30
1980 Texas	AL	5	0	0	2	7	30	5	2	2	0	0	2	0	4	0	2	0	0	0	0	.000	0	0	2.57
1981 Seattle	AL	20	13	1	3	85	369	88	50	45	10	3	4	2	38	2	31	3	0	4	7	.364	0	0	4.76
1982 Seattle	AL	3	0	0	1	4.2	24	7	7	7	3	0	0	1	2	0	1	0	0	0	0	.000	0	0	13.50

Year Team	Lg	G	GS	CG	GF	IP	BFP	H	R	ER	HR	SH	SF	HB	TBB	IBB	SO	WP	Bk	W	L	Pct.	ShO	Sv	ERA
1984 Chicago	AL	11	1	0	4	18.1	81	20	12	7	2	0	4	1	6	0	4	4	0	1	2	.333	0	2	3.44
1985 Chicago	AL	31	0	0	9	29.2	135	37	19	19	3	4	1	0	13	3	22	3	0	1	0	1.000	0	1	5.76
1987 Kansas City	AL	48	0	0	22	50.2	210	38	28	24	4	3	3	0	28	3	44	4	1	4	4	.500	0	5	4.26
1988 Kansas City	AL	42	0	0	20	38	164	33	17	15	2	2	0	3	17	1	29	2	0	0	4	.000	0	3	3.55
1989 Kansas City	AL	15	0	0	5	14.1	66	20	10	9	0	0	2	0	6	0	9	0	1	0	0	.000	0	0	5.65
1990 Detroit	AL	57	0	0	34	82.2	325	62	27	27	5	2	4	3	25	2	56	2	1	1	3	.250	0	13	2.94
1991 Detroit	AL	47	0	0	16	75.1	319	74	37	34	7	1	4	0	39	8	47	1	1	3	2	.600	0	2	4.06
1992 Pittsburgh	NL	23	0	0	6	31.2	142	34	16	15	4	2	1	0	19	3	18	1	0	1	0	1.000	0	2	4.26
12 ML YEARS		307	16	1	123	447.1	1910	433	232	211	40	18	26	11	199	22	265	21	4	15	23	.395	0	26	4.25

Jerry Goff

Bats: Left **Throws:** Right **Pos:** PH **Ht:** 6' 3" **Wt:** 210 **Born:** 04/12/64 **Age:** 29

					BATTING															BASERUNNING				PERCENTAGES		
Year Team	Lg	G	AB	H	2B	3B	HR	(Hm	Rd)	TB	R	RBI	TBB	IBB	SO	HBP	SH	SF	SB	CS	SB%	GDP	Avg	OBP	SLG
1990 Montreal	NL	52	119	27	1	0	3	(0	3)	37	14	7	21	4	36	0	1	0	0	2	.00	0	.227	.343	.311
1992 Montreal	NL	3	3	0	0	0	0	(0	0)	0	0	0	0	0	3	0	0	0	0	0	.00	0	.000	.000	.000
2 ML YEARS		55	122	27	1	0	3	(0	3)	37	14	7	21	4	39	0	1	0	0	2	.00	0	.221	.336	.303

Leo Gomez

Bats: Right **Throws:** Right **Pos:** 3B **Ht:** 6' 0" **Wt:** 180 **Born:** 03/02/67 **Age:** 26

					BATTING															BASERUNNING				PERCENTAGES		
Year Team	Lg	G	AB	H	2B	3B	HR	(Hm	Rd)	TB	R	RBI	TBB	IBB	SO	HBP	SH	SF	SB	CS	SB%	GDP	Avg	OBP	SLG
1990 Baltimore	AL	12	39	9	0	0	0	(0	0)	9	3	1	8	0	7	0	1	0	0	0	.00	2	.231	.362	.231
1991 Baltimore	AL	118	391	91	17	2	16	(7	9)	160	40	45	40	0	82	2	5	7	1	1	.50	11	.233	.302	.409
1992 Baltimore	AL	137	468	124	24	0	17	(6	11)	199	62	64	63	4	78	8	5	8	2	3	.40	14	.265	.356	.425
3 ML YEARS		267	898	224	41	2	33	(13	20)	368	105	110	111	4	167	10	11	15	3	4	.43	27	.249	.334	.410

Rene Gonzales

Bats: Right **Throws:** Right **Pos:** 3B/1B/2B **Ht:** 6' 3" **Wt:** 195 **Born:** 09/03/61 **Age:** 31

					BATTING															BASERUNNING				PERCENTAGES		
Year Team	Lg	G	AB	H	2B	3B	HR	(Hm	Rd)	TB	R	RBI	TBB	IBB	SO	HBP	SH	SF	SB	CS	SB%	GDP	Avg	OBP	SLG
1984 Montreal	NL	29	30	7	1	0	0	(0	0)	8	5	2	2	0	5	1	0	0	0	0	.00	0	.233	.303	.267
1986 Montreal	NL	11	26	3	0	0	0	(0	0)	3	1	0	2	0	7	0	0	0	0	2	.00	0	.115	.179	.115
1987 Baltimore	AL	37	60	16	2	1	1	(1	0)	23	14	7	3	0	11	0	2	0	1	0	1.00	2	.267	.302	.383
1988 Baltimore	AL	92	237	51	6	0	2	(1	1)	63	13	15	13	0	32	3	5	2	2	0	1.00	5	.215	.263	.266
1989 Baltimore	AL	71	166	36	4	0	1	(0	1)	43	16	11	12	0	30	0	6	1	5	3	.63	6	.217	.268	.259
1990 Baltimore	AL	67	103	22	3	1	1	(1	0)	30	13	12	12	0	14	0	6	0	1	2	.33	3	.214	.296	.291
1991 Toronto	AL	71	118	23	3	0	1	(1	0)	29	16	6	12	0	22	4	6	1	0	0	.00	5	.195	.289	.246
1992 California	AL	104	329	91	17	1	7	(6	1)	131	47	38	41	1	46	4	5	1	7	4	.64	17	.277	.363	.398
8 ML YEARS		482	1069	249	36	3	13	(10	3)	330	125	91	97	1	167	12	30	5	16	11	.59	38	.233	.303	.309

Jose Gonzalez

Bats: Right **Throws:** Right **Pos:** LF **Ht:** 6' 2" **Wt:** 200 **Born:** 11/23/64 **Age:** 28

					BATTING															BASERUNNING				PERCENTAGES		
Year Team	Lg	G	AB	H	2B	3B	HR	(Hm	Rd)	TB	R	RBI	TBB	IBB	SO	HBP	SH	SF	SB	CS	SB%	GDP	Avg	OBP	SLG
1985 Los Angeles	NL	23	11	3	2	0	0	(0	0)	5	6	0	1	0	3	0	0	0	1	1	.50	1	.273	.333	.455
1986 Los Angeles	NL	57	93	20	5	1	2	(1	1)	33	15	6	7	0	29	0	2	0	4	3	.57	0	.215	.270	.355
1987 Los Angeles	NL	19	16	3	2	0	0	(0	0)	5	2	1	1	0	2	0	0	1	5	0	1.00	0	.188	.222	.313
1988 Los Angeles	NL	37	24	2	1	0	0	(0	0)	3	7	0	2	0	10	0	0	0	3	0	1.00	0	.083	.154	.125
1989 Los Angeles	NL	95	261	70	11	2	3	(2	1)	94	31	18	23	5	53	0	1	1	9	3	.75	2	.268	.326	.360
1990 Los Angeles	NL	106	99	23	5	3	2	(2	0)	40	15	8	6	1	27	1	1	1	3	1	.75	1	.232	.280	.404
1991 3 ML Teams		91	117	13	2	1	2	(1	1)	23	15	7	13	0	42	1	2	1	8	0	1.00	2	.111	.205	.197
1992 California	AL	33	55	10	2	0	0	(0	0)	12	4	2	7	1	20	0	1	1	0	0	.00	2	.182	.270	.218
1991 Los Angeles	NL	42	28	0	0	0	0	(0	0)	0	3	0	2	0	9	0	0	0	0	0	.00	0	.000	.067	.000
Pittsburgh	NL	16	20	2	0	0	1	(1	0)	5	2	3	0	0	6	0	2	1	0	0	.00	0	.100	.095	.250
Cleveland	AL	33	69	11	2	1	1	(0	1)	18	10	4	11	0	27	1	0	0	8	0	1.00	2	.159	.284	.261
8 ML YEARS		461	676	144	30	7	9	(6	3)	215	95	42	60	7	186	2	7	5	33	9	.79	8	.213	.277	.318

Juan Gonzalez

Bats: Right **Throws:** Right **Pos:** CF/LF **Ht:** 6' 3" **Wt:** 210 **Born:** 10/16/69 **Age:** 23

					BATTING															BASERUNNING				PERCENTAGES		
Year Team	Lg	G	AB	H	2B	3B	HR	(Hm	Rd)	TB	R	RBI	TBB	IBB	SO	HBP	SH	SF	SB	CS	SB%	GDP	Avg	OBP	SLG
1989 Texas	AL	24	60	9	3	0	1	(1	0)	15	6	7	6	0	17	0	2	0	0	0	.00	4	.150	.227	.250
1990 Texas	AL	25	90	26	7	1	4	(3	1)	47	11	12	2	0	18	2	0	1	0	1	.00	2	.289	.316	.522
1991 Texas	AL	142	545	144	34	1	27	(7	20)	261	78	102	42	7	118	5	0	3	4	4	.50	10	.264	.321	.479
1992 Texas	AL	155	584	152	24	2	43	(19	24)	309	77	109	35	1	143	5	0	8	0	0	.00	16	.260	.304	.529

| | 4 ML YEARS | 346 | 1279 | 331 | 68 | 4 | 75 | (30 | 45) | 632 | 172 | 230 | 85 | 8 | 296 | 12 | 2 | 12 | 4 | 6 | .40 | 32 | .259 | .308 | .494 |

Luis Gonzalez

Bats: Left **Throws:** Right **Pos:** LF　　　　**Ht:** 6' 2" **Wt:** 180 **Born:** 09/03/67 **Age:** 25

			BATTING																	BASERUNNING				PERCENTAGES		
Year Team	Lg	G	AB	H	2B	3B	HR	(Hm	Rd)	TB	R	RBI	TBB	IBB	SO	HBP	SH	SF	SB	CS	SB%	GDP	Avg	OBP	SLG
1990 Houston	NL	12	21	4	2	0	0	(0	0)	6	1	0	2	1	5	0	0	0	0	0	.00	0	.190	.261	.286
1991 Houston	NL	137	473	120	28	9	13	(4	9)	205	51	69	40	4	101	8	1	4	10	7	.59	9	.254	.320	.433
1992 Houston	NL	122	387	94	19	3	10	(4	6)	149	40	55	24	3	52	2	1	2	7	7	.50	6	.243	.289	.385
3 ML YEARS		271	881	218	49	12	23	(8	15)	360	92	124	66	8	158	10	2	6	17	14	.55	15	.247	.305	.409

Dwight Gooden

Pitches: Right **Bats:** Right **Pos:** SP　　　　**Ht:** 6' 3" **Wt:** 210 **Born:** 11/16/64 **Age:** 28

		HOW MUCH HE PITCHED						WHAT HE GAVE UP									THE RESULTS					
Year Team	Lg	G	GS	CG	GF	IP	BFP	H	R	ER	HR	SH	SF	HB	TBB	IBB	SO	WP	Bk	W	L	Pct.	ShO	Sv	ERA
1984 New York	NL	31	31	7	0	218	879	161	72	63	7	3	2	2	73	2	276	3	7	17	9	.654	3	0	2.60
1985 New York	NL	35	35	16	0	276.2	1065	198	51	47	13	6	2	2	69	4	268	6	2	24	4	.857	8	0	1.53
1986 New York	NL	33	33	12	0	250	1020	197	92	79	17	10	8	4	80	3	200	4	4	17	6	.739	2	0	2.84
1987 New York	NL	25	25	7	0	179.2	730	162	68	64	11	5	5	2	53	2	148	1	1	15	7	.682	3	0	3.21
1988 New York	NL	34	34	10	0	248.1	1024	242	98	88	8	10	6	6	57	4	175	5	5	18	9	.667	3	0	3.19
1989 New York	NL	19	17	0	1	118.1	497	93	42	38	9	4	3	2	47	2	101	7	5	9	4	.692	0	1	2.89
1990 New York	NL	34	34	2	0	232.2	983	229	106	99	10	10	7	7	70	3	223	6	3	19	7	.731	1	0	3.83
1991 New York	NL	27	27	3	0	190	789	185	80	76	12	5	4	3	56	2	150	5	2	13	7	.650	1	0	3.60
1992 New York	NL	31	31	3	0	206	863	197	93	84	11	10	7	3	70	7	145	3	1	10	13	.435	0	0	3.67
9 ML YEARS		269	267	60	1	1919.2	7850	1664	702	638	98	63	44	31	575	29	1686	40	30	142	66	.683	21	2	2.99

Tom Goodwin

Bats: Left **Throws:** Right **Pos:** LF　　　　**Ht:** 6' 1" **Wt:** 165 **Born:** 07/27/68 **Age:** 24

			BATTING																	BASERUNNING				PERCENTAGES		
Year Team	Lg	G	AB	H	2B	3B	HR	(Hm	Rd)	TB	R	RBI	TBB	IBB	SO	HBP	SH	SF	SB	CS	SB%	GDP	Avg	OBP	SLG
1989 Great Falls	R	63	240	74	12	3	2	--	--	98	55	33	28	1	30	2	1	2	60	8	.88	3	.308	.382	.408
1990 Bakersfield	A	32	134	39	6	2	0	--	--	49	24	13	11	0	22	0	1	0	22	4	.85	0	.291	.345	.366
San Antonio	AA	102	428	119	14	4	0	--	--	141	76	28	38	2	72	1	8	3	60	11	.85	3	.278	.336	.329
1991 Albuquerque	AAA	132	509	139	19	4	1	--	--	169	84	45	59	0	83	2	10	3	48	22	.69	5	.273	.349	.332
1992 Albuquerque	AAA	82	319	96	10	4	2	--	--	120	48	28	37	2	47	1	6	3	27	10	.73	3	.301	.372	.376
1991 Los Angeles	NL	16	7	1	0	0	0	(0	0)	1	3	0	0	0	0	0	0	0	1	1	.50	0	.143	.143	.143
1992 Los Angeles	NL	57	73	17	1	1	0	(0	0)	20	15	3	6	0	10	0	0	0	7	3	.70	0	.233	.291	.274
2 ML YEARS		73	80	18	1	1	0	(0	0)	21	18	3	6	0	10	0	0	0	8	4	.67	0	.225	.279	.263

Tom Gordon

Pitches: Right **Bats:** Right **Pos:** RP/SP　　　　**Ht:** 5' 9" **Wt:** 180 **Born:** 11/18/67 **Age:** 25

		HOW MUCH HE PITCHED						WHAT HE GAVE UP									THE RESULTS					
Year Team	Lg	G	GS	CG	GF	IP	BFP	H	R	ER	HR	SH	SF	HB	TBB	IBB	SO	WP	Bk	W	L	Pct.	ShO	Sv	ERA
1988 Kansas City	AL	5	2	0	0	15.2	67	16	9	9	1	0	0	0	7	0	18	0	0	0	2	.000	0	0	5.17
1989 Kansas City	AL	49	16	1	16	163	677	122	67	66	10	4	4	1	86	4	153	12	0	17	9	.654	1	1	3.64
1990 Kansas City	AL	32	32	6	0	195.1	858	192	99	81	17	8	2	3	99	1	175	11	0	12	11	.522	1	0	3.73
1991 Kansas City	AL	45	14	1	11	158	684	129	76	68	16	5	3	4	87	6	167	5	0	9	14	.391	0	1	3.87
1992 Kansas City	AL	40	11	0	13	117.2	516	116	67	60	9	2	6	4	55	4	98	5	2	6	10	.375	0	0	4.59
5 ML YEARS		171	75	8	40	649.2	2802	575	318	284	53	19	15	12	334	15	611	33	2	44	46	.489	2	2	3.93

Goose Gossage

Pitches: Right **Bats:** Right **Pos:** RP　　　　**Ht:** 6' 3" **Wt:** 225 **Born:** 07/05/51 **Age:** 41

		HOW MUCH HE PITCHED						WHAT HE GAVE UP									THE RESULTS					
Year Team	Lg	G	GS	CG	GF	IP	BFP	H	R	ER	HR	SH	SF	HB	TBB	IBB	SO	WP	Bk	W	L	Pct.	ShO	Sv	ERA
1972 Chicago	AL	36	1	0	9	80	352	72	44	38	2	10	2	4	44	3	57	7	0	7	1	.875	0	2	4.28
1973 Chicago	AL	20	4	1	4	50	232	57	44	41	9	5	4	3	37	2	33	6	0	0	4	.000	0	0	7.38
1974 Chicago	AL	39	3	0	19	89	397	92	45	41	4	6	4	2	47	7	64	2	1	4	6	.400	0	1	4.15
1975 Chicago	AL	62	0	0	49	142	582	99	32	29	3	15	0	5	70	15	130	3	0	9	8	.529	0	26	1.84
1976 Chicago	AL	31	29	15	1	224	956	214	104	98	16	8	7	9	90	3	135	6	0	9	17	.346	0	1	3.94
1977 Pittsburgh	NL	72	0	0	55	133	523	78	27	24	9	7	6	2	49	6	151	2	0	11	9	.550	0	26	1.62
1978 New York	AL	63	0	0	55	134	543	87	41	30	9	9	8	2	59	8	122	5	0	10	11	.476	0	27	2.01
1979 New York	AL	36	0	0	33	58	234	48	18	17	5	4	0	0	19	4	41	3	0	5	3	.625	0	18	2.64
1980 New York	AL	64	0	0	58	99	401	74	29	25	5	8	4	1	37	3	103	4	0	6	2	.750	0	33	2.27
1981 New York	AL	32	0	0	30	47	173	22	6	4	2	1	1	1	14	1	48	1	0	3	2	.600	0	20	0.77
1982 New York	AL	56	0	0	43	93	356	63	23	23	5	5	2	0	28	5	102	1	0	4	5	.444	0	30	2.23
1983 New York	AL	57	0	0	47	87.1	367	82	27	22	5	5	6	1	25	5	90	0	0	13	5	.722	0	22	2.27
1984 San Diego	NL	62	0	0	51	102.1	412	75	34	33	6	4	3	1	36	4	84	2	2	10	6	.625	0	25	2.90

Year	Team	Lg	G	GS	CG	GF	IP	BFP	H	R	ER	HR	SH	SF	HB	TBB	IBB	SO	WP	Bk	W	L	Pct.	ShO	Sv	ERA
1985	San Diego	NL	50	0	0	38	79	308	64	21	16	1	3	4	1	17	1	52	0	0	5	3	.625	0	26	1.82
1986	San Diego	NL	45	0	0	38	64.2	281	69	36	32	8	2	4	2	20	0	63	4	0	5	7	.417	0	21	4.45
1987	San Diego	NL	40	0	0	30	52	217	47	18	18	4	2	3	0	19	6	44	2	0	5	4	.556	0	11	3.12
1988	Chicago	NL	46	0	0	33	43.2	194	50	23	21	3	3	1	3	15	5	30	3	2	4	4	.500	0	13	4.33
1989	2 ML Teams		42	0	0	28	58	238	46	22	19	2	3	2	1	30	4	30	3	0	3	1	.750	0	5	2.95
1991	Texas	AL	44	0	0	16	40.1	167	33	16	16	4	3	0	1	16	1	28	3	0	4	2	.667	0	1	3.57
1992	Oakland	AL	30	0	0	13	38	163	32	13	12	5	1	2	2	19	4	26	0	0	0	2	.000	0	0	2.84
1989	San Francisco	NL	31	0	0	22	43.2	182	32	16	13	2	2	2	0	27	3	24	2	0	2	1	.667	0	4	2.68
	New York	AL	11	0	0	6	14.1	56	14	6	6	0	1	0	1	3	1	6	1	0	1	0	1.000	0	1	3.77
20	ML YEARS		927	37	16	648	1714.1	7096	1404	623	559	107	104	63	43	691	87	1433	57	5	117	102	.534	0	308	2.93

Jim Gott

Pitches: Right   Bats: Right   Pos: RP **Ht: 6' 4"   Wt: 220   Born: 08/03/59   Age: 33**

			HOW MUCH HE PITCHED						WHAT HE GAVE UP												THE RESULTS					
Year	Team	Lg	G	GS	CG	GF	IP	BFP	H	R	ER	HR	SH	SF	HB	TBB	IBB	SO	WP	Bk	W	L	Pct.	ShO	Sv	ERA
1982	Toronto	AL	30	23	1	4	136	600	134	76	67	15	3	2	3	66	0	82	8	0	5	10	.333	1	0	4.43
1983	Toronto	AL	34	30	6	2	176.2	776	195	103	93	15	4	3	5	68	5	121	2	0	9	14	.391	1	0	4.74
1984	Toronto	AL	35	12	1	11	109.2	464	93	54	49	7	7	6	3	49	3	73	1	0	7	6	.538	1	2	4.02
1985	San Francisco	NL	26	26	2	0	148.1	629	144	73	64	10	6	4	1	51	3	78	3	2	7	10	.412	0	0	3.88
1986	San Francisco	NL	9	2	0	3	13	66	16	12	11	0	1	1	0	13	2	9	1	1	0	0	.000	0	1	7.62
1987	2 ML Teams		55	3	0	30	87	382	81	43	33	4	2	1	2	40	7	90	5	0	1	2	.333	0	13	3.41
1988	Pittsburgh	NL	67	0	0	59	77.1	314	68	30	30	9	7	3	2	22	5	76	1	6	6	6	.500	0	34	3.49
1989	Pittsburgh	NL	1	0	0	0	0.2	4	1	0	0	0	0	0	0	1	0	1	0	0	0	0	.000	0	0	0.00
1990	Los Angeles	NL	50	0	0	24	62	270	59	27	20	5	2	4	0	34	7	44	4	0	3	5	.375	0	3	2.90
1991	Los Angeles	NL	55	0	0	26	76	322	63	28	25	5	6	1	1	32	7	73	6	3	4	3	.571	0	2	2.96
1992	Los Angeles	NL	68	0	0	28	88	369	72	27	24	4	6	1	1	41	13	75	9	3	3	3	.500	0	6	2.45
1987	San Francisco	NL	30	3	0	8	56	253	53	32	28	4	1	1	2	32	5	63	3	0	1	0	1.000	0	0	4.50
	Pittsburgh	NL	25	0	0	22	31	129	28	11	5	0	1	0	0	8	2	27	2	0	0	2	.000	0	13	1.45
11	ML YEARS		430	96	10	187	974.2	4196	926	473	416	74	44	26	18	417	52	722	40	15	45	59	.433	3	61	3.84

Mauro Gozzo

Pitches: Right   Bats: Right   Pos: RP **Ht: 6' 3"   Wt: 212   Born: 03/07/66   Age: 27**

			HOW MUCH HE PITCHED						WHAT HE GAVE UP												THE RESULTS					
Year	Team	Lg	G	GS	CG	GF	IP	BFP	H	R	ER	HR	SH	SF	HB	TBB	IBB	SO	WP	Bk	W	L	Pct.	ShO	Sv	ERA
1989	Toronto	AL	9	3	0	2	31.2	133	35	19	17	1	0	2	1	9	1	10	0	0	4	1	.800	0	0	4.83
1990	Cleveland	AL	2	0	0	1	3	13	2	0	0	0	0	0	0	2	0	2	0	0	0	0	.000	0	0	0.00
1991	Cleveland	AL	2	2	0	0	4.2	28	9	10	10	0	0	1	0	7	0	3	2	0	0	0	.000	0	0	19.29
1992	Minnesota	AL	2	0	0	0	1.2	12	7	5	5	2	0	0	0	0	0	1	1	0	0	0	.000	0	0	27.00
4	ML YEARS		15	5	0	3	41	186	53	34	32	3	0	3	1	18	1	16	3	0	4	1	.800	0	0	7.02

Mark Grace

Bats: Left   Throws: Left   Pos: 1B **Ht: 6' 2"   Wt: 190   Born: 06/28/64   Age: 29**

						BATTING														BASERUNNING			PERCENTAGES		
Year	Team	Lg	G	AB	H	2B	3B	HR	(Hm	Rd)	TB	R	RBI	TBB	IBB	SO	HBP	SH	SF	SB	CS	SB%	GDP	Avg	OBP	SLG
1988	Chicago	NL	134	486	144	23	4	7	(0	7)	196	65	57	60	5	43	0	0	4	3	3	.50	12	.296	.371	.403
1989	Chicago	NL	142	510	160	28	3	13	(8	5)	233	74	79	80	13	42	0	3	3	14	7	.67	13	.314	.405	.457
1990	Chicago	NL	157	589	182	32	1	9	(4	5)	243	72	82	59	5	54	5	1	8	15	6	.71	10	.309	.372	.413
1991	Chicago	NL	160	619	169	28	5	8	(5	3)	231	87	58	70	7	53	3	4	7	3	4	.43	6	.273	.346	.373
1992	Chicago	NL	158	603	185	37	5	9	(5	4)	259	72	79	72	8	36	4	2	8	6	1	.86	14	.307	.380	.430
5	ML YEARS		751	2807	840	148	18	46	(22	24)	1162	370	355	341	38	228	12	10	30	41	21	.66	55	.299	.374	.414

Joe Grahe

Pitches: Right   Bats: Right   Pos: RP/SP **Ht: 6' 0"   Wt: 200   Born: 08/14/67   Age: 25**

			HOW MUCH HE PITCHED						WHAT HE GAVE UP												THE RESULTS					
Year	Team	Lg	G	GS	CG	GF	IP	BFP	H	R	ER	HR	SH	SF	HB	TBB	IBB	SO	WP	Bk	W	L	Pct.	ShO	Sv	ERA
1990	California	AL	8	8	0	0	43.1	200	51	30	24	3	0	0	3	23	1	25	1	0	3	4	.429	0	0	4.98
1991	California	AL	18	10	1	2	73	330	84	43	39	2	1	1	3	33	0	40	2	0	3	7	.300	0	0	4.81
1992	California	AL	46	7	0	31	94.2	399	85	37	37	5	4	4	6	39	2	39	4	0	5	6	.455	0	21	3.52
3	ML YEARS		72	25	1	33	211	929	220	110	100	10	5	5	12	95	3	104	6	0	11	17	.393	0	21	4.27

Mark Grant

Pitches: Right   Bats: Right   Pos: RP/SP **Ht: 6' 2"   Wt: 215   Born: 10/24/63   Age: 29**

			HOW MUCH HE PITCHED						WHAT HE GAVE UP												THE RESULTS					
Year	Team	Lg	G	GS	CG	GF	IP	BFP	H	R	ER	HR	SH	SF	HB	TBB	IBB	SO	WP	Bk	W	L	Pct.	ShO	Sv	ERA
1984	San Francisco	NL	11	10	0	1	53.2	231	56	40	38	6	2	3	1	19	0	32	3	0	1	4	.200	0	1	6.37
1986	San Francisco	NL	4	1	0	3	10	39	6	4	4	0	0	0	0	5	0	5	0	1	0	1	.000	0	0	3.60
1987	2 ML Teams		33	25	2	2	163.1	720	170	88	77	22	15	1	1	73	8	90	8	3	7	9	.438	1	1	4.24

Year	Team	Lg	G	GS	CG	GF	IP	BFP	H	R	ER	HR	SH	SF	HB	TBB	IBB	SO	WP	Bk	W	L	Pct.	ShO	Sv	ERA
1988	San Diego	NL	33	11	0	9	97.2	410	97	41	40	14	6	4	2	36	6	61	5	0	2	8	.200	0	0	3.69
1989	San Diego	NL	50	0	0	19	116.1	466	105	45	43	11	5	2	3	32	6	69	2	0	8	2	.800	0	2	3.33
1990	2 ML Teams		59	1	0	21	91.1	411	108	53	48	9	6	5	1	37	11	69	2	1	2	3	.400	0	3	4.73
1992	Seattle	AL	23	10	0	4	81	352	100	39	35	6	5	1	2	22	2	42	2	0	2	4	.333	0	0	3.89
1987	San Francisco	NL	16	8	0	2	61	264	66	29	24	6	7	1	1	21	5	32	2	2	1	2	.333	0	1	3.54
	San Diego	NL	17	17	2	0	102.1	456	104	59	53	16	8	0	0	52	3	58	6	1	6	7	.462	1	0	4.66
1990	San Diego	NL	26	0	0	5	39	180	47	23	21	5	4	3	0	19	8	29	1	1	1	1	.500	0	0	4.85
	Atlanta	NL	33	1	0	16	52.1	231	61	30	27	4	2	2	1	18	3	40	1	0	1	1	.333	0	0	4.64
	7 ML YEARS		213	58	2	59	613.1	2629	642	310	285	68	39	16	10	224	33	368	22	5	22	31	.415	1	7	4.18

Craig Grebeck

Bats: Right **Throws:** Right **Pos:** SS **Ht:** 5' 7" **Wt:** 160 **Born:** 12/29/64 **Age:** 28

							BATTING											BASERUNNING				PERCENTAGES		
Year	Team	Lg	G	AB	H	2B	3B	HR	(Hm | Rd)	TB	R	RBI	TBB	IBB	SO	HBP	SH	SF	SB	CS	SB%	GDP	Avg	OBP	SLG
1990	Chicago	AL	59	119	20	3	1	1	(1 | 0)	28	7	9	8	0	24	2	3	3	0	0	.00	2	.168	.227	.235
1991	Chicago	AL	107	224	63	16	3	6	(3 | 3)	103	37	31	38	0	40	1	4	1	1	3	.25	3	.281	.386	.460
1992	Chicago	AL	88	287	77	21	2	3	(2 | 1)	111	24	35	30	0	34	3	10	3	0	3	.00	5	.268	.341	.387
	3 ML YEARS		254	630	160	40	6	10	(6 | 4)	242	68	75	76	0	98	6	17	7	1	6	.14	10	.254	.337	.384

Gary Green

Bats: Right **Throws:** Right **Pos:** SS **Ht:** 6' 3" **Wt:** 175 **Born:** 01/14/62 **Age:** 31

							BATTING											BASERUNNING				PERCENTAGES		
Year	Team	Lg	G	AB	H	2B	3B	HR	(Hm | Rd)	TB	R	RBI	TBB	IBB	SO	HBP	SH	SF	SB	CS	SB%	GDP	Avg	OBP	SLG
1986	San Diego	NL	13	33	7	1	0	0	(0 | 0)	8	2	2	1	0	11	0	1	0	0	0	.00	0	.212	.235	.242
1989	San Diego	NL	15	27	7	3	0	0	(0 | 0)	10	4	0	1	0	1	0	0	0	0	1	.00	0	.259	.286	.370
1990	Texas	AL	62	88	19	3	0	0	(0 | 0)	22	10	8	6	0	18	0	4	1	1	1	.50	2	.216	.263	.250
1991	Texas	AL	8	20	3	1	0	0	(0 | 0)	4	0	1	1	0	6	0	2	0	0	0	.00	0	.150	.190	.200
1992	Cincinnati	NL	8	12	4	1	0	0	(0 | 0)	5	3	0	0	0	2	0	0	0	0	0	.00	0	.333	.333	.417
	5 ML YEARS		106	180	40	9	0	0	(0 | 0)	49	19	11	9	0	38	0	7	1	1	2	.33	2	.222	.258	.272

Tommy Greene

Pitches: Right **Bats:** Right **Pos:** SP **Ht:** 6' 5" **Wt:** 225 **Born:** 04/06/67 **Age:** 26

			HOW MUCH HE PITCHED						WHAT HE GAVE UP											THE RESULTS					
Year	Team	Lg	G	GS	CG	GF	IP	BFP	H	R	ER	HR	SH	SF	HB	TBB	IBB	SO	WP	Bk	W	L	Pct.	ShO	Sv	ERA
1989	Atlanta	NL	4	4	1	0	26.1	103	22	12	12	5	1	2	0	6	1	17	1	0	1	2	.333	1	0	4.10
1990	2 ML Teams		15	9	0	1	51.1	227	50	31	29	8	5	0	1	26	1	21	1	0	3	3	.500	0	0	5.08
1991	Philadelphia	NL	36	27	3	3	207.2	857	177	85	78	19	9	11	3	66	4	154	9	1	13	7	.650	2	0	3.38
1992	Philadelphia	NL	13	12	0	0	64.1	298	75	39	38	5	4	2	0	34	2	39	1	0	3	3	.500	0	0	5.32
1990	Atlanta	NL	5	2	0	0	12.1	61	14	11	11	3	2	0	1	9	0	4	0	0	1	0	1.000	0	0	8.03
	Philadelphia	NL	10	7	0	1	39	166	36	20	18	5	3	0	0	17	1	17	1	0	2	3	.400	0	0	4.15
	4 ML YEARS		68	52	4	4	349.2	1485	324	167	157	37	19	15	4	132	8	231	12	1	20	15	.571	3	0	4.04

Willie Greene

Bats: Left **Throws:** Right **Pos:** 3B **Ht:** 5'11" **Wt:** 165 **Born:** 09/23/71 **Age:** 21

							BATTING											BASERUNNING				PERCENTAGES		
Year	Team	Lg	G	AB	H	2B	3B	HR	(Hm | Rd)	TB	R	RBI	TBB	IBB	SO	HBP	SH	SF	SB	CS	SB%	GDP	Avg	OBP	SLG
1989	Pirates	R	23	86	24	3	3	5	--	--	48	17	11	9	1	6	1	0	0	4	3	.57	0	.279	.354	.558
	Princeton	R	39	136	44	6	4	2	--	--	64	22	24	9	1	29	2	0	0	4	4	.50	0	.324	.374	.471
1990	Augusta	A	86	291	75	12	4	11	--	--	128	59	47	61	3	58	3	1	5	6	5	.55	5	.258	.386	.440
	Salem	A	17	60	11	1	1	3	--	--	23	9	9	7	1	18	1	0	1	0	1	.00	1	.183	.275	.383
	Rockford	A	11	35	14	3	0	0	--	--	17	4	2	6	0	7	0	0	0	2	1	.67	0	.400	.488	.486
1991	Wst Plm Bch	A	99	322	70	9	3	12	--	--	121	46	43	50	2	92	3	1	3	9	7	.56	3	.217	.325	.376
1992	Cedar Rapds	A	34	120	34	8	2	12	--	--	82	26	40	18	0	27	2	0	2	2	4	.33	3	.283	.380	.683
	Chattanooga	AA	96	349	97	19	2	15	--	--	165	47	66	46	3	90	3	1	5	8	9	.47	8	.278	.362	.473
1992	Cincinnati	NL	29	93	25	5	2	2	(2 | 0)	40	10	13	10	0	23	0	0	1	0	2	.00	1	.269	.337	.430

Mike Greenwell

Bats: Left **Throws:** Right **Pos:** LF **Ht:** 6' 0" **Wt:** 205 **Born:** 07/18/63 **Age:** 29

							BATTING											BASERUNNING				PERCENTAGES		
Year	Team	Lg	G	AB	H	2B	3B	HR	(Hm | Rd)	TB	R	RBI	TBB	IBB	SO	HBP	SH	SF	SB	CS	SB%	GDP	Avg	OBP	SLG
1985	Boston	AL	17	31	10	1	0	4	(1 | 3)	23	7	8	3	1	4	0	0	0	1	0	1.00	0	.323	.382	.742
1986	Boston	AL	31	35	11	2	0	0	(0 | 0)	13	4	4	5	0	7	0	0	0	0	0	.00	0	.314	.400	.371
1987	Boston	AL	125	412	135	31	6	19	(8 | 11)	235	71	89	35	1	40	6	0	3	5	4	.56	7	.328	.386	.570
1988	Boston	AL	158	590	192	39	8	22	(12 | 10)	313	86	119	87	18	38	9	0	7	16	8	.67	11	.325	.416	.531
1989	Boston	AL	145	578	178	36	0	14	(6 | 8)	256	87	95	56	15	44	3	0	4	13	5	.72	21	.308	.370	.443
1990	Boston	AL	159	610	181	30	6	14	(6 | 8)	265	71	73	65	12	43	4	0	3	8	7	.53	19	.297	.367	.434
1991	Boston	AL	147	544	163	26	6	9	(5 | 4)	228	76	83	43	6	35	3	1	7	15	5	.75	11	.300	.350	.419

Year Team	Lg	G	AB	H	2B	3B	HR	(Hm	Rd)	TB	R	RBI	TBB	IBB	SO	HBP	SH	SF	SB	CS	SB%	GDP	Avg	OBP	SLG
1992 Boston	AL	49	180	42	2	0	2	(0	2)	50	16	18	18	1	19	2	0	2	2	3	.40	8	.233	.307	.278
8 ML YEARS		831	2980	912	167	26	84	(38	46)	1383	418	489	312	54	230	27	1	26	60	32	.65	78	.306	.374	.464

Tommy Gregg

Bats: Left **Throws:** Left **Pos:** CF **Ht:** 6' 1" **Wt:** 190 **Born:** 07/29/63 **Age:** 29

				BATTING															BASERUNNING				PERCENTAGES		
Year Team	Lg	G	AB	H	2B	3B	HR	(Hm	Rd)	TB	R	RBI	TBB	IBB	SO	HBP	SH	SF	SB	CS	SB%	GDP	Avg	OBP	SLG
1987 Pittsburgh	NL	10	8	2	1	0	0	(0	0)	3	3	0	0	0	2	0	0	0	0	0	.00	2	.250	.250	.375
1988 2 ML Teams		25	44	13	4	0	1	(0	1)	20	5	7	3	1	6	0	0	1	0	1	.00	1	.295	.333	.455
1989 Atlanta	NL	102	276	67	8	0	6	(2	4)	93	24	23	18	2	45	0	3	1	3	4	.43	4	.243	.288	.337
1990 Atlanta	NL	124	239	63	13	1	5	(2	3)	93	18	32	20	4	39	1	0	1	4	3	.57	1	.264	.322	.389
1991 Atlanta	NL	72	107	20	8	1	1	(1	0)	33	13	4	12	2	24	1	0	0	2	2	.50	1	.187	.275	.308
1992 Atlanta	NL	18	19	5	0	0	1	(1	0)	8	1	1	1	0	7	0	0	0	1	0	1.00	1	.263	.300	.421
1988 Pittsburgh	NL	14	15	3	1	0	1	(0	1)	7	4	3	1	0	4	0	0	1	0	1	.00	0	.200	.235	.467
Atlanta	NL	11	29	10	3	0	0	(0	0)	13	1	4	2	1	2	0	0	0	0	0	.00	1	.345	.387	.448
6 ML YEARS		351	693	170	34	2	14	(6	8)	250	64	67	54	9	123	2	3	3	10	10	.50	10	.245	.301	.361

Ken Griffey Jr

Bats: Left **Throws:** Left **Pos:** CF **Ht:** 6' 3" **Wt:** 195 **Born:** 11/21/69 **Age:** 23

				BATTING															BASERUNNING				PERCENTAGES		
Year Team	Lg	G	AB	H	2B	3B	HR	(Hm	Rd)	TB	R	RBI	TBB	IBB	SO	HBP	SH	SF	SB	CS	SB%	GDP	Avg	OBP	SLG
1989 Seattle	AL	127	455	120	23	0	16	(10	6)	191	61	61	44	8	83	2	1	4	16	7	.70	4	.264	.329	.420
1990 Seattle	AL	155	597	179	28	7	22	(8	14)	287	91	80	63	12	81	2	0	4	16	11	.59	12	.300	.366	.481
1991 Seattle	AL	154	548	179	42	1	22	(16	6)	289	76	100	71	21	82	1	4	9	18	6	.75	10	.327	.399	.527
1992 Seattle	AL	142	565	174	39	4	27	(16	11)	302	83	103	44	15	67	5	0	3	10	5	.67	15	.308	.361	.535
4 ML YEARS		578	2165	652	132	12	87	(50	37)	1069	311	344	222	56	313	10	5	20	60	29	.67	41	.301	.366	.494

Alfredo Griffin

Bats: Both **Throws:** Right **Pos:** SS/2B **Ht:** 5'11" **Wt:** 166 **Born:** 03/06/57 **Age:** 36

				BATTING															BASERUNNING				PERCENTAGES		
Year Team	Lg	G	AB	H	2B	3B	HR	(Hm	Rd)	TB	R	RBI	TBB	IBB	SO	HBP	SH	SF	SB	CS	SB%	GDP	Avg	OBP	SLG
1976 Cleveland	AL	12	4	1	0	0	0	(0	0)	1	0	0	0	0	2	0	0	0	0	1	.00	0	.250	.250	.250
1977 Cleveland	AL	14	41	6	1	0	0	(0	0)	7	5	3	3	0	5	0	0	0	2	2	.50	1	.146	.205	.171
1978 Cleveland	AL	5	4	2	1	0	0	(0	0)	3	1	0	2	0	1	0	0	0	0	0	.00	0	.500	.667	.750
1979 Toronto	AL	153	624	179	22	10	2	(2	0)	227	81	31	40	0	59	5	16	4	21	16	.57	10	.287	.333	.364
1980 Toronto	AL	155	653	166	26	15	2	(1	1)	228	63	41	24	2	58	4	10	5	18	23	.44	8	.254	.283	.349
1981 Toronto	AL	101	388	81	19	6	0	(0	0)	112	30	21	17	1	38	1	6	2	8	12	.40	6	.209	.243	.289
1982 Toronto	AL	162	539	130	20	8	1	(0	1)	169	57	48	22	0	48	0	11	4	10	8	.56	7	.241	.269	.314
1983 Toronto	AL	162	528	132	22	9	4	(2	2)	184	62	47	27	0	44	3	11	3	8	11	.42	5	.250	.289	.348
1984 Toronto	AL	140	419	101	8	2	4	(1	3)	125	53	30	4	0	33	1	13	4	11	3	.79	5	.241	.248	.298
1985 Oakland	AL	162	614	166	18	7	2	(0	2)	204	75	64	20	1	50	0	5	7	24	9	.73	6	.270	.290	.332
1986 Oakland	AL	162	594	169	23	6	4	(1	3)	216	74	51	35	6	52	2	12	6	33	16	.67	5	.285	.323	.364
1987 Oakland	AL	144	494	130	23	5	3	(2	1)	172	69	60	28	2	41	4	10	3	26	13	.67	9	.263	.306	.348
1988 Los Angeles	NL	95	316	63	8	3	1	(0	0)	80	39	27	24	7	30	2	11	1	7	5	.58	3	.199	.259	.253
1989 Los Angeles	NL	136	506	125	27	2	0	(0	0)	156	49	29	29	2	57	0	11	1	10	7	.59	5	.247	.287	.308
1990 Los Angeles	NL	141	461	97	11	3	1	(0	1)	117	38	35	29	11	65	2	6	4	6	3	.67	5	.210	.258	.254
1991 Los Angeles	NL	109	350	85	6	2	0	(0	0)	95	27	27	22	5	49	1	7	5	5	4	.56	5	.243	.286	.271
1992 Los Angeles	AL	63	150	35	7	0	0	(0	0)	42	21	10	9	0	19	0	3	2	3	1	.75	3	.233	.273	.280
17 ML YEARS		1916	6685	1668	242	78	24	(9	15)	2138	744	524	335	37	651	25	132	51	192	134	.59	83	.250	.286	.320

Marquis Grissom

Bats: Right **Throws:** Right **Pos:** CF **Ht:** 5'11" **Wt:** 190 **Born:** 04/17/67 **Age:** 26

				BATTING															BASERUNNING				PERCENTAGES		
Year Team	Lg	G	AB	H	2B	3B	HR	(Hm	Rd)	TB	R	RBI	TBB	IBB	SO	HBP	SH	SF	SB	CS	SB%	GDP	Avg	OBP	SLG
1989 Montreal	NL	26	74	19	2	0	1	(0	1)	24	16	2	12	0	21	0	1	0	1	0	1.00	1	.257	.360	.324
1990 Montreal	NL	98	288	74	14	2	3	(2	1)	101	42	29	27	2	40	0	4	1	22	2	.92	3	.257	.320	.351
1991 Montreal	NL	148	558	149	23	9	6	(3	3)	208	73	39	34	0	89	1	4	0	76	17	.82	8	.267	.310	.373
1992 Montreal	NL	159	653	180	39	6	14	(8	6)	273	99	66	42	6	81	5	3	4	78	13	.86	12	.276	.322	.418
4 ML YEARS		431	1573	422	78	17	24	(13	11)	606	230	136	115	8	231	6	12	5	177	32	.85	24	.268	.320	.385

Buddy Groom

Pitches: Left **Bats:** Left **Pos:** SP/RP **Ht:** 6' 2" **Wt:** 200 **Born:** 07/10/65 **Age:** 27

		HOW MUCH HE PITCHED						WHAT HE GAVE UP											THE RESULTS					
Year Team	Lg	G	GS	CG	GF	IP	BFP	H	R	ER	HR	SH	SF	HB	TBB	IBB	SO	WP	Bk	W	L	Pct.	ShO	Sv	ERA
1987 White Sox	R	4	1	0	1	12	48	12	1	1	0	1	0	1	2	0	8	0	0	1	0	1.000	0	1	0.75
Daytona Bch	A	11	10	2	0	67.2	290	60	30	27	4	1	0	2	33	1	29	2	0	7	2	.778	0	0	3.59

Year	Team	Lg	G	GS	CG	GF	IP	BFP	H	R	ER	HR	SH	SF	HB	TBB	IBB	SO	WP	Bk	W	L	Pct.	ShO	Sv	ERA
1988	Tampa	A	27	27	8	0	195	801	181	69	55	7	2	10	6	51	1	118	11	6	13	10	.565	0	0	2.54
1989	Birmingham	AA	26	26	3	0	167.1	735	172	101	84	13	10	8	2	78	1	94	11	3	13	8	.619	1	0	4.52
1990	Birmingham	AA	20	20	0	0	115.1	519	135	81	65	10	3	1	2	48	1	66	6	2	6	8	.429	0	0	5.07
1991	London	AA	11	7	0	2	51.2	220	51	20	20	7	0	0	2	12	1	39	2	0	7	1	.875	0	0	3.48
	Toledo	AAA	24	6	0	4	75	320	73	39	36	7	5	2	4	25	2	49	1	1	2	5	.286	0	1	4.32
1992	Toledo	AAA	16	16	1	0	109.1	443	102	41	34	8	3	4	1	23	1	71	5	0	7	7	.500	0	0	2.80
1992	Detroit	AL	12	7	0	3	38.2	177	48	28	25	4	3	2	0	22	4	15	0	1	0	5	.000	0	1	5.82

Kevin Gross

Pitches: Right **Bats:** Right **Pos:** SP **Ht:** 6' 5" **Wt:** 215 **Born:** 06/08/61 **Age:** 32

			HOW MUCH HE PITCHED						WHAT HE GAVE UP												THE RESULTS					
Year	Team	Lg	G	GS	CG	GF	IP	BFP	H	R	ER	HR	SH	SF	HB	TBB	IBB	SO	WP	Bk	W	L	Pct.	ShO	Sv	ERA
1983	Philadelphia	NL	17	17	1	0	96	418	100	46	38	13	2	1	3	35	3	66	4	1	4	6	.400	1	0	3.56
1984	Philadelphia	NL	44	14	1	9	129	566	140	66	59	8	9	3	5	44	4	84	4	0	8	5	.615	0	1	4.12
1985	Philadelphia	NL	38	31	6	0	205.2	873	194	86	78	11	7	5	7	81	6	151	2	0	15	13	.536	2	0	3.41
1986	Philadelphia	NL	37	36	7	0	241.2	1040	240	115	108	28	8	5	8	94	2	154	2	1	12	12	.500	2	0	4.02
1987	Philadelphia	NL	34	33	3	1	200.2	878	205	107	97	26	8	6	10	87	7	110	3	7	9	16	.360	1	0	4.35
1988	Philadelphia	NL	33	33	5	0	231.2	989	209	101	95	18	9	4	11	89	5	162	5	7	12	14	.462	1	0	3.69
1989	Montreal	NL	31	31	4	0	201.1	867	188	105	98	20	10	3	6	88	6	158	5	5	11	12	.478	3	0	4.38
1990	Montreal	NL	31	26	2	3	163.1	712	171	86	83	9	6	9	4	65	7	111	4	1	9	12	.429	1	0	4.57
1991	Los Angeles	NL	46	10	0	16	115.2	509	112	56	46	10	6	4	2	50	6	95	3	0	10	11	.476	0	3	3.58
1992	Los Angeles	NL	34	30	4	0	204.2	856	182	82	72	11	14	6	3	77	10	158	4	2	8	13	.381	3	0	3.17
10 ML YEARS			345	261	33	29	1789.2	7708	1752	849	774	154	79	46	59	710	56	1249	36	28	98	114	.462	14	4	3.89

Kip Gross

Pitches: Right **Bats:** Right **Pos:** RP **Ht:** 6' 2" **Wt:** 190 **Born:** 08/24/64 **Age:** 28

			HOW MUCH HE PITCHED						WHAT HE GAVE UP												THE RESULTS					
Year	Team	Lg	G	GS	CG	GF	IP	BFP	H	R	ER	HR	SH	SF	HB	TBB	IBB	SO	WP	Bk	W	L	Pct.	ShO	Sv	ERA
1990	Cincinnati	NL	5	0	0	2	6.1	25	6	3	3	0	0	1	0	2	0	3	0	0	0	0	.000	0	0	4.26
1991	Cincinnati	NL	29	9	1	6	85.2	381	93	43	33	8	6	2	0	40	2	40	5	1	6	4	.600	0	0	3.47
1992	Los Angeles	NL	16	1	0	7	23.2	109	32	14	11	1	0	0	0	10	1	14	1	1	1	1	.500	0	0	4.18
3 ML YEARS			50	10	1	15	115.2	515	131	60	47	9	6	3	0	52	3	57	6	2	7	5	.583	0	0	3.66

Jeff Grotewold

Bats: Left **Throws:** Right **Pos:** C **Ht:** 6' 0" **Wt:** 215 **Born:** 12/08/65 **Age:** 27

			BATTING																	BASERUNNING				PERCENTAGES		
Year	Team	Lg	G	AB	H	2B	3B	HR	(Hm	Rd)	TB	R	RBI	TBB	IBB	SO	HBP	SH	SF	SB	CS	SB%	GDP	Avg	OBP	SLG
1987	Spartanburg	A	113	381	96	22	2	15	--	--	167	56	54	47	10	114	4	0	3	4	6	.40	5	.252	.338	.438
1988	Clearwater	A	125	442	97	23	2	6	--	--	142	35	39	42	9	103	1	1	1	2	1	.67	16	.219	.288	.321
1989	Clearwater	A	91	301	84	17	2	6	--	--	123	32	55	32	4	43	1	0	4	8	2	.80	12	.279	.346	.409
	Reading	AA	25	80	16	2	0	0	--	--	18	9	11	8	0	14	0	0	2	0	0	.00	2	.200	.267	.225
1990	Reading	AA	127	412	111	33	1	15	--	--	191	56	72	62	5	83	1	2	4	2	2	.50	11	.269	.363	.464
1991	Scranton-Wb	AAA	87	276	71	13	5	5	--	--	109	33	38	25	1	61	1	2	0	0	2	.00	6	.257	.321	.395
1992	Scranton/wb	AAA	17	51	15	1	1	1	--	--	21	8	8	7	1	10	2	0	0	0	0	.00	1	.294	.400	.412
1992	Philadelphia	NL	72	65	13	2	0	3	(0	3)	24	7	5	9	0	16	1	0	0	0	0		4	.200	.307	.369

Kelly Gruber

Bats: Right **Throws:** Right **Pos:** 3B **Ht:** 6' 0" **Wt:** 185 **Born:** 02/26/62 **Age:** 31

			BATTING																	BASERUNNING				PERCENTAGES		
Year	Team	Lg	G	AB	H	2B	3B	HR	(Hm	Rd)	TB	R	RBI	TBB	IBB	SO	HBP	SH	SF	SB	CS	SB%	GDP	Avg	OBP	SLG
1984	Toronto	AL	15	16	1	0	0	1	(0	1)	4	1	2	0	0	5	0	0	0	0	0	.00	1	.063	.063	.250
1985	Toronto	AL	5	13	3	0	0	0	(0	0)	3	0	1	0	0	3	0	0	0	0	0	.00	0	.231	.231	.231
1986	Toronto	AL	87	143	28	4	1	5	(4	1)	49	20	15	5	0	27	0	2	2	2	5	.29	4	.196	.220	.343
1987	Toronto	AL	138	341	80	14	3	12	(5	7)	136	50	36	17	2	70	7	1	2	12	2	.86	11	.235	.283	.399
1988	Toronto	AL	158	569	158	33	5	16	(5	11)	249	75	81	38	1	92	7	5	4	23	5	.82	20	.278	.328	.438
1989	Toronto	AL	135	545	158	24	4	18	(8	10)	244	83	73	30	0	60	3	0	5	10	5	.67	13	.290	.328	.448
1990	Toronto	AL	150	592	162	36	6	31	(23	8)	303	92	118	48	2	94	8	1	13	14	2	.88	14	.274	.330	.512
1991	Toronto	AL	113	429	108	18	2	20	(8	12)	190	58	65	31	5	70	6	3	5	12	7	.63	7	.252	.308	.443
1992	Toronto	AL	120	446	102	16	3	11	(7	4)	157	42	43	26	3	72	4	1	4	7	7	.50	14	.229	.275	.352
9 ML YEARS			921	3094	800	145	24	114	(60	54)	1335	421	434	195	13	493	35	13	35	80	33	.71	84	.259	.307	.431

Mark Gubicza

Pitches: Right **Bats:** Right **Pos:** SP **Ht:** 6' 5" **Wt:** 225 **Born:** 08/14/62 **Age:** 30

			HOW MUCH HE PITCHED						WHAT HE GAVE UP												THE RESULTS					
Year	Team	Lg	G	GS	CG	GF	IP	BFP	H	R	ER	HR	SH	SF	HB	TBB	IBB	SO	WP	Bk	W	L	Pct.	ShO	Sv	ERA
1984	Kansas City	AL	29	29	4	0	189	800	172	90	85	13	4	9	5	75	0	111	3	1	10	14	.417	2	0	4.05

Year	Team	Lg	G	GS	CG	GF	IP	BFP	H	R	ER	HR	SH	SF	HB	TBB	IBB	SO	WP	Bk	W	L	Pct.	ShO	Sv	ERA
1985	Kansas City	AL	29	28	0	0	177.1	760	160	88	80	14	1	6	5	77	0	99	12	0	14	10	.583	0	0	4.06
1986	Kansas City	AL	35	24	3	2	180.2	765	155	77	73	8	4	8	5	84	2	118	15	0	12	6	.667	2	0	3.64
1987	Kansas City	AL	35	35	10	0	241.2	1036	231	114	107	18	6	11	6	120	3	166	14	1	13	18	.419	2	0	3.98
1988	Kansas City	AL	35	35	8	0	269.2	1111	237	94	81	11	3	6	6	83	3	183	12	4	20	8	.714	4	0	2.70
1989	Kansas City	AL	36	36	8	0	255	1060	252	100	86	10	11	8	5	63	8	173	9	0	15	11	.577	2	0	3.04
1990	Kansas City	AL	16	16	2	0	94	409	101	48	47	5	6	4	4	38	4	71	2	1	4	7	.364	0	0	4.50
1991	Kansas City	AL	26	26	0	0	133	601	168	90	84	10	3	5	6	42	1	89	5	0	9	12	.429	0	0	5.68
1992	Kansas City	AL	18	18	2	0	111.1	470	110	47	46	8	5	3	1	36	3	81	5	1	7	6	.538	1	0	3.72
9 ML YEARS			259	247	37	2	1651.2	7012	1586	748	689	97	43	60	43	618	24	1091	77	8	104	92	.531	13	0	3.75

Juan Guerrero

Bats: Right **Throws:** Right **Pos:** SS/3B   **Ht:** 5'11" **Wt:** 160 **Born:** 02/01/67 **Age:** 26

					BATTING															BASERUNNING				PERCENTAGES		
Year	Team	Lg	G	AB	H	2B	3B	HR	(Hm	Rd)	TB	R	RBI	TBB	IBB	SO	HBP	SH	SF	SB	CS	SB%	GDP	Avg	OBP	SLG
1987	Pocatello	R	34	81	17	5	1	1	--	--	27	13	7	17	0	28	1	0	0	1	1	.50		.210	.354	.333
1988	Clinton	A	111	385	106	17	3	13	--	--	168	57	54	17	0	95	5	1	5	7	4	.64	5	.275	.304	.436
1989	San Jose	A	108	409	115	24	2	13	--	--	182	61	78	36	1	68	7	0	5	5	5	.58	13	.281	.346	.445
1990	Shreveport	AA	118	390	94	21	1	16	--	--	165	55	47	26	0	74	5	2	2	4	8	.33	9	.241	.296	.423
1991	Shreveport	AA	128	479	160	40	2	19	--	--	261	78	94	46	2	88	5	0	4	14	9	.61	12	.334	.395	.545
1992	Houston	NL	79	125	25	4	2	1	(1	0)	36	8	14	10	2	32	1	1	2	1	0	1.00	0	.200	.261	.288

Pedro Guerrero

Bats: Right **Throws:** Right **Pos:** 1B   **Ht:** 6' 0" **Wt:** 199 **Born:** 06/29/56 **Age:** 37

					BATTING															BASERUNNING				PERCENTAGES		
Year	Team	Lg	G	AB	H	2B	3B	HR	(Hm	Rd)	TB	R	RBI	TBB	IBB	SO	HBP	SH	SF	SB	CS	SB%	GDP	Avg	OBP	SLG
1978	Los Angeles	NL	5	8	5	0	1	0	(0	0)	7	3	1	0	0	0	0	0	0	0	0	.00	0	.625	.625	.875
1979	Los Angeles	NL	25	62	15	2	0	2	(0	2)	23	7	9	1	1	14	0	0	1	2	0	1.00	1	.242	.250	.371
1980	Los Angeles	NL	75	183	59	9	1	7	(3	4)	91	27	31	12	3	31	0	1	3	2	1	.67	2	.322	.359	.497
1981	Los Angeles	NL	98	347	104	17	2	12	(5	7)	161	46	48	34	3	57	2	3	1	5	9	.36	12	.300	.365	.464
1982	Los Angeles	NL	150	575	175	27	5	32	(15	17)	308	87	100	65	16	89	5	4	3	22	5	.81	7	.304	.378	.536
1983	Los Angeles	NL	160	584	174	28	6	32	(13	19)	310	87	103	72	12	110	2	0	6	23	7	.77	11	.298	.373	.531
1984	Los Angeles	NL	144	535	162	29	4	16	(7	9)	247	85	72	49	7	105	1	1	8	9	8	.53	7	.303	.358	.462
1985	Los Angeles	NL	137	487	156	22	2	33	(13	20)	281	99	87	83	14	68	6	0	5	12	4	.75	13	.320	**.422**	.577
1986	Los Angeles	NL	31	61	15	3	0	5	(1	4)	33	7	10	2	0	19	1	0	0	0	0	.00	1	.246	.281	.541
1987	Los Angeles	NL	152	545	184	25	2	27	(12	15)	294	89	89	74	18	85	4	0	7	9	7	.56	16	.338	.416	.539
1988	2 ML Teams		103	364	104	14	2	10	(5	5)	152	40	65	46	9	59	5	0	7	4	1	.80	5	.286	.367	.418
1989	St. Louis	NL	162	570	177	42	1	17	(3	14)	272	60	117	79	13	84	4	0	12	2	0	1.00	17	.311	.391	.477
1990	St. Louis	NL	136	498	140	31	1	13	(3	10)	225	42	80	44	14	70	1	0	11	1	1	.50	14	.281	.334	.426
1991	St. Louis	NL	115	427	116	12	1	8	(4	4)	154	41	70	37	2	46	1	0	7	4	2	.67	12	.272	.326	.361
1992	St. Louis	NL	43	146	32	6	1	1	(1	0)	43	10	16	11	3	25	0	0	2	2	2	.50	4	.219	.270	.295
1988	Los Angeles	NL	59	215	64	7	1	5	(3	2)	88	24	35	25	2	33	3	0	3	2	1	.67	2	.298	.374	.409
	St. Louis	NL	44	149	40	7	1	5	(2	3)	64	16	30	21	7	26	2	0	4	2	0	1.00	3	.268	.358	.430
15 ML YEARS			1536	5392	1618	267	29	215	(90	125)	2588	730	898	609	115	862	32	9	73	97	47	67	122	.300	.370	.480

Lee Guetterman

Pitches: Left **Bats:** Left **Pos:** RP   **Ht:** 6' 8" **Wt:** 230 **Born:** 11/22/58 **Age:** 34

				HOW MUCH HE PITCHED						WHAT HE GAVE UP											THE RESULTS				
Year	Team	Lg	G	GS	CG	GF	IP	BFP	H	R	ER	HR	SH	SF	HB	TBB	IBB	SO	WP	Bk	W	L	Pct.	ShO	Sv	ERA
1984	Seattle	AL	3	0	0	1	4.1	22	9	2	2	0	0	0	0	2	0	2	1	0	0	0	.000	0	0	4.15
1986	Seattle	AL	41	4	1	8	76	353	108	67	62	7	3	5	4	30	3	38	2	0	0	4	.000	0	0	7.34
1987	Seattle	AL	25	17	2	3	113.1	483	117	60	48	13	2	5	2	35	2	42	3	0	11	4	.733	1	0	3.81
1988	New York	AL	20	2	0	7	40.2	177	49	21	21	2	1	1	1	14	0	15	2	0	1	2	.333	0	0	4.65
1989	New York	AL	70	0	0	38	103	412	98	31	28	6	4	2	0	26	9	51	4	0	5	5	.500	0	13	2.45
1990	New York	AL	64	0	0	21	93	376	80	37	35	6	8	3	0	26	7	48	1	1	11	7	.611	0	2	3.39
1991	New York	AL	64	0	0	37	88	376	91	42	36	6	4	4	3	25	5	35	4	0	3	4	.429	0	6	3.68
1992	2 ML Teams		58	0	0	22	66	310	92	52	52	10	2	5	1	27	8	20	4	0	4	5	.444	0	2	7.09
1992	New York	AL	15	0	0	7	22.2	114	35	24	24	5	0	2	0	13	3	5	1	0	1	1	.500	0	0	9.53
	New York	NL	43	0	0	15	43.1	196	57	28	28	5	2	3	1	14	5	15	3	0	3	4	.429	0	2	5.82
8 ML YEARS			345	23	3	137	584.1	2509	644	312	284	50	24	25	11	185	34	251	21	1	35	31	.530	1	23	4.37

Ozzie Guillen

Bats: Left **Throws:** Right **Pos:** SS   **Ht:** 5'11" **Wt:** 150 **Born:** 01/20/64 **Age:** 29

					BATTING															BASERUNNING				PERCENTAGES		
Year	Team	Lg	G	AB	H	2B	3B	HR	(Hm	Rd)	TB	R	RBI	TBB	IBB	SO	HBP	SH	SF	SB	CS	SB%	GDP	Avg	OBP	SLG
1985	Chicago	AL	150	491	134	21	9	1	(1	0)	176	71	33	12	1	36	1	8	1	7	4	.64	5	.273	.291	.358
1986	Chicago	AL	159	547	137	19	4	2	(1	1)	170	58	47	12	1	52	1	12	5	8	4	.67	14	.250	.265	.311
1987	Chicago	AL	149	560	156	22	7	2	(2	0)	198	64	51	22	2	52	1	13	8	25	8	.76	10	.279	.303	.354
1988	Chicago	AL	156	566	148	16	7	0	(0	0)	178	58	39	25	3	40	2	10	3	25	13	.66	14	.261	.294	.314

80

Year	Team	Lg	G																									
1989	Chicago	AL	155	597	151	20	8	1	(0	1)	190	63	54	15	3	48	0	11	3	36	17	.68	8	.253	.270	.318
1990	Chicago	AL	160	516	144	21	4	1	(1	0)	176	61	58	26	8	37	1	15	5	13	17	.43	6	.279	.312	.341
1991	Chicago	AL	154	524	143	20	3	3	(1	2)	178	52	49	11	1	38	0	13	7	21	15	.58	7	.273	.284	.340
1992	Chicago	AL	12	40	8	4	0	0	(0	0)	12	5	7	1	0	5	0	1	1	1	0	1.00	1	.200	.214	.300
	8 ML YEARS		1095	3841	1021	143	42	10	(6	4)	1278	432	338	124	19	308	6	83	33	136	78	.64	65	.266	.287	.333

Bill Gullickson

Pitches: Right **Bats:** Right **Pos:** SP **Ht:** 6' 3" **Wt:** 225 **Born:** 02/20/59 **Age:** 34

			HOW MUCH HE PITCHED					WHAT HE GAVE UP									THE RESULTS					
Year	Team	Lg	G	GS	CG	GF	IP	BFP	H	R	ER	HR	SH	SF	HB	TBB	IBB	SO	WP	Bk	W	L	Pct.	ShO	Sv	ERA
1979	Montreal	NL	1	0	0	1	1	4	2	0	0	0	0	0	0	0	0	0	0	0	0	0	.000	0	0	0.00
1980	Montreal	NL	24	19	5	1	141	593	127	53	47	6	3	4	2	50	2	120	5	0	10	5	.667	2	0	3.00
1981	Montreal	NL	22	22	3	0	157	640	142	54	49	3	5	2	4	34	4	115	4	0	7	9	.438	2	0	2.81
1982	Montreal	NL	34	34	6	0	236.2	990	231	101	94	25	9	6	4	61	2	155	11	3	12	14	.462	0	0	3.57
1983	Montreal	NL	34	34	10	0	242.1	990	230	108	101	19	4	7	4	59	4	120	4	1	17	12	.586	1	0	3.75
1984	Montreal	NL	32	32	3	0	226.2	919	230	100	91	27	8	4	1	37	7	100	5	0	12	9	.571	0	0	3.61
1985	Montreal	NL	29	29	4	0	181.1	759	187	78	71	8	12	8	1	47	9	68	1	1	14	12	.538	1	0	3.52
1986	Cincinnati	NL	37	37	6	0	244.2	1014	245	103	92	24	12	13	2	60	10	121	3	0	15	12	.556	2	0	3.38
1987	2 ML Teams		35	35	4	0	213	896	218	128	115	40	8	8	3	50	7	117	4	1	14	13	.519	1	0	4.86
1990	Houston	NL	32	32	2	0	193.1	846	221	100	82	21	6	8	2	61	14	73	3	2	10	14	.417	1	0	3.82
1991	Detroit	AL	35	35	4	0	226.1	954	256	109	98	22	8	8	4	44	13	91	4	0	20	9	.690	0	0	3.90
1992	Detroit	AL	34	34	4	0	221.2	919	228	109	107	35	7	9	0	50	5	64	6	0	14	13	.519	0	0	4.34
1987	Cincinnati	NL	27	27	3	0	165	698	172	99	89	33	6	6	2	39	6	89	4	1	10	11	.476	1	0	4.85
	New York	AL	8	8	1	0	48	198	46	29	26	7	2	2	1	11	1	28	0	0	4	2	.667	0	0	4.88
	12 ML YEARS		349	343	51	2	2285	9524	2317	1043	947	230	82	77	27	553	77	1144	50	8	145	122	.543	11	0	3.73

Eric Gunderson

Pitches: Left **Bats:** Right **Pos:** RP **Ht:** 6' 0" **Wt:** 175 **Born:** 03/29/66 **Age:** 27

			HOW MUCH HE PITCHED					WHAT HE GAVE UP									THE RESULTS					
Year	Team	Lg	G	GS	CG	GF	IP	BFP	H	R	ER	HR	SH	SF	HB	TBB	IBB	SO	WP	Bk	W	L	Pct.	ShO	Sv	ERA
1987	Everett	A	15	15	5	0	98.2	406	80	34	27	4	2	2	3	34	1	99	4	3	8	4	.667	3	0	2.46
1988	San Jose	A	20	20	5	0	149.1	640	131	56	44	2	7	3	17	52	0	151	14	6	12	5	.706	4	0	2.65
	Shreveport	AA	7	6	0	1	36.2	166	45	25	21	1	1	1	1	13	0	28	0	1	1	2	.333	0	0	5.15
1989	Shreveport	AA	11	11	2	0	72.2	298	68	24	22	1	1	3	1	23	0	61	1	1	8	2	.800	1	0	2.72
	Phoenix	AAA	14	14	2	0	85.2	375	93	51	48	7	5	6	2	36	2	56	7	1	2	4	.333	1	0	5.04
1990	Phoenix	AAA	16	16	0	0	82	418	137	87	75	11	5	3	3	46	1	41	4	2	5	7	.417	0	0	8.23
	Shreveport	AA	8	8	1	0	52.2	225	51	24	19	7	1	3	2	17	1	44	1	0	2	2	.500	1	0	3.25
1991	Phoenix	AAA	40	14	0	8	107	511	153	85	73	10	3	4	3	44	4	53	3	0	7	6	.538	0	3	6.14
1992	Jacksnville	AA	15	0	0	8	23.1	93	18	10	6	2	1	0	0	7	0	23	0	0	2	0	1.000	0	2	2.31
	Calgary	AAA	27	1	0	12	52.1	244	57	37	35	6	4	3	5	31	3	50	5	0	0	2	.000	0	5	6.02
1990	San Francisco	NL	7	4	0	1	19.2	94	24	14	12	2	1	0	0	11	1	14	0	0	1	2	.333	0	0	5.49
1991	San Francisco	NL	2	0	0	1	3.1	18	6	4	2	0	0	0	0	1	0	2	0	0	0	0	.000	0	1	5.40
1992	Seattle	AL	9	0	0	4	9.1	45	12	12	9	1	0	2	1	5	3	2	0	2	2	1	.667	0	0	8.68
	3 ML YEARS		18	4	0	6	32.1	157	42	30	23	3	1	2	1	17	4	18	0	2	3	3	.500	0	1	6.40

Mark Guthrie

Pitches: Left **Bats:** Both **Pos:** RP **Ht:** 6' 4" **Wt:** 200 **Born:** 09/22/65 **Age:** 27

			HOW MUCH HE PITCHED					WHAT HE GAVE UP									THE RESULTS					
Year	Team	Lg	G	GS	CG	GF	IP	BFP	H	R	ER	HR	SH	SF	HB	TBB	IBB	SO	WP	Bk	W	L	Pct.	ShO	Sv	ERA
1989	Minnesota	AL	13	8	0	2	57.1	254	66	32	29	7	1	5	1	21	1	38	1	0	2	4	.333	0	0	4.55
1990	Minnesota	AL	24	21	3	0	144.2	603	154	65	61	8	6	0	1	39	3	101	9	0	7	9	.438	1	0	3.79
1991	Minnesota	AL	41	12	0	13	98	432	116	52	47	11	4	3	1	41	2	72	7	0	7	5	.583	0	2	4.32
1992	Minnesota	AL	54	0	0	15	75	303	59	27	24	7	4	2	0	23	7	76	2	0	2	3	.400	0	5	2.88
	4 ML YEARS		132	41	3	30	375	1592	395	176	161	33	15	10	3	124	13	287	19	0	18	21	.462	1	7	3.86

Johnny Guzman

Pitches: Left **Bats:** Right **Pos:** RP **Ht:** 5'10" **Wt:** 155 **Born:** 01/21/71 **Age:** 22

			HOW MUCH HE PITCHED					WHAT HE GAVE UP									THE RESULTS					
Year	Team	Lg	G	GS	CG	GF	IP	BFP	H	R	ER	HR	SH	SF	HB	TBB	IBB	SO	WP	Bk	W	L	Pct.	ShO	Sv	ERA
1988	Athletics	R	16	1	0	7	23	116	37	27	22	1	2	2	1	8	0	18	1	4	0	2	.000	0	1	8.61
1989	Modesto	A	5	3	0	1	16.2	81	23	11	9	0	0	0	0	13	0	12	2	1	0	2	.000	0	0	4.86
	Madison	A	9	9	1	0	45.2	201	41	26	19	3	0	1	2	21	0	36	1	4	3	3	.500	0	0	3.74
1990	Modesto	A	13	13	1	0	84.2	337	67	25	18	3	4	2	4	23	2	58	2	1	7	4	.636	1	0	1.91
	Huntsville	AA	16	16	0	0	105.2	458	89	52	42	9	4	1	7	54	1	63	6	2	5	6	.455	0	0	3.58
1991	Tacoma	AAA	17	13	0	2	79.2	394	113	74	60	8	3	4	2	51	0	40	4	6	2	5	.286	0	0	6.78
	Huntsville	AA	7	7	0	0	44	194	46	17	17	3	2	1	1	25	0	23	4	5	2	1	.667	0	0	3.48
1992	Huntsville	AA	14	14	2	0	89.2	378	87	43	37	8	2	0	8	26	0	55	8	1	8	2	.800	1	0	3.71

		G	GS	CG	GF	IP	BFP	H	R	ER	HR	SH	SF	HB	TBB	IBB	SO	WP	Bk	W	L	Pct.	ShO	Sv	ERA
Tacoma	AAA	20	9	0	4	68.2	294	70	43	39	6	3	2	0	24	4	45	1	3	3	6	.333	0	0	5.11
1991 Oakland	AL	5	0	0	1	5	24	11	5	5	0	0	0	0	2	0	3	0	0	1	0	1.000	0	0	9.00
1992 Oakland	AL	2	0	0	2	3	18	8	4	4	0	0	0	1	0	0	0	0	0	0	0	.000	0	0	12.00
2 ML YEARS		7	0	0	3	8	42	19	9	9	0	0	0	1	2	0	3	0	0	1	0	1.000	0	0	10.13

Jose Guzman

Pitches: Right **Bats:** Right **Pos:** SP **Ht:** 6' 3" **Wt:** 195 **Born:** 04/09/63 **Age:** 30

		HOW MUCH HE PITCHED						WHAT HE GAVE UP												THE RESULTS					
Year Team	Lg	G	GS	CG	GF	IP	BFP	H	R	ER	HR	SH	SF	HB	TBB	IBB	SO	WP	Bk	W	L	Pct.	ShO	Sv	ERA
1985 Texas	AL	5	5	0	0	32.2	140	27	13	10	3	0	0	0	14	1	24	1	0	3	2	.600	0	0	2.76
1986 Texas	AL	29	29	2	0	172.1	757	199	101	87	23	7	4	6	60	2	87	3	0	9	15	.375	0	0	4.54
1987 Texas	AL	37	30	6	1	208.1	880	196	115	108	30	6	8	3	82	0	143	6	5	14	14	.500	0	0	4.67
1988 Texas	AL	30	30	6	0	206.2	876	180	99	85	20	4	6	5	82	3	157	10	12	11	13	.458	2	0	3.70
1991 Texas	AL	25	25	5	0	169.2	730	152	67	58	10	2	3	4	84	1	125	8	1	13	7	.650	1	0	3.08
1992 Texas	AL	33	33	5	0	224	947	229	103	91	17	9	7	4	73	0	179	6	0	16	11	.593	0	0	3.66
6 ML YEARS		159	152	24	1	1013.2	4330	983	498	439	103	28	28	22	395	7	715	34	18	66	62	.516	3	0	3.90

Juan Guzman

Pitches: Right **Bats:** Right **Pos:** SP **Ht:** 5'11" **Wt:** 195 **Born:** 10/28/66 **Age:** 26

		HOW MUCH HE PITCHED						WHAT HE GAVE UP												THE RESULTS					
Year Team	Lg	G	GS	CG	GF	IP	BFP	H	R	ER	HR	SH	SF	HB	TBB	IBB	SO	WP	Bk	W	L	Pct.	ShO	Sv	ERA
1985 Dodgers	R	21	3	0	12	42	189	39	26	18	2	3	2	1	25	3	43	15	3	5	1	.833	0	4	3.86
1986 Vero Beach	A	26	24	3	0	131.1	594	114	69	51	3	4	3	4	90	4	96	16	2	10	9	.526	0	0	3.49
1987 Bakersfield	A	22	21	0	0	110	508	106	71	58	4	0	1	1	84	0	113	19	1	5	6	.455	0	0	4.75
1988 Knoxville	AA	46	2	0	23	84	363	52	29	22	1	4	4	1	61	5	90	6	6	4	5	.444	0	0	2.36
1989 Syracuse	AAA	14	0	0	4	20.1	99	13	9	9	0	0	1	0	30	5	28	5	0	1	1	.500	0	0	3.98
Knoxville	AA	22	8	0	7	47.2	232	34	36	33	2	2	1	2	60	0	50	8	5	1	4	.200	0	0	6.23
1990 Knoxville	AA	37	21	2	7	157	685	145	84	74	10	6	11	3	80	6	138	21	8	11	9	.550	0	1	4.24
1991 Syracuse	AAA	12	11	0	0	67	287	46	39	30	4	1	3	2	42	0	67	7	2	4	5	.444	0	0	4.03
1992 Syracuse	AAA	1	1	0	0	3	16	6	2	2	0	0	0	0	1	0	3	0	0	0	0	.000	0	0	6.00
1991 Toronto	AL	23	23	1	0	138.2	574	98	53	46	6	2	5	4	66	0	123	10	0	10	3	.769	0	0	2.99
1992 Toronto	AL	28	28	1	0	180.2	733	135	56	53	6	5	3	1	72	2	165	14	2	16	5	.762	0	0	2.64
2 ML YEARS		51	51	2	0	319.1	1307	233	109	99	12	7	8	5	138	2	288	24	2	26	8	.765	0	0	2.79

Chris Gwynn

Bats: Left **Throws:** Left **Pos:** RF **Ht:** 6' 0" **Wt:** 210 **Born:** 10/13/64 **Age:** 28

		BATTING																	BASERUNNING				PERCENTAGES		
Year Team	Lg	G	AB	H	2B	3B	HR	(Hm	Rd)	TB	R	RBI	TBB	IBB	SO	HBP	SH	SF	SB	CS	SB%	GDP	Avg	OBP	SLG
1987 Los Angeles	NL	17	32	7	1	0	0	(0	0)	8	2	2	1	0	7	0	1	0	0	0	.00	0	.219	.242	.250
1988 Los Angeles	NL	12	11	2	0	0	0	(0	0)	2	1	0	1	0	2	0	0	0	0	0	.00	0	.182	.250	.182
1989 Los Angeles	NL	32	68	16	4	1	0	(0	0)	22	8	7	2	0	9	0	2	1	1	0	1.00	1	.235	.254	.324
1990 Los Angeles	NL	101	141	40	2	1	5	(0	5)	59	19	22	7	2	28	0	0	3	0	1	.00	2	.284	.311	.418
1991 Los Angeles	NL	94	139	35	5	1	5	(3	2)	57	18	22	10	1	23	1	1	3	1	0	1.00	5	.252	.301	.410
1992 Kansas City	AL	34	84	24	3	2	1	(0	1)	34	10	7	3	0	10	0	1	2	0	0	.00	1	.286	.303	.405
6 ML YEARS		290	475	124	15	5	11	(3	8)	182	58	60	24	3	79	1	5	9	2	1	.67	9	.261	.293	.383

Tony Gwynn

Bats: Left **Throws:** Left **Pos:** RF **Ht:** 5'11" **Wt:** 215 **Born:** 05/09/60 **Age:** 33

		BATTING																	BASERUNNING				PERCENTAGES		
Year Team	Lg	G	AB	H	2B	3B	HR	(Hm	Rd)	TB	R	RBI	TBB	IBB	SO	HBP	SH	SF	SB	CS	SB%	GDP	Avg	OBP	SLG
1982 San Diego	NL	54	190	55	12	2	1	(0	1)	74	33	17	14	0	16	0	4	1	8	3	.73	5	.289	.337	.389
1983 San Diego	NL	86	304	94	12	2	1	(0	1)	113	34	37	23	3	21	0	4	3	7	4	.64	9	.309	.355	.372
1984 San Diego	NL	158	606	213	21	10	5	(3	2)	269	88	71	59	13	23	2	6	2	33	18	.65	15	.351	.410	.444
1985 San Diego	NL	154	622	197	29	5	6	(3	3)	254	90	46	45	4	33	2	1	1	14	11	.56	17	.317	.364	.408
1986 San Diego	NL	160	642	211	33	7	14	(8	6)	300	107	59	52	11	35	3	2	2	37	9	.80	20	.329	.381	.467
1987 San Diego	NL	157	589	218	36	13	7	(5	2)	301	119	54	82	26	35	3	2	4	56	12	.82	13	.370	.447	.511
1988 San Diego	NL	133	521	163	22	5	7	(3	4)	216	64	70	51	13	40	0	4	2	26	11	.70	11	.313	.373	.415
1989 San Diego	NL	158	604	203	27	7	4	(3	1)	256	82	62	56	16	30	1	11	7	40	16	.71	12	.336	.389	.424
1990 San Diego	NL	141	573	177	29	10	4	(2	2)	238	79	72	44	20	23	1	7	4	17	8	.68	13	.309	.357	.415
1991 San Diego	NL	134	530	168	27	11	4	(1	3)	229	69	62	34	8	19	0	0	5	8	8	.50	11	.317	.355	.432
1992 San Diego	NL	128	520	165	27	3	6	(4	2)	216	77	41	46	12	16	0	0	3	3	6	.33	13	.317	.371	.415
11 ML YEARS		1463	5701	1864	275	75	59	(32	27)	2466	842	591	506	128	291	12	41	34	249	106	.70	139	.327	.381	.433

Dave Haas

Pitches: Right **Bats:** Right **Pos:** SP **Ht:** 6' 1" **Wt:** 200 **Born:** 10/19/65 **Age:** 27

Year	Team	Lg	G	GS	CG	GF	IP	BFP	H	R	ER	HR	SH	SF	HB	TBB	IBB	SO	WP	Bk	W	L	Pct.	ShO	Sv	ERA
1988	Fayetteville	A	11	11	0	0	54.2	243	59	20	11	0	1	1	6	19	1	46	2	4	4	3	.571	0	0	1.81
1989	Lakeland	A	10	10	1	0	62	247	50	16	14	1	0	1	6	16	0	46	1	1	4	1	.800	1	0	2.03
	London	AA	18	18	2	0	103.2	460	107	69	65	13	5	2	11	51	1	75	5	1	3	11	.214	1	0	5.64
1990	London	AA	27	27	3	0	177.2	740	151	64	59	10	4	3	10	74	1	116	14	1	13	8	.619	1	0	2.99
1991	Toledo	AAA	28	28	1	0	158.1	718	187	103	92	11	8	3	8	77	3	133	8	1	8	10	.444	0	0	5.23
1992	Toledo	AAA	22	22	2	0	148.2	636	149	72	69	11	5	5	9	53	1	112	5	0	9	8	.529	0	0	4.18
1991	Detroit	AL	11	0	0	0	10.2	50	8	8	8	1	2	2	1	12	3	6	1	0	1	0	1.000	0	0	6.75
1992	Detroit	AL	12	11	0	0	61.2	264	68	30	27	8	1	0	1	16	1	29	2	0	5	3	.625	1	0	3.94
2 ML YEARS			23	11	1	1	72.1	314	76	38	35	9	3	2	2	28	4	35	3	0	6	3	.667	1	0	4.35

John Habyan

Pitches: Right **Bats:** Right **Pos:** RP **Ht:** 6' 2" **Wt:** 191 **Born:** 01/29/64 **Age:** 29

Year	Team	Lg	G	GS	CG	GF	IP	BFP	H	R	ER	HR	SH	SF	HB	TBB	IBB	SO	WP	Bk	W	L	Pct.	ShO	Sv	ERA
1985	Baltimore	AL	2	0	0	1	2.2	12	3	1	0	0	0	0	0	0	0	2	0	0	1	0	1.000	0	0	0.00
1986	Baltimore	AL	6	5	0	1	26.1	117	24	17	13	3	2	1	0	18	2	14	1	0	1	3	.250	0	0	4.44
1987	Baltimore	AL	27	13	0	4	116.1	493	110	67	62	20	4	4	2	40	1	64	3	0	6	7	.462	0	1	4.80
1988	Baltimore	AL	7	0	0	1	14.2	68	22	10	7	2	0	2	0	4	0	4	1	1	1	0	1.000	0	0	4.30
1990	New York	AL	6	0	0	1	8.2	37	10	2	2	0	0	0	1	2	0	4	1	0	0	0	.000	0	0	2.08
1991	New York	AL	66	0	0	16	90	349	73	28	23	2	2	1	2	20	2	70	1	2	4	2	.667	0	2	2.30
1992	New York	AL	56	0	0	20	72.2	316	84	32	31	6	5	3	2	21	5	44	2	1	5	6	.455	0	7	3.84
7 ML YEARS			170	18	0	44	331.1	1392	326	157	138	33	13	11	7	105	10	202	9	4	18	18	.500	0	10	3.75

Mel Hall

Bats: Left **Throws:** Left **Pos:** LF/RF **Ht:** 6' 1" **Wt:** 214 **Born:** 09/16/60 **Age:** 32

Year	Team	Lg	G	AB	H	2B	3B	HR	(Hm	Rd)	TB	R	RBI	TBB	IBB	SO	HBP	SH	SF	SB	CS	SB%	GDP	Avg	OBP	SLG
1981	Chicago	NL	10	11	1	0	0	1	(1	0)	4	1	2	1	0	4	0	0	0	0	0	.00	0	.091	.167	.364
1982	Chicago	NL	24	80	21	3	2	0	(0	0)	28	6	4	5	1	17	2	0	1	0	1	.00	0	.263	.318	.350
1983	Chicago	NL	112	410	116	23	5	17	(6	11)	200	60	56	42	6	101	3	1	2	6	6	.50	4	.283	.352	.488
1984	2 ML Teams		131	407	108	24	4	11	(7	4)	173	68	52	47	8	78	2	0	7	3	2	.60	5	.265	.339	.425
1985	Cleveland	AL	23	66	21	6	0	0	(0	0)	27	7	12	8	0	12	0	0	0	0	1	.00	2	.318	.387	.409
1986	Cleveland	AL	140	442	131	29	2	18	(8	10)	218	68	77	33	8	65	2	0	3	6	2	.75	8	.296	.346	.493
1987	Cleveland	AL	142	485	136	21	1	18	(8	10)	213	57	76	20	6	68	1	0	2	5	4	.56	7	.280	.309	.439
1988	Cleveland	AL	150	515	144	32	4	6	(3	3)	202	69	71	28	12	50	0	2	8	7	3	.70	8	.280	.312	.392
1989	New York	AL	113	361	94	9	0	17	(11	6)	154	54	58	21	4	37	0	1	8	0	0	.00	9	.260	.295	.427
1990	New York	AL	113	360	93	23	2	12	(3	9)	156	41	46	6	2	46	2	0	3	0	0	.00	7	.258	.272	.433
1991	New York	AL	141	492	140	23	2	19	(13	6)	224	67	80	26	6	40	3	0	6	0	1	.00	6	.285	.321	.455
1992	New York	AL	152	583	163	36	3	15	(7	8)	250	67	81	29	4	53	1	0	9	4	2	.67	13	.280	.310	.429
1984	Chicago	NL	48	150	42	11	3	4	(3	1)	71	25	22	12	3	23	0	0	2	2	1	.67	2	.280	.329	.473
	Cleveland	AL	83	257	66	13	1	7	(4	3)	102	43	30	35	5	55	2	0	5	1	1	.50	3	.257	.344	.397
12 ML YEARS			1251	4212	1168	229	25	134	(67	67)	1849	565	615	266	57	571	16	4	50	31	22	.58	69	.277	.319	.439

Darryl Hamilton

Bats: Left **Throws:** Right **Pos:** RF/LF/CF **Ht:** 6' 1" **Wt:** 180 **Born:** 12/03/64 **Age:** 28

Year	Team	Lg	G	AB	H	2B	3B	HR	(Hm	Rd)	TB	R	RBI	TBB	IBB	SO	HBP	SH	SF	SB	CS	SB%	GDP	Avg	OBP	SLG
1988	Milwaukee	AL	44	103	19	4	0	1	(1	0)	26	14	11	12	0	9	1	0	1	7	3	.70	2	.184	.274	.252
1990	Milwaukee	AL	89	156	46	5	0	1	(1	0)	54	27	18	9	0	12	0	3	0	10	3	.77	2	.295	.333	.346
1991	Milwaukee	AL	122	405	126	15	6	1	(0	1)	156	64	57	33	2	38	0	7	3	16	6	.73	10	.311	.361	.385
1992	Milwaukee	AL	128	470	140	19	7	5	(1	4)	188	67	62	45	0	42	1	4	7	41	14	.75	10	.298	.356	.400
4 ML YEARS			383	1134	331	43	13	8	(3	5)	424	172	148	99	2	101	2	14	11	74	26	.74	24	.292	.347	.374

Chris Hammond

Pitches: Left **Bats:** Left **Pos:** SP **Ht:** 6' 1" **Wt:** 190 **Born:** 01/21/66 **Age:** 27

Year	Team	Lg	G	GS	CG	GF	IP	BFP	H	R	ER	HR	SH	SF	HB	TBB	IBB	SO	WP	Bk	W	L	Pct.	ShO	Sv	ERA
1990	Cincinnati	NL	3	3	0	0	11.1	56	13	9	8	2	1	0	0	12	1	4	1	3	0	2	.000	0	0	6.35
1991	Cincinnati	NL	20	18	0	0	99.2	425	92	51	45	4	6	1	2	48	3	50	3	0	7	7	.500	0	0	4.06
1992	Cincinnati	NL	28	26	0	1	147.1	627	149	75	69	13	5	3	3	55	6	79	6	0	7	10	.412	0	0	4.21
3 ML YEARS			51	47	0	1	258.1	1108	254	135	122	19	12	4	5	115	10	133	10	3	14	19	.424	0	0	4.25

Chris Haney

Pitches: Left **Bats:** Left **Pos:** SP

Ht: 6' 3" **Wt:** 185 **Born:** 11/16/68 **Age:** 24

Year	Team	Lg	G	GS	CG	GF	IP	BFP	H	R	ER	HR	SH	SF	HB	TBB	IBB	SO	WP	Bk	W	L	Pct.	ShO	Sv	ERA
1990	Jamestown	A	6	5	0	1	28	109	17	3	3	1	1	0	4	11	0	26	0	1	3	0	1.000	0	1	0.96
	Rockford	A	8	8	3	0	53	204	40	15	13	1	3	2	1	6	0	45	0	0	2	4	.333	0	0	2.21
	Jacksnville	AA	1	1	0	0	6	25	6	0	0	0	0	0	0	3	0	6	0	0	1	0	1.000	0	0	0.00
1991	Harrisburg	AA	12	12	3	0	83.1	334	65	21	20	4	8	2	3	31	1	68	3	1	5	3	.625	0	0	2.16
	Indianapolis	AAA	2	2	0	0	10.1	50	14	10	5	2	0	0	1	6	0	8	2	0	1	1	.500	0	0	4.35
1992	Indianapols	AAA	15	15	0	0	84	368	88	50	48	4	3	2	3	42	0	61	2	0	5	2	.714	0	0	5.14
1991	Montreal	NL	16	16	0	0	84.2	387	94	49	38	6	6	1	1	43	1	51	9	0	3	7	.300	0	0	4.04
1992	2 ML Teams		16	13	2	2	80	339	75	43	41	11	0	6	4	26	2	54	5	1	4	6	.400	2	0	4.61
1992	Montreal	NL	9	6	1	2	38	165	40	25	23	6	0	3	4	10	0	27	5	1	2	3	.400	1	0	5.45
	Kansas City	AL	7	7	1	0	42	174	35	18	18	5	0	3	0	16	2	27	0	0	2	3	.400	1	0	3.86
	2 ML YEARS		32	29	2	2	164.2	726	169	92	79	17	6	7	5	69	3	105	14	1	7	13	.350	2	0	4.32

Todd Haney

Bats: Right **Throws:** Right **Pos:** 2B

Ht: 5' 9" **Wt:** 165 **Born:** 07/30/65 **Age:** 27

Year	Team	Lg	G	AB	H	2B	3B	HR	(Hm	Rd)	TB	R	RBI	TBB	IBB	SO	HBP	SH	SF	SB	CS	SB%	GDP	Avg	OBP	SLG
1987	Bellingham	A	66	252	64	11	2	5	--	--	94	57	27	44	0	33	2	1	2	18	10	.64	1	.254	.367	.373
1988	Wausau	A	132	452	127	23	2	7	--	--	175	66	52	56	0	54	7	8	2	35	10	.78	7	.281	.368	.387
1989	San Berndno	A	25	107	27	5	0	0	--	--	32	10	7	7	0	14	0	0	1	2	3	.40	2	.252	.296	.299
	Williamsprt	AA	115	401	108	20	4	2	--	--	142	59	31	49	2	43	5	7	3	13	8	.62	7	.269	.354	.354
1990	Williamsprt	AA	2	1	1	1	0	0	--	--	2	0	0	1	0	0	0	0	0	0	0	.00	1	.500	.667	1.000
	Calgary	AAA	108	419	142	15	6	1	--	--	172	81	36	37	1	38	4	6	0	16	11	.59	11	.339	.398	.411
1991	Indianapols	AAA	132	510	159	32	3	2	--	--	203	68	39	47	3	49	9	7	4	11	10	.52	7	.312	.377	.398
1992	Indianapols	AAA	57	200	53	14	0	6	--	--	85	30	33	37	0	34	1	3	2	0	1	1.00	2	.265	.379	.425
1992	Montreal	NL	7	10	3	1	0	0	(0	0)	4	0	1	0	0	0	0	1	0	0	0	.00	0	.300	.300	.400

Dave Hansen

Bats: Left **Throws:** Right **Pos:** 3B

Ht: 6' 0" **Wt:** 180 **Born:** 11/24/68 **Age:** 24

Year	Team	Lg	G	AB	H	2B	3B	HR	(Hm	Rd)	TB	R	RBI	TBB	IBB	SO	HBP	SH	SF	SB	CS	SB%	GDP	Avg	OBP	SLG
1990	Los Angeles	NL	5	7	1	0	0	0	(0	0)	1	0	1	0	0	3	0	0	0	0	0	.00	0	.143	.143	.143
1991	Los Angeles	NL	53	56	15	4	0	1	(0	1)	22	3	5	2	0	12	0	0	0	1	0	1.00	0	.268	.293	.393
1992	Los Angeles	NL	132	341	73	11	0	6	(1	5)	102	30	22	34	3	49	1	0	2	0	2	.00	9	.214	.286	.299
	3 ML YEARS		190	404	89	15	0	7	(1	6)	125	33	28	36	3	64	1	0	2	1	2	.33	11	.220	.284	.309

Erik Hanson

Pitches: Right **Bats:** Right **Pos:** SP

Ht: 6' 6" **Wt:** 210 **Born:** 05/18/65 **Age:** 28

Year	Team	Lg	G	GS	CG	GF	IP	BFP	H	R	ER	HR	SH	SF	HB	TBB	IBB	SO	WP	Bk	W	L	Pct.	ShO	Sv	ERA
1988	Seattle	AL	6	6	0	0	41.2	168	35	17	15	4	3	0	1	12	1	36	2	2	2	3	.400	0	0	3.24
1989	Seattle	AL	17	17	1	0	113.1	465	103	44	40	7	4	1	5	32	1	75	3	0	9	5	.643	0	0	3.18
1990	Seattle	AL	33	33	5	0	236	964	205	88	85	15	5	6	2	68	6	211	10	1	18	9	.667	1	0	3.24
1991	Seattle	AL	27	27	2	0	174.2	744	182	82	74	16	2	8	2	56	2	143	14	1	8	8	.500	1	0	3.81
1992	Seattle	AL	31	30	6	0	186.2	809	209	110	100	14	8	9	7	57	1	112	6	0	8	17	.320	1	0	4.82
	5 ML YEARS		114	113	14	0	752.1	3150	734	341	314	56	22	24	17	225	11	577	35	6	45	42	.517	3	0	3.76

Shawn Hare

Bats: Left **Throws:** Left **Pos:** RF

Ht: 6' 2" **Wt:** 190 **Born:** 03/26/67 **Age:** 26

Year	Team	Lg	G	AB	H	2B	3B	HR	(Hm	Rd)	TB	R	RBI	TBB	IBB	SO	HBP	SH	SF	SB	CS	SB%	GDP	Avg	OBP	SLG
1989	Lakeland	A	93	290	94	16	4	2	--	--	124	32	36	41	4	32	2	2	1	11	5	.69	7	.324	.410	.428
1990	Toledo	AAA	127	429	109	25	4	9	--	--	169	53	55	49	9	77	4	0	3	9	6	.60	10	.254	.334	.394
1991	London	AA	31	125	34	12	0	4	--	--	58	20	28	12	1	23	1	0	0	2	2	.50	5	.272	.341	.464
	Toledo	AAA	80	252	78	18	2	9	--	--	127	44	42	30	1	53	2	1	5	1	2	.33	6	.310	.381	.504
1992	Toledo	AAA	57	203	67	12	2	5	--	--	98	31	34	31	2	28	0	0	4	6	1	.86	8	.330	.412	.483
1991	Detroit	AL	9	19	1	1	0	0	(0	0)	2	0	0	2	0	1	0	0	0	0	0	.00	3	.053	.143	.105
1992	Detroit	AL	15	26	3	1	0	0	(0	0)	4	0	5	2	0	4	0	0	1	0	0	.00	0	.115	.172	.154
	2 ML YEARS		24	45	4	2	0	0	(0	0)	6	0	5	4	0	5	0	0	1	0	0	.00	3	.089	.160	.133

Mike Harkey

Pitches: Right **Bats:** Right **Pos:** SP **Ht:** 6' 5" **Wt:** 220 **Born:** 10/25/66 **Age:** 26

Year	Team	Lg	G	GS	CG	GF	IP	BFP	H	R	ER	HR	SH	SF	HB	TBB	IBB	SO	WP	Bk	W	L	Pct.	ShO	Sv	ERA
1988	Chicago	NL	5	5	0	0	34.2	155	33	14	10	0	5	0	2	15	3	18	2	1	0	3	.000	0	0	2.60
1990	Chicago	NL	27	27	2	0	173.2	728	153	71	63	14	5	4	7	59	8	94	8	1	12	6	.667	1	0	3.26
1991	Chicago	NL	4	4	0	0	18.2	84	21	11	11	3	0	1	0	6	1	15	1	0	0	2	.000	0	0	5.30
1992	Chicago	NL	7	7	0	0	38	159	34	13	8	4	1	2	1	15	0	21	3	1	4	0	1.000	0	0	1.89
	4 ML YEARS		43	43	2	0	265	1126	241	109	92	21	11	7	10	95	12	148	14	3	16	11	.593	1	0	3.12

Pete Harnisch

Pitches: Right **Bats:** Right **Pos:** SP **Ht:** 6' 0" **Wt:** 207 **Born:** 09/23/66 **Age:** 26

Year	Team	Lg	G	GS	CG	GF	IP	BFP	H	R	ER	HR	SH	SF	HB	TBB	IBB	SO	WP	Bk	W	L	Pct.	ShO	Sv	ERA
1988	Baltimore	AL	2	2	0	0	13	61	13	8	8	1	2	0	0	9	1	10	1	0	0	2	.000	0	0	5.54
1989	Baltimore	AL	18	17	2	1	103.1	468	97	55	53	10	4	5	5	64	3	70	5	1	5	9	.357	0	0	4.62
1990	Baltimore	AL	31	31	3	0	188.2	821	189	96	91	17	6	5	1	86	5	122	2	2	11	11	.500	0	0	4.34
1991	Houston	NL	33	33	4	0	216.2	900	169	71	65	14	9	7	5	83	3	172	5	2	12	9	.571	2	0	2.70
1992	Houston	NL	34	34	0	0	206.2	859	182	92	85	18	5	5	5	64	3	164	4	1	9	10	.474	0	0	3.70
	5 ML YEARS		118	117	9	1	728.1	3109	650	322	302	60	26	22	16	306	15	538	17	6	37	41	.474	2	0	3.73

Brian Harper

Bats: Right **Throws:** Right **Pos:** C **Ht:** 6' 2" **Wt:** 205 **Born:** 10/16/59 **Age:** 33

Year	Team	Lg	G	AB	H	2B	3B	HR	(Hm	Rd)	TB	R	RBI	TBB	IBB	SO	HBP	SH	SF	SB	CS	SB%	GDP	Avg	OBP	SLG
1979	California	AL	1	2	0	0	0	0	(0	0)	0	0	0	0	0	1	0	0	0	0	0	.00	0	.000	.000	.000
1981	California	AL	4	11	3	0	0	0	(0	0)	3	1	1	0	0	0	0	0	1	1	0	1.00	0	.273	.250	.273
1982	Pittsburgh	NL	20	29	8	1	0	2	(0	2)	15	4	4	1	1	4	0	1	0	0	0	.00	1	.276	.300	.517
1983	Pittsburgh	NL	61	131	29	4	1	7	(5	2)	56	16	20	2	0	15	1	2	4	0	0	.00	3	.221	.232	.427
1984	Pittsburgh	NL	46	112	29	4	0	2	(1	1)	39	4	11	5	0	11	2	1	1	0	0	.00	4	.259	.300	.348
1985	St. Louis	NL	43	52	13	4	0	0	(0	0)	17	5	8	2	0	3	0	0	1	0	0	.00	2	.250	.273	.327
1986	Detroit	AL	19	36	5	1	0	0	(0	0)	6	2	3	3	0	3	0	1	1	0	0	.00	1	.139	.200	.167
1987	Oakland	AL	11	17	4	1	0	0	(0	0)	5	1	3	0	0	4	0	1	1	0	0	.00	1	.235	.222	.294
1988	Minnesota	AL	60	166	49	11	1	3	(0	3)	71	15	20	10	1	12	3	2	1	0	3	.00	12	.295	.344	.428
1989	Minnesota	AL	126	385	125	24	0	8	(4	4)	173	43	57	13	3	16	6	4	4	2	4	.33	11	.325	.353	.449
1990	Minnesota	AL	134	479	141	42	3	6	(1	5)	207	61	54	19	2	27	7	0	4	3	2	.60	20	.294	.328	.432
1991	Minnesota	AL	123	441	137	28	1	10	(4	6)	197	54	69	14	3	22	6	2	6	1	2	.33	14	.311	.336	.447
1992	Minnesota	AL	140	502	154	25	0	9	(3	6)	206	58	73	26	7	22	7	1	10	0	1	.00	15	.307	.343	.410
	13 ML YEARS		788	2363	697	145	6	47	(18	29)	995	264	323	95	17	140	32	15	34	7	12	.37	84	.295	.326	.421

Donald Harris

Bats: Right **Throws:** Right **Pos:** CF **Ht:** 6' 1" **Wt:** 185 **Born:** 11/12/67 **Age:** 25

Year	Team	Lg	G	AB	H	2B	3B	HR	(Hm	Rd)	TB	R	RBI	TBB	IBB	SO	HBP	SH	SF	SB	CS	SB%	GDP	Avg	OBP	SLG
1989	Butte	R	65	264	75	7	8	6	--	--	116	50	37	12	0	54	6	0	3	14	4	.78	6	.284	.326	.439
1990	Tulsa	AA	64	213	34	5	1	1	--	--	44	16	15	7	0	69	3	3	0	7	3	.70	0	.160	.197	.207
	Gastonia	A	58	221	46	10	0	3	--	--	65	27	13	14	0	63	2	4	0	15	8	.65	2	.208	.262	.294
1991	Tulsa	AA	130	450	102	17	8	11	--	--	168	47	53	26	1	118	7	7	2	9	6	.60	11	.227	.278	.373
1992	Tulsa	AA	83	303	77	15	2	11	--	--	129	39	39	9	1	85	7	3	1	4	3	.57	11	.254	.291	.426
1991	Texas	AL	18	8	3	0	0	1	(0	1)	6	4	2	1	0	3	0	0	0	1	0	1.00	0	.375	.444	.750
1992	Texas	AL	24	33	6	1	0	0	(0	0)	7	3	1	0	0	15	0	0	0	1	0	1.00	0	.182	.182	.212
	2 ML YEARS		42	41	9	1	0	1	(0	1)	13	7	3	1	0	18	0	0	0	2	0	1.00	0	.220	.238	.317

Gene Harris

Pitches: Right **Bats:** Right **Pos:** RP **Ht:** 5'11" **Wt:** 190 **Born:** 12/05/64 **Age:** 28

Year	Team	Lg	G	GS	CG	GF	IP	BFP	H	R	ER	HR	SH	SF	HB	TBB	IBB	SO	WP	Bk	W	L	Pct.	ShO	Sv	ERA
1989	2 ML Teams		21	6	0	9	53.1	236	63	38	35	4	7	4	1	25	1	25	3	0	2	5	.286	0	1	5.91
1990	Seattle	AL	25	0	0	12	38	176	31	25	20	5	0	2	1	30	5	43	2	0	1	2	.333	0	0	4.74
1991	Seattle	AL	8	0	0	3	13.1	66	15	8	6	1	1	0	0	10	3	6	1	0	0	0	.000	0	1	4.05
1992	2 ML Teams		22	1	0	4	30.1	130	23	15	14	3	3	0	1	15	0	25	1	2	0	2	.000	0	0	4.15
1989	Montreal	NL	11	0	0	7	20	84	16	11	11	1	7	1	0	10	0	11	3	0	1	1	.500	0	0	4.95
	Seattle	AL	10	6	0	2	33.1	152	47	27	24	3	0	3	1	15	1	14	0	0	1	4	.200	0	1	6.48
1992	Seattle	AL	8	0	0	2	9	40	8	7	7	3	0	0	0	6	0	6	0	1	0	0	.000	0	0	7.00
	San Diego	NL	14	1	0	2	21.1	90	15	8	7	0	3	0	1	9	0	19	1	1	0	2	.000	0	0	2.95
	4 ML YEARS		76	7	0	28	135	608	132	86	75	13	11	6	3	80	9	99	7	2	3	9	.250	0	2	5.00

Greg Harris

Pitches: Right **Bats:** Both **Pos:** RP **Ht:** 6' 0" **Wt:** 175 **Born:** 11/02/55 **Age:** 37

Year	Team	Lg	G	GS	CG	GF	IP	BFP	H	R	ER	HR	SH	SF	HB	TBB	IBB	SO	WP	Bk	W	L	Pct.	ShO	Sv	ERA
1981	New York	NL	16	14	0	2	69	300	65	36	34	8	4	1	2	28	2	54	3	2	3	5	.375	0	1	4.43
1982	Cincinnati	NL	34	10	1	9	91.1	398	96	56	49	12	5	3	2	37	1	67	2	2	2	6	.250	0	1	4.83
1983	San Diego	NL	1	0	0	0	1	9	2	3	3	0	1	0	1	3	2	1	0	0	0	0	.000	0	0	27.00
1984	2 ML Teams		34	1	0	14	54.1	226	38	18	15	3	2	3	4	25	1	45	3	0	2	2	.500	0	3	2.48
1985	Texas	AL	58	0	0	35	113	450	74	35	31	7	3	2	5	43	3	111	2	1	5	4	.556	0	11	2.47
1986	Texas	AL	73	0	0	63	111.1	462	103	40	35	12	3	6	1	42	6	95	2	1	10	8	.556	0	20	2.83
1987	Texas	AL	42	19	0	14	140.2	629	157	92	76	18	7	3	4	56	3	106	4	2	5	10	.333	0	0	4.86
1988	Philadelphia	NL	66	1	0	19	107	446	80	34	28	7	6	2	4	52	14	71	8	2	4	6	.400	0	1	2.36
1989	2 ML Teams		59	0	0	24	103.1	442	85	46	38	8	4	3	2	58	9	76	12	0	4	4	.500	0	1	3.31
1990	Boston	AL	34	30	1	3	184.1	803	186	90	82	13	8	9	6	77	7	117	8	1	13	9	.591	0	0	4.00
1991	Boston	AL	53	21	0	15	173	731	157	79	74	13	4	8	5	69	5	127	6	1	11	12	.478	0	2	3.85
1992	Boston	AL	70	2	1	22	107.2	459	82	38	30	6	8	5	4	60	11	73	5	0	4	9	.308	0	4	2.51
1984	Montreal	NL	15	0	0	4	17.2	68	10	4	4	0	1	0	2	7	1	15	0	0	0	1	.000	0	2	2.04
	San Diego	NL	19	1	0	10	36.2	158	28	14	11	3	1	3	2	18	0	30	3	0	2	1	.667	0	1	2.70
1989	Philadelphia	NL	44	0	0	17	75.1	324	64	34	30	7	3	2	2	43	7	51	10	0	2	2	.500	0	1	3.58
	Boston	AL	15	0	0	7	28	118	21	12	8	1	1	1	0	15	2	25	2	0	2	2	.500	0	0	2.57
	12 ML YEARS		540	98	4	220	1256	5355	1125	567	495	107	55	45	40	550	64	943	55	12	63	75	.457	0	44	3.55

Greg W. Harris

Pitches: Right **Bats:** Right **Pos:** SP **Ht:** 6' 2" **Wt:** 195 **Born:** 12/01/63 **Age:** 29

Year	Team	Lg	G	GS	CG	GF	IP	BFP	H	R	ER	HR	SH	SF	HB	TBB	IBB	SO	WP	Bk	W	L	Pct.	ShO	Sv	ERA
1988	San Diego	NL	3	1	1	2	18	68	13	3	3	0	0	0	0	3	0	15	0	0	2	0	1.000	0	0	1.50
1989	San Diego	NL	56	8	0	25	135	554	106	43	39	8	5	2	2	52	9	106	3	3	8	9	.471	0	6	2.60
1990	San Diego	NL	73	0	0	33	117.1	488	92	35	30	6	9	7	4	49	13	97	2	3	8	8	.500	0	9	2.30
1991	San Diego	NL	20	20	3	0	133	537	116	42	33	16	9	2	1	27	6	95	2	0	9	5	.643	2	0	2.23
1992	San Diego	NL	20	20	1	0	118	496	113	62	54	13	8	3	2	35	2	66	2	1	4	8	.333	0	0	4.12
	5 ML YEARS		172	49	5	60	521.1	2143	440	185	159	43	31	14	9	166	30	379	9	7	31	30	.508	2	15	2.74

Lenny Harris

Bats: Left **Throws:** Right **Pos:** 2B/3B **Ht:** 5'10" **Wt:** 205 **Born:** 10/28/64 **Age:** 28

Year	Team	Lg	G	AB	H	2B	3B	HR	(Hm	Rd)	TB	R	RBI	TBB	IBB	SO	HBP	SH	SF	SB	CS	SB%	GDP	Avg	OBP	SLG
1988	Cincinnati	NL	16	43	16	1	0	0	(0	0)	17	7	8	5	0	4	0	1	2	4	1	.80	0	.372	.420	.395
1989	2 ML Teams		115	335	79	10	1	3	(1	2)	100	36	26	20	0	33	2	1	0	14	9	.61	14	.236	.283	.299
1990	Los Angeles	NL	137	431	131	16	4	2	(0	2)	161	61	29	29	2	31	1	3	1	15	10	.60	8	.304	.348	.374
1991	Los Angeles	NL	145	429	123	16	1	3	(1	2)	150	59	38	37	5	32	5	12	2	12	3	.80	16	.287	.349	.350
1992	Los Angeles	NL	135	347	94	11	0	0	(0	0)	105	28	30	24	3	24	1	6	2	19	7	.73	10	.271	.318	.303
1989	Cincinnati	NL	61	188	42	4	0	2	(0	2)	52	17	11	9	0	20	1	1	0	10	6	.63	5	.223	.263	.277
	Los Angeles	NL	54	147	37	6	1	1	(1	0)	48	19	15	11	0	13	1	0	0	4	3	.57	9	.252	.308	.327
	5 ML YEARS		548	1585	443	54	6	8	(2	6)	533	191	131	115	10	124	9	23	7	64	30	.68	48	.279	.330	.336

Mike Hartley

Pitches: Right **Bats:** Right **Pos:** RP **Ht:** 6' 1" **Wt:** 197 **Born:** 08/31/61 **Age:** 31

Year	Team	Lg	G	GS	CG	GF	IP	BFP	H	R	ER	HR	SH	SF	HB	TBB	IBB	SO	WP	Bk	W	L	Pct.	ShO	Sv	ERA
1989	Los Angeles	NL	5	0	0	3	6	20	2	1	1	0	0	0	0	0	0	4	0	0	0	1	.000	0	0	1.50
1990	Los Angeles	NL	32	6	1	8	79.1	325	58	32	26	7	2	1	2	30	2	76	3	0	6	3	.667	1	1	2.95
1991	2 ML Teams		58	0	0	16	83.1	368	74	40	39	11	2	1	6	47	8	63	10	2	4	1	.800	0	2	4.21
1992	Philadelphia	NL	46	0	0	15	55	243	54	23	21	5	5	1	2	23	6	53	4	0	7	6	.538	0	0	3.44
1991	Los Angeles	NL	40	0	0	11	57	258	53	29	28	7	1	1	3	37	7	44	8	1	2	0	1.000	0	1	4.42
	Philadelphia	NL	18	0	0	5	26.1	110	21	11	11	4	1	0	3	10	1	19	2	1	2	1	.667	0	1	3.76
	4 ML YEARS		141	6	1	42	223.2	956	188	96	87	23	9	3	10	100	16	196	17	2	17	11	.607	1	3	3.50

Jeff Hartsock

Pitches: Right **Bats:** Right **Pos:** RP **Ht:** 6' 0" **Wt:** 190 **Born:** 11/19/66 **Age:** 26

Year	Team	Lg	G	GS	CG	GF	IP	BFP	H	R	ER	HR	SH	SF	HB	TBB	IBB	SO	WP	Bk	W	L	Pct.	ShO	Sv	ERA
1988	Great Falls	R	14	13	1	0	81	334	62	30	24	3	1	0	2	26	1	108	8	4	7	2	.778	0	0	2.67
1989	Bakersfield	A	26	26	5	0	164	670	123	64	48	5	4	2	4	62	0	146	11	2	12	5	.706	2	0	2.63
1990	San Antonio	AA	16	16	0	0	94	401	88	42	41	2	3	2	2	42	2	68	4	2	6	4	.600	0	0	3.93
	Albuquerque	AAA	11	10	0	0	46.1	226	62	38	32	5	1	0	0	30	1	33	4	2	3	3	.500	0	0	6.22
1991	Albuquerque	AAA	29	26	0	0	154	678	153	80	65	12	2	5	3	78	0	123	9	1	12	6	.667	0	0	3.80
1992	Iowa	AAA	27	27	2	0	173.1	744	177	91	84	13	9	8	10	61	2	87	3	1	5	12	.294	0	0	4.36

| 1992 Chicago | NL | 4 | 0 | 0 | 0 | 9.1 | 46 | 15 | 7 | 7 | 2 | 1 | 1 | 0 | 4 | 0 | 6 | 2 | 0 | 0 | 0 | .000 | 0 | 0 | 6.75 |

Bryan Harvey

Pitches: Right **Bats:** Right **Pos:** RP   **Ht:** 6' 2" **Wt:** 212 **Born:** 06/02/63 **Age:** 30

		HOW MUCH HE PITCHED						WHAT HE GAVE UP										THE RESULTS					
Year Team	Lg	G	GS	CG	GF	IP	BFP	H	R	ER	HR	SH	SF	HB	TBB	IBB	SO	WP	Bk	W	L	Pct.	ShO	Sv	ERA
1987 California	AL	3	0	0	2	5	22	6	0	0	0	0	0	0	2	0	3	3	0	0	0	.000	0	0	0.00
1988 California	AL	50	0	0	38	76	303	59	22	18	4	3	3	1	20	6	67	4	1	7	5	.583	0	17	2.13
1989 California	AL	51	0	0	42	55	245	36	21	21	6	5	2	0	41	1	78	5	0	3	3	.500	0	25	3.44
1990 California	AL	54	0	0	47	64.1	267	45	24	23	4	4	4	0	35	6	82	7	1	4	4	.500	0	25	3.22
1991 California	AL	67	0	0	63	78.2	309	51	20	14	6	3	2	1	17	3	101	2	2	2	4	.333	0	46	1.60
1992 California	AL	25	0	0	22	28.2	122	22	12	9	4	2	3	0	11	1	34	4	0	0	4	.000	0	13	2.83
6 ML YEARS		250	0	0	214	307.2	1268	219	99	85	24	17	14	2	126	17	365	25	4	16	20	.444	0	126	2.49

Bill Haselman

Bats: Right **Throws:** Right **Pos:** C   **Ht:** 6' 3" **Wt:** 205 **Born:** 05/25/66 **Age:** 27

		BATTING																BASERUNNING				PERCENTAGES		
Year Team	Lg	G	AB	H	2B	3B	HR	(Hm	Rd)	TB	R	RBI	TBB	IBB	SO	HBP	SH	SF	SB	CS	SB%	GDP	Avg	OBP	SLG
1990 Texas	AL	7	13	2	0	0	0	(0	0)	2	0	3	1	0	5	0	0	0	0	0	.00	0	.154	.214	.154
1992 Seattle	AL	8	19	5	0	0	0	(0	0)	5	1	0	0	0	7	0	0	0	0	0	.00	1	.263	.263	.263
2 ML YEARS		15	32	7	0	0	0	(0	0)	7	1	3	1	0	12	0	0	0	0	0	.00	1	.219	.242	.219

Billy Hatcher

Bats: Right **Throws:** Right **Pos:** LF/CF   **Ht:** 5'10" **Wt:** 190 **Born:** 10/04/60 **Age:** 32

		BATTING																BASERUNNING				PERCENTAGES		
Year Team	Lg	G	AB	H	2B	3B	HR	(Hm	Rd)	TB	R	RBI	TBB	IBB	SO	HBP	SH	SF	SB	CS	SB%	GDP	Avg	OBP	SLG
1984 Chicago	NL	8	9	1	0	0	0	(0	0)	1	1	0	1	1	0	0	0	0	1	0	1.00	0	.111	.200	.111
1985 Chicago	NL	53	163	40	12	1	2	(2	0)	60	24	10	8	0	12	3	2	2	2	4	.33	9	.245	.290	.368
1986 Houston	NL	127	419	108	15	4	6	(2	4)	149	55	36	22	1	52	5	6	1	38	14	.73	3	.258	.302	.356
1987 Houston	NL	141	564	167	28	3	11	(3	8)	234	96	63	42	1	70	9	7	5	53	9	.85	11	.296	.352	.415
1988 Houston	NL	145	530	142	25	4	7	(3	4)	196	79	52	37	4	56	8	8	8	32	13	.71	6	.268	.321	.370
1989 2 ML Teams		135	481	111	19	3	4	(0	4)	148	59	51	30	2	62	2	3	4	24	7	.77	4	.231	.277	.308
1990 Cincinnati	NL	139	504	139	28	5	5	(2	3)	192	68	25	33	5	42	6	1	1	30	10	.75	4	.276	.327	.381
1991 Cincinnati	NL	138	442	116	25	3	4	(2	2)	159	45	41	26	4	55	7	4	3	11	9	.55	9	.262	.312	.360
1992 2 ML Teams		118	409	102	19	2	3	(1	2)	134	47	33	22	1	52	3	6	4	4	8	.33	11	.249	.290	.328
1989 Houston	NL	108	395	90	15	3	3	(0	3)	120	49	44	30	2	53	1	3	4	22	6	.79	3	.228	.281	.304
Pittsburgh	NL	27	86	21	4	0	1	(0	1)	28	10	7	0	0	9	1	0	0	2	1	.67	1	.244	.253	.326
1992 Cincinnati	NL	43	94	27	3	0	2	(0	2)	36	10	10	5	0	11	0	0	3	0	2	.00	2	.287	.314	.383
Boston	AL	75	315	75	16	2	1	(1	0)	98	37	23	17	1	41	3	6	1	4	6	.40	9	.238	.283	.311
9 ML YEARS		1004	3521	926	171	25	42	(15	27)	1273	474	311	221	19	401	43	37	28	196	74	.73	57	.263	.312	.362

Hilly Hathaway

Pitches: Left **Bats:** Left **Pos:** SP   **Ht:** 6' 4" **Wt:** 195 **Born:** 09/12/69 **Age:** 23

		HOW MUCH HE PITCHED						WHAT HE GAVE UP										THE RESULTS					
Year Team	Lg	G	GS	CG	GF	IP	BFP	H	R	ER	HR	SH	SF	HB	TBB	IBB	SO	WP	Bk	W	L	Pct.	ShO	Sv	ERA
1990 Boise	A	15	15	0	0	86.1	337	57	18	14	1	1	3	2	25	0	113	7	5	8	2	.800	0	0	1.46
1991 Quad City	A	20	20	1	0	129	545	126	58	48	5	4	1	7	41	1	110	11	3	9	6	.600	0	0	3.35
1992 Palm Sprngs	A	3	3	2	0	24	98	25	5	4	1	0	0	0	3	0	17	0	0	2	1	.667	1	0	1.50
Midland	AA	14	14	1	0	95.1	378	90	39	34	2	1	1	8	10	0	69	2	2	7	2	.778	0	0	3.21
1992 California	AL	2	1	0	0	5.2	29	8	5	5	1	1	1	1	3	0	1	0	0	0	1	.000	0	0	7.94

Charlie Hayes

Bats: Right **Throws:** Right **Pos:** 3B   **Ht:** 6' 0" **Wt:** 205 **Born:** 05/29/65 **Age:** 28

		BATTING																BASERUNNING				PERCENTAGES		
Year Team	Lg	G	AB	H	2B	3B	HR	(Hm	Rd)	TB	R	RBI	TBB	IBB	SO	HBP	SH	SF	SB	CS	SB%	GDP	Avg	OBP	SLG
1988 San Francisco	NL	7	11	1	0	0	0	(0	0)	1	0	0	0	0	3	0	0	0	0	0	.00	0	.091	.091	.091
1989 2 ML Teams		87	304	78	15	1	8	(3	5)	119	26	43	11	1	50	0	2	3	3	1	.75	6	.257	.280	.391
1990 Philadelphia	NL	152	561	145	20	0	10	(3	7)	195	56	57	28	3	91	2	0	6	4	4	.50	12	.258	.293	.348
1991 Philadelphia	NL	142	460	106	23	1	12	(6	6)	167	34	53	16	3	75	1	2	1	3	3	.50	13	.230	.257	.363
1992 New York	AL	142	509	131	19	2	18	(7	11)	208	52	66	28	0	100	3	3	6	3	5	.38	12	.257	.297	.409
1989 San Francisco	NL	3	5	1	0	0	0	(0	0)	1	0	0	0	0	1	0	0	0	0	0	.00	0	.200	.200	.200
Philadelphia	NL	84	299	77	15	1	8	(3	5)	118	26	43	11	1	49	0	2	3	3	1	.75	6	.258	.281	.395
5 ML YEARS		530	1845	461	77	4	48	(19	29)	690	168	219	83	7	319	6	7	16	13	13	.50	43	.250	.282	.374

Von Hayes

Bats: Left **Throws:** Right **Pos:** RF **Ht:** 6' 5" **Wt:** 186 **Born:** 08/31/58 **Age:** 34

Year	Team	Lg	G	AB	H	2B	3B	HR	(Hm	Rd)	TB	R	RBI	TBB	IBB	SO	HBP	SH	SF	SB	CS	SB%	GDP	Avg	OBP	SLG
1981	Cleveland	AL	43	109	28	8	2	1	(0	1)	43	21	17	14	1	10	2	4	2	8	1	.89	2	.257	.346	.394
1982	Cleveland	AL	150	527	132	25	3	14	(3	11)	205	65	82	42	3	63	4	8	2	32	13	.71	10	.250	.310	.389
1983	Philadelphia	NL	124	351	93	9	5	6	(3	3)	130	45	32	36	7	55	3	0	2	20	12	.63	11	.265	.337	.370
1984	Philadelphia	NL	152	561	164	27	6	16	(10	6)	251	85	67	59	4	84	0	0	2	48	13	.79	10	.292	.359	.447
1985	Philadelphia	NL	152	570	150	30	4	13	(12	1)	227	76	70	61	6	99	0	2	4	21	8	.72	6	.263	.332	.398
1986	Philadelphia	NL	158	610	186	46	2	19	(11	8)	293	107	98	74	9	77	1	1	4	24	12	.67	14	.305	.379	.480
1987	Philadelphia	NL	158	556	154	36	5	21	(14	7)	263	84	84	121	12	77	0	0	4	16	7	.70	12	.277	.404	.473
1988	Philadelphia	NL	104	367	100	28	2	6	(2	4)	150	43	45	49	5	59	1	1	5	20	9	.69	3	.272	.355	.409
1989	Philadelphia	NL	154	540	140	27	2	26	(15	11)	249	93	78	101	14	103	4	0	7	28	7	.80	7	.259	.376	.461
1990	Philadelphia	NL	129	467	122	14	3	17	(10	7)	193	70	73	87	16	81	4	0	10	16	7	.70	10	.261	.375	.413
1991	Philadelphia	NL	77	284	64	15	1	0	(0	0)	81	43	21	31	1	42	3	0	5	9	2	.82	6	.225	.303	.285
1992	California	AL	94	307	69	17	1	4	(2	2)	100	35	29	37	4	54	0	3	3	11	6	.65	9	.225	.305	.326
	12 ML YEARS		1495	5249	1402	282	36	143	(82	61)	2185	767	696	712	82	804	22	19	50	253	97	.72	100	.267	.354	.416

Neal Heaton

Pitches: Left **Bats:** Left **Pos:** RP **Ht:** 6' 0" **Wt:** 200 **Born:** 03/03/60 **Age:** 33

Year	Team	Lg	G	GS	CG	GF	IP	BFP	H	R	ER	HR	SH	SF	HB	TBB	IBB	SO	WP	Bk	W	L	Pct.	ShO	Sv	ERA
1982	Cleveland	AL	8	4	0	0	31	142	32	21	18	1	1	2	0	16	0	14	4	0	0	2	.000	0	0	5.23
1983	Cleveland	AL	39	16	4	19	149.1	637	157	79	69	11	3	5	1	44	10	75	1	0	11	7	.611	3	7	4.16
1984	Cleveland	AL	38	34	4	2	198.2	880	231	128	115	21	6	10	0	75	5	75	3	1	12	15	.444	1	0	5.21
1985	Cleveland	AL	36	33	5	2	207.2	921	244	119	113	19	7	8	7	80	2	82	2	2	9	17	.346	1	0	4.90
1986	2 ML Teams		33	29	5	2	198.2	850	201	102	90	26	6	5	2	81	8	90	4	0	7	15	.318	0	1	4.08
1987	Montreal	NL	32	32	3	0	193.1	807	207	103	97	25	5	5	3	37	3	105	2	5	13	10	.565	1	0	4.52
1988	Montreal	NL	32	11	0	7	97.1	415	98	54	54	14	5	3	3	43	5	43	1	5	3	10	.231	0	2	4.99
1989	Pittsburgh	NL	42	18	1	5	147.1	620	127	55	50	12	12	3	6	55	12	67	4	5	6	7	.462	0	0	3.05
1990	Pittsburgh	NL	30	24	0	2	146	599	143	66	56	17	10	6	2	38	1	68	4	1	12	9	.571	0	0	3.45
1991	Pittsburgh	NL	42	1	0	5	68.2	293	72	37	33	6	3	3	4	21	2	34	0	1	3	3	.500	0	0	4.33
1992	2 ML Teams		32	0	0	9	42	189	43	21	19	5	2	3	1	23	2	31	3	1	3	1	.750	0	0	4.07
1986	Cleveland	AL	12	12	2	0	74.1	324	73	42	35	8	2	0	1	34	4	24	2	0	3	6	.333	0	0	4.24
	Minnesota	AL	21	17	3	2	124.1	526	128	60	55	18	4	5	1	47	4	66	2	0	4	9	.308	0	1	3.98
1992	Kansas City	AL	31	0	0	8	41	185	43	21	19	5	2	3	1	22	2	29	3	1	3	1	.750	0	0	4.17
	Milwaukee	AL	1	0	0	0	1	4	0	0	0	0	0	0	0	1	0	2	0	0	0	0	.000	0	0	0.00
	11 ML YEARS		364	202	22	53	1480	6353	1555	785	714	157	60	53	29	513	50	684	28	21	79	96	.451	6	10	4.34

Bert Heffernan

Bats: Left **Throws:** Right **Pos:** C **Ht:** 5'10" **Wt:** 185 **Born:** 03/03/65 **Age:** 28

Year	Team	Lg	G	AB	H	2B	3B	HR	(Hm	Rd)	TB	R	RBI	TBB	IBB	SO	HBP	SH	SF	SB	CS	SB%	GDP	Avg	OBP	SLG
1988	Beloit	A	5	14	3	0	0	0	--	--	3	1	0	5	0	0	0	0	0	0	0	.00	1	.214	.421	.214
	Helena	R	65	196	55	13	0	4	--	--	80	47	31	61	1	40	0	2	4	14	5	.74	2	.281	.444	.408
1989	Beloit	A	127	425	126	20	1	4	--	--	160	53	59	70	4	57	4	3	4	9	8	.53	7	.296	.398	.376
1990	El Paso	AA	110	390	109	18	2	1	--	--	134	49	42	60	4	68	1	7	3	6	3	.67	16	.279	.374	.344
1991	Albuquerque	AAA	67	161	39	10	1	0	--	--	51	17	13	22	1	19	0	3	2	1	3	.25	7	.242	.317	.317
1992	Calgary	AAA	15	46	14	2	0	1	--	--	19	8	4	7	0	7	0	0	0	1	1	.50	1	.304	.396	.413
	Jacksnville	AA	58	196	56	9	0	2	--	--	71	16	23	29	0	28	2	2	2	4	7	.36	5	.286	.380	.362
1992	Seattle	AL	8	11	1	1	0	0	(0	0)	2	0	1	0	0	1	0	0	0	0	0	.00	1	.091	.091	.182

Scott Hemond

Bats: Right **Throws:** Right **Pos:** C **Ht:** 6' 0" **Wt:** 205 **Born:** 11/18/65 **Age:** 27

Year	Team	Lg	G	AB	H	2B	3B	HR	(Hm	Rd)	TB	R	RBI	TBB	IBB	SO	HBP	SH	SF	SB	CS	SB%	GDP	Avg	OBP	SLG
1989	Oakland	AL	4	0	0	0	0	0	(0	0)	0	2	0	0	0	0	0	0	0	0	0	.00	0	.000	.000	.000
1990	Oakland	AL	7	13	2	0	0	0	(0	0)	2	0	1	0	0	5	0	0	0	0	0	.00	0	.154	.154	.154
1991	Oakland	AL	23	23	5	0	0	0	(0	0)	5	4	0	1	0	7	0	0	0	1	2	.33	0	.217	.250	.217
1992	2 ML Teams		25	40	9	2	0	0	(0	0)	11	8	2	4	0	13	0	0	1	1	0	1.00	2	.225	.289	.275
1992	Oakland	AL	17	27	6	1	0	0	(0	0)	7	7	1	3	0	7	0	0	1	1	0	1.00	2	.222	.300	.259
	Chicago	AL	8	13	3	1	0	0	(0	0)	4	1	1	1	0	6	0	0	0	0	0	.00	0	.231	.267	.308
	4 ML YEARS		59	76	16	2	0	0	(0	0)	18	14	3	5	0	25	0	0	1	2	2	.50	2	.211	.256	.237

Dave Henderson

Bats: Right **Throws:** Right **Pos:** CF **Ht:** 6' 2" **Wt:** 220 **Born:** 07/21/58 **Age:** 34

						BATTING														BASERUNNING				PERCENTAGES		
Year	Team	Lg	G	AB	H	2B	3B	HR	(Hm	Rd)	TB	R	RBI	TBB	IBB	SO	HBP	SH	SF	SB	CS	SB%	GDP	Avg	OBP	SLG
1981	Seattle	AL	59	126	21	3	0	6	(5	1)	42	17	13	16	1	24	1	1	1	2	1	.67	4	.167	.264	.333
1982	Seattle	AL	104	324	82	17	1	14	(8	6)	143	47	48	36	2	67	0	1	1	2	5	.29	5	.253	.327	.441
1983	Seattle	AL	137	484	130	24	5	17	(9	8)	215	50	55	28	3	93	1	2	6	9	3	.75	5	.269	.306	.444
1984	Seattle	AL	112	350	98	23	0	14	(8	6)	163	42	43	19	0	56	2	2	1	5	5	.50	4	.280	.320	.466
1985	Seattle	AL	139	502	121	28	2	14	(8	6)	195	70	68	48	2	104	3	1	2	6	1	.86	11	.241	.310	.388
1986	2 ML Teams		139	388	103	22	4	15	(10	5)	178	59	47	39	4	110	2	2	1	2	3	.40	6	.265	.335	.459
1987	2 ML Teams		90	205	48	12	0	8	(4	4)	84	32	26	30	0	53	0	1	2	3	1	.75	3	.234	.329	.410
1988	Oakland	AL	146	507	154	38	1	24	(12	12)	266	100	94	47	1	92	4	5	7	2	4	.33	14	.304	.363	.525
1989	Oakland	AL	152	579	145	24	3	15	(10	5)	220	77	80	54	1	131	3	1	6	8	5	.62	13	.250	.315	.380
1990	Oakland	AL	127	450	122	28	0	20	(11	9)	210	65	63	40	1	105	1	1	2	3	1	.75	5	.271	.331	.467
1991	Oakland	AL	150	572	158	33	0	25	(15	10)	266	86	85	58	3	113	4	1	2	6	6	.50	9	.276	.346	.465
1992	Oakland	AL	20	63	9	1	0	0	(0	0)	10	1	2	2	0	16	0	0	0	0	0	.00	0	.143	.169	.159
1986	Seattle	AL	103	337	93	19	4	14	(10	4)	162	51	44	37	4	95	2	1	1	1	3	.25	5	.276	.350	.481
	Boston	AL	36	51	10	3	0	1	(0	1)	16	8	3	2	0	15	0	1	0	1	0	1.00	1	.196	.226	.314
1987	Boston	AL	75	184	43	10	0	8	(4	4)	77	30	25	22	0	48	0	1	2	1	1	.50	3	.234	.313	.418
	San Francisco	NL	15	21	5	2	0	0	(0	0)	7	2	1	8	0	5	0	0	0	2	0	1.00	0	.238	.448	.333
12 ML YEARS			1375	4550	1191	253	16	172	(100	72)	1992	646	624	417	18	964	21	18	31	48	35	.58	79	.262	.325	.438

Rickey Henderson

Bats: Right **Throws:** Left **Pos:** LF **Ht:** 5'10" **Wt:** 190 **Born:** 12/25/58 **Age:** 34

						BATTING														BASERUNNING				PERCENTAGES		
Year	Team	Lg	G	AB	H	2B	3B	HR	(Hm	Rd)	TB	R	RBI	TBB	IBB	SO	HBP	SH	SF	SB	CS	SB%	GDP	Avg	OBP	SLG
1979	Oakland	AL	89	351	96	13	3	1	(1	0)	118	49	26	34	0	39	2	8	3	33	11	.75	4	.274	.338	.336
1980	Oakland	AL	158	591	179	22	4	9	(3	6)	236	111	53	117	7	54	5	6	3	100	26	.79	6	.303	.420	.399
1981	Oakland	AL	108	423	135	18	7	6	(5	1)	185	89	35	64	4	68	2	0	4	56	22	.72	7	.319	.408	.437
1982	Oakland	AL	149	536	143	24	4	10	(5	5)	205	119	51	116	1	94	2	0	2	130	42	.76	5	.267	.398	.382
1983	Oakland	AL	145	513	150	25	7	9	(5	4)	216	105	48	103	8	80	4	1	1	108	19	.85	11	.292	.414	.421
1984	Oakland	AL	142	502	147	27	4	16	(7	9)	230	113	58	86	1	81	5	1	3	66	18	.79	7	.293	.399	.458
1985	New York	AL	143	547	172	28	5	24	(8	16)	282	146	72	99	1	65	3	0	5	80	10	.89	8	.314	.419	.516
1986	New York	AL	153	608	160	31	5	28	(13	15)	285	130	74	89	2	81	2	0	2	87	18	.83	12	.263	.358	.469
1987	New York	AL	95	358	104	17	3	17	(10	7)	178	78	37	80	1	52	2	0	0	41	8	.84	10	.291	.423	.497
1988	New York	AL	140	554	169	30	2	6	(2	4)	221	118	50	82	1	54	3	2	6	93	13	.88	6	.305	.394	.399
1989	2 ML Teams		150	541	148	26	3	12	(7	5)	216	113	57	126	5	68	3	0	4	77	14	.85	8	.274	.411	.399
1990	Oakland	AL	136	489	159	33	3	28	(8	20)	282	119	61	97	2	60	4	2	2	65	10	.87	13	.325	.439	.577
1991	Oakland	AL	134	470	126	17	1	18	(8	10)	199	105	57	98	7	73	7	0	3	58	18	.76	7	.268	.400	.423
1992	Oakland	AL	117	396	112	18	3	15	(10	5)	181	77	46	95	5	56	6	0	3	48	11	.81	5	.283	.426	.457
1989	New York	AL	65	235	58	13	1	3	(1	2)	82	41	22	56	0	29	1	0	1	25	8	.76	0	.247	.392	.349
	Oakland	AL	85	306	90	13	2	9	(6	3)	134	72	35	70	5	39	2	0	3	52	6	.90	8	.294	.425	.438
14 ML YEARS			1859	6879	2000	329	54	199	(92	107)	3034	1472	725	1286	45	925	50	20	41	1042	240	.81	109	.291	.404	.441

Tom Henke

Pitches: Right **Bats:** Right **Pos:** RP **Ht:** 6' 5" **Wt:** 225 **Born:** 12/21/57 **Age:** 35

			HOW MUCH HE PITCHED						WHAT HE GAVE UP										THE RESULTS					
Year	Team	Lg	G	GS	CG	GF	IP	BFP	H	R	ER	HR	SH	SF	HB	TBB	IBB	SO	WP	Bk	W	L	Pct.	ShO	Sv	ERA
1982	Texas	AL	8	0	0	6	15.2	67	14	2	2	0	1	0	1	8	2	9	0	0	1	0	1.000	0	0	1.15
1983	Texas	AL	8	0	0	5	16	65	16	6	6	1	0	0	0	4	0	17	0	0	1	0	1.000	0	1	3.38
1984	Texas	AL	25	0	0	13	28.1	141	36	21	20	0	1	4	1	20	2	25	2	2	1	1	.500	0	2	6.35
1985	Toronto	AL	28	0	0	22	40	153	29	12	9	4	2	2	0	8	2	42	0	0	3	3	.500	0	13	2.03
1986	Toronto	AL	63	0	0	51	91.1	370	63	39	34	6	2	6	1	32	4	118	3	1	9	5	.643	0	27	3.35
1987	Toronto	AL	72	0	0	62	94	363	62	27	26	10	3	5	0	25	3	128	5	0	0	6	.000	0	34	2.49
1988	Toronto	AL	52	0	0	44	68	285	60	23	22	6	4	2	2	24	4	66	0	0	4	4	.500	0	25	2.91
1989	Toronto	AL	64	0	0	56	89	356	66	20	19	5	4	3	2	25	4	116	2	0	8	3	.727	0	20	1.92
1990	Toronto	AL	61	0	0	58	74.2	297	58	18	18	8	4	1	1	19	2	75	6	0	2	4	.333	0	32	2.17
1991	Toronto	AL	49	0	0	43	50.1	190	33	13	13	4	0	0	0	11	2	53	1	0	0	2	.000	0	32	2.32
1992	Toronto	AL	57	0	0	50	55.2	228	40	19	14	5	0	3	0	22	2	46	4	0	3	2	.600	0	34	2.26
11 ML YEARS			487	0	0	410	623	2515	477	200	183	49	21	26	8	198	26	695	23	3	32	30	.516	0	220	2.64

Mike Henneman

Pitches: Right **Bats:** Right **Pos:** RP **Ht:** 6' 4" **Wt:** 205 **Born:** 12/11/61 **Age:** 31

			HOW MUCH HE PITCHED						WHAT HE GAVE UP										THE RESULTS					
Year	Team	Lg	G	GS	CG	GF	IP	BFP	H	R	ER	HR	SH	SF	HB	TBB	IBB	SO	WP	Bk	W	L	Pct.	ShO	Sv	ERA
1987	Detroit	AL	55	0	0	28	96.2	399	86	36	32	8	2	2	3	30	5	75	7	0	11	3	.786	0	7	2.98

Year Team	Lg	G	GS	CG	GF	IP	BFP	H	R	ER	HR	SH	SF	HB	TBB	IBB	SO	WP	Bk	W	L	Pct.	ShO	Sv	ERA
1988 Detroit	AL	65	0	0	51	91.1	364	72	23	19	7	5	2	2	24	10	58	8	1	9	6	.600	0	22	1.87
1989 Detroit	AL	60	0	0	35	90	401	84	46	37	4	7	3	5	51	15	69	0	1	11	4	.733	0	8	3.70
1990 Detroit	AL	69	0	0	53	94.1	399	90	36	32	4	5	2	3	33	12	50	3	0	8	6	.571	0	22	3.05
1991 Detroit	AL	60	0	0	50	84.1	358	81	29	27	2	5	5	0	34	8	61	5	0	10	2	.833	0	21	2.88
1992 Detroit	AL	60	0	0	53	77.1	321	75	36	34	6	3	5	0	20	10	58	7	0	2	6	.250	0	24	3.96
6 ML YEARS		369	0	0	270	534	2242	488	206	181	31	27	19	13	192	60	371	30	2	51	27	.654	0	104	3.05

Butch Henry

Pitches: Left **Bats:** Left **Pos:** SP **Ht:** 6' 1" **Wt:** 195 **Born:** 10/07/68 **Age:** 24

| | | HOW MUCH HE PITCHED | | | | | | WHAT HE GAVE UP | | | | | | | | | | | | THE RESULTS | | | | | |
Year Team	Lg	G	GS	CG	GF	IP	BFP	H	R	ER	HR	SH	SF	HB	TBB	IBB	SO	WP	Bk	W	L	Pct.	ShO	Sv	ERA
1987 Billings	R	9	5	0	2	35	151	37	21	18	3	0	1	1	12	1	38	4	1	4	0	1.000	0	1	4.63
1988 Cedar Rapds	A	27	27	1	0	187	745	144	59	47	14	7	4	6	56	2	163	6	8	16	2	.889	1	0	2.26
1989 Chattanooga	AA	7	7	0	0	26.1	110	22	12	10	2	1	1	0	12	1	19	2	0	1	3	.250	0	0	3.42
1990 Chattanooga	AA	24	22	2	0	143	622	151	74	67	15	9	5	3	58	0	95	12	2	8	8	.500	0	0	4.22
1991 Tucson	AAA	27	27	2	0	153.2	671	192	92	82	10	8	5	1	42	2	97	5	4	10	11	.476	0	0	4.80
1992 Houston	NL	28	28	2	0	165.2	710	185	81	74	16	12	7	1	41	7	96	2	2	6	9	.400	1	0	4.02

Doug Henry

Pitches: Right **Bats:** Right **Pos:** RP **Ht:** 6' 4" **Wt:** 185 **Born:** 12/10/63 **Age:** 29

| | | HOW MUCH HE PITCHED | | | | | | WHAT HE GAVE UP | | | | | | | | | | | | THE RESULTS | | | | | |
Year Team	Lg	G	GS	CG	GF	IP	BFP	H	R	ER	HR	SH	SF	HB	TBB	IBB	SO	WP	Bk	W	L	Pct.	ShO	Sv	ERA
1986 Beloit	A	27	24	4	1	143.1	639	153	95	74	16	3	5	6	56	4	115	9	4	7	8	.467	1	1	4.65
1987 Beloit	A	31	15	1	5	132.2	593	145	83	72	6	2	4	5	51	5	106	7	0	8	9	.471	0	2	4.88
1988 Stockton	A	23	1	0	14	70.2	280	46	19	14	1	1	1	1	31	1	71	5	4	7	1	.875	0	7	1.78
El Paso	AA	14	3	3	1	45.2	182	33	16	16	4	0	1	1	19	0	50	3	3	4	0	1.000	1	0	3.15
1989 El Paso	AA	1	1	0	0	2	11	3	3	3	1	0	0	0	3	0	2	0	0	0	0	.000	0	0	13.50
Stockton	A	4	3	0	0	11	43	9	4	0	0	0	0	0	3	0	9	0	0	0	1	.000	0	0	0.00
1990 Stockton	A	4	0	0	3	8	35	4	1	1	0	0	1	2	3	0	13	1	0	1	0	1.000	0	1	1.13
El Paso	AA	15	0	0	12	30.2	131	31	13	10	1	0	1	0	11	0	25	0	2	1	0	1.000	0	9	2.93
Denver	AAA	27	0	0	15	50.2	219	46	26	25	4	3	1	0	27	2	54	3	0	2	3	.400	0	8	4.44
1991 Denver	AAA	32	0	0	27	57.2	234	47	16	14	4	4	2	3	20	3	47	4	2	3	2	.600	0	14	2.18
1991 Milwaukee	AL	32	0	0	25	36	137	16	4	4	1	1	2	0	14	1	28	0	0	2	1	.667	0	15	1.00
1992 Milwaukee	AL	68	0	0	56	65	277	64	34	29	6	1	2	0	24	4	52	4	0	1	4	.200	0	29	4.02
2 ML YEARS		100	0	0	81	101	414	80	38	33	7	2	4	0	38	5	80	4	0	3	5	.375	0	44	2.94

Dwayne Henry

Pitches: Right **Bats:** Right **Pos:** RP **Ht:** 6' 3" **Wt:** 230 **Born:** 02/16/62 **Age:** 31

| | | HOW MUCH HE PITCHED | | | | | | WHAT HE GAVE UP | | | | | | | | | | | | THE RESULTS | | | | | |
Year Team	Lg	G	GS	CG	GF	IP	BFP	H	R	ER	HR	SH	SF	HB	TBB	IBB	SO	WP	Bk	W	L	Pct.	ShO	Sv	ERA
1984 Texas	AL	3	0	0	1	4.1	25	5	4	4	0	1	0	0	7	0	2	0	0	0	1	.000	0	0	8.31
1985 Texas	AL	16	0	0	10	21	86	16	7	6	0	2	1	0	7	0	20	1	0	2	2	.500	0	3	2.57
1986 Texas	AL	19	0	0	4	19.1	93	14	11	10	1	1	2	1	22	0	17	7	1	1	0	1.000	0	0	4.66
1987 Texas	AL	5	0	0	1	10	50	12	10	10	2	0	0	0	9	0	7	1	0	0	0	.000	0	0	9.00
1988 Texas	AL	11	0	0	5	10.1	59	15	10	10	1	0	1	3	9	1	10	3	1	0	1	.000	0	1	8.71
1989 Atlanta	NL	12	0	0	6	12.2	55	12	6	6	2	2	0	0	5	1	16	1	0	0	2	.000	0	1	4.26
1990 Atlanta	NL	34	0	0	14	38.1	176	41	26	24	3	0	1	0	25	0	34	2	1	2	2	.500	0	0	5.63
1991 Houston	NL	52	0	0	25	67.2	282	51	25	24	7	6	2	2	39	7	51	5	0	3	2	.600	0	2	3.19
1992 Cincinnati	NL	60	0	0	11	83.2	352	59	31	31	4	7	3	1	44	6	72	12	0	3	3	.500	0	0	3.33
9 ML YEARS		212	0	0	77	267.1	1178	225	130	125	20	19	10	7	167	15	229	32	3	11	13	.458	0	7	4.21

Pat Hentgen

Pitches: Right **Bats:** Right **Pos:** RP **Ht:** 6' 2" **Wt:** 200 **Born:** 11/13/68 **Age:** 24

| | | HOW MUCH HE PITCHED | | | | | | WHAT HE GAVE UP | | | | | | | | | | | | THE RESULTS | | | | | |
Year Team	Lg	G	GS	CG	GF	IP	BFP	H	R	ER	HR	SH	SF	HB	TBB	IBB	SO	WP	Bk	W	L	Pct.	ShO	Sv	ERA
1986 St.Cathrnes	A	13	11	0	2	40	191	38	27	20	3	2	1	2	30	1	30	3	0	0	4	.000	0	1	4.50
1987 Myrtle Bch	A	32	31	2	0	188	753	145	62	49	5	4	2	8	60	0	131	14	3	11	5	.688	2	0	2.35
1988 Dunedin	A	31	30	0	1	151.1	651	139	80	58	10	4	6	4	65	1	125	14	2	3	12	.200	0	0	3.45
1989 Dunedin	A	29	28	0	0	151.1	633	123	53	45	5	6	7	2	71	1	148	16	4	9	8	.529	0	0	2.68
1990 Knoxville	AA	28	26	0	0	153.1	633	121	57	52	10	3	5	3	68	0	142	9	5	9	5	.643	0	0	3.05
1991 Syracuse	AAA	31	28	1	2	171	729	146	91	85	17	5	6	2	90	1	155	11	2	8	9	.471	0	0	4.47
1992 Syracuse	AAA	4	4	0	0	20.1	81	15	6	6	1	2	0	0	8	0	17	0	1	1	2	.333	0	0	2.66
1991 Toronto	AL	3	1	0	1	7.1	30	5	2	2	1	1	0	2	3	0	3	1	0	0	0	.000	0	0	2.45
1992 Toronto	AL	28	2	0	10	50.1	229	49	30	30	7	2	2	0	32	5	39	2	1	5	2	.714	0	0	5.36
2 ML YEARS		31	3	0	11	57.2	259	54	32	32	8	3	2	2	35	5	42	3	1	5	2	.714	0	0	4.99

90

Gil Heredia

Pitches: Right **Bats:** Right **Pos:** RP/SP   **Ht:** 6' 1" **Wt:** 190 **Born:** 10/26/65 **Age:** 27

				HOW MUCH HE PITCHED				WHAT HE GAVE UP										THE RESULTS				
Year	Team	Lg	G	GS	CG	GF	IP	BFP	H	R	ER	HR	SH	SF	HB	TBB	IBB	SO	WP	Bk	W	L	Pct.	ShO	Sv	ERA
1987	Everett	A	3	3	1	0	20	80	24	8	8	2	0	0	0	1	0	14	1	0	2	0	1.000	0	0	3.60
	Fresno	A	11	11	5	0	80.2	321	62	28	26	8	2	5	0	23	1	60	2	2	5	3	.625	2	0	2.90
1988	San Jose	A	27	27	9	0	206.1	863	216	107	80	9	9	7	4	46	0	121	9	0	13	12	.520	0	0	3.49
1989	Shreveport	AA	7	2	1	1	24.2	104	28	10	7	1	1	0	1	4	0	8	2	0	1	0	1.000	0	0	2.55
1990	Phoenix	AAA	29	19	0	2	147	626	159	81	67	7	6	6	3	37	0	75	4	1	9	7	.563	0	1	4.10
1991	Phoenix	AAA	33	15	5	7	140.1	592	155	60	44	3	9	2	2	28	5	75	4	0	9	11	.450	1	1	2.82
1992	Phoenix	AAA	22	7	1	7	80.2	325	83	30	18	3	2	1	1	13	1	37	2	0	5	5	.500	1	1	2.01
	Indianapols	AAA	3	3	0	0	17.2	72	18	2	2	1	0	0	1	3	0	10	0	1	2	0	1.000	0	0	1.02
1991	San Francisco	NL	7	4	0	1	33	126	27	14	14	4	2	1	0	7	2	13	1	0	0	2	.000	0	0	3.82
1992	2 ML Teams		20	5	0	4	44.2	187	44	23	21	4	2	1	1	20	1	22	1	0	2	3	.400	0	0	4.23
1992	San Francisco	NL	13	4	0	3	30	132	32	20	18	3	0	0	1	16	1	15	1	0	2	3	.400	0	0	5.40
	Montreal	NL	7	1	0	1	14.2	55	12	3	3	1	2	1	0	4	0	7	0	0	0	0	.000	0	0	1.84
	2 ML YEARS		27	9	0	5	77.2	313	71	37	35	8	4	2	1	27	3	35	2	0	2	5	.286	0	0	4.06

Carlos Hernandez

Bats: Right **Throws:** Right **Pos:** C   **Ht:** 5'11" **Wt:** 185 **Born:** 05/24/67 **Age:** 26

							BATTING												BASERUNNING				PERCENTAGES		
Year	Team	Lg	G	AB	H	2B	3B	HR	(Hm | Rd)	TB	R	RBI	TBB	IBB	SO	HBP	SH	SF	SB	CS	SB%	GDP	Avg	OBP	SLG
1985	Dodgers	R	22	49	12	1	0	0	--	--	13	3	6	3	0	8	0	0	0	0	0	.00	4	.245	.288	.265
1986	Dodgers	R	57	205	64	7	0	1	--	--	74	19	31	5	2	18	2	1	1	1	2	.33	7	.312	.333	.361
1987	Bakersfield	A	48	162	37	6	1	3	--	--	54	22	22	14	0	23	3	1	2	8	4	.67	6	.228	.298	.333
1988	Bakersfield	A	92	333	103	15	2	5	--	--	137	37	52	16	2	39	1	3	4	3	2	.60	18	.309	.339	.411
	Albuquerque	AAA	3	8	1	0	0	0	--	--	1	0	1	0	0	0	0	0	0	0	0	.00	1	.125	.125	.125
1989	San Antonio	AA	99	370	111	16	3	8	--	--	157	37	41	12	0	46	7	1	3	2	3	.40	12	.300	.332	.424
	Albuquerque	AAA	4	14	3	0	0	0	--	--	3	1	1	2	1	1	0	0	0	0	0	.00	1	.214	.313	.214
1990	Albuquerque	AAA	52	143	45	8	1	0	--	--	55	11	16	8	1	25	1	0	3	2	2	.50	5	.315	.348	.385
1991	Albuquerque	AAA	95	345	119	24	2	8	--	--	171	60	44	24	5	36	1	0	2	5	5	.50	10	.345	.387	.496
1990	Los Angeles	NL	10	20	4	1	0	0	(0 | 0)	5	2	1	0	0	2	0	0	0	0	0	.00	0	.200	.200	.250
1991	Los Angeles	NL	15	14	3	1	0	0	(0 | 0)	4	1	1	0	0	5	1	0	1	1	0	1.00	2	.214	.250	.286
1992	Los Angeles	NL	69	173	45	4	0	3	(1 | 2)	58	11	17	11	1	21	4	0	2	0	1	.00	8	.260	.316	.335
	3 ML YEARS		94	207	52	6	0	3	(1 | 2)	67	14	19	11	1	28	5	0	3	1	1	.50	10	.251	.301	.324

Cesar Hernandez

Bats: Right **Throws:** Right **Pos:** LF   **Ht:** 6' 0" **Wt:** 160 **Born:** 09/28/66 **Age:** 26

							BATTING												BASERUNNING				PERCENTAGES		
Year	Team	Lg	G	AB	H	2B	3B	HR	(Hm | Rd)	TB	R	RBI	TBB	IBB	SO	HBP	SH	SF	SB	CS	SB%	GDP	Avg	OBP	SLG
1986	Burlington	A	38	104	26	11	0	1	--	--	40	12	12	7	0	24	4	1	2	7	0	1.00	2	.250	.316	.385
1987	Wst Plm Bch	A	32	106	25	3	1	2	--	--	36	14	6	4	0	29	1	0	1	6	1	.86	1	.236	.268	.340
1988	Rockford	A	117	411	101	20	4	19	--	--	186	71	60	25	1	109	4	1	1	28	8	.78	11	.246	.295	.453
1989	Wst Plm Bch	A	42	158	45	8	3	1	--	--	62	16	15	8	1	32	5	1	2	16	4	.80	2	.285	.335	.392
	Jacksnville	AA	81	222	47	9	1	3	--	--	67	25	13	22	2	60	0	1	0	11	4	.73	3	.212	.283	.302
1990	Jacksnville	AA	118	393	94	21	7	10	--	--	159	58	50	18	3	75	7	1	6	16	11	.59	4	.239	.281	.405
1991	Harrisburg	AA	128	418	106	16	2	13	--	--	165	58	52	25	2	106	8	1	6	34	8	.81	7	.254	.304	.395
1992	Nashville	AAA	1	2	2	0	0	0	--	--	2	0	0	0	0	0	0	0	0	1	0	1.00	0	1.000	1.000	1.000
	Chattanooga	AA	93	328	91	23	4	3	--	--	131	50	27	19	1	65	4	2	0	12	9	.57	5	.277	.325	.399
1992	Cincinnati	NL	34	51	14	4	0	0	(0 | 0)	18	6	4	0	0	10	0	0	0	3	1	.75	1	.275	.275	.353

Jeremy Hernandez

Pitches: Right **Bats:** Right **Pos:** RP   **Ht:** 6' 6" **Wt:** 205 **Born:** 07/07/66 **Age:** 26

				HOW MUCH HE PITCHED				WHAT HE GAVE UP										THE RESULTS				
Year	Team	Lg	G	GS	CG	GF	IP	BFP	H	R	ER	HR	SH	SF	HB	TBB	IBB	SO	WP	Bk	W	L	Pct.	ShO	Sv	ERA
1987	Erie	A	16	16	1	0	99.1	412	87	36	31	7	2	3	2	41	3	62	7	1	5	4	.556	0	0	2.81
1988	Springfield	A	24	24	3	0	147.1	615	133	73	58	8	0	3	7	34	2	97	4	8	12	6	.667	1	0	3.54
1989	St.Pete	A	3	3	0	0	14	63	17	14	12	0	2	1	0	5	0	5	2	0	0	2	.000	0	0	7.71
	Chston-Sc	A	10	10	2	0	58.2	260	65	37	23	2	2	0	3	16	1	39	1	3	3	5	.375	1	0	3.53
	Riverside	A	9	9	4	0	67	264	55	17	13	2	0	0	4	11	0	65	2	0	5	2	.714	1	0	1.75
	Wichita	AA	4	3	0	0	19	91	30	18	18	6	1	1	0	8	0	9	4	0	2	1	.667	0	0	8.53
1990	Wichita	AA	26	26	1	0	155	675	163	92	78	18	7	7	7	50	0	101	6	1	7	6	.538	0	0	4.53
1991	Las Vegas	AAA	56	0	0	45	68.1	309	76	36	36	1	5	2	4	25	10	67	2	0	4	8	.333	0	13	4.74
1992	Las Vegas	AAA	42	0	0	33	55.2	236	53	19	18	2	5	3	4	20	4	38	3	0	2	4	.333	0	11	2.91
1991	San Diego	NL	9	0	0	7	14.1	56	8	1	0	0	0	0	0	5	0	9	2	0	0	0	.000	0	2	0.00
1992	San Diego	NL	26	0	0	11	36.2	157	39	17	17	4	6	5	1	11	5	25	0	0	1	4	.200	0	1	4.17
	2 ML YEARS		35	0	0	18	51	213	47	18	17	4	6	5	1	16	5	34	2	0	1	4	.200	0	3	3.00

Jose Hernandez

Bats: Right Throws: Right Pos: SS   Ht: 6' 1" Wt: 180 Born: 07/14/69 Age: 23

								BATTING											BASERUNNING				PERCENTAGES		
Year Team	Lg	G	AB	H	2B	3B	HR	(Hm Rd)	TB	R	RBI	TBB	IBB	SO	HBP	SH	SF	SB	CS	SB%	GDP	Avg	OBP	SLG
1987 Rangers	R	24	52	9	1	1	0	-- --	12	5	2	9	0	25	1	1	0	2	1	.67	1	.173	.306	.231
1988 Rangers	R	55	162	26	7	1	1	-- --	38	19	13	12	0	36	0	0	1	4	1	.80	5	.160	.217	.235
1989 Gastonia	A	91	215	47	7	6	1	-- --	69	35	16	33	0	67	0	8	0	9	2	.82	3	.219	.323	.321
1990 Charlotte	A	121	388	99	14	7	1	-- --	130	43	44	50	4	122	4	11	2	11	8	.58	8	.255	.345	.335
1991 Okla City	AAA	14	46	14	1	1	1	-- --	20	6	3	4	0	10	0	3	1	0	0	.00	1	.304	.353	.435
Tulsa	AA	91	301	72	17	4	1	-- --	100	36	20	26	0	75	1	5	4	4	3	.57	6	.239	.298	.332
1991 Texas	AL	45	98	18	2	1	0	(0 0)	22	8	4	3	0	31	0	6	0	0	1	.00	2	.184	.208	.224
1992 Cleveland	AL	3	4	0	0	0	0	(0 0)	0	0	0	0	0	2	0	0	0	0	0	.00	0	.000	.000	.000
2 ML YEARS		48	102	18	2	1	0	(0 0)	22	8	4	3	0	33	0	6	0	0	1	.00	2	.176	.200	.216

Roberto Hernandez

Pitches: Right Bats: Right Pos: RP   Ht: 6' 4" Wt: 220 Born: 11/11/64 Age: 28

			HOW	MUCH	HE	PITCHED				WHAT	HE	GAVE	UP							THE	RESULTS				
Year Team	Lg	G	GS	CG	GF	IP	BFP	H	R	ER	HR	SH	SF	HB	TBB	IBB	SO	WP	Bk	W	L	Pct.	ShO	Sv	ERA
1986 Salem	A	10	10	0	0	55	0	57	37	28	3	0	0	1	42	1	38	6	0	2	2	.500	0	0	4.58
1987 Quad City	A	7	6	0	1	21	102	24	21	16	2	0	0	2	12	0	21	5	0	3	3	.400	0	1	6.86
1988 Quad City	A	24	24	6	0	164.2	699	157	70	58	8	6	4	6	48	0	114	7	5	9	10	.474	1	0	3.17
Midland	AA	3	3	0	0	12.1	59	16	13	9	0	0	0	1	8	0	7	1	0	0	2	.000	0	0	6.57
1989 Midland	AA	12	12	0	0	64	305	94	54	49	4	1	5	2	30	0	42	4	1	2	7	.222	0	0	6.89
Palm Sprngs	A	7	7	0	0	42.2	188	49	27	22	2	3	1	2	16	0	33	4	0	1	4	.200	0	0	4.64
South Bend	A	4	4	0	0	24.1	95	19	9	9	1	2	0	0	7	0	17	0	0	1	1	.500	0	0	3.33
1990 Birmingham	AA	17	17	1	0	108	469	103	57	44	6	5	5	6	43	2	62	3	1	8	5	.615	0	0	3.67
Vancouver	AAA	11	11	3	0	79.1	329	73	33	25	4	3	3	2	26	0	49	3	0	3	5	.375	1	0	2.84
1991 Vancouver	AAA	7	7	0	0	44.2	195	41	17	16	2	1	1	0	23	0	40	1	0	4	1	.800	0	0	3.22
White Sox	R	1	1	0	0	6	18	2	0	0	0	0	0	0	0	0	7	0	0	0	0	.000	0	0	0.00
Birmingham	AA	4	4	0	0	22.2	85	11	5	5	2	0	1	2	6	0	25	2	0	2	1	.667	0	0	1.99
1992 Vancouver	AAA	9	0	0	9	20.2	86	13	9	6	0	0	0	0	11	1	23	0	0	3	3	.500	0	2	2.61
1991 Chicago	AL	9	3	0	1	15	69	18	15	13	1	0	0	0	7	0	6	1	0	1	0	1.000	0	0	7.80
1992 Chicago	AL	43	0	0	27	71	277	45	15	13	4	0	3	4	20	1	68	2	0	7	3	.700	0	12	1.65
2 ML YEARS		52	3	0	28	86	346	63	30	26	5	0	3	4	27	1	74	3	0	8	3	.727	0	12	2.72

Xavier Hernandez

Pitches: Right Bats: Left Pos: RP   Ht: 6' 2" Wt: 185 Born: 08/16/65 Age: 27

			HOW	MUCH	HE	PITCHED				WHAT	HE	GAVE	UP							THE	RESULTS				
Year Team	Lg	G	GS	CG	GF	IP	BFP	H	R	ER	HR	SH	SF	HB	TBB	IBB	SO	WP	Bk	W	L	Pct.	ShO	Sv	ERA
1989 Toronto	AL	7	0	0	2	22.2	101	25	12	12	2	0	2	1	8	0	7	1	0	1	0	1.000	0	0	4.76
1990 Houston	NL	34	1	0	10	62.1	268	60	34	32	8	2	4	4	24	5	24	6	0	2	1	.667	0	0	4.62
1991 Houston	NL	32	6	0	8	63	285	66	34	33	6	1	1	0	32	7	55	0	0	2	7	.222	0	3	4.71
1992 Houston	NL	77	0	0	25	111	454	81	31	26	5	3	2	3	42	7	96	5	0	9	1	.900	0	7	2.11
4 ML YEARS		150	7	0	45	259	1108	232	114	103	21	6	9	8	106	19	182	12	0	14	9	.609	0	10	3.58

Orel Hershiser

Pitches: Right Bats: Right Pos: SP   Ht: 6' 3" Wt: 192 Born: 09/16/58 Age: 34

			HOW	MUCH	HE	PITCHED				WHAT	HE	GAVE	UP							THE	RESULTS				
Year Team	Lg	G	GS	CG	GF	IP	BFP	H	R	ER	HR	SH	SF	HB	TBB	IBB	SO	WP	Bk	W	L	Pct.	ShO	Sv	ERA
1983 Los Angeles	NL	8	0	0	4	8	37	7	6	3	1	1	0	0	6	0	5	1	0	0	0	.000	0	1	3.38
1984 Los Angeles	NL	45	20	8	10	189.2	771	160	65	56	9	2	3	4	50	8	150	8	1	11	8	.579	4	2	2.66
1985 Los Angeles	NL	36	34	9	1	239.2	953	179	72	54	8	5	4	6	68	5	157	5	0	19	3	.864	5	0	2.03
1986 Los Angeles	NL	35	35	8	0	231.1	988	213	112	99	13	14	6	5	86	11	153	12	3	14	14	.500	1	0	3.85
1987 Los Angeles	NL	37	35	10	2	264.2	1093	247	105	90	17	8	2	9	74	5	190	11	2	16	16	.500	1	1	3.06
1988 Los Angeles	NL	35	34	15	1	267	1068	208	73	67	18	9	6	4	73	10	178	6	5	23	8	.742	8	1	2.26
1989 Los Angeles	NL	35	33	8	0	256.2	1047	226	75	66	9	19	6	3	77	14	178	8	4	15	15	.500	4	0	2.31
1990 Los Angeles	NL	4	4	0	0	25.1	106	26	12	12	1	1	0	1	4	0	16	0	1	1	1	.500	0	0	4.26
1991 Los Angeles	NL	21	21	0	0	112	473	112	43	43	3	2	1	5	32	6	73	2	4	7	2	.778	0	0	3.46
1992 Los Angeles	NL	33	33	1	0	210.2	910	209	101	86	15	15	6	8	69	13	130	10	0	10	15	.400	0	0	3.67
10 ML YEARS		289	249	59	18	1805	7446	1587	664	576	94	76	34	45	539	72	1230	63	20	116	82	.586	23	5	2.87

Joe Hesketh

Pitches: Left Bats: Left Pos: SP/RP   Ht: 6' 2" Wt: 173 Born: 02/15/59 Age: 34

			HOW	MUCH	HE	PITCHED				WHAT	HE	GAVE	UP							THE	RESULTS				
Year Team	Lg	G	GS	CG	GF	IP	BFP	H	R	ER	HR	SH	SF	HB	TBB	IBB	SO	WP	Bk	W	L	Pct.	ShO	Sv	ERA
1984 Montreal	NL	11	5	1	0	45	182	38	12	9	2	2	2	0	15	3	32	1	3	2	2	.500	1	1	1.80
1985 Montreal	NL	25	25	2	0	155.1	618	125	52	43	10	8	2	0	45	2	113	3	3	10	5	.667	1	0	2.49

Year Team	Lg	G	GS	CG	GF	IP	BFP	H	R	ER	HR	SH	SF	HB	TBB	IBB	SO	WP	Bk	W	L	Pct.	ShO	Sv	ERA
1986 Montreal	NL	15	15	0	0	82.2	362	92	46	46	11	2	2	2	31	4	67	4	3	6	5	.545	0	0	5.01
1987 Montreal	NL	18	0	0	3	28.2	128	23	12	10	2	2	0	2	15	3	31	1	0	0	0	.000	0	1	3.14
1988 Montreal	NL	60	0	0	23	72.2	304	63	30	23	1	5	4	0	35	9	64	5	1	4	3	.571	0	9	2.85
1989 Montreal	NL	43	0	0	17	48.1	219	54	34	31	5	6	2	0	26	6	44	1	3	6	4	.600	0	3	5.77
1990 3 ML Teams		45	2	0	19	59.2	269	69	35	30	7	0	1	1	25	2	50	8	0	1	6	.143	0	5	4.53
1991 Boston	AL	39	17	0	5	153.1	631	142	59	56	19	7	3	0	53	3	104	8	0	12	4	.750	0	0	3.29
1992 Boston	AL	30	25	1	1	148.2	659	162	84	72	15	5	6	2	58	9	104	6	0	8	9	.471	0	1	4.36
1990 Montreal	NL	2	0	0	0	3	12	2	0	0	0	0	0	0	2	1	3	0	0	1	0	1.000	0	0	0.00
Atlanta	NL	31	0	0	15	31	135	30	23	20	5	0	1	1	12	0	21	5	0	0	2	.000	0	5	5.81
Boston	AL	12	2	0	4	25.2	122	37	12	10	2	0	0	0	11	1	26	3	0	0	4	.000	0	0	3.51
9 ML YEARS		286	89	4	70	794.1	3372	768	364	320	72	37	22	7	303	41	609	37	13	49	38	.563	2	20	3.63

Greg Hibbard

Pitches: Left **Bats:** Left **Pos:** SP   **Ht:** 6' 0" **Wt:** 190 **Born:** 09/13/64 **Age:** 28

		HOW MUCH HE PITCHED						WHAT HE GAVE UP											THE RESULTS					
Year Team	Lg	G	GS	CG	GF	IP	BFP	H	R	ER	HR	SH	SF	HB	TBB	IBB	SO	WP	Bk	W	L	Pct.	ShO	Sv	ERA
1989 Chicago	AL	23	23	2	0	137.1	581	142	58	49	5	5	4	2	41	0	55	4	0	6	7	.462	0	0	3.21
1990 Chicago	AL	33	33	3	0	211	871	202	80	74	11	8	10	6	55	2	92	2	1	14	9	.609	1	0	3.16
1991 Chicago	AL	32	29	5	1	194	806	196	107	93	23	8	2	2	57	1	71	1	0	11	11	.500	0	0	4.31
1992 Chicago	AL	31	28	0	2	176	755	187	92	86	17	10	6	7	57	2	69	1	1	10	7	.588	0	1	4.40
4 ML YEARS		119	113	10	3	718.1	3013	727	337	302	56	31	22	17	210	5	287	8	2	41	34	.547	1	1	3.78

Bryan Hickerson

Pitches: Left **Bats:** Left **Pos:** RP   **Ht:** 6' 2" **Wt:** 195 **Born:** 10/13/63 **Age:** 29

		HOW MUCH HE PITCHED						WHAT HE GAVE UP											THE RESULTS					
Year Team	Lg	G	GS	CG	GF	IP	BFP	H	R	ER	HR	SH	SF	HB	TBB	IBB	SO	WP	Bk	W	L	Pct.	ShO	Sv	ERA
1986 Visalia	A	11	11	3	0	72.1	302	72	37	34	3	9	3	1	25	1	69	2	0	4	3	.571	0	0	4.23
1987 Clinton	A	17	10	2	3	94	371	60	17	13	1	3	1	1	37	0	103	5	0	11	0	1.000	1	1	1.24
Shreveport	AA	4	3	0	0	16	70	20	7	7	0	1	1	0	4	0	23	1	0	1	2	.333	0	0	3.94
1989 San Jose	A	21	21	1	0	134	561	111	52	38	1	6	5	1	57	0	110	3	2	11	6	.647	1	0	2.55
1990 Shreveport	AA	27	6	0	7	66	294	71	37	31	2	4	2	1	26	2	63	2	2	3	6	.333	0	1	4.23
Phoenix	AAA	12	4	0	3	34.1	162	48	25	21	2	2	2	0	16	2	26	0	1	0	4	.000	0	0	5.50
1991 Shreveport	AA	23	0	0	6	39	165	36	15	13	2	6	0	0	14	3	41	2	1	3	4	.429	0	2	3.00
Phoenix	AAA	12	0	0	7	21.1	97	29	10	9	1	1	1	0	5	1	21	1	0	1	1	.500	0	2	3.80
1991 San Francisco	NL	17	6	0	4	50	212	53	20	20	3	2	0	0	17	3	43	2	0	2	2	.500	0	0	3.60
1992 San Francisco	NL	61	1	0	8	87.1	345	74	31	30	7	4	5	1	21	2	68	4	1	5	3	.625	0	0	3.09
2 ML YEARS		78	7	0	12	137.1	557	127	51	50	10	6	5	1	38	5	111	6	1	7	5	.583	0	0	3.28

Donnie Hill

Bats: Both **Throws:** Right **Pos:** SS   **Ht:** 5'10" **Wt:** 161 **Born:** 11/12/60 **Age:** 32

		BATTING																	BASERUNNING				PERCENTAGES		
Year Team	Lg	G	AB	H	2B	3B	HR	(Hm	Rd)	TB	R	RBI	TBB	IBB	SO	HBP	SH	SF	SB	CS	SB%	GDP	Avg	OBP	SLG
1983 Oakland	AL	53	158	42	7	0	2	(1	1)	55	20	15	4	0	21	0	5	2	1	1	.50	3	.266	.280	.348
1984 Oakland	AL	73	174	40	6	0	2	(0	2)	52	21	16	5	0	12	0	4	2	1	1	.50	3	.230	.249	.299
1985 Oakland	AL	123	393	112	13	2	3	(0	3)	138	45	48	23	2	33	0	16	4	9	4	.69	7	.285	.321	.351
1986 Oakland	AL	108	339	96	16	2	4	(0	4)	128	37	29	23	1	38	0	4	0	5	2	.71	9	.283	.329	.378
1987 Chicago	AL	111	410	98	14	6	9	(1	8)	151	57	46	30	1	35	1	4	4	1	0	1.00	11	.239	.290	.368
1988 Chicago	AL	83	221	48	6	1	2	(1	1)	62	17	20	26	1	32	0	3	3	3	1	.75	3	.217	.296	.281
1990 California	AL	103	352	93	18	2	3	(0	3)	124	36	32	29	1	27	1	6	4	1	2	.33	10	.264	.319	.352
1991 California	AL	77	209	50	8	1	1	(1	0)	63	36	20	30	1	21	0	3	0	1	0	1.00	1	.239	.335	.301
1992 Minnesota	AL	25	51	15	3	0	0	(0	0)	18	7	2	5	0	6	1	2	0	0	0	.00	0	.294	.368	.353
9 ML YEARS		756	2307	594	91	14	26	(4	22)	791	276	228	175	7	225	3	47	19	22	11	.67	47	.257	.308	.343

Glenallen Hill

Bats: Right **Throws:** Right **Pos:** LF/DH   **Ht:** 6' 2" **Wt:** 210 **Born:** 03/22/65 **Age:** 28

		BATTING																	BASERUNNING				PERCENTAGES		
Year Team	Lg	G	AB	H	2B	3B	HR	(Hm	Rd)	TB	R	RBI	TBB	IBB	SO	HBP	SH	SF	SB	CS	SB%	GDP	Avg	OBP	SLG
1989 Toronto	AL	19	52	15	0	0	1	(1	0)	18	4	7	3	0	12	0	0	0	2	1	.67	0	.288	.327	.346
1990 Toronto	AL	84	260	60	11	3	12	(7	5)	113	47	32	18	0	62	0	0	0	8	3	.73	5	.231	.281	.435
1991 2 ML Teams		72	221	57	8	2	8	(3	5)	93	29	25	23	0	54	0	1	3	6	4	.60	7	.258	.324	.421
1992 Cleveland	AL	102	369	89	16	1	18	(7	11)	161	38	49	20	0	73	4	0	1	9	6	.60	11	.241	.287	.436
1991 Toronto	AL	35	99	25	5	2	3	(2	1)	43	14	11	7	0	24	0	0	2	2	2	.50	2	.253	.296	.434
Cleveland	AL	37	122	32	3	0	5	(1	4)	50	15	14	16	0	30	0	1	1	4	2	.67	5	.262	.345	.410
4 ML YEARS		277	902	221	35	6	39	(18	21)	385	118	113	64	0	201	4	1	4	25	14	.64	23	.245	.297	.427

Ken Hill

Pitches: Right **Bats:** Right **Pos:** SP   Ht: 6' 2"   Wt: 175   Born: 12/14/65   Age: 27

Year Team	Lg	G	GS	CG	GF	IP	BFP	H	R	ER	HR	SH	SF	HB	TBB	IBB	SO	WP	Bk	W	L	Pct.	ShO	Sv	ERA
1988 St. Louis	NL	4	1	0	0	14	62	16	9	8	0	0	0	0	6	0	6	1	0	0	1	.000	0	0	5.14
1989 St. Louis	NL	33	33	2	0	196.2	862	186	92	83	9	14	5	5	99	6	112	11	2	7	15	.318	1	0	3.80
1990 St. Louis	NL	17	14	1	1	78.2	343	79	49	48	7	5	5	1	33	1	58	5	0	5	6	.455	0	0	5.49
1991 St. Louis	NL	30	30	0	0	181.1	743	147	76	72	15	7	7	6	67	4	121	7	1	11	10	.524	0	0	3.57
1992 Montreal	NL	33	33	3	0	218	908	187	76	65	13	15	3	3	75	4	150	11	4	16	9	.640	3	0	2.68
5 ML YEARS		117	111	6	1	688.2	2918	615	302	276	44	41	20	15	280	15	447	35	7	39	41	.488	4	0	3.61

Milt Hill

Pitches: Right **Bats:** Right **Pos:** RP   Ht: 6' 0"   Wt: 180   Born: 08/22/65   Age: 27

Year Team	Lg	G	GS	CG	GF	IP	BFP	H	R	ER	HR	SH	SF	HB	TBB	IBB	SO	WP	Bk	W	L	Pct.	ShO	Sv	ERA
1987 Billings	R	21	0	0	19	32.2	125	25	10	6	1	1	0	0	4	2	40	5	0	3	1	.750	0	7	1.65
1988 Cedar Rapds	A	44	0	0	38	78.1	300	52	21	18	3	3	1	1	17	7	69	4	8	9	4	.692	0	13	2.07
1989 Chattanooga	AA	51	0	0	42	70	281	49	19	16	4	1	5	0	28	6	63	1	4	6	5	.545	0	13	2.06
1990 Nashville	AAA	48	0	0	11	71.1	276	51	20	18	4	1	5	2	18	1	58	4	2	4	4	.500	0	3	2.27
1991 Nashville	AAA	37	0	0	16	67.1	269	59	26	22	3	3	3	0	15	1	62	3	3	3	3	.500	0	3	2.94
1992 Nashville	AAA	53	0	0	39	74.1	292	56	30	22	7	3	1	1	17	4	70	4	1	0	5	.000	0	18	2.66
1991 Cincinnati	NL	22	0	0	8	33.1	137	36	14	14	1	4	3	0	8	2	20	1	0	1	1	.500	0	0	3.78
1992 Cincinnati	NL	14	0	0	5	20	80	15	9	7	1	2	1	1	5	2	10	0	0	0	0	.000	0	1	3.15
2 ML YEARS		36	0	0	13	53.1	217	51	23	21	2	6	4	1	13	4	30	1	0	1	1	.500	0	1	3.54

Shawn Hillegas

Pitches: Right **Bats:** Right **Pos:** RP/SP   Ht: 6' 2"   Wt: 223   Born: 08/21/64   Age: 28

Year Team	Lg	G	GS	CG	GF	IP	BFP	H	R	ER	HR	SH	SF	HB	TBB	IBB	SO	WP	Bk	W	L	Pct.	ShO	Sv	ERA
1987 Los Angeles	NL	12	10	0	1	58	252	52	27	23	5	4	1	0	31	0	51	4	0	4	3	.571	0	0	3.57
1988 2 ML Teams		17	16	0	0	96.2	405	84	42	40	9	1	4	4	35	1	56	3	0	6	6	.500	0	0	3.72
1989 Chicago	AL	50	16	0	12	119.2	533	132	67	63	12	4	2	3	51	4	76	4	1	7	11	.389	0	3	4.74
1990 Chicago	AL	7	0	0	3	11.1	43	4	1	1	0	1	1	0	5	1	5	2	0	0	0	.000	0	0	0.79
1991 Cleveland	AL	51	3	0	31	83	359	67	42	40	7	4	7	2	46	7	66	5	0	3	4	.429	0	7	4.34
1992 2 ML Teams		26	9	1	6	86	385	104	57	50	13	2	3	0	37	2	49	2	0	1	8	.111	1	0	5.23
1988 Los Angeles	NL	11	10	0	0	56.2	239	54	26	26	5	1	2	3	17	1	30	3	0	3	4	.429	0	0	4.13
Chicago	AL	6	6	0	0	40	166	30	16	14	4	0	2	1	18	0	26	0	0	3	2	.600	0	0	3.15
1992 New York	AL	21	9	1	4	78.1	351	96	52	48	12	1	3	0	33	1	46	2	0	1	8	.111	1	0	5.51
Oakland	AL	5	0	0	2	7.2	34	8	5	2	1	1	0	0	4	1	3	0	0	0	0	.000	0	0	2.35
6 ML YEARS		163	51	1	53	454.2	1977	443	236	217	46	16	18	9	205	15	303	20	1	21	32	.396	1	10	4.30

Eric Hillman

Pitches: Left **Bats:** Left **Pos:** SP   Ht: 6'10"   Wt: 225   Born: 04/27/66   Age: 27

Year Team	Lg	G	GS	CG	GF	IP	BFP	H	R	ER	HR	SH	SF	HB	TBB	IBB	SO	WP	Bk	W	L	Pct.	ShO	Sv	ERA
1987 Little Fls	A	13	13	2	0	79	346	84	44	37	4	2	5	3	30	2	80	8	1	6	4	.600	1	0	4.22
1988 Columbia	A	17	13	0	4	73	320	54	45	32	2	2	2	6	43	0	60	5	3	1	6	.143	0	1	3.95
1989 Columbia	A	9	7	0	2	33.2	151	28	17	7	1	1	2	4	21	0	33	1	0	2	1	.667	0	1	1.87
St.Lucie	A	19	14	1	1	88.1	404	96	59	54	3	3	2	3	53	0	67	15	1	6	6	.500	0	0	5.50
1990 St. Lucie	A	4	3	0	0	27	99	15	2	2	0	1	0	1	8	0	23	3	0	2	0	1.000	0	0	0.67
Jackson	AA	15	15	0	0	89.1	386	93	42	39	2	1	1	4	30	1	61	7	2	6	5	.545	0	0	3.93
1991 Tidewater	AAA	27	27	2	0	161.2	710	184	89	72	9	15	6	10	58	0	91	12	3	5	12	.294	0	0	4.01
1992 Tidewater	AAA	34	9	0	7	91.1	380	93	39	37	6	2	4	2	27	1	49	6	2	9	2	.818	0	0	3.65
1992 New York	NL	11	8	0	2	52.1	227	67	31	31	9	3	1	2	10	2	16	1	0	2	2	.500	0	0	5.33

Sterling Hitchcock

Pitches: Left **Bats:** Left **Pos:** SP   Ht: 6' 1"   Wt: 195   Born: 04/29/71   Age: 22

Year Team	Lg	G	GS	CG	GF	IP	BFP	H	R	ER	HR	SH	SF	HB	TBB	IBB	SO	WP	Bk	W	L	Pct.	ShO	Sv	ERA
1989 Yankees	R	13	13	0	0	76.2	299	48	16	14	1	3	1	4	27	0	98	5	0	9	1	.900	0	0	1.64
1990 Greensboro	A	27	27	6	0	173.1	694	122	68	56	7	5	2	8	60	1	171	6	2	12	12	.500	5	0	2.91
1991 Pr William	A	19	19	2	0	119.1	500	111	49	35	2	3	4	3	26	0	101	5	2	7	7	.500	0	0	2.64
1992 Albany	AA	24	24	2	0	146.2	600	116	51	42	6	3	1	9	42	0	155	9	2	6	9	.400	0	0	2.58
1992 New York	AL	3	3	0	0	13	68	23	12	12	2	0	0	1	6	0	6	0	0	0	2	.000	0	0	8.31

Chris Hoiles

Bats: Right **Throws:** Right **Pos:** C   **Ht:** 6' 0" **Wt:** 206 **Born:** 03/20/65 **Age:** 28

						BATTING										BASERUNNING				PERCENTAGES		
Year Team	Lg	G	AB	H	2B	3B	HR	(Hm Rd)	TB	R	RBI	TBB	IBB	SO	HBP	SH	SF	SB	CS	SB%	GDP	Avg	OBP	SLG
1989 Baltimore	AL	6	9	1	1	0	0	(0 0)	2	0	1	1	0	3	0	0	0	0	0	.00	0	.111	.200	.222
1990 Baltimore	AL	23	63	12	3	0	1	(1 0)	18	7	6	5	1	12	0	0	0	0	0	.00	0	.190	.250	.286
1991 Baltimore	AL	107	341	83	15	0	11	(5 6)	131	36	31	29	1	61	1	0	1	0	2	.00	11	.243	.304	.384
1992 Baltimore	AL	96	310	85	10	1	20	(8 12)	157	49	40	55	2	60	2	1	3	0	2	.00	8	.274	.384	.506
4 ML YEARS		232	723	181	29	1	32	(14 18)	308	92	78	90	4	136	3	1	4	0	4	.00	19	.250	.334	.426

Dave Hollins

Bats: Both **Throws:** Right **Pos:** 3B   **Ht:** 6' 1" **Wt:** 205 **Born:** 05/25/66 **Age:** 27

						BATTING										BASERUNNING				PERCENTAGES		
Year Team	Lg	G	AB	H	2B	3B	HR	(Hm Rd)	TB	R	RBI	TBB	IBB	SO	HBP	SH	SF	SB	CS	SB%	GDP	Avg	OBP	SLG
1990 Philadelphia	NL	72	114	21	0	0	5	(2 3)	36	14	15	10	3	28	1	0	2	0	0	.00	1	.184	.252	.316
1991 Philadelphia	NL	56	151	45	10	2	6	(3 3)	77	18	21	17	1	26	3	0	1	1	1	.50	2	.298	.378	.510
1992 Philadelphia	NL	156	586	158	28	4	27	(14 13)	275	104	93	76	4	110	19	0	4	9	6	.60	8	.270	.369	.469
3 ML YEARS		284	851	224	38	6	38	(19 19)	388	136	129	103	8	164	23	0	7	10	7	.59	11	.263	.356	.456

Jessie Hollins

Pitches: Right **Bats:** Right **Pos:** RP   **Ht:** 6' 3" **Wt:** 190 **Born:** 01/27/70 **Age:** 23

		HOW MUCH HE PITCHED						WHAT HE GAVE UP										THE RESULTS					
Year Team	Lg	G	GS	CG	GF	IP	BFP	H	R	ER	HR	SH	SF	HB	TBB	IBB	SO	WP	Bk	W	L	Pct.	ShO	Sv	ERA
1989 Wytheville	R	22	3	0	6	48.1	240	59	44	26	4	2	1	6	23	0	31	12	7	3	1	.750	0	0	4.84
1990 Peoria	A	5	0	0	1	9.2	49	12	9	6	2	0	0	1	5	0	8	1	0	0	0	.000	0	0	5.59
Geneva	A	17	16	1	1	97.1	434	87	49	30	4	3	2	3	49	1	115	21	4	10	3	.769	0	0	2.77
1991 Winston-Sal	A	41	13	0	15	98.1	480	107	78	62	9	2	3	6	83	1	74	13	3	4	8	.333	0	5	5.67
1992 Charlotte	AA	63	0	0	56	70.1	300	60	28	25	4	3	3	1	32	1	73	14	3	3	4	.429	0	25	3.20
1992 Chicago	NL	4	0	0	3	4.2	27	8	7	7	1	0	2	0	5	0	0	1	0	0	0	.000	0	0	13.50

Brian Holman

Pitches: Right **Bats:** Right **Pos:** SP   **Ht:** 6' 4" **Wt:** 185 **Born:** 01/25/65 **Age:** 28

		HOW MUCH HE PITCHED						WHAT HE GAVE UP										THE RESULTS					
Year Team	Lg	G	GS	CG	GF	IP	BFP	H	R	ER	HR	SH	SF	HB	TBB	IBB	SO	WP	Bk	W	L	Pct.	ShO	Sv	ERA
1988 Montreal	NL	18	16	1	1	100.1	422	101	39	36	3	4	1	0	34	2	58	2	0	4	8	.333	1	0	3.23
1989 2 ML Teams		33	25	6	1	191.1	833	194	86	78	11	6	4	7	77	6	105	8	1	9	12	.429	2	0	3.67
1990 Seattle	AL	28	28	3	0	189.2	804	188	92	85	17	1	7	6	66	2	121	8	2	11	11	.500	0	0	4.03
1991 Seattle	AL	30	30	5	0	195.1	839	199	86	80	16	6	3	10	77	0	108	8	1	13	14	.481	3	0	3.69
1989 Montreal	NL	10	3	0	0	31.2	145	34	18	17	2	2	1	1	15	0	23	3	1	1	2	.333	0	0	4.83
Seattle	AL	23	22	6	1	159.2	688	160	68	61	9	4	3	6	62	6	82	5	0	8	10	.444	2	0	3.44
4 ML YEARS		109	99	15	2	676.2	2898	682	303	279	47	17	15	23	254	10	392	26	4	37	45	.451	6	0	3.71

Darren Holmes

Pitches: Right **Bats:** Right **Pos:** RP   **Ht:** 6' 0" **Wt:** 199 **Born:** 04/25/66 **Age:** 27

		HOW MUCH HE PITCHED						WHAT HE GAVE UP										THE RESULTS					
Year Team	Lg	G	GS	CG	GF	IP	BFP	H	R	ER	HR	SH	SF	HB	TBB	IBB	SO	WP	Bk	W	L	Pct.	ShO	Sv	ERA
1990 Los Angeles	NL	14	0	0	1	17.1	77	15	10	10	1	1	2	0	11	3	19	1	0	0	1	.000	0	0	5.19
1991 Milwaukee	AL	40	0	0	9	76.1	344	90	43	40	6	8	3	1	27	1	59	6	0	1	4	.200	0	3	4.72
1992 Milwaukee	AL	41	0	0	25	42.1	173	35	12	12	1	4	0	2	11	4	31	0	0	4	4	.500	0	6	2.55
3 ML YEARS		95	0	0	35	136	594	140	65	62	8	13	5	3	49	8	109	7	0	5	9	.357	0	9	4.10

Rick Honeycutt

Pitches: Left **Bats:** Left **Pos:** RP   **Ht:** 6' 1" **Wt:** 191 **Born:** 06/29/54 **Age:** 39

		HOW MUCH HE PITCHED						WHAT HE GAVE UP										THE RESULTS					
Year Team	Lg	G	GS	CG	GF	IP	BFP	H	R	ER	HR	SH	SF	HB	TBB	IBB	SO	WP	Bk	W	L	Pct.	ShO	Sv	ERA
1977 Seattle	AL	10	3	0	3	29	125	26	16	14	7	0	2	3	11	2	17	2	1	0	1	.000	0	0	4.34
1978 Seattle	AL	26	24	4	0	134	594	150	81	73	12	9	7	3	49	5	50	3	0	5	11	.313	1	0	4.90
1979 Seattle	AL	33	28	8	2	194	839	201	103	87	22	11	6	6	67	7	83	5	1	11	12	.478	1	0	4.04
1980 Seattle	AL	30	30	9	0	203	871	221	99	89	22	11	7	3	60	7	79	4	0	10	17	.370	1	0	3.95
1981 Texas	AL	20	20	8	0	128	509	120	49	47	12	5	0	0	17	1	40	1	0	11	6	.647	2	0	3.30
1982 Texas	AL	30	26	4	3	164	728	201	103	96	20	4	8	3	54	4	64	3	1	5	17	.227	1	0	5.27
1983 2 ML Teams		34	32	6	0	213.2	865	214	85	72	15	5	6	8	50	6	74	1	3	16	11	.593	2	0	3.03
1984 Los Angeles	NL	29	28	6	0	183.2	762	180	72	58	11	6	5	2	51	11	75	1	2	10	9	.526	2	0	2.84
1985 Los Angeles	NL	31	25	1	2	142	600	141	71	54	9	5	4	1	49	7	67	2	0	8	12	.400	0	1	3.42
1986 Los Angeles	NL	32	28	0	2	171	713	164	71	63	9	6	1	3	45	4	100	4	1	11	9	.550	0	0	3.32
1987 2 ML Teams		34	24	1	1	139.1	631	158	91	73	13	1	3	4	54	4	102	5	1	3	16	.158	1	0	4.72
1988 Oakland	AL	55	0	0	17	79.2	330	74	36	31	6	3	6	3	25	2	47	3	8	3	2	.600	0	7	3.50

Year	Team	Lg	G	GS	CG	GF	IP	BFP	H	R	ER	HR	SH	SF	HB	TBB	IBB	SO	WP	Bk	W	L	Pct.	ShO	Sv	ERA
1989	Oakland	AL	64	0	0	24	76.2	305	56	26	20	5	5	2	1	26	3	52	6	1	2	2	.500	0	12	2.35
1990	Oakland	AL	63	0	0	13	63.1	256	46	23	19	2	2	6	1	22	2	38	1	1	2	2	.500	0	7	2.70
1991	Oakland	AL	43	0	0	7	37.2	167	37	16	15	3	2	1	2	20	3	26	0	0	2	4	.333	0	0	3.58
1992	Oakland	AL	54	0	0	7	39	169	41	19	16	2	4	1	3	10	3	32	2	0	1	4	.200	0	3	3.69
1983	Texas		25	25	5	0	174.2	693	168	59	47	9	3	6	6	37	2	56	1	2	14	8	.636	2	0	2.42
	Los Angeles	NL	9	7	1	0	39	172	46	26	25	6	2	0	2	13	4	18	0	1	2	3	.400	1	0	5.77
1987	Los Angeles	NL	27	20	1	0	115.2	525	133	74	59	10	0	0	2	45	4	92	4	0	2	12	.143	1	0	4.59
	Oakland	AL	7	4	0	1	23.2	106	25	17	14	3	1	3	2	9	0	10	1	1	1	4	.200	0	0	5.32
	16 ML YEARS		588	268	47	81	1998	8464	2030	961	827	170	79	65	46	610	71	946	43	20	100	135	.426	11	30	3.73

Sam Horn

Bats: Left **Throws:** Left **Pos:** DH   **Ht:** 6' 5" **Wt:** 247 **Born:** 11/02/63 **Age:** 29

					BATTING															BASERUNNING				PERCENTAGES		
Year	Team	Lg	G	AB	H	2B	3B	HR	(Hm	Rd)	TB	R	RBI	TBB	IBB	SO	HBP	SH	SF	SB	CS	SB%	GDP	Avg	OBP	SLG
1987	Boston	AL	46	158	44	7	1	14	(6	8)	93	31	34	17	0	55	2	0	0	0	1	.00	5	.278	.356	.589
1988	Boston	AL	24	61	9	0	0	2	(2	0)	15	4	8	11	3	20	0	0	1	0	0	.00	1	.148	.274	.246
1989	Boston	AL	33	54	8	2	0	0	(0	0)	10	1	4	8	1	16	0	0	0	0	0	.00	4	.148	.258	.185
1990	Baltimore	AL	79	246	61	13	0	14	(8	6)	116	30	45	32	1	62	0	0	2	0	0	.00	8	.248	.332	.472
1991	Baltimore	AL	121	317	74	16	0	23	(12	11)	159	45	61	41	4	99	3	0	1	0	0	.00	10	.233	.326	.502
1992	Baltimore	AL	63	162	38	10	1	5	(2	3)	65	13	19	21	2	60	1	0	1	0	0	.00	8	.235	.324	.401
	6 ML YEARS		366	998	234	48	1	58	(30	28)	458	124	171	130	11	312	6	0	5	0	1	.00	36	.234	.325	.459

Vince Horsman

Pitches: Left **Bats:** Right **Pos:** RP   **Ht:** 6' 2" **Wt:** 180 **Born:** 03/09/67 **Age:** 26

				HOW MUCH HE PITCHED					WHAT HE GAVE UP											THE RESULTS					
Year	Team	Lg	G	GS	CG	GF	IP	BFP	H	R	ER	HR	SH	SF	HB	TBB	IBB	SO	WP	Bk	W	L	Pct.	ShO	Sv	ERA
1985	Medicne Hat	R	18	1	0	2	40.1	0	56	31	28	1	0	0	0	23	3	30	1	0	0	3	.000	0	1	6.25
1986	Florence	A	29	9	1	10	90.2	419	93	56	41	8	1	6	1	49	0	64	5	4	4	3	.571	1	1	4.07
1987	Myrtle Bch	A	30	28	0	1	149	621	144	74	55	20	6	5	2	37	2	109	5	2	7	7	.500	0	0	3.32
1988	Knoxville	AA	20	6	1	6	58.1	260	57	34	30	5	4	4	3	28	3	40	4	1	3	2	.600	0	0	4.63
	Dunedin	A	14	2	0	3	39.2	159	28	7	6	1	1	1	1	13	2	34	1	1	3	1	.750	0	1	1.36
1989	Dunedin	A	35	1	0	23	79	330	72	24	22	3	5	1	1	27	3	60	3	4	5	6	.455	0	8	2.51
	Knoxville	AA	4	0	0	3	5	19	3	1	1	0	0	0	0	2	1	3	0	0	0	0	.000	0	1	1.80
1990	Dunedin	A	28	0	0	14	50	209	53	21	18	0	2	2	1	15	2	41	2	0	4	7	.364	0	1	3.24
	Knoxville	AA	8	0	0	2	11.2	51	11	7	6	1	1	0	0	5	2	10	1	0	2	1	.667	0	0	4.63
1991	Knoxville	AA	42	2	0	17	80.2	335	80	23	21	2	3	1	0	19	5	80	3	1	4	1	.800	0	3	2.34
1991	Toronto	AL	4	0	0	2	4	16	2	0	0	0	1	0	0	3	1	2	0	0	0	0	.000	0	0	0.00
1992	Oakland	AL	58	0	0	9	43.1	180	39	13	12	3	3	1	0	21	4	18	1	0	2	1	.667	0	1	2.49
	2 ML YEARS		62	0	0	11	47.1	196	41	13	12	3	4	1	0	24	5	20	1	0	2	1	.667	0	1	2.28

Steve Hosey

Bats: Right **Throws:** Right **Pos:** RF   **Ht:** 6' 3" **Wt:** 218 **Born:** 04/02/69 **Age:** 24

					BATTING															BASERUNNING				PERCENTAGES		
Year	Team	Lg	G	AB	H	2B	3B	HR	(Hm	Rd)	TB	R	RBI	TBB	IBB	SO	HBP	SH	SF	SB	CS	SB%	GDP	Avg	OBP	SLG
1989	Everett	A	73	288	83	14	3	13	--	--	142	44	59	27	2	84	10	0	2	15	3	.83	3	.288	.367	.493
1990	San Jose	A	139	479	111	13	6	16	--	--	184	85	78	71	2	139	5	1	4	16	17	.48	7	.232	.335	.384
1991	Shreveport	AA	126	409	120	21	5	17	--	--	202	79	74	56	5	87	6	5	4	24	11	.69	7	.293	.383	.494
1992	Phoenix	AAA	125	462	132	28	7	10	--	--	204	64	65	39	4	98	6	0	5	15	15	.50	11	.286	.346	.442
1992	San Francisco	NL	21	56	14	1	0	1	(1	0)	18	6	6	0	0	15	0	0	2	1	1	.50	1	.250	.241	.321

Charlie Hough

Pitches: Right **Bats:** Right **Pos:** SP   **Ht:** 6' 2" **Wt:** 190 **Born:** 01/05/48 **Age:** 45

				HOW MUCH HE PITCHED					WHAT HE GAVE UP											THE RESULTS					
Year	Team	Lg	G	GS	CG	GF	IP	BFP	H	R	ER	HR	SH	SF	HB	TBB	IBB	SO	WP	Bk	W	L	Pct.	ShO	Sv	ERA
1970	Los Angeles	NL	8	0	0	5	17	79	18	11	10	7	0	0	0	11	0	8	0	0	0	0	.000	0	2	5.29
1971	Los Angeles	NL	4	0	0	3	4	19	3	3	2	1	1	0	0	3	0	4	0	0	0	0	.000	0	0	4.50
1972	Los Angeles	NL	2	0	0	2	3	13	2	1	1	0	0	0	1	2	0	4	0	0	0	0	.000	0	0	3.00
1973	Los Angeles	NL	37	0	0	18	72	309	52	24	22	3	4	3	6	45	2	70	2	0	4	2	.667	0	5	2.75
1974	Los Angeles	NL	49	0	0	16	96	389	65	45	40	12	6	8	4	40	2	63	4	0	9	4	.692	0	1	3.75
1975	Los Angeles	NL	38	0	0	24	61	266	43	25	20	3	3	0	8	34	0	34	4	1	3	7	.300	0	4	2.95
1976	Los Angeles	NL	77	0	0	55	143	600	102	43	35	6	4	1	8	77	3	81	9	0	12	8	.600	0	18	2.20
1977	Los Angeles	NL	70	1	0	53	127	551	98	53	47	10	10	4	7	70	6	105	8	0	6	12	.333	0	22	3.33
1978	Los Angeles	NL	55	0	0	31	93	390	69	38	34	6	0	0	5	48	4	66	6	0	5	5	.500	0	7	3.29
1979	Los Angeles	NL	42	14	0	10	151	662	152	88	80	16	9	4	8	66	2	76	9	1	7	5	.583	0	0	4.77
1980	2 ML Teams		35	3	2	12	93	426	91	51	47	6	7	4	5	58	2	72	11	0	3	5	.375	1	1	4.55
1981	Texas	AL	21	5	2	9	82	330	61	30	27	4	1	1	3	31	1	69	4	0	4	1	.800	0	1	2.96
1982	Texas	AL	34	34	12	0	228	954	217	111	100	21	7	4	7	72	5	128	9	0	16	13	.552	2	0	3.95

Year	Team	Lg	G	GS	CG	GF	IP	BFP	H	R	ER	HR	SH	SF	HB	TBB	IBB	SO	WP	Bk	W	L	Pct.	ShO	Sv	ERA
1983	Texas	AL	34	33	11	1	252	1030	219	96	89	22	5	5	3	95	0	152	6	1	15	13	.536	3	0	3.18
1984	Texas	AL	36	36	17	0	266	1133	260	127	111	26	5	7	9	94	3	164	12	2	16	14	.533	1	0	3.76
1985	Texas	AL	34	34	14	0	250.1	1018	198	102	92	23	1	7	7	83	1	141	11	3	14	16	.467	1	0	3.31
1986	Texas	AL	33	33	7	0	230.1	958	188	115	97	32	9	1	9	89	2	146	16	0	17	10	.630	2	0	3.79
1987	Texas	AL	40	40	13	0	285.1	1231	238	159	120	36	5	14	19	124	1	223	12	9	18	13	.581	0	0	3.79
1988	Texas	AL	34	34	10	0	252	1067	202	111	93	20	8	8	12	126	1	174	10	10	15	16	.484	0	0	3.32
1989	Texas	AL	30	30	5	0	182	795	168	97	88	28	3	6	6	95	2	94	7	5	10	13	.435	1	0	4.35
1990	Texas	AL	32	32	5	0	218.2	950	190	108	99	24	2	11	11	119	2	114	4	0	12	12	.500	0	0	4.07
1991	Chicago	AL	31	29	4	1	199.1	858	167	98	89	21	8	16	11	94	0	107	5	1	9	10	.474	1	0	4.02
1992	Chicago	AL	27	27	4	0	176.1	751	160	88	77	19	2	6	7	66	2	76	10	1	7	12	.368	0	0	3.93
1980	Los Angeles	NL	19	1	0	5	32	156	37	21	20	4	3	3	2	21	0	25	3	0	1	3	.250	0	1	5.63
	Texas	AL	16	2	2	7	61	270	54	30	27	2	4	1	3	37	2	47	8	0	2	2	.500	1	0	3.98
23 ML YEARS			803	385	106	240	3482.1	14779	2963	1624	1420	346	100	110	156	1542	41	2171	159	34	202	191	.514	12	61	3.67

Dave Howard

Bats: Both   **Throws:** Right   **Pos:** SS   **Ht:** 6' 0"   **Wt:** 165   **Born:** 02/26/67   **Age:** 26

							BATTING											BASERUNNING			PERCENTAGES		
Year	Team	Lg	G	AB	H	2B	3B	HR	(Hm	Rd)	TB	R	RBI	TBB	IBB	SO	HBP	SH	SF	SB	CS	SB%	GDP	Avg	OBP	SLG
1987	Ft. Myers	A	89	289	56	9	4	1	--	--	76	26	19	30	0	68	0	7	0	11	10	.52	3	.194	.270	.263
1988	Appleton	A	110	368	82	9	4	1	--	--	102	48	22	25	0	80	2	4	3	7	5	.58	3	.223	.274	.277
1989	Baseball Cy	A	83	267	63	7	3	3	--	--	85	36	30	23	1	44	1	3	2	12	2	.86	1	.236	.297	.318
1990	Memphis	AA	116	384	96	10	4	5	--	--	129	41	44	39	0	73	1	10	6	15	4	.79	8	.250	.316	.336
1991	Omaha	AAA	14	41	5	0	0	0	--	--	5	2	2	7	0	11	1	2	0	1	1	.50	0	.122	.265	.122
1992	Baseball Cy	A	3	9	4	1	0	0	--	--	5	3	0	2	0	0	0	0	0	0	0	.00	0	.444	.545	.556
	Omaha	AAA	19	68	8	1	0	0	--	--	9	5	3	3	0	8	0	2	2	1	0	1.00	5	.118	.151	.132
1991	Kansas City	AL	94	236	51	7	0	1	(0	1)	61	20	17	16	0	45	1	9	2	3	2	.60	1	.216	.267	.258
1992	Kansas City	AL	74	219	49	6	2	1	(1	0)	62	19	18	15	0	43	0	8	2	3	4	.43	3	.224	.271	.283
2 ML YEARS			168	455	100	13	2	2	(1	1)	123	39	35	31	0	88	1	17	4	6	6	.50	4	.220	.269	.270

Thomas Howard

Bats: Both   **Throws:** Right   **Pos:** LF/CF/RF   **Ht:** 6' 2"   **Wt:** 205   **Born:** 12/11/64   **Age:** 28

							BATTING											BASERUNNING			PERCENTAGES		
Year	Team	Lg	G	AB	H	2B	3B	HR	(Hm | Rd)	TB	R	RBI	TBB	IBB	SO	HBP	SH	SF	SB	CS	SB%	GDP	Avg	OBP	SLG
1990	San Diego	NL	20	44	12	2	0	0	(0 | 0)	14	4	0	0	0	11	0	1	0	0	1	.00	1	.273	.273	.318
1991	San Diego	NL	106	281	70	12	3	4	(4 | 0)	100	30	22	24	4	57	1	2	1	10	7	.59	4	.249	.309	.356
1992	2 ML Teams		122	361	100	15	2	2	(1 | 1)	125	37	32	17	0	60	0	11	2	15	8	.65	4	.277	.308	.346
1992	San Diego	NL	5	3	1	0	0	0	(0 | 0)	1	1	0	0	0	0	0	1	0	0	0	.00	0	.333	.333	.333
	Cleveland	AL	117	358	99	15	2	2	(1 | 1)	124	36	32	17	1	60	0	10	2	15	8	.65	4	.277	.308	.346
3 ML YEARS			248	686	182	29	5	6	(5 | 1)	239	71	54	41	5	128	1	14	3	25	16	.61	9	.265	.306	.348

Steve Howe

Pitches: Left   **Bats:** Left   **Pos:** RP   **Ht:** 5'11"   **Wt:** 198   **Born:** 03/10/58   **Age:** 35

			HOW MUCH HE PITCHED						WHAT HE GAVE UP									THE RESULTS					
Year	Team	Lg	G	GS	CG	GF	IP	BFP	H	R	ER	HR	SH	SF	HB	TBB	IBB	SO	WP	Bk	W	L	Pct.	ShO	Sv	ERA
1980	Los Angeles	NL	59	0	0	36	85	359	83	33	25	1	8	3	2	22	10	39	1	0	7	9	.438	0	17	2.65
1981	Los Angeles	NL	41	0	0	25	54	227	51	17	15	2	4	4	0	18	7	32	0	0	5	3	.625	0	8	2.50
1982	Los Angeles	NL	66	0	0	41	99.1	393	87	27	23	3	10	3	1	17	11	49	1	0	7	5	.583	0	13	2.08
1983	Los Angeles	NL	46	0	0	33	68.2	274	55	15	11	2	5	3	1	12	7	52	3	0	4	7	.364	0	18	1.44
1985	2 ML Teams		32	0	0	19	41	198	58	33	25	3	2	5	1	12	4	21	3	0	3	4	.429	0	3	5.49
1987	Texas	AL	24	0	0	15	31.1	131	33	15	15	2	2	0	3	8	1	19	2	1	3	3	.500	0	1	4.31
1991	New York	AL	37	0	0	10	48.1	189	39	12	9	1	2	1	3	7	2	34	2	0	3	1	.750	0	3	1.68
1992	New York	AL	20	0	0	10	22	79	9	7	6	1	1	1	0	3	1	12	1	0	3	0	1.000	0	6	2.45
1985	Los Angeles	NL	19	0	0	14	22	104	30	17	12	2	2	2	1	5	2	11	2	0	1	1	.500	0	3	4.91
	Minnesota	AL	13	0	0	5	19	94	28	16	13	1	0	3	0	7	2	10	1	0	2	3	.400	0	0	6.16
8 ML YEARS			325	0	0	189	449.2	1850	415	159	129	15	34	20	10	99	43	258	13	1	35	32	.522	0	69	2.58

Jay Howell

Pitches: Right   **Bats:** Right   **Pos:** RP   **Ht:** 6' 3"   **Wt:** 212   **Born:** 11/26/55   **Age:** 37

			HOW MUCH HE PITCHED						WHAT HE GAVE UP									THE RESULTS					
Year	Team	Lg	G	GS	CG	GF	IP	BFP	H	R	ER	HR	SH	SF	HB	TBB	IBB	SO	WP	Bk	W	L	Pct.	ShO	Sv	ERA
1980	Cincinnati	NL	5	0	0	1	3	19	8	5	5	0	0	1	1	0	0	1	0	0	0	0	.000	0	0	15.00
1981	Chicago	NL	10	2	0	1	22	97	23	13	12	3	1	1	2	10	2	10	0	0	2	0	1.000	0	0	4.91
1982	New York	AL	6	6	0	0	28	138	42	25	24	1	0	2	0	13	0	21	1	0	2	3	.400	0	0	7.71
1983	New York	AL	19	12	2	3	82	368	89	53	49	7	1	5	3	35	0	61	2	1	1	5	.167	0	0	5.38
1984	New York	AL	61	1	0	23	103.2	426	86	33	31	5	3	3	0	34	3	109	4	0	9	4	.692	0	7	2.69
1985	Oakland	AL	63	0	0	58	98	414	98	32	31	5	3	4	1	31	3	68	4	1	9	8	.529	0	29	2.85
1986	Oakland	AL	38	0	0	33	53.1	230	53	23	20	3	3	1	1	23	4	42	4	0	3	6	.333	0	16	3.38

97

Year	Team	Lg	G	GS	CG	GF	IP	BFP	H	R	ER	HR	SH	SF	HB	TBB	IBB	SO	WP	Bk	W	L	Pct.	ShO	Sv	ERA
1987	Oakland	AL	36	0	0	27	44.1	200	48	30	29	6	3	2	1	21	1	35	4	0	3	4	.429	0	16	5.89
1988	Los Angeles	NL	50	0	0	38	65	262	44	16	15	1	3	3	1	21	2	70	2	2	5	3	.625	0	21	2.08
1989	Los Angeles	NL	56	0	0	41	79.2	312	60	15	14	3	4	2	0	22	6	55	1	0	5	3	.625	0	28	1.58
1990	Los Angeles	NL	45	0	0	35	66	271	59	17	16	5	1	0	6	20	3	59	4	1	3	3	.500	0	16	2.18
1991	Los Angeles	NL	44	0	0	35	51	202	39	19	18	3	5	2	1	11	3	40	0	0	6	5	.545	0	16	3.18
1992	Los Angeles	NL	41	0	0	26	46.2	203	41	9	8	2	5	1	1	18	5	36	3	1	1	3	.250	0	4	1.54
	13 ML YEARS		474	21	2	321	742.2	3142	690	290	272	44	32	27	18	259	32	607	29	6	51	49	.510	0	153	3.30

Pat Howell

Bats: Both **Throws:** Right **Pos:** CF **Ht:** 5'11" **Wt:** 155 **Born:** 08/31/68 **Age:** 24

					BATTING															BASERUNNING				PERCENTAGES		
Year	Team	Lg	G	AB	H	2B	3B	HR	(Hm	Rd)	TB	R	RBI	TBB	IBB	SO	HBP	SH	SF	SB	CS	SB%	GDP	Avg	OBP	SLG
1987	Kingsport	R	34	92	20	2	0	1	--	--	25	14	5	10	0	28	2	0	0	8	2	.80	0	.217	.308	.272
1988	Kingsport	R	66	251	67	6	3	0	--	--	79	43	16	12	0	52	1	2	3	27	6	.82	0	.267	.300	.315
1989	Pittsfield	A	56	231	67	4	3	1	--	--	80	41	26	7	0	46	3	6	1	45	10	.82	0	.290	.318	.346
1990	Columbia	A	135	573	151	15	5	1	--	--	179	97	37	22	2	111	7	10	3	79	11	.88	2	.264	.298	.312
1991	St. Lucie	A	62	246	54	8	2	0	--	--	66	36	10	14	0	47	3	6	0	37	9	.80	0	.220	.270	.268
	Williamsprt	AA	70	274	77	5	1	1	--	--	87	43	26	21	0	50	6	8	0	27	11	.71	2	.281	.346	.318
1992	Tidewater	AAA	104	405	99	8	3	1	--	--	116	46	22	22	1	98	5	4	2	21	10	.68	2	.244	.290	.286
1992	New York	NL	31	75	14	1	0	0	(0	0)	15	9	1	2	0	15	1	1	0	4	2	.67	0	.187	.218	.200

Dann Howitt

Bats: Left **Throws:** Right **Pos:** LF/RF **Ht:** 6'5" **Wt:** 205 **Born:** 02/13/64 **Age:** 29

					BATTING															BASERUNNING				PERCENTAGES		
Year	Team	Lg	G	AB	H	2B	3B	HR	(Hm	Rd)	TB	R	RBI	TBB	IBB	SO	HBP	SH	SF	SB	CS	SB%	GDP	Avg	OBP	SLG
1986	Medford	A	66	208	66	9	2	6	--	--	97	36	37	49	3	37	1	1	5	1	.83	7	.317	.448	.466
1987	Modesto	A	109	336	70	11	2	8	--	--	109	44	42	59	1	110	4	3	3	7	9	.44	8	.208	.331	.324
1988	Modesto	A	132	480	121	20	2	18	--	--	199	75	86	81	3	106	2	0	2	11	5	.69	9	.252	.361	.415
	Tacoma	AAA	4	15	2	1	0	0	--	--	3	1	0	0	0	4	0	0	0	0	0	.00	0	.133	.133	.200
1989	Huntsville	AA	138	509	143	28	2	26	--	--	253	78	111	68	7	107	3	2	6	2	1	.67	6	.281	.365	.497
1990	Tacoma	AAA	118	437	116	30	1	11	--	--	181	58	69	38	3	95	2	0	4	4	4	.50	16	.265	.324	.414
1991	Tacoma	AAA	122	449	120	28	6	14	--	--	202	58	73	49	2	92	2	1	5	5	2	.71	14	.267	.339	.450
1992	Tacoma	AAA	43	140	41	13	1	1	--	--	59	25	27	23	0	20	2	0	5	5	3	.63	3	.293	.388	.421
	Calgary	AAA	50	178	54	9	5	6	--	--	91	29	33	12	1	38	1	2	1	4	0	1.00	7	.303	.349	.511
1989	Oakland	AL	3	3	0	0	0	0	(0	0)	0	0	0	0	0	2	0	0	0	0	0	.00	0	.000	.000	.000
1990	Oakland	AL	14	22	3	0	1	0	(0	0)	5	3	1	3	0	12	0	0	0	0	0	.00	0	.136	.240	.227
1991	Oakland	AL	21	42	7	1	0	1	(0	1)	11	5	3	1	0	12	0	0	1	0	0	.00	0	.167	.182	.262
1992	2 ML Teams		35	85	16	4	1	2	(1	1)	28	7	10	8	1	9	0	0	3	1	1	.50	6	.188	.250	.329
1992	Oakland	AL	22	48	6	0	0	1	(0	1)	9	1	2	5	1	4	0	1	0	0	0	.00	4	.125	.208	.188
	Seattle	AL	13	37	10	4	1	1	(1	0)	19	6	8	3	0	5	0	0	3	1	1	.50	2	.270	.302	.514
	4 ML YEARS		73	152	26	5	2	3	(1	2)	44	15	14	12	1	35	0	0	4	1	1	.50	7	.171	.226	.289

Peter Hoy

Pitches: Right **Bats:** Left **Pos:** RP **Ht:** 6'7" **Wt:** 220 **Born:** 06/29/66 **Age:** 27

					HOW MUCH HE PITCHED					WHAT HE GAVE UP											THE RESULTS				
Year	Team	Lg	G	GS	CG	GF	IP	BFP	H	R	ER	HR	SH	SF	HB	TBB	IBB	SO	WP	Bk	W	L	Pct.	ShO	Sv	ERA
1989	Elmira	A	26	12	3	6	118	486	109	52	37	6	6	2	4	37	1	73	3	4	6	10	.375	0	1	2.82
1990	Winter Havn	A	52	3	0	30	108.2	460	110	54	43	3	10	5	3	30	1	48	5	5	2	10	.167	0	7	3.56
1991	New Britain	AA	47	0	0	40	68	269	47	20	11	2	9	1	3	22	8	39	1	2	4	4	.500	0	15	1.46
	Pawtucket	AAA	15	0	0	13	22.2	93	18	8	6	2	2	0	0	10	1	12	2	0	1	2	.333	0	5	2.38
1992	Pawtucket	AAA	45	0	0	22	73	317	83	41	39	9	3	3	0	25	5	38	5	3	3	2	.600	0	5	4.81
1992	Boston	AL	5	0	0	2	3.2	19	8	3	3	0	0	0	0	2	1	2	0	0	0	0	.000	0	0	7.36

Kent Hrbek

Bats: Left **Throws:** Right **Pos:** 1B **Ht:** 6'4" **Wt:** 245 **Born:** 05/21/60 **Age:** 33

					BATTING															BASERUNNING				PERCENTAGES		
Year	Team	Lg	G	AB	H	2B	3B	HR	(Hm	Rd)	TB	R	RBI	TBB	IBB	SO	HBP	SH	SF	SB	CS	SB%	GDP	Avg	OBP	SLG
1981	Minnesota	AL	24	67	16	5	0	1	(0	1)	24	5	7	5	1	9	1	0	0	0	0	.00	0	.239	.301	.358
1982	Minnesota	AL	140	532	160	21	4	23	(11	12)	258	82	92	54	12	80	0	1	4	3	1	.75	17	.301	.363	.485
1983	Minnesota	AL	141	515	153	41	5	16	(7	9)	252	75	84	57	5	71	3	0	7	4	6	.40	12	.297	.366	.489
1984	Minnesota	AL	149	559	174	31	3	27	(15	12)	292	80	107	65	15	87	4	1	6	1	1	.50	17	.311	.383	.522
1985	Minnesota	AL	158	593	165	31	2	21	(10	11)	263	78	93	67	12	87	2	0	4	1	1	.50	12	.278	.351	.444
1986	Minnesota	AL	149	550	147	27	1	29	(18	11)	263	85	91	71	9	81	6	0	7	2	2	.50	15	.267	.353	.478
1987	Minnesota	AL	143	477	136	20	1	34	(20	14)	260	85	90	84	12	60	0	0	5	5	2	.71	13	.285	.389	.545
1988	Minnesota	AL	143	510	159	31	0	25	(13	12)	265	75	76	67	7	54	0	2	0	0	3	.00	15	.312	.387	.520
1989	Minnesota	AL	109	375	102	17	0	25	(17	8)	194	59	84	53	4	35	1	1	4	3	0	1.00	6	.272	.360	.517
1990	Minnesota	AL	143	492	141	26	0	22	(8	14)	233	61	79	69	8	45	7	2	8	5	2	.71	17	.287	.377	.474

Year	Team	Lg	G	AB	H	2B	3B	HR	(Hm	Rd)	TB	R	RBI	TBB	IBB	SO	HBP	SH	SF	SB	CS	SB%	GDP	Avg	OBP	SLG
1991	Minnesota	AL	132	462	131	20	1	20	(11	9)	213	72	89	67	4	48	0	3	2	4	4	.50	15	.284	.373	.461
1992	Minnesota	AL	112	394	96	20	0	15	(10	5)	161	52	58	71	9	56	0	2	3	5	2	.71	13	.244	.357	.409
	12 ML YEARS		1543	5526	1580	290	17	258	(140	118)	2678	809	950	730	98	713	24	12	57	33	24	.58	146	.286	.368	.485

Rex Hudler

Bats: Right **Throws:** Right **Pos:** 2B   **Ht:** 6' 0" **Wt:** 195 **Born:** 09/02/60 **Age:** 32

									BATTING											BASERUNNING				PERCENTAGES		
Year	Team	Lg	G	AB	H	2B	3B	HR	(Hm	Rd)	TB	R	RBI	TBB	IBB	SO	HBP	SH	SF	SB	CS	SB%	GDP	Avg	OBP	SLG
1984	New York	AL	9	7	1	1	0	0	(0	0)	2	2	0	1	0	5	1	0	0	0	0	.00	0	.143	.333	.286
1985	New York	AL	20	51	8	0	1	0	(0	0)	10	4	1	1	0	9	0	5	0	0	1	.00	0	.157	.173	.196
1986	Baltimore	AL	14	1	0	0	0	0	(0	0)	0	1	0	0	0	0	0	0	0	1	0	1.00	0	.000	.000	.000
1988	Montreal	NL	77	216	59	14	2	4	(1	3)	89	38	14	10	6	34	0	1	2	29	7	.81	2	.273	.303	.412
1989	Montreal	NL	92	155	38	7	0	6	(3	3)	63	21	13	6	2	23	1	0	0	15	4	.79	2	.245	.278	.406
1990	2 ML Teams		93	220	62	11	2	7	(2	5)	98	31	22	12	1	32	2	2	1	18	10	.64	3	.282	.323	.445
1991	St. Louis	NL	101	207	47	10	2	1	(1	0)	64	21	15	10	1	29	0	2	2	12	8	.60	1	.227	.260	.309
1992	St. Louis	NL	61	98	24	4	0	3	(2	1)	37	17	5	2	0	23	1	1	1	2	6	.25	0	.245	.265	.378
1990	Montreal	NL	4	3	1	0	0	0	(0	0)	1	1	0	0	0	1	0	0	0	0	0	.00	0	.333	.333	.333
	St. Louis	NL	89	217	61	11	2	7	(2	5)	97	30	22	12	1	31	2	2	1	18	10	.64	3	.281	.323	.447
	8 ML YEARS		467	955	239	47	7	21	(9	12)	363	135	70	42	10	155	5	11	6	77	36	.68	8	.250	.284	.380

Mike Huff

Bats: Right **Throws:** Right **Pos:** RF   **Ht:** 6' 1" **Wt:** 180 **Born:** 08/11/63 **Age:** 29

									BATTING											BASERUNNING				PERCENTAGES		
Year	Team	Lg	G	AB	H	2B	3B	HR	(Hm	Rd)	TB	R	RBI	TBB	IBB	SO	HBP	SH	SF	SB	CS	SB%	GDP	Avg	OBP	SLG
1989	Los Angeles	NL	12	25	5	1	0	1	(0	1)	9	4	2	3	0	6	1	1	0	0	1	.00	0	.200	.310	.360
1991	2 ML Teams		102	243	61	10	2	3	(1	2)	84	42	25	37	2	48	6	6	2	14	4	.78	7	.251	.361	.346
1992	Chicago	AL	60	115	24	5	0	0	(0	0)	29	13	8	10	1	24	1	2	2	1	2	.33	2	.209	.273	.252
1991	Cleveland	AL	51	146	35	6	1	2	(1	1)	49	28	10	25	0	30	4	3	1	11	2	.85	2	.240	.364	.336
	Chicago	AL	51	97	26	4	1	1	(0	1)	35	14	15	12	2	18	2	3	1	3	2	.60	5	.268	.357	.361
	3 ML YEARS		174	383	90	16	2	4	(1	3)	122	59	35	50	3	78	8	9	4	15	7	.68	9	.235	.333	.319

Tim Hulett

Bats: Right **Throws:** Right **Pos:** 3B/DH   **Ht:** 6' 0" **Wt:** 199 **Born:** 01/12/60 **Age:** 33

									BATTING											BASERUNNING				PERCENTAGES		
Year	Team	Lg	G	AB	H	2B	3B	HR	(Hm	Rd)	TB	R	RBI	TBB	IBB	SO	HBP	SH	SF	SB	CS	SB%	GDP	Avg	OBP	SLG
1983	Chicago	AL	6	5	1	0	0	0	(0	0)	1	0	0	0	0	0	0	0	0	1	0	1.00	0	.200	.200	.200
1984	Chicago	AL	8	7	0	0	0	0	(0	0)	0	1	0	1	0	4	0	0	0	1	0	1.00	0	.000	.125	.000
1985	Chicago	AL	141	395	106	19	4	5	(2	3)	148	52	37	30	1	81	4	4	3	6	4	.60	8	.268	.324	.375
1986	Chicago	AL	150	520	120	16	5	17	(7	10)	197	53	44	21	0	91	1	6	4	4	1	.80	11	.231	.260	.379
1987	Chicago	AL	68	240	52	10	0	7	(3	4)	83	20	28	10	1	41	0	5	2	0	2	.00	6	.217	.246	.346
1989	Baltimore	AL	33	97	27	5	0	3	(2	1)	41	12	18	10	0	17	0	1	1	0	0	.00	3	.278	.343	.423
1990	Baltimore	AL	53	153	39	7	1	3	(2	1)	57	16	16	15	0	41	0	1	0	1	0	1.00	2	.255	.321	.373
1991	Baltimore	AL	79	206	42	9	0	7	(1	6)	72	29	18	13	0	49	1	1	0	0	1	.00	3	.204	.255	.350
1992	Baltimore	AL	57	142	41	7	2	2	(1	1)	58	11	21	10	1	31	1	0	0	0	1	.00	7	.289	.340	.408
	9 ML YEARS		595	1765	428	73	12	44	(18	26)	657	194	182	110	3	355	7	18	10	13	9	.59	40	.242	.288	.372

David Hulse

Bats: Left **Throws:** Left **Pos:** CF   **Ht:** 5'11" **Wt:** 170 **Born:** 02/25/68 **Age:** 25

									BATTING											BASERUNNING				PERCENTAGES		
Year	Team	Lg	G	AB	H	2B	3B	HR	(Hm	Rd)	TB	R	RBI	TBB	IBB	SO	HBP	SH	SF	SB	CS	SB%	GDP	Avg	OBP	SLG
1990	Butte	R	64	257	92	2	2	2	--	--	114	54	34	25	1	31	2	2	0	24	5	.83	4	.358	.419	.444
1991	Charlotte	A	88	310	86	4	5	0	--	--	100	41	17	36	2	75	1	6	0	44	7	.86	4	.277	.354	.323
1992	Tulsa	AA	88	354	101	14	3	3	--	--	130	40	20	20	2	86	3	1	0	17	10	.63	2	.285	.329	.367
	Okla City	AAA	8	30	7	1	1	0	--	--	10	7	3	1	0	4	1	1	0	2	2	.50	0	.233	.281	.333
1992	Texas	AL	32	92	28	4	0	0	(0	0)	32	14	2	3	0	18	0	2	0	3	1	.75	0	.304	.326	.348

Mike Humphreys

Bats: Right **Throws:** Right **Pos:** LF   **Ht:** 6' 0" **Wt:** 185 **Born:** 04/10/67 **Age:** 26

									BATTING											BASERUNNING				PERCENTAGES		
Year	Team	Lg	G	AB	H	2B	3B	HR	(Hm	Rd)	TB	R	RBI	TBB	IBB	SO	HBP	SH	SF	SB	CS	SB%	GDP	Avg	OBP	SLG
1988	Spokane	A	76	303	93	16	5	6	--	--	137	67	59	46	1	57	0	0	4	21	4	.84	9	.307	.394	.452
1989	Riverside	A	117	420	121	26	1	13	--	--	188	77	66	72	4	79	7	3	5	23	10	.70	9	.288	.397	.448
1990	Wichita	AA	116	421	116	21	4	17	--	--	196	92	79	67	4	79	5	2	4	37	9	.80	6	.276	.378	.466
	Las Vegas	AAA	12	42	10	1	0	2	--	--	17	7	6	4	0	11	1	2	0	1	0	1.00	4	.238	.319	.405
1991	Columbus	AAA	117	413	117	23	5	9	--	--	177	71	53	63	3	61	3	1	6	34	9	.79	10	.283	.377	.429
1992	Columbus	AAA	114	408	115	18	6	6	--	--	163	83	46	59	0	69	1	3	5	37	13	.74	9	.282	.370	.400
1991	New York	AL	25	40	8	0	0	0	(0	0)	8	9	3	9	0	7	0	1	0	2	0	1.00	0	.200	.347	.200

Year	Team	Lg	G	AB	H	2B	3B	HR	(Hm	Rd)	TB	R	RBI	TBB	IBB	SO	HBP	SH	SF	SB	CS	SB%	GDP	Avg	OBP	SLG
1992	New York	AL	4	10	1	0	0	0	(0	0)	1	0	0	0	0	1	0	0	0	0	0	.00	2	.100	.100	.100
	2 ML YEARS		29	50	9	0	0	0	(0	0)	9	9	3	9	0	8	0	1	0	2	0	1.00	2	.180	.305	.180

Todd Hundley

Bats: Both **Throws:** Right **Pos:** C   **Ht:** 5'11" **Wt:** 185 **Born:** 05/27/69 **Age:** 24

							BATTING													BASERUNNING				PERCENTAGES		
Year	Team	Lg	G	AB	H	2B	3B	HR	(Hm	Rd)	TB	R	RBI	TBB	IBB	SO	HBP	SH	SF	SB	CS	SB%	GDP	Avg	OBP	SLG
1987	Little Fls	A	34	103	15	4	0	1	--	--	22	12	10	12	2	27	3	0	0	0	0	.00	7	.146	.254	.214
1988	Little Fls	A	52	176	33	8	0	2	--	--	47	23	18	16	1	31	4	2	1	1	1	.50	2	.188	.269	.267
	St. Lucie	A	1	1	0	0	0	0			0	0	0	2	0	1	0	0	0	0	0	.00	0	.000	.667	.000
1989	Columbia	A	125	439	118	23	4	11	--	--	182	67	66	54	10	67	8	1	5	6	3	.67	20	.269	.356	.415
1990	Jackson	AA	81	279	74	12	2	1	--	--	93	27	35	34	3	44	1	0	3	5	3	.63	5	.265	.344	.333
1991	Tidewater	AAA	125	454	124	24	4	14	--	--	198	62	66	51	2	95	2	4	8	1	2	.33	12	.273	.344	.436
1990	New York	NL	36	67	14	6	0	0	(0	0)	20	8	2	6	0	18	0	1	0	0	0	.00	1	.209	.274	.299
1991	New York	NL	21	60	8	0	1	1	(1	0)	13	5	7	6	0	14	1	1	1	0	0	.00	3	.133	.221	.217
1992	New York	NL	123	358	75	17	0	7	(2	5)	113	32	32	19	4	76	4	7	2	3	0	1.00	8	.209	.256	.316
	3 ML YEARS		180	485	97	23	1	8	(3	5)	146	45	41	31	4	108	5	9	3	3	0	1.00	12	.200	.254	.301

Brian Hunter

Bats: Right **Throws:** Left **Pos:** 1B   **Ht:** 6' 0" **Wt:** 195 **Born:** 03/04/68 **Age:** 25

							BATTING													BASERUNNING				PERCENTAGES		
Year	Team	Lg	G	AB	H	2B	3B	HR	(Hm	Rd)	TB	R	RBI	TBB	IBB	SO	HBP	SH	SF	SB	CS	SB%	GDP	Avg	OBP	SLG
1987	Pulaski	R	65	251	58	10	2	8	--	--	96	38	30	18	0	47	5	0	1	3	2	.60	7	.231	.295	.382
1988	Burlington	A	117	417	108	17	0	22	--	--	191	58	71	45	2	90	8	1	7	7	2	.78	7	.259	.338	.458
	Durham	A	13	49	17	3	0	3	--	--	29	13	9	7	0	8	0	0	0	2	0	1.00	0	.347	.429	.592
1989	Greenville	AA	124	451	114	19	2	19	--	--	194	57	82	33	2	61	7	1	9	5	4	.56	4	.253	.308	.430
1990	Richmond	AAA	43	137	27	4	0	5	--	--	46	13	16	18	0	37	0	1	1	2	1	.67	0	.197	.288	.336
1991	Greenville	AA	88	320	77	13	1	14	--	--	134	45	55	43	1	62	3	0	4	3	4	.43	6	.241	.332	.419
1991	Richmond	AAA	48	181	47	7	0	10	--	--	84	28	30	11	1	24	1	2	3	3	2	.60	6	.260	.301	.464
1991	Atlanta	NL	97	271	68	16	1	12	(7	5)	122	32	50	17	0	48	1	0	2	0	2	.00	6	.251	.296	.450
1992	Atlanta	NL	102	238	57	13	2	14	(9	5)	116	34	41	21	3	50	0	1	8	1	2	.33	2	.239	.292	.487
	2 ML YEARS		199	509	125	29	3	26	(16	10)	238	66	91	38	3	98	1	1	10	1	4	.20	8	.246	.294	.468

Bruce Hurst

Pitches: Left **Bats:** Left **Pos:** SP   **Ht:** 6' 3" **Wt:** 220 **Born:** 03/24/58 **Age:** 35

			HOW MUCH HE PITCHED					WHAT HE GAVE UP										THE RESULTS					
Year	Team	Lg	G	GS	CG	GF	IP	BFP	H	R	ER	HR	SH	SF	HB	TBB	IBB	SO	WP	Bk	W	L	Pct.	ShO	Sv	ERA
1980	Boston	AL	12	7	0	2	31	147	39	33	31	4	0	2	2	16	0	16	4	2	2	2	.500	0	0	9.00
1981	Boston	AL	5	5	0	0	23	104	23	11	11	1	0	2	1	12	2	11	2	0	2	0	1.000	0	0	4.30
1982	Boston	AL	28	19	0	3	117	535	161	87	75	16	2	7	3	40	2	53	5	0	3	7	.300	0	0	5.77
1983	Boston	AL	33	32	6	0	211.1	903	241	102	96	22	3	4	3	62	5	115	1	2	12	12	.500	2	0	4.09
1984	Boston	AL	33	33	9	0	218	958	232	106	95	25	3	4	6	88	3	136	1	1	12	12	.500	2	0	3.92
1985	Boston	AL	35	31	6	0	229.1	973	243	123	115	31	6	4	3	70	4	189	3	4	11	13	.458	1	0	4.51
1986	Boston	AL	25	25	11	0	174.1	721	169	63	58	18	5	3	3	50	2	167	6	0	13	8	.619	4	0	2.99
1987	Boston	AL	33	33	15	0	238.2	1001	239	124	117	35	5	8	1	76	5	190	3	1	15	13	.536	3	0	4.41
1988	Boston	AL	33	32	7	0	216.2	922	222	98	88	21	8	5	2	65	1	166	5	3	18	6	.750	1	0	3.66
1989	San Diego	NL	33	33	10	0	244.2	990	214	84	73	16	18	3	0	66	7	179	8	0	15	11	.577	2	0	2.69
1990	San Diego	NL	33	33	9	0	223.2	903	188	85	78	21	15	1	1	63	5	162	7	1	11	9	.550	4	0	3.14
1991	San Diego	NL	31	31	4	0	221.2	909	201	89	81	17	8	4	3	59	3	141	5	1	15	8	.652	0	0	3.29
1992	San Diego	NL	32	32	6	0	217.1	902	223	96	93	22	12	4	0	51	3	131	4	3	14	9	.609	4	0	3.85
	13 ML YEARS		366	346	83	5	2366.2	9968	2395	1101	1011	249	85	51	28	718	42	1656	54	18	143	110	.565	23	0	3.84

Jon Hurst

Pitches: Right **Bats:** Right **Pos:** SP   **Ht:** 6' 3" **Wt:** 175 **Born:** 10/20/66 **Age:** 26

			HOW MUCH HE PITCHED					WHAT HE GAVE UP										THE RESULTS					
Year	Team	Lg	G	GS	CG	GF	IP	BFP	H	R	ER	HR	SH	SF	HB	TBB	IBB	SO	WP	Bk	W	L	Pct.	ShO	Sv	ERA
1987	Rangers	R	12	12	0	0	57.1	233	34	19	12	0	1	2	2	32	1	59	0	0	4	3	.571	0	0	1.88
1988	Rangers	R	5	5	0	3	15.1	53	5	1	1	0	1	0	1	4	1	13	0	0	1	0	1.000	0	0	0.59
	Charlotte	A	7	2	0	1	16	62	8	4	3	0	0	2	3	6	0	20	2	2	1	0	1.000	0	0	1.69
	Okla City	AAA	1	1	0	0	1.2	11	1	2	2	0	0	0	0	5	0	2	0	0	0	0	.000	0	0	10.80
1989	Charlotte	A	19	11	0	4	58.2	270	67	44	29	5	3	4	3	32	0	37	6	0	4	6	.400	0	1	4.45
1990	Gastonia	A	15	7	0	3	61.1	247	48	21	18	2	1	3	4	19	0	49	3	0	8	1	.889	0	1	2.64
	Tulsa	AA	8	3	0	2	25.2	124	29	30	27	4	2	1	0	16	1	23	1	0	0	2	.000	0	0	9.47
	Charlotte	A	6	0	0	3	12.1	50	8	3	3	1	1	0	0	5	1	8	0	0	0	1	.000	0	0	2.19
1991	Miami	A	15	15	0	0	99.1	413	89	41	32	6	7	5	6	31	2	91	2	0	8	2	.800	0	0	2.90
	Tulsa	AA	5	2	1	3	25	92	18	6	6	1	1	0	2	6	0	17	1	0	2	1	.667	0	1	2.16

Team	Lg	G	GS	CG	GF	IP	BFP	H	R	ER	HR	SH	SF	HB	TBB	IBB	SO	WP	Bk	W	L	Pct.	ShO	Sv	ERA
Harrisburg	AA	6	6	1	0	42	160	26	4	4	3	1	1	1	12	1	34	1	0	5	0	1.000	0	0	0.86
1992 Indianapols	AAA	23	23	2	0	119.1	511	135	59	50	7	9	3	3	29	1	70	3	0	4	8	.333	0	0	3.77
1992 Montreal	NL	3	3	0	0	16.1	72	18	10	10	1	0	0	1	7	0	4	1	0	1	1	.500	0	0	5.51

Jeff Huson

Bats: Left **Throws:** Right **Pos:** SS/2B   **Ht:** 6' 3" **Wt:** 180 **Born:** 08/15/64 **Age:** 28

Year Team	Lg	G	AB	H	2B	3B	HR	(Hm	Rd)	TB	R	RBI	TBB	IBB	SO	HBP	SH	SF	SB	CS	SB%	GDP	Avg	OBP	SLG
1988 Montreal	NL	20	42	13	2	0	0	(0	0)	15	7	3	4	2	3	0	0	0	2	1	.67	2	.310	.370	.357
1989 Montreal	NL	32	74	12	5	0	0	(0	0)	17	1	2	6	3	6	0	3	0	3	0	1.00	6	.162	.225	.230
1990 Texas	AL	145	396	95	12	2	0	(0	0)	111	57	28	46	0	54	2	7	3	12	4	.75	8	.240	.320	.280
1991 Texas	AL	119	268	57	8	3	2	(0	1)	77	36	26	39	0	32	0	9	1	8	3	.73	6	.213	.312	.287
1992 Texas	AL	123	318	83	14	3	4	(0	4)	115	49	24	41	2	43	1	8	6	18	6	.75	7	.261	.342	.362
5 ML YEARS		439	1098	260	41	8	6	(1	5)	335	150	83	136	7	138	3	27	10	43	14	.75	29	.237	.320	.305

Pete Incaviglia

Bats: Right **Throws:** Right **Pos:** LF/RF   **Ht:** 6' 1" **Wt:** 225 **Born:** 04/02/64 **Age:** 29

Year Team	Lg	G	AB	H	2B	3B	HR	(Hm	Rd)	TB	R	RBI	TBB	IBB	SO	HBP	SH	SF	SB	CS	SB%	GDP	Avg	OBP	SLG
1986 Texas	AL	153	540	135	21	2	30	(17	13)	250	82	88	55	2	185	4	0	7	3	2	.60	9	.250	.320	.463
1987 Texas	AL	139	509	138	26	4	27	(11	16)	253	85	80	48	1	168	1	0	5	9	3	.75	8	.271	.332	.497
1988 Texas	AL	116	418	104	19	3	22	(12	10)	195	59	54	39	3	153	7	0	3	6	4	.60	6	.249	.321	.467
1989 Texas	AL	133	453	107	27	4	21	(13	8)	205	48	81	32	0	136	6	0	4	5	7	.42	12	.236	.293	.453
1990 Texas	AL	153	529	123	27	0	24	(15	9)	222	59	85	45	5	146	9	0	4	3	4	.43	18	.233	.302	.420
1991 Detroit	AL	97	337	72	12	1	11	(6	5)	119	38	38	36	0	92	1	1	2	1	3	.25	6	.214	.290	.353
1992 Houston	NL	113	349	93	22	1	11	(6	5)	150	31	44	25	2	99	3	0	2	2	2	.50	6	.266	.319	.430
7 ML YEARS		904	3135	772	154	15	146	(80	66)	1394	402	470	280	13	979	31	1	27	29	25	.54	65	.246	.312	.445

Jeff Innis

Pitches: Right **Bats:** Right **Pos:** RP   **Ht:** 6' 1" **Wt:** 168 **Born:** 07/05/62 **Age:** 30

Year Team	Lg	G	GS	CG	GF	IP	BFP	H	R	ER	HR	SH	SF	HB	TBB	IBB	SO	WP	Bk	W	L	Pct.	ShO	Sv	ERA
1987 New York	NL	17	1	0	8	25.2	109	29	9	9	5	0	0	1	4	1	28	1	1	0	1	.000	0	0	3.16
1988 New York	NL	12	0	0	7	19	80	19	6	4	0	1	1	0	2	1	14	0	0	0	1	.500	0	0	1.89
1989 New York	NL	29	0	0	12	39.2	160	38	16	14	2	1	1	1	8	0	16	0	0	0	1	.000	0	0	3.18
1990 New York	NL	18	0	0	12	26.1	104	19	9	7	4	0	2	1	10	3	12	1	1	1	3	.250	0	1	2.39
1991 New York	NL	69	0	0	29	84.2	336	66	30	25	2	6	5	0	23	6	47	4	0	0	2	.000	0	0	2.66
1992 New York	NL	76	0	0	28	88	373	85	32	28	4	7	4	6	36	4	39	1	0	6	9	.400	0	1	2.86
6 ML YEARS		221	1	0	96	283.1	1162	256	102	87	17	15	13	9	83	15	156	7	2	8	17	.320	0	2	2.76

Daryl Irvine

Pitches: Right **Bats:** Right **Pos:** RP   **Ht:** 6' 3" **Wt:** 195 **Born:** 11/15/64 **Age:** 28

Year Team	Lg	G	GS	CG	GF	IP	BFP	H	R	ER	HR	SH	SF	HB	TBB	IBB	SO	WP	Bk	W	L	Pct.	ShO	Sv	ERA
1990 Boston	AL	11	0	0	6	17.1	75	15	10	9	0	1	3	0	10	3	9	1	1	1	1	.500	0	0	4.67
1991 Boston	AL	9	0	0	5	18	90	25	13	12	2	1	0	2	9	1	8	1	0	0	0	.000	0	0	6.00
1992 Boston	AL	21	0	0	8	28	128	31	20	19	1	1	3	2	14	2	10	3	0	3	4	.429	0	0	6.11
3 ML YEARS		41	0	0	19	63.1	293	71	43	40	3	3	6	4	33	6	27	5	1	4	5	.444	0	0	5.68

Bo Jackson

Bats: Right **Throws:** Right **Pos:** DH   **Ht:** 6' 1" **Wt:** 235 **Born:** 11/30/62 **Age:** 30

Year Team	Lg	G	AB	H	2B	3B	HR	(Hm	Rd)	TB	R	RBI	TBB	IBB	SO	HBP	SH	SF	SB	CS	SB%	GDP	Avg	OBP	SLG
1986 Kansas City	AL	25	82	17	2	1	2	(1	1)	27	9	9	7	0	34	2	0	0	3	1	.75	1	.207	.286	.329
1987 Kansas City	AL	116	396	93	17	2	22	(14	8)	180	46	53	30	0	158	5	1	2	10	4	.71	3	.235	.296	.455
1988 Kansas City	AL	124	439	108	16	4	25	(10	15)	207	63	68	25	6	146	1	1	2	26	6	.82	6	.246	.287	.472
1989 Kansas City	AL	135	515	132	15	6	32	(11	21)	255	86	105	39	8	172	3	0	4	26	9	.74	10	.256	.310	.495
1990 Kansas City	AL	111	405	110	16	1	28	(12	16)	212	74	78	44	2	128	2	0	5	15	9	.63	10	.272	.342	.523
1991 Chicago	AL	23	71	16	4	0	3	(3	0)	29	8	14	12	1	25	0	0	1	0	1	.00	3	.225	.333	.408
6 ML YEARS		534	1908	476	70	14	112	(51	61)	910	286	327	157	17	663	13	2	14	81	30	.73	33	.249	.309	.477

Danny Jackson

Pitches: Left **Bats:** Right **Pos:** SP **Ht:** 6' 0" **Wt:** 205 **Born:** 01/05/62 **Age:** 31

			HOW MUCH HE PITCHED							WHAT HE GAVE UP												THE RESULTS					
Year Team	Lg	G	GS	CG	GF	IP	BFP	H	R	ER	HR	SH	SF	HB	TBB	IBB	SO	WP	Bk	W	L	Pct.	ShO	Sv	ERA
1983 Kansas City	AL	4	3	0	0	19	87	26	12	11	1	1	0	0	6	0	9	0	0	1	1	.500	0	0	5.21
1984 Kansas City	AL	15	11	1	3	76	338	84	41	36	4	3	0	5	35	0	40	3	2	2	6	.250	0	0	4.26
1985 Kansas City	AL	32	32	4	0	208	893	209	94	79	7	5	4	6	76	2	114	4	2	14	12	.538	3	0	3.42
1986 Kansas City	AL	32	27	4	3	185.2	789	177	83	66	13	10	4	4	79	1	115	7	0	11	12	.478	1	1	3.20
1987 Kansas City	AL	36	34	11	1	224	981	219	115	100	11	8	7	7	109	1	152	5	0	9	18	.333	2	0	4.02
1988 Cincinnati	NL	35	35	15	0	260.2	1034	206	86	79	13	13	5	2	71	6	161	5	2	23	8	.742	6	0	2.73
1989 Cincinnati	NL	20	20	1	0	115.2	519	122	78	72	10	6	4	1	57	7	70	3	2	6	11	.353	0	0	5.60
1990 Cincinnati	NL	22	21	0	1	117.1	499	119	54	47	11	4	5	2	40	4	76	3	1	6	6	.500	0	0	3.61
1991 Chicago	NL	17	14	0	0	70.2	347	89	59	53	8	8	2	1	48	4	31	1	1	1	5	.167	0	0	6.75
1992 2 ML Teams		34	34	0	0	201.1	883	211	99	86	6	17	10	4	77	6	97	2	2	8	13	.381	0	0	3.84
1992 Chicago	NL	19	19	0	0	113	501	117	59	53	5	11	5	3	48	3	51	1	2	4	9	.308	0	0	4.22
Pittsburgh	NL	15	15	0	0	88.1	382	94	40	33	1	6	5	1	29	3	46	1	0	4	4	.500	0	0	3.36
10 ML YEARS		247	231	36	8	1478.1	6370	1462	721	629	84	75	41	32	598	31	865	33	12	81	92	.468	12	0	3.83

Darrin Jackson

Bats: Right **Throws:** Right **Pos:** CF **Ht:** 6' 0" **Wt:** 185 **Born:** 08/22/63 **Age:** 29

					BATTING														BASERUNNING				PERCENTAGES		
Year Team	Lg	G	AB	H	2B	3B	HR	(Hm	Rd)	TB	R	RBI	TBB	IBB	SO	HBP	SH	SF	SB	CS	SB%	GDP	Avg	OBP	SLG
1985 Chicago	NL	5	11	1	0	0	0	(0	0)	1	0	0	0	0	3	0	0	0	0	0	.00	0	.091	.091	.091
1987 Chicago	NL	7	5	4	1	0	0	(0	0)	5	2	0	0	0	0	0	0	0	0	0	.00	0	.800	.800	1.000
1988 Chicago	NL	100	188	50	11	3	6	(3	3)	85	29	20	5	1	28	1	2	1	4	1	.80	3	.266	.287	.452
1989 2 ML Teams		70	170	37	7	0	4	(1	3)	56	17	20	13	5	34	0	0	2	1	4	.20	2	.218	.270	.329
1990 San Diego	NL	58	113	29	3	0	3	(1	2)	41	10	9	5	1	24	0	1	1	3	0	1.00	1	.257	.286	.363
1991 San Diego	NL	122	359	94	12	1	21	(12	9)	171	51	49	27	2	66	2	3	3	5	3	.63	5	.262	.315	.476
1992 San Diego	NL	155	587	146	23	5	17	(11	6)	230	72	70	26	4	106	4	6	5	14	3	.82	21	.249	.283	.392
1989 Chicago	NL	45	83	19	4	0	1	(0	1)	26	7	8	6	1	17	0	0	1	1	2	.33	1	.229	.281	.313
San Diego	NL	25	87	18	3	0	3	(1	2)	30	10	12	7	4	17	0	0	2	2	0	.00	1	.207	.260	.345
7 ML YEARS		517	1433	361	57	9	51	(28	23)	589	181	168	76	13	261	7	12	12	27	11	.71	32	.252	.291	.411

Mike Jackson

Pitches: Right **Bats:** Right **Pos:** RP **Ht:** 6' 0" **Wt:** 200 **Born:** 12/22/64 **Age:** 28

			HOW MUCH HE PITCHED							WHAT HE GAVE UP												THE RESULTS					
Year Team	Lg	G	GS	CG	GF	IP	BFP	H	R	ER	HR	SH	SF	HB	TBB	IBB	SO	WP	Bk	W	L	Pct.	ShO	Sv	ERA
1986 Philadelphia	NL	9	0	0	4	13.1	54	12	5	5	2	0	0	2	4	1	3	0	0	0	0	.000	0	0	3.38
1987 Philadelphia	NL	55	7	0	8	109.1	468	88	55	51	16	3	4	3	56	6	93	6	8	3	10	.231	0	1	4.20
1988 Seattle	AL	62	0	0	29	99.1	412	74	37	29	10	3	10	2	43	10	76	6	6	6	5	.545	0	4	2.63
1989 Seattle	AL	65	0	0	27	99.1	431	81	43	35	8	6	2	6	54	6	94	1	2	4	6	.400	0	7	3.17
1990 Seattle	AL	63	0	0	28	77.1	338	64	42	39	8	8	5	2	44	12	69	9	2	5	7	.417	0	3	4.54
1991 Seattle	AL	72	0	0	35	88.2	363	64	35	32	5	4	0	6	34	11	74	3	0	7	7	.500	0	14	3.25
1992 San Francisco	NL	67	0	0	24	82	346	76	35	34	7	5	2	4	33	10	80	1	0	6	6	.500	0	2	3.73
7 ML YEARS		393	7	0	155	569.1	2412	459	252	225	56	29	23	25	268	56	489	26	18	31	41	.431	0	31	3.56

Brook Jacoby

Bats: Right **Throws:** Right **Pos:** 3B **Ht:** 5'11" **Wt:** 195 **Born:** 11/23/59 **Age:** 33

					BATTING														BASERUNNING				PERCENTAGES		
Year Team	Lg	G	AB	H	2B	3B	HR	(Hm	Rd)	TB	R	RBI	TBB	IBB	SO	HBP	SH	SF	SB	CS	SB%	GDP	Avg	OBP	SLG
1981 Atlanta	NL	11	10	2	0	0	0	(0	0)	2	0	1	0	0	3	0	0	0	0	0	.00	1	.200	.200	.200
1983 Atlanta	NL	4	8	0	0	0	0	(0	0)	0	0	0	0	0	1	0	1	0	0	0	.00	0	.000	.000	.000
1984 Cleveland	AL	126	439	116	19	3	7	(2	5)	162	64	40	32	0	73	3	2	7	3	2	.60	13	.264	.314	.369
1985 Cleveland	AL	161	606	166	26	3	20	(9	11)	258	72	87	48	3	120	0	1	7	2	3	.40	17	.274	.324	.426
1986 Cleveland	AL	158	583	168	30	4	17	(10	7)	257	83	80	56	5	137	0	1	1	2	1	.67	15	.288	.350	.441
1987 Cleveland	AL	155	540	162	26	4	32	(21	11)	292	73	69	75	2	73	3	0	2	2	3	.40	19	.300	.387	.541
1988 Cleveland	AL	152	552	133	25	0	9	(3	6)	185	59	49	48	2	101	1	0	5	2	3	.40	12	.241	.300	.335
1989 Cleveland	AL	147	519	141	26	5	13	(7	6)	216	49	64	62	3	90	3	0	8	2	5	.29	15	.272	.348	.416
1990 Cleveland	AL	155	553	162	24	4	14	(10	4)	236	77	75	63	6	58	2	2	4	1	4	.20	20	.293	.365	.427
1991 2 ML Teams		122	419	94	21	1	4	(2	2)	129	28	44	27	3	54	3	0	4	2	1	.67	13	.224	.274	.308
1992 Cleveland	AL	120	291	76	7	0	4	(3	1)	95	30	36	28	2	54	1	3		0	3	.00	13	.261	.324	.326
1991 Cleveland	AL	66	231	54	9	1	4	(2	2)	77	14	24	16	2	32	2	0	0	2	0	.00	7	.234	.289	.333
Oakland	AL	56	188	40	12	0	0	(0	0)	52	14	20	11	1	22	1	0	4	2	0	1.00	6	.213	.255	.277
11 ML YEARS		1311	4520	1220	204	24	120	(67	53)	1832	535	545	439	26	764	16	10	42	16	25	.39	138	.270	.334	.405

John Jaha

Bats: Right **Throws:** Right **Pos:** 1B **Ht:** 6' 1" **Wt:** 195 **Born:** 05/27/66 **Age:** 27

BATTING / BASERUNNING / PERCENTAGES

Year Team	Lg	G	AB	H	2B	3B	HR	(Hm	Rd)	TB	R	RBI	TBB	IBB	SO	HBP	SH	SF	SB	CS	SB%	GDP	Avg	OBP	SLG
1985 Helena	R	24	68	18	3	0	2	--	--	27	13	14	14	0	23	0	0	1	4	0	1.00	0	.265	.386	.397
1986 Tri-Cities	A	73	258	82	13	2	15	--	--	144	65	67	70	4	75	5	0	2	9	4	.69	2	.318	.469	.558
1987 Beloit	A	122	376	101	22	0	7	--	--	144	68	47	102	2	86	4	2	3	10	5	.67	11	.269	.427	.383
1988 Stockton	A	99	302	77	14	6	8	--	--	127	58	54	69	0	85	2	2	1	10	6	.63	10	.255	.396	.421
1989 Stockton	A	140	479	140	26	5	25	--	--	251	83	91	112	6	115	5	2	13	8	11	.42	15	.292	.422	.524
1990 Stockton	A	26	84	22	5	0	4	--	--	39	12	19	18	0	25	2	0	0	0	0	.00	1	.262	.404	.464
1991 El Paso	AA	130	486	167	38	3	30	--	--	301	121	134	78	6	101	8	1	5	12	6	.67	9	.344	.438	.619
1992 Denver	AAA	79	274	88	18	2	18	--	--	164	61	69	50	1	60	6	1	2	6	4	.60	3	.321	.434	.599
1992 Milwaukee	AL	47	133	30	3	1	2	(1	1)	41	17	10	12	1	30	2	1	4	10	0	1.00	1	.226	.291	.308

Chris James

Bats: Right **Throws:** Right **Pos:** LF **Ht:** 6' 1" **Wt:** 190 **Born:** 10/04/62 **Age:** 30

BATTING / BASERUNNING / PERCENTAGES

Year Team	Lg	G	AB	H	2B	3B	HR	(Hm	Rd)	TB	R	RBI	TBB	IBB	SO	HBP	SH	SF	SB	CS	SB%	GDP	Avg	OBP	SLG
1986 Philadelphia	NL	16	46	13	3	0	1	(0	1)	19	5	5	1	0	13	0	1	0	0	0	.00	1	.283	.298	.413
1987 Philadelphia	NL	115	358	105	20	6	17	(9	8)	188	48	54	27	0	67	2	1	3	3	1	.75	4	.293	.344	.525
1988 Philadelphia	NL	150	566	137	24	1	19	(10	9)	220	57	66	31	2	73	3	0	5	7	4	.64	15	.242	.283	.389
1989 2 ML Teams		132	482	117	17	2	13	(7	6)	177	55	65	26	2	68	1	4	3	5	2	.71	20	.243	.281	.367
1990 Cleveland	AL	140	528	158	32	4	12	(6	6)	234	62	70	31	4	71	4	3	3	4	3	.57	11	.299	.341	.443
1991 Cleveland	AL	115	437	104	16	2	5	(1	4)	139	31	41	18	2	61	4	2	2	3	4	.43	9	.238	.273	.318
1992 San Francisco	NL	111	248	60	10	4	5	(3	2)	93	25	32	14	2	45	2	0	3	2	3	.40	2	.242	.285	.375
1989 Philadelphia	NL	45	179	37	4	0	2	(1	1)	47	14	19	4	0	23	0	1	1	3	1	.75	9	.207	.223	.263
San Diego	NL	87	303	80	13	2	11	(6	5)	130	41	46	22	2	45	1	3	2	2	1	.67	11	.264	.314	.429
7 ML YEARS		779	2665	694	122	19	72	(36	36)	1070	283	333	148	12	398	16	11	19	24	17	.59	62	.260	.301	.402

Dion James

Bats: Left **Throws:** Left **Pos:** RF/CF **Ht:** 6' 1" **Wt:** 175 **Born:** 11/09/62 **Age:** 30

BATTING / BASERUNNING / PERCENTAGES

Year Team	Lg	G	AB	H	2B	3B	HR	(Hm	Rd)	TB	R	RBI	TBB	IBB	SO	HBP	SH	SF	SB	CS	SB%	GDP	Avg	OBP	SLG
1983 Milwaukee	AL	11	20	2	0	0	0	(0	0)	2	1	1	2	0	2	0	0	0	1	0	1.00	0	.100	.182	.100
1984 Milwaukee	AL	128	387	114	19	5	1	(1	0)	146	52	30	32	1	41	3	6	3	10	10	.50	7	.295	.351	.377
1985 Milwaukee	AL	18	49	11	1	0	0	(0	0)	12	5	3	6	0	6	0	0	0	0	0	.00	0	.224	.309	.245
1987 Atlanta	NL	134	494	154	37	6	10	(5	5)	233	80	61	70	2	63	2	5	3	10	8	.56	8	.312	.397	.472
1988 Atlanta	NL	132	386	99	17	5	3	(1	2)	135	46	30	58	5	59	1	2	2	9	9	.50	12	.256	.353	.350
1989 2 ML Teams		134	415	119	18	0	5	(1	4)	152	41	40	49	6	49	1	3	1	2	7	.22	9	.287	.363	.366
1990 Cleveland	AL	87	248	68	15	2	1	(0	1)	90	28	22	27	3	23	1	3	1	5	3	.63	6	.274	.347	.363
1992 New York	AL	67	145	38	8	0	3	(2	1)	55	24	17	22	0	15	1	0	2	1	0	1.00	3	.262	.359	.379
1989 Atlanta	NL	63	170	44	7	0	1	(0	1)	54	15	11	25	2	23	1	3	1	1	3	.25	4	.259	.355	.318
Cleveland	AL	71	245	75	11	0	4	(1	3)	98	26	29	24	4	26	0	0	0	1	4	.20	5	.306	.368	.385
8 ML YEARS		711	2144	605	115	18	23	(10	13)	825	277	204	266	17	258	9	21	12	38	37	.51	45	.282	.362	.385

Stan Javier

Bats: Both **Throws:** Right **Pos:** CF/LF/RF **Ht:** 6' 0" **Wt:** 185 **Born:** 01/09/64 **Age:** 29

BATTING / BASERUNNING / PERCENTAGES

Year Team	Lg	G	AB	H	2B	3B	HR	(Hm	Rd)	TB	R	RBI	TBB	IBB	SO	HBP	SH	SF	SB	CS	SB%	GDP	Avg	OBP	SLG
1984 New York	AL	7	7	1	0	0	0	(0	0)	1	1	0	0	0	1	0	0	0	0	0	.00	0	.143	.143	.143
1986 Oakland	AL	59	114	23	0	0	0	(0	0)	31	13	8	16	0	27	1	0	0	8	0	1.00	2	.202	.305	.272
1987 Oakland	AL	81	151	28	3	1	2	(1	1)	39	22	9	19	3	33	0	6	0	3	2	.60	2	.185	.276	.258
1988 Oakland	AL	125	397	102	13	3	2	(0	2)	127	49	35	32	1	63	2	6	3	20	1	.95	13	.257	.313	.320
1989 Oakland	AL	112	310	77	12	3	1	(1	0)	98	42	28	31	1	45	1	4	2	12	2	.86	6	.248	.317	.316
1990 2 ML Teams		123	309	92	9	6	3	(1	2)	122	60	27	40	2	50	0	6	2	15	7	.68	6	.298	.376	.395
1991 Los Angeles	NL	121	176	36	5	3	1	(0	1)	50	21	11	16	0	36	0	2	2	7	1	.88	4	.205	.268	.284
1992 2 ML Teams		130	334	83	17	1	1	(1	0)	105	42	29	37	2	54	3	3	2	18	3	.86	4	.249	.327	.314
1990 Oakland	AL	19	33	8	0	2	0	(0	0)	12	4	3	3	0	6	0	0	0	0	0	.00	0	.242	.306	.364
Los Angeles	NL	104	276	84	9	4	3	(1	2)	110	56	24	37	2	44	0	6	2	15	7	.68	6	.304	.384	.399
1992 Los Angeles	NL	56	58	11	3	0	1	(1	0)	17	6	5	6	2	11	1	1	0	1	2	.33	0	.190	.277	.293
Philadelphia	NL	74	276	72	14	1	0	(0	0)	88	36	24	31	0	43	2	2	2	17	1	.94	4	.261	.338	.319
8 ML YEARS		758	1798	442	67	17	10	(4	6)	573	250	147	191	9	309	7	28	11	83	16	.84	37	.246	.319	.319

Mike Jeffcoat

Pitches: Left **Bats:** Left **Pos:** SP **Ht:** 6' 2" **Wt:** 190 **Born:** 08/03/59 **Age:** 33

Year Team	Lg	G	GS	CG	GF	IP	BFP	H	R	ER	HR	SH	SF	HB	TBB	IBB	SO	WP	Bk	W	L	Pct.	ShO	Sv	ERA
1983 Cleveland	AL	11	2	0	1	32.2	140	32	13	12	1	1	0	1	13	1	9	1	1	1	3	.250	0	0	3.31
1984 Cleveland	AL	63	1	0	12	75.1	327	82	28	25	7	3	7	1	24	7	41	8	1	5	2	.714	0	1	2.99
1985 2 ML Teams		28	1	0	10	31.2	143	35	18	16	5	4	3	2	12	4	14	1	0	0	2	.000	0	0	4.55
1987 Texas	AL	2	2	0	0	7	35	11	10	10	4	0	0	0	4	0	1	0	0	0	1	.000	0	0	12.86
1988 Texas	AL	5	2	0	2	10	52	19	13	13	1	1	0	2	5	1	5	0	0	0	2	.000	0	0	11.70
1989 Texas	AL	22	22	2	0	130.2	559	139	65	52	7	3	5	4	33	0	64	0	1	9	6	.600	2	0	3.58
1990 Texas	AL	44	12	1	11	110.2	466	122	57	55	12	3	2	2	28	5	58	1	0	5	6	.455	0	5	4.47
1991 Texas	AL	70	0	0	21	79.2	363	104	46	41	8	5	4	4	25	3	43	3	1	5	3	.625	0	1	4.63
1992 Texas	AL	6	3	0	2	19.2	89	28	17	16	2	2	2	0	5	0	6	0	0	0	1	.000	0	0	7.32
1985 Cleveland	AL	9	0	0	3	9.2	44	8	5	3	1	2	2	0	6	1	4	0	0	0	0	.000	0	0	2.79
San Francisco	NL	19	1	0	7	22	99	27	13	13	4	2	1	2	6	3	10	1	0	0	2	.000	0	0	5.32
9 ML YEARS		251	45	3	59	497.1	2174	572	267	240	47	22	23	16	149	21	241	14	3	25	26	.490	2	7	4.34

Gregg Jefferies

Bats: Both **Throws:** Right **Pos:** 3B **Ht:** 5'10" **Wt:** 185 **Born:** 08/01/67 **Age:** 25

Year Team	Lg	G	AB	H	2B	3B	HR	(Hm	Rd)	TB	R	RBI	TBB	IBB	SO	HBP	SH	SF	SB	CS	SB%	GDP	Avg	OBP	SLG
1987 New York	NL	6	6	3	1	0	0	(0	0)	4	0	2	0	0	0	0	0	0	0	0	.00	0	.500	.500	.667
1988 New York	NL	29	109	35	8	2	6	(3	3)	65	19	17	8	0	10	0	0	1	5	1	.83	1	.321	.364	.596
1989 New York	NL	141	508	131	28	2	12	(7	5)	199	72	56	39	8	46	5	2	5	21	6	.78	16	.258	.314	.392
1990 New York	NL	153	604	171	40	3	15	(9	6)	262	96	68	46	2	40	5	0	4	11	2	.85	12	.283	.337	.434
1991 New York	NL	136	486	132	19	2	9	(5	4)	182	59	62	47	2	38	2	1	3	26	5	.84	12	.272	.336	.374
1992 Kansas City	AL	152	604	172	36	3	10	(3	7)	244	66	75	43	4	29	1	0	9	19	9	.68	24	.285	.329	.404
6 ML YEARS		617	2317	644	132	12	52	(27	25)	956	312	280	183	16	163	13	3	22	82	23	.78	65	.278	.331	.413

Reggie Jefferson

Bats: Both **Throws:** Left **Pos:** 1B **Ht:** 6' 4" **Wt:** 210 **Born:** 09/25/68 **Age:** 24

Year Team	Lg	G	AB	H	2B	3B	HR	(Hm	Rd)	TB	R	RBI	TBB	IBB	SO	HBP	SH	SF	SB	CS	SB%	GDP	Avg	OBP	SLG
1986 Reds	R	59	208	54	4	5	3	--	--	77	28	33	24	1	40	2	1	2	10	9	.53	3	.260	.339	.370
1987 Cedar Rapds	A	15	54	12	5	0	3	--	--	26	9	11	1	0	12	3	0	0	1	1	.50	2	.222	.276	.481
Billings	R	8	22	8	1	0	1	--	--	12	10	9	4	1	2	1	0	0	1	0	1.00	1	.364	.481	.545
1988 Cedar Rapds	A	135	517	149	26	2	18	--	--	233	76	90	40	6	89	13	0	5	2	1	.67	12	.288	.351	.451
1989 Chattanooga	AA	135	487	140	19	3	17	--	--	216	66	80	43	5	73	7	0	4	2	3	.40	11	.287	.351	.444
1990 Nashville	AAA	37	126	34	11	2	5	--	--	64	24	23	14	1	30	1	0	0	1	0	1.00	3	.270	.348	.508
1991 Nashville	AAA	28	103	33	3	1	3	--	--	47	15	20	10	1	22	4	0	0	3	1	.75	3	.320	.402	.456
Canton-Akrn	AA	6	25	7	1	0	0	--	--	8	2	4	1	0	5	0	0	0	0	0	.00	0	.280	.308	.320
Colo Spngs	AAA	39	136	42	11	0	3	--	--	62	29	21	9	1	28	1	0	2	0	0	.00	1	.309	.381	.456
1992 Colo Spngs	AAA	57	218	68	11	4	11	--	--	120	44	44	29	3	50	1	0	2	0	1	1.00	7	.312	.390	.550
1991 2 ML Teams		31	108	21	3	0	3	(2	1)	33	11	13	4	0	24	0	0	1	0	0	.00	3	.194	.221	.306
1992 Cleveland	AL	24	89	30	6	2	1	(1	0)	43	8	6	1	0	17	1	0	0	0	0	.00	2	.337	.352	.483
1991 Cincinnati	NL	5	7	1	0	0	1	(1	0)	4	1	1	1	0	2	0	0	0	0	0	.00	0	.143	.250	.571
Cleveland	AL	26	101	20	3	0	2	(1	1)	29	10	12	3	0	22	0	0	1	0	0	.00	3	.198	.219	.287
2 ML YEARS		55	197	51	9	2	4	(3	1)	76	19	19	5	0	41	1	0	1	0	0	.00	3	.259	.279	.386

Shawn Jeter

Bats: Left **Throws:** Right **Pos:** RF **Ht:** 6' 2" **Wt:** 185 **Born:** 06/28/66 **Age:** 27

Year Team	Lg	G	AB	H	2B	3B	HR	(Hm	Rd)	TB	R	RBI	TBB	IBB	SO	HBP	SH	SF	SB	CS	SB%	GDP	Avg	OBP	SLG
1985 Blue Jays	R	56	219	45	2	3	1	--	--	56	25	16	22	0	50	1	0	0	8	6	.57	3	.205	.281	.256
1986 St.Cathrnes	A	70	241	57	5	4	3	--	--	79	29	19	34	0	79	1	4	0	9	6	.60	5	.237	.333	.328
1987 Dunedin	A	127	468	127	22	5	9	--	--	186	59	56	54	3	107	6	2	4	8	8	.50	9	.271	.352	.397
1988 Dunedin	A	13	32	9	1	0	2	--	--	16	4	3	3	0	7	0	0	1	0	1	.00	1	.281	.333	.500
Knoxville	AA	80	238	59	7	4	3	--	--	83	31	25	24	1	46	0	3	1	10	5	.67	4	.248	.316	.349
1989 Knoxville	AA	101	308	84	9	2	3	--	--	106	39	25	27	0	65	1	2	1	8	4	.67	6	.273	.332	.344
1990 Knoxville	AA	131	461	126	25	2	4	--	--	167	67	43	39	5	95	2	6	7	25	14	.64	6	.273	.328	.362
1991 Syracuse	AAA	70	242	64	15	1	3	--	--	90	36	26	15	5	55	0	6	0	5	5	.50	8	.264	.307	.372
Vancouver	AAA	43	144	43	5	1	1	--	--	53	24	13	11	2	27	2	1	1	4	2	.67	1	.299	.354	.368
1992 Vancouver	AAA	96	379	114	18	5	2	--	--	148	61	34	38	6	63	2	6	1	26	11	.70	6	.301	.367	.391
1992 Chicago	AL	13	18	2	0	0	0	(0	0)	2	1	0	0	0	7	0	0	0	0	0	.00	0	.111	.111	.111

Howard Johnson

Bats: Both **Throws:** Right **Pos:** CF/LF   **Ht:** 5'10" **Wt:** 195 **Born:** 11/29/60 **Age:** 32

Year	Team	Lg	G	AB	H	2B	3B	HR	(Hm	Rd)	TB	R	RBI	TBB	IBB	SO	HBP	SH	SF	SB	CS	SB%	GDP	Avg	OBP	SLG
1982	Detroit	AL	54	155	49	5	0	4	(1	3)	66	23	14	16	1	30	1	1	0	7	4	.64	3	.316	.384	.426
1983	Detroit	AL	27	66	14	0	0	3	(2	1)	23	11	5	7	0	10	1	0	0	0	0	.00	1	.212	.297	.348
1984	Detroit	AL	116	355	88	14	1	12	(4	8)	140	43	50	40	1	67	1	4	2	10	6	.63	6	.248	.324	.394
1985	New York	NL	126	389	94	18	4	11	(5	6)	153	38	46	34	10	78	0	1	4	6	4	.60	6	.242	.300	.393
1986	New York	NL	88	220	54	14	0	10	(5	5)	98	30	39	31	8	64	1	1	0	8	1	.89	2	.245	.341	.445
1987	New York	NL	157	554	147	22	1	36	(13	23)	279	93	99	83	18	113	5	0	3	32	10	.76	8	.265	.364	.504
1988	New York	NL	148	495	114	21	1	24	(9	15)	209	85	68	86	25	104	3	2	8	23	7	.77	6	.230	.343	.422
1989	New York	NL	153	571	164	41	3	36	(19	17)	319	104	101	77	8	126	1	0	6	41	8	.84	4	.287	.369	.559
1990	New York	NL	154	590	144	37	3	23	(13	10)	256	89	90	69	12	100	0	0	9	34	8	.81	7	.244	.319	.434
1991	New York	NL	156	564	146	34	4	38	(21	17)	302	108	117	78	12	120	1	0	15	30	16	.65	4	.259	.342	.535
1992	New York	NL	100	350	78	19	0	7	(2	5)	118	48	43	55	5	79	2	0	3	22	5	.81	7	.223	.329	.337
11 ML YEARS			1279	4309	1092	225	17	204	(94	110)	1963	672	672	576	100	891	16	9	50	213	69	.76	54	.253	.340	.456

Jeff Johnson

Pitches: Left **Bats:** Right **Pos:** SP/RP   **Ht:** 6'3" **Wt:** 206 **Born:** 08/04/66 **Age:** 26

Year	Team	Lg	G	GS	CG	GF	IP	BFP	H	R	ER	HR	SH	SF	HB	TBB	IBB	SO	WP	Bk	W	L	Pct.	ShO	Sv	ERA
1988	Oneonta	A	14	14	0	0	87.2	371	67	35	29	2	3	3	2	39	0	91	3	2	6	1	.857	0	0	2.98
1989	Pr William	A	25	24	0	0	138.2	578	125	59	45	7	8	2	0	55	1	99	14	2	4	10	.286	0	0	2.92
1990	Ft.Laurdrle	A	17	17	1	0	103.2	439	101	55	42	2	5	2	3	25	0	84	5	2	4	8	.429	0	0	3.65
	Albany	AA	9	9	3	0	60.2	239	44	14	11	0	2	0	2	15	0	41	1	0	4	3	.571	1	0	1.63
1991	Columbus	AAA	10	10	0	0	62	261	58	27	18	1	4	1	1	25	0	40	1	3	4	0	1.000	0	0	2.61
1992	Columbus	AAA	11	11	0	0	58	229	41	15	14	0	2	2	2	18	0	38	3	1			.667	0	0	2.17
1991	New York	AL	23	23	0	0	127	562	156	89	83	15	7	4	6	33	1	62	5	1	6	11	.353	0	0	5.88
1992	New York	AL	13	8	0	3	52.2	245	71	44	39	4	2	2	2	23	0	14	1	0	2	3	.400	0	0	6.66
2 ML YEARS			36	31	0	3	179.2	807	227	133	122	19	9	6	8	56	1	76	6	1	8	14	.364	0	0	6.11

Lance Johnson

Bats: Left **Throws:** Left **Pos:** CF   **Ht:** 5'11" **Wt:** 160 **Born:** 07/06/63 **Age:** 29

Year	Team	Lg	G	AB	H	2B	3B	HR	(Hm	Rd)	TB	R	RBI	TBB	IBB	SO	HBP	SH	SF	SB	CS	SB%	GDP	Avg	OBP	SLG
1987	St. Louis	NL	33	59	13	2	1	0	(0	0)	17	4	7	4	1	6	0	0	0	6	1	.86	2	.220	.270	.288
1988	Chicago	AL	33	124	23	4	1	0	(0	0)	29	11	6	6	0	11	0	2	0	6	2	.75	1	.185	.223	.234
1989	Chicago	AL	50	180	54	8	2	0	(0	0)	66	28	16	17	0	24	0	2	0	16	3	.84	1	.300	.360	.367
1990	Chicago	AL	151	541	154	18	9	1	(0	1)	193	76	51	33	2	45	1	8	4	36	22	.62	12	.285	.325	.357
1991	Chicago	AL	160	588	161	14	13	0	(0	0)	201	72	49	26	2	58	1	6	3	26	11	.70	14	.274	.304	.342
1992	Chicago	AL	157	567	158	15	12	3	(2	1)	206	67	47	34	4	33	1	4	5	41	14	.75	20	.279	.318	.363
6 ML YEARS			584	2059	563	61	38	4	(2	2)	712	258	176	120	9	177	3	22	12	131	53	.71	50	.273	.313	.346

Randy Johnson

Pitches: Left **Bats:** Right **Pos:** SP   **Ht:** 6'10" **Wt:** 225 **Born:** 09/10/63 **Age:** 29

Year	Team	Lg	G	GS	CG	GF	IP	BFP	H	R	ER	HR	SH	SF	HB	TBB	IBB	SO	WP	Bk	W	L	Pct.	ShO	Sv	ERA
1988	Montreal	NL	4	4	1	0	26	109	23	8	7	3	0	0	0	7	0	25	3	0	3	0	1.000	0	0	2.42
1989	2 ML Teams		29	28	2	1	160.2	715	147	100	86	13	10	13	3	96	2	130	7	7	7	13	.350	0	0	4.82
1990	Seattle	AL	33	33	5	0	219.2	944	174	103	89	26	7	6	5	120	2	194	4	2	14	11	.560	2	0	3.65
1991	Seattle	AL	33	33	2	0	201.1	889	151	96	89	15	9	8	2	152	0	228	12	0	13	10	.565	1	0	3.98
1992	Seattle	AL	31	31	6	0	210.1	922	154	104	89	13	3	8	18	144	1	241	13	1	12	14	.462	2	0	3.77
1989	Montreal	NL	7	6	0	1	29.2	143	29	25	22	2	3	4	0	26	1	26	2	2	0	4	.000	0	0	6.67
	Seattle	AL	22	22	2	0	131	572	118	75	64	11	7	9	3	70	1	104	5	5	7	9	.438	0	0	4.40
5 ML YEARS			130	129	16	1	818	3579	649	411	359	70	29	35	38	519	5	818	39	12	49	48	.505	5	0	3.95

Joel Johnston

Pitches: Right **Bats:** Right **Pos:** RP   **Ht:** 6'4" **Wt:** 220 **Born:** 03/08/67 **Age:** 26

Year	Team	Lg	G	GS	CG	GF	IP	BFP	H	R	ER	HR	SH	SF	HB	TBB	IBB	SO	WP	Bk	W	L	Pct.	ShO	Sv	ERA
1988	Eugene	A	14	14	0	0	64	295	64	49	37	1	4	3	7	34	0	64	7	6	4	7	.364	0	0	5.20
1989	Baseball Cy	A	26	26	0	0	131.2	586	135	84	72	6	2	6	11	63	2	76	8	5	9	4	.692	0	0	4.92
1990	Memphis	AA	4	3	0	1	12	40	5	9	5	1	0	0	0	6	0	6	3	0	0	0	.000	0	0	6.75
	Baseball Cy	A	31	7	1	18	55.1	251	36	37	30	2	6	3	3	49	0	60	6	1	2	4	.333	0	7	4.88
	Omaha	AAA	2	0	0	0	3	9	1	0	0	0	0	0	0	1	0	3	0	0	0	0	.000	0	0	0.00
1991	Omaha	AAA	47	0	0	27	74.1	318	60	43	43	12	4	0	1	42	2	63	6	0	4	7	.364	0	8	5.21

Year Team	Lg	G	GS	CG	GF	IP	BFP	H	R	ER	HR	SH	SF	HB	TBB	IBB	SO	WP	Bk	W	L	Pct.	ShO	Sv	ERA
1992 Omaha	AAA	42	0	0	22	74.2	342	80	54	53	9	5	5	4	45	2	48	6	1	5	2	.714	0	2	6.39
1991 Kansas City	AL	13	0	0	1	22.1	85	9	1	1	0	1	0	0	9	3	21	0	0	1	0	1.000	0	0	0.40
1992 Kansas City	AL	5	0	0	1	2.2	13	3	4	4	2	0	0	0	2	0	0	1	0	0	0	.000	0	0	13.50
2 ML YEARS		18	0	0	2	25	98	12	5	5	2	1	0	0	11	3	21	1	0	1	0	1.000	0	0	1.80

Barry Jones

Pitches: Right **Bats:** Right **Pos:** RP

Ht: 6' 4" **Wt:** 225 **Born:** 02/15/63 **Age:** 30

		HOW MUCH HE PITCHED						WHAT HE GAVE UP												THE RESULTS					
Year Team	Lg	G	GS	CG	GF	IP	BFP	H	R	ER	HR	SH	SF	HB	TBB	IBB	SO	WP	Bk	W	L	Pct.	ShO	Sv	ERA
1986 Pittsburgh	NL	26	0	0	10	37.1	159	29	16	12	3	2	1	0	21	2	29	2	0	3	4	.429	0	3	2.89
1987 Pittsburgh	NL	32	0	0	10	43.1	203	55	34	27	6	3	2	0	23	6	28	3	0	2	4	.333	0	1	5.61
1988 2 ML Teams		59	0	0	25	82.1	347	72	28	26	6	5	5	1	38	7	48	13	2	3	3	.500	0	3	2.84
1989 Chicago	AL	22	0	0	9	30.1	121	22	12	8	2	4	2	1	8	0	17	1	0	3	2	.600	0	1	2.37
1990 Chicago	AL	65	0	0	9	74	310	62	20	19	2	7	5	1	33	7	45	0	1	11	4	.733	0	1	2.31
1991 Montreal	NL	77	0	0	46	88.2	353	76	35	33	8	7	3	1	33	8	46	1	1	4	9	.308	0	13	3.35
1992 2 ML Teams		61	0	0	17	69.2	319	85	46	44	3	3	3	2	35	7	30	2	2	7	6	.538	0	1	5.68
1988 Pittsburgh	NL	42	0	0	15	56.1	241	57	21	19	3	5	4	1	21	6	31	7	1	1	1	.500	0	2	3.04
Chicago	AL	17	0	0	10	26	106	15	7	7	3	0	1	0	17	1	17	6	1	2	2	.500	0	1	2.42
1992 Philadelphia	NL	44	0	0	10	54.1	243	65	30	28	3	2	2	2	24	4	19	1	2	5	6	.455	0	0	4.64
New York	NL	17	0	0	7	15.1	76	20	16	16	0	1	1	0	11	3	11	1	0	2	0	1.000	0	1	9.39
7 ML YEARS		342	0	0	125	425.2	1812	401	191	169	30	31	21	6	191	37	243	22	6	33	32	.508	0	23	3.57

Calvin Jones

Pitches: Right **Bats:** Right **Pos:** RP

Ht: 6' 3" **Wt:** 185 **Born:** 09/26/63 **Age:** 29

		HOW MUCH HE PITCHED						WHAT HE GAVE UP												THE RESULTS					
Year Team	Lg	G	GS	CG	GF	IP	BFP	H	R	ER	HR	SH	SF	HB	TBB	IBB	SO	WP	Bk	W	L	Pct.	ShO	Sv	ERA
1984 Bellingham	A	10	9	0	0	59.2	0	29	23	16	0	0	0	7	36	0	59	8	1	5	0	1.000	0	0	2.41
1985 Wausau	A	20	19	1	0	106	473	96	59	46	10	0	2	5	65	1	71	9	2	4	11	.267	0	0	3.91
1986 Salinas	A	26	25	2	0	157.1	680	141	76	63	9	4	4	4	90	2	137	15	2	11	8	.579	0	0	3.60
1987 Chattanooga	AA	26	10	0	12	81.1	372	90	58	45	5	5	1	2	38	0	77	4	0	2	9	.182	0	2	4.98
1988 Vermont	AA	24	4	0	6	74.2	312	52	26	22	1	0	2	0	47	2	58	4	3	7	5	.583	0	0	2.65
1989 San Berndno	A	5	0	0	4	12.1	49	8	1	1	0	0	1	0	7	0	15	0	2	2	0	1.000	0	1	0.73
Williamsprt	AA	5	0	0	3	6.2	34	13	9	9	1	0	0	0	4	0	5	1	0	0	0	.000	0	0	12.15
1990 San Berndno	A	53	0	0	27	67	298	43	32	22	4	1	3	4	54	2	94	6	0	5	3	.625	0	8	2.96
1991 Calgary	AAA	20	0	0	15	23	109	19	12	10	1	0	0	2	19	1	25	6	2	1	1	.500	0	7	3.91
1992 Calgary	AAA	21	1	0	13	32.2	145	23	15	14	3	1	3	0	22	0	32	3	0	2	0	1.000	0	3	3.86
1991 Seattle	AL	27	0	0	6	46.1	194	33	14	13	0	6	0	1	29	5	42	6	0	2	2	.500	0	2	2.53
1992 Seattle	AL	38	1	0	14	61.2	275	50	39	39	8	1	4	2	47	1	49	10	0	3	5	.375	0	0	5.69
2 ML YEARS		65	1	0	20	108	469	83	53	52	8	7	4	3	76	6	91	16	0	5	7	.417	0	2	4.33

Chris Jones

Bats: Right **Throws:** Right **Pos:** RF/LF

Ht: 6' 2" **Wt:** 205 **Born:** 12/16/65 **Age:** 27

		BATTING															BASERUNNING				PERCENTAGES		
Year Team	Lg	G	AB	H	2B	3B	HR	(Hm | Rd)	TB	R	RBI	TBB	IBB	SO	HBP	SH	SF	SB	CS	SB%	GDP	Avg	OBP	SLG
1984 Billings	R	21	73	11	2	0	2	--	--	19	8	13	2	0	24	0	0	1	4	0	1.00	0	.151	.171	.260
1985 Billings	R	63	240	62	12	5	4	--	--	96	43	33	19	0	72	1	1	1	13	0	1.00	6	.258	.314	.400
1986 Cedar Rapds	A	128	473	117	13	9	20	--	--	208	65	78	20	1	126	3	0	4	23	17	.58	7	.247	.280	.440
1987 Vermont	AA	113	383	88	11	4	10	--	--	137	50	39	23	4	99	4	2	3	13	10	.57	12	.230	.278	.358
1988 Chattanooga	AA	116	410	111	20	7	4	--	--	157	50	61	29	1	102	2	0	7	11	9	.55	4	.271	.317	.383
1989 Nashville	AAA	21	49	8	1	0	2	--	--	15	8	5	0	0	16	0	1	0	2	0	1.00	1	.163	.163	.306
Chattanooga	AA	103	378	95	18	2	10	--	--	147	47	54	23	1	68	3	0	1	10	2	.83	13	.251	.299	.389
1990 Nashville	AAA	134	436	114	23	3	10	--	--	173	53	52	23	3	86	2	5	1	12	8	.60	18	.261	.301	.397
1991 Nashville	AAA	73	267	65	5	4	9	--	--	105	29	33	19	1	60	2	0	1	10	5	.67	6	.243	.298	.393
1992 Tucson	AAA	45	170	55	9	8	3	--	--	89	25	28	18	2	34	0	1	2	7	1	.88	6	.324	.384	.524
1991 Cincinnati	NL	52	89	26	1	2	2	(0 | 2)	37	14	6	2	0	31	0	0	1	2	1	.67	2	.292	.304	.416
1992 Houston	NL	54	63	12	2	1	1	(1 | 0)	19	7	4	7	0	21	0	3	0	1	0	1.00	1	.190	.271	.302
2 ML YEARS		106	152	38	3	3	3	(1 | 2)	56	21	10	9	0	52	0	3	1	3	1	.83	3	.250	.290	.368

Doug Jones

Pitches: Right **Bats:** Right **Pos:** RP

Ht: 6' 2" **Wt:** 195 **Born:** 06/24/57 **Age:** 36

		HOW MUCH HE PITCHED						WHAT HE GAVE UP												THE RESULTS					
Year Team	Lg	G	GS	CG	GF	IP	BFP	H	R	ER	HR	SH	SF	HB	TBB	IBB	SO	WP	Bk	W	L	Pct.	ShO	Sv	ERA
1982 Milwaukee	AL	4	0	0	2	2.2	14	5	3	3	1	0	0	0	1	0	1	0	0	0	0	.000	0	0	10.13
1986 Cleveland	AL	11	0	0	5	18	79	18	5	5	0	1	1	1	6	1	12	0	0	1	0	1.000	0	1	2.50
1987 Cleveland	AL	49	0	0	29	91.1	400	101	45	32	4	5	5	6	24	5	87	0	0	6	5	.545	0	8	3.15
1988 Cleveland	AL	51	0	0	46	83.1	338	69	26	21	1	3	0	2	16	3	72	2	3	3	4	.429	0	37	2.27
1989 Cleveland	AL	59	0	0	53	80.2	331	76	25	21	4	8	6	1	13	4	65	1	1	7	10	.412	0	32	2.34
1990 Cleveland	AL	66	0	0	64	84.1	331	66	26	24	5	2	2	2	22	4	55	2	0	5	5	.500	0	43	2.56

Year	Team	Lg	G	GS	CG	GF	IP	BFP	H	R	ER	HR	SH	SF	HB	TBB	IBB	SO	WP	Bk	W	L	Pct.	ShO	Sv	ERA
1991	Cleveland	AL	36	4	0	29	63.1	293	87	42	39	7	2	2	0	17	5	48	1	0	4	8	.333	0	7	5.54
1992	Houston	NL	80	0	0	70	111.2	440	96	29	23	5	9	0	5	17	5	93	2	1	11	8	.579	0	36	1.85
8 ML YEARS			356	4	0	298	535.1	2226	518	201	168	27	30	16	17	116	27	433	8	5	37	40	.481	0	164	2.82

Jimmy Jones

Pitches: Right **Bats:** Right **Pos:** SP **Ht:** 6' 2" **Wt:** 190 **Born:** 04/20/64 **Age:** 29

			HOW MUCH HE PITCHED						WHAT HE GAVE UP										THE RESULTS						
Year	Team	Lg	G	GS	CG	GF	IP	BFP	H	R	ER	HR	SH	SF	HB	TBB	IBB	SO	WP	Bk	W	L	Pct.	ShO	Sv	ERA
1986	San Diego	NL	3	3	1	0	18	65	10	6	5	1	1	0	0	3	0	15	0	0	2	0	1.000	1	0	2.50
1987	San Diego	NL	30	22	2	4	145.2	639	154	85	67	14	5	5	5	54	2	51	3	2	9	7	.563	1	0	4.14
1988	San Diego	NL	29	29	3	0	179	760	192	98	82	14	11	9	3	44	3	82	4	1	9	14	.391	0	0	4.12
1989	New York	AL	11	6	0	3	48	211	56	29	28	7	1	1	2	16	1	25	1	0	2	1	.667	0	0	5.25
1990	New York	AL	17	7	0	9	50	238	72	42	35	8	1	4	1	23	0	25	3	0	1	2	.333	0	0	6.30
1991	Houston	NL	26	22	1	0	135.1	593	143	73	66	9	7	2	3	51	3	88	4	0	6	8	.429	1	0	4.39
1992	Houston	NL	25	23	0	1	139.1	579	135	64	63	13	7	4	5	39	3	69	4	1	10	6	.625	0	0	4.07
7 ML YEARS			141	112	7	17	715.1	3085	762	397	346	66	33	25	19	230	12	355	19	4	39	38	.506	3	0	4.35

Tim Jones

Bats: Left **Throws:** Right **Pos:** SS/2B **Ht:** 5'10" **Wt:** 175 **Born:** 12/01/62 **Age:** 30

			BATTING															BASERUNNING				PERCENTAGES		
Year	Team	Lg	G	AB	H	2B	3B	HR	(Hm | Rd)	TB	R	RBI	TBB	IBB	SO	HBP	SH	SF	SB	CS	SB%	GDP	Avg	OBP	SLG
1988	St. Louis	NL	31	52	14	0	0	0	(0 | 0)	14	2	3	4	0	10	0	1	0	4	1	.80	1	.269	.321	.269
1989	St. Louis	NL	42	75	22	6	0	0	(0 | 0)	28	11	7	7	1	8	1	1	2	1	0	1.00	1	.293	.353	.373
1990	St. Louis	NL	67	128	28	7	1	1	(1 | 0)	40	9	12	12	1	20	1	4	0	3	4	.43	1	.219	.291	.313
1991	St. Louis	NL	16	24	4	2	0	0	(0 | 0)	6	1	2	2	1	6	0	0	1	0	1	.00	0	.167	.222	.250
1992	St. Louis	NL	67	145	29	4	0	0	(0 | 0)	33	9	3	11	1	29	0	2	0	5	2	.71	5	.200	.256	.228
5 ML YEARS			223	424	97	19	1	1	(1 | 0)	121	32	27	36	4	73	2	7	3	13	8	.62	5	.229	.290	.285

Brian Jordan

Bats: Right **Throws:** Right **Pos:** LF/RF **Ht:** 6' 1" **Wt:** 205 **Born:** 03/29/67 **Age:** 26

			BATTING															BASERUNNING				PERCENTAGES		
Year	Team	Lg	G	AB	H	2B	3B	HR	(Hm | Rd)	TB	R	RBI	TBB	IBB	SO	HBP	SH	SF	SB	CS	SB%	GDP	Avg	OBP	SLG
1988	Hamilton	A	19	71	22	3	1	4	--	--	39	12	12	6	1	15	3	1	0	3	3	.50	1	.310	.388	.549
1989	St.Pete	A	11	43	15	4	1	2	--	--	27	7	11	0	0	8	2	0	0	0	2	.00	1	.349	.378	.628
1990	Arkansas	AA	16	50	8	1	0	0	--	--	9	4	0	0	0	11	1	0	0	0	2	.00	1	.160	.176	.180
	St. Pete	A	9	30	5	0	1	0	--	--	7	3	1	2	0	11	0	0	0	0	2	.00	1	.167	.219	.233
1991	Louisville	AAA	61	212	56	11	4	4	--	--	87	35	24	17	1	41	8	1	0	10	4	.71	5	.264	.342	.410
1992	Louisville	AAA	43	155	45	3	1	4	--	--	62	23	16	8	1	21	4	0	2	13	2	.87	1	.290	.337	.400
1992	St. Louis	NL	55	193	40	9	4	5	(3 | 2)	72	17	22	10	1	48	1	0	0	7	2	.78	6	.207	.250	.373

Ricky Jordan

Bats: Right **Throws:** Right **Pos:** 1B/LF **Ht:** 6' 3" **Wt:** 208 **Born:** 05/26/65 **Age:** 28

			BATTING															BASERUNNING				PERCENTAGES		
Year	Team	Lg	G	AB	H	2B	3B	HR	(Hm | Rd)	TB	R	RBI	TBB	IBB	SO	HBP	SH	SF	SB	CS	SB%	GDP	Avg	OBP	SLG
1988	Philadelphia	NL	69	273	84	15	1	11	(6 | 5)	134	41	43	7	2	39	0	0	1	1	1	.50	5	.308	.324	.491
1989	Philadelphia	NL	144	523	149	22	3	12	(7 | 5)	213	63	75	23	5	62	5	0	8	4	3	.57	19	.285	.317	.407
1990	Philadelphia	NL	92	324	78	21	0	5	(2 | 3)	114	32	44	13	6	39	5	0	4	2	0	1.00	9	.241	.277	.352
1991	Philadelphia	NL	101	301	82	21	3	9	(5 | 4)	136	38	49	14	2	49	2	0	5	0	2	.00	11	.272	.304	.452
1992	Philadelphia	NL	94	276	84	19	0	4	(2 | 2)	115	33	34	5	0	44	0	0	3	3	0	1.00	8	.304	.313	.417
5 ML YEARS			500	1697	477	98	7	41	(22 | 19)	712	207	245	62	15	233	12	0	21	10	6	.63	52	.281	.307	.420

Terry Jorgensen

Bats: Right **Throws:** Right **Pos:** 1B **Ht:** 6' 4" **Wt:** 213 **Born:** 09/02/66 **Age:** 26

			BATTING															BASERUNNING				PERCENTAGES		
Year	Team	Lg	G	AB	H	2B	3B	HR	(Hm | Rd)	TB	R	RBI	TBB	IBB	SO	HBP	SH	SF	SB	CS	SB%	GDP	Avg	OBP	SLG
1987	Kenosha	A	67	254	80	17	0	7	--	--	118	37	33	18	0	43	2	0	1	1	0	1.00	7	.315	.364	.465
1988	Orlando	AA	135	472	116	27	4	3	--	--	160	53	43	40	3	62	6	2	6	4	1	.80	11	.246	.309	.339
1989	Orlando	AA	135	514	135	27	5	13	--	--	211	84	101	76	4	78	5	0	9	1	1	.50	6	.263	.358	.411
1990	Portland	AAA	123	440	114	28	3	10	--	--	178	43	50	44	2	83	0	1	4	0	0	.00	11	.259	.324	.405
1991	Portland	AAA	126	456	136	29	0	11	--	--	198	74	59	54	1	41	4	2	2	1	0	1.00	22	.298	.376	.434
1992	Portland	AAA	135	505	149	32	2	14	--	--	227	78	71	54	3	58	4	3	5	2	0	1.00	22	.295	.364	.450
1989	Minnesota	AL	10	23	4	1	0	0	(0 | 0)	5	1	2	4	0	5	0	0	0	0	0	.00	1	.174	.296	.217
1992	Minnesota	AL	22	58	18	1	0	0	(0 | 0)	19	5	5	3	0	11	1	0	1	2	1	.33	4	.310	.349	.328
2 ML YEARS			32	81	22	2	0	0	(0 | 0)	24	6	7	7	0	16	1	0	1	2	1	.33	5	.272	.333	.296

Felix Jose

Bats: Both **Throws:** Right **Pos:** RF   **Ht:** 6' 1" **Wt:** 221 **Born:** 05/08/65 **Age:** 28

Year	Team	Lg	G	AB	H	2B	3B	HR	(Hm	Rd)	TB	R	RBI	TBB	IBB	SO	HBP	SH	SF	SB	CS	SB%	GDP	Avg	OBP	SLG
1988	Oakland	AL	8	6	2	1	0	0	(0	0)	3	2	1	0	0	1	0	0	0	1	0	1.00	0	.333	.333	.500
1989	Oakland	AL	20	57	11	2	0	0	(0	0)	13	3	5	4	0	13	0	0	0	1	0	1.00	2	.193	.246	.228
1990	2 ML Teams		126	426	113	16	1	11	(5	6)	164	54	52	24	0	81	5	2	1	12	6	.67	9	.265	.311	.385
1991	St. Louis	NL	154	568	173	40	6	8	(3	5)	249	69	77	50	8	113	2	0	5	20	12	.63	12	.305	.360	.438
1992	St. Louis	NL	131	509	150	22	3	14	(12	2)	220	62	75	40	8	100	1	0	1	28	12	.70	9	.295	.347	.432
1990	Oakland	AL	101	341	90	12	0	8	(3	5)	126	42	39	16	0	65	5	2	1	8	2	.80	8	.264	.306	.370
	St. Louis	NL	25	85	23	4	1	3	(2	1)	38	12	13	8	0	16	0	0	0	4	4	.50	1	.271	.333	.447
	5 ML YEARS		439	1566	449	81	10	33	(20	13)	649	190	210	118	16	308	8	2	7	61	31	.66	32	.287	.338	.414

Wally Joyner

Bats: Left **Throws:** Left **Pos:** 1B   **Ht:** 6' 2" **Wt:** 205 **Born:** 06/16/62 **Age:** 31

Year	Team	Lg	G	AB	H	2B	3B	HR	(Hm	Rd)	TB	R	RBI	TBB	IBB	SO	HBP	SH	SF	SB	CS	SB%	GDP	Avg	OBP	SLG
1986	California	AL	154	593	172	27	3	22	(11	11)	271	82	100	57	8	58	2	10	12	5	2	.71	11	.290	.348	.457
1987	California	AL	149	564	161	33	1	34	(19	15)	298	100	117	72	12	64	5	2	10	8	2	.80	14	.285	.366	.528
1988	California	AL	158	597	176	31	2	13	(6	7)	250	81	85	55	14	51	5	0	6	8	2	.80	16	.295	.356	.419
1989	California	AL	159	593	167	30	2	16	(8	8)	249	78	79	46	7	58	6	1	8	3	2	.60	15	.282	.335	.420
1990	California	AL	83	310	83	15	0	8	(5	3)	122	35	41	41	4	34	1	1	5	2	1	.67	10	.268	.350	.394
1991	California	AL	143	551	166	34	3	21	(10	11)	269	79	96	52	4	66	1	2	5	2	0	1.00	11	.301	.360	.488
1992	Kansas City	AL	149	572	154	36	2	9	(1	8)	221	66	66	55	4	50	4	0	2	11	5	.69	19	.269	.336	.386
	7 ML YEARS		995	3780	1079	206	13	123	(60	63)	1680	521	584	378	53	381	24	16	48	39	14	.74	96	.285	.350	.444

Dave Justice

Bats: Left **Throws:** Left **Pos:** RF   **Ht:** 6' 3" **Wt:** 200 **Born:** 04/14/66 **Age:** 27

Year	Team	Lg	G	AB	H	2B	3B	HR	(Hm	Rd)	TB	R	RBI	TBB	IBB	SO	HBP	SH	SF	SB	CS	SB%	GDP	Avg	OBP	SLG
1989	Atlanta	NL	16	51	12	3	0	1	(1	0)	18	7	3	3	1	9	1	1	0	2	1	.67	1	.235	.291	.353
1990	Atlanta	NL	127	439	124	23	2	28	(19	9)	235	76	78	64	4	92	0	0	1	11	6	.65	2	.282	.373	.535
1991	Atlanta	NL	109	396	109	25	1	21	(11	10)	199	67	87	65	9	81	3	0	5	8	8	.50	4	.275	.377	.503
1992	Atlanta	NL	144	484	124	19	5	21	(10	11)	216	78	72	79	8	85	2	0	6	2	4	.33	1	.256	.359	.446
	4 ML YEARS		396	1370	369	70	8	71	(41	30)	668	228	240	211	22	267	6	1	12	23	19	.55	8	.269	.366	.488

Scott Kamieniecki

Pitches: Right **Bats:** Right **Pos:** SP   **Ht:** 6' 0" **Wt:** 197 **Born:** 04/19/64 **Age:** 29

Year	Team	Lg	G	GS	CG	GF	IP	BFP	H	R	ER	HR	SH	SF	HB	TBB	IBB	SO	WP	Bk	W	L	Pct.	ShO	Sv	ERA
1987	Pr William	A	19	19	1	0	112.1	499	91	61	52	7	1	2	5	78	3	84	9	2	9	5	.643	0	0	4.17
	Albany	AA	10	7	0	1	37	176	41	25	22	0	5	0	1	33	3	19	3	1	1	3	.250	0	0	5.35
1988	Pr William	A	15	15	7	0	100.1	451	115	62	49	3	2	0	2	50	1	72	10	1	6	7	.462	2	0	4.40
	Ft.Laudrdle	A	12	11	1	0	77	329	71	36	31	0	1	2	1	40	1	51	7	0	3	6	.333	1	0	3.62
1989	Albany	AA	24	23	6	1	151	636	142	67	62	13	1	3	2	57	1	140	5	0	10	9	.526	3	0	3.70
1990	Albany	AA	22	21	3	0	132	562	113	55	47	5	6	6	0	61	2	99	6	1	10	9	.526	1	0	3.20
1991	Columbus	AAA	11	11	3	0	76.1	308	61	25	20	2	3	2	3	20	0	58	2	3	6	3	.667	1	0	2.36
1992	Ft. Laud	A	1	1	1	0	7	28	8	1	1	0	0	0	0	0	0	3	0	0	1	0	1.000	0	0	1.29
	Columbus	AAA	2	2	0	0	13	50	6	1	1	1	0	0	0	4	0	12	0	0	1	0	1.000	0	0	0.69
1991	New York	AL	9	9	0	0	55.1	239	54	24	24	8	2	1	3	22	1	34	1	0	4	4	.500	0	0	3.90
1992	New York	AL	28	28	4	0	188	804	193	100	91	13	3	5	5	74	9	88	9	1	6	14	.300	0	0	4.36
	2 ML YEARS		37	37	4	0	243.1	1043	247	124	115	21	5	6	8	96	10	122	10	1	10	18	.357	0	0	4.25

Ron Karkovice

Bats: Right **Throws:** Right **Pos:** C   **Ht:** 6' 1" **Wt:** 215 **Born:** 08/08/63 **Age:** 29

Year	Team	Lg	G	AB	H	2B	3B	HR	(Hm	Rd)	TB	R	RBI	TBB	IBB	SO	HBP	SH	SF	SB	CS	SB%	GDP	Avg	OBP	SLG
1986	Chicago	AL	37	97	24	7	0	4	(1	3)	43	13	13	9	0	37	1	1	1	1	0	1.00	3	.247	.315	.443
1987	Chicago	AL	39	85	6	0	0	2	(1	1)	12	7	7	7	0	40	2	1	0	3	0	1.00	2	.071	.160	.141
1988	Chicago	AL	46	115	20	4	0	3	(1	2)	33	10	9	7	0	30	1	3	0	4	2	.67	1	.174	.228	.287
1989	Chicago	AL	71	182	48	9	2	3	(0	3)	70	21	24	10	0	56	2	7	2	0	0	.00	0	.264	.306	.385
1990	Chicago	AL	68	183	45	10	0	6	(0	6)	73	30	20	16	1	52	1	7	1	2	0	1.00	1	.246	.308	.399
1991	Chicago	AL	75	167	41	13	0	5	(0	5)	69	25	22	15	1	42	1	9	1	0	0	.00	2	.246	.310	.413
1992	Chicago	AL	123	342	81	12	1	13	(5	8)	134	39	50	30	1	89	3	4	2	10	4	.71	3	.237	.302	.392
	7 ML YEARS		459	1171	265	55	3	36	(8	28)	434	145	145	94	3	346	11	32	7	20	6	.77	12	.226	.288	.371

Eric Karros

Bats: Right **Throws:** Right **Pos:** 1B **Ht:** 6' 4" **Wt:** 205 **Born:** 11/04/67 **Age:** 25

							BATTING										BASERUNNING				PERCENTAGES		
Year Team	Lg	G	AB	H	2B	3B	HR	(Hm	Rd)	TB	R	RBI	TBB	IBB	SO	HBP	SH	SF	SB	CS	SB%	GDP	Avg	OBP	SLG
1988 Great Falls	R	66	268	98	12	1	12	--	--	148	68	55	32	0	35	3	0	4	9	2	.82	7	.366	.433	.552
1989 Bakersfield	A	142	545	165	40	1	15	--	--	252	86	86	63	3	99	2	0	4	18	7	.72	15	.303	.375	.462
1990 San Antonio	AA	131	509	179	45	2	18	--	--	282	90	78	57	5	80	6	1	6	8	10	.44	18	.352	.419	.554
1991 Albuquerque	AAA	132	488	154	33	8	22	--	--	269	88	101	58	8	80	6	0	5	3	2	.60	6	.316	.391	.551
1991 Los Angeles	NL	14	14	1	1	0	0	(0	0)	2	0	1	1	0	6	0	0	0	0	0	.00	0	.071	.133	.143
1992 Los Angeles	NL	149	545	140	30	1	20	(6	14)	232	63	88	37	3	103	2	0	5	2	4	.33	15	.257	.304	.426
2 ML YEARS		163	559	141	31	1	20	(6	14)	234	63	89	38	3	109	2	0	5	2	4	.33	15	.252	.300	.419

Pat Kelly

Bats: Right **Throws:** Right **Pos:** 2B **Ht:** 6' 0" **Wt:** 180 **Born:** 10/14/67 **Age:** 25

							BATTING										BASERUNNING				PERCENTAGES		
Year Team	Lg	G	AB	H	2B	3B	HR	(Hm | Rd)	TB	R	RBI	TBB	IBB	SO	HBP	SH	SF	SB	CS	SB%	GDP	Avg	OBP	SLG
1988 Oneonta	A	71	280	92	11	6	2	--	--	121	49	34	16	0	45	5	5	1	25	6	.81	0	.329	.374	.432
1989 Pr William	A	124	436	116	21	7	3	--	--	160	61	45	32	1	79	8	4	7	31	9	.78	3	.266	.323	.367
1990 Albany	AA	126	418	113	19	6	8	--	--	168	67	44	37	1	79	6	5	4	31	14	.69	7	.270	.335	.402
1991 Columbus	AAA	31	116	39	9	2	3	--	--	61	27	19	9	1	16	0	1	0	8	2	.80	1	.336	.384	.526
1992 Albany	AA	2	6	0	0	0	0	--	--	0	1	0	2	0	4	0	0	0	0	0	.00	0	.000	.250	.000
1991 New York	AL	96	298	72	12	4	3	(3 | 0)	101	35	23	15	0	52	5	2	2	12	1	.92	5	.242	.288	.339
1992 New York	AL	106	318	72	22	2	7	(3 | 4)	119	38	27	25	1	72	10	6	3	8	5	.62	6	.226	.301	.374
2 ML YEARS		202	616	144	34	6	10	(6 | 4)	220	73	50	40	1	124	15	8	5	20	6	.77	11	.234	.294	.357

Roberto Kelly

Bats: Right **Throws:** Right **Pos:** CF/LF **Ht:** 6' 2" **Wt:** 192 **Born:** 10/01/64 **Age:** 28

							BATTING										BASERUNNING				PERCENTAGES		
Year Team	Lg	G	AB	H	2B	3B	HR	(Hm | Rd)	TB	R	RBI	TBB	IBB	SO	HBP	SH	SF	SB	CS	SB%	GDP	Avg	OBP	SLG
1987 New York	AL	23	52	14	3	0	1	(0 | 1)	20	12	7	5	0	15	0	1	1	9	3	.75	0	.269	.328	.385
1988 New York	AL	38	77	19	4	1	1	(1 | 0)	28	9	7	3	0	15	0	3	1	5	2	.71	0	.247	.272	.364
1989 New York	AL	137	441	133	18	3	9	(2 | 7)	184	65	48	41	3	89	6	8	0	35	12	.74	9	.302	.369	.417
1990 New York	AL	162	641	183	32	4	15	(5 | 10)	268	85	61	33	0	148	4	4	4	42	17	.71	7	.285	.323	.418
1991 New York	AL	126	486	130	22	2	20	(11 | 9)	216	68	69	45	2	77	5	2	5	32	9	.78	14	.267	.333	.444
1992 New York	AL	152	580	158	31	2	10	(6 | 4)	223	81	66	41	4	96	4	1	6	28	5	.85	19	.272	.322	.384
6 ML YEARS		638	2277	637	110	12	56	(25 | 31)	939	320	258	168	9	440	19	19	17	151	48	.76	49	.280	.332	.412

Jeff Kent

Bats: Right **Throws:** Right **Pos:** 2B/3B **Ht:** 6' 1" **Wt:** 185 **Born:** 03/07/68 **Age:** 25

							BATTING										BASERUNNING				PERCENTAGES		
Year Team	Lg	G	AB	H	2B	3B	HR	(Hm | Rd)	TB	R	RBI	TBB	IBB	SO	HBP	SH	SF	SB	CS	SB%	GDP	Avg	OBP	SLG
1989 St.Cathrnes	A	73	268	60	14	1	13	--	--	115	34	37	33	2	81	6	0	4	5	1	.83	2	.224	.318	.429
1990 Dunedin	A	132	447	124	32	2	16	--	--	208	72	60	53	5	98	6	3	3	17	7	.71	4	.277	.360	.465
1991 Knoxville	AA	139	445	114	34	1	12	--	--	186	68	61	80	2	104	10	2	3	25	6	.81	3	.256	.379	.418
1992 2 ML Teams		102	305	73	21	2	11	(4 | 7)	131	52	50	27	0	76	7	0	4	2	3	.40	5	.239	.312	.430
1992 Toronto	AL	65	192	46	13	1	8	(2 | 6)	85	36	35	20	0	47	6	0	4	2	1	.67	3	.240	.324	.443
New York	NL	37	113	27	8	1	3	(2 | 1)	46	16	15	7	0	29	1	0	0	0	2	.00	2	.239	.289	.407

Jimmy Key

Pitches: Left **Bats:** Right **Pos:** SP **Ht:** 6' 1" **Wt:** 185 **Born:** 04/22/61 **Age:** 32

		HOW MUCH HE PITCHED						WHAT HE GAVE UP											THE RESULTS				
Year Team	Lg	G	GS	CG	GF	IP	BFP	H	R	ER	HR	SH	SF	HB	TBB	IBB	SO	WP	Bk	W	L	Pct.	ShO	Sv	ERA
1984 Toronto	AL	63	0	0	24	62	285	70	37	32	8	6	1	1	32	8	44	3	1	4	5	.444	0	10	4.65
1985 Toronto	AL	35	32	3	0	212.2	856	188	77	71	22	5	5	2	50	1	85	6	1	14	6	.700	0	0	3.00
1986 Toronto	AL	36	35	4	0	232	959	222	98	92	24	10	6	3	74	1	141	3	0	14	11	.560	2	0	3.57
1987 Toronto	AL	36	36	8	0	261	1033	210	93	80	24	11	3	2	66	6	161	8	5	17	8	.680	1	0	2.76
1988 Toronto	AL	21	21	2	0	131.1	551	127	55	48	13	4	3	5	30	2	65	1	0	12	5	.706	2	0	3.29
1989 Toronto	AL	33	33	5	0	216	886	226	99	93	18	9	9	3	27	2	118	4	1	13	14	.481	1	0	3.88
1990 Toronto	AL	27	27	0	0	154.2	636	169	79	73	20	5	6	1	22	2	88	0	1	13	7	.650	0	0	4.25
1991 Toronto	AL	33	33	2	0	209.1	877	207	84	71	12	10	5	3	44	3	125	1	0	16	12	.571	2	0	3.05
1992 Toronto	AL	33	33	4	0	216.2	900	205	88	85	24	2	7	4	59	0	117	5	0	13	13	.500	2	0	3.53
9 ML YEARS		317	250	28	24	1695.2	6983	1624	710	645	165	62	45	24	404	25	944	31	9	116	81	.589	10	10	3.42

John Kiely

Pitches: Right **Bats:** Right **Pos:** RP   **Ht:** 6' 3" **Wt:** 210 **Born:** 10/04/64 **Age:** 28

			HOW MUCH HE PITCHED						WHAT HE GAVE UP										THE RESULTS					
Year Team	Lg	G	GS	CG	GF	IP	BFP	H	R	ER	HR	SH	SF	HB	TBB	IBB	SO	WP	Bk	W	L	Pct.	ShO	Sv	ERA
1988 Bristol	R	8	0	0	6	11.2	53	9	9	8	0	2	0	0	7	0	14	2	0	2	2	.500	0	1	6.17
1989 Lakeland	A	36	0	0	22	63.2	267	52	26	17	2	4	3	0	27	4	56	1	2	4	3	.571	0	8	2.40
1990 London	AA	46	0	0	25	76.2	321	63	17	15	2	2	4	2	42	6	52	2	0	3	0	1.000	0	12	1.76
1991 Toledo	AAA	42	0	0	27	72	301	57	25	17	3	4	2	3	35	3	60	2	0	4	2	.667	0	6	2.13
1992 Toledo	AAA	21	0	0	17	31.2	125	25	11	10	1	0	0	0	7	0	31	1	0	1	1	.500	0	9	2.84
1991 Detroit	AL	7	0	0	3	6.2	42	13	11	11	0	2	1	1	9	2	1	1	0	0	1	.000	0	0	14.85
1992 Detroit	AL	39	0	0	20	55	231	44	14	13	2	4	3	0	28	3	18	0	0	4	2	.667	0	0	2.13
2 ML YEARS		46	0	0	23	61.2	273	57	25	24	2	6	4	1	37	5	19	1	0	4	3	.571	0	0	3.50

Darryl Kile

Pitches: Right **Bats:** Right **Pos:** SP   **Ht:** 6' 5" **Wt:** 185 **Born:** 12/02/68 **Age:** 24

			HOW MUCH HE PITCHED						WHAT HE GAVE UP										THE RESULTS					
Year Team	Lg	G	GS	CG	GF	IP	BFP	H	R	ER	HR	SH	SF	HB	TBB	IBB	SO	WP	Bk	W	L	Pct.	ShO	Sv	ERA
1988 Astros	R	12	12	0	0	59.2	263	48	34	21	1	3	1	3	33	0	54	9	8	5	3	.625	0	0	3.17
1989 Columbus	AA	20	20	6	0	125.2	508	74	47	36	5	3	4	6	68	1	108	5	6	11	6	.647	2	0	2.58
Tucson	AAA	6	6	1	0	25.2	122	33	20	17	1	0	0	1	13	0	18	1	1	2	1	.667	1	0	5.96
1990 Tucson	AAA	26	23	1	1	123.1	575	147	97	91	16	2	5	5	68	1	77	13	4	5	10	.333	0	0	6.64
1992 Tucson	AAA	9	9	0	0	56.1	250	50	31	25	3	0	2	3	32	0	43	4	2	4	1	.800	0	0	3.99
1991 Houston	NL	37	22	0	5	153.2	689	144	63	63	16	9	5	6	84	4	100	5	4	7	11	.389	0	0	3.69
1992 Houston	NL	22	22	2	0	125.1	554	124	61	55	8	5	6	4	63	4	90	3	4	5	10	.333	0	0	3.95
2 ML YEARS		59	44	2	5	279	1243	268	142	118	24	14	11	10	147	8	190	8	8	12	21	.364	0	0	3.81

Eric King

Pitches: Right **Bats:** Right **Pos:** SP   **Ht:** 6' 2" **Wt:** 218 **Born:** 04/10/64 **Age:** 29

			HOW MUCH HE PITCHED						WHAT HE GAVE UP										THE RESULTS					
Year Team	Lg	G	GS	CG	GF	IP	BFP	H	R	ER	HR	SH	SF	HB	TBB	IBB	SO	WP	Bk	W	L	Pct.	ShO	Sv	ERA
1986 Detroit	AL	33	16	3	9	138.1	579	108	54	54	11	6	1	8	63	3	79	4	3	11	4	.733	1	3	3.51
1987 Detroit	AL	55	4	0	26	116	513	111	67	63	15	3	3	4	60	10	89	5	1	6	9	.400	0	9	4.89
1988 Detroit	AL	23	5	0	8	68.2	303	60	28	26	5	5	2	5	34	2	45	4	2	4	1	.800	0	3	3.41
1989 Chicago	AL	25	25	1	0	159.1	666	144	69	60	13	3	4	4	64	1	72	5	4	9	10	.474	1	0	3.39
1990 Chicago	AL	25	25	2	0	151	623	135	59	55	6	1		6	40	0	70	2	3	12	4	.750	2	0	3.28
1991 Cleveland	AL	25	24	2	0	150.2	656	166	83	77	7	7	8	3	44	4	59	2	2	6	11	.353	1	0	4.60
1992 Detroit	AL	17	14	0	2	79.1	348	90	47	46	12	1	2	1	28	1	45	3	0	4	6	.400	0	1	5.22
7 ML YEARS		203	113	8	45	863.1	3688	814	407	381	73	31	21	31	333	21	459	25	15	52	45	.536	5	16	3.97

Jeff King

Bats: Right **Throws:** Right **Pos:** 3B/1B/2B   **Ht:** 6' 1" **Wt:** 180 **Born:** 12/26/64 **Age:** 28

			BATTING															BASERUNNING				PERCENTAGES		
Year Team	Lg	G	AB	H	2B	3B	HR	(Hm	Rd)	TB	R	RBI	TBB	IBB	SO	HBP	SH	SF	SB	CS	SB%	GDP	Avg	OBP	SLG
1989 Pittsburgh	NL	75	215	42	13	3	5	(3	2)	76	31	19	20	1	34	2	2	4	4	2	.67	3	.195	.266	.353
1990 Pittsburgh	NL	127	371	91	17	1	14	(9	5)	152	46	53	21	1	50	1	2	7	3	3	.50	12	.245	.283	.410
1991 Pittsburgh	NL	33	109	26	4	1	4	(3	1)	41	16	18	14	3	15	1	0	1	3	1	.75	3	.239	.328	.376
1992 Pittsburgh	NL	130	480	111	21	2	14	(6	8)	178	56	65	27	3	56	2	8	5	4	6	.40	8	.231	.272	.371
4 ML YEARS		365	1175	270	52	7	37	(21	16)	447	149	155	82	8	155	6	12	17	14	12	.54	26	.230	.280	.380

Mike Kingery

Bats: Left **Throws:** Left **Pos:** CF   **Ht:** 6' 0" **Wt:** 185 **Born:** 03/29/61 **Age:** 32

			BATTING															BASERUNNING				PERCENTAGES		
Year Team	Lg	G	AB	H	2B	3B	HR	(Hm	Rd)	TB	R	RBI	TBB	IBB	SO	HBP	SH	SF	SB	CS	SB%	GDP	Avg	OBP	SLG
1986 Kansas City	AL	62	209	54	8	5	3	(1	2)	81	25	14	12	2	30	0	0	2	7	3	.70	4	.258	.296	.388
1987 Seattle	AL	120	354	99	25	4	9	(5	4)	159	38	52	27	0	43	2	1	6	7	9	.44	4	.280	.329	.449
1988 Seattle	AL	57	123	25	6	0	1	(1	0)	34	21	9	19	1	23	1	1	1	3	1	.75	1	.203	.313	.276
1989 Seattle	AL	31	76	17	3	0	2	(2	0)	26	14	6	7	0	14	0	0	1	1	1	.50	2	.224	.286	.342
1990 San Francisco	NL	105	207	61	7	1	0	(0	0)	70	24	24	12	0	19	1	5	1	6	1	.86	1	.295	.335	.338
1991 San Francisco	NL	91	110	20	2	2	0	(0	0)	26	13	8	15	1	21	0	0	0	1	0	1.00	3	.182	.280	.236
1992 Oakland	AL	12	28	3	0	0	0	(0	0)	3	3	1	1	0	3	0	0	0	0	0	.00	1	.107	.138	.107
7 ML YEARS		478	1107	279	51	12	15	(9	6)	399	138	114	93	4	153	4	7	11	25	15	.63	16	.252	.309	.360

Bob Kipper

Pitches: Left **Bats:** Right **Pos:** RP   **Ht:** 6' 2" **Wt:** 185 **Born:** 07/08/64 **Age:** 28

			HOW MUCH HE PITCHED						WHAT HE GAVE UP										THE RESULTS					
Year Team	Lg	G	GS	CG	GF	IP	BFP	H	R	ER	HR	SH	SF	HB	TBB	IBB	SO	WP	Bk	W	L	Pct.	ShO	Sv	ERA
1985 2 ML Teams		7	5	0	1	28	124	28	24	22	5	1	3	0	10	0	13	0	0	1	3	.250	0	0	7.07

Year	Team	Lg	G	GS	CG	GF	IP	BFP	H	R	ER	HR	SH	SF	HB	TBB	IBB	SO	WP	Bk	W	L	Pct.	ShO	Sv	ERA
1986	Pittsburgh	NL	20	19	0	1	114	496	123	60	51	17	3	3	2	34	3	81	3	3	6	8	.429	0	0	4.03
1987	Pittsburgh	NL	24	20	1	0	110.2	493	117	74	73	25	4	3	2	52	4	83	5	0	5	9	.357	1	0	5.94
1988	Pittsburgh	NL	50	0	0	15	65	267	54	33	27	7	5	3	2	26	4	39	1	1	2	6	.250	0	0	3.74
1989	Pittsburgh	NL	52	0	0	15	83	334	55	29	27	5	5	3	0	33	6	58	5	2	3	4	.429	0	4	2.93
1990	Pittsburgh	NL	41	1	0	7	62.2	260	44	24	21	7	2	3	3	26	1	35	1	5	5	2	.714	0	3	3.02
1991	Pittsburgh	NL	52	0	0	18	60	264	66	34	31	7	1	2	0	22	3	38	0	1	2	2	.500	0	4	4.65
1992	Minnesota	AL	25	0	0	12	38.2	168	40	23	19	8	2	0	3	14	3	22	1	0	3	3	.500	0	0	4.42
1985	California	AL	2	1	0	0	3.1	20	7	8	8	1	0	2	0	3	0	0	0	0	0	1	.000	0	0	21.60
	Pittsburgh	NL	5	4	0	1	24.2	104	21	16	14	4	1	1	0	7	0	13	0	0	1	2	.333	0	0	5.11
	8 ML YEARS		271	45	1	69	562	2406	527	301	271	81	23	20	12	217	24	369	16	12	27	37	.422	1	11	4.34

Wayne Kirby

Bats: Left **Throws:** Right **Pos:** DH **Ht:** 5'10" **Wt:** 185 **Born:** 01/22/64 **Age:** 29

						BATTING												BASERUNNING				PERCENTAGES		
Year	Team	Lg	G	AB	H	2B	3B	HR	(Hm | Rd)	TB	R	RBI	TBB	IBB	SO	HBP	SH	SF	SB	CS	SB%	GDP	Avg	OBP	SLG
1984	Vero Beach	A	76	224	61	6	3	0	--	--	73	39	21	21	2	30	6	5	2	11	9	.55	3	.272	.348	.326
	Great Falls	R	20	84	26	2	2	1	--	--	35	19	11	12	2	9	0	1	1	19	3	.86	2	.310	.392	.417
	Bakersfield	A	23	84	23	3	0	0	--	--	26	14	10	4	0	5	0	2	1	8	3	.73	0	.274	.303	.310
1985	Vero Beach	A	122	437	123	9	3	0	--	--	138	70	28	41	1	41	3	4	3	31	14	.69	3	.281	.345	.316
1986	Vero Beach	A	114	387	101	9	4	2	--	--	124	60	31	37	3	30	1	2	2	28	17	.62	5	.261	.326	.320
1987	San Antonio	AA	24	80	19	1	2	1	--	--	27	7	9	4	0	7	0	3	0	6	4	.60	0	.238	.274	.338
	Bakersfield	A	105	416	112	14	3	0	--	--	132	77	34	49	1	41	3	5	2	56	21	.73	3	.269	.349	.317
1988	Bakersfield	A	12	47	13	0	1	0	--	--	15	12	4	11	0	4	0	0	0	9	2	.82	0	.277	.414	.319
	San Antonio	AA	100	334	80	9	2	0	--	--	93	50	21	21	2	42	3	10	1	26	10	.72	5	.240	.290	.278
1989	San Antonio	AA	44	140	30	3	1	0	--	--	35	14	7	18	0	17	1	2	1	11	6	.65	4	.214	.306	.250
	Albuquerque	AAA	78	310	106	18	8	0	--	--	140	62	30	26	1	27	1	5	1	29	14	.67	2	.342	.393	.452
1990	Albuquerque	AAA	119	342	95	14	5	0	--	--	119	56	30	28	1	36	3	4	3	29	7	.81	2	.278	.335	.348
1991	Colo Spmgs	AAA	118	385	113	14	4	1	--	--	138	66	39	34	2	36	2	5	3	29	14	.67	3	.294	.351	.358
1992	Colo Spmgs	AAA	123	470	162	18	16	11	--	--	245	101	74	36	4	28	2	4	2	51	20	.72	7	.345	.392	.521
1991	Cleveland	AL	21	43	9	2	0	1	(0 | 0)	11	4	5	2	0	6	0	1	1	1	2	.33	2	.209	.239	.256
1992	Cleveland	AL	21	18	3	1	0	1	(0 | 1)	7	9	1	3	0	2	0	0	0	0	3	.00	1	.167	.286	.389
	2 ML YEARS		42	61	12	3	0	1	(0 | 1)	18	13	6	5	0	8	0	1	1	1	5	.17	3	.197	.254	.295

Ryan Klesko

Bats: Left **Throws:** Left **Pos:** 1B **Ht:** 6'3" **Wt:** 220 **Born:** 06/12/71 **Age:** 22

						BATTING												BASERUNNING				PERCENTAGES		
Year	Team	Lg	G	AB	H	2B	3B	HR	(Hm | Rd)	TB	R	RBI	TBB	IBB	SO	HBP	SH	SF	SB	CS	SB%	GDP	Avg	OBP	SLG
1989	Braves	R	17	57	23	5	4	1	--	--	39	14	16	6	2	6	0	0	1	4	3	.57	2	.404	.453	.684
	Sumter	A	25	90	26	6	0	1	--	--	35	17	12	11	1	14	0	1	1	1	0	1.00	6	.289	.363	.389
1990	Sumter	A	63	231	85	15	1	10	--	--	132	41	38	31	5	30	1	0	5	13	1	.93	6	.368	.437	.571
	Durham	A	77	292	80	16	1	7	--	--	119	40	47	32	4	53	2	0	6	10	5	.67	8	.274	.343	.408
1991	Greenville	AA	126	419	122	22	3	14	--	--	192	64	67	75	14	60	6	3	3	14	17	.45	5	.291	.404	.458
1992	Richmond	AAA	123	418	105	22	2	17	--	--	182	63	59	41	6	72	4	1	2	3	5	.38	14	.251	.323	.435
1992	Atlanta	NL	13	14	0	0	0	0	(0 | 0)	0	0	1	1	0	5	0	0	0	0	0	.00	0	.000	.067	.000

Joe Klink

Pitches: Left **Bats:** Left **Pos:** RP **Ht:** 5'11" **Wt:** 175 **Born:** 02/03/62 **Age:** 31

						HOW MUCH HE PITCHED				WHAT HE GAVE UP									THE RESULTS				
Year	Team	Lg	G	GS	CG	GF	IP	BFP	H	R	ER	HR	SH	SF	HB	TBB	IBB	SO	WP	Bk	W	L	Pct.	ShO	Sv	ERA
1987	Minnesota	AL	23	0	0	5	23	116	37	18	17	4	1	1	0	11	0	17	1	0	0	0	.000	0	0	6.65
1990	Oakland	AL	40	0	0	19	39.2	165	34	9	9	1	1	0	0	18	0	19	3	1	0	0	.000	0	1	2.04
1991	Oakland	AL	62	0	0	10	62	266	60	30	30	4	8	0	5	21	5	34	4	0	10	3	.769	0	2	4.35
	3 ML YEARS		114	0	0	34	124.2	547	131	57	56	9	10	1	5	50	5	70	8	1	10	4	.714	0	3	4.04

Chuck Knoblauch

Bats: Right **Throws:** Right **Pos:** 2B **Ht:** 5'9" **Wt:** 179 **Born:** 07/07/68 **Age:** 24

						BATTING												BASERUNNING				PERCENTAGES		
Year	Team	Lg	G	AB	H	2B	3B	HR	(Hm | Rd)	TB	R	RBI	TBB	IBB	SO	HBP	SH	SF	SB	CS	SB%	GDP	Avg	OBP	SLG
1989	Kenosha	A	51	196	56	13	1	2	--	--	77	29	19	32	0	23	1	1	1	9	7	.56	5	.286	.387	.393
	Visalia	A	18	77	28	10	0	0	--	--	38	20	21	6	0	11	1	1	1	4	0	1.00	0	.364	.412	.494
1990	Orlando	AA	118	432	125	24	6	2	--	--	167	74	53	63	0	31	9	2	3	23	7	.77	13	.289	.389	.387
1991	Minnesota	AL	151	565	159	24	6	1	(1 | 0)	198	78	50	59	0	40	4	1	5	25	5	.83	8	.281	.351	.350
1992	Minnesota	AL	155	600	178	19	6	2	(0 | 2)	215	104	56	88	1	60	5	2	12	34	13	.72	8	.297	.384	.358
	2 ML YEARS		306	1165	337	43	12	3	(1 | 2)	413	182	106	147	1	100	9	3	17	59	18	.77	16	.289	.368	.355

Randy Knorr

Bats: Right **Throws:** Right **Pos:** C　　　　**Ht:** 6' 2" **Wt:** 205 **Born:** 11/12/68 **Age:** 24

							BATTING												BASERUNNING				PERCENTAGES		
Year	Team	Lg	G	AB	H	2B	3B	HR	(Hm	Rd)	TB	R	RBI	TBB	IBB	SO	HBP	SH	SF	SB	CS	SB%	GDP	Avg	OBP	SLG
1986	Medicne Hat	R	55	215	58	13	0	4	--	--	83	21	32	17	0	53	0	3	3	0	0	.00	6	.270	.319	.386
1987	Medicne Hat	R	26	106	31	7	0	10	--	--	68	21	24	5	3	26	1	0	3	0	0	.00	1	.292	.322	.642
	Myrtle Bch	A	46	129	34	4	0	6	--	--	56	17	21	6	0	46	0	0	0	0	0	.00	1	.264	.292	.434
1988	Myrtle Bch	A	117	364	85	13	0	9	--	--	125	43	42	41	0	91	0	9	2	0	1	.00	7	.234	.310	.343
1989	Dunedin	A	33	122	32	6	0	6	--	--	56	13	23	6	0	21	0	0	2	0	2	.00	0	.262	.292	.459
1990	Knoxville	AA	116	392	108	12	1	13	--	--	161	51	64	31	2	83	2	4	6	0	3	.00	7	.276	.327	.411
1991	Knoxville	AA	24	74	13	4	0	0	--	--	17	7	4	10	1	18	1	0	1	2	0	1.00	0	.176	.279	.230
	Syracuse	AAA	91	342	89	20	0	5	--	--	124	29	44	23	3	58	3	0	4	1	0	1.00	17	.260	.309	.363
1992	Syracuse	AAA	61	228	62	13	1	11	--	--	110	27	27	17	1	38	0	0	3	1	0	1.00	5	.272	.319	.482
1991	Toronto	AL	3	1	0	0	0	0	(0	0)	0	0	0	1	0	1	0	0	0	0	0	.00	0	.000	.500	.000
1992	Toronto	AL	8	19	5	0	0	1	(0	1)	8	1	2	1	1	5	0	0	0	0	0	.00	0	.263	.300	.421
	2 ML YEARS		11	20	5	0	0	1	(0	1)	8	1	2	2	1	6	0	0	0	0	0	.00	0	.250	.318	.400

Kurt Knudsen

Pitches: Right **Bats:** Right **Pos:** RP　　　　**Ht:** 6' 3" **Wt:** 200 **Born:** 02/20/67 **Age:** 26

			HOW MUCH HE PITCHED						WHAT HE GAVE UP									THE RESULTS				
Year	Team	Lg	G	GS	CG	GF	IP	BFP	H	R	ER	HR	SH	SF	HB	TBB	IBB	SO	WP	Bk	W	L	Pct.	ShO	Sv	ERA
1988	Bristol	R	2	0	0	2	2.1	14	4	3	0	0	0	0	0	1	0	0	0	0	0	0	.000	0	0	0.00
	Fayettevlle	A	12	0	0	5	20	77	8	4	3	1	2	1	1	9	1	22	1	1	3	1	.750	0	1	1.35
	Lakeland	A	7	0	0	4	9.1	39	7	2	1	0	0	0	0	7	0	6	2	0	0	0	.000	0	0	0.96
1989	Lakeland	A	45	0	0	26	54.1	225	43	16	13	1	5	2	1	22	7	68	2	3	3	2	.600	0	10	2.15
1990	Lakeland	A	14	8	0	5	67	253	42	18	17	2	2	1	0	22	0	70	5	2	5	0	1.000	0	3	2.28
	London	AA	15	0	0	8	26	102	15	6	6	1	0	1	2	11	0	26	2	1	2	1	.667	0	1	2.08
1991	London	AA	34	0	0	18	51.2	226	42	29	20	1	4	5	1	30	2	56	4	1	2	3	.400	0	6	3.48
	Toledo	AAA	12	0	0	3	18.1	79	13	3	3	1	0	0	0	10	1	28	2	0	1	2	.333	0	0	1.47
1992	Toledo	AAA	12	0	0	8	21.2	82	11	5	5	1	1	1	1	6	0	19	1	0	3	1	.750	0	1	2.08
1992	Detroit	AL	48	1	0	14	70.2	313	70	39	36	9	4	2	1	41	9	51	5	0	2	3	.400	0	5	4.58

Kevin Koslofski

Bats: Left **Throws:** Right **Pos:** RF/LF/CF　　　　**Ht:** 5' 8" **Wt:** 165 **Born:** 09/24/66 **Age:** 26

							BATTING												BASERUNNING				PERCENTAGES		
Year	Team	Lg	G	AB	H	2B	3B	HR	(Hm	Rd)	TB	R	RBI	TBB	IBB	SO	HBP	SH	SF	SB	CS	SB%	GDP	Avg	OBP	SLG
1984	Eugene	A	53	155	29	2	2	1	--	--	38	23	10	25	0	37	0	1	1	10	2	.83	3	.187	.298	.245
1985	Royals	R	33	108	27	4	2	0	--	--	35	17	11	12	0	19	3	2	0	7	2	.78	1	.250	.341	.324
1986	Ft. Myers	A	103	331	84	13	5	0	--	--	107	44	29	47	2	59	2	7	4	12	6	.67	6	.254	.346	.323
1987	Ft. Myers	A	109	330	80	12	3	0	--	--	98	46	25	46	3	64	7	3	2	25	9	.74	4	.242	.345	.297
1988	Baseball Cy	A	108	368	97	7	8	3	--	--	129	52	30	44	5	71	4	4	2	32	11	.74	4	.264	.347	.351
1989	Baseball Cy	A	116	343	89	10	3	4	--	--	117	65	33	51	2	57	5	5	3	41	14	.75	9	.259	.361	.341
1990	Memphis	AA	118	367	78	11	5	3	--	--	108	52	32	54	1	89	2	7	3	12	7	.63	4	.213	.315	.294
1991	Memphis	AA	81	287	93	15	3	7	--	--	135	41	39	33	3	56	4	4	4	10	13	.43	2	.324	.396	.470
	Omaha	AAA	25	94	28	3	2	2	--	--	41	13	19	15	0	19	1	2	1	4	3	.57	1	.298	.396	.436
1992	Omaha	AAA	78	280	87	12	5	4	--	--	121	29	32	21	3	47	2	7	1	8	3	.73	2	.311	.362	.432
1992	Kansas City	AL	55	133	33	0	2	3	(1	2)	46	20	13	12	0	23	1	3	1	2	1	.67	2	.248	.313	.346

Randy Kramer

Pitches: Right **Bats:** Right **Pos:** SP　　　　**Ht:** 6' 2" **Wt:** 180 **Born:** 09/20/60 **Age:** 32

			HOW MUCH HE PITCHED						WHAT HE GAVE UP									THE RESULTS				
Year	Team	Lg	G	GS	CG	GF	IP	BFP	H	R	ER	HR	SH	SF	HB	TBB	IBB	SO	WP	Bk	W	L	Pct.	ShO	Sv	ERA
1988	Pittsburgh	NL	5	1	0	1	10	42	12	6	6	1	1	1	1	1	0	7	1	0	1	2	.333	0	0	5.40
1989	Pittsburgh	NL	35	15	1	7	111.1	482	90	53	49	10	9	4	7	61	4	52	1	0	5	9	.357	1	2	3.96
1990	2 ML Teams		22	4	0	6	46	207	47	25	23	6	5	0	3	21	6	27	0	0	0	3	.000	0	0	4.50
1992	Seattle	AL	4	4	0	0	16.1	84	30	14	14	2	1	0	1	7	0	6	0	0	0	1	.000	0	0	7.71
1990	Pittsburgh	NL	12	2	0	2	25.2	112	27	15	14	3	2	0	2	9	4	15	0	0	0	1	.000	0	0	4.91
	Chicago	NL	10	2	0	4	20.1	95	20	10	9	3	3	0	1	12	2	12	0	0	0	2	.000	0	0	3.98
	4 ML YEARS		66	24	1	14	183.2	815	179	98	92	19	16	5	12	90	10	92	2	0	6	15	.286	1	2	4.51

Chad Kreuter

Bats: Both **Throws:** Right **Pos:** C　　　　**Ht:** 6' 2" **Wt:** 190 **Born:** 08/26/64 **Age:** 28

							BATTING												BASERUNNING				PERCENTAGES		
Year	Team	Lg	G	AB	H	2B	3B	HR	(Hm	Rd)	TB	R	RBI	TBB	IBB	SO	HBP	SH	SF	SB	CS	SB%	GDP	Avg	OBP	SLG
1988	Texas	AL	16	51	14	2	1	1	(0	1)	21	3	5	7	0	13	0	0	0	0	0	.00	1	.275	.362	.412
1989	Texas	AL	87	158	24	3	0	5	(2	3)	42	16	9	27	0	40	0	6	1	0	1	.00	4	.152	.274	.266
1990	Texas	AL	22	22	1	1	0	0	(0	0)	2	2	2	8	0	9	0	1	1	0	0	.00	0	.045	.290	.091
1991	Texas	AL	3	4	0	0	0	0	(0	0)	0	0	0	0	0	1	0	0	0	0	0	.00	0	.000	.000	.000

Year	Team	Lg	G	AB	H	2B	3B	HR	(Hm	Rd)	TB	R	RBI	TBB	IBB	SO	HBP	SH	SF	SB	CS	SB%	GDP	Avg	OBP	SLG
1992	Detroit	AL	67	190	48	9	0	2	(2	0)	63	22	16	20	1	38	0	3	2	0	1	.00	8	.253	.321	.332
	5 ML YEARS		195	425	87	15	1	8	(4	4)	128	43	32	62	1	101	0	10	4	0	2	.00	13	.205	.303	.301

Bill Krueger

Pitches: Left Bats: Left Pos: SP/RP **Ht: 6' 5" Wt: 205 Born: 04/24/58 Age: 35**

Year	Team	Lg	G	GS	CG	GF	IP	BFP	H	R	ER	HR	SH	SF	HB	TBB	IBB	SO	WP	Bk	W	L	Pct.	ShO	Sv	ERA
1983	Oakland	AL	17	16	2	0	109.2	473	104	54	44	7	0	5	2	53	1	58	1	1	7	6	.538	0	0	3.61
1984	Oakland	AL	26	24	1	0	142	647	156	95	75	9	4	8	2	85	2	61	5	1	10	10	.500	0	0	4.75
1985	Oakland	AL	32	23	2	4	151.1	674	165	95	76	13	1	5	2	69	1	56	6	3	9	10	.474	0	0	4.52
1986	Oakland	AL	11	3	0	4	34.1	149	40	25	23	4	1	2	0	13	0	10	3	1	1	2	.333	0	1	6.03
1987	2 ML Teams		11	0	0	1	8	46	12	9	6	0	0	0	0	9	3	4	0	1	0	3	.000	0	0	6.75
1988	Los Angeles	NL	1	1	0	0	2.1	14	4	3	3	0	0	0	1	2	1	1	0	0	0	0	.000	0	0	11.57
1989	Milwaukee	AL	34	5	0	8	93.2	403	96	43	40	9	5	1	0	33	3	72	10	1	3	2	.600	0	3	3.84
1990	Milwaukee	AL	30	17	0	4	129	566	137	70	57	10	3	10	3	54	6	64	8	0	6	8	.429	0	0	3.98
1991	Seattle	AL	35	25	1	2	175	751	194	82	70	15	6	9	4	60	4	91	10	1	11	8	.579	0	0	3.60
1992	2 ML Teams		36	29	2	3	178.2	765	189	95	90	18	4	1	4	53	2	99	12	0	10	8	.556	2	0	4.53
1987	Oakland	AL	9	0	0	1	5.2	33	9	7	6	0	0	0	0	8	3	2	0	1	0	3	.000	0	0	9.53
	Los Angeles	NL	2	0	0	0	2.1	13	3	2	0	0	0	0	0	1	0	2	0	0	0	0	.000	0	0	0.00
1992	Minnesota	AL	27	27	2	0	161.1	684	166	82	77	18	4	1	3	46	2	86	11	0	10	6	.625	2	0	4.30
	Montreal	NL	9	2	0	3	17.1	81	23	13	13	0	0	0	1	7	0	13	1	0	0	2	.000	0	0	6.75
	10 ML YEARS		233	143	8	26	1024	4488	1097	571	484	85	24	41	18	431	23	516	55	9	57	57	.500	2	4	4.25

John Kruk

Bats: Left Throws: Left Pos: 1B/RF **Ht: 5'10" Wt: 200 Born: 02/09/61 Age: 32**

Year	Team	Lg	G	AB	H	2B	3B	HR	(Hm	Rd)	TB	R	RBI	TBB	IBB	SO	HBP	SH	SF	SB	CS	SB%	GDP	Avg	OBP	SLG
1986	San Diego	NL	122	278	86	16	2	4	(1	3)	118	33	38	45	0	58	0	2	2	2	4	.33	11	.309	.403	.424
1987	San Diego	NL	138	447	140	14	2	20	(8	12)	218	72	91	73	15	93	0	3	4	18	10	.64	6	.313	.406	.488
1988	San Diego	NL	120	378	91	17	1	9	(8	1)	137	54	44	80	12	68	0	3	5	5	3	.63	7	.241	.369	.362
1989	2 ML Teams		112	357	107	13	6	8	(6	2)	156	53	44	44	2	53	0	2	3	3	0	1.00	10	.300	.374	.437
1990	Philadelphia	NL	142	443	129	25	8	7	(2	5)	191	52	67	69	16	70	0	2	1	10	5	.67	11	.291	.386	.431
1991	Philadelphia	NL	152	538	158	27	6	21	(8	13)	260	84	92	67	16	100	1	0	9	7	0	1.00	11	.294	.367	.483
1992	Philadelphia	NL	144	507	164	30	4	10	(7	3)	232	86	70	92	8	88	1	0	7	3	5	.38	11	.323	.423	.458
1989	San Diego	NL	31	76	14	0	0	3	(2	1)	23	7	6	17	0	14	0	1	0	0	0	.00	5	.184	.333	.303
	Philadelphia	NL	81	281	93	13	6	5	(4	1)	133	46	38	27	2	39	0	1	3	3	0	1.00	5	.331	.386	.473
	7 ML YEARS		930	2948	875	142	29	79	(40	39)	1312	434	446	470	69	530	2	12	31	48	27	.64	67	.297	.390	.445

Jeff Kunkel

Bats: Right Throws: Right Pos: SS **Ht: 6' 2" Wt: 180 Born: 03/25/62 Age: 31**

Year	Team	Lg	G	AB	H	2B	3B	HR	(Hm	Rd)	TB	R	RBI	TBB	IBB	SO	HBP	SH	SF	SB	CS	SB%	GDP	Avg	OBP	SLG
1984	Texas	AL	50	142	29	2	3	3	(1	2)	46	13	7	2	0	35	1	3	2	4	3	.57	2	.204	.218	.324
1985	Texas	AL	2	4	1	0	0	0	(0	0)	1	1	0	0	0	3	0	0	0	0	0	.00	0	.250	.250	.250
1986	Texas	AL	8	13	3	0	0	1	(1	0)	6	3	2	0	0	2	0	0	0	0	0	.00	0	.231	.231	.462
1987	Texas	AL	15	32	7	0	0	1	(0	1)	10	1	2	0	0	10	1	1	0	0	1	.00	0	.219	.242	.313
1988	Texas	AL	55	154	35	8	3	2	(2	0)	55	14	15	4	1	35	1	1	1	0	1	.00	5	.227	.250	.357
1989	Texas	AL	108	293	79	21	2	8	(8	0)	128	39	29	20	0	75	3	10	0	3	2	.60	6	.270	.323	.437
1990	Texas	AL	99	200	34	11	1	3	(1	2)	56	17	17	11	0	66	2	5	0	2	1	.67	7	.170	.221	.280
1992	Chicago	NL	20	29	4	2	0	0	(0	0)	6	0	1	0	0	8	0	0	0	0	0	.00	1	.138	.138	.207
	8 ML YEARS		357	867	192	44	9	18	(13	5)	308	88	73	37	1	234	8	20	3	9	8	.53	21	.221	.259	.355

Steve Lake

Bats: Right Throws: Right Pos: C **Ht: 6' 1" Wt: 202 Born: 03/14/57 Age: 36**

Year	Team	Lg	G	AB	H	2B	3B	HR	(Hm	Rd)	TB	R	RBI	TBB	IBB	SO	HBP	SH	SF	SB	CS	SB%	GDP	Avg	OBP	SLG
1983	Chicago	NL	38	85	22	4	1	1	(1	0)	31	9	7	2	2	6	1	0	0	0	0	.00	4	.259	.284	.365
1984	Chicago	NL	25	54	12	4	0	2	(1	1)	22	4	7	0	0	7	1	1	1	0	0	.00	0	.222	.232	.407
1985	Chicago	NL	58	119	18	2	0	1	(1	0)	23	5	11	3	1	21	1	4	1	1	0	1.00	3	.151	.177	.193
1986	2 ML Teams		36	68	20	2	0	2	(0	2)	28	8	14	3	1	7	0	1	0	0	0	.00	3	.294	.324	.412
1987	St. Louis	NL	74	179	45	7	2	2	(1	1)	62	19	19	10	4	18	0	5	1	0	0	.00	2	.251	.289	.346
1988	St. Louis	NL	36	54	15	3	0	1	(1	0)	21	5	4	3	0	15	2	0	0	0	0	.00	0	.278	.339	.389
1989	Philadelphia	NL	58	155	39	5	1	2	(1	1)	52	19	14	12	4	20	0	1	1	0	0	.00	6	.252	.304	.335
1990	Philadelphia	NL	29	80	20	2	0	0	(0	0)	22	4	6	3	1	12	1	0	0	0	0	.00	0	.250	.286	.275
1991	Philadelphia	NL	58	158	36	4	1	1	(0	1)	45	12	11	7	2	26	0	4	0	0	0	.00	9	.228	.238	.285
1992	Philadelphia	NL	20	53	13	2	0	1	(0	1)	18	3	2	1	0	9	0	0	0	0	0	.00	0	.245	.255	.340
1986	Chicago	NL	10	19	8	1	0	0	(0	0)	9	4	4	1	1	2	0	1	0	0	0	.00	1	.421	.450	.474
	St. Louis	NL	26	49	12	1	0	2	(0	2)	19	4	10	2	0	5	0	0	0	0	0	.00	2	.245	.275	.388

| 10 ML YEARS | 432 1005 240 | 35 5 13 | (7 6) 324 | 78 95 39 14 140 | 6 16 5 | 1 0 1.00 25 | .239 .270 .322 |

Tim Laker

Bats: Right **Throws:** Right **Pos:** C **Ht:** 6' 2" **Wt:** 175 **Born:** 11/27/69 **Age:** 23

						BATTING											BASERUNNING			PERCENTAGES		
Year Team	Lg	G	AB	H	2B	3B	HR	(Hm	Rd)	TB	R	RBI	TBB	IBB	SO	HBP	SH	SF	SB	CS	SB%	GDP	Avg	OBP	SLG
1988 Jamestown	A	47	152	34	9	0	0	--	--	43	14	17	8	0	30	0	2	1	2	1	.67	4	.224	.261	.283
1989 Rockford	A	14	48	11	1	1	0	--	--	14	4	4	3	0	6	0	0	0	1	0	1.00	1	.229	.275	.292
Jamestown	A	58	216	48	9	1	2	--	--	65	25	24	16	1	40	2	0	3	8	4	.67	4	.222	.278	.301
1990 Rockford	A	120	425	94	18	3	7	--	--	139	46	57	32	1	83	1	1	8	7	2	.78	9	.221	.273	.327
Wst Plm Bch	A	2	3	0	0	0	0	--	--	0	0	0	0	0	1	0	0	0	0	0	.00	0	.000	.000	.000
1991 Harrisburg	AA	11	35	10	1	0	1	--	--	14	4	5	2	0	5	1	0	0	0	1	.00	1	.286	.342	.400
Wst Plm Bch	A	100	333	77	15	2	5	--	--	111	36	33	22	0	52	2	0	4	10	1	.91	9	.231	.280	.333
1992 Harrisburg	AA	117	409	99	19	3	15	--	--	169	55	68	39	2	89	5	0	5	3	1	.75	10	.242	.312	.413
1992 Montreal	NL	28	46	10	3	0	0	(0	0)	13	8	4	2	0	14	0	0	0	1	1	.50	1	.217	.250	.283

Dennis Lamp

Pitches: Right **Bats:** Right **Pos:** RP **Ht:** 6' 3" **Wt:** 215 **Born:** 09/23/52 **Age:** 40

			HOW MUCH HE PITCHED					WHAT HE GAVE UP										THE RESULTS					
Year Team	Lg	G	GS	CG	GF	IP	BFP	H	R	ER	HR	SH	SF	HB	TBB	IBB	SO	WP	Bk	W	L	Pct.	ShO	Sv	ERA
1977 Chicago	NL	11	3	0	4	30	137	43	21	21	3	1	1	2	8	4	12	0	1	0	2	.000	0	0	6.30
1978 Chicago	NL	37	36	6	0	224	928	221	96	82	16	10	3	4	56	8	73	2	2	7	15	.318	3	0	3.29
1979 Chicago	NL	38	32	6	3	200	843	223	96	78	14	9	5	5	46	9	86	1	0	11	10	.524	1	0	3.51
1980 Chicago	NL	41	37	2	3	203	921	259	123	117	16	17	4	1	82	7	83	10	0	10	14	.417	1	0	5.19
1981 Chicago	AL	27	10	3	5	127	514	103	41	34	4	5	0	1	43	1	71	4	1	7	6	.538	0	0	2.41
1982 Chicago	AL	44	27	3	11	189.2	817	206	96	84	9	12	2	6	59	3	78	5	0	11	8	.579	2	5	3.99
1983 Chicago	AL	49	5	1	31	116.1	483	123	52	48	6	2	1	4	29	7	44	0	0	7	7	.500	0	15	3.71
1984 Toronto	AL	56	4	0	37	85	387	97	53	43	9	7	1	1	38	7	45	2	0	8	8	.500	0	9	4.55
1985 Toronto	AL	53	1	0	11	105.2	426	96	42	39	7	5	6	0	27	3	68	5	0	11	0	1.000	0	2	3.32
1986 Toronto	AL	40	2	0	11	73	329	93	50	41	5	4	1	0	23	6	30	2	0	2	6	.250	0	2	5.05
1987 Oakland	AL	36	5	0	10	56.2	262	76	38	32	5	3	3	1	22	3	36	4	0	1	3	.250	0	0	5.08
1988 Boston	AL	46	0	0	14	82.2	350	92	39	32	3	3	2	2	19	3	49	5	8	7	6	.538	0	0	3.48
1989 Boston	AL	42	0	0	14	112.1	445	96	37	29	4	5	5	0	27	6	61	1	1	4	2	.667	0	2	2.32
1990 Boston	AL	47	1	0	5	105.2	453	114	61	55	10	8	4	3	30	8	49	2	0	3	5	.375	0	0	4.68
1991 Boston	AL	51	0	0	12	92	403	100	54	48	8	3	2	3	31	7	57	1	0	6	3	.667	0	0	4.70
1992 Pittsburgh	NL	21	0	0	2	28	125	33	16	16	3	1	0	2	9	4	15	0	1	1	1	.500	0	0	5.14
16 ML YEARS		639	163	21	173	1831	7823	1975	915	799	122	95	40	35	549	86	857	44	14	96	96	.500	7	35	3.93

Tom Lampkin

Bats: Left **Throws:** Right **Pos:** C **Ht:** 5'11" **Wt:** 183 **Born:** 03/04/64 **Age:** 29

						BATTING											BASERUNNING			PERCENTAGES		
Year Team	Lg	G	AB	H	2B	3B	HR	(Hm | Rd)	TB	R	RBI	TBB	IBB	SO	HBP	SH	SF	SB	CS	SB%	GDP	Avg	OBP	SLG
1988 Cleveland	AL	4	4	0	0	0	0	(0 | 0)	0	0	0	1	0	0	0	0	0	0	0	.00	1	.000	.200	.000
1990 San Diego	NL	26	63	14	0	1	1	(1 | 0)	19	4	4	4	1	9	0	0	0	0	1	.00	2	.222	.269	.302
1991 San Diego	NL	38	58	11	3	1	0	(0 | 0)	16	4	3	3	0	9	0	0	0	0	0	.00	0	.190	.230	.276
1992 San Diego	NL	9	17	4	0	0	0	(0 | 0)	4	3	0	6	0	1	1	0	0	2	0	1.00	0	.235	.458	.235
4 ML YEARS		77	142	29	3	2	1	(1 | 0)	39	11	7	14	1	19	1	0	0	2	1	.67	3	.204	.280	.275

Les Lancaster

Pitches: Right **Bats:** Right **Pos:** RP **Ht:** 6' 2" **Wt:** 200 **Born:** 04/21/62 **Age:** 31

			HOW MUCH HE PITCHED					WHAT HE GAVE UP										THE RESULTS					
Year Team	Lg	G	GS	CG	GF	IP	BFP	H	R	ER	HR	SH	SF	HB	TBB	IBB	SO	WP	Bk	W	L	Pct.	ShO	Sv	ERA
1987 Chicago	NL	27	18	0	4	132.1	578	138	76	72	14	5	6	1	51	5	78	7	8	8	3	.727	0	0	4.90
1988 Chicago	NL	44	3	1	15	85.2	371	89	42	36	4	3	7	1	34	7	36	3	3	4	6	.400	0	5	3.78
1989 Chicago	NL	42	0	0	15	72.2	288	60	12	11	2	3	4	0	15	1	56	2	1	4	2	.667	0	8	1.36
1990 Chicago	NL	55	6	1	26	109	479	121	57	56	11	6	5	1	40	8	65	7	0	9	5	.643	1	6	4.62
1991 Chicago	NL	64	11	1	21	156	653	150	68	61	13	9	4	4	49	7	102	2	2	9	7	.563	0	3	3.52
1992 Detroit	AL	41	1	0	17	86.2	404	101	66	61	11	2	4	3	51	12	35	2	0	3	4	.429	0	0	6.33
6 ML YEARS		273	39	3	98	642.1	2773	659	321	297	55	28	30	10	240	40	372	23	14	37	27	.578	1	22	4.16

Bill Landrum

Pitches: Right **Bats:** Right **Pos:** RP **Ht:** 6' 2" **Wt:** 205 **Born:** 08/17/58 **Age:** 34

			HOW MUCH HE PITCHED					WHAT HE GAVE UP										THE RESULTS					
Year Team	Lg	G	GS	CG	GF	IP	BFP	H	R	ER	HR	SH	SF	HB	TBB	IBB	SO	WP	Bk	W	L	Pct.	ShO	Sv	ERA
1986 Cincinnati	NL	10	0	0	4	13.1	65	23	11	10	0	1	1	0	4	0	14	0	0	0	0	.000	0	0	6.75

Year	Team	Lg	G	GS	CG	GF	IP	BFP	H	R	ER	HR	SH	SF	HB	TBB	IBB	SO	WP	Bk	W	L	Pct.	ShO	Sv	ERA
1987	Cincinnati	NL	44	2	0	14	65	276	68	35	34	3	7	2	0	34	6	42	4	1	3	2	.600	0	2	4.71
1988	Chicago	NL	7	0	0	5	12.1	55	19	8	8	1	0	0	0	3	0	6	1	1	1	0	1.000	0	0	5.84
1989	Pittsburgh	NL	56	0	0	40	81	325	60	18	15	2	3	2	0	28	8	51	2	0	2	3	.400	0	26	1.67
1990	Pittsburgh	NL	54	0	0	41	71.2	292	69	22	17	4	5	3	0	21	5	39	1	1	7	3	.700	0	13	2.13
1991	Pittsburgh	NL	61	0	0	43	76.1	322	76	32	27	4	1	1	0	19	5	45	3	2	4	4	.500	0	17	3.18
1992	Montreal	NL	18	0	0	6	20	95	27	16	16	3	1	0	2	9	2	7	0	0	1	1	.500	0	0	7.20
	7 ML YEARS		250	2	0	153	339.2	1430	342	142	127	17	18	9	2	118	26	204	11	5	18	13	.581	0	58	3.37

Mark Langston

Pitches: Left   **Bats:** Right   **Pos:** SP   **Ht:** 6' 2"   **Wt:** 184   **Born:** 08/20/60   **Age:** 32

			HOW MUCH HE PITCHED							WHAT HE GAVE UP								THE RESULTS				
Year	Team	Lg	G	GS	CG	GF	IP	BFP	H	R	ER	HR	SH	SF	HB	TBB	IBB	SO	WP	Bk	W	L	Pct.	ShO	Sv	ERA
1984	Seattle	AL	35	33	5	0	225	965	188	99	85	16	13	7	8	118	5	204	4	2	17	10	.630	2	0	3.40
1985	Seattle	AL	24	24	2	0	126.2	577	122	85	77	22	3	2	2	91	2	72	3	3	7	14	.333	0	0	5.47
1986	Seattle	AL	37	36	9	1	239.1	1057	234	142	129	30	5	8	4	123	1	245	10	3	12	14	.462	0	0	4.85
1987	Seattle	AL	35	35	14	0	272	1152	242	132	116	30	12	6	5	114	0	262	9	2	19	13	.594	3	0	3.84
1988	Seattle	AL	35	35	9	0	261.1	1078	222	108	97	32	6	5	3	110	2	235	7	4	15	11	.577	3	0	3.34
1989	2 ML Teams		34	34	8	0	250	1037	198	87	76	16	9	7	4	112	6	235	6	4	16	14	.533	5	0	2.74
1990	California	AL	33	33	5	0	223	950	215	120	109	13	6	6	5	104	1	195	8	0	10	17	.370	1	0	4.40
1991	California	AL	34	34	7	0	246.1	992	190	89	82	30	4	6	2	96	3	183	6	0	19	8	.704	0	0	3.00
1992	California	AL	32	32	9	0	229	941	206	103	93	14	4	5	6	74	2	174	5	0	13	14	.481	2	0	3.66
1989	Seattle	AL	10	10	2	0	73.1	297	60	30	29	3	0	3	4	19	0	60	1	2	4	5	.444	1	0	3.56
	Montreal	NL	24	24	6	0	176.2	740	138	57	47	13	9	4	0	93	6	175	5	2	12	9	.571	4	0	2.39
	9 ML YEARS		299	296	68	1	2072.2	8749	1817	965	864	203	62	52	39	942	22	1805	58	18	128	115	.527	16	0	3.75

Ray Lankford

Bats: Left   **Throws:** Left   **Pos:** CF   **Ht:** 5'11"   **Wt:** 198   **Born:** 06/05/67   **Age:** 26

			BATTING																BASERUNNING				PERCENTAGES		
Year	Team	Lg	G	AB	H	2B	3B	HR	(Hm | Rd)	TB	R	RBI	TBB	IBB	SO	HBP	SH	SF	SB	CS	SB%	GDP	Avg	OBP	SLG
1990	St. Louis	NL	39	126	36	10	1	3	(2 | 1)	57	12	12	13	0	27	0	0	0	8	2	.80	1	.286	.353	.452
1991	St. Louis	NL	151	566	142	23	15	9	(4 | 5)	222	83	69	41	1	114	1	4	3	44	20	.69	4	.251	.301	.392
1992	St. Louis	NL	153	598	175	40	6	20	(13 | 7)	287	87	86	72	6	147	5	2	5	42	24	.64	6	.293	.371	.480
	3 ML YEARS		343	1290	353	73	22	32	(19 | 13)	566	182	167	126	7	288	6	6	8	94	46	.67	11	.274	.339	.439

Carney Lansford

Bats: Right   **Throws:** Right   **Pos:** 3B/1B   **Ht:** 6' 2"   **Wt:** 195   **Born:** 02/07/57   **Age:** 36

			BATTING																BASERUNNING				PERCENTAGES		
Year	Team	Lg	G	AB	H	2B	3B	HR	(Hm | Rd)	TB	R	RBI	TBB	IBB	SO	HBP	SH	SF	SB	CS	SB%	GDP	Avg	OBP	SLG
1978	California	AL	121	453	133	23	2	8	(4 | 4)	184	63	52	31	2	67	4	5	7	20	9	.69	4	.294	.339	.406
1979	California	AL	157	654	188	30	5	19	(14 | 5)	285	114	79	39	2	115	3	12	4	20	8	.71	16	.287	.329	.436
1980	California	AL	151	602	157	27	3	15	(8 | 7)	235	87	80	50	2	93	0	7	11	14	5	.74	12	.261	.312	.390
1981	Boston	AL	102	399	134	23	3	4	(1 | 3)	175	61	52	34	3	28	2	1	2	15	10	.60	6	.336	.389	.439
1982	Boston	AL	128	482	145	28	4	11	(4 | 7)	214	65	63	46	2	48	2	1	8	9	4	.69	15	.301	.359	.444
1983	Oakland	AL	80	299	92	16	2	10	(4 | 6)	142	43	45	22	4	33	3	0	4	3	8	.27	8	.308	.357	.475
1984	Oakland	AL	151	597	179	31	5	14	(7 | 7)	262	70	74	40	6	62	3	2	9	9	3	.75	12	.300	.342	.439
1985	Oakland	AL	98	401	111	18	2	13	(7 | 6)	172	51	46	18	1	27	4	4	5	2	3	.40	6	.277	.311	.429
1986	Oakland	AL	151	591	168	16	4	19	(10 | 9)	249	80	72	39	2	51	5	1	4	16	7	.70	16	.284	.332	.421
1987	Oakland	AL	151	554	160	27	4	19	(9 | 10)	252	89	76	60	11	44	9	5	3	27	8	.77	9	.289	.366	.455
1988	Oakland	AL	150	556	155	20	2	7	(1 | 6)	200	80	57	35	4	35	7	5	4	29	8	.78	17	.279	.327	.360
1989	Oakland	AL	148	551	185	28	2	2	(1 | 1)	223	81	52	51	2	25	9	1	4	37	15	.71	21	.336	.398	.405
1990	Oakland	AL	134	507	136	15	1	3	(1 | 2)	162	58	50	45	4	50	6	2	4	16	14	.53	10	.268	.333	.320
1991	Oakland	AL	5	16	1	0	0	0	(0 | 0)	1	0	1	0	0	2	0	0	0	0	0	.00	0	.063	.063	.063
1992	Oakland	AL	135	496	130	30	1	7	(4 | 3)	183	65	75	43	0	39	7	7	8	7	2	.78	14	.262	.325	.369
	15 ML YEARS		1862	7158	2074	332	40	151	(66 | 85)	2939	1007	874	553	45	719	64	53	77	224	104	.68	166	.290	.343	.411

Barry Larkin

Bats: Right   **Throws:** Right   **Pos:** SS   **Ht:** 6' 0"   **Wt:** 190   **Born:** 04/28/64   **Age:** 29

			BATTING																BASERUNNING				PERCENTAGES		
Year	Team	Lg	G	AB	H	2B	3B	HR	(Hm | Rd)	TB	R	RBI	TBB	IBB	SO	HBP	SH	SF	SB	CS	SB%	GDP	Avg	OBP	SLG
1986	Cincinnati	NL	41	159	45	4	3	3	(3 | 0)	64	27	19	9	1	21	0	0	1	8	0	1.00	2	.283	.320	.403
1987	Cincinnati	NL	125	439	107	16	2	12	(6 | 6)	163	64	43	36	3	52	5	5	3	21	6	.78	16	.244	.306	.371
1988	Cincinnati	NL	151	588	174	32	5	12	(9 | 3)	252	91	56	41	9	24	8	10	5	40	7	.85	7	.296	.347	.429
1989	Cincinnati	NL	97	325	111	14	4	4	(1 | 3)	145	47	36	20	5	23	2	2	8	10	5	.67	7	.342	.375	.446
1990	Cincinnati	NL	158	614	185	25	6	7	(4 | 3)	243	85	67	49	3	49	7	7	4	30	5	.86	14	.301	.358	.396
1991	Cincinnati	NL	123	464	140	27	4	20	(16 | 4)	235	88	69	55	1	64	3	3	2	24	6	.80	7	.302	.378	.506
1992	Cincinnati	NL	140	533	162	32	6	12	(8 | 4)	242	76	78	63	8	58	4	2	7	15	4	.79	13	.304	.377	.454
	7 ML YEARS		835	3122	924	150	30	70	(47 | 23)	1344	478	368	273	24	291	29	29	30	148	33	.82	58	.296	.355	.430

Gene Larkin

Bats: Both **Throws:** Right **Pos:** 1B/RF   **Ht:** 6' 3" **Wt:** 207 **Born:** 10/24/62 **Age:** 30

Year Team	Lg	G	AB	H	2B	3B	HR	(Hm	Rd)	TB	R	RBI	TBB	IBB	SO	HBP	SH	SF	SB	CS	SB%	GDP	Avg	OBP	SLG
1987 Minnesota	AL	85	233	62	11	2	4	(0	4)	89	23	28	25	3	31	2	0	2	1	4	.20	4	.266	.340	.382
1988 Minnesota	AL	149	505	135	30	2	8	(5	3)	193	56	70	68	8	55	15	1	5	3	2	.60	12	.267	.368	.382
1989 Minnesota	AL	136	446	119	25	1	6	(3	3)	164	61	46	54	6	55	9	5	6	5	2	.71	13	.267	.353	.368
1990 Minnesota	AL	119	401	108	26	4	5	(5	0)	157	46	42	42	2	55	5	5	4	5	3	.63	6	.269	.343	.392
1991 Minnesota	AL	98	255	73	14	1	2	(0	2)	95	34	19	30	3	21	1	3	2	2	3	.40	9	.286	.361	.373
1992 Minnesota	AL	115	337	83	18	1	6	(5	1)	121	38	42	28	6	43	4	0	4	7	2	.78	7	.246	.308	.359
6 ML YEARS		702	2177	580	124	11	31	(18	13)	819	258	247	247	28	262	36	14	23	23	16	.59	51	.266	.348	.376

Mike LaValliere

Bats: Left **Throws:** Right **Pos:** C   **Ht:** 5' 9" **Wt:** 210 **Born:** 08/18/60 **Age:** 32

Year Team	Lg	G	AB	H	2B	3B	HR	(Hm	Rd)	TB	R	RBI	TBB	IBB	SO	HBP	SH	SF	SB	CS	SB%	GDP	Avg	OBP	SLG
1984 Philadelphia	NL	6	7	0	0	0	0	(0	0)	0	0	0	2	0	2	0	0	0	0	0	.00	0	.000	.222	.000
1985 St. Louis	NL	12	34	5	1	0	0	(0	0)	6	2	6	7	0	3	0	0	3	0	0	.00	2	.147	.273	.176
1986 St. Louis	NL	110	303	71	10	2	3	(1	2)	94	18	30	36	5	37	1	10	0	0	1	.00	7	.234	.318	.310
1987 Pittsburgh	NL	121	340	102	19	0	1	(1	0)	124	33	36	43	9	32	1	3	3	0	0	.00	7	.300	.377	.365
1988 Pittsburgh	NL	120	352	92	18	0	2	(0	2)	116	24	47	50	10	34	2	1	4	3	2	.60	8	.261	.353	.330
1989 Pittsburgh	NL	68	190	60	10	0	2	(2	0)	76	15	23	29	7	24	0	4	0	0	2	.00	4	.316	.406	.400
1990 Pittsburgh	NL	96	279	72	15	0	3	(2	1)	96	27	31	44	8	20	2	4	1	0	3	.00	6	.258	.362	.344
1991 Pittsburgh	NL	108	336	97	11	2	3	(1	2)	121	25	41	33	4	27	2	1	5	2	1	.67	10	.289	.351	.360
1992 Pittsburgh	NL	95	293	75	13	1	2	(1	1)	96	22	29	44	14	21	1	0	5	0	3	.00	8	.256	.350	.328
9 ML YEARS		736	2134	574	97	5	16	(8	8)	729	166	243	288	57	200	9	23	21	5	12	.29	49	.269	.355	.342

Terry Leach

Pitches: Right **Bats:** Right **Pos:** RP   **Ht:** 6' 0" **Wt:** 190 **Born:** 03/13/54 **Age:** 39

Year Team	Lg	G	GS	CG	GF	IP	BFP	H	R	ER	HR	SH	SF	HB	TBB	IBB	SO	WP	Bk	W	L	Pct.	ShO	Sv	ERA
1981 New York	NL	21	1	0	3	35	139	26	11	10	2	0	0	0	12	1	16	0	0	1	1	.500	0	0	2.57
1982 New York	NL	21	1	1	12	45.1	194	46	22	21	2	5	1	0	18	5	30	0	0	2	1	.667	0	3	4.17
1985 New York	NL	22	4	1	4	55.2	226	48	19	18	3	5	2	1	14	3	30	0	0	3	4	.429	1	1	2.91
1986 New York	NL	6	0	0	1	6.2	30	6	3	2	0	0	0	0	3	0	4	0	0	0	0	.000	0	0	2.70
1987 New York	NL	44	12	1	7	131.1	542	132	54	47	14	8	1	1	29	5	61	0	1	11	1	.917	0	1	3.22
1988 New York	NL	52	0	0	21	92	392	95	32	26	5	8	3	3	24	4	51	0	0	7	2	.778	0	3	2.54
1989 2 ML Teams		40	3	0	10	95	413	97	57	44	5	6	6	2	40	9	36	1	1	5	6	.455	0	0	4.17
1990 Minnesota	AL	55	0	0	29	81.2	344	84	31	29	2	7	2	1	21	10	46	1	1	2	5	.286	0	2	3.20
1991 Minnesota	AL	50	0	0	22	67.1	292	82	28	27	3	3	1	0	14	5	32	1	0	1	2	.333	0	1	3.61
1992 Chicago	AL	51	0	0	21	73.2	292	57	17	16	2	2	1	4	20	5	22	0	0	6	5	.545	0	0	1.95
1989 New York	NL	10	0	0	4	21.1	85	19	11	10	1	0	2	1	4	0	2	0	0	0	0	.000	0	0	4.22
Kansas City	Al	30	3	0	6	73.2	328	78	46	34	4	6	4	1	36	9	34	1	1	5	6	.455	0	0	4.15
10 ML YEARS		362	21	3	130	683.2	2864	673	274	240	38	44	17	12	195	47	328	3	3	38	27	.585	3	9	3.16

Tim Leary

Pitches: Right **Bats:** Right **Pos:** SP   **Ht:** 6' 3" **Wt:** 218 **Born:** 12/23/58 **Age:** 34

Year Team	Lg	G	GS	CG	GF	IP	BFP	H	R	ER	HR	SH	SF	HB	TBB	IBB	SO	WP	Bk	W	L	Pct.	ShO	Sv	ERA
1981 New York	NL	1	1	0	0	2	7	0	0	0	0	0	0	0	1	0	3	1	0	0	0	.000	0	0	0.00
1983 New York	NL	2	2	1	0	10.2	53	15	10	4	0	1	1	0	4	0	9	0	1	1	1	.500	0	0	3.38
1984 New York	NL	20	7	0	3	53.2	237	61	28	24	2	1	2	2	18	3	29	2	3	3	3	.500	0	0	4.02
1985 Milwaukee	AL	5	5	0	0	33.1	146	40	18	15	5	2	0	1	8	0	29	1	0	1	4	.200	0	0	4.05
1986 Milwaukee	AL	33	30	3	2	188.1	817	216	97	88	20	4	6	7	53	4	110	7	0	12	12	.500	2	0	4.21
1987 Los Angeles	NL	39	12	0	11	107.2	469	121	62	57	15	6	1	2	36	5	61	3	1	3	11	.214	0	1	4.76
1988 Los Angeles	NL	35	34	9	0	228.2	932	201	87	74	13	7	3	6	56	4	180	9	6	17	11	.607	6	0	2.91
1989 2 ML Teams		33	31	2	0	207	874	205	84	81	17	7	8	5	68	15	123	10	0	8	14	.364	0	0	3.52
1990 New York	AL	31	31	6	0	208	881	202	105	95	18	7	4	7	78	1	138	23	0	9	19	.321	1	0	4.11
1991 New York	AL	28	18	1	4	120.2	551	150	89	87	20	7	2	4	57	1	83	10	0	4	10	.286	0	0	6.49
1992 2 ML Teams		26	23	3	2	141	624	131	89	84	12	6	11	9	87	5	46	7	0	8	10	.444	0	0	5.36
1989 Los Angeles	NL	19	17	2	0	117.1	481	107	45	44	9	4	4	2	37	7	59	4	0	6	7	.462	0	0	3.38
Cincinnati	NL	14	14	0	0	89.2	393	98	39	37	8	3	4	3	31	8	64	6	0	2	7	.222	0	0	3.71
1992 New York	AL	18	15	2	2	97	414	84	62	60	9	4	6	4	57	2	34	7	0	5	6	.455	0	0	5.57
Seattle	AL	8	8	1	0	44	210	47	27	24	3	2	5	2	30	3	12	2	0	3	4	.429	0	0	4.91
11 ML YEARS		253	194	25	22	1301	5591	1342	669	609	122	48	38	43	466	38	811	75	11	66	95	.410	9	1	4.21

Manuel Lee

Bats: Both **Throws: Right** **Pos: SS** — **Ht: 5' 9"** **Wt: 166** **Born: 06/17/65** **Age: 28**

									BATTING											BASERUNNING				PERCENTAGES		
Year	Team	Lg	G	AB	H	2B	3B	HR	(Hm	Rd)	TB	R	RBI	TBB	IBB	SO	HBP	SH	SF	SB	CS	SB%	GDP	Avg	OBP	SLG
1985	Toronto	AL	64	40	8	0	0	0	(0	0)	8	9	0	2	0	9	0	1	0	1	4	.20	2	.200	.238	.200
1986	Toronto	AL	35	78	16	0	1	1	(1	0)	21	8	7	4	0	10	0	2	1	0	1	.00	5	.205	.241	.269
1987	Toronto	AL	56	121	31	2	3	1	(0	1)	42	14	11	6	0	13	0	1	1	2	0	1.00	1	.256	.289	.347
1988	Toronto	AL	116	381	111	16	3	2	(2	0)	139	38	38	26	1	64	0	4	4	3	3	.50	13	.291	.333	.365
1989	Toronto	AL	99	300	78	9	2	3	(1	2)	100	27	34	20	1	60	0	1	1	4	2	.67	8	.260	.305	.333
1990	Toronto	AL	117	391	95	12	4	6	(2	4)	133	45	41	26	0	90	0	1	3	3	1	.75	9	.243	.288	.340
1991	Toronto	AL	138	445	104	18	3	0	(0	0)	128	41	29	24	0	107	2	10	4	7	2	.78	11	.234	.274	.288
1992	Toronto	AL	128	396	104	10	1	3	(1	2)	125	49	39	50	0	73	0	8	3	6	2	.75	8	.263	.343	.316
	8 ML YEARS		753	2152	547	67	17	16	(7	9)	696	231	199	158	2	426	2	28	17	26	15	.63	57	.254	.304	.323

Craig Lefferts

Pitches: Left **Bats: Left** **Pos: SP** — **Ht: 6' 1"** **Wt: 210** **Born: 09/29/57** **Age: 35**

			HOW MUCH HE PITCHED						WHAT HE GAVE UP												THE RESULTS					
Year	Team	Lg	G	GS	CG	GF	IP	BFP	H	R	ER	HR	SH	SF	HB	TBB	IBB	SO	WP	Bk	W	L	Pct.	ShO	Sv	ERA
1983	Chicago	NL	56	5	0	10	89	367	80	35	31	13	7	0	2	29	3	60	2	0	3	4	.429	0	1	3.13
1984	San Diego	NL	62	0	0	29	105.2	420	88	29	25	4	4	6	1	24	1	56	2	2	3	4	.429	0	10	2.13
1985	San Diego	NL	60	0	0	24	83.1	345	75	34	31	7	7	1	0	30	4	48	2	0	7	6	.538	0	2	3.35
1986	San Diego	NL	83	0	0	36	107.2	446	98	41	37	7	9	5	1	44	11	72	1	1	9	8	.529	0	4	3.09
1987	2 ML Teams		77	0	0	22	98.2	416	92	47	42	13	6	2	2	33	11	57	6	3	5	5	.500	0	6	3.83
1988	San Francisco	NL	64	0	0	30	92.1	362	74	33	30	7	6	3	1	23	5	58	4	0	3	8	.273	0	11	2.92
1989	San Francisco	NL	70	0	0	32	107	430	93	38	32	11	4	4	1	22	5	71	4	1	2	4	.333	0	20	2.69
1990	San Diego	NL	56	0	0	44	78.2	327	68	26	22	10	5	1	1	22	4	60	1	0	7	5	.583	0	23	2.52
1991	San Diego	NL	54	0	0	40	69	290	74	35	30	5	10	5	1	14	3	48	3	1	1	6	.143	0	23	3.91
1992	2 ML Teams		32	32	0	1	196.1	820	214	95	82	19	14	6	0	41	2	104	5	1	14	12	.538	0	0	3.76
1987	San Diego	NL	33	0	0	8	51.1	225	56	29	25	9	2	0	2	15	5	39	5	2	2	2	.500	0	2	4.38
	San Francisco	NL	44	0	0	14	47.1	191	36	18	17	4	4	2	0	18	6	18	1	1	3	3	.500	0	4	3.23
1992	San Diego	NL	27	27	0	0	163.1	684	180	76	67	16	12	5	0	35	2	81	4	1	13	9	.591	0	0	3.69
	Baltimore	AL	5	5	1	0	33	136	34	19	15	3	2	1	0	6	0	23	1	0	1	3	.250	0	0	4.09
	10 ML YEARS		614	37	1	267	1027.2	4223	956	413	362	96	72	33	10	282	49	634	30	9	54	62	.466	0	100	3.17

Charlie Leibrandt

Pitches: Left **Bats: Right** **Pos: SP** — **Ht: 6' 3"** **Wt: 200** **Born: 10/04/56** **Age: 36**

			HOW MUCH HE PITCHED						WHAT HE GAVE UP												THE RESULTS					
Year	Team	Lg	G	GS	CG	GF	IP	BFP	H	R	ER	HR	SH	SF	HB	TBB	IBB	SO	WP	Bk	W	L	Pct.	ShO	Sv	ERA
1979	Cincinnati	NL	3	0	0	1	4	16	2	2	0	0	0	1	0	2	0	1	0	0	0	0	.000	0	0	0.00
1980	Cincinnati	NL	36	27	5	3	174	754	200	84	82	15	12	2	2	54	4	62	1	6	10	9	.526	2	0	4.24
1981	Cincinnati	NL	7	4	1	0	30	128	28	12	12	0	4	2	0	15	2	9	0	0	1	1	.500	1	0	3.60
1982	Cincinnati	NL	36	11	0	10	107.2	484	130	68	61	4	10	2	2	48	9	34	6	1	5	7	.417	0	2	5.10
1984	Kansas City	AL	23	23	0	0	143.2	621	158	65	58	11	3	7	3	38	2	53	5	1	11	7	.611	0	0	3.63
1985	Kansas City	AL	33	33	8	0	237.2	983	223	86	71	17	8	5	5	68	3	108	4	3	17	9	.654	3	0	2.69
1986	Kansas City	AL	35	34	8	0	231.1	975	238	112	105	18	14	5	4	63	0	108	2	1	14	11	.560	1	0	4.09
1987	Kansas City	AL	35	35	8	0	240.1	1015	235	104	91	23	5	5	1	74	2	151	9	3	16	11	.593	3	0	3.41
1988	Kansas City	AL	35	35	7	0	243	1002	244	98	86	20	5	7	4	62	3	125	10	4	13	12	.520	2	0	3.19
1989	Kansas City	AL	33	27	3	3	161	712	196	98	92	13	8	4	2	54	4	73	9	2	5	11	.313	1	0	5.14
1990	Atlanta	NL	24	24	5	0	162.1	680	164	72	57	9	7	6	4	35	3	76	4	3	9	11	.450	2	0	3.16
1991	Atlanta	NL	36	36	1	0	229.2	949	212	105	89	18	19	6	4	56	3	128	5	3	15	13	.536	1	0	3.49
1992	Atlanta	NL	32	31	5	0	193	799	191	78	72	9	7	4	5	42	4	104	3	2	15	7	.682	2	0	3.36
	13 ML YEARS		368	320	51	17	2157.2	9118	2221	984	876	157	102	56	33	611	39	1032	58	29	131	109	.546	18	2	3.65

Al Leiter

Pitches: Left **Bats: Left** **Pos: RP** — **Ht: 6' 3"** **Wt: 215** **Born: 10/23/65** **Age: 27**

			HOW MUCH HE PITCHED						WHAT HE GAVE UP												THE RESULTS					
Year	Team	Lg	G	GS	CG	GF	IP	BFP	H	R	ER	HR	SH	SF	HB	TBB	IBB	SO	WP	Bk	W	L	Pct.	ShO	Sv	ERA
1987	New York	AL	4	4	0	0	22.2	104	24	16	16	2	1	0	0	15	0	28	4	0	2	2	.500	0	0	6.35
1988	New York	AL	14	14	0	0	57.1	251	49	27	25	7	1	0	5	33	0	60	1	4	4	4	.500	0	0	3.92
1989	2 ML Teams		5	5	0	0	33.1	154	32	23	21	2	1	1	2	23	0	26	2	1	1	2	.333	0	0	5.67
1990	Toronto	AL	4	0	0	2	6.1	22	1	0	0	0	0	0	0	2	0	5	0	0	0	0	.000	0	0	0.00
1991	Toronto	AL	3	0	0	1	1.2	13	3	5	5	0	1	0	0	5	0	1	0	0	0	0	.000	0	0	27.00
1992	Toronto	AL	1	0	0	0	1	7	1	1	1	0	0	0	0	2	0	0	0	0	0	0	.000	0	0	9.00
1989	New York	AL	4	4	0	0	26.2	123	23	20	18	1	1	1	2	21	0	22	1	1	1	2	.333	0	0	6.08
	Toronto	AL	1	1	0	0	6.2	31	9	3	3	1	0	0	0	2	0	4	1	0	0	0	.000	0	0	4.05
	6 ML YEARS		31	23	0	3	122.1	551	110	72	68	11	4	1	7	80	0	120	7	5	7	8	.467	0	0	5.00

Mark Leiter

Pitches: Right **Bats:** Right **Pos:** RP/SP   **Ht:** 6' 3" **Wt:** 210 **Born:** 04/13/63 **Age:** 30

Year Team	Lg	G	GS	CG	GF	IP	BFP	H	R	ER	HR	SH	SF	HB	TBB	IBB	SO	WP	Bk	W	L	Pct.	ShO	Sv	ERA
1990 New York	AL	8	3	0	2	26.1	119	33	20	20	5	2	1	2	9	0	21	0	0	1	1	.500	0	0	6.84
1991 Detroit	AL	38	15	1	7	134.2	578	125	66	63	16	5	6	6	50	4	103	2	0	9	7	.563	0	1	4.21
1992 Detroit	AL	35	14	1	7	112	475	116	57	52	9	2	8	3	43	5	75	3	0	8	5	.615	0	0	4.18
3 ML YEARS		81	32	2	16	273	1172	274	143	135	30	9	15	11	102	9	199	5	0	18	13	.581	0	1	4.45

Scott Leius

Bats: Right **Throws:** Right **Pos:** 3B   **Ht:** 6' 3" **Wt:** 190 **Born:** 09/24/65 **Age:** 27

Year Team	Lg	G	AB	H	2B	3B	HR	(Hm	Rd)	TB	R	RBI	TBB	IBB	SO	HBP	SH	SF	SB	CS	SB%	GDP	Avg	OBP	SLG
1990 Minnesota	AL	14	25	6	1	0	1	(0	1)	10	4	4	2	0	2	0	1	0	0	0	.00	2	.240	.296	.400
1991 Minnesota	AL	109	199	57	7	2	5	(2	3)	83	35	20	30	1	35	0	5	1	5	5	.50	4	.286	.378	.417
1992 Minnesota	AL	129	409	102	18	2	2	(2	0)	130	50	35	34	0	61	1	5	0	6	5	.55	10	.249	.309	.318
3 ML YEARS		252	633	165	26	4	8	(4	4)	223	89	59	66	1	98	1	11	1	11	10	.52	16	.261	.331	.352

Mark Lemke

Bats: Both **Throws:** Right **Pos:** 2B/3B   **Ht:** 5' 9" **Wt:** 167 **Born:** 08/13/65 **Age:** 27

Year Team	Lg	G	AB	H	2B	3B	HR	(Hm	Rd)	TB	R	RBI	TBB	IBB	SO	HBP	SH	SF	SB	CS	SB%	GDP	Avg	OBP	SLG
1988 Atlanta	NL	16	58	13	4	0	0	(0	0)	17	8	2	4	0	5	0	2	0	0	2	.00	1	.224	.274	.293
1989 Atlanta	NL	14	55	10	2	1	2	(1	1)	20	4	10	5	0	7	0	0	0	0	1	.00	1	.182	.250	.364
1990 Atlanta	NL	102	239	54	13	0	0	(0	0)	67	22	21	21	3	22	0	4	2	0	1	.00	6	.226	.286	.280
1991 Atlanta	NL	136	269	63	11	2	2	(2	0)	84	36	23	29	2	27	0	6	4	1	2	.33	9	.234	.305	.312
1992 Atlanta	NL	155	427	97	7	4	6	(4	2)	130	38	26	50	11	39	0	12	2	3	0	.00	9	.227	.307	.304
5 ML YEARS		423	1048	237	37	7	10	(7	3)	318	108	82	109	16	100	0	24	8	1	9	.10	26	.226	.297	.303

Patrick Lennon

Bats: Right **Throws:** Right **Pos:** 1B   **Ht:** 6' 2" **Wt:** 200 **Born:** 04/27/68 **Age:** 25

Year Team	Lg	G	AB	H	2B	3B	HR	(Hm	Rd)	TB	R	RBI	TBB	IBB	SO	HBP	SH	SF	SB	CS	SB%	GDP	Avg	OBP	SLG
1986 Bellingham	A	51	169	41	5	2	3	--	--	59	35	27	36	0	50	0	1	1	8	6	.57	3	.243	.374	.349
1987 Wausau	A	98	319	80	21	3	7	--	--	128	54	34	46	1	82	1	1	2	25	8	.76	10	.251	.345	.401
1988 Vermont	AA	95	321	83	9	3	9	--	--	125	44	40	21	1	87	3	3	4	15	6	.71	9	.259	.307	.389
1989 Williamsprt	AA	66	248	65	14	2	3	--	--	92	32	31	23	2	53	0	0	5	7	4	.64	9	.262	.319	.371
1990 San Berndno	A	44	163	47	6	2	8	--	--	81	29	30	15	1	51	0	0	1	6	0	1.00	4	.288	.346	.497
Williamsprt	AA	49	167	49	6	4	5	--	--	78	24	22	10	0	37	2	0	3	10	4	.71	2	.293	.335	.467
1991 Calgary	AAA	112	416	137	29	5	15	--	--	221	75	74	46	4	68	4	1	1	12	5	.71	9	.329	.400	.531
1992 Calgary	AAA	13	48	17	3	0	1	--	--	23	8	9	6	0	10	0	0	0	4	1	.80	1	.354	.426	.479
1991 Seattle	AL	9	8	1	1	0	0	(0	0)	2	2	1	3	0	1	0	0	0	0	0	.00	0	.125	.364	.250
1992 Seattle	AL	1	2	0	0	0	0	(0	0)	0	0	0	0	0	0	0	0	0	0	0	.00	0	.000	.000	.000
2 ML YEARS		10	10	1	1	0	0	(0	0)	2	2	1	3	0	1	0	0	0	0	0	.00	0	.100	.308	.200

Danilo Leon

Pitches: Right **Bats:** Right **Pos:** RP   **Ht:** 6' 1" **Wt:** 170 **Born:** 04/03/67 **Age:** 26

Year Team	Lg	G	GS	CG	GF	IP	BFP	H	R	ER	HR	SH	SF	HB	TBB	IBB	SO	WP	Bk	W	L	Pct.	ShO	Sv	ERA
1992 Charlotte	A	4	0	0	0	9.1	35	5	2	2	0	0	0	1	2	0	7	0	2	0	0	.000	0	0	1.93
Tulsa	AA	12	0	0	4	30	113	15	4	2	0	1	1	1	8	1	34	3	1	5	0	1.000	0	1	0.60
Okla City	AAA	3	0	0	1	4.2	19	2	0	0	0	0	0	0	3	0	4	0	0	1	0	1.000	0	0	0.00
1992 Texas	AL	15	0	0	3	18.1	84	18	14	12	5	0	0	3	10	0	15	0	0	1	1	.500	0	0	5.89

Mark Leonard

Bats: Left **Throws:** Right **Pos:** LF   **Ht:** 6' 0" **Wt:** 195 **Born:** 08/14/64 **Age:** 28

Year Team	Lg	G	AB	H	2B	3B	HR	(Hm	Rd)	TB	R	RBI	TBB	IBB	SO	HBP	SH	SF	SB	CS	SB%	GDP	Avg	OBP	SLG
1990 San Francisco	NL	11	17	3	1	0	1	(0	1)	7	3	2	3	0	8	0	0	0	0	0	.00	0	.176	.300	.412
1991 San Francisco	NL	64	129	31	7	1	2	(0	2)	46	14	14	12	1	25	1	1	2	0	1	.00	3	.240	.306	.357
1992 San Francisco	NL	55	128	30	7	0	4	(3	1)	49	13	16	16	0	31	3	0	1	0	1	.00	3	.234	.331	.383
3 ML YEARS		130	274	64	15	1	7	(3	4)	102	30	32	31	1	64	4	1	3	0	2	.00	6	.234	.317	.372

Jesse Levis

Bats: Left **Throws:** Right **Pos:** C **Ht:** 5' 9" **Wt:** 180 **Born:** 04/14/68 **Age:** 25

Year	Team	Lg	G	AB	H	2B	3B	HR	(Hm	Rd)	TB	R	RBI	TBB	IBB	SO	HBP	SH	SF	SB	CS	SB%	GDP	Avg	OBP	SLG
1989	Colo Sprngs	AAA	1	1	0	0	0	0	--	--	0	0	0	0	0	0	0	0	0	0	0	.00	1	.000	.000	.000
	Burlington	R	27	93	32	4	0	4	--	--	48	11	16	10	3	7	2	0	1	1	0	1.00	2	.344	.415	.516
	Kinston	A	27	87	26	6	0	2	--	--	38	11	11	12	0	15	2	0	0	1	0	1.00	3	.299	.396	.437
1990	Kinston	A	107	382	113	18	3	7	--	--	158	63	64	64	1	42	5	1	6	4	1	.80	5	.296	.398	.372
1991	Canton-Akrn	AA	115	382	101	17	3	6	--	--	142	31	45	40	5	36	0	4	2	2	5	.29	11	.264	.333	.372
1992	Colo Sprngs	AAA	87	253	92	20	1	6	--	--	132	39	44	37	0	25	1	3	2	1	3	.25	9	.364	.444	.522
1992	Cleveland	AL	28	43	12	4	0	1	(0	1)	19	2	3	0	0	5	0	0	0	0	0	.00	1	.279	.279	.442

Darren Lewis

Bats: Right **Throws:** Right **Pos:** CF **Ht:** 6' 0" **Wt:** 175 **Born:** 08/28/67 **Age:** 25

Year	Team	Lg	G	AB	H	2B	3B	HR	(Hm	Rd)	TB	R	RBI	TBB	IBB	SO	HBP	SH	SF	SB	CS	SB%	GDP	Avg	OBP	SLG
1990	Oakland	AL	25	35	8	0	0	0	(0	0)	8	4	1	7	0	4	1	3	0	2	0	1.00	2	.229	.372	.229
1991	San Francisco	NL	72	222	55	5	3	1	(0	1)	69	41	15	36	0	30	2	7	0	13	7	.65	1	.248	.358	.311
1992	San Francisco	NL	100	320	74	8	1	1	(1	0)	87	38	18	29	0	46	1	10	2	28	8	.78	3	.231	.295	.272
	3 ML YEARS		197	577	137	13	4	2	(1	1)	164	83	34	72	0	80	4	20	2	43	15	.74	6	.237	.325	.284

Mark Lewis

Bats: Right **Throws:** Right **Pos:** SS **Ht:** 6' 1" **Wt:** 190 **Born:** 11/30/69 **Age:** 23

Year	Team	Lg	G	AB	H	2B	3B	HR	(Hm	Rd)	TB	R	RBI	TBB	IBB	SO	HBP	SH	SF	SB	CS	SB%	GDP	Avg	OBP	SLG
1988	Burlington	R	61	227	60	13	1	7	--	--	96	39	43	25	0	44	5	0	5	14	6	.70	2	.264	.344	.423
1989	Kinston	A	93	349	94	16	3	1	--	--	119	50	32	34	4	50	2	3	5	17	9	.65	7	.269	.333	.341
	Canton-Akrn	AA	7	25	5	1	0	0	--	--	6	4	1	1	0	3	0	0	0	0	0	.00	1	.200	.231	.240
1990	Canton-Akrn	AA	102	390	106	19	3	10	--	--	161	55	60	23	3	49	4	2	5	8	7	.53	10	.272	.315	.413
	Colo Sprngs	AAA	34	124	38	8	1	1	--	--	51	16	21	9	0	13	0	1	1	2	3	.40	4	.306	.351	.411
1991	Colo Sprngs	AAA	46	179	50	10	3	2	--	--	72	29	31	18	0	23	0	0	6	2	1	.67	4	.279	.335	.402
1991	Cleveland	AL	84	314	83	15	1	0	(0	0)	100	29	30	15	0	45	0	2	5	2	2	.50	12	.264	.293	.318
1992	Cleveland	AL	122	413	109	21	0	5	(2	3)	145	44	30	25	1	69	3	1	4	4	5	.44	12	.264	.308	.351
	2 ML YEARS		206	727	192	36	1	5	(2	3)	245	73	60	40	1	114	3	3	9	6	7	.46	24	.264	.302	.337

Richie Lewis

Pitches: Right **Bats:** Right **Pos:** SP **Ht:** 5'10" **Wt:** 175 **Born:** 01/25/66 **Age:** 27

Year	Team	Lg	G	GS	CG	GF	IP	BFP	H	R	ER	HR	SH	SF	HB	TBB	IBB	SO	WP	Bk	W	L	Pct.	ShO	Sv	ERA
1987	Indianapolis	AAA	2	0	0	2	3.2	19	6	4	4	2	0	0	0	2	0	3	0	0	0	0	.000	0	0	9.82
1988	Jacksnville	AA	12	12	1	0	61.1	275	37	32	23	2	0	3	3	56	0	60	7	4	5	3	.625	0	0	3.38
1989	Jacksnville	AA	17	17	0	0	94.1	414	80	37	27	2	7	1	2	55	0	105	8	2	5	4	.556	0	0	2.58
1990	Wst Plm Bch	A	10	0	0	0	15	68	12	8	5	0	1	0	0	11	0	14	1	0	0	1	.000	0	2	3.00
	Jacksnville	AA	11	0	0	8	14.1	54	7	2	2	0	0	1	0	5	0	14	3	0	0	0	.000	0	5	1.26
1991	Harrisburg	AA	34	6	0	16	74.2	318	67	33	31	2	3	2	2	40	1	82	5	2	6	5	.545	0	5	3.74
	Indianapolis	AAA	5	4	0	0	27.2	131	35	12	11	1	0	1	0	20	1	22	2	0	1	0	1.000	0	0	3.58
	Rochester	AAA	2	2	0	0	16	62	13	5	5	1	0	0	0	7	0	18	1	0	1	0	1.000	0	0	2.81
1992	Rochester	AAA	24	23	6	1	159.1	668	136	63	58	15	1	4	3	61	2	154	13	2	10	9	.526	1	0	3.28
1992	Baltimore	AL	2	2	0	0	6.2	40	13	8	8	1	0	1	0	7	0	4	0	0	1	1	.500	0	0	10.80

Scott Lewis

Pitches: Right **Bats:** Right **Pos:** RP **Ht:** 6' 3" **Wt:** 178 **Born:** 12/05/65 **Age:** 27

Year	Team	Lg	G	GS	CG	GF	IP	BFP	H	R	ER	HR	SH	SF	HB	TBB	IBB	SO	WP	Bk	W	L	Pct.	ShO	Sv	ERA
1990	California	AL	2	2	1	0	16.1	60	10	4	4	2	0	0	0	2	0	9	0	0	1	1	.500	0	0	2.20
1991	California	AL	16	11	0	0	60.1	281	81	43	42	9	2	0	2	21	0	37	3	0	3	5	.375	0	0	6.27
1992	California	AL	21	2	0	7	38.1	160	36	18	17	3	0	3	2	14	1	18	1	1	4	0	1.000	0	0	3.99
	3 ML YEARS		39	15	1	7	115	501	127	65	63	14	2	3	4	37	1	64	4	1	8	6	.571	0	0	4.93

Jim Leyritz

Bats: Right **Throws:** Right **Pos:** DH/C **Ht:** 6' 0" **Wt:** 190 **Born:** 12/27/63 **Age:** 29

Year	Team	Lg	G	AB	H	2B	3B	HR	(Hm	Rd)	TB	R	RBI	TBB	IBB	SO	HBP	SH	SF	SB	CS	SB%	GDP	Avg	OBP	SLG
1990	New York	AL	92	303	78	13	1	5	(1	4)	108	28	25	27	1	51	7	1	1	2	3	.40	11	.257	.331	.356
1991	New York	AL	32	77	14	3	0	0	(0	0)	17	8	4	13	0	15	0	1	0	0	0	.00	0	.182	.300	.221
1992	New York	AL	63	144	37	6	0	7	(3	4)	64	17	26	14	1	22	6	0	3	0	1	.00	2	.257	.341	.444

		G	AB	H	2B	3B	HR	(Hm	Rd)	TB	R	RBI	TBB	IBB	SO	HBP	SH	SF	SB	CS	SB%	GDP	Avg	OBP	SLG
3 ML YEARS		187	524	129	22	1	12	(4	8)	189	53	55	54	2	88	13	2	4	2	5	.29	13	.246	.329	.361

Derek Lilliquist

Pitches: Left **Bats:** Left **Pos:** RP **Ht:** 6' 0" **Wt:** 214 **Born:** 02/20/66 **Age:** 27

Year Team	Lg	G	GS	CG	GF	IP	BFP	H	R	ER	HR	SH	SF	HB	TBB	IBB	SO	WP	Bk	W	L	Pct.	ShO	Sv	ERA
1989 Atlanta	NL	32	30	0	0	165.2	718	202	87	73	16	8	3	2	34	5	79	4	3	8	10	.444	0	0	3.97
1990 2 ML Teams		28	18	1	3	122	537	136	74	72	16	9	5	3	42	5	63	2	3	5	11	.313	1	0	5.31
1991 San Diego	NL	6	2	0	1	14.1	70	25	14	14	3	0	0	0	4	1	7	0	0	0	2	.000	0	0	8.79
1992 Cleveland	AL	71	0	0	22	61.2	239	39	13	12	5	5	4	2	18	6	47	2	0	5	3	.625	0	6	1.75
1990 Atlanta	NL	12	11	0	1	61.2	279	75	45	43	10	6	4	1	19	4	34	0	2	2	8	.200	0	0	6.28
San Diego	NL	16	7	1	2	60.1	258	61	29	29	6	3	1	2	23	1	29	2	1	3	3	.500	1	0	4.33
4 ML YEARS		137	50	1	26	363.2	1564	402	188	171	40	22	12	7	98	17	196	8	6	18	26	.409	1	6	4.23

Jose Lind

Bats: Right **Throws:** Right **Pos:** 2B **Ht:** 5'11" **Wt:** 170 **Born:** 05/01/64 **Age:** 29

Year Team	Lg	G	AB	H	2B	3B	HR	(Hm	Rd)	TB	R	RBI	TBB	IBB	SO	HBP	SH	SF	SB	CS	SB%	GDP	Avg	OBP	SLG
1987 Pittsburgh	NL	35	143	46	8	4	0	(0	0)	62	21	11	8	1	12	0	6	0	2	1	.67	5	.322	.358	.434
1988 Pittsburgh	NL	154	611	160	24	4	2	(1	1)	198	82	49	42	0	75	0	12	3	15	4	.79	11	.262	.308	.324
1989 Pittsburgh	NL	153	578	134	21	3	2	(2	0)	167	52	48	39	7	64	2	13	5	15	1	.94	13	.232	.280	.289
1990 Pittsburgh	NL	152	514	134	28	5	1	(1	0)	175	46	48	35	19	52	1	4	7	8	0	1.00	20	.261	.305	.340
1991 Pittsburgh	NL	150	502	133	16	6	3	(2	1)	170	53	54	30	10	56	2	5	6	7	4	.64	20	.265	.306	.339
1992 Pittsburgh	NL	135	468	110	14	1	0	(0	0)	126	38	39	26	12	29	1	7	4	3	1	.75	14	.235	.275	.269
6 ML YEARS		779	2816	717	111	23	8	(6	2)	898	292	249	180	49	288	6	47	25	50	11	.82	83	.255	.298	.319

Jim Lindeman

Bats: Right **Throws:** Right **Pos:** RF **Ht:** 6' 1" **Wt:** 200 **Born:** 01/10/62 **Age:** 31

Year Team	Lg	G	AB	H	2B	3B	HR	(Hm	Rd)	TB	R	RBI	TBB	IBB	SO	HBP	SH	SF	SB	CS	SB%	GDP	Avg	OBP	SLG
1986 St. Louis	NL	19	55	14	1	0	1	(0	1)	18	7	6	2	0	10	0	0	1	1	1	.50	2	.255	.276	.327
1987 St. Louis	NL	75	207	43	13	0	8	(2	6)	80	20	28	11	0	56	3	2	4	3	1	.75	4	.208	.253	.386
1988 St. Louis	NL	17	43	9	1	0	2	(0	2)	16	3	7	2	0	9	0	1	0	0	0	.00	1	.209	.244	.372
1989 St. Louis	NL	73	45	5	1	0	0	(0	0)	6	8	2	3	0	18	0	1	1	0	0	.00	2	.111	.163	.133
1990 Detroit	AL	12	32	7	1	0	2	(2	0)	14	5	8	2	0	13	0	0	0	0	0	.00	0	.219	.265	.438
1991 Philadelphia	NL	65	95	32	5	0	0	(0	0)	37	13	12	13	1	14	0	2	1	0	1	.00	1	.337	.413	.389
1992 Philadelphia	NL	29	39	10	1	0	1	(1	0)	14	6	6	3	0	11	0	0	0	0	0	.00	1	.256	.310	.359
7 ML YEARS		290	516	120	23	0	14	(5	9)	185	62	69	36	1	131	3	6	7	4	3	.57	11	.233	.283	.359

Doug Linton

Pitches: Right **Bats:** Right **Pos:** RP/SP **Ht:** 6' 1" **Wt:** 180 **Born:** 02/09/65 **Age:** 28

Year Team	Lg	G	GS	CG	GF	IP	BFP	H	R	ER	HR	SH	SF	HB	TBB	IBB	SO	WP	Bk	W	L	Pct.	ShO	Sv	ERA
1987 Myrtle Bch	A	20	19	2	1	122	480	94	34	21	9	0	2	2	25	0	155	8	1	14	2	.875	0	1	1.55
Knoxville	AA	1	1	0	0	3	15	5	3	3	0	0	0	1	1	0	1	0	1	0	0	.000	0	0	9.00
1988 Dunedin	A	12	0	0	6	27.2	111	19	5	5	0	1	1	0	9	1	28	2	2	2	1	.667	0	2	1.63
1989 Dunedin	A	9	1	0	5	27.1	117	27	12	9	1	0	1	0	9	0	35	1	0	1	2	.333	0	2	2.96
Knoxville	AA	14	13	3	0	90	355	68	28	26	2	3	1	2	23	2	93	6	1	5	4	.556	2	0	2.60
1990 Syracuse	AAA	26	26	8	0	177.1	753	174	77	67	14	2	10	8	67	3	113	4		10	10	.500	3	0	3.40
1991 Syracuse	AAA	30	26	3	1	161.2	710	181	108	90	21	6	10	10	56	2	93	5	0	10	12	.455	1	0	5.01
1992 Syracuse	AAA	25	25	7	0	170.2	741	176	83	70	17	5	4	7	70	3	126	12	1	12	10	.545	1	0	3.69
1992 Toronto	AL	8	3	0	2	24	116	31	23	23	5	1	2	0	17	0	16	2	0	1	3	.250	0	0	8.63

Pat Listach

Bats: Both **Throws:** Right **Pos:** SS **Ht:** 5' 9" **Wt:** 170 **Born:** 09/12/67 **Age:** 25

Year Team	Lg	G	AB	H	2B	3B	HR	(Hm	Rd)	TB	R	RBI	TBB	IBB	SO	HBP	SH	SF	SB	CS	SB%	GDP	Avg	OBP	SLG
1988 Beloit	A	53	200	48	5	1	1	--	--	58	40	14	18	0	20	6	4	2	20	9	.69	6	.240	.319	.290
1989 Stockton	A	132	480	110	11	4	2	--	--	135	73	34	58	1	106	4	7	1	37	19	.66	10	.229	.317	.281
1990 Stockton	A	139	503	137	21	6	2	--	--	176	116	39	105	2	122	6	3	1	78	28	.74	8	.272	.403	.350
1991 El Paso	AA	49	186	47	5	2	0	--	--	56	40	14	25	0	56	5	2	0	14	2	.88	3	.253	.356	.301
Denver	AAA	89	286	72	10	4	1	--	--	93	51	31	45	1	67	0	3	4	23	7	.77	2	.252	.349	.325
1992 Milwaukee	AL	149	579	168	19	6	1	(0	1)	202	93	47	55	0	124	1	12	2	54	18	.75	3	.290	.352	.349

Greg Litton

Bats: Right **Throws:** Right **Pos:** 2B **Ht:** 6' 0" **Wt:** 190 **Born:** 07/13/64 **Age:** 28

Year Team	Lg	G	AB	H	2B	3B	HR	(Hm	Rd)	TB	R	RBI	TBB	IBB	SO	HBP	SH	SF	SB	CS	SB%	GDP	Avg	OBP	SLG
1989 San Francisco	NL	71	143	36	5	3	4	(3	1)	59	12	17	7	0	29	1	4	0	0	2	.00	3	.252	.291	.413
1990 San Francisco	NL	93	204	50	9	1	1	(0	1)	64	17	24	11	0	45	1	2	2	1	0	1.00	5	.245	.284	.314
1991 San Francisco	NL	59	127	23	7	1	1	(0	1)	35	13	15	11	0	25	1	3	1	0	2	.00	2	.181	.250	.276
1992 San Francisco	NL	68	140	32	5	0	4	(2	2)	49	9	15	11	0	33	0	3	0	0	1	.00	2	.229	.285	.350
4 ML YEARS		291	614	141	26	5	10	(5	5)	207	51	71	40	0	132	3	12	3	1	5	.17	12	.230	.279	.337

Scott Livingstone

Bats: Left **Throws:** Right **Pos:** 3B **Ht:** 6' 0" **Wt:** 198 **Born:** 07/15/65 **Age:** 27

Year Team	Lg	G	AB	H	2B	3B	HR	(Hm	Rd)	TB	R	RBI	TBB	IBB	SO	HBP	SH	SF	SB	CS	SB%	GDP	Avg	OBP	SLG
1988 Lakeland	A	53	180	51	8	1	2	--	--	67	28	25	11	3	25	3	2	2	1	1	.50	3	.283	.332	.372
1989 London	AA	124	452	98	18	1	14	--	--	160	46	71	52	4	67	2	0	6	1	1	.50	4	.217	.297	.354
1990 Toledo	AAA	103	345	94	19	0	6	--	--	131	44	36	21	0	40	1	0	1	1	5	.17	7	.272	.315	.380
1991 Toledo	AAA	92	331	100	13	3	3	--	--	128	48	62	40	3	52	2	3	6	2	1	.67	9	.302	.375	.387
1991 Detroit	AL	44	127	37	5	0	2	(1	1)	48	19	11	10	0	25	0	1	1	2	1	.67	0	.291	.341	.378
1992 Detroit	AL	117	354	100	21	0	4	(2	2)	133	43	46	21	1	36	0	3	4	1	3	.25	8	.282	.319	.376
2 ML YEARS		161	481	137	26	0	6	(3	3)	181	62	57	31	1	61	0	4	5	3	4	.43	8	.285	.325	.376

Kenny Lofton

Bats: Left **Throws:** Left **Pos:** CF **Ht:** 6' 0" **Wt:** 180 **Born:** 05/31/67 **Age:** 26

Year Team	Lg	G	AB	H	2B	3B	HR	(Hm	Rd)	TB	R	RBI	TBB	IBB	SO	HBP	SH	SF	SB	CS	SB%	GDP	Avg	OBP	SLG
1988 Auburn	A	48	187	40	6	1	1	--	--	51	23	14	19	0	51	0	1	0	26	4	.87	3	.214	.286	.273
1989 Auburn	A	34	110	29	3	1	0	--	--	34	21	8	14	0	30	0	1	4	26	5	.84	1	.264	.336	.309
Asheville	A	22	82	27	2	0	1	--	--	32	14	9	12	0	10	1	2	0	14	6	.70	1	.329	.421	.390
1990 Osceola	A	124	481	159	15	5	2	--	--	190	98	35	61	2	77	3	8	3	62	16	.79	4	.331	.407	.395
1991 Tucson	AAA	130	545	168	19	17	2	--	--	227	93	52	52	5	95	0	8	2	40	23	.63	2	.308	.367	.417
1991 Houston	NL	20	74	15	1	0	0	(0	0)	16	9	0	5	0	19	0	0	0	2	1	.67	0	.203	.253	.216
1992 Cleveland	AL	148	576	164	15	8	5	(3	2)	210	96	42	68	3	54	2	4	1	66	12	.85	7	.285	.362	.365
2 ML YEARS		168	650	179	16	8	5	(3	2)	226	105	42	73	3	73	2	4	1	68	13	.84	7	.275	.350	.348

Javier Lopez

Bats: Right **Throws:** Right **Pos:** C **Ht:** 6' 3" **Wt:** 210 **Born:** 11/05/70 **Age:** 22

Year Team	Lg	G	AB	H	2B	3B	HR	(Hm	Rd)	TB	R	RBI	TBB	IBB	SO	HBP	SH	SF	SB	CS	SB%	GDP	Avg	OBP	SLG
1988 Braves	R	31	94	18	4	0	1	--	--	25	8	9	3	0	19	0	1	1	1	0	1.00	0	.191	.214	.266
1989 Pulaski	R	51	153	40	8	1	3	--	--	59	27	27	5	0	35	1	0	3	3	2	.60	8	.261	.284	.386
1990 Burlington	A	116	422	112	17	3	11	--	--	168	48	55	14	2	84	5	4	0	0	2	.00	10	.265	.297	.398
1991 Durham	A	113	384	94	14	2	11	--	--	145	43	51	25	4	87	3	0	3	10	3	.77	10	.245	.294	.378
1992 Greenville	AA	115	442	142	28	3	16	--	--	224	64	60	24	1	47	5	1	2	7	3	.70	8	.321	.362	.507
1992 Atlanta	NL	9	16	6	2	0	0	(0	0)	8	3	2	0	0	1	0	0	0	0	0	.00	0	.375	.375	.500

Steve Lyons

Bats: Left **Throws:** Right **Pos:** 1B **Ht:** 6' 3" **Wt:** 205 **Born:** 06/03/60 **Age:** 33

Year Team	Lg	G	AB	H	2B	3B	HR	(Hm	Rd)	TB	R	RBI	TBB	IBB	SO	HBP	SH	SF	SB	CS	SB%	GDP	Avg	OBP	SLG
1985 Boston	AL	133	371	98	14	3	5	(4	1)	133	52	30	32	0	64	1	2	3	12	9	.57	2	.264	.322	.358
1986 2 ML Teams		101	247	56	9	3	1	(1	0)	74	30	20	19	2	47	1	4	4	4	6	.40	4	.227	.280	.300
1987 Chicago	AL	76	193	54	11	1	1	(1	0)	70	26	19	12	0	37	0	4	1	3	1	.75	4	.280	.320	.363
1988 Chicago	AL	146	472	127	28	3	5	(1	4)	176	59	45	32	1	59	1	15	6	1	2	.33	6	.269	.313	.373
1989 Chicago	AL	140	443	117	21	3	2	(0	2)	150	51	50	35	3	68	1	12	3	9	6	.60	3	.264	.317	.339
1990 Chicago	AL	94	146	28	6	1	1	(0	1)	39	22	11	10	1	41	1	4	2	1	0	1.00	1	.192	.245	.267
1991 Boston	AL	87	212	51	10	1	4	(2	2)	75	15	17	11	2	35	0	3	1	10	3	.77	1	.241	.277	.354
1992 3 ML Teams		48	55	11	0	2	0	(0	0)	15	5	4	3	0	8	0	1	0	1	3	.25	2	.200	.241	.273
1986 Boston	AL	59	124	31	7	2	1	(1	0)	45	20	14	12	2	23	0	1	2	2	3	.40	3	.250	.312	.363
Chicago	AL	42	123	25	2	1	0	(0	0)	29	10	6	7	0	24	1	3	2	2	3	.40	1	.203	.248	.236
1992 Atlanta	NL	11	14	1	0	0	0	(0	0)	3	0	1	0	0	4	0	0	0	0	0	.00	1	.071	.071	.214
Montreal	NL	16	13	3	0	0	0	(0	0)	3	2	1	1	0	3	0	1	0	1	2	.33	1	.231	.286	.231
Boston	AL	21	28	7	0	1	0	(0	0)	9	3	2	2	0	1	0	0	0	0	1	.00	0	.250	.300	.321
8 ML YEARS		825	2139	542	99	17	19	(8	11)	732	260	196	154	9	359	5	45	20	41	30	.58	23	.253	.302	.342

Kevin Maas

Bats: Left   **Throws:** Left   **Pos:** DH/1B   **Ht:** 6' 3"   **Wt:** 209   **Born:** 01/20/65   **Age:** 28

Year	Team	Lg	G	AB	H	2B	3B	HR	(Hm	Rd)	TB	R	RBI	TBB	IBB	SO	HBP	SH	SF	SB	CS	SB%	GDP	Avg	OBP	SLG
1990	New York	AL	79	254	64	9	0	21	(12	9)	136	42	41	43	10	76	3	0	0	1	2	.33	2	.252	.367	.535
1991	New York	AL	148	500	110	14	1	23	(8	15)	195	69	63	83	3	128	4	0	5	5	1	.83	4	.220	.333	.390
1992	New York	AL	98	286	71	12	0	11	(7	4)	116	35	35	25	4	63	0	0	4	3	1	.75	1	.248	.305	.406
	3 ML YEARS		325	1040	245	35	1	55	(27	28)	447	146	139	151	17	267	7	0	9	9	4	.69	7	.236	.334	.430

Bob MacDonald

Pitches: Left   **Bats:** Left   **Pos:** RP   **Ht:** 6' 3"   **Wt:** 208   **Born:** 04/27/65   **Age:** 28

Year	Team	Lg	G	GS	CG	GF	IP	BFP	H	R	ER	HR	SH	SF	HB	TBB	IBB	SO	WP	Bk	W	L	Pct.	ShO	Sv	ERA
1990	Toronto	AL	4	0	0	1	2.1	8	0	0	0	0	0	0	0	2	0	0	0	0	0	0	.000	0	0	0.00
1991	Toronto	AL	45	0	0	10	53.2	231	51	19	17	5	2	2	0	25	4	24	1	1	3	3	.500	0	0	2.85
1992	Toronto	AL	27	0	0	9	47.1	204	50	24	23	4	1	1	1	16	3	26	0	0	1	0	1.000	0	0	4.37
	3 ML YEARS		76	0	0	20	103.1	443	101	43	40	9	3	3	1	43	7	50	1	1	4	3	.571	0	0	3.48

Mike Macfarlane

Bats: Right   **Throws:** Right   **Pos:** C/DH   **Ht:** 6' 1"   **Wt:** 205   **Born:** 04/12/64   **Age:** 29

Year	Team	Lg	G	AB	H	2B	3B	HR	(Hm	Rd)	TB	R	RBI	TBB	IBB	SO	HBP	SH	SF	SB	CS	SB%	GDP	Avg	OBP	SLG
1987	Kansas City	AL	8	19	4	1	0	0	(0	0)	5	0	3	2	0	2	0	0	0	0	0	.00	1	.211	.286	.263
1988	Kansas City	AL	70	211	56	15	0	4	(2	2)	83	25	26	21	2	37	1	1	2	0	0	.00	5	.265	.332	.393
1989	Kansas City	AL	69	157	35	6	0	2	(0	2)	47	13	19	7	0	27	2	0	1	0	0	.00	8	.223	.263	.299
1990	Kansas City	AL	124	400	102	24	4	6	(1	5)	152	37	58	25	2	69	7	1	6	1	0	1.00	9	.255	.306	.380
1991	Kansas City	AL	84	267	74	18	2	13	(6	7)	135	34	41	17	0	52	6	1	4	1	0	1.00	4	.277	.330	.506
1992	Kansas City	AL	129	402	94	28	3	17	(7	10)	179	51	48	30	2	89	15	1	2	1	5	.17	8	.234	.310	.445
	6 ML YEARS		484	1456	365	92	9	42	(16	26)	601	160	195	102	6	276	31	4	15	3	5	.38	35	.251	.310	.413

Shane Mack

Bats: Right   **Throws:** Right   **Pos:** LF   **Ht:** 6' 0"   **Wt:** 185   **Born:** 12/07/63   **Age:** 29

Year	Team	Lg	G	AB	H	2B	3B	HR	(Hm	Rd)	TB	R	RBI	TBB	IBB	SO	HBP	SH	SF	SB	CS	SB%	GDP	Avg	OBP	SLG
1987	San Diego	NL	105	238	57	11	3	4	(2	2)	86	28	25	18	0	47	3	6	2	4	6	.40	11	.239	.299	.361
1988	San Diego	NL	56	119	29	3	0	0	(0	0)	32	13	12	14	0	21	3	3	1	5	1	.83	2	.244	.336	.269
1990	Minnesota	AL	125	313	102	10	4	8	(5	3)	144	50	44	29	1	69	5	6	0	13	4	.76	7	.326	.392	.460
1991	Minnesota	AL	143	442	137	27	8	18	(4	14)	234	79	74	34	1	79	6	2	5	13	9	.59	11	.310	.363	.529
1992	Minnesota	AL	156	600	189	31	6	16	(10	6)	280	101	75	64	1	106	15	11	2	26	14	.65	8	.315	.394	.467
	5 ML YEARS		585	1712	514	82	21	46	(21	25)	776	271	230	159	3	322	32	28	10	61	34	.64	39	.300	.369	.453

Greg Maddux

Pitches: Right   **Bats:** Right   **Pos:** SP   **Ht:** 6' 0"   **Wt:** 175   **Born:** 04/14/66   **Age:** 27

Year	Team	Lg	G	GS	CG	GF	IP	BFP	H	R	ER	HR	SH	SF	HB	TBB	IBB	SO	WP	Bk	W	L	Pct.	ShO	Sv	ERA
1986	Chicago	NL	6	5	1	1	31	144	44	20	19	3	1	0	1	11	2	20	2	0	2	4	.333	0	0	5.52
1987	Chicago	NL	30	27	1	2	155.2	701	181	111	97	17	7	1	4	74	13	101	4	7	6	14	.300	1	0	5.61
1988	Chicago	NL	34	34	9	0	249	1047	230	97	88	13	11	2	9	81	16	140	3	6	18	8	.692	3	0	3.18
1989	Chicago	NL	35	35	7	0	238.1	1002	222	90	78	13	18	6	6	82	13	135	5	3	19	12	.613	1	0	2.95
1990	Chicago	NL	35	35	8	0	237	1011	242	116	91	11	18	5	4	71	10	144	3	3	15	15	.500	2	0	3.46
1991	Chicago	NL	37	37	7	0	263	1070	232	113	98	18	16	3	6	66	9	198	6	3	15	11	.577	2	0	3.35
1992	Chicago	NL	35	35	9	0	268	1061	201	68	65	7	15	3	14	70	7	199	5	0	20	11	.645	4	0	2.18
	7 ML YEARS		212	208	42	3	1442	6036	1352	615	536	82	86	20	44	455	70	937	28	22	95	75	.559	13	0	3.35

Mike Maddux

Pitches: Right   **Bats:** Left   **Pos:** RP   **Ht:** 6' 2"   **Wt:** 190   **Born:** 08/27/61   **Age:** 31

Year	Team	Lg	G	GS	CG	GF	IP	BFP	H	R	ER	HR	SH	SF	HB	TBB	IBB	SO	WP	Bk	W	L	Pct.	ShO	Sv	ERA
1986	Philadelphia	NL	16	16	0	0	78	351	88	56	47	6	3	3	3	34	4	44	4	2	3	7	.300	0	0	5.42
1987	Philadelphia	NL	7	2	0	0	17	72	17	5	5	0	0	0	0	5	0	15	1	0	2	0	1.000	0	0	2.65
1988	Philadelphia	NL	25	11	0	4	88.2	380	91	41	37	6	7	3	5	34	4	59	4	2	4	3	.571	0	0	3.76
1989	Philadelphia	NL	16	4	2	1	43.2	191	52	29	25	3	3	1	2	14	3	26	3	1	1	3	.250	1	0	5.15
1990	Los Angeles	NL	11	2	0	3	20.2	88	24	15	15	0	0	1	1	4	0	11	2	0	0	1	.000	0	0	6.53
1991	San Diego	NL	64	1	0	27	98.2	388	78	30	27	4	5	2	1	27	3	57	5	0	7	2	.778	0	5	2.46
1992	San Diego	NL	50	1	0	14	79.2	330	71	25	21	2	2	3	0	24	4	60	4	1	2	2	.500	0	5	2.37
	7 ML YEARS		189	37	2	49	426.1	1800	421	201	177	24	20	13	12	142	18	272	23	6	19	18	.514	1	11	3.74

122

Dave Magadan

Bats: Left **Throws:** Right **Pos:** 3B **Ht:** 6' 3" **Wt:** 205 **Born:** 09/30/62 **Age:** 30

							BATTING											BASERUNNING				PERCENTAGES		
Year	Team	Lg	G	AB	H	2B	3B	HR	(Hm | Rd)	TB	R	RBI	TBB	IBB	SO	HBP	SH	SF	SB	CS	SB%	GDP	Avg	OBP	SLG
1986	New York	NL	10	18	8	0	0	0	(0 | 0)	8	3	3	3	0	1	0	0	0	0	0	.00	1	.444	.524	.444
1987	New York	NL	85	192	61	13	1	3	(2 | 1)	85	21	24	22	2	22	0	1	1	0	0	.00	5	.318	.386	.443
1988	New York	NL	112	314	87	15	0	1	(1 | 0)	105	39	35	60	4	39	2	1	3	0	1	.00	9	.277	.393	.334
1989	New York	NL	127	374	107	22	3	4	(3 | 1)	147	47	41	49	6	37	1	1	4	1	0	1.00	2	.286	.367	.393
1990	New York	NL	144	451	148	28	6	6	(2 | 4)	206	74	72	74	4	55	2	4	10	2	1	.67	11	.328	.417	.457
1991	New York	NL	124	418	108	23	0	4	(2 | 2)	143	58	51	83	3	50	2	7	7	1	1	.50	5	.258	.378	.342
1992	New York	NL	99	321	91	9	1	3	(2 | 1)	111	33	28	56	3	44	0	2	0	1	0	1.00	6	.283	.390	.346
	7 ML YEARS		701	2088	610	110	11	21	(12 | 9)	805	275	254	347	22	248	7	16	25	5	3	.63	39	.292	.391	.386

Mike Magnante

Pitches: Left **Bats:** Left **Pos:** RP/SP **Ht:** 6' 1" **Wt:** 180 **Born:** 06/17/65 **Age:** 28

			HOW MUCH HE PITCHED					WHAT HE GAVE UP										THE RESULTS					
Year	Team	Lg	G	GS	CG	GF	IP	BFP	H	R	ER	HR	SH	SF	HB	TBB	IBB	SO	WP	Bk	W	L	Pct.	ShO	Sv	ERA
1988	Eugene	A	3	3	0	0	16	59	10	6	1	0	0	0	0	2	0	26	0	0	1	1	.500	0	0	0.56
	Appleton	A	9	8	0	0	47.2	199	48	20	17	3	4	1	0	15	0	40	3	0	3	2	.600	0	0	3.21
	Baseball Cy	A	4	4	1	0	24	95	19	12	11	1	1	0	0	8	0	19	0	0	1	1	.500	0	0	4.13
1989	Memphis	AA	26	26	4	0	157.1	659	137	70	64	10	6	2	9	53	3	118	8	0	8	9	.471	1	0	3.66
1990	Omaha	AAA	13	13	2	0	76.2	320	72	39	35	6	3	0	2	25	0	56	3	1	2	5	.286	0	0	4.11
1991	Omaha	AAA	10	10	2	1	65.2	264	53	23	22	2	2	2	1	23	0	50	0	0	6	1	.857	0	0	3.02
1991	Kansas City	AL	38	0	0	10	55	236	55	19	15	3	2	1	0	23	3	42	1	0	0	1	.000	0	0	2.45
1992	Kansas City	AL	44	12	0	11	89.1	403	115	53	49	5	5	7	2	35	5	31	2	0	4	9	.308	0	0	4.94
	2 ML YEARS		82	12	0	21	144.1	639	170	72	64	8	7	8	2	58	8	73	3	0	4	10	.286	0	0	3.99

Joe Magrane

Pitches: Left **Bats:** Right **Pos:** SP **Ht:** 6' 6" **Wt:** 230 **Born:** 07/02/64 **Age:** 28

			HOW MUCH HE PITCHED					WHAT HE GAVE UP										THE RESULTS					
Year	Team	Lg	G	GS	CG	GF	IP	BFP	H	R	ER	HR	SH	SF	HB	TBB	IBB	SO	WP	Bk	W	L	Pct.	ShO	Sv	ERA
1987	St. Louis	NL	27	26	4	0	170.1	722	157	75	67	9	9	3	10	60	6	101	9	7	9	7	.563	2	0	3.54
1988	St. Louis	NL	24	24	4	0	165.1	677	133	57	40	8	6	4	2	51	4	100	8	8	5	9	.357	3	0	2.18
1989	St. Louis	NL	34	33	9	1	234.2	971	219	81	76	5	14	8	6	72	7	127	14	5	18	9	.667	3	0	2.91
1990	St. Louis	NL	31	31	3	0	203.1	855	204	86	81	10	8	6	8	59	7	100	11	1	10	17	.370	2	0	3.59
1992	St. Louis	NL	5	5	0	0	31.1	143	34	15	14	2	3	1	2	15	0	20	4	0	1	2	.333	0	0	4.02
	5 ML YEARS		121	119	20	1	805	3368	747	314	278	32	42	22	28	257	24	448	46	21	43	44	.494	10	0	3.11

Pat Mahomes

Pitches: Right **Bats:** Right **Pos:** SP **Ht:** 6' 1" **Wt:** 175 **Born:** 08/09/70 **Age:** 22

			HOW MUCH HE PITCHED					WHAT HE GAVE UP										THE RESULTS					
Year	Team	Lg	G	GS	CG	GF	IP	BFP	H	R	ER	HR	SH	SF	HB	TBB	IBB	SO	WP	Bk	W	L	Pct.	ShO	Sv	ERA
1988	Elizabethtn	R	13	13	3	0	78	344	66	45	32	4	3	1	0	51	0	93	9	2	6	3	.667	0	0	3.69
1989	Kenosha	A	25	25	3	0	156.1	668	120	66	57	4	0	9	2	100	3	167	9	3	13	7	.650	1	0	3.28
1990	Visalia	A	28	28	5	0	185.1	784	136	77	68	14	3	4	4	118	1	178	19	1	11	11	.500	1	0	3.30
1991	Orlando	AA	18	17	2	0	116	463	77	30	23	5	0	3	3	57	0	136	3	0	8	5	.615	0	0	1.78
	Portland	AAA	9	9	2	0	55	244	50	26	21	2	2	3	0	36	1	41	2	1	3	5	.375	0	0	3.44
1992	Portland	AAA	17	16	3	1	111	455	97	43	42	7	0	0	0	43	1	87	4	0	9	5	.643	3	1	3.41
1992	Minnesota	AL	14	13	0	1	69.2	302	73	41	39	5	0	3	0	37	0	44	2	1	3	4	.429	0	0	5.04

Mike Maksudian

Bats: Left **Throws:** Right **Pos:** 1B **Ht:** 5'11" **Wt:** 220 **Born:** 05/28/66 **Age:** 27

							BATTING											BASERUNNING				PERCENTAGES		
Year	Team	Lg	G	AB	H	2B	3B	HR	(Hm	Rd)	TB	R	RBI	TBB	IBB	SO	HBP	SH	SF	SB	CS	SB%	GDP	Avg	OBP	SLG
1987	White Sox	R	34	109	38	11	3	1	--	--	58	23	28	19	4	13	1	0	2	7	2	.78	2	.349	.443	.532
1988	South Bend	A	102	366	111	26	3	4	--	--	155	51	50	60	9	59	3	0	2	5	3	.63	5	.303	.404	.423
	Tampa	A	1	3	2	1	0	0	--	--	3	1	2	0	0	1	0	0	0	0	0	.00	0	.667	.667	1.000
	St. Lucie	A	13	42	9	2	1	0	--	--	13	7	1	8	0	6	0	0	1	0	0	.00	1	.214	.333	.310
1989	Miami	A	83	288	90	18	4	9	--	--	143	36	42	28	2	42	0	0	2	6	4	.60	11	.313	.371	.497
1990	Knoxville	AA	121	422	121	22	5	8	--	--	177	51	55	50	6	66	2	0	1	6	4	.60	9	.287	.364	.419
1991	Syracuse	AAA	31	97	32	6	3	1	--	--	47	13	13	10	0	17	0	1	0	0	0	.00	2	.330	.393	.485
	Knoxville	AA	71	231	59	12	3	5	--	--	92	32	35	37	5	43	0	0	5	2	2	.50	3	.255	.352	.398
1992	Syracuse	AAA	101	339	95	17	1	13	--	--	153	38	58	32	6	63	1	0	1	4	1	.80	7	.280	.343	.451
1992	Toronto	AL	3	3	0	0	0	0	(0	0)	0	0	0	0	0	0	0	0	0	0	0	.00	0	.000	.000	.000

Candy Maldonado

Bats: Right **Throws:** Right **Pos:** LF **Ht:** 6' 0" **Wt:** 195 **Born:** 09/05/60 **Age:** 32

Year	Team	Lg	G	AB	H	2B	3B	HR	(Hm	Rd)	TB	R	RBI	TBB	IBB	SO	HBP	SH	SF	SB	CS	SB%	GDP	Avg	OBP	SLG
1981	Los Angeles	NL	11	12	1	0	0	0	(0	0)	1	0	0	0	0	5	0	0	0	0	0	.00	0	.083	.083	.083
1982	Los Angeles	NL	6	4	0	0	0	0	(0	0)	0	0	0	1	1	2	0	0	0	0	0	.00	0	.000	.200	.000
1983	Los Angeles	NL	42	62	12	1	1	1	(1	0)	18	5	6	5	0	14	0	1	0	0	0	.00	0	.194	.254	.290
1984	Los Angeles	NL	116	254	68	14	0	5	(1	4)	97	25	28	19	0	29	1	1	3	0	3	.00	6	.268	.318	.382
1985	Los Angeles	NL	121	213	48	7	1	5	(2	3)	72	20	19	19	4	40	0	2	1	1	1	.50	3	.225	.288	.338
1986	San Francisco	NL	133	405	102	31	3	18	(6	12)	193	49	85	20	4	77	3	0	4	4	4	.50	12	.252	.289	.477
1987	San Francisco	NL	118	442	129	28	4	20	(14	6)	225	69	85	34	4	78	6	0	7	8	8	.50	9	.292	.346	.509
1988	San Francisco	NL	142	499	127	23	1	12	(5	7)	188	53	68	37	1	89	7	3	6	6	5	.55	13	.255	.311	.377
1989	San Francisco	NL	129	345	75	23	0	9	(1	8)	125	39	41	37	4	69	3	1	3	4	1	.80	8	.217	.296	.362
1990	Cleveland	AL	155	590	161	32	2	22	(12	10)	263	76	95	49	4	134	5	0	7	3	5	.38	13	.273	.330	.446
1991	2 ML Teams		86	288	72	15	0	12	(7	5)	123	37	48	36	4	76	6	0	3	4	0	1.00	8	.250	.342	.427
1992	Toronto	AL	137	489	133	25	4	20	(8	12)	226	64	66	59	3	112	7	2	3	2	2	.50	13	.272	.357	.462
1991	Milwaukee	AL	34	111	23	6	0	5	(3	2)	44	11	20	13	0	23	0	0	1	1	0	1.00	4	.207	.288	.396
	Toronto	AL	52	177	49	9	0	7	(4	3)	79	26	28	23	4	53	6	0	2	3	0	1.00	4	.277	.375	.446
12 ML YEARS			1196	3603	928	199	16	124	(57	67)	1531	437	541	316	29	725	38	10	37	32	29	.52	86	.258	.321	.425

Rob Mallicoat

Pitches: Left **Bats:** Left **Pos:** RP **Ht:** 6' 3" **Wt:** 180 **Born:** 11/16/64 **Age:** 28

Year	Team	Lg	G	GS	CG	GF	IP	BFP	H	R	ER	HR	SH	SF	HB	TBB	IBB	SO	WP	Bk	W	L	Pct.	ShO	Sv	ERA
1987	Houston	NL	4	1	0	0	6.2	31	8	5	5	0	0	0	0	6	0	4	0	0	0	0	.000	0	0	6.75
1991	Houston	NL	24	0	0	4	23.1	103	22	10	10	2	1	2	2	13	1	18	1	0	0	2	.000	0	0	3.86
1992	Houston	NL	23	0	0	6	23.2	120	26	19	19	2	3	1	5	19	2	20	2	0	0	0	.000	0	0	7.23
3 ML YEARS			51	1	0	10	53.2	254	56	34	34	4	4	3	7	38	3	42	3	0	0	2	.000	0	1	5.70

Barry Manuel

Pitches: Right **Bats:** Right **Pos:** RP **Ht:** 5'11" **Wt:** 185 **Born:** 08/12/65 **Age:** 27

Year	Team	Lg	G	GS	CG	GF	IP	BFP	H	R	ER	HR	SH	SF	HB	TBB	IBB	SO	WP	Bk	W	L	Pct.	ShO	Sv	ERA
1987	Rangers	R	1	0	0	0	1	7	3	2	2	0	0	0	0	1	0	1	2	0	0	0	.000	0	0	18.00
	Charlotte	A	13	5	0	3	30	138	33	24	22	2	1	2	3	18	0	19	4	0	1	2	.333	0	0	6.60
1988	Charlotte	A	37	0	0	22	60.1	259	47	24	17	4	6	1	4	32	0	55	8	3	4	3	.571	0	4	2.54
1989	Tulsa	AA	11	11	0	0	49.1	237	49	44	41	5	3	6	9	39	0	40	3	3	3	4	.429	0	0	7.48
	Charlotte	A	15	14	0	0	76.1	330	77	43	40	6	4	3	8	30	0	51	6	1	4	7	.364	0	0	4.72
1990	Charlotte	A	57	0	0	56	56.1	238	39	23	18	2	4	2	3	30	2	60	1	0	1	5	.167	0	36	2.88
1991	Tulsa	AA	56	0	0	48	68.1	300	63	29	25	5	4	2	5	34	1	45	0	1	2	7	.222	0	25	3.29
1992	Okla City	AAA	27	0	0	22	27.1	143	32	24	16	1	1	2	2	26	0	11	1	0	1	8	.111	0	5	5.27
	Tulsa	AA	16	1	0	8	27	122	28	12	12	4	0	1	1	16	0	28	0	0	2	0	1.000	0	0	4.00
1991	Texas	AL	8	0	0	5	16	58	7	2	2	0	0	3	0	6	0	5	2	0	1	0	1.000	0	0	1.13
1992	Texas	AL	3	0	0	0	5.2	25	6	3	3	2	0	0	1	1	0	9	0	0	1	0	1.000	0	0	4.76
2 ML YEARS			11	0	0	5	21.2	83	13	5	5	2	0	3	1	7	0	14	2	0	2	0	1.000	0	0	2.08

Kirt Manwaring

Bats: Right **Throws:** Right **Pos:** C **Ht:** 5'11" **Wt:** 190 **Born:** 07/15/65 **Age:** 27

Year	Team	Lg	G	AB	H	2B	3B	HR	(Hm	Rd)	TB	R	RBI	TBB	IBB	SO	HBP	SH	SF	SB	CS	SB%	GDP	Avg	OBP	SLG
1987	San Francisco	NL	6	7	1	0	0	0	(0	0)	1	0	0	0	0	1	1	0	0	0	0	.00	1	.143	.250	.143
1988	San Francisco	NL	40	116	29	7	0	1	(0	1)	39	12	15	2	0	21	3	1	1	0	1	.00	1	.250	.279	.336
1989	San Francisco	NL	85	200	42	4	2	0	(0	0)	50	14	18	11	1	28	4	7	1	2	1	.67	5	.210	.264	.250
1990	San Francisco	NL	8	13	2	0	1	0	(0	0)	4	0	1	0	0	3	0	0	0	0	0	.00	0	.154	.154	.308
1991	San Francisco	NL	67	178	40	9	0	0	(0	0)	49	16	19	9	0	22	3	7	2	1	1	.50	2	.225	.271	.275
1992	San Francisco	NL	109	349	85	10	5	4	(1	3)	117	24	26	29	0	42	5	6	0	2	1	.67	12	.244	.311	.335
6 ML YEARS			315	863	199	30	8	5	(1	4)	260	66	79	51	1	117	16	21	4	5	4	.56	21	.231	.285	.301

Tom Marsh

Bats: Right **Throws:** Right **Pos:** LF/RF **Ht:** 6' 2" **Wt:** 180 **Born:** 12/27/65 **Age:** 27

Year	Team	Lg	G	AB	H	2B	3B	HR	(Hm	Rd)	TB	R	RBI	TBB	IBB	SO	HBP	SH	SF	SB	CS	SB%	GDP	Avg	OBP	SLG
1988	Batavia	A	62	216	55	14	1	8	--	--	95	35	27	16	0	54	3	1	2	6	4	.60	2	.255	.318	.440
1989	Spartanburg	A	79	288	73	18	1	10	--	--	123	42	42	29	2	66	3	2	5	8	5	.62	2	.253	.323	.427
	Clearwater	A	43	141	24	2	1	1	--	--	31	12	10	7	0	30	2	4	0	5	2	.71	3	.170	.220	.220
1990	Spartanburg	A	24	75	21	2	1	1	--	--	37	14	15	8	1	21	3	0	0	5	2	.71	0	.280	.372	.493
	Reading	AA	41	132	34	6	1	1	--	--	45	13	10	8	0	27	3	4	1	5	0	1.00	3	.258	.313	.341

124

1991	Reading	AA	67	236	62	12	5	7	--	--	105	27	35	11	0	47	1	3	3	8	4	.67	7	.263	.295	.445
1992	Scranton/wb	AAA	45	158	38	7	2	8	--	--	73	26	25	10	0	30	2	1	0	5	4	.56	5	.241	.294	.462
1992	Philadelphia	NL	42	125	25	3	2	2	(1	1)	38	7	16	2	0	23	1	2	2	0	1	.00	2	.200	.215	.304

Al Martin

Bats: Left **Throws:** Left **Pos:** LF　　　　　　　**Ht:** 6' 2" **Wt:** 220 **Born:** 11/24/67 **Age:** 25

								BATTING												BASERUNNING				PERCENTAGES		
Year	Team	Lg	G	AB	H	2B	3B	HR	(Hm	Rd)	TB	R	RBI	TBB	IBB	SO	HBP	SH	SF	SB	CS	SB%	GDP	Avg	OBP	SLG
1985	Braves	R	40	138	32	3	0	0	--	--	35	16	9	19	2	36	2	0	1	1	4	.20	4	.232	.331	.254
1986	Sumter	A	44	156	38	5	0	1	--	--	46	23	24	23	1	36	0	0	0	6	2	.75	6	.244	.341	.295
	Idaho Falls	R	63	242	80	17	6	4	--	--	121	39	44	20	0	53	2	0	0	11	2	.85	1	.331	.386	.500
1987	Sumter	A	117	375	95	18	5	12	--	--	159	59	64	44	5	69	2	1	4	27	8	.77	5	.253	.332	.424
1988	Burlington	A	123	480	134	21	3	7	--	--	182	69	42	30	5	88	4	5	5	40	12	.77	6	.279	.324	.379
1989	Durham	A	128	457	124	26	3	9	--	--	183	84	48	34	0	107	3	0	3	27	14	.66	6	.271	.324	.400
1990	Greenville	AA	133	455	110	17	5	10	--	--	167	64	50	43	4	102	3	1	3	20	7	.74	9	.242	.310	.367
1991	Greenville	AA	86	301	73	13	3	7	--	--	113	38	38	32	4	84	8	1	1	19	7	.73	2	.243	.330	.375
	Richmond	AAA	44	151	42	11	1	5	--	--	70	20	18	7	0	33	1	0	0	11	2	.85	0	.278	.314	.464
1992	Buffalo	AAA	125	420	128	16	15	20	--	--	234	85	59	35	4	93	6	3	5	20	5	.80	1	.305	.363	.557
1992	Pittsburgh	NL	12	12	2	0	1	0	(0	0)	4	1	2	0	0	5	0	0	1	0	0	.00	0	.167	.154	.333

Carlos Martinez

Bats: Right **Throws:** Right **Pos:** 1B/3B　　　　　**Ht:** 6' 5" **Wt:** 175 **Born:** 08/11/65 **Age:** 27

								BATTING												BASERUNNING				PERCENTAGES		
Year	Team	Lg	G	AB	H	2B	3B	HR	(Hm	Rd)	TB	R	RBI	TBB	IBB	SO	HBP	SH	SF	SB	CS	SB%	GDP	Avg	OBP	SLG
1988	Chicago	AL	17	55	9	1	0	0	(0	0)	10	5	0	0	0	12	0	0	0	1	0	1.00	1	.164	.164	.182
1989	Chicago	AL	109	350	105	22	0	5	(2	3)	142	44	32	21	2	57	1	6	1	4	1	.80	14	.300	.340	.406
1990	Chicago	AL	92	272	61	6	5	4	(2	2)	89	18	24	10	2	40	0	1	0	0	4	.00	8	.224	.252	.327
1991	Cleveland	AL	72	257	73	14	0	5	(3	2)	102	22	30	10	2	43	2	1	5	3	2	.60	10	.284	.310	.397
1992	Cleveland	AL	69	228	60	9	1	5	(2	3)	86	23	35	7	0	21	1	1	4	1	2	.33	5	.263	.283	.377
	5 ML YEARS		359	1162	308	52	6	19	(9	10)	429	112	121	48	6	173	4	9	10	9	9	.50	38	.265	.294	.369

Chito Martinez

Bats: Left **Throws:** Left **Pos:** RF　　　　　　　**Ht:** 5'10" **Wt:** 182 **Born:** 12/19/65 **Age:** 27

								BATTING												BASERUNNING				PERCENTAGES		
Year	Team	Lg	G	AB	H	2B	3B	HR	(Hm	Rd)	TB	R	RBI	TBB	IBB	SO	HBP	SH	SF	SB	CS	SB%	GDP	Avg	OBP	SLG
1984	Eugene	A	59	176	53	12	3	0	--	--	71	18	26	24	2	38	0	1	0	4	4	.50	3	.301	.385	.403
1985	Ft. Myers	A	76	248	65	9	5	0	--	--	84	35	29	31	3	42	1	1	3	11	5	.69	8	.262	.343	.339
1986	Memphis	AA	93	283	86	16	5	11	--	--	145	48	44	42	4	58	2	2	1	4	4	.50	2	.304	.396	.512
1987	Omaha	AAA	35	121	26	10	1	2	--	--	44	14	14	11	0	43	0	0	0	0	0	.00	0	.215	.280	.364
	Memphis	AA	78	283	74	10	3	9	--	--	117	34	43	33	0	94	1	0	2	5	3	.63	4	.261	.339	.413
1988	Memphis	AA	141	485	110	16	4	13	--	--	173	67	65	66	4	130	1	2	6	20	3	.87	6	.227	.317	.357
1989	Memphis	AA	127	399	97	20	2	23	--	--	190	55	62	63	7	137	1	4	4	3	3	.50	8	.243	.345	.476
1990	Omaha	AAA	122	364	96	12	8	21	--	--	187	59	67	54	5	129	3	0	3	6	6	.50	3	.264	.361	.514
1991	Rochester	AAA	60	211	68	8	1	20	--	--	138	42	50	26	3	69	0	0	2	2	2	.50	3	.322	.393	.654
1991	Baltimore	AL	67	216	58	12	1	13	(8	5)	111	32	33	11	0	51	0	0	1	1	1	.50	2	.269	.303	.514
1992	Baltimore	AL	83	198	53	10	1	5	(2	3)	80	26	25	31	4	47	2	0	4	0	1	.00	9	.268	.366	.404
	2 ML YEARS		150	414	111	22	2	18	(10	8)	191	58	58	42	4	98	2	0	5	1	2	.33	11	.268	.335	.461

Dave Martinez

Bats: Left **Throws:** Left **Pos:** CF/1B　　　　　**Ht:** 5'10" **Wt:** 175 **Born:** 09/26/64 **Age:** 28

								BATTING												BASERUNNING				PERCENTAGES		
Year	Team	Lg	G	AB	H	2B	3B	HR	(Hm	Rd)	TB	R	RBI	TBB	IBB	SO	HBP	SH	SF	SB	CS	SB%	GDP	Avg	OBP	SLG
1986	Chicago	NL	53	108	15	1	1	1	(1	0)	21	13	7	6	0	22	1	0	1	4	2	.67	1	.139	.190	.194
1987	Chicago	NL	142	459	134	18	8	8	(5	3)	192	70	36	57	4	96	2	1	1	16	8	.67	4	.292	.372	.418
1988	2 ML Teams		138	447	114	13	6	6	(2	4)	157	51	46	38	8	94	2	2	5	23	9	.72	3	.255	.313	.351
1989	Montreal	NL	126	361	99	16	7	3	--	--	138	41	27	27	2	57	0	7	1	23	4	.85	1	.274	.324	.382
1990	Montreal	NL	118	391	109	13	5	11	(5	6)	165	60	39	24	2	48	1	3	2	13	11	.54	8	.279	.321	.422
1991	Montreal	NL	124	396	117	18	5	7	(3	4)	166	47	42	20	3	54	3	5	3	16	7	.70	3	.295	.332	.419
1992	Cincinnati	NL	135	393	100	20	5	3	(3	0)	139	47	31	42	4	54	0	6	4	12	8	.60	6	.254	.323	.354
1988	Chicago	NL	75	256	65	10	1	4	(2	2)	89	27	34	21	5	46	2	0	4	7	3	.70	2	.254	.311	.348
	Montreal		63	191	49	3	5	2	(0	2)	68	24	12	17	3	48	0	2	1	16	6	.73	1	.257	.316	.356
	7 ML YEARS		836	2555	688	99	37	39	(20	19)	978	329	228	214	23	425	9	24	17	107	49	.69	26	.269	.326	.383

Dennis Martinez

Pitches: Right **Bats:** Right **Pos:** SP **Ht:** 6' 1" **Wt:** 180 **Born:** 05/14/55 **Age:** 38

Year Team	Lg	G	GS	CG	GF	IP	BFP	H	R	ER	HR	SH	SF	HB	TBB	IBB	SO	WP	Bk	W	L	Pct.	ShO	Sv	ERA
1976 Baltimore	AL	4	2	1	1	28	106	23	8	8	1	1	0	0	8	0	18	1	0	1	2	.333	0	0	2.57
1977 Baltimore	AL	42	13	5	19	167	709	157	86	76	10	8	8	8	64	5	107	5	0	14	7	.667	0	4	4.10
1978 Baltimore	AL	40	38	15	0	276	1140	257	121	108	20	8	7	3	93	4	142	8	0	16	11	.593	2	0	3.52
1979 Baltimore	AL	40	39	18	0	292	1206	279	129	119	28	12	12	1	78	1	132	9	2	15	16	.484	3	0	3.67
1980 Baltimore	AL	25	12	2	8	100	428	103	44	44	12	1	3	2	44	6	42	0	1	6	4	.600	0	1	3.96
1981 Baltimore	AL	25	24	9	0	179	753	173	84	66	10	2	5	2	62	1	88	6	1	14	5	.737	2	0	3.32
1982 Baltimore	AL	40	39	10	0	252	1093	262	123	118	30	11	7	7	87	2	111	7	1	16	12	.571	2	0	4.21
1983 Baltimore	AL	32	25	4	3	153	688	209	108	94	21	3	5	2	45	0	71	2	0	7	16	.304	0	0	5.53
1984 Baltimore	AL	34	20	2	4	141.2	599	145	81	79	26	0	5	5	37	2	77	13	0	6	9	.400	0	0	5.02
1985 Baltimore	AL	33	31	3	1	180	789	203	110	103	29	0	11	9	63	3	68	4	1	13	11	.542	1	0	5.15
1986 2 ML Teams		23	15	1	2	104.2	449	114	57	55	11	8	2	3	30	4	65	3	2	3	6	.333	1	0	4.73
1987 Montreal	NL	22	22	2	0	144.2	599	133	59	53	9	4	3	6	40	2	84	4	2	11	4	.733	1	0	3.30
1988 Montreal	NL	34	34	9	0	235.1	968	215	94	71	21	2	6	6	55	3	120	5	10	15	13	.536	2	0	2.72
1989 Montreal	NL	34	33	5	1	232	950	227	88	82	21	8	2	7	49	4	142	5	2	16	7	.696	2	0	3.18
1990 Montreal	NL	32	32	7	0	226	908	191	80	74	16	11	3	6	49	9	156	1	1	10	11	.476	2	0	2.95
1991 Montreal	NL	31	31	9	0	222	905	187	70	59	9	7	3	4	62	3	123	3	0	14	11	.560	5	0	2.39
1992 Montreal	NL	32	32	6	0	226.1	900	172	75	62	12	12	5	9	60	3	147	2	0	16	11	.593	0	0	2.47
1986 Baltimore	AL	4	0	0	1	6.2	33	11	5	5	0	0	1	0	2	0	2	1	0	0	0	.000	0	0	6.75
Montreal	NL	19	15	1	1	98	416	103	52	50	11	8	1	3	28	4	63	2	2	3	6	.333	1	0	4.59
17 ML YEARS		523	442	108	39	3159.2	13190	3050	1417	1271	286	98	87	80	926	52	1693	78	23	193	156	.553	23	5	3.62

Domingo Martinez

Bats: Right **Throws:** Right **Pos:** 1B **Ht:** 6' 2" **Wt:** 210 **Born:** 08/04/67 **Age:** 25

Year Team	Lg	G	AB	H	2B	3B	HR	(Hm	Rd)	TB	R	RBI	TBB	IBB	SO	HBP	SH	SF	SB	CS	SB%	GDP	Avg	OBP	SLG
1985 Blue Jays	R	58	219	65	10	2	4	--	--	91	36	19	12	0	42	2	0	0	3	4	.43	3	.297	.339	.416
1986 Ventura	A	129	455	113	19	6	9	--	--	171	51	57	36	2	127	4	3	3	9	9	.50	15	.248	.307	.376
1987 Dunedin	A	118	435	112	32	2	8	--	--	172	53	65	41	2	88	3	0	2	8	3	.73	9	.257	.324	.395
1988 Knoxville	AA	143	516	136	25	2	13	--	--	204	54	70	40	3	88	5	0	7	2	7	.22	13	.264	.319	.395
1989 Knoxville	AA	120	415	102	19	2	10	--	--	155	56	53	42	3	82	9	1	5	2	2	.50	7	.246	.325	.373
1990 Knoxville	AA	128	463	119	20	3	17	--	--	196	52	67	51	1	81	5	1	2	2	3	.40	24	.257	.336	.423
1991 Syracuse	AAA	126	467	146	16	2	17	--	--	217	61	83	41	0	107	6	5	6	6	4	.60	10	.313	.371	.465
1992 Syracuse	AAA	116	438	120	22	2	21	--	--	205	55	62	33	5	95	8	0	4	6	0	1.00	11	.274	.333	.468
1992 Toronto	AL	7	8	5	0	0	1	(1	0)	8	2	3	0	0	0	0	0	0	0	0	.00	0	.625	.625	1.000

Edgar Martinez

Bats: Right **Throws:** Right **Pos:** 3B/DH **Ht:** 5'11" **Wt:** 175 **Born:** 01/02/63 **Age:** 30

Year Team	Lg	G	AB	H	2B	3B	HR	(Hm	Rd)	TB	R	RBI	TBB	IBB	SO	HBP	SH	SF	SB	CS	SB%	GDP	Avg	OBP	SLG
1987 Seattle	AL	13	43	16	5	2	0	(0	0)	25	6	5	2	0	5	1	0	0	0	0	.00	0	.372	.413	.581
1988 Seattle	AL	14	32	9	4	0	0	(0	0)	13	0	5	4	0	7	0	1	1	0	0	.00	0	.281	.351	.406
1989 Seattle	AL	65	171	41	5	0	2	(0	2)	52	20	20	17	1	26	3	2	3	2	1	.67	3	.240	.314	.304
1990 Seattle	AL	144	487	147	27	2	11	(3	8)	211	71	49	74	3	62	5	1	3	1	4	.20	13	.302	.397	.433
1991 Seattle	AL	150	544	167	35	1	14	(8	6)	246	98	52	84	9	72	8	2	4	0	3	.00	19	.307	.405	.452
1992 Seattle	AL	135	528	181	46	3	18	(11	7)	287	100	73	54	2	61	4	1	5	14	4	.78	15	.343	.404	.544
6 ML YEARS		521	1805	561	122	8	45	(22	23)	834	295	204	235	15	233	21	7	16	17	12	.59	50	.311	.393	.462

Pedro Martinez

Pitches: Right **Bats:** Right **Pos:** SP **Ht:** 5'11" **Wt:** 150 **Born:** 07/25/71 **Age:** 21

Year Team	Lg	G	GS	CG	GF	IP	BFP	H	R	ER	HR	SH	SF	HB	TBB	IBB	SO	WP	Bk	W	L	Pct.	ShO	Sv	ERA
1990 Great Falls	R	14	14	0	0	77	346	74	39	31	5	2	2	8	40	1	82	6	1	8	3	.727	0	0	3.62
1991 Bakersfield	A	10	10	0	0	61.1	243	41	17	14	3	0	2	5	19	0	83	1	1	8	0	1.000	0	0	2.05
San Antonio	AA	12	12	4	0	76.2	310	57	21	15	1	5	0	3	31	1	74	5	1	7	5	.583	3	0	1.76
Albuquerque	AAA	6	6	0	0	39.1	157	28	17	16	3	1	1	0	16	0	35	0	2	3	3	.500	0	0	3.66
1992 Albuquerque	AAA	20	20	3	0	125.1	527	104	57	53	10	4	2	9	57	0	124	2	0	7	6	.538	1	0	3.81
1992 Los Angeles	NL	2	1	0	1	8	31	6	2	2	0	0	0	0	1	0	8	0	0	0	1	.000	0	0	2.25

Ramon Martinez

Pitches: Right **Bats:** Left **Pos:** SP   **Ht:** 6' 4" **Wt:** 173 **Born:** 03/22/68 **Age:** 25

Year	Team	Lg	G	GS	CG	GF	IP	BFP	H	R	ER	HR	SH	SF	HB	TBB	IBB	SO	WP	Bk	W	L	Pct.	ShO	Sv	ERA
1988	Los Angeles	NL	9	6	0	0	35.2	151	27	17	15	0	4	0	0	22	1	23	1	0	1	3	.250	0	0	3.79
1989	Los Angeles	NL	15	15	2	0	98.2	410	79	39	35	11	4	0	5	41	1	89	1	0	6	4	.600	2	0	3.19
1990	Los Angeles	NL	33	33	12	0	234.1	950	191	89	76	22	7	5	4	67	5	223	3	3	20	6	.769	3	0	2.92
1991	Los Angeles	NL	33	33	6	0	220.1	916	190	89	80	18	8	4	7	69	4	150	6	0	17	13	.567	4	0	3.27
1992	Los Angeles	NL	25	25	1	0	150.2	662	141	82	67	11	12	1	5	69	4	101	9	0	8	11	.421	1	0	4.00
	5 ML YEARS		115	112	21	0	739.2	3089	628	316	273	62	35	10	21	268	15	586	20	3	52	37	.584	10	0	3.32

Tino Martinez

Bats: Left **Throws:** Right **Pos:** 1B/DH   **Ht:** 6' 2" **Wt:** 205 **Born:** 12/07/67 **Age:** 25

Year	Team	Lg	G	AB	H	2B	3B	HR	(Hm	Rd)	TB	R	RBI	TBB	IBB	SO	HBP	SH	SF	SB	CS	SB%	GDP	Avg	OBP	SLG
1990	Seattle	AL	24	68	15	4	0	0	(0	0)	19	4	5	9	0	9	0	0	1	0	0	.00	0	.221	.308	.279
1991	Seattle	AL	36	112	23	2	0	4	(3	1)	37	11	9	11	0	24	0	0	2	0	0	.00	2	.205	.272	.330
1992	Seattle	AL	136	460	118	19	2	16	(10	6)	189	53	66	42	9	77	2	1	8	2	1	.67	24	.257	.316	.411
	3 ML YEARS		196	640	156	25	2	20	(13	7)	245	68	80	62	9	110	2	1	11	2	1	.67	26	.244	.308	.383

John Marzano

Bats: Right **Throws:** Right **Pos:** C   **Ht:** 5'11" **Wt:** 195 **Born:** 02/14/63 **Age:** 30

Year	Team	Lg	G	AB	H	2B	3B	HR	(Hm	Rd)	TB	R	RBI	TBB	IBB	SO	HBP	SH	SF	SB	CS	SB%	GDP	Avg	OBP	SLG
1987	Boston	AL	52	168	41	11	0	5	(4	1)	67	20	24	7	0	41	3	2	2	0	1	.00	3	.244	.283	.399
1988	Boston	AL	10	29	4	1	0	0	(0	0)	5	3	1	1	0	3	0	0	0	0	0	.00	1	.138	.167	.172
1989	Boston	AL	7	18	8	3	0	1	(1	0)	14	5	3	0	0	2	0	1	1	0	0	.00	1	.444	.421	.778
1990	Boston	AL	32	83	20	4	0	0	(0	0)	24	8	6	5	0	10	0	2	1	0	1	.00	0	.241	.281	.289
1991	Boston	AL	49	114	30	8	0	0	(0	0)	38	10	9	1	0	16	1	1	2	0	0	.00	5	.263	.271	.333
1992	Boston	AL	19	50	4	2	1	0	(0	0)	8	4	1	2	0	12	1	1	0	0	0	.00	0	.080	.132	.160
	6 ML YEARS		169	462	107	29	1	6	(5	1)	156	50	44	16	0	84	5	7	6	0	2	.00	10	.232	.262	.338

Roger Mason

Pitches: Right **Bats:** Right **Pos:** RP   **Ht:** 6' 6" **Wt:** 220 **Born:** 09/18/58 **Age:** 34

Year	Team	Lg	G	GS	CG	GF	IP	BFP	H	R	ER	HR	SH	SF	HB	TBB	IBB	SO	WP	Bk	W	L	Pct.	ShO	Sv	ERA
1984	Detroit	AL	5	2	0	2	22	97	23	11	11	1	0	2	0	10	0	15	2	0	1	1	.500	0	1	4.50
1985	San Francisco	NL	5	5	1	0	29.2	128	28	13	7	1	2	0	0	11	1	26	0	0	1	3	.250	1	0	2.12
1986	San Francisco	NL	11	11	1	0	60	262	56	35	32	5	2	3	3	30	3	43	1	0	3	4	.429	0	0	4.80
1987	San Francisco	NL	5	5	0	0	26	110	30	15	13	4	1	0	0	10	0	18	1	1	1	1	.500	0	0	4.50
1989	Houston	NL	2	0	0	1	1.1	8	2	3	3	0	0	0	0	2	0	3	0	0	0	0	.000	0	0	20.25
1991	Pittsburgh	NL	24	0	0	9	29.2	114	21	11	10	2	1	1	1	6	1	21	2	0	3	2	.600	0	3	3.03
1992	Pittsburgh	NL	65	0	0	26	88	374	80	41	40	11	8	4	4	33	8	56	3	0	5	7	.417	0	8	4.09
	7 ML YEARS		117	23	2	35	256.2	1093	240	129	116	24	14	10	8	102	13	182	9	1	14	18	.438	1	12	4.07

Greg Mathews

Pitches: Left **Bats:** Right **Pos:** SP/RP   **Ht:** 6' 2" **Wt:** 180 **Born:** 05/17/62 **Age:** 31

Year	Team	Lg	G	GS	CG	GF	IP	BFP	H	R	ER	HR	SH	SF	HB	TBB	IBB	SO	WP	Bk	W	L	Pct.	ShO	Sv	ERA
1986	St. Louis	NL	23	22	1	1	145.1	591	139	61	59	15	7	1	2	44	3	67	5	6	11	8	.579	0	0	3.65
1987	St. Louis	NL	32	32	2	0	197.2	822	184	87	82	17	9	2	0	71	5	108	7	2	11	11	.500	1	0	3.73
1988	St. Louis	NL	13	13	1	0	68	286	61	34	32	4	1	3	2	33	5	31	4	4	4	6	.400	0	0	4.24
1990	St. Louis	NL	11	10	0	0	50.2	229	53	34	30	2	4	2	2	30	1	18	2	1	0	5	.000	0	0	5.33
1992	Philadelphia	NL	14	7	0	1	52.1	228	54	31	30	7	2	1	1	24	2	27	1	2	2	3	.400	1	0	5.16
	5 ML YEARS		93	84	4	2	514	2156	491	247	233	45	23	9	7	202	16	251	19	15	28	33	.459	1	0	4.08

Terry Mathews

Pitches: Right **Bats:** Left **Pos:** RP   **Ht:** 6' 2" **Wt:** 225 **Born:** 10/05/64 **Age:** 28

Year	Team	Lg	G	GS	CG	GF	IP	BFP	H	R	ER	HR	SH	SF	HB	TBB	IBB	SO	WP	Bk	W	L	Pct.	ShO	Sv	ERA
1987	Gastonia	A	34	1	0	13	48.1	234	53	35	30	5	4	5	2	32	4	46	7	1	3	3	.500	0	0	5.59
1988	Charlotte	A	27	26	2	0	163.2	672	141	68	51	6	3	3	4	49	2	94	11	3	13	6	.684	1	0	2.80
1989	Tulsa	AA	10	10	1	0	45.1	211	53	40	31	3	2	6	2	24	1	32	6	3	2	5	.286	0	0	6.15
	Charlotte	A	10	10	0	0	59.1	241	55	28	24	2	1	3	2	17	0	30	2	0	4	2	.667	0	0	3.64
1990	Tulsa	AA	14	14	4	0	86.1	375	88	50	41	1	1	6	2	36	2	48	9	0	5	7	.417	2	0	4.27
	Okla City	AAA	12	11	1	0	70.2	307	81	39	29	4	3	4	3	15	0	36	2	0	2	7	.222	1	0	3.69

Year	Team	Lg	G	GS	CG	GF	IP	BFP	H	R	ER	HR	SH	SF	HB	TBB	IBB	SO	WP	Bk	W	L	Pct.	ShO	Sv	ERA
1991	Okla City	AAA	18	13	1	2	95.1	410	98	39	37	2	3	3	2	34	3	63	4	1	5	6	.455	0	1	3.49
1992	Okla City	AAA	9	2	0	3	16.2	73	17	8	8	1	0	0	1	7	0	13	2	0	1	1	.500	0	1	4.32
1991	Texas	AL	34	2	0	0	57.1	236	54	24	23	5	2	0	1	18	3	51	5	0	4	0	1.000	0	1	3.61
1992	Texas	AL	40	0	0	11	42.1	199	48	29	28	4	1	3	1	31	3	26	2	1	2	4	.333	0	0	5.95
	2 ML YEARS		74	2	0	19	99.2	435	102	53	51	9	3	3	2	49	6	77	7	1	6	4	.600	0	1	4.61

Don Mattingly

Bats: Left **Throws:** Left **Pos:** 1B/DH **Ht:** 6' 0" **Wt:** 192 **Born:** 04/20/61 **Age:** 32

								BATTING												BASERUNNING				PERCENTAGES		
Year	Team	Lg	G	AB	H	2B	3B	HR	(Hm	Rd)	TB	R	RBI	TBB	IBB	SO	HBP	SH	SF	SB	CS	SB%	GDP	Avg	OBP	SLG
1982	New York	AL	7	12	2	0	0	0	(0	0)	2	0	1	0	0	1	0	0	1	0	0	.00	2	.167	.154	.167
1983	New York	AL	91	279	79	15	4	4	(0	4)	114	34	32	21	5	31	1	2	2	0	0	.00	8	.283	.333	.409
1984	New York	AL	153	603	207	44	2	23	(12	11)	324	91	110	41	8	33	1	8	9	1	1	.50	15	.343	.381	.537
1985	New York	AL	159	652	211	48	3	35	(22	13)	370	107	145	56	13	41	2	2	15	2	2	.50	15	.324	.371	.567
1986	New York	AL	162	677	238	53	2	31	(17	14)	388	117	113	53	11	35	1	1	10	0	0	.00	17	.352	.394	.573
1987	New York	AL	141	569	186	38	2	30	(17	13)	318	93	115	51	13	38	1	0	8	1	4	.20	16	.327	.378	.559
1988	New York	AL	144	599	186	37	0	18	(11	7)	277	94	88	41	14	29	3	0	8	1	0	1.00	13	.311	.353	.462
1989	New York	AL	158	631	191	37	2	23	(19	4)	301	79	113	51	18	30	1	0	10	3	0	1.00	15	.303	.351	.477
1990	New York	AL	102	394	101	16	0	5	(4	1)	132	40	42	28	13	20	3	0	3	1	0	1.00	13	.256	.308	.335
1991	New York	AL	152	587	169	35	0	9	(7	2)	231	64	68	46	11	42	4	0	9	2	0	1.00	21	.288	.339	.394
1992	New York	AL	157	640	184	40	0	14	(6	8)	266	89	86	39	7	43	1	0	6	3	0	1.00	11	.288	.327	.416
	11 ML YEARS		1426	5643	1754	363	15	192	(115	77)	2723	808	913	427	113	343	18	13	81	14	7	.67	146	.311	.356	.483

Rob Maurer

Bats: Left **Throws:** Left **Pos:** 1B **Ht:** 6' 3" **Wt:** 210 **Born:** 01/07/67 **Age:** 26

								BATTING												BASERUNNING				PERCENTAGES		
Year	Team	Lg	G	AB	H	2B	3B	HR	(Hm	Rd)	TB	R	RBI	TBB	IBB	SO	HBP	SH	SF	SB	CS	SB%	GDP	Avg	OBP	SLG
1988	Butte	R	63	233	91	18	3	8	--	--	139	65	60	35	3	33	3	0	2	0	0	.00	2	.391	.473	.597
1989	Charlotte	A	132	456	126	18	9	6	--	--	180	69	51	86	6	109	8	0	4	3	4	.43	9	.276	.397	.395
1990	Tulsa	AA	104	367	110	31	4	21	--	--	212	55	78	54	6	112	6	0	2	4	2	.67	5	.300	.396	.578
1991	Okla City	AAA	132	459	138	41	3	20	--	--	245	76	77	96	8	134	3	0	6	2	3	.40	5	.301	.420	.534
1992	Okla City	AAA	135	493	142	34	2	10	--	--	210	76	82	75	3	117	4	1	7	1	1	.50	9	.288	.382	.426
1991	Texas	AL	13	16	1	1	0	0	(0	0)	2	0	2	2	0	6	1	0	0	0	0	.00	0	.063	.211	.125
1992	Texas	AL	8	9	2	0	0	0	(0	0)	2	1	1	1	0	2	0	0	0	0	0	.00	0	.222	.300	.222
	2 ML YEARS		21	25	3	1	0	0	(0	0)	4	1	3	3	0	8	1	0	0	0	0	.00	0	.120	.241	.160

Derrick May

Bats: Left **Throws:** Right **Pos:** LF/RF **Ht:** 6' 4" **Wt:** 205 **Born:** 07/14/68 **Age:** 24

								BATTING												BASERUNNING				PERCENTAGES		
Year	Team	Lg	G	AB	H	2B	3B	HR	(Hm	Rd)	TB	R	RBI	TBB	IBB	SO	HBP	SH	SF	SB	CS	SB%	GDP	Avg	OBP	SLG
1986	Wytheville	R	54	178	57	6	1	0	--	--	65	25	24	16	1	52	2	0	1	17	4	.81	5	.320	.381	.365
1987	Peoria	A	128	439	131	19	8	9	--	--	193	60	52	42	4	106	1	0	5	5	7	.42	5	.298	.357	.440
1988	Winston-Sal	A	130	485	148	29	9	8	--	--	219	76	65	37	4	82	5	0	5	13	8	.62	3	.305	.357	.452
1989	Charlotte	AA	136	491	145	26	5	9	--	--	208	72	70	33	4	76	5	1	0	19	7	.73	8	.295	.346	.424
1990	Iowa	AAA	119	459	136	27	1	8	--	--	189	55	69	23	4	50	0	1	6	5	6	.45	11	.296	.326	.412
1991	Iowa	AAA	82	310	92	18	4	3	--	--	127	47	49	19	4	38	4	1	3	7	9	.44	9	.297	.342	.410
1992	Iowa	AAA	3	30	11	4	1	2	--	--	23	6	8	3	0	3	0	0	0	0	0	.00	1	.367	.424	.767
1990	Chicago	NL	17	61	15	3	0	1	(1	0)	21	8	11	2	0	7	0	0	0	1	0	1.00	1	.246	.270	.344
1991	Chicago	NL	15	22	5	2	0	1	(1	0)	10	4	3	2	0	1	0	0	0	0	0	.00	1	.227	.280	.455
1992	Chicago	NL	124	351	96	11	0	8	(3	5)	131	33	45	14	4	40	3	2	1	5	3	.63	9	.274	.306	.373
	3 ML YEARS		156	434	116	16	0	10	(5	5)	162	45	59	18	4	48	3	2	2	6	3	.67	11	.267	.300	.373

Brent Mayne

Bats: Left **Throws:** Right **Pos:** C **Ht:** 6' 1" **Wt:** 190 **Born:** 04/19/68 **Age:** 25

								BATTING												BASERUNNING				PERCENTAGES		
Year	Team	Lg	G	AB	H	2B	3B	HR	(Hm	Rd)	TB	R	RBI	TBB	IBB	SO	HBP	SH	SF	SB	CS	SB%	GDP	Avg	OBP	SLG
1990	Kansas City	AL	5	13	3	0	0	0	(0	0)	3	2	1	3	0	3	0	0	0	0	1	.00	0	.231	.375	.231
1991	Kansas City	AL	85	231	58	8	0	3	(2	1)	75	22	31	23	4	42	0	2	3	2	4	.33	6	.251	.315	.325
1992	Kansas City	AL	82	213	48	10	0	0	(0	0)	58	16	18	11	0	26	0	2	3	0	4	.00	5	.225	.260	.272
	3 ML YEARS		172	457	109	18	0	3	(2	1)	136	40	50	37	4	71	0	4	6	2	9	.18	11	.239	.292	.298

Matt Maysey

Pitches: Right **Bats:** Right **Pos:** RP **Ht:** 6' 4" **Wt:** 225 **Born:** 01/08/67 **Age:** 26

								HOW MUCH HE PITCHED		WHAT HE GAVE UP										THE RESULTS					
Year	Team	Lg	G	GS	CG	GF	IP	BFP	H	R	ER	HR	SH	SF	HB	TBB	IBB	SO	WP	Bk	W	L	Pct.	ShO	Sv	ERA
1985	Spokane	A	7	4	0	2	29		27	18	15	3	0	0	1	16	0	18	5	0	0	3	.000	0	0	4.66
1986	Charleston	A	18	5	0	11	43	196	43	28	24	5	3	0	3	24	2	39	5	2	3	2	.600	0	1	5.02

Year	Team	Lg	G	GS	CG	GF	IP	BFP	H	R	ER	HR	SH	SF	HB	TBB	IBB	SO	WP	Bk	W	L	Pct.	ShO	Sv	ERA
1987	Chston-Sc	A	41	18	5	21	150.1	623	112	71	53	13	8	7	5	59	4	143	13	3	14	11	.560	0	7	3.17
1988	Wichita	AA	28	28	4	0	187	789	180	88	77	15	7	6	5	68	1	120	18	5	9	9	.500	0	0	3.71
1989	Las Vegas	AAA	28	28	4	0	176.1	773	173	94	80	19	3	1	2	84	3	96	12	3	8	12	.400	1	0	4.08
1990	Las Vegas	AAA	26	25	1	1	137.2	634	155	97	86	10	6	5	5	88	5	72	12	1	6	10	.375	0	0	5.62
1991	Harrisburg	AA	15	15	2	0	104.2	419	90	26	22	3	2	3	2	28	0	86	8	0	6	5	.545	2	0	1.89
	Indianapols	AAA	12	12	0	0	63	272	60	45	36	7	0	1	2	33	2	45	6	0	3	6	.333	0	0	5.14
1992	Indianapols	AAA	35	1	0	14	67	286	63	32	32	9	4	2	0	28	5	38	2	1	5	3	.625	0	5	4.30
1992	Montreal	NL	2	0	0	1	2.1	12	4	1	1	0	0	1	0	0	0	0	1	0	0	0	.000	0	0	3.86

Kirk McCaskill

Pitches: Right **Bats:** Right **Pos:** SP **Ht:** 6' 1" **Wt:** 205 **Born:** 04/09/61 **Age:** 32

			HOW MUCH HE PITCHED						WHAT HE GAVE UP											THE RESULTS					
Year	Team	Lg	G	GS	CG	GF	IP	BFP	H	R	ER	HR	SH	SF	HB	TBB	IBB	SO	WP	Bk	W	L	Pct.	ShO	Sv	ERA
1985	California	AL	30	29	6	0	189.2	807	189	105	99	23	2	5	4	64	1	102	5	0	12	12	.500	1	0	4.70
1986	California	AL	34	33	10	1	246.1	1013	207	98	92	19	6	5	5	92	1	202	10	2	17	10	.630	2	0	3.36
1987	California	AL	14	13	1	0	74.2	334	84	52	47	14	3	1	2	34	0	56	1	0	4	6	.400	0	0	5.67
1988	California	AL	23	23	4	0	146.1	635	155	78	70	9	1	6	1	61	3	98	13	2	8	6	.571	2	0	4.31
1989	California	AL	32	32	6	0	212	864	202	73	69	16	3	4	3	59	1	107	7	2	15	10	.600	4	0	2.93
1990	California	AL	29	29	2	0	174.1	738	161	77	63	9	3	1	2	72	1	78	6	1	12	11	.522	1	0	3.25
1991	California	AL	30	30	1	0	177.2	762	193	93	84	19	6	6	3	66	1	71	6	0	10	19	.345	0	0	4.26
1992	Chicago	AL	34	34	0	0	209	911	193	116	97	11	7	7	6	95	5	109	6	2	12	13	.480	0	0	4.18
	8 ML YEARS		226	223	30	1	1430	6064	1384	692	621	120	31	35	26	543	13	823	54	9	90	87	.508	11	0	3.91

Lloyd McClendon

Bats: Right **Throws:** Right **Pos:** RF/1B **Ht:** 6' 0" **Wt:** 212 **Born:** 01/11/59 **Age:** 34

			BATTING															BASERUNNING				PERCENTAGES		
Year	Team	Lg	G	AB	H	2B	3B	HR	(Hm | Rd)	TB	R	RBI	TBB	IBB	SO	HBP	SH	SF	SB	CS	SB%	GDP	Avg	OBP	SLG
1987	Cincinnati	NL	45	72	15	5	0	2	(0 | 2)	26	8	13	4	0	15	0	0	1	1	0	1.00	1	.208	.247	.361
1988	Cincinnati	NL	72	137	30	4	0	3	(0 | 3)	43	9	14	15	1	22	2	1	2	4	0	1.00	6	.219	.301	.314
1989	Chicago	NL	92	259	74	12	1	12	(9 | 3)	124	47	40	37	3	31	1	1	7	6	4	.60	3	.286	.368	.479
1990	2 ML Teams		53	110	18	3	0	2	(0 | 2)	27	6	12	14	2	22	0	0	1	1	0	1.00	2	.164	.256	.245
1991	Pittsburgh	NL	85	163	47	7	0	7	(2 | 5)	75	24	24	18	0	23	2	0	0	2	1	.67	2	.288	.366	.460
1992	Pittsburgh	NL	84	190	48	8	1	3	(3 | 0)	67	26	20	28	0	24	2	1	3	3	1	.25	5	.253	.350	.353
1990	Chicago	NL	49	107	17	3	0	1	(0 | 1)	23	5	10	14	2	21	0	0	1	1	0	1.00	2	.159	.254	.215
	Pittsburgh	NL	4	3	1	0	0	1	(0 | 1)	4	1	2	0	0	1	0	0	0	0	0	.00	0	.333	.333	1.333
	6 ML YEARS		431	931	232	39	2	29	(14 | 15)	362	120	123	116	6	137	7	3	14	15	8	.65	19	.249	.332	.389

Bob McClure

Pitches: Left **Bats:** Right **Pos:** RP **Ht:** 5'11" **Wt:** 188 **Born:** 04/29/53 **Age:** 40

			HOW MUCH HE PITCHED						WHAT HE GAVE UP											THE RESULTS					
Year	Team	Lg	G	GS	CG	GF	IP	BFP	H	R	ER	HR	SH	SF	HB	TBB	IBB	SO	WP	Bk	W	L	Pct.	ShO	Sv	ERA
1975	Kansas City	AL	12	0	0	4	15	66	4	0	0	0	0	0	0	14	2	15	0	2	1	0	1.000	0	1	0.00
1976	Kansas City	AL	8	0	0	4	4	22	3	4	4	0	0	0	0	8	0	3	0	0	0	0	.000	0	0	9.00
1977	Milwaukee	AL	68	0	0	31	71	302	64	25	20	2	5	5	1	34	5	57	1	2	2	1	.667	0	6	2.54
1978	Milwaukee	AL	44	0	0	29	65	283	53	30	27	8	7	2	6	30	4	47	1	1	2	6	.250	0	9	3.74
1979	Milwaukee	AL	36	0	0	16	51	229	53	29	22	6	2	3	3	24	0	37	5	0	5	2	.714	0	5	3.88
1980	Milwaukee	AL	52	5	2	23	91	390	83	34	31	6	1	5	2	37	2	47	0	2	5	8	.385	1	10	3.07
1981	Milwaukee	AL	4	0	0	1	8	34	7	3	3	1	0	0	0	4	1	6	0	0	0	0	.000	0	0	3.38
1982	Milwaukee	AL	34	26	5	5	172.2	734	160	90	81	21	6	4	4	74	4	99	5	5	12	7	.632	0	0	4.22
1983	Milwaukee	AL	24	23	4	0	142	625	152	75	71	11	0	4	5	68	1	68	4	6	9	9	.500	0	0	4.50
1984	Milwaukee	AL	39	18	1	5	139.2	616	154	76	68	9	8	8	2	52	4	68	1	3	4	8	.333	0	1	4.38
1985	Milwaukee	AL	38	1	0	12	85.2	370	91	43	41	10	3	2	3	30	2	57	5	0	4	1	.800	0	3	4.31
1986	2 ML Teams		65	0	0	22	79	332	71	29	28	4	4	3	1	33	3	53	1	1	4	6	.400	0	6	3.19
1987	Montreal	NL	52	0	0	16	52.1	222	47	30	20	8	5	2	0	20	3	33	0	1	6	1	.857	0	5	3.44
1988	2 ML Teams		33	0	0	13	30	133	35	18	18	4	3	2	2	8	0	19	1	3	2	3	.400	0	3	5.40
1989	California	AL	48	0	0	27	52.1	205	39	14	9	2	1	4	1	15	1	36	2	2	6	1	.857	0	3	1.55
1990	California	AL	11	0	0	1	7	30	7	6	5	0	1	0	0	3	0	6	0	1	2	0	1.000	0	0	6.43
1991	2 ML Teams		45	0	0	11	32.2	146	37	19	18	4	1	4	2	13	2	20	2	1	1	1	.500	0	0	4.96
1992	St. Louis	NL	71	0	0	16	54	230	51	21	19	6	1	3	2	25	5	24	1	0	2	2	.500	0	0	3.17
1986	Milwaukee	AL	13	0	0	7	16.1	75	18	7	7	2	1	1	0	10	1	11	0	0	2	1	.667	0	0	3.86
	Montreal	NL	52	0	0	15	62.2	257	53	22	21	2	3	2	1	23	2	42	1	1	2	5	.286	0	6	3.02
1988	Montreal	NL	19	0	0	8	19	87	23	13	13	3	3	2	1	6	0	12	0	3	1	3	.250	0	2	6.16
	New York	NL	14	0	0	5	11	46	12	5	5	1	0	0	1	2	0	7	1	0	1	0	1.000	0	1	4.09
1991	California	AL	13	0	0	2	9.2	48	13	11	10	2	1	1	1	5	0	5	2	1	0	1	.000	0	0	9.31
	St. Louis	NL	32	0	0	9	23	98	24	8	8	1	0	3	1	8	2	15	0	0	1	0	.500	0	0	3.13
	18 ML YEARS		684	73	12	232	1152.1	4969	1112	546	485	102	48	51	34	492	39	695	29	30	67	56	.545	1	52	3.79

Rodney McCray

Bats: Both   **Throws:** Right   **Pos:** RF   **Ht:** 5'10"   **Wt:** 175   **Born:** 09/13/63   **Age:** 29

Year	Team	Lg	G	AB	H	2B	3B	HR	(Hm	Rd)	TB	R	RBI	TBB	IBB	SO	HBP	SH	SF	SB	CS	SB%	GDP	Avg	OBP	SLG
1984	Spokane	A	71	244	50	6	1	1	--	--	61	40	20	65	0	50	2	0	4	25	5	.83	8	.205	.371	.250
1985	Charleston	A	117	373	77	8	1	1	--	--	90	81	27	80	2	88	6	5	1	49	7	.88	6	.206	.354	.241
1986	Charleston	A	123	417	107	13	3	4	--	--	138	88	33	108	2	80	5	6	2	81	32	.72	3	.257	.414	.331
1987	Reno	A	117	413	87	11	5	0	--	--	108	69	26	69	3	96	10	9	3	65	16	.80	4	.211	.335	.262
1988	South Bend	A	107	306	65	10	2	1	--	--	82	48	24	56	0	72	10	7	2	55	12	.82	5	.212	.350	.268
1989	Sarasota	A	124	422	112	19	4	1	--	--	142	81	34	96	3	81	9	4	2	44	22	.67	6	.265	.410	.336
1990	Birmingham	AA	60	188	37	2	2	1	--	--	46	36	16	36	0	42	5	6	2	25	10	.71	2	.197	.338	.245
	Vancouver	AAA	19	53	12	4	2	0	--	--	20	7	6	10	0	20	2	1	0	4	3	.57	0	.226	.369	.377
1991	Vancouver	AAA	83	222	51	9	5	0	--	--	70	37	13	26	0	48	8	2	2	14	10	.58	4	.230	.329	.315
1992	Tidewater	AAA	8	10	0	0	0	0	--	--	0	1	0	1	0	5	0	0	0	3	0	1.00	0	.000	.091	.000
1990	Chicago	AL	32	6	0	0	0	0	(0	0)	0	8	0	1	0	4	0	0	0	6	0	1.00	0	.000	.143	.000
1991	Chicago	AL	17	7	2	0	0	0	(0	0)	2	2	0	0	0	2	0	0	0	1	1	.50	0	.286	.286	.286
1992	New York	NL	18	1	1	0	0	0	(0	0)	1	3	1	0	0	0	0	0	0	2	0	1.00	0	1.000	1.000	1.000
	3 ML YEARS		67	14	3	0	0	0	(0	0)	3	13	1	1	0	6	0	0	0	9	1	.90	0	.214	.267	.214

Lance McCullers

Pitches: Right   **Bats:** Both   **Pos:** RP   **Ht:** 6'1"   **Wt:** 210   **Born:** 03/08/64   **Age:** 29

Year	Team	Lg	G	GS	CG	GF	IP	BFP	H	R	ER	HR	SH	SF	HB	TBB	IBB	SO	WP	Bk	W	L	Pct.	ShO	Sv	ERA
1985	San Diego	NL	21	0	0	11	35	142	23	15	9	3	7	0	1	16	3	27	0	1	0	2	.000	0	5	2.31
1986	San Diego	NL	70	7	0	29	136	550	103	46	42	12	8	3	4	58	9	92	5	3	10	10	.500	0	5	2.78
1987	San Diego	NL	78	0	0	41	123.1	540	115	60	51	11	6	2	2	59	11	126	5	1	8	10	.444	0	16	3.72
1988	San Diego	NL	60	0	0	39	97.2	407	70	29	27	8	7	3	0	55	12	81	4	2	3	6	.333	0	10	2.49
1989	New York	AL	52	1	0	20	84.2	373	83	46	43	9	3	5	3	37	4	82	2	0	4	3	.571	0	3	4.57
1990	2 ML Teams		20	1	0	14	44.2	186	32	19	15	4	0	3	0	19	3	31	5	0	2	0	1.000	0	0	3.02
1992	Texas	AL	5	0	0	1	5	23	1	4	3	0	0	0	0	8	0	3	0	0	1	0	1.000	0	0	5.40
1990	New York	AL	11	0	0	7	15	65	14	8	6	2	0	1	0	6	2	11	3	0	1	0	1.000	0	0	3.60
	Detroit	AL	9	1	0	7	29.2	121	18	11	9	2	0	2	0	13	1	20	2	0	1	0	1.000	0	0	2.73
	7 ML YEARS		306	9	0	155	526.1	2221	427	219	190	47	31	16	10	252	42	442	21	7	28	31	.475	0	39	3.25

Ben McDonald

Pitches: Right   **Bats:** Right   **Pos:** SP   **Ht:** 6'7"   **Wt:** 214   **Born:** 11/24/67   **Age:** 25

Year	Team	Lg	G	GS	CG	GF	IP	BFP	H	R	ER	HR	SH	SF	HB	TBB	IBB	SO	WP	Bk	W	L	Pct.	ShO	Sv	ERA
1989	Baltimore	AL	6	0	0	2	7.1	33	8	7	7	2	0	1	0	4	0	3	1	1	1	0	1.000	0	0	8.59
1990	Baltimore	AL	21	15	3	2	118.2	472	88	36	32	9	3	5	0	35	0	65	5	0	8	5	.615	2	0	2.43
1991	Baltimore	AL	21	21	1	0	126.1	541	126	71	68	16	2	3	1	43	2	85	3	0	6	8	.429	0	0	4.84
1992	Baltimore	AL	35	35	4	0	227	958	213	113	107	32	6	6	9	74	5	158	3	2	13	13	.500	2	0	4.24
	4 ML YEARS		83	71	8	4	479.1	1995	435	227	214	59	11	15	10	156	7	311	12	3	28	26	.519	4	0	4.02

Jack McDowell

Pitches: Right   **Bats:** Right   **Pos:** SP   **Ht:** 6'5"   **Wt:** 180   **Born:** 01/16/66   **Age:** 27

Year	Team	Lg	G	GS	CG	GF	IP	BFP	H	R	ER	HR	SH	SF	HB	TBB	IBB	SO	WP	Bk	W	L	Pct.	ShO	Sv	ERA
1987	Chicago	AL	4	4	0	0	28	103	16	6	6	1	0	0	2	6	0	15	0	0	3	0	1.000	0	0	1.93
1988	Chicago	AL	26	26	1	0	158.2	687	147	85	70	12	6	7	7	68	5	84	11	1	5	10	.333	0	0	3.97
1990	Chicago	AL	33	33	4	0	205	866	189	93	87	20	1	5	7	77	0	165	7	1	14	9	.609	0	0	3.82
1991	Chicago	AL	35	35	15	0	253.2	1028	212	97	96	19	8	4	4	82	2	191	10	1	17	10	.630	3	0	3.41
1992	Chicago	AL	34	34	13	0	260.2	1079	247	95	92	21	8	6	7	75	9	178	6	0	20	10	.667	1	0	3.18
	5 ML YEARS		132	132	33	0	906	3763	811	376	351	73	23	22	27	308	16	633	34	3	59	39	.602	4	0	3.49

Roger McDowell

Pitches: Right   **Bats:** Right   **Pos:** RP   **Ht:** 6'1"   **Wt:** 182   **Born:** 12/21/60   **Age:** 32

Year	Team	Lg	G	GS	CG	GF	IP	BFP	H	R	ER	HR	SH	SF	HB	TBB	IBB	SO	WP	Bk	W	L	Pct.	ShO	Sv	ERA
1985	New York	NL	62	2	0	36	127.1	516	108	43	40	9	6	2	1	37	8	70	6	2	6	5	.545	0	17	2.83
1986	New York	NL	75	0	0	52	128	524	107	48	43	4	7	3	3	42	5	65	3	3	14	9	.609	0	22	3.02
1987	New York	NL	56	0	0	45	88.2	384	95	41	41	7	5	5	2	28	4	32	3	1	7	5	.583	0	25	4.16
1988	New York	NL	62	0	0	41	89	378	80	31	26	1	3	5	2	31	7	46	6	1	5	5	.500	0	16	2.63
1989	2 ML Teams		69	0	0	56	92	387	79	36	20	3	6	1	3	38	8	47	3	1	4	8	.333	0	23	1.96
1990	Philadelphia	NL	72	0	0	60	86.1	373	92	44	37	2	10	4	2	35	9	39	1	1	6	8	.429	0	22	3.86
1991	2 ML Teams		71	0	0	34	101.1	445	100	40	33	4	11	3	2	48	20	50	2	0	9	9	.500	0	10	2.93
1992	Los Angeles	NL	65	0	0	39	83.2	393	103	46	38	3	10	3	1	42	13	50	4	1	6	10	.375	0	14	4.09
1989	New York	NL	25	0	0	15	35.1	156	34	21	13	1	3	1	2	16	3	15	3	1	1	5	.167	0	4	3.31

	Lg	G	GS	CG	GF	IP	BFP	H	R	ER	HR	SH	SF	HB	TBB	IBB	SO	WP	Bk	W	L	Pct.	ShO	Sv	ERA
Philadelphia	NL	44	0	0	41	56.2	231	45	15	7	2	3	0	1	22	5	32	0	0	3	3	.500	0	19	1.11
1991 Philadelphia	NL	38	0	0	16	59	271	61	28	21	1	7	1	2	32	12	28	1	0	3	6	.333	0	3	3.20
Los Angeles	NL	33	0	0	18	42.1	174	39	12	12	3	4	2	0	16	8	22	1	0	6	3	.667	0	7	2.55
8 ML YEARS		532	2	0	363	796.1	3400	764	326	278	33	58	26	17	301	74	399	28	10	57	59	.491	0	149	3.14

Chuck McElroy

Pitches: Left   **Bats:** Left   **Pos:** RP   **Ht:** 6' 0"   **Wt:** 180   **Born:** 10/01/67   **Age:** 25

		HOW MUCH HE PITCHED						WHAT HE GAVE UP											THE RESULTS					
Year Team	Lg	G	GS	CG	GF	IP	BFP	H	R	ER	HR	SH	SF	HB	TBB	IBB	SO	WP	Bk	W	L	Pct.	ShO	Sv	ERA
1989 Philadelphia	NL	11	0	0	4	10.1	46	12	2	2	1	0	0	0	4	1	8	0	0	0	0	.000	0	0	1.74
1990 Philadelphia	NL	16	0	0	8	14	76	24	13	12	0	0	1	0	10	2	16	0	0	0	1	.000	0	3	7.71
1991 Chicago	NL	71	0	0	12	101.1	419	73	33	22	7	9	6	0	57	7	92	1	0	6	2	.750	0	3	1.95
1992 Chicago	NL	72	0	0	30	83.2	369	73	40	33	5	5	5	0	51	10	83	3	0	4	7	.364	0	6	3.55
4 ML YEARS		170	0	0	54	209.1	910	182	88	69	13	14	12	0	122	20	199	4	0	10	10	.500	0	9	2.97

Willie McGee

Bats: Both   **Throws:** Right   **Pos:** RF/CF   **Ht:** 6' 1"   **Wt:** 195   **Born:** 11/02/58   **Age:** 34

		BATTING																BASERUNNING				PERCENTAGES		
Year Team	Lg	G	AB	H	2B	3B	HR	(Hm	Rd)	TB	R	RBI	TBB	IBB	SO	HBP	SH	SF	SB	CS	SB%	GDP	Avg	OBP	SLG
1982 St. Louis	NL	123	422	125	12	8	4	(2	2)	165	43	56	12	2	58	2	2	1	24	12	.67	9	.296	.318	.391
1983 St. Louis	NL	147	601	172	22	8	5	(4	1)	225	75	75	26	2	98	0	1	3	39	8	.83	8	.286	.314	.374
1984 St. Louis	NL	145	571	166	19	11	6	(2	4)	225	82	50	29	2	80	1	0	3	43	10	.81	12	.291	.325	.394
1985 St. Louis	NL	152	612	216	26	18	10	(3	7)	308	114	82	34	2	86	0	1	5	56	16	.78	3	.353	.384	.503
1986 St. Louis	NL	124	497	127	22	7	7	(7	0)	184	65	48	37	7	82	1	0	4	19	16	.54	8	.256	.306	.370
1987 St. Louis	NL	153	620	177	37	11	11	(6	5)	269	76	105	24	5	90	2	1	5	16	4	.80	24	.285	.312	.434
1988 St. Louis	NL	137	562	164	24	6	3	(1	2)	209	73	50	32	5	84	1	2	3	41	6	.87	10	.292	.329	.372
1989 St. Louis	NL	58	199	47	10	2	3	(1	2)	70	23	17	10	0	34	1	0	1	8	6	.57	2	.236	.275	.352
1990 2 ML Teams		154	614	199	35	7	3	(1	2)	257	99	77	48	6	104	1	0	2	31	9	.78	13	.324	.373	.419
1991 San Francisco	NL	131	497	155	30	3	4	(2	2)	203	67	43	34	3	74	2	8	2	17	9	.65	11	.312	.357	.408
1992 San Francisco	NL	138	474	141	20	2	1	(0	1)	168	56	36	29	3	88	1	5	1	13	4	.76	7	.297	.339	.354
1990 St. Louis	NL	125	501	168	32	5	3	(1	2)	219	76	62	38	6	86	1	0	2	28	9	.76	9	.335	.382	.437
Oakland	AL	29	113	31	3	2	0	(0	0)	38	23	15	10	0	18	0	0	0	3	0	1.00	4	.274	.333	.336
11 ML YEARS		1462	5669	1689	257	83	57	(29	28)	2283	773	639	315	37	878	12	20	30	307	100	.75	107	.298	.335	.403

Russ McGinnis

Bats: Right   **Throws:** Right   **Pos:** C   **Ht:** 6' 3"   **Wt:** 225   **Born:** 06/18/63   **Age:** 30

		BATTING																BASERUNNING				PERCENTAGES		
Year Team	Lg	G	AB	H	2B	3B	HR	(Hm	Rd)	TB	R	RBI	TBB	IBB	SO	HBP	SH	SF	SB	CS	SB%	GDP	Avg	OBP	SLG
1985 Helena	R	48	150	46	7	0	5	--	--	68	33	38	31	1	19	4	0	2	2	2	.50	5	.307	.433	.453
1986 Beloit	A	124	413	102	24	2	16	--	--	178	62	59	52	2	79	12	3	4	5	2	.71	13	.247	.345	.431
1987 Beloit	A	51	189	58	10	0	13	--	--	107	34	35	19	2	36	2	1	0	1	2	.33	4	.307	.376	.566
Modesto	A	47	165	42	9	0	8	--	--	75	24	31	23	1	33	2	3	3	1	1	.50	4	.255	.347	.455
1988 Huntsville	AA	23	77	20	9	0	2	--	--	35	9	15	7	0	13	0	0	1	1	0	1.00	1	.260	.321	.455
Tacoma	AAA	63	186	47	13	1	2	--	--	68	25	22	21	0	38	1	3	1	1	0	1.00	7	.253	.330	.366
1989 Tacoma	AAA	110	380	105	25	0	7	--	--	151	42	60	45	0	78	6	2	5	0	1	.00	9	.276	.358	.397
1990 Tacoma	AAA	110	359	89	19	1	13	--	--	149	57	77	75	2	70	6	1	7	2	1	.67	15	.248	.380	.415
1991 Iowa	AAA	111	374	105	18	2	15	--	--	172	70	70	63	6	68	6	1	4	3	1	.75	12	.281	.389	.460
1992 Okla City	AAA	99	330	87	19	1	18	--	--	162	63	51	79	1	52	7	2	2	0	6	.00	15	.264	.414	.491
1992 Texas	AL	14	33	8	4	0	0	(0	0)	12	2	4	3	0	7	0	0	0	0	0	.00	1	.242	.306	.364

Fred McGriff

Bats: Left   **Throws:** Left   **Pos:** 1B   **Ht:** 6' 3"   **Wt:** 210   **Born:** 10/31/63   **Age:** 29

		BATTING																BASERUNNING				PERCENTAGES		
Year Team	Lg	G	AB	H	2B	3B	HR	(Hm	Rd)	TB	R	RBI	TBB	IBB	SO	HBP	SH	SF	SB	CS	SB%	GDP	Avg	OBP	SLG
1986 Toronto	AL	3	5	1	0	0	0	(0	0)	1	1	0	0	0	2	0	0	0	0	0	.00	0	.200	.200	.200
1987 Toronto	AL	107	295	73	16	0	20	(7	13)	149	58	43	60	4	104	1	0	0	3	2	.60	3	.247	.376	.505
1988 Toronto	AL	154	536	151	35	4	34	(18	16)	296	100	82	79	3	149	4	0	4	6	1	.86	15	.282	.376	.552
1989 Toronto	AL	161	551	148	27	3	36	(18	18)	289	98	92	119	12	132	4	1	5	7	4	.64	14	.269	.399	.525
1990 Toronto	AL	153	557	167	21	1	35	(14	21)	295	91	88	94	12	108	2	1	4	5	3	.63	7	.300	.400	.530
1991 San Diego	NL	153	528	147	19	1	31	(18	13)	261	84	106	105	26	135	2	0	7	4	1	.80	14	.278	.396	.494
1992 San Diego	NL	152	531	152	30	4	35	(21	14)	295	79	104	96	23	108	1	0	4	8	6	.57	14	.286	.394	.556
7 ML YEARS		883	3003	839	148	13	191	(96	95)	1586	511	515	553	80	738	14	2	24	33	17	.66	67	.279	.391	.528

131

Mark McGwire

Bats: Right **Throws:** Right **Pos:** 1B **Ht:** 6' 5" **Wt:** 225 **Born:** 10/01/63 **Age:** 29

Year Team	Lg	G	AB	H	2B	3B	HR	(Hm	Rd)	TB	R	RBI	TBB	IBB	SO	HBP	SH	SF	SB	CS	SB%	GDP	Avg	OBP	SLG
1986 Oakland	AL	18	53	10	1	0	3	(1	2)	20	10	9	4	0	18	1	0	0	0	1	.00	0	.189	.259	.377
1987 Oakland	AL	151	557	161	28	4	49	(21	28)	344	97	118	71	8	131	5	0	8	0	1	.50	6	.289	.370	.618
1988 Oakland	AL	155	550	143	22	1	32	(12	20)	263	87	99	76	4	117	4	1	4	0	0	.00	15	.260	.352	.478
1989 Oakland	AL	143	490	113	17	0	33	(12	21)	229	74	95	83	5	94	3	0	11	1	1	.50	23	.231	.339	.467
1990 Oakland	AL	156	523	123	16	0	39	(14	25)	256	87	108	110	9	116	7	1	9	2	1	.67	13	.235	.370	.489
1991 Oakland	AL	154	483	97	22	0	22	(15	7)	185	62	75	93	3	116	3	1	5	2	1	.67	13	.201	.330	.383
1992 Oakland	AL	139	467	125	22	0	42	(24	18)	273	87	104	90	12	105	5	0	9	0	1	.00	10	.268	.385	.585
7 ML YEARS		916	3123	772	128	5	220	(99	121)	1570	504	608	527	41	697	28	3	46	6	6	.50	80	.247	.356	.503

Tim McIntosh

Bats: Right **Throws:** Right **Pos:** C **Ht:** 5'11" **Wt:** 195 **Born:** 03/21/65 **Age:** 28

Year Team	Lg	G	AB	H	2B	3B	HR	(Hm	Rd)	TB	R	RBI	TBB	IBB	SO	HBP	SH	SF	SB	CS	SB%	GDP	Avg	OBP	SLG
1986 Beloit	A	49	173	45	3	2	4	--	--	64	26	21	18	0	33	2	0	3	0	0	.00	3	.260	.332	.370
1987 Beloit	A	130	461	139	30	3	20	--	--	235	83	85	49	2	96	7	1	3	7	4	.64	4	.302	.375	.510
1988 Stockton	A	138	519	147	32	6	15	--	--	236	81	92	57	1	96	11	6	5	10	5	.67	6	.283	.363	.455
1989 El Paso	AA	120	463	139	30	3	17	--	--	226	72	93	29	3	72	8	2	6	5	4	.56	8	.300	.346	.488
1990 Denver	AAA	116	416	120	20	3	18	--	--	200	72	74	26	0	58	14	3	7	6	2	.75	9	.288	.346	.481
1991 Denver	AAA	122	462	135	19	9	18	--	--	226	69	91	37	4	59	11	0	7	2	5	.29	13	.292	.354	.489
1990 Milwaukee	AL	5	5	1	0	0	1	(1	0)	4	1	1	0	0	2	0	0	0	0	0	.00	0	.200	.200	.800
1991 Milwaukee	AL	7	11	4	1	0	1	(1	0)	8	2	1	0	0	4	0	0	0	0	0	.00	0	.364	.364	.727
1992 Milwaukee	AL	35	77	14	3	0	0	(0	0)	17	7	6	3	0	9	2	1	1	1	3	.25	1	.182	.229	.221
3 ML YEARS		47	93	19	4	0	2	(2	0)	29	10	8	3	0	15	2	1	1	1	3	.25	1	.204	.242	.312

Jeff McKnight

Bats: Both **Throws:** Right **Pos:** 2B **Ht:** 6' 0" **Wt:** 180 **Born:** 02/18/63 **Age:** 30

Year Team	Lg	G	AB	H	2B	3B	HR	(Hm	Rd)	TB	R	RBI	TBB	IBB	SO	HBP	SH	SF	SB	CS	SB%	GDP	Avg	OBP	SLG
1984 Columbia	A	95	251	64	10	1	1	--	--	79	31	27	26	2	17	1	1	1	9	1	.90	5	.255	.326	.315
1985 Columbia	A	67	159	42	6	1	1	--	--	53	26	24	21	2	18	1	0	2	6	2	.75	2	.264	.350	.333
Lynchburg	A	49	150	33	6	1	0	--	--	41	19	21	29	0	19	0	4	3	0	0	.00	1	.220	.341	.273
1986 Jackson	AA	132	469	118	24	3	4	--	--	160	71	55	76	3	58	3	5	9	5	2	.71	10	.252	.354	.341
1987 Jackson	AA	16	59	12	3	0	2	--	--	21	5	8	4	0	12	1	0	1	1	1	.50	3	.203	.266	.356
Tidewater	AAA	87	184	47	7	3	2	--	--	66	21	25	24	1	22	1	1	4	0	1	.00	6	.255	.338	.359
1988 Tidewater	AAA	113	345	88	14	0	2	--	--	108	36	25	36	5	32	0	1	3	0	4	.00	3	.255	.323	.313
1989 Tidewater	AAA	116	425	106	19	2	9	--	--	156	84	48	79	1	56	1	3	4	3	0	1.00	13	.249	.368	.367
1990 Rochester	AAA	100	339	95	21	3	7	--	--	143	56	45	41	3	58	0	4	6	7	5	.58	4	.280	.352	.422
1991 Rochester	AAA	22	81	31	7	2	1	--	--	45	19	18	14	0	10	0	0	1	1	2	.33	3	.383	.469	.556
1992 Tidewater	AAA	102	352	108	21	1	4	--	--	143	43	43	51	3	52	1	1	1	3	3	.50	14	.307	.395	.406
1989 New York	NL	6	12	3	0	0	0	(0	0)	3	2	0	2	0	1	0	0	0	0	0	.00	1	.250	.357	.250
1990 Baltimore	AL	29	75	15	2	0	1	(1	0)	20	11	4	5	0	17	1	3	0	0	0	.00	0	.200	.259	.267
1991 Baltimore	AL	16	41	7	1	0	0	(0	0)	8	2	2	2	0	7	0	0	0	1	0	1.00	0	.171	.209	.195
1992 New York	NL	31	85	23	3	1	2	(1	1)	34	10	13	2	0	8	0	0	0	0	1	.00	2	.271	.287	.400
4 ML YEARS		82	213	48	6	1	3	(2	1)	65	25	19	11	0	33	1	3	0	1	1	.50	5	.225	.267	.305

Mark McLemore

Bats: Both **Throws:** Right **Pos:** 2B/DH **Ht:** 5'11" **Wt:** 195 **Born:** 10/04/64 **Age:** 28

Year Team	Lg	G	AB	H	2B	3B	HR	(Hm	Rd)	TB	R	RBI	TBB	IBB	SO	HBP	SH	SF	SB	CS	SB%	GDP	Avg	OBP	SLG
1986 California	AL	5	4	0	0	0	0	(0	0)	0	0	0	1	0	2	0	1	0	0	1	.00	0	.000	.200	.000
1987 California	AL	138	433	102	13	3	3	(3	0)	130	61	41	48	0	72	0	15	3	25	8	.76	7	.236	.310	.300
1988 California	AL	77	233	56	11	2	2	(1	1)	77	38	16	25	0	28	0	5	2	13	7	.65	6	.240	.312	.330
1989 California	AL	32	103	25	3	1	0	(0	0)	30	12	14	7	0	19	1	3	1	6	1	.86	2	.243	.295	.291
1990 2 ML Teams		28	60	9	2	0	0	(0	0)	11	6	2	4	0	15	0	1	0	1	0	1.00	1	.150	.203	.183
1991 Houston	NL	21	61	9	1	0	0	(0	0)	10	6	2	6	0	13	0	0	1	0	1	.00	1	.148	.221	.164
1992 Baltimore	AL	101	228	56	7	2	0	(0	0)	67	40	27	21	1	26	0	6	1	11	5	.69	6	.246	.308	.294
1990 California	AL	20	48	7	2	0	0	(0	0)	9	4	2	4	0	9	0	1	0	1	0	1.00	1	.146	.212	.188
Cleveland	AL	8	12	2	0	0	0	(0	0)	2	2	0	0	0	6	0	0	0	0	0	.00	0	.167	.167	.167
7 ML YEARS		402	1122	257	37	8	5	(4	1)	325	163	102	112	1	175	1	31	8	56	23	.71	23	.229	.298	.290

Jim McNamara

Bats: Left **Throws:** Right **Pos:** C **Ht:** 6' 4" **Wt:** 210 **Born:** 06/10/65 **Age:** 28

										BATTING										BASERUNNING				PERCENTAGES		
Year	Team	Lg	G	AB	H	2B	3B	HR	(Hm	Rd)	TB	R	RBI	TBB	IBB	SO	HBP	SH	SF	SB	CS	SB%	GDP	Avg	OBP	SLG
1986	Everett	A	46	158	39	1	2	8	--	--	68	23	30	18	2	39	3	0	2	0	0	.00	3	.247	.331	.430
1987	Clinton	A	110	385	95	22	1	5	--	--	134	43	53	19	1	52	2	0	7	4	2	.67	15	.247	.277	.348
1988	San Jose	A	93	315	59	9	0	1	--	--	71	27	41	43	1	76	2	0	2	3	4	.43	18	.187	.287	.225
1989	Salinas	A	49	155	37	8	0	0	--	--	45	9	10	22	2	24	0	1	0	3	1	.75	3	.239	.333	.290
	Phoenix	AAA	27	69	12	3	0	0	--	--	15	3	4	4	0	13	0	2	0	1	2	.33	2	.174	.219	.217
	San Jose	A	19	65	18	2	0	1	--	--	23	2	8	1	0	13	0	0	1	0	1	.00	3	.277	.284	.354
1990	San Jose	A	53	158	32	2	2	1	--	--	41	20	22	18	0	30	1	1	1	0	4	.00	3	.203	.287	.259
	Phoenix	AAA	6	20	9	0	0	0	--	--	9	2	1	3	0	4	0	0	0	0	0	.00	0	.450	.522	.450
	Shreveport	AA	28	79	19	7	0	0	--	--	26	2	13	7	0	9	0	0	0	0	1	.00	7	.241	.302	.329
1991	Phoenix	AAA	17	53	9	1	0	0	--	--	10	3	2	6	0	12	0	1	0	0	0	.00	1	.170	.254	.189
	Shreveport	AA	39	109	30	8	2	2	--	--	48	13	20	21	3	11	0	1	1	2	1	.67	2	.275	.389	.440
1992	Phoenix	AAA	23	67	14	3	0	0	--	--	17	5	3	14	3	13	0	0	0	0	0	.00	5	.209	.346	.254
1992	San Francisco	NL	30	74	16	1	0	1	(1	0)	20	6	9	6	2	25	0	2	0	0	0	.00	1	.216	.275	.270

Brian McRae

Bats: Both **Throws:** Right **Pos:** CF **Ht:** 6' 0" **Wt:** 185 **Born:** 08/27/67 **Age:** 25

										BATTING										BASERUNNING				PERCENTAGES		
Year	Team	Lg	G	AB	H	2B	3B	HR	(Hm	Rd)	TB	R	RBI	TBB	IBB	SO	HBP	SH	SF	SB	CS	SB%	GDP	Avg	OBP	SLG
1990	Kansas City	AL	46	168	48	8	3	2	(1	1)	68	21	23	9	0	29	0	3	2	4	3	.57	5	.286	.318	.405
1991	Kansas City	AL	152	629	164	28	9	8	(3	5)	234	86	64	24	1	99	2	3	5	20	11	.65	12	.261	.288	.372
1992	Kansas City	AL	149	533	119	23	5	4	(2	2)	164	63	52	42	1	88	6	7	4	18	5	.78	10	.223	.285	.308
	3 ML YEARS		347	1330	331	59	17	14	(6	8)	466	170	139	75	2	216	8	13	11	42	19	.69	27	.249	.291	.350

Kevin McReynolds

Bats: Right **Throws:** Right **Pos:** LF/RF **Ht:** 6' 1" **Wt:** 215 **Born:** 10/16/59 **Age:** 33

										BATTING										BASERUNNING				PERCENTAGES		
Year	Team	Lg	G	AB	H	2B	3B	HR	(Hm	Rd)	TB	R	RBI	TBB	IBB	SO	HBP	SH	SF	SB	CS	SB%	GDP	Avg	OBP	SLG
1983	San Diego	NL	39	140	31	3	1	4	(3	1)	48	15	14	12	1	29	0	0	3	2	1	.67	1	.221	.277	.343
1984	San Diego	NL	147	525	146	26	6	20	(10	10)	244	68	75	34	8	69	0	3	9	3	6	.33	14	.278	.317	.465
1985	San Diego	NL	152	564	132	24	4	15	(6	9)	209	61	75	43	6	81	3	2	4	4	0	1.00	17	.234	.290	.371
1986	San Diego	NL	158	560	161	31	6	26	(14	12)	282	89	96	66	6	83	1	5	9	8	6	.57	9	.288	.358	.504
1987	New York	NL	151	590	163	32	5	29	(18	11)	292	86	95	39	5	70	1	1	8	14	1	.93	13	.276	.318	.495
1988	New York	NL	147	552	159	30	2	27	(13	14)	274	82	99	38	3	56	4	1	5	21	0	1.00	6	.288	.336	.496
1989	New York	NL	148	545	148	25	3	22	(12	10)	245	74	85	46	10	74	1	0	7	15	7	.68	8	.272	.326	.450
1990	New York	NL	147	521	140	23	1	24	(11	13)	237	75	82	71	11	61	1	0	8	9	2	.82	8	.269	.353	.455
1991	New York	NL	143	522	135	32	1	16	(7	9)	217	65	74	49	7	46	2	1	4	6	6	.50	8	.259	.322	.416
1992	Kansas City	AL	109	373	92	25	0	13	(4	9)	156	45	49	67	3	48	0	0	5	7	1	.88	6	.247	.357	.418
	10 ML YEARS		1341	4892	1307	251	29	196	(98	98)	2204	660	744	465	60	617	13	13	62	89	30	.75	90	.267	.329	.451

Rusty Meacham

Pitches: Right **Bats:** Right **Pos:** RP **Ht:** 6' 2" **Wt:** 165 **Born:** 01/27/68 **Age:** 25

								HOW MUCH HE PITCHED				WHAT HE GAVE UP									THE RESULTS					
Year	Team	Lg	G	GS	CG	GF	IP	BFP	H	R	ER	HR	SH	SF	HB	TBB	IBB	SO	WP	Bk	W	L	Pct.	ShO	Sv	ERA
1988	Fayetteville	A	6	5	0	0	24.2	117	37	19	17	3	0	1	2	6	1	16	2	5	0	3	.000	0	0	6.20
	Bristol	R	13	9	2	1	75.1	303	55	14	12	2	1	1	7	22	0	85	5	1	9	1	.900	2	0	1.43
1989	Fayetteville	A	16	15	2	1	102	413	103	33	26	4	1	4	1	23	0	74	2	3	10	3	.769	0	0	2.29
	Lakeland	A	11	9	4	1	64.2	259	59	15	14	3	3	0	2	12	2	39	0	0	5	4	.556	2	0	1.95
1990	London	AA	26	26	9	0	178	722	160	70	62	11	3	7	4	36	0	123	5	1	15	9	.625	3	0	3.13
1991	Toledo	AAA	26	17	3	4	125.1	517	117	53	43	8	2	5	1	40	3	70	6	0	9	7	.563	1	2	3.09
1991	Detroit	AL	10	4	0	1	27.2	126	35	17	16	4	1	3	0	11	0	14	0	1	2	1	.667	0	0	5.20
1992	Kansas City	AL	64	0	0	20	101.2	412	88	39	31	5	3	9	1	21	5	64	4	0	10	4	.714	0	2	2.74
	2 ML YEARS		74	4	0	21	129.1	538	123	56	47	9	4	12	1	32	5	78	4	1	12	5	.706	0	2	3.27

Jose Melendez

Pitches: Right **Bats:** Right **Pos:** RP/SP **Ht:** 6' 2" **Wt:** 175 **Born:** 09/02/65 **Age:** 27

								HOW MUCH HE PITCHED				WHAT HE GAVE UP									THE RESULTS					
Year	Team	Lg	G	GS	CG	GF	IP	BFP	H	R	ER	HR	SH	SF	HB	TBB	IBB	SO	WP	Bk	W	L	Pct.	ShO	Sv	ERA
1990	Seattle	AL	3	0	0	1	5.1	28	8	8	7	2	0	0	1	3	0	7	1	0	0	0	.000	0	0	11.81
1991	San Diego	NL	31	9	0	10	93.2	381	77	35	34	11	2	6	1	24	3	60	3	2	8	5	.615	0	3	3.27
1992	San Diego	NL	56	3	0	18	89.1	363	82	32	29	9	7	4	3	20	7	82	1	1	6	7	.462	0	0	2.92
	3 ML YEARS		90	12	0	29	188.1	772	167	75	70	22	9	10	5	47	10	149	5	3	14	12	.538	0	3	3.35

Bob Melvin

Bats: Right **Throws:** Right **Pos:** C **Ht:** 6' 4" **Wt:** 205 **Born:** 10/28/61 **Age:** 31

Year	Team	Lg	G	AB	H	2B	3B	HR	(Hm	Rd)	TB	R	RBI	TBB	IBB	SO	HBP	SH	SF	SB	CS	SB%	GDP	Avg	OBP	SLG
1985	Detroit	AL	41	82	18	4	1	0	(0	0)	24	10	4	3	0	21	0	2	0	0	0	.00	1	.220	.247	.293
1986	San Francisco	NL	89	268	60	14	2	5	(2	3)	93	24	25	15	1	69	0	3	3	3	2	.60	7	.224	.262	.347
1987	San Francisco	NL	84	246	49	8	0	11	(6	5)	90	31	31	17	3	44	0	0	2	0	0	.00	7	.199	.249	.366
1988	San Francisco	NL	92	273	64	13	1	8	(4	4)	103	23	27	13	0	46	0	1	1	0	2	.00	5	.234	.268	.377
1989	Baltimore	AL	85	278	67	10	1	1	(0	1)	82	22	32	15	3	53	0	7	1	1	4	.20	10	.241	.279	.295
1990	Baltimore	AL	93	301	73	14	1	5	(3	2)	104	30	37	11	1	53	0	3	3	0	1	.00	8	.243	.267	.346
1991	Baltimore	AL	79	228	57	10	0	1	(0	1)	70	11	23	11	2	46	0	1	5	0	0	.00	5	.250	.279	.307
1992	Kansas City	AL	32	70	22	5	0	0	(0	0)	27	5	6	5	0	13	0	0	2	0	0	.00	3	.314	.351	.386
	8 ML YEARS		595	1746	410	78	6	31	(15	16)	593	156	185	90	10	345	0	17	17	4	13	.24	46	.235	.270	.340

Tony Menendez

Pitches: Right **Bats:** Right **Pos:** RP **Ht:** 6' 2" **Wt:** 189 **Born:** 02/20/65 **Age:** 28

Year	Team	Lg	G	GS	CG	GF	IP	BFP	H	R	ER	HR	SH	SF	HB	TBB	IBB	SO	WP	Bk	W	L	Pct.	ShO	Sv	ERA
1984	White Sox	R	6	6	0	0	37	148	26	19	13	2	0	1	0	13	0	30	2	0	3	2	.600	0	0	3.16
1985	Buffalo	AAA	1	1	0	0	2.1	15	9	5	5	0	0	0	0	1	1	2	0	0	0	1	.000	0	0	19.29
	Appleton	A	24	24	2	0	148	620	134	67	45	8	6	3	4	55	0	100	11	1	13	4	.765	0	0	2.74
1986	Peninsula	A	11	10	1	1	63	279	58	35	32	9	1	6	4	29	0	43	6	0	4	4	.500	1	0	4.57
	Birmingham	AA	17	17	0	0	96.1	470	132	71	61	17	0	3	7	50	0	52	14	0	7	8	.467	0	0	5.70
1987	Birmingham	AA	27	27	4	0	173.1	776	193	111	93	19	3	7	7	76	1	102	12	2	10	10	.500	1	0	4.83
1988	Birmingham	AA	24	24	3	0	153	642	131	79	67	14	4	8	2	64	0	112	6	4	6	11	.353	0	0	3.94
1989	Birmingham	AA	27	18	2	6	144	596	123	61	51	14	5	1	4	53	2	115	7	2	10	4	.714	1	0	3.19
1990	Vancouver	AAA	24	9	2	2	72.2	307	63	34	30	6	3	5	6	28	1	48	1	0	2	5	.286	1	0	3.72
1991	Tulsa	AA	3	2	0	1	14	54	9	2	2	0	0	0	0	4	0	14	0	0	3	0	1.000	0	0	1.29
	Okla City	AAA	21	19	0	1	116	504	107	70	67	6	5	8	6	62	3	82	8	1	5	5	.500	0	0	5.20
1992	Nashville	AAA	50	2	0	11	106.2	458	98	53	48	10	8	5	3	47	6	92	3	0	3	5	.375	0	1	4.05
1992	Cincinnati	NL	3	0	0	1	4.2	15	1	1	1	1	0	0	0	0	0	5	0	0	1	0	1.000	0	0	1.93

Orlando Merced

Bats: Both **Throws:** Right **Pos:** 1B/RF **Ht:** 5'11" **Wt:** 170 **Born:** 11/02/66 **Age:** 26

Year	Team	Lg	G	AB	H	2B	3B	HR	(Hm	Rd)	TB	R	RBI	TBB	IBB	SO	HBP	SH	SF	SB	CS	SB%	GDP	Avg	OBP	SLG
1990	Pittsburgh	NL	25	24	5	1	0	0	(0	0)	6	3	0	1	0	9	0	0	0	0	0	.00	1	.208	.240	.250
1991	Pittsburgh	NL	120	411	113	17	2	10	(5	5)	164	83	50	64	4	81	1	1	1	8	4	.67	6	.275	.373	.399
1992	Pittsburgh	NL	134	405	100	28	5	6	(4	2)	156	50	60	52	8	63	2	1	5	5	4	.56	6	.247	.332	.385
	3 ML YEARS		279	840	218	46	7	16	(9	7)	326	136	110	117	12	153	3	2	6	13	8	.62	13	.260	.350	.388

Henry Mercedes

Bats: Right **Throws:** Right **Pos:** C **Ht:** 5'11" **Wt:** 185 **Born:** 07/23/69 **Age:** 23

Year	Team	Lg	G	AB	H	2B	3B	HR	(Hm	Rd)	TB	R	RBI	TBB	IBB	SO	HBP	SH	SF	SB	CS	SB%	GDP	Avg	OBP	SLG
1988	Athletics	R	2	5	2	0	0	0	--	--	2	1	0	0	0	0	0	0	0	0	0	.00	0	.400	.400	.400
1989	Madison	A	51	152	32	3	0	2	--	--	41	11	13	22	1	46	1	3	0	0	0	.00	1	.211	.314	.270
	Modesto	A	16	37	3	0	0	1	--	--	6	6	3	7	0	22	0	0	0	0	0	.00	2	.081	.227	.162
	Sou Oregon	A	22	61	10	0	1	0	--	--	12	6	1	10	0	24	1	0	0	0	2	.00	0	.164	.292	.197
1990	Tacoma	AAA	12	31	6	1	0	0	--	--	7	3	2	3	0	7	0	2	0	0	1	.00	2	.194	.265	.226
	Madison	A	90	282	64	13	2	3	--	--	90	29	38	30	0	100	1	6	2	6	0	1.00	5	.227	.302	.319
1991	Modesto	A	116	388	100	17	3	4	--	--	135	55	61	68	1	110	2	3	3	5	8	.38	6	.258	.369	.348
1992	Tacoma	AAA	85	246	57	9	2	0	--	--	70	36	20	26	0	60	0	4	0	1	3	.25	8	.232	.305	.285
1992	Oakland	AL	9	5	4	0	1	0	(0	0)	6	1	1	1	0	1	0	0	0	0	0	.00	0	.800	.800	1.200

Luis Mercedes

Bats: Right **Throws:** Right **Pos:** RF **Ht:** 6' 3" **Wt:** 193 **Born:** 02/20/68 **Age:** 25

Year	Team	Lg	G	AB	H	2B	3B	HR	(Hm	Rd)	TB	R	RBI	TBB	IBB	SO	HBP	SH	SF	SB	CS	SB%	GDP	Avg	OBP	SLG
1988	Bluefield	R	59	215	59	8	4	0	--	--	75	36	20	32	0	39	2	3	1	16	11	.59	6	.274	.372	.349
1989	Frederick	A	108	401	124	12	5	3	--	--	155	62	36	30	2	62	3	2	2	29	11	.73	7	.309	.360	.387
1990	Hagerstown	AA	108	416	139	12	4	3	--	--	168	71	37	34	2	70	6	6	2	38	14	.73	13	.334	.391	.404
1991	Rochester	AAA	102	374	125	14	5	2	--	--	155	68	36	65	0	63	5	6	4	23	14	.62	10	.334	.435	.414
1992	Rochester	AAA	103	409	128	15	1	3	--	--	154	62	29	44	2	56	1	3	3	35	14	.71	11	.313	.379	.377
1991	Baltimore	AL	19	54	11	2	0	0	(0	0)	13	10	2	4	0	9	0	1	0	0	0	.00	1	.204	.259	.241
1992	Baltimore	AL	23	50	7	2	0	0	(0	0)	9	7	4	8	0	9	1	2	1	0	1	.00	2	.140	.267	.180

	G	AB	H	2B	3B	HR	(Hm	Rd)	TB	R	RBI	TBB	IBB	SO	HBP	SH	SF	SB	CS	SB%	GDP	Avg	OBP	SLG
2 ML YEARS	42	104	18	4	0	0	(0	0)	22	17	6	12	0	18	1	3	1	0	1	.00	3	.173	.263	.212

Kent Mercker

Pitches: Left **Bats:** Left **Pos:** RP **Ht:** 6' 2" **Wt:** 195 **Born:** 02/01/68 **Age:** 25

		HOW MUCH HE PITCHED						WHAT HE GAVE UP										THE RESULTS					
Year Team	Lg	G	GS	CG	GF	IP	BFP	H	R	ER	HR	SH	SF	HB	TBB	IBB	SO	WP	Bk	W	L	Pct.	ShO	Sv	ERA
1989 Atlanta	NL	2	1	0	1	4.1	26	8	6	6	0	0	0	0	6	0	4	0	0	0	0	.000	0	0	12.46
1990 Atlanta	NL	36	0	0	28	48.1	211	43	22	17	6	1	2	2	24	3	39	2	0	4	7	.364	0	7	3.17
1991 Atlanta	NL	50	4	0	28	73.1	306	56	23	21	5	2	2	1	35	3	62	4	1	5	3	.625	0	6	2.58
1992 Atlanta	NL	53	0	0	18	68.1	289	51	27	26	4	4	1	3	35	1	49	6	0	3	2	.600	0	6	3.42
4 ML YEARS		141	5	0	75	194.1	832	158	78	70	15	7	5	6	100	7	154	12	1	12	12	.500	0	19	3.24

Matt Merullo

Bats: Left **Throws:** Right **Pos:** C **Ht:** 6' 2" **Wt:** 200 **Born:** 08/04/65 **Age:** 27

		BATTING																BASERUNNING				PERCENTAGES		
Year Team	Lg	G	AB	H	2B	3B	HR	(Hm | Rd)	TB	R	RBI	TBB	IBB	SO	HBP	SH	SF	SB	CS	SB%	GDP	Avg	OBP	SLG
1989 Chicago	AL	31	81	18	1	0	1	(1 | 0)	22	5	8	6	0	14	0	2	1	0	1	.00	2	.222	.273	.272
1991 Chicago	AL	80	140	32	1	0	5	(1 | 4)	48	8	21	9	1	18	0	1	4	0	0	.00	0	.229	.268	.343
1992 Chicago	AL	24	50	9	1	1	0	(0 | 0)	12	3	3	1	0	8	1	0	1	0	0	.00	0	.180	.208	.240
3 ML YEARS		135	271	59	3	1	6	(2 | 4)	82	16	32	16	1	40	1	3	6	0	1	.00	3	.218	.259	.303

Jose Mesa

Pitches: Right **Bats:** Right **Pos:** SP **Ht:** 6' 3" **Wt:** 222 **Born:** 05/22/66 **Age:** 27

		HOW MUCH HE PITCHED						WHAT HE GAVE UP										THE RESULTS					
Year Team	Lg	G	GS	CG	GF	IP	BFP	H	R	ER	HR	SH	SF	HB	TBB	IBB	SO	WP	Bk	W	L	Pct.	ShO	Sv	ERA
1987 Baltimore	AL	6	5	0	0	31.1	143	38	23	21	7	0	0	0	15	0	17	4	0	1	3	.250	0	0	6.03
1990 Baltimore	AL	7	7	0	0	46.2	202	37	20	20	2	2	2	1	27	2	24	1	1	3	2	.600	0	0	3.86
1991 Baltimore	AL	23	23	2	0	123.2	566	151	86	82	11	5	4	3	62	2	64	3	0	6	11	.353	1	0	5.97
1992 2 ML Teams		28	27	1	1	160.2	700	169	86	82	14	2	5	4	70	1	62	2	0	7	12	.368	1	0	4.59
1992 Baltimore	AL	13	12	0	1	67.2	300	77	41	39	9	0	3	2	27	1	22	2	0	3	8	.273	0	0	5.19
Cleveland	AL	15	15	1	0	93	400	92	45	43	5	2	2	2	43	0	40	0	0	4	4	.500	1	0	4.16
4 ML YEARS		64	62	3	1	362.1	1611	395	215	205	34	9	11	8	174	5	167	10	1	17	28	.378	2	0	5.09

Hensley Meulens

Bats: Right **Throws:** Right **Pos:** 3B **Ht:** 6' 3" **Wt:** 212 **Born:** 06/23/67 **Age:** 26

		BATTING																BASERUNNING				PERCENTAGES		
Year Team	Lg	G	AB	H	2B	3B	HR	(Hm | Rd)	TB	R	RBI	TBB	IBB	SO	HBP	SH	SF	SB	CS	SB%	GDP	Avg	OBP	SLG
1989 New York	AL	8	28	5	0	0	0	(0	0)	5	2	1	2	0	8	0	0	0	1	.00	1	.179	.233	.179
1990 New York	AL	23	83	20	7	0	3	(2 | 1)	36	12	10	9	0	25	3	0	0	1	0	1.00	3	.241	.337	.434
1991 New York	AL	96	288	64	8	1	6	(4 | 2)	92	37	29	18	1	97	4	1	2	3	0	1.00	7	.222	.276	.319
1992 New York	AL	2	5	3	0	0	1	(1 | 0)	6	1	1	1	0	0	0	0	0	0	0	.00	0	.600	.667	1.200
4 ML YEARS		129	404	92	15	1	10	(7 | 3)	139	52	41	30	1	130	7	1	2	4	1	.80	13	.228	.291	.344

Bob Milacki

Pitches: Right **Bats:** Right **Pos:** SP **Ht:** 6' 4" **Wt:** 232 **Born:** 07/28/64 **Age:** 28

		HOW MUCH HE PITCHED						WHAT HE GAVE UP										THE RESULTS					
Year Team	Lg	G	GS	CG	GF	IP	BFP	H	R	ER	HR	SH	SF	HB	TBB	IBB	SO	WP	Bk	W	L	Pct.	ShO	Sv	ERA
1988 Baltimore	AL	3	3	1	0	25	91	9	2	2	1	0	0	0	9	0	18	0	0	2	0	1.000	1	0	0.72
1989 Baltimore	AL	37	36	3	1	243	1022	233	105	101	21	7	6	2	88	4	113	1	1	14	12	.538	2	0	3.74
1990 Baltimore	AL	27	24	1	0	135.1	594	143	73	67	18	5	5	0	61	2	60	2	1	5	8	.385	1	0	4.46
1991 Baltimore	AL	31	26	3	1	184	758	175	86	82	17	7	5	1	53	3	108	1	2	10	9	.526	1	0	4.01
1992 Baltimore	AL	23	20	0	1	115.2	525	140	78	75	16	3	3	2	44	2	51	7	1	6	8	.429	0	1	5.84
5 ML YEARS		121	109	8	3	703	2990	700	344	327	73	22	19	5	255	11	350	11	5	37	37	.500	5	1	4.19

Sam Militello

Pitches: Right **Bats:** Right **Pos:** SP **Ht:** 6' 3" **Wt:** 200 **Born:** 11/26/69 **Age:** 23

		HOW MUCH HE PITCHED						WHAT HE GAVE UP										THE RESULTS					
Year Team	Lg	G	GS	CG	GF	IP	BFP	H	R	ER	HR	SH	SF	HB	TBB	IBB	SO	WP	Bk	W	L	Pct.	ShO	Sv	ERA
1990 Oneonta	A	13	13	3	0	88.2	332	53	14	12	2	0	2	1	24	0	119	0	2	8	2	.800	2	0	1.22
1991 Pr William	A	16	16	1	0	103.1	397	65	19	14	1	1	4	4	27	1	113	1	1	12	2	.857	0	0	1.22
Albany	AA	7	7	0	0	46	191	40	14	12	3	1	1	3	19	1	55	0	0	2	2	.500	0	0	2.35
1992 Columbus	AAA	22	21	3	0	141.1	576	105	45	36	5	2	5	11	46	1	152	4	1	12	2	.857	2	0	2.29
1992 New York	AL	9	9	0	0	60	255	43	24	23	6	0	0	2	32	1	42	1	0	3	3	.500	0	0	3.45

Keith Miller

Bats: Right **Throws:** Right **Pos:** 2B/LF   **Ht:** 5'11" **Wt:** 185 **Born:** 06/12/63 **Age:** 30

Year Team	Lg	G	AB	H	2B	3B	HR	(Hm	Rd)	TB	R	RBI	TBB	IBB	SO	HBP	SH	SF	SB	CS	SB%	GDP	Avg	OBP	SLG
1987 New York	NL	25	51	19	2	2	0	(0	0)	25	14	1	2	0	6	1	3	0	8	1	.89	1	.373	.407	.490
1988 New York	NL	40	70	15	1	1	1	(1	0)	21	9	5	6	0	10	0	3	0	0	5	.00	1	.214	.276	.300
1989 New York	NL	57	143	33	7	0	1	(0	1)	43	15	7	5	0	27	1	3	0	6	0	1.00	3	.231	.262	.301
1990 New York	NL	88	233	60	8	0	1	(1	0)	71	42	12	23	1	46	2	2	2	16	3	.84	2	.258	.327	.305
1991 New York	NL	98	275	77	22	1	4	(2	2)	113	41	23	23	2	44	5	0	1	14	4	.78	2	.280	.345	.411
1992 Kansas City	AL	106	416	118	24	4	4	(1	3)	162	57	38	31	0	46	14	1	2	16	6	.73	1	.284	.352	.389
6 ML YEARS		414	1188	322	64	8	11	(5	6)	435	178	86	90	1	179	23	12	5	60	19	.76	10	.271	.333	.366

Paul Miller

Pitches: Right **Bats:** Right **Pos:** RP   **Ht:** 6'5" **Wt:** 220 **Born:** 04/27/65 **Age:** 28

Year Team	Lg	G	GS	CG	GF	IP	BFP	H	R	ER	HR	SH	SF	HB	TBB	IBB	SO	WP	Bk	W	L	Pct.	ShO	Sv	ERA
1987 Pirates	R	12	12	1	0	70.1	292	55	34	25	3	4	1	2	26	0	62	3	0	3	6	.333	1	0	3.20
1988 Augusta	A	15	15	2	0	90.1	374	80	34	29	3	3	5	4	28	1	51	8	5	6	5	.545	2	0	2.89
1989 Salem	A	26	20	2	0	133.2	599	138	86	62	17	2	4	8	64	0	82	8	1	6	12	.333	1	0	4.17
1990 Salem	A	22	22	5	0	150.2	628	145	58	41	6	3	6	7	33	1	83	5	1	8	6	.571	1	0	2.45
Harrisburg	AA	5	5	2	0	37	148	27	9	9	1	1	2	2	10	0	11	0	0	2	1	.667	1	0	2.19
1991 Carolina	AA	15	15	1	0	89.1	369	69	29	24	4	7	1	3	35	4	69	5	1	7	2	.778	0	0	2.42
Buffalo	AAA	10	10	2	0	67	272	41	17	11	2	4	0	5	29	0	30	1	1	5	2	.714	0	0	1.48
1992 Buffalo	AAA	8	7	0	0	32.1	150	38	23	14	3	3	1	1	16	0	18	0	0	2	3	.400	0	0	3.90
1991 Pittsburgh	NL	1	1	0	0	5	21	4	3	3	0	0	0	0	3	0	2	0	0	0	0	.000	0	0	5.40
1992 Pittsburgh	NL	6	0	0	1	11.1	46	11	3	3	0	1	0	0	1	0	5	1	0	1	0	1.000	0	0	2.38
2 ML YEARS		7	1	0	1	16.1	67	15	6	6	0	1	1	0	4	0	7	1	0	1	0	1.000	0	0	3.31

Joe Millette

Bats: Right **Throws:** Right **Pos:** SS   **Ht:** 6'1" **Wt:** 175 **Born:** 08/12/66 **Age:** 26

Year Team	Lg	G	AB	H	2B	3B	HR	(Hm	Rd)	TB	R	RBI	TBB	IBB	SO	HBP	SH	SF	SB	CS	SB%	GDP	Avg	OBP	SLG
1989 Batavia	A	11	42	10	3	0	0	--	--	13	4	4	4	0	6	0	0	0	3	0	1.00	0	.238	.304	.310
Spartanburg	A	60	209	50	4	3	0	--	--	60	27	18	28	0	36	7	3	3	4	2	.67	5	.239	.344	.287
1990 Clearwater	A	108	295	54	5	0	0	--	--	59	31	18	29	0	53	7	7	6	4	4	.50	5	.183	.267	.200
1991 Clearwater	A	18	55	14	2	0	0	--	--	16	6	6	7	0	6	1	3	2	1	2	.33	1	.255	.338	.291
Reading	AA	115	353	87	9	4	3	--	--	113	52	28	36	2	54	7	10	3	6	6	.50	5	.246	.326	.320
1992 Scranton/wb	AAA	78	256	68	11	1	1	--	--	84	24	23	15	0	30	6	7	0	3	2	.60	8	.266	.321	.328
1992 Philadelphia	NL	33	78	16	0	0	0	(0	0)	16	5	2	5	2	10	2	2	0	1	0	1.00	8	.205	.271	.205

Randy Milligan

Bats: Right **Throws:** Right **Pos:** 1B   **Ht:** 6'1" **Wt:** 234 **Born:** 11/27/61 **Age:** 31

Year Team	Lg	G	AB	H	2B	3B	HR	(Hm	Rd)	TB	R	RBI	TBB	IBB	SO	HBP	SH	SF	SB	CS	SB%	GDP	Avg	OBP	SLG
1987 New York	NL	3	1	0	0	0	0	(0	0)	0	0	0	1	0	1	0	0	0	0	0	.00	0	.000	.500	.000
1988 Pittsburgh	NL	40	82	18	5	0	3	(1	2)	32	10	8	20	0	24	1	0	0	1	2	.33	2	.220	.379	.390
1989 Baltimore	AL	124	365	98	23	5	12	(6	6)	167	56	45	74	2	75	3	0	2	9	5	.64	12	.268	.394	.458
1990 Baltimore	AL	109	362	96	20	1	20	(11	9)	178	64	60	88	3	68	2	0	4	6	3	.67	11	.265	.408	.492
1991 Baltimore	AL	141	483	127	17	2	16	(8	8)	196	57	70	84	4	108	2	0	2	0	5	.00	23	.263	.373	.406
1992 Baltimore	AL	137	462	111	21	1	11	(7	4)	167	71	53	106	0	81	4	0	5	0	1	.00	15	.240	.373	.361
6 ML YEARS		554	1755	450	86	9	62	(33	29)	740	258	236	373	9	357	12	0	13	16	16	.50	63	.256	.388	.422

Alan Mills

Pitches: Right **Bats:** Both **Pos:** RP/SP   **Ht:** 6'1" **Wt:** 190 **Born:** 10/18/66 **Age:** 26

Year Team	Lg	G	GS	CG	GF	IP	BFP	H	R	ER	HR	SH	SF	HB	TBB	IBB	SO	WP	Bk	W	L	Pct.	ShO	Sv	ERA
1990 New York	AL	36	0	0	18	41.2	200	48	21	19	4	4	1	1	33	6	24	3	0	1	5	.167	0	0	4.10
1991 New York	AL	6	2	0	3	16.1	72	16	9	8	1	0	1	0	8	0	11	2	0	1	1	.500	0	0	4.41
1992 Baltimore	AL	35	3	0	12	103.1	428	78	33	30	5	6	5	1	54	10	60	2	0	10	4	.714	0	2	2.61
3 ML YEARS		77	5	0	33	161.1	700	142	63	57	10	10	7	2	95	16	95	7	0	12	10	.545	0	2	3.18

Blas Minor

Pitches: Right **Bats:** Right **Pos:** RP
Ht: 6' 3" **Wt:** 195 **Born:** 03/20/66 **Age:** 27

		HOW MUCH HE PITCHED				WHAT HE GAVE UP						THE RESULTS			
Year Team	Lg	G	GS	CG	GF	IP	BFP	H	R	ER	HR	SH	SF	HB	TBB	IBB	SO	WP	Bk	W	L	Pct.	ShO	Sv	ERA

Year Team	Lg	G	GS	CG	GF	IP	BFP	H	R	ER	HR	SH	SF	HB	TBB	IBB	SO	WP	Bk	W	L	Pct.	ShO	Sv	ERA
1988 Princeton	R	15	0	0	14	16.1	77	18	10	8	2	0	0	0	5	0	23	0	0	0	1	.000	0	7	4.41
1989 Salem	A	39	4	0	25	86.2	377	91	43	35	6	4	1	2	31	6	62	3	1	3	5	.375	0	0	3.63
1990 Harrisburg	AA	38	6	0	23	94	391	81	41	32	5	8	4	0	29	7	98	3	1	6	4	.600	0	5	3.06
Buffalo	AAA	1	0	0	0	2.2	12	2	1	1	0	0	0	0	2	0	2	0	0	0	1	.000	0	0	3.38
1991 Buffalo	AAA	17	3	0	3	36	168	46	27	23	7	2	1	0	15	0	25	1	0	2	2	.500	0	0	5.75
Carolina	AA	3	2	0	1	12.2	52	9	4	4	0	1	0	0	7	0	18	1	0	0	0	.000	0	0	2.84
1992 Buffalo	AAA	45	8	0	29	96.1	379	72	30	26	7	4	2	1	26	2	60	2	1	5	4	.556	0	18	2.43
1992 Pittsburgh	NL	1	0	0	0	2	9	3	2	1	0	0	0	0	0	0	0	1	0	0	0	.000	0	0	4.50

Kevin Mitchell

Bats: Right **Throws:** Right **Pos:** LF/DH
Ht: 5'11" **Wt:** 210 **Born:** 01/13/62 **Age:** 31

		BATTING																	BASERUNNING				PERCENTAGES		
Year Team	Lg	G	AB	H	2B	3B	HR	(Hm	Rd)	TB	R	RBI	TBB	IBB	SO	HBP	SH	SF	SB	CS	SB%	GDP	Avg	OBP	SLG
1984 New York	NL	7	14	3	0	0	0	(0	0)	3	0	1	0	0	3	0	0	0	0	1	.00	0	.214	.214	.214
1986 New York	NL	108	328	91	22	2	12	(4	8)	153	51	43	33	0	61	1	1	1	3	3	.50	6	.277	.344	.466
1987 2 ML Teams		131	464	130	20	2	22	(9	13)	220	68	70	48	4	88	2	0	1	9	6	.60	10	.280	.350	.474
1988 San Francisco	NL	148	505	127	25	7	19	(10	9)	223	60	80	48	7	85	5	1	7	5	5	.50	9	.251	.319	.442
1989 San Francisco	NL	154	543	158	34	6	47	(22	25)	345	100	125	87	32	115	3	0	7	3	4	.43	6	.291	.388	.635
1990 San Francisco	NL	140	524	152	24	2	35	(15	20)	285	90	93	58	9	87	2	0	5	4	7	.36	8	.290	.360	.544
1991 San Francisco	NL	113	371	95	13	1	27	(9	18)	191	52	69	43	8	57	5	0	4	2	3	.40	6	.256	.338	.428
1992 Seattle	Al	99	360	103	24	0	9	(5	4)	154	48	67	35	4	46	3	0	4	0	2	.00	5	.286	.351	.428
1987 San Diego	NL	62	196	48	7	1	7	(2	5)	78	19	26	20	3	38	0	0	1	0	0	.00	5	.245	.313	.398
San Francisco	NL	69	268	82	13	1	15	(7	8)	142	49	44	28	1	50	2	0	0	9	6	.60	5	.306	.376	.530
8 ML YEARS		900	3109	859	162	20	171	(74	97)	1574	469	548	352	64	542	21	2	29	26	31	.46	49	.276	.351	.506

Dave Mlicki

Pitches: Right **Bats:** Right **Pos:** SP
Ht: 6' 4" **Wt:** 185 **Born:** 06/08/68 **Age:** 25

		HOW MUCH HE PITCHED						WHAT HE GAVE UP											THE RESULTS					
Year Team	Lg	G	GS	CG	GF	IP	BFP	H	R	ER	HR	SH	SF	HB	TBB	IBB	SO	WP	Bk	W	L	Pct.	ShO	Sv	ERA
1990 Burlington	R	8	1	0	2	18	81	16	11	7	1	0	1	1	6	0	17	0	0	3	1	.750	0	0	3.50
Watertown	A	7	4	0	3	32	139	33	15	12	3	0	1	0	11	0	28	2	0	3	0	1.000	0	0	3.38
1991 Columbus	A	22	19	2	1	115.2	516	101	70	54	3	0	1	6	70	1	136	10	2	8	6	.571	0	0	4.20
1992 Canton-Akrn	AA	27	27	2	0	172.2	720	143	77	69	8	5	7	3	80	1	146	9	1	11	9	.550	0	0	3.60
1992 Cleveland	Al	4	4	0	0	21.2	101	23	14	12	3	2	0	1	16	0	16	1	0	0	2	.000	0	0	4.98

Dennis Moeller

Pitches: Left **Bats:** Right **Pos:** SP
Ht: 6' 2" **Wt:** 180 **Born:** 09/15/67 **Age:** 25

		HOW MUCH HE PITCHED						WHAT HE GAVE UP											THE RESULTS					
Year Team	Lg	G	GS	CG	GF	IP	BFP	H	R	ER	HR	SH	SF	HB	TBB	IBB	SO	WP	Bk	W	L	Pct.	ShO	Sv	ERA
1986 Eugene	A	14	11	0	0	61.2	0	54	22	21	1	0	0	2	34	0	65	7	2	4	0	1.000	0	0	3.06
1987 Appleton	A	18	13	0	0	55	292	72	63	44	5	2	3	1	45	3	49	6	0	2	5	.286	0	0	7.20
1988 Appleton	A	20	18	0	1	99	421	94	46	35	4	4	3	4	34	1	88	5	2	3	5	.375	0	0	3.18
1989 Baseball Cy	A	12	11	2	1	71	280	59	17	14	2	0	3	1	20	1	64	1	1	9	0	1.000	0	0	1.77
Memphis	AA	5	5	0	0	25.1	100	16	9	8	2	2	0	1	10	0	21	0	0	1	1	.500	0	0	2.84
1990 Memphis	AA	14	14	0	0	67.2	307	79	55	47	11	3	3	2	30	1	42	3	2	7	6	.538	0	0	6.25
Omaha	AAA	11	11	1	0	65	274	63	29	29	8	1	0	1	30	0	53	0	5	5	2	.714	1	0	4.02
1991 Memphis	AA	10	10	0	0	53	224	52	24	15	6	1	1	1	21	0	54	1	1	4	5	.444	0	0	2.55
Omaha	AAA	14	14	0	0	78.1	342	70	36	28	4	3	1	3	40	0	51	3	3	7	3	.700	0	0	3.22
1992 Omaha	AAA	23	16	3	2	120.2	496	121	36	33	4	3	1	3	34	1	56	5	3	8	5	.615	1	2	2.46
1992 Kansas City	Al	5	4	0	1	18	89	24	17	14	5	3	3	0	11	2	6	1	1	0	3	.000	0	0	7.00

Paul Molitor

Bats: Right **Throws:** Right **Pos:** DH/1B
Ht: 6' 0" **Wt:** 185 **Born:** 08/22/56 **Age:** 36

		BATTING																	BASERUNNING				PERCENTAGES		
Year Team	Lg	G	AB	H	2B	3B	HR	(Hm	Rd)	TB	R	RBI	TBB	IBB	SO	HBP	SH	SF	SB	CS	SB%	GDP	Avg	OBP	SLG
1978 Milwaukee	AL	125	521	142	26	4	6	(4	2)	194	73	45	19	2	54	4	7	5	30	12	.71	6	.273	.301	.372
1979 Milwaukee	AL	140	584	188	27	16	9	(3	6)	274	88	62	48	5	48	2	6	5	33	13	.72	9	.322	.372	.469
1980 Milwaukee	AL	111	450	137	29	2	9	(2	7)	197	81	37	48	4	48	3	6	5	34	7	.83	9	.304	.372	.438
1981 Milwaukee	AL	64	251	67	11	0	2	(1	1)	84	45	19	25	1	29	3	5	0	10	6	.63	3	.267	.341	.335
1982 Milwaukee	AL	160	666	201	26	8	19	(9	10)	300	136	71	69	1	93	1	10	5	41	9	.82	9	.302	.366	.450
1983 Milwaukee	AL	152	608	164	28	6	15	(9	6)	249	95	47	59	4	74	2	7	6	41	8	.84	12	.270	.333	.410
1984 Milwaukee	AL	13	46	10	1	0	0	(0	0)	11	3	6	2	0	8	0	0	1	1	0	1.00	0	.217	.245	.239
1985 Milwaukee	AL	140	576	171	28	3	10	(6	4)	235	93	48	54	6	80	1	7	4	21	7	.75	12	.297	.356	.408

		G	AB	H	2B	3B	HR	(Hm	Rd)	TB	R	RBI	TBB	IBB	SO				SB	CS	SB%	GDP	Avg	OBP	SLG
1986 Milwaukee	AL	105	437	123	24	6	9	(5	4)	186	62	55	40	0	81	0	2	3	20	5	.80	9	.281	.340	.426
1987 Milwaukee	AL	118	465	164	41	5	16	(7	9)	263	114	75	69	2	67	2	5	1	45	10	.82	4	.353	.438	.566
1988 Milwaukee	AL	154	609	190	34	6	13	(9	4)	275	115	60	71	8	54	2	5	3	41	10	.80	10	.312	.384	.452
1989 Milwaukee	AL	155	615	194	35	4	11	(6	5)	270	84	56	64	4	67	4	4	9	27	11	.71	11	.315	.379	.439
1990 Milwaukee	AL	103	418	119	27	6	12	(6	6)	194	64	45	37	4	51	1	0	2	18	3	.86	7	.285	.343	.464
1991 Milwaukee	AL	158	665	216	32	13	17	(7	10)	325	133	75	77	16	62	6	0	1	19	8	.70	11	.325	.399	.489
1992 Milwaukee	AL	158	609	195	36	7	12	(4	8)	281	89	89	73	12	66	3	4	11	31	6	.84	13	.320	.389	.461
15 ML YEARS		1856	7520	2281	405	86	160	(78	82)	3338	1275	790	755	69	882	34	68	61	412	115	.78	125	.303	.367	.444

Rich Monteleone

Pitches: Right **Bats:** Right **Pos:** RP   **Ht:** 6' 3" **Wt:** 236 **Born:** 03/22/63 **Age:** 30

		HOW MUCH HE PITCHED						WHAT HE GAVE UP											THE RESULTS					
Year Team	Lg	G	GS	CG	GF	IP	BFP	H	R	ER	HR	SH	SF	HB	TBB	IBB	SO	WP	Bk	W	L	Pct.	ShO	Sv	ERA
1987 California	AL	3	0	0	1	7	34	10	5	5	2	0	0	1	4	0	2	0	0	0	0	.000	0	0	6.43
1988 California	AL	3	0	0	2	4.1	20	4	0	0	0	0	0	1	1	1	3	0	1	0	0	.000	0	0	0.00
1989 California	AL	24	0	0	8	39.2	170	39	15	14	3	1	2	1	13	1	27	2	0	2	2	.500	0	0	3.18
1990 New York	AL	5	0	0	2	7.1	31	8	5	5	0	0	0	0	2	0	8	0	0	0	1	.000	0	0	6.14
1991 New York	AL	26	0	0	10	47	201	42	27	19	5	2	2	0	19	3	34	1	1	3	1	.750	0	0	3.64
1992 New York	AL	47	0	0	15	92.2	380	82	35	34	7	3	1	0	27	3	62	0	3	7	3	.700	0	0	3.30
6 ML YEARS		108	0	0	38	198	836	185	87	77	17	6	5	3	66	8	136	3	5	12	7	.632	0	0	3.50

Jeff Montgomery

Pitches: Right **Bats:** Right **Pos:** RP   **Ht:** 5'11" **Wt:** 180 **Born:** 01/07/62 **Age:** 31

		HOW MUCH HE PITCHED						WHAT HE GAVE UP											THE RESULTS					
Year Team	Lg	G	GS	CG	GF	IP	BFP	H	R	ER	HR	SH	SF	HB	TBB	IBB	SO	WP	Bk	W	L	Pct.	ShO	Sv	ERA
1987 Cincinnati	NL	14	0	0	6	19.1	89	25	15	14	2	0	0	0	9	1	13	1	1	2	2	.500	0	0	6.52
1988 Kansas City	AL	45	0	0	13	62.2	271	54	25	24	6	3	2	2	30	1	47	3	6	7	2	.778	0	1	3.45
1989 Kansas City	AL	63	0	0	39	92	363	66	16	14	3	1	1	2	25	4	94	6	1	7	3	.700	0	18	1.37
1990 Kansas City	AL	73	0	0	59	94.1	400	81	36	25	6	2	2	5	34	8	94	3	0	6	5	.545	0	24	2.39
1991 Kansas City	AL	67	0	0	55	90	376	83	32	29	6	2	2	2	28	2	77	6	0	4	4	.500	0	33	2.90
1992 Kansas City	AL	65	0	0	62	82.2	333	61	23	20	5	4	2	3	27	2	69	2	0	1	6	.143	0	39	2.18
6 ML YEARS		327	1	0	234	441	1832	370	147	126	28	16	9	14	153	18	394	21	8	27	22	.551	0	115	2.57

Mike Moore

Pitches: Right **Bats:** Right **Pos:** SP   **Ht:** 6' 4" **Wt:** 205 **Born:** 11/26/59 **Age:** 33

		HOW MUCH HE PITCHED						WHAT HE GAVE UP											THE RESULTS					
Year Team	Lg	G	GS	CG	GF	IP	BFP	H	R	ER	HR	SH	SF	HB	TBB	IBB	SO	WP	Bk	W	L	Pct.	ShO	Sv	ERA
1982 Seattle	AL	28	27	1	0	144.1	651	159	91	86	21	8	4	2	79	0	73	6	0	7	14	.333	1	0	5.36
1983 Seattle	AL	22	21	3	1	128	556	130	75	67	10	1	6	3	60	4	108	7	0	6	8	.429	2	0	4.71
1984 Seattle	AL	34	33	6	0	212	937	236	127	117	16	5	6	6	85	10	158	7	2	7	17	.292	0	0	4.97
1985 Seattle	AL	35	34	14	1	247	1016	230	100	95	18	2	7	4	70	2	155	10	3	17	10	.630	2	0	3.46
1986 Seattle	AL	38	37	11	1	266	1145	279	141	127	28	10	6	12	94	6	146	4	1	11	13	.458	1	1	4.30
1987 Seattle	AL	33	33	12	0	231	1020	268	145	121	29	9	8	0	84	3	115	4	2	9	19	.321	0	0	4.71
1988 Seattle	AL	37	32	9	3	228.2	918	196	104	96	24	3	3	3	63	6	182	4	3	9	15	.375	3	1	3.78
1989 Oakland	AL	35	35	6	0	241.2	976	193	82	70	14	5	6	2	83	1	172	17	0	19	11	.633	3	0	2.61
1990 Oakland	AL	33	33	3	0	199.1	862	204	113	103	14	4	7	3	84	2	73	13	0	13	15	.464	0	0	4.65
1991 Oakland	AL	33	33	3	0	210	887	176	75	69	11	5	4	5	105	1	153	14	0	17	8	.680	1	0	2.96
1992 Oakland	AL	36	36	3	0	223	982	229	113	102	20	7	11	8	103	5	117	22	0	17	12	.586	0	0	4.12
11 ML YEARS		364	354	70	6	2331	9950	2300	1166	1053	205	59	68	47	910	40	1452	108	11	132	142	.482	13	2	4.07

Mickey Morandini

Bats: Left **Throws:** Right **Pos:** 2B   **Ht:** 5'11" **Wt:** 175 **Born:** 04/22/66 **Age:** 27

		BATTING																	BASERUNNING				PERCENTAGES		
Year Team	Lg	G	AB	H	2B	3B	HR	(Hm	Rd)	TB	R	RBI	TBB	IBB	SO	HBP	SH	SF	SB	CS	SB%	GDP	Avg	OBP	SLG
1990 Philadelphia	NL	25	79	19	4	0	1	(1	0)	26	9	3	6	0	19	0	2	0	3	1	1.00	1	.241	.294	.329
1991 Philadelphia	NL	98	325	81	11	4	1	(1	0)	103	38	20	29	0	45	2	6	2	13	2	.87	7	.249	.313	.317
1992 Philadelphia	NL	127	422	112	8	8	3	(2	1)	145	47	30	25	2	64	0	6	2	8	3	.73	4	.265	.305	.344
3 ML YEARS		250	826	212	23	12	5	(4	1)	274	94	53	60	2	128	2	14	4	24	5	.83	12	.257	.307	.332

Mike Morgan

Pitches: Right **Bats:** Right **Pos:** SP   **Ht:** 6' 2" **Wt:** 210 **Born:** 10/08/59 **Age:** 33

		HOW MUCH HE PITCHED						WHAT HE GAVE UP											THE RESULTS					
Year Team	Lg	G	GS	CG	GF	IP	BFP	H	R	ER	HR	SH	SF	HB	TBB	IBB	SO	WP	Bk	W	L	Pct.	ShO	Sv	ERA
1978 Oakland	AL	3	3	1	0	12	60	19	12	10	1	1	0	0	8	0	0	0	0	0	3	.000	0	0	7.50
1979 Oakland	AL	13	13	2	0	77	368	102	57	51	7	4	3	3	50	0	17	7	0	2	10	.167	0	0	5.96

Year	Team	Lg	G	GS	CG	GF	IP	BFP	H	R	ER	HR	SH	SF	HB	TBB	IBB	SO	WP	Bk	W	L	Pct.	ShO	Sv	ERA
1982	New York	AL	30	23	2	2	150.1	661	167	77	73	15	2	4	2	67	5	71	6	0	7	11	.389	0	0	4.37
1983	Toronto	AL	16	4	0	2	45.1	198	48	26	26	6	0	1	0	21	0	22	3	0	0	3	.000	0	0	5.16
1985	Seattle	AL	2	2	0	0	6	33	11	8	8	2	0	0	0	5	0	2	1	0	1	1	.500	0	0	12.00
1986	Seattle	AL	37	33	9	2	216.1	951	243	122	109	24	7	3	4	86	3	116	8	1	11	17	.393	1	1	4.53
1987	Seattle	AL	34	31	8	2	207	898	245	117	107	25	8	5	5	53	3	85	11	0	12	17	.414	2	0	4.65
1988	Baltimore	AL	22	10	2	6	71.1	299	70	45	43	6	1	0	1	23	1	29	5	0	1	6	.143	1	1	5.43
1989	Los Angeles	NL	40	19	0	7	152.2	604	130	51	43	6	8	6	2	33	8	72	6	0	8	11	.421	0	0	2.53
1990	Los Angeles	NL	33	33	6	0	211	891	216	100	88	19	11	4	5	60	5	106	4	1	11	15	.423	4	0	3.75
1991	Los Angeles	NL	34	33	5	1	236.1	949	197	85	73	12	10	4	3	61	10	140	6	0	14	10	.583	1	1	2.78
1992	Chicago	NL	34	34	6	0	240	966	203	80	68	14	10	5	3	79	10	123	11	0	16	8	.667	0	0	2.55
	12 ML YEARS		298	238	41	22	1625.1	6878	1651	780	699	137	62	36	28	546	45	783	68	2	83	112	.426	9	3	3.87

Hal Morris

Bats: Left   Throws: Left   Pos: 1B   Ht: 6' 4" Wt: 215 Born: 04/09/65 Age: 28

						BATTING												BASERUNNING				PERCENTAGES		
Year	Team	Lg	G	AB	H	2B	3B	HR	(Hm | Rd)	TB	R	RBI	TBB	IBB	SO	HBP	SH	SF	SB	CS	SB%	GDP	Avg	OBP	SLG
1988	New York	AL	15	20	2	0	0	0	(0 | 0)	2	1	0	0	0	9	0	0	0	0	0	.00	0	.100	.100	.100
1989	New York	AL	15	18	5	0	0	0	(0 | 0)	5	2	4	1	0	4	0	0	0	0	0	.00	2	.278	.316	.278
1990	Cincinnati	NL	107	309	105	22	3	7	(3 | 4)	154	50	36	21	4	32	1	3	2	9	3	.75	12	.340	.381	.498
1991	Cincinnati	NL	136	478	152	33	1	14	(9 | 5)	229	72	59	46	7	61	1	5	7	10	4	.71	4	.318	.374	.479
1992	Cincinnati	NL	115	395	107	21	3	6	(3 | 3)	152	41	53	45	8	53	2	2	2	6	6	.50	12	.271	.347	.385
	5 ML YEARS		388	1220	371	76	7	27	(15 | 12)	542	166	152	113	19	159	4	10	11	25	13	.66	30	.304	.362	.444

Jack Morris

Pitches: Right   Bats: Right   Pos: SP   Ht: 6' 3" Wt: 200 Born: 05/16/55 Age: 38

			HOW MUCH HE PITCHED						WHAT HE GAVE UP											THE RESULTS					
Year	Team	Lg	G	GS	CG	GF	IP	BFP	H	R	ER	HR	SH	SF	HB	TBB	IBB	SO	WP	Bk	W	L	Pct.	ShO	Sv	ERA
1977	Detroit	AL	7	6	1	0	46	189	38	20	19	4	3	1	0	23	0	28	2	0	1	1	.500	0	0	3.72
1978	Detroit	AL	28	7	0	10	106	469	107	57	51	8	8	9	3	49	5	48	4	0	3	5	.375	0	0	4.33
1979	Detroit	AL	27	27	9	0	198	806	179	76	72	19	3	6	4	59	4	113	9	1	17	7	.708	1	0	3.27
1980	Detroit	AL	36	36	11	0	250	1074	252	125	116	20	10	13	4	87	5	112	6	2	16	15	.516	2	0	4.18
1981	Detroit	AL	25	25	15	0	198	798	153	69	67	14	8	9	2	78	11	97	2	2	14	7	.667	1	0	3.05
1982	Detroit	AL	37	37	17	0	266.1	1107	247	131	120	37	4	5	0	96	7	135	10	0	17	16	.515	3	0	4.06
1983	Detroit	AL	37	37	20	0	293.2	1204	257	117	109	30	8	9	3	83	5	232	18	0	20	13	.606	1	0	3.34
1984	Detroit	AL	35	35	9	0	240.1	1015	221	108	96	20	5	3	2	87	7	148	14	0	19	11	.633	1	0	3.60
1985	Detroit	AL	35	35	13	0	257	1077	212	102	95	21	11	7	5	110	7	191	15	3	16	11	.593	4	0	3.33
1986	Detroit	AL	35	35	15	0	267	1092	229	105	97	40	7	3	0	82	7	223	12	0	21	8	.724	6	0	3.27
1987	Detroit	AL	34	34	13	0	266	1101	227	111	100	39	6	5	1	93	7	208	24	1	18	11	.621	0	0	3.38
1988	Detroit	AL	34	34	10	0	235	997	225	115	103	20	12	3	4	83	7	168	11	11	15	13	.536	2	0	3.94
1989	Detroit	AL	24	24	10	0	170.1	743	189	102	92	23	6	7	2	59	3	115	12	1	6	14	.300	0	0	4.86
1990	Detroit	AL	36	36	11	0	249.2	1073	231	144	125	26	7	10	6	97	13	162	16	2	15	18	.455	3	0	4.51
1991	Minnesota	AL	35	35	10	0	246.2	1032	226	107	94	18	5	8	5	92	5	163	15	1	18	12	.600	2	0	3.43
1992	Toronto	AL	34	34	6	0	240.2	1005	222	114	108	18	4	7	10	80	2	132	9	2	21	6	.778	1	0	4.04
	16 ML YEARS		499	477	170	10	3530.2	14782	3215	1603	1464	357	107	105	51	1258	95	2275	179	26	237	168	.585	27	0	3.73

John Morris

Bats: Left   Throws: Left   Pos: RF   Ht: 6' 1" Wt: 185 Born: 02/23/61 Age: 32

						BATTING												BASERUNNING				PERCENTAGES		
Year	Team	Lg	G	AB	H	2B	3B	HR	(Hm	Rd)	TB	R	RBI	TBB	IBB	SO	HBP	SH	SF	SB	CS	SB%	GDP	Avg	OBP	SLG
1986	St. Louis	NL	39	100	24	0	1	1	(1	0)	29	8	14	7	2	15	0	0	1	6	2	.75	2	.240	.287	.290
1987	St. Louis	NL	101	157	41	6	4	3	(1	2)	64	22	23	11	4	22	1	1	0	5	2	.71	2	.261	.314	.408
1988	St. Louis	NL	20	38	11	2	1	0	(0	0)	15	3	3	1	0	7	0	0	0	0	0	.00	0	.289	.308	.395
1989	St. Louis	NL	96	117	28	4	1	2	(2	0)	40	8	14	4	0	22	0	3	0	1	0	1.00	4	.239	.264	.342
1990	St. Louis	NL	18	18	2	0	0	0	(0	0)	2	0	0	3	0	6	0	0	0	0	0	.00	0	.111	.238	.111
1991	Philadelphia	NL	85	127	28	2	1	1	(1	0)	35	15	6	12	4	25	1	0	0	2	0	1.00	1	.220	.293	.276
1992	California	AL	43	57	11	1	0	1	(0	1)	15	4	3	4	1	11	1	1	0	1	0	1.00	1	.193	.258	.263
	7 ML YEARS		402	614	145	15	8	8	(5	3)	200	60	63	42	11	108	3	5	1	15	4	.79	9	.236	.288	.326

John Moses

Bats: Both   Throws: Left   Pos: LF   Ht: 5'10" Wt: 175 Born: 08/09/57 Age: 35

						BATTING												BASERUNNING				PERCENTAGES		
Year	Team	Lg	G	AB	H	2B	3B	HR	(Hm	Rd)	TB	R	RBI	TBB	IBB	SO	HBP	SH	SF	SB	CS	SB%	GDP	Avg	OBP	SLG
1982	Seattle	AL	22	44	14	5	1	1	(1	0)	24	7	3	4	0	5	0	0	0	5	1	.83	0	.318	.375	.545
1983	Seattle	AL	93	130	27	4	1	0	(0	0)	33	19	6	12	0	20	1	0	0	11	5	.69	4	.208	.280	.254
1984	Seattle	AL	19	35	12	1	1	0	(0	0)	15	3	2	2	0	1	1	0	0	1	0	1.00	0	.343	.395	.429
1985	Seattle	AL	33	62	12	0	0	0	(0	0)	12	4	3	2	0	8	0	1	0	5	2	.71	3	.194	.219	.194

Year	Team	Lg	G	AB	H	2B	3B	HR	(Hm	Rd)	TB	R	RBI	TBB	IBB	SO	HBP	SH	SF	SB	CS	SB%	GDP	Avg	OBP	SLG
1986	Seattle	AL	103	399	102	16	3	3	(2	1)	133	56	34	34	3	65	0	5	4	25	18	.58	7	.256	.311	.333
1987	Seattle	AL	116	390	96	16	4	3	(2	1)	129	58	38	29	2	49	3	8	3	23	15	.61	6	.246	.301	.331
1988	Minnesota	AL	105	206	65	10	3	2	(0	2)	87	33	12	15	2	21	2	1	1	11	6	.65	4	.316	.366	.422
1989	Minnesota	AL	129	242	68	12	3	1	(0	1)	89	33	31	19	1	23	1	3	2	14	7	.67	5	.281	.333	.368
1990	Minnesota	AL	115	172	38	3	1	1	(0	1)	46	26	14	19	1	19	2	0	2	2	3	.40	4	.221	.303	.267
1991	Detroit	AL	13	21	1	1	0	0	(0	0)	2	5	1	2	0	7	0	1	0	4	0	1.00	0	.048	.130	.095
1992	Seattle	AL	21	22	3	1	0	0	(0	0)	4	3	1	5	0	4	0	2	0	0	0	.00	0	.136	.296	.182
11 ML YEARS			769	1723	438	69	17	11	(5	6)	574	247	145	143	9	226	10	22	12	101	57	.64	33	.254	.313	.333

Terry Mulholland

Pitches: Left **Bats:** Right **Pos:** SP **Ht:** 6' 3" **Wt:** 208 **Born:** 03/09/63 **Age:** 30

			HOW MUCH HE PITCHED					WHAT HE GAVE UP									THE RESULTS				
Year	Team	Lg	G	GS	CG	GF	IP	BFP	H	R	ER	HR	SH	SF	HB	TBB	IBB	SO	WP	Bk	W	L	Pct.	ShO	Sv	ERA
1986	San Francisco	NL	15	10	0	1	54.2	245	51	33	30	3	5	1	1	35	2	27	6	0	1	7	.125	0	0	4.94
1988	San Francisco	NL	9	6	2	1	46	191	50	20	19	3	5	0	1	7	0	18	1	0	2	1	.667	1	0	3.72
1989	2 ML Teams		25	18	2	4	115.1	513	137	66	63	8	7	1	4	36	3	66	3	0	4	7	.364	1	0	4.92
1990	Philadelphia	NL	33	26	6	2	180.2	746	172	78	67	15	7	12	2	42	7	75	7	2	9	10	.474	1	0	3.34
1991	Philadelphia	NL	34	34	8	0	232	956	231	100	93	15	11	6	3	49	2	142	3	0	16	13	.552	3	0	3.61
1992	Philadelphia	NL	32	32	12	0	229	937	227	101	97	14	10	7	3	46	3	125	3	0	13	11	.542	2	0	3.81
1989	San Francisco	NL	5	1	0	2	11	51	15	5	5	0	0	0	0	4	0	6	0	0	0	0	.000	0	0	4.09
	Philadelphia	NL	20	17	2	2	104.1	462	122	61	58	8	7	1	4	32	3	60	3	0	4	7	.364	1	0	5.00
6 ML YEARS			148	126	30	8	857.2	3588	868	398	369	58	45	27	14	215	17	453	23	2	45	49	.479	8	0	3.87

Rance Mulliniks

Bats: Left **Throws:** Right **Pos:** DH **Ht:** 6' 0" **Wt:** 175 **Born:** 01/15/56 **Age:** 37

			BATTING																BASERUNNING				PERCENTAGES		
Year	Team	Lg	G	AB	H	2B	3B	HR	(Hm	Rd)	TB	R	RBI	TBB	IBB	SO	HBP	SH	SF	SB	CS	SB%	GDP	Avg	OBP	SLG
1977	California	AL	78	271	73	13	2	3	(2	1)	99	36	21	23	2	36	1	8	0	1	1	.50	2	.269	.329	.365
1978	California	AL	50	119	22	3	1	1	(1	0)	30	6	6	8	0	23	1	0	2	2	0	1.00	3	.185	.238	.252
1979	California	AL	22	68	10	0	0	1	(0	1)	13	7	6	4	0	14	1	0	5	0	0	.00	2	.147	.192	.191
1980	Kansas City	AL	36	54	14	3	0	0	(0	0)	17	8	6	7	0	10	0	0	1	0	0	.00	2	.259	.339	.315
1981	Kansas City	AL	24	44	10	3	0	0	(0	0)	13	6	5	2	0	7	0	0	0	0	1	.00	2	.227	.261	.295
1982	Toronto	AL	112	311	76	25	0	4	(2	2)	113	32	35	37	1	49	1	3	1	3	2	.60	10	.244	.326	.363
1983	Toronto	AL	129	364	100	34	3	10	(4	6)	170	54	49	57	5	43	1	3	2	2	0	.00	14	.275	.373	.467
1984	Toronto	AL	125	343	111	21	5	3	(1	2)	151	41	42	33	3	44	1	0	2	2	3	.40	5	.324	.383	.440
1985	Toronto	AL	129	366	108	26	1	10	(4	6)	166	55	57	55	2	54	0	1	5	2	0	1.00	10	.295	.383	.454
1986	Toronto	AL	117	348	90	22	0	11	(5	6)	145	50	45	43	1	60	1	1	2	1	1	.50	12	.259	.340	.417
1987	Toronto	AL	124	332	103	28	1	11	(6	5)	166	37	44	34	1	55	0	3	3	1	1	.50	10	.310	.371	.500
1988	Toronto	AL	119	337	101	21	1	12	(7	5)	160	49	48	56	3	57	0	2	4	1	0	1.00	10	.300	.395	.475
1989	Toronto	AL	103	273	65	11	2	3	(1	2)	89	25	29	34	6	40	0	0	2	0	0	.00	12	.238	.320	.326
1990	Toronto	AL	57	97	28	4	0	2	(1	1)	38	11	16	22	2	19	0	0	1	2	1	.67	2	.289	.417	.392
1991	Toronto	AL	97	240	60	12	1	2	(1	1)	80	27	24	44	2	44	0	0	2	0	0	.00	9	.250	.364	.333
1992	Toronto	AL	3	2	1	0	0	0	(0	0)	1	1	0	1	0	0	0	0	0	0	0	.00	0	.500	.667	.500
16 ML YEARS			1325	3569	972	226	17	73	(35	38)	1451	445	435	460	28	555	7	21	32	15	12	.56	105	.272	.354	.407

Mike Munoz

Pitches: Left **Bats:** Left **Pos:** RP **Ht:** 6' 2" **Wt:** 200 **Born:** 07/12/65 **Age:** 27

			HOW MUCH HE PITCHED					WHAT HE GAVE UP									THE RESULTS				
Year	Team	Lg	G	GS	CG	GF	IP	BFP	H	R	ER	HR	SH	SF	HB	TBB	IBB	SO	WP	Bk	W	L	Pct.	ShO	Sv	ERA
1989	Los Angeles	NL	3	0	0	1	2.2	14	5	5	5	1	0	0	0	2	0	3	0	0	0	0	.000	0	0	16.88
1990	Los Angeles	NL	8	0	0	3	5.2	24	6	2	2	0	1	0	0	3	0	2	0	0	0	1	.000	0	0	3.18
1991	Detroit	AL	6	0	0	4	9.1	46	14	10	10	0	0	1	0	5	0	3	1	0	0	0	.000	0	0	9.64
1992	Detroit	AL	65	0	0	15	48	210	44	16	16	3	4	2	0	25	6	23	2	0	1	2	.333	0	2	3.00
4 ML YEARS			82	0	0	23	65.2	294	69	33	33	4	5	3	0	35	6	31	3	0	1	3	.250	0	2	4.52

Pedro Munoz

Bats: Right **Throws:** Right **Pos:** RF **Ht:** 5'10" **Wt:** 205 **Born:** 09/19/68 **Age:** 24

			BATTING																BASERUNNING				PERCENTAGES		
Year	Team	Lg	G	AB	H	2B	3B	HR	(Hm	Rd)	TB	R	RBI	TBB	IBB	SO	HBP	SH	SF	SB	CS	SB%	GDP	Avg	OBP	SLG
1990	Minnesota	AL	22	85	23	4	1	0	(0	0)	29	13	5	2	0	16	0	1	2	3	0	1.00	3	.271	.281	.341
1991	Minnesota	AL	51	138	39	7	1	7	(4	3)	69	15	26	9	0	31	1	0	3	3	0	1.00	2	.283	.327	.500
1992	Minnesota	AL	127	418	113	16	3	12	(8	4)	171	44	71	17	1	90	1	0	3	4	5	.44	18	.270	.298	.409
3 ML YEARS			200	641	175	27	5	19	(12	7)	269	72	102	28	1	137	2	2	7	10	5	.67	23	.273	.302	.420

140

Dale Murphy

Bats: Right **Throws:** Right **Pos:** RF **Ht:** 6' 4" **Wt:** 221 **Born:** 03/12/56 **Age:** 37

Year Team	Lg	G	AB	H	2B	3B	HR	(Hm	Rd)	TB	R	RBI	TBB	IBB	SO	HBP	SH	SF	SB	CS	SB%	GDP	Avg	OBP	SLG
1976 Atlanta	NL	19	65	17	6	0	0	(0	0)	23	3	9	7	0	9	0	0	0	0	0	.00	0	.262	.333	.354
1977 Atlanta	NL	18	76	24	8	1	2	(0	2)	40	5	14	0	0	8	0	0	0	0	1	.00	3	.316	.316	.526
1978 Atlanta	NL	151	530	120	14	3	23	(17	6)	209	66	79	42	3	145	3	3	5	11	7	.61	15	.226	.284	.394
1979 Atlanta	NL	104	384	106	7	2	21	(12	9)	180	53	57	38	5	67	2	0	5	6	1	.86	12	.276	.340	.469
1980 Atlanta	NL	156	569	160	27	2	33	(17	16)	290	98	89	59	9	133	1	2	2	9	6	.60	8	.281	.349	.510
1981 Atlanta	NL	104	369	91	12	1	13	(8	5)	144	43	50	44	8	72	0	1	2	14	5	.74	10	.247	.325	.390
1982 Atlanta	NL	162	598	168	23	2	36	(24	12)	303	113	109	93	9	134	3	0	4	23	11	.68	10	.281	.378	.507
1983 Atlanta	NL	162	589	178	24	4	36	(17	19)	318	131	121	90	12	110	2	0	6	30	4	.88	15	.302	.393	.540
1984 Atlanta	NL	162	607	176	32	8	36	(18	18)	332	94	100	79	20	134	2	0	3	19	7	.73	13	.290	.372	.547
1985 Atlanta	NL	162	616	185	32	2	37	(19	18)	332	118	111	90	15	141	1	0	5	10	3	.77	14	.300	.388	.539
1986 Atlanta	NL	160	614	163	29	7	29	(17	12)	293	89	83	75	5	141	2	0	1	7	7	.50	10	.265	.347	.477
1987 Atlanta	NL	159	566	167	27	1	44	(25	19)	328	115	105	115	29	136	7	0	5	16	6	.73	11	.295	.417	.580
1988 Atlanta	NL	156	592	134	35	4	24	(14	10)	249	77	77	74	16	125	2	0	3	3	5	.38	24	.226	.313	.421
1989 Atlanta	NL	154	574	131	16	0	20	(9	11)	207	60	84	65	10	142	2	0	6	3	2	.60	14	.228	.306	.361
1990 2 ML Teams		154	563	138	23	1	24	(9	15)	235	60	83	61	14	130	1	0	4	9	3	.75	22	.245	.318	.417
1991 Philadelphia	NL	153	544	137	33	1	18	(9	9)	226	66	81	48	3	93	0	0	7	1	0	1.00	20	.252	.309	.415
1992 Philadelphia	NL	18	62	10	1	0	2	(2	0)	17	5	7	1	0	13	0	0	0	0	0	.00	3	.161	.175	.274
1990 Atlanta	NL	97	349	81	14	0	17	(8	9)	146	38	55	41	11	84	1	0	3	9	2	.82	11	.232	.312	.418
Philadelphia		57	214	57	9	1	7	(1	6)	89	22	28	20	3	46	0	0	1	0	1	.00	11	.266	.328	.416
17 ML YEARS		2154	7918	2105	349	39	398	(217	181)	3726	1196	1259	981	158	1733	28	6	58	161	68	.70	204	.266	.347	.471

Rob Murphy

Pitches: Left **Bats:** Left **Pos:** RP **Ht:** 6' 2" **Wt:** 215 **Born:** 05/26/60 **Age:** 33

Year Team	Lg	G	GS	CG	GF	IP	BFP	H	R	ER	HR	SH	SF	HB	TBB	IBB	SO	WP	Bk	W	L	Pct.	ShO	Sv	ERA
1985 Cincinnati	NL	2	0	0	2	3	12	2	2	2	1	0	0	0	2	0	1	0	0	0	0	.000	0	0	6.00
1986 Cincinnati	NL	34	0	0	12	50.1	195	26	4	4	0	3	3	0	21	2	36	5	0	6	0	1.000	0	1	0.72
1987 Cincinnati	NL	87	0	0	21	100.2	415	91	37	34	7	1	2	0	32	5	99	1	0	8	5	.615	0	3	3.04
1988 Cincinnati	NL	76	0	0	28	84.2	350	69	31	29	3	9	1	1	38	6	74	5	1	0	6	.000	0	3	3.08
1989 Boston	AL	74	0	0	27	105	438	97	38	32	7	7	3	1	41	8	107	6	0	5	7	.417	0	9	2.74
1990 Boston	AL	68	0	0	20	57	285	85	46	40	10	4	4	1	32	3	54	4	0	0	6	.000	0	7	6.32
1991 Seattle	AL	57	0	0	26	48	211	47	17	16	4	3	0	1	19	4	34	4	0	0	1	.000	0	4	3.00
1992 Houston	NL	59	0	0	6	55.2	242	56	28	25	2	3	3	0	21	4	42	4	0	3	1	.750	0	0	4.04
8 ML YEARS		457	0	0	142	504.1	2148	473	203	182	34	30	16	4	206	32	447	29	1	22	26	.458	0	27	3.25

Eddie Murray

Bats: Both **Throws:** Right **Pos:** 1B **Ht:** 6' 2" **Wt:** 222 **Born:** 02/24/56 **Age:** 37

Year Team	Lg	G	AB	H	2B	3B	HR	(Hm	Rd)	TB	R	RBI	TBB	IBB	SO	HBP	SH	SF	SB	CS	SB%	GDP	Avg	OBP	SLG
1977 Baltimore	AL	160	611	173	29	2	27	(14	13)	287	81	88	48	6	104	1	0	6	0	1	.00	22	.283	.333	.470
1978 Baltimore	AL	161	610	174	32	3	27	(10	17)	293	85	95	70	7	97	1	1	8	6	5	.55	15	.285	.356	.480
1979 Baltimore	AL	159	606	179	30	2	25	(10	15)	288	90	99	72	9	78	2	1	6	10	2	.83	16	.295	.369	.475
1980 Baltimore	AL	158	621	186	36	2	32	(10	22)	322	100	116	54	10	71	2	0	6	7	2	.78	18	.300	.354	.519
1981 Baltimore	AL	99	378	111	21	2	22	(12	10)	202	57	78	40	10	43	1	0	3	2	3	.40	10	.294	.360	.534
1982 Baltimore	AL	151	550	174	30	1	32	(18	14)	302	87	110	70	18	82	1	0	6	7	2	.78	17	.316	.391	.549
1983 Baltimore	AL	156	582	178	30	3	33	(16	17)	313	115	111	86	13	90	3	0	9	5	1	.83	13	.306	.393	.538
1984 Baltimore	AL	162	588	180	26	3	29	(18	11)	299	97	110	107	25	87	2	0	8	10	2	.83	9	.306	.410	.509
1985 Baltimore	AL	156	583	173	37	1	31	(15	16)	305	111	124	84	12	68	2	0	8	5	2	.71	8	.297	.383	.523
1986 Baltimore	AL	137	495	151	25	1	17	(9	8)	229	61	84	78	7	49	0	0	5	3	0	1.00	15	.305	.396	.463
1987 Baltimore	AL	160	618	171	28	3	30	(14	16)	295	89	91	73	6	80	0	0	3	1	2	.33	15	.277	.352	.477
1988 Baltimore	AL	161	603	171	27	2	28	(14	14)	286	75	84	75	8	78	0	0	3	5	2	.71	20	.284	.361	.474
1989 Los Angeles	NL	160	594	147	29	1	20	(4	16)	238	66	88	87	24	85	2	0	7	7	2	.78	12	.247	.342	.401
1990 Los Angeles	NL	155	558	184	22	3	26	(12	14)	290	96	95	82	21	64	1	0	4	8	5	.62	19	.330	.414	.520
1991 Los Angeles	NL	153	576	150	23	1	19	(11	8)	232	69	96	55	17	74	0	0	8	10	3	.77	17	.260	.321	.403
1992 New York	NL	156	551	144	37	2	16	(7	9)	233	64	93	66	8	74	0	0	8	4	2	.67	15	.261	.336	.423
16 ML YEARS		2444	9124	2646	462	32	414	(194	220)	4414	1343	1562	1147	201	1224	18	2	98	90	36	.71	243	.290	.367	.484

Mike Mussina

Pitches: Right **Bats:** Right **Pos:** SP   **Ht:** 6' 2" **Wt:** 182 **Born:** 12/08/68 **Age:** 24

Year Team	Lg	G	GS	CG	GF	IP	BFP	H	R	ER	HR	SH	SF	HB	TBB	IBB	SO	WP	Bk	W	L	Pct.	ShO	Sv	ERA
1990 Hagerstown	AA	7	7	2	0	42.1	168	34	10	7	1	1	1	0	7	0	40	3	1	3	0	1.000	1	0	1.49
Rochester	AAA	2	2	0	0	13.1	50	8	2	2	2	0	0	0	4	0	15	0	0	0	0	.000	0	0	1.35
1991 Rochester	AAA	19	19	3	0	122.1	497	108	42	39	9	3	1	2	31	0	107	6	1	10	4	.714	1	0	2.87
1991 Baltimore	AL	12	12	2	0	87.2	349	77	31	28	7	3	2	1	21	0	52	3	1	4	5	.444	0	0	2.87
1992 Baltimore	AL	32	32	8	0	241	957	212	70	68	16	13	6	2	48	2	130	6	0	18	5	.783	4	0	2.54
2 ML YEARS		44	44	10	0	328.2	1306	289	101	96	23	16	8	3	69	2	182	9	1	22	10	.688	4	0	2.63

Jeff Mutis

Pitches: Left **Bats:** Left **Pos:** SP   **Ht:** 6' 2" **Wt:** 185 **Born:** 12/20/66 **Age:** 26

Year Team	Lg	G	GS	CG	GF	IP	BFP	H	R	ER	HR	SH	SF	HB	TBB	IBB	SO	WP	Bk	W	L	Pct.	ShO	Sv	ERA
1988 Burlington	R	3	3	0	0	22	79	8	1	1	0	0	0	0	6	0	20	1	2	3	0	1.000	0	0	0.41
Kinston	A	1	1	0	0	5.2	24	6	1	1	0	1	0	0	3	0	2	1	0	1	0	1.000	0	0	1.59
1989 Kinston	A	16	15	5	1	99.2	406	87	42	29	6	1	4	2	20	0	68	3	2	7	3	.700	2	0	2.62
1990 Canton-Akrn	AA	26	26	7	0	165	702	178	73	58	6	3	2	3	44	2	94	5	1	11	10	.524	3	0	3.16
1991 Canton-Akrn	AA	25	24	7	0	169.2	682	138	42	34	0	8	4	6	51	2	89	3	1	11	5	.688	4	0	1.80
1992 Colo Spngs	AAA	25	24	4	0	145.1	652	177	99	82	8	6	8	5	57	1	77	8	4	9	9	.500	0	0	5.08
1991 Cleveland	AL	3	3	0	0	12.1	68	23	16	16	1	2	1	0	7	1	6	1	0	0	3	.000	0	0	11.68
1992 Cleveland	AL	3	2	0	0	11.1	64	24	14	12	4	0	2	0	6	0	8	2	0	0	2	.000	0	0	9.53
2 ML YEARS		6	5	0	0	23.2	132	47	30	28	5	2	3	0	13	1	14	3	0	0	5	.000	0	0	10.65

Greg Myers

Bats: Left **Throws:** Right **Pos:** C   **Ht:** 6' 2" **Wt:** 205 **Born:** 04/14/66 **Age:** 27

Year Team	Lg	G	AB	H	2B	3B	HR	(Hm	Rd)	TB	R	RBI	TBB	IBB	SO	HBP	SH	SF	SB	CS	SB%	GDP	Avg	OBP	SLG
1987 Toronto	AL	7	9	1	0	0	0	(0	0)	1	1	0	0	0	3	0	0	0	0	0	.00	2	.111	.111	.111
1989 Toronto	AL	17	44	5	2	0	0	(0	0)	7	1	2	0	9	0	0	0	0	0	1	.00	1	.114	.152	.159
1990 Toronto	AL	87	250	59	7	1	5	(3	2)	83	33	22	22	0	33	0	0	1	0	1	.00	12	.236	.293	.332
1991 Toronto	AL	107	309	81	22	0	8	(5	3)	127	25	36	21	4	45	0	0	3	0	0	.00	13	.262	.306	.411
1992 2 ML Teams		30	78	18	7	0	1	(0	1)	28	4	13	5	0	11	0	1	2	0	0	.00	2	.231	.271	.359
1992 Toronto	AL	22	61	14	6	0	1	(0	1)	23	4	13	5	0	5	0	0	2	0	0	.00	2	.230	.279	.377
California	AL	8	17	4	1	0	0	(0	0)	5	0	0	0	0	6	0	0	0	0	0	.00	0	.235	.235	.294
5 ML YEARS		248	690	164	38	1	14	(8	6)	246	63	72	50	4	101	0	2	9	0	2	.00	31	.238	.286	.357

Randy Myers

Pitches: Left **Bats:** Left **Pos:** RP   **Ht:** 6' 1" **Wt:** 215 **Born:** 09/19/62 **Age:** 30

Year Team	Lg	G	GS	CG	GF	IP	BFP	H	R	ER	HR	SH	SF	HB	TBB	IBB	SO	WP	Bk	W	L	Pct.	ShO	Sv	ERA
1985 New York	NL	1	0	0	1	2	7	0	0	0	0	0	0	0	1	0	2	0	0	0	0	.000	0	0	0.00
1986 New York	NL	10	0	0	5	10.2	53	11	5	5	1	0	0	1	9	1	13	0	0	0	0	.000	0	0	4.22
1987 New York	NL	54	0	0	18	75	314	61	36	33	6	7	6	0	30	5	92	3	0	3	6	.333	0	6	3.96
1988 New York	NL	55	0	0	44	68	261	45	15	13	5	3	2	2	17	2	69	2	0	7	3	.700	0	26	1.72
1989 New York	NL	65	0	0	47	84.1	349	62	23	22	4	6	2	0	40	4	88	3	0	7	4	.636	0	24	2.35
1990 Cincinnati	NL	66	0	0	59	86.2	353	59	24	20	6	4	2	3	38	8	98	2	1	4	6	.400	0	31	2.08
1991 Cincinnati	NL	58	12	1	18	132	575	116	61	52	8	8	6	1	80	5	108	2	1	6	13	.316	0	6	3.55
1992 San Diego	NL	66	0	0	57	79.2	348	84	38	38	7	7	5	1	34	3	66	5	0	3	6	.333	0	38	4.29
8 ML YEARS		375	12	1	249	538.1	2260	438	202	183	37	35	23	8	249	28	536	17	2	30	38	.441	0	131	3.06

Chris Nabholz

Pitches: Left **Bats:** Left **Pos:** SP   **Ht:** 6' 5" **Wt:** 210 **Born:** 01/05/67 **Age:** 26

Year Team	Lg	G	GS	CG	GF	IP	BFP	H	R	ER	HR	SH	SF	HB	TBB	IBB	SO	WP	Bk	W	L	Pct.	ShO	Sv	ERA
1990 Montreal	NL	11	11	1	0	70	282	43	23	22	6	1	2	2	32	1	53	1	1	6	2	.750	1	0	2.83
1991 Montreal	NL	24	24	1	0	153.2	631	134	66	62	5	2	4	2	57	4	99	3	1	8	7	.533	0	0	3.63
1992 Montreal	NL	32	32	1	0	195	812	176	80	72	11	7	4	5	74	2	130	5	1	11	12	.478	1	0	3.32
3 ML YEARS		67	67	3	0	418.2	1725	353	169	156	22	10	10	9	163	7	282	9	3	25	21	.543	2	0	3.35

Tim Naehring

Bats: Right **Throws:** Right **Pos:** SS/2B   **Ht:** 6' 2" **Wt:** 190 **Born:** 02/01/67 **Age:** 26

Year Team	Lg	G	AB	H	2B	3B	HR	(Hm	Rd)	TB	R	RBI	TBB	IBB	SO	HBP	SH	SF	SB	CS	SB%	GDP	Avg	OBP	SLG
1990 Boston	AL	24	85	23	6	0	2	(2	0)	35	10	12	8	1	15	0	0	0	0	0	.00	2	.271	.333	.412
1991 Boston	AL	20	55	6	1	0	0	(0	0)	7	1	3	6	0	15	0	4	0	0	0	.00	0	.109	.197	.127

Year	Team	Lg	G	AB	H	2B	3B	HR	(Hm	Rd)	TB	R	RBI	TBB	IBB	SO	HBP	SH	SF	SB	CS	SB%	GDP	Avg	OBP	SLG
1992	Boston	AL	72	186	43	8	0	3	(0	3)	60	12	14	18	0	31	3	6	1	0	0	.00	1	.231	.308	.323
	3 ML YEARS		116	326	72	15	0	5	(2	3)	102	23	29	32	1	61	3	10	1	0	0	.00	3	.221	.296	.313

Charles Nagy

Pitches: Right **Bats:** Left **Pos:** SP **Ht:** 6' 3" **Wt:** 200 **Born:** 05/05/67 **Age:** 26

			HOW MUCH HE PITCHED					WHAT HE GAVE UP										THE RESULTS					
Year	Team	Lg	G	GS	CG	GF	IP	BFP	H	R	ER	HR	SH	SF	HB	TBB	IBB	SO	WP	Bk	W	L	Pct.	ShO	Sv	ERA
1990	Cleveland	AL	9	8	0	1	45.2	208	58	31	30	7	1	1	1	21	1	26	1	1	2	4	.333	0	0	5.91
1991	Cleveland	AL	33	33	6	0	211.1	914	228	103	97	15	5	9	6	66	7	109	6	2	10	15	.400	1	0	4.13
1992	Cleveland	AL	33	33	10	0	252	1018	245	91	83	11	6	9	2	57	1	169	7	0	17	10	.630	3	0	2.96
	3 ML YEARS		75	74	16	1	509	2140	531	225	210	33	12	19	9	144	9	304	14	3	29	29	.500	4	0	3.71

Bob Natal

Bats: Right **Throws:** Right **Pos:** C **Ht:** 5'11" **Wt:** 190 **Born:** 11/13/65 **Age:** 27

									BATTING										BASERUNNING				PERCENTAGES		
Year	Team	Lg	G	AB	H	2B	3B	HR	(Hm	Rd)	TB	R	RBI	TBB	IBB	SO	HBP	SH	SF	SB	CS	SB%	GDP	Avg	OBP	SLG
1987	Jamestown	A	57	180	58	8	4	7	--	--	95	26	32	12	1	25	3	0	3	6	4	.60	3	.322	.369	.528
1988	Wst Plm Bch	A	113	387	93	17	0	6	--	--	128	47	51	29	0	50	3	3	3	3	2	.60	8	.240	.306	.331
1989	Jacksnville	AA	46	141	29	8	1	0	--	--	39	12	11	9	0	24	0	2	3	2	1	.67	1	.206	.248	.277
	Wst Plm Bch	A	15	48	6	0	0	1	--	--	9	5	2	9	1	9	2	0	0	1	0	1.00	1	.125	.288	.188
1990	Jacksnville	AA	62	171	42	7	1	7	--	--	72	23	25	14	2	42	5	1	2	0	1	.00	2	.246	.318	.421
1991	Indianapols	AAA	16	41	13	4	0	0	--	--	17	2	9	6	1	9	0	0	1	1	0	1.00	0	.317	.396	.415
	Harrisburg	AA	100	336	86	16	3	13	--	--	147	47	53	49	3	90	8	2	5	1	1	.50	5	.256	.359	.438
1992	Indianapols	AAA	96	344	104	19	3	12	--	--	165	50	50	28	1	42	4	1	3	3	0	1.00	7	.302	.359	.480
1992	Montreal	NL	5	6	0	0	0	0	(0	0)	0	0	1	0	1	0	0	0	0	0	0	.00	1	.000	.143	.000

Jaime Navarro

Pitches: Right **Bats:** Right **Pos:** SP **Ht:** 6' 4" **Wt:** 210 **Born:** 03/27/67 **Age:** 26

			HOW MUCH HE PITCHED					WHAT HE GAVE UP										THE RESULTS					
Year	Team	Lg	G	GS	CG	GF	IP	BFP	H	R	ER	HR	SH	SF	HB	TBB	IBB	SO	WP	Bk	W	L	Pct.	ShO	Sv	ERA
1989	Milwaukee	AL	19	17	1	1	109.2	470	119	47	38	6	5	2	1	32	3	56	3	0	7	8	.467	0	0	3.12
1990	Milwaukee	AL	32	22	3	2	149.1	654	176	83	74	11	4	5	4	41	3	75	6	5	8	7	.533	0	1	4.46
1991	Milwaukee	AL	34	34	10	0	234	1002	237	117	102	18	7	8	6	73	3	114	10	0	15	12	.556	2	0	3.92
1992	Milwaukee	AL	34	34	5	0	246	1004	224	98	91	14	9	13	6	64	4	100	6	0	17	11	.607	3	0	3.33
	4 ML YEARS		119	107	19	3	739	3130	756	345	305	49	25	28	17	210	13	345	25	5	47	38	.553	5	1	3.71

Denny Neagle

Pitches: Left **Bats:** Left **Pos:** RP/SP **Ht:** 6' 4" **Wt:** 205 **Born:** 09/13/68 **Age:** 24

			HOW MUCH HE PITCHED					WHAT HE GAVE UP										THE RESULTS					
Year	Team	Lg	G	GS	CG	GF	IP	BFP	H	R	ER	HR	SH	SF	HB	TBB	IBB	SO	WP	Bk	W	L	Pct.	ShO	Sv	ERA
1989	Elizabethtn	R	6	3	0	3	22	91	20	11	11	1	1	1	1	8	0	32	1	1	1	2	.333	0	1	4.50
	Kenosha	A	6	6	1	0	43.2	166	25	9	8	3	5	1	1	16	0	40	1	0	2	1	.667	1	0	1.65
1990	Visalia	A	10	10	0	0	63	241	39	13	10	2	1	1	0	16	0	92	0	2	8	0	1.000	0	0	1.43
	Orlando	AA	17	17	4	0	121.1	486	94	40	33	11	4	2	5	31	0	94	2	0	12	3	.800	1	0	2.45
1991	Portland	AAA	19	17	1	1	104.2	438	101	41	38	6	4	2	2	32	1	94	4	0	9	4	.692	1	0	3.27
1991	Minnesota	AL	7	3	0	2	20	92	28	9	9	3	0	0	0	7	2	14	1	0	0	1	.000	0	0	4.05
1992	Pittsburgh	NL	55	6	0	8	86.1	380	81	46	43	9	4	3	2	43	8	77	3	2	4	6	.400	0	2	4.48
	2 ML YEARS		62	9	0	10	106.1	472	109	55	52	12	4	3	2	50	10	91	4	2	4	7	.364	0	2	4.40

Troy Neel

Bats: Left **Throws:** Right **Pos:** LF **Ht:** 6' 4" **Wt:** 210 **Born:** 09/14/65 **Age:** 27

									BATTING										BASERUNNING				PERCENTAGES		
Year	Team	Lg	G	AB	H	2B	3B	HR	(Hm	Rd)	TB	R	RBI	TBB	IBB	SO	HBP	SH	SF	SB	CS	SB%	GDP	Avg	OBP	SLG
1986	Batavia	A	4	13	0	0	0	0	--	--	0	0	1	0	0	8	0	0	0	0	0	.00	0	.000	.000	.000
1987	Burlington	R	59	192	54	17	0	10	--	--	101	36	59	25	4	59	3	0	5	0	0	.00	3	.281	.364	.526
1988	Waterloo	A	91	331	96	20	1	8	--	--	142	49	57	38	3	76	6	0	3	0	1	.00	11	.290	.370	.429
1989	Canton-Akrn	AA	124	404	118	21	2	21	--	--	206	58	73	51	6	87	9	0	5	5	9	.36	10	.292	.380	.510
1990	Colo Sprngs	AAA	98	288	81	15	0	6	--	--	114	39	50	43	1	52	2	0	4	5	4	.56	5	.281	.374	.396
1991	Tacoma	AAA	18	59	14	3	1	0	--	--	19	7	7	7	0	14	1	0	0	0	0	.00	0	.237	.328	.322
	Huntsville	AA	110	364	101	21	0	23	--	--	191	64	68	82	18	75	5	0	7	1	3	.25	7	.277	.410	.525
1992	Tacoma	AAA	112	396	139	36	3	17	--	--	232	61	74	60	11	84	6	0	5	2	5	.29	8	.351	.439	.586
1992	Oakland	AL	24	53	14	3	0	3	(2	1)	26	8	9	5	0	15	1	0	0	0	1	.00	1	.264	.339	.491

Gene Nelson

Pitches: Right **Bats:** Right **Pos:** RP **Ht:** 6' 0" **Wt:** 174 **Born:** 12/03/60 **Age:** 32

Year	Team	Lg	G	GS	CG	GF	IP	BFP	H	R	ER	HR	SH	SF	HB	TBB	IBB	SO	WP	Bk	W	L	Pct.	ShO	Sv	ERA
1981	New York	AL	8	7	0	0	39	179	40	24	21	5	0	2	1	23	1	16	2	0	3	1	.750	0	0	4.85
1982	Seattle	AL	22	19	2	2	122.2	545	133	70	63	16	4	2	2	60	1	71	4	2	6	9	.400	1	0	4.62
1983	Seattle	AL	10	5	1	2	32	153	38	29	28	6	2	0	1	21	2	11	1	0	0	3	.000	0	0	7.88
1984	Chicago	AL	20	9	2	4	74.2	304	72	38	37	9	1	2	1	17	0	36	4	1	3	5	.375	0	1	4.46
1985	Chicago	AL	46	18	1	11	145.2	643	144	74	69	23	9	2	7	67	4	101	11	1	10	10	.500	0	2	4.26
1986	Chicago	AL	54	1	0	26	114.2	488	118	52	49	7	7	1	3	41	5	70	3	0	6	6	.500	0	6	3.85
1987	Oakland	AL	54	6	0	15	123.2	530	120	58	54	12	3	5	5	35	0	94	7	0	6	5	.545	0	3	3.93
1988	Oakland	AL	54	1	0	20	111.2	456	93	42	38	9	3	4	3	38	4	67	4	6	9	6	.600	0	3	3.06
1989	Oakland	AL	50	0	0	15	80	335	60	33	29	5	3	4	2	30	3	70	5	0	3	5	.375	0	3	3.26
1990	Oakland	AL	51	0	0	17	74.2	291	55	14	13	5	1	5	3	17	1	38	1	0	3	3	.500	0	5	1.57
1991	Oakland	AL	44	0	0	11	48.2	229	60	38	37	12	3	4	3	23	1	23	0	0	1	5	.167	0	0	6.84
1992	Oakland	AL	28	2	0	8	51.2	234	68	37	37	5	4	5	0	22	5	23	2	0	3	1	.750	0	0	6.45
	12 ML YEARS		441	68	6	131	1019	4387	1001	509	475	114	40	36	31	394	27	620	44	10	53	59	.473	1	23	4.20

Jeff Nelson

Pitches: Right **Bats:** Right **Pos:** RP **Ht:** 6' 8" **Wt:** 225 **Born:** 11/17/66 **Age:** 26

Year	Team	Lg	G	GS	CG	GF	IP	BFP	H	R	ER	HR	SH	SF	HB	TBB	IBB	SO	WP	Bk	W	L	Pct.	ShO	Sv	ERA
1984	Great Falls	R	1	0	0	0	0.2	0	3	4	4	1	0	0	1	3	0	1	0	0	0	0	.000	0	0	54.00
	Dodgers	R	9	0	0	3	13.1	56	6	3	2	0	0	0	1	6	0	7	1	1	0	0	.000	0	0	1.35
1985	Dodgers	R	14	7	0	3	47.1	242	72	50	29	1	0	1	0	32	0	31	8	1	0	5	.000	0	0	5.51
1986	Great Falls	R	3	0	0	2	2	0	5	3	3	0	0	0	0	3	2	1	2	0	0	0	.000	0	0	13.50
	Bakersfield	A	24	11	0	6	71.1	412	79	83	53	9	1	9	4	84	1	37	10	0	0	7	.000	0	0	6.69
1987	Salinas	A	17	16	1	0	80	389	80	61	51	2	4	3	4	71	0	43	17	0	3	7	.300	0	0	5.74
1988	San Berndno	A	27	27	1	0	149.1	677	163	115	92	9	2	8	8	91	2	94	20	0	8	9	.471	1	0	5.54
1989	Williamsprt	AA	15	15	2	0	92.1	392	72	41	34	2	0	3	4	53	1	61	9	1	7	5	.583	0	0	3.31
1990	Williamsprt	AA	10	10	0	0	43.1	203	65	35	31	2	0	2	2	18	1	14	2	0	1	4	.200	0	0	6.44
	Peninsula	A	18	7	1	8	60	247	47	21	21	5	1	0	1	25	1	49	2	0	2	2	.500	1	6	3.15
1991	Jacksnville	AA	21	0	0	20	28.1	113	23	5	4	0	2	0	0	9	0	34	2	0	4	0	1.000	0	12	1.27
	Calgary	AAA	28	0	0	21	32.1	146	39	19	14	1	2	3	0	15	3	26	2	1	3	4	.429	0	7	3.90
1992	Calgary	AAA	2	0	0	0	3.2	10	0	0	0	0	0	0	0	1	0	0	0	0	1	0	1.000	0	0	0.00
1992	Seattle	AL	66	0	0	27	81	352	71	34	31	7	9	3	6	44	12	46	2	0	1	7	.125	0	6	3.44

Al Newman

Bats: Both **Throws:** Right **Pos:** 2B/3B/SS **Ht:** 5' 9" **Wt:** 212 **Born:** 06/30/60 **Age:** 33

Year	Team	Lg	G	AB	H	2B	3B	HR	(Hm	Rd)	TB	R	RBI	TBB	IBB	SO	HBP	SH	SF	SB	CS	SB%	GDP	Avg	OBP	SLG
1985	Montreal	NL	25	29	5	1	0	0	(0	0)	6	7	1	3	0	4	0	0	0	2	1	.67	0	.172	.250	.207
1986	Montreal	NL	95	185	37	3	0	1	(0	1)	43	23	8	21	2	20	0	4	2	11	11	.50	4	.200	.279	.232
1987	Minnesota	AL	110	307	68	15	5	0	(0	0)	93	44	29	34	0	27	0	7	1	15	11	.58	5	.221	.298	.303
1988	Minnesota	AL	105	260	58	7	0	0	(0	0)	65	35	19	29	0	34	0	6	0	12	3	.80	5	.223	.301	.250
1989	Minnesota	AL	141	446	113	18	2	0	(0	0)	135	62	38	59	0	46	2	10	4	25	12	.68	3	.253	.341	.303
1990	Minnesota	AL	144	388	94	14	0	0	(0	0)	108	43	30	33	0	34	2	8	2	13	6	.68	7	.242	.304	.278
1991	Minnesota	AL	118	246	47	5	0	0	(0	0)	52	25	19	23	0	21	1	5	3	4	5	.44	5	.191	.260	.211
1992	Texas	AL	116	246	54	5	0	0	(0	0)	59	25	12	34	0	26	1	8	0	9	6	.60	5	.220	.317	.240
	8 ML YEARS		854	2107	476	68	7	1	(0	1)	561	264	156	236	2	212	6	48	12	91	55	.62	33	.226	.304	.266

Warren Newson

Bats: Left **Throws:** Left **Pos:** RF/LF **Ht:** 5' 7" **Wt:** 190 **Born:** 07/03/64 **Age:** 28

Year	Team	Lg	G	AB	H	2B	3B	HR	(Hm	Rd)	TB	R	RBI	TBB	IBB	SO	HBP	SH	SF	SB	CS	SB%	GDP	Avg	OBP	SLG
1986	Spokane	A	54	159	37	8	1	2	--	--	53	29	31	47	1	37	0	1	1	3	1	.75	5	.233	.406	.333
1987	Chston-Sc	A	58	191	66	12	2	7	--	--	103	50	32	52	1	35	0	2	1	13	7	.65	5	.346	.484	.539
	Reno	A	51	165	51	7	2	6	--	--	80	44	28	39	0	34	0	2	1	2	6	.25	1	.309	.439	.485
1988	Riverside	A	130	438	130	23	7	22	--	--	233	99	91	107	3	102	0	0	3	36	19	.65	11	.297	.432	.532
1989	Wichita	AA	128	427	130	20	6	18	--	--	216	94	70	103	10	99	0	1	5	20	9	.69	9	.304	.436	.506
1990	Las Vegas	AAA	123	404	123	20	3	13	--	--	188	80	58	83	3	110	0	1	4	13	5	.72	10	.304	.420	.465
1991	Vancouver	AAA	33	111	41	12	1	2	--	--	61	19	19	30	1	26	0	0	2	5	4	.56	2	.369	.497	.550
1992	Vancouver	AAA	19	59	15	0	0	0	--	--	15	7	9	16	1	21	1	0	0	3	2	.60	0	.254	.421	.254
1991	Chicago	AL	71	132	39	5	0	4	(1	3)	56	20	25	28	1	34	0	0	0	2	2	.50	4	.295	.419	.424
1992	Chicago	AL	63	136	30	3	0	1	(1	0)	36	19	11	37	2	38	0	0	0	3	0	1.00	4	.221	.387	.265
	2 ML YEARS		134	268	69	8	0	5	(2	3)	92	39	36	65	3	72	0	0	0	5	2	.71	8	.257	.402	.343

Rod Nichols

Pitches: Right **Bats:** Right **Pos:** RP/SP **Ht:** 6' 2" **Wt:** 190 **Born:** 12/29/64 **Age:** 28

Year Team	Lg	G	GS	CG	GF	IP	BFP	H	R	ER	HR	SH	SF	HB	TBB	IBB	SO	WP	Bk	W	L	Pct.	ShO	Sv	ERA
1988 Cleveland	AL	11	10	3	1	69.1	297	73	41	39	5	2	2	2	23	1	31	2	3	1	7	.125	0	0	5.06
1989 Cleveland	AL	15	11	0	2	71.2	315	81	42	35	9	3	2	2	24	0	42	0	0	4	6	.400	0	0	4.40
1990 Cleveland	AL	4	2	0	0	16	79	24	14	14	5	1	0	2	6	0	3	0	0	0	3	.000	0	0	7.88
1991 Cleveland	AL	31	16	3	4	137.1	578	145	63	54	6	6	4	6	30	3	76	3	0	2	11	.154	1	1	3.54
1992 Cleveland	AL	30	9	0	5	105.1	456	114	58	53	13	1	5	2	31	1	56	3	0	4	3	.571	0	0	4.53
5 ML YEARS		91	48	6	12	399.2	1725	437	218	195	38	13	13	14	114	5	208	8	3	11	30	.268	1	1	4.39

Dave Nied

Pitches: Right **Bats:** Right **Pos:** RP **Ht:** 6' 2" **Wt:** 185 **Born:** 12/22/68 **Age:** 24

Year Team	Lg	G	GS	CG	GF	IP	BFP	H	R	ER	HR	SH	SF	HB	TBB	IBB	SO	WP	Bk	W	L	Pct.	ShO	Sv	ERA
1988 Sumter	A	27	27	3	0	165.1	701	156	78	69	15	7	3	12	53	1	133	6	2	12	9	.571	1	0	3.76
1989 Durham	A	12	12	0	0	58.1	275	74	47	43	10	2	1	5	23	1	38	1	0	5	2	.714	0	0	6.63
Burlington	A	13	12	2	0	80	341	78	38	34	3	3	2	5	23	0	73	3	1	5	6	.455	1	0	3.83
1990 Durham	A	10	10	0	0	42.1	176	38	19	18	3	2	1	1	14	0	27	4	0	1	1	.500	0	0	3.83
Burlington	A	10	9	1	1	64	252	55	21	16	2	2	2	1	10	0	66	3	0	5	3	.625	1	0	2.25
1991 Durham	A	13	12	2	1	80.2	312	46	19	14	2	1	1	3	23	0	77	0	0	8	3	.727	2	0	1.56
Greenville	AA	15	15	1	0	89.2	367	79	26	24	0	3	2	6	20	3	101	1	0	7	3	.700	0	0	2.41
1992 Richmond	AAA	26	26	7	0	168	680	144	73	53	15	8	7	3	44	2	159	1	0	14	9	.609	2	0	2.84
1992 Atlanta	NL	6	2	0	0	23	83	10	3	3	0	1	0	0	5	0	19	0	0	3	0	1.000	0	0	1.17

Jerry Nielsen

Pitches: Left **Bats:** Left **Pos:** RP **Ht:** 6' 1" **Wt:** 180 **Born:** 08/05/66 **Age:** 26

Year Team	Lg	G	GS	CG	GF	IP	BFP	H	R	ER	HR	SH	SF	HB	TBB	IBB	SO	WP	Bk	W	L	Pct.	ShO	Sv	ERA
1988 Oneonta	A	19	1	0	8	38	158	27	6	3	0	3	0	3	18	0	35	0	4	6	2	.750	0	0	0.71
1989 Pr William	A	39	0	0	16	49.1	198	26	14	12	0	2	4	6	25	0	45	6	0	3	2	.600	0	4	2.19
1990 Pr William	A	26	26	1	0	151.2	665	149	76	66	9	4	2	11	79	1	119	9	2	7	12	.368	1	0	3.92
1991 Ft.Laudrdle	A	42	0	0	14	64.2	275	50	29	20	2	5	5	3	31	4	66	7	0	3	3	.500	0	4	2.78
Albany	AA	6	0	0	2	8	38	9	6	5	1	1	0	0	8	0	5	0	0	0	1	.000	0	0	5.63
1992 Albany	AA	36	0	0	21	53	207	38	8	7	1	1	0	1	15	2	59	5	0	3	5	.375	0	11	1.19
Columbus	AAA	4	0	0	2	5	18	2	1	1	0	0	2	1	2	0	5	1	0	0	0	.000	0	1	1.80
1992 New York	AL	20	0	0	12	19.2	90	17	10	10	1	1	1	0	18	2	12	1	0	1	0	1.000	0	0	4.58

Melvin Nieves

Bats: Both **Throws:** Right **Pos:** LF **Ht:** 6' 2" **Wt:** 200 **Born:** 12/28/71 **Age:** 21

Year Team	Lg	G	AB	H	2B	3B	HR	(Hm	Rd)	TB	R	RBI	TBB	IBB	SO	HBP	SH	SF	SB	CS	SB%	GDP	Avg	OBP	SLG
1988 Braves	R	56	176	30	6	0	1	--	--	39	16	12	20	0	53	2	1	1	5	4	.56	2	.170	.261	.222
1989 Pulaski	R	64	231	64	16	3	9	--	--	113	43	46	30	4	59	1	3	4	6	4	.60	2	.277	.357	.489
1990 Sumter	A	126	459	130	24	7	9	--	--	195	60	59	53	4	125	9	1	9	10	6	.63	7	.283	.362	.425
1991 Durham	A	64	201	53	11	0	9	--	--	91	31	25	40	2	53	5	0	1	3	8	.27	1	.264	.397	.453
1992 Durham	A	31	106	32	9	1	8	--	--	67	18	32	17	3	33	2	0	4	4	2	.67	1	.302	.395	.632
Greenville	AA	100	350	99	23	5	18	--	--	186	61	76	52	2	98	6	2	4	6	4	.60	4	.283	.381	.531
1992 Atlanta	NL	12	19	4	1	0	0	(0	0)	5	0	1	2	0	7	0	0	0	0	0	.00	0	.211	.286	.263

Dave Nilsson

Bats: Left **Throws:** Right **Pos:** C **Ht:** 6' 3" **Wt:** 185 **Born:** 12/14/69 **Age:** 23

Year Team	Lg	G	AB	H	2B	3B	HR	(Hm	Rd)	TB	R	RBI	TBB	IBB	SO	HBP	SH	SF	SB	CS	SB%	GDP	Avg	OBP	SLG
1987 Helena	R	55	188	74	13	0	1	--	--	90	36	21	22	2	14	0	1	2	0	1	.00	4	.394	.453	.479
1988 Beloit	A	95	332	74	15	2	4	--	--	105	28	41	25	2	49	2	0	5	2	5	.29	10	.223	.277	.316
1989 Stockton	A	125	472	115	16	6	5	--	--	158	59	56	51	1	75	1	4	4	2	1	.67	20	.244	.316	.335
1990 Stockton	A	107	359	104	22	3	7	--	--	153	70	47	43	3	36	0	0	4	6	5	.55	6	.290	.362	.426
1991 El Paso	AA	65	249	104	24	3	5	--	--	149	52	57	27	4	14	1	0	2	4	0	1.00	4	.418	.473	.598
Denver	AAA	28	95	22	8	0	1	--	--	33	10	14	17	0	16	0	0	0	1	1	.50	2	.232	.348	.347
1992 Denver	AAA	66	240	76	16	7	3	--	--	115	38	39	23	2	19	0	0	2	10	4	.71	3	.317	.369	.479
1992 Milwaukee	AL	51	164	38	8	0	4	(1	3)	58	15	25	17	1	18	0	2	0	2	2	.50	1	.232	.304	.354

Otis Nixon

Bats: Both **Throws:** Right **Pos:** CF/RF **Ht:** 6' 2" **Wt:** 180 **Born:** 01/09/59 **Age:** 34

Year Team	Lg	G	AB	H	2B	3B	HR	(Hm	Rd)	TB	R	RBI	TBB	IBB	SO	HBP	SH	SF	SB	CS	SB%	GDP	Avg	OBP	SLG
1983 New York	AL	13	14	2	0	0	0	(0	0)	2	2	0	1	0	5	0	0	0	2	0	1.00	0	.143	.200	.143
1984 Cleveland	AL	49	91	14	0	0	0	(0	0)	14	16	1	8	0	11	0	3	1	12	6	.67	2	.154	.220	.154
1985 Cleveland	AL	104	162	38	4	0	3	(1	2)	51	34	9	8	0	27	0	4	0	20	11	.65	2	.235	.271	.315
1986 Cleveland	AL	105	95	25	4	1	0	(0	0)	31	33	8	13	0	12	0	2	0	23	6	.79	1	.263	.352	.326
1987 Cleveland	AL	19	17	1	0	0	0	(0	0)	1	2	1	3	0	4	0	0	0	2	3	.40	0	.059	.200	.059
1988 Montreal	NL	90	271	66	8	2	0	(0	0)	78	47	15	28	0	42	0	4	2	46	13	.78	0	.244	.312	.288
1989 Montreal	NL	126	258	56	7	2	0	(0	0)	67	41	21	33	1	36	0	2	0	37	12	.76	4	.217	.306	.260
1990 Montreal	NL	119	231	58	6	2	1	(0	1)	71	46	20	28	0	33	0	3	1	50	13	.79	2	.251	.331	.307
1991 Atlanta	NL	124	401	119	10	1	0	(0	0)	131	81	26	47	3	40	2	7	3	72	21	.77	5	.297	.371	.327
1992 Atlanta	NL	120	456	134	14	2	2	(1	1)	158	79	22	39	0	54	0	5	2	41	18	.69	4	.294	.348	.346
10 ML YEARS		869	1996	513	53	10	6	(2	4)	604	381	123	208	4	264	2	30	9	305	103	.75	20	.257	.326	.303

Junior Noboa

Bats: Right **Throws:** Right **Pos:** 2B **Ht:** 5'10" **Wt:** 170 **Born:** 11/10/64 **Age:** 28

Year Team	Lg	G	AB	H	2B	3B	HR	(Hm	Rd)	TB	R	RBI	TBB	IBB	SO	HBP	SH	SF	SB	CS	SB%	GDP	Avg	OBP	SLG
1984 Cleveland	AL	23	11	4	0	0	0	(0	0)	4	3	0	0	0	2	0	1	0	1	0	1.00	1	.364	.364	.364
1987 Cleveland	AL	39	80	18	2	1	0	(0	0)	22	7	7	3	1	6	0	5	0	1	0	1.00	1	.225	.253	.275
1988 California	AL	21	16	1	0	0	0	(0	0)	1	4	0	0	0	1	0	0	0	0	0	.00	2	.063	.063	.063
1989 Montreal	NL	21	44	10	0	0	0	(0	0)	10	3	1	1	0	3	0	0	0	0	0	.00	0	.227	.244	.227
1990 Montreal	NL	81	158	42	7	2	0	(0	0)	53	15	14	7	2	14	1	3	4	4	1	.80	2	.266	.294	.335
1991 Montreal	NL	67	95	23	3	0	1	(0	1)	29	5	2	1	1	8	0	0	0	2	3	.40	1	.242	.250	.305
1992 New York	NL	46	47	7	0	0	0	(0	0)	7	7	3	3	0	8	1	0	1	0	0	.00	2	.149	.212	.149
7 ML YEARS		298	451	105	12	3	1	(0	1)	126	44	27	15	4	42	2	9	5	8	4	.67	9	.233	.258	.279

Matt Nokes

Bats: Left **Throws:** Right **Pos:** C **Ht:** 6' 1" **Wt:** 198 **Born:** 10/31/63 **Age:** 29

Year Team	Lg	G	AB	H	2B	3B	HR	(Hm	Rd)	TB	R	RBI	TBB	IBB	SO	HBP	SH	SF	SB	CS	SB%	GDP	Avg	OBP	SLG
1985 San Francisco	NL	19	53	11	2	0	2	(1	1)	19	3	5	1	0	9	1	0	0	0	0	.00	2	.208	.236	.358
1986 Detroit	AL	7	24	8	1	0	1	(0	1)	12	2	2	1	1	1	0	0	0	0	0	.00	0	.333	.360	.500
1987 Detroit	AL	135	461	133	14	2	32	(14	18)	247	69	87	35	2	70	6	3	3	2	1	.67	13	.289	.345	.536
1988 Detroit	AL	122	382	96	18	0	16	(9	7)	162	53	53	34	3	58	1	6	2	0	1	.00	11	.251	.313	.424
1989 Detroit	AL	87	268	67	10	0	9	(7	2)	104	15	39	17	1	37	2	1	2	1	0	1.00	11	.250	.298	.388
1990 2 ML Teams		136	351	87	9	1	11	(4	7)	131	33	40	24	6	47	6	0	1	2	2	.50	11	.248	.306	.373
1991 New York	AL	135	456	122	20	0	24	(13	11)	214	52	77	25	5	49	5	0	7	3	2	.60	6	.268	.308	.469
1992 New York	AL	121	384	86	9	1	22	(18	4)	163	42	59	37	11	62	3	0	6	0	1	.00	13	.224	.293	.424
1990 Detroit	AL	44	111	30	5	1	3	(1	2)	46	12	8	4	3	14	2	0	1	0	0	.00	5	.270	.305	.414
New York	AL	92	240	57	4	0	8	(3	5)	85	21	32	20	3	33	4	0	0	2	2	.50	6	.238	.307	.354
8 ML YEARS		762	2379	610	83	4	117	(66	51)	1052	269	362	174	29	333	24	10	21	8	7	.53	64	.256	.311	.442

Edwin Nunez

Pitches: Right **Bats:** Right **Pos:** RP **Ht:** 6' 5" **Wt:** 240 **Born:** 05/27/63 **Age:** 30

Year Team	Lg	G	GS	CG	GF	IP	BFP	H	R	ER	HR	SH	SF	HB	TBB	IBB	SO	WP	Bk	W	L	Pct.	ShO	Sv	ERA
1982 Seattle	AL	8	5	0	0	35.1	153	36	18	18	7	3	0	0	16	0	27	0	2	1	2	.333	0	0	4.58
1983 Seattle	AL	14	5	0	4	37	170	40	21	18	3	1	0	3	22	1	35	0	2	0	4	.000	0	0	4.38
1984 Seattle	AL	37	0	0	23	67.2	280	55	26	24	8	1	3	3	21	2	57	1	0	2	2	.500	0	7	3.19
1985 Seattle	AL	70	0	0	53	90.1	378	79	36	31	13	4	3	0	34	5	58	2	1	7	3	.700	0	16	3.09
1986 Seattle	AL	14	1	0	6	21.2	93	25	15	14	5	0	0	0	5	1	17	0	1	1	2	.333	0	0	5.82
1987 Seattle	AL	48	0	0	40	47.1	198	45	20	20	7	3	4	1	18	3	34	2	0	3	4	.429	0	12	3.80
1988 2 ML Teams		24	3	0	6	43.1	210	66	40	33	5	2	4	2	17	3	27	1	1	2	4	.333	0	0	6.85
1989 Detroit	AL	27	0	0	12	54	238	49	33	25	6	6	3	0	36	13	41	2	1	3	4	.429	0	1	4.17
1990 Detroit	AL	42	0	0	15	80.1	343	65	26	20	4	5	1	2	37	6	66	4	0	3	1	.750	0	6	2.24
1991 Milwaukee	AL	23	0	0	18	25.1	119	28	20	17	6	3	2	0	13	2	24	0	1	2	1	.667	0	8	6.04
1992 2 ML Teams		49	0	0	16	59.1	263	63	34	32	6	0	4	2	22	0	49	5	0	1	3	.250	0	3	4.85
1988 Seattle	AL	14	3	0	2	29.1	145	45	33	26	4	2	4	2	14	3	19	0	1	1	4	.200	0	0	7.98
New York	NL	10	0	0	4	14	65	21	7	7	1	0	0	0	3	0	8	1	0	1	0	1.000	0	0	4.50
1992 Milwaukee	AL	10	0	0	5	13.2	58	12	5	4	1	0	0	0	6	0	10	0	0	1	1	.500	0	0	2.63
Texas	AL	39	0	0	11	45.2	205	51	29	28	5	0	4	2	16	0	39	5	0	0	2	.000	0	3	5.52
11 ML YEARS		356	14	0	193	561.2	2445	551	289	252	70	28	24	13	241	36	435	17	8	25	30	.455	0	53	4.04

Charlie O'Brien

Bats: Right **Throws:** Right **Pos:** C   **Ht:** 6' 2" **Wt:** 200 **Born:** 05/01/61 **Age:** 32

Year	Team	Lg	G	AB	H	2B	3B	HR	(Hm	Rd)	TB	R	RBI	TBB	IBB	SO	HBP	SH	SF	SB	CS	SB%	GDP	Avg	OBP	SLG
1985	Oakland	AL	16	11	3	1	0	0	(0	0)	4	3	1	3	0	3	0	0	0	0	0	.00	0	.273	.429	.364
1987	Milwaukee	AL	10	35	7	3	1	0	(0	0)	12	2	0	4	0	4	0	1	0	0	1	.00	0	.200	.282	.343
1988	Milwaukee	AL	40	118	26	6	0	2	(2	0)	38	12	9	5	0	16	0	4	0	0	1	.00	3	.220	.252	.322
1989	Milwaukee	AL	62	188	44	10	0	6	(4	2)	72	22	35	21	1	11	9	8	0	0	0	.00	11	.234	.339	.383
1990	2 ML Teams		74	213	38	10	2	0	(0	0)	52	17	20	21	3	34	3	10	2	0	0	.00	4	.178	.259	.244
1991	New York	NL	69	168	31	6	0	2	(1	1)	43	16	14	17	1	25	4	0	2	0	2	.00	5	.185	.272	.256
1992	New York	NL	68	156	33	12	0	2	(1	1)	51	15	13	16	1	18	1	4	0	0	1	.00	4	.212	.289	.327
1990	New York	NL	46	145	27	7	2	0	(0	0)	38	11	11	11	1	26	2	8	0	0	0	.00	3	.186	.253	.262
	New York	NL	28	68	11	3	0	0	(0	0)	14	6	9	10	2	8	1	2	2	0	0	.00	1	.162	.272	.206
	7 ML YEARS		339	889	182	48	3	12	(8	4)	272	87	92	87	6	111	17	27	4	0	5	.00	27	.205	.287	.306

Pete O'Brien

Bats: Left **Throws:** Left **Pos:** 1B/DH   **Ht:** 6' 2" **Wt:** 195 **Born:** 02/09/58 **Age:** 35

Year	Team	Lg	G	AB	H	2B	3B	HR	(Hm	Rd)	TB	R	RBI	TBB	IBB	SO	HBP	SH	SF	SB	CS	SB%	GDP	Avg	OBP	SLG
1982	Texas	AL	20	67	16	4	1	4	(2	2)	34	13	13	6	0	8	0	0	1	1	0	1.00	0	.239	.297	.507
1983	Texas	AL	154	524	124	24	5	8	(4	4)	182	53	53	58	2	62	1	3	2	5	4	.56	12	.237	.313	.347
1984	Texas	AL	142	520	149	26	2	18	(7	11)	233	57	80	53	8	50	0	1	7	3	5	.38	11	.287	.348	.448
1985	Texas	AL	159	573	153	34	3	22	(12	10)	259	69	92	69	4	53	1	3	9	5	10	.33	18	.267	.342	.452
1986	Texas	AL	156	551	160	23	3	23	(11	12)	258	86	90	87	11	66	0	0	3	4	4	.50	19	.290	.385	.468
1987	Texas	AL	159	569	163	26	1	23	(9	14)	260	84	88	59	6	61	0	0	10	0	4	.00	9	.286	.348	.457
1988	Texas	AL	156	547	149	24	1	16	(6	10)	223	57	71	72	9	73	0	1	8	1	4	.20	12	.272	.352	.408
1989	Cleveland	AL	155	554	144	24	1	12	(5	7)	206	75	55	83	17	48	2	2	5	3	1	.75	10	.260	.356	.372
1990	Seattle	AL	108	366	82	18	0	5	(3	2)	115	32	27	44	1	33	2	1	4	0	0	.00	12	.224	.308	.314
1991	Seattle	AL	152	560	139	29	3	17	(12	5)	225	58	88	44	7	61	1	3	9	0	1	.00	14	.248	.300	.402
1992	Seattle	AL	134	396	88	15	1	14	(6	8)	147	40	52	40	8	27	0	1	7	2	1	.67	8	.222	.289	.371
	11 ML YEARS		1495	5227	1367	247	21	162	(77	85)	2142	624	709	615	73	542	7	15	65	24	34	.41	125	.262	.336	.410

Paul O'Neill

Bats: Left **Throws:** Left **Pos:** RF   **Ht:** 6' 4" **Wt:** 215 **Born:** 02/25/63 **Age:** 30

Year	Team	Lg	G	AB	H	2B	3B	HR	(Hm	Rd)	TB	R	RBI	TBB	IBB	SO	HBP	SH	SF	SB	CS	SB%	GDP	Avg	OBP	SLG
1985	Cincinnati	NL	5	12	4	1	0	0	(0	0)	5	1	1	0	0	2	0	0	0	0	0	.00	0	.333	.333	.417
1986	Cincinnati	NL	3	2	0	0	0	0	(0	0)	0	0	0	0	0	1	0	0	0	0	0	.00	0	.000	.333	.000
1987	Cincinnati	NL	84	160	41	14	1	7	(4	3)	78	24	28	18	1	29	0	0	0	2	1	.67	3	.256	.331	.488
1988	Cincinnati	NL	145	485	122	25	3	16	(12	4)	201	58	73	38	5	65	2	3	5	8	6	.57	7	.252	.306	.414
1989	Cincinnati	NL	117	428	118	24	2	15	(11	4)	191	49	74	46	8	64	2	0	4	20	5	.80	7	.276	.346	.446
1990	Cincinnati	NL	145	503	136	28	0	16	(10	6)	212	59	78	53	13	103	2	1	5	13	11	.54	12	.270	.339	.421
1991	Cincinnati	NL	152	532	136	36	0	28	(20	8)	256	71	91	73	14	107	1	0	1	12	7	.63	8	.256	.346	.481
1992	Cincinnati	NL	148	496	122	19	1	14	(6	8)	185	59	66	77	15	85	2	3	6	6	3	.67	10	.246	.346	.373
	8 ML YEARS		799	2618	679	147	7	96	(63	33)	1128	321	411	306	56	456	9	7	21	61	33	.65	47	.259	.336	.431

Ken Oberkfell

Bats: Left **Throws:** Right **Pos:** 2B   **Ht:** 6' 1" **Wt:** 210 **Born:** 05/04/56 **Age:** 37

Year	Team	Lg	G	AB	H	2B	3B	HR	(Hm	Rd)	TB	R	RBI	TBB	IBB	SO	HBP	SH	SF	SB	CS	SB%	GDP	Avg	OBP	SLG
1977	St. Louis	NL	9	9	1	0	0	0	(0	0)	1	0	1	0	0	3	0	0	0	0	0	.00	0	.111	.111	.111
1978	St. Louis	NL	24	50	6	1	0	0	(0	0)	7	7	0	3	0	1	0	1	0	0	0	.00	1	.120	.170	.140
1979	St. Louis	NL	135	369	111	19	5	1	(1	0)	143	53	35	57	9	35	4	1	4	4	1	.80	9	.301	.396	.388
1980	St. Louis	NL	116	422	128	27	6	3	(0	3)	176	58	46	51	8	23	1	9	3	4	4	.50	11	.303	.377	.417
1981	St. Louis	NL	102	376	110	12	6	2	(0	2)	140	43	45	37	6	28	0	3	4	13	5	.72	11	.293	.353	.372
1982	St. Louis	NL	137	470	136	22	5	2	(1	1)	174	55	34	40	6	31	1	3	2	11	9	.55	11	.289	.345	.370
1983	St. Louis	NL	151	488	143	26	5	3	(0	3)	188	62	38	61	5	27	1	4	3	12	6	.67	12	.293	.371	.385
1984	2 ML Teams		100	324	87	19	2	1	(1	0)	113	38	21	31	3	27	1	3	3	2	5	.29	7	.269	.331	.349
1985	Atlanta	NL	134	412	112	19	4	3	(2	1)	148	30	35	51	6	38	6	1	2	1	2	.33	10	.272	.359	.359
1986	Atlanta	NL	151	503	136	24	3	5	(2	3)	181	62	48	83	6	40	2	4	4	7	4	.64	11	.270	.373	.360
1987	Atlanta	NL	135	508	142	29	2	3	(2	1)	184	59	48	48	5	29	2	5	3	3	3	.50	13	.280	.342	.362
1988	2 ML Teams		140	476	129	22	4	3	(1	2)	168	49	42	37	7	34	2	6	8	4	5	.44	8	.271	.321	.353
1989	2 ML Teams		97	156	42	6	1	2	(1	1)	56	19	17	10	0	10	2	2	3	0	0	.00	4	.269	.316	.359
1990	Houston	NL	77	150	31	6	1	1	(0	1)	42	10	12	15	1	17	1	1	1	1	1	.50	2	.207	.281	.280
1991	Houston	NL	53	70	16	4	0	0	(0	0)	20	7	14	14	4	8	0	0	0	0	0	.00	0	.229	.357	.286

Year	Team	Lg	G	AB	H	2B	3B	HR	(Hm	Rd)	TB	R	RBI	TBB	IBB	SO	HBP	SH	SF	SB	CS	SB%	GDP	Avg	OBP	SLG
1992	California	AL	41	91	24	1	0	0	(0	0)	25	6	10	8	2	5	0	0	2	0	1	.00	2	.264	.317	.275
1984	St. Louis	NL	50	152	47	11	1	0	(0	0)	60	17	11	16	2	10	1	0	0	1	2	.33	3	.309	.379	.395
	Atlanta	NL	50	172	40	8	1	1	(1	0)	53	21	10	15	1	17	0	3	3	1	3	.25	4	.233	.289	.308
1988	Atlanta	NL	120	422	117	20	4	3	(1	2)	154	42	40	32	6	28	2	5	8	4	5	.44	6	.277	.325	.365
	Pittsburgh	NL	20	54	12	2	0	0	(0	0)	14	7	2	5	1	6	0	1	0	0	0	.00	0	.222	.288	.259
1989	Pittsburgh	NL	14	40	5	1	0	0	(0	0)	6	2	2	2	0	2	0	1	0	0	0	.00	0	.125	.163	.150
	San Francisco	NL	83	116	37	5	1	2	(1	1)	50	17	15	8	0	8	2	1	2	0	1	.00	4	.319	.367	.431
16 ML YEARS			1602	4874	1354	237	44	29	(11	18)	1766	558	446	546	68	356	23	43	42	62	47	.57	112	.278	.351	.362

Jose Offerman

Bats: Both **Throws:** Right **Pos:** SS **Ht:** 6' 0" **Wt:** 160 **Born:** 11/08/68 **Age:** 24

				BATTING																	BASERUNNING			PERCENTAGES		
Year	Team	Lg	G	AB	H	2B	3B	HR	(Hm	Rd)	TB	R	RBI	TBB	IBB	SO	HBP	SH	SF	SB	CS	SB%	GDP	Avg	OBP	SLG
1990	Los Angeles	NL	29	58	9	0	0	1	(1	0)	12	7	7	4	1	14	0	1	0	1	0	1.00	0	.155	.210	.207
1991	Los Angeles	NL	52	113	22	2	0	0	(0	0)	24	10	3	25	2	32	1	1	0	3	2	.60	5	.195	.345	.212
1992	Los Angeles	NL	149	534	139	20	8	1	(1	0)	178	67	30	57	4	98	0	5	2	23	16	.59	5	.260	.331	.333
3 ML YEARS			230	705	170	22	8	2	(2	0)	214	84	40	86	7	144	1	7	2	27	18	.60	10	.241	.324	.304

Bobby Ojeda

Pitches: Left **Bats:** Left **Pos:** SP **Ht:** 6' 1" **Wt:** 195 **Born:** 12/17/57 **Age:** 35

			HOW MUCH HE PITCHED					WHAT HE GAVE UP										THE RESULTS					
Year	Team	Lg	G	GS	CG	GF	IP	BFP	H	R	ER	HR	SH	SF	HB	TBB	IBB	SO	WP	Bk	W	L	Pct.	ShO	Sv	ERA
1980	Boston	AL	7	7	0	0	26	122	39	20	20	2	0	0	0	14	1	12	1	0	1	1	.500	0	0	6.92
1981	Boston	AL	10	10	2	0	66	267	50	25	23	6	3	1	2	25	2	28	0	0	6	2	.750	0	0	3.14
1982	Boston	AL	22	14	0	6	78.1	352	95	53	49	13	0	1	1	29	0	52	5	0	4	6	.400	0	0	5.63
1983	Boston	AL	29	28	5	0	173.2	746	173	85	78	15	6	11	3	73	2	94	2	0	12	7	.632	0	0	4.04
1984	Boston	AL	33	32	8	0	216.2	928	211	106	96	17	8	6	2	96	2	137	0	1	12	12	.500	5	0	3.99
1985	Boston	AL	39	22	5	10	157.2	671	166	74	70	11	10	3	2	48	9	102	3	3	9	11	.450	0	1	4.00
1986	New York	NL	32	30	7	1	217.1	871	185	72	62	15	10	3	2	52	3	148	2	1	18	5	.783	2	0	2.57
1987	New York	NL	10	7	0	0	46.1	192	45	23	20	5	3	1	0	10	1	21	1	0	3	5	.375	0	0	3.88
1988	New York	NL	29	29	5	0	190.1	752	158	74	61	6	6	6	4	33	2	133	4	7	10	13	.435	5	0	2.88
1989	New York	NL	31	31	5	0	192	824	179	83	74	16	6	7	2	78	5	95	0	2	13	11	.542	2	0	3.47
1990	New York	NL	38	12	0	9	118	500	123	53	48	10	3	3	2	40	4	62	2	3	7	6	.538	0	0	3.66
1991	Los Angeles	NL	31	31	2	0	189.1	802	181	78	67	15	15	9	3	70	9	120	4	2	12	9	.571	1	0	3.18
1992	Los Angeles	NL	29	29	2	0	166.1	731	169	80	67	8	11	7	1	81	8	94	3	0	6	9	.400	1	0	3.63
13 ML YEARS			340	282	41	26	1838	7758	1774	826	735	139	81	58	24	649	48	1098	27	19	113	97	.538	16	1	3.60

John Olerud

Bats: Left **Throws:** Left **Pos:** 1B **Ht:** 6' 5" **Wt:** 218 **Born:** 08/05/68 **Age:** 24

				BATTING																	BASERUNNING			PERCENTAGES		
Year	Team	Lg	G	AB	H	2B	3B	HR	(Hm	Rd)	TB	R	RBI	TBB	IBB	SO	HBP	SH	SF	SB	CS	SB%	GDP	Avg	OBP	SLG
1989	Toronto	AL	6	8	3	0	0	0	(0	0)	3	2	0	0	0	1	0	0	0	0	0	.00	0	.375	.375	.375
1990	Toronto	AL	111	358	95	15	1	14	(11	3)	154	43	48	57	6	75	1	1	4	0	2	.00	0	.265	.364	.430
1991	Toronto	AL	139	454	116	30	1	17	(7	10)	199	64	68	68	9	84	6	3	10	0	2	.00	12	.256	.353	.438
1992	Toronto	AL	138	458	130	28	0	16	(4	12)	206	68	66	70	11	61	1	1	7	1	0	1.00	15	.284	.375	.450
4 ML YEARS			394	1278	344	73	2	47	(22	25)	562	177	182	195	26	221	8	5	21	1	4	.20	32	.269	.364	.440

Steve Olin

Pitches: Right **Bats:** Right **Pos:** RP **Ht:** 6' 2" **Wt:** 190 **Born:** 10/04/65 **Age:** 27

			HOW MUCH HE PITCHED					WHAT HE GAVE UP										THE RESULTS					
Year	Team	Lg	G	GS	CG	GF	IP	BFP	H	R	ER	HR	SH	SF	HB	TBB	IBB	SO	WP	Bk	W	L	Pct.	ShO	Sv	ERA
1989	Cleveland	AL	25	0	0	8	36	152	35	16	15	1	1	0	0	14	2	24	2	0	1	4	.200	0	1	3.75
1990	Cleveland	AL	50	1	0	16	92.1	394	96	41	35	3	5	2	6	26	2	64	0	0	4	4	.500	0	1	3.41
1991	Cleveland	AL	48	0	0	32	56.1	249	61	26	21	2	2	0	1	23	7	38	0	0	3	6	.333	0	17	3.36
1992	Cleveland	AL	72	0	0	62	88.1	360	80	25	23	8	5	2	4	27	6	47	1	1	8	5	.615	0	29	2.34
4 ML YEARS			195	1	0	118	273	1155	272	108	94	14	13	4	11	90	17	173	3	1	16	19	.457	0	48	3.10

Omar Olivares

Pitches: Right **Bats:** Right **Pos:** SP **Ht:** 6' 1" **Wt:** 193 **Born:** 07/06/67 **Age:** 25

			HOW MUCH HE PITCHED					WHAT HE GAVE UP										THE RESULTS					
Year	Team	Lg	G	GS	CG	GF	IP	BFP	H	R	ER	HR	SH	SF	HB	TBB	IBB	SO	WP	Bk	W	L	Pct.	ShO	Sv	ERA
1990	St. Louis	NL	9	9	0	0	49.1	201	45	17	16	2	1	0	2	17	0	20	1	1	1	1	.500	0	0	2.92
1991	St. Louis	NL	28	24	0	2	167.1	688	148	72	69	13	11	2	5	61	1	91	3	1	11	7	.611	0	1	3.71
1992	St. Louis	NL	32	30	1	1	197	818	189	84	84	20	8	7	4	63	5	124	2	0	9	9	.500	0	0	3.84
3 ML YEARS			69	60	1	3	413.2	1707	382	173	169	35	20	9	11	141	6	235	6	2	21	17	.553	0	1	3.68

148

Joe Oliver

Bats: Right **Throws:** Right **Pos:** C   **Ht:** 6' 3" **Wt:** 210 **Born:** 07/24/65 **Age:** 27

							BATTING											BASERUNNING				PERCENTAGES		
Year	Team	Lg	G	AB	H	2B	3B	HR	(Hm | Rd)	TB	R	RBI	TBB	IBB	SO	HBP	SH	SF	SB	CS	SB%	GDP	Avg	OBP	SLG
1989	Cincinnati	NL	49	151	41	8	0	3	(1 | 2)	58	13	23	6	1	28	1	1	2	0	0	.00	3	.272	.300	.384
1990	Cincinnati	NL	121	364	84	23	0	8	(3 | 5)	131	34	52	37	15	75	2	5	1	1	1	.50	6	.231	.304	.360
1991	Cincinnati	NL	94	269	58	11	0	11	(7 | 4)	102	21	41	18	5	53	0	4	0	0	0	.00	14	.216	.265	.379
1992	Cincinnati	NL	143	485	131	25	1	10	(7 | 3)	188	42	57	35	19	75	1	6	7	2	3	.40	12	.270	.316	.388
	4 ML YEARS		407	1269	314	67	1	32	(18 | 14)	479	110	173	96	40	231	4	16	10	3	4	.43	35	.247	.300	.377

Francisco Oliveras

Pitches: Right **Bats:** Right **Pos:** RP/SP   **Ht:** 5'10" **Wt:** 170 **Born:** 01/31/63 **Age:** 30

			HOW MUCH HE PITCHED						WHAT HE GAVE UP									THE RESULTS					
Year	Team	Lg	G	GS	CG	GF	IP	BFP	H	R	ER	HR	SH	SF	HB	TBB	IBB	SO	WP	Bk	W	L	Pct.	ShO	Sv	ERA
1989	Minnesota	AL	12	8	1	1	55.2	239	64	28	28	8	0	1	1	15	0	24	0	2	3	4	.429	0	1	4.53
1990	San Francisco	NL	33	2	0	9	55.1	231	47	22	17	5	1	3	2	21	6	41	2	1	2	2	.500	0	2	2.77
1991	San Francisco	NL	55	1	0	17	79.1	316	69	36	34	12	5	3	1	22	4	48	2	2	6	6	.500	0	3	3.86
1992	San Francisco	NL	16	7	0	3	44.2	179	41	19	18	11	2	2	1	10	2	17	0	0	0	3	.000	0	0	3.63
	4 ML YEARS		116	18	1	30	235	965	221	105	97	36	8	9	5	68	12	130	4	5	11	15	.423	0	5	3.71

Greg Olson

Bats: Right **Throws:** Right **Pos:** C   **Ht:** 6' 0" **Wt:** 200 **Born:** 09/06/60 **Age:** 32

							BATTING											BASERUNNING				PERCENTAGES		
Year	Team	Lg	G	AB	H	2B	3B	HR	(Hm | Rd)	TB	R	RBI	TBB	IBB	SO	HBP	SH	SF	SB	CS	SB%	GDP	Avg	OBP	SLG
1989	Minnesota	AL	3	2	1	0	0	0	(0 | 0)	1	0	0	0	0	0	0	0	0	0	0	.00	0	.500	.500	.500
1990	Atlanta	NL	100	298	78	12	1	7	(4 | 3)	113	36	36	30	4	51	2	1	1	1	1	.50	8	.262	.332	.379
1991	Atlanta	NL	133	411	99	25	0	6	(6 | 0)	142	46	44	44	3	48	3	2	4	1	1	.50	13	.241	.316	.345
1992	Atlanta	NL	95	302	72	14	2	3	(3 | 0)	99	27	27	34	4	31	1	1	2	2	1	.67	8	.238	.316	.328
	4 ML YEARS		331	1013	250	51	3	16	(10 | 6)	355	109	107	108	11	130	6	4	7	4	3	.57	29	.247	.321	.350

Gregg Olson

Pitches: Right **Bats:** Right **Pos:** RP   **Ht:** 6' 4" **Wt:** 206 **Born:** 10/11/66 **Age:** 26

			HOW MUCH HE PITCHED						WHAT HE GAVE UP									THE RESULTS					
Year	Team	Lg	G	GS	CG	GF	IP	BFP	H	R	ER	HR	SH	SF	HB	TBB	IBB	SO	WP	Bk	W	L	Pct.	ShO	Sv	ERA
1988	Baltimore	AL	10	0	0	4	11	51	10	4	4	1	0	0	0	10	1	9	0	1	1	1	.500	0	0	3.27
1989	Baltimore	AL	64	0	0	52	85	356	57	17	16	1	4	1	1	46	10	90	9	3	5	2	.714	0	27	1.69
1990	Baltimore	AL	64	0	0	58	74.1	305	57	20	20	3	1	2	3	31	3	74	5	0	6	5	.545	0	37	2.42
1991	Baltimore	AL	72	0	0	62	73.2	319	74	28	26	1	5	1	1	29	5	72	8	1	4	6	.400	0	31	3.18
1992	Baltimore	AL	60	0	0	56	61.1	244	46	14	14	3	0	2	0	24	0	58	4	0	1	5	.167	0	36	2.05
	5 ML YEARS		270	0	0	232	305.1	1275	244	83	80	9	10	6	5	140	19	303	26	5	17	19	.472	0	131	2.36

Jose Oquendo

Bats: Both **Throws:** Right **Pos:** 2B   **Ht:** 5'10" **Wt:** 171 **Born:** 07/04/63 **Age:** 29

							BATTING											BASERUNNING				PERCENTAGES		
Year	Team	Lg	G	AB	H	2B	3B	HR	(Hm | Rd)	TB	R	RBI	TBB	IBB	SO	HBP	SH	SF	SB	CS	SB%	GDP	Avg	OBP	SLG
1983	New York	NL	120	328	70	7	0	1	(0 | 1)	80	29	17	19	2	60	2	3	1	8	9	.47	10	.213	.244	.244
1984	New York	NL	81	189	42	5	0	0	(0 | 0)	47	23	10	15	2	26	2	3	2	10	1	.91	2	.222	.284	.249
1986	St. Louis	NL	76	138	41	4	1	0	(0 | 0)	47	20	13	15	4	20	0	2	3	2	3	.40	3	.297	.359	.341
1987	St. Louis	NL	116	248	71	9	0	1	(0 | 1)	83	43	24	54	6	29	0	6	4	4	4	.50	6	.286	.408	.335
1988	St. Louis	NL	148	451	125	10	1	7	(4 | 3)	158	36	46	52	7	40	0	12	3	4	6	.40	8	.277	.350	.350
1989	St. Louis	NL	163	556	162	28	7	1	(0 | 1)	207	59	48	79	7	59	0	7	8	3	5	.38	12	.291	.375	.372
1990	St. Louis	NL	156	469	118	17	5	1	(1 | 0)	148	38	37	74	8	46	0	5	5	1	1	.50	7	.252	.350	.316
1991	St. Louis	NL	127	366	88	11	4	1	(0 | 1)	110	37	26	67	13	48	1	4	3	1	2	.33	5	.240	.357	.301
1992	St. Louis	NL	14	35	9	3	1	0	(0 | 0)	14	3	5	1	1	3	0	0	0	0	0	.00	0	.257	.350	.400
	9 ML YEARS		1001	2780	726	94	19	12	(5 | 7)	894	288	224	380	50	331	5	42	29	33	31	.52	53	.261	.348	.322

Jesse Orosco

Pitches: Left **Bats:** Right **Pos:** RP   **Ht:** 6' 2" **Wt:** 185 **Born:** 04/21/57 **Age:** 36

			HOW MUCH HE PITCHED						WHAT HE GAVE UP									THE RESULTS					
Year	Team	Lg	G	GS	CG	GF	IP	BFP	H	R	ER	HR	SH	SF	HB	TBB	IBB	SO	WP	Bk	W	L	Pct.	ShO	Sv	ERA
1979	New York	NL	18	0	0	6	35	154	33	20	19	4	3	0	2	22	0	22	0	0	1	2	.333	0	0	4.89
1981	New York	NL	8	0	0	4	17	69	13	4	3	2	2	0	0	6	2	18	0	1	0	1	.000	0	1	1.59
1982	New York	NL	54	2	0	22	109.1	451	92	37	33	7	5	4	2	40	2	89	3	2	4	10	.286	0	4	2.72
1983	New York	NL	62	0	0	42	110	432	76	27	18	3	4	3	1	38	7	84	1	2	13	7	.650	0	17	1.47
1984	New York	NL	60	0	0	52	87	355	58	29	25	7	3	4	2	34	6	85	1	1	10	6	.625	0	31	2.59
1985	New York	NL	54	0	0	39	79	331	66	26	24	6	1	1	0	34	7	68	4	0	8	6	.571	0	17	2.73
1986	New York	NL	58	0	0	40	81	338	64	23	21	6	2	3	3	35	3	62	2	0	8	6	.571	0	21	2.33

149

Year	Team	Lg	G	GS	CG	GF	IP	BFP	H	R	ER	HR	SH	SF	HB	TBB	IBB	SO	WP	Bk	W	L	Pct.	ShO	Sv	ERA
1987	New York	NL	58	0	0	41	77	335	78	41	38	5	5	4	2	31	9	78	2	0	3	9	.250	0	16	4.44
1988	Los Angeles	NL	55	0	0	21	53	229	41	18	16	4	3	3	2	30	3	43	1	0	3	2	.600	0	9	2.72
1989	Cleveland	AL	69	0	0	29	78	312	54	20	18	7	8	3	2	26	4	79	0	0	3	4	.429	0	3	2.08
1990	Cleveland	AL	55	0	0	28	64.2	289	58	35	28	9	5	3	0	38	7	55	1	0	5	4	.556	0	2	3.90
1991	Cleveland	AL	47	0	0	20	45.2	202	52	20	19	4	1	3	1	15	8	36	1	1	2	0	1.000	0	0	3.74
1992	Milwaukee	AL	59	0	0	14	39	158	33	15	14	5	0	2	1	13	1	40	2	0	3	1	.750	0	1	3.23
	13 ML YEARS		657	4	0	358	875.2	3655	718	315	276	69	42	32	18	362	59	759	18	7	63	58	.521	0	122	2.84

Joe Orsulak

Bats: Left **Throws:** Left **Pos:** RF/LF **Ht:** 6' 1" **Wt:** 210 **Born:** 05/31/62 **Age:** 31

Year	Team	Lg	G	AB	H	2B	3B	HR	(Hm	Rd)	TB	R	RBI	TBB	IBB	SO	HBP	SH	SF	SB	CS	SB%	GDP	Avg	OBP	SLG
1983	Pittsburgh	NL	7	11	2	0	0	0	(0	0)	2	0	1	0	0	2	0	0	1	0	1	.00	0	.182	.167	.182
1984	Pittsburgh	NL	32	67	17	1	2	0	(0	0)	22	12	3	1	0	7	1	3	1	3	1	.75	0	.254	.271	.328
1985	Pittsburgh	NL	121	397	119	14	6	0	(0	0)	145	54	21	26	3	27	1	9	3	24	11	.69	5	.300	.342	.365
1986	Pittsburgh	NL	138	401	100	19	6	2	(0	2)	137	60	19	28	2	38	1	6	1	24	11	.69	4	.249	.299	.342
1988	Baltimore	AL	125	379	109	21	3	8	(3	5)	160	48	27	23	2	30	3	8	3	9	8	.53	7	.288	.331	.422
1989	Baltimore	AL	123	390	111	22	5	7	(0	7)	164	59	55	41	6	35	2	7	6	5	3	.63	8	.285	.351	.421
1990	Baltimore	AL	124	413	111	14	3	11	(9	2)	164	49	57	46	9	48	1	4	1	6	8	.43	7	.269	.343	.397
1991	Baltimore	AL	143	486	135	22	1	5	(3	2)	174	57	43	28	1	45	4	0	3	6	2	.75	9	.278	.321	.358
1992	Baltimore	AL	117	391	113	18	3	4	(2	2)	149	45	39	28	5	34	4	4	1	5	4	.56	3	.289	.342	.381
	9 ML YEARS		930	2935	817	131	29	37	(17	20)	1117	384	265	221	28	266	17	41	20	82	49	.63	43	.278	.330	.381

Junior Ortiz

Bats: Right **Throws:** Right **Pos:** C **Ht:** 5'11" **Wt:** 185 **Born:** 10/24/59 **Age:** 33

Year	Team	Lg	G	AB	H	2B	3B	HR	(Hm	Rd)	TB	R	RBI	TBB	IBB	SO	HBP	SH	SF	SB	CS	SB%	GDP	Avg	OBP	SLG
1982	Pittsburgh	NL	7	15	3	1	0	0	(0	0)	4	1	0	1	0	3	0	0	0	0	0	.00	1	.200	.250	.267
1983	2 ML Teams		73	193	48	5	0	0	(0	0)	53	11	12	4	0	34	1	2	0	1	0	1.00	1	.249	.268	.275
1984	New York	NL	40	91	18	3	0	0	(0	0)	21	6	11	5	0	15	0	0	2	1	0	1.00	2	.198	.235	.231
1985	Pittsburgh	NL	23	72	21	2	0	1	(0	0)	26	4	5	3	1	17	0	1	0	1	0	1.00	1	.292	.320	.361
1986	Pittsburgh	NL	49	110	37	6	0	0	(0	0)	43	11	14	9	0	13	0	1	2	0	1	.00	4	.336	.380	.391
1987	Pittsburgh	NL	75	192	52	8	1	1	(0	1)	65	16	22	15	1	23	0	5	1	0	2	.00	6	.271	.322	.339
1988	Pittsburgh	NL	49	118	33	6	0	2	(1	1)	45	8	18	9	0	9	2	1	2	1	4	.20	6	.280	.336	.381
1989	Pittsburgh	NL	91	230	50	6	1	1	(0	1)	61	16	22	20	4	20	2	3	3	2	2	.50	9	.217	.282	.265
1990	Minnesota	AL	71	170	57	7	1	0	(0	0)	66	18	18	12	0	16	2	2	1	0	4	.00	4	.335	.384	.388
1991	Minnesota	AL	61	134	28	5	1	0	(0	0)	35	9	11	15	0	12	1	1	0	0	1	.00	6	.209	.293	.261
1992	Cleveland	AL	86	244	61	7	0	0	(0	0)	68	20	24	12	0	23	4	2	0	1	3	.25	7	.250	.296	.279
1983	Pittsburgh	NL	5	8	1	0	0	0	(0	0)	1	1	0	1	0	0	0	1	0	0	0	.00	0	.125	.222	.125
	New York	NL	68	185	47	5	0	0	(0	0)	52	10	12	3	0	34	1	1	0	1	0	1.00	1	.254	.270	.281
	11 ML YEARS		625	1569	408	56	4	5	(1	4)	487	120	157	105	6	185	12	18	11	7	17	.29	47	.260	.309	.310

John Orton

Bats: Right **Throws:** Right **Pos:** C **Ht:** 6' 1" **Wt:** 192 **Born:** 12/08/65 **Age:** 27

Year	Team	Lg	G	AB	H	2B	3B	HR	(Hm	Rd)	TB	R	RBI	TBB	IBB	SO	HBP	SH	SF	SB	CS	SB%	GDP	Avg	OBP	SLG
1989	California	AL	16	39	7	1	0	0	(0	0)	8	4	4	2	0	17	0	1	0	0	0	.00	0	.179	.220	.205
1990	California	AL	31	84	16	5	0	1	(0	1)	24	8	6	5	0	31	1	2	0	0	1	.00	2	.190	.244	.286
1991	California	AL	29	69	14	4	0	0	(0	0)	18	7	3	10	0	17	1	4	0	0	1	.00	2	.203	.313	.261
1992	California	AL	43	114	25	3	0	2	(1	1)	34	11	12	7	0	32	2	2	0	1	1	.50	1	.219	.276	.298
	4 ML YEARS		119	306	62	13	0	3	(1	2)	84	30	25	24	0	97	4	9	0	1	3	.25	5	.203	.269	.275

Donovan Osborne

Pitches: Left **Bats:** Both **Pos:** SP/RP **Ht:** 6' 2" **Wt:** 195 **Born:** 06/21/69 **Age:** 24

Year	Team	Lg	G	GS	CG	GF	IP	BFP	H	R	ER	HR	SH	SF	HB	TBB	IBB	SO	WP	Bk	W	L	Pct.	ShO	Sv	ERA
1990	Hamilton	A	4	4	0	0	20	86	21	8	8	0	1	1	0	5	1	14	1	2	0	2	.000	0	0	3.60
	Savannah	A	6	6	1	0	41.1	169	40	20	12	2	1	1	3	7	0	28	2	3	2	2	.500	0	0	2.61
1991	Arkansas	AA	26	26	3	0	166	696	177	82	67	6	9	4	4	43	3	130	4	4	8	12	.400	0	0	3.63
1992	St. Louis	NL	34	29	0	2	179	754	193	91	75	14	7	4	2	38	2	104	6	0	11	9	.550	0	0	3.77

Al Osuna

Pitches: Left **Bats:** Right **Pos:** RP **Ht:** 6' 3" **Wt:** 200 **Born:** 08/10/65 **Age:** 27

Year	Team	Lg	G	GS	CG	GF	IP	BFP	H	R	ER	HR	SH	SF	HB	TBB	IBB	SO	WP	Bk	W	L	Pct.	ShO	Sv	ERA
1990	Houston	NL	12	0	0	2	11.1	48	10	6	6	1	0	2	3	6	1	6	3	0	2	0	1.000	0	0	4.76

150

Year	Team	Lg	G	GS	CG	GF	IP	BFP	H	R	ER	HR	SH	SF	HB	TBB	IBB	SO	WP	Bk	W	L	Pct.	ShO	Sv	ERA
1991	Houston	NL	71	0	0	32	81.2	353	59	39	31	5	6	5	3	46	5	68	3	1	7	6	.538	0	12	3.42
1992	Houston	NL	66	0	0	17	61.2	270	52	29	29	8	5	6	1	38	5	37	3	1	6	3	.667	0	0	4.23
3 ML YEARS			149	0	0	51	154.2	671	121	74	66	14	11	13	7	90	11	111	9	2	15	9	.625	0	12	3.84

Dave Otto

Pitches: Left **Bats:** Left **Pos:** SP   **Ht:** 6' 7" **Wt:** 210 **Born:** 11/12/64 **Age:** 28

			HOW MUCH HE PITCHED						WHAT HE GAVE UP											THE RESULTS					
Year	Team	Lg	G	GS	CG	GF	IP	BFP	H	R	ER	HR	SH	SF	HB	TBB	IBB	SO	WP	Bk	W	L	Pct.	ShO	Sv	ERA
1987	Oakland	AL	3	0	0	3	6	24	7	6	6	1	0	0	0	1	0	3	0	0	0	0	.000	0	0	9.00
1988	Oakland	AL	3	2	0	1	10	43	9	2	2	0	0	0	0	6	0	7	0	1	0	0	.000	0	0	1.80
1989	Oakland	AL	1	1	0	0	6.2	26	6	2	2	0	1	0	0	2	0	4	0	0	0	0	.000	0	0	2.70
1990	Oakland	AL	2	0	0	2	2.1	13	3	3	2	0	0	0	0	3	0	2	0	0	0	0	.000	0	0	7.71
1991	Cleveland	AL	18	14	1	0	100	425	108	52	47	7	8	4	4	27	6	47	3	0	2	8	.200	0	0	4.23
1992	Cleveland	AL	18	16	0	0	80.1	368	110	64	63	12	3	1	1	33	0	32	5	0	5	9	.357	0	0	7.06
6 ML YEARS			45	33	1	6	205.1	899	243	129	122	20	12	5	5	72	6	95	8	1	7	17	.292	0	0	5.35

Spike Owen

Bats: Both **Throws:** Right **Pos:** SS   **Ht:** 5'10" **Wt:** 170 **Born:** 04/19/61 **Age:** 32

						BATTING													BASERUNNING				PERCENTAGES		
Year	Team	Lg	G	AB	H	2B	3B	HR	(Hm	Rd)	TB	R	RBI	TBB	IBB	SO	HBP	SH	SF	SB	CS	SB%	GDP	Avg	OBP	SLG
1983	Seattle	AL	80	306	60	11	3	2	(1	1)	83	36	21	24	0	44	2	5	3	10	6	.63	2	.196	.257	.271
1984	Seattle	AL	152	530	130	18	8	3	(2	1)	173	67	43	46	0	63	3	9	2	16	8	.67	5	.245	.308	.326
1985	Seattle	AL	118	352	91	10	6	6	(3	3)	131	41	37	34	0	27	0	5	2	11	5	.69	5	.259	.322	.372
1986	2 ML Teams		154	528	122	24	7	1	(0	1)	163	67	45	51	1	51	2	9	3	4	4	.50	13	.231	.300	.309
1987	Boston	AL	132	437	113	17	7	2	(2	0)	150	50	48	53	2	43	1	9	4	11	8	.58	9	.259	.337	.343
1988	Boston	AL	89	257	64	14	1	5	(2	3)	95	40	18	27	0	27	2	7	1	0	1	.00	7	.249	.324	.370
1989	Montreal	NL	142	437	102	17	4	6	(5	1)	145	52	41	76	25	44	3	3	3	3	2	.60	11	.233	.349	.332
1990	Montreal	NL	149	453	106	24	5	5	(2	3)	155	55	35	70	12	60	0	5	5	8	6	.57	6	.234	.333	.342
1991	Montreal	NL	139	424	108	22	8	3	(1	2)	155	39	26	42	11	61	1	4	4	2	6	.25	11	.255	.321	.366
1992	Montreal	NL	122	386	104	16	3	7	(3	4)	147	52	40	50	3	30	0	4	6	9	4	.69	10	.269	.348	.381
1986	Seattle	AL	112	402	99	22	6	0	(0	0)	133	46	35	34	1	42	1	7	2	1	3	.25	11	.246	.305	.331
	Boston	AL	42	126	23	2	1	1	(0	1)	30	21	10	17	0	9	1	2	1	3	1	.75	2	.183	.283	.238
10 ML YEARS			1277	4110	1000	173	52	40	(21	19)	1397	499	354	473	54	450	14	60	33	74	50	.60	79	.243	.321	.340

Mike Pagliarulo

Bats: Left **Throws:** Right **Pos:** 3B   **Ht:** 6' 2" **Wt:** 201 **Born:** 03/15/60 **Age:** 33

						BATTING													BASERUNNING				PERCENTAGES		
Year	Team	Lg	G	AB	H	2B	3B	HR	(Hm	Rd)	TB	R	RBI	TBB	IBB	SO	HBP	SH	SF	SB	CS	SB%	GDP	Avg	OBP	SLG
1984	New York	AL	67	201	48	15	3	7	(4	3)	90	24	34	15	0	46	0	0	3	0	0	.00	5	.239	.288	.448
1985	New York	AL	138	380	91	16	2	19	(8	11)	168	55	62	45	4	86	4	3	3	0	0	.00	6	.239	.324	.442
1986	New York	AL	149	504	120	24	3	28	(14	14)	234	71	71	54	10	120	4	1	2	4	1	.80	10	.238	.316	.464
1987	New York	AL	150	522	122	26	3	32	(17	15)	250	76	87	53	9	111	2	2	3	1	3	.25	9	.234	.305	.479
1988	New York	AL	125	444	96	20	1	15	(8	7)	163	46	67	37	9	104	2	1	6	1	0	1.00	5	.216	.276	.367
1989	2 ML Teams		124	371	73	17	0	7	(5	2)	111	31	30	37	4	82	3	1	0	3	1	.75	5	.197	.275	.299
1990	San Diego	NL	128	398	101	23	2	7	(1	6)	149	29	38	39	3	66	3	2	4	1	3	.25	12	.254	.322	.374
1991	Minnesota	AL	121	365	102	20	0	6	(4	2)	140	38	36	21	3	55	3	2	2	1	2	.33	9	.279	.322	.384
1992	Minnesota	AL	42	105	21	4	0	0	(0	0)	25	10	9	1	0	17	1	0	1	0	1	.00	2	.200	.213	.238
1989	New York	AL	74	223	44	10	0	4	(3	1)	66	19	16	19	0	43	2	0	0	1	1	.50	2	.197	.266	.296
	San Diego		50	148	29	7	0	3	(2	1)	45	12	14	18	4	39	1	1	0	2	0	1.00	3	.196	.287	.304
9 ML YEARS			1044	3290	774	165	14	121	(61	60)	1330	380	434	302	42	687	22	12	24	12	10	.55	62	.235	.302	.404

Tom Pagnozzi

Bats: Right **Throws:** Right **Pos:** C   **Ht:** 6' 1" **Wt:** 190 **Born:** 07/30/62 **Age:** 30

						BATTING													BASERUNNING				PERCENTAGES		
Year	Team	Lg	G	AB	H	2B	3B	HR	(Hm	Rd)	TB	R	RBI	TBB	IBB	SO	HBP	SH	SF	SB	CS	SB%	GDP	Avg	OBP	SLG
1987	St. Louis	NL	27	48	9	1	0	2	(2	0)	16	8	9	4	2	13	0	1	0	1	0	1.00	0	.188	.250	.333
1988	St. Louis	NL	81	195	55	9	0	0	(0	0)	64	17	15	11	1	32	0	2	1	0	0	.00	6	.282	.319	.328
1989	St. Louis	NL	52	80	12	2	0	0	(0	0)	14	3	3	6	2	19	1	0	1	0	0	.00	7	.150	.216	.175
1990	St. Louis	NL	69	220	61	15	0	2	(2	0)	82	20	23	14	1	37	1	0	2	1	1	.50	0	.277	.321	.373
1991	St. Louis	NL	140	459	121	24	5	2	(2	0)	161	38	57	36	6	63	4	6	5	9	13	.41	10	.264	.319	.351
1992	St. Louis	NL	139	485	121	26	3	7	(3	4)	174	33	44	28	9	64	1	6	3	2	5	.29	15	.249	.290	.359
6 ML YEARS			508	1487	379	77	8	13	(9	4)	511	119	151	99	21	228	7	15	12	13	19	.41	37	.255	.302	.344

Vince Palacios

Pitches: Right **Bats:** Right **Pos:** RP/SP **Ht:** 6' 3" **Wt:** 175 **Born:** 07/19/63 **Age:** 29

Year Team	Lg	G	GS	CG	GF	IP	BFP	H	R	ER	HR	SH	SF	HB	TBB	IBB	SO	WP	Bk	W	L	Pct.	ShO	Sv	ERA
1987 Pittsburgh	NL	6	4	0	0	29.1	120	27	14	14	1	2	0	1	9	1	13	0	2	2	1	.667	0	0	4.30
1988 Pittsburgh	NL	7	3	0	0	24.1	113	28	18	18	3	2	1	0	15	1	15	2	3	1	2	.333	0	0	6.66
1990 Pittsburgh	NL	7	0	0	4	15	50	4	0	0	0	0	0	0	2	0	8	2	0	0	0	.000	0	3	0.00
1991 Pittsburgh	NL	36	7	1	8	81.2	347	69	34	34	12	4	1	1	38	2	64	6	2	6	3	.667	1	3	3.75
1992 Pittsburgh	NL	20	8	0	4	53	232	56	25	25	1	4	1	0	27	1	33	7	0	3	2	.600	0	0	4.25
5 ML YEARS		76	22	1	16	203.1	862	184	91	91	17	12	3	2	91	5	133	17	7	12	8	.600	1	6	4.03

Donn Pall

Pitches: Right **Bats:** Right **Pos:** RP **Ht:** 6' 1" **Wt:** 183 **Born:** 01/11/62 **Age:** 31

Year Team	Lg	G	GS	CG	GF	IP	BFP	H	R	ER	HR	SH	SF	HB	TBB	IBB	SO	WP	Bk	W	L	Pct.	ShO	Sv	ERA
1988 Chicago	AL	17	0	0	6	28.2	130	39	11	11	1	2	1	0	8	1	16	1	0	0	2	.000	0	0	3.45
1989 Chicago	AL	53	0	0	27	87	370	90	35	32	9	8	2	8	19	3	58	4	1	4	5	.444	0	6	3.31
1990 Chicago	AL	56	0	0	11	76	306	63	33	28	7	4	2	4	24	8	39	2	0	3	5	.375	0	2	3.32
1991 Chicago	AL	51	0	0	7	71	282	59	22	19	7	4	0	3	20	3	40	2	0	7	2	.778	0	0	2.41
1992 Chicago	AL	39	0	0	12	73	323	79	43	40	9	1	3	2	27	8	27	1	2	5	2	.714	0	1	4.93
5 ML YEARS		216	0	0	63	335.2	1411	330	144	130	33	19	8	17	98	23	180	10	3	19	16	.543	0	9	3.49

Rafael Palmeiro

Bats: Left **Throws:** Left **Pos:** 1B **Ht:** 6' 0" **Wt:** 188 **Born:** 09/24/64 **Age:** 28

Year Team	Lg	G	AB	H	2B	3B	HR	(Hm	Rd)	TB	R	RBI	TBB	IBB	SO	HBP	SH	SF	SB	CS	SB%	GDP	Avg	OBP	SLG
1986 Chicago	NL	22	73	18	4	0	3	(1	2)	31	9	12	4	0	6	1	0	0	1	1	.50	4	.247	.295	.425
1987 Chicago	NL	84	221	61	15	1	14	(5	9)	120	32	30	20	1	26	1	0	2	2	2	.50	4	.276	.336	.543
1988 Chicago	NL	152	580	178	41	5	8	(8	0)	253	75	53	38	6	34	3	2	6	12	2	.86	11	.307	.349	.436
1989 Texas	AL	156	559	154	23	4	8	(4	4)	209	76	64	63	3	48	6	2	2	4	3	.57	18	.275	.354	.374
1990 Texas	AL	154	598	191	35	6	14	(9	5)	280	72	89	40	6	59	3	2	8	3	3	.50	24	.319	.361	.468
1991 Texas	AL	159	631	203	49	3	26	(12	14)	336	115	88	68	10	72	6	2	7	4	3	.57	17	.322	.389	.532
1992 Texas	AL	159	608	163	27	4	22	(8	14)	264	84	85	72	8	83	10	5	6	2	3	.40	10	.268	.352	.434
7 ML YEARS		886	3270	968	194	23	95	(47	48)	1493	463	421	305	34	328	30	13	31	28	17	.62	88	.296	.358	.457

Dean Palmer

Bats: Right **Throws:** Right **Pos:** 3B **Ht:** 6' 2" **Wt:** 195 **Born:** 12/27/68 **Age:** 24

Year Team	Lg	G	AB	H	2B	3B	HR	(Hm	Rd)	TB	R	RBI	TBB	IBB	SO	HBP	SH	SF	SB	CS	SB%	GDP	Avg	OBP	SLG
1989 Texas	AL	16	19	2	2	0	0	(0	0)	4	0	1	0	0	12	0	0	1	0	0	.00	0	.105	.100	.211
1991 Texas	AL	81	268	50	9	2	15	(6	9)	108	38	37	32	0	98	3	1	0	0	2	.00	4	.187	.281	.403
1992 Texas	AL	152	541	124	25	0	26	(11	15)	227	74	72	62	2	154	4	2	4	10	4	.71	9	.229	.311	.420
3 ML YEARS		249	828	176	36	2	41	(17	24)	339	112	110	94	2	264	7	3	5	10	6	.63	13	.213	.297	.409

Mark Parent

Bats: Right **Throws:** Right **Pos:** C **Ht:** 6' 5" **Wt:** 225 **Born:** 09/16/61 **Age:** 31

Year Team	Lg	G	AB	H	2B	3B	HR	(Hm	Rd)	TB	R	RBI	TBB	IBB	SO	HBP	SH	SF	SB	CS	SB%	GDP	Avg	OBP	SLG
1986 San Diego	NL	8	14	2	0	0	0	(0	0)	2	1	0	1	0	3	0	0	0	0	0	.00	1	.143	.200	.143
1987 San Diego	NL	12	25	2	0	0	0	(0	0)	2	0	2	0	0	9	0	0	0	0	0	.00	0	.080	.080	.080
1988 San Diego	NL	41	118	23	3	0	6	(4	2)	44	9	15	6	0	23	0	0	1	0	0	.00	1	.195	.232	.373
1989 San Diego	NL	52	141	27	4	0	7	(6	1)	52	12	21	8	2	34	0	1	4	1	0	1.00	5	.191	.229	.369
1990 San Diego	NL	65	189	42	11	0	3	(1	2)	62	13	16	16	3	29	0	3	0	1	0	1.00	2	.222	.283	.328
1991 Texas	AL	3	1	0	0	0	0	(0	0)	0	0	0	0	0	1	0	0	0	0	0	.00	0	.000	.000	.000
1992 Baltimore	AL	17	34	8	1	0	2	(0	2)	15	4	4	3	0	7	1	2	0	0	0	.00	0	.235	.316	.441
7 ML YEARS		198	522	104	19	0	18	(11	7)	177	39	58	34	5	106	1	6	5	2	0	1.00	9	.199	.247	.339

Clay Parker

Pitches: Right **Bats:** Right **Pos:** SP **Ht:** 6' 1" **Wt:** 175 **Born:** 12/19/62 **Age:** 30

Year Team	Lg	G	GS	CG	GF	IP	BFP	H	R	ER	HR	SH	SF	HB	TBB	IBB	SO	WP	Bk	W	L	Pct.	ShO	Sv	ERA
1987 Seattle	AL	3	1	0	1	7.2	43	15	10	9	2	0	1	1	4	0	8	0	0	0	0	.000	0	0	10.57
1989 New York	AL	22	17	2	1	120	507	123	53	49	12	6	2	2	31	3	53	2	2	4	5	.444	0	0	3.68
1990 2 ML Teams		29	3	0	8	73	308	64	29	29	11	3	3	4	32	6	40	4	0	3	3	.500	0	3	3.58
1992 Seattle	AL	8	6	0	1	33.1	154	47	28	28	6	0	2	2	11	0	20	1	0	0	2	.000	0	0	7.56
1990 New York	AL	5	2	0	1	22	91	19	11	11	5	0	1	0	7	1	20	1	0	1	1	.500	0	0	4.50
Detroit	AL	24	1	0	7	51	217	45	18	18	6	3	2	1	25	5	20	3	0	2	2	.500	0	0	3.18

152

| 4 ML YEARS | 62 | 27 | 2 | 11 | 234 | 1012 | 249 | 120 | 115 | 31 | 9 | 8 | 6 | 78 | 9 | 121 | 7 | 2 | 7 | 10 | .412 | 0 | 0 | 4.42 |

Derek Parks

Bats: Right **Throws:** Right **Pos:** C   **Ht:** 6' 0" **Wt:** 205 **Born:** 09/29/68 **Age:** 24

								BATTING											BASERUNNING				PERCENTAGES		
Year Team	Lg	G	AB	H	2B	3B	HR	(Hm	Rd)	TB	R	RBI	TBB	IBB	SO	HBP	SH	SF	SB	CS	SB%	GDP	Avg	OBP	SLG
1986 Elizabethtn	R	62	224	53	10	1	10	--	--	95	39	40	23	0	58	5	0	3	1	0	1.00	3	.237	.318	.424
1987 Kenosha	A	129	466	115	19	2	24	--	--	210	70	94	77	5	111	10	0	6	1	1	.50	12	.247	.361	.451
1988 Orlando	AA	118	400	94	15	0	7	--	--	130	52	42	49	1	81	15	0	5	1	1	.50	12	.235	.337	.325
1989 Orlando	AA	31	95	18	3	0	2	--	--	27	16	10	19	0	27	6	0	1	0	0	1.00	1	.189	.358	.284
1990 Portland	AAA	76	231	41	8	1	11	--	--	84	27	27	18	0	56	8	0	1	0	0	.00	6	.177	.260	.364
1991 Orlando	AA	92	256	55	14	0	6	--	--	87	31	31	31	1	64	12	2	3	0	0	.00	4	.215	.325	.340
1992 Portland	AAA	79	249	61	12	0	12	--	--	109	33	49	25	0	47	4	4	6	0	1	.00	6	.245	.317	.438
1992 Minnesota	AL	7	6	2	0	0	0	(0	0)	2	1	0	1	0	1	1	0	0	0	0	.00	0	.333	.500	.333

Jeff Parrett

Pitches: Right **Bats:** Right **Pos:** RP   **Ht:** 6' 3" **Wt:** 195 **Born:** 08/26/61 **Age:** 31

		HOW MUCH HE PITCHED						WHAT HE GAVE UP										THE RESULTS					
Year Team	Lg	G	GS	CG	GF	IP	BFP	H	R	ER	HR	SH	SF	HB	TBB	IBB	SO	WP	Bk	W	L	Pct.	ShO	Sv	ERA
1986 Montreal	NL	12	0	0	6	20.1	91	19	11	11	3	0	1	0	13	0	21	2	0	0	1	.000	0	0	4.87
1987 Montreal	NL	45	0	0	26	62	267	53	33	29	8	5	1	0	30	4	56	6	1	7	6	.538	0	6	4.21
1988 Montreal	NL	61	0	0	34	91.2	369	66	29	27	8	9	6	1	45	9	62	4	1	12	4	.750	0	6	2.65
1989 Philadelphia	NL	72	0	0	34	105.2	444	90	43	35	6	7	5	0	44	13	98	7	3	12	6	.667	0	6	2.98
1990 2 ML Teams		67	5	0	19	108.2	479	119	62	56	11	7	5	2	55	10	86	5	1	5	10	.333	0	2	4.64
1991 Atlanta	NL	18	0	0	9	21.1	109	31	18	15	2	2	0	0	12	2	14	4	0	1	2	.333	0	1	6.33
1992 Oakland	AL	66	0	0	14	98.1	410	81	35	33	7	4	4	2	42	3	78	13	0	9	1	.900	0	0	3.02
1990 Philadelphia	NL	47	5	0	14	81.2	355	92	51	47	10	3	1	1	36	8	69	3	1	4	9	.308	0	1	5.18
Atlanta	NL	20	0	0	5	27	124	27	11	9	1	4	4	1	19	2	17	2	0	1	1	.500	0	1	3.00
7 ML YEARS		341	5	0	142	508	2169	459	231	206	45	34	22	5	241	41	415	41	6	46	30	.605	0	21	3.65

Lance Parrish

Bats: Right **Throws:** Right **Pos:** C/1B/DH   **Ht:** 6' 3" **Wt:** 224 **Born:** 06/15/56 **Age:** 37

								BATTING											BASERUNNING				PERCENTAGES		
Year Team	Lg	G	AB	H	2B	3B	HR	(Hm	Rd)	TB	R	RBI	TBB	IBB	SO	HBP	SH	SF	SB	CS	SB%	GDP	Avg	OBP	SLG
1977 Detroit	AL	12	46	9	2	0	3	(2	1)	20	10	7	5	0	12	0	0	0	0	0	.00	2	.196	.275	.435
1978 Detroit	AL	85	288	63	11	3	14	(7	7)	122	37	41	11	0	71	3	1	1	0	0	.00	8	.219	.254	.424
1979 Detroit	AL	143	493	136	26	3	19	(8	11)	225	65	65	49	2	105	2	3	1	6	7	.46	15	.276	.343	.456
1980 Detroit	AL	144	553	158	34	6	24	(7	17)	276	79	82	31	3	109	3	2	3	6	4	.60	24	.286	.325	.499
1981 Detroit	AL	96	348	85	18	2	10	(8	2)	137	39	46	34	6	52	0	1	1	2	3	.40	16	.244	.311	.394
1982 Detroit	AL	133	486	138	19	2	32	(22	10)	257	75	87	40	5	99	1	0	2	3	4	.43	5	.284	.338	.529
1983 Detroit	AL	155	605	163	42	3	27	(12	15)	292	80	114	44	7	106	1	0	13	1	3	.25	21	.269	.314	.483
1984 Detroit	AL	147	578	137	16	2	33	(13	20)	256	75	98	41	6	120	2	2	6	2	3	.40	12	.237	.287	.443
1985 Detroit	AL	140	549	150	27	1	28	(11	17)	263	64	98	41	5	90	2	3	5	2	6	.25	10	.273	.323	.479
1986 Detroit	AL	91	327	84	6	1	22	(8	14)	158	53	62	38	3	83	5	1	3	0	0	.00	3	.257	.340	.483
1987 Philadelphia	NL	130	466	114	21	0	17	(5	12)	186	42	67	47	2	104	1	1	1	0	0	.00	23	.245	.313	.399
1988 Philadelphia	NL	123	424	91	17	2	15	(11	4)	157	44	60	47	7	93	2	0	5	0	0	.00	11	.215	.293	.370
1989 California	AL	124	433	103	12	1	17	(8	9)	168	48	50	42	6	104	2	1	4	1	1	.50	10	.238	.306	.388
1990 California	AL	133	470	126	14	0	24	(14	10)	212	54	70	46	4	107	5	0	2	2	2	.50	12	.268	.338	.451
1991 California	AL	119	402	87	12	0	19	(9	10)	156	38	51	35	2	117	5	0	1	0	1	.00	7	.216	.285	.388
1992 2 ML Teams		93	275	64	13	1	12	(7	5)	115	26	32	24	3	70	1	1	3	1	1	.50	7	.233	.294	.418
1992 California	AL	24	83	19	2	0	4	(1	3)	33	7	11	5	1	22	0	1	1	0	0	.00	1	.229	.270	.398
Seattle	AL	69	192	45	11	1	8	(6	2)	82	19	21	19	2	48	1	0	2	1	1	.50	6	.234	.304	.427
16 ML YEARS		1868	6743	1708	290	27	316	(152	164)	3000	829	1030	575	61	1442	35	16	55	26	36	.42	186	.253	.313	.445

Dan Pasqua

Bats: Left **Throws:** Left **Pos:** RF   **Ht:** 6' 0" **Wt:** 203 **Born:** 10/17/61 **Age:** 31

								BATTING											BASERUNNING				PERCENTAGES		
Year Team	Lg	G	AB	H	2B	3B	HR	(Hm	Rd)	TB	R	RBI	TBB	IBB	SO	HBP	SH	SF	SB	CS	SB%	GDP	Avg	OBP	SLG
1985 New York	AL	60	148	31	3	1	9	(7	2)	63	17	25	16	4	38	1	0	1	0	0	.00	1	.209	.289	.426
1986 New York	AL	102	280	82	17	0	16	(9	7)	147	44	45	47	3	78	3	1	1	2	0	1.00	4	.293	.399	.525
1987 New York	AL	113	318	74	7	1	17	(6	11)	134	42	42	40	3	99	1	2	1	0	2	.00	7	.233	.319	.421
1988 Chicago	AL	129	422	96	16	2	20	(11	9)	176	48	50	46	5	100	3	2	2	1	0	1.00	10	.227	.307	.417
1989 Chicago	AL	73	246	61	9	1	11	(5	6)	105	26	47	25	1	58	1	1	4	1	2	.33	0	.248	.315	.427
1990 Chicago	AL	112	325	89	27	3	13	(4	9)	161	43	58	37	7	66	2	0	5	1	1	.50	4	.274	.347	.495
1991 Chicago	AL	134	417	108	22	5	18	(10	8)	194	71	66	62	4	86	3	1	1	0	0	.00	9	.259	.358	.465
1992 Chicago	AL	93	265	56	16	1	6	(2	4)	92	26	33	36	1	57	1	1	3	0	1	.00	4	.211	.305	.347

Bob Patterson

Pitches: Left **Bats: Right** **Pos: RP**   **Ht: 6' 2"** **Wt: 185** **Born: 05/16/59** **Age: 34**

		HOW MUCH HE PITCHED						WHAT HE GAVE UP												THE RESULTS					
Year Team	Lg	G	GS	CG	GF	IP	BFP	H	R	ER	HR	SH	SF	HB	TBB	IBB	SO	WP	Bk	W	L	Pct.	ShO	Sv	ERA
1985 San Diego	NL	3	0	0	2	4	26	13	11	11	2	0	0	0	3	0	1	0	1	0	0	.000	0	0	24.75
1986 Pittsburgh	NL	11	5	0	2	36.1	159	49	20	20	0	1	1	0	5	2	20	0	1	2	3	.400	0	0	4.95
1987 Pittsburgh	NL	15	7	0	2	43	201	49	34	32	5	6	3	1	22	4	27	1	0	1	4	.200	0	0	6.70
1989 Pittsburgh	NL	12	3	0	2	26.2	109	23	13	12	3	1	1	0	8	2	20	0	0	4	3	.571	0	0	4.05
1990 Pittsburgh	NL	55	5	0	19	94.2	386	88	33	31	9	5	3	3	21	7	70	1	2	8	5	.615	0	5	2.95
1991 Pittsburgh	NL	54	1	0	19	65.2	270	67	32	30	7	2	2	0	15	1	57	0	0	4	3	.571	0	2	4.11
1992 Pittsburgh	NL	60	0	0	26	64.2	268	59	22	21	7	3	2	0	23	6	43	3	0	6	3	.667	0	9	2.92
7 ML YEARS		210	21	0	72	335	1419	348	165	157	33	18	12	4	97	22	238	5	4	25	21	.543	0	17	4.22

John Patterson

Bats: Both **Throws: Right** **Pos: 2B**   **Ht: 5' 9"** **Wt: 160** **Born: 02/11/67** **Age: 26**

		BATTING																BASERUNNING				PERCENTAGES		
Year Team	Lg	G	AB	H	2B	3B	HR	(Hm	Rd)	TB	R	RBI	TBB	IBB	SO	HBP	SH	SF	SB	CS	SB%	GDP	Avg	OBP	SLG
1988 Everett	A	58	232	58	10	4	0	--	--	76	37	26	18	0	27	0	0	1	21	3	.88	1	.250	.303	.328
1990 San Jose	A	131	530	160	23	6	4	--	--	207	91	66	46	2	74	9	5	6	29	17	.63	7	.302	.364	.391
1991 Shreveport	AA	117	464	137	31	13	4	--	--	206	81	56	30	3	63	11	3	3	40	19	.68	9	.295	.350	.444
1992 Phoenix	AAA	94	362	109	20	6	2	--	--	147	52	37	33	4	45	5	0	2	22	18	.55	3	.301	.366	.406
1992 San Francisco	NL	32	103	19	1	1	0	(0	0)	22	10	4	5	0	24	1	0	0	5	1	.83	2	.184	.229	.214

Ken Patterson

Pitches: Left **Bats: Left** **Pos: RP**   **Ht: 6' 4"** **Wt: 210** **Born: 07/08/64** **Age: 28**

		HOW MUCH HE PITCHED						WHAT HE GAVE UP												THE RESULTS					
Year Team	Lg	G	GS	CG	GF	IP	BFP	H	R	ER	HR	SH	SF	HB	TBB	IBB	SO	WP	Bk	W	L	Pct.	ShO	Sv	ERA
1988 Chicago	AL	9	2	0	3	20.2	92	25	11	11	2	0	0	0	7	0	8	1	1	0	2	.000	0	1	4.79
1989 Chicago	AL	50	1	0	18	66.1	284	64	37	33	11	4	4	2	28	3	43	3	1	6	1	.857	0	0	4.52
1990 Chicago	AL	43	0	0	15	66.1	283	58	27	25	6	2	5	2	34	1	40	2	0	2	1	.667	0	2	3.39
1991 Chicago	AL	43	0	0	13	63.2	265	48	22	20	5	3	2	1	35	1	32	2	0	3	0	1.000	0	1	2.83
1992 Chicago	NL	32	1	0	4	41.2	191	41	25	18	7	6	4	1	27	6	23	3	1	2	3	.400	0	0	3.89
5 ML YEARS		177	4	0	53	258	1115	236	122	107	31	12	15	6	131	11	146	11	3	13	7	.650	0	4	3.73

Roger Pavlik

Pitches: Right **Bats: Right** **Pos: SP**   **Ht: 6' 2"** **Wt: 220** **Born: 10/04/67** **Age: 25**

		HOW MUCH HE PITCHED						WHAT HE GAVE UP												THE RESULTS					
Year Team	Lg	G	GS	CG	GF	IP	BFP	H	R	ER	HR	SH	SF	HB	TBB	IBB	SO	WP	Bk	W	L	Pct.	ShO	Sv	ERA
1987 Gastonia	A	15	14	0	0	67.1	303	66	46	37	3	1	4	5	42	0	55	6	0	2	7	.222	0	0	4.95
1988 Gastonia	A	18	16	0	1	84.1	408	94	65	43	3	4	0	6	58	2	89	10	3	2	12	.143	0	0	4.59
Butte	R	8	8	1	0	49	223	45	29	25	2	2	1	7	34	0	56	3	0	4	0	1.000	1	0	4.59
1989 Charlotte	A	26	22	1	2	118.2	511	92	60	45	5	4	4	8	72	1	98	12	4	3	8	.273	1	1	3.41
1990 Charlotte	A	11	11	1	0	66.1	279	50	21	18	1	2	0	5	40	3	76	6	1	5	3	.625	0	0	2.44
Tulsa	AA	16	16	2	0	100.1	418	66	29	26	4	3	1	5	71	2	91	7	2	6	5	.545	1	0	2.33
1991 Okla City	AAA	8	7	0	0	26	126	19	21	15	1	0	1	1	26	1	43	5	1	0	5	.000	0	0	5.19
1992 Okla City	AAA	18	18	0	0	117.2	485	90	44	39	7	3	8	4	51	0	104	14	1	7	5	.583	0	0	2.98
1992 Texas	AL	13	12	1	0	62	275	66	32	29	3	0	2	3	34	0	45	9	0	4	4	.500	0	0	4.21

Bill Pecota

Bats: Right **Throws: Right** **Pos: 3B/2B/SS**   **Ht: 6' 2"** **Wt: 195** **Born: 02/16/60** **Age: 33**

		BATTING																BASERUNNING				PERCENTAGES		
Year Team	Lg	G	AB	H	2B	3B	HR	(Hm	Rd)	TB	R	RBI	TBB	IBB	SO	HBP	SH	SF	SB	CS	SB%	GDP	Avg	OBP	SLG
1986 Kansas City	AL	12	29	6	2	0	0	(0	0)	8	3	2	3	0	3	1	0	1	0	2	.00	1	.207	.294	.276
1987 Kansas City	AL	66	156	43	5	1	3	(0	3)	59	22	14	15	0	25	1	0	0	5	0	1.00	3	.276	.343	.378
1988 Kansas City	AL	90	178	37	3	3	1	(0	1)	49	25	15	18	0	34	2	7	1	7	2	.78	1	.208	.286	.275
1989 Kansas City	AL	65	83	17	4	2	3	(0	3)	34	21	5	7	1	9	1	1	0	5	0	1.00	4	.205	.275	.410
1990 Kansas City	AL	87	240	58	15	2	5	(3	2)	92	43	20	33	0	39	1	6	0	8	5	.62	5	.242	.336	.383
1991 Kansas City	AL	125	398	114	23	2	6	(4	2)	159	53	45	41	6	45	2	7	0	16	7	.70	12	.286	.356	.399
1992 New York	NL	117	269	61	13	0	2	(1	1)	80	28	26	25	3	40	1	5	2	9	3	.75	7	.227	.293	.297
7 ML YEARS		562	1353	336	65	10	20	(8	12)	481	195	127	142	10	195	9	26	4	50	19	.72	33	.248	.323	.356

Jorge Pedre

Bats: Right **Throws:** Right **Pos:** C   **Ht:** 5'11" **Wt:** 210 **Born:** 10/12/66 **Age:** 26

					BATTING														BASERUNNING				PERCENTAGES		
Year	Team	Lg	G	AB	H	2B	3B	HR	(Hm	Rd)	TB	R	RBI	TBB	IBB	SO	HBP	SH	SF	SB	CS	SB%	GDP	Avg	OBP	SLG
1987	Eugene	A	64	233	63	15	0	13	--	--	117	28	66	16	2	48	12	0	1	2	1	.67	10	.270	.347	.502
1988	Appleton	A	111	412	112	20	2	6	--	--	154	44	54	23	1	76	4	0	6	4	2	.67	7	.272	.312	.374
1989	Baseball Cy	A	55	208	68	17	2	5	--	--	104	39	40	13	1	31	4	0	3	1	2	.33	2	.327	.373	.500
	Memphis	AA	38	141	33	5	0	2	--	--	44	17	16	9	0	18	0	1	2	0	0	.00	4	.234	.276	.312
1990	Memphis	AA	99	360	93	14	1	9	--	--	136	55	54	27	1	47	6	0	7	6	1	.86	17	.258	.315	.378
1991	Memphis	AA	100	363	92	28	1	9	--	--	149	43	59	24	4	72	7	1	3	1	2	.33	7	.253	.310	.410
	Omaha	AAA	31	116	25	4	0	1	--	--	32	12	4	4	0	18	0	0	0	2	1	.67	1	.216	.242	.276
1992	Iowa	AAA	98	296	75	17	0	6	--	--	112	31	34	26	1	62	1	5	1	2	0	1.00	10	.253	.315	.378
1991	Kansas City	AL	10	19	5	1	1	0	(0	0)	8	2	3	3	0	5	0	0	0	0	0	.00	0	.263	.364	.421
1992	Chicago	NL	4	4	0	0	0	0	(0	0)	0	0	0	0	0	1	0	0	0	0	0	.00	0	.000	.000	.000
	2 ML YEARS		14	23	5	1	1	0	(0	0)	8	2	3	3	0	6	0	0	0	0	0	.00	0	.217	.308	.348

Julio Peguero

Bats: Both **Throws:** Right **Pos:** CF   **Ht:** 6'0" **Wt:** 160 **Born:** 09/07/68 **Age:** 24

					BATTING														BASERUNNING				PERCENTAGES		
Year	Team	Lg	G	AB	H	2B	3B	HR	(Hm	Rd)	TB	R	RBI	TBB	IBB	SO	HBP	SH	SF	SB	CS	SB%	GDP	Avg	OBP	SLG
1987	Macon	A	132	520	148	11	6	4	--	--	183	88	53	56	3	76	1	1	4	23	9	.72	5	.285	.353	.352
1988	Salem	A	128	517	135	17	5	5	--	--	177	86	50	64	3	81	5	2	1	43	11	.80	11	.261	.348	.342
1989	Harrisburg	AA	76	284	70	14	1	2	--	--	92	34	21	29	0	39	2	1	0	14	12	.54	5	.246	.321	.324
1990	Harrisburg	AA	104	411	116	14	9	1	--	--	151	40	26	29	1	53	0	0	2	8	12	.40	17	.282	.328	.367
	Reading	AA	3	12	1	0	0	0	--	--	1	0	2	2	0	1	0	0	0	0	0	.00	0	.083	.214	.083
1991	Scranton-Wb	AAA	133	506	138	20	9	2	--	--	182	71	39	40	3	71	1	5	2	21	14	.60	12	.273	.326	.360
1992	Scranton/wb	AAA	74	289	74	14	2	1	--	--	95	41	21	24	2	56	2	2	2	14	14	.50	5	.256	.315	.329
	Albuquerque	AAA	30	76	20	4	0	1	--	--	27	13	8	13	0	13	2	2	1	1	1	.50	1	.263	.380	.355
1992	Philadelphia	NL	14	9	2	0	0	0	(0	0)	2	3	0	3	0	3	0	0	0	0	0	.00	0	.222	.417	.222

Dan Peltier

Bats: Left **Throws:** Left **Pos:** RF   **Ht:** 6'1" **Wt:** 200 **Born:** 06/30/68 **Age:** 25

					BATTING														BASERUNNING				PERCENTAGES		
Year	Team	Lg	G	AB	H	2B	3B	HR	(Hm	Rd)	TB	R	RBI	TBB	IBB	SO	HBP	SH	SF	SB	CS	SB%	GDP	Avg	OBP	SLG
1989	Butte	R	33	122	49	7	1	7	--	--	79	35	28	25	2	16	1	0	0	10	1	.91	4	.402	.507	.648
1990	Tulsa	AA	117	448	125	19	4	11	--	--	185	66	57	40	2	67	6	1	2	8	6	.57	8	.279	.345	.413
1991	Okla City	AAA	94	345	79	16	4	3	--	--	112	38	31	43	2	71	0	2	2	6	5	.55	8	.229	.313	.325
1992	Okla City	AAA	125	450	133	30	7	7	--	--	198	65	53	60	3	72	3	3	1	1	7	.13	14	.296	.381	.440
1992	Texas	AL	12	24	4	0	0	0	(0	0)	4	1	2	0	0	3	0	0	0	0	0	.00	0	.167	.167	.167

Alejandro Pena

Pitches: Right **Bats:** Right **Pos:** RP   **Ht:** 6'1" **Wt:** 203 **Born:** 06/25/59 **Age:** 34

			HOW MUCH HE PITCHED					WHAT HE GAVE UP											THE RESULTS					
Year	Team	Lg	G	GS	CG	GF	IP	BFP	H	R	ER	HR	SH	SF	HB	TBB	IBB	SO	WP	Bk	W	L	Pct.	ShO	Sv	ERA
1981	Los Angeles	NL	14	0	0	7	25	104	18	8	8	2	0	0	0	11	1	14	0	0	1	1	.500	0	2	2.88
1982	Los Angeles	NL	29	0	0	11	35.2	160	37	24	19	2	2	0	1	21	7	20	1	1	0	2	.000	0	0	4.79
1983	Los Angeles	NL	34	26	4	4	177	730	152	67	54	7	8	5	1	51	7	120	2	1	12	9	.571	3	1	2.75
1984	Los Angeles	NL	28	28	8	0	199.1	813	186	67	55	7	6	2	3	46	7	135	5	1	12	6	.667	4	0	2.48
1985	Los Angeles	NL	2	1	0	0	4.1	23	7	5	4	1	0	0	0	3	1	2	0	0	0	1	.000	0	0	8.31
1986	Los Angeles	NL	24	10	0	6	70	309	74	40	38	6	3	1	1	30	5	46	1	1	1	2	.333	0	1	4.89
1987	Los Angeles	NL	37	7	0	17	87.1	377	82	41	34	9	5	6	2	37	5	76	0	1	2	7	.222	0	11	3.50
1988	Los Angeles	NL	60	0	0	31	94.1	378	75	29	20	4	3	3	1	27	6	83	3	2	6	7	.462	0	12	1.91
1989	Los Angeles	NL	53	0	0	28	76	306	62	20	18	6	3	1	2	18	4	75	1	1	4	3	.571	0	5	2.13
1990	New York	NL	52	0	0	32	76	320	71	31	27	4	1	6	1	22	5	76	0	0	3	3	.500	0	5	3.20
1991	2 ML Teams		59	0	0	36	82.1	331	74	23	22	6	3	4	0	22	4	62	1	2	8	1	.889	0	15	2.40
1992	Atlanta	NL	41	0	0	31	42	173	40	19	19	7	2	1	0	13	5	34	0	0	1	6	.143	0	15	4.07
1991	New York	NL	44	0	0	24	63	261	63	20	19	5	2	4	0	19	4	49	1	2	6	1	.857	0	4	2.71
	Atlanta	NL	15	0	0	12	19.1	70	11	3	3	1	1	0	0	3	0	13	0	0	2	0	1.000	0	11	1.40
	12 ML YEARS		433	72	12	203	969.1	4024	878	374	318	61	36	29	12	301	57	743	14	10	50	48	.510	7	67	2.95

Geronimo Pena

Bats: Both **Throws:** Right **Pos:** 2B   **Ht:** 6'1" **Wt:** 170 **Born:** 03/29/67 **Age:** 26

					BATTING														BASERUNNING				PERCENTAGES		
Year	Team	Lg	G	AB	H	2B	3B	HR	(Hm	Rd)	TB	R	RBI	TBB	IBB	SO	HBP	SH	SF	SB	CS	SB%	GDP	Avg	OBP	SLG
1990	St. Louis	NL	18	45	11	2	0	0	(0	0)	13	5	2	4	0	14	1	0	1	1	1	.50	0	.244	.314	.289
1991	St. Louis	NL	104	185	45	8	3	5	(1	4)	74	38	17	18	1	45	5	1	3	15	5	.75	0	.243	.322	.400
1992	St. Louis	NL	62	203	62	12	1	7	(4	3)	97	31	31	24	0	37	5	0	4	13	8	.62	1	.305	.386	.478

155

| 3 ML YEARS | 184 | 433 | 118 | 22 | 4 | 12 | (5 | 7) | 184 | 74 | 50 | 46 | 1 | 96 | 11 | 1 | 8 | 29 | 14 | .67 | 1 | .273 | .351 | .425 |

Jim Pena

Pitches: Left   **Bats:** Left   **Pos:** RP   **Ht:** 6' 0"   **Wt:** 175   **Born:** 09/17/64   **Age:** 28

			HOW MUCH HE PITCHED						WHAT HE GAVE UP											THE RESULTS					
Year Team	Lg	G	GS	CG	GF	IP	BFP	H	R	ER	HR	SH	SF	HB	TBB	IBB	SO	WP	Bk	W	L	Pct.	ShO	Sv	ERA
1986 Everett	A	14	14	4	0	101.2	0	86	40	33	7	0	0	0	54	0	92	2	2	10	2	.833	0	0	2.92
1987 Clinton	A	26	26	6	0	161	690	158	90	71	15	6	5	3	80	0	142	6	2	10	11	.476	2	0	3.97
1989 Salinas	A	8	6	0	1	42.2	165	28	15	11	3	0	3	0	14	0	47	1	0	3	4	.429	0	0	2.32
San Jose	A	16	15	1	0	97.1	408	84	45	33	9	1	2	2	35	0	71	2	4	4	8	.333	1	0	3.05
1990 Shreveport	AA	25	24	1	0	139	593	138	70	57	9	3	9	2	57	2	101	8	2	10	7	.588	0	0	3.69
1991 Shreveport	AA	45	3	1	16	83	362	84	56	44	9	3	5	0	41	5	51	3	2	7	4	.636	0	2	4.77
1992 Phoenix	AAA	33	2	0	12	39	174	45	22	18	4	4	0	0	20	6	27	0	0	7	3	.700	0	1	4.15
1992 San Francisco	NL	25	2	0	4	44	204	49	19	17	4	8	1	1	20	5	32	0	0	1	1	.500	0	0	3.48

Tony Pena

Bats: Right   **Throws:** Right   **Pos:** C   **Ht:** 6' 0"   **Wt:** 185   **Born:** 06/04/57   **Age:** 36

								BATTING											BASERUNNING				PERCENTAGES		
Year Team	Lg	G	AB	H	2B	3B	HR	(Hm	Rd)	TB	R	RBI	TBB	IBB	SO	HBP	SH	SF	SB	CS	SB%	GDP	Avg	OBP	SLG
1980 Pittsburgh	NL	8	21	9	1	1	0	(0	0)	12	1	1	0	0	4	0	0	0	0	1	.00	1	.429	.429	.571
1981 Pittsburgh	NL	66	210	63	9	1	2	(1	1)	80	16	17	8	2	23	1	2	2	1	2	.33	4	.300	.326	.381
1982 Pittsburgh	NL	138	497	147	28	4	11	(5	6)	216	53	63	17	3	57	4	3	2	2	5	.29	17	.296	.323	.435
1983 Pittsburgh	NL	151	542	163	22	3	15	(8	7)	236	51	70	31	8	73	0	6	1	6	7	.46	13	.301	.338	.435
1984 Pittsburgh	NL	147	546	156	27	2	15	(7	8)	232	77	78	36	5	79	4	4	2	12	8	.60	14	.286	.333	.425
1985 Pittsburgh	NL	147	546	136	27	2	10	(2	8)	197	53	59	29	4	67	0	7	5	12	8	.60	19	.249	.284	.361
1986 Pittsburgh	NL	144	510	147	26	2	10	(5	5)	207	56	52	53	6	69	1	0	1	9	10	.47	21	.288	.356	.406
1987 St. Louis	NL	116	384	82	13	4	5	(1	4)	118	40	44	36	9	54	1	2	2	6	1	.86	19	.214	.281	.307
1988 St. Louis	NL	149	505	133	23	1	10	(4	6)	188	55	51	33	11	60	1	3	4	6	2	.75	12	.263	.308	.372
1989 St. Louis	NL	141	424	110	17	2	4	(3	1)	143	36	37	35	19	33	2	2	1	5	3	.63	19	.259	.318	.337
1990 Boston	AL	143	491	129	19	1	7	(3	4)	171	62	56	43	3	71	1	2	3	8	6	.57	23	.263	.322	.348
1991 Boston	AL	141	464	107	23	2	5	(2	3)	149	45	48	37	1	53	4	4	3	8	3	.73	23	.231	.291	.321
1992 Boston	AL	133	410	99	21	1	1	(1	0)	125	39	38	24	0	61	1	13	2	3	2	.60	11	.241	.284	.305
13 ML YEARS		1624	5550	1481	256	26	95	(42	53)	2074	584	614	382	71	704	20	48	28	78	58	.57	196	.267	.315	.374

Terry Pendleton

Bats: Both   **Throws:** Right   **Pos:** 3B   **Ht:** 5' 9"   **Wt:** 195   **Born:** 07/16/60   **Age:** 32

								BATTING											BASERUNNING				PERCENTAGES		
Year Team	Lg	G	AB	H	2B	3B	HR	(Hm	Rd)	TB	R	RBI	TBB	IBB	SO	HBP	SH	SF	SB	CS	SB%	GDP	Avg	OBP	SLG
1984 St. Louis	NL	67	262	85	16	3	1	(0	1)	110	37	33	16	3	32	0	0	5	20	5	.80	7	.324	.357	.420
1985 St. Louis	NL	149	559	134	16	3	5	(3	2)	171	56	69	37	4	75	0	3	3	17	12	.59	18	.240	.285	.306
1986 St. Louis	NL	159	578	138	26	5	1	(0	1)	177	56	59	34	10	59	1	6	7	24	6	.80	12	.239	.279	.306
1987 St. Louis	NL	159	583	167	29	4	12	(5	7)	240	82	96	70	6	74	2	3	9	19	12	.61	18	.286	.360	.412
1988 St. Louis	NL	110	391	99	20	2	6	(3	3)	141	44	53	21	4	51	2	4	3	3	3	.50	9	.253	.293	.361
1989 St. Louis	NL	162	613	162	28	5	13	(8	5)	239	83	74	44	3	81	0	2	2	9	5	.64	16	.264	.313	.390
1990 St. Louis	NL	121	447	103	20	2	6	(6	0)	145	46	58	30	8	58	1	0	6	7	5	.58	12	.230	.277	.324
1991 Atlanta	NL	153	586	187	34	8	22	(13	9)	303	94	86	43	8	70	1	7	7	10	2	.83	16	.319	.363	.517
1992 Atlanta	NL	160	640	199	39	1	21	(13	8)	303	98	105	37	8	67	0	5	7	5	2	.71	16	.311	.345	.473
9 ML YEARS		1240	4659	1274	228	33	87	(51	36)	1829	596	633	332	54	567	7	30	49	114	52	.69	124	.273	.320	.393

William Pennyfeather

Bats: Right   **Throws:** Right   **Pos:** CF   **Ht:** 6' 2"   **Wt:** 195   **Born:** 05/25/68   **Age:** 25

								BATTING											BASERUNNING				PERCENTAGES		
Year Team	Lg	G	AB	H	2B	3B	HR	(Hm	Rd)	TB	R	RBI	TBB	IBB	SO	HBP	SH	SF	SB	CS	SB%	GDP	Avg	OBP	SLG
1988 Pirates	R	17	74	18	2	1	1	--	--	25	6	7	2	0	18	0	0	1	3	3	.50	0	.243	.260	.338
Princeton	R	16	57	19	2	0	1	--	--	24	11	5	6	0	15	0	0	0	2	2	.78	0	.333	.397	.421
1989 Welland	A	75	289	55	10	1	3	--	--	76	34	26	12	1	75	2	1	6	18	5	.78	6	.190	.223	.263
1990 Augusta	A	122	465	122	14	4	4	--	--	156	69	48	23	0	85	3	3	3	21	10	.68	7	.262	.300	.335
1991 Salem	A	81	319	85	17	3	8	--	--	132	35	46	8	0	52	1	1	2	11	8	.58	9	.266	.285	.414
Carolina	AA	42	149	41	5	0	0	--	--	46	13	9	7	0	17	1	1	1	3	2	.60	8	.275	.310	.309
1992 Carolina	AA	51	199	67	13	1	6	--	--	100	28	25	9	1	34	0	0	3	7	6	.54	5	.337	.360	.503
Buffalo	AAA	55	160	38	6	2	1	--	--	51	19	12	2	0	24	3	2	3	3	2	.60	4	.238	.261	.319
1992 Pittsburgh	NL	15	9	2	0	0	0	(0	0)	2	2	0	0	0	0	0	0	0	0	0	.00	1	.222	.222	.222

Melido Perez

Pitches: Right **Bats:** Right **Pos:** SP **Ht:** 6' 4" **Wt:** 180 **Born:** 02/15/66 **Age:** 27

			HOW MUCH HE PITCHED						WHAT HE GAVE UP										THE RESULTS					
Year Team	Lg	G	GS	CG	GF	IP	BFP	H	R	ER	HR	SH	SF	HB	TBB	IBB	SO	WP	Bk	W	L	Pct.	ShO	Sv	ERA
1987 Kansas City	AL	3	3	0	0	10.1	53	18	12	9	2	0	0	0	5	0	5	0	0	1	1	.500	0	0	7.84
1988 Chicago	AL	32	32	3	0	197	836	186	105	83	26	5	8	2	72	0	138	13	3	12	10	.545	1	0	3.79
1989 Chicago	AL	31	31	2	0	183.1	810	187	106	102	23	5	4	3	90	3	141	12	5	11	14	.440	0	0	5.01
1990 Chicago	AL	35	35	3	0	197	833	177	111	101	14	4	6	2	86	1	161	8	4	13	14	.481	3	0	4.61
1991 Chicago	AL	49	8	0	16	135.2	553	111	49	47	15	4	1	1	52	0	128	11	1	8	7	.533	0	1	3.12
1992 New York	AL	33	33	10	0	247.2	1013	212	94	79	16	6	8	5	93	5	218	13	0	13	16	.448	1	0	2.87
6 ML YEARS		183	142	18	16	971	4098	891	477	421	96	24	27	13	398	9	791	57	13	58	62	.483	5	1	3.90

Mike Perez

Pitches: Right **Bats:** Right **Pos:** RP **Ht:** 6' 0" **Wt:** 187 **Born:** 10/19/64 **Age:** 28

			HOW MUCH HE PITCHED						WHAT HE GAVE UP										THE RESULTS					
Year Team	Lg	G	GS	CG	GF	IP	BFP	H	R	ER	HR	SH	SF	HB	TBB	IBB	SO	WP	Bk	W	L	Pct.	ShO	Sv	ERA
1986 Johnson Cty	R	18	8	2	6	72.2	314	69	35	24	3	1	2	5	22	0	72	1	0	3	5	.375	0	3	2.97
1987 Springfield	A	58	0	0	51	84.1	321	47	12	8	2	3	2	2	21	3	119	2	0	6	2	.750	0	41	0.85
1988 Arkansas	AA	11	0	0	6	14.1	75	18	18	18	2	1	2	1	13	2	17	2	3	1	3	.250	0	0	11.30
St. Pete	A	35	0	0	28	43.1	173	24	12	10	0	2	3	4	16	1	45	2	4	2	2	.500	0	17	2.08
1989 Arkansas	AA	57	0	0	51	76.2	329	68	34	31	5	0	2	2	32	2	74	3	1	4	6	.400	0	33	3.64
1990 Louisville	AAA	57	0	0	50	67.1	298	64	34	32	9	4	1	2	33	4	69	3	0	7	7	.500	0	31	4.28
1991 Louisville	AAA	37	0	0	23	47	225	54	38	32	5	5	2	2	25	6	38	5	0	3	5	.375	0	4	6.13
1990 St. Louis	NL	13	0	0	7	13.2	55	12	6	6	0	0	2	0	3	0	5	0	0	1	0	1.000	0	1	3.95
1991 St. Louis	NL	14	0	0	2	17	75	19	11	11	1	1	0	1	7	2	7	0	1	0	2	.000	0	0	5.82
1992 St. Louis	NL	77	0	0	22	93	377	70	23	19	4	7	4	1	32	9	46	4	0	9	3	.750	0	1	1.84
3 ML YEARS		104	0	0	31	123.2	507	101	40	36	5	8	6	2	42	11	58	4	1	10	5	.667	0	2	2.62

Tony Perezchica

Bats: Right **Throws:** Right **Pos:** 3B **Ht:** 5'11" **Wt:** 165 **Born:** 04/20/66 **Age:** 27

					BATTING														BASERUNNING				PERCENTAGES		
Year Team	Lg	G	AB	H	2B	3B	HR	(Hm	Rd)	TB	R	RBI	TBB	IBB	SO	HBP	SH	SF	SB	CS	SB%	GDP	Avg	OBP	SLG
1988 San Francisco	NL	7	8	1	0	0	0	(0	0)	1	1	1	2	0	1	0	0	1	0	0	.00	0	.125	.273	.125
1990 San Francisco	NL	4	3	1	0	0	0	(0	0)	1	1	0	1	0	2	0	0	0	0	0	.00	0	.333	.500	.333
1991 2 ML Teams		40	70	19	6	1	0	(0	0)	27	6	3	5	0	17	0	0	0	0	1	.00	0	.271	.320	.386
1992 Cleveland		18	20	2	1	0	0	(0	0)	3	2	1	2	0	6	0	0	2	0	0	.00	0	.100	.182	.150
1991 San Francisco	NL	23	48	11	4	1	0	(0	0)	17	2	3	2	0	12	0	0	0	0	1	.00	0	.229	.260	.354
Cleveland	AL	17	22	8	2	0	0	(0	0)	10	4	0	3	0	5	0	0	0	0	0	.00	0	.364	.440	.455
4 ML YEARS		69	101	23	7	1	0	(0	0)	32	10	5	10	0	26	0	0	3	0	1	.00	0	.228	.295	.317

Gerald Perry

Bats: Left **Throws:** Right **Pos:** 1B **Ht:** 6' 0" **Wt:** 201 **Born:** 10/30/60 **Age:** 32

					BATTING														BASERUNNING				PERCENTAGES		
Year Team	Lg	G	AB	H	2B	3B	HR	(Hm	Rd)	TB	R	RBI	TBB	IBB	SO	HBP	SH	SF	SB	CS	SB%	GDP	Avg	OBP	SLG
1983 Atlanta	NL	27	39	14	2	0	1	(0	1)	19	5	6	5	0	4	0	0	1	0	1	.00	1	.359	.422	.487
1984 Atlanta	NL	122	347	92	12	2	7	(3	4)	129	52	47	61	5	38	2	2	7	15	12	.56	9	.265	.372	.372
1985 Atlanta	NL	110	238	51	5	0	3	(3	0)	65	22	13	23	1	28	0	0	1	9	5	.64	7	.214	.282	.273
1986 Atlanta	NL	29	70	19	2	0	2	(0	2)	27	6	11	8	1	4	0	1	1	0	1	.00	4	.271	.342	.386
1987 Atlanta	NL	142	533	144	35	2	12	(2	10)	219	77	74	48	1	63	1	3	5	42	16	.72	18	.270	.329	.411
1988 Atlanta	NL	141	547	164	29	1	8	(4	4)	219	61	74	36	9	49	1	1	10	29	14	.67	18	.300	.338	.400
1989 Atlanta	NL	72	266	67	11	0	4	(2	2)	90	24	21	32	5	28	3	0	2	10	6	.63	5	.252	.337	.338
1990 Kansas City	AL	133	465	118	22	2	8	(3	5)	168	57	57	39	4	56	3	0	5	17	4	.81	14	.254	.313	.361
1991 St. Louis	NL	109	242	58	8	4	6	(1	5)	92	29	36	22	1	34	0	0	3	15	8	.65	2	.240	.300	.380
1992 St. Louis	NL	87	143	34	8	0	1	(1	0)	45	13	18	15	4	23	1	0	2	3	6	.33	3	.238	.311	.315
10 ML YEARS		972	2890	761	134	11	52	(21	31)	1073	346	357	289	31	327	11	7	37	140	73	.66	81	.263	.329	.371

Geno Petralli

Bats: Left **Throws:** Right **Pos:** C **Ht:** 6' 1" **Wt:** 200 **Born:** 09/25/59 **Age:** 33

					BATTING														BASERUNNING				PERCENTAGES		
Year Team	Lg	G	AB	H	2B	3B	HR	(Hm	Rd)	TB	R	RBI	TBB	IBB	SO	HBP	SH	SF	SB	CS	SB%	GDP	Avg	OBP	SLG
1982 Toronto	AL	16	44	16	2	0	0	(0	0)	18	3	1	4	0	6	0	1	0	0	0	.00	1	.364	.417	.409
1983 Toronto	AL	6	4	0	0	0	0	(0	0)	0	0	0	1	0	1	0	0	0	0	0	.00	0	.000	.200	.000
1984 Toronto	AL	3	3	0	0	0	0	(0	0)	0	0	0	0	0	0	0	0	0	0	0	.00	0	.000	.000	.000
1985 Texas	AL	42	100	27	2	0	0	(0	0)	29	7	11	8	0	12	1	3	4	1	0	1.00	4	.270	.319	.290
1986 Texas	AL	69	137	35	9	3	2	(1	1)	56	17	18	5	0	14	0	0	0	3	0	1.00	7	.255	.282	.409
1987 Texas	AL	101	202	61	11	2	7	(4	3)	97	28	31	27	2	29	2	0	1	0	2	.00	4	.302	.388	.480
1988 Texas	AL	129	351	99	14	2	7	(1	6)	138	35	36	41	5	52	2	1	5	0	1	.00	12	.282	.356	.393

Year Team	Lg	G	AB	H	2B	3B	HR	(Hm	Rd)	TB	R	RBI	TBB	IBB	SO	HBP	SH	SF	SB	CS	SB%	GDP	Avg	OBP	SLG
1989 Texas	AL	70	184	56	7	0	4	(1	3)	75	18	23	17	1	24	2	1	1	0	0	.00	5	.304	.368	.408
1990 Texas	AL	133	325	83	13	1	0	(0	0)	98	28	21	50	3	49	3	1	3	0	2	.00	12	.255	.357	.302
1991 Texas	AL	87	199	54	8	1	2	(0	2)	70	21	20	21	1	25	0	7	1	2	1	.67	4	.271	.339	.352
1992 Texas	AL	94	192	38	12	0	1	(0	1)	53	11	18	20	2	34	0	1	0	0	0	.00	8	.198	.274	.276
11 ML YEARS		750	1741	469	78	9	23	(7	16)	634	168	179	194	14	246	10	15	15	6	6	.50	57	.269	.343	.364

Gary Pettis

Bats: Both **Throws:** Right **Pos:** CF **Ht:** 6' 1" **Wt:** 160 **Born:** 04/03/58 **Age:** 35

		BATTING																	BASERUNNING				PERCENTAGES		
Year Team	Lg	G	AB	H	2B	3B	HR	(Hm	Rd)	TB	R	RBI	TBB	IBB	SO	HBP	SH	SF	SB	CS	SB%	GDP	Avg	OBP	SLG
1982 California	AL	10	5	1	0	0	1	(1	0)	4	5	1	0	0	2	0	0	0	0	0	.00	0	.200	.200	.800
1983 California	AL	22	85	25	2	3	3	(0	3)	42	19	6	7	0	15	0	1	0	8	3	.73	1	.294	.348	.494
1984 California	AL	140	397	90	11	6	2	(1	1)	119	63	29	60	1	115	3	5	1	48	17	.74	4	.227	.332	.300
1985 California	AL	125	443	114	10	8	1	(0	1)	143	67	32	62	0	125	0	9	2	56	9	.86	5	.257	.347	.323
1986 California	AL	154	539	139	23	4	5	(1	4)	185	93	58	69	2	132	0	15	5	50	13	.79	7	.258	.339	.343
1987 California	AL	133	394	82	13	2	1	(1	0)	102	49	17	52	0	124	1	1	0	24	5	.83	8	.208	.302	.259
1988 Detroit	AL	129	458	96	14	4	3	(0	3)	127	65	36	47	0	85	1	6	0	44	10	.81	3	.210	.285	.277
1989 Detroit	AL	119	444	114	8	6	1	(1	0)	137	77	18	84	0	106	0	8	0	43	15	.74	14	.257	.375	.309
1990 Texas	AL	136	423	101	16	8	3	(3	0)	142	66	31	57	0	118	4	11	3	38	15	.72	6	.239	.333	.336
1991 Texas	AL	137	282	61	7	5	0	(0	0)	78	37	19	54	0	91	0	6	1	29	13	.69	4	.216	.341	.277
1992 2 ML Teams		78	159	32	5	3	1	(1	0)	46	27	12	29	0	45	0	3	1	14	4	.78	3	.201	.323	.289
1992 San Diego	NL	30	30	6	1	0	0	(0	0)	7	0	0	2	0	11	0	0	0	1	0	1.00	0	.200	.250	.233
Detroit	AL	48	129	26	4	3	1	(1	0)	39	27	12	27	0	34	0	3	1	13	4	.76	3	.202	.338	.302
11 ML YEARS		1183	3629	855	109	49	21	(12	9)	1125	568	259	521	3	958	9	65	13	354	104	.77	55	.236	.332	.310

Tony Phillips

Bats: Both **Throws:** Right **Pos:** 2B/3B/LF/CF/RF/DH **Ht:** 5'10" **Wt:** 175 **Born:** 04/25/59 **Age:** 34

		BATTING																	BASERUNNING				PERCENTAGES		
Year Team	Lg	G	AB	H	2B	3B	HR	(Hm	Rd)	TB	R	RBI	TBB	IBB	SO	HBP	SH	SF	SB	CS	SB%	GDP	Avg	OBP	SLG
1982 Oakland	AL	40	81	17	2	2	0	(0	0)	23	11	8	12	0	26	2	5	0	2	3	.40	0	.210	.326	.284
1983 Oakland	AL	148	412	102	12	3	4	(1	3)	132	54	35	48	1	70	2	11	3	16	5	.76	5	.248	.327	.320
1984 Oakland	AL	154	451	120	24	3	4	(2	2)	162	62	37	42	1	86	0	7	5	10	6	.63	5	.266	.325	.359
1985 Oakland	AL	42	161	45	12	2	4	(2	2)	73	23	17	13	0	34	0	3	1	3	2	.60	1	.280	.331	.453
1986 Oakland	AL	118	441	113	14	5	5	(3	2)	152	76	52	76	0	82	3	9	3	15	10	.60	2	.256	.367	.345
1987 Oakland	AL	111	379	91	20	0	10	(5	5)	141	48	46	57	1	76	0	2	3	7	6	.54	9	.240	.337	.372
1988 Oakland	AL	79	212	43	8	4	2	(2	0)	65	32	17	36	0	50	1	1	1	0	2	.00	6	.203	.320	.307
1989 Oakland	AL	143	451	118	15	6	4	(2	2)	157	48	47	58	2	66	3	5	7	3	8	.27	17	.262	.345	.348
1990 Detroit	AL	152	573	144	23	5	8	(4	4)	201	97	55	99	0	85	4	9	2	19	9	.68	10	.251	.364	.351
1991 Detroit	AL	146	564	160	28	4	17	(9	8)	247	87	72	79	5	95	3	3	6	10	5	.67	8	.284	.371	.438
1992 Detroit	AL	159	606	167	32	3	10	(3	7)	235	114	64	114	2	93	1	5	7	12	10	.55	13	.276	.387	.388
11 ML YEARS		1292	4331	1120	190	37	68	(33	35)	1588	652	450	634	12	763	19	60	38	97	66	.60	76	.259	.353	.367

Mike Piazza

Bats: Right **Throws:** Right **Pos:** C **Ht:** 6' 3" **Wt:** 200 **Born:** 09/04/68 **Age:** 24

		BATTING																	BASERUNNING				PERCENTAGES		
Year Team	Lg	G	AB	H	2B	3B	HR	(Hm	Rd)	TB	R	RBI	TBB	IBB	SO	HBP	SH	SF	SB	CS	SB%	GDP	Avg	OBP	SLG
1989 Salem	A	57	198	53	11	0	8	--	--	88	22	25	13	0	51	2	0	1	0	0	.00	11	.268	.318	.444
1990 Vero Beach	A	88	272	68	20	0	6	--	--	106	27	45	11	0	68	1	0	1	0	1	.00	9	.250	.281	.390
1991 Bakersfield	A	117	448	124	27	2	29	--	--	242	71	80	47	2	83	3	0	8	0	3	.00	19	.277	.344	.540
1992 San Antonio	AA	31	114	43	11	0	7	--	--	75	18	20	13	2	18	0	0	0	0	0	.00	2	.377	.441	.658
Albuquerque	AAA	94	358	122	22	5	16	--	--	202	54	69	37	4	57	2	0	1	1	3	.25	9	.341	.405	.564
1992 Los Angeles	NL	21	69	16	3	0	1	(1	0)	22	5	7	4	0	12	1	0	0	0	0	.00	1	.232	.284	.319

Hipolito Pichardo

Pitches: Right **Bats:** Right **Pos:** SP/RP **Ht:** 6' 1" **Wt:** 160 **Born:** 08/22/69 **Age:** 23

		HOW MUCH HE PITCHED						WHAT HE GAVE UP										THE RESULTS					
Year Team	Lg	G	GS	CG	GF	IP	BFP	H	R	ER	HR	SH	SF	HB	TBB	IBB	SO	WP	Bk	W	L	Pct.	ShO	Sv	ERA
1988 Royals	R	1	0	0	0	1.1	9	3	2	2	0	0	0	1	1	0	3	0	0	0	0	.000	0	0	13.50
1989 Appleton	A	12	12	2	0	75.2	300	58	29	25	4	2	1	5	18	0	50	5	4	5	4	.556	0	0	2.97
1990 Baseball Cy	A	11	10	0	0	45	201	47	28	19	1	2	2	1	25	0	40	4	2	1	6	.143	0	0	3.80
1991 Memphis	AA	34	11	0	5	99	447	116	56	47	4	7	4	4	38	5	75	6	1	3	11	.214	0	0	4.27
1992 Memphis	AA	2	2	0	0	14	55	13	2	1	0	1	0	0	1	0	10	0	0	0	0	.000	0	0	0.64
1992 Kansas City	AL	31	24	1	0	143.2	615	148	71	63	9	4	5	3	49	1	59	3	1	9	6	.600	1	0	3.95

Eddie Pierce

Pitches: Left   **Bats:** Left   **Pos:** SP   **Ht:** 6' 1"   **Wt:** 185   **Born:** 10/06/68   **Age:** 24

Year Team	Lg	G	GS	CG	GF	IP	BFP	H	R	ER	HR	SH	SF	HB	TBB	IBB	SO	WP	Bk	W	L	Pct.	ShO	Sv	ERA
1989 Eugene	A	27	0	0	24	39	175	24	19	12	0	0	0	3	26	0	71	9	2	2	2	.500	0	4	2.77
1990 Baseball Cy	A	37	0	0	22	50	228	49	21	18	3	3	0	0	32	0	52	7	2	3	1	.750	0	5	3.24
Memphis	AA	1	0	0	0	1	3	0	0	0	0	0	0	0	1	0	1	0	0	0	0	.000	0	0	0.00
1991 Memphis	AA	31	20	2	4	136	595	136	73	58	6	6	1	2	61	1	90	3	1	5	11	.313	0		3.84
1992 Memphis	AA	25	25	1	0	153.2	662	159	74	65	11	8	3	3	51	1	131	8	1	10	10	.500	1	0	3.81
1992 Kansas City	AL	2	1	0	0	5.1	26	9	2	2	1	0	1	0	4	0	3	0	0	0	0	.000	0	0	3.38

Phil Plantier

Bats: Left   **Throws:** Right   **Pos:** RF/LF/DH   **Ht:** 5'11"   **Wt:** 195   **Born:** 01/27/69   **Age:** 24

Year Team	Lg	G	AB	H	2B	3B	HR	(Hm	Rd)	TB	R	RBI	TBB	IBB	SO	HBP	SH	SF	SB	CS	SB%	GDP	Avg	OBP	SLG
1990 Boston	AL	14	15	2	1	0	0	(0	0)	3	1	4	0	6	1	0	1	0	0	0	.00	1	.133	.333	.200
1991 Boston	AL	53	148	49	7	1	11	(6	5)	91	27	35	23	2	38	1	0	1	1	0	1.00	2	.331	.420	.615
1992 Boston	AL	108	349	86	19	0	7	(5	2)	126	46	30	44	8	83	2	2	2	2	3	.40	9	.246	.332	.361
3 ML YEARS		175	512	137	27	1	18	(11	7)	220	74	68	71	10	127	4	2	5	3	3	.50	12	.268	.358	.430

Dan Plesac

Pitches: Left   **Bats:** Left   **Pos:** RP/SP   **Ht:** 6' 5"   **Wt:** 215   **Born:** 02/04/62   **Age:** 31

Year Team	Lg	G	GS	CG	GF	IP	BFP	H	R	ER	HR	SH	SF	HB	TBB	IBB	SO	WP	Bk	W	L	Pct.	ShO	Sv	ERA
1986 Milwaukee	AL	51	0	0	33	91	377	81	34	30	5	6	5	0	29	1	75	4	0	10	7	.588	0	14	2.97
1987 Milwaukee	AL	57	0	0	47	79.1	325	63	30	23	8	1	2	3	23	1	89	6	0	5	6	.455	0	23	2.61
1988 Milwaukee	AL	50	0	0	48	52.1	211	46	14	14	2	2	0	0	12	2	52	4	6	1	2	.333	0	30	2.41
1989 Milwaukee	AL	52	0	0	51	61.1	242	47	16	16	6	0	4	0	17	1	52	5	0	3	4	.429	0	33	2.35
1990 Milwaukee	AL	66	0	0	52	69	299	67	36	34	5	2	2	3	31	6	65	2	0	3	7	.300	0	24	4.43
1991 Milwaukee	AL	45	10	0	25	92.1	402	92	49	44	12	3	7	3	39	1	61	2	1	2	7	.222	0	8	4.29
1992 Milwaukee	AL	44	4	0	13	79	330	64	28	26	5	8	4	3	35	5	54	3	1	5	4	.556	0	1	2.96
7 ML YEARS		365	14	0	269	524.1	2186	460	207	187	43	22	24	12	186	17	448	21	8	29	37	.439	0	133	3.21

Eric Plunk

Pitches: Right   **Bats:** Right   **Pos:** RP   **Ht:** 6' 5"   **Wt:** 217   **Born:** 09/03/63   **Age:** 29

Year Team	Lg	G	GS	CG	GF	IP	BFP	H	R	ER	HR	SH	SF	HB	TBB	IBB	SO	WP	Bk	W	L	Pct.	ShO	Sv	ERA
1986 Oakland	AL	26	15	0	2	120.1	537	91	75	71	14	2	3	5	102	2	98	9	6	4	7	.364	0	0	5.31
1987 Oakland	AL	32	11	0	11	95	432	91	53	50	8	3	5	2	62	3	90	5	2	4	6	.400	0	2	4.74
1988 Oakland	AL	49	0	0	22	78	331	62	27	26	6	3	2	1	39	4	79	4	7	7	2	.778	0	5	3.00
1989 2 ML Teams		50	7	0	17	104.1	445	82	43	38	10	3	4	1	64	2	85	10	3	8	6	.571	0	1	3.28
1990 New York	AL	47	0	0	16	72.2	310	58	27	22	6	7	0	2	43	1	67	4	2	6	3	.667	0	0	2.72
1991 New York	AL	43	8	0	14	111.2	521	128	69	59	18	6	4	1	62	1	103	6	2	2	5	.286	0	0	4.76
1992 Cleveland	AL	58	0	0	20	71.2	309	61	31	29	5	3	2	0	38	2	50	5	0	9	6	.600	0	4	3.64
1989 Oakland	AL	23	0	0	12	28.2	113	17	7	7	1	1	0	1	12	0	24	4	0	1	1	.500	0	1	2.20
New York	AL	27	7	0	5	75.2	332	65	36	31	9	2	4	0	52	2	61	6	3	7	5	.583	0	0	3.69
7 ML YEARS		305	41	0	94	653.2	2885	573	325	295	67	27	20	12	410	18	572	43	22	40	45	.533	0	12	4.06

Luis Polonia

Bats: Left   **Throws:** Left   **Pos:** LF/DH   **Ht:** 5' 8"   **Wt:** 150   **Born:** 10/12/64   **Age:** 28

Year Team	Lg	G	AB	H	2B	3B	HR	(Hm	Rd)	TB	R	RBI	TBB	IBB	SO	HBP	SH	SF	SB	CS	SB%	GDP	Avg	OBP	SLG
1987 Oakland	AL	125	435	125	16	10	4	(1	3)	173	78	49	32	1	64	0	1	1	29	7	.81	4	.287	.335	.398
1988 Oakland	AL	84	288	84	11	4	2	(1	1)	109	51	27	21	0	40	0	2	2	24	9	.73	3	.292	.338	.378
1989 2 ML Teams		125	433	130	17	6	3	(1	2)	168	70	46	25	1	44	2	2	4	22	8	.73	13	.300	.338	.388
1990 2 ML Teams		120	403	135	7	9	2	(2	0)	166	52	35	25	1	43	1	3	4	21	14	.60	9	.335	.372	.412
1991 California	AL	150	604	179	28	8	2	(1	1)	229	92	50	52	4	74	1	2	3	48	23	.68	11	.296	.352	.379
1992 California	AL	149	577	165	17	4	0	(0	0)	190	83	35	45	6	64	1	8	4	51	21	.71	18	.286	.337	.329
1989 Oakland	AL	59	206	59	6	4	1	(0	1)	76	31	17	9	0	15	0	2	1	13	4	.76	5	.286	.315	.369
New York	AL	66	227	71	11	2	2	(1	1)	92	39	29	16	1	29	2	0	3	9	4	.69	8	.313	.359	.405
1990 New York	AL	11	22	7	0	0	0	(0	0)	7	2	3	0	0	1	0	0	1	1	0	1.00	1	.318	.304	.318
California	AL	109	381	128	7	9	2	(2	0)	159	50	32	25	1	42	1	3	3	20	14	.59	8	.336	.376	.417
6 ML YEARS		753	2740	818	96	41	13	(6	7)	1035	426	242	200	13	329	5	18	18	195	82	.70	58	.299	.345	.378

159

Jim Poole

Pitches: Left **Bats:** Left **Pos:** RP   **Ht:** 6' 2" **Wt:** 203 **Born:** 04/28/66 **Age:** 27

Year Team	Lg	G	GS	CG	GF	IP	BFP	H	R	ER	HR	SH	SF	HB	TBB	IBB	SO	WP	Bk	W	L	Pct.	ShO	Sv	ERA
1990 Los Angeles	NL	16	0	0	4	10.2	46	7	5	5	1	0	0	0	8	4	6	1	0	0	0	.000	0	0	4.22
1991 2 ML Teams		29	0	0	5	42	166	29	14	11	3	3	3	0	12	2	38	2	0	3	2	.600	0	1	2.36
1992 Baltimore	AL	6	0	0	1	3.1	14	3	3	0	0	0	0	0	1	0	3	0	0	0	0	.000	0	0	0.00
1991 Texas	AL	5	0	0	2	6	31	10	4	3	0	0	1	0	3	0	4	0	0	0	0	.000	0	1	4.50
Baltimore	AL	24	0	0	3	36	135	19	10	8	3	3	2	0	9	2	34	2	0	3	2	.600	0	0	2.00
3 ML YEARS		51	0	0	10	56	226	39	22	16	4	3	3	0	21	6	47	3	0	3	2	.600	0	1	2.57

Mark Portugal

Pitches: Right **Bats:** Right **Pos:** SP   **Ht:** 6' 0" **Wt:** 190 **Born:** 10/30/62 **Age:** 30

Year Team	Lg	G	GS	CG	GF	IP	BFP	H	R	ER	HR	SH	SF	HB	TBB	IBB	SO	WP	Bk	W	L	Pct.	ShO	Sv	ERA
1985 Minnesota	AL	6	4	0	0	24.1	105	24	16	15	3	0	2	0	14	0	12	1	1	1	3	.250	0	0	5.55
1986 Minnesota	AL	27	15	3	7	112.2	481	112	56	54	10	5	3	1	50	1	67	5	0	6	10	.375	0	1	4.31
1987 Minnesota	AL	13	7	0	3	44	204	58	40	38	13	0	1	1	24	1	28	2	0	1	3	.250	0	0	7.77
1988 Minnesota	AL	26	0	0	9	57.2	242	60	30	29	11	2	3	1	17	1	31	2	2	3	3	.500	0	3	4.53
1989 Houston	NL	20	15	2	1	108	440	91	34	33	7	8	1	2	37	0	86	3	0	7	1	.875	1	0	2.75
1990 Houston	NL	32	32	1	0	196.2	831	187	90	79	21	7	6	4	67	4	136	6	0	11	10	.524	0	0	3.62
1991 Houston	NL	32	27	1	3	168.1	710	163	91	84	19	6	6	2	59	5	120	4	1	10	12	.455	0	1	4.49
1992 Houston	NL	18	16	1	0	101.1	405	76	32	30	7	5	1	1	41	3	62	1	1	6	3	.667	1	0	2.66
8 ML YEARS		174	116	8	23	813	3418	771	389	362	91	33	23	12	309	15	542	24	5	45	45	.500	2	5	4.01

Dennis Powell

Pitches: Left **Bats:** Right **Pos:** RP   **Ht:** 6' 3" **Wt:** 200 **Born:** 08/13/63 **Age:** 29

Year Team	Lg	G	GS	CG	GF	IP	BFP	H	R	ER	HR	SH	SF	HB	TBB	IBB	SO	WP	Bk	W	L	Pct.	ShO	Sv	ERA
1985 Los Angeles	NL	16	2	0	6	29.1	133	30	19	17	7	4	1	1	13	3	19	3	0	1	1	.500	0	1	5.22
1986 Los Angeles	NL	27	6	0	5	65.1	272	65	32	31	5	5	2	1	25	7	31	7	2	2	7	.222	0	0	4.27
1987 Seattle	AL	16	3	0	1	34.1	147	32	13	12	3	2	2	0	15	0	17	0	0	1	3	.250	0	0	3.15
1988 Seattle	AL	12	2	0	1	18.2	95	29	20	18	2	0	2	2	11	2	15	0	0	1	3	.250	0	0	8.68
1989 Seattle	AL	43	1	0	9	45	201	49	25	25	6	3	3	2	21	0	27	1	0	2	2	.500	0	2	5.00
1990 2 ML Teams		11	7	0	2	42.1	214	64	40	33	0	2	2	2	21	0	23	2	0	0	4	.000	0	0	7.02
1992 Seattle	AL	49	0	0	11	57	243	49	30	29	5	5	0	3	29	2	35	2	0	4	2	.667	0	0	4.58
1990 Seattle	AL	2	0	0	1	3	17	5	3	3	0	0	0	1	2	0	0	0	0	0	0	.000	0	0	9.00
Milwaukee	AL	9	7	0	1	39.1	197	59	37	30	0	2	2	1	19	0	23	2	0	0	4	.000	0	0	6.86
7 ML YEARS		174	21	0	35	292	1305	318	179	165	28	21	12	11	135	14	167	15	2	11	22	.333	0	3	5.09

Ted Power

Pitches: Right **Bats:** Right **Pos:** RP   **Ht:** 6' 4" **Wt:** 220 **Born:** 01/31/55 **Age:** 38

Year Team	Lg	G	GS	CG	GF	IP	BFP	H	R	ER	HR	SH	SF	HB	TBB	IBB	SO	WP	Bk	W	L	Pct.	ShO	Sv	ERA
1981 Los Angeles	NL	5	2	0	1	14	66	16	6	5	0	0	2	1	7	2	7	0	0	1	3	.250	0	0	3.21
1982 Los Angeles	NL	12	4	0	4	33.2	160	38	27	25	4	4	1	0	23	1	15	3	3	1	1	.500	0	0	6.68
1983 Cincinnati	NL	49	6	1	14	111	480	120	62	56	10	4	6	1	49	3	57	1	0	5	6	.455	0	2	4.54
1984 Cincinnati	NL	78	0	0	42	108.2	456	93	37	34	4	9	8	0	46	8	81	3	0	9	7	.563	0	11	2.82
1985 Cincinnati	NL	64	0	0	50	80	342	65	27	24	2	6	4	1	45	8	42	1	0	8	6	.571	0	27	2.70
1986 Cincinnati	NL	56	10	0	30	129	537	115	59	53	13	9	6	1	52	10	95	5	1	10	6	.625	0	1	3.70
1987 Cincinnati	NL	34	34	2	0	204	887	213	115	102	28	8	7	3	71	7	133	3	2	10	13	.435	1	0	4.50
1988 2 ML Teams		26	14	2	3	99	443	121	67	65	8	2	4	3	38	7	57	4	2	6	7	.462	2	0	5.91
1989 St. Louis	NL	23	15	0	2	97	407	96	47	40	7	5	3	1	21	3	43	1	0	7	7	.500	0	0	3.71
1990 Pittsburgh	NL	40	0	0	25	51.2	218	50	23	21	5	3	2	0	17	6	42	1	0	1	3	.250	0	7	3.66
1991 Cincinnati	NL	68	0	0	22	87	371	87	37	35	6	6	4	2	31	5	51	6	1	5	3	.625	0	3	3.62
1992 Cleveland	AL	64	0	0	16	99.1	409	88	33	28	7	7	8	4	35	9	51	2	1	3	3	.500	0	6	2.54
1988 Kansas City	AL	22	12	2	3	80.1	360	98	54	53	7	2	4	3	30	3	44	3	2	5	6	.455	2	0	5.94
Detroit	AL	4	2	0	0	18.2	83	23	13	12	1	0	0	0	8	4	13	1	0	1	1	.500	0	0	5.79
12 ML YEARS		519	85	5	209	1114.1	4776	1102	540	488	94	63	55	17	435	69	674	30	10	66	65	.504	3	57	3.94

Todd Pratt

Bats: Right **Throws:** Right **Pos:** C   **Ht:** 6' 3" **Wt:** 195 **Born:** 02/09/67 **Age:** 26

Year Team	Lg	G	AB	H	2B	3B	HR	(Hm	Rd)	TB	R	RBI	TBB	IBB	SO	HBP	SH	SF	SB	CS	SB%	GDP	Avg	OBP	SLG
1985 Elmira	A	39	119	16	1	1	0	--	--	19	7	5	10	0	27	1	3	1	0	1	.00	6	.134	.206	.160
1986 Greensboro	A	107	348	84	16	1	12	--	--	136	63	56	74	0	114	5	4	4	0	1	.00	10	.241	.378	.391
1987 Winter Havn	A	118	407	105	22	0	12	--	--	163	57	65	70	4	94	1	0	6	0	1	.00	10	.258	.364	.400

160

Year	Team	Lg	G	AB	H	2B	3B	HR	(Hm	Rd)	TB	R	RBI	TBB	IBB	SO	HBP	SH	SF	SB	CS	SB%	GDP	Avg	OBP	SLG
1988	New Britain	AA	124	395	89	15	2	8	--	--	132	41	49	41	2	110	3	1	6	1	4	.20	7	.225	.299	.334
1989	New Britain	AA	109	338	77	17	1	2	--	--	102	30	35	44	1	66	7	1	5	1	2	.33	10	.228	.325	.302
1990	New Britain	AA	70	195	45	14	1	2	--	--	67	15	22	18	0	56	0	3	2	0	1	.00	7	.231	.293	.344
1991	Pawtucket	AAA	68	219	64	16	0	11	--	--	113	27	41	23	2	42	3	5	0	3	0	.00	9	.292	.367	.516
1992	Reading	AA	41	132	44	6	1	6	--	--	70	20	26	24	0	28	0	0	0	2	0	1.00	1	.333	.436	.530
	Scranton/wb	AAA	41	125	40	9	1	7	--	--	72	20	28	30	0	14	0	1	2	1	0	1.00	5	.320	.446	.576
1992	Philadelphia	NL	16	46	13	1	0	2	(2	0)	20	6	10	4	0	12	0	0	0	0	0	.00	2	.283	.340	.435

Tom Prince

Bats: Right **Throws:** Right **Pos:** C   **Ht:** 5'11" **Wt:** 185 **Born:** 08/13/64 **Age:** 28

			BATTING																BASERUNNING				PERCENTAGES		
Year	Team	Lg	G	AB	H	2B	3B	HR	(Hm	Rd)	TB	R	RBI	TBB	IBB	SO	HBP	SH	SF	SB	CS	SB%	GDP	Avg	OBP	SLG
1987	Pittsburgh	NL	4	9	2	1	0	1	(0	1)	6	1	2	0	0	2	0	0	0	0	0	.00	0	.222	.222	.667
1988	Pittsburgh	NL	29	74	13	2	0	0	(0	0)	15	3	6	4	0	15	0	2	0	0	0	.00	5	.176	.218	.203
1989	Pittsburgh	NL	21	52	7	4	0	0	(0	0)	11	1	5	6	1	12	0	0	1	1	1	.50	1	.135	.220	.212
1990	Pittsburgh	NL	4	10	1	0	0	0	(0	0)	1	1	0	1	0	2	0	0	0	0	1	.00	0	.100	.182	.100
1991	Pittsburgh	NL	26	34	9	3	0	1	(0	1)	15	4	2	7	0	3	1	0	0	0	0	.00	3	.265	.405	.441
1992	Pittsburgh	NL	27	44	4	2	0	0	(0	0)	6	1	5	6	0	9	0	0	2	1	1	.50	2	.091	.192	.136
	6 ML YEARS		111	223	36	12	0	2	(0	2)	54	11	20	24	1	43	1	2	3	2	3	.40	11	.161	.243	.242

Kirby Puckett

Bats: Right **Throws:** Right **Pos:** CF   **Ht:** 5' 8" **Wt:** 215 **Born:** 03/14/61 **Age:** 32

			BATTING																BASERUNNING				PERCENTAGES		
Year	Team	Lg	G	AB	H	2B	3B	HR	(Hm	Rd)	TB	R	RBI	TBB	IBB	SO	HBP	SH	SF	SB	CS	SB%	GDP	Avg	OBP	SLG
1984	Minnesota	AL	128	557	165	12	5	0	(0	0)	187	63	31	16	1	69	4	4	2	14	7	.67	11	.296	.320	.336
1985	Minnesota	AL	161	691	199	29	13	4	(2	2)	266	80	74	41	0	87	4	5	3	21	12	.64	9	.288	.330	.385
1986	Minnesota	AL	161	680	223	37	6	31	(14	17)	365	119	96	34	4	99	7	2	0	20	12	.63	14	.328	.366	.537
1987	Minnesota	AL	157	624	207	32	5	28	(18	10)	333	96	99	32	7	91	6	0	6	12	7	.63	16	.332	.367	.534
1988	Minnesota	AL	158	657	234	42	5	24	(13	11)	358	109	121	23	4	83	2	0	9	6	7	.46	17	.356	.375	.545
1989	Minnesota	AL	159	635	215	45	4	9	(7	2)	295	75	85	41	9	59	3	0	5	11	4	.73	21	.339	.379	.465
1990	Minnesota	AL	146	551	164	40	3	12	(6	6)	246	82	80	57	11	73	3	1	3	5	4	.56	15	.298	.365	.446
1991	Minnesota	AL	152	611	195	29	6	15	(7	8)	281	92	89	31	4	78	4	8	7	11	5	.69	27	.319	.352	.460
1992	Minnesota	AL	160	639	210	38	4	19	(9	10)	313	104	110	44	13	97	6	1	6	17	7	.71	17	.329	.374	.490
	9 ML YEARS		1382	5645	1812	304	51	142	(76	66)	2644	820	785	319	53	736	39	21	41	117	65	.64	147	.321	.359	.468

Tim Pugh

Pitches: Right **Bats:** Right **Pos:** SP   **Ht:** 6' 6" **Wt:** 225 **Born:** 01/26/67 **Age:** 26

			HOW MUCH HE PITCHED					WHAT HE GAVE UP										THE RESULTS					
Year	Team	Lg	G	GS	CG	GF	IP	BFP	H	R	ER	HR	SH	SF	HB	TBB	IBB	SO	WP	Bk	W	L	Pct.	ShO	Sv	ERA
1989	Billings	R	13	13	2	0	77.2	333	81	44	34	4	6	2	5	25	0	72	4	6	2	6	.250	0	0	3.94
1990	Chston-Wv	A	27	27	8	0	177.1	733	142	58	37	5	5	3	7	56	0	154	10	0	15	6	.714	2	0	1.88
1991	Chattanooga	AA	5	5	0	0	38.1	143	20	7	7	2	1	1	4	11	0	24	0	0	3	1	.750	0	0	1.64
	Nashville	AAA	23	23	3	0	148.2	612	130	68	63	9	3	6	10	56	2	89	9	1	7	11	.389	1	0	3.81
1992	Nashville	AAA	27	27	3	0	169.2	725	165	75	67	10	6	5	8	65	3	117	4	0	12	9	.571	2	0	3.55
1992	Cincinnati	NL	7	7	0	0	45.1	187	47	15	13	2	2	1	1	13	3	18	0	0	4	2	.667	0	0	2.58

Harvey Pulliam

Bats: Right **Throws:** Right **Pos:** DH   **Ht:** 6' 0" **Wt:** 210 **Born:** 10/20/67 **Age:** 25

			BATTING																BASERUNNING				PERCENTAGES		
Year	Team	Lg	G	AB	H	2B	3B	HR	(Hm	Rd)	TB	R	RBI	TBB	IBB	SO	HBP	SH	SF	SB	CS	SB%	GDP	Avg	OBP	SLG
1986	Royals	R	48	168	35	3	0	4	--	--	50	14	23	8	1	33	3	2	3	3	2	.60	9	.208	.253	.298
1987	Appleton	A	110	395	109	20	1	9	--	--	158	54	55	26	0	79	3	1	3	21	7	.75	10	.276	.323	.400
1988	Baseball Cy	A	132	457	111	19	4	4	--	--	150	56	42	34	4	87	5	2	3	21	11	.66	13	.243	.301	.328
1989	Omaha	AAA	7	22	4	2	0	0	--	--	6	3	2	3	0	6	0	0	0	0	0	.00	0	.182	.280	.273
	Memphis	AA	116	417	121	28	8	10	--	--	195	67	67	44	4	65	5	0	3	5	5	.50	12	.290	.362	.468
1990	Omaha	AAA	123	436	117	18	5	16	--	--	193	72	72	49	0	82	3	2	4	9	3	.75	14	.268	.343	.443
1991	Omaha	AAA	104	346	89	18	2	6	--	--	129	35	39	31	0	62	1	1	3	2	4	.33	4	.257	.318	.373
1992	Omaha	AAA	100	359	97	12	2	16	--	--	161	55	60	32	1	53	6	1	3	4	2	.67	15	.270	.338	.448
1991	Kansas City	AL	18	33	9	1	0	3	(2	1)	19	4	4	1	0	9	0	1	0	0	0	.00	1	.273	.333	.576
1992	Kansas City	AL	4	5	1	1	0	0	(0	0)	2	2	0	1	0	3	0	0	0	0	0	.00	0	.200	.333	.400
	2 ML YEARS		22	38	10	2	0	3	(2	1)	21	6	4	1	1	12	0	1	0	0	0	.00	1	.263	.333	.553

Paul Quantrill

Pitches: Right **Bats:** Left **Pos:** RP 　　　　**Ht:** 6' 1" **Wt:** 175 **Born:** 11/03/68 **Age:** 24

			HOW MUCH HE PITCHED						WHAT HE GAVE UP											THE RESULTS					
Year Team	Lg	G	GS	CG	GF	IP	BFP	H	R	ER	HR	SH	SF	HB	TBB	IBB	SO	WP	Bk	W	L	Pct.	ShO	Sv	ERA
1989 Red Sox	R	2	0	0	2	5	18	2	0	0	0	0	0	0	0	0	5	0	0	0	0	.000	0	2	0.00
Elmira	A	20	7	5	7	76	326	90	37	29	5	4	3	6	12	2	57	1	2	5	4	.556	0	2	3.43
1990 Winter Havn	A	7	7	1	0	45.2	182	46	24	21	3	0	2	0	6	0	14	3	0	2	5	.286	0	0	4.14
New Britain	AA	22	22	1	0	132.2	549	149	65	52	3	4	7	4	23	2	53	3	2	7	11	.389	1	0	3.53
1991 New Britain	AA	5	5	1	0	35	142	32	14	8	2	3	1	1	8	0	18	0	0	2	1	.667	0	0	2.06
Pawtucket	AAA	25	23	6	0	155.2	645	169	81	77	14	9	2	4	30	1	75	2	2	10	7	.588	2	0	4.45
1992 Pawtucket	AAA	19	18	4	1	119	504	143	63	59	16	3	1	4	20	1	56	1	1	6	8	.429	1	0	4.46
1992 Boston	AL	27	0	0	10	49.1	213	55	18	12	1	4	2	1	15	5	24	1	0	2	3	.400	0	1	2.19

Tom Quinlan

Bats: Right **Throws:** Right **Pos:** 3B 　　　　**Ht:** 6' 3" **Wt:** 210 **Born:** 03/27/68 **Age:** 25

							BATTING												BASERUNNING				PERCENTAGES		
Year Team	Lg	G	AB	H	2B	3B	HR	(Hm	Rd)	TB	R	RBI	TBB	IBB	SO	HBP	SH	SF	SB	CS	SB%	GDP	Avg	OBP	SLG
1987 Myrtle Bch	A	132	435	97	20	3	5	--	--	138	42	51	34	0	130	6	3	6	0	2	.00	4	.223	.285	.317
1988 Knoxville	AA	98	326	71	19	1	8	--	--	116	33	47	35	1	99	5	3	2	4	9	.31	5	.218	.302	.356
1989 Knoxville	AA	139	452	95	21	3	16	--	--	170	62	57	41	0	118	9	3	4	6	4	.60	11	.210	.287	.376
1990 Knoxville	AA	141	481	124	24	6	15	--	--	205	70	51	49	2	157	14	7	1	8	9	.47	5	.258	.343	.426
1991 Syracuse	AAA	132	466	112	24	6	10	--	--	178	56	49	72	3	163	5	3	2	9	4	.69	7	.240	.347	.382
1992 Syracuse	AAA	107	349	75	17	1	6	--	--	112	43	36	43	0	112	10	1	2	1	3	.25	11	.215	.317	.321
1990 Toronto	AL	1	2	1	0	0	0	(0	0)	1	0	0	0	0	1	1	0	0	0	0	.00	0	.500	.667	.500
1992 Toronto	AL	13	15	1	1	0	0	(0	0)	2	2	2	2	0	9	0	0	0	0	0	.00	0	.067	.176	.133
2 ML YEARS		14	17	2	1	0	0	(0	0)	3	2	2	2	0	10	1	0	0	0	0	.00	0	.118	.250	.176

Luis Quinones

Bats: Both **Throws:** Right **Pos:** 3B 　　　　**Ht:** 5'11" **Wt:** 185 **Born:** 04/28/62 **Age:** 31

							BATTING												BASERUNNING				PERCENTAGES		
Year Team	Lg	G	AB	H	2B	3B	HR	(Hm	Rd)	TB	R	RBI	TBB	IBB	SO	HBP	SH	SF	SB	CS	SB%	GDP	Avg	OBP	SLG
1983 Oakland	AL	19	42	8	2	1	0	(0	0)	12	5	4	1	0	4	0	1	1	1	1	.50	0	.190	.205	.286
1986 San Francisco	NL	71	106	19	1	3	0	(0	0)	26	13	11	3	1	17	1	4	1	3	1	.75	1	.179	.207	.245
1987 Chicago	NL	49	101	22	6	0	0	(0	0)	28	12	8	10	0	16	0	0	0	0	0	.00	0	.218	.288	.277
1988 Cincinnati	NL	23	52	12	3	0	1	(0	1)	18	4	11	2	1	11	0	2	1	1	1	.50	0	.231	.255	.346
1989 Cincinnati	NL	97	340	83	13	4	12	(5	7)	140	43	34	25	0	46	3	8	2	2	4	.33	3	.244	.300	.412
1990 Cincinnati	NL	83	145	35	7	0	2	(1	1)	48	10	17	13	3	29	1	1	4	1	0	1.00	3	.241	.301	.331
1991 Cincinnati	NL	97	212	47	4	3	4	(2	2)	69	15	20	21	3	31	2	1	1	1	2	.33	2	.222	.297	.325
1992 Minnesota	AL	3	5	1	0	0	0	(0	0)	1	0	1	0	0	0	0	0	0	0	0	.00	0	.200	.167	.200
8 ML YEARS		442	1003	227	36	11	19	(8	11)	342	102	106	75	8	154	7	17	11	9	9	.50	9	.226	.282	.341

Carlos Quintana

Bats: Right **Throws:** Right **Pos:** 1B/RF 　　　　**Ht:** 6' 2" **Wt:** 220 **Born:** 08/26/65 **Age:** 27

							BATTING												BASERUNNING				PERCENTAGES		
Year Team	Lg	G	AB	H	2B	3B	HR	(Hm	Rd)	TB	R	RBI	TBB	IBB	SO	HBP	SH	SF	SB	CS	SB%	GDP	Avg	OBP	SLG
1988 Boston	AL	5	6	2	0	0	0	(0	0)	2	1	2	2	0	3	0	0	0	0	0	.00	0	.333	.500	.333
1989 Boston	AL	34	77	16	5	0	0	(0	0)	21	6	6	7	0	12	0	0	0	0	0	.00	5	.208	.274	.273
1990 Boston	AL	149	512	147	28	0	7	(3	4)	196	56	67	52	0	74	2	4	2	1	2	.33	19	.287	.354	.383
1991 Boston	AL	149	478	141	21	1	11	(2	9)	197	69	71	61	2	66	2	6	3	1	0	1.00	17	.295	.375	.412
4 ML YEARS		337	1073	306	54	1	18	(5	13)	416	132	146	122	2	155	4	10	5	2	2	.50	41	.285	.359	.388

Jamie Quirk

Bats: Left **Throws:** Right **Pos:** C 　　　　**Ht:** 6' 4" **Wt:** 200 **Born:** 10/22/54 **Age:** 38

							BATTING												BASERUNNING				PERCENTAGES		
Year Team	Lg	G	AB	H	2B	3B	HR	(Hm	Rd)	TB	R	RBI	TBB	IBB	SO	HBP	SH	SF	SB	CS	SB%	GDP	Avg	OBP	SLG
1975 Kansas City	AL	14	39	10	0	0	1	(1	0)	13	2	5	2	1	7	0	0	0	0	0	.00	1	.256	.293	.333
1976 Kansas City	AL	64	114	28	6	0	1	(1	0)	37	11	15	2	0	22	0	0	3	0	0	.00	1	.246	.252	.325
1977 Milwaukee	AL	93	221	48	14	1	3	(2	1)	73	16	13	8	2	47	2	2	0	0	1	.00	4	.217	.251	.330
1978 Kansas City	AL	17	29	6	2	0	0	(0	0)	8	3	2	5	0	4	0	0	0	0	0	.00	0	.207	.324	.277
1979 Kansas City	AL	51	79	24	6	1	1	(1	0)	35	8	11	5	0	13	1	0	0	0	0	.00	0	.304	.353	.443
1980 Kansas City	AL	62	163	45	5	0	5	(3	2)	65	13	21	7	2	24	1	3	3	3	2	.60	7	.276	.305	.399
1981 Kansas City	AL	46	100	25	7	0	0	(0	0)	32	8	10	6	1	17	1	0	0	0	2	.00	5	.250	.299	.320
1982 Kansas City	AL	36	78	18	3	0	1	(1	0)	24	8	5	3	0	15	0	0	1	0	0	.00	2	.231	.256	.308
1983 St. Louis	NL	48	86	18	2	1	2	(0	2)	28	3	11	6	0	27	1	0	0	0	0	.00	2	.209	.269	.326
1984 2 ML Teams		4	3	1	0	0	0	(1	0)	4	1	2	0	0	2	0	0	1	0	0	.00	0	.333	.250	1.333
1985 Kansas City	AL	19	57	16	3	1	0	(0	0)	21	3	4	2	0	9	0	0	0	0	0	.00	1	.281	.305	.368

Year Team	Lg	G	AB	H	2B	3B	HR	(Hm	Rd)	TB	R	RBI	TBB	IBB	SO	HBP	SH	SF	SB	CS	SB%	GDP	Avg	OBP	SLG
1986 Kansas City	AL	80	219	47	10	0	8	(5	3)	81	24	26	17	3	41	1	0	1	0	1	.00	4	.215	.273	.370
1987 Kansas City	AL	109	296	70	17	0	5	(0	5)	102	24	33	28	1	56	4	2	4	1	0	1.00	8	.236	.307	.345
1988 Kansas City	AL	84	196	47	7	1	8	(2	6)	80	22	25	28	2	41	1	4	3	1	5	.17	2	.240	.333	.408
1989 3 ML Teams	AL	47	85	15	2	0	1	(0	1)	20	6	10	12	0	20	0	1	1	0	2	.00	4	.176	.276	.235
1990 Oakland	AL	56	121	34	5	1	3	(1	2)	50	12	26	14	1	34	1	5	3	0	0	.00	1	.281	.353	.413
1991 Oakland	AL	76	203	53	4	0	1	(0	1)	60	16	17	16	1	28	2	3	0	0	3	.00	7	.261	.321	.296
1992 Oakland	AL	78	177	39	7	1	2	(2	0)	54	13	11	16	3	28	3	5	1	0	0	.00	4	.220	.294	.305
1984 Chicago	AL	3	2	0	0	0	0	(0	0)	0	0	1	0	0	2	0	0	1	0	0	.00	0	.000	.000	.000
Cleveland	AL	1	1	1	0	0	1	(1	0)	4	1	1	0	0	0	0	0	0	0	0	.00	0	1.000	1.000	4.000
1989 New York	AL	13	24	2	0	0	0	(0	0)	2	0	0	3	0	5	0	0	0	0	1	.00	1	.083	.185	.083
Oakland	AL	9	10	2	0	0	0	(0	1)	5	1	1	0	0	4	0	0	0	0	1	.00	3	.200	.200	.500
Baltimore	AL	25	51	11	2	0	0	(0	0)	13	5	9	9	0	11	0	1	1	0	1	.00	3	.216	.328	.255
18 ML YEARS		984	2266	544	100	7	43	(20	23)	787	193	247	177	17	435	18	25	21	5	16	.24	57	.240	.298	.347

Mike Raczka

Pitches: Left   **Bats:** Left   **Pos:** RP   Ht: 6' 0"   Wt: 200   Born: 11/16/62   Age: 30

Year Team	Lg	G	GS	CG	GF	IP	BFP	H	R	ER	HR	SH	SF	HB	TBB	IBB	SO	WP	Bk	W	L	Pct.	ShO	Sv	ERA
1990 Las Vegas	AAA	4	2	0	0	11.2	52	11	10	10	2	1	0	0	9	0	7	1	0	1	0	1.000	0	0	7.71
Tacoma	AAA	42	0	0	18	55.2	238	48	27	22	3	5	1	3	35	3	54	2	0	6	5	.545	0	2	3.56
1992 Modesto	A	6	0	0	3	9.1	43	13	9	7	1	1	0	1	3	0	5	1	0	1	1	.500	0	0	6.75
Tacoma	AAA	31	1	0	11	48.2	196	38	22	19	3	3	4	0	24	6	26	2	1	0	1	.000	0	0	3.51
1992 Oakland	AL	8	0	0	1	6.1	33	8	7	6	0	0	2	0	5	0	2	0	0	0	0	.000	0	0	8.53

Scott Radinsky

Pitches: Left   **Bats:** Left   **Pos:** RP   Ht: 6' 3"   Wt: 190   Born: 03/03/68   Age: 25

Year Team	Lg	G	GS	CG	GF	IP	BFP	H	R	ER	HR	SH	SF	HB	TBB	IBB	SO	WP	Bk	W	L	Pct.	ShO	Sv	ERA
1990 Chicago	AL	62	0	0	18	52.1	237	47	29	28	1	2	2	2	36	1	46	2	1	6	1	.857	0	4	4.82
1991 Chicago	AL	67	0	0	19	71.1	289	53	18	16	4	4	4	1	23	2	49	0	0	5	5	.500	0	8	2.02
1992 Chicago	AL	68	0	0	33	59.1	261	54	21	18	3	2	1	2	34	5	48	3	0	3	7	.300	0	15	2.73
3 ML YEARS		197	0	0	70	183	787	154	68	62	8	8	7	5	93	8	143	5	1	14	13	.519	0	27	3.05

Tim Raines

Bats: Both   **Throws:** Right   **Pos:** LF/DH   Ht: 5' 8"   Wt: 185   Born: 09/16/59   Age: 33

Year Team	Lg	G	AB	H	2B	3B	HR	(Hm	Rd)	TB	R	RBI	TBB	IBB	SO	HBP	SH	SF	SB	CS	SB%	GDP	Avg	OBP	SLG
1979 Montreal	NL	6	0	0	0	0	0	(0	0)	0	3	0	0	0	0	0	0	0	2	0	1.00	0	.000	.000	.000
1980 Montreal	NL	15	20	1	0	0	0	(0	0)	1	5	0	6	0	3	0	1	0	5	0	1.00	0	.050	.269	.050
1981 Montreal	NL	88	313	95	13	7	5	(3	2)	137	61	37	45	5	31	2	0	3	71	11	.87	7	.304	.391	.438
1982 Montreal	NL	156	647	179	32	8	4	(1	3)	239	90	43	75	9	83	2	6	1	78	16	.83	6	.277	.353	.369
1983 Montreal	NL	156	615	183	32	8	11	(5	6)	264	133	71	97	9	70	2	2	4	90	14	.87	12	.298	.393	.429
1984 Montreal	NL	160	622	192	**38**	9	8	(2	6)	272	106	60	87	7	69	2	3	4	75	10	.88	7	.309	.393	.437
1985 Montreal	NL	150	575	184	30	13	11	(4	7)	273	115	41	81	13	60	3	3	3	70	9	.89	9	.320	.405	.475
1986 Montreal	NL	151	580	194	35	10	9	(4	5)	276	91	62	78	9	60	2	1	3	70	9	.89	6	**.334**	**.413**	.476
1987 Montreal	NL	139	530	175	34	8	18	(9	9)	279	**123**	68	90	26	52	4	0	3	50	5	.91	9	.330	.429	.526
1988 Montreal	NL	109	429	116	19	7	12	(5	7)	185	66	48	53	14	44	2	0	4	33	7	.83	8	.270	.350	.431
1989 Montreal	NL	145	517	148	29	6	9	(6	3)	216	76	60	93	18	48	3	0	5	41	9	.82	8	.286	.395	.418
1990 Montreal	NL	130	457	131	11	5	9	(6	3)	179	65	62	70	8	43	3	0	8	49	16	.75	9	.287	.379	.392
1991 Chicago	AL	155	609	163	20	6	5	(1	4)	210	102	50	83	9	68	5	9	3	51	15	.77	7	.268	.359	.345
1992 Chicago	AL	144	551	162	22	9	7	(4	3)	223	102	54	81	4	48	0	4	8	45	6	.88	5	.294	.380	.405
14 ML YEARS		1704	6465	1923	315	96	108	(50	58)	2754	1138	656	939	131	679	30	29	49	730	127	.85	93	.297	.386	.426

Rafael Ramirez

Bats: Right   **Throws:** Right   **Pos:** SS   Ht: 5'11"   Wt: 190   Born: 02/18/59   Age: 34

Year Team	Lg	G	AB	H	2B	3B	HR	(Hm	Rd)	TB	R	RBI	TBB	IBB	SO	HBP	SH	SF	SB	CS	SB%	GDP	Avg	OBP	SLG
1980 Atlanta	NL	50	165	44	6	1	2	(2	0)	58	17	11	2	0	33	4	3	0	2	1	.67	2	.267	.292	.352
1981 Atlanta	NL	95	307	67	16	2	2	(1	1)	93	30	20	24	3	47	1	9	0	7	3	.70	3	.218	.276	.303
1982 Atlanta	NL	157	609	169	24	4	10	(7	3)	231	74	52	36	7	49	3	16	5	27	14	.66	10	.278	.319	.379
1983 Atlanta	NL	152	622	185	13	5	7	(2	5)	229	82	58	36	4	48	2	6	2	16	12	.57	8	.297	.337	.368
1984 Atlanta	NL	145	591	157	22	4	2	(1	1)	193	51	48	26	1	70	1	5	6	14	17	.45	9	.266	.295	.327
1985 Atlanta	NL	138	568	141	25	4	5	(4	1)	189	54	58	20	1	63	0	2	5	2	6	.25	21	.248	.272	.333
1986 Atlanta	NL	134	496	119	21	1	8	(1	7)	166	57	33	21	1	60	3	7	3	19	8	.70	16	.240	.273	.335
1987 Atlanta	NL	56	179	47	12	0	1	(0	1)	62	22	21	8	0	16	2	4	1	6	3	.67	3	.263	.300	.346
1988 Houston	NL	155	566	156	30	5	6	(2	4)	214	51	59	18	6	61	3	6	6	3	2	.60	16	.276	.298	.378
1989 Houston	NL	151	537	132	20	2	6	(3	3)	174	46	54	29	3	64	0	6	3	3	1	.75	8	.246	.283	.324

Year	Team	Lg	G	AB	H	2B	3B	HR	(Hm	Rd)	TB	R	RBI	TBB	IBB	SO	HBP	SH	SF	SB	CS	SB%	GDP	Avg	OBP	SLG
1990	Houston	NL	132	445	116	19	3	2	(1	1)	147	44	37	24	9	46	1	9	1	10	5	.67	9	.261	.299	.330
1991	Houston	NL	101	233	55	10	0	1	(0	1)	68	17	20	13	1	40	0	1	2	3	3	.50	3	.236	.274	.292
1992	Houston	NL	73	176	44	6	0	1	(0	1)	53	17	13	7	1	24	1	1	0	0	0	.00	5	.250	.283	.301
13 ML YEARS			1539	5494	1432	224	31	53	(24	29)	1877	562	484	264	37	621	21	73	35	112	75	.60	113	.261	.295	.342

Fernando Ramsey

Bats: Right **Throws:** Right **Pos:** CF **Ht:** 6' 1" **Wt:** 175 **Born:** 12/20/65 **Age:** 27

			BATTING																BASERUNNING				PERCENTAGES		
Year	Team	Lg	G	AB	H	2B	3B	HR	(Hm	Rd)	TB	R	RBI	TBB	IBB	SO	HBP	SH	SF	SB	CS	SB%	GDP	Avg	OBP	SLG
1987	Geneva	A	39	56	9	1	0	0	--	--	10	9	3	5	1	10	0	2	0	2	0	1.00	0	.161	.230	.179
1988	Chston-Wv	A	121	381	92	5	1	0	--	--	99	36	15	14	1	68	4	6	0	15	7	.68	4	.241	.276	.260
1989	Peoria	A	131	410	100	7	5	0	--	--	117	56	34	25	0	70	10	11	3	16	10	.62	6	.244	.301	.285
1990	Winston-Sal	A	124	428	109	12	4	5	--	--	144	52	48	19	0	50	3	9	2	43	7	.86	4	.255	.290	.336
1991	Charlotte	AA	139	547	151	18	6	6	--	--	199	78	49	36	0	90	3	7	2	37	17	.69	8	.276	.323	.364
1992	Iowa	AAA	133	480	129	9	5	1	--	--	151	62	38	23	0	78	2	11	0	39	12	.76	14	.269	.305	.315
1992	Chicago	NL	18	25	3	0	0	0	(0	0)	3	0	2	0	0	6	0	0	0	0	0	.00	0	.120	.120	.120

Willie Randolph

Bats: Right **Throws:** Right **Pos:** 2B **Ht:** 5'11" **Wt:** 170 **Born:** 07/06/54 **Age:** 38

			BATTING																BASERUNNING				PERCENTAGES		
Year	Team	Lg	G	AB	H	2B	3B	HR	(Hm	Rd)	TB	R	RBI	TBB	IBB	SO	HBP	SH	SF	SB	CS	SB%	GDP	Avg	OBP	SLG
1975	Pittsburgh	NL	30	61	10	1	0	0	(0	0)	11	9	3	7	1	6	0	1	1	1	0	1.00	3	.164	.246	.180
1976	New York	AL	125	430	115	15	4	1	(0	1)	141	59	40	58	5	39	3	6	3	37	12	.76	10	.267	.356	.328
1977	New York	AL	147	551	151	28	11	4	(2	2)	213	91	40	64	1	53	1	2	6	13	6	.68	11	.274	.347	.387
1978	New York	AL	134	499	139	18	6	3	(2	1)	178	87	42	82	1	51	4	6	5	36	7	.84	12	.279	.381	.357
1979	New York	AL	153	574	155	15	13	5	(2	3)	211	98	61	95	5	39	3	5	5	33	12	.73	23	.270	.374	.368
1980	New York	AL	138	513	151	23	7	7	(2	5)	209	99	46	119	4	45	2	5	3	30	5	.86	6	.294	.427	.407
1981	New York	AL	93	357	83	14	3	2	(1	1)	109	59	24	57	0	24	0	5	3	14	5	.74	10	.232	.336	.305
1982	New York	AL	144	553	155	21	4	3	(1	2)	193	85	36	75	3	35	3	10	2	16	9	.64	13	.280	.368	.349
1983	New York	AL	104	420	117	21	1	2	(1	1)	146	73	38	53	0	32	1	3	0	12	4	.75	11	.279	.361	.348
1984	New York	AL	142	564	162	24	2	2	(1	1)	196	86	31	86	4	42	0	7	7	10	6	.63	15	.287	.377	.348
1985	New York	AL	143	497	137	21	2	5	(3	2)	177	75	40	85	3	39	4	5	6	16	9	.64	24	.276	.382	.356
1986	New York	AL	141	492	136	15	2	5	(2	3)	170	76	50	94	0	49	3	8	4	15	2	.88	11	.276	.393	.346
1987	New York	AL	120	449	137	24	2	7	(3	4)	186	96	67	82	1	25	2	5	5	11	1	.92	15	.305	.411	.414
1988	New York	AL	110	404	93	20	1	2	(1	1)	121	43	34	55	2	39	2	8	5	8	4	.67	10	.230	.322	.300
1989	Los Angeles	NL	145	549	155	18	0	2	(0	2)	179	62	36	71	2	51	4	4	5	7	6	.54	10	.282	.366	.326
1990	2 ML Teams		119	388	101	13	3	2	(1	1)	126	52	30	45	1	34	2	10	1	7	1	.88	14	.260	.339	.325
1991	Milwaukee	AL	124	431	141	14	3	0	(0	0)	161	60	54	75	3	38	0	3	3	4	2	.67	14	.327	.424	.374
1992	New York	NL	90	286	72	11	1	2	(2	0)	91	29	15	40	1	34	4	6	0	1	3	.25	6	.252	.352	.318
1990	Los Angeles	NL	26	96	26	4	0	1	(0	1)	33	15	9	13	0	9	1	3	0	1	0	1.00	3	.271	.364	.344
	Oakland	AL	93	292	75	9	3	1	(1	0)	93	37	21	32	1	25	1	7	1	6	1	.86	11	.257	.331	.318
18 ML YEARS			2202	8018	2210	316	65	54	(24	30)	2818	1239	687	1243	37	675	38	99	64	271	94	.74	218	.276	.373	.351

Pat Rapp

Pitches: Right **Bats:** Right **Pos:** SP **Ht:** 6' 3" **Wt:** 195 **Born:** 07/13/67 **Age:** 25

			HOW MUCH HE PITCHED						WHAT HE GAVE UP											THE RESULTS				
Year	Team	Lg	G	GS	CG	GF	IP	BFP	H	R	ER	HR	SH	SF	HB	TBB	IBB	SO	WP	Bk	W	L	Pct.	ShO	Sv	ERA
1989	Pocatello	R	16	12	1	1	73	333	90	54	43	5	3	2	8	29	1	40	6	0	4	6	.400	0	0	5.30
1990	Clinton	A	27	26	4	1	167.1	692	132	60	49	2	6	2	7	79	2	132	8	3	14	10	.583	0	0	2.64
1991	San Jose	A	16	15	1	0	90	396	88	41	25	1	1	2	10	37	0	73	1	0	7	5	.583	0	0	2.50
	Shreveport	AA	10	10	1	0	60.1	257	52	23	18	1	4	2	3	22	0	46	1	0	6	2	.750	1	0	2.69
1992	Phoenix	AAA	39	12	2	17	121	516	115	54	41	2	8	10	2	40	1	79	1	1	7	8	.467	0	3	3.05
1992	San Francisco	NL	3	2	0	1	10	43	8	8	8	0	2	0	1	6	1	3	0	0	0	2	.000	0	0	7.20

Dennis Rasmussen

Pitches: Left **Bats:** Left **Pos:** SP **Ht:** 6' 7" **Wt:** 233 **Born:** 04/18/59 **Age:** 34

			HOW MUCH HE PITCHED						WHAT HE GAVE UP											THE RESULTS				
Year	Team	Lg	G	GS	CG	GF	IP	BFP	H	R	ER	HR	SH	SF	HB	TBB	IBB	SO	WP	Bk	W	L	Pct.	ShO	Sv	ERA
1983	San Diego	NL	4	1	0	1	13.2	58	10	5	3	1	0	0	0	8	0	13	1	0	0	0	.000	0	0	1.98
1984	New York	AL	24	24	1	0	147.2	616	127	79	75	16	3	7	4	60	0	110	8	2	9	6	.600	0	0	4.57
1985	New York	AL	22	16	2	1	101.2	429	97	56	45	10	1	5	1	42	1	63	3	1	3	5	.375	0	0	3.98
1986	New York	AL	31	31	3	0	202	819	160	91	87	28	1	5	2	74	0	131	5	0	18	6	.750	1	0	3.88
1987	2 ML Teams		33	32	2	0	191.1	814	184	100	97	36	8	6	5	67	1	128	7	2	13	8	.619	0	0	4.56
1988	2 ML Teams		31	31	7	0	204.2	854	199	84	78	17	10	4	4	58	4	112	7	5	16	10	.615	1	0	3.43
1989	San Diego	NL	33	33	1	0	183.2	799	190	100	87	18	9	11	3	72	6	87	4	2	10	10	.500	1	0	4.26
1990	San Diego	NL	32	32	3	0	187.2	825	217	110	94	28	14	4	3	62	4	86	9	1	11	15	.423	1	0	4.51
1991	San Diego	NL	24	24	1	0	146.2	633	155	74	61	12	4	6	2	49	3	75	1	1	6	13	.316	1	0	3.74

Year	Team	Lg	G	GS	CG	GF	IP	BFP	H	R	ER	HR	SH	SF	HB	TBB	IBB	SO	WP	Bk	W	L	Pct.	ShO	Sv	ERA
1992	2 ML Teams		8	6	1	1	42.2	158	32	13	12	2	1	1	1	8	1	12	3	0	4	1	.800	1	0	2.53
1987	New York	AL	26	25	2	0	146	627	145	78	77	31	5	5	4	55	1	89	6	0	9	7	.563	0	0	4.75
	Cincinnati	NL	7	7	0	0	45.1	187	39	22	20	5	3	1	1	12	0	39	1	2	4	1	.800	0	0	3.97
1988	Cincinnati	NL	11	11	1	0	56.1	255	68	36	36	8	2	2	2	22	4	27	1	5	2	6	.250	1	0	5.75
	San Diego	NL	20	20	6	0	148.1	599	131	48	42	9	8	2	2	36	0	85	6	0	14	4	.778	0	0	2.55
1992	Chicago	NL	3	1	0	1	5	24	7	6	6	2	0	1	1	2	1	0	0	0	0	0	.000	0	0	10.80
	Kansas City	AL	5	5	1	0	37.2	134	25	7	6	0	1	0	0	6	0	12	3	0	4	1	.800	1	0	1.43
10	ML YEARS		242	230	21	3	1421.2	6005	1371	712	639	168	51	49	25	500	20	817	48	14	90	74	.549	5	0	4.05

Randy Ready

Bats: Right **Throws:** Right **Pos:** LF/DH   **Ht:** 5'11" **Wt:** 180 **Born:** 01/08/60 **Age:** 33

						BATTING														BASERUNNING				PERCENTAGES		
Year	Team	Lg	G	AB	H	2B	3B	HR	(Hm	Rd)	TB	R	RBI	TBB	IBB	SO	HBP	SH	SF	SB	CS	SB%	GDP	Avg	OBP	SLG
1983	Milwaukee	AL	12	37	15	3	2	1	(0	1)	25	8	6	6	1	3	0	0	0	0	1	.00	0	.405	.488	.676
1984	Milwaukee	AL	37	123	23	6	1	3	(3	0)	40	13	13	14	0	18	0	3	0	0	0	.00	2	.187	.270	.325
1985	Milwaukee	AL	48	181	48	9	5	1	(0	1)	70	29	21	14	0	23	1	2	2	0	0	.00	6	.265	.318	.387
1986	2 ML Teams		24	82	15	4	0	1	(0	1)	22	8	4	9	0	10	0	1	0	2	0	1.00	3	.183	.264	.268
1987	San Diego	NL	124	350	108	26	6	12	(7	5)	182	69	54	67	2	44	3	2	1	7	3	.70	7	.309	.423	.520
1988	San Diego	NL	114	331	88	16	2	7	(3	4)	129	43	39	39	1	38	3	4	3	6	2	.75	3	.266	.346	.390
1989	2 ML Teams		100	254	67	13	2	8	(3	5)	108	37	26	42	0	37	2	1	4	4	3	.57	4	.264	.368	.425
1990	Philadelphia	NL	101	217	53	9	1	1	(0	1)	67	26	26	29	0	35	1	3	3	2	2	.60	3	.244	.332	.309
1991	Philadelphia	NL	76	205	51	10	1	1	(1	0)	66	32	20	47	3	25	1	1	4	2	1	.67	5	.249	.385	.322
1992	Oakland	AL	61	125	25	2	0	3	(1	2)	36	17	17	25	1	23	0	2	2	1	0	1.00	1	.200	.329	.288
1986	Milwaukee	AL	23	79	15	4	0	1	(0	1)	22	8	4	9	0	9	0	1	0	2	0	1.00	3	.190	.273	.278
	San Diego	NL	1	3	0	0	0	0	(0	0)	0	0	0	0	0	1	0	0	0	0	0	.00	0	.000	.000	.000
1989	San Diego	NL	28	67	17	2	1	0	(0	0)	21	4	5	11	0	6	0	1	1	0	0	.00	2	.254	.354	.313
	Philadelphia	NL	72	187	50	11	1	8	(3	5)	87	33	21	31	0	31	2	0	3	4	3	.57	2	.267	.372	.465
10	ML YEARS		697	1905	493	98	20	38	(18	20)	745	282	226	292	8	256	11	19	19	25	12	.68	34	.259	.357	.391

Jeff Reardon

Pitches: Right **Bats:** Right **Pos:** RP   **Ht:** 6'0" **Wt:** 205 **Born:** 10/01/55 **Age:** 37

			HOW MUCH HE PITCHED						WHAT HE GAVE UP										THE RESULTS						
Year	Team	Lg	G	GS	CG	GF	IP	BFP	H	R	ER	HR	SH	SF	HB	TBB	IBB	SO	WP	Bk	W	L	Pct.	ShO	Sv	ERA
1979	New York	NL	18	0	0	10	21	81	12	7	4	2	2	1	0	9	3	10	2	0	1	2	.333	0	2	1.71
1980	New York	NL	61	0	0	35	110	475	96	36	32	10	8	5	0	47	15	101	2	0	8	7	.533	0	6	2.62
1981	2 ML Teams		43	0	0	33	70.1	279	48	17	17	5	3	1	2	21	4	49	1	0	3	0	1.000	0	8	2.18
1982	Montreal	NL	75	0	0	53	109	444	87	28	25	6	8	4	2	36	4	86	2	0	7	4	.636	0	26	2.06
1983	Montreal	NL	66	0	0	53	92	403	87	34	31	7	8	2	1	44	9	78	2	0	7	9	.438	0	21	3.03
1984	Montreal	NL	68	0	0	58	87	363	70	31	28	5	3	2	3	37	7	79	4	0	7	7	.500	0	23	2.90
1985	Montreal	NL	63	0	0	50	87.2	356	68	31	31	7	3	1	1	26	4	67	2	0	2	8	.200	0	41	3.18
1986	Montreal	NL	62	0	0	48	89	368	83	42	39	12	9	1	1	26	2	67	0	0	7	9	.438	0	35	3.94
1987	Minnesota	AL	63	0	0	58	80.1	337	70	41	40	14	1	3	3	28	4	83	2	0	8	8	.500	0	31	4.48
1988	Minnesota	AL	63	0	0	58	73	299	68	21	20	6	4	1	2	15	2	56	0	3	2	4	.333	0	42	2.47
1989	Minnesota	AL	65	0	0	61	73	297	68	33	33	8	1	5	3	12	3	46	1	1	5	4	.556	0	31	4.07
1990	Boston	AL	47	0	0	37	51.1	210	39	19	18	5	1	0	1	19	4	33	0	0	5	3	.625	0	21	3.16
1991	Boston	AL	57	0	0	51	59.1	248	54	21	20	9	0	2	1	16	3	44	0	0	1	4	.200	0	40	3.03
1992	2 ML Teams		60	0	0	50	58	245	67	22	22	6	2	2	2	9	1	39			5	2	.714	0	30	3.41
1981	New York	NL	18	0	0	14	28.2	124	27	11	11	2	0	1	1	12	4	28	0	0	1	0	1.000	0	2	3.45
	Montreal	NL	25	0	0	19	41.2	155	21	6	6	3	3	0	1	9	0	21	1	0	2	0	1.000	0	6	1.30
1992	Boston	AL	46	0	0	39	42.1	183	53	20	20	6	1	2	1	7	0	32	0	0	2	2	.500	0	27	4.25
	Atlanta	NL	14	0	0	11	15.2	62	14	2	2	0	1	0	1	2	1	7	0	0	3	0	1.000	0	3	1.15
14	ML YEARS		811	0	0	655	1061	4405	917	383	360	102	53	30	22	345	65	838	18	4	68	71	.489	0	357	3.05

Jeff Reboulet

Bats: Right **Throws:** Right **Pos:** SS/2B/3B   **Ht:** 6'0" **Wt:** 167 **Born:** 04/30/64 **Age:** 29

						BATTING														BASERUNNING				PERCENTAGES		
Year	Team	Lg	G	AB	H	2B	3B	HR	(Hm	Rd)	TB	R	RBI	TBB	IBB	SO	HBP	SH	SF	SB	CS	SB%	GDP	Avg	OBP	SLG
1986	Visalia	A	72	254	73	13	1	0	--	--	88	54	29	54	1	33	1	5	2	14	11	.56	4	.287	.412	.346
1987	Orlando	AA	129	422	108	15	1	1	--	--	128	52	35	58	0	56	1	5	0	9	5	.64	9	.256	.347	.303
1988	Orlando	AA	125	439	112	24	2	4	--	--	152	57	41	53	0	55	3	7	2	18	8	.69	9	.255	.338	.346
	Portland	AAA	4	12	1	0	0	0	--	--	1	0	1	3	0	2	0	0	0	0	0	.00	0	.083	.267	.083
1989	Portland	AAA	26	65	16	1	0	0	--	--	17	9	3	12	0	11	0	0	2	2	1	.67	2	.246	.354	.262
	Orlando	AA	81	291	63	5	1	0	--	--	70	43	26	49	0	33	1	2	3	11	6	.65	7	.216	.328	.241
1990	Orlando	AA	97	287	66	12	2	2	--	--	88	43	28	57	1	37	2	5	4	10	5	.67	5	.230	.357	.307
1991	Portland	AAA	134	391	97	27	3	3	--	--	139	50	46	57	2	52	2	17	2	5	2	.71	9	.248	.345	.355
1992	Portland	AAA	48	161	46	11	1	2	--	--	65	21	21	35	0	18	1	4	1	3	3	.50	7	.286	.414	.404
1992	Minnesota	AL	73	137	26	7	1	1	(1	0)	38	15	16	23	0	26	1	7	0	3	2	.60	0	.190	.311	.277

Gary Redus

Bats: Right **Throws:** Right **Pos:** 1B/RF 　　**Ht:** 6' 1" **Wt:** 185 **Born:** 11/01/56 **Age:** 36

Year	Team	Lg	G	AB	H	2B	3B	HR	(Hm	Rd)	TB	R	RBI	TBB	IBB	SO	HBP	SH	SF	SB	CS	SB%	GDP	Avg	OBP	SLG
1982	Cincinnati	NL	20	83	18	3	2	1	(1	0)	28	12	7	5	0	21	0	0	1	11	2	.85	0	.217	.258	.337
1983	Cincinnati	NL	125	453	112	20	9	17	(6	11)	201	90	51	71	4	111	3	2	2	39	14	.74	6	.247	.352	.444
1984	Cincinnati	NL	123	394	100	21	3	7	(4	3)	148	69	22	52	3	71	1	3	5	48	11	.81	4	.254	.338	.376
1985	Cincinnati	NL	101	246	62	14	4	6	(4	2)	102	51	28	44	2	52	1	2	1	48	12	.80	0	.252	.366	.415
1986	Philadelphia	NL	90	340	84	22	4	11	(8	3)	147	62	33	47	4	78	3	1	1	25	7	.78	2	.247	.343	.432
1987	Chicago	AL	130	475	112	26	6	12	(4	8)	186	78	48	69	0	90	0	3	7	52	11	.83	7	.236	.328	.392
1988	2 ML Teams		107	333	83	12	4	8	(3	5)	127	54	38	48	1	71	3	0	8	31	4	.89	6	.249	.342	.381
1989	Pittsburgh	NL	98	279	79	18	7	6	(3	3)	129	42	33	40	3	51	1	1	3	25	6	.81	5	.283	.372	.462
1990	Pittsburgh	NL	96	227	56	15	3	6	(2	4)	95	32	23	33	0	38	2	1	5	11	5	.69	1	.247	.341	.419
1991	Pittsburgh	NL	98	252	62	12	2	7	(3	4)	99	45	24	28	2	39	3	1	4	17	3	.85	0	.246	.324	.393
1992	Pittsburgh	NL	76	176	45	7	3	3	(1	2)	67	26	12	17	0	25	0	0	0	11	4	.73	1	.256	.321	.381
1988	Chicago	AL	77	262	69	10	4	6	(1	5)	105	42	34	33	1	52	2	0	7	26	2	.93	5	.263	.342	.401
	Pittsburgh	NL	30	71	14	2	0	2	(2	0)	22	12	4	15	0	19	1	0	1	5	2	.71	1	.197	.341	.310
11	ML YEARS		1064	3258	813	170	47	84	(39	45)	1329	561	319	454	19	647	17	14	37	318	79	.80	32	.250	.341	.408

Darren Reed

Bats: Right **Throws:** Right **Pos:** RF/LF 　　**Ht:** 6' 1" **Wt:** 205 **Born:** 10/16/65 **Age:** 27

Year	Team	Lg	G	AB	H	2B	3B	HR	(Hm	Rd)	TB	R	RBI	TBB	IBB	SO	HBP	SH	SF	SB	CS	SB%	GDP	Avg	OBP	SLG
1984	Oneonta	A	40	113	26	7	0	2	--	--	39	17	9	10	0	19	0	1	1	2	1	.67	2	.230	.290	.345
1985	Ft.Laudrdle	A	100	369	117	21	4	10	--	--	176	63	61	36	3	56	7	0	1	13	3	.81	9	.317	.382	.477
1986	Albany	AA	51	196	45	11	1	4	--	--	70	22	27	15	0	24	1	1	5	1	0	1.00	2	.230	.281	.357
1987	Columbus	AAA	21	79	26	3	3	8	--	--	59	15	16	4	0	9	0	0	0	2	2	.00	2	.329	.361	.747
	Albany	AA	107	404	129	23	4	20	--	--	220	68	79	51	9	50	8	0	3	9	6	.60	10	.319	.403	.545
1988	Tidewater	AAA	101	345	83	26	0	9	--	--	136	31	47	32	2	66	3	3	4	0	3	.00	9	.241	.307	.394
1989	Tidewater	AAA	133	444	119	30	6	4	--	--	173	57	50	60	1	70	11	1	4	11	2	.85	15	.268	.366	.390
1990	Tidewater	AAA	104	359	95	21	6	17	--	--	179	58	74	51	4	62	6	0	4	15	4	.79	11	.265	.362	.499
1992	Indianapols	AAA	1	3	1	1	0	0	--	--	2	0	0	0	0	1	0	0	0	0	0	.00	0	.333	.333	.667
	Wst Plm Bch	A	10	40	10	4	0	2	--	--	20	6	12	1	0	14	4	0	0	0	0	.00	0	.250	.326	.500
1990	New York	NL	26	39	8	4	1	1	(1	0)	17	5	2	3	0	11	0	0	0	1	0	1.00	3	.205	.262	.436
1992	2 ML Teams		56	114	20	4	0	5	(1	4)	39	12	14	8	2	34	1	0	2	0	0	.00	3	.175	.232	.342
1992	Montreal	NL	42	81	14	2	0	5	(1	4)	31	10	10	6	2	23	1	0	0	0	0	.00	3	.173	.239	.383
	Minnesota	AL	14	33	6	2	0	0	(0	0)	8	2	4	2	0	11	0	0	2	0	0	.00	0	.182	.216	.242
2	ML YEARS		82	153	28	8	1	6	(2	4)	56	17	16	11	2	45	1	0	2	1	0	1.00	3	.183	.240	.366

Jeff Reed

Bats: Left **Throws:** Right **Pos:** C 　　**Ht:** 6' 2" **Wt:** 190 **Born:** 11/12/62 **Age:** 30

Year	Team	Lg	G	AB	H	2B	3B	HR	(Hm	Rd)	TB	R	RBI	TBB	IBB	SO	HBP	SH	SF	SB	CS	SB%	GDP	Avg	OBP	SLG
1984	Minnesota	AL	18	21	3	3	0	0	(0	0)	6	3	1	2	0	6	0	1	0	0	0	.00	0	.143	.217	.286
1985	Minnesota	AL	7	10	2	0	0	0	(0	0)	2	2	0	0	0	3	0	0	0	0	0	.00	0	.200	.200	.200
1986	Minnesota	AL	68	165	39	6	1	2	(1	1)	53	13	9	16	0	19	1	3	0	1	0	1.00	2	.236	.308	.321
1987	Montreal	NL	75	207	44	11	0	1	(1	0)	58	15	21	12	1	20	1	4	4	0	1	.00	4	.213	.254	.280
1988	2 ML Teams		92	265	60	9	2	1	(1	0)	76	20	16	28	1	41	0	1	1	1	0	1.00	5	.226	.299	.287
1989	Cincinnati	NL	102	287	64	11	0	3	(1	2)	84	16	23	34	5	46	2	3	4	0	0	.00	6	.223	.306	.293
1990	Cincinnati	NL	72	175	44	8	1	3	(2	1)	63	12	16	24	5	26	0	0	5	0	0	.00	4	.251	.340	.360
1991	Cincinnati	NL	91	270	72	15	2	3	(1	2)	100	20	31	23	3	38	1	1	5	0	1	.00	6	.267	.321	.370
1992	Cincinnati	NL	15	25	4	0	0	0	(0	0)	4	2	2	1	1	4	0	0	0	0	0	.00	0	.160	.192	.160
1988	Montreal	NL	43	123	27	3	2	0	(1	0)	34	10	9	13	1	22	0	1	1	1	0	1.00	3	.220	.294	.276
	Cincinnati	NL	49	142	33	6	0	1	(1	0)	42	10	7	15	0	19	0	0	0	0	0	.00	2	.232	.306	.296
9	ML YEARS		540	1425	332	63	6	13	(7	6)	446	103	119	140	16	203	5	13	15	2	2	.50	32	.233	.301	.313

Jody Reed

Bats: Right **Throws:** Right **Pos:** 2B 　　**Ht:** 5' 9" **Wt:** 165 **Born:** 07/26/62 **Age:** 30

Year	Team	Lg	G	AB	H	2B	3B	HR	(Hm	Rd)	TB	R	RBI	TBB	IBB	SO	HBP	SH	SF	SB	CS	SB%	GDP	Avg	OBP	SLG
1987	Boston	AL	9	30	9	1	1	0	(0	0)	12	4	8	4	0	0	0	1	0	1	1	.50	0	.300	.382	.400
1988	Boston	AL	109	338	99	23	1	1	(0	1)	127	60	28	45	1	21	4	11	2	1	3	.25	5	.293	.380	.376
1989	Boston	AL	146	524	151	42	2	3	(2	1)	206	76	40	73	0	44	4	13	5	4	5	.44	12	.288	.376	.393
1990	Boston	AL	155	598	173	45	0	5	(3	2)	233	70	51	75	4	65	4	11	3	4	4	.50	19	.289	.371	.390
1991	Boston	AL	153	618	175	42	2	5	(3	2)	236	87	60	60	2	53	4	11	3	6	5	.55	15	.283	.349	.382
1992	Boston	AL	143	550	136	27	1	3	(2	1)	174	64	40	62	2	44	0	10	4	7	8	.47	17	.247	.321	.316
6	ML YEARS		715	2658	743	180	7	17	(11	6)	988	361	227	319	9	227	16	57	17	23	26	.47	68	.280	.358	.372

166

Rick Reed

Pitches: Right **Bats:** Right **Pos:** SP **Ht:** 6' 0" **Wt:** 195 **Born:** 08/16/64 **Age:** 28

		HOW MUCH HE PITCHED						WHAT HE GAVE UP												THE RESULTS					
Year Team	Lg	G	GS	CG	GF	IP	BFP	H	R	ER	HR	SH	SF	HB	TBB	IBB	SO	WP	Bk	W	L	Pct.	ShO	Sv	ERA
1988 Pittsburgh	NL	2	2	0	0	12	47	10	4	4	1	2	0	0	2	0	6	0	0	1	0	1.000	0	0	3.00
1989 Pittsburgh	NL	15	7	0	2	54.2	232	62	35	34	5	2	3	2	11	3	34	0	3	1	4	.200	0	0	5.60
1990 Pittsburgh	NL	13	8	1	2	53.2	238	62	32	26	6	2	1	1	12	6	27	0	0	2	3	.400	1	1	4.36
1991 Pittsburgh	NL	1	1	0	0	4.1	21	8	6	5	1	0	0	0	1	0	2	0	0	0	0	.000	0	0	10.38
1992 Kansas City	AL	19	18	1	0	100.1	419	105	47	41	10	2	5	5	20	3	49	0	0	3	7	.300	1	0	3.68
5 ML YEARS		50	36	2	4	225	957	247	124	110	23	8	9	8	46	12	118	0	3	7	14	.333	2	1	4.40

Steve Reed

Pitches: Right **Bats:** Right **Pos:** RP **Ht:** 6' 2" **Wt:** 195 **Born:** 03/11/66 **Age:** 27

		HOW MUCH HE PITCHED						WHAT HE GAVE UP												THE RESULTS					
Year Team	Lg	G	GS	CG	GF	IP	BFP	H	R	ER	HR	SH	SF	HB	TBB	IBB	SO	WP	Bk	W	L	Pct.	ShO	Sv	ERA
1988 Pocatello	R	31	0	0	29	46	192	42	20	13	3	3	2	2	8	1	49	0	1	4	1	.800	0	13	2.54
1989 Clinton	A	60	0	0	50	94.2	370	54	16	11	1	4	5	7	38	10	104	0	0	5	3	.625	0	26	1.05
San Jose	A	2	0	0	1	2	7	0	0	0	0	0	0	0	1	0	3	0	0	0	0	.000	0	0	0.00
1990 Shreveport	AA	45	0	0	28	60.1	255	53	20	11	2	2	1	2	20	6	59	0	1	3	1	.750	0	8	1.64
1991 Shreveport	AA	15	0	0	14	21.2	81	17	2	2	1	0	0	0	3	0	26	0	0	2	0	1.000	0	7	0.83
Phoenix	AAA	41	0	0	24	56.1	241	62	33	27	5	3	2	2	12	0	46	1	0	2	3	.400	0	6	4.31
1992 Shreveport	AA	27	0	0	25	29	105	18	3	2	1	0	1	1	0	0	33	0	0	1	0	1.000	0	23	0.62
Phoenix	AAA	29	0	0	28	31	128	27	13	12	2	2	2	0	10	3	30	1	0	0	1	.000	0	20	3.48
1992 San Francisco	NL	18	0	0	2	15.2	63	13	5	4	2	0	0	0	3	0	11	0	0	1	0	1.000	0	0	2.30

Kevin Reimer

Bats: Left **Throws:** Right **Pos:** LF/DH **Ht:** 6' 2" **Wt:** 230 **Born:** 06/28/64 **Age:** 29

		BATTING																BASERUNNING				PERCENTAGES		
Year Team	Lg	G	AB	H	2B	3B	HR	(Hm Rd)	TB	R	RBI	TBB	IBB	SO	HBP	SH	SF	SB	CS	SB%	GDP	Avg	OBP	SLG
1988 Texas	AL	12	25	3	0	0	1	(0 1)	6	2	2	0	0	6	0	0	1	0	0	.00	0	.120	.115	.240
1989 Texas	AL	3	5	0	0	0	0	(0 0)	0	0	0	0	0	1	0	0	0	0	0	.00	1	.000	.000	.000
1990 Texas	AL	64	100	26	9	1	2	(0 2)	43	5	15	10	0	22	1	0	0	0	1	.00	3	.260	.333	.430
1991 Texas	AL	136	394	106	22	0	20	(13 7)	188	46	69	33	6	93	7	0	0	0	3	.00	10	.269	.332	.477
1992 Texas	AL	148	494	132	32	2	16	(10 6)	216	56	58	42	5	103	10	0	1	2	4	.33	10	.267	.336	.437
5 ML YEARS		363	1018	267	63	3	39	(23 16)	453	109	144	85	11	225	18	0	8	2	8	20	24	.262	.328	.445

Todd Revenig

Pitches: Right **Bats:** Right **Pos:** RP **Ht:** 6' 1" **Wt:** 185 **Born:** 06/28/69 **Age:** 24

		HOW MUCH HE PITCHED						WHAT HE GAVE UP												THE RESULTS					
Year Team	Lg	G	GS	CG	GF	IP	BFP	H	R	ER	HR	SH	SF	HB	TBB	IBB	SO	WP	Bk	W	L	Pct.	ShO	Sv	ERA
1990 Sou Oregon	A	24	0	0	14	44.2	176	33	13	4	2	4	1	0	9	2	46	1	2	3	2	.600	0	6	0.81
1991 Madison	A	26	0	0	22	28.2	109	13	6	3	1	3	0	0	10	2	27	1	1	1	0	1.000	0	13	0.94
Huntsville	AA	12	0	0	6	18.1	68	11	3	2	1	0	1	2	4	0	10	0	0	1	2	.333	0	0	0.98
1992 Huntsville	AA	53	0	0	48	63.2	233	32	14	12	8	2	2	0	11	0	49	1	0	1	1	.500	0	33	1.70
1992 Oakland	AL	2	0	0	2	2	7	2	0	0	0	0	0	0	0	0	1	0	0	0	0	.000	0	0	0.00

Harold Reynolds

Bats: Both **Throws:** Right **Pos:** 2B **Ht:** 5'11" **Wt:** 165 **Born:** 11/26/60 **Age:** 32

		BATTING																BASERUNNING				PERCENTAGES		
Year Team	Lg	G	AB	H	2B	3B	HR	(Hm Rd)	TB	R	RBI	TBB	IBB	SO	HBP	SH	SF	SB	CS	SB%	GDP	Avg	OBP	SLG
1983 Seattle	AL	20	59	12	4	1	0	(0 0)	18	8	1	2	0	9	0	1	1	0	2	.00	0	.203	.226	.305
1984 Seattle	AL	10	10	3	0	0	0	(0 0)	3	3	0	0	0	1	1	1	0	1	1	.50	0	.300	.364	.300
1985 Seattle	AL	67	104	15	3	1	0	(0 0)	20	15	6	17	0	14	0	1	0	3	2	.60	0	.144	.264	.192
1986 Seattle	AL	126	445	99	19	4	1	(1 0)	129	46	24	29	0	42	3	9	0	30	12	.71	6	.222	.275	.290
1987 Seattle	AL	160	530	146	31	8	1	(1 0)	196	73	35	39	0	34	2	8	5	60	20	.75	7	.275	.325	.370
1988 Seattle	AL	158	598	169	26	11	4	(4 0)	229	61	41	51	1	51	2	10	2	35	29	.55	9	.283	.340	.383
1989 Seattle	AL	153	613	184	24	9	0	(0 0)	226	87	43	55	1	45	3	3	3	25	18	.58	4	.300	.359	.369
1990 Seattle	AL	160	642	162	36	5	5	(0 5)	223	100	55	81	3	52	3	5	6	31	16	.66	9	.252	.336	.347
1991 Seattle	AL	161	631	160	34	6	3	(1 2)	215	95	57	72	2	63	5	14	6	28	8	.78	11	.254	.332	.341
1992 Seattle	AL	140	458	113	23	3	3	(2 1)	151	55	33	45	1	41	3	11	4	15	12	.56	12	.247	.316	.330
10 ML YEARS		1155	4090	1063	200	48	17	(9 8)	1410	543	295	391	8	352	22	63	27	228	120	.66	59	.260	.326	.345

Shane Reynolds

Pitches: Right **Bats:** Right **Pos:** SP   **Ht:** 6' 3" **Wt:** 210 **Born:** 03/26/68 **Age:** 25

Year Team	Lg	G	GS	CG	GF	IP	BFP	H	R	ER	HR	SH	SF	HB	TBB	IBB	SO	WP	Bk	W	L	Pct.	ShO	Sv	ERA
1989 Auburn	A	6	6	1	0	35	150	36	16	9	1	1	0	4	14	0	23	1	1	3	2	.600	0	0	2.31
Asheville	A	8	8	2	0	51.1	224	53	25	21	2	2	2	1	21	0	33	1	4	5	3	.625	1	0	3.68
1990 Columbus	AA	29	27	2	1	155.1	710	182	104	83	14	11	5	5	70	1	92	6	6	9	10	.474	1	0	4.81
1991 Jackson	AA	27	27	2	0	151	673	165	93	75	8	8	7	2	62	1	116	3	3	8	9	.471	0	0	4.47
1992 Tucson	AAA	25	22	2	1	142	605	156	73	58	4	3	3	4	34	2	106	4	1	9	8	.529	0	1	3.68
1992 Houston	NL	8	5	0	0	25.1	122	42	22	20	2	6	1	0	6	1	10	1	1	1	3	.250	0	0	7.11

Armando Reynoso

Pitches: Right **Bats:** Right **Pos:** RP   **Ht:** 6' 0" **Wt:** 186 **Born:** 05/01/66 **Age:** 27

Year Team	Lg	G	GS	CG	GF	IP	BFP	H	R	ER	HR	SH	SF	HB	TBB	IBB	SO	WP	Bk	W	L	Pct.	ShO	Sv	ERA
1990 Richmond	AAA	4	3	0	0	24	102	26	7	6	3	1	1	0	7	0	15	0	3	3	1	.750	0	0	2.25
1991 Richmond	AAA	22	19	3	1	131	544	117	44	38	9	7	3	10	39	1	97	8	6	10	6	.625	3	0	2.61
1992 Richmond	AAA	28	27	4	1	169.1	693	156	65	50	12	3	5	7	52	6	108	8	5	12	9	.571	1	0	2.66
1991 Atlanta	NL	6	5	0	1	23.1	103	26	18	16	4	3	0	3	10	1	10	2	0	2	1	.667	0	0	6.17
1992 Atlanta	NL	3	1	0	1	7.2	32	11	4	4	2	1	0	1	2	1	2	0	0	1	0	1.000	0	1	4.70
2 ML YEARS		9	6	0	2	31	135	37	22	20	6	4	0	4	12	2	12	2	0	3	1	.750	0	1	5.81

Arthur Rhodes

Pitches: Left **Bats:** Left **Pos:** SP   **Ht:** 6' 2" **Wt:** 204 **Born:** 10/24/69 **Age:** 23

Year Team	Lg	G	GS	CG	GF	IP	BFP	H	R	ER	HR	SH	SF	HB	TBB	IBB	SO	WP	Bk	W	L	Pct.	ShO	Sv	ERA
1988 Bluefield	R	11	7	0	3	35.1	155	29	17	13	1	0	1	1	15	0	44	9	2	3	4	.429	0	0	3.31
1989 Erie	A	5	5	1	0	31	115	13	7	4	1	0	0	0	10	0	45	2	1	2	0	1.000	0	0	1.16
Frederick	A	7	6	0	0	24.1	109	19	16	14	2	0	1	0	19	0	28	4	1	2	2	.500	0	0	5.18
1990 Frederick	A	13	13	4	0	80.2	322	62	25	19	6	0	1	1	21	0	103	3	1	4	6	.400	0	0	2.12
Hagerstown	AA	12	12	0	0	72.1	303	62	32	30	3	1	3	0	39	0	60	5	0	3	4	.429	0	0	3.73
1991 Hagerstown	AA	19	19	2	0	106.2	428	73	37	32	2	1	3	0	47	1	115	10	0	7	4	.636	2	0	2.70
1992 Rochester	AAA	17	17	1	0	101.2	434	84	48	42	7	3	3	0	46	0	115	4	0	6	6	.500	0	0	3.72
1991 Baltimore	AL	8	8	0	0	36	174	47	35	32	4	1	3	0	23	0	23	2	0	0	3	.000	0	0	8.00
1992 Baltimore	AL	15	15	2	0	94.1	394	87	39	38	6	5	1	1	38	2	77	2	1	7	5	.583	1	0	3.63
2 ML YEARS		23	23	2	0	130.1	568	134	74	70	10	6	4	1	61	2	100	4	1	7	8	.467	1	0	4.83

Karl Rhodes

Bats: Left **Throws:** Left **Pos:** LF   **Ht:** 5'11" **Wt:** 170 **Born:** 08/21/68 **Age:** 24

Year Team	Lg	G	AB	H	2B	3B	HR	(Hm	Rd)	TB	R	RBI	TBB	IBB	SO	HBP	SH	SF	SB	CS	SB%	GDP	Avg	OBP	SLG
1990 Houston	NL	38	86	21	6	1	1	(0	1)	32	12	3	13	3	12	0	1	1	4	1	.80	1	.244	.340	.372
1991 Houston	NL	44	136	29	3	1	1	(0	1)	37	7	12	14	3	26	1	0	1	2	2	.50	3	.213	.289	.272
1992 Houston	NL	5	4	0	0	0	0	(0	0)	0	0	0	0	0	2	0	0	0	0	0	.00	0	.000	.000	.000
3 ML YEARS		87	226	50	9	2	2	(0	2)	69	19	15	27	6	40	1	1	2	6	3	.67	4	.221	.305	.305

Dave Righetti

Pitches: Left **Bats:** Left **Pos:** RP/SP   **Ht:** 6' 4" **Wt:** 212 **Born:** 11/28/58 **Age:** 34

Year Team	Lg	G	GS	CG	GF	IP	BFP	H	R	ER	HR	SH	SF	HB	TBB	IBB	SO	WP	Bk	W	L	Pct.	ShO	Sv	ERA
1979 New York	AL	3	3	0	0	17	67	10	7	7	2	1	1	0	10	0	13	0	0	0	1	.000	0	0	3.71
1981 New York	AL	15	15	2	0	105	422	75	25	24	1	0	2	0	38	0	89	1	1	8	4	.667	0	0	2.06
1982 New York	AL	33	27	4	3	183	804	155	88	77	11	8	5	6	108	4	163	9	5	11	10	.524	0	1	3.79
1983 New York	AL	31	31	7	0	217	900	194	96	83	12	10	4	2	67	2	169	10	1	14	8	.636	2	0	3.44
1984 New York	AL	64	0	0	53	96.1	400	79	29	25	5	4	4	0	37	7	90	0	2	5	6	.455	0	31	2.34
1985 New York	AL	74	0	0	60	107	452	96	36	33	5	6	3	0	45	3	92	7	0	12	7	.632	0	29	2.78
1986 New York	AL	74	0	0	68	106.2	435	88	31	29	4	5	4	2	35	7	83	1	0	8	8	.500	0	46	2.45
1987 New York	AL	60	0	0	54	95	419	95	45	37	9	6	5	2	44	4	77	1	3	8	6	.571	0	31	3.51
1988 New York	AL	60	0	0	41	87	377	86	35	34	5	4	0	1	37	2	70	2	4	5	4	.556	0	25	3.52
1989 New York	AL	55	0	0	53	69	300	73	32	23	3	7	2	1	26	6	51	0	0	2	6	.250	0	25	3.00
1990 New York	AL	53	0	0	47	53	235	48	24	21	8	1	1	2	26	2	43	2	0	1	1	.500	0	36	3.57
1991 San Francisco	NL	61	0	0	49	71.2	304	64	29	27	4	4	2	3	28	6	51	1	1	2	7	.222	0	24	3.39
1992 San Francisco	NL	54	4	0	0	78.1	340	79	47	44	6	4	0	0	36	5	47	6	2	2	7	.222	0	3	5.06
13 ML YEARS		637	80	13	451	1286	5455	1142	524	464	73	62	37	19	537	48	1038	40	19	78	75	.510	2	251	3.25

Jose Rijo

Pitches: Right **Bats:** Right **Pos:** SP **Ht:** 6' 2" **Wt:** 210 **Born:** 05/13/65 **Age:** 28

		HOW MUCH HE PITCHED						WHAT HE GAVE UP												THE RESULTS					
Year Team	Lg	G	GS	CG	GF	IP	BFP	H	R	ER	HR	SH	SF	HB	TBB	IBB	SO	WP	Bk	W	L	Pct.	ShO	Sv	ERA
1984 New York	AL	24	5	0	8	62.1	289	74	40	33	5	6	1	1	33	1	47	2	1	2	8	.200	0	0	4.76
1985 Oakland	AL	12	9	0	1	63.2	272	57	26	25	6	5	0	0	28	2	65	0	0	6	4	.600	0	0	3.53
1986 Oakland	AL	39	26	4	9	193.2	856	172	116	100	24	10	9	4	108	7	176	6	4	9	11	.450	0	1	4.65
1987 Oakland	AL	21	14	1	3	82.1	394	106	67	54	10	0	3	2	41	1	67	5	2	2	7	.222	0	0	5.90
1988 Cincinnati	NL	49	19	0	12	162	653	120	47	43	7	8	5	3	63	7	160	1	4	13	8	.619	0	0	2.39
1989 Cincinnati	NL	19	19	1	0	111	464	101	39	35	6	3	6	2	48	3	86	4	3	7	6	.538	1	0	2.84
1990 Cincinnati	NL	29	29	7	0	197	801	151	65	59	10	8	1	2	78	1	152	2	5	14	8	.636	1	0	2.70
1991 Cincinnati	NL	30	30	3	0	204.1	825	165	69	57	8	4	8	3	55	4	172	2	4	15	6	.714	1	0	2.51
1992 Cincinnati	NL	33	33	2	0	211	836	185	67	60	15	9	4	3	44	1	171	2	1	15	10	.600	0	0	2.56
9 ML YEARS		256	184	18	33	1287.1	5390	1131	536	466	91	53	37	21	498	27	1096	24	24	83	68	.550	3	3	3.26

Ernest Riles

Bats: Left **Throws:** Right **Pos:** SS **Ht:** 6' 1" **Wt:** 180 **Born:** 10/02/60 **Age:** 32

					BATTING														BASERUNNING				PERCENTAGES		
Year Team	Lg	G	AB	H	2B	3B	HR	(Hm	Rd)	TB	R	RBI	TBB	IBB	SO	HBP	SH	SF	SB	CS	SB%	GDP	Avg	OBP	SLG
1985 Milwaukee	AL	116	448	128	12	7	5	(2	3)	169	54	45	36	0	54	2	6	3	2	2	.50	16	.286	.339	.377
1986 Milwaukee	AL	145	524	132	24	2	9	(2	7)	187	69	47	54	0	80	1	6	3	7	7	.50	14	.252	.321	.357
1987 Milwaukee	AL	83	276	72	11	1	4	(1	3)	97	38	38	30	1	47	1	3	6	3	4	.43	6	.261	.329	.351
1988 2 ML Teams		120	314	87	13	3	4	(4	0)	118	33	37	17	2	59	0	1	4	3	4	.43	8	.277	.310	.376
1989 San Francisco	NL	122	302	84	13	2	7	(5	2)	122	43	40	28	3	50	2	1	4	0	6	.00	7	.278	.339	.404
1990 San Francisco	NL	92	155	31	2	1	8	(7	1)	59	22	21	26	3	26	0	2	1	0	0	.00	2	.200	.313	.381
1991 Oakland	AL	108	281	60	8	4	5	(3	2)	91	30	32	31	3	42	1	4	4	3	2	.60	3	.214	.290	.324
1992 Houston	NL	39	61	16	1	0	1	(0	1)	20	5	4	2	0	11	0	0	1	1	0	1.00	2	.262	.281	.328
1988 Milwaukee	AL	41	127	32	6	1	1	(1	0)	43	7	9	7	0	26	0	1	0	2	2	.50	5	.252	.291	.339
San Francisco	NL	79	187	55	7	2	3	(3	0)	75	26	28	10	2	33	0	0	4	1	2	.33	5	.294	.323	.401
8 ML YEARS		825	2361	610	84	20	43	(24	19)	863	294	264	224	12	369	7	23	26	19	25	.43	61	.258	.321	.366

Billy Ripken

Bats: Right **Throws:** Right **Pos:** 2B **Ht:** 6' 1" **Wt:** 186 **Born:** 12/16/64 **Age:** 28

					BATTING														BASERUNNING				PERCENTAGES		
Year Team	Lg	G	AB	H	2B	3B	HR	(Hm	Rd)	TB	R	RBI	TBB	IBB	SO	HBP	SH	SF	SB	CS	SB%	GDP	Avg	OBP	SLG
1987 Baltimore	AL	58	234	72	9	0	2	(0	2)	87	27	20	21	0	23	0	1	1	4	1	.80	3	.308	.363	.372
1988 Baltimore	AL	150	512	106	18	1	2	(0	2)	132	52	34	33	0	63	5	6	3	8	2	.80	14	.207	.260	.258
1989 Baltimore	AL	115	318	76	11	2	2	(0	2)	97	31	26	22	0	53	0	19	5	1	2	.33	12	.239	.284	.305
1990 Baltimore	AL	129	406	118	28	1	3	(2	1)	157	48	38	28	2	43	4	17	1	5	2	.71	7	.291	.342	.387
1991 Baltimore	AL	104	287	62	11	1	0	(0	0)	75	24	14	15	0	31	0	11	2	0	1	.00	14	.216	.253	.261
1992 Baltimore	AL	111	330	76	15	0	4	(3	1)	103	35	36	18	1	26	3	10	2	2	2	.40	10	.230	.275	.312
6 ML YEARS		667	2087	510	92	5	13	(5	8)	651	217	168	137	3	239	12	64	14	20	11	.65	60	.244	.293	.312

Cal Ripken

Bats: Right **Throws:** Right **Pos:** SS **Ht:** 6' 4" **Wt:** 224 **Born:** 08/24/60 **Age:** 32

					BATTING														BASERUNNING				PERCENTAGES		
Year Team	Lg	G	AB	H	2B	3B	HR	(Hm	Rd)	TB	R	RBI	TBB	IBB	SO	HBP	SH	SF	SB	CS	SB%	GDP	Avg	OBP	SLG
1981 Baltimore	AL	23	39	5	0	0	0	(0	0)	5	1	0	1	0	8	0	0	0	0	0	.00	4	.128	.150	.128
1982 Baltimore	AL	160	598	158	32	5	28	(11	17)	284	90	93	46	3	95	3	2	6	3	3	.50	16	.264	.317	.475
1983 Baltimore	AL	162	663	211	47	2	27	(12	15)	343	121	102	58	0	97	0	0	5	0	4	.00	24	.318	.371	.517
1984 Baltimore	AL	162	641	195	37	7	27	(16	11)	327	103	86	71	1	89	2	0	2	2	1	.67	16	.304	.374	.510
1985 Baltimore	AL	161	642	181	32	5	26	(15	11)	301	116	110	67	1	68	1	0	8	2	3	.40	32	.282	.347	.469
1986 Baltimore	AL	162	627	177	35	1	25	(10	15)	289	98	81	70	5	60	4	0	6	4	2	.67	19	.282	.355	.461
1987 Baltimore	AL	162	624	157	28	3	27	(17	10)	272	97	98	81	0	77	1	0	11	3	5	.38	19	.252	.333	.436
1988 Baltimore	AL	161	575	152	25	1	23	(11	12)	248	87	81	102	7	69	2	0	10	2	2	.50	10	.264	.372	.431
1989 Baltimore	AL	162	646	166	30	0	21	(13	8)	259	80	93	57	5	72	3	0	6	3	2	.60	22	.257	.317	.401
1990 Baltimore	AL	161	600	150	28	4	21	(8	13)	249	78	84	82	18	66	5	0	7	3	1	.75	12	.250	.341	.415
1991 Baltimore	AL	162	650	210	46	5	34	(16	18)	368	99	114	53	15	46	5	0	9	6	1	.86	19	.323	.374	.566
1992 Baltimore	AL	162	637	160	29	1	14	(5	9)	233	73	72	64	14	50	7	0	7	4	3	.57	13	.251	.323	.366
12 ML YEARS		1800	6942	1922	369	34	273	(134	139)	3178	1043	1014	752	69	797	33	3	77	32	27	.54	206	.277	.347	.458

Bill Risley

Pitches: Right **Bats:** Right **Pos:** SP **Ht:** 6' 2" **Wt:** 210 **Born:** 05/29/67 **Age:** 26

		HOW MUCH HE PITCHED						WHAT HE GAVE UP												THE RESULTS					
Year Team	Lg	G	GS	CG	GF	IP	BFP	H	R	ER	HR	SH	SF	HB	TBB	IBB	SO	WP	Bk	W	L	Pct.	ShO	Sv	ERA
1987 Reds	R	11	11	0	0	52.1	226	38	24	11	0	1	3	3	26	3	50	6	2	1	4	.200	0	0	1.89

Year Team	Lg	G	GS	CG	GF	IP	BFP	H	R	ER	HR	SH	SF	HB	TBB	IBB	SO	WP	Bk	W	L	Pct.	ShO	Sv	ERA
1988 Greensboro	A	23	23	3	0	120.1	515	82	60	55	2	3	9	11	84	0	135	9	19	8	4	.667	3	0	4.11
1989 Cedar Rapds	A	27	27	2	0	140.2	581	87	72	61	9	1	9	6	81	2	128	19	8	9	10	.474	0	0	3.90
1990 Cedar Rapds	A	22	22	7	0	137.2	579	99	51	43	8	6	4	7	68	1	123	13	3	8	9	.471	1	0	2.81
1991 Chattanooga	AA	19	19	3	0	108.1	465	81	48	38	3	3	6	9	60	2	77	5	5	5	7	.417	0	0	3.16
Nashville	AAA	8	8	1	0	44	199	45	27	24	7	3	1	1	26	1	32	3	0	3	5	.375	0	0	4.91
1992 Indianapols	AAA	25	15	0	1	95.2	434	105	69	68	11	3	5	4	47	0	64	1	4	5	8	.385	0	0	6.40
1992 Montreal	NL	1	1	0	0	5	19	4	1	1	0	1	0	0	1	0	2	0	0	1	0	1.000	0	0	1.80

Wally Ritchie

Pitches: Left **Bats:** Left **Pos:** RP **Ht:** 6' 2" **Wt:** 180 **Born:** 07/12/65 **Age:** 27

Year Team	Lg	G	GS	CG	GF	IP	BFP	H	R	ER	HR	SH	SF	HB	TBB	IBB	SO	WP	Bk	W	L	Pct.	ShO	Sv	ERA
1987 Philadelphia	NL	49	0	0	13	62.1	273	60	27	26	8	5	2	1	29	11	45	2	3	3	2	.600	0	3	3.75
1988 Philadelphia	NL	19	0	0	8	26	115	19	14	9	1	2	3	1	17	2	8	2	0	0	0	.000	0	0	3.12
1991 Philadelphia	NL	39	0	0	15	50.1	213	44	17	14	4	2	4	2	17	5	26	1	0	1	2	.333	0	0	2.50
1992 Philadelphia	NL	40	0	0	13	39	174	44	17	13	3	4	0	0	17	3	19	0	0	2	1	.667	0	0	3.00
4 ML YEARS		147	0	0	47	177.2	775	167	75	62	16	13	9	4	80	21	98	5	3	6	5	.545	0	4	3.14

Kevin Ritz

Pitches: Right **Bats:** Right **Pos:** RP/SP **Ht:** 6' 4" **Wt:** 220 **Born:** 06/08/65 **Age:** 28

Year Team	Lg	G	GS	CG	GF	IP	BFP	H	R	ER	HR	SH	SF	HB	TBB	IBB	SO	WP	Bk	W	L	Pct.	ShO	Sv	ERA
1989 Detroit	AL	12	12	1	0	74	334	75	41	36	2	1	5	1	44	5	56	6	0	4	6	.400	0	0	4.38
1990 Detroit	AL	4	4	0	0	7.1	52	14	12	9	0	3	0	0	14	2	3	3	0	0	4	.000	0	0	11.05
1991 Detroit	AL	11	5	0	3	15.1	86	17	22	20	1	1	2	2	22	1	9	0	0	0	3	.000	0	0	11.74
1992 Detroit	AL	23	11	0	4	80.1	368	88	52	50	4	1	4	3	44	4	57	7	1	2	5	.286	0	0	5.60
4 ML YEARS		50	32	1	7	177	840	194	127	115	7	6	11	6	124	12	125	16	1	6	18	.250	0	0	5.85

Ben Rivera

Pitches: Right **Bats:** Right **Pos:** SP/RP **Ht:** 6' 6" **Wt:** 210 **Born:** 01/11/69 **Age:** 24

Year Team	Lg	G	GS	CG	GF	IP	BFP	H	R	ER	HR	SH	SF	HB	TBB	IBB	SO	WP	Bk	W	L	Pct.	ShO	Sv	ERA
1987 Braves	R	16	5	0	2	49.2	220	55	26	18	0	1	2	2	19	1	29	2	2	1	5	.167	0	0	3.26
1988 Sumter	A	27	27	3	0	173.1	724	167	77	61	12	2	5	7	52	0	99	6	7	9	11	.450	2	0	3.17
1989 Durham	A	23	22	1	0	102.1	462	113	55	51	6	4	3	5	51	1	58	10	3	5	7	.417	0	0	4.49
1990 Greenville	AA	13	13	0	0	52	243	68	40	38	6	2	1	3	26	0	32	10	0	1	4	.200	*	0	6.58
Durham	A	16	13	1	3	75	327	69	41	30	7	2	3	5	33	1	64	4	2	5	3	.625	1	1	3.60
1991 Greenville	AA	26	26	3	0	158.2	683	155	76	63	13	2	1	3	75	4	116	8	4	11	8	.579	2	0	3.57
1992 Scranton/wb	AAA	2	2	1	0	12	41	4	0	0	0	0	0	1	2	0	10	0	1	2	0	1.000	1	0	0.00
1992 2 ML Teams		28	14	4	7	117.1	487	99	40	40	9	5	2	4	45	4	77	5	0	7	4	.636	1	0	3.07
1992 Atlanta	NL	8	0	0	3	15.1	78	21	8	8	1	0	1	2	13	2	11	0	0	0	1	.000	0	0	4.70
Philadelphia	NL	20	14	4	4	102	409	78	32	32	8	5	1	2	32	2	66	5	0	7	3	.700	1	0	2.82

Luis Rivera

Bats: Right **Throws:** Right **Pos:** SS **Ht:** 5'10" **Wt:** 175 **Born:** 01/03/64 **Age:** 29

								BATTING											BASERUNNING				PERCENTAGES		
Year Team	Lg	G	AB	H	2B	3B	HR	(Hm	Rd)	TB	R	RBI	TBB	IBB	SO	HBP	SH	SF	SB	CS	SB%	GDP	Avg	OBP	SLG
1986 Montreal	NL	55	166	34	11	1	0	(0	0)	47	20	13	17	0	33	2	1	1	1	1	.50	1	.205	.285	.283
1987 Montreal	NL	18	32	5	2	0	0	(0	0)	7	0	1	1	0	8	0	0	0	0	0	.00	0	.156	.182	.219
1988 Montreal	NL	123	371	83	17	3	4	(2	2)	118	35	30	24	4	69	1	3	3	3	4	.43	9	.224	.271	.318
1989 Boston	AL	93	323	83	17	1	5	(4	1)	117	35	29	20	1	60	1	4	1	2	3	.40	7	.257	.301	.362
1990 Boston	AL	118	346	78	20	0	7	(4	3)	119	38	45	25	0	58	1	12	1	4	3	.57	10	.225	.279	.344
1991 Boston	AL	129	414	107	22	3	8	(4	4)	159	64	40	35	0	86	3	12	4	4	4	.50	10	.258	.318	.384
1992 Boston	AL	102	288	62	11	1	0	(0	0)	75	17	29	26	0	56	3	5	4	4	3	.57	5	.215	.287	.260
7 ML YEARS		638	1940	452	100	9	24	(14	10)	642	209	187	148	5	370	11	37	10	18	18	.50	42	.233	.290	.331

Bip Roberts

Bats: Both **Throws:** Right **Pos:** LF/2B/3B/CF **Ht:** 5' 7" **Wt:** 165 **Born:** 10/27/63 **Age:** 29

								BATTING											BASERUNNING				PERCENTAGES		
Year Team	Lg	G	AB	H	2B	3B	HR	(Hm	Rd)	TB	R	RBI	TBB	IBB	SO	HBP	SH	SF	SB	CS	SB%	GDP	Avg	OBP	SLG
1986 San Diego	NL	101	241	61	5	2	1	(0	1)	73	34	12	14	1	29	0	2	1	14	12	.54	2	.253	.293	.303
1988 San Diego	NL	5	9	3	0	0	0	(0	0)	3	1	0	1	0	2	0	0	0	0	2	.00	0	.333	.400	.333
1989 San Diego	NL	117	329	99	15	8	3	(2	1)	139	81	25	49	0	45	1	6	2	21	11	.66	9	.301	.391	.422
1990 San Diego	NL	149	556	172	36	3	9	(4	5)	241	104	44	55	1	65	6	8	4	46	12	.79	8	.309	.375	.433
1991 San Diego	NL	117	424	119	13	3	3	(3	0)	147	66	32	37	0	71	4	4	3	26	11	.70	6	.281	.342	.347
1992 Cincinnati	NL	147	532	172	34	6	4	(3	1)	230	92	45	62	4	54	2	1	4	44	16	.73	7	.323	.393	.432

6 ML YEARS		636	2091	626	103	22	20	(12	8)	833	378	158	218	6	266	13	21	14	151	64	70	26	.299	.367	.398

Don Robinson

Pitches: Right **Bats:** Right **Pos:** SP   **Ht:** 6' 4" **Wt:** 235 **Born:** 06/08/57 **Age:** 36

		HOW MUCH HE PITCHED						WHAT HE GAVE UP												THE RESULTS					
Year Team	Lg	G	GS	CG	GF	IP	BFP	H	R	ER	HR	SH	SF	HB	TBB	IBB	SO	WP	Bk	W	L	Pct.	ShO	Sv	ERA
1978 Pittsburgh	NL	35	32	9	1	228	937	203	98	88	20	8	8	3	57	4	135	9	4	14	6	.700	1	1	3.47
1979 Pittsburgh	NL	29	25	4	1	161	684	171	74	69	12	6	5	4	52	5	96	6	1	8	8	.500	0	0	3.86
1980 Pittsburgh	NL	29	24	3	1	160	671	157	74	71	14	8	3	5	45	5	103	7	2	7	10	.412	2	1	3.99
1981 Pittsburgh	NL	16	2	0	4	38	182	47	27	25	4	7	2	0	23	4	17	3	0	0	3	.000	0	2	5.92
1982 Pittsburgh	NL	38	30	6	3	227	977	213	123	108	26	12	8	3	103	11	165	17	0	15	13	.536	0	0	4.28
1983 Pittsburgh	NL	9	6	0	2	36.1	168	43	21	18	5	2	0	0	21	3	28	2	0	2	2	.500	0	0	4.46
1984 Pittsburgh	NL	51	1	0	28	122	500	99	45	41	6	4	9	0	49	4	110	5	0	5	6	.455	0	10	3.02
1985 Pittsburgh	NL	44	6	0	22	95.1	418	95	45	41	6	2	0	2	42	11	65	2	0	5	11	.313	0	3	3.87
1986 Pittsburgh	NL	50	0	0	41	69.1	295	61	27	26	5	5	4	2	27	3	53	4	1	3	4	.429	0	14	3.37
1987 2 ML Teams		67	0	0	54	108	460	105	42	41	7	7	3	0	40	6	79	7	1	11	7	.611	0	19	3.42
1988 San Francisco	NL	51	19	3	19	176.2	725	152	63	48	11	7	8	3	49	12	122	4	2	10	5	.667	2	6	2.45
1989 San Francisco	NL	34	32	5	2	197	793	184	80	75	22	6	5	2	37	6	96	4	4	12	11	.522	1	0	3.43
1990 San Francisco	NL	26	25	4	0	157.2	667	173	84	80	18	4	3	1	41	8	78	2	0	10	7	.588	0	0	4.57
1991 San Francisco	NL	34	16	0	7	121.1	525	123	64	59	12	4	5	1	50	7	78	1	0	5	9	.357	0	1	4.38
1992 2 ML Teams		11	11	0	0	60	252	56	36	34	7	4	6	1	7	0	26	1	0	2	4	.333	0	0	5.10
1987 Pittsburgh	NL	42	0	0	37	65.1	276	66	29	28	6	6	1	0	22	3	53	6	1	6	6	.500	0	12	3.86
San Francisco	NL	25	0	0	17	42.2	184	39	13	13	1	1	2	0	18	3	26	1	0	5	1	.833	0	7	2.74
1992 California	AL	3	3	0	0	16.1	69	19	4	4	1	4	1	0	3	0	9	1	0	1	0	1.000	0	0	2.20
Philadelphia	NL	8	8	0	0	43.2	183	49	32	30	6	3	6	1	4	0	17	0	0	1	4	.200	0	0	6.18
15 ML YEARS		524	229	34	185	1957.2	8254	1894	907	824	175	86	69	27	643	89	1251	74	15	109	106	.507	6	57	3.79

Jeff Robinson

Pitches: Right **Bats:** Right **Pos:** RP/SP   **Ht:** 6' 4" **Wt:** 200 **Born:** 12/13/60 **Age:** 32

		HOW MUCH HE PITCHED						WHAT HE GAVE UP												THE RESULTS					
Year Team	Lg	G	GS	CG	GF	IP	BFP	H	R	ER	HR	SH	SF	HB	TBB	IBB	SO	WP	Bk	W	L	Pct.	ShO	Sv	ERA
1984 San Francisco	NL	34	33	1	0	171.2	749	195	99	87	12	5	8	7	52	4	102	7	2	7	15	.318	1	0	4.56
1985 San Francisco	NL	8	0	0	0	12.1	59	16	11	7	2	0	1	0	10	1	8	1	0	0	0	.000	0	0	5.11
1986 San Francisco	NL	64	1	0	22	104.1	431	92	46	39	8	1	3	1	32	7	90	11	0	6	3	.667	0	8	3.36
1987 2 ML Teams		81	0	0	40	123.1	495	89	43	39	11	10	4	1	54	11	101	5	2	8	9	.471	0	14	2.85
1988 Pittsburgh	NL	75	0	0	35	124.2	513	113	44	42	6	2	6	3	39	5	87	11	0	11	5	.688	0	9	3.03
1989 Pittsburgh	NL	50	19	0	18	141.1	643	161	92	72	14	7	7	1	59	11	95	14	2	7	13	.350	0	4	4.58
1990 New York	AL	54	4	1	12	88.2	372	82	35	34	8	5	1	1	34	3	43	2	0	3	6	.333	0	0	3.45
1991 California	AL	39	0	0	16	57	252	56	34	34	9	3	2	2	29	4	57	10	0	0	3	.000	0	3	5.37
1992 Chicago	AL	49	5	0	12	78	335	76	29	26	5	2	2	2	40	7	46	8	1	4	3	.571	0	1	3.00
1987 San Francisco	NL	63	0	0	33	96.2	395	69	34	30	10	9	4	1	48	10	82	3	2	6	8	.429	0	10	2.79
Pittsburgh	NL	18	0	0	7	26.2	100	20	9	9	1	1	0	0	6	1	19	2	0	2	1	.667	0	4	3.04
9 ML YEARS		454	62	2	155	901.1	3849	880	433	380	75	35	34	18	349	53	629	69	7	46	57	.447	1	39	3.79

Jeff M. Robinson

Pitches: Right **Bats:** Right **Pos:** RP/SP   **Ht:** 6' 6" **Wt:** 235 **Born:** 12/14/61 **Age:** 31

		HOW MUCH HE PITCHED						WHAT HE GAVE UP												THE RESULTS					
Year Team	Lg	G	GS	CG	GF	IP	BFP	H	R	ER	HR	SH	SF	HB	TBB	IBB	SO	WP	Bk	W	L	Pct.	ShO	Sv	ERA
1987 Detroit	AL	29	21	2	2	127.1	569	132	86	76	16	2	2	7	54	3	98	4	3	9	6	.600	1	0	5.37
1988 Detroit	AL	24	23	6	0	172	698	121	61	57	19	2	6	3	72	5	114	8	1	13	6	.684	2	0	2.98
1989 Detroit	AL	16	16	1	0	78	347	76	47	41	10	3	3	1	46	1	40	5	0	4	5	.444	1	0	4.73
1990 Detroit	AL	27	27	1	0	145	654	141	101	96	23	3	5	6	88	9	76	16	1	10	9	.526	1	0	5.96
1991 Baltimore	AL	21	19	0	0	104.1	472	119	66	60	12	3	0	6	51	2	65	8	0	4	9	.308	0	0	5.18
1992 2 ML Teams		24	11	0	2	82	355	83	48	47	8	1	4	1	36	1	32	6	1	7	5	.583	0	0	5.16
1992 Texas	AL	16	4	0	2	45.2	203	50	30	29	6	1	3	0	21	1	18	6	1	4	4	.500	0	0	5.72
Pittsburgh	NL	8	7	0	0	36.1	152	33	18	18	2	0	1	1	15	0	14	0	0	3	1	.750	0	0	4.46
6 ML YEARS		141	117	10	4	708.2	3095	672	405	377	88	14	20	24	347	21	425	47	6	47	40	.540	5	0	4.79

Ron Robinson

Pitches: Right **Bats:** Right **Pos:** SP   **Ht:** 6' 4" **Wt:** 235 **Born:** 03/24/62 **Age:** 31

		HOW MUCH HE PITCHED						WHAT HE GAVE UP												THE RESULTS					
Year Team	Lg	G	GS	CG	GF	IP	BFP	H	R	ER	HR	SH	SF	HB	TBB	IBB	SO	WP	Bk	W	L	Pct.	ShO	Sv	ERA
1984 Cincinnati	NL	12	5	1	2	39.2	166	35	18	12	3	1	1	0	13	3	24	0	2	1	2	.333	0	0	2.72
1985 Cincinnati	NL	33	12	0	9	108.1	453	107	53	48	11	3	4	1	32	3	76	3	0	7	7	.500	0	1	3.99
1986 Cincinnati	NL	70	0	0	32	116.2	487	110	44	42	10	4	3	2	43	8	117	3	0	10	3	.769	0	14	3.24
1987 Cincinnati	NL	48	18	0	14	154	638	148	71	63	14	8	7	1	43	8	99	2	0	7	5	.583	0	4	3.68
1988 Cincinnati	NL	17	16	0	0	78.2	347	88	47	36	5	5	5	2	26	4	38	3	0	3	7	.300	0	0	4.12

Year	Team	Lg	G	GS	CG	GF	IP	BFP	H	R	ER	HR	SH	SF	HB	TBB	IBB	SO	WP	Bk	W	L	Pct.	ShO	Sv	ERA
1989	Cincinnati	NL	15	15	0	0	83.1	353	80	36	31	8	5	1	2	28	2	36	2	0	5	3	.625	0	0	3.35
1990	2 ML Teams		28	27	7	0	179.2	764	194	78	65	7	4	7	6	51	1	71	3	0	14	7	.667	2	0	3.26
1991	Milwaukee	AL	1	1	0	0	4.1	21	6	3	3	0	0	0	1	3	1	0	0	0	0	1	.000	0	0	6.23
1992	Milwaukee	AL	8	8	0	0	35.1	171	51	26	23	3	0	1	2	14	0	12	0	0	1	4	.200	0	0	5.86
1990	Cincinnati	NL	6	5	0	0	31.1	137	36	18	17	2	1	0	0	14	0	14	1	0	2	2	.500	0	0	4.88
	Milwaukee	AL	22	22	7	0	148.1	627	158	60	48	5	3	7	6	37	1	57	2	0	12	5	.706	2	0	2.91
	9 ML YEARS		232	102	8	57	800	3400	819	376	323	61	30	29	17	253	30	473	16	2	48	39	.552	2	19	3.63

Henry Rodriguez

Bats: Left **Throws:** Left **Pos:** RF/LF **Ht:** 6' 1" **Wt:** 180 **Born:** 11/08/67 **Age:** 25

							BATTING													BASERUNNING				PERCENTAGES		
Year	Team	Lg	G	AB	H	2B	3B	HR	(Hm	Rd)	TB	R	RBI	TBB	IBB	SO	HBP	SH	SF	SB	CS	SB%	GDP	Avg	OBP	SLG
1987	Dodgers	R	49	148	49	7	3	0	--	--	62	23	15	16	7	15	3	1	2	3	1	.75	5	.331	.402	.419
1988	Salem	A	72	291	84	14	4	2	--	--	112	47	39	21	1	42	4	1	6	14	2	.88	7	.289	.339	.385
1989	Vero Beach	A	126	433	123	33	1	10	--	--	188	53	73	46	1	58	2	1	6	7	6	.54	12	.284	.354	.434
	Bakersfield	A	3	9	2	0	0	1	--	--	5	2	2	0	0	3	0	0	0	0	0	.00	0	.222	.222	.556
1990	San Antonio	AA	129	495	144	21	9	28	--	--	267	82	109	61	9	66	2	1	14	5	4	.56	10	.291	.362	.539
1991	Albuquerque	AAA	121	446	121	22	5	10	--	--	183	61	67	25	3	62	1	1	5	4	5	.44	11	.271	.308	.410
1992	Albuquerque	AAA	94	365	111	21	5	14	--	--	184	59	72	31	5	57	1	2	10	1	5	.17	11	.304	.351	.504
1992	Los Angeles	NL	53	146	32	7	0	3	(2	1)	48	11	14	8	0	30	0	1	1	0	0	.00	2	.219	.258	.329

Ivan Rodriguez

Bats: Right **Throws:** Right **Pos:** C **Ht:** 5' 9" **Wt:** 205 **Born:** 11/30/71 **Age:** 21

							BATTING													BASERUNNING				PERCENTAGES		
Year	Team	Lg	G	AB	H	2B	3B	HR	(Hm	Rd)	TB	R	RBI	TBB	IBB	SO	HBP	SH	SF	SB	CS	SB%	GDP	Avg	OBP	SLG
1989	Gastonia	A	112	386	92	22	1	7	--	--	137	38	42	21	0	58	2	5	4	2	5	.29	6	.238	.278	.355
1990	Charlotte	A	109	408	117	17	7	2	--	--	154	48	55	12	2	50	7	1	4	1	0	1.00	6	.287	.316	.377
1991	Tulsa	AA	50	175	48	7	2	3	--	--	68	16	28	6	0	27	1	1	5	1	2	.33	5	.274	.294	.389
1991	Texas	AL	88	280	74	16	0	3	(3	0)	99	24	27	5	0	42	0	2	1	0	1	.00	10	.264	.276	.354
1992	Texas	AL	123	420	109	16	1	8	(4	4)	151	39	37	24	2	73	1	7	2	0	0	.00	15	.260	.300	.360
	2 ML YEARS		211	700	183	32	1	11	(7	4)	250	63	64	29	2	115	1	9	3	0	1	.00	25	.261	.291	.357

Rich Rodriguez

Pitches: Left **Bats:** Right **Pos:** RP **Ht:** 6' 0" **Wt:** 200 **Born:** 03/01/63 **Age:** 30

			HOW MUCH HE PITCHED						WHAT HE GAVE UP											THE RESULTS					
Year	Team	Lg	G	GS	CG	GF	IP	BFP	H	R	ER	HR	SH	SF	HB	TBB	IBB	SO	WP	Bk	W	L	Pct.	ShO	Sv	ERA
1990	San Diego	NL	32	0	0	15	47.2	201	52	17	15	2	2	1	1	16	4	22	1	1	1	1	.500	0	1	2.83
1991	San Diego	NL	64	1	0	19	80	335	66	31	29	8	7	2	0	44	8	40	4	1	3	1	.750	0	0	3.26
1992	San Diego	NL	61	1	0	15	91	369	77	28	24	4	2	2	0	29	4	64	1	1	6	3	.667	0	0	2.37
	3 ML YEARS		157	2	0	49	218.2	905	195	76	68	14	11	5	1	89	16	126	6	3	10	5	.667	0	1	2.80

Kenny Rogers

Pitches: Left **Bats:** Left **Pos:** RP **Ht:** 6' 1" **Wt:** 205 **Born:** 11/10/64 **Age:** 28

			HOW MUCH HE PITCHED						WHAT HE GAVE UP											THE RESULTS					
Year	Team	Lg	G	GS	CG	GF	IP	BFP	H	R	ER	HR	SH	SF	HB	TBB	IBB	SO	WP	Bk	W	L	Pct.	ShO	Sv	ERA
1989	Texas	AL	73	0	0	24	73.2	314	60	28	24	2	6	3	4	42	9	63	6	0	3	4	.429	0	2	2.93
1990	Texas	AL	69	3	0	46	97.2	428	93	40	34	6	7	4	1	42	5	74	5	0	10	6	.625	0	15	3.13
1991	Texas	AL	63	9	0	20	109.2	511	121	80	66	14	9	5	6	61	7	73	3	1	10	10	.500	0	5	5.42
1992	Texas	AL	81	0	0	38	78.2	337	80	32	27	7	4	1	0	26	8	70	4	1	3	6	.333	0	6	3.09
	4 ML YEARS		286	12	0	128	359.2	1590	354	180	151	29	26	13	11	171	29	280	18	2	26	26	.500	0	28	3.78

Kevin Rogers

Pitches: Left **Bats:** Both **Pos:** SP **Ht:** 6' 2" **Wt:** 190 **Born:** 08/20/68 **Age:** 24

			HOW MUCH HE PITCHED						WHAT HE GAVE UP											THE RESULTS					
Year	Team	Lg	G	GS	CG	GF	IP	BFP	H	R	ER	HR	SH	SF	HB	TBB	IBB	SO	WP	Bk	W	L	Pct.	ShO	Sv	ERA
1988	Pocatello	R	13	13	1	0	69.2	314	73	51	48	4	0	3	2	35	0	71	5	4	2	8	.200	0	0	6.20
1989	Clinton	A	29	28	4	0	169.1	722	128	74	48	4	2	6	6	78	1	168	5	7	13	8	.619	0	0	2.55
1990	San Jose	A	28	26	1	1	172	731	143	86	69	9	6	8	11	68	1	186	19	3	14	5	.737	1	0	3.61
1991	Shreveport	AA	22	22	2	0	118	528	124	63	44	8	5	5	2	54	4	108	11	2	4	6	.400	0	0	3.36
1992	Shreveport	AA	16	16	2	0	101	413	87	34	29	3	2	1	4	29	0	110	7	0	8	5	.615	2	0	2.58
	Phoenix	AAA	11	11	1	0	69.2	287	63	34	31	0	5	3	1	22	1	62	2	1	3	3	.500	1	0	4.00
1992	San Francisco	NL	6	6	0	0	34	148	37	17	16	4	2	0	1	13	1	26	2	0	0	2	.000	0	0	4.24

Dave Rohde

Bats: Both **Throws:** Right **Pos:** 3B   **Ht:** 6' 2" **Wt:** 182 **Born:** 05/08/64 **Age:** 29

Year Team	Lg	G	AB	H	2B	3B	HR	(Hm	Rd)	TB	R	RBI	TBB	IBB	SO	HBP	SH	SF	SB	CS	SB%	GDP	Avg	OBP	SLG
1990 Houston	NL	59	98	18	4	0	0	(0	0)	22	8	5	9	2	20	5	4	1	0	0	.00	3	.184	.283	.224
1991 Houston	NL	29	41	5	0	0	0	(0	0)	5	3	0	5	0	8	0	2	0	0	0	.00	1	.122	.217	.122
1992 Cleveland	AL	5	7	0	0	0	0	(0	0)	0	0	0	2	1	3	0	0	0	0	0	.00	0	.000	.222	.000
3 ML YEARS		93	146	23	4	0	0	(0	0)	27	11	5	16	3	31	5	6	1	0	0	.00	4	.158	.262	.185

Mel Rojas

Pitches: Right **Bats:** Right **Pos:** RP   **Ht:** 5'11" **Wt:** 185 **Born:** 12/10/66 **Age:** 26

Year Team	Lg	G	GS	CG	GF	IP	BFP	H	R	ER	HR	SH	SF	HB	TBB	IBB	SO	WP	Bk	W	L	Pct.	ShO	Sv	ERA
1990 Montreal	NL	23	0	0	5	40	173	34	17	16	5	2	0	2	24	4	26	2	0	3	1	.750	0	1	3.60
1991 Montreal	NL	37	0	0	13	48	200	42	21	20	4	0	2	1	13	1	37	3	0	3	3	.500	0	6	3.75
1992 Montreal	NL	68	0	0	26	100.2	399	71	17	16	2	4	2	2	34	8	70	2	0	7	1	.875	0	10	1.43
3 ML YEARS		128	0	0	44	188.2	772	147	55	52	11	6	4	5	71	13	133	7	0	13	5	.722	0	17	2.48

Bobby Rose

Bats: Right **Throws:** Right **Pos:** 2B   **Ht:** 5'11" **Wt:** 185 **Born:** 03/15/67 **Age:** 26

Year Team	Lg	G	AB	H	2B	3B	HR	(Hm	Rd)	TB	R	RBI	TBB	IBB	SO	HBP	SH	SF	SB	CS	SB%	GDP	Avg	OBP	SLG
1989 California	AL	14	38	8	1	2	1	(1	0)	16	4	3	2	0	10	1	1	0	0	0	.00	2	.211	.268	.421
1990 California	AL	7	13	5	0	0	1	(1	0)	8	5	2	2	0	1	0	1	0	0	0	.00	0	.385	.467	.615
1991 California	AL	22	65	18	5	1	1	(0	1)	28	5	8	3	0	13	0	0	1	0	0	.00	1	.277	.304	.431
1992 California	AL	30	84	18	5	0	2	(1	1)	29	10	10	8	1	9	2	1	1	1	1	.50	2	.214	.295	.345
4 ML YEARS		73	200	49	11	3	5	(3	2)	81	24	23	15	1	33	3	3	2	1	1	.50	5	.245	.305	.405

Wayne Rosenthal

Pitches: Right **Bats:** Right **Pos:** RP   **Ht:** 6' 5" **Wt:** 240 **Born:** 02/19/65 **Age:** 28

Year Team	Lg	G	GS	CG	GF	IP	BFP	H	R	ER	HR	SH	SF	HB	TBB	IBB	SO	WP	Bk	W	L	Pct.	ShO	Sv	ERA
1986 Rangers	R	23	3	1	16	61.2	234	36	9	5	0	1	0	0	11	0	73	4	0	4	2	.667	1	9	0.73
1987 Gastonia	A	56	0	0	55	68.2	273	44	19	13	6	5	3	0	25	5	101	10	0	1	5	.167	0	30	1.70
1988 Charlotte	A	23	0	0	19	26.1	98	20	6	6	1	1	0	0	4	0	21	1	1	1	2	.333	0	7	2.05
1989 Charlotte	A	20	0	0	16	24.1	95	13	8	6	1	4	1	0	8	1	26	1	1	2	1	.667	0	10	2.22
Tulsa	AA	31	0	0	22	50	209	40	20	17	2	1	3	0	21	3	47	0	0	2	4	.333	0	10	3.06
1990 Tulsa	AA	12	0	0	10	15	62	9	6	4	1	1	1	0	9	1	18	3	1	2	2	.500	0	4	2.40
Okla City	AAA	42	0	0	33	48	200	40	24	16	1	2	1	2	18	3	39	5	1	3	4	.429	0	14	3.00
1991 Okla City	AAA	32	0	0	16	51.2	226	52	24	23	2	3	3	3	22	2	59	3	1	3	2	.600	0	5	4.01
1992 Okla City	AAA	57	0	0	33	61.2	282	72	42	39	5	2	2	2	29	3	54	11	0	1	6	.143	0	11	5.69
1991 Texas	AL	36	0	0	8	70.1	321	72	43	41	9	1	3	1	36	1	61	8	1	1	4	.200	0	1	5.25
1992 Texas	AL	6	0	0	2	4.2	24	7	4	4	1	0	0	0	2	0	1	1	0	0	0	.000	0	0	7.71
2 ML YEARS		42	0	0	10	75	345	79	47	45	10	1	3	1	38	1	62	9	1	1	4	.200	0	1	5.40

Rico Rossy

Bats: Right **Throws:** Right **Pos:** SS   **Ht:** 5'10" **Wt:** 175 **Born:** 02/16/64 **Age:** 29

Year Team	Lg	G	AB	H	2B	3B	HR	(Hm	Rd)	TB	R	RBI	TBB	IBB	SO	HBP	SH	SF	SB	CS	SB%	GDP	Avg	OBP	SLG
1985 Newark	A	73	246	53	14	2	3	--	--	80	38	25	32	1	22	1	3	1	17	7	.71	13	.215	.307	.325
1986 Miami	A	38	134	34	7	1	1	--	--	46	26	9	24	0	8	1	6	1	10	6	.63	4	.254	.369	.343
Charlotte	AA	77	232	68	16	2	3	--	--	97	40	25	26	0	19	2	8	1	13	5	.72	2	.293	.368	.418
1987 Charlotte	AA	127	471	135	22	3	4	--	--	175	69	50	43	0	38	3	3	1	20	9	.69	20	.287	.349	.372
1988 Buffalo	AAA	68	187	46	4	0	1	--	--	53	12	20	13	0	17	0	0	1	1	5	.17	4	.246	.294	.283
1989 Harrisburg	AA	78	238	60	16	1	2	--	--	84	20	25	27	0	19	3	0	2	2	4	.33	5	.252	.333	.353
Buffalo	AAA	38	109	21	5	0	0	--	--	26	11	10	18	1	11	1	1	2	4	0	1.00	4	.193	.308	.239
1990 Buffalo	AAA	8	17	3	0	1	0	--	--	5	3	2	4	0	2	0	1	1	1	0	1.00	1	.176	.318	.294
Greenville	AA	5	21	4	1	0	0	--	--	5	4	0	1	0	2	0	0	0	0	2	.00	1	.190	.227	.238
Richmond	AAA	107	380	88	13	0	4	--	--	113	58	32	69	1	43	3	7	2	11	6	.65	12	.232	.352	.297
1991 Richmond	AAA	139	482	124	25	1	2	--	--	157	58	48	67	1	46	5	13	3	4	8	.33	12	.257	.352	.326
1992 Omaha	AAA	48	174	55	10	1	4	--	--	79	29	17	34	0	14	0	2	3	3	5	.38	5	.316	.422	.454
1991 Atlanta	NL	5	1	0	0	0	0	(0	0)	0	0	0	0	0	1	0	0	0	0	0	.00	0	.000	.000	.000
1992 Kansas City	AL	59	149	32	8	1	1	(0	1)	45	21	12	20	1	20	1	1	1	0	3	.00	6	.215	.310	.302
2 ML YEARS		64	150	32	8	1	1	(0	1)	45	21	12	20	1	21	1	1	1	0	3	.00	6	.213	.308	.300

173

Rich Rowland

Bats: Right **Throws:** Right **Pos:** C **Ht:** 6' 1" **Wt:** 215 **Born:** 02/25/67 **Age:** 26

								BATTING												BASERUNNING				PERCENTAGES		
Year Team	Lg	G	AB	H	2B	3B	HR	(Hm	Rd)	TB	R	RBI	TBB	IBB	SO	HBP	SH	SF	SB	CS	SB%	GDP	Avg	OBP	SLG
1988 Bristol	R	56	186	51	10	1	4	--	--	75	29	41	27	1	39	1	0	3	1	2	.33	2	.274	.364	.403
1989 Fayetteville	A	108	375	102	17	1	9	--	--	148	43	59	54	2	98	3	3	3	4	1	.80	8	.272	.366	.395
1990 London	AA	47	161	46	10	0	8	--	--	80	22	30	20	3	33	3	0	1	1	1	.50	7	.286	.373	.497
Toledo	AAA	62	192	50	12	0	7	--	--	83	28	22	15	0	33	1	3	2	2	3	.40	3	.260	.314	.432
1991 Toledo	AAA	109	383	104	25	0	13	--	--	168	56	68	60	3	77	3	0	1	4	2	.67	8	.272	.374	.439
1992 Toledo	AAA	136	473	111	19	1	25	--	--	207	75	82	56	6	112	3	0	4	9	3	.75	20	.235	.317	.438
1990 Detroit	AL	7	19	3	1	0	0	(0	0)	4	3	0	2	1	4	0	0	0	0	0	.00	1	.158	.238	.211
1991 Detroit	AL	4	4	1	0	0	0	(0	0)	1	0	1	1	0	2	0	0	1	0	0	.00	0	.250	.333	.250
1992 Detroit	AL	6	14	3	0	0	0	(0	0)	3	2	0	3	0	3	0	0	0	0	0	.00	1	.214	.353	.214
3 ML YEARS		17	37	7	1	0	0	(0	0)	8	5	1	6	1	9	0	0	1	0	0	.00	2	.189	.295	.216

Stan Royer

Bats: Right **Throws:** Right **Pos:** 3B **Ht:** 6' 3" **Wt:** 195 **Born:** 08/31/67 **Age:** 25

								BATTING												BASERUNNING				PERCENTAGES		
Year Team	Lg	G	AB	H	2B	3B	HR	(Hm	Rd)	TB	R	RBI	TBB	IBB	SO	HBP	SH	SF	SB	CS	SB%	GDP	Avg	OBP	SLG
1988 Sou Oregon	A	73	286	91	19	3	6	--	--	134	47	48	33	1	71	2	1	4	0	1	1.00	6	.318	.388	.469
1989 Tacoma	AAA	6	19	5	1	0	0	--	--	6	2	2	2	0	6	0	0	0	0	0	.00	1	.263	.333	.316
Modesto	A	127	476	120	28	1	11	--	--	183	54	69	58	3	132	1	2	2	3	2	.60	11	.252	.333	.384
1990 Huntsville	AA	137	527	136	29	3	14	--	--	213	69	89	43	0	113	3	8	4	4	1	.80	13	.258	.315	.404
Louisville	AAA	4	15	4	1	1	0	--	--	7	1	4	2	0	5	0	0	0	0	0	.00	0	.267	.353	.467
1991 Louisville	AAA	138	523	133	29	6	14	--	--	216	48	74	43	1	126	3	0	6	1	2	.33	13	.254	.311	.413
1992 Louisville	AAA	124	444	125	31	2	11	--	--	193	55	77	32	2	74	4	4	4	0	0	.00	17	.282	.333	.435
1991 St. Louis	NL	9	21	6	1	0	0	(0	0)	7	1	1	1	0	2	0	0	0	0	0	.00	0	.286	.318	.333
1992 St. Louis	NL	13	31	10	2	0	2	(1	1)	18	6	9	1	0	4	0	0	1	0	0	.00	0	.323	.333	.581
2 ML YEARS		22	52	16	3	0	2	(1	1)	25	7	10	2	0	6	0	0	1	0	0	.00	0	.308	.327	.481

Bruce Ruffin

Pitches: Left **Bats:** Both **Pos:** RP/SP **Ht:** 6' 2" **Wt:** 213 **Born:** 10/04/63 **Age:** 29

		HOW MUCH HE PITCHED						WHAT HE GAVE UP											THE RESULTS					
Year Team	Lg	G	GS	CG	GF	IP	BFP	H	R	ER	HR	SH	SF	HB	TBB	IBB	SO	WP	Bk	W	L	Pct.	ShO	Sv	ERA
1986 Philadelphia	NL	21	21	6	0	146.1	600	138	53	40	6	2	4	1	44	6	70	0	1	9	4	.692	0	0	2.46
1987 Philadelphia	NL	35	35	3	0	204.2	884	236	118	99	17	8	10	4	73	4	93	6	0	11	14	.440	1	0	4.35
1988 Philadelphia	NL	55	15	3	14	144.1	646	151	86	71	7	10	3	3	80	4	82	12	0	6	10	.375	0	3	4.43
1989 Philadelphia	NL	24	23	1	0	125.2	576	152	69	62	10	8	1	0	62	6	70	8	0	6	10	.375	0	0	4.44
1990 Philadelphia	NL	32	25	2	1	149	678	178	99	89	14	10	6	1	62	7	79	3	2	6	13	.316	1	0	5.38
1991 Philadelphia	NL	31	15	1	2	119	508	125	52	50	6	6	4	1	38	3	85	4	0	4	7	.364	1	0	3.78
1992 Milwaukee	AL	25	6	1	6	58	272	66	43	43	7	3	3	0	41	3	45	2	0	1	6	.143	0	0	6.67
7 ML YEARS		223	140	17	23	947	4164	1046	520	454	67	47	31	8	400	35	524	35	3	43	64	.402	3	3	4.31

Scott Ruskin

Pitches: Left **Bats:** Right **Pos:** RP **Ht:** 6' 2" **Wt:** 195 **Born:** 06/08/63 **Age:** 30

		HOW MUCH HE PITCHED						WHAT HE GAVE UP											THE RESULTS					
Year Team	Lg	G	GS	CG	GF	IP	BFP	H	R	ER	HR	SH	SF	HB	TBB	IBB	SO	WP	Bk	W	L	Pct.	ShO	Sv	ERA
1990 2 ML Teams		67	0	0	12	75.1	336	75	28	23	4	5	2	2	38	6	57	3	1	3	2	.600	0	2	2.75
1991 Montreal	NL	64	0	0	24	63.2	275	57	31	30	4	5	0	3	30	2	46	5	0	4	4	.500	0	6	4.24
1992 Cincinnati	NL	57	0	0	19	53.2	234	56	31	30	6	7	2	1	20	4	43	1	0	4	3	.571	0	0	5.03
1990 Pittsburgh	NL	44	0	0	8	47.2	221	50	21	16	2	3	2	2	28	3	34	3	1	2	2	.500	0	2	3.02
Montreal	NL	23	0	0	4	27.2	115	25	7	7	2	2	0	0	10	3	23	0	0	1	0	1.000	0	0	2.28
3 ML YEARS		188	0	0	55	192.2	845	188	90	83	14	17	4	6	88	12	146	9	1	11	9	.550	0	8	3.88

Jeff Russell

Pitches: Right **Bats:** Right **Pos:** RP **Ht:** 6' 3" **Wt:** 205 **Born:** 09/02/61 **Age:** 31

		HOW MUCH HE PITCHED						WHAT HE GAVE UP											THE RESULTS					
Year Team	Lg	G	GS	CG	GF	IP	BFP	H	R	ER	HR	SH	SF	HB	TBB	IBB	SO	WP	Bk	W	L	Pct.	ShO	Sv	ERA
1983 Cincinnati	NL	10	10	2	0	68.1	282	58	30	23	7	6	5	0	22	3	40	1	1	4	5	.444	0	0	3.03
1984 Cincinnati	NL	33	30	4	1	181.2	787	186	97	86	15	8	3	4	65	8	101	3	3	6	**18**	.250	2	0	4.26
1985 Texas	AL	13	13	0	0	62	295	85	55	52	10	1	3	2	27	1	44	2	0	3	6	.333	0	0	7.55
1986 Texas	AL	37	0	0	9	82	338	74	40	31	11	3	2	1	31	2	54	5	0	5	2	.714	0	2	3.40
1987 Texas	AL	52	2	0	12	97.1	442	109	56	48	9	0	5	2	52	5	56	6	1	5	4	.556	0	3	4.44
1988 Texas	AL	34	24	5	1	188.2	793	183	86	80	15	4	3	7	66	3	88	5	7	10	9	.526	0	0	3.82
1989 Texas	AL	71	0	0	**66**	72.2	278	45	21	16	4	1	3	3	24	5	77	6	0	6	4	.600	0	**38**	1.98
1990 Texas	AL	27	0	0	25	25.1	111	23	15	12	1	3	1	0	16	5	16	2	0	1	5	.167	0	10	4.26
1991 Texas	AL	68	0	0	56	79.1	336	71	36	29	11	3	4	1	26	1	52	6	0	6	4	.600	0	30	3.29

Year Team	Lg	G	GS	CG	GF	IP	BFP	H	R	ER	HR	SH	SF	HB	TBB	IBB	SO	WP	Bk	W	L	Pct.	ShO	Sv	ERA
1992 2 ML Teams		59	0	0	46	66.1	276	55	14	12	3	1	2	2	25	3	48	3	0	4	3	.571	0	30	1.63
1992 Texas	AL	51	0	0	42	56.2	241	51	14	12	3	1	2	2	22	3	43	3	0	2	3	.400	0	28	1.91
Oakland	AI	8	0	0	4	9.2	35	4	0	0	0	0	0	0	3	0	5	0	0	2	0	1.000	0	2	0.00
10 ML YEARS		404	79	11	213	923.2	3938	889	450	389	86	28	31	22	354	36	576	39	12	50	60	.455	2	113	3.79

John Russell

Bats: Right **Throws:** Right **Pos:** C **Ht:** 6' 0" **Wt:** 195 **Born:** 01/05/61 **Age:** 32

							BATTING												BASERUNNING			PERCENTAGES		
Year Team	Lg	G	AB	H	2B	3B	HR	(Hm	Rd)	TB	R	RBI	TBB	IBB	SO	HBP	SH	SF	SB	CS	SB%	GDP	Avg	OBP	SLG
1984 Philadelphia	NL	39	99	28	8	1	2	(1	1)	44	11	11	12	2	33	0	0	3	0	1	.00	2	.283	.351	.444
1985 Philadelphia	NL	81	216	47	12	0	9	(6	3)	86	22	23	18	0	72	0	0	0	2	0	1.00	5	.218	.278	.398
1986 Philadelphia	NL	93	315	76	21	2	13	(8	5)	140	35	60	25	2	103	3	1	4	0	1	.00	6	.241	.300	.444
1987 Philadelphia	NL	24	62	9	1	0	3	(1	2)	19	5	8	3	0	17	0	0	0	0	1	.00	4	.145	.185	.306
1988 Philadelphia	NL	22	49	12	1	0	2	(1	1)	19	5	4	3	0	15	1	0	0	0	0	.00	0	.245	.302	.388
1989 Atlanta	NL	74	159	29	2	0	2	(1	1)	37	14	9	8	1	53	1	0	1	0	0	.00	4	.182	.225	.233
1990 Texas	AL	68	128	35	4	0	2	(0	2)	45	16	8	11	2	41	0	1	0	1	0	1.00	3	.273	.331	.352
1991 Texas	AL	22	27	3	0	0	0	(0	0)	3	3	1	1	0	7	0	0	1	0	0	.00	0	.111	.138	.111
1992 Texas	AI	7	10	1	0	0	0	(0	0)	1	1	2	1	0	4	1	0	1	0	0	.00	0	.100	.231	.100
9 ML YEARS		430	1065	240	49	3	33	(18	15)	394	112	126	82	7	345	6	2	10	3	3	.50	26	.225	.282	.370

Ken Ryan

Pitches: Right **Bats:** Right **Pos:** RP **Ht:** 6' 3" **Wt:** 200 **Born:** 10/24/68 **Age:** 24

		HOW MUCH HE PITCHED						WHAT HE GAVE UP												THE RESULTS					
Year Team	Lg	G	GS	CG	GF	IP	BFP	H	R	ER	HR	SH	SF	HB	TBB	IBB	SO	WP	Bk	W	L	Pct.	ShO	Sv	ERA
1986 Elmira	A	13	1	0	10	21.2	103	20	14	14	0	2	2	1	21	2	22	1	0	2	2	.500	0	0	5.82
1987 Greensboro	A	28	19	2	8	121.1	554	139	88	74	10	1	7	3	63	8	75	10	3	3	12	.200	0	0	5.49
1988 Lynchburg	A	19	14	0	2	71.1	344	92	51	49	4	2	1	3	45	5	49	5	3	2	7	.222	0	0	6.18
1989 Winter Havn	A	24	22	3	1	137	586	114	58	48	5	4	4	7	81	0	78	8	4	8	8	.500	0	0	3.15
1990 Lynchburg	A	28	28	3	0	161.1	735	182	104	92	10	6	5	6	82	0	109	19	1	6	14	.300	1	0	5.13
1991 Winter Havn	A	21	1	0	11	52.2	213	40	15	12	1	0	0	2	19	0	53	3	1	1	3	.250	0	1	2.05
New Britain	AA	14	0	0	6	26	116	23	7	5	2	4	0	1	12	1	26	2	0	1	2	.333	0	1	1.73
Pawtucket	AAA	9	0	0	4	18.1	80	15	11	10	2	2	2	1	11	1	14	2	0	1	0	1.000	0	1	4.91
1992 New Britain	AA	44	0	0	42	50.2	220	44	17	11	0	0	2	1	24	2	51	4	0	1	4	.200	0	22	1.95
Pawtucket	AAA	9	0	0	9	8.2	36	6	2	2	1	0	0	0	4	0	6	0	0	2	0	1.000	0	7	2.08
1992 Boston	AL	7	0	0	6	7	30	4	5	5	1	2	1	0	5	0	5	0	0	0	0	.000	0	1	6.43

Nolan Ryan

Pitches: Right **Bats:** Right **Pos:** SP **Ht:** 6' 2" **Wt:** 212 **Born:** 01/31/47 **Age:** 46

		HOW MUCH HE PITCHED						WHAT HE GAVE UP												THE RESULTS					
Year Team	Lg	G	GS	CG	GF	IP	BFP	H	R	ER	HR	SH	SF	HB	TBB	IBB	SO	WP	Bk	W	L	Pct.	ShO	Sv	ERA
1966 New York	NL	2	1	0	0	3	17	5	5	5	1	0	0	0	3	1	6	1	0	0	1	.000	0	0	15.00
1968 New York	NL	21	18	3	1	134	559	93	50	46	12	12	4	4	75	4	133	7	0	6	9	.400	0	0	3.09
1969 New York	NL	25	10	2	4	89	375	60	38	35	3	2	2	1	53	3	92	1	3	6	3	.667	0	1	3.54
1970 New York	NL	27	19	5	4	132	570	86	59	50	10	8	4	4	97	2	125	8	0	7	11	.389	2	1	3.41
1971 New York	NL	30	26	3	1	152	705	125	78	67	8	3	0	15	116	4	137	6	1	10	14	.417	0	0	3.97
1972 California	AL	39	39	20	0	284	1154	166	80	72	14	11	3	10	157	4	329	18	0	19	16	.543	9	0	2.28
1973 California	AL	41	39	26	2	326	1355	238	113	104	18	7	7	7	162	2	383	15	0	21	16	.568	4	1	2.87
1974 California	AL	42	41	26	1	332.2	1392	221	127	107	18	12	4	9	202	3	367	9	0	22	16	.579	3	0	2.89
1975 California	AL	28	28	10	0	198	864	152	90	76	13	6	7	7	132	0	186	12	0	14	12	.538	5	0	3.45
1976 California	AL	39	39	21	0	284	1196	193	117	106	13	13	4	5	183	2	327	5	2	17	18	.486	7	0	3.36
1977 California	AL	37	37	22	0	299	1272	198	110	92	12	22	10	9	204	7	341	21	3	19	16	.543	4	0	2.77
1978 California	AL	31	31	14	0	235	1008	183	106	97	12	11	14	3	148	7	260	13	2	10	13	.435	3	0	3.71
1979 California	AL	34	34	17	0	223	937	169	104	89	15	8	10	6	114	3	223	9	0	16	14	.533	5	0	3.59
1980 Houston	NL	35	35	4	0	234	982	205	100	87	10	7	7	3	98	1	200	10	1	11	10	.524	2	0	3.35
1981 Houston	NL	21	21	5	0	149	605	99	34	28	2	5	3	1	68	1	140	16	2	11	5	.688	3	0	1.69
1982 Houston	NL	35	35	10	0	250.1	1050	196	100	88	20	9	3	8	109	3	245	18	2	16	12	.571	3	0	3.16
1983 Houston	NL	29	29	5	0	196.1	804	134	74	65	9	7	5	4	101	3	183	5	1	14	9	.609	2	0	2.98
1984 Houston	NL	30	30	5	0	183.2	760	143	78	62	12	4	6	4	69	2	197	6	3	12	11	.522	2	0	3.04
1985 Houston	NL	35	35	4	0	232	983	205	108	98	12	11	12	9	95	8	209	14	2	10	12	.455	0	0	3.80
1986 Houston	NL	30	30	1	0	178	729	119	72	66	14	5	4	4	82	5	194	15	0	12	8	.600	0	0	3.34
1987 Houston	NL	34	34	0	0	211.2	873	154	75	65	14	9	1	4	87	2	270	10	2	8	16	.333	0	0	2.76
1988 Houston	NL	33	33	4	0	220	930	186	98	86	18	10	8	7	87	6	228	10	7	12	11	.522	1	0	3.52
1989 Texas	AL	32	32	6	0	239.1	988	162	96	85	17	9	5	9	98	3	301	19	1	16	10	.615	2	0	3.20
1990 Texas	AL	30	30	5	0	204	818	137	86	78	18	3	5	7	74	2	232	9	1	13	9	.591	2	0	3.44
1991 Texas	AL	27	27	2	0	173	683	102	58	53	12	3	9	5	72	0	203	8	0	12	6	.667	2	0	2.91
1992 Texas	AL	27	27	2	0	157.1	675	138	75	65	9	6	7	12	69	0	157	9	0	5	9	.357	0	0	3.72
26 ML YEARS		794	760	222	13	5320.1	22284	3869	2131	1875	316	203	144	157	2755	78	5668	274	33	319	287	.526	61	3	3.17

Bret Saberhagen

Pitches: Right **Bats:** Right **Pos:** SP **Ht:** 6' 1" **Wt:** 200 **Born:** 04/11/64 **Age:** 29

		HOW MUCH HE PITCHED						WHAT HE GAVE UP												THE RESULTS					
Year Team	Lg	G	GS	CG	GF	IP	BFP	H	R	ER	HR	SH	SF	HB	TBB	IBB	SO	WP	Bk	W	L	Pct.	ShO	Sv	ERA
1984 Kansas City	AL	38	18	2	9	157.2	634	138	71	61	13	8	5	2	36	4	73	7	1	10	11	.476	1	1	3.48
1985 Kansas City	AL	32	32	10	0	235.1	931	211	79	75	19	9	7	1	38	1	158	1	3	20	6	.769	1	0	2.87
1986 Kansas City	AL	30	25	4	4	156	652	165	77	72	15	3	3	2	29	1	112	1	1	7	12	.368	2	0	4.15
1987 Kansas City	AL	33	33	15	0	257	1048	246	99	96	27	8	5	6	53	2	163	6	1	18	10	.643	4	0	3.36
1988 Kansas City	AL	35	35	9	0	260.2	1089	271	122	110	18	8	10	4	59	5	171	9	0	14	16	.467	0	0	3.80
1989 Kansas City	AL	36	35	12	0	262.1	1021	209	74	63	13	9	6	2	43	6	193	8	1	23	6	.793	4	0	2.16
1990 Kansas City	AL	20	20	5	0	135	561	146	52	49	9	4	4	1	28	1	87	1	0	5	9	.357	0	0	3.27
1991 Kansas City	AL	28	28	7	0	196.1	789	165	76	67	12	8	3	9	45	5	136	8	1	13	8	.619	2	0	3.07
1992 New York	NL	17	15	1	0	97.2	397	84	39	38	6	3	3	4	27	1	81	1	2	3	5	.375	1	0	3.50
9 ML YEARS		269	241	65	13	1758	7122	1635	689	631	132	60	46	31	358	26	1174	42	10	113	83	.577	15	1	3.23

Chris Sabo

Bats: Right **Throws:** Right **Pos:** 3B **Ht:** 6' 0" **Wt:** 185 **Born:** 01/19/62 **Age:** 31

		BATTING																	BASERUNNING				PERCENTAGES		
Year Team	Lg	G	AB	H	2B	3B	HR	(Hm	Rd)	TB	R	RBI	TBB	IBB	SO	HBP	SH	SF	SB	CS	SB%	GDP	Avg	OBP	SLG
1988 Cincinnati	NL	137	538	146	40	2	11	(8	3)	223	74	44	29	1	52	6	5	4	46	14	.77	12	.271	.314	.414
1989 Cincinnati	NL	82	304	79	21	1	6	(3	3)	120	40	29	25	2	33	1	4	2	14	9	.61	2	.260	.316	.395
1990 Cincinnati	NL	148	567	153	38	2	25	(15	10)	270	95	71	61	7	58	4	1	3	25	10	.71	8	.270	.343	.476
1991 Cincinnati	NL	153	582	175	35	3	26	(15	11)	294	91	88	44	3	79	6	5	3	19	6	.76	13	.301	.354	.505
1992 Cincinnati	NL	96	344	84	19	3	12	(8	4)	145	42	43	30	1	54	1	1	6	4	5	.44	12	.244	.302	.422
5 ML YEARS		616	2335	637	153	11	80	(49	31)	1052	342	275	189	14	276	18	16	18	108	44	.71	47	.273	.330	.451

Luis Salazar

Bats: Right **Throws:** Right **Pos:** 3B/SS/LF **Ht:** 5'10" **Wt:** 190 **Born:** 05/19/56 **Age:** 37

		BATTING																	BASERUNNING				PERCENTAGES		
Year Team	Lg	G	AB	H	2B	3B	HR	(Hm	Rd)	TB	R	RBI	TBB	IBB	SO	HBP	SH	SF	SB	CS	SB%	GDP	Avg	OBP	SLG
1980 San Diego	NL	44	169	57	4	7	1	(0	1)	78	28	25	9	1	25	1	3	1	11	2	.85	4	.337	.372	.462
1981 San Diego	NL	109	400	121	19	6	3	(2	1)	161	37	38	16	2	72	1	5	2	11	8	.58	7	.303	.329	.403
1982 San Diego	NL	145	524	127	15	5	8	(6	2)	176	55	62	23	10	80	2	5	5	32	9	.78	10	.242	.274	.336
1983 San Diego	NL	134	481	124	16	2	14	(10	4)	186	52	45	17	8	80	2	8	2	24	9	.73	4	.258	.285	.387
1984 San Diego	NL	93	228	55	7	2	3	(1	2)	75	20	17	6	1	38	0	2	0	11	7	.61	5	.241	.261	.329
1985 Chicago	AL	122	327	80	18	2	10	(4	6)	132	39	45	12	2	60	0	9	5	14	4	.78	5	.245	.267	.404
1986 Chicago	AL	4	7	1	0	0	0	(0	0)	1	1	0	1	0	3	0	0	0	0	0	.00	0	.143	.250	.143
1987 San Diego	NL	84	189	48	5	0	3	(1	2)	62	13	17	14	2	30	0	1	2	3	3	.50	2	.254	.302	.328
1988 Detroit	AL	130	452	122	14	1	12	(5	7)	174	61	62	21	2	70	3	10	3	6	0	1.00	13	.270	.305	.385
1989 2 ML Teams		121	326	92	12	2	9	(6	3)	135	34	34	15	3	57	1	7	0	1	4	.20	6	.282	.316	.414
1990 Chicago	NL	115	410	104	13	3	12	(7	5)	159	44	47	19	3	59	4	0	1	3	1	.75	4	.254	.293	.388
1991 Chicago	NL	103	333	86	14	1	14	(8	6)	144	34	38	15	1	45	1	2	0	3	0	.00	8	.258	.292	.432
1992 Chicago	NL	98	255	53	7	2	5	(3	2)	79	20	25	11	2	34	0	3	4	1	1	.50	10	.208	.237	.310
1989 San Diego	NL	95	246	66	7	2	8	(5	3)	101	27	22	11	3	44	1	7	0	1	3	.25	4	.268	.302	.411
Chicago	NL	26	80	26	5	0	1	(1	0)	34	7	12	4	0	13	0	0	0	0	0	.00	2	.325	.357	.425
13 ML YEARS		1302	4101	1070	144	33	94	(53	41)	1562	438	455	179	37	653	15	55	25	117	51	.70	78	.261	.293	.381

Tim Salmon

Bats: Right **Throws:** Right **Pos:** RF **Ht:** 6' 3" **Wt:** 210 **Born:** 08/24/68 **Age:** 24

		BATTING																	BASERUNNING				PERCENTAGES		
Year Team	Lg	G	AB	H	2B	3B	HR	(Hm	Rd)	TB	R	RBI	TBB	IBB	SO	HBP	SH	SF	SB	CS	SB%	GDP	Avg	OBP	SLG
1989 Bend	A	55	196	48	6	5	6	(--	--)	82	37	31	33	0	61	6	1	2	2	4	.33	2	.245	.367	.418
1990 Palm Sprngs	A	36	118	34	6	0	2	(--	--)	46	19	21	21	0	44	4	0	0	11	1	.92	1	.288	.413	.390
Midland	AA	27	97	26	3	1	3	(--	--)	40	17	16	18	0	38	1	0	1	1	0	1.00	1	.268	.385	.412
1991 Midland	AA	131	465	114	26	4	23	(--	--)	217	100	94	89	1	166	6	3	2	12	6	.67	6	.245	.372	.467
1992 Edmonton	AAA	118	409	142	38	4	29	(--	--)	275	101	105	91	11	103	6	0	4	9	7	.56	9	.347	.469	.672
1992 California	AL	23	79	14	1	0	2	(1	1)	21	8	6	11	1	23	1	0	1	1	1	.50	1	.177	.283	.266

Bill Sampen

Pitches: Right **Bats:** Right **Pos:** RP **Ht:** 6' 2" **Wt:** 195 **Born:** 01/18/63 **Age:** 30

		HOW MUCH HE PITCHED						WHAT HE GAVE UP												THE RESULTS					
Year Team	Lg	G	GS	CG	GF	IP	BFP	H	R	ER	HR	SH	SF	HB	TBB	IBB	SO	WP	Bk	W	L	Pct.	ShO	Sv	ERA
1990 Montreal	NL	59	4	0	26	90.1	394	94	34	30	7	5	3	2	33	6	69	4	0	12	7	.632	0	2	2.99
1991 Montreal	NL	43	8	0	8	92.1	409	96	49	41	13	4	4	3	46	7	52	3	1	9	5	.643	0	0	4.00
1992 2 ML Teams		52	2	0	13	83	348	83	32	30	4	6	3	3	32	7	37	2	2	1	6	.143	0	0	3.25
1992 Montreal	NL	44	1	0	10	63.1	267	62	22	22	4	5	1	1	29	6	23	1	2	1	4	.200	0	0	3.13
Kansas City	AL	8	1	0	3	19.2	81	21	10	8	0	1	2	3	3	1	14	1	0	0	2	.000	0	0	3.66

3 ML YEARS	154	14	0	47	265.2	1151	273	115	101	24	15	10	9	111	20	158	9	3	22	18	.550	0	2	3.42

Juan Samuel

Bats: Right **Throws:** Right **Pos:** 2B/RF   **Ht:** 5'11" **Wt:** 183 **Born:** 12/09/60 **Age:** 32

								BATTING											BASERUNNING				PERCENTAGES		
Year Team	Lg	G	AB	H	2B	3B	HR	(Hm Rd)	TB	R	RBI	TBB	IBB	SO	HBP	SH	SF	SB	CS	SB%	GDP	Avg	OBP	SLG
1983 Philadelphia	NL	18	65	18	1	2	2	(1 1)	29	14	5	4	1	16	1	0	1	3	2	.60	1	.277	.324	.446
1984 Philadelphia	NL	160	701	191	36	19	15	(8 7)	310	105	69	28	2	168	7	0	1	72	15	.83	6	.272	.307	.442
1985 Philadelphia	NL	161	663	175	31	13	19	(8 11)	289	101	74	33	2	141	6	2	5	53	19	.74	8	.264	.303	.436
1986 Philadelphia	NL	145	591	157	36	12	16	(10 6)	265	90	78	26	3	142	8	1	7	42	14	.75	8	.266	.302	.448
1987 Philadelphia	NL	160	655	178	37	15	28	(15 13)	329	113	100	60	5	162	5	0	6	35	15	.70	12	.272	.335	.502
1988 Philadelphia	NL	157	629	153	32	9	12	(7 5)	239	68	67	39	6	151	12	0	5	33	10	.77	8	.243	.298	.380
1989 2 ML Teams		137	532	125	16	2	11	(5 6)	178	69	48	42	2	120	11	2	2	42	12	.78	7	.235	.303	.335
1990 Los Angeles	NL	143	492	119	24	3	13	(6 7)	188	62	52	51	5	126	5	5	5	38	20	.66	8	.242	.316	.382
1991 Los Angeles	NL	153	594	161	22	6	12	(4 8)	231	74	58	49	4	133	3	10	3	23	8	.73	8	.271	.328	.389
1992 2 ML Teams		76	224	61	8	4	0	(0 0)	77	22	23	14	4	49	2	4	2	8	3	.73	2	.272	.318	.344
1989 Philadelphia	NL	51	199	49	3	1	8	(3 5)	78	32	20	18	1	45	1	0	1	11	3	.79	2	.246	.311	.392
New York	NL	86	333	76	13	1	3	(2 1)	100	37	28	24	1	75	10	2	1	31	9	.78	5	.228	.299	.300
1992 Los Angeles	NL	47	122	32	3	1	0	(0 0)	37	7	15	7	3	22	1	4	2	2	2	.50	0	.262	.303	.303
Kansas City	AL	29	102	29	5	3	0	(0 0)	40	15	8	7	1	27	1	0	0	6	1	.86	2	.284	.336	.392
10 ML YEARS		1310	5146	1338	243	85	128	(64 64)	2135	718	574	346	34	1208	60	24	37	349	118	.75	68	.260	.312	.415

Rey Sanchez

Bats: Right **Throws:** Right **Pos:** SS   **Ht:** 5'10" **Wt:** 180 **Born:** 10/05/67 **Age:** 25

								BATTING											BASERUNNING				PERCENTAGES		
Year Team	Lg	G	AB	H	2B	3B	HR	(Hm Rd)	TB	R	RBI	TBB	IBB	SO	HBP	SH	SF	SB	CS	SB%	GDP	Avg	OBP	SLG
1986 Rangers	R	52	169	49	3	1	0	-- --	54	27	23	41	0	18	3	3	1	10	10	.50	3	.290	.435	.320
1987 Gastonia	A	50	160	35	1	2	1	-- --	43	19	10	22	0	17	2	3	0	6	3	.67	9	.219	.321	.269
Butte	R	49	189	69	10	6	0	-- --	91	36	25	21	1	11	2	3	2	22	6	.79	6	.365	.430	.481
1988 Charlotte	A	128	418	128	6	5	0	-- --	144	60	38	35	4	24	5	1	3	29	11	.73	14	.306	.364	.344
1989 Okla City	AAA	134	464	104	10	4	1	-- --	125	38	39	21	0	50	2	5	3	4	4	.50	14	.224	.259	.269
1991 Iowa	AAA	126	417	121	16	5	2	-- --	153	60	46	37	1	27	7	11	2	13	7	.65	11	.290	.356	.367
1992 Iowa	AAA	20	76	26	3	0	0	-- --	29	12	3	4	0	1	0	1	0	6	3	.67	3	.342	.375	.382
1991 Chicago	NL	13	23	6	0	0	0	(0 0)	6	1	2	4	0	3	0	0	0	0	0	.00	0	.261	.370	.261
1992 Chicago	NL	74	255	64	14	3	1	(1 0)	87	24	19	10	1	17	3	5	2	2	1	.67	7	.251	.285	.341
2 ML YEARS		87	278	70	14	3	1	(1 0)	93	25	21	14	1	20	3	5	2	2	1	.67	7	.252	.293	.335

Ryne Sandberg

Bats: Right **Throws:** Right **Pos:** 2B   **Ht:** 6' 2" **Wt:** 185 **Born:** 09/18/59 **Age:** 33

								BATTING											BASERUNNING				PERCENTAGES		
Year Team	Lg	G	AB	H	2B	3B	HR	(Hm Rd)	TB	R	RBI	TBB	IBB	SO	HBP	SH	SF	SB	CS	SB%	GDP	Avg	OBP	SLG
1981 Philadelphia	NL	13	6	1	0	0	0	(0 0)	1	2	0	0	0	1	0	0	0	0	0	.00	0	.167	.167	.167
1982 Chicago	NL	156	635	172	33	5	7	(5 2)	236	103	54	36	3	90	4	7	5	32	12	.73	7	.271	.312	.372
1983 Chicago	NL	158	633	165	25	4	8	(4 4)	222	94	48	51	3	79	3	7	5	37	11	.77	8	.261	.316	.351
1984 Chicago	NL	156	636	200	36	19	19	(11 8)	331	114	84	52	3	101	3	5	4	32	7	.82	7	.314	.367	.520
1985 Chicago	NL	153	609	186	31	6	26	(17 9)	307	113	83	57	5	97	1	2	4	54	11	.83	10	.305	.364	.504
1986 Chicago	NL	154	627	178	28	5	14	(8 6)	258	68	76	46	6	79	0	3	6	34	11	.76	11	.284	.330	.411
1987 Chicago	NL	132	523	154	25	2	16	(8 8)	231	81	59	59	4	79	2	1	2	21	2	.91	11	.294	.367	.442
1988 Chicago	NL	155	618	163	23	8	19	(10 9)	259	77	69	54	3	91	1	1	5	25	10	.71	14	.264	.322	.419
1989 Chicago	NL	157	606	176	25	5	30	(16 14)	301	104	76	59	8	85	4	1	2	15	5	.75	9	.290	.356	.497
1990 Chicago	NL	155	615	188	30	3	40	(25 15)	344	116	100	50	8	84	1	0	9	25	7	.78	4	.306	.354	.559
1991 Chicago	NL	158	585	170	32	2	26	(15 11)	284	104	100	87	4	89	2	1	9	22	8	.73	9	.291	.379	.485
1992 Chicago	NL	158	612	186	32	8	26	(16 10)	312	100	87	68	4	73	1	0	6	17	6	.74	13	.304	.371	.510
12 ML YEARS		1705	6705	1939	320	67	231	(135 96)	3086	1076	836	619	51	948	22	28	57	314	90	.78	107	.289	.349	.460

Deion Sanders

Bats: Left **Throws:** Left **Pos:** CF/LF   **Ht:** 6' 1" **Wt:** 195 **Born:** 08/09/67 **Age:** 25

								BATTING											BASERUNNING				PERCENTAGES		
Year Team	Lg	G	AB	H	2B	3B	HR	(Hm Rd)	TB	R	RBI	TBB	IBB	SO	HBP	SH	SF	SB	CS	SB%	GDP	Avg	OBP	SLG
1989 New York	AL	14	47	11	2	0	2	(0 2)	19	7	7	3	1	8	0	0	0	1	0	1.00	0	.234	.280	.404
1990 New York	AL	57	133	21	2	3	3	(1 2)	36	24	9	13	0	27	1	1	1	8	2	.80	2	.158	.236	.271
1991 Atlanta	NL	54	110	21	1	2	4	(2 2)	38	16	13	12	0	23	0	0	0	11	3	.79	1	.191	.270	.345
1992 Atlanta	NL	97	303	92	6	14	8	(5 3)	150	54	28	18	0	52	2	1	1	26	9	.74	5	.304	.346	.495
4 ML YEARS		222	593	145	11	18	17	(8 9)	243	101	57	46	1	110	3	2	2	46	14	.77	8	.245	.301	.410

Reggie Sanders

Bats: Right **Throws:** Right **Pos:** CF/LF   **Ht:** 6' 1" **Wt:** 180 **Born:** 12/01/67 **Age:** 25

Year Team	Lg	G	AB	H	2B	3B	HR	(Hm	Rd)	TB	R	RBI	TBB	IBB	SO	HBP	SH	SF	SB	CS	SB%	GDP	Avg	OBP	SLG
1988 Billings	R	17	64	15	1	1	0	--	--	18	11	3	6	0	4	0	1	1	10	2	.83	1	.234	.296	.281
1989 Greensboro	A	81	315	91	18	5	9	--	--	146	53	53	29	2	63	3	1	1	21	7	.75	3	.289	.353	.463
1990 Cedar Rapds	A	127	466	133	21	4	17	--	--	213	89	63	59	2	95	4	2	1	40	15	.73	8	.285	.370	.457
1991 Chattanooga	AA	86	302	95	15	8	8	--	--	150	50	49	41	5	67	1	1	4	15	2	.88	5	.315	.394	.497
1991 Cincinnati	NL	9	40	8	0	0	1	(0	1)	11	6	3	0	0	9	0	0	0	1	1	.50	1	.200	.200	.275
1992 Cincinnati	NL	116	385	104	26	6	12	(6	6)	178	62	36	48	2	98	4	0	1	16	7	.70	6	.270	.356	.462
2 ML YEARS		125	425	112	26	6	13	(6	7)	189	68	39	48	2	107	4	0	1	17	8	.68	7	.264	.343	.445

Scott Sanderson

Pitches: Right **Bats:** Right **Pos:** SP   **Ht:** 6' 5" **Wt:** 192 **Born:** 07/22/56 **Age:** 36

Year Team	Lg	G	GS	CG	GF	IP	BFP	H	R	ER	HR	SH	SF	HB	TBB	IBB	SO	WP	Bk	W	L	Pct.	ShO	Sv	ERA
1978 Montreal	NL	17	9	1	1	61	251	52	20	17	3	3	2	1	21	0	50	2	0	4	2	.667	1	0	2.51
1979 Montreal	NL	34	24	5	3	168	696	148	69	64	16	5	7	3	54	4	138	2	3	9	8	.529	3	1	3.43
1980 Montreal	NL	33	33	7	0	211	875	206	76	73	18	11	5	3	56	3	125	6	0	16	11	.593	3	0	3.11
1981 Montreal	NL	22	22	4	0	137	560	122	50	45	10	7	4	1	31	2	77	2	0	9	7	.563	1	0	2.96
1982 Montreal	NL	32	32	7	0	224	922	212	98	86	24	9	6	3	58	5	158	2	1	12	12	.500	0	0	3.46
1983 Montreal	NL	18	16	0	1	81.1	346	98	50	42	12	2	1	0	20	0	55	0	0	6	7	.462	0	1	4.65
1984 Chicago	NL	24	24	3	0	140.2	571	140	54	49	5	6	8	2	24	3	76	3	2	8	5	.615	0	0	3.14
1985 Chicago	NL	19	19	2	0	121	480	100	49	42	13	7	7	0	27	4	80	1	0	5	6	.455	0	0	3.12
1986 Chicago	NL	37	28	1	2	169.2	697	165	85	79	21	6	5	2	37	2	124	3	1	9	11	.450	1	1	4.19
1987 Chicago	NL	32	22	0	5	144.2	631	156	72	69	23	4	5	3	50	5	106	1	0	8	9	.471	0	2	4.29
1988 Chicago	NL	11	0	0	3	15.1	62	13	9	9	1	0	3	0	3	1	6	0	0	1	2	.333	0	0	5.28
1989 Chicago	NL	37	23	2	2	146.1	611	155	69	64	16	8	3	2	31	6	86	1	3	11	9	.550	0	0	3.94
1990 Oakland	AL	34	34	2	0	206.1	885	205	99	89	27	4	8	4	66	2	128	7	1	17	11	.607	1	0	3.88
1991 New York	AL	34	34	2	0	208	837	200	95	88	22	5	5	3	29	0	130	4	1	16	10	.615	2	0	3.81
1992 New York	AL	33	33	0	0	193.1	851	220	116	106	28	3	11	4	64	5	104	4	1	12	11	.522	1	0	4.93
15 ML YEARS		410	353	38	17	2227.2	9275	2192	1011	922	239	80	80	31	571	42	1443	38	13	143	121	.542	13	5	3.72

Benito Santiago

Bats: Right **Throws:** Right **Pos:** C   **Ht:** 6' 1" **Wt:** 185 **Born:** 03/09/65 **Age:** 28

Year Team	Lg	G	AB	H	2B	3B	HR	(Hm	Rd)	TB	R	RBI	TBB	IBB	SO	HBP	SH	SF	SB	CS	SB%	GDP	Avg	OBP	SLG
1986 San Diego	NL	17	62	18	2	0	3	(2	1)	29	10	6	2	0	12	0	0	1	0	1	.00	0	.290	.308	.468
1987 San Diego	NL	146	546	164	33	2	18	(11	7)	255	64	79	16	2	112	5	1	4	21	12	.64	12	.300	.324	.467
1988 San Diego	NL	139	492	122	22	2	10	(3	7)	178	49	46	24	2	82	1	5	5	15	7	.68	18	.248	.282	.362
1989 San Diego	NL	129	462	109	16	3	16	(8	8)	179	50	62	26	6	89	1	3	2	11	6	.65	9	.236	.277	.387
1990 San Diego	NL	100	344	93	8	5	11	(5	6)	144	42	53	27	2	55	3	1	7	5	5	.50	4	.270	.323	.419
1991 San Diego	NL	152	580	155	22	3	17	(6	11)	234	60	87	23	5	114	4	0	7	8	10	.44	21	.267	.296	.403
1992 San Diego	NL	106	386	97	21	0	10	(8	2)	148	37	42	21	1	52	0	0	4	2	5	.29	14	.251	.287	.383
7 ML YEARS		789	2872	758	124	15	85	(43	42)	1167	312	375	139	18	516	14	10	30	62	46	.57	78	.264	.298	.406

Nelson Santovenia

Bats: Right **Throws:** Right **Pos:** C   **Ht:** 6' 3" **Wt:** 210 **Born:** 07/27/61 **Age:** 31

Year Team	Lg	G	AB	H	2B	3B	HR	(Hm	Rd)	TB	R	RBI	TBB	IBB	SO	HBP	SH	SF	SB	CS	SB%	GDP	Avg	OBP	SLG
1987 Montreal	NL	2	1	0	0	0	0	(0	0)	0	0	0	0	0	0	0	0	0	0	0	.00	0	.000	.000	.000
1988 Montreal	NL	92	309	73	20	2	8	(6	2)	121	26	41	24	3	77	3	4	4	2	3	.40	4	.236	.294	.392
1989 Montreal	NL	97	304	76	14	1	5	(4	1)	107	30	31	24	2	37	3	2	4	2	1	.67	12	.250	.307	.352
1990 Montreal	NL	59	163	31	3	1	6	(4	2)	54	13	28	8	0	31	0	0	5	0	3	.00	5	.190	.222	.331
1991 Montreal	NL	41	96	24	5	0	2	(1	1)	35	7	14	2	2	18	0	0	4	0	0	.00	4	.250	.255	.365
1992 Chicago	AL	2	3	1	0	0	0	(0	0)	1	1	2	0	0	0	0	0	0	0	0	.00	0	.333	.333	1.333
6 ML YEARS		293	876	205	42	4	22	(15	7)	321	77	116	58	7	163	6	6	17	4	7	.36	25	.234	.281	.366

Mackey Sasser

Bats: Left **Throws:** Right **Pos:** C/1B   **Ht:** 6' 1" **Wt:** 210 **Born:** 08/03/62 **Age:** 30

Year Team	Lg	G	AB	H	2B	3B	HR	(Hm	Rd)	TB	R	RBI	TBB	IBB	SO	HBP	SH	SF	SB	CS	SB%	GDP	Avg	OBP	SLG
1987 2 ML Teams		14	27	5	0	0	0	(0	0)	5	2	2	0	0	2	0	0	0	0	0	.00	0	.185	.185	.185
1988 New York	NL	60	123	35	10	1	1	(0	1)	50	9	17	6	4	9	0	0	2	0	0	.00	4	.285	.313	.407
1989 New York	NL	72	182	53	14	2	1	(0	1)	74	17	22	7	4	15	0	1	1	0	1	.00	3	.291	.316	.407
1990 New York	NL	100	270	83	14	0	6	(3	3)	115	31	41	15	9	19	1	0	2	0	0	.00	7	.307	.344	.426
1991 New York	NL	96	228	62	14	2	5	(3	2)	95	18	35	9	2	19	1	1	4	0	2	.00	6	.272	.298	.417

Year Team	Lg	G	AB	H	2B	3B	HR	(Hm	Rd)	TB	R	RBI	TBB	IBB	SO	HBP	SH	SF	SB	CS	SB%	GDP	Avg	OBP	SLG
1992 New York	NL	92	141	34	6	0	2	(1	1)	46	7	18	3	0	10	0	0	5	0	0	.00	4	.241	.248	.326
1987 San Francisco	NL	2	4	0	0	0	0	(0	0)	0	0	0	0	0	0	0	0	0	0	0	.00	0	.000	.000	.000
Pittsburgh	NL	12	23	5	0	0	0	(0	0)	5	2	2	0	0	2	0	0	0	0	0	.00	1	.217	.217	.217
6 ML YEARS		434	971	272	58	5	15	(8	7)	385	84	135	40	19	74	2	2	14	0	3	.00	25	.280	.306	.396

Rich Sauveur

Pitches: Left Bats: Left Pos: RP Ht: 6' 4" Wt: 170 Born: 11/23/63 Age: 29

		HOW MUCH HE PITCHED						WHAT HE GAVE UP										THE RESULTS					
Year Team	Lg	G	GS	CG	GF	IP	BFP	H	R	ER	HR	SH	SF	HB	TBB	IBB	SO	WP	Bk	W	L	Pct.	ShO	Sv	ERA
1986 Pittsburgh	NL	3	3	0	0	12	57	17	8	8	3	1	0	2	6	0	6	0	2	0	0	.000	0	0	6.00
1988 Montreal	NL	4	0	0	0	3	14	3	2	2	1	0	0	0	2	0	3	0	0	0	0	.000	0	0	6.00
1991 New York	NL	6	0	0	0	3.1	19	7	4	4	1	2	0	0	2	0	4	0	0	0	0	.000	0	0	10.80
1992 Kansas City	AL	8	0	0	2	14.1	65	15	7	7	1	0	0	2	8	1	7	0	1	0	1	.000	0	0	4.40
4 ML YEARS		21	3	0	2	32.2	155	42	21	21	6	3	0	4	18	1	20	0	3	0	1	.000	0	0	5.79

Steve Sax

Bats: Right Throws: Right Pos: 2B Ht: 5'11" Wt: 188 Born: 01/29/60 Age: 33

		BATTING																	BASERUNNING				PERCENTAGES		
Year Team	Lg	G	AB	H	2B	3B	HR	(Hm	Rd)	TB	R	RBI	TBB	IBB	SO	HBP	SH	SF	SB	CS	SB%	GDP	Avg	OBP	SLG
1981 Los Angeles	NL	31	119	33	2	0	2	(0	2)	41	15	9	7	1	14	0	1	0	5	7	.42	0	.277	.317	.345
1982 Los Angeles	NL	150	638	180	23	7	4	(2	2)	229	88	47	49	1	53	2	10	0	49	19	.72	10	.282	.335	.359
1983 Los Angeles	NL	155	623	175	18	5	5	(3	2)	218	94	41	58	3	73	1	8	2	56	30	.65	8	.281	.342	.350
1984 Los Angeles	NL	145	569	138	24	4	1	(1	0)	173	70	35	47	3	53	1	2	3	34	19	.64	12	.243	.300	.304
1985 Los Angeles	NL	136	488	136	8	4	1	(1	0)	155	62	42	54	12	43	3	3	3	27	11	.71	15	.279	.352	.318
1986 Los Angeles	NL	157	633	210	43	4	6	(1	5)	279	91	56	59	5	58	3	6	3	40	17	.70	12	.332	.390	.441
1987 Los Angeles	NL	157	610	171	22	7	6	(2	4)	225	84	46	44	5	61	3	5	1	37	11	.77	13	.280	.331	.369
1988 Los Angeles	NL	160	632	175	19	4	5	(2	3)	217	70	57	45	6	51	1	7	2	42	12	.78	11	.277	.325	.343
1989 New York	AL	158	651	205	26	3	5	(2	3)	252	88	63	52	2	44	1	8	5	43	17	.72	19	.315	.364	.387
1990 New York	AL	155	615	160	24	2	4	(3	1)	200	70	42	49	3	46	4	6	6	43	9	.83	13	.260	.316	.325
1991 New York	AL	158	652	198	38	2	10	(6	4)	270	85	56	41	2	38	3	5	6	31	11	.74	15	.304	.345	.414
1992 Chicago	AL	143	567	134	26	4	4	(1	3)	180	74	47	43	4	42	2	12	6	30	12	.71	17	.236	.290	.317
12 ML YEARS		1705	6797	1915	273	46	53	(24	29)	2439	891	541	548	47	576	24	73	37	437	175	.71	145	.282	.336	.359

Bob Scanlan

Pitches: Right Bats: Right Pos: RP Ht: 6' 8" Wt: 215 Born: 08/09/66 Age: 26

		HOW MUCH HE PITCHED						WHAT HE GAVE UP										THE RESULTS					
Year Team	Lg	G	GS	CG	GF	IP	BFP	H	R	ER	HR	SH	SF	HB	TBB	IBB	SO	WP	Bk	W	L	Pct.	ShO	Sv	ERA
1984 Phillies	R	13	6	0	2	33.1	173	43	31	24	0	3	2	0	30	0	17	4	1	0	2	.000	0	0	6.48
1985 Spartanburg	A	26	25	4	0	152.1	669	160	95	70	7	3	6	4	53	0	108	8	0	8	12	.400	1	0	4.14
1986 Clearwater	A	24	22	5	0	125.2	559	146	73	58	1	6	4	5	45	4	51	4	1	8	12	.400	0	0	4.15
1987 Reading	AA	27	26	3	0	164	718	187	98	93	12	9	9	11	55	3	91	4	1	15	5	.750	1	0	5.10
1988 Maine	AAA	28	27	4	0	161	713	181	110	100	10	13	7	8	50	7	79	17	8	5	18	.217	1	0	5.59
1989 Reading	AA	31	17	4	8	118.1	531	124	88	76	9	3	5	6	58	1	63	12	1	6	10	.375	1	0	5.78
1990 Scr Wil-Bar	AAA	23	23	1	0	130	565	128	79	70	11	3	4	7	59	3	74	3	0	8	11	.421	0	0	4.85
1991 Iowa	AAA	4	3	0	1	18.1	79	14	8	6	0	2	0	0	10	1	15	3	0	2	0	1.000	0	0	2.95
1991 Chicago	NL	40	13	0	16	111	482	114	60	48	5	8	6	3	40	3	44	5	1	7	8	.467	0	1	3.89
1992 Chicago	NL	69	0	0	41	87.1	360	76	32	28	4	4	2	1	30	6	42	6	4	3	6	.333	0	14	2.89
2 ML YEARS		109	13	0	57	198.1	842	190	92	76	9	12	8	4	70	9	86	11	5	10	14	.417	0	15	3.45

Steve Scarsone

Bats: Right Throws: Right Pos: 2B Ht: 6' 2" Wt: 170 Born: 04/11/66 Age: 27

		BATTING																	BASERUNNING				PERCENTAGES		
Year Team	Lg	G	AB	H	2B	3B	HR	(Hm	Rd)	TB	R	RBI	TBB	IBB	SO	HBP	SH	SF	SB	CS	SB%	GDP	Avg	OBP	SLG
1986 Bend	A	65	219	48	10	4	4	--	--	78	42	21	30	0	51	4	1	2	11	2	.85	2	.219	.322	.356
1987 Chston-Wv	A	95	259	56	11	1	1	--	--	72	35	17	31	0	64	3	3	0	8	5	.62	1	.216	.307	.278
1988 Clearwater	A	125	456	120	21	4	8	--	--	173	51	46	18	0	93	8	6	6	14	4	.78	3	.263	.299	.379
1989 Reading	AA	75	240	43	5	0	4	--	--	60	30	22	15	2	67	1	5	4	2	2	.50	5	.179	.227	.250
1990 Clearwater	A	59	211	58	9	5	3	--	--	86	20	23	19	1	57	4	5	1	3	4	.43	2	.275	.345	.408
Reading	AA	74	245	65	12	1	3	--	--	88	26	23	14	0	63	1	4	0	0	0	.00	0	.265	.308	.359
1991 Reading	AA	15	49	15	0	0	3	--	--	24	6	3	4	0	15	0	0	0	2	0	1.00	0	.306	.358	.490
Scranton-Wb	AAA	111	405	111	20	6	6	--	--	161	52	38	19	1	81	7	2	7	10	5	.67	4	.274	.313	.398
1992 Scranton/wb	AAA	89	325	89	23	4	11	--	--	153	43	48	24	3	74	4	5	3	10	7	.59	7	.274	.329	.471
Rochester	AAA	23	82	21	3	0	1	--	--	27	13	12	6	1	12	1	1	3	3	2	.60	3	.256	.304	.329
1992 2 ML Teams		18	30	5	0	0	0	(0	0)	5	3	0	2	0	12	0	1	0	0	0	.00	0	.167	.219	.167
1992 Philadelphia	NL	7	13	2	0	0	0	(0	0)	2	1	0	1	0	6	0	0	0	0	0	.00	0	.154	.214	.154
Baltimore	AL	11	17	3	0	0	0	(0	0)	3	2	0	1	0	6	0	1	0	0	0	.00	0	.176	.222	.176

Jeff Schaefer

Bats: Right **Throws:** Right **Pos:** SS/3B   **Ht:** 5'10" **Wt:** 170 **Born:** 05/31/60 **Age:** 33

Year	Team	Lg	G	AB	H	2B	3B	HR	(Hm	Rd)	TB	R	RBI	TBB	IBB	SO	HBP	SH	SF	SB	CS	SB%	GDP	Avg	OBP	SLG
1989	Chicago	AL	15	10	1	0	0	0	(0	0)	1	2	0	0	0	2	0	1	0	1	1	.50	0	.100	.100	.100
1990	Seattle	AL	55	107	22	3	0	0	(0	0)	25	11	6	3	0	11	2	2	1	4	1	.80	1	.206	.239	.234
1991	Seattle	AL	84	164	41	7	1	1	(0	1)	53	19	11	5	0	25	0	6	0	3	1	.75	7	.250	.272	.323
1992	Seattle	AL	65	70	8	2	0	1	(0	1)	13	5	3	2	0	10	0	6	0	0	1	.00	2	.114	.139	.186
	4 ML YEARS		219	351	72	12	1	2	(0	2)	92	37	20	10	0	48	2	15	1	8	4	.67	10	.205	.231	.262

Rich Scheid

Pitches: Left **Bats:** Left **Pos:** RP   **Ht:** 6'3" **Wt:** 185 **Born:** 02/03/65 **Age:** 28

Year	Team	Lg	G	GS	CG	GF	IP	BFP	H	R	ER	HR	SH	SF	HB	TBB	IBB	SO	WP	Bk	W	L	Pct.	ShO	Sv	ERA
1986	Oneonta	A	15	15	3	0	93	368	62	30	23	1	1	0	3	32	1	100	6	2	9	3	.750	1	0	2.23
1987	Ft.Laudrdle	A	9	8	1	1	55	236	43	25	18	1	1	3	0	29	0	49	3	0	7	0	1.000	0	0	2.95
	Albany	AA	9	9	1	0	48	221	44	33	29	2	1	4	5	33	1	33	5	3	2	3	.400	1	0	5.44
	Pittsfield	AA	11	6	0	2	28	145	44	27	23	1	0	2	1	19	0	13	2	0	2	0	1.000	0	0	7.39
1988	Pittsfield	AA	24	20	1	1	118.1	522	119	58	49	6	9	6	1	62	3	75	10	10	6	6	.500	0	1	3.73
1989	Iowa	AAA	7	0	0	2	7.1	42	8	6	4	0	0	0	0	10	1	7	0	1	0	0	.000	0	0	4.91
	Charlotte	AA	17	6	1	2	46.1	209	43	30	21	8	1	1	2	27	2	37	7	7	4	1	.800	0	0	4.08
1990	Birmingham	AA	25	0	0	13	44.2	192	37	17	11	0	0	5	1	21	4	37	4	3	2	1	.667	0	4	2.22
	Vancouver	AAA	20	2	0	10	39.1	173	37	19	14	2	1	0	0	24	1	38	2	3	2	2	.500	0	0	3.20
1991	Vancouver	AAA	47	0	0	20	66.2	293	65	46	45	7	4	1	2	33	4	57	6	0	6	7	.462	0	3	6.08
1992	Vancouver	AAA	29	0	0	6	35.1	160	29	13	11	0	2	1	0	28	4	24	3	0	1	2	.333	0	0	2.80
	Tucson	AAA	12	8	0	1	57	236	49	23	16	4	2	2	1	23	2	34	4	3	2	3	.400	0	1	2.53
1992	Houston	NL	7	1	0	3	12	56	14	8	8	2	0	0	0	6	1	8	1	1	0	1	.000	0	0	6.00

Curt Schilling

Pitches: Right **Bats:** Right **Pos:** SP/RP   **Ht:** 6'4" **Wt:** 215 **Born:** 11/14/66 **Age:** 26

Year	Team	Lg	G	GS	CG	GF	IP	BFP	H	R	ER	HR	SH	SF	HB	TBB	IBB	SO	WP	Bk	W	L	Pct.	ShO	Sv	ERA
1988	Baltimore	AL	4	4	0	0	14.2	76	22	19	16	3	0	3	1	10	1	4	2	0	0	3	.000	0	0	9.82
1989	Baltimore	AL	5	1	0	0	8.2	38	10	6	6	2	0	0	0	3	0	6	1	0	0	1	.000	0	0	6.23
1990	Baltimore	AL	35	0	0	16	46	191	38	13	13	1	2	4	0	19	0	32	0	0	1	2	.333	0	3	2.54
1991	Houston	NL	56	0	0	34	75.2	336	79	35	32	2	5	1	0	39	7	71	4	1	3	5	.375	0	8	3.81
1992	Philadelphia	NL	42	26	10	10	226.1	895	165	67	59	11	7	8	1	59	4	147	4	0	14	11	.560	4	2	2.35
	5 ML YEARS		142	31	10	60	371.1	1536	314	140	126	19	14	16	2	130	12	260	11	1	18	22	.450	4	13	3.05

Dave Schmidt

Pitches: Right **Bats:** Right **Pos:** RP   **Ht:** 6'1" **Wt:** 194 **Born:** 04/22/57 **Age:** 36

Year	Team	Lg	G	GS	CG	GF	IP	BFP	H	R	ER	HR	SH	SF	HB	TBB	IBB	SO	WP	Bk	W	L	Pct.	ShO	Sv	ERA
1981	Texas	AL	14	1	0	8	32	132	31	11	11	1	0	0	1	11	3	13	3	1	0	1	.000	0	1	3.09
1982	Texas	AL	33	8	0	14	109.2	462	118	45	39	5	6	3	5	25	5	69	2	0	4	6	.400	0	6	3.20
1983	Texas	AL	31	0	0	20	46.1	191	42	20	20	3	1	1	1	14	1	29	2	0	3	3	.500	0	2	3.88
1984	Texas	AL	43	0	0	37	70.1	293	69	30	20	3	7	3	0	20	9	46	4	0	6	6	.500	0	12	2.56
1985	Texas	AL	51	4	1	35	85.2	356	81	36	30	6	3	2	0	22	8	46	2	1	7	6	.538	1	5	3.15
1986	Chicago	AL	49	1	0	21	92.1	394	94	37	34	10	3	3	5	27	7	67	5	0	3	6	.333	0	8	3.31
1987	Baltimore	AL	35	14	2	7	124	515	128	57	52	13	0	1	1	26	2	70	2	0	10	5	.667	2	1	3.77
1988	Baltimore	AL	41	9	0	11	129.2	541	129	58	49	14	5	3	3	38	5	67	3	0	8	5	.615	0	2	3.40
1989	Baltimore	AL	38	26	2	5	156.2	686	196	102	99	24	9	7	2	36	2	46	3	1	10	13	.435	0	0	5.69
1990	Montreal	NL	34	0	0	20	48	213	58	26	23	3	4	1	0	13	5	22	1	0	3	3	.500	0	13	4.31
1991	Montreal	NL	4	0	0	1	4.1	24	9	5	5	2	1	0	0	2	0	3	0	0	0	1	.000	0	0	10.38
1992	Seattle	AL	3	0	0	0	3.1	19	7	7	7	1	0	0	0	3	0	1	0	0	0	0	.000	0	0	18.90
	12 ML YEARS		376	63	5	179	902.1	3826	962	434	389	85	39	24	18	237	47	479	27	3	54	55	.495	3	50	3.88

Dick Schofield

Bats: Right **Throws:** Right **Pos:** SS   **Ht:** 5'10" **Wt:** 179 **Born:** 11/21/62 **Age:** 30

Year	Team	Lg	G	AB	H	2B	3B	HR	(Hm	Rd)	TB	R	RBI	TBB	IBB	SO	HBP	SH	SF	SB	CS	SB%	GDP	Avg	OBP	SLG
1983	California	AL	21	54	11	2	0	3	(2	1)	22	4	4	6	0	8	1	1	0	0	0	.00	2	.204	.295	.407
1984	California	AL	140	400	77	10	3	4	(0	4)	105	39	21	33	0	79	6	13	0	5	2	.71	7	.193	.264	.263
1985	California	AL	147	438	96	19	3	8	(5	3)	145	50	41	35	0	70	8	12	3	11	4	.73	6	.219	.287	.331
1986	California	AL	139	458	114	17	6	13	(7	6)	182	67	57	48	2	55	5	9	9	23	5	.82	8	.249	.321	.397
1987	California	AL	134	479	120	17	3	9	(4	5)	170	52	46	37	0	63	2	10	3	19	3	.86	4	.251	.305	.355

Year	Team	Lg	G	AB	H	2B	3B	HR	(Hm	Rd)	TB	R	RBI	TBB	IBB	SO	HBP	SH	SF	SB	CS	SB%	GDP	Avg	OBP	SLG
1988	California	AL	155	527	126	11	6	6	(3	3)	167	61	34	40	0	57	9	11	2	20	5	.80	5	.239	.303	.317
1989	California	AL	91	302	69	11	2	4	(1	3)	96	42	26	28	0	47	3	11	2	9	3	.75	4	.228	.299	.318
1990	California	AL	99	310	79	8	1	1	(1	0)	92	41	18	52	3	61	2	13	2	3	4	.43	3	.255	.363	.297
1991	California	AL	134	427	96	9	3	0	(0	0)	111	44	31	50	2	69	3	7	0	8	4	.67	3	.225	.310	.260
1992	2 ML Teams		143	423	87	18	2	4	(3	1)	121	52	36	61	4	82	5	10	3	11	4	.73	11	.206	.311	.286
1992	California	AL	1	3	1	0	0	0	(0	0)	1	0	1	0	0	0	0	0	0	0	0	.00	0	.333	.500	.333
	New York	NL	142	420	86	18	2	4	(3	1)	120	52	36	60	4	82	5	10	3	11	4	.73	11	.205	.309	.286
	10 ML YEARS		1203	3818	875	122	29	52	(26	26)	1211	452	314	390	11	591	44	97	24	109	34	.76	55	.229	.306	.317

Mike Schooler

Pitches: Right **Bats:** Right **Pos:** RP Ht: 6' 3" Wt: 220 Born: 08/10/62 Age: 30

			HOW MUCH HE PITCHED						WHAT HE GAVE UP											THE RESULTS					
Year	Team	Lg	G	GS	CG	GF	IP	BFP	H	R	ER	HR	SH	SF	HB	TBB	IBB	SO	WP	Bk	W	L	Pct.	ShO	Sv	ERA
1988	Seattle	AL	40	0	0	33	48.1	214	45	21	19	4	2	3	1	24	4	54	4	1	5	8	.385	0	15	3.54
1989	Seattle	AL	67	0	0	60	77	329	81	27	24	2	3	1	2	19	3	69	6	1	1	7	.125	0	33	2.81
1990	Seattle	AL	49	0	0	45	56	229	47	18	14	5	3	2	1	16	5	45	1	0	1	4	.200	0	30	2.25
1991	Seattle	AL	34	0	0	23	34.1	138	25	14	14	2	1	1	0	10	0	31	2	1	3	3	.500	0	7	3.67
1992	Seattle	AL	53	0	0	36	51.2	232	55	29	27	7	4	3	1	24	6	33	0	0	2	7	.222	0	13	4.70
	5 ML YEARS		243	0	0	197	267.1	1142	253	109	98	20	13	10	5	93	18	232	13	3	12	29	.293	0	98	3.30

Pete Schourek

Pitches: Left **Bats:** Left **Pos:** SP Ht: 6' 5" Wt: 205 Born: 05/10/69 Age: 24

			HOW MUCH HE PITCHED						WHAT HE GAVE UP											THE RESULTS					
Year	Team	Lg	G	GS	CG	GF	IP	BFP	H	R	ER	HR	SH	SF	HB	TBB	IBB	SO	WP	Bk	W	L	Pct.	ShO	Sv	ERA
1987	Kingsport	R	12	12	2	0	78.1	336	70	37	32	7	4	1	2	34	0	57	2	1	4	5	.444	0	0	3.68
1989	Columbia	A	27	19	5	3	136	593	120	66	43	11	7	4	2	66	2	131	5	3	5	9	.357	1	1	2.85
	St.Lucie	A	2	1	0	1	4	16	3	1	1	0	0	0	0	2	0	4	0	0	0	0	.000	0	0	2.25
1990	Tidewater	AAA	2	2	1	0	14	54	9	4	4	0	2	0	1	5	0	14	0	0	1	0	1.000	1	0	2.57
	St. Lucie	A	5	5	2	0	37	143	29	4	4	1	0	0	2	8	0	28	0	0	4	1	.800	2	0	0.97
	Jackson	AA	19	19	1	0	124.1	518	109	53	42	8	5	7	8	39	2	94	5	1	11	4	.733	0	0	3.04
1991	Tidewater	AAA	4	4	0	0	25	100	18	7	7	3	1	0	0	10	0	17	0	0	1	1	.500	0	0	2.52
1992	Tidewater	AAA	8	8	2	0	52.2	228	46	20	16	2	0	0	0	23	0	42	3	1	2	5	.286	1	0	2.73
1991	New York	NL	35	8	1	7	86.1	385	82	49	41	7	5	4	2	43	4	67	1	0	5	4	.556	1	2	4.27
1992	New York	NL	22	21	0	0	136	578	137	60	55	9	4	4	2	44	6	60	4	2	6	8	.429	0	0	3.64
	2 ML YEARS		57	29	1	7	222.1	963	219	109	96	16	9	8	4	87	10	127	5	2	11	12	.478	1	2	3.89

Mike Scioscia

Bats: Left **Throws:** Right **Pos:** C Ht: 6' 2" Wt: 220 Born: 11/27/58 Age: 34

			BATTING																	BASERUNNING			PERCENTAGES		
Year	Team	Lg	G	AB	H	2B	3B	HR	(Hm	Rd)	TB	R	RBI	TBB	IBB	SO	HBP	SH	SF	SB	CS	SB%	GDP	Avg	OBP	SLG
1980	Los Angeles	NL	54	134	34	5	1	1	(1	0)	44	8	8	12	2	9	0	5	1	1	0	1.00	2	.254	.313	.328
1981	Los Angeles	NL	93	290	80	10	0	2	(0	2)	96	27	29	36	8	18	1	4	4	0	2	.00	8	.276	.353	.331
1982	Los Angeles	NL	129	365	80	11	1	5	(2	3)	108	31	38	44	11	31	1	5	4	2	0	1.00	8	.219	.302	.296
1983	Los Angeles	NL	12	35	11	3	0	1	(0	1)	17	3	7	5	1	2	0	0	0	0	0	.00	1	.314	.400	.486
1984	Los Angeles	NL	114	341	93	18	0	5	(0	5)	126	29	38	52	10	26	1	1	1	2	1	.67	10	.273	.367	.370
1985	Los Angeles	NL	141	429	127	26	3	7	(1	6)	180	47	53	77	9	21	5	11	3	3	3	.50	10	.296	.407	.420
1986	Los Angeles	NL	122	374	94	18	1	5	(2	3)	129	36	26	62	4	23	3	6	4	3	3	.50	11	.251	.359	.345
1987	Los Angeles	NL	142	461	122	26	1	6	(2	4)	168	44	38	55	9	23	1	4	2	7	4	.64	13	.265	.343	.364
1988	Los Angeles	NL	130	408	105	18	0	3	(1	2)	132	29	35	38	12	31	0	3	3	0	3	.00	14	.257	.318	.324
1989	Los Angeles	NL	133	408	102	16	0	10	(4	6)	148	40	44	52	14	29	3	7	1	0	2	.00	4	.250	.338	.363
1990	Los Angeles	NL	135	435	115	25	0	12	(5	7)	176	46	66	55	14	31	3	1	4	4	1	.80	11	.264	.348	.405
1991	Los Angeles	NL	119	345	91	16	2	8	(3	5)	135	39	40	47	3	32	3	5	4	4	3	.57	5	.264	.353	.391
1992	Los Angeles	NL	117	348	77	6	3	3	(1	2)	98	19	24	32	4	31	1	5	3	3	2	.60	9	.221	.286	.282
	13 ML YEARS		1441	4373	1131	198	12	68	(22	46)	1557	398	446	567	101	307	22	57	37	29	24	.55	106	.259	.344	.356

Gary Scott

Bats: Right **Throws:** Right **Pos:** 3B Ht: 6' 0" Wt: 175 Born: 08/22/68 Age: 24

			BATTING																	BASERUNNING			PERCENTAGES		
Year	Team	Lg	G	AB	H	2B	3B	HR	(Hm	Rd)	TB	R	RBI	TBB	IBB	SO	HBP	SH	SF	SB	CS	SB%	GDP	Avg	OBP	SLG
1989	Geneva	A	48	175	49	10	1	10	--	--	91	33	42	22	2	23	9	0	2	4	1	.80	2	.280	.385	.520
1990	Winston-Sal	A	102	380	112	22	0	12	--	--	170	63	70	29	4	66	14	5	6	17	3	.85	7	.295	.361	.447
	Charlotte	AA	35	143	44	9	0	4	--	--	65	21	17	7	1	17	0	0	3	3	4	.43	3	.308	.333	.455
1991	Iowa	AAA	63	231	48	10	2	3	--	--	71	21	34	20	2	45	6	3	2	0	6	.00	11	.208	.286	.307
1992	Iowa	AAA	95	354	93	26	0	10	--	--	149	48	48	37	1	48	6	4	5	3	1	.75	8	.263	.338	.421
1991	Chicago	NL	31	79	13	3	0	1	(1	0)	19	8	5	13	4	14	3	1	0	0	1	.00	2	.165	.305	.241
1992	Chicago	NL	36	96	15	2	0	2	(1	1)	23	8	11	5	1	14	0	1	0	2	1	.00	3	.156	.198	.240
	2 ML YEARS		67	175	28	5	0	3	(2	1)	42	16	16	18	5	28	3	2	0	2	2	.00	5	.160	.250	.240

Tim Scott

Pitches: Right **Bats:** Right **Pos:** RP **Ht:** 6' 2" **Wt:** 185 **Born:** 11/16/66 **Age:** 26

		HOW MUCH HE PITCHED						WHAT HE GAVE UP										THE RESULTS					
Year Team	Lg	G	GS	CG	GF	IP	BFP	H	R	ER	HR	SH	SF	HB	TBB	IBB	SO	WP	Bk	W	L	Pct.	ShO	Sv	ERA
1984 Great Falls	R	13	13	3	0	78	0	90	58	38	4	0	0	2	38	1	44	5	2	5	4	.556	2	0	4.38
1985 Bakersfield	A	12	10	2	1	63.2	0	84	46	41	4	0	0	1	28	0	31	2	4	3	4	.429	0	0	5.80
1986 Vero Beach	A	20	13	3	2	95.1	418	113	44	36	2	4	9	2	34	2	37	5	5	5	4	.556	1	0	3.40
1987 San Antonio	AA	2	2	0	0	5.1	33	14	10	10	2	0	0	1	2	0	6	1	0	0	1	.000	0	0	16.88
Bakersfield	A	7	5	1	1	32.1	137	33	19	16	2	0	1	1	10	1	29	2	0	2	3	.400	0	0	4.45
1988 Bakersfield	A	36	2	0	25	64.1	272	52	34	26	3	4	4	2	26	5	59	2	0	4	7	.364	0	7	3.64
1989 San Antonio	AA	48	0	0	28	68	308	71	30	28	3	5	3	0	36	5	64	1	4	4	2	.667	0	3	3.71
1990 Albuquerque	AAA	17	0	0	8	15	73	14	9	7	1	0	0	0	14	2	15	0	0	2	1	.667	0	3	4.20
San Antonio	AA	30	0	0	20	47.1	186	35	17	15	5	0	1	1	14	0	52	0	0	3	3	.500	0	7	2.85
1991 Las Vegas	AAA	41	11	0	9	111	497	133	78	64	8	5	2	1	39	8	74	1	0	8	8	.500	0	0	5.19
1992 Las Vegas	AAA	24	0	0	23	28	106	20	8	7	1	1	1	1	3	0	28	2	0	1	2	.333	0	15	2.25
1991 San Diego	NL	2	0	0	0	1	5	2	2	1	0	0	0	0	0	0	1	0	0	0	0	.000	0	0	9.00
1992 San Diego	NL	34	0	0	16	37.2	173	39	24	22	4	4	1	1	21	6	30	0	1	4	1	.800	0	0	5.26
2 ML YEARS		36	0	0	16	38.2	178	41	26	23	4	4	1	1	21	6	31	0	1	4	1	.800	0	0	5.35

Scott Scudder

Pitches: Right **Bats:** Right **Pos:** SP **Ht:** 6' 2" **Wt:** 185 **Born:** 02/14/68 **Age:** 25

		HOW MUCH HE PITCHED						WHAT HE GAVE UP										THE RESULTS					
Year Team	Lg	G	GS	CG	GF	IP	BFP	H	R	ER	HR	SH	SF	HB	TBB	IBB	SO	WP	Bk	W	L	Pct.	ShO	Sv	ERA
1989 Cincinnati	NL	23	17	0	3	100.1	451	91	54	50	14	7	2	1	61	11	66	0	1	4	9	.308	0	0	4.49
1990 Cincinnati	NL	21	10	0	3	71.2	316	74	41	39	12	3	1	3	30	4	42	2	2	5	5	.500	0	0	4.90
1991 Cincinnati	NL	27	14	0	4	101.1	443	91	52	49	6	8	3	6	56	4	51	7	0	6	9	.400	0	1	4.35
1992 Cleveland	AL	23	22	0	0	109	509	134	80	64	10	6	4	2	55	0	66	7	0	6	10	.375	0	0	5.28
4 ML YEARS		94	63	0	10	382.1	1719	390	227	202	42	24	10	12	202	19	225	16	3	21	33	.389	0	1	4.76

Rudy Seanez

Pitches: Right **Bats:** Right **Pos:** RP **Ht:** 5'10" **Wt:** 185 **Born:** 10/20/68 **Age:** 24

		HOW MUCH HE PITCHED						WHAT HE GAVE UP										THE RESULTS					
Year Team	Lg	G	GS	CG	GF	IP	BFP	H	R	ER	HR	SH	SF	HB	TBB	IBB	SO	WP	Bk	W	L	Pct.	ShO	Sv	ERA
1989 Cleveland	AL	5	0	0	2	5	20	1	2	2	0	0	2	0	4	1	7	1	1	0	0	.000	0	0	3.60
1990 Cleveland	AL	24	0	0	12	27.1	127	22	17	17	2	0	1	1	25	1	24	5	0	2	1	.667	0	0	5.60
1991 Cleveland	AL	5	0	0	0	5	33	10	12	9	2	0	0	0	7	0	7	2	0	0	0	.000	0	0	16.20
3 ML YEARS		34	0	0	14	37.1	180	33	31	28	4	0	3	1	36	2	38	8	1	2	1	.667	0	0	6.75

Steve Searcy

Pitches: Left **Bats:** Left **Pos:** RP **Ht:** 6' 1" **Wt:** 195 **Born:** 06/04/64 **Age:** 29

		HOW MUCH HE PITCHED						WHAT HE GAVE UP										THE RESULTS					
Year Team	Lg	G	GS	CG	GF	IP	BFP	H	R	ER	HR	SH	SF	HB	TBB	IBB	SO	WP	Bk	W	L	Pct.	ShO	Sv	ERA
1988 Detroit	AL	2	2	0	0	8	37	8	6	5	3	0	0	0	4	0	5	0	0	0	2	.000	0	0	5.63
1989 Detroit	AL	8	2	0	3	22.1	100	27	16	15	3	0	0	0	12	1	11	0	0	1	1	.500	0	0	6.04
1990 Detroit	AL	16	12	1	2	75.1	341	76	44	39	9	2	6	0	51	3	66	3	0	2	7	.222	0	0	4.66
1991 2 ML Teams		34	5	0	8	71	335	81	56	52	10	5	5	0	44	1	53	5	1	3	3	.500	0	0	6.59
1992 Philadelphia	NL	10	0	0	3	10.1	50	13	9	7	0	1	1	0	8	0	5	0	0	0	0	.000	0	0	6.10
1991 Detroit	AL	16	5	0	4	40.2	201	52	40	38	8	2	3	0	30	0	32	4	0	1	2	.333	0	0	8.41
Philadelphia	NL	18	0	0	4	30.1	134	29	16	14	2	3	2	0	14	1	21	1	1	2	1	.667	0	0	4.15
5 ML YEARS		70	21	1	16	187	863	205	131	118	25	8	12	0	119	5	140	8	1	6	13	.316	0	0	5.68

David Segui

Bats: Both **Throws:** Left **Pos:** 1B/RF **Ht:** 6' 1" **Wt:** 200 **Born:** 07/19/66 **Age:** 26

		BATTING																	BASERUNNING				PERCENTAGES		
Year Team	Lg	G	AB	H	2B	3B	HR	(Hm	Rd)	TB	R	RBI	TBB	IBB	SO	HBP	SH	SF	SB	CS	SB%	GDP	Avg	OBP	SLG
1990 Baltimore	AL	40	123	30	7	0	2	(1	1)	43	14	15	11	2	15	1	1	0	0	0	.00	12	.244	.311	.350
1991 Baltimore	AL	86	212	59	7	0	2	(1	1)	72	15	22	12	2	19	0	3	1	1	1	.50	7	.278	.316	.340
1992 Baltimore	AL	115	189	44	9	0	1	(1	0)	56	21	17	20	3	23	0	2	0	1	0	1.00	4	.233	.306	.296
3 ML YEARS		241	524	133	23	0	5	(3	2)	171	50	54	43	7	57	1	6	1	2	1	.67	23	.254	.311	.326

Kevin Seitzer

Bats: Right **Throws:** Right **Pos:** 3B **Ht:** 5'11" **Wt:** 190 **Born:** 03/26/62 **Age:** 31

		BATTING																	BASERUNNING				PERCENTAGES		
Year Team	Lg	G	AB	H	2B	3B	HR	(Hm	Rd)	TB	R	RBI	TBB	IBB	SO	HBP	SH	SF	SB	CS	SB%	GDP	Avg	OBP	SLG
1986 Kansas City	AL	28	96	31	4	1	2	(1	1)	43	16	11	19	0	14	1	0	0	0	0	.00	0	.323	.440	.448
1987 Kansas City	AL	161	641	207	33	8	15	(7	8)	301	105	83	80	0	85	2	1	1	12	7	.63	18	.323	.399	.470
1988 Kansas City	AL	149	559	170	32	5	5	(4	1)	227	90	60	72	4	64	6	3	3	10	8	.56	15	.304	.388	.406

182

Year	Team	Lg	G	AB	H	2B	3B	HR	(Hm	Rd)	TB	R	RBI	TBB	IBB	SO	HBP	SH	SF	SB	CS	SB%	GDP	Avg	OBP	SLG
1989	Kansas City	AL	160	597	168	17	2	4	(2	2)	201	78	48	102	7	76	5	4	7	17	8	.68	16	.281	.387	.337
1990	Kansas City	AL	158	622	171	31	5	6	(5	1)	230	91	38	67	2	66	2	4	2	7	5	.58	11	.275	.346	.370
1991	Kansas City	AL	85	234	62	11	3	1	(0	1)	82	28	25	29	3	21	2	1	1	4	1	.80	4	.265	.350	.350
1992	Milwaukee	AL	148	540	146	35	1	5	(2	3)	198	74	71	57	4	44	2	7	9	13	11	.54	16	.270	.337	.367
	7 ML YEARS		889	3289	955	163	25	38	(21	17)	1282	482	336	426	20	370	20	20	23	63	40	.61	80	.290	.373	.390

Frank Seminara

Pitches: Right **Bats:** Right **Pos:** SP   **Ht:** 6' 2" **Wt:** 205 **Born:** 05/16/67 **Age:** 26

Year	Team	Lg	G	GS	CG	GF	IP	BFP	H	R	ER	HR	SH	SF	HB	TBB	IBB	SO	WP	Bk	W	L	Pct.	ShO	Sv	ERA
1988	Oneonta	A	16	13	0	2	78.1	350	86	49	38	2	3	2	5	32	2	60	11	6	4	7	.364	0	1	4.37
1989	Pr William	A	21	0	0	12	36.2	158	26	23	15	0	1	3	5	22	3	23	5	4	2	4	.333	0	2	3.68
	Oneonta	A	11	10	3	0	70	280	51	25	16	0	3	0	3	18	0	70	1	3	7	2	.778	1	0	2.06
1990	Pr William	A	25	25	4	0	170.1	692	136	51	36	5	1	2	10	52	1	132	12	2	16	8	.667	2	0	1.90
1991	Wichita	AA	27	27	6	0	176	761	173	86	66	10	9	5	9	68	0	107	12	3	15	10	.600	1	0	3.38
1992	Las Vegas	AAA	13	13	1	0	80.2	357	92	46	37	2	2	4	3	33	3	48	2	5	6	4	.600	1	0	4.13
1992	San Diego	NL	19	18	0	0	100.1	435	98	46	41	5	3	2	3	46	3	61	1	1	9	4	.692	0	0	3.68

Scott Servais

Bats: Right **Throws:** Right **Pos:** C   **Ht:** 6' 2" **Wt:** 195 **Born:** 06/04/67 **Age:** 26

Year	Team	Lg	G	AB	H	2B	3B	HR	(Hm	Rd)	TB	R	RBI	TBB	IBB	SO	HBP	SH	SF	SB	CS	SB%	GDP	Avg	OBP	SLG
1989	Osceola	A	46	153	41	9	0	2	--	--	56	16	23	16	2	35	2	0	5	0	2	.00	1	.268	.335	.366
	Columbus	AA	63	199	47	5	0	1	--	--	55	20	22	19	0	42	3	1	4	0	3	.00	5	.236	.307	.276
1990	Tucson	AAA	89	303	66	11	3	5	--	--	98	37	37	18	1	61	4	3	4	0	0	.00	6	.218	.267	.323
1991	Tucson	AAA	60	219	71	12	0	2	--	--	89	34	27	13	2	19	6	3	1	0	4	.00	9	.324	.377	.406
1991	Houston	NL	16	37	6	3	0	0	(0	0)	9	0	6	4	0	8	0	1	0	0	0	.00	0	.162	.244	.243
1992	Houston	NL	77	205	49	9	0	0	(0	0)	58	12	15	11	2	25	5	6	0	0	0	.00	7	.239	.294	.283
	2 ML YEARS		93	242	55	12	0	0	(0	0)	67	12	21	15	2	33	5	7	0	0	0	.00	7	.227	.286	.277

Scott Service

Pitches: Right **Bats:** Right **Pos:** RP   **Ht:** 6' 6" **Wt:** 240 **Born:** 07/27/67 **Age:** 25

Year	Team	Lg	G	GS	CG	GF	IP	BFP	H	R	ER	HR	SH	SF	HB	TBB	IBB	SO	WP	Bk	W	L	Pct.	ShO	Sv	ERA
1986	Spartanburg	A	14	9	1	1	58.2	281	68	44	38	3	2	1	7	34	0	49	6	1	1	6	.143	0	0	5.83
	Utica	A	10	10	2	0	70.2	299	65	30	21	1	3	2	5	18	0	43	5	1	5	4	.556	0	0	2.67
	Clearwater	A	4	4	1	0	25.1	105	20	10	9	2	1	0	0	15	0	19	1	1	1	2	.333	1	0	3.20
1987	Reading	AA	5	4	0	0	19.2	95	22	19	17	5	0	0	0	16	1	12	1	0	0	3	.000	0	0	7.78
	Clearwater	A	21	21	5	0	137.2	557	127	46	38	8	2	3	4	32	0	73	1	1	13	4	.765	2	0	2.48
1988	Reading	AA	10	9	1	0	56.2	240	52	25	18	4	1	1	0	22	2	39	1	6	3	4	.429	1	0	2.86
	Maine	AAA	19	18	1	0	110.1	470	109	51	45	10	6	6	2	31	3	87	0	2	8	8	.500	0	0	3.67
1989	Reading	AA	23	10	1	9	85.2	349	71	36	31	8	1	3	8	23	0	82	3	0	6	6	.500	1	1	3.26
	Scr Wil-Bar	AAA	23	0	0	15	33.1	148	27	8	8	2	4	0	2	23	6	23	0	0	3	1	.750	0	6	2.16
1990	Scr Wil-Bar	AAA	45	9	0	11	96.1	427	95	56	51	10	4	2	5	44	1	94	4	0	5	4	.556	0	2	4.76
1991	Indianapols	AAA	18	17	3	1	121.1	477	83	42	40	7	2	3	6	39	0	91	5	1	6	7	.462	1	0	2.97
1992	Indianapols	AAA	13	0	0	7	24.1	95	12	3	2	0	2	0	3	9	0	25	0	0	2	0	1.000	0	2	0.74
	Nashville	AAA	39	2	0	15	70.2	299	54	22	18	2	4	0	2	35	3	87	2	0	6	2	.750	0	4	2.29
1988	Philadelphia	NL	5	0	0	1	5.1	23	7	1	1	0	0	0	1	1	0	6	0	0	0	0	.000	0	0	1.69
1992	Montreal	NL	5	0	0	0	7	41	15	11	11	1	0	0	0	5	0	11	0	0	0	0	.000	0	0	14.14
	2 ML YEARS		10	0	0	1	12.1	64	22	12	12	1	0	0	1	6	0	17	0	0	0	0	.000	0	0	8.76

Mike Sharperson

Bats: Right **Throws:** Right **Pos:** 2B/3B   **Ht:** 6' 3" **Wt:** 190 **Born:** 10/04/61 **Age:** 31

Year	Team	Lg	G	AB	H	2B	3B	HR	(Hm	Rd)	TB	R	RBI	TBB	IBB	SO	HBP	SH	SF	SB	CS	SB%	GDP	Avg	OBP	SLG
1987	2 ML Teams		42	129	29	6	1	0	(0	0)	37	11	10	11	1	20	1	1	0	2	1	.67	3	.225	.291	.287
1988	Los Angeles	NL	46	59	16	1	0	0	(0	0)	17	8	4	1	0	12	1	2	1	0	1	.00	1	.271	.290	.288
1989	Los Angeles	NL	27	28	7	3	0	0	(0	0)	10	2	5	4	1	7	0	1	1	0	1	.00	1	.250	.333	.357
1990	Los Angeles	NL	129	357	106	14	2	3	(1	2)	133	42	36	46	6	39	1	8	3	15	6	.71	5	.297	.376	.373
1991	Los Angeles	NL	105	216	60	11	2	2	(1	1)	81	24	20	25	0	24	1	10	0	1	3	.25	2	.278	.355	.375
1992	Los Angeles	NL	128	317	95	21	0	3	(2	1)	125	48	36	47	1	33	0	5	3	2	2	.50	9	.300	.387	.394
1987	Toronto	AL	32	96	20	4	1	0	(0	0)	26	4	9	7	0	15	1	1	0	2	1	.67	2	.208	.269	.271
	Los Angeles	NL	10	33	9	2	0	0	(0	0)	11	7	1	4	1	5	0	0	0	0	0	.00	1	.273	.351	.333
	6 ML YEARS		477	1106	313	56	5	8	(4	4)	403	135	111	134	9	135	4	27	8	20	14	.59	21	.283	.360	.364

Jeff Shaw

Pitches: Right **Bats:** Right **Pos:** SP   **Ht:** 6' 2" **Wt:** 185 **Born:** 07/07/66 **Age:** 26

		HOW MUCH HE PITCHED							WHAT HE GAVE UP									THE RESULTS					
Year Team	Lg	G	GS	CG	GF	IP	BFP	H	R	ER	HR	SH	SF	HB	TBB	IBB	SO	WP	Bk	W	L	Pct.	ShO	Sv	ERA
1990 Cleveland	AL	12	9	0	0	48.2	229	73	38	36	11	1	3	0	20	0	25	3	0	3	4	.429	0	0	6.66
1991 Cleveland	AL	29	1	0	9	72.1	311	72	34	27	6	1	4	4	27	5	31	6	0	0	5	.000	0	1	3.36
1992 Cleveland	AL	2	1	0	1	7.2	33	7	7	7	2	2	0	0	4	0	3	0	0	0	0	.000	0	0	8.22
3 ML YEARS		43	11	0	10	128.2	573	152	79	70	19	4	7	4	51	5	59	9	0	3	10	.231	0	1	4.90

Gary Sheffield

Bats: Right **Throws:** Right **Pos:** 3B   **Ht:** 5'11" **Wt:** 190 **Born:** 11/18/68 **Age:** 24

			BATTING															BASERUNNING				PERCENTAGES		
Year Team	Lg	G	AB	H	2B	3B	HR	(Hm	Rd)	TB	R	RBI	TBB	IBB	SO	HBP	SH	SF	SB	CS	SB%	GDP	Avg	OBP	SLG
1988 Milwaukee	AL	24	80	19	1	0	4	(1	3)	32	12	12	7	0	7	0	1	1	3	1	.75	5	.238	.295	.400
1989 Milwaukee	AL	95	368	91	18	0	5	(2	3)	124	34	32	27	0	33	4	3	3	10	6	.63	4	.247	.303	.337
1990 Milwaukee	AL	125	487	143	30	1	10	(3	7)	205	67	67	44	1	41	3	4	9	25	10	.71	11	.294	.350	.421
1991 Milwaukee	AL	50	175	34	12	2	2	(2	0)	56	25	22	19	1	15	3	1	5	5	5	.50	3	.194	.277	.320
1992 San Diego	NL	146	557	184	34	3	33	(23	10)	323	87	100	48	5	40	6	0	7	5	6	.45	19	.330	.385	.580
5 ML YEARS		440	1667	471	95	6	54	(31	23)	740	225	233	145	7	136	16	9	25	48	28	.63	42	.283	.341	.444

Keith Shepherd

Pitches: Right **Bats:** Right **Pos:** RP   **Ht:** 6' 2" **Wt:** 205 **Born:** 01/21/68 **Age:** 25

		HOW MUCH HE PITCHED							WHAT HE GAVE UP									THE RESULTS					
Year Team	Lg	G	GS	CG	GF	IP	BFP	H	R	ER	HR	SH	SF	HB	TBB	IBB	SO	WP	Bk	W	L	Pct.	ShO	Sv	ERA
1990 Reno	A	5	5	0	0	25	120	22	25	15	1	3	1	2	18	0	16	6	1	1	4	.200	0	0	5.40
Watertown	A	24	0	0	19	54.1	235	41	22	15	1	4	0	4	29	1	55	9	1	3	3	.500	0	3	2.48
1991 South Bend	A	31	0	0	21	35.1	140	17	4	2	0	3	0	1	19	2	38	5	1	1	2	.333	0	10	0.51
Sarasota	A	18	0	0	8	39.2	166	33	16	12	0	3	1	2	20	0	24	1	0	1	1	.500	0	2	2.72
1992 Birmingham	AA	40	0	0	30	71.1	282	50	19	17	1	4	1	1	20	2	64	7	1	3	3	.500	0	7	2.14
Reading	AA	4	3	0	1	22.2	87	17	7	7	1	2	0		4	1	9	0	0	0	1	.000	0	0	2.78
1992 Philadelphia	NL	12	0	0	6	22	91	19	10	8	0	4	3	0	6	1	10	1	0	1	1	.500	0	2	3.27

Tommy Shields

Bats: Right **Throws:** Right **Pos:** PR   **Ht:** 6' 0" **Wt:** 180 **Born:** 08/14/64 **Age:** 28

			BATTING															BASERUNNING				PERCENTAGES		
Year Team	Lg	G	AB	H	2B	3B	HR	(Hm	Rd)	TB	R	RBI	TBB	IBB	SO	HBP	SH	SF	SB	CS	SB%	GDP	Avg	OBP	SLG
1986 Watertown	A	43	153	44	6	1	4	--	--	64	25	25	17	0	36	7	1	3	15	6	.71	3	.288	.378	.418
Pr William	A	30	112	31	7	1	1	--	--	43	17	12	9	0	16	5	1	1	4	1	.80	5	.277	.354	.384
1988 Salem	A	45	156	49	5	0	3	--	--	63	20	25	16	0	24	6	1	2	10	3	.77	5	.314	.394	.404
Harrisburg	AA	57	198	61	4	2	2	--	--	75	30	21	14	1	25	3	2	1	7	3	.70	5	.308	.361	.379
1989 Harrisburg	AA	123	417	120	13	4	5	--	--	156	66	47	25	3	62	9	2	3	17	5	.77	11	.288	.339	.374
1990 Buffalo	AAA	123	380	94	20	3	2	--	--	126	42	30	21	1	72	2	6	3	12	6	.67	11	.247	.288	.332
1991 Rochester	AAA	116	412	119	18	3	6	--	--	161	69	52	32	1	73	11	5	3	16	8	.67	11	.289	.354	.391
1992 Rochester	AAA	121	431	130	23	3	10	--	--	189	58	59	30	1	72	6	4	4	13	7	.65	5	.302	.352	.439
1992 Baltimore	AL	2	0	0	0	0	0	(0	0)	0	0	0	0	0	0	0	0	0	0	0	.00	0	.000	.000	.000

Steve Shifflett

Pitches: Right **Bats:** Right **Pos:** RP   **Ht:** 6' 1" **Wt:** 200 **Born:** 01/05/66 **Age:** 27

		HOW MUCH HE PITCHED							WHAT HE GAVE UP									THE RESULTS					
Year Team	Lg	G	GS	CG	GF	IP	BFP	H	R	ER	HR	SH	SF	HB	TBB	IBB	SO	WP	Bk	W	L	Pct.	ShO	Sv	ERA
1989 Appleton	A	18	2	0	5	39	171	34	25	18	1	1	1	2	19	2	13	8	3	3	3	.500	0	0	4.15
1990 Appleton	A	57	0	0	34	82.2	330	67	35	27	3	6	2	3	28	4	40	1	1	6	5	.545	0	10	2.94
1991 Memphis	AA	59	1	0	35	113	460	105	34	27	4	8	3	5	22	6	78	1	3	11	5	.688	0	9	2.15
1992 Omaha	AAA	32	0	0	29	43.2	165	30	8	8	0	4	3	0	15	1	19	0	2	3	2	.600	0	14	1.65
1992 Kansas City	AL	34	0	0	15	52	221	55	15	15	6	4	1	2	17	6	25	2	1	1	4	.200	0	0	2.60

Craig Shipley

Bats: Right **Throws:** Right **Pos:** SS/2B   **Ht:** 6' 1" **Wt:** 185 **Born:** 01/07/63 **Age:** 30

			BATTING															BASERUNNING				PERCENTAGES		
Year Team	Lg	G	AB	H	2B	3B	HR	(Hm	Rd)	TB	R	RBI	TBB	IBB	SO	HBP	SH	SF	SB	CS	SB%	GDP	Avg	OBP	SLG
1986 Los Angeles	NL	12	27	3	1	0	0	(0	0)	4	3	4	2	1	5	1	1	0	0	0	.00	1	.111	.200	.148
1987 Los Angeles	NL	26	35	9	1	0	0	(0	0)	10	3	2	0	0	6	0	0	0	0	0	.00	2	.257	.257	.286
1989 New York	NL	4	7	1	0	0	0	(0	0)	1	3	0	0	0	1	0	0	0	0	0	.00	0	.143	.143	.143
1991 San Diego	NL	37	91	25	3	0	1	(0	1)	31	6	6	2	0	14	1	1	0	0	1	.00	1	.275	.298	.341
1992 San Diego	NL	52	105	26	6	0	0	(0	0)	32	7	7	2	1	21	0	1	0	1	1	.50	2	.248	.262	.305
5 ML YEARS		131	265	64	11	0	1	(0	1)	78	22	19	6	2	47	2	3	0	1	2	.33	6	.242	.264	.294

Terry Shumpert

Bats: Right **Throws:** Right **Pos:** 2B 　　　　　　**Ht:** 5'11" **Wt:** 190 **Born:** 08/16/66 **Age:** 26

Year Team	Lg	G	AB	H	2B	3B	HR	(Hm	Rd)	TB	R	RBI	TBB	IBB	SO	HBP	SH	SF	SB	CS	SB%	GDP	Avg	OBP	SLG
1990 Kansas City	AL	32	91	25	6	1	0	(0	0)	33	7	8	2	0	17	1	0	2	3	3	.50	4	.275	.292	.363
1991 Kansas City	AL	144	369	80	16	4	5	(1	4)	119	45	34	30	0	75	5	10	3	17	11	.61	10	.217	.283	.322
1992 Kansas City	AL	36	94	14	5	1	1	(0	1)	24	6	11	3	0	17	0	2	0	2	2	.50	2	.149	.175	.255
3 ML YEARS		212	554	119	27	6	6	(1	5)	176	58	53	35	0	109	6	12	5	22	16	.58	16	.215	.267	.318

Ruben Sierra

Bats: Both **Throws:** Right **Pos:** RF 　　　　　　**Ht:** 6' 1" **Wt:** 200 **Born:** 10/06/65 **Age:** 27

Year Team	Lg	G	AB	H	2B	3B	HR	(Hm	Rd)	TB	R	RBI	TBB	IBB	SO	HBP	SH	SF	SB	CS	SB%	GDP	Avg	OBP	SLG
1986 Texas	AL	113	382	101	13	10	16	(8	8)	182	50	55	22	3	65	1	1	5	7	8	.47	8	.264	.302	.476
1987 Texas	AL	158	643	169	35	4	30	(15	15)	302	97	109	39	4	114	2	0	12	16	11	.59	18	.263	.302	.470
1988 Texas	AL	156	615	156	32	2	23	(15	8)	261	77	91	44	10	91	1	0	8	18	4	.82	15	.254	.301	.424
1989 Texas	AL	162	634	194	35	14	29	(21	8)	344	101	119	43	2	82	2	0	10	8	2	.80	7	.306	.347	.543
1990 Texas	AL	159	608	170	37	2	16	(10	6)	259	70	96	49	13	86	1	0	8	9	0	1.00	15	.280	.330	.426
1991 Texas	AL	161	661	203	44	5	25	(12	13)	332	110	116	56	7	91	0	0	9	16	4	.80	17	.307	.357	.502
1992 2 ML Teams		151	601	167	34	7	17	(10	7)	266	83	87	45	12	68	0	0	10	14	4	.78	11	.278	.323	.443
1992 Texas	AL	124	500	139	30	6	14	(8	6)	223	66	70	31	6	59	0	0	8	12	4	.75	9	.278	.315	.446
Oakland	AL	27	101	28	4	1	3	(2	1)	43	17	17	14	6	9	0	0	2	2	0	1.00	2	.277	.359	.426
7 ML YEARS		1060	4144	1160	230	44	156	(91	65)	1946	588	673	298	51	597	7	1	62	88	33	.73	91	.280	.325	.470

Dave Silvestri

Bats: Right **Throws:** Right **Pos:** SS 　　　　　　**Ht:** 6' 0" **Wt:** 180 **Born:** 09/29/67 **Age:** 25

Year Team	Lg	G	AB	H	2B	3B	HR	(Hm	Rd)	TB	R	RBI	TBB	IBB	SO	HBP	SH	SF	SB	CS	SB%	GDP	Avg	OBP	SLG
1989 Osceola	A	129	437	111	20	1	2	--	--	139	67	50	68	1	72	6	8	10	28	13	.68	15	.254	.355	.318
1990 Pr William	A	131	465	120	30	7	5	--	--	179	74	56	77	0	90	6	5	5	37	13	.74	9	.258	.367	.385
Albany	AA	2	7	2	0	0	0	--	--	2	0	2	0	0	1	0	0	0	0	0	.00	0	.286	.286	.286
1991 Albany	AA	140	512	134	31	8	19	--	--	238	97	83	83	3	126	2	2	2	20	13	.61	18	.262	.366	.465
1992 Columbus	AAA	118	420	117	25	5	13	--	--	191	83	73	58	1	110	8	0	5	19	11	.63	10	.279	.373	.455
1992 New York	AL	7	13	4	0	2	0	(0	0)	8	3	1	0	0	3	0	0	0	0	0	.00	1	.308	.308	.615

Mike Simms

Bats: Right **Throws:** Right **Pos:** RF 　　　　　　**Ht:** 6' 4" **Wt:** 185 **Born:** 01/12/67 **Age:** 26

Year Team	Lg	G	AB	H	2B	3B	HR	(Hm	Rd)	TB	R	RBI	TBB	IBB	SO	HBP	SH	SF	SB	CS	SB%	GDP	Avg	OBP	SLG
1990 Houston	NL	12	13	4	1	0	1	(0	1)	8	3	2	0	0	4	0	0	0	0	0	.00	0	.308	.308	.615
1991 Houston	NL	49	123	25	5	0	3	(1	2)	39	18	16	18	0	38	0	0	2	1	0	1.00	2	.203	.301	.317
1992 Houston	NL	15	24	6	1	0	1	(0	1)	10	1	3	2	0	9	1	0	0	0	0	.00	1	.250	.333	.417
3 ML YEARS		76	160	35	7	0	5	(1	4)	57	22	21	20	0	51	1	0	2	1	0	1.00	4	.219	.306	.356

Doug Simons

Pitches: Left **Bats:** Left **Pos:** RP 　　　　　　**Ht:** 6' 0" **Wt:** 170 **Born:** 09/15/66 **Age:** 26

| | | HOW MUCH HE PITCHED | | | | | | WHAT HE GAVE UP | | | | | | | | | | | | THE RESULTS | | | | | |
Year Team	Lg	G	GS	CG	GF	IP	BFP	H	R	ER	HR	SH	SF	HB	TBB	IBB	SO	WP	Bk	W	L	Pct.	ShO	Sv	ERA
1988 Visalia	A	17	16	5	1	107.1	467	100	59	47	10	4	3	5	46	0	123	6	1	6	5	.545	2	0	3.94
1989 Visalia	A	14	14	1	0	90.2	372	77	33	15	4	1	4	5	33	1	79	4	1	6	2	.750	0	0	1.49
Orlando	AA	14	14	3	0	87.1	374	83	39	37	7	2	2	2	37	0	58	1	2	7	3	.700	0	0	3.81
1990 Orlando	AA	29	28	5	0	188	765	160	76	53	13	9	4	6	43	2	109	7	1	15	12	.556	0	0	2.54
1992 Indianapolis	AAA	32	14	2	6	120	481	114	45	41	7	2	6	2	25	1	66	3	0	11	4	.733	1	0	3.08
1991 New York	NL	42	1	0	11	60.2	258	55	40	35	5	9	4	2	19	5	38	3	0	2	3	.400	0	1	5.19
1992 Montreal	NL	7	0	0	2	5.1	35	15	14	14	3	1	1	1	2	0	6	1	0	0	0	.000	0	0	23.63
2 ML YEARS		49	1	0	13	66	293	70	54	49	8	10	5	3	21	5	44	4	0	2	3	.400	0	1	6.68

Matt Sinatro

Bats: Right **Throws:** Right **Pos:** C 　　　　　　**Ht:** 5' 9" **Wt:** 175 **Born:** 03/22/60 **Age:** 33

Year Team	Lg	G	AB	H	2B	3B	HR	(Hm	Rd)	TB	R	RBI	TBB	IBB	SO	HBP	SH	SF	SB	CS	SB%	GDP	Avg	OBP	SLG
1981 Atlanta	NL	12	32	9	1	1	0	(0	0)	12	4	4	5	1	4	0	0	0	1	0	1.00	0	.281	.378	.375
1982 Atlanta	NL	37	81	11	2	0	1	(0	1)	16	10	4	4	0	9	0	2	0	0	1	.00	3	.136	.176	.198
1983 Atlanta	NL	7	12	2	0	0	0	(0	0)	2	0	2	2	0	1	0	0	0	0	0	.00	0	.167	.286	.167
1984 Atlanta	NL	2	4	0	0	0	0	(0	0)	0	0	0	0	0	0	0	0	0	0	0	.00	0	.000	.000	.000
1987 Oakland	AL	6	3	0	0	0	0	(0	0)	0	0	0	0	0	1	0	0	0	0	0	.00	1	.000	.000	.000
1988 Oakland	AL	10	9	3	2	0	0	(0	0)	5	1	5	0	0	1	0	0	1	0	0	.00	2	.333	.300	.556

Year	Team	Lg	G	AB	H	2B	3B	HR	(Hm	Rd)	TB	R	RBI	TBB	IBB	SO	HBP	SH	SF	SB	CS	SB%	GDP	Avg	OBP	SLG
1989	Detroit	AL	13	25	3	0	0	0	(0	0)	3	2	1	1	0	3	1	0	0	0	0	.00	1	.120	.185	.120
1990	Seattle	AL	30	50	15	1	0	0	(0	0)	16	2	4	4	0	10	0	3	0	1	0	1.00	3	.300	.352	.320
1991	Seattle	AL	5	8	2	0	0	0	(0	0)	2	1	1	1	0	1	0	0	0	0	0	.00	0	.250	.333	.250
1992	Seattle	AL	18	28	3	0	0	0	(0	0)	3	0	0	0	0	5	0	0	0	0	0	.00	1	.107	.107	.107
10	ML YEARS		140	252	48	6	1	1	(0	1)	59	20	21	17	1	35	1	5	1	2	1	.67	11	.190	.244	.234

Don Slaught

Bats: Right **Throws:** Right **Pos:** C **Ht:** 6' 1" **Wt:** 190 **Born:** 09/11/58 **Age:** 34

									BATTING											BASERUNNING				PERCENTAGES		
Year	Team	Lg	G	AB	H	2B	3B	HR	(Hm	Rd)	TB	R	RBI	TBB	IBB	SO	HBP	SH	SF	SB	CS	SB%	GDP	Avg	OBP	SLG
1982	Kansas City	AL	43	115	32	6	0	3	(0	3)	47	14	8	9	0	12	0	2	0	0	0	.00	3	.278	.331	.409
1983	Kansas City	AL	83	276	86	13	4	0	(0	0)	107	21	28	11	0	27	0	1	2	3	1	.75	8	.312	.336	.388
1984	Kansas City	AL	124	409	108	27	4	4	(1	3)	155	48	42	20	4	55	2	8	7	0	0	.00	8	.264	.297	.379
1985	Texas	AL	102	343	96	17	4	8	(4	4)	145	34	35	20	1	41	6	1	0	5	4	.56	8	.280	.331	.423
1986	Texas	AL	95	314	83	17	1	13	(5	8)	141	39	46	16	0	59	5	3	3	3	2	.60	8	.264	.308	.449
1987	Texas	AL	95	237	53	15	2	8	(5	3)	96	25	16	24	3	51	1	4	0	0	3	.00	7	.224	.298	.405
1988	New York	AL	97	322	91	25	1	9	(7	2)	145	33	43	24	3	54	3	5	4	1	0	1.00	10	.283	.334	.450
1989	New York	AL	117	350	88	21	3	5	(3	2)	130	34	38	30	3	57	5	2	5	1	1	.50	9	.251	.315	.371
1990	Pittsburgh	NL	84	230	69	18	3	4	(1	3)	105	27	29	27	2	27	3	3	4	0	1	.00	2	.300	.375	.457
1991	Pittsburgh	NL	77	220	65	17	1	1	(0	1)	87	19	29	21	1	32	3	5	1	1	0	1.00	6	.295	.363	.395
1992	Pittsburgh	NL	87	255	88	17	3	4	(2	2)	123	26	37	17	5	23	2	6	5	2	2	.50	6	.345	.384	.482
11	ML YEARS		1004	3071	859	193	26	59	(28	31)	1281	320	351	219	22	438	30	40	31	16	14	.53	75	.280	.331	.417

Heathcliff Slocumb

Pitches: Right **Bats:** Right **Pos:** RP **Ht:** 6' 3" **Wt:** 210 **Born:** 06/07/66 **Age:** 27

			HOW MUCH HE PITCHED						WHAT HE GAVE UP									THE RESULTS					
Year	Team	Lg	G	GS	CG	GF	IP	BFP	H	R	ER	HR	SH	SF	HB	TBB	IBB	SO	WP	Bk	W	L	Pct.	ShO	Sv	ERA
1984	Kingsport	R	1	0	0	0	0.1	3	0	1	0	0	1	0	0	1	0	0	0	0	0	0	.000	0	0	0.00
	Little Fls	A	4	1	0	0	9	51	8	11	11	0	0	1	0	16	0	10	4	0	0	0	.000	0	0	11.00
1985	Kingsport	R	11	9	1	0	52.1	232	47	32	22	0	2	1	1	31	0	29	15	0	3	2	.600	0	0	3.78
1986	Little Fls	A	25	0	0	13	43.2	186	24	17	8	3	1	0	0	36	1	41	8	0	3	1	.750	0	1	1.65
1987	Winston-Sal	A	9	4	0	1	27.1	135	26	25	19	1	2	3	0	26	0	27	0	1	1	2	.333	0	0	6.26
	Peoria	A	16	16	3	0	103.2	455	97	44	30	2	0	2	3	42	3	81	15	0	10	4	.714	1	0	2.60
1988	Winston-Sal	A	25	19	2	3	119.2	567	122	75	66	5	2	5	3	90	1	78	19	2	6	6	.500	1	1	4.96
1989	Peoria	A	49	0	0	43	55.2	233	31	16	11	0	5	3	1	33	4	52	6	0	5	3	.625	0	22	1.78
1990	Charlotte	AA	43	0	0	37	50.1	232	50	20	12	0	6	2	3	32	5	37	4	0	3	1	.750	0	12	2.15
	Iowa	AAA	20	0	0	10	27	115	16	10	6	1	2	1	2	18	2	21	3	0	3	2	.600	0	1	2.00
1991	Iowa	AAA	12	0	0	6	13.1	59	10	8	6	0	1	0	1	6	0	9	1	0	1	0	1.000	0	1	4.05
1992	Iowa	AAA	36	1	0	23	41.2	177	36	13	12	0	1	1	0	16	1	47	4	0	1	3	.250	0	7	2.59
1991	Chicago	NL	52	0	0	21	62.2	274	53	29	24	3	6	6	3	30	6	34	9	0	2	1	.667	0	1	3.45
1992	Chicago	NL	30	0	0	11	36	174	52	27	26	3	2	2	1	21	3	27	1	0	0	3	.000	0	1	6.50
2	ML YEARS		82	0	0	32	98.2	448	105	56	50	6	8	8	4	51	9	61	10	0	2	4	.333	0	2	4.56

Joe Slusarski

Pitches: Right **Bats:** Right **Pos:** SP **Ht:** 6' 4" **Wt:** 195 **Born:** 12/19/66 **Age:** 26

			HOW MUCH HE PITCHED						WHAT HE GAVE UP									THE RESULTS					
Year	Team	Lg	G	GS	CG	GF	IP	BFP	H	R	ER	HR	SH	SF	HB	TBB	IBB	SO	WP	Bk	W	L	Pct.	ShO	Sv	ERA
1989	Modesto	A	27	27	4	0	184	753	155	78	65	15	5	3	8	50	0	160	13	1	13	10	.565	1	0	3.18
1990	Huntsville	AA	17	17	2	0	108.2	471	114	65	54	9	2	9	3	35	0	75	5	0	6	8	.429	0	0	4.47
	Tacoma	AAA	9	9	0	0	55.2	241	54	24	21	3	1	3	2	22	0	37	1	1	4	2	.667	0	0	3.40
1991	Tacoma	AAA	7	7	0	0	46.1	182	42	20	14	4	0	0	0	10	0	25	0	2	4	2	.667	0	0	2.72
1992	Tacoma	AAA	11	10	0	0	57.1	249	67	30	24	6	0	5	1	18	1	26	1	0	2	4	.333	0	0	3.77
1991	Oakland	AL	20	19	1	0	109.1	486	121	69	64	14	0	3	4	52	1	60	4	0	5	7	.417	0	0	5.27
1992	Oakland	AL	15	14	0	1	76	338	85	52	46	15	1	5	6	27	0	38	0	1	5	5	.500	0	0	5.45
2	ML YEARS		35	33	1	1	185.1	824	206	121	110	29	1	8	10	79	1	98	4	1	10	12	.455	0	0	5.34

John Smiley

Pitches: Left **Bats:** Left **Pos:** SP **Ht:** 6' 4" **Wt:** 200 **Born:** 03/17/65 **Age:** 28

			HOW MUCH HE PITCHED						WHAT HE GAVE UP									THE RESULTS					
Year	Team	Lg	G	GS	CG	GF	IP	BFP	H	R	ER	HR	SH	SF	HB	TBB	IBB	SO	WP	Bk	W	L	Pct.	ShO	Sv	ERA
1986	Pittsburgh	NL	12	0	0	2	11.2	42	4	6	5	2	0	0	0	4	0	9	0	0	1	0	1.000	0	0	3.86
1987	Pittsburgh	NL	63	0	0	19	75	336	69	49	48	7	0	3	0	50	8	58	5	1	5	5	.500	0	4	5.76
1988	Pittsburgh	NL	34	32	5	0	205	835	185	81	74	15	11	8	3	46	4	129	6	6	13	11	.542	1	0	3.25
1989	Pittsburgh	NL	28	28	8	0	205.1	835	174	78	64	22	5	7	4	49	5	123	5	2	12	8	.600	1	0	2.81
1990	Pittsburgh	NL	26	25	2	0	149.1	632	161	83	77	15	5	4	2	36	1	86	2	2	9	10	.474	0	0	4.64
1991	Pittsburgh	NL	33	32	2	0	207.2	836	194	78	71	17	11	4	3	44	0	129	3	1	20	8	.714	1	0	3.08
1992	Minnesota	AL	34	34	5	0	241	970	205	93	86	17	4	9	6	65	0	163	4	0	16	9	.640	2	0	3.21

Bryn Smith

Pitches: Right **Bats: Right** **Pos: RP** **Ht: 6' 2"** **Wt: 205** **Born: 08/11/55** **Age: 37**

			HOW	MUCH	HE	PITCHED		WHAT	HE	GAVE	UP							THE	RESULTS				
Year Team	Lg	G	GS	CG	GF	IP	BFP	H	R	ER	HR	SH	SF	HB	TBB	IBB	SO	WP	Bk	W	L	Pct.	ShO	Sv	ERA
1981 Montreal	NL	7	0	0	1	13	53	14	4	4	1	0	0	0	3	0	9	2	0	1	0	1.000	0	0	2.77
1982 Montreal	NL	47	1	0	16	79.1	335	81	43	37	5	1	4	0	23	5	50	5	1	2	4	.333	0	3	4.20
1983 Montreal	NL	49	12	5	17	155.1	636	142	51	43	13	14	2	5	43	6	101	5	3	6	11	.353	3	3	2.49
1984 Montreal	NL	28	28	4	0	179	751	178	72	66	15	7	2	3	51	7	101	2	2	12	13	.480	2	0	3.32
1985 Montreal	NL	32	32	4	0	222.1	890	193	85	72	12	13	4	1	41	3	127	1	1	18	5	.783	2	0	2.91
1986 Montreal	NL	30	30	1	0	187.1	807	182	101	82	15	10	3	6	63	6	105	4	2	10	8	.556	0	0	3.94
1987 Montreal	NL	26	26	2	0	150.1	643	164	81	73	16	7	5	2	31	4	94	2	0	10	9	.526	0	0	4.37
1988 Montreal	NL	32	32	1	0	198	791	179	79	66	15	7	6	10	32	2	122	2	5	12	10	.545	0	0	3.00
1989 Montreal	NL	33	32	3	0	215.2	864	177	76	68	16	7	5	4	54	4	129	3	1	10	11	.476	1	0	2.84
1990 St. Louis	NL	26	25	0	0	141.1	605	160	81	67	11	7	5	4	30	1	78	2	0	9	8	.529	0	0	4.27
1991 St. Louis	NL	31	31	3	0	198.2	818	188	95	85	16	10	7	7	45	3	94	3	1	12	9	.571	0	0	3.85
1992 St. Louis	NL	13	1	0	3	21.1	91	20	11	11	3	2	0	3	5	1	9	1	0	4	2	.667	0	0	4.64
12 ML YEARS		354	250	23	37	1761.2	7284	1678	779	674	138	85	43	45	421	42	1019	32	16	106	90	.541	8	6	3.44

Dan Smith

Pitches: Left **Bats: Left** **Pos: SP** **Ht: 6' 5"** **Wt: 190** **Born: 08/20/69** **Age: 23**

			HOW	MUCH	HE	PITCHED		WHAT	HE	GAVE	UP							THE	RESULTS				
Year Team	Lg	G	GS	CG	GF	IP	BFP	H	R	ER	HR	SH	SF	HB	TBB	IBB	SO	WP	Bk	W	L	Pct.	ShO	Sv	ERA
1990 Butte	R	5	5	0	0	24.2	102	23	10	10	3	2	0	2	6	0	27	3	1	2	0	1.000	0	0	3.65
Tulsa	AA	7	7	0	0	38.1	151	27	16	16	2	0	3	0	16	0	32	0	0	3	2	.600	0	0	3.76
1991 Okla City	AAA	28	27	3	1	151.2	713	195	114	93	10	6	8	4	75	1	85	5	5	4	17	.190	0	0	5.52
1992 Tulsa	AA	24	23	4	0	146.1	571	110	48	41	4	9	3	6	34	0	122	3	3	11	7	.611	3	0	2.52
1992 Texas	AL	4	2	0	1	14.1	67	18	8	8	1	2	1	0	8	1	5	0	0	0	3	.000	0	0	5.02

Dave Smith

Pitches: Right **Bats: Right** **Pos: RP** **Ht: 6' 1"** **Wt: 195** **Born: 01/21/55** **Age: 38**

			HOW	MUCH	HE	PITCHED		WHAT	HE	GAVE	UP							THE	RESULTS				
Year Team	Lg	G	GS	CG	GF	IP	BFP	H	R	ER	HR	SH	SF	HB	TBB	IBB	SO	WP	Bk	W	L	Pct.	ShO	Sv	ERA
1980 Houston	NL	57	0	0	35	103	422	90	24	22	1	6	1	4	32	7	85	3	1	7	5	.583	0	10	1.92
1981 Houston	NL	42	0	0	22	75	305	54	26	23	2	6	1	2	23	4	52	4	0	5	3	.625	0	8	2.76
1982 Houston	NL	49	1	0	29	63.1	286	69	30	27	4	9	4	0	31	4	28	2	4	5	4	.556	0	11	3.84
1983 Houston	NL	42	0	0	24	72.2	323	72	32	25	2	3	5	0	36	4	41	1	1	3	1	.750	0	6	3.10
1984 Houston	NL	53	0	0	24	77.1	304	60	22	19	5	2	1	1	20	3	45	1	1	5	4	.556	0	5	2.21
1985 Houston	NL	64	0	0	46	79.1	315	69	26	20	3	3	1	1	17	5	40	4	1	9	5	.643	0	27	2.27
1986 Houston	NL	54	0	0	51	56	223	39	17	17	5	4	1	1	22	3	46	2	0	4	7	.364	0	33	2.73
1987 Houston	NL	50	0	0	44	60	240	39	13	11	0	3	1	1	21	8	73	2	2	2	3	.400	0	24	1.65
1988 Houston	NL	51	0	0	39	57.1	249	60	26	17	1	4	1	1	19	8	38	1	3	4	5	.444	0	27	2.67
1989 Houston	NL	52	0	0	44	58	239	49	20	17	1	8	1	1	19	7	31	2	2	3	4	.429	0	25	2.64
1990 Houston	NL	49	0	0	42	60.1	239	45	18	16	4	4	1	0	20	4	50	5	5	6	6	.500	0	23	2.39
1991 Chicago	NL	35	0	0	28	33	151	39	22	22	6	2	0	1	19	5	16	1	1	0	6	.000	0	17	6.00
1992 Chicago	NL	11	0	0	4	14.1	61	15	4	4	0	1	1	0	4	2	3	0	1	0	0	.000	0	0	2.51
13 ML YEARS		609	1	0	432	809.2	3357	700	280	240	34	55	19	13	283	64	548	28	22	53	53	.500	0	216	2.67

Dwight Smith

Bats: Left **Throws: Right** **Pos: CF/LF/RF** **Ht: 5'11"** **Wt: 175** **Born: 11/08/63** **Age: 29**

						BATTING										BASERUNNING				PERCENTAGES		
Year Team	Lg	G	AB	H	2B	3B	HR	(Hm | Rd)	TB	R	RBI	TBB	IBB	SO	HBP	SH	SF	SB	CS	SB%	GDP	Avg	OBP	SLG
1989 Chicago	NL	109	343	111	19	6	9	(5 | 4)	169	52	52	31	0	51	2	4	1	9	4	.69	4	.324	.382	.493
1990 Chicago	NL	117	290	76	15	0	6	(3 | 3)	109	34	27	28	2	46	2	0	2	11	6	.65	7	.262	.329	.376
1991 Chicago	NL	90	167	38	7	2	3	(2 | 1)	58	16	21	11	2	32	1	1	0	2	3	.40	2	.228	.279	.347
1992 Chicago	NL	109	217	60	10	3	3	(3 | 0)	85	28	24	13	0	40	1	0	2	9	8	.53	1	.276	.318	.392
4 ML YEARS		425	1017	285	51	11	21	(13 | 8)	421	130	124	83	4	169	6	5	5	31	21	.60	14	.280	.337	.414

Lee Smith

Pitches: Right **Bats: Right** **Pos: RP** **Ht: 6' 6"** **Wt: 269** **Born: 12/04/57** **Age: 35**

			HOW	MUCH	HE	PITCHED		WHAT	HE	GAVE	UP							THE	RESULTS				
Year Team	Lg	G	GS	CG	GF	IP	BFP	H	R	ER	HR	SH	SF	HB	TBB	IBB	SO	WP	Bk	W	L	Pct.	ShO	Sv	ERA
1980 Chicago	NL	18	0	0	6	22	97	21	9	7	0	1	1	0	14	5	17	0	0	2	0	1.000	0	0	2.86
1981 Chicago	NL	40	1	0	12	67	280	57	31	26	2	8	2	1	31	8	50	7	1	3	6	.333	0	1	3.49
1982 Chicago	NL	72	5	0	38	117	480	105	38	35	5	6	5	3	37	5	99	6	1	2	5	.286	0	17	2.69

187

Year Team	Lg	G	GS	CG	GF	IP	BFP	H	R	ER	HR	SH	SF	HB	TBB	IBB	SO	WP	Bk	W	L	Pct.	ShO	Sv	ERA
1983 Chicago	NL	66	0	0	56	103.1	413	70	23	19	5	9	2	1	41	14	91	5	2	4	10	.286	0	29	1.65
1984 Chicago	NL	69	0	0	59	101	428	98	42	41	6	4	5	0	35	7	86	6	0	9	7	.563	0	33	3.65
1985 Chicago	NL	65	0	0	57	97.2	397	87	35	33	9	3	1	1	32	6	112	4	0	7	4	.636	0	33	3.04
1986 Chicago	NL	66	0	0	59	90.1	372	69	32	31	7	6	3	0	42	11	93	2	0	9	9	.500	0	31	3.09
1987 Chicago	NL	62	0	0	55	83.2	360	84	30	29	4	4	0	0	32	5	96	4	0	4	10	.286	0	36	3.12
1988 Boston	AL	64	0	0	57	83.2	363	72	34	26	7	3	2	1	37	6	96	2	0	4	5	.444	0	29	2.80
1989 Boston	AL	64	0	0	50	70.2	290	53	30	28	6	2	2	0	33	6	96	1	0	6	1	.857	0	25	3.57
1990 2 ML Teams		64	0	0	53	83	344	71	24	19	3	2	3	0	29	7	87	2	0	5	5	.500	0	31	2.06
1991 St. Louis	NL	67	0	0	61	73	300	70	19	19	5	5	1	0	13	5	67	1	0	6	3	.667	0	47	2.34
1992 St. Louis	NL	70	0	0	55	75	310	62	28	26	4	2	1	0	26	4	60	2	0	4	9	.308	0	43	3.12
1990 Boston	AL	11	0	0	8	14.1	64	13	4	3	0	0	0	0	9	2	17	1	0	2	1	.667	0	4	1.88
St. Louis	NL	53	0	0	45	68.2	280	58	20	16	3	2	3	0	20	5	70	1	0	3	4	.429	0	27	2.10
13 ML YEARS		787	6	0	618	1067.1	4434	919	375	339	63	55	28	7	402	89	1050	42	4	65	74	.468	0	355	2.86

Lonnie Smith

Bats: Right **Throws:** Right **Pos:** LF **Ht:** 5' 9" **Wt:** 190 **Born:** 12/22/55 **Age:** 37

								BATTING											BASERUNNING				PERCENTAGES		
Year Team	Lg	G	AB	H	2B	3B	HR	(Hm	Rd)	TB	R	RBI	TBB	IBB	SO	HBP	SH	SF	SB	CS	SB%	GDP	Avg	OBP	SLG
1978 Philadelphia	NL	17	4	0	0	0	0	(0	0)	0	6	0	4	0	3	0	0	0	4	0	1.00	0	.000	.500	.000
1979 Philadelphia	NL	17	30	5	2	0	0	(0	0)	7	4	3	1	0	7	0	0	0	2	1	.67	0	.167	.194	.233
1980 Philadelphia	NL	100	298	101	14	4	3	(2	1)	132	69	20	26	2	48	4	1	2	33	13	.72	5	.339	.397	.443
1981 Philadelphia	NL	62	176	57	14	3	2	(1	1)	83	40	11	18	1	14	5	3	0	21	10	.68	1	.324	.402	.472
1982 St. Louis	NL	156	592	182	35	8	8	(3	5)	257	120	69	64	2	74	9	3	4	68	26	.72	11	.307	.381	.434
1983 St. Louis	NL	130	492	158	31	5	8	(4	4)	223	83	45	41	2	55	9	1	4	43	18	.70	11	.321	.381	.453
1984 St. Louis	NL	145	504	126	20	4	6	(3	3)	172	77	49	70	0	90	9	3	4	50	13	.79	7	.250	.349	.341
1985 2 ML Teams		148	544	140	25	6	6	(2	4)	195	92	48	56	0	89	7	1	5	52	13	.80	4	.257	.332	.358
1986 Kansas City	AL	134	508	146	25	7	8	(2	6)	209	80	44	46	0	78	10	2	2	26	9	.74	10	.287	.357	.411
1987 Kansas City	AL	48	167	42	7	1	3	(1	2)	60	26	8	24	0	31	4	0	2	9	4	.69	1	.251	.355	.359
1988 Atlanta	NL	43	114	27	3	0	3	(2	1)	39	14	9	10	0	25	0	0	1	4	2	.67	0	.237	.296	.342
1989 Atlanta	NL	134	482	152	34	4	21	(10	11)	257	89	79	76	3	95	11	1	7	25	12	.68	7	.315	.415	.533
1990 Atlanta	NL	135	466	142	27	9	9	(2	7)	214	72	42	58	3	69	6	1	6	10	10	.50	2	.305	.384	.459
1991 Atlanta	NL	122	353	97	19	1	7	(6	1)	139	58	44	50	3	64	9	2	2	9	5	.64	4	.275	.377	.394
1992 Atlanta	NL	84	158	39	8	2	6	(3	3)	69	23	33	17	1	37	3	0	4	4	0	1.00	1	.247	.324	.437
1985 St. Louis	NL	28	96	25	2	2	0	(0	0)	31	15	7	15	0	20	3	1	0	12	6	.67	2	.260	.377	.323
Kansas City	AL	120	448	115	23	4	6	(2	4)	164	77	41	41	0	69	4	0	5	40	7	.85	2	.257	.321	.366
15 ML YEARS		1475	4888	1414	264	54	90	(41	49)	2056	853	504	561	17	779	86	18	43	360	136	.73	64	.289	.369	.421

Ozzie Smith

Bats: Both **Throws:** Right **Pos:** SS **Ht:** 5'10" **Wt:** 168 **Born:** 12/26/54 **Age:** 38

								BATTING											BASERUNNING				PERCENTAGES		
Year Team	Lg	G	AB	H	2B	3B	HR	(Hm	Rd)	TB	R	RBI	TBB	IBB	SO	HBP	SH	SF	SB	CS	SB%	GDP	Avg	OBP	SLG
1978 San Diego	NL	159	590	152	17	6	1	(0	1)	184	69	46	47	0	43	0	28	3	40	12	.77	11	.258	.311	.312
1979 San Diego	NL	156	587	124	18	6	0	(0	0)	154	77	27	37	5	37	2	22	1	28	7	.80	11	.211	.260	.262
1980 San Diego	NL	158	609	140	18	5	0	(0	0)	168	67	35	71	1	49	5	23	4	57	15	.79	9	.230	.313	.276
1981 San Diego	NL	110	450	100	11	2	0	(0	0)	115	53	21	41	1	37	5	10	1	22	12	.65	9	.222	.294	.256
1982 St. Louis	NL	140	488	121	24	1	2	(0	2)	153	58	43	68	12	32	2	4	5	25	5	.83	10	.248	.339	.314
1983 St. Louis	NL	159	552	134	30	6	3	(1	2)	185	69	50	64	9	36	1	7	2	34	7	.83	10	.243	.321	.335
1984 St. Louis	NL	124	412	106	20	5	1	(1	0)	139	53	44	56	5	17	2	11	3	35	7	.83	8	.257	.347	.337
1985 St. Louis	NL	158	537	148	22	3	6	(2	4)	194	70	54	65	11	27	2	9	2	31	8	.79	13	.276	.355	.361
1986 St. Louis	NL	153	514	144	19	4	0	(0	0)	171	67	54	79	13	27	2	11	3	31	7	.82	9	.280	.376	.333
1987 St. Louis	NL	158	600	182	40	4	0	(0	0)	230	104	75	89	3	36	1	12	4	43	9	.83	9	.303	.392	.383
1988 St. Louis	NL	153	575	155	27	1	3	(2	1)	193	80	51	74	2	43	1	12	7	57	9	.86	7	.270	.350	.336
1989 St. Louis	NL	155	593	162	30	8	2	(1	1)	214	82	50	55	3	37	2	11	3	29	7	.81	10	.273	.335	.361
1990 St. Louis	NL	143	512	130	21	1	1	(0	1)	156	61	50	61	4	33	2	7	10	32	6	.84	8	.254	.330	.305
1991 St. Louis	NL	150	550	157	30	3	3	(2	1)	202	96	50	83	2	36	1	6	1	35	9	.80	8	.285	.380	.367
1992 St. Louis	NL	132	518	153	20	2	0	(0	0)	177	73	31	59	4	34	0	12	1	43	9	.83	11	.295	.367	.342
15 ML YEARS		2208	8087	2108	347	57	22	(9	13)	2635	1079	681	949	75	524	28	185	50	542	129	.81	142	.261	.338	.326

Pete Smith

Pitches: Right **Bats:** Right **Pos:** SP **Ht:** 6' 2" **Wt:** 200 **Born:** 02/27/66 **Age:** 27

				HOW MUCH HE PITCHED					WHAT HE GAVE UP										THE RESULTS					
Year Team	Lg	G	GS	CG	GF	IP	BFP	H	R	ER	HR	SH	SF	HB	TBB	IBB	SO	WP	Bk	W	L	Pct.	ShO	Sv	ERA
1987 Atlanta	NL	6	6	0	0	31.2	143	39	21	17	3	0	2	0	14	0	11	3	1	1	2	.333	0	0	4.83
1988 Atlanta	NL	32	32	5	0	195.1	837	183	89	80	15	12	4	1	88	3	124	3	1	7	15	.318	3	0	3.69
1989 Atlanta	NL	28	27	1	0	142	613	144	83	75	13	4	5	0	57	2	115	3	7	5	14	.263	0	0	4.75
1990 Atlanta	NL	13	13	0	0	77	327	77	45	41	11	4	3	0	24	2	56	2	1	5	6	.455	0	0	4.79
1991 Atlanta	NL	14	10	0	2	48	211	48	33	27	5	2	4	0	22	3	29	1	4	1	3	.250	0	0	5.06

Year	Team	Lg	G	GS	CG	GF	IP	BFP	H	R	ER	HR	SH	SF	HB	TBB	IBB	SO	WP	Bk	W	L	Pct.	ShO	Sv	ERA
1992	Atlanta	NL	12	11	2	0	79	323	63	19	18	3	4	1	0	28	2	43	2	1	7	0	1.000	1	0	2.05
	6 ML YEARS		105	99	11	2	573	2454	554	290	258	50	26	19	1	233	12	378	16	21	26	40	.394	4	0	4.05

Zane Smith

Pitches: Left **Bats: Left** **Pos: SP**   **Ht: 6' 1"** **Wt: 205** **Born: 12/28/60** **Age: 32**

			HOW MUCH HE PITCHED						WHAT HE GAVE UP												THE RESULTS					
Year	Team	Lg	G	GS	CG	GF	IP	BFP	H	R	ER	HR	SH	SF	HB	TBB	IBB	SO	WP	Bk	W	L	Pct.	ShO	Sv	ERA
1984	Atlanta	NL	3	3	0	0	20	87	16	7	5	1	1	0	0	13	2	16	0	0	1	0	1.000	0	0	2.25
1985	Atlanta	NL	42	18	2	3	147	631	135	70	62	4	16	1	3	80	5	85	2	0	9	10	.474	2	0	3.80
1986	Atlanta	NL	38	32	3	2	204.2	889	209	109	92	8	13	6	5	105	6	139	8	0	8	16	.333	1	1	4.05
1987	Atlanta	NL	36	36	9	0	242	1035	245	130	110	19	12	5	5	91	6	130	5	1	15	10	.600	3	0	4.09
1988	Atlanta	NL	23	22	3	0	140.1	609	159	72	67	8	15	2	3	44	4	59	2	2	5	10	.333	0	0	4.30
1989	2 ML Teams		48	17	0	10	147	634	141	76	57	7	15	5	3	52	7	93	4	0	1	13	.071	0	2	3.49
1990	2 ML Teams		33	31	4	1	215.1	860	196	77	61	15	3	3	3	50	4	130	2	0	12	9	.571	2	0	2.55
1991	Pittsburgh	NL	35	35	6	0	228	916	234	95	81	15	7	5	2	29	3	120	1	0	16	10	.615	3	0	3.20
1992	Pittsburgh	NL	23	22	4	0	141	566	138	56	48	8	12	4	2	19	3	56	0	0	8	8	.500	3	0	3.06
1989	Atlanta	NL	17	17	0	0	99	432	102	65	49	5	10	5	2	33	3	58	3	0	1	12	.077	0	0	4.45
	Montreal	NL	31	0	0	10	48	202	39	11	8	2	5	0	1	19	4	35	1	0	0	1	.000	0	2	1.50
1990	Montreal	NL	22	21	1	0	139.1	578	141	57	50	11	2	2	3	41	3	80	1	0	6	7	.462	0	0	3.23
	Pittsburgh	NL	11	10	3	1	76	282	55	20	11	4	1	1	0	9	1	50	1	0	6	2	.750	2	0	1.30
	9 ML YEARS		281	216	31	16	1485.1	6227	1473	692	583	85	94	31	26	483	40	828	24	3	75	86	.466	14	3	3.53

John Smoltz

Pitches: Right **Bats: Right** **Pos: SP**   **Ht: 6' 3"** **Wt: 185** **Born: 05/15/67** **Age: 26**

			HOW MUCH HE PITCHED						WHAT HE GAVE UP												THE RESULTS					
Year	Team	Lg	G	GS	CG	GF	IP	BFP	H	R	ER	HR	SH	SF	HB	TBB	IBB	SO	WP	Bk	W	L	Pct.	ShO	Sv	ERA
1988	Atlanta	NL	12	12	0	0	64	297	74	40	39	10	2	0	2	33	4	37	2	1	2	7	.222	0	0	5.48
1989	Atlanta	NL	29	29	5	0	208	847	160	79	68	15	10	7	2	72	2	168	8	3	12	11	.522	0	0	2.94
1990	Atlanta	NL	34	34	6	0	231.1	966	206	109	99	20	9	8	1	90	3	170	14	3	14	11	.560	2	0	3.85
1991	Atlanta	NL	36	36	5	0	229.2	947	206	101	97	16	9	9	3	77	1	148	20	2	14	13	.519	0	0	3.80
1992	Atlanta	NL	35	35	9	0	246.2	1021	206	90	78	17	7	8	5	80	5	215	17	1	15	12	.556	3	0	2.85
	5 ML YEARS		146	146	25	0	979.2	4078	852	419	381	78	37	32	13	352	15	738	61	10	57	54	.514	5	0	3.50

J.T. Snow

Bats: Both **Throws: Left** **Pos: 1B**   **Ht: 6' 2"** **Wt: 202** **Born: 02/26/68** **Age: 25**

			BATTING																	BASERUNNING				PERCENTAGES		
Year	Team	Lg	G	AB	H	2B	3B	HR	(Hm	Rd)	TB	R	RBI	TBB	IBB	SO	HBP	SH	SF	SB	CS	SB%	GDP	Avg	OBP	SLG
1989	Oneonta	A	73	274	80	18	2	8	--	--	126	41	51	29	6	35	2	2	4	4	1	.80	9	.292	.359	.460
1990	Pr William	A	138	520	133	25	1	8	--	--	184	57	72	46	3	65	5	0	7	2	0	1.00	20	.256	.318	.354
1991	Albany	AA	132	477	133	33	3	13	--	--	211	78	76	67	3	78	3	2	10	5	1	.83	10	.279	.364	.442
1992	Columbus	AAA	135	492	154	26	4	15	--	--	233	81	78	70	11	65	1	1	6	3	3	.50	9	.313	.395	.474
1992	New York	AL	7	14	2	1	0	0	(0	0)	3	1	2	5	1	5	0	0	0	0	0	.00	0	.143	.368	.214

Cory Snyder

Bats: Right **Throws: Right** **Pos: RF/1B/3B/LF/CF**   **Ht: 6' 3"** **Wt: 185** **Born: 11/11/62** **Age: 30**

			BATTING																	BASERUNNING				PERCENTAGES		
Year	Team	Lg	G	AB	H	2B	3B	HR	(Hm	Rd)	TB	R	RBI	TBB	IBB	SO	HBP	SH	SF	SB	CS	SB%	GDP	Avg	OBP	SLG
1986	Cleveland	AL	103	416	113	21	1	24	(12	12)	208	58	69	16	0	123	0	1	0	2	3	.40	8	.272	.299	.500
1987	Cleveland	AL	157	577	136	24	2	33	(17	16)	263	74	82	31	4	166	1	0	6	5	1	.83	3	.236	.273	.456
1988	Cleveland	AL	142	511	139	24	3	26	(11	15)	247	71	75	42	7	101	1	0	4	5	1	.83	12	.272	.326	.483
1989	Cleveland	AL	132	489	105	17	0	18	(6	12)	176	49	59	23	1	134	2	0	4	6	5	.55	11	.215	.251	.360
1990	Cleveland	AL	123	438	102	27	3	14	(3	11)	177	46	55	21	3	118	2	1	6	1	4	.20	11	.233	.268	.404
1991	2 ML Teams		71	166	29	4	1	3	(2	1)	44	14	17	9	1	60	0	4	1	0	0	.00	6	.175	.216	.265
1992	San Francisco	NL	124	390	105	22	2	14	(8	6)	173	48	57	23	2	96	2	2	3	4	4	.50	10	.269	.311	.444
1991	Chicago	AL	50	117	22	4	0	3	(2	1)	35	10	11	6	1	41	0	3	0	0	0	.00	5	.188	.228	.299
	Toronto	AL	21	49	7	0	1	0	(0	0)	9	4	6	3	0	19	0	1	1	0	0	.00	1	.143	.189	.184
	7 ML YEARS		852	2987	729	139	12	132	(59	73)	1288	360	414	165	18	798	8	8	24	23	18	.56	61	.244	.283	.431

Luis Sojo

Bats: Right **Throws: Right** **Pos: 2B**   **Ht: 5'11"** **Wt: 174** **Born: 01/03/66** **Age: 27**

			BATTING																	BASERUNNING				PERCENTAGES		
Year	Team	Lg	G	AB	H	2B	3B	HR	(Hm	Rd)	TB	R	RBI	TBB	IBB	SO	HBP	SH	SF	SB	CS	SB%	GDP	Avg	OBP	SLG
1990	Toronto	AL	33	80	18	3	0	1	(0	1)	24	14	9	5	0	5	0	0	0	1	1	.50	1	.225	.271	.300
1991	California	AL	113	364	94	14	1	3	(1	2)	119	38	20	14	0	26	5	19	0	4	2	.67	12	.258	.295	.327
1992	California	AL	106	368	100	12	3	7	(2	5)	139	37	43	14	0	24	1	7	1	7	11	.39	14	.272	.299	.378
	3 ML YEARS		252	812	212	29	4	11	(3	8)	282	89	72	33	0	55	6	26	2	12	14	.46	27	.261	.295	.347

Paul Sorrento

Bats: Left **Throws:** Right **Pos:** 1B/DH   **Ht:** 6' 2" **Wt:** 223 **Born:** 11/17/65 **Age:** 27

Year	Team	Lg	G	AB	H	2B	3B	HR	(Hm	Rd)	TB	R	RBI	TBB	IBB	SO	HBP	SH	SF	SB	CS	SB%	GDP	Avg	OBP	SLG
1989	Minnesota	AL	14	21	5	0	0	0	(0	0)	5	2	1	5	1	4	0	0	1	0	0	.00	0	.238	.370	.238
1990	Minnesota	AL	41	121	25	4	1	5	(2	3)	46	11	13	12	0	31	1	0	1	1	1	.50	3	.207	.281	.380
1991	Minnesota	AL	26	47	12	2	0	4	(2	2)	26	6	13	4	2	11	0	0	0	0	0	.00	3	.255	.314	.553
1992	Cleveland	AL	140	458	123	24	1	18	(11	7)	203	52	60	51	7	89	1	1	3	0	3	.00	13	.269	.341	.443
	4 ML YEARS		221	647	165	30	2	27	(15	12)	280	71	87	72	10	135	2	1	5	1	4	.20	19	.255	.329	.433

Sammy Sosa

Bats: Right **Throws:** Right **Pos:** CF   **Ht:** 6' 0" **Wt:** 175 **Born:** 11/12/68 **Age:** 24

Year	Team	Lg	G	AB	H	2B	3B	HR	(Hm	Rd)	TB	R	RBI	TBB	IBB	SO	HBP	SH	SF	SB	CS	SB%	GDP	Avg	OBP	SLG
1989	2 ML Teams		58	183	47	8	0	4	(1	3)	67	27	13	11	2	47	2	5	2	7	5	.58	6	.257	.303	.366
1990	Chicago	AL	153	532	124	26	10	15	(10	5)	215	72	70	33	4	150	6	2	6	32	16	.67	10	.233	.282	.404
1991	Chicago	AL	116	316	64	10	1	10	(3	7)	106	39	33	14	2	98	2	5	1	13	6	.68	5	.203	.240	.335
1992	Chicago	NL	67	262	68	7	2	8	(4	4)	103	41	25	19	1	63	4	4	2	15	7	.68	4	.260	.317	.393
1989	Texas	AL	25	84	20	3	0	1	(0	1)	26	8	3	0	0	20	0	4	0	0	2	.00	3	.238	.238	.310
	Chicago	AL	33	99	27	5	0	3	(1	2)	41	19	10	11	2	27	2	1	2	7	3	.70	3	.273	.351	.414
	4 ML YEARS		394	1293	303	51	13	37	(18	19)	491	179	141	77	9	358	14	16	11	67	34	.66	25	.234	.282	.380

Bill Spiers

Bats: Left **Throws:** Right **Pos:** SS   **Ht:** 6' 2" **Wt:** 190 **Born:** 06/05/66 **Age:** 27

Year	Team	Lg	G	AB	H	2B	3B	HR	(Hm	Rd)	TB	R	RBI	TBB	IBB	SO	HBP	SH	SF	SB	CS	SB%	GDP	Avg	OBP	SLG
1989	Milwaukee	AL	114	345	88	9	3	4	(1	3)	115	44	33	21	1	63	1	4	2	10	2	.83	2	.255	.298	.333
1990	Milwaukee	AL	112	363	88	15	3	2	(2	0)	115	44	36	16	0	45	1	6	3	11	6	.65	12	.242	.274	.317
1991	Milwaukee	AL	133	414	117	13	6	8	(1	7)	166	71	54	34	0	55	2	10	4	14	8	.64	9	.283	.337	.401
1992	Milwaukee	AL	12	16	5	2	0	0	(0	0)	7	2	2	1	0	4	0	1	0	1	1	.50	0	.313	.353	.438
	4 ML YEARS		371	1138	298	39	12	14	(4	10)	403	161	125	72	1	167	4	21	9	36	17	.68	23	.262	.306	.354

Ed Sprague

Bats: Right **Throws:** Right **Pos:** C   **Ht:** 6' 2" **Wt:** 215 **Born:** 07/25/67 **Age:** 25

Year	Team	Lg	G	AB	H	2B	3B	HR	(Hm	Rd)	TB	R	RBI	TBB	IBB	SO	HBP	SH	SF	SB	CS	SB%	GDP	Avg	OBP	SLG
1989	Dunedin	A	52	192	42	9	2	7	--	--	76	21	23	16	2	40	7	0	2	1	1	.50	1	.219	.300	.396
	Syracuse	AAA	86	288	60	14	1	5	--	--	91	28	23	18	2	73	5	1	3	0	0	.00	1	.208	.264	.316
1990	Syracuse	AAA	142	519	124	23	5	20	--	--	217	60	75	31	1	100	10	3	4	4	2	.67	9	.239	.293	.418
1991	Syracuse	AAA	23	88	32	8	0	5	--	--	55	24	25	10	0	21	2	0	2	2	0	1.00	1	.364	.431	.625
1992	Syracuse	AAA	100	369	102	18	2	16	--	--	172	49	50	44	3	73	4	0	2	0	2	.00	7	.276	.358	.466
1991	Toronto	AL	61	160	44	7	0	4	(3	1)	63	17	20	19	2	43	3	0	1	0	3	.00	0	.275	.361	.394
1992	Toronto	AL	22	47	11	2	0	1	(1	0)	16	6	7	3	0	7	0	0	0	0	0	.00	0	.234	.280	.340
	2 ML YEARS		83	207	55	9	0	5	(4	1)	79	23	27	22	2	50	3	0	1	0	3	.00	2	.266	.343	.382

Russ Springer

Pitches: Right **Bats:** Right **Pos:** RP   **Ht:** 6' 4" **Wt:** 195 **Born:** 11/07/68 **Age:** 24

Year	Team	Lg	G	GS	CG	GF	IP	BFP	H	R	ER	HR	SH	SF	HB	TBB	IBB	SO	WP	Bk	W	L	Pct.	ShO	Sv	ERA
1989	Yankees	R	6	6	0	0	24	95	14	8	4	0	0	0	1	10	0	34	1	0	3	0	1.000	0	0	1.50
1990	Yankees	R	4	4	0	0	15	62	10	6	2	0	0	0	0	4	0	17	1	1	0	2	.000	0	0	1.20
	Greensboro	A	10	10	0	0	56.1	249	51	33	22	3	0	1	1	31	0	51	3	1	2	3	.400	0	0	3.51
1991	Ft.Laurdrle	A	25	25	2	0	152.1	634	118	68	59	9	5	6	6	62	1	138	6	3	5	9	.357	0	0	3.49
	Albany	AA	2	2	0	0	15	60	9	4	3	0	0	0	0	6	1	16	0	0	1	0	1.000	0	0	1.80
1992	Columbus	AAA	20	20	1	0	123.2	499	89	46	37	11	1	3	5	54	0	95	4	0	8	5	.615	0	0	2.69
1992	New York	AL	14	0	0	5	16	75	18	11	11	0	0	0	1	10	0	12	0	0	0	0	.000	0	0	6.19

Steve Springer

Bats: Right **Throws:** Right **Pos:** 2B   **Ht:** 6' 0" **Wt:** 190 **Born:** 02/11/61 **Age:** 32

Year	Team	Lg	G	AB	H	2B	3B	HR	(Hm	Rd)	TB	R	RBI	TBB	IBB	SO	HBP	SH	SF	SB	CS	SB%	GDP	Avg	OBP	SLG
1984	Jackson	AA	103	362	99	21	3	5	--	--	141	41	40	24	3	50	2	0	0	6	4	.60	16	.273	.322	.390
1985	Tidewater	AAA	126	479	125	20	4	7	--	--	174	59	56	34	2	72	1	6	5	9	5	.64	16	.261	.308	.363
1986	Tidewater	AAA	117	440	120	19	6	4	--	--	163	52	46	30	0	74	1	5	0	10	5	.67	16	.273	.321	.370
1987	Tidewater	AAA	132	467	131	23	4	7	--	--	183	65	54	41	6	78	3	4	5	6	3	.67	10	.281	.339	.392
1988	Tidewater	AAA	97	337	88	15	0	2	--	--	109	42	25	29	0	66	0	2	1	4	0	1.00	7	.261	.319	.323
	Vancouver	AAA	27	105	28	4	1	2	--	--	40	15	9	4	1	17	0	2	0	1	2	.33	4	.267	.294	.381

Year	Team	Lg	G	AB	H	2B	3B	HR	(Hm	Rd)	TB	R	RBI	TBB	IBB	SO	HBP	SH	SF	SB	CS	SB%	GDP	Avg	OBP	SLG
1989	Vancouver	AAA	137	520	144	21	3	8	--	--	195	61	56	26	1	83	3	7	5	8	8	.50	11	.277	.312	.375
1990	Colo Sprngs	AAA	73	252	70	21	5	6	--	--	119	39	42	17	1	48	0	0	8	6	3	.67	6	.278	.314	.472
	Las Vegas	AAA	22	72	18	5	0	2	--	--	29	7	10	7	0	19	0	1	2	0	1	.00	2	.250	.309	.403
1991	Calgary	AAA	109	412	106	25	2	17	--	--	186	62	70	28	5	76	0	3	2	8	2	.80	14	.257	.303	.451
1992	Tidewater	AAA	117	427	124	16	0	16	--	--	188	57	70	22	1	84	0	0	3	9	4	.69	12	.290	.323	.440
1990	Cleveland	AL	4	12	2	0	0	0	(0	0)	2	1	1	0	0	6	0	0	1	0	0	.00	0	.167	.154	.167
1992	2 ML Teams		4	5	2	1	0	0	(0	0)	3	0	0	0	0	1	0	0	0	0	0	.00	0	.400	.400	.600
1992	Texas	AL	0	0	0	0	0	0	(0	0)	0	0	0	0	0	0	0	0	0	0	0	.00	0	.000	.000	.000
	New York	NL	4	5	2	1	0	0	(0	0)	3	0	0	0	0	1	0	0	0	0	0	.00	0	.400	.400	.600
	2 ML YEARS		8	17	4	1	0	0	(0	0)	5	1	1	0	0	7	0	0	1	0	0	.00	0	.235	.222	.294

Randy St. Claire

Pitches: Right **Bats:** Right **Pos:** RP   **Ht:** 6' 2" **Wt:** 190 **Born:** 08/23/60 **Age:** 32

			HOW MUCH HE PITCHED					WHAT HE GAVE UP										THE RESULTS						
Year	Team	Lg	G	GS	CG	GF	IP	BFP	H	R	ER	HR	SH	SF	HB	TBB	IBB	SO	WP	Bk	W	L	Pct.	ShO	Sv	ERA
1984	Montreal	NL	4	0	0	4	8	38	11	4	4	0	1	2	1	2	1	4	0	0	0	0	.000	0	0	4.50
1985	Montreal	NL	42	0	0	14	68.2	294	69	32	30	3	6	1	1	26	7	25	1	0	5	3	.625	0	0	3.93
1986	Montreal	NL	11	0	0	2	19	76	13	5	5	2	0	0	0	6	1	21	1	0	2	0	1.000	0	1	2.37
1987	Montreal	NL	44	0	0	24	67	282	64	31	30	9	1	3	1	20	4	43	4	0	3	3	.500	0	7	4.03
1988	2 ML Teams		16	0	0	9	21	98	24	13	9	5	0	2	0	10	3	14	0	1	1	0	1.000	0	0	3.86
1989	Minnesota	AL	14	0	0	8	22.1	98	19	13	13	4	1	1	2	10	2	14	1	0	1	0	1.000	0	1	5.24
1991	Atlanta	NL	19	0	0	5	28.2	123	31	17	13	4	3	1	0	9	3	30	4	0	0	0	.000	0	0	4.08
1992	Atlanta	NL	10	0	0	1	15.1	68	17	11	10	1	0	0	0	8	3	7	0	0	0	0	.000	0	0	5.87
1988	Montreal	NL	6	0	0	3	7.1	38	11	5	5	2	0	1	0	5	1	6	0	1	0	0	.000	0	0	6.14
	Cincinnati	NL	10	0	0	6	13.2	60	13	8	4	3	0	1	0	5	2	8	0	0	1	0	1.000	0	0	2.63
	8 ML YEARS		160	0	0	67	250	1077	248	126	114	28	12	10	5	91	24	158	11	1	12	6	.667	0	9	4.10

Matt Stairs

Bats: Left **Throws:** Right **Pos:** LF   **Ht:** 5' 9" **Wt:** 175 **Born:** 02/27/69 **Age:** 24

			BATTING																BASERUNNING				PERCENTAGES		
Year	Team	Lg	G	AB	H	2B	3B	HR	(Hm	Rd)	TB	R	RBI	TBB	IBB	SO	HBP	SH	SF	SB	CS	SB%	GDP	Avg	OBP	SLG
1989	Jamestown	A	14	43	11	1	0	1	--	--	15	8	5	3	0	5	0	0	0	1	2	.33	0	.256	.304	.349
	Wst Plm Bch	A	36	111	21	3	1	1	--	--	29	12	9	9	0	18	0	1	1	0	0	.00	3	.189	.248	.261
	Rockford	A	44	141	40	9	2	2	--	--	59	20	14	15	3	29	2	2	1	5	4	.56	4	.284	.358	.418
1990	Wst Plm Bch	A	55	184	62	9	3	3	--	--	86	30	30	40	4	19	5	0	2	15	2	.88	5	.337	.463	.467
	Jacksnville	AA	79	280	71	17	0	3	--	--	97	26	34	22	1	42	3	0	5	5	3	.63	6	.254	.310	.346
1991	Harrisburg	AA	129	505	168	30	10	13	--	--	257	87	78	66	8	47	3	2	3	23	11	.68	14	.333	.411	.509
1992	Indianapols	AAA	110	401	107	23	4	11	--	--	171	57	56	49	3	61	4	4	2	11	11	.50	10	.267	.351	.426
1992	Montreal	NL	13	30	5	2	0	0	(0	0)	7	2	5	7	0	7	0	0	0	0	0	.00	0	.167	.316	.233

Andy Stankiewicz

Bats: Right **Throws:** Right **Pos:** SS/2B   **Ht:** 5' 9" **Wt:** 165 **Born:** 08/10/64 **Age:** 28

			BATTING																BASERUNNING				PERCENTAGES		
Year	Team	Lg	G	AB	H	2B	3B	HR	(Hm	Rd)	TB	R	RBI	TBB	IBB	SO	HBP	SH	SF	SB	CS	SB%	GDP	Avg	OBP	SLG
1986	Oneonta	A	59	216	64	8	3	0	--	--	78	51	17	38	0	41	5	4	4	14	3	.82	2	.296	.407	.361
1987	Ft.Laudrdle	A	119	456	140	18	7	2	--	--	178	80	47	62	1	84	4	7	1	26	13	.67	9	.307	.394	.390
1988	Albany	AA	109	414	111	20	2	1	--	--	138	63	33	39	0	53	9	9	2	15	10	.60	6	.268	.343	.333
	Columbus	AAA	29	114	25	0	0	0	--	--	25	4	4	6	0	25	0	1	0	2	0	1.00	4	.219	.258	.219
1989	Albany	AA	133	498	133	26	2	4	--	--	175	74	49	57	2	59	8	3	11	41	9	.82	8	.267	.345	.351
1990	Columbus	AAA	135	446	102	14	4	1	--	--	127	68	48	71	1	63	10	7	4	25	8	.76	11	.229	.345	.285
1991	Columbus	AAA	125	372	101	12	4	1	--	--	124	47	41	29	0	45	8	8	5	29	16	.64	9	.272	.333	.333
1992	New York	AL	116	400	107	22	2	2	(2	0)	139	52	25	38	0	42	5	7	1	9	5	.64	13	.268	.338	.348

Mike Stanley

Bats: Right **Throws:** Right **Pos:** C   **Ht:** 6' 0" **Wt:** 190 **Born:** 06/25/63 **Age:** 30

			BATTING																BASERUNNING				PERCENTAGES		
Year	Team	Lg	G	AB	H	2B	3B	HR	(Hm	Rd)	TB	R	RBI	TBB	IBB	SO	HBP	SH	SF	SB	CS	SB%	GDP	Avg	OBP	SLG
1986	Texas	AL	15	30	10	3	0	1	(0	1)	16	4	1	3	0	7	0	0	0	1	0	1.00	0	.333	.394	.533
1987	Texas	AL	78	216	59	8	1	6	(3	3)	87	34	37	31	0	48	1	1	4	3	0	1.00	6	.273	.361	.403
1988	Texas	AL	94	249	57	8	0	3	(1	2)	74	21	27	37	0	62	0	1	5	0	0	.00	6	.229	.323	.297
1989	Texas	AL	67	122	30	3	1	1	(1	0)	38	9	11	12	1	29	2	1	0	1	0	1.00	6	.246	.324	.311
1990	Texas	AL	103	189	47	8	1	2	(1	1)	63	21	19	30	2	25	0	6	1	1	0	1.00	4	.249	.350	.333
1991	Texas	AL	95	181	45	13	1	3	(1	2)	69	25	25	34	0	44	2	5	1	0	0	.00	2	.249	.372	.381
1992	New York	AL	68	173	43	7	0	8	(5	3)	74	24	27	33	0	45	1	0	0	0	0	.00	6	.249	.372	.428
	7 ML YEARS		520	1160	291	50	4	24	(12	12)	421	138	147	180	3	260	6	14	11	6	0	1.00	29	.251	.352	.363

Mike Stanton

Pitches: Left **Bats:** Left **Pos:** RP

Ht: 6' 1" **Wt:** 190 **Born:** 06/02/67 **Age:** 26

			HOW MUCH HE PITCHED						WHAT HE GAVE UP											THE RESULTS					
Year	Team	Lg	G	GS	CG	GF	IP	BFP	H	R	ER	HR	SH	SF	HB	TBB	IBB	SO	WP	Bk	W	L	Pct.	ShO	Sv	ERA
1989	Atlanta	NL	20	0	0	10	24	94	17	4	4	0	4	0	0	8	1	27	1	0	0	1	.000	0	7	1.50
1990	Atlanta	NL	7	0	0	4	7	42	16	16	14	1	1	0	1	4	2	7	1	0	0	3	.000	0	2	18.00
1991	Atlanta	NL	74	0	0	20	78	314	62	27	25	6	6	0	1	21	6	54	0	0	5	5	.500	0	7	2.88
1992	Atlanta	NL	65	0	0	23	63.2	264	59	32	29	6	1	2	2	20	2	44	3	0	5	4	.556	0	8	4.10
	4 ML YEARS		166	0	0	57	172.2	714	154	79	72	13	12	2	4	53	11	132	5	0	10	13	.435	0	24	3.75

Terry Steinbach

Bats: Right **Throws:** Right **Pos:** C

Ht: 6' 1" **Wt:** 195 **Born:** 03/02/62 **Age:** 31

								BATTING												BASERUNNING				PERCENTAGES		
Year	Team	Lg	G	AB	H	2B	3B	HR	(Hm	Rd)	TB	R	RBI	TBB	IBB	SO	HBP	SH	SF	SB	CS	SB%	GDP	Avg	OBP	SLG
1986	Oakland	AL	6	15	5	0	0	2	(0	2)	11	3	4	1	0	0	0	0	0	0	0	.00	0	.333	.375	.733
1987	Oakland	AL	122	391	111	16	3	16	(6	10)	181	66	56	32	2	66	9	3	3	1	2	.33	10	.284	.349	.463
1988	Oakland	AL	104	351	93	19	1	9	(6	3)	141	42	51	33	2	47	6	3	5	3	0	1.00	13	.265	.334	.402
1989	Oakland	AL	130	454	124	13	1	7	(5	2)	160	37	42	30	2	66	2	2	3	1	2	.33	14	.273	.319	.352
1990	Oakland	AL	114	379	95	15	2	9	(3	6)	141	32	57	19	1	66	4	5	3	0	1	.00	11	.251	.291	.372
1991	Oakland	AL	129	456	125	31	1	6	(1	5)	176	50	67	22	4	70	7	0	9	2	2	.50	15	.274	.312	.386
1992	Oakland	AL	128	438	122	20	1	12	(3	9)	180	48	53	45	3	58	1	0	3	2	3	.40	20	.279	.345	.411
	7 ML YEARS		733	2484	675	114	9	61	(24	37)	990	278	330	182	14	373	29	13	26	9	10	.47	83	.272	.326	.399

Ray Stephens

Bats: Right **Throws:** Right **Pos:** C

Ht: 6' 0" **Wt:** 190 **Born:** 09/22/62 **Age:** 30

								BATTING												BASERUNNING				PERCENTAGES		
Year	Team	Lg	G	AB	H	2B	3B	HR	(Hm	Rd)	TB	R	RBI	TBB	IBB	SO	HBP	SH	SF	SB	CS	SB%	GDP	Avg	OBP	SLG
1985	Erie	A	9	31	9	1	1	1	--	--	15	3	5	7	0	6	0	0	0	0	0	.00	1	.290	.421	.484
	Savannah	A	39	127	26	6	0	0	--	--	32	11	6	14	0	32	1	1	1	1	1	.50	3	.205	.287	.252
1986	Savannah	A	95	325	71	10	0	13	--	--	120	52	56	57	1	76	3	1	2	2	4	.33	6	.218	.339	.369
	Louisville	AAA	12	31	6	1	0	1	--	--	10	2	2	1	0	13	1	0	1	0	0	.00	0	.194	.235	.323
1987	Arkansas	AA	100	307	77	20	0	8	--	--	121	35	42	37	4	68	3	2	2	6	2	.75	10	.251	.335	.394
	Louisville	AAA	9	30	4	0	0	0	--	--	4	1	2	5	1	9	0	0	1	0	1	.00	3	.133	.250	.133
1988	Louisville	AAA	115	355	67	13	2	3	--	--	93	26	25	45	3	78	1	0	3	2	0	1.00	3	.189	.280	.262
1989	Arkansas	AA	112	363	95	14	0	7	--	--	130	49	44	44	2	61	4	4	3	2	1	.67	11	.262	.345	.358
1990	Louisville	AAA	98	294	65	8	1	3	--	--	84	20	27	27	3	74	4	9	1	0	1	.00	12	.221	.294	.286
1991	Louisville	AAA	60	165	46	7	0	7	--	--	74	16	28	24	1	39	4	2	0	0	3	.00	4	.279	.383	.448
1992	Scranton/wb	AAA	17	44	9	1	0	1	--	--	13	4	2	3	0	10	0	2	0	0	0	.00	0	.205	.255	.295
	Okla City	AAA	54	191	58	8	0	6	--	--	84	22	32	15	1	39	0	0	3	2	0	1.00	10	.304	.351	.440
1990	St. Louis	NL	5	15	2	1	0	1	(1	0)	6	2	1	0	0	3	0	0	0	0	0	.00	2	.133	.133	.400
1991	St. Louis	NL	6	7	2	0	0	0	(0	0)	2	0	0	1	0	3	0	0	0	0	0	.00	0	.286	.375	.286
1992	Texas	AL	8	13	2	0	0	0	(0	0)	2	0	0	0	0	5	0	1	0	0	0	.00	0	.154	.154	.154
	3 ML YEARS		19	35	6	1	0	1	(1	0)	10	2	1	1	0	11	0	1	0	0	0	.00	2	.171	.194	.286

Phil Stephenson

Bats: Left **Throws:** Left **Pos:** LF

Ht: 6' 1" **Wt:** 200 **Born:** 09/19/60 **Age:** 32

								BATTING												BASERUNNING				PERCENTAGES		
Year	Team	Lg	G	AB	H	2B	3B	HR	(Hm	Rd)	TB	R	RBI	TBB	IBB	SO	HBP	SH	SF	SB	CS	SB%	GDP	Avg	OBP	SLG
1989	2 ML Teams		27	38	9	0	0	2	(2	0)	15	4	2	5	0	5	0	2	0	1	0	1.00	0	.237	.326	.395
1990	San Diego	NL	103	182	38	9	1	4	(2	2)	61	26	19	30	1	43	0	0	1	2	1	.67	3	.209	.319	.335
1991	San Diego	NL	11	7	2	0	0	0	(0	0)	2	0	0	2	0	3	0	0	0	0	0	.00	0	.286	.444	.286
1992	San Diego	NL	53	71	11	2	1	0	(0	0)	15	5	8	10	0	11	0	3	0	0	0	.00	0	.155	.259	.211
1989	Chicago	NL	17	21	3	0	0	0	(0	0)	3	0	0	2	0	3	0	0	0	0	1	1.00	0	.143	.217	.143
	San Diego	NL	10	17	6	0	0	2	(2	0)	12	4	2	3	0	2	0	2	0	0	0	.00	0	.353	.450	.706
	4 ML YEARS		194	298	60	11	2	6	(4	2)	93	35	29	47	1	62	0	5	1	3	1	.75	3	.201	.309	.312

Lee Stevens

Bats: Left **Throws:** Left **Pos:** 1B

Ht: 6' 4" **Wt:** 219 **Born:** 07/10/67 **Age:** 25

								BATTING												BASERUNNING				PERCENTAGES		
Year	Team	Lg	G	AB	H	2B	3B	HR	(Hm	Rd)	TB	R	RBI	TBB	IBB	SO	HBP	SH	SF	SB	CS	SB%	GDP	Avg	OBP	SLG
1990	California	AL	67	248	53	10	0	7	(4	3)	84	28	32	22	3	75	0	2	3	1	1	.50	8	.214	.275	.339
1991	California	AL	18	58	17	7	0	0	(0	0)	24	8	9	6	2	12	0	1	1	0	2	.33	0	.293	.354	.414
1992	California	AL	106	312	69	19	0	7	(2	5)	109	25	37	29	6	64	1	1	2	1	4	.20	4	.221	.288	.349
	3 ML YEARS		191	618	139	36	0	14	(6	8)	217	61	78	57	11	151	1	4	6	3	7	.30	12	.225	.289	.351

Dave Stewart

Pitches: Right Bats: Right Pos: SP Ht: 6' 2" Wt: 200 Born: 02/19/57 Age: 36

Year	Team	Lg	G	GS	CG	GF	IP	BFP	H	R	ER	HR	SH	SF	HB	TBB	IBB	SO	WP	Bk	W	L	Pct.	ShO	Sv	ERA
1978	Los Angeles	NL	1	0	0	1	2	6	1	0	0	0	0	0	0	0	0	1	0	0	0	0	.000	0	0	0.00
1981	Los Angeles	NL	32	0	0	14	43	184	40	13	12	3	7	3	0	14	5	29	4	0	4	3	.571	0	6	2.51
1982	Los Angeles	NL	45	14	0	9	146.1	616	137	72	62	14	10	5	2	49	11	80	3	0	9	8	.529	0	1	3.81
1983	2 ML Teams		54	9	2	25	135	565	117	43	39	6	9	4	4	50	7	78	3	0	10	4	.714	0	8	2.60
1984	Texas	AL	32	27	3	2	192.1	847	193	106	101	26	4	5	4	87	3	119	12	0	7	14	.333	0	0	4.73
1985	2 ML Teams		46	5	0	32	85.2	383	91	57	52	13	5	2	2	41	5	66	7	1	0	6	.000	0	4	5.46
1986	2 ML Teams		37	17	4	4	161.2	700	152	76	71	16	4	7	3	69	0	111	10	3	9	5	.643	1	0	3.95
1987	Oakland	AL	37	37	8	0	261.1	1103	224	121	107	24	7	5	6	105	2	205	11	0	20	13	.606	1	0	3.68
1988	Oakland	AL	37	37	14	0	275.2	1156	240	111	99	14	7	9	3	110	5	192	14	16	21	12	.636	2	0	3.23
1989	Oakland	AL	36	36	8	0	257.2	1081	260	105	95	23	9	10	6	69	0	155	13	0	21	9	.700	0	0	3.32
1990	Oakland	AL	36	36	11	0	267	1088	226	84	76	16	10	10	5	83	1	166	8	0	22	11	.667	4	0	2.56
1991	Oakland	AL	35	35	2	0	226	1014	245	135	130	24	5	15	9	105	1	144	12	0	11	11	.500	1	0	5.18
1992	Oakland		31	31	2	0	199.1	838	175	96	81	25	5	8	8	79	1	130	3	1	12	10	.545	0	0	3.66
1983	Los Angeles	NL	46	1	0	25	76	328	67	28	25	4	7	3	2	33	7	54	2	0	5	2	.714	0	8	2.96
	Texas	AL	8	8	2	0	59	237	50	15	14	2	2	1	2	17	0	24	1	0	5	2	.714	0	0	2.14
1985	Texas	AL	42	5	0	29	81.1	361	86	53	49	13	5	2	2	37	5	64	5	1	0	6	.000	0	4	5.42
	Philadelphia	NL	4	0	0	3	4.1	22	5	4	3	0	0	0	0	4	0	2	2	0	0	0	.000	0	0	6.23
1986	Philadelphia	NL	8	0	0	2	12.1	56	15	9	9	1	0	3	0	4	0	9	1	3	0	0	.000	0	0	6.57
	Oakland	AL	29	17	4	2	149.1	644	137	67	62	15	4	4	3	65	0	102	9	0	9	5	.643	1	0	3.74
	13 ML YEARS		459	284	54	87	2253	9581	2101	1019	925	204	82	83	52	861	41	1476	100	21	146	106	.579	9	19	3.70

Dave Stieb

Pitches: Right Bats: Right Pos: SP/RP Ht: 6' 1" Wt: 195 Born: 07/22/57 Age: 35

Year	Team	Lg	G	GS	CG	GF	IP	BFP	H	R	ER	HR	SH	SF	HB	TBB	IBB	SO	WP	Bk	W	L	Pct.	ShO	Sv	ERA
1979	Toronto	AL	18	18	7	0	129	563	139	70	62	11	4	4	4	48	3	52	3	1	8	8	.500	1	0	4.33
1980	Toronto	AL	34	32	14	0	243	1004	232	108	100	12	12	9	6	83	6	108	6	2	12	15	.444	4	0	3.70
1981	Toronto	AL	25	25	11	0	184	748	148	70	65	10	5	7	11	61	2	89	1	2	11	10	.524	2	0	3.18
1982	Toronto	AL	38	38	19	0	288.1	1187	271	116	104	27	10	3	5	75	4	141	3	1	17	14	.548	5	0	3.25
1983	Toronto	AL	36	36	14	0	278	1141	223	105	94	21	6	9	14	93	6	187	5	1	17	12	.586	4	0	3.04
1984	Toronto	AL	35	35	11	0	267	1085	215	87	84	19	8	6	11	88	1	198	2	0	16	8	.667	2	0	2.83
1985	Toronto	AL	36	36	8	0	265	1087	206	89	73	22	14	2	9	96	3	167	4	1	14	13	.519	2	0	2.48
1986	Toronto	AL	37	34	1	2	205	919	239	128	108	29	6	6	15	87	1	127	7	0	7	12	.368	1	4	4.74
1987	Toronto	AL	33	31	3	1	185	789	164	92	84	16	5	5	7	87	4	115	4	0	13	9	.591	1	0	4.09
1988	Toronto	AL	32	31	8	1	207.1	844	157	76	70	11	4	4	13	79	0	147	4	5	16	8	.667	4	0	3.04
1989	Toronto	AL	33	33	3	0	206.2	850	164	83	77	12	10	3	13	76	2	101	3	1	17	8	.680	2	0	3.35
1990	Toronto	AL	33	33	2	0	208.2	861	179	73	68	16	6	3	10	64	0	125	5	0	18	6	.750	2	0	2.93
1991	Toronto	AL	9	9	1	0	59.2	244	52	22	21	4	4	1	2	23	0	29	0	0	4	3	.571	0	0	3.17
1992	Toronto	AL	21	14	1	3	96.1	415	98	58	54	9	6	5	4	43	3	45	4	0	4	6	.400	0	1	5.04
	14 ML YEARS		420	405	103	7	2823	11737	2487	1177	1064	218	96	67	124	1003	35	1631	51	14	174	132	.569	30	1	3.39

Kurt Stillwell

Bats: Both Throws: Right Pos: 2B Ht: 5'11" Wt: 185 Born: 06/04/65 Age: 28

Year	Team	Lg	G	AB	H	2B	3B	HR	(Hm	Rd)	TB	R	RBI	TBB	IBB	SO	HBP	SH	SF	SB	CS	SB%	GDP	Avg	OBP	SLG
1986	Cincinnati	NL	104	279	64	6	1	0	(0	0)	72	31	26	30	1	47	2	4	0	6	2	.75	5	.229	.309	.258
1987	Cincinnati	NL	131	395	102	20	7	4	(3	1)	148	54	33	32	2	50	2	2	2	4	6	.40	5	.258	.316	.375
1988	Kansas City	AL	128	459	115	28	5	10	(4	6)	183	63	53	47	0	76	3	6	3	6	5	.55	7	.251	.322	.399
1989	Kansas City	AL	130	463	121	20	7	7	(2	5)	176	52	54	42	2	64	3	5	3	9	6	.60	3	.261	.325	.380
1990	Kansas City	AL	144	506	126	35	4	3	(3	0)	178	60	51	39	1	60	4	4	7	0	2	.00	11	.249	.304	.352
1991	Kansas City	AL	122	385	102	17	1	6	(1	5)	139	44	51	33	5	56	1	5	4	3	4	.43	8	.265	.322	.361
1992	San Diego	NL	114	379	86	15	3	2	(1	1)	113	35	24	26	9	58	1	4	6	4	1	.80	6	.227	.274	.298
	7 ML YEARS		873	2866	716	141	28	32	(14	18)	1009	339	292	249	20	411	16	30	25	32	26	.55	45	.250	.311	.352

Todd Stottlemyre

Pitches: Right Bats: Left Pos: SP Ht: 6' 3" Wt: 195 Born: 05/20/65 Age: 28

Year	Team	Lg	G	GS	CG	GF	IP	BFP	H	R	ER	HR	SH	SF	HB	TBB	IBB	SO	WP	Bk	W	L	Pct.	ShO	Sv	ERA
1988	Toronto	AL	28	16	0	2	98	443	109	70	62	15	5	3	4	46	5	67	2	3	4	8	.333	0	0	5.69
1989	Toronto	AL	27	18	0	4	127.2	545	137	56	55	11	3	7	5	44	4	63	4	1	7	7	.500	0	0	3.88
1990	Toronto	AL	33	33	4	0	203	866	214	101	98	18	3	5	8	69	4	115	6	1	13	17	.433	0	0	4.34
1991	Toronto	AL	34	34	1	0	219	921	194	97	92	21	0	8	12	75	3	116	4	0	15	8	.652	0	0	3.78
1992	Toronto	AL	28	27	6	0	174	755	175	99	87	20	2	11	10	63	4	98	7	0	12	11	.522	2	0	4.50

| 5 ML YEARS | | 150 | 128 | 11 | 6 | 821.2 | 3530 | 829 | 423 | 394 | 85 | 13 | 34 | 39 | 297 | 20 | 459 | 23 | 5 | 51 | 51 | .500 | 2 | 0 | 4.32 |

Doug Strange

Bats: Both   **Throws:** Right   **Pos:** 3B/2B   **Ht:** 6' 2"   **Wt:** 170   **Born:** 04/13/64   **Age:** 29

								BATTING											BASERUNNING				PERCENTAGES		
Year	Team	Lg	G	AB	H	2B	3B	HR	(Hm | Rd)	TB	R	RBI	TBB	IBB	SO	HBP	SH	SF	SB	CS	SB%	GDP	Avg	OBP	SLG
1989	Detroit	AL	64	196	42	4	1	1	(1 | 0)	51	16	14	17	0	36	1	3	0	3	3	.50	6	.214	.280	.260
1991	Chicago	NL	3	9	4	1	0	0	(0 | 0)	5	0	1	0	0	1	1	0	1	1	0	1.00	0	.444	.455	.556
1992	Chicago	NL	52	94	15	1	0	1	(0 | 1)	19	7	5	10	2	15	0	2	0	1	0	1.00	2	.160	.240	.202
	3 ML YEARS		119	299	61	6	1	2	(1 | 1)	75	23	20	27	2	52	2	5	1	5	3	.63	8	.204	.274	.251

Darryl Strawberry

Bats: Left   **Throws:** Left   **Pos:** RF   **Ht:** 6' 6"   **Wt:** 200   **Born:** 03/12/62   **Age:** 31

								BATTING											BASERUNNING				PERCENTAGES		
Year	Team	Lg	G	AB	H	2B	3B	HR	(Hm | Rd)	TB	R	RBI	TBB	IBB	SO	HBP	SH	SF	SB	CS	SB%	GDP	Avg	OBP	SLG
1983	New York	NL	122	420	108	15	7	26	(10 | 16)	215	63	74	47	9	128	4	0	2	19	6	.76	5	.257	.336	.512
1984	New York	NL	147	522	131	27	4	26	(8 | 18)	244	75	97	75	15	131	0	1	4	27	8	.77	8	.251	.343	.467
1985	New York	NL	111	393	109	15	4	29	(14 | 15)	219	78	79	73	13	96	1	0	3	26	11	.70	9	.277	.389	.557
1986	New York	NL	136	475	123	27	5	27	(11 | 16)	241	76	93	72	9	141	6	0	9	28	12	.70	4	.259	.358	.507
1987	New York	NL	154	532	151	32	5	39	(20 | 19)	310	108	104	97	13	122	7	0	4	36	12	.75	4	.284	.398	.583
1988	New York	NL	153	543	146	27	3	39	(21 | 18)	296	101	101	85	21	127	3	0	9	29	14	.67	6	.269	.366	**.545**
1989	New York	NL	134	476	107	26	1	29	(15 | 14)	222	69	77	61	13	105	1	0	3	11	4	.73	4	.225	.312	.466
1990	New York	NL	152	542	150	18	1	37	(24 | 13)	281	92	108	70	15	110	4	0	5	15	8	.65	5	.277	.361	.518
1991	Los Angeles	NL	139	505	134	22	4	28	(14 | 14)	248	86	99	75	4	125	3	0	5	10	8	.56	8	.265	.361	.491
1992	Los Angeles	NL	43	156	37	8	0	5	(3 | 2)	60	20	25	19	4	34	1	0	1	3	1	.75	2	.237	.322	.385
	10 ML YEARS		1291	4564	1196	217	34	285	(140 | 145)	2336	768	857	674	116	1119	30	1	45	204	84	.71	55	.262	.358	.512

Franklin Stubbs

Bats: Left   **Throws:** Left   **Pos:** 1B/DH   **Ht:** 6' 2"   **Wt:** 208   **Born:** 10/21/60   **Age:** 32

								BATTING											BASERUNNING				PERCENTAGES		
Year	Team	Lg	G	AB	H	2B	3B	HR	(Hm | Rd)	TB	R	RBI	TBB	IBB	SO	HBP	SH	SF	SB	CS	SB%	GDP	Avg	OBP	SLG
1984	Los Angeles	NL	87	217	42	2	3	8	(4 | 4)	74	22	17	24	3	63	0	3	1	2	2	.50	0	.194	.273	.341
1985	Los Angeles	NL	10	9	2	0	0	0	(0 | 0)	2	0	2	0	0	3	0	0	0	0	0	.00	0	.222	.222	.222
1986	Los Angeles	NL	132	420	95	11	1	23	(12 | 11)	177	55	58	37	11	107	2	4	2	7	1	.88	9	.226	.291	.421
1987	Los Angeles	NL	129	386	90	16	3	16	(6 | 10)	160	48	52	31	9	85	1	3	2	8	1	.89	7	.233	.290	.415
1988	Los Angeles	NL	115	242	54	13	0	8	(3 | 5)	91	30	34	23	3	61	1	2	5	11	3	.79	4	.223	.288	.376
1989	Los Angeles	NL	69	103	30	6	0	4	(1 | 3)	48	11	15	16	2	27	0	1	0	3	2	.60	3	.291	.387	.466
1990	Houston	NL	146	448	117	23	2	23	(9 | 14)	213	59	71	48	3	114	2	1	2	19	6	.76	4	.261	.334	.475
1991	Milwaukee	AL	103	362	77	16	2	11	(8 | 3)	130	42	38	35	3	71	2	0	5	13	4	.76	4	.213	.282	.359
1992	Milwaukee	AL	92	288	66	11	1	9	(3 | 6)	106	37	42	27	3	68	1	5	1	11	8	.58	2	.229	.297	.368
	9 ML YEARS		883	2475	573	98	12	102	(46 | 56)	1001	310	329	241	37	599	9	19	18	74	27	.73	33	.232	.300	.404

William Suero

Bats: Right   **Throws:** Right   **Pos:** 2B   **Ht:** 5' 9"   **Wt:** 175   **Born:** 11/07/66   **Age:** 26

								BATTING											BASERUNNING				PERCENTAGES		
Year	Team	Lg	G	AB	H	2B	3B	HR	(Hm | Rd)	TB	R	RBI	TBB	IBB	SO	HBP	SH	SF	SB	CS	SB%	GDP	Avg	OBP	SLG
1986	Medicne Hat	R	64	273	76	7	5	2	--	--	99	39	28	15	0	36	3	4	2	13	4	.76	7	.278	.321	.363
1987	St.Cathmes	A	77	297	94	12	4	4	--	--	126	43	24	35	1	35	1	2	1	23	11	.68	3	.316	.389	.424
1988	Myrtle Bch	A	125	493	140	21	6	6	--	--	191	88	52	49	2	72	4	3	6	21	7	.75	4	.284	.350	.387
1989	Dunedin	A	51	206	60	10	5	2	--	--	86	35	17	16	0	32	3	1	0	9	3	.75	3	.291	.351	.417
	Knoxville	AA	87	324	84	17	5	4	--	--	123	42	29	34	0	50	3	2	0	7	4	.64	2	.259	.335	.380
1990	Knoxville	AA	133	483	127	29	7	16	--	--	218	80	60	78	3	78	7	6	2	40	21	.66	5	.263	.372	.451
1991	Syracuse	AAA	98	393	78	18	1	1	--	--	101	49	28	38	0	51	7	4	3	17	13	.57	9	.198	.279	.257
	Denver	AAA	20	70	27	3	2	0	--	--	34	20	15	10	0	8	0	2	1	3	0	1.00	3	.386	.457	.486
1992	Denver	AAA	75	276	71	10	9	1	--	--	102	42	25	31	1	33	1	3	2	16	9	.64	5	.257	.332	.370
1992	Milwaukee	AL	18	16	3	1	0	0	(0 | 0)	4	4	0	2	0	1	1	0	0	1	1	.50	2	.188	.316	.250

B.J. Surhoff

Bats: Left   **Throws:** Right   **Pos:** C/1B   **Ht:** 6' 1"   **Wt:** 200   **Born:** 08/04/64   **Age:** 28

								BATTING											BASERUNNING				PERCENTAGES		
Year	Team	Lg	G	AB	H	2B	3B	HR	(Hm | Rd)	TB	R	RBI	TBB	IBB	SO	HBP	SH	SF	SB	CS	SB%	GDP	Avg	OBP	SLG
1987	Milwaukee	AL	115	395	118	22	3	7	(5 | 2)	167	50	68	36	1	30	0	5	9	11	10	.52	13	.299	.350	.423
1988	Milwaukee	AL	139	493	121	21	0	5	(2 | 3)	157	47	38	31	9	49	3	11	3	21	6	.78	12	.245	.292	.318
1989	Milwaukee	AL	126	436	108	17	4	5	(3 | 2)	148	42	55	25	1	29	3	3	10	14	12	.54	8	.248	.287	.339
1990	Milwaukee	AL	135	474	131	21	4	6	(4 | 2)	178	55	59	41	5	37	1	7	7	18	7	.72	8	.276	.331	.376
1991	Milwaukee	AL	143	505	146	19	4	5	(3 | 2)	188	57	68	26	2	33	0	13	9	5	8	.38	21	.289	.319	.372

Year Team	Lg	G	AB	H	2B	3B	HR	(Hm	Rd)	TB	R	RBI	TBB	IBB	SO	HBP	SH	SF	SB	CS	SB%	GDP	Avg	OBP	SLG
1992 Milwaukee	AL	139	480	121	19	1	4	(3	1)	154	63	62	46	8	41	2	5	10	14	8	64	9	.252	.314	.321
6 ML YEARS		797	2783	745	119	16	32	(20	12)	992	314	350	205	26	219	9	44	48	83	51	62	71	.268	.315	.356

Rick Sutcliffe

Pitches: Right Bats: Left Pos: SP **Ht: 6' 7" Wt: 215 Born: 06/21/56 Age: 37**

		HOW MUCH HE PITCHED						WHAT HE GAVE UP											THE RESULTS					
Year Team	Lg	G	GS	CG	GF	IP	BFP	H	R	ER	HR	SH	SF	HB	TBB	IBB	SO	WP	Bk	W	L	Pct.	ShO	Sv	ERA
1976 Los Angeles	NL	1	1	0	0	5	17	2	0	0	0	0	0	0	1	0	3	0	0	0	0	.000	0	0	0.00
1978 Los Angeles	NL	2	0	0	0	2	9	2	0	0	0	0	0	1	1	0	0	0	0	0	0	.000	0	0	0.00
1979 Los Angeles	NL	39	30	5	2	242	1016	217	104	93	16	16	9	2	97	6	117	8	6	17	10	.630	1	0	3.46
1980 Los Angeles	NL	42	10	1	19	110	491	122	73	68	10	4	3	1	55	2	59	4	5	3	9	.250	1	5	5.56
1981 Los Angeles	NL	14	6	0	5	47	197	41	24	21	5	1	2	2	20	2	16	0	0	2	2	.500	0	0	4.02
1982 Cleveland	AL	34	27	6	3	216	887	174	81	71	16	7	8	4	98	2	142	6	1	14	8	.636	1	1	2.96
1983 Cleveland	AL	36	35	10	0	243.1	1061	251	131	116	23	8	9	6	102	5	160	7	3	17	11	.607	2	0	4.29
1984 2 ML Teams		35	35	9	0	244.2	1030	234	113	99	16	5	4	3	85	3	213	6	3	20	6	.769	3	0	3.64
1985 Chicago	NL	20	20	6	0	130	549	119	51	46	12	3	4	3	44	3	102	6	0	8	8	.500	3	0	3.18
1986 Chicago	NL	28	27	4	0	176.2	764	166	92	91	18	6	2	1	96	8	122	13	1	5	14	.263	1	0	4.64
1987 Chicago	NL	34	34	6	0	237.1	1012	223	106	97	24	9	8	4	106	14	174	9	4	18	10	.643	1	0	3.68
1988 Chicago	NL	32	32	12	0	226	958	232	97	97	18	17	5	2	70	9	144	11	4	13	14	.481	2	0	3.86
1989 Chicago	NL	35	34	5	0	229	938	202	98	93	18	15	10	2	69	8	153	12	6	16	11	.593	1	0	3.66
1990 Chicago	NL	5	5	0	0	21.1	97	17	14	14	2	1	2	0	12	0	7	4	0	0	2	.000	0	0	5.91
1991 Chicago	NL	19	18	0	0	96.2	422	96	52	44	4	5	8	0	45	2	52	2	2	6	5	.545	0	0	4.10
1992 Baltimore	AL	36	36	5	0	237.1	1018	251	123	118	20	6	11	7	74	4	109	7	2	16	15	.516	2	0	4.47
1984 Cleveland	AL	15	15	2	0	94.1	428	111	60	54	7	4	3	2	46	3	58	3	1	4	5	.444	0	0	5.15
Chicago	NL	20	20	7	0	150.1	602	123	53	45	9	1	1	1	39	0	155	3	2	16	1	.941	3	0	2.69
16 ML YEARS		412	350	69	29	2464.1	10466	2357	1159	1068	202	103	85	38	975	68	1573	95	37	155	125	.554	18	6	3.90

Dale Sveum

Bats: Both Throws: Right Pos: SS **Ht: 6' 3" Wt: 185 Born: 11/23/63 Age: 29**

		BATTING																	BASERUNNING				PERCENTAGES		
Year Team	Lg	G	AB	H	2B	3B	HR	(Hm	Rd)	TB	R	RBI	TBB	IBB	SO	HBP	SH	SF	SB	CS	SB%	GDP	Avg	OBP	SLG
1986 Milwaukee	AL	91	317	78	13	2	7	(4	3)	116	35	35	32	0	63	1	5	1	4	3	.57	7	.246	.316	.366
1987 Milwaukee	AL	153	535	135	27	3	25	(9	16)	243	86	95	40	4	133	1	5	5	2	6	.25	11	.252	.303	.454
1988 Milwaukee	AL	129	467	113	14	4	9	(2	7)	162	41	51	21	0	122	1	3	3	1	0	1.00	6	.242	.274	.347
1990 Milwaukee	AL	48	117	23	7	0	1	(1	0)	33	15	12	12	0	30	2	0	2	0	1	.00	2	.197	.278	.282
1991 Milwaukee	AL	90	266	64	19	1	4	(3	1)	97	33	43	32	0	78	1	5	4	2	4	.33	8	.241	.320	.365
1992 2 ML Teams		94	249	49	13	0	4	(1	3)	74	28	28	28	4	68	0	2	5	1	1	.50	6	.197	.273	.297
1992 Philadelphia	NL	54	135	24	4	0	2	(0	2)	34	13	16	16	4	39	0	0	2	0	0	.00	5	.178	.261	.252
Chicago	AL	40	114	25	9	0	2	(1	1)	40	15	12	12	0	29	0	2	3	1	1	.50	1	.219	.287	.351
6 ML YEARS		605	1951	462	93	10	50	(20	30)	725	238	264	165	8	494	6	20	20	10	15	.40	40	.237	.296	.372

Russ Swan

Pitches: Left Bats: Left Pos: RP/SP **Ht: 6' 4" Wt: 215 Born: 01/03/64 Age: 29**

		HOW MUCH HE PITCHED						WHAT HE GAVE UP											THE RESULTS					
Year Team	Lg	G	GS	CG	GF	IP	BFP	H	R	ER	HR	SH	SF	HB	TBB	IBB	SO	WP	Bk	W	L	Pct.	ShO	Sv	ERA
1989 San Francisco	NL	2	2	0	0	6.2	34	11	10	8	4	2	0	0	4	0	2	0	0	0	2	.000	0	0	10.80
1990 2 ML Teams		13	9	0	0	49.1	213	48	26	20	3	2	3	0	22	2	16	1	1	2	4	.333	0	0	3.65
1991 Seattle	AL	63	0	0	11	78.2	336	81	35	30	8	6	1	0	28	7	33	6	0	6	2	.750	0	2	3.43
1992 Seattle	AL	55	9	1	26	104.1	457	104	60	55	8	7	5	3	45	7	45	6	0	3	10	.231	0	9	4.74
1990 San Francisco	NL	2	1	0	0	2.1	18	6	4	1	0	0	0	0	4	0	1	0	0	0	0	.000	0	0	3.86
Seattle	AL	11	8	0	0	47	195	42	22	19	3	2	3	0	18	2	15	0	1	2	3	.400	0	0	3.64
4 ML YEARS		133	20	1	37	239	1040	244	131	113	23	17	9	3	99	16	96	15	1	11	18	.379	0	11	4.26

Bill Swift

Pitches: Right Bats: Right Pos: SP/RP **Ht: 6' 0" Wt: 180 Born: 10/27/61 Age: 31**

		HOW MUCH HE PITCHED						WHAT HE GAVE UP											THE RESULTS					
Year Team	Lg	G	GS	CG	GF	IP	BFP	H	R	ER	HR	SH	SF	HB	TBB	IBB	SO	WP	Bk	W	L	Pct.	ShO	Sv	ERA
1985 Seattle	AL	23	21	0	0	120.2	532	131	71	64	8	6	3	5	48	5	55	5	3	6	10	.375	0	0	4.77
1986 Seattle	AL	29	17	1	3	115.1	534	148	85	70	5	5	3	7	55	2	55	2	1	2	9	.182	0	0	5.46
1988 Seattle	AL	38	24	6	4	174.2	757	199	99	89	10	5	3	8	65	3	47	6	2	8	12	.400	1	0	4.59
1989 Seattle	AL	37	16	0	7	130	551	140	72	64	7	4	3	2	38	4	45	4	1	7	3	.700	0	1	4.43
1990 Seattle	AL	55	8	0	18	128	533	135	46	34	4	5	4	7	21	6	42	8	3	6	4	.600	0	2	2.39
1991 Seattle	AL	71	0	0	30	90.1	359	74	22	20	3	2	0	1	26	4	48	2	1	1	2	.333	0	17	1.99
1992 San Francisco	NL	30	22	3	2	164.2	655	144	41	38	6	5	2	3	43	3	77	0	1	10	4	.714	2	1	2.08
7 ML YEARS		283	108	10	64	923.2	3921	971	436	379	43	32	18	33	296	27	369	27	12	40	44	.476	3	25	3.69

Greg Swindell

Pitches: Left **Bats:** Right **Pos:** SP   **Ht:** 6' 3" **Wt:** 225 **Born:** 01/02/65 **Age:** 28

Year Team	Lg	G	GS	CG	GF	IP	BFP	H	R	ER	HR	SH	SF	HB	TBB	IBB	SO	WP	Bk	W	L	Pct.	ShO	Sv	ERA
1986 Cleveland	AL	9	9	1	0	61.2	255	57	35	29	9	3	1	1	15	0	46	3	2	5	2	.714	0	0	4.23
1987 Cleveland	AL	16	15	4	0	102.1	441	112	62	58	18	4	3	1	37	1	97	0	1	3	8	.273	1	0	5.10
1988 Cleveland	AL	33	33	12	0	242	988	234	97	86	18	9	5	1	45	3	180	5	0	18	14	.563	4	0	3.20
1989 Cleveland	AL	28	28	5	0	184.1	749	170	71	69	16	4	4	0	51	1	129	3	1	13	6	.684	2	0	3.37
1990 Cleveland	AL	34	34	3	0	214.2	912	245	110	105	27	8	6	1	47	2	135	3	2	12	9	.571	0	0	4.40
1991 Cleveland	AL	33	33	7	0	238	971	241	112	92	21	13	8	3	31	1	169	3	1	9	16	.360	0	0	3.48
1992 Cincinnati	NL	31	30	5	0	213.2	867	210	72	64	14	9	7	2	41	4	138	3	2	12	8	.600	3	0	2.70
7 ML YEARS		184	182	37	0	1256.2	5183	1269	559	503	123	50	34	9	267	12	894	20	9	72	63	.533	10	0	3.60

Pat Tabler

Bats: Right **Throws:** Right **Pos:** 1B   **Ht:** 6' 2" **Wt:** 200 **Born:** 02/02/58 **Age:** 35

Year Team	Lg	G	AB	H	2B	3B	HR	(Hm	Rd)	TB	R	RBI	TBB	IBB	SO	HBP	SH	SF	SB	CS	SB%	GDP	Avg	OBP	SLG
1981 Chicago	NL	35	101	19	3	1	1	(1	0)	27	11	5	13	0	26	0	3	0	0	1	.00	4	.188	.281	.267
1982 Chicago	NL	25	85	20	4	2	1	(0	1)	31	9	7	6	0	20	1	0	2	0	0	.00	3	.235	.287	.365
1983 Cleveland	AL	124	430	125	23	5	6	(3	3)	176	56	65	56	1	63	1	0	5	2	4	.33	18	.291	.370	.409
1984 Cleveland	AL	144	473	137	21	3	10	(5	5)	194	66	68	47	2	62	3	0	5	3	1	.75	16	.290	.354	.410
1985 Cleveland	AL	117	404	111	18	3	5	(5	0)	150	47	59	27	2	55	2	2	3	0	6	.00	15	.275	.321	.371
1986 Cleveland	AL	130	473	154	29	2	6	(5	1)	205	61	48	29	3	75	3	2	1	3	1	.75	11	.326	.368	.433
1987 Cleveland	AL	151	553	170	34	3	11	(5	6)	243	66	86	51	6	84	6	3	5	5	2	.71	6	.307	.369	.439
1988 2 ML Teams		130	444	125	22	3	2	(0	2)	159	53	66	46	1	68	3	0	5	5	3	.50	9	.282	.349	.358
1989 Kansas City	AL	123	390	101	11	1	2	(2	0)	120	36	42	37	0	42	2	3	2	0	0	.00	14	.259	.325	.308
1990 2 ML Teams		92	238	65	15	1	2	(1	1)	88	18	29	23	2	29	2	0	3	0	2	.00	8	.273	.338	.370
1991 Toronto	AL	82	185	40	5	1	1	(1	0)	50	20	21	29	5	21	1	2	5	0	0	.00	3	.216	.318	.270
1992 Toronto	AL	49	135	34	5	0	0	(0	0)	39	11	16	11	0	14	0	1	0	0	0	.00	6	.252	.306	.289
1988 Cleveland	AL	41	143	32	5	1	1	(1	0)	42	16	17	23	1	27	1	0	1	1	0	1.00	3	.224	.333	.294
Kansas City		89	301	93	17	2	1	(0	1)	117	37	49	23	0	41	2	0	4	2	3	.40	6	.309	.358	.389
1990 Kansas City	AL	75	195	53	14	0	1	(0	1)	70	12	19	20	2	21	1	0	0	2	0	.00	8	.272	.338	.359
New York	NL	17	43	12	1	1	1	(1	0)	18	6	10	3	0	8	1	0	0	0	0	.00	0	.279	.340	.419
12 ML YEARS		1202	3911	1101	190	25	47	(28	19)	1482	454	512	375	22	559	24	15	37	16	20	.44	113	.282	.345	.379

Jeff Tackett

Bats: Right **Throws:** Right **Pos:** C   **Ht:** 6' 2" **Wt:** 206 **Born:** 12/01/65 **Age:** 27

Year Team	Lg	G	AB	H	2B	3B	HR	(Hm	Rd)	TB	R	RBI	TBB	IBB	SO	HBP	SH	SF	SB	CS	SB%	GDP	Avg	OBP	SLG
1984 Bluefield	R	34	98	16	2	0	0	--	--	18	9	12	23	0	28	0	0	2	1	1	.50	1	.163	.317	.184
1985 Daytona Bch	A	40	103	20	5	2	0	--	--	29	8	10	13	0	16	1	0	1	1	3	.25	6	.194	.288	.282
Newark	A	62	187	39	6	0	0	--	--	45	21	22	22	0	33	2	3	1	2	2	.50	4	.209	.297	.241
1986 Hagerstown	A	83	246	70	15	1	0	--	--	87	53	34	36	0	36	5	0	1	16	5	.76	2	.285	.385	.354
1987 Charlotte	AA	61	205	46	6	1	0	--	--	54	18	13	12	0	34	2	1	1	5	5	.50	2	.224	.273	.263
1988 Charlotte	AA	81	272	56	9	0	0	--	--	65	24	18	42	0	46	2	0	1	6	4	.60	7	.206	.315	.239
1989 Rochester	AAA	67	199	36	3	1	2	--	--	47	13	17	19	0	45	1	2	2	3	1	.75	3	.181	.253	.236
1990 Rochester	AAA	108	306	73	8	3	4	--	--	99	37	33	47	0	50	7	3	0	4	8	.33	3	.239	.353	.324
1991 Rochester	AAA	126	433	102	18	2	6	--	--	142	64	50	54	0	60	2	4	3	3	3	.50	15	.236	.321	.328
1991 Baltimore	AL	6	8	1	0	0	0	(0	0)	1	1	0	2	0	2	0	1	0	0	0	.00	0	.125	.300	.125
1992 Baltimore	AL	65	179	43	8	1	5	(4	1)	68	21	24	17	1	28	2	6	4	0	0	.00	11	.240	.307	.380
2 ML YEARS		71	187	44	8	1	5	(4	1)	69	22	24	19	1	30	2	7	4	0	0	.00	11	.235	.307	.369

Frank Tanana

Pitches: Left **Bats:** Left **Pos:** SP   **Ht:** 6' 3" **Wt:** 200 **Born:** 07/03/53 **Age:** 39

Year Team	Lg	G	GS	CG	GF	IP	BFP	H	R	ER	HR	SH	SF	HB	TBB	IBB	SO	WP	Bk	W	L	Pct.	ShO	Sv	ERA
1973 California	AL	4	4	2	0	26	108	20	11	9	2	0	0	0	8	0	22	2	0	2	2	.500	1	0	3.12
1974 California	AL	39	35	12	2	269	1127	262	104	93	27	10	4	8	77	4	180	4	2	14	19	.424	4	0	3.11
1975 California	AL	34	33	16	1	257	1029	211	80	75	21	13	4	7	73	6	269	8	1	16	9	.640	5	0	2.63
1976 California	AL	34	34	23	0	288	1142	212	88	78	24	14	3	9	73	5	261	5	0	19	10	.655	2	0	2.44
1977 California	AL	31	31	20	0	241	973	201	72	68	19	8	7	12	61	2	205	8	1	15	9	.625	7	0	2.54
1978 California	AL	33	33	10	0	239	1014	239	108	97	26	8	10	9	60	7	137	5	8	18	12	.600	4	0	3.65
1979 California	AL	18	17	2	0	90	382	93	44	39	9	1	2	2	25	0	46	6	1	7	5	.583	1	0	3.90
1980 California	AL	32	31	7	1	204	870	223	107	94	18	8	4	8	45	0	113	3	1	11	12	.478	0	0	4.15
1981 Boston	AL	24	23	5	0	141	596	142	70	63	17	9	4	4	43	4	78	2	0	4	10	.286	2	0	4.02
1982 Texas	AL	30	30	7	0	194.1	832	199	102	91	16	13	4	7	55	10	87	0	1	7	18	.280	0	0	4.21

Year	Team	Lg	G	GS	CG	GF	IP	BFP	H	R	ER	HR	SH	SF	HB	TBB	IBB	SO	WP	Bk	W	L	Pct.	ShO	Sv	ERA
1983	Texas	AL	29	22	3	1	159.1	667	144	70	56	14	7	3	7	49	5	108	6	1	7	9	.438	0	0	3.16
1984	Texas	AL	35	35	9	0	246.1	1054	234	117	89	30	6	5	6	81	3	141	12	4	15	15	.500	1	0	3.25
1985	2 ML Teams		33	33	4	0	215	907	220	112	102	28	5	8	3	57	8	159	5	1	12	14	.462	0	0	4.27
1986	Detroit	AL	32	31	3	1	188.1	812	196	95	87	23	8	5	3	65	9	119	7	1	12	9	.571	1	0	4.16
1987	Detroit	AL	34	34	5	0	218.2	924	216	106	95	27	8	11	5	56	5	146	6	0	15	10	.600	3	0	3.91
1988	Detroit	AL	32	32	2	0	203	876	213	105	95	25	6	3	4	64	7	127	6	0	14	11	.560	0	0	4.21
1989	Detroit	AL	33	33	6	0	223.2	955	227	105	89	21	7	10	8	74	8	147	8	0	10	14	.417	1	0	3.58
1990	Detroit	AL	34	29	1	4	176.1	763	190	104	104	25	3	7	9	66	7	114	5	1	9	8	.529	0	1	5.31
1991	Detroit	AL	33	33	3	0	217.1	920	217	98	89	26	12	9	2	78	9	107	3	1	13	12	.520	2	0	3.69
1992	Detroit	AL	32	31	3	0	186.2	818	188	102	91	22	7	10	7	90	9	91	11	1	13	11	.542	0	0	4.39
1985	Texas	AL	13	13	0	0	77.2	340	89	53	51	15	2	4	1	23	2	52	3	0	2	7	.222	0	0	5.91
	Detroit		20	20	4	0	137.1	567	131	59	51	13	3	4	2	34	6	107	2	1	10	7	.588	0	0	3.34
20 ML YEARS			606	584	143	10	3984	16769	3847	1800	1604	420	153	113	120	1200	108	2657	112	25	233	219	.515	34	1	3.62

Kevin Tapani

Pitches: Right **Bats:** Right **Pos:** SP **Ht:** 6' 0" **Wt:** 183 **Born:** 02/18/64 **Age:** 29

			HOW MUCH HE PITCHED						WHAT HE GAVE UP											THE RESULTS					
Year	Team	Lg	G	GS	CG	GF	IP	BFP	H	R	ER	HR	SH	SF	HB	TBB	IBB	SO	WP	Bk	W	L	Pct.	ShO	Sv	ERA
1989	2 ML Teams		8	5	0	1	40	169	39	18	17	3	1	2	0	12	1	23	0	1	2	2	.500	0	0	3.83
1990	Minnesota	AL	28	28	1	0	159.1	659	164	75	72	12	3	4	2	29	2	101	1	2	12	8	.600	1	0	4.07
1991	Minnesota	AL	34	34	4	0	244	974	225	84	81	23	9	6	2	40	0	135	3	3	16	9	.640	1	0	2.99
1992	Minnesota	AL	34	34	4	0	220	911	226	103	97	17	8	11	5	48	2	138	4	0	16	11	.593	1	0	3.97
1989	New York	NL	3	0	0	1	7.1	31	5	3	3	1	0	1	0	4	0	2	0	1	0	0	.000	0	0	3.68
	Minnesota	AL	5	5	0	0	32.2	138	34	15	14	2	1	1	0	8	1	21	0	0	2	2	.500	0	0	3.86
4 ML YEARS			104	101	9	1	663.1	2713	654	280	267	55	21	23	9	129	5	397	8	4	46	30	.605	3	0	3.62

Danny Tartabull

Bats: Right **Throws:** Right **Pos:** RF/DH **Ht:** 6' 1" **Wt:** 210 **Born:** 10/30/62 **Age:** 30

			BATTING																BASERUNNING				PERCENTAGES		
Year	Team	Lg	G	AB	H	2B	3B	HR	(Hm	Rd)	TB	R	RBI	TBB	IBB	SO	HBP	SH	SF	SB	CS	SB%	GDP	Avg	OBP	SLG
1984	Seattle	AL	10	20	6	1	0	2	(1	1)	13	3	7	2	0	3	1	0	1	0	0	.00	0	.300	.375	.650
1985	Seattle	AL	19	61	20	7	1	1	(0	1)	32	8	7	8	0	14	0	0	0	1	0	1.00	1	.328	.406	.525
1986	Seattle	AL	137	511	138	25	6	25	(13	12)	250	76	96	61	2	157	1	2	3	4	8	.33	10	.270	.347	.489
1987	Kansas City	AL	158	582	180	27	3	34	(15	19)	315	95	101	79	2	136	1	0	5	9	4	.69	14	.309	.390	.541
1988	Kansas City	AL	146	507	139	38	3	26	(15	11)	261	80	102	76	4	119	4	0	6	8	5	.62	10	.274	.369	.515
1989	Kansas City	AL	133	441	118	22	0	18	(9	9)	194	54	62	69	2	123	3	0	2	4	2	.67	12	.268	.369	.440
1990	Kansas City	AL	88	313	84	19	0	15	(5	10)	148	41	60	36	0	93	0	0	3	1	1	.50	9	.268	.341	.473
1991	Kansas City	AL	132	484	153	35	3	31	(13	18)	287	78	100	65	6	121	3	0	5	6	3	.67	9	.316	.397	.593
1992	New York	AL	123	421	112	19	0	25	(11	14)	206	72	85	103	14	115	0	0	2	2	2	.50	7	.266	.409	.489
9 ML YEARS			946	3340	950	193	16	177	(82	95)	1706	507	620	499	30	881	13	2	27	35	25	.58	72	.284	.377	.511

Jimmy Tatum

Bats: Right **Throws:** Right **Pos:** 3B **Ht:** 6' 2" **Wt:** 200 **Born:** 10/09/67 **Age:** 25

			BATTING																BASERUNNING				PERCENTAGES		
Year	Team	Lg	G	AB	H	2B	3B	HR	(Hm	Rd)	TB	R	RBI	TBB	IBB	SO	HBP	SH	SF	SB	CS	SB%	GDP	Avg	OBP	SLG
1985	Spokane	A	74	281	64	9	1	1	--	--	78	21	32	20	0	60	5	4	1	0	1	.00	7	.228	.290	.278
1986	Charleston	A	120	431	112	19	2	10	--	--	165	55	62	41	2	83	2	4	.33	2	4	.33	11	.260	.324	.383
1987	Chston-Sc	A	128	468	131	22	2	9	--	--	184	52	72	46	2	65	8	4	9	8	5	.62	16	.280	.348	.393
1988	Wichita	AA	118	402	105	26	1	8	--	--	157	38	54	30	2	73	5	6	3	2	3	.40	5	.261	.318	.391
1990	Canton-Akrn	AA	30	106	19	6	0	2	--	--	31	6	11	6	1	19	1	0	2	1	0	1.00	2	.179	.226	.292
	Stockton	A	70	260	68	16	0	12	--	--	120	41	59	13	0	49	8	0	4	4	5	.44	7	.262	.312	.517
1991	El Paso	A	130	493	158	27	8	18	--	--	255	99	128	63	5	79	15	2	20	5	7	.42	21	.320	.399	.517
1992	Denver	AAA	130	492	162	36	3	19	--	--	261	74	101	40	3	87	9	4	11	8	9	.47	12	.329	.382	.530
1992	Milwaukee	AL	5	8	1	0	0	0	(0	0)	1	0	0	1	0	2	0	0	0	0	0	.00	0	.125	.222	.125

Eddie Taubensee

Bats: Left **Throws:** Right **Pos:** C **Ht:** 6' 4" **Wt:** 205 **Born:** 10/31/68 **Age:** 24

			BATTING																BASERUNNING				PERCENTAGES		
Year	Team	Lg	G	AB	H	2B	3B	HR	(Hm	Rd)	TB	R	RBI	TBB	IBB	SO	HBP	SH	SF	SB	CS	SB%	GDP	Avg	OBP	SLG
1986	Reds	R	35	107	21	3	0	1	--	--	27	8	11	11	0	33	0	0	0	0	1	.00	2	.196	.271	.252
1987	Billings	R	55	162	43	7	0	5	--	--	65	24	28	25	5	47	1	0	2	2	2	.50	2	.265	.363	.401
1988	Chattanooga	AA	5	12	2	0	0	1	--	--	5	2	1	3	0	4	0	0	0	0	0	.00	0	.167	.333	.417
	Greensboro	A	103	330	85	16	1	10	--	--	133	36	41	44	5	93	4	1	1	8	4	.67	2	.258	.351	.403
1989	Cedar Rapds	A	59	196	39	5	0	8	--	--	68	25	22	25	4	55	2	0	0	4	1	.80	3	.199	.296	.347
	Chattanooga	AA	45	127	24	2	0	3	--	--	35	11	13	11	2	28	0	1	3	0	0	.00	3	.189	.248	.276
1990	Cedar Rapds	A	122	417	108	22	1	16	--	--	180	57	62	51	5	98	4	1	4	11	4	.73	8	.259	.342	.432
1991	Colo Sprngs	AAA	91	287	89	23	3	13	--	--	157	53	39	31	5	61	0	0	0	0	0	.00	6	.310	.377	.547
1992	Tucson	AAA	20	74	25	8	1	1	--	--	38	13	10	8	1	17	0	1	0	0	1	.00	0	.338	.402	.514

Year Team	Lg	G	AB	H	2B	3B	HR	(Hm	Rd)	TB	R	RBI	TBB	IBB	SO	HBP	SH	SF	SB	CS	SB%	GDP	Avg	OBP	SLG
1991 Cleveland	AL	26	66	16	2	1	0	(0	0)	20	5	8	5	1	16	0	0	2	0	0	.00	1	.242	.288	.303
1992 Houston	NL	104	297	66	15	0	5	(2	3)	96	23	28	31	3	78	2	0	1	2	0	.67	4	.222	.299	.323
2 ML YEARS		130	363	82	17	1	5	(2	3)	116	28	36	36	4	94	2	0	3	2	1	.67	5	.226	.297	.320

Scott Taylor

Pitches: Left **Bats:** Left **Pos:** RP   **Ht:** 6' 1" **Wt:** 190 **Born:** 08/02/67 **Age:** 25

		HOW MUCH HE PITCHED						WHAT HE GAVE UP												THE RESULTS					
Year Team	Lg	G	GS	CG	GF	IP	BFP	H	R	ER	HR	SH	SF	HB	TBB	IBB	SO	WP	Bk	W	L	Pct.	ShO	Sv	ERA
1988 Elmira	A	2	1	0	1	3.2	16	2	0	0	0	0	0	0	3	0	8	0	0	1	0	1.000	0	0	0.00
1989 Lynchburg	A	19	9	0	4	81	332	61	33	26	7	2	2	1	25	3	99	3	3	5	3	.625	0	1	2.89
1990 Lynchburg	A	13	13	1	0	89	372	76	36	27	2	3	0	2	30	2	120	7	3	5	6	.455	0	0	2.73
New Britain	AA	5	5	1	0	27.1	117	23	8	5	0	3	0	1	13	1	27	1	0	0	2	.000	0	0	1.65
1991 New Britain	AA	4	4	0	0	29	109	20	2	2	0	0	0	0	9	0	38	1	0	2	0	1.000	0	0	0.62
Pawtucket	AAA	7	7	1	0	39	161	32	19	15	3	0	2	1	17	0	35	1	1	3	3	.500	0	0	3.46
1992 Pawtucket	AAA	26	26	5	0	162	694	168	73	66	16	3	5	2	61	1	91	17	0	9	11	.450	0	0	3.67
1992 Boston	AL	4	1	0	1	14.2	57	13	8	8	4	0	0	0	4	0	7	0	0	1	1	.500	0	0	4.91

Walt Terrell

Pitches: Right **Bats:** Left **Pos:** RP/SP   **Ht:** 6' 2" **Wt:** 205 **Born:** 05/11/58 **Age:** 35

		HOW MUCH HE PITCHED						WHAT HE GAVE UP												THE RESULTS					
Year Team	Lg	G	GS	CG	GF	IP	BFP	H	R	ER	HR	SH	SF	HB	TBB	IBB	SO	WP	Bk	W	L	Pct.	ShO	Sv	ERA
1982 New York	NL	3	3	0	0	21	97	22	12	8	2	1	0	0	14	2	8	1	1	0	3	.000	0	0	3.43
1983 New York	NL	21	20	4	1	133.2	561	123	57	53	7	9	5	2	55	7	59	5	0	8	8	.500	2	0	3.57
1984 New York	NL	33	33	3	0	215	926	232	99	84	16	11	8	4	80	1	114	6	0	11	12	.478	1	0	3.52
1985 Detroit	AL	34	34	5	0	229	983	221	107	98	9	11	7	4	95	5	130	5	0	15	10	.600	3	0	3.85
1986 Detroit	AL	34	33	9	1	217.1	918	199	116	110	30	2	3	3	98	5	93	5	0	15	12	.556	2	0	4.56
1987 Detroit	AL	35	35	10	0	244.2	1057	254	123	110	30	3	10	3	94	7	143	8	0	17	10	.630	1	0	4.05
1988 Detroit	AL	29	29	11	0	206.1	870	199	101	91	20	13	6	2	78	8	84	7	2	7	16	.304	1	0	3.97
1989 2 ML Teams		32	32	5	0	206.1	882	236	117	103	23	10	4	2	50	1	93	6	0	11	18	.379	2	0	4.49
1990 2 ML Teams		29	28	0	0	158	710	184	98	92	20	9	3	12	57	4	64	7	2	8	11	.421	0	0	5.24
1991 Detroit	AL	35	33	8	1	218.2	954	257	115	103	16	10	9	2	79	10	80	8	0	12	14	.462	2	0	4.24
1992 Detroit	AL	36	14	1	7	136.2	611	163	86	79	14	6	7	3	48	10	61	3	0	7	10	.412	0	0	5.20
1989 San Diego	NL	19	19	4	0	123.1	520	134	65	55	14	8	2	0	26	1	63	4	0	5	13	.278	1	0	4.01
New York	AL	13	13	1	0	83	362	102	52	48	9	2	2	2	24	0	30	2	0	6	5	.545	1	0	5.20
1990 Pittsburgh	NL	16	16	0	0	82.2	377	98	59	54	13	6	2	4	33	1	34	7	2	2	7	.222	0	0	5.88
Detroit	AL	13	12	0	0	75.1	333	86	39	38	7	3	1	8	24	3	30	0	0	6	4	.600	0	0	4.54
11 ML YEARS		321	294	56	10	1986.2	8569	2090	1031	931	187	85	62	37	748	60	929	61	5	111	124	.472	14	0	4.22

Mickey Tettleton

Bats: Both **Throws:** Right **Pos:** C/DH   **Ht:** 6' 2" **Wt:** 212 **Born:** 09/16/60 **Age:** 32

		BATTING																	BASERUNNING				PERCENTAGES		
Year Team	Lg	G	AB	H	2B	3B	HR	(Hm	Rd)	TB	R	RBI	TBB	IBB	SO	HBP	SH	SF	SB	CS	SB%	GDP	Avg	OBP	SLG
1984 Oakland	AL	33	76	20	2	1	1	(1	0)	27	10	5	11	0	21	0	0	1	0	0	.00	3	.263	.352	.355
1985 Oakland	AL	78	211	53	12	0	3	(1	2)	74	23	15	28	0	59	2	5	0	2	2	.50	6	.251	.344	.351
1986 Oakland	AL	90	211	43	9	0	10	(4	6)	82	26	35	39	0	51	1	7	4	7	1	.88	3	.204	.325	.389
1987 Oakland	AL	82	211	41	3	0	8	(5	3)	68	19	26	30	0	65	0	5	4	1	1	.50	3	.194	.292	.322
1988 Baltimore	AL	86	283	74	11	1	11	(7	4)	120	31	37	28	2	70	2	1	2	0	1	.00	9	.261	.330	.424
1989 Baltimore	AL	117	411	106	21	2	26	(15	11)	209	72	65	73	4	117	1	1	3	3	2	.60	8	.258	.369	.509
1990 Baltimore	AL	135	444	99	21	2	15	(8	7)	169	68	51	106	3	160	5	0	4	2	4	.33	7	.223	.376	.381
1991 Detroit	AL	154	501	132	17	2	31	(15	16)	246	85	89	101	9	131	2	0	4	3	3	.50	12	.263	.387	.491
1992 Detroit	AL	157	525	125	25	0	32	(18	14)	246	82	83	122	18	137	1	0	6	0	6	.00	5	.238	.379	.469
9 ML YEARS		932	2873	693	121	8	137	(74	63)	1241	416	406	538	36	811	14	19	26	18	20	.47	56	.241	.361	.432

Tim Teufel

Bats: Right **Throws:** Right **Pos:** 2B/3B   **Ht:** 6' 0" **Wt:** 175 **Born:** 07/07/58 **Age:** 34

		BATTING																	BASERUNNING				PERCENTAGES		
Year Team	Lg	G	AB	H	2B	3B	HR	(Hm	Rd)	TB	R	RBI	TBB	IBB	SO	HBP	SH	SF	SB	CS	SB%	GDP	Avg	OBP	SLG
1983 Minnesota	AL	21	78	24	7	1	3	(3	0)	42	11	6	2	0	8	0	2	0	0	0	.00	1	.308	.325	.538
1984 Minnesota	AL	157	568	149	30	3	14	(9	5)	227	76	61	76	8	73	2	2	4	1	3	.25	18	.262	.349	.400
1985 Minnesota	AL	138	434	113	24	3	10	(6	4)	173	58	50	48	2	70	3	7	4	4	2	.67	14	.260	.335	.399
1986 New York	NL	93	279	69	20	1	4	(2	2)	103	35	31	32	1	42	1	3	3	1	2	.33	6	.247	.324	.369
1987 New York	NL	97	299	92	29	0	14	(4	10)	163	55	61	44	2	53	2	3	2	3	2	.60	7	.308	.398	.545
1988 New York	NL	90	273	64	20	0	4	(1	3)	96	35	31	29	1	41	1	2	4	0	1	.00	6	.234	.306	.352
1989 New York	NL	83	219	56	7	2	2	(1	1)	73	27	15	32	1	50	1	0	2	1	3	.25	4	.256	.350	.333
1990 New York	NL	80	175	43	11	0	10	(4	6)	84	28	24	15	1	33	0	1	0	0	0	.00	5	.246	.304	.480
1991 2 ML Teams		117	341	74	16	0	12	(6	6)	126	41	44	51	4	77	1	4	2	9	3	.75	8	.217	.319	.370
1992 San Diego	NL	101	246	55	10	0	6	(2	4)	83	23	25	31	3	45	1	0	1	2	1	.67	7	.224	.312	.337

Year	Team	Lg	G	AB	H	2B	3B	HR	(Hm	Rd)	TB	R	RBI	TBB	IBB	SO	HBP	SH	SF	SB	CS	SB%	GDP	Avg	OBP	SLG
1991	New York	NL	20	34	4	0	0	1	(1	0)	7	2	2	2	0	8	0	0	0	1	1	.50	0	.118	.167	.206
	San Diego	NL	97	307	70	16	0	11	(5	6)	119	39	42	49	4	69	1	4	2	8	2	.80	8	.228	.334	.388
	10 ML YEARS		977	2912	739	174	10	79	(38	41)	1170	389	348	360	23	492	12	24	23	21	17	.55	76	.254	.336	.402

Bob Tewksbury

Pitches: Right **Bats:** Right **Pos:** SP   **Ht:** 6' 4" **Wt:** 208 **Born:** 11/30/60 **Age:** 32

			HOW MUCH HE PITCHED						WHAT HE GAVE UP										THE RESULTS					
Year	Team	Lg	G	GS	CG	GF	IP	BFP	H	R	ER	HR	SH	SF	HB	TBB	IBB	SO	WP	Bk	W	L	Pct.	ShO	Sv	ERA
1986	New York	AL	23	20	2	0	130.1	558	144	58	48	8	4	7	5	31	0	49	3	2	9	5	.643	0	0	3.31
1987	2 ML Teams		15	9	0	4	51.1	242	79	41	38	6	5	1	1	20	3	22	1	2	1	8	.111	0	0	6.66
1988	Chicago	NL	1	1	0	0	3.1	18	6	5	3	1	0	1	0	2	0	1	0	0	0	0	.000	0	0	8.10
1989	St. Louis	NL	7	4	1	2	30	125	25	12	11	2	1	1	2	10	3	17	0	0	1	0	1.000	1	0	3.30
1990	St. Louis	NL	28	20	3	1	145.1	595	151	67	56	7	5	7	3	15	3	50	2	0	10	9	.526	2	1	3.47
1991	St. Louis	NL	30	30	3	0	191	798	206	86	69	13	12	10	5	38	2	75	0	0	11	12	.478	0	0	3.25
1992	St. Louis	NL	33	32	5	1	233	915	217	63	56	15	9	7	3	20	0	91	2	0	16	5	.762	0	0	2.16
1987	New York	AL	8	6	0	1	33.1	149	47	26	25	5	2	0	1	7	0	12	0	0	1	4	.200	0	0	6.75
	Chicago	NL	7	3	0	3	18	93	32	15	13	1	3	1	0	13	3	10	1	2	0	4	.000	0	0	6.50
	7 ML YEARS		137	116	14	8	784.1	3251	828	332	281	52	36	34	19	136	11	305	8	4	48	39	.552	3	1	3.22

Bobby Thigpen

Pitches: Right **Bats:** Right **Pos:** RP   **Ht:** 6' 3" **Wt:** 195 **Born:** 07/17/63 **Age:** 29

			HOW MUCH HE PITCHED						WHAT HE GAVE UP										THE RESULTS					
Year	Team	Lg	G	GS	CG	GF	IP	BFP	H	R	ER	HR	SH	SF	HB	TBB	IBB	SO	WP	Bk	W	L	Pct.	ShO	Sv	ERA
1986	Chicago	AL	20	0	0	14	35.2	142	26	7	7	1	1	1	1	12	0	20	0	0	2	0	1.000	0	7	1.77
1987	Chicago	AL	51	0	0	37	89	369	86	30	27	10	6	0	3	24	5	52	0	0	7	5	.583	0	16	2.73
1988	Chicago	AL	68	0	0	59	90	398	96	38	33	6	4	5	4	33	3	62	6	2	5	8	.385	0	34	3.30
1989	Chicago	AL	61	0	0	56	79	336	62	34	33	10	5	5	1	40	3	47	2	1	2	6	.250	0	34	3.76
1990	Chicago	AL	77	0	0	73	88.2	347	60	20	18	5	4	3	1	32	3	70	2	0	4	6	.400	0	57	1.83
1991	Chicago	AL	67	0	0	58	69.2	309	63	32	27	10	7	3	4	38	8	47	2	0	7	5	.583	0	30	3.49
1992	Chicago	AL	55	0	0	40	55	253	58	29	29	4	2	4	3	33	5	45	0	0	1	3	.250	0	22	4.75
	7 ML YEARS		399	0	0	337	507	2154	451	190	174	46	29	21	17	212	27	343	12	3	28	33	.459	0	200	3.09

Frank Thomas

Bats: Right **Throws:** Right **Pos:** 1B   **Ht:** 6' 5" **Wt:** 240 **Born:** 05/27/68 **Age:** 25

			BATTING																BASERUNNING				PERCENTAGES		
Year	Team	Lg	G	AB	H	2B	3B	HR	(Hm	Rd)	TB	R	RBI	TBB	IBB	SO	HBP	SH	SF	SB	CS	SB%	GDP	Avg	OBP	SLG
1990	Chicago	AL	60	191	63	11	3	7	(2	5)	101	39	31	44	0	54	2	0	3	0	1	.00	5	.330	.454	.529
1991	Chicago	AL	158	559	178	31	2	32	(24	8)	309	104	109	138	13	112	1	0	2	1	2	.33	20	.318	.453	.553
1992	Chicago	AL	160	573	185	46	2	24	(10	14)	307	108	115	122	6	88	5	0	11	6	3	.67	19	.323	.439	.536
	3 ML YEARS		378	1323	426	88	7	63	(36	27)	717	251	255	304	19	254	8	0	16	7	6	.54	44	.322	.447	.542

Jim Thome

Bats: Left **Throws:** Right **Pos:** 3B   **Ht:** 6' 3" **Wt:** 200 **Born:** 08/27/70 **Age:** 22

			BATTING																BASERUNNING				PERCENTAGES		
Year	Team	Lg	G	AB	H	2B	3B	HR	(Hm	Rd)	TB	R	RBI	TBB	IBB	SO	HBP	SH	SF	SB	CS	SB%	GDP	Avg	OBP	SLG
1989	Indians	R	55	186	44	5	3	0	--	--	55	22	22	21	1	33	1	3	2	6	4	.60	5	.237	.314	.296
1990	Burlington	R	34	118	44	7	1	12	--	--	89	31	34	27	3	18	4	0	0	6	3	.67	2	.373	.503	.754
	Kinston	A	33	117	36	4	1	4	--	--	54	19	16	24	0	26	1	0	1	4	1	.80	4	.308	.427	.462
1991	Canton-Akrn	AA	84	294	99	20	2	5	--	--	138	47	45	44	4	58	4	0	3	8	2	.80	7	.337	.426	.469
	Colo Sprngs	AAA	41	151	43	7	3	2	--	--	62	20	28	12	0	29	0	0	3	0	0	.00	4	.285	.331	.411
1992	Canton-Akrn	AA	30	107	36	9	2	1	--	--	52	16	14	24	3	30	1	0	0	2	0	.00	3	.336	.462	.486
	Colo Sprngs	AAA	12	48	15	4	1	2	--	--	27	11	14	6	1	16	1	0	0	0	0	.00	0	.313	.400	.563
1991	Cleveland	AL	27	98	25	4	2	1	(0	1)	36	7	9	5	1	16	1	0	0	1	1	.50	4	.255	.298	.367
1992	Cleveland	AL	40	117	24	3	1	2	(1	1)	35	8	12	10	2	34	2	0	2	2	0	1.00	3	.205	.275	.299
	2 ML YEARS		67	215	49	7	3	3	(1	2)	71	15	21	15	3	50	3	0	2	3	1	.75	7	.228	.285	.330

Milt Thompson

Bats: Left **Throws:** Right **Pos:** LF/RF   **Ht:** 5'11" **Wt:** 200 **Born:** 01/05/59 **Age:** 34

			BATTING																BASERUNNING				PERCENTAGES		
Year	Team	Lg	G	AB	H	2B	3B	HR	(Hm	Rd)	TB	R	RBI	TBB	IBB	SO	HBP	SH	SF	SB	CS	SB%	GDP	Avg	OBP	SLG
1984	Atlanta	NL	25	99	30	1	0	2	(1	2)	37	16	4	11	1	11	0	1	0	14	2	.88	1	.303	.373	.374
1985	Atlanta	NL	73	182	55	7	2	0	(0	0)	66	17	6	7	0	36	3	1	0	9	4	.69	1	.302	.339	.363
1986	Philadelphia	NL	96	299	75	7	1	6	(4	2)	102	38	23	26	1	62	1	4	2	19	4	.83	4	.251	.311	.341
1987	Philadelphia	NL	150	527	159	26	9	7	(3	4)	224	86	43	42	2	87	0	3	3	46	10	.82	5	.302	.351	.425
1988	Philadelphia	NL	122	378	109	16	2	2	(1	1)	135	53	33	39	6	59	1	2	3	17	9	.65	8	.288	.354	.357
1989	St. Louis	NL	155	545	158	28	8	4	(2	2)	214	60	68	39	5	91	4	0	3	27	8	.77	12	.290	.340	.393

Year Team	Lg	G	AB	H	2B	3B	HR	(Hm	Rd)	TB	R	RBI	TBB	IBB	SO	HBP	SH	SF	SB	CS	SB%	GDP	Avg	OBP	SLG
1990 St. Louis	NL	135	418	91	14	7	6	(3	3)	137	42	30	39	5	60	5	1	0	25	5	.83	4	.218	.292	.328
1991 St. Louis	NL	115	326	100	16	5	6	(4	2)	144	55	34	32	7	53	0	2	1	16	9	.64	4	.307	.368	.442
1992 St. Louis	NL	109	208	61	9	1	4	(1	3)	84	31	17	16	3	39	2	0	0	18	6	.75	3	.293	.350	.404
9 ML YEARS		980	2982	838	124	35	37	(18	19)	1143	398	258	251	30	498	16	14	12	191	57	.77	42	.281	.339	.383

Robby Thompson

Bats: Right **Throws:** Right **Pos:** 2B **Ht:** 5'11" **Wt:** 170 **Born:** 05/10/62 **Age:** 31

Year Team	Lg	G	AB	H	2B	3B	HR	(Hm	Rd)	TB	R	RBI	TBB	IBB	SO	HBP	SH	SF	SB	CS	SB%	GDP	Avg	OBP	SLG
1986 San Francisco	NL	149	549	149	27	3	7	(0	7)	203	73	47	42	0	112	5	18	1	12	15	.44	11	.271	.328	.370
1987 San Francisco	NL	132	420	110	26	5	10	(7	3)	176	62	44	40	3	91	8	6	0	16	11	.59	8	.262	.338	.419
1988 San Francisco	NL	138	477	126	24	6	7	(3	4)	183	66	48	40	0	111	4	14	5	14	5	.74	7	.264	.323	.384
1989 San Francisco	NL	148	547	132	26	11	13	(7	6)	219	91	50	51	0	133	13	9	0	12	2	.86	6	.241	.321	.400
1990 San Francisco	NL	144	498	122	22	3	15	(8	7)	195	67	56	34	1	96	6	8	3	14	4	.78	9	.245	.299	.392
1991 San Francisco	NL	144	492	129	24	5	19	(11	8)	220	74	48	63	2	95	6	11	1	14	7	.67	5	.262	.352	.447
1992 San Francisco	NL	128	443	115	25	1	14	(8	6)	184	54	49	43	1	75	8	7	4	5	9	.36	8	.260	.333	.415
7 ML YEARS		983	3426	883	174	34	85	(44	41)	1380	487	342	313	7	713	50	73	14	87	53	.62	54	.258	.328	.403

Ryan Thompson

Bats: Right **Throws:** Right **Pos:** CF **Ht:** 6'3" **Wt:** 200 **Born:** 11/04/67 **Age:** 25

Year Team	Lg	G	AB	H	2B	3B	HR	(Hm	Rd)	TB	R	RBI	TBB	IBB	SO	HBP	SH	SF	SB	CS	SB%	GDP	Avg	OBP	SLG
1987 Medcine Hat	R	40	110	27	3	1	1	--	--	35	13	9	6	0	34	0	0	0	1	2	.33	1	.245	.284	.318
1988 St.Cathrnes	A	23	57	10	4	0	0	--	--	14	13	2	24	0	21	4	1	0	2	2	.50	0	.175	.447	.246
Dunedin	A	17	29	4	0	0	1	--	--	7	2	2	2	0	12	1	0	0	0	0	.00	0	.138	.219	.241
1989 St.Cathrnes	A	74	278	76	14	1	6	--	--	110	39	36	16	0	60	4	0	3	9	6	.60	8	.273	.319	.396
1990 Dunedin	A	117	438	101	15	5	6	--	--	144	56	37	20	1	100	2	3	4	18	5	.78	5	.231	.265	.329
1991 Knoxville	AA	114	403	97	14	3	8	--	--	141	48	40	26	2	88	4	5	3	17	10	.63	11	.241	.291	.350
1992 Syracuse	AAA	112	429	121	20	7	14	--	--	197	74	46	43	1	114	3	2	1	10	4	.71	5	.282	.351	.459
1992 New York	NL	30	108	24	7	1	3	(3	0)	42	15	10	8	0	24	0	0	1	2	2	.50	2	.222	.274	.389

Dickie Thon

Bats: Right **Throws:** Right **Pos:** SS **Ht:** 5'11" **Wt:** 178 **Born:** 06/20/58 **Age:** 35

Year Team	Lg	G	AB	H	2B	3B	HR	(Hm	Rd)	TB	R	RBI	TBB	IBB	SO	HBP	SH	SF	SB	CS	SB%	GDP	Avg	OBP	SLG
1979 California	AL	35	56	19	3	0	0	(0	0)	22	6	8	5	0	10	0	1	0	0	0	.00	2	.339	.393	.393
1980 California	AL	80	267	68	12	2	0	(0	0)	84	32	15	10	0	28	1	5	2	7	5	.58	5	.255	.282	.315
1981 Houston	NL	49	95	26	6	0	0	(0	0)	32	13	3	9	1	13	0	1	0	6	1	.86	3	.274	.337	.337
1982 Houston	NL	136	496	137	31	10	3	(1	2)	197	73	36	37	2	48	1	5	1	37	8	.82	4	.276	.327	.397
1983 Houston	NL	154	619	177	28	9	20	(4	16)	283	81	79	54	10	73	2	3	8	34	16	.68	12	.286	.341	.457
1984 Houston	NL	5	17	6	0	1	0	(0	0)	8	3	1	0	0	4	1	0	0	0	1	.00	1	.353	.389	.471
1985 Houston	NL	84	251	63	6	1	6	(3	3)	89	26	29	18	4	50	0	1	2	8	3	.73	2	.251	.299	.355
1986 Houston	NL	106	278	69	13	1	3	(0	3)	93	24	21	29	5	49	0	1	1	6	5	.55	8	.248	.318	.335
1987 Houston	NL	32	66	14	1	0	1	(0	1)	18	6	3	16	3	13	0	1	0	3	0	1.00	1	.212	.366	.273
1988 San Diego	NL	95	258	68	12	2	1	(0	1)	87	36	18	33	0	49	1	2	2	19	4	.83	4	.264	.347	.337
1989 Philadelphia	NL	136	435	118	18	4	15	(8	7)	189	45	60	33	6	81	0	1	3	6	3	.67	6	.271	.321	.434
1990 Philadelphia	NL	149	552	141	20	4	8	(3	5)	193	54	48	37	10	77	3	1	2	12	5	.71	14	.255	.305	.350
1991 Philadelphia	NL	146	539	136	18	4	9	(4	5)	189	44	44	25	6	84	0	2	4	11	5	.69	9	.252	.283	.351
1992 Texas	AL	95	275	68	15	3	4	(2	2)	101	30	37	20	1	40	0	3	2	12	2	.86	2	.247	.293	.367
14 ML YEARS		1302	4204	1110	183	41	70	(25	45)	1585	473	402	326	48	619	9	27	30	161	58	.74	73	.264	.316	.377

Gary Thurman

Bats: Right **Throws:** Right **Pos:** RF **Ht:** 5'10" **Wt:** 175 **Born:** 11/12/64 **Age:** 28

Year Team	Lg	G	AB	H	2B	3B	HR	(Hm	Rd)	TB	R	RBI	TBB	IBB	SO	HBP	SH	SF	SB	CS	SB%	GDP	Avg	OBP	SLG
1987 Kansas City	AL	27	81	24	2	0	0	(0	0)	26	12	5	8	0	20	0	1	0	7	2	.78	1	.296	.360	.321
1988 Kansas City	AL	35	66	11	1	0	0	(0	0)	12	6	2	4	0	20	0	0	0	5	1	.83	0	.167	.214	.182
1989 Kansas City	AL	72	87	17	2	1	0	(0	0)	21	24	5	15	0	26	0	2	1	16	0	1.00	0	.195	.311	.241
1990 Kansas City	AL	23	60	14	3	0	0	(0	0)	17	5	3	2	0	12	0	1	0	1	1	.50	2	.233	.258	.283
1991 Kansas City	AL	80	184	51	9	0	2	(1	1)	66	24	13	11	0	42	1	3	1	15	5	.75	4	.277	.320	.359
1992 Kansas City	AL	88	200	49	6	3	0	(0	0)	61	25	20	9	0	34	1	6	0	9	6	.60	3	.245	.281	.305
6 ML YEARS		325	678	166	23	4	2	(1	1)	203	96	48	49	0	154	2	13	2	53	15	.78	10	.245	.297	.299

Mike Timlin

Pitches: Right Bats: Right Pos: RP   Ht: 6' 4" Wt: 205 Born: 03/10/66 Age: 27

Year	Team	Lg	G	GS	CG	GF	IP	BFP	H	R	ER	HR	SH	SF	HB	TBB	IBB	SO	WP	Bk	W	L	Pct.	ShO	Sv	ERA
							HOW MUCH HE PITCHED				WHAT HE GAVE UP												THE RESULTS			
1987	Medicne Hat	R	13	12	2	0	75.1	326	79	50	43	4	1	2	5	26	0	66	9	5	4	8	.333	0	0	5.14
1988	Myrtle Bch	A	35	22	0	1	151	653	119	68	48	4	2	2	19	77	2	106	8	4	10	6	.625	0	0	2.86
1989	Dunedin	A	33	7	1	16	88.2	397	90	44	32	2	9	3	5	36	2	64	10	3	5	8	.385	0	7	3.25
1990	Dunedin	A	42	0	0	40	50.1	203	36	11	8	0	3	0	1	16	2	46	3	0	7	2	.778	0	22	1.43
	Knoxville	AA	17	0	0	15	26	105	20	6	5	0	0	0	1	7	1	21	0	0	1	2	.333	0	8	1.73
1992	Dunedin	A	6	1	0	1	10	39	9	2	1	0	0	0	0	2	0	7	1	0	0	0	.000	0	1	0.90
	Syracuse	AAA	7	1	0	4	11.1	51	15	11	11	3	0	0	0	5	1	7	0	0	0	1	.000	0	3	8.74
1991	Toronto	AL	63	3	0	17	108.1	463	94	43	38	6	6	2	1	50	11	85	5	0	11	6	.647	0	3	3.16
1992	Toronto	AL	26	0	0	14	43.2	190	45	23	20	0	2	1	1	20	5	35	0	0	0	0	.000	0	4	4.12
	2 ML YEARS		89	3	0	31	152	653	139	66	58	6	8	3	2	70	16	120	5	0	11	8	.579	0	4	3.43

Ron Tingley

Bats: Right Throws: Right Pos: C   Ht: 6' 2" Wt: 194 Born: 05/27/59 Age: 34

Year	Team	Lg	G	AB	H	2B	3B	HR	(Hm	Rd)	TB	R	RBI	TBB	IBB	SO	HBP	SH	SF	SB	CS	SB%	GDP	Avg	OBP	SLG
								BATTING													BASERUNNING			PERCENTAGES		
1982	San Diego	NL	8	20	2	0	0	0	(0	0)	2	0	0	0	0	7	0	1	0	0	0	.00	0	.100	.100	.100
1988	Cleveland	AL	9	24	4	0	0	1	(0	1)	7	1	2	2	0	8	0	0	0	0	0	.00	1	.167	.231	.292
1989	California	AL	4	3	1	0	0	0	(0	0)	1	0	0	1	0	0	0	0	0	0	0	.00	1	.333	.500	.333
1990	California	AL	5	3	0	0	0	0	(0	0)	0	0	0	1	0	1	0	0	0	0	0	.00	1	.000	.250	.000
1991	California	AL	45	115	23	7	1	0	(1	0)	33	11	13	8	0	34	1	4	0	1	1	.50	1	.200	.258	.287
1992	California	AL	71	127	25	2	1	3	(2	1)	38	15	8	13	0	35	2	5	0	0	1	.00	4	.197	.282	.299
	6 ML YEARS		142	292	55	9	1	5	(3	2)	81	27	23	25	0	85	3	10	0	1	2	.33	7	.188	.259	.277

Randy Tomlin

Pitches: Left Bats: Left Pos: SP   Ht: 5'10" Wt: 170 Born: 06/14/66 Age: 27

Year	Team	Lg	G	GS	CG	GF	IP	BFP	H	R	ER	HR	SH	SF	HB	TBB	IBB	SO	WP	Bk	W	L	Pct.	ShO	Sv	ERA
							HOW MUCH HE PITCHED				WHAT HE GAVE UP												THE RESULTS			
1990	Pittsburgh	NL	12	12	2	0	77.2	297	62	24	22	5	2	2	1	12	1	42	1	3	4	4	.500	0	0	2.55
1991	Pittsburgh	NL	31	27	4	0	175	736	170	75	58	9	5	2	6	54	4	104	2	3	8	7	.533	2	0	2.98
1992	Pittsburgh	NL	35	33	1	0	208.2	866	226	85	79	11	13	5	5	42	4	90	7	2	14	9	.609	1	0	3.41
	3 ML YEARS		78	72	7	0	461.1	1899	458	184	159	25	20	9	12	108	9	236	10	8	26	20	.565	3	0	3.10

Alan Trammell

Bats: Right Throws: Right Pos: SS   Ht: 6' 0" Wt: 185 Born: 02/21/58 Age: 35

Year	Team	Lg	G	AB	H	2B	3B	HR	(Hm	Rd)	TB	R	RBI	TBB	IBB	SO	HBP	SH	SF	SB	CS	SB%	GDP	Avg	OBP	SLG
								BATTING													BASERUNNING			PERCENTAGES		
1977	Detroit	AL	19	43	8	0	0	0	(0	0)	8	6	0	12	0	12	0	1	0	0	0	.00	1	.186	.255	.186
1978	Detroit	AL	139	448	120	14	6	2	(0	2)	152	49	34	45	0	56	2	6	3	3	1	.75	12	.268	.335	.339
1979	Detroit	AL	142	460	127	11	4	6	(4	2)	164	68	50	43	0	55	0	12	5	17	14	.55	6	.276	.335	.357
1980	Detroit	AL	146	560	168	21	5	9	(5	4)	226	107	65	69	2	63	3	13	7	12	12	.50	10	.300	.376	.404
1981	Detroit	AL	105	392	101	15	3	2	(2	0)	128	52	31	49	2	31	3	16	3	10	3	.77	10	.258	.342	.327
1982	Detroit	AL	157	489	126	34	3	9	(5	4)	193	66	57	52	0	47	0	9	6	19	8	.70	5	.258	.325	.395
1983	Detroit	AL	142	505	161	31	2	14	(8	6)	238	83	66	57	2	64	0	15	4	30	10	.75	7	.319	.385	.471
1984	Detroit	AL	139	555	174	34	5	14	(7	7)	260	85	69	60	2	63	3	6	2	19	13	.59	8	.314	.382	.468
1985	Detroit	AL	149	605	156	21	7	13	(7	6)	230	79	57	50	4	71	2	11	9	14	5	.74	6	.258	.312	.380
1986	Detroit	AL	151	574	159	33	7	21	(8	13)	269	107	75	59	4	57	5	11	4	25	12	.68	7	.277	.347	.469
1987	Detroit	AL	151	597	205	34	3	28	(13	15)	329	109	105	60	8	47	3	2	6	21	2	.91	11	.343	.402	.551
1988	Detroit	AL	128	466	145	24	1	15	(7	8)	216	73	69	46	8	46	4	0	7	7	4	.64	14	.311	.373	.464
1989	Detroit	AL	121	449	109	20	3	5	(2	3)	150	54	43	45	1	45	4	3	5	10	2	.83	9	.243	.314	.334
1990	Detroit	AL	146	559	170	37	1	14	(9	5)	251	71	89	68	7	55	1	3	6	12	10	.55	11	.304	.377	.449
1991	Detroit	AL	101	375	93	20	0	9	(6	3)	140	57	55	37	1	39	3	5	1	11	2	.85	7	.248	.320	.373
1992	Detroit	AL	29	102	28	7	1	1	(0	1)	40	11	11	15	0	4	1	1	1	2	2	.50	6	.275	.370	.392
	16 ML YEARS		1965	7179	2050	356	51	162	(83	79)	2994	1077	876	759	41	755	34	114	69	212	100	.68	130	.286	.354	.417

Jeff Treadway

Bats: Left Throws: Right Pos: 2B   Ht: 5'11" Wt: 170 Born: 01/22/63 Age: 30

Year	Team	Lg	G	AB	H	2B	3B	HR	(Hm	Rd)	TB	R	RBI	TBB	IBB	SO	HBP	SH	SF	SB	CS	SB%	GDP	Avg	OBP	SLG
								BATTING													BASERUNNING			PERCENTAGES		
1987	Cincinnati	NL	23	84	28	4	0	2	(2	0)	38	9	4	2	0	6	1	3	0	1	0	1.00	1	.333	.356	.452
1988	Cincinnati	NL	103	301	76	19	4	2	(2	0)	109	30	23	27	7	30	3	4	6	3	2	.60	9	.252	.315	.362
1989	Atlanta	NL	134	473	131	18	3	8	(2	6)	179	58	40	30	3	38	0	6	5	3	2	.60	9	.277	.317	.378
1990	Atlanta	NL	128	474	134	20	2	11	(5	6)	191	56	59	25	1	42	3	5	4	3	4	.43	10	.283	.320	.403

						(Hm	Rd)													SB%		Avg	OBP	SLG
1991 Atlanta	NL	106	306	98	17	2	3	(1 | 2)	128	41	32	23	1	19	2	2	3	2	2	.50	8	.320	.368	.418
1992 Atlanta	NL	61	126	28	6	1	0	(0 | 0)	36	5	5	9	4	16	0	0	0	1	2	.33	3	.222	.274	.286
6 ML YEARS		555	1764	495	84	12	26	(12 | 14)	681	199	163	116	16	151	9	21	18	12	10	.55	35	.281	.325	.386

Ricky Trlicek

Pitches: Right **Bats:** Right **Pos:** RP · **Ht:** 6' 2" **Wt:** 200 **Born:** 04/26/69 **Age:** 24

		HOW MUCH HE PITCHED						WHAT HE GAVE UP										THE RESULTS					
Year Team	Lg	G	GS	CG	GF	IP	BFP	H	R	ER	HR	SH	SF	HB	TBB	IBB	SO	WP	Bk	W	L	Pct.	ShO	Sv	ERA
1987 Utica	A	10	8	1	0	37.1	177	43	28	17	2	0	0	1	31	2	22	5	1	2	5	.286	1	0	4.10
1988 Batavia	A	8	8	0	0	31.2	151	27	32	26	2	0	3	4	31	0	26	7	2	2	3	.400	0	0	7.39
1989 Sumter	A	15	15	0	0	93.2	385	73	40	27	7	3	3	4	40	1	72	3	3	6	5	.545	0	0	2.59
Durham	A	1	1	0	0	8	30	3	2	1	0	0	0	1	1	0	4	2	0	0	0	.000	0	0	1.13
1990 Dunedin	A	26	26	0	0	154.1	649	128	74	64	2	6	3	6	72	0	125	22	6	5	8	.385	0	0	3.73
1991 Knoxville	AA	41	0	0	38	51.1	218	36	26	14	3	2	3	0	22	3	55	4	0	2	5	.286	0	16	2.45
1992 Syracuse	AAA	35	0	0	23	43.1	195	37	22	21	2	2	2	0	31	1	35	7	1	1	1	.500	0	10	4.36
1992 Toronto	AL	2	0	0	0	1.2	9	2	2	2	0	0	0	0	2	0	1	0	0	0	0	.000	0	0	10.80

Mike Trombley

Pitches: Right **Bats:** Right **Pos:** SP · **Ht:** 6' 2" **Wt:** 200 **Born:** 04/14/67 **Age:** 26

		HOW MUCH HE PITCHED						WHAT HE GAVE UP										THE RESULTS					
Year Team	Lg	G	GS	CG	GF	IP	BFP	H	R	ER	HR	SH	SF	HB	TBB	IBB	SO	WP	Bk	W	L	Pct.	ShO	Sv	ERA
1989 Kenosha	A	12	3	0	6	49	202	45	23	17	1	1	0	3	13	0	41	4	3	5	1	.833	0	2	3.12
Visalia	A	6	6	2	0	42	165	31	12	10	2	2	0	3	11	0	36	2	0	2	2	.500	1	0	2.14
1990 Visalia	A	27	25	3	1	176	739	163	79	67	12	3	3	11	50	0	164	8	1	14	6	.700	1	0	3.43
1991 Orlando	AA	27	27	7	0	191	773	153	65	54	12	7	6	7	57	3	175	2	1	12	7	.632	2	0	2.54
1992 Portland	AAA	25	25	2	0	165	695	149	70	67	18	5	2	6	58	1	138	1	2	10	8	.556	0	0	3.65
1992 Minnesota	AL	10	7	0	0	46.1	194	43	20	17	5	2	0	1	17	0	38	0	0	3	2	.600	0	0	3.30

Scooter Tucker

Bats: Right **Throws:** Right **Pos:** C · **Ht:** 6' 2" **Wt:** 205 **Born:** 11/18/66 **Age:** 26

		BATTING																BASERUNNING				PERCENTAGES		
Year Team	Lg	G	AB	H	2B	3B	HR	(Hm	Rd)	TB	R	RBI	TBB	IBB	SO	HBP	SH	SF	SB	CS	SB%	GDP	Avg	OBP	SLG
1988 Everett	A	45	153	40	5	0	3	--	--	54	24	23	30	0	34	3	0	3	0	0	.00	8	.261	.386	.353
1989 Clinton	A	126	426	105	20	2	3	--	--	138	44	43	58	2	80	9	3	4	6	5	.55	11	.246	.346	.324
1990 San Jose	A	123	439	123	28	2	5	--	--	170	59	71	71	4	69	13	2	6	9	3	.75	14	.280	.391	.387
1991 Shreveport	AA	110	352	100	29	1	4	--	--	143	49	49	48	1	58	5	6	2	3	4	.43	8	.284	.374	.406
1992 Tucson	AAA	83	288	87	15	1	1	--	--	107	36	29	28	1	35	3	1	2	5	1	.83	12	.302	.368	.372
1992 Houston	NL	20	50	6	1	0	0	(0	0)	7	5	3	3	0	13	2	1	0	1	1	.50	2	.120	.200	.140

Shane Turner

Bats: Left **Throws:** Right **Pos:** 3B/LF · **Ht:** 5'10" **Wt:** 190 **Born:** 01/08/63 **Age:** 30

		BATTING																BASERUNNING				PERCENTAGES		
Year Team	Lg	G	AB	H	2B	3B	HR	(Hm	Rd)	TB	R	RBI	TBB	IBB	SO	HBP	SH	SF	SB	CS	SB%	GDP	Avg	OBP	SLG
1985 Oneonta	A	64	228	56	7	3	0	--	--	69	35	26	35	2	44	3	1	2	12	0	1.00	2	.246	.351	.303
1986 Ft.Laudrdle	A	66	222	71	12	2	2	--	--	93	48	36	51	.1	35	3	4	3	12	8	.60	6	.320	.448	.419
1987 Columbus	AAA	25	76	17	0	2	0	--	--	21	10	7	5	0	16	0	1	0	2	1	.67	2	.224	.272	.276
Albany	AA	20	73	23	3	1	1	--	--	31	19	8	12	0	3	1	1	1	2	1	.67	3	.315	.414	.425
Reading	AA	74	283	96	16	6	3	--	--	133	50	47	21	1	35	3	1	1	3	6	.33	5	.339	.390	.470
1988 Maine	AAA	38	117	21	3	1	0	--	--	26	10	9	7	0	21	1	3	2	2	2	.50	1	.179	.228	.222
Reading	AA	78	295	88	11	6	3	--	--	120	52	21	26	3	53	7	6	2	14	2	.88	3	.298	.367	.407
1989 Reading	AA	46	141	28	5	1	1	--	--	38	18	11	27	1	27	2	0	0	13	3	.81	2	.199	.335	.270
Rochester	AAA	59	194	43	6	1	2	--	--	57	31	19	19	1	33	1	4	1	6	4	.60	5	.222	.293	.294
1990 Hagerstown	AA	10	38	9	1	0	0	--	--	10	5	1	0	0	10	0	0	0	1	0	1.00	1	.237	.237	.263
Rochester	AAA	86	209	59	7	0	1	--	--	69	29	19	25	2	41	0	7	2	3	5	.38	4	.282	.356	.330
1991 Rochester	AAA	110	404	114	13	2	1	--	--	134	49	57	47	1	75	3	1	2	6	7	.46	13	.282	.360	.332
1992 Calgary	AAA	76	242	68	17	3	0	--	--	91	31	26	35	1	46	3	2	1	10	8	.56	7	.281	.377	.376
1988 Philadelphia	NL	18	35	6	0	0	0	(0	0)	6	1	1	5	0	9	0	0	0	0	0	.00	1	.171	.275	.171
1991 Baltimore	AL	4	1	0	0	0	0	(0	0)	0	0	0	0	0	0	0	0	0	0	0	.00	0	.000	.000	.000
1992 Seattle	AL	34	74	20	5	0	0	(0	0)	25	8	5	9	0	15	0	2	2	2	1	.67	4	.270	.341	.338
3 ML YEARS		56	110	26	5	0	0	(0	0)	31	9	6	14	0	24	0	2	2	2	1	.67	5	.236	.317	.282

Jose Uribe

Bats: Both **Throws:** Right **Pos:** SS · **Ht:** 5'10" **Wt:** 165 **Born:** 01/21/59 **Age:** 34

		BATTING																BASERUNNING				PERCENTAGES		
Year Team	Lg	G	AB	H	2B	3B	HR	(Hm	Rd)	TB	R	RBI	TBB	IBB	SO	HBP	SH	SF	SB	CS	SB%	GDP	Avg	OBP	SLG
1984 St. Louis	NL	8	19	4	0	0	0	(0	0)	4	4	3	0	0	2	0	1	0	1	0	1.00	1	.211	.211	.211

Year	Team	Lg	G	AB	H	2B	3B	HR	(Hm	Rd)	TB	R	RBI	TBB	IBB	SO	HBP	SH	SF	SB	CS	SB%	GDP	Avg	OBP	SLG
1985	San Francisco	NL	147	476	113	20	4	3	(2	1)	150	46	26	30	8	57	2	5	0	8	2	.80	5	.237	.285	.315
1986	San Francisco	NL	157	453	101	15	1	3	(1	2)	127	46	43	61	19	76	0	3	0	22	11	.67	2	.223	.315	.280
1987	San Francisco	NL	95	309	90	16	5	5	(4	1)	131	44	30	24	9	35	1	5	1	12	2	.86	1	.291	.343	.424
1988	San Francisco	NL	141	493	124	10	7	3	(1	2)	157	47	35	36	10	69	0	4	2	14	10	.58	3	.252	.301	.318
1989	San Francisco	NL	151	453	100	12	6	1	(0	1)	127	34	30	34	12	74	0	6	4	6	6	.50	7	.221	.273	.280
1990	San Francisco	NL	138	415	103	8	6	1	(0	1)	126	35	24	29	13	49	0	4	0	5	9	.36	8	.248	.297	.304
1991	San Francisco	NL	90	231	51	8	4	1	(0	1)	70	23	12	20	6	33	0	1	0	3	4	.43	2	.221	.283	.303
1992	San Francisco	NL	66	162	39	9	1	2	(0	2)	56	24	13	14	3	25	0	4	1	2	2	.50	3	.241	.299	.346
	9 ML YEARS		993	3011	725	98	34	19	(8	11)	948	303	216	248	80	420	3	33	8	73	46	.61	32	.241	.298	.315

Sergio Valdez

Pitches: Right   Bats: Right   Pos: RP   Ht: 6' 1"   Wt: 190   Born: 09/07/65   Age: 27

Year	Team	Lg	G	GS	CG	GF	IP	BFP	H	R	ER	HR	SH	SF	HB	TBB	IBB	SO	WP	Bk	W	L	Pct.	ShO	Sv	ERA
1986	Montreal	NL	5	5	0	0	25	120	39	20	19	2	0	0	1	11	0	20	2	0	0	4	.000	0	0	6.84
1989	Atlanta	NL	19	1	0	8	32.2	145	31	24	22	5	2	0	0	17	3	26	2	0	1	2	.333	0	0	6.06
1990	2 ML Teams		30	3	0	7	107.2	466	115	66	58	17	5	5	1	38	2	66	4	0	6	6	.500	0	0	4.85
1991	Cleveland	AL	6	0	0	1	16.1	70	15	11	10	3	1	1	0	5	1	11	1	0	1	0	1.000	0	0	5.51
1992	Montreal	NL	27	0	0	9	37.1	148	25	12	10	2	1	0	0	12	1	32	4	0	0	2	.000	0	0	2.41
1990	Atlanta	NL	6	0	0	3	5.1	26	6	4	4	0	1	0	0	3	0	3	1	0	0	0	.000	0	0	6.75
	Cleveland	AL	24	13	0	4	102.1	440	109	62	54	17	4	5	1	35	2	63	3	0	6	6	.500	0	0	4.75
	5 ML YEARS		87	19	0	25	219	949	225	133	119	29	9	6	2	83	7	155	13	0	8	14	.364	0	0	4.89

John Valentin

Bats: Right   Throws: Right   Pos: SS   Ht: 6' 0"   Wt: 170   Born: 02/18/67   Age: 26

Year	Team	Lg	G	AB	H	2B	3B	HR	(Hm	Rd)	TB	R	RBI	TBB	IBB	SO	HBP	SH	SF	SB	CS	SB%	GDP	Avg	OBP	SLG
1988	Elmira	A	60	207	45	5	1	2	--	--	58	18	16	36	1	35	0	5	2	5	4	.56	6	.217	.331	.280
1989	Winter Havn	A	55	215	58	13	1	3	--	--	82	27	18	13	0	29	1	2	3	4	4	.50	7	.270	.310	.381
	Lynchburg	A	75	264	65	7	2	8	--	--	100	47	34	41	1	40	2	2	2	5	2	.71	8	.246	.350	.379
1990	New Britain	AA	94	312	68	18	1	2	--	--	94	20	31	25	1	46	0	11	3	1	2	.33	5	.218	.274	.301
1991	New Britain	AA	23	81	16	3	0	0	--	--	19	8	5	9	0	14	0	1	0	1	1	.50	2	.198	.278	.235
	Pawtucket	AAA	100	329	87	22	4	9	--	--	144	52	49	60	2	42	0	6	4	0	1	.00	4	.264	.374	.438
1992	Pawtucket	AAA	97	331	86	18	1	9	--	--	133	47	29	48	1	50	3	5	1	1	2	.33	9	.260	.358	.402
1992	Boston	AL	58	185	51	13	0	5	(1	4)	79	21	25	20	0	17	2	4	1	1	0	1.00	5	.276	.351	.427

Jose Valentin

Bats: Both   Throws: Right   Pos: 2B   Ht: 5'10"   Wt: 175   Born: 10/12/69   Age: 23

Year	Team	Lg	G	AB	H	2B	3B	HR	(Hm	Rd)	TB	R	RBI	TBB	IBB	SO	HBP	SH	SF	SB	CS	SB%	GDP	Avg	OBP	SLG
1987	Spokane	A	70	244	61	8	2	2	--	--	79	52	24	35	2	38	1	3	0	8	5	.62	4	.250	.346	.324
1988	Chston-Sc	A	133	444	102	20	1	6	--	--	143	56	44	45	1	83	3	9	4	11	4	.73	10	.232	.304	.322
1989	Riverside	A	114	381	74	10	5	10	--	--	124	40	41	37	1	93	5	5	2	8	7	.53	4	.194	.273	.325
	Wichita	AA	18	49	12	1	0	2	--	--	19	8	5	5	1	12	0	3	0	1	0	1.00	1	.245	.315	.388
1990	Wichita	AA	11	36	10	2	0	0	--	--	12	4	2	5	0	7	0	1	1	2	1	.67	1	.278	.366	.333
1991	Wichita	AA	129	447	112	22	5	17	--	--	195	73	68	55	1	115	4	4	5	8	6	.57	5	.251	.335	.436
1992	Denver	AAA	139	492	118	19	11	3	--	--	168	78	45	53	2	99	5	9	6	9	4	.69	8	.240	.317	.341
1992	Milwaukee	AL	4	3	0	0	0	0	(0	0)	0	1	1	0	0	0	0	0	0	1	0	.00	0	.000	.000	.000

Julio Valera

Pitches: Right   Bats: Right   Pos: SP   Ht: 6' 2"   Wt: 215   Born: 10/13/68   Age: 24

Year	Team	Lg	G	GS	CG	GF	IP	BFP	H	R	ER	HR	SH	SF	HB	TBB	IBB	SO	WP	Bk	W	L	Pct.	ShO	Sv	ERA
1986	Kingsport	R	13	13	2	0	76.1	356	91	58	44	5	4	0	0	29	2	64	4	1	3	10	.231	1	0	5.19
1987	Columbia	A	22	22	2	0	125.1	522	114	53	39	7	2	1	4	31	0	97	6	0	8	7	.533	2	0	2.80
1988	Columbia	A	30	27	8	3	191	775	171	77	68	8	5	7	4	51	3	144	9	6	15	11	.577	0	1	3.20
1989	St.Lucie	A	6	6	3	0	45	173	34	5	5	1	2	0	0	6	1	45	0	0	4	2	.667	2	0	1.00
	Jackson	AA	19	19	6	0	137.1	566	123	47	38	4	7	3	8	36	2	107	10	0	10	6	.625	2	0	2.49
	Tidewater	AAA	2	2	0	0	13	52	8	3	3	1	0	0	1	5	0	10	1	0	1	1	.500	0	0	2.08
1990	Tidewater	AAA	24	24	9	0	168	648	146	66	53	12	6	5	5	39	3	133	7	5	10	10	.500	2	0	3.02
1991	Tidewater	AAA	26	26	3	0	176.1	739	152	79	75	12	8	6	6	70	4	117	8	3	10	10	.500	1	0	3.83
1992	Tidewater	AAA	1	1	0	0	6	25	5	0	0	0	0	0	0	2	0	7	2	0	1	0	1.000	0	0	0.00
1990	New York	NL	3	3	0	0	13	64	20	11	10	1	0	0	0	7	0	11	0	0	1	1	.500	0	0	6.92
1991	New York	NL	2	0	0	1	2	11	1	0	0	0	0	0	0	4	1	3	0	0	0	0	.000	0	0	0.00
1992	California	AL	30	28	4	0	188	792	188	82	78	15	6	2	2	64	5	113	5	0	8	11	.421	2	0	3.73
	3 ML YEARS		35	31	4	1	203	867	209	93	88	16	6	2	2	75	6	120	5	0	9	12	.429	2	0	3.90

Dave Valle

Bats: Right **Throws:** Right **Pos:** C **Ht:** 6' 2" **Wt:** 200 **Born:** 10/30/60 **Age:** 32

Year Team	Lg	G	AB	H	2B	3B	HR	(Hm	Rd)	TB	R	RBI	TBB	IBB	SO	HBP	SH	SF	SB	CS	SB%	GDP	Avg	OBP	SLG
1984 Seattle	AL	13	27	8	1	0	1	(1	0)	12	4	4	1	0	5	0	0	0	0	0	.00	0	.296	.321	.444
1985 Seattle	AL	31	70	11	1	0	0	(0	0)	12	2	4	1	0	17	1	1	0	0	0	.00	1	.157	.181	.171
1986 Seattle	AL	22	53	18	3	0	5	(4	1)	36	10	15	7	0	7	0	0	0	0	0	.00	2	.340	.417	.679
1987 Seattle	AL	95	324	83	16	3	12	(8	4)	141	40	53	15	2	46	3	0	4	2	0	1.00	13	.256	.292	.435
1988 Seattle	AL	93	290	67	15	2	10	(5	5)	116	29	50	18	0	38	9	3	2	0	1	.00	13	.231	.295	.400
1989 Seattle	AL	94	316	75	10	3	7	(1	6)	112	32	34	29	2	32	6	1	3	0	0	.00	13	.237	.311	.354
1990 Seattle	AL	107	308	66	15	0	7	(1	6)	102	37	33	45	0	48	7	4	0	1	2	.33	11	.214	.328	.331
1991 Seattle	AL	132	324	63	8	1	8	(0	8)	97	38	32	34	0	49	9	6	3	0	0	.00	19	.194	.286	.299
1992 Seattle	AL	124	367	88	16	1	9	(7	2)	133	39	30	27	1	58	8	7	1	0	0	.00	7	.240	.305	.362
9 ML YEARS		711	2079	479	85	10	59	(27	32)	761	231	255	177	5	300	43	22	13	3	5	.38	79	.230	.302	.366

Andy Van Slyke

Bats: Left **Throws:** Right **Pos:** CF **Ht:** 6' 2" **Wt:** 195 **Born:** 12/21/60 **Age:** 32

Year Team	Lg	G	AB	H	2B	3B	HR	(Hm	Rd)	TB	R	RBI	TBB	IBB	SO	HBP	SH	SF	SB	CS	SB%	GDP	Avg	OBP	SLG
1983 St. Louis	NL	101	309	81	15	5	8	(3	5)	130	51	38	46	5	64	1	2	3	21	7	.75	4	.262	.357	.421
1984 St. Louis	NL	137	361	88	16	4	7	(3	4)	133	45	50	63	9	71	0	0	2	28	5	.85	5	.244	.354	.368
1985 St. Louis	NL	146	424	110	25	6	13	(6	8)	186	61	55	47	6	54	2	1	1	34	6	.85	7	.259	.335	.439
1986 St. Louis	NL	137	418	113	23	7	13	(6	7)	189	48	61	47	5	85	1	1	3	21	8	.72	2	.270	.343	.452
1987 Pittsburgh	NL	157	564	165	36	11	21	(11	10)	286	93	82	56	4	122	4	3	3	34	8	.81	6	.293	.359	.507
1988 Pittsburgh	NL	154	587	169	23	15	25	(16	9)	297	101	100	57	2	126	1	1	13	30	9	.77	8	.288	.345	.506
1989 Pittsburgh	NL	130	476	113	18	9	9	(4	5)	176	64	53	47	3	100	3	1	4	16	4	.80	13	.237	.308	.370
1990 Pittsburgh	NL	136	493	140	26	6	17	(6	11)	229	67	77	66	2	89	1	3	4	14	4	.78	6	.284	.367	.465
1991 Pittsburgh	NL	138	491	130	24	7	17	(9	8)	219	87	83	71	1	85	4	0	11	10	3	.77	5	.265	.355	.446
1992 Pittsburgh	NL	154	614	**199**	45	12	14	(6	8)	310	103	89	58	4	99	4	0	9	12	3	.80	9	.324	.381	.505
10 ML YEARS		1390	4737	1308	251	82	144	(69	75)	2155	720	688	558	41	895	21	12	53	220	57	.79	65	.276	.351	.455

John VanderWal

Bats: Left **Throws:** Left **Pos:** LF **Ht:** 6' 2" **Wt:** 190 **Born:** 04/29/66 **Age:** 27

Year Team	Lg	G	AB	H	2B	3B	HR	(Hm	Rd)	TB	R	RBI	TBB	IBB	SO	HBP	SH	SF	SB	CS	SB%	GDP	Avg	OBP	SLG
1987 Jamestown	A	18	69	33	12	3	3	--	--	60	24	15	3	0	14	0	0	1	3	2	.60	2	.478	.548	.870
Wst Plm Bch	A	50	189	54	11	2	2	--	--	75	29	22	30	0	25	0	1	3	8	3	.73	2	.286	.378	.397
1988 Wst Plm Bch	A	62	231	64	15	2	10	--	--	113	50	33	32	2	40	3	3	3	11	4	.73	0	.277	.368	.489
Jacksnville	AA	58	208	54	14	0	3	--	--	77	22	14	17	1	49	1	0	2	3	4	.43	3	.260	.317	.370
1989 Jacksnville	AA	71	217	55	9	2	6	--	--	86	30	24	22	1	51	1	0	2	2	3	.40	5	.253	.322	.396
1990 Jacksnville	AA	77	277	84	25	3	8	--	--	139	45	40	39	2	46	3	0	2	6	3	.67	7	.303	.393	.502
Indianapols	AAA	51	135	40	6	0	2	--	--	52	16	14	13	0	28	0	0	0	0	1	.00	3	.296	.358	.385
1991 Indianapols	AAA	133	478	140	36	8	15	--	--	237	84	71	79	4	118	2	1	4	8	1	.89	10	.293	.393	.496
1991 Montreal	NL	21	61	13	4	1	1	(0	1)	22	4	8	1	0	18	0	0	1	0	0	.00	2	.213	.222	.361
1992 Montreal	NL	105	213	51	8	2	4	(2	2)	75	21	20	24	2	36	0	0	0	3	0	1.00	2	.239	.316	.352
2 ML YEARS		126	274	64	12	3	5	(2	3)	97	25	28	25	2	54	0	0	1	3	0	1.00	4	.234	.297	.354

Gary Varsho

Bats: Left **Throws:** Right **Pos:** RF/LF **Ht:** 5'11" **Wt:** 188 **Born:** 06/20/61 **Age:** 32

Year Team	Lg	G	AB	H	2B	3B	HR	(Hm	Rd)	TB	R	RBI	TBB	IBB	SO	HBP	SH	SF	SB	CS	SB%	GDP	Avg	OBP	SLG
1988 Chicago	NL	46	73	20	3	0	0	(0	0)	23	6	5	1	0	6	0	0	1	5	0	1.00	0	.274	.280	.315
1989 Chicago	NL	61	87	16	4	2	0	(0	0)	24	10	6	4	1	13	0	0	0	3	0	1.00	0	.184	.220	.276
1990 Chicago	NL	46	48	12	4	0	0	(0	0)	16	10	1	1	1	6	0	0	0	2	0	1.00	1	.250	.265	.333
1991 Pittsburgh	NL	99	187	51	11	2	4	(1	3)	78	23	23	19	2	34	2	1	1	9	2	.82	2	.273	.344	.417
1992 Pittsburgh	NL	103	162	36	6	3	4	(3	1)	60	22	22	10	2	32	0	0	1	5	2	.71	2	.222	.266	.370
5 ML YEARS		355	557	135	28	7	8	(4	4)	201	71	57	35	5	91	2	1	3	24	4	.86	5	.242	.288	.361

Jim Vatcher

Bats: Right **Throws:** Right **Pos:** RF **Ht:** 5' 9" **Wt:** 165 **Born:** 05/27/66 **Age:** 27

Year Team	Lg	G	AB	H	2B	3B	HR	(Hm	Rd)	TB	R	RBI	TBB	IBB	SO	HBP	SH	SF	SB	CS	SB%	GDP	Avg	OBP	SLG
1990 2 ML Teams		57	73	19	2	1	1	(1	0)	26	7	7	5	0	15	0	0	0	0	0	.00	1	.260	.308	.356
1991 San Diego	NL	17	20	4	0	0	0	(0	0)	4	3	2	4	0	6	0	0	0	1	0	1.00	0	.200	.333	.200
1992 San Diego	NL	13	16	4	1	0	0	(0	0)	5	1	2	3	0	6	0	1	0	0	0	.00	0	.250	.368	.313
1990 Philadelphia	NL	36	46	12	1	0	1	(1	0)	16	5	4	4	0	6	0	0	0	0	0	.00	1	.261	.320	.348
Atlanta	NL	21	27	7	1	1	0	(0	0)	10	2	3	1	0	9	0	0	0	0	0	.00	0	.259	.286	.370
3 ML YEARS		87	109	27	3	1	1	(1	0)	35	11	11	12	0	27	0	1	0	1	0	1.00	1	.248	.322	.321

Greg Vaughn

Bats: Right **Throws:** Right **Pos:** LF **Ht:** 6' 0" **Wt:** 193 **Born:** 07/03/65 **Age:** 27

Year Team	Lg	G	AB	H	2B	3B	HR	(Hm	Rd)	TB	R	RBI	TBB	IBB	SO	HBP	SH	SF	SB	CS	SB%	GDP	Avg	OBP	SLG
1989 Milwaukee	AL	38	113	30	3	0	5	(1	4)	48	18	23	13	0	23	0	0	2	4	1	.80	0	.265	.336	.425
1990 Milwaukee	AL	120	382	84	26	2	17	(9	8)	165	51	61	33	1	91	1	7	6	7	4	.64	11	.220	.280	.432
1991 Milwaukee	AL	145	542	132	24	5	27	(16	11)	247	81	98	62	2	125	1	2	7	2	2	.50	5	.244	.319	.456
1992 Milwaukee	AL	141	501	114	18	2	23	(11	12)	205	77	78	60	1	123	5	2	5	15	15	.50	8	.228	.313	.409
4 ML YEARS		444	1538	360	71	9	72	(37	35)	665	227	260	168	4	362	7	11	20	28	22	.56	24	.234	.309	.432

Mo Vaughn

Bats: Left **Throws:** Right **Pos:** 1B/DH **Ht:** 6' 1" **Wt:** 230 **Born:** 12/15/67 **Age:** 25

Year Team	Lg	G	AB	H	2B	3B	HR	(Hm	Rd)	TB	R	RBI	TBB	IBB	SO	HBP	SH	SF	SB	CS	SB%	GDP	Avg	OBP	SLG
1989 New Britain	AA	73	245	68	15	0	8	--	--	107	28	38	25	3	47	3	1	1	1	3	.25	7	.278	.350	.437
1990 Pawtucket	AAA	108	386	114	26	1	22	--	--	208	62	72	44	2	87	6	0	2	3	2	.60	10	.295	.374	.539
1991 Pawtucket	AAA	69	234	64	10	0	14	--	--	116	35	50	60	7	44	3	0	4	2	1	.67	6	.274	.422	.496
1992 Pawtucket	AAA	39	149	42	6	0	6	--	--	66	15	28	18	1	35	0	0	1	1	0	1.00	5	.282	.357	.443
1991 Boston	AL	74	219	57	12	0	4	(1	3)	81	21	32	26	2	43	2	0	4	2	1	.67	7	.260	.339	.370
1992 Boston	AL	113	355	83	16	2	13	(8	5)	142	42	57	47	7	67	3	0	3	3	3	.50	8	.234	.326	.400
2 ML YEARS		187	574	140	28	2	17	(9	8)	223	63	89	73	9	110	5	0	7	5	4	.56	15	.244	.331	.389

Randy Velarde

Bats: Right **Throws:** Right **Pos:** SS/3B/LF **Ht:** 6' 0" **Wt:** 190 **Born:** 11/24/62 **Age:** 30

Year Team	Lg	G	AB	H	2B	3B	HR	(Hm	Rd)	TB	R	RBI	TBB	IBB	SO	HBP	SH	SF	SB	CS	SB%	GDP	Avg	OBP	SLG
1987 New York	AL	8	22	4	0	0	0	(0	0)	4	1	1	0	0	6	0	0	0	0	0	.00	1	.182	.182	.182
1988 New York	AL	48	115	20	6	0	5	(2	3)	41	18	12	8	0	24	2	0	0	1	1	.50	3	.174	.240	.357
1989 New York	AL	33	100	34	4	2	2	(1	1)	48	12	11	7	0	14	1	3	0	0	3	.00	6	.340	.389	.480
1990 New York	AL	95	229	48	6	2	5	(1	4)	73	21	19	20	0	53	1	2	1	0	3	.00	6	.210	.275	.319
1991 New York	AL	80	184	45	11	1	1	(0	1)	61	19	15	18	0	43	3	5	0	3	1	.75	6	.245	.322	.332
1992 New York	AL	121	412	112	24	1	7	(2	5)	159	57	46	38	1	78	2	4	5	7	2	.78	13	.272	.333	.386
6 ML YEARS		385	1062	263	51	6	20	(6	14)	386	128	104	91	1	218	9	14	6	11	10	.52	29	.248	.311	.363

Guillermo Velasquez

Bats: Left **Throws:** Right **Pos:** 1B **Ht:** 6' 0" **Wt:** 170 **Born:** 04/23/68 **Age:** 25

Year Team	Lg	G	AB	H	2B	3B	HR	(Hm	Rd)	TB	R	RBI	TBB	IBB	SO	HBP	SH	SF	SB	CS	SB%	GDP	Avg	OBP	SLG
1987 Chston-Sc	A	102	295	65	12	0	3	--	--	86	32	30	16	0	65	0	1	0	2	0	1.00	13	.220	.260	.292
1988 Chston-Sc	A	135	520	149	28	3	11	--	--	216	55	90	34	9	110	1	3	9	1	1	.50	6	.287	.326	.415
1989 Riverside	A	139	544	152	30	2	9	--	--	213	73	69	51	4	91	2	0	10	4	3	.57	14	.279	.338	.392
1990 Wichita	AA	105	377	102	21	2	12	--	--	163	48	72	35	5	66	1	0	4	1	1	.50	9	.271	.331	.432
1991 Wichita	AA	130	501	148	26	3	21	--	--	243	72	100	48	6	75	1	0	7	4	2	.67	6	.295	.354	.485
1992 Las Vegas	AAA	136	512	158	44	4	7	--	--	231	68	99	44	8	94	1	0	9	3	1	.75	7	.309	.359	.451
1992 San Diego	NL	15	23	7	0	0	1	(1	0)	10	1	5	1	0	7	0	0	0	0	0	.00	0	.304	.333	.435

Robin Ventura

Bats: Left **Throws:** Right **Pos:** 3B **Ht:** 6' 1" **Wt:** 192 **Born:** 07/14/67 **Age:** 25

Year Team	Lg	G	AB	H	2B	3B	HR	(Hm	Rd)	TB	R	RBI	TBB	IBB	SO	HBP	SH	SF	SB	CS	SB%	GDP	Avg	OBP	SLG
1989 Chicago	AL	16	45	8	3	0	0	(0	0)	11	5	7	8	0	6	1	1	3	0	0	.00	1	.178	.298	.244
1990 Chicago	AL	150	493	123	17	1	5	(2	3)	157	48	54	55	2	53	1	13	3	1	4	.20	5	.249	.324	.318
1991 Chicago	AL	157	606	172	25	1	23	(16	7)	268	92	100	80	3	67	4	8	7	2	4	.33	22	.284	.367	.442
1992 Chicago	AL	157	592	167	38	1	16	(7	9)	255	85	93	93	9	71	0	1	8	2	4	.33	14	.282	.375	.431
4 ML YEARS		480	1736	470	83	3	44	(25	19)	691	230	254	236	14	197	6	23	21	5	12	.29	42	.271	.356	.398

Hector Villanueva

Bats: Right **Throws:** Right **Pos:** C **Ht:** 6' 1" **Wt:** 220 **Born:** 10/02/64 **Age:** 28

Year Team	Lg	G	AB	H	2B	3B	HR	(Hm	Rd)	TB	R	RBI	TBB	IBB	SO	HBP	SH	SF	SB	CS	SB%	GDP	Avg	OBP	SLG
1990 Chicago	NL	52	114	31	4	1	7	(2	5)	58	14	18	4	2	27	2	0	0	1	0	1.00	3	.272	.308	.509
1991 Chicago	NL	71	192	53	10	1	13	(11	2)	104	23	32	21	1	30	0	0	0	0	0	.00	3	.276	.346	.542
1992 Chicago	NL	51	112	17	6	0	2	(2	0)	29	9	13	11	2	24	0	0	0	0	0	.00	5	.152	.228	.259
3 ML YEARS		174	418	101	20	2	22	(15	7)	191	46	63	36	5	81	2	0	1	1	0	1.00	11	.242	.304	.457

Frank Viola

Pitches: Left **Bats:** Left **Pos:** SP **Ht:** 6' 4" **Wt:** 210 **Born:** 04/19/60 **Age:** 33

Year	Team	Lg	G	GS	CG	GF	IP	BFP	H	R	ER	HR	SH	SF	HB	TBB	IBB	SO	WP	Bk	W	L	Pct.	ShO	Sv	ERA
1982	Minnesota	AL	22	22	3	0	126	543	152	77	73	22	2	0	0	38	2	84	4	1	4	10	.286	1	0	5.21
1983	Minnesota	AL	35	34	4	0	210	949	242	141	128	34	5	2	8	92	7	127	6	2	7	15	.318	0	0	5.49
1984	Minnesota	AL	35	35	10	0	257.2	1047	225	101	92	28	1	5	4	73	1	149	6	1	18	12	.600	4	0	3.21
1985	Minnesota	AL	36	36	9	0	250.2	1059	262	136	114	26	5	5	2	68	3	135	6	2	18	14	.563	0	0	4.09
1986	Minnesota	AL	37	37	7	0	245.2	1053	257	136	123	37	4	5	3	83	0	191	12	0	16	13	.552	1	0	4.51
1987	Minnesota	AL	36	36	7	0	251.2	1037	230	91	81	29	7	3	6	66	1	197	1	1	17	10	.630	1	0	2.90
1988	Minnesota	AL	35	35	7	0	255.1	1031	236	80	75	20	6	6	3	54	2	193	5	1	24	7	.774	2	0	2.64
1989	2 ML Teams		36	36	9	0	261	1082	246	115	106	22	12	6	4	74	4	211	8	1	13	17	.433	2	0	3.66
1990	New York	NL	35	35	7	0	249.2	1016	227	83	74	15	13	3	2	60	2	182	11	0	20	12	.625	3	0	2.67
1991	New York	NL	35	35	3	0	231.1	980	259	112	102	25	15	5	1	54	4	132	6	1	13	15	.464	0	0	3.97
1992	Boston	AL	35	35	6	0	238	999	214	99	91	13	7	10	4	89	4	121	12	2	13	12	.520	1	0	3.44
1989	Minnesota	AL	24	24	7	0	175.2	731	171	80	74	17	9	4	3	47	1	138	5	1	8	12	.400	1	0	3.79
	New York	NL	12	12	2	0	85.1	351	75	35	32	5	3	2	1	27	3	73	3	0	5	5	.500	1	0	3.38
	11 ML YEARS		377	376	72	0	2577	10796	2550	1171	1059	271	77	50	40	751	30	1722	77	12	163	137	.543	15	0	3.70

Joe Vitko

Pitches: Right **Bats:** Right **Pos:** RP **Ht:** 6' 8" **Wt:** 210 **Born:** 02/01/70 **Age:** 23

Year	Team	Lg	G	GS	CG	GF	IP	BFP	H	R	ER	HR	SH	SF	HB	TBB	IBB	SO	WP	Bk	W	L	Pct.	ShO	Sv	ERA
1989	Mets	R	8	5	1	2	41	170	28	15	15	0	0	2	1	16	0	33	4	3	4	1	.800	0	0	3.29
	Pittsfield	A	5	5	1	0	29.2	119	24	6	3	1	0	0	2	8	0	29	1	0	2	1	.667	1	0	0.91
1990	Columbia	A	16	12	4	2	90.1	367	70	29	25	3	3	2	1	30	0	72	12	1	8	1	.889	2	1	2.49
1991	St. Lucie	A	22	22	5	0	140.1	549	102	40	35	6	2	1	4	39	1	105	6	1	11	8	.579	2	0	2.24
1992	Binghamton	AA	26	26	4	0	165	696	163	76	64	11	2	1	12	53	0	89	7	0	12	8	.600	3	0	3.49
1992	New York	NL	3	1	0	1	4.2	29	12	11	7	1	0	1	0	1	0	6	1	0	0	1	.000	0	0	13.50

Jose Vizcaino

Bats: Both **Throws:** Right **Pos:** SS/3B **Ht:** 6' 1" **Wt:** 180 **Born:** 03/26/68 **Age:** 25

Year	Team	Lg	G	AB	H	2B	3B	HR	(Hm	Rd)	TB	R	RBI	TBB	IBB	SO	HBP	SH	SF	SB	CS	SB%	GDP	Avg	OBP	SLG
1989	Los Angeles	NL	7	10	2	0	0	0	(0	0)	2	2	0	0	0	1	0	1	0	0	0	.00	0	.200	.200	.200
1990	Los Angeles	NL	37	51	14	1	1	0	(0	0)	17	3	2	4	1	8	0	0	0	1	1	.50	1	.275	.327	.333
1991	Chicago	NL	93	145	38	5	0	0	(0	0)	43	7	10	5	0	18	0	2	2	2	1	.67	1	.262	.283	.297
1992	Chicago	NL	86	285	64	10	4	1	(0	1)	85	25	17	14	2	35	0	5	1	3	0	1.00	4	.225	.260	.298
	4 ML YEARS		223	491	118	16	5	1	(0	1)	147	37	29	23	3	62	0	8	3	6	2	.75	6	.240	.273	.299

Omar Vizquel

Bats: Both **Throws:** Right **Pos:** SS **Ht:** 5' 9" **Wt:** 165 **Born:** 04/24/67 **Age:** 26

Year	Team	Lg	G	AB	H	2B	3B	HR	(Hm	Rd)	TB	R	RBI	TBB	IBB	SO	HBP	SH	SF	SB	CS	SB%	GDP	Avg	OBP	SLG
1989	Seattle	AL	143	387	85	7	3	1	(1	0)	101	45	20	28	0	40	1	13	2	1	4	.20	6	.220	.273	.261
1990	Seattle	AL	81	255	63	3	2	2	(0	2)	76	19	18	18	0	22	0	10	2	4	1	.80	7	.247	.295	.298
1991	Seattle	AL	142	426	98	16	4	1	(1	0)	125	42	41	45	0	37	0	8	3	7	2	.78	8	.230	.302	.293
1992	Seattle	AL	136	483	142	20	4	0	(0	0)	170	49	21	32	0	38	2	9	1	15	13	.54	14	.294	.340	.352
	4 ML YEARS		502	1551	388	46	13	4	(2	2)	472	155	100	123	0	137	3	40	8	27	20	.57	35	.250	.305	.304

Jack Voigt

Bats: Right **Throws:** Right **Pos:** PH **Ht:** 6' 1" **Wt:** 175 **Born:** 05/17/66 **Age:** 27

Year	Team	Lg	G	AB	H	2B	3B	HR	(Hm	Rd)	TB	R	RBI	TBB	IBB	SO	HBP	SH	SF	SB	CS	SB%	GDP	Avg	OBP	SLG
1987	Newark	A	63	219	70	10	1	11	--	--	115	41	52	33	0	45	0	1	1	1	3	.25	3	.320	.407	.525
	Hagerstown	A	2	9	1	0	0	0	--	--	1	0	1	1	0	4	0	0	0	0	0	.00	0	.111	.200	.111
1988	Hagerstown	A	115	367	83	18	2	12	--	--	141	62	42	66	2	92	6	3	2	5	2	.71	7	.226	.351	.384
1989	Frederick	A	127	406	107	26	5	10	--	--	173	61	77	62	4	106	4	2	5	17	2	.89	5	.264	.363	.426
1990	Hagerstown	AA	126	418	106	26	2	12	--	--	172	55	70	59	1	97	5	6	11	5	3	.63	7	.254	.345	.411
1991	Hagerstown	AA	29	90	22	3	0	0	--	--	25	15	6	15	1	19	2	1	0	6	0	1.00	2	.244	.364	.278
	Rochester	AAA	83	267	72	11	4	6	--	--	109	46	35	40	2	53	1	5	2	9	1	.90	8	.270	.365	.408
1992	Rochester	AAA	129	443	126	23	4	16	--	--	205	74	64	58	3	102	4	3	0	9	2	.82	10	.284	.372	.463
1992	Baltimore	AL	1	0	0	0	0	0	(0	0)	0	0	0	0	0	0	0	0	0	0	0	.00	0	.000	.000	.000

Paul Wagner

Pitches: Right **Bats: Right** **Pos: RP**   **Ht: 6' 3"** **Wt: 205** **Born: 11/14/67** **Age: 25**

			HOW MUCH HE PITCHED						WHAT HE GAVE UP										THE RESULTS					
Year Team	Lg	G	GS	CG	GF	IP	BFP	H	R	ER	HR	SH	SF	HB	TBB	IBB	SO	WP	Bk	W	L	Pct.	ShO	Sv	ERA
1989 Welland	A	13	10	0	1	50.1	220	54	34	25	4	1	1	1	15	0	34	4	0	4	5	.444	0	0	4.47
1990 Augusta	A	35	1	0	20	72	313	71	30	22	3	3	3	2	30	3	71	7	0	7	7	.500	0	4	2.75
Salem	A	11	4	0	3	36	159	39	22	20	7	0	0	0	17	1	28	3	0	0	1	.000	0	2	5.00
1991 Salem	A	25	25	5	0	158.2	660	124	70	55	14	4	2	8	60	0	113	11	1	11	6	.647	2	0	3.12
1992 Carolina	AA	19	19	2	0	121.2	513	104	52	41	3	6	5	3	47	2	101	6	0	6	6	.500	1	0	3.03
Buffalo	AAA	8	8	0	0	39.1	181	51	27	24	1	2	1	1	14	0	19	2	0	3	3	.500	0	0	5.49
1992 Pittsburgh	NL	6	1	0	1	13	52	9	1	1	0	0	0	0	5	0	5	1	0	2	0	1.000	0	0	0.69

Tim Wakefield

Pitches: Right **Bats: Right** **Pos: SP**   **Ht: 6' 2"** **Wt: 195** **Born: 08/02/66** **Age: 26**

			HOW MUCH HE PITCHED						WHAT HE GAVE UP										THE RESULTS					
Year Team	Lg	G	GS	CG	GF	IP	BFP	H	R	ER	HR	SH	SF	HB	TBB	IBB	SO	WP	Bk	W	L	Pct.	ShO	Sv	ERA
1989	A	18	1	0	11	39.2	168	30	17	15	1	2	1	2	21	0	42	9	0	1	1	.500	0	2	3.40
1990 Salem	A	28	28	0	1	190.1	824	187	109	100	24	7	6	10	85	2	127	11	0	10	14	.417	0	0	4.73
1991 Buffalo	AAA	1	1	0	0	4.2	23	8	6	6	3	0	0	0	1	0	4	0	0	0	1	.000	0	0	11.57
Carolina	AA	26	25	8	1	183	741	155	68	59	13	6	3	9	51	6	120	2	1	15	8	.652	1	0	2.90
1992 Buffalo	AAA	20	20	6	0	135.1	559	122	52	46	10	3	7	3	51	1	71	9	0	10	3	.769	1	0	3.06
1992 Pittsburgh	NL	13	13	4	0	92	373	76	26	22	3	6	4	1	35	1	51	3	1	8	1	.889	1	0	2.15

Bob Walk

Pitches: Right **Bats: Right** **Pos: SP/RP**   **Ht: 6' 3"** **Wt: 217** **Born: 11/26/56** **Age: 36**

			HOW MUCH HE PITCHED						WHAT HE GAVE UP										THE RESULTS					
Year Team	Lg	G	GS	CG	GF	IP	BFP	H	R	ER	HR	SH	SF	HB	TBB	IBB	SO	WP	Bk	W	L	Pct.	ShO	Sv	ERA
1980 Philadelphia	NL	27	27	2	0	152	673	163	82	77	8	5	5	2	71	2	94	6	3	11	7	.611	0	0	4.56
1981 Atlanta	NL	12	8	0	1	43	189	41	25	22	6	2	0	0	23	0	16	1	0	1	4	.200	0	0	4.60
1982 Atlanta	NL	32	27	3	1	164.1	717	179	101	89	19	8	5	6	59	2	84	7	0	11	9	.550	1	0	4.87
1983 Atlanta	NL	1	1	0	0	3.2	20	7	3	3	0	1	0	0	2	0	4	0	0	0	0	.000	0	0	7.36
1984 Pittsburgh	NL	2	2	0	0	10.1	44	8	5	3	1	0	0	0	4	1	10	0	0	1	1	.500	0	0	2.61
1985 Pittsburgh	NL	9	9	1	0	58.2	248	60	27	24	3	3	1	0	18	2	40	2	3	2	3	.400	1	0	3.68
1986 Pittsburgh	NL	44	15	1	7	141.2	592	129	66	59	14	6	5	3	64	7	78	12	1	7	8	.467	1	2	3.75
1987 Pittsburgh	NL	39	12	1	6	117	498	107	52	43	11	6	2	3	51	2	78	7	3	8	2	.800	1	0	3.31
1988 Pittsburgh	NL	32	32	1	0	212.2	881	183	75	64	6	14	5	2	65	5	81	13	9	12	10	.545	1	0	2.71
1989 Pittsburgh	NL	33	31	2	1	196	843	208	106	96	15	4	2	4	65	1	83	7	4	13	10	.565	0	0	4.41
1990 Pittsburgh	NL	26	24	1	0	129.2	549	136	59	54	17	3	3	4	36	2	73	5	3	7	5	.583	1	1	3.75
1991 Pittsburgh	NL	25	20	0	0	115	484	104	53	46	10	7	4	5	35	2	67	11	2	9	2	.818	0	0	3.60
1992 Pittsburgh	NL	36	19	1	7	135	567	132	54	48	10	5	1	6	43	5	60	7	2	10	6	.625	0	2	3.20
13 ML YEARS		318	227	13	24	1479	6305	1457	708	628	120	64	33	35	536	31	768	78	30	92	67	.579	6	5	3.82

Chico Walker

Bats: Both **Throws: Right** **Pos: 3B/2B/LF**   **Ht: 5' 9"** **Wt: 185** **Born: 11/26/58** **Age: 34**

					BATTING														BASERUNNING				PERCENTAGES		
Year Team	Lg	G	AB	H	2B	3B	HR	(Hm	Rd)	TB	R	RBI	TBB	IBB	SO	HBP	SH	SF	SB	CS	SB%	GDP	Avg	OBP	SLG
1980 Boston	AL	19	57	12	0	0	1	(1	0)	15	5	3	5	6	1	10	1	1	3	2	.60	1	.211	.292	.263
1981 Boston	AL	6	17	6	0	0	0	(0	0)	6	3	2	1	0	2	0	0	0	0	2	.00	0	.353	.389	.353
1983 Boston	AL	4	5	2	0	2	0	(0	0)	6	2	1	0	0	0	0	0	0	0	0	.00	0	.400	.400	1.200
1984 Boston	AL	3	2	0	0	0	0	(0	0)	0	0	1	0	0	1	0	0	1	0	0	.00	0	.000	.000	.000
1985 Chicago	NL	21	12	1	0	0	0	(0	0)	1	3	0	0	0	5	0	0	0	1	0	1.00	0	.083	.083	.083
1986 Chicago	NL	28	101	28	3	2	1	(0	1)	38	21	7	10	0	20	0	0	1	15	4	.79	3	.277	.339	.376
1987 Chicago	NL	47	105	21	4	0	0	(0	0)	25	15	7	12	1	23	0	2	2	11	4	.73	1	.200	.277	.238
1988 California	AL	33	78	12	1	0	0	(0	0)	13	8	2	6	0	15	0	2	0	2	1	.67	2	.154	.214	.167
1991 Chicago	NL	124	374	96	10	1	6	(4	2)	126	51	34	33	2	57	0	1	3	13	5	.72	3	.257	.315	.337
1992 2 ML Teams		126	253	73	12	0	4	(0	4)	99	26	38	27	3	50	0	0	9	15	1	.94	9	.289	.351	.391
1992 Chicago	NL	19	26	3	0	0	0	(0	0)	3	2	2	3	0	4	0	0	1	1	0	1.00	0	.115	.200	.115
New York	NL	107	227	70	12	0	4	(0	4)	96	24	36	24	3	46	0	0	4	14	1	.93	9	.308	.369	.423
10 ML YEARS		411	1004	251	30	6	12	(5	7)	329	132	97	95	7	183	1	6	13	60	19	.76	19	.250	.312	.328

Larry Walker

Bats: Left **Throws: Right** **Pos: RF**   **Ht: 6' 3"** **Wt: 215** **Born: 12/01/66** **Age: 26**

					BATTING														BASERUNNING				PERCENTAGES		
Year Team	Lg	G	AB	H	2B	3B	HR	(Hm	Rd)	TB	R	RBI	TBB	IBB	SO	HBP	SH	SF	SB	CS	SB%	GDP	Avg	OBP	SLG
1989 Montreal	NL	20	47	8	0	0	0	(0	0)	8	4	4	5	0	13	1	3	0	1	1	.50	0	.170	.264	.170
1990 Montreal	NL	133	419	101	18	3	19	(9	10)	182	59	51	49	5	112	5	3	2	21	7	.75	8	.241	.326	.434
1991 Montreal	NL	137	487	141	30	2	16	(5	11)	223	59	64	42	2	102	5	1	4	14	9	.61	7	.290	.349	.458

| 1992 Montreal | NL | 143 | 528 | 159 | 31 | 4 | 23 | (13 | 10) | 267 | 85 | 93 | 41 | 10 | 97 | 6 | 0 | 8 | 18 | 6 | .75 | 9 | .301 | .353 | .506 |
| 4 ML YEARS | | 433 | 1481 | 409 | 79 | 9 | 58 | (27 | 31) | 680 | 207 | 212 | 137 | 17 | 324 | 17 | 7 | 14 | 54 | 23 | .70 | 24 | .276 | .341 | .459 |

Mike Walker

Pitches: Right **Bats:** Right **Pos:** SP **Ht:** 6' 3" **Wt:** 205 **Born:** 06/23/65 **Age:** 28

| | | | HOW MUCH HE PITCHED | | | | | WHAT HE GAVE UP | | | | | | | | | | THE RESULTS | | | | |
Year Team	Lg	G	GS	CG	GF	IP	BFP	H	R	ER	HR	SH	SF	HB	TBB	IBB	SO	WP	Bk	W	L	Pct.	ShO	Sv	ERA
1986 Watertown	A	16	16	2	0	103.1	477	116	71	52	8	4	5	7	46	1	81	8	1	4	10	.286	0	0	4.53
1987 Harrisburg	AA	4	4	0	0	15	74	20	17	15	2	0	0	0	9	0	9	4	1	0	2	.000	0	0	9.00
Salem	A	21	21	4	0	135.2	581	140	67	56	14	6	2	0	57	1	91	8	0	12	5	.706	1	0	3.71
1988 Harrisburg	AA	13	13	2	0	74.1	308	76	40	29	8	3	2	2	15	0	47	4	4	2	7	.222	2	0	3.51
Salem	A	5	5	1	0	37	160	42	17	13	3	1	0	1	9	0	29	3	0	2	2	.500	0	0	3.16
Buffalo	AAA	8	8	2	0	55	217	52	18	17	3	3	3	1	8	1	26	1	0	2	3	.400	0	0	2.78
1989 Buffalo	AAA	3	3	0	0	17	74	12	13	10	2	2	0	0	13	0	5	2	0	0	1	.000	0	0	5.29
Calgary	AAA	18	17	2	0	88	412	119	74	63	15	4	4	2	37	3	46	7	2	6	7	.462	1	0	6.44
1990 Calgary	AAA	25	24	3	0	144.2	637	176	92	86	16	4	6	3	45	0	64	7	0	5	11	.313	0	0	5.35
1992 Jacksonville	AA	11	11	0	0	62	261	63	38	33	6	2	1	3	18	0	40	3	1	3	3	.500	0	0	4.79
Calgary	AAA	12	6	1	1	41	189	50	26	24	5	3	0	1	19	1	24	2	0	5	1	.833	0	0	5.27
1992 Seattle	AL	5	3	0	1	14.2	74	21	14	12	4	1	1	0	9	3	5	1	0	0	3	.000	0	0	7.36

Tim Wallach

Bats: Right **Throws:** Right **Pos:** 3B/1B **Ht:** 6' 3" **Wt:** 202 **Born:** 09/14/57 **Age:** 35

| | | | | | | | | BATTING | | | | | | | | | | | BASERUNNING | | | | PERCENTAGES | | |
Year Team	Lg	G	AB	H	2B	3B	HR	(Hm	Rd)	TB	R	RBI	TBB	IBB	SO	HBP	SH	SF	SB	CS	SB%	GDP	Avg	OBP	SLG
1980 Montreal	NL	5	11	2	0	0	1	(0	1)	5	1	2	1	0	5	0	0	0	0	0	.00	0	.182	.250	.455
1981 Montreal	NL	71	212	50	9	1	4	(1	3)	73	19	13	15	2	37	4	0	0	0	1	.00	3	.236	.299	.344
1982 Montreal	NL	158	596	160	31	3	28	(11	17)	281	89	97	36	4	81	4	5	4	6	4	.60	15	.268	.313	.471
1983 Montreal	NL	156	581	156	33	3	19	(9	10)	252	54	70	55	8	97	6	0	5	0	3	.00	9	.269	.335	.434
1984 Montreal	NL	160	582	143	25	4	18	(4	14)	230	55	72	50	6	101	7	0	4	3	7	.30	12	.246	.311	.395
1985 Montreal	NL	155	569	148	36	3	22	(9	13)	256	70	81	38	8	79	5	0	5	9	9	.50	17	.260	.310	.450
1986 Montreal	NL	134	480	112	22	1	18	(6	12)	190	50	71	44	8	72	10	0	5	8	4	.67	16	.233	.308	.396
1987 Montreal	NL	153	593	177	42	4	26	(13	13)	305	89	123	37	5	98	7	0	7	9	5	.64	14	.298	.343	.514
1988 Montreal	NL	159	592	152	32	5	12	(3	9)	230	52	69	38	7	88	3	0	7	2	6	.25	19	.257	.302	.389
1989 Montreal	NL	154	573	159	42	0	13	(6	7)	240	76	77	58	10	81	1	0	7	3	7	.30	21	.277	.341	.419
1990 Montreal	NL	161	626	185	37	5	21	(9	12)	295	69	98	42	11	80	3	0	7	6	9	.40	12	.296	.339	.471
1991 Montreal	NL	151	577	130	22	1	13	(5	8)	193	60	73	50	8	100	6	0	4	2	4	.33	12	.225	.292	.334
1992 Montreal	NL	150	537	120	29	1	9	(5	4)	178	53	59	50	2	90	8	0	7	2	2	.50	10	.223	.296	.331
13 ML YEARS		1767	6529	1694	360	31	204	(81	123)	2728	737	905	514	79	1009	64	5	62	50	61	.45	152	.259	.317	.418

Denny Walling

Bats: Left **Throws:** Right **Pos:** PH **Ht:** 6' 1" **Wt:** 185 **Born:** 04/17/54 **Age:** 39

| | | | | | | | | BATTING | | | | | | | | | | | BASERUNNING | | | | PERCENTAGES | | |
Year Team	Lg	G	AB	H	2B	3B	HR	(Hm	Rd)	TB	R	RBI	TBB	IBB	SO	HBP	SH	SF	SB	CS	SB%	GDP	Avg	OBP	SLG
1975 Oakland	AL	6	8	1	1	0	0	(0	0)	2	0	2	0	0	4	0	0	0	0	0	.00	0	.125	.125	.250
1976 Oakland	AL	3	11	3	0	0	0	(0	0)	3	1	0	0	0	3	0	0	0	0	0	.00	0	.273	.273	.273
1977 Houston	NL	6	21	6	0	1	0	(0	0)	8	1	6	2	0	4	0	0	0	0	1	.00	0	.286	.348	.381
1978 Houston	NL	120	247	62	11	3	3	(2	1)	88	30	36	30	3	24	1	0	2	9	2	.82	2	.251	.332	.356
1979 Houston	NL	82	147	48	8	4	3	(3	0)	73	21	31	17	2	21	0	0	1	3	2	.60	2	.327	.394	.497
1980 Houston	NL	100	284	85	6	5	3	(1	2)	110	30	29	35	4	26	0	0	2	4	3	.57	2	.299	.374	.387
1981 Houston	NL	65	158	37	6	0	5	(2	3)	58	23	23	28	1	17	0	1	2	2	1	.67	3	.234	.346	.367
1982 Houston	NL	85	146	30	4	1	1	(1	0)	39	22	14	23	3	19	0	0	1	4	2	.67	6	.205	.312	.267
1983 Houston	NL	100	135	40	5	3	3	(1	2)	60	24	19	15	1	16	0	1	1	2	2	.50	1	.296	.364	.444
1984 Houston	NL	87	249	70	11	5	3	(0	3)	100	37	31	16	2	28	1	0	2	7	1	.88	4	.281	.325	.402
1985 Houston	NL	119	345	93	20	1	7	(2	5)	136	44	45	25	2	26	0	0	4	5	2	.71	8	.270	.316	.394
1986 Houston	NL	130	382	119	23	1	13	(5	8)	183	54	58	36	5	31	0	0	4	1	1	.50	8	.312	.367	.479
1987 Houston	NL	110	325	92	21	4	5	(2	3)	136	45	33	39	1	37	0	2	4	5	1	.83	9	.283	.356	.418
1988 2 ML Teams		84	234	56	13	2	1	(0	1)	76	22	21	17	3	25	0	1	0	2	0	1.00	3	.239	.291	.325
1989 St. Louis	NL	69	79	24	7	0	1	(0	1)	34	9	11	14	2	12	0	0	0	0	0	.00	1	.304	.409	.430
1990 St. Louis	NL	78	127	28	5	0	1	(1	0)	36	7	19	8	0	15	0	1	1	0	0	.00	5	.220	.265	.283
1991 Texas	AL	24	44	4	1	0	0	(0	0)	5	1	2	3	0	8	2	0	0	0	0	.00	3	.091	.184	.114
1992 Houston	NL	3	3	1	0	0	0	(0	0)	1	1	0	0	0	0	0	0	0	0	0	.00	0	.333	.333	.333
1988 St. Louis	NL	65	176	43	10	2	1	(0	1)	60	19	20	15	3	18	0	1	0	1	0	1.00	2	.244	.304	.341
St. Louis	NL	19	58	13	3	0	0	(0	0)	16	3	1	2	0	7	0	0	0	1	0	1.00	1	.224	.250	.276
18 ML YEARS		1271	2945	799	142	30	49	(20	29)	1148	372	380	308	29	316	4	6	24	44	18	.71	57	.271	.339	.390

Dan Walters

Bats: Right **Throws:** Right **Pos:** C **Ht:** 6' 4" **Wt:** 225 **Born:** 08/15/66 **Age:** 26

							BATTING													BASERUNNING				PERCENTAGES		
Year	Team	Lg	G	AB	H	2B	3B	HR	(Hm	Rd)	TB	R	RBI	TBB	IBB	SO	HBP	SH	SF	SB	CS	SB%	GDP	Avg	OBP	SLG
1985	Asheville	A	15	28	1	0	0	0	--	--	1	1	1	1	0	11	0	1	0	0	0	.00	1	.036	.069	.036
	Auburn	A	44	144	30	6	0	0	--	--	36	15	10	8	0	23	1	0	3	1	0	1.00	6	.208	.250	.250
1986	Asheville	A	101	366	96	21	1	8	--	--	143	42	46	14	0	59	1	1	2	1	1	.50	12	.262	.290	.391
1987	Osceola	A	99	338	84	8	0	1	--	--	95	23	30	33	2	42	0	5	5	2	4	.33	15	.249	.311	.281
1988	Tucson	AAA	2	7	0	0	0	0	--	--	0	0	0	0	0	2	0	0	0	0	0	.00	0	.000	.000	.000
	Columbus	AA	98	305	71	10	1	7	--	--	104	31	28	26	0	42	3	3	4	1	0	1.00	11	.233	.296	.341
1989	Wichita	AA	89	300	82	15	0	6	--	--	115	30	45	25	2	31	3	3	2	0	2	.00	5	.273	.333	.383
1990	Wichita	AA	58	199	59	12	0	7	--	--	92	25	40	21	2	21	1	0	2	0	0	.00	8	.296	.363	.462
	Las Vegas	AAA	53	184	47	9	0	3	--	--	65	19	26	13	0	24	0	0	3	0	0	.00	10	.255	.300	.353
1991	Las Vegas	AAA	96	293	93	22	0	4	--	--	127	39	44	22	5	35	0	0	0	0	0	.00	12	.317	.365	.433
1992	Las Vegas	AAA	35	127	50	9	0	2	--	--	65	16	25	10	1	12	2	1	2	0	0	.00	5	.394	.440	.512
1992	San Diego	NL	57	179	45	11	1	4	(3	1)	70	14	22	10	0	28	2	1	2	1	0	1.00	3	.251	.295	.391

Bruce Walton

Pitches: Right **Bats:** Right **Pos:** RP **Ht:** 6' 2" **Wt:** 195 **Born:** 12/25/62 **Age:** 30

			HOW MUCH HE PITCHED					WHAT HE GAVE UP									THE RESULTS					
Year	Team	Lg	G	GS	CG	GF	IP	BFP	H	R	ER	HR	SH	SF	HB	TBB	IBB	SO	WP	Bk	W	L	Pct.	ShO	Sv	ERA
1985	Pocatello	R	18	9	2	6	76.2	0	89	46	35	2	0	0	1	27	3	69	2	0	3	7	.300	0	3	4.11
1986	Modesto	A	27	27	4	0	176	778	204	96	80	16	10	5	9	41	1	107	7	1	13	7	.650	0	0	4.09
	Madison	A	1	1	0	0	5	21	5	3	3	0	0	0	0	1	0	1	0	0	0	0	.000	0	0	5.40
1987	Modesto	A	16	16	3	0	106.1	437	97	44	34	6	1	3	4	27	0	84	2	0	8	6	.571	1	0	2.88
	Huntsville	AA	18	2	0	6	58	248	61	24	20	4	2	3	1	13	1	40	4	2	2	2	.500	0	2	3.10
1988	Huntsville	AA	42	3	0	17	116.1	502	126	64	59	10	5	3	5	23	7	82	2	6	4	5	.444	0	3	4.56
1989	Tacoma	AAA	32	14	1	7	107.2	461	118	59	45	7	4	4	1	27	1	76	3	2	8	6	.571	1	0	3.76
1990	Tacoma	AAA	46	5	0	21	98.1	403	103	42	34	12	4	7	2	23	5	67	1	5	5	5	.500	0	7	3.11
1991	Tacoma	AAA	38	0	0	38	46.2	184	39	11	7	0	2	0	0	5	1	49	2	0	1	1	.500	0	20	1.35
1992	Tacoma	AAA	35	7	2	22	81.1	333	76	29	25	6	1	2	3	21	4	60	1	0	8	2	.800	1	8	2.77
1991	Oakland	AL	12	0	0	5	13	56	13	9	9	3	0	1	0	6	0	10	3	0	1	0	1.000	0	0	6.23
1992	Oakland	AL	7	0	0	2	10	49	17	11	11	1	0	1	0	3	0	7	0	1	0	0	.000	0	0	9.90
	2 ML YEARS		19	0	0	7	23	105	28	20	20	4	0	2	0	9	0	17	3	1	1	0	1.000	0	0	7.83

Jerome Walton

Bats: Right **Throws:** Right **Pos:** LF **Ht:** 6' 1" **Wt:** 175 **Born:** 07/08/65 **Age:** 27

							BATTING													BASERUNNING				PERCENTAGES		
Year	Team	Lg	G	AB	H	2B	3B	HR	(Hm	Rd)	TB	R	RBI	TBB	IBB	SO	HBP	SH	SF	SB	CS	SB%	GDP	Avg	OBP	SLG
1989	Chicago	NL	116	475	139	23	3	5	(3	2)	183	64	46	27	1	77	6	2	5	24	7	.77	6	.293	.335	.385
1990	Chicago	NL	101	392	103	16	2	2	(2	0)	129	63	21	50	1	70	4	1	2	14	7	.67	4	.263	.350	.329
1991	Chicago	NL	123	270	59	13	1	5	(3	2)	89	42	17	19	0	55	3	3	3	7	3	.70	7	.219	.275	.330
1992	Chicago	NL	30	55	7	0	1	0	(0	0)	9	7	1	9	0	13	2	3	0	1	2	.33	1	.127	.273	.164
	4 ML YEARS		370	1192	308	52	7	12	(8	4)	410	176	85	105	2	215	15	9	10	46	19	.71	18	.258	.324	.344

Duane Ward

Pitches: Right **Bats:** Right **Pos:** RP **Ht:** 6' 4" **Wt:** 215 **Born:** 05/28/64 **Age:** 29

			HOW MUCH HE PITCHED					WHAT HE GAVE UP									THE RESULTS					
Year	Team	Lg	G	GS	CG	GF	IP	BFP	H	R	ER	HR	SH	SF	HB	TBB	IBB	SO	WP	Bk	W	L	Pct.	ShO	Sv	ERA
1986	2 ML Teams		12	1	0	7	18	88	25	17	16	2	2	0	1	12	0	9	1	1	0	2	.000	0	0	8.00
1987	Toronto	AL	12	1	0	4	11.2	57	14	9	9	0	1	1	0	12	2	10	0	0	1	0	1.000	0	0	6.94
1988	Toronto	AL	64	0	0	32	111.2	487	101	46	41	5	4	5	5	60	8	91	10	3	9	3	.750	0	15	3.30
1989	Toronto	AL	66	0	0	39	114.2	494	94	55	48	4	12	11	5	58	11	122	13	0	4	10	.286	0	15	3.77
1990	Toronto	AL	73	0	0	39	127.2	508	101	51	49	9	6	2	1	42	10	112	5	0	2	8	.200	0	11	3.45
1991	Toronto	AL	81	0	0	46	107.1	428	80	36	33	3	3	4	2	33	3	132	6	0	7	6	.538	0	23	2.77
1992	Toronto	AL	79	0	0	35	101.1	414	76	27	22	5	3	4	1	39	3	103	7	0	7	4	.636	0	12	1.95
1986	Atlanta	NL	10	0	0	6	16	73	22	13	13	2	2	0	0	8	0	8	0	1	0	1	.000	0	0	7.31
	Toronto	AL	2	1	0	1	2	15	3	4	3	0	0	0	1	4	0	1	1	0	0	1	.000	0	0	13.50
	7 ML YEARS		387	2	0	202	592.1	2476	491	241	218	28	31	27	15	256	37	579	42	4	30	33	.476	0	76	3.31

Kevin Ward

Bats: Right **Throws:** Right **Pos:** LF **Ht:** 6' 1" **Wt:** 195 **Born:** 09/28/61 **Age:** 31

							BATTING													BASERUNNING				PERCENTAGES		
Year	Team	Lg	G	AB	H	2B	3B	HR	(Hm	Rd)	TB	R	RBI	TBB	IBB	SO	HBP	SH	SF	SB	CS	SB%	GDP	Avg	OBP	SLG
1984	Peninsula	A	130	456	119	18	5	13	--	--	186	84	69	53	3	90	6	4	7	21	3	.88	11	.261	.341	.408
1985	Reading	AA	42	132	40	9	6	1	--	--	64	23	21	23	1	19	5	0	2	7	5	.58	2	.303	.420	.485
1986	Reading	AA	119	398	109	27	6	7	--	--	169	79	59	66	1	66	6	1	7	28	14	.67	9	.274	.379	.425

209

Year	Team	Lg	G	AB	H	2B	3B	HR	(Hm	Rd)	TB	R	RBI	TBB	IBB	SO	HBP	SH	SF	SB	CS	SB%	GDP	Avg	OBP	SLG
1987	Reading	AA	16	56	14	5	1	0	--	--	21	9	6	6	0	12	1	0	1	5	2	.71	0	.250	.328	.375
	Maine	AAA	106	326	68	13	3	13	--	--	126	48	37	30	0	68	5	1	2	14	8	.64	9	.209	.284	.387
1988	Maine	AAA	134	456	105	22	8	11	--	--	176	60	63	62	1	118	7	9	3	17	11	.61	9	.230	.330	.386
1989	Huntsville	AA	27	84	26	4	4	3	--	--	47	20	18	29	0	18	1	0	3	15	0	1.00	1	.310	.479	.560
1990	Tacoma	AAA	123	421	125	30	14	10	--	--	213	83	60	44	1	72	14	4	4	24	10	.71	8	.297	.379	.506
1991	Las Vegas	AAA	83	276	89	17	6	6	--	--	136	51	43	58	2	53	7	1	5	10	4	.71	4	.322	.445	.493
1991	San Diego	NL	44	107	26	7	2	2	(0	2)	43	13	8	9	0	27	1	1	0	1	4	.20	1	.243	.308	.402
1992	San Diego	NL	81	147	29	5	0	3	(0	3)	43	12	12	14	0	38	2	1	1	2	3	.40	8	.197	.274	.293
	2 ML YEARS		125	254	55	12	2	5	(0	5)	86	25	20	23	0	65	3	2	1	3	7	.30	11	.217	.288	.339

Turner Ward

Bats: Both **Throws:** Right **Pos:** RF **Ht:** 6' 2" **Wt:** 200 **Born:** 04/11/65 **Age:** 28

							BATTING													BASERUNNING				PERCENTAGES		
Year	Team	Lg	G	AB	H	2B	3B	HR	(Hm	Rd)	TB	R	RBI	TBB	IBB	SO	HBP	SH	SF	SB	CS	SB%	GDP	Avg	OBP	SLG
1990	Cleveland	AL	14	46	16	2	1	1	(0	1)	23	10	10	3	0	8	0	0	0	3	0	1.00	1	.348	.388	.500
1991	2 ML Teams		48	113	27	7	0	0	(0	0)	34	12	7	11	0	18	0	4	0	0	1	.00	2	.239	.306	.301
1992	Toronto	AL	18	29	10	3	0	1	(0	1)	16	7	3	4	0	4	0	0	0	0	1	.00	1	.345	.424	.552
1991	Cleveland	AL	40	100	23	7	0	0	(0	0)	30	11	5	10	0	16	0	4	0	0	0	.00	1	.230	.300	.300
	Toronto	AL	8	13	4	0	0	0	(0	0)	4	1	2	1	0	2	0	0	0	0	0	.00	1	.308	.357	.308
	3 ML YEARS		80	188	53	12	1	2	(0	2)	73	29	20	18	0	30	0	4	0	3	1	.75	4	.282	.345	.388

Gary Wayne

Pitches: Left **Bats:** Left **Pos:** RP **Ht:** 6' 3" **Wt:** 195 **Born:** 11/30/62 **Age:** 30

				HOW MUCH HE PITCHED					WHAT HE GAVE UP									THE RESULTS					
Year	Team	Lg	G	GS	CG	GF	IP	BFP	H	R	ER	HR	SH	SF	HB	TBB	IBB	SO	WP	Bk	W	L	Pct.	ShO	Sv	ERA
1989	Minnesota	AL	60	0	0	21	71	302	55	28	26	4	4	2	1	36	4	41	7	0	3	4	.429	0	1	3.30
1990	Minnesota	AL	38	0	0	12	38.2	166	38	19	18	5	1	2	1	13	0	28	4	0	1	1	.500	0	1	4.19
1991	Minnesota	AL	8	0	0	2	12.1	52	11	7	7	1	1	1	1	4	0	7	0	0	1	0	1.000	0	1	5.11
1992	Minnesota	AL	41	0	0	13	48	210	46	18	14	2	8	3	3	19	5	29	1	1	3	3	.500	0	0	2.63
	4 ML YEARS		147	0	0	48	170	730	150	72	65	12	14	8	6	72	9	105	12	1	8	8	.500	0	3	3.44

Dave Weathers

Pitches: Right **Bats:** Right **Pos:** RP **Ht:** 6' 3" **Wt:** 205 **Born:** 09/25/69 **Age:** 23

				HOW MUCH HE PITCHED					WHAT HE GAVE UP									THE RESULTS					
Year	Team	Lg	G	GS	CG	GF	IP	BFP	H	R	ER	HR	SH	SF	HB	TBB	IBB	SO	WP	Bk	W	L	Pct.	ShO	Sv	ERA
1988	St.Cathrnes	A	15	12	0	0	62.2	267	58	30	21	3	2	0	2	26	0	36	5	4	4	4	.500	0	0	3.02
1989	Myrtle Bch	A	31	31	2	0	172.2	759	163	99	74	3	5	2	7	86	2	111	12	1	11	13	.458	0	0	3.86
1990	Dunedin	A	27	27	2	0	158	675	158	82	65	2	4	7	9	59	0	96	10	9	10	7	.588	0	0	3.70
1991	Knoxville	AA	24	22	5	0	139.1	575	121	51	38	3	1	3	8	49	1	114	7	2	10	7	.588	2	0	2.45
1992	Syracuse	AAA	12	10	0	1	48.1	215	48	29	25	3	2	1	2	21	2	30	2	0	1	4	.200	0	0	4.66
1991	Toronto	AL	15	0	0	4	14.2	79	15	9	8	1	2	1	2	17	3	13	0	0	1	0	1.000	0	0	4.91
1992	Toronto	AL	2	0	0	0	3.1	15	5	3	3	1	0	0	0	2	0	3	0	0	0	0	.000	0	0	8.10
	2 ML YEARS		17	0	0	4	18	94	20	12	11	2	2	1	2	19	3	16	0	0	1	0	1.000	0	0	5.50

Lenny Webster

Bats: Right **Throws:** Right **Pos:** C **Ht:** 5' 9" **Wt:** 185 **Born:** 02/10/65 **Age:** 28

							BATTING													BASERUNNING				PERCENTAGES		
Year	Team	Lg	G	AB	H	2B	3B	HR	(Hm	Rd)	TB	R	RBI	TBB	IBB	SO	HBP	SH	SF	SB	CS	SB%	GDP	Avg	OBP	SLG
1986	Kenosha	A	22	65	10	2	0	0	--	--	12	2	8	10	0	12	0	1	0	0	0	.00	3	.154	.267	.185
	Elizabethtn	R	48	152	35	4	0	3	--	--	48	29	14	22	0	21	2	0	0	1	0	1.00	6	.230	.335	.316
1987	Kenosha	A	52	140	35	7	0	3	--	--	51	17	17	17	0	20	0	0	3	2	0	1.00	1	.250	.325	.364
1988	Kenosha	A	129	465	134	23	2	11	--	--	194	82	87	71	5	47	1	2	7	3	2	.60	13	.288	.379	.417
1989	Visalia	A	63	231	62	7	0	5	--	--	84	36	39	27	1	27	1	0	5	2	1	.67	9	.268	.341	.364
	Orlando	AA	59	191	45	7	0	2	--	--	58	29	17	44	1	20	3	2	2	2	0	1.00	3	.236	.383	.304
1990	Orlando	AA	126	455	119	31	0	8	--	--	174	69	71	68	5	57	0	0	3	0	0	.00	11	.262	.356	.382
1991	Portland	AAA	87	325	82	18	0	7	--	--	121	43	34	24	2	32	1	0	3	1	4	.20	14	.252	.303	.372
1989	Minnesota	AL	14	20	6	2	0	0	(0	0)	8	3	1	3	0	2	0	0	0	0	0	.00	0	.300	.391	.400
1990	Minnesota	AL	2	6	2	1	0	0	(0	0)	3	1	0	1	0	1	0	0	0	0	0	.00	0	.333	.429	.500
1991	Minnesota	AL	18	34	10	1	0	3	(1	2)	20	7	8	6	0	10	0	0	1	0	0	.00	2	.294	.390	.588
1992	Minnesota	AL	53	118	33	10	1	1	(1	0)	48	10	13	9	0	11	0	2	0	0	2	.00	3	.280	.331	.407
	4 ML YEARS		87	178	51	14	1	4	(2	2)	79	21	22	19	0	24	0	2	1	0	2	.00	5	.287	.354	.444

Mitch Webster

Bats: Both **Throws:** Left **Pos:** RF/LF **Ht:** 6' 1" **Wt:** 185 **Born:** 05/16/59 **Age:** 34

							BATTING													BASERUNNING				PERCENTAGES		
Year	Team	Lg	G	AB	H	2B	3B	HR	(Hm	Rd)	TB	R	RBI	TBB	IBB	SO	HBP	SH	SF	SB	CS	SB%	GDP	Avg	OBP	SLG
1983	Toronto	AL	11	11	2	0	0	0	(0	0)	2	2	0	1	0	1	0	0	0	0	0	.00	0	.182	.250	.182
1984	Toronto	AL	26	22	5	2	1	0	(0	0)	9	9	4	1	0	7	0	0	0	0	0	.00	1	.227	.261	.409

1985 2 ML Teams		78	213	58	8	2	11	(3	8)	103	32	30	20	3	33	0	1	1	15	10	.60	3	.272	.333	.484
1986 Montreal	NL	151	576	167	31	13	8	(2	6)	248	89	49	57	4	78	4	3	5	36	15	.71	9	.290	.355	.431
1987 Montreal	NL	156	588	165	30	8	15	(9	6)	256	101	63	70	5	95	6	8	4	33	10	.77	6	.281	.361	.435
1988 2 ML Teams		151	523	136	16	8	6	(3	3)	186	69	39	55	2	87	8	5	4	22	14	.61	5	.260	.337	.356
1989 Chicago	NL	98	272	70	12	4	3	(1	2)	99	40	19	30	5	55	1	3	2	14	2	.88	3	.257	.331	.364
1990 Cleveland	AL	128	437	110	20	6	12	(6	6)	178	58	55	20	1	61	3	11	6	22	6	.79	5	.252	.285	.407
1991 3 ML Teams		107	203	42	8	5	2	(2	0)	66	23	19	21	1	61	0	2	0	2	3	.40	3	.207	.281	.325
1992 Los Angeles	NL	135	262	70	12	5	6	(1	5)	110	33	35	27	3	49	2	8	5	11	5	.69	1	.267	.334	.420
1985 Toronto	AL	4	1	0	0	0	0	(0	0)	0	0	0	0	0	0	0	0	0	0	1	.00	0	.000	.000	.000
Montreal	NL	74	212	58	8	2	11	(3	8)	103	32	30	20	3	33	0	1	1	15	9	.63	3	.274	.335	.486
1988 Montreal	NL	81	259	66	5	2	2	(0	2)	81	33	13	36	2	37	5	4	2	12	10	.55	3	.255	.354	.313
Chicago	NL	70	264	70	11	6	4	(3	1)	105	36	26	19	0	50	3	1	2	10	4	.71	2	.265	.319	.398
1991 Cleveland	AL	13	32	4	0	0	0	(0	0)	4	2	0	3	0	9	0	1	0	2	2	.50	0	.125	.200	.125
Pittsburgh	NL	36	97	17	3	4	1	(1	0)	31	9	9	9	1	31	0	0	0	0	0	.00	3	.175	.245	.320
Los Angeles	NL	58	74	21	5	1	1	(0	0)	31	12	10	9	0	21	0	1	0	1	1	1.00	0	.284	.361	.419
10 ML YEARS		1041	3107	825	139	52	63	(27	36)	1257	456	313	302	24	527	24	41	27	155	65	.70	36	.266	.333	.405

Eric Wedge

Bats: Right **Throws:** Right **Pos:** DH   **Ht:** 6' 3" **Wt:** 215 **Born:** 01/27/68 **Age:** 25

								BATTING												BASERUNNING				PERCENTAGES		
Year Team	Lg	G	AB	H	2B	3B	HR	(Hm	Rd)	TB	R	RBI	TBB	IBB	SO	HBP	SH	SF	SB	CS	SB%	GDP	Avg	OBP	SLG
1989 Elmira	A	41	145	34	6	2	7	--	--	65	20	22	15	0	21	0	0	0	1	1	.50	3	.234	.306	.448
New Britain	AA	14	40	8	2	0	0	--	--	10	3	2	5	0	10	0	2	0	0	0	.00	1	.200	.289	.250
1990 New Britain	AA	103	339	77	13	1	5	--	--	107	36	48	51	2	54	1	0	5	1	3	.25	14	.227	.326	.316
1991 New Britain	AA	2	8	2	0	0	0	--	--	2	0	2	0	0	2	0	0	1	0	0	.00	0	.250	.222	.250
Winter Havn	A	8	21	5	0	0	1	--	--	8	2	1	3	0	7	0	1	0	1	0	1.00	1	.238	.333	.381
Pawtucket	AAA	53	163	38	14	1	5	--	--	69	24	18	25	0	26	1	2	5	1	2	.33	3	.233	.330	.423
1992 Pawtucket	AAA	65	211	63	9	0	11	--	--	105	28	40	32	3	40	1	0	3	0	0	.00	6	.299	.389	.498
1991 Boston	AL	1	1	1	0	0	0	(0	0)	1	0	0	0	0	0	0	0	0	0	0	.00	0	1.000	1.000	1.000
1992 Boston	AL	27	68	17	2	0	5	(3	2)	34	11	11	13	0	18	0	0	0	0	0	.00	0	.250	.370	.500
2 ML YEARS		28	69	18	2	0	5	(3	2)	35	11	11	13	0	18	0	0	0	0	0	.00	0	.261	.378	.507

Bill Wegman

Pitches: Right **Bats:** Right **Pos:** SP   **Ht:** 6' 5" **Wt:** 220 **Born:** 12/19/62 **Age:** 30

		HOW MUCH HE PITCHED						WHAT HE GAVE UP										THE RESULTS					
Year Team	Lg	G	GS	CG	GF	IP	BFP	H	R	ER	HR	SH	SF	HB	TBB	IBB	SO	WP	Bk	W	L	Pct.	ShO	Sv	ERA
1985 Milwaukee	AL	3	3	0	0	17.2	73	17	8	7	3	0	1	0	3	0	6	0	1	2	0	1.000	0	0	3.57
1986 Milwaukee	AL	35	32	2	1	198.1	836	217	120	113	32	4	5	7	43	2	82	5	2	5	12	.294	0	0	5.13
1987 Milwaukee	AL	34	33	7	0	225	934	229	113	106	31	4	6	6	53	2	102	0	2	12	11	.522	0	0	4.24
1988 Milwaukee	AL	32	31	4	0	199	847	207	104	91	24	3	10	4	50	5	84	1	1	13	13	.500	1	0	4.12
1989 Milwaukee	AL	11	8	0	1	51	240	69	44	38	6	0	4	0	21	2	27	2	0	2	6	.250	0	0	6.71
1990 Milwaukee	AL	8	5	1	0	29.2	132	37	21	16	6	1	1	0	6	1	20	0	0	2	2	.500	1	0	4.85
1991 Milwaukee	AL	28	28	7	0	193.1	785	176	76	61	16	6	4	7	40	0	89	6	0	15	7	.682	2	0	2.84
1992 Milwaukee	AL	35	35	7	0	261.2	1079	251	104	93	28	7	4	9	55	3	127	1	2	13	14	.481	0	0	3.20
8 ML YEARS		186	175	28	2	1175.2	4926	1203	590	525	146	25	35	33	271	15	537	15	8	64	65	.496	4	0	4.02

John Wehner

Bats: Right **Throws:** Right **Pos:** 3B/1B   **Ht:** 6' 3" **Wt:** 205 **Born:** 06/29/67 **Age:** 26

								BATTING												BASERUNNING				PERCENTAGES		
Year Team	Lg	G	AB	H	2B	3B	HR	(Hm	Rd)	TB	R	RBI	TBB	IBB	SO	HBP	SH	SF	SB	CS	SB%	GDP	Avg	OBP	SLG
1988 Watertown	A	70	265	73	6	0	3	--	--	88	41	31	21	0	39	2	1	4	18	6	.75	4	.275	.329	.332
1989 Salem	A	137	515	155	32	6	14	--	--	241	69	73	42	4	81	1	0	1	21	10	.68	14	.301	.354	.468
1990 Harrisburg	AA	138	511	147	27	1	4	--	--	188	72	62	40	4	51	4	4	6	24	11	.69	12	.288	.340	.368
1991 Carolina	AA	61	234	62	5	1	3	--	--	78	30	21	24	1	32	2	3	5	17	5	.77	7	.265	.332	.333
Buffalo	AAA	31	112	34	9	2	1	--	--	50	18	15	14	1	12	0	0	2	6	4	.60	5	.304	.375	.446
1992 Buffalo	AAA	60	223	60	13	2	7	--	--	98	37	27	29	0	30	2	1	3	10	7	.59	6	.269	.354	.439
1991 Pittsburgh	NL	37	106	36	7	0	0	(0	0)	43	15	7	7	0	17	0	0	0	3	0	1.00	4	.340	.381	.406
1992 Pittsburgh	NL	55	123	22	6	0	0	(0	0)	28	11	4	12	2	22	0	2	0	3	0	1.00	4	.179	.252	.228
2 ML YEARS		92	229	58	13	0	0	(0	0)	71	26	11	19	2	39	0	2	0	6	0	1.00	4	.253	.310	.310

Walt Weiss

Bats: Both **Throws:** Right **Pos:** SS   **Ht:** 6' 0" **Wt:** 175 **Born:** 11/28/63 **Age:** 29

								BATTING												BASERUNNING				PERCENTAGES		
Year Team	Lg	G	AB	H	2B	3B	HR	(Hm	Rd)	TB	R	RBI	TBB	IBB	SO	HBP	SH	SF	SB	CS	SB%	GDP	Avg	OBP	SLG
1987 Oakland	AL	16	26	12	4	0	0	(0	0)	16	3	1	2	0	2	0	1	0	1	2	.33	0	.462	.500	.615
1988 Oakland	AL	147	452	113	17	3	3	(0	3)	145	44	39	35	1	56	9	8	7	4	4	.50	9	.250	.312	.321
1989 Oakland	AL	84	236	55	11	0	3	(2	1)	75	30	21	21	0	39	1	5	0	6	1	.86	5	.233	.298	.318
1990 Oakland	AL	138	445	118	17	1	2	(1	1)	143	50	35	46	5	53	4	6	4	9	3	.75	7	.265	.337	.321

Year	Team	Lg	G																									
1991	Oakland	AL	40	133	30	6	1	0	(0	0)	38	15	13	12	0	14	0	1	2	6	0	1.00	3	.226	.286	.286
1992	Oakland	AL	103	316	67	5	2	0	(0	0)	76	36	21	43	1	39	1	11	4	6	3	.67	10	.212	.305	.241
	6 ML YEARS		528	1608	395	60	7	8	(3	5)	493	178	130	159	7	203	15	32	17	32	13	.71	34	.246	.316	.307

Bob Welch

Pitches: Right **Bats:** Right **Pos:** SP **Ht:** 6' 3" **Wt:** 198 **Born:** 11/03/56 **Age:** 36

			HOW MUCH HE PITCHED						WHAT HE GAVE UP										THE RESULTS					
Year	Team	Lg	G	GS	CG	GF	IP	BFP	H	R	ER	HR	SH	SF	HB	TBB	IBB	SO	WP	Bk	W	L	Pct.	ShO	Sv	ERA
1978	Los Angeles	NL	23	13	4	6	111	439	92	28	25	6	4	6	1	26	2	66	2	2	7	4	.636	3	3	2.03
1979	Los Angeles	NL	25	12	1	10	81	349	82	42	36	7	4	1	3	32	4	64	0	0	5	6	.455	0	5	4.00
1980	Los Angeles	NL	32	32	3	0	214	889	190	85	78	15	12	10	3	79	6	141	7	5	14	9	.609	2	0	3.28
1981	Los Angeles	NL	23	23	2	0	141	601	141	56	54	11	9	4	3	41	0	88	2	0	9	5	.643	1	0	3.45
1982	Los Angeles	NL	36	36	9	0	235.2	965	199	94	88	19	7	4	5	81	5	176	5	1	16	11	.593	3	0	3.36
1983	Los Angeles	NL	31	31	4	0	204	828	164	73	60	13	8	7	3	72	4	156	4	6	15	12	.556	3	0	2.65
1984	Los Angeles	NL	31	29	3	0	178.2	771	191	86	75	11	10	2	2	58	7	126	4	2	13	13	.500	1	0	3.78
1985	Los Angeles	NL	23	23	8	0	167.1	675	141	49	43	16	6	2	6	35	2	96	7	4	14	4	.778	3	0	2.31
1986	Los Angeles	NL	33	33	7	0	235.2	981	227	95	86	14	7	8	7	55	6	183	2	1	7	13	.350	3	0	3.28
1987	Los Angeles	NL	35	35	6	0	251.2	1027	204	94	90	21	10	6	4	86	6	196	4	4	15	9	.625	4	0	3.22
1988	Oakland	AL	36	36	4	0	244.2	1034	237	107	99	22	12	8	10	81	1	158	3	13	17	9	.654	2	0	3.64
1989	Oakland	AL	33	33	1	0	209.2	884	191	82	70	13	3	4	6	78	3	137	5	0	17	8	.680	0	0	3.00
1990	Oakland	AL	35	35	2	0	238	979	214	90	78	26	6	5	5	77	4	127	2	2	27	6	.818	2	0	2.95
1991	Oakland	AL	35	35	7	0	220	950	220	124	112	25	6	6	11	91	3	101	3	2	12	13	.480	1	0	4.58
1992	Oakland	AL	20	20	0	0	123.2	513	114	47	45	13	3	3	2	43	0	47	1	0	11	7	.611	0	0	3.27
	15 ML YEARS		451	426	61	16	2856	11885	2607	1152	1039	232	107	76	71	935	53	1862	51	42	199	129	.607	28	8	3.27

David Wells

Pitches: Left **Bats:** Left **Pos:** RP/SP **Ht:** 6' 4" **Wt:** 225 **Born:** 05/20/63 **Age:** 30

			HOW MUCH HE PITCHED						WHAT HE GAVE UP										THE RESULTS					
Year	Team	Lg	G	GS	CG	GF	IP	BFP	H	R	ER	HR	SH	SF	HB	TBB	IBB	SO	WP	Bk	W	L	Pct.	ShO	Sv	ERA
1987	Toronto	AL	18	2	0	6	29.1	132	37	14	13	0	1	0	0	12	0	32	4	0	4	3	.571	0	1	3.99
1988	Toronto	AL	41	0	0	15	64.1	279	65	36	33	12	2	2	2	31	9	56	6	2	3	5	.375	0	4	4.62
1989	Toronto	AL	54	0	0	19	86.1	352	66	25	23	5	3	2	0	28	7	78	6	3	7	4	.636	0	2	2.40
1990	Toronto	AL	43	25	0	8	189	759	165	72	66	14	9	2	2	45	3	115	7	1	11	6	.647	0	3	3.14
1991	Toronto	AL	40	28	2	3	198.1	811	188	88	82	24	6	6	2	49	1	106	10	3	15	10	.600	0	1	3.72
1992	Toronto	AL	41	14	0	14	120	529	138	84	72	16	3	4	8	36	6	62	3	1	7	9	.438	0	2	5.40
	6 ML YEARS		237	69	2	65	687.1	2862	659	319	289	71	24	16	14	201	26	449	36	10	47	37	.560	0	13	3.78

David West

Pitches: Left **Bats:** Left **Pos:** RP/SP **Ht:** 6' 6" **Wt:** 230 **Born:** 09/01/64 **Age:** 28

			HOW MUCH HE PITCHED						WHAT HE GAVE UP										THE RESULTS					
Year	Team	Lg	G	GS	CG	GF	IP	BFP	H	R	ER	HR	SH	SF	HB	TBB	IBB	SO	WP	Bk	W	L	Pct.	ShO	Sv	ERA
1988	New York	NL	2	1	0	0	6	25	6	2	2	0	0	0	0	3	0	3	0	2	1	0	1.000	0	0	3.00
1989	2 ML Teams		21	7	0	4	63.2	294	73	49	48	9	2	3	3	33	3	50	2	0	3	4	.429	0	0	6.79
1990	Minnesota	AL	29	27	2	0	146.1	646	142	88	83	21	6	4	4	78	1	92	4	1	7	9	.438	0	0	5.10
1991	Minnesota	AL	15	12	0	0	71.1	305	66	37	36	13	2	3	4	28	0	52	3	0	4	4	.500	0	0	4.54
1992	Minnesota	AL	9	3	0	1	28.1	139	32	24	22	3	0	2	1	20	0	19	2	0	1	3	.250	0	0	6.99
1989	New York	NL	11	2	0	0	24.1	112	25	20	20	4	0	1	1	14	2	19	1	0	0	2	.000	0	0	7.40
	Minnesota	AL	10	5	0	4	39.1	182	48	29	28	5	2	2	2	19	1	31	1	0	3	2	.600	0	0	6.41
	5 ML YEARS		76	50	2	5	315.2	1409	319	200	191	46	10	12	9	162	4	216	11	3	16	20	.444	0	0	5.45

Mickey Weston

Pitches: Right **Bats:** Right **Pos:** SP **Ht:** 6' 1" **Wt:** 180 **Born:** 03/26/61 **Age:** 32

			HOW MUCH HE PITCHED						WHAT HE GAVE UP										THE RESULTS					
Year	Team	Lg	G	GS	CG	GF	IP	BFP	H	R	ER	HR	SH	SF	HB	TBB	IBB	SO	WP	Bk	W	L	Pct.	ShO	Sv	ERA
1989	Baltimore	AL	7	0	0	2	13	55	18	8	8	1	0	0	1	2	0	7	0	0	1	0	1.000	0	1	5.54
1990	Baltimore	AL	9	2	0	4	21	94	28	20	18	6	1	0	0	6	1	9	1	0	0	1	.000	0	0	7.71
1991	Toronto	AL	2	0	0	2	2	8	1	0	0	0	0	0	0	1	1	1	0	0	0	0	.000	0	0	0.00
1992	Philadelphia	NL	1	1	0	0	3.2	19	7	5	5	1	0	0	1	1	0	0	0	0	0	1	.000	0	0	12.27
	4 ML YEARS		19	3	0	8	39.2	176	54	33	31	8	1	0	2	10	2	17	1	0	1	2	.333	0	1	7.03

John Wetteland

Pitches: Right **Bats:** Right **Pos:** RP **Ht:** 6' 2" **Wt:** 195 **Born:** 08/21/66 **Age:** 26

			HOW MUCH HE PITCHED						WHAT HE GAVE UP										THE RESULTS					
Year	Team	Lg	G	GS	CG	GF	IP	BFP	H	R	ER	HR	SH	SF	HB	TBB	IBB	SO	WP	Bk	W	L	Pct.	ShO	Sv	ERA
1989	Los Angeles	NL	31	12	0	7	102.2	411	81	46	43	8	4	2	0	34	4	96	16	1	5	8	.385	0	1	3.77
1990	Los Angeles	NL	22	5	0	7	43	190	44	28	23	6	1	1	4	17	3	36	8	0	2	4	.333	0	0	4.81

212

212

Year	Team	Lg	G	GS	CG	GF	IP	BFP	H	R	ER	HR	SH	SF	HB	TBB	IBB	SO	WP	Bk	W	L	Pct.	ShO	Sv	ERA
1991	Los Angeles	NL	6	0	0	3	9	36	5	2	0	0	0	1	1	3	0	9	1	0	1	0	1.000	0	0	0.00
1992	Montreal	NL	67	0	0	58	83.1	347	64	27	27	6	5	1	4	36	3	99	4	0	4	4	.500	0	37	2.92
	4 ML YEARS		126	17	0	75	238	984	194	103	93	20	10	5	9	90	10	240	29	1	12	16	.429	0	38	3.52

Lou Whitaker

Bats: Left **Throws:** Right **Pos:** 2B **Ht:** 5'11" **Wt:** 180 **Born:** 05/12/57 **Age:** 36

					BATTING														BASERUNNING				PERCENTAGES		
Year	Team	Lg	G	AB	H	2B	3B	HR	(Hm	Rd)	TB	R	RBI	TBB	IBB	SO	HBP	SH	SF	SB	CS	SB%	GDP	Avg	OBP	SLG
1977	Detroit	AL	11	32	8	1	0	0	(0	0)	9	5	2	4	0	6	0	1	0	2	2	.50	0	.250	.333	.281
1978	Detroit	AL	139	484	138	12	7	3	(2	1)	173	71	58	61	0	65	1	13	8	7	7	.50	9	.285	.361	.357
1979	Detroit	AL	127	423	121	14	8	3	(3	0)	160	75	42	78	2	66	1	14	4	20	10	.67	10	.286	.395	.378
1980	Detroit	AL	145	477	111	19	1	1	(1	0)	135	68	45	73	0	79	0	12	6	8	4	.67	9	.233	.331	.283
1981	Detroit	AL	109	335	88	14	4	5	(4	1)	125	48	36	40	3	42	1	3	3	5	3	.63	5	.263	.340	.373
1982	Detroit	AL	152	560	160	22	8	15	(9	6)	243	76	65	48	4	58	1	6	4	11	3	.79	8	.286	.341	.434
1983	Detroit	AL	161	643	206	40	6	12	(7	5)	294	94	72	67	8	70	0	2	8	17	10	.63	9	.320	.380	.457
1984	Detroit	AL	143	558	161	25	1	13	(8	5)	227	90	56	62	5	63	0	4	5	6	5	.55	9	.289	.357	.407
1985	Detroit	AL	152	609	170	29	8	21	(11	10)	278	102	73	80	9	56	2	5	5	6	4	.60	3	.279	.362	.456
1986	Detroit	AL	144	584	157	26	6	20	(8	12)	255	95	73	63	5	70	0	0	4	13	8	.62	20	.269	.338	.437
1987	Detroit	AL	149	604	160	38	6	16	(10	6)	258	110	59	71	2	108	1	4	4	13	5	.72	5	.265	.341	.427
1988	Detroit	AL	115	403	111	18	2	12	(8	4)	169	54	55	66	5	61	0	6	2	2	0	1.00	8	.275	.376	.419
1989	Detroit	AL	148	509	128	21	1	28	(17	11)	235	77	85	89	6	59	3	1	9	6	3	.67	7	.251	.361	.462
1990	Detroit	AL	132	472	112	22	2	18	(8	10)	192	75	60	74	7	71	0	1	5	8	2	.80	10	.237	.338	.407
1991	Detroit	AL	138	470	131	26	2	23	(15	8)	230	94	78	90	6	45	2	2	8	4	2	.67	3	.279	.391	.489
1992	Detroit	AL	130	453	126	26	0	19	(11	8)	209	77	71	81	5	46	1	5	4	6	4	.60	9	.278	.386	.461
	16 ML YEARS		2095	7616	2088	353	62	209	(122	87)	3192	1211	930	1047	67	965	13	79	79	134	72	.65	124	.274	.360	.419

Devon White

Bats: Both **Throws:** Right **Pos:** CF **Ht:** 6'2" **Wt:** 182 **Born:** 12/29/62 **Age:** 30

					BATTING														BASERUNNING				PERCENTAGES		
Year	Team	Lg	G	AB	H	2B	3B	HR	(Hm	Rd)	TB	R	RBI	TBB	IBB	SO	HBP	SH	SF	SB	CS	SB%	GDP	Avg	OBP	SLG
1985	California	AL	21	7	1	0	0	0	(0	0)	1	7	0	1	0	3	1	0	0	3	1	.75	0	.143	.333	.143
1986	California	AL	29	51	12	1	1	1	(0	1)	18	8	3	6	0	8	0	0	0	6	0	1.00	0	.235	.316	.353
1987	California	AL	159	639	168	33	5	24	(11	13)	283	103	87	39	2	135	2	14	2	32	11	.74	8	.263	.306	.443
1988	California	AL	122	455	118	22	2	11	(3	8)	177	76	51	23	1	84	2	5	1	17	8	.68	5	.259	.297	.389
1989	California	AL	156	636	156	18	13	12	(9	3)	236	86	56	31	3	129	2	7	2	44	16	.73	12	.245	.282	.371
1990	California	AL	125	443	96	17	3	11	(5	6)	152	57	44	44	5	116	3	10	3	21	6	.78	6	.217	.290	.343
1991	Toronto	AL	156	642	181	40	10	17	(9	8)	292	110	60	55	1	135	7	5	6	33	10	.77	7	.282	.342	.455
1992	Toronto	AL	153	641	159	26	7	17	(7	10)	250	98	60	47	0	133	5	0	3	37	4	.90	9	.248	.303	.390
	8 ML YEARS		921	3514	891	157	41	93	(44	49)	1409	545	361	246	12	743	22	41	17	193	56	.78	47	.254	.305	.401

Wally Whitehurst

Pitches: Right **Bats:** Right **Pos:** RP/SP **Ht:** 6'3" **Wt:** 195 **Born:** 04/11/64 **Age:** 29

			HOW MUCH HE PITCHED						WHAT HE GAVE UP										THE RESULTS					
Year	Team	Lg	G	GS	CG	GF	IP	BFP	H	R	ER	HR	SH	SF	HB	TBB	IBB	SO	WP	Bk	W	L	Pct.	ShO	Sv	ERA
1989	New York	NL	9	1	0	4	14	64	17	7	7	2	0	1	0	5	0	9	1	0	0	1	.000	0	0	4.50
1990	New York	NL	38	0	0	16	65.2	263	63	27	24	5	3	0	0	9	2	46	2	0	1	0	1.000	0	2	3.29
1991	New York	NL	36	20	0	3	133.1	556	142	67	62	12	6	3	4	25	3	87	3	4	7	12	.368	0	1	4.18
1992	New York	NL	44	11	0	7	97	421	99	45	39	4	6	3	4	33	5	70	2	1	3	9	.250	0	0	3.62
	4 ML YEARS		127	32	0	33	310	1304	321	146	132	23	15	7	8	72	10	212	8	5	11	22	.333	0	3	3.83

Mark Whiten

Bats: Both **Throws:** Right **Pos:** RF **Ht:** 6'3" **Wt:** 215 **Born:** 11/25/66 **Age:** 26

					BATTING														BASERUNNING				PERCENTAGES		
Year	Team	Lg	G	AB	H	2B	3B	HR	(Hm	Rd)	TB	R	RBI	TBB	IBB	SO	HBP	SH	SF	SB	CS	SB%	GDP	Avg	OBP	SLG
1990	Toronto	AL	33	88	24	1	1	2	(1	1)	33	12	7	7	0	14	0	0	1	2	0	1.00	0	.273	.323	.375
1991	2 ML Teams		116	407	99	18	7	9	(4	5)	158	46	45	30	2	85	3	0	5	4	3	.57	13	.243	.297	.388
1992	Cleveland	AL	148	508	129	19	4	9	(6	3)	183	73	43	72	10	102	2	3	3	16	12	.57	12	.254	.347	.360
1991	Toronto	AL	46	149	33	4	3	2	(2	0)	49	12	19	11	1	35	1	0	3	0	1	.00	5	.221	.274	.329
	Cleveland	AL	70	258	66	14	4	7	(2	5)	109	34	26	19	1	50	2	0	2	4	2	.67	8	.256	.310	.422
	3 ML YEARS		297	1003	252	38	12	20	(11	9)	374	131	95	109	12	201	5	3	9	22	15	.59	27	.251	.325	.373

Matt Whiteside

Pitches: Right **Bats:** Right **Pos:** RP **Ht:** 6'0" **Wt:** 185 **Born:** 08/08/67 **Age:** 25

			HOW MUCH HE PITCHED						WHAT HE GAVE UP										THE RESULTS					
Year	Team	Lg	G	GS	CG	GF	IP	BFP	H	R	ER	HR	SH	SF	HB	TBB	IBB	SO	WP	Bk	W	L	Pct.	ShO	Sv	ERA
1990	Butte	R	18	5	0	5	57.1	255	57	33	22	4	0	0	9	25	0	45	4	6	4	4	.500	0	2	3.45

Year	Team		G	GS	CG	GF	IP	BFP	H	R	ER	HR	SH	SF	HB	TBB	IBB	SO	WP	Bk	W	L	Pct.	ShO	Sv	ERA
1991	Gastonia	A	48	0	0	42	62.2	255	44	19	15	1	1	3	5	21	0	71	3	0	3	1	.750	0	29	2.15
1992	Tulsa	AA	33	0	0	32	33.2	134	31	9	9	2	0	0	1	3	1	30	2	0	0	1	.000	0	21	2.41
	Okla City	AAA	12	0	0	12	11.1	44	7	1	1	1	0	0	0	3	1	13	0	0	1	0	1.000	0	8	0.79
1992	Texas	AL	20	0	0	8	28	118	26	8	6	1	0	1	0	11	2	13	2	0	1	1	.500	0	4	1.93

Kevin Wickander

Pitches: Left **Bats:** Left **Pos:** RP **Ht:** 6' 2" **Wt:** 202 **Born:** 01/04/65 **Age:** 28

			HOW MUCH HE PITCHED						WHAT HE GAVE UP											THE RESULTS					
Year	Team	Lg	G	GS	CG	GF	IP	BFP	H	R	ER	HR	SH	SF	HB	TBB	IBB	SO	WP	Bk	W	L	Pct.	ShO	Sv	ERA
1989	Cleveland	AL	2	0	0	1	2.2	15	6	1	1	0	0	0	0	2	1	0	0	0	0	0	.000	0	0	3.38
1990	Cleveland	AL	10	0	0	3	12.1	53	14	6	5	0	0	2	1	4	0	10	0	0	0	1	.000	0	0	3.65
1992	Cleveland	AL	44	0	0	10	41	187	39	14	14	1	2	2	4	28	3	38	1	1	2	0	1.000	0	1	3.07
	3 ML YEARS		56	0	0	14	56	255	59	21	20	1	2	4	5	34	4	48	1	1	2	1	.667	0	1	3.21

Bob Wickman

Pitches: Right **Bats:** Right **Pos:** SP **Ht:** 6' 1" **Wt:** 207 **Born:** 02/06/69 **Age:** 24

			HOW MUCH HE PITCHED						WHAT HE GAVE UP											THE RESULTS					
Year	Team	Lg	G	GS	CG	GF	IP	BFP	H	R	ER	HR	SH	SF	HB	TBB	IBB	SO	WP	Bk	W	L	Pct.	ShO	Sv	ERA
1990	White Sox	R	2	2	0	0	11	42	7	4	3	0	0	1	0	1	0	15	2	3	2	0	1.000	0	0	2.45
	Sarasota	A	2	2	0	0	13.2	61	17	7	3	0	0	1	0	4	0	8	0	0	0	1	.000	0	0	1.98
	South Bend	A	9	9	3	0	65.1	256	50	16	10	1	3	0	1	16	0	50	0	3	7	2	.778	0	0	1.38
1991	Sarasota	A	7	7	1	0	44	188	43	16	10	2	1	0	1	11	0	32	1	2	5	1	.833	1	0	2.05
	Birmingham	AA	20	20	4	0	131.1	572	127	68	52	5	3	5	5	50	0	81	4	2	6	10	.375	1	0	3.56
1992	Columbus	AAA	23	23	2	0	157	641	131	61	51	12	1	2	5	55	0	108	10	1	12	5	.706	1	0	2.92
1992	New York	AL	8	8	0	0	50.1	213	51	25	23	2	1	3	2	20	0	21	3	0	6	1	.857	0	0	4.11

Curt Wilkerson

Bats: Both **Throws:** Right **Pos:** SS/2B **Ht:** 5' 9" **Wt:** 175 **Born:** 04/26/61 **Age:** 32

			BATTING															BASERUNNING				PERCENTAGES		
Year	Team	Lg	G	AB	H	2B	3B	HR	(Hm | Rd)	TB	R	RBI	TBB	IBB	SO	HBP	SH	SF	SB	CS	SB%	GDP	Avg	OBP	SLG
1983	Texas	AL	16	35	6	0	1	0	(0 | 0)	8	7	1	2	0	5	0	0	0	3	0	1.00	0	.171	.216	.229
1984	Texas	AL	153	484	120	12	0	1	(0 | 1)	135	47	26	22	0	72	2	12	2	12	10	.55	7	.248	.282	.279
1985	Texas	AL	129	360	88	11	6	0	(0 | 0)	111	35	22	22	0	63	4	6	3	14	7	.67	7	.244	.293	.308
1986	Texas	AL	110	236	56	10	3	0	(0 | 0)	72	27	15	11	0	42	1	0	1	9	7	.56	2	.237	.273	.305
1987	Texas	AL	85	138	37	5	3	2	(1 | 1)	54	28	14	6	0	16	2	0	0	6	3	.67	2	.268	.308	.391
1988	Texas	AL	117	338	99	12	5	0	(0 | 0)	121	41	28	26	3	43	2	3	2	9	4	.69	7	.293	.345	.358
1989	Chicago	NL	77	160	39	4	2	1	(1 | 0)	50	18	10	8	0	33	0	1	1	4	2	.67	3	.244	.278	.313
1990	Chicago	NL	77	186	41	5	1	0	(0 | 0)	48	21	16	7	2	36	0	3	0	2	2	.50	4	.220	.249	.258
1991	Pittsburgh	NL	85	191	36	9	1	2	(2 | 0)	53	20	18	15	0	40	0	0	4	2	1	.67	2	.188	.243	.277
1992	Kansas City	AL	111	296	74	10	1	2	(2 | 0)	92	27	29	18	3	47	1	7	4	18	7	.72	4	.250	.292	.311
	10 ML YEARS		960	2424	596	78	23	8	(6 | 2)	744	271	179	137	8	397	12	32	17	79	43	.65	38	.246	.288	.307

Rick Wilkins

Bats: Left **Throws:** Right **Pos:** C **Ht:** 6' 2" **Wt:** 210 **Born:** 06/04/67 **Age:** 26

			BATTING															BASERUNNING				PERCENTAGES		
Year	Team	Lg	G	AB	H	2B	3B	HR	(Hm | Rd)	TB	R	RBI	TBB	IBB	SO	HBP	SH	SF	SB	CS	SB%	GDP	Avg	OBP	SLG
1987	Geneva	A	75	243	61	8	2	8	--	--	97	35	43	58	8	40	1	0	0	7	2	.78	3	.251	.397	.399
1988	Peoria	A	137	490	119	30	1	8	--	--	175	54	63	67	6	110	7	2	9	4	6	.40	12	.243	.337	.357
1989	Winston-Sal	A	132	445	111	24	1	12	--	--	173	61	54	50	6	87	8	2	7	6	3	.67	11	.249	.331	.389
1990	Charlotte	AA	127	449	102	17	1	17	--	--	172	48	71	43	5	97	5	1	3	4	5	.44	9	.227	.300	.383
1991	Iowa	AAA	38	107	29	3	1	5	--	--	49	12	14	11	1	17	1	2	2	1	2	.33	1	.271	.339	.458
1992	Iowa	AAA	47	155	43	11	2	5			73	20	28	19	2	42	2	1	1	0	0	.00	1	.277	.362	.471
1991	Chicago	NL	86	203	45	9	0	6	(2 | 4)	72	21	22	19	2	56	6	7	0	3	3	.50	3	.222	.307	.355
1992	Chicago	NL	83	244	66	9	1	8	(3 | 5)	101	20	22	28	7	53	0	1	1	0	2	.00	6	.270	.344	.414
	2 ML YEARS		169	447	111	18	1	14	(5 | 9)	173	41	44	47	9	109	6	8	1	3	5	.38	9	.248	.327	.387

Jerry Willard

Bats: Left **Throws:** Right **Pos:** 1B **Ht:** 6' 2" **Wt:** 195 **Born:** 03/14/60 **Age:** 33

			BATTING															BASERUNNING				PERCENTAGES		
Year	Team	Lg	G	AB	H	2B	3B	HR	(Hm | Rd)	TB	R	RBI	TBB	IBB	SO	HBP	SH	SF	SB	CS	SB%	GDP	Avg	OBP	SLG
1984	Cleveland	AL	87	246	55	8	1	10	(5 | 5)	95	21	37	26	0	55	0	0	3	1	0	1.00	6	.224	.295	.386
1985	Cleveland	AL	104	300	81	13	0	7	(4 | 3)	115	39	36	28	1	59	1	4	1	0	0	.00	3	.270	.333	.383
1986	Oakland	AL	75	161	43	7	0	4	(2 | 2)	62	17	26	22	0	28	2	4	4	0	1	.00	4	.267	.354	.385
1987	Oakland	AL	7	6	1	0	0	0	(0 | 0)	1	1	0	2	0	1	0	0	0	0	0	.00	0	.167	.375	.167
1990	Chicago	AL	3	3	0	0	0	0	(0 | 0)	0	0	0	0	0	2	0	0	0	0	0	.00	0	.000	.000	.000
1991	Atlanta	NL	17	14	3	0	0	1	(1 | 0)	6	1	4	2	0	5	0	0	0	0	0	.00	0	.214	.313	.429

Year Team	Lg	G	AB	H	2B	3B	HR	(Hm	Rd)	TB	R	RBI	TBB	IBB	SO	HBP	SH	SF	SB	CS	SB%	GDP	Avg	OBP	SLG
1992 2 ML Teams		47	48	11	1	0	2	(1	1)	18	2	8	2	1	10	0	0	0	0	0	.00	5	.229	.260	.375
1992 Atlanta	NL	26	23	8	1	0	2	(1	1)	15	2	7	1	1	3	0	0	0	0	0	.00	3	.348	.375	.652
Montreal	NL	21	25	3	0	0	0	(0	0)	3	0	1	1	0	7	0	0	0	0	0	.00	2	.120	.154	.120
7 ML YEARS		340	778	194	29	1	24	(13	11)	297	81	111	82	2	160	3	8	8	1	1	.50	18	.249	.320	.382

Bernie Williams

Bats: Both **Throws:** Right **Pos:** CF   **Ht:** 6' 2" **Wt:** 196 **Born:** 09/13/68 **Age:** 24

								BATTING												BASERUNNING				PERCENTAGES		
Year Team	Lg	G	AB	H	2B	3B	HR	(Hm	Rd)	TB	R	RBI	TBB	IBB	SO	HBP	SH	SF	SB	CS	SB%	GDP	Avg	OBP	SLG
1986 Yankees	R	61	230	62	5	3	2	--	--	79	45	25	39	0	40	1	1	3	33	12	.73	3	.270	.374	.343
1987 Ft.Lauderdle	A	25	71	11	3	0	0	--	--	14	11	4	18	1	22	3	2	0	9	1	.90	1	.155	.348	.197
Oneonta	A	25	93	32	4	0	0	--	--	36	13	15	10	0	14	1	1	1	9	3	.75	0	.344	.410	.387
1988 Pr William	A	92	337	113	16	7	7	--	--	164	72	45	66	6	66	4	0	1	29	11	.73	5	.335	.449	.487
1989 Columbus	AAA	50	162	35	8	1	2	--	--	51	21	16	25	1	38	2	3	2	11	5	.69	3	.216	.325	.315
Albany	AA	91	314	79	11	8	11	--	--	139	63	42	60	4	72	6	3	1	26	13	.67	9	.252	.381	.443
1990 Albany	AA	134	466	131	28	5	8	--	--	193	91	54	98	6	97	4	1	2	39	18	.68	12	.281	.409	.414
1991 Columbus	AAA	78	306	90	14	6	8	--	--	140	52	37	38	2	43	2	4	3	9	8	.53	5	.294	.372	.458
1992 Columbus	AAA	95	363	111	23	9	8	--	--	176	68	50	52	5	61	1	1	6	20	8	.71	8	.306	.389	.485
1991 New York	AL	85	320	76	19	4	3	(1	2)	112	43	34	48	0	57	1	2	3	10	5	.67	4	.238	.336	.350
1992 New York	AL	62	261	73	14	2	5	(3	2)	106	39	26	29	1	36	1	2	0	7	6	.54	5	.280	.354	.406
2 ML YEARS		147	581	149	33	6	8	(4	4)	218	82	60	77	1	93	2	4	3	17	11	.61	9	.256	.344	.375

Brian Williams

Pitches: Right **Bats:** Right **Pos:** SP   **Ht:** 6' 2" **Wt:** 195 **Born:** 02/15/69 **Age:** 24

			HOW MUCH HE PITCHED					WHAT HE GAVE UP										THE RESULTS					
Year Team	Lg	G	GS	CG	GF	IP	BFP	H	R	ER	HR	SH	SF	HB	TBB	IBB	SO	WP	Bk	W	L	Pct.	ShO	Sv	ERA
1990 Auburn	A	3	3	0	0	6.2	34	6	5	3	0	1	0	1	6	0	7	1	1	0	0	.000	0	0	4.05
1991 Osceola	A	15	15	0	0	89.2	378	72	41	29	0	3	6	2	40	1	67	3	5	6	4	.600	0	0	2.91
Jackson	AA	3	3	0	0	15	66	17	8	7	1	0	0	0	7	0	15	3	0	2	1	.667	0	0	4.20
Tucson	AAA	7	7	0	0	38.1	177	39	25	21	3	4	0	2	22	0	29	3	4	0	1	.000	0	0	4.93
1992 Tucson	AAA	12	12	0	0	70	315	78	37	35	3	3	4	6	26	0	58	5	4	6	1	.857	0	0	4.50
1991 Houston	NL	2	2	0	0	12	49	11	5	5	2	0	0	1	4	0	4	0	0	0	1	.000	0	0	3.75
1992 Houston	NL	16	16	0	0	96.1	413	92	44	42	10	7	3	0	42	1	54	2	1	7	6	.538	0	0	3.92
2 ML YEARS		18	18	0	0	108.1	462	103	49	47	12	7	3	1	46	1	58	2	1	7	7	.500	0	0	3.90

Gerald Williams

Bats: Right **Throws:** Right **Pos:** RF   **Ht:** 6' 2" **Wt:** 185 **Born:** 08/10/66 **Age:** 26

								BATTING												BASERUNNING				PERCENTAGES		
Year Team	Lg	G	AB	H	2B	3B	HR	(Hm	Rd)	TB	R	RBI	TBB	IBB	SO	HBP	SH	SF	SB	CS	SB%	GDP	Avg	OBP	SLG
1987 Oneonta	A	29	115	42	6	2	2	--	--	58	26	29	16	0	18	1	1	0	6	2	.75	3	.365	.447	.504
1988 Pr William	A	54	159	29	3	0	2	--	--	38	20	18	15	0	47	0	1	1	6	1	.86	4	.182	.251	.239
Ft.Lauderdle	A	63	212	40	7	2	2	--	--	57	21	17	16	0	56	3	1	0	4	3	.57	4	.189	.255	.269
1989 Pr William	A	134	454	104	19	6	13	--	--	174	63	69	51	1	120	7	5	1	15	10	.60	7	.229	.316	.383
1990 Ft.Lauderdle	A	50	204	59	4	5	7	--	--	94	25	43	16	1	52	2	0	2	19	5	.79	1	.289	.344	.461
Albany	AA	96	324	81	17	2	13	--	--	141	54	58	35	1	75	2	1	3	18	8	.69	7	.250	.324	.435
1991 Albany	AA	45	175	50	15	0	5	--	--	80	28	32	18	2	26	0	1	3	18	3	.86	5	.286	.347	.457
Columbus	AAA	61	198	51	8	3	2	--	--	71	20	27	16	1	39	1	0	5	9	12	.43	3	.258	.309	.359
1992 Columbus	AAA	142	547	156	31	6	16	--	--	247	92	86	38	2	98	5	0	5	36	14	.72	12	.285	.334	.452
1992 New York	AL	15	27	8	2	0	3	(2	1)	19	7	6	0	0	3	0	0	0	2	0	1.00	0	.296	.296	.704

Matt D. Williams

Bats: Right **Throws:** Right **Pos:** 3B   **Ht:** 6' 2" **Wt:** 210 **Born:** 11/28/65 **Age:** 27

								BATTING												BASERUNNING				PERCENTAGES		
Year Team	Lg	G	AB	H	2B	3B	HR	(Hm	Rd)	TB	R	RBI	TBB	IBB	SO	HBP	SH	SF	SB	CS	SB%	GDP	Avg	OBP	SLG
1987 San Francisco	NL	84	245	46	9	2	8	(5	3)	83	28	21	16	4	68	1	3	1	4	3	.57	5	.188	.240	.339
1988 San Francisco	NL	52	156	32	6	1	8	(7	1)	64	17	19	8	0	41	2	3	1	0	1	.00	7	.205	.251	.410
1989 San Francisco	NL	84	292	59	18	1	18	(10	8)	133	31	50	14	1	72	2	1	2	1	2	.33	5	.202	.242	.455
1990 San Francisco	NL	159	617	171	27	2	33	(20	13)	301	87	**122**	33	9	138	7	2	5	7	4	.64	13	.277	.319	.488
1991 San Francisco	NL	157	589	158	24	5	34	(17	17)	294	72	98	33	6	128	6	0	7	5	5	.50	11	.268	.310	.499
1992 San Francisco	NL	146	529	120	13	5	20	(9	11)	203	58	66	39	11	109	6	0	2	7	7	.50	15	.227	.286	.384
6 ML YEARS		682	2428	586	97	16	121	(68	53)	1078	293	376	143	31	556	24	9	18	24	22	.52	56	.241	.288	.444

Mike Williams

Pitches: Right **Bats:** Right **Pos:** SP   **Ht:** 6' 2" **Wt:** 190 **Born:** 07/29/68 **Age:** 24

			HOW MUCH HE PITCHED					WHAT HE GAVE UP										THE RESULTS					
Year Team	Lg	G	GS	CG	GF	IP	BFP	H	R	ER	HR	SH	SF	HB	TBB	IBB	SO	WP	Bk	W	L	Pct.	ShO	Sv	ERA
1990 Batavia	A	27	0	0	21	47	195	39	17	12	0	3	3	1	14	4	42	1	1	2	3	.400	0	11	2.30

1991	Clearwater	A	14	14	2	0	93.1	348	65	23	18	5	3	1	3	14	0	76	2	6	7	3	.700	1	0	1.74
	Reading	AA	16	15	2	0	102.1	414	93	44	42	1	3	3	2	36	0	51	2	0	7	5	.583	1	0	3.69
1992	Reading	AA	3	3	0	0	15.2	68	17	10	9	1	0	1	0	7	0	12	3	0	1	2	.333	0	0	5.17
	Scranton/wb	AAA	16	16	3	0	92.2	381	84	26	25	4	4	0	0	30	2	59	2	0	9	1	.900	1	0	2.43
1992	Philadelphia	NL	5	5	1	0	28.2	121	29	20	17	3	1	1	0	7	0	5	0	0	1	1	.500	0	0	5.34

Mitch Williams

Pitches: Left **Bats:** Left **Pos:** RP   **Ht:** 6' 4" **Wt:** 205 **Born:** 11/17/64 **Age:** 28

			HOW MUCH HE PITCHED						WHAT HE GAVE UP										THE RESULTS					
Year	Team	Lg	G	GS	CG	GF	IP	BFP	H	R	ER	HR	SH	SF	HB	TBB	IBB	SO	WP	Bk	W	L	Pct.	ShO	Sv	ERA
1986	Texas	AL	80	0	0	38	98	435	69	39	39	8	1	3	11	79	8	90	5	5	8	6	.571	0	8	3.58
1987	Texas	AL	85	1	0	32	108.2	469	63	47	39	9	4	3	7	94	7	129	4	2	8	6	.571	0	6	3.23
1988	Texas	AL	67	0	0	51	68	296	48	38	35	4	3	4	6	47	3	61	5	6	2	7	.222	0	18	4.63
1989	Chicago	NL	76	0	0	61	81.2	365	71	27	24	6	2	5	8	52	4	67	6	4	4	4	.500	0	36	2.64
1990	Chicago	NL	59	2	0	39	66.1	310	60	38	29	4	5	3	1	50	6	55	4	2	1	8	.111	0	16	3.93
1991	Philadelphia	NL	69	0	0	60	88.1	386	56	24	23	4	4	4	8	62	5	84	4	1	12	5	.706	0	30	2.34
1992	Philadelphia	NL	66	0	0	56	81	368	69	39	34	4	8	3	6	64	2	74	5	3	5	8	.385	0	29	3.78
	7 ML YEARS		502	3	0	337	592	2629	436	252	223	39	27	25	47	448	35	560	33	23	40	44	.476	0	143	3.39

Reggie Williams

Bats: Both **Throws:** Right **Pos:** CF   **Ht:** 6' 1" **Wt:** 185 **Born:** 05/05/66 **Age:** 27

			BATTING															BASERUNNING				PERCENTAGES		
Year	Team	Lg	G	AB	H	2B	3B	HR	(Hm	Rd)	TB	R	RBI	TBB	IBB	SO	HBP	SH	SF	SB	CS	SB%	GDP	Avg	OBP	SLG
1988	Everett	A	60	223	56	8	1	3	--	--	75	52	29	47	0	43	3	0	2	36	10	.78	5	.251	.385	.336
1989	Clinton	A	68	236	46	9	2	3	--	--	68	38	18	29	0	66	3	5	1	14	9	.61	1	.195	.290	.288
	Boise	A	42	153	41	5	1	3	--	--	57	33	14	24	0	29	2	0	1	18	5	.78	2	.268	.372	.373
1990	Quad City	A	58	189	46	11	2	3	--	--	70	50	12	39	0	60	4	2	1	24	6	.80	2	.243	.382	.370
1991	Palm Sprngs	A	14	44	13	1	0	1	--	--	17	10	2	21	0	15	1	1	0	6	5	.55	0	.295	.530	.386
	Midland	AA	83	319	99	12	3	1	--	--	120	77	30	62	2	67	0	5	3	21	9	.70	3	.310	.419	.376
1992	Edmonton	AAA	139	519	141	26	9	3	--	--	194	96	64	88	1	110	3	7	8	44	14	.76	9	.272	.375	.374
1992	California	AL	14	26	6	1	1	0	(0	0)	9	5	2	1	0	10	0	0	0	0	2	.00	0	.231	.259	.346

Mark Williamson

Pitches: Right **Bats:** Right **Pos:** RP   **Ht:** 6' 0" **Wt:** 177 **Born:** 07/21/59 **Age:** 33

			HOW MUCH HE PITCHED						WHAT HE GAVE UP										THE RESULTS					
Year	Team	Lg	G	GS	CG	GF	IP	BFP	H	R	ER	HR	SH	SF	HB	TBB	IBB	SO	WP	Bk	W	L	Pct.	ShO	Sv	ERA
1987	Baltimore	AL	61	2	0	36	125	520	122	59	56	12	5	3	3	41	15	73	3	0	8	9	.471	0	3	4.03
1988	Baltimore	AL	37	10	2	11	117.2	507	125	70	64	14	4	2	2	40	8	69	5	3	5	8	.385	0	2	4.90
1989	Baltimore	AL	65	0	0	38	107.1	445	105	35	35	4	7	3	2	30	9	55	0	0	10	5	.667	0	9	2.93
1990	Baltimore	AL	49	0	0	15	85.1	343	65	25	21	8	6	7	0	28	2	60	1	0	8	2	.800	0	1	2.21
1991	Baltimore	AL	65	0	0	21	80.1	357	87	42	40	9	1	5	0	35	7	53	7	0	5	5	.500	0	4	4.48
1992	Baltimore	AL	12	0	0	5	18.2	78	16	3	2	1	1	0	0	10	1	14	1	0	0	0	.000	0	1	0.96
	6 ML YEARS		289	12	2	126	534.1	2250	520	234	218	48	24	20	7	184	42	324	17	3	36	29	.554	0	20	3.67

Carl Willis

Pitches: Right **Bats:** Left **Pos:** RP   **Ht:** 6' 4" **Wt:** 213 **Born:** 12/28/60 **Age:** 32

			HOW MUCH HE PITCHED						WHAT HE GAVE UP										THE RESULTS					
Year	Team	Lg	G	GS	CG	GF	IP	BFP	H	R	ER	HR	SH	SF	HB	TBB	IBB	SO	WP	Bk	W	L	Pct.	ShO	Sv	ERA
1984	2 ML Teams		17	2	0	5	25.2	113	33	17	17	2	1	0	0	7	2	7	0	0	0	3	.000	0	1	5.96
1985	Cincinnati	NL	11	0	0	6	13.2	69	21	18	14	3	1	2	0	5	0	6	1	0	1	0	1.000	0	0	9.22
1986	Cincinnati	NL	29	0	0	7	52.1	233	54	29	26	4	5	1	1	32	9	24	3	1	1	3	.250	0	0	4.47
1988	Chicago	AL	6	0	0	0	12	55	17	12	11	3	0	1	0	7	1	6	2	0	0	0	.000	0	0	8.25
1991	Minnesota	AL	40	0	0	9	89	355	76	31	26	4	4	3	4	19	2	53	4	1	8	3	.727	0	2	2.63
1992	Minnesota	AL	59	0	0	21	79.1	313	73	25	24	4	2	3	0	11	1	45	2	1	7	3	.700	0	1	2.72
1984	Detroit	AL	10	2	0	4	16	74	25	13	13	1	0	0	0	5	2	4	0	0	0	2	.000	0	0	7.31
	Cincinnati	NL	7	0	0	1	9.2	39	8	4	4	1	1	0	0	2	0	3	0	0	0	1	.000	0	1	3.72
	6 ML YEARS		162	2	0	48	272	1138	274	132	118	20	12	11	2	81	15	141	12	3	17	12	.586	0	5	3.90

Craig Wilson

Bats: Right **Throws:** Right **Pos:** 3B/2B   **Ht:** 5'11" **Wt:** 208 **Born:** 11/28/64 **Age:** 28

			BATTING															BASERUNNING				PERCENTAGES		
Year	Team	Lg	G	AB	H	2B	3B	HR	(Hm | Rd)	TB	R	RBI	TBB	IBB	SO	HBP	SH	SF	SB	CS	SB%	GDP	Avg	OBP	SLG
1989	St. Louis	NL	6	4	1	0	0	0	(0 | 0)	1	1	1	1	0	2	0	0	0	0	0	.00	0	.250	.400	.250
1990	St. Louis	NL	55	121	30	2	0	0	(0 | 0)	32	13	7	8	0	14	0	0	2	0	2	.00	7	.248	.290	.264
1991	St. Louis	NL	60	82	14	2	0	0	(0 | 0)	16	5	13	6	2	10	0	0	2	0	0	.00	2	.171	.222	.195
1992	St. Louis	NL	61	106	33	6	0	0	(0 | 0)	39	6	13	10	2	18	0	2	1	1	2	.33	4	.311	.368	.368

4 ML YEARS	182	313	78	10	0	0	(0	0)	88	25	34	25	4	44	0	2	5	1	4	.20	13	.249	.300	.281

Dan Wilson

Bats: Right **Throws:** Right **Pos:** C **Ht:** 6' 3" **Wt:** 190 **Born:** 03/25/69 **Age:** 24

						BATTING													BASERUNNING				PERCENTAGES		
Year Team	Lg	G	AB	H	2B	3B	HR	(Hm	Rd)	TB	R	RBI	TBB	IBB	SO	HBP	SH	SF	SB	CS	SB%	GDP	Avg	OBP	SLG
1990 Chston-Wv	A	32	113	28	9	1	2	--	--	45	16	17	13	0	18	0	1	1	0	0	.00	1	.248	.323	.398
1991 Chston-Wv	A	52	197	62	11	1	3	--	--	84	25	29	25	0	21	2	0	1	1	1	.50	6	.315	.396	.426
Chattanooga	AA	81	292	75	19	2	2	--	--	104	32	38	21	0	39	0	1	4	2	2	.50	10	.257	.303	.356
1992 Nashville	AAA	106	366	92	16	1	4	--	--	122	27	34	31	3	58	2	2	4	1	4	.20	7	.251	.310	.333
1992 Cincinnati	NL	12	25	9	1	0	0	(0	0)	10	2	3	3	0	8	0	0	0	0	0	.00	2	.360	.429	.400

Steve Wilson

Pitches: Left **Bats:** Left **Pos:** RP **Ht:** 6' 4" **Wt:** 195 **Born:** 12/13/64 **Age:** 28

		HOW MUCH HE PITCHED						WHAT HE GAVE UP										THE RESULTS					
Year Team	Lg	G	GS	CG	GF	IP	BFP	H	R	ER	HR	SH	SF	HB	TBB	IBB	SO	WP	Bk	W	L	Pct.	ShO	Sv	ERA
1988 Texas	AL	3	0	0	1	7.2	31	7	5	5	1	0	0	0	4	1	1	0	0	0	0	.000	0	0	5.87
1989 Chicago	NL	53	8	0	9	85.2	364	83	43	40	6	5	4	1	31	5	65	0	1	6	4	.600	0	2	4.20
1990 Chicago	NL	45	15	1	5	139	597	140	77	74	17	9	3	2	43	6	95	2	1	4	9	.308	0	1	4.79
1991 2 ML Teams		19	0	0	5	20.2	81	14	7	6	1	0	1	0	9	1	14	0	0	0	0	.000	0	2	2.61
1992 Los Angeles	NL	60	0	0	18	66.2	301	74	37	31	6	5	4	1	29	7	54	7	0	2	5	.286	0	0	4.18
1991 Chicago	NL	8	0	0	2	12.1	53	13	7	6	1	0	1	0	5	1	9	0	0	0	0	.000	0	0	4.38
Los Angeles	NL	11	0	0	3	8.1	28	1	0	0	0	0	0	0	4	0	5	0	0	0	0	.000	0	2	0.00
5 ML YEARS		180	23	1	38	319.2	1374	318	169	156	31	19	12	4	116	20	229	9	2	12	18	.400	0	5	4.39

Trevor Wilson

Pitches: Left **Bats:** Left **Pos:** SP **Ht:** 6' 0" **Wt:** 195 **Born:** 06/07/66 **Age:** 27

		HOW MUCH HE PITCHED						WHAT HE GAVE UP										THE RESULTS					
Year Team	Lg	G	GS	CG	GF	IP	BFP	H	R	ER	HR	SH	SF	HB	TBB	IBB	SO	WP	Bk	W	L	Pct.	ShO	Sv	ERA
1988 San Francisco	NL	4	4	0	0	22	96	25	14	10	1	3	1	0	8	0	15	0	1	0	2	.000	0	0	4.09
1989 San Francisco	NL	14	4	0	2	39.1	167	28	20	19	2	3	1	4	24	0	22	0	1	2	3	.400	0	0	4.35
1990 San Francisco	NL	27	17	3	3	110.1	457	87	52	49	11	6	2	1	49	3	66	5	2	8	7	.533	2	0	4.00
1991 San Francisco	NL	44	29	3	6	202	841	173	87	80	13	14	5	5	77	4	139	5	3	13	11	.542	1	0	3.56
1992 San Francisco	NL	26	26	1	0	154	661	152	82	72	18	11	6	6	64	5	88	2	7	8	14	.364	1	0	4.21
5 ML YEARS		115	80	6	11	527.2	2222	465	255	230	45	37	15	16	222	12	330	12	14	31	37	.456	4	0	3.92

Willie Wilson

Bats: Both **Throws:** Right **Pos:** CF **Ht:** 6' 3" **Wt:** 200 **Born:** 07/09/55 **Age:** 37

						BATTING													BASERUNNING				PERCENTAGES		
Year Team	Lg	G	AB	H	2B	3B	HR	(Hm	Rd)	TB	R	RBI	TBB	IBB	SO	HBP	SH	SF	SB	CS	SB%	GDP	Avg	OBP	SLG
1976 Kansas City	AL	12	6	1	0	0	0	(0	0)	1	0	0	0	0	2	0	0	0	2	1	.67	0	.167	.167	.167
1977 Kansas City	AL	13	34	11	2	0	0	(0	0)	13	10	1	1	0	8	0	2	0	6	3	.67	1	.324	.343	.382
1978 Kansas City	AL	127	198	43	8	2	0	(0	0)	55	43	16	16	0	33	2	5	2	46	12	.79	2	.217	.280	.278
1979 Kansas City	AL	154	588	185	18	13	6	(3	3)	247	113	49	28	3	92	7	13	4	83	12	.87	1	.315	.351	.420
1980 Kansas City	AL	161	705	230	28	15	3	(2	1)	297	133	49	28	3	81	6	5	1	79	10	.89	4	.326	.357	.421
1981 Kansas City	AL	102	439	133	10	7	1	(0	1)	160	54	32	18	3	42	4	3	1	34	8	.81	5	.303	.335	.364
1982 Kansas City	AL	136	585	194	19	15	3	(2	1)	252	87	46	26	2	81	6	2	2	37	11	.77	4	.332	.365	.431
1983 Kansas City	AL	137	576	159	22	8	2	(2	0)	203	90	33	33	2	75	1	1	0	59	8	.88	4	.276	.316	.352
1984 Kansas City	AL	128	541	163	24	9	2	(1	1)	211	81	44	39	2	56	3	2	3	47	5	.90	7	.301	.350	.390
1985 Kansas City	AL	141	605	168	25	21	4	(1	3)	247	87	43	29	3	94	5	2	1	43	11	.80	6	.278	.316	.408
1986 Kansas City	AL	156	631	170	20	7	9	(5	4)	231	77	44	31	1	97	9	3	1	34	8	.81	6	.269	.313	.366
1987 Kansas City	AL	146	610	170	18	15	4	(0	4)	230	97	30	32	2	88	6	4	1	59	11	.84	9	.279	.320	.377
1988 Kansas City	AL	147	591	155	17	11	1	(0	1)	197	81	37	22	1	106	2	8	5	35	7	.83	5	.262	.289	.333
1989 Kansas City	AL	112	383	97	17	7	3	(1	2)	137	58	43	27	0	78	1	6	6	24	6	.80	8	.253	.300	.358
1990 Kansas City	AL	115	307	89	13	3	2	(1	1)	114	49	42	30	1	57	2	3	2	24	6	.80	4	.290	.354	.371
1991 Oakland	AL	113	294	70	14	4	0	(0	0)	92	38	28	18	1	43	4	1	0	20	5	.80	11	.238	.290	.313
1992 Oakland	AL	132	396	107	15	5	0	(0	0)	132	38	37	35	2	65	1	2	3	28	8	.78	11	.270	.329	.333
17 ML YEARS		2032	7489	2145	270	142	40	(18	22)	2819	1136	574	413	26	1098	59	62	34	660	132	.83	88	.286	.327	.376

Dave Winfield

Bats: Right **Throws:** Right **Pos:** DH/RF **Ht:** 6' 6" **Wt:** 245 **Born:** 10/03/51 **Age:** 41

						BATTING													BASERUNNING				PERCENTAGES		
Year Team	Lg	G	AB	H	2B	3B	HR	(Hm	Rd)	TB	R	RBI	TBB	IBB	SO	HBP	SH	SF	SB	CS	SB%	GDP	Avg	OBP	SLG
1973 San Diego	NL	56	141	39	4	1	3	(2	1)	54	9	12	12	1	19	0	0	1	0	0	.00	5	.277	.331	.383
1974 San Diego	NL	145	498	132	18	4	20	(12	8)	218	57	75	40	2	96	1	0	5	9	7	.56	14	.265	.318	.438
1975 San Diego	NL	143	509	136	20	2	15	(7	8)	205	74	76	69	14	82	3	3	7	23	4	.85	11	.267	.354	.403
1976 San Diego	NL	137	492	139	26	4	13	(4	9)	212	81	69	65	8	78	3	2	5	26	7	.79	14	.283	.366	.431

Year	Team	Lg	G	AB	H	2B	3B	HR	(Hm	Rd)	TB	R	RBI	TBB	IBB	SO	HBP	SH	SF	SB	CS	SB%	GDP	Avg	OBP	SLG
1977	San Diego	NL	157	615	169	29	7	25	(12	13)	287	104	92	58	10	75	0	0	5	16	7	.70	12	.275	.335	.467
1978	San Diego	NL	158	587	181	30	5	24	(11	13)	293	88	97	55	20	81	2	0	5	21	9	.70	13	.308	.367	.499
1979	San Diego	NL	159	597	184	27	10	34	(16	18)	**333**	97	**118**	85	**24**	71	2	0	2	15	9	.63	9	.308	.395	.558
1980	San Diego	NL	162	558	154	25	6	20	(7	13)	251	89	87	79	14	83	2	0	4	23	7	.77	13	.276	.365	.450
1981	New York	AL	105	388	114	25	1	13	(4	9)	180	52	68	43	3	41	1	1	7	11	1	.92	13	.294	.360	.464
1982	New York	AL	140	539	151	24	8	37	(14	**23**)	302	84	106	45	7	64	0	5	8	5	3	.63	20	.280	.331	.560
1983	New York	AL	152	598	169	26	8	32	(13	19)	307	99	116	58	2	77	2	0	6	15	6	.71	30	.283	.345	.513
1984	New York	AL	141	567	193	34	4	19	(9	10)	292	106	100	53	9	71	0	0	6	6	4	.60	14	.340	.393	.515
1985	New York	AL	155	633	174	34	6	26	(15	11)	298	105	114	52	8	96	0	0	4	19	7	.73	17	.275	.328	.471
1986	New York	AL	154	565	148	31	5	24	(12	12)	261	90	104	77	9	106	2	2	6	6	5	.55	20	.262	.349	.462
1987	New York	AL	156	575	158	22	1	27	(11	16)	263	83	97	76	5	96	0	1	3	5	6	.45	20	.275	.358	.457
1988	New York	AL	149	559	180	37	2	25	(12	13)	296	96	107	69	10	88	2	0	1	9	4	.69	19	.322	.398	.530
1990	2 ML Teams		132	475	127	21	2	21	(13	8)	215	70	78	52	3	81	2	1	7	0	1	.00	17	.267	.338	.453
1991	California	AL	150	568	149	27	4	28	(13	15)	268	75	86	56	4	109	1	2	6	7	2	.78	21	.262	.326	.472
1992	Toronto	AL	156	583	169	33	3	26	(13	13)	286	92	108	82	10	89	1	1	3	2	3	.40	10	.290	.377	.491
1990	New York	AL	20	61	13	3	0	2	(0	2)	22	7	6	4	0	13	1	0	1	0	0	.00	2	.213	.269	.361
	California	AL	112	414	114	18	2	19	(13	6)	193	63	72	48	3	68	1	1	6	0	1	.00	15	.275	.348	.466
19 ML YEARS			2707	10047	2866	493	83	432	(200	232)	4821	1551	1710	1126	163	1503	24	18	91	218	92	.70	292	.285	.356	.480

Herm Winningham

Bats: Left **Throws:** Right **Pos:** LF/CF   **Ht:** 5'11" **Wt:** 190 **Born:** 12/01/61 **Age:** 31

			BATTING																BASERUNNING				PERCENTAGES		
Year	Team	Lg	G	AB	H	2B	3B	HR	(Hm	Rd)	TB	R	RBI	TBB	IBB	SO	HBP	SH	SF	SB	CS	SB%	GDP	Avg	OBP	SLG
1984	New York	NL	14	27	11	1	1	0	(0	0)	14	5	5	1	0	7	0	0	0	2	1	.67	0	.407	.429	.519
1985	Montreal	NL	125	312	74	6	5	3	(0	3)	99	30	21	28	3	72	0	1	4	20	9	.69	1	.237	.297	.317
1986	Montreal	NL	90	185	40	6	3	4	(1	3)	64	23	11	18	3	51	0	1	0	12	7	.63	4	.216	.286	.346
1987	Montreal	NL	137	347	83	20	3	4	(2	2)	121	34	41	34	7	68	0	1	4	29	10	.74	10	.239	.304	.349
1988	2 ML Teams		100	203	47	3	4	0	(0	0)	58	16	21	17	1	45	0	3	2	12	8	.60	2	.232	.288	.286
1989	Cincinnati	NL	115	251	63	11	3	3	(1	2)	89	40	13	24	1	50	0	3	0	14	5	.74	5	.251	.316	.355
1990	Cincinnati	NL	84	160	41	8	5	3	(0	3)	68	20	17	14	1	31	0	2	1	6	4	.60	0	.256	.314	.425
1991	Cincinnati	NL	98	169	38	6	1	1	(1	0)	49	17	4	11	1	40	0	2	0	4	4	.50	2	.225	.272	.290
1992	Boston	AL	105	234	55	8	1	1	(1	0)	68	27	14	10	0	53	0	0	0	6	5	.55	3	.235	.266	.291
1988	Montreal	NL	47	90	21	2	1	0	(0	0)	25	10	6	12	1	18	0	0	1	4	5	.44	2	.233	.320	.278
	Cincinnati	NL	53	113	26	1	3	0	(0	0)	33	6	15	5	0	27	0	3	1	8	3	.73	0	.230	.261	.292
9 ML YEARS			868	1888	452	69	26	19	(6	13)	630	212	147	157	17	417	0	13	11	105	53	.66	27	.239	.296	.334

Bobby Witt

Pitches: Right **Bats:** Right **Pos:** SP   **Ht:** 6' 2" **Wt:** 205 **Born:** 05/11/64 **Age:** 29

			HOW MUCH HE PITCHED					WHAT HE GAVE UP											THE RESULTS					
Year	Team	Lg	G	GS	CG	GF	IP	BFP	H	R	ER	HR	SH	SF	HB	TBB	IBB	SO	WP	Bk	W	L	Pct.	ShO	Sv	ERA
1986	Texas	AL	31	31	0	0	157.2	741	130	104	96	18	3	9	3	**143**	2	174	**22**	3	11	9	.550	0	0	5.48
1987	Texas	AL	26	25	1	0	143	673	114	82	78	10	5	5	3	**140**	1	160	7	2	8	10	.444	0	0	4.91
1988	Texas	AL	22	22	13	0	174.1	736	134	83	76	13	7	6	1	101	2	148	**16**	8	8	10	.444	2	0	3.92
1989	Texas	AL	31	31	5	0	194.1	869	182	123	**111**	14	11	8	2	**114**	3	166	7	4	12	13	.480	1	0	5.14
1990	Texas	AL	33	32	7	1	222	954	197	98	83	12	5	6	4	110	3	221	11	2	17	10	.630	1	0	3.36
1991	Texas	AL	17	16	1	0	88.2	413	84	66	60	4	3	4	1	74	1	82	8	0	3	7	.300	1	0	6.09
1992	2 ML Teams		31	31	0	0	193	848	183	99	92	16	7	10	2	114	2	125	9	1	10	14	.417	0	0	4.29
1992	Texas	AL	25	25	0	0	161.1	708	152	87	80	14	5	8	2	95	1	100	6	1	9	13	.409	0	0	4.46
	Oakland	AL	6	6	0	0	31.2	140	31	12	12	2	2	2	0	19	1	25	3	0	1	1	.500	0	0	3.41
7 ML YEARS			191	188	27	1	1173	5234	1024	655	596	87	41	48	16	796	14	1076	80	20	69	73	.486	5	0	4.57

Mark Wohlers

Pitches: Right **Bats:** Right **Pos:** RP   **Ht:** 6' 4" **Wt:** 207 **Born:** 01/23/70 **Age:** 23

			HOW MUCH HE PITCHED					WHAT HE GAVE UP											THE RESULTS					
Year	Team	Lg	G	GS	CG	GF	IP	BFP	H	R	ER	HR	SH	SF	HB	TBB	IBB	SO	WP	Bk	W	L	Pct.	ShO	Sv	ERA
1988	Pulaski	R	13	9	1	4	59.2	275	47	37	22	0	1	3	0	50	0	49	6	2	5	3	.625	0	0	3.32
1989	Sumter	A	14	14	0	0	68	326	74	55	49	3	3	3	4	59	0	51	10	1	2	7	.222	0	0	6.49
	Pulaski	R	14	8	0	2	46	219	48	36	28	5	1	0	2	28	0	50	2	0	1	1	.500	0	0	5.48
1990	Sumter	A	37	2	0	16	52.2	208	27	13	11	1	1	2	4	20	0	85	0	2	5	4	.556	0	5	1.88
	Greenville	AA	14	0	0	11	15.2	72	14	7	7	0	0	1	1	14	0	20	1	0	0	1	.000	0	6	4.02
1991	Greenville	AA	28	0	0	27	31.1	116	9	4	2	0	3	2	0	13	0	44	3	0	0	0	.000	0	21	0.57
	Richmond	AAA	23	0	0	21	26.1	111	23	4	3	1	4	0	1	12	1	22	1	1	1	0	1.000	0	11	1.03
1992	Richmond	AAA	27	2	0	20	34.1	151	32	16	15	5	4	1	0	17	3	33	6	0	0	2	.000	0	9	3.93
1991	Atlanta	NL	17	0	0	4	19.2	89	17	7	7	1	2	1	2	13	3	13	0	0	3	1	.750	0	2	3.20
1992	Atlanta	NL	32	0	0	16	35.1	140	28	11	10	0	5	1	1	14	4	17	1	0	1	2	.333	0	4	2.55
2 ML YEARS			49	0	0	20	55	229	45	18	17	1	7	2	3	27	7	30	1	0	4	3	.571	0	6	2.78

Ted Wood

Bats: Left **Throws:** Left **Pos:** RF **Ht:** 6' 2" **Wt:** 178 **Born:** 01/04/67 **Age:** 26

								BATTING												BASERUNNING				PERCENTAGES		
Year	Team	Lg	G	AB	H	2B	3B	HR	(Hm	Rd)	TB	R	RBI	TBB	IBB	SO	HBP	SH	SF	SB	CS	SB%	GDP	Avg	OBP	SLG
1989	Shreveport	AA	114	349	90	13	1	0	--	--	105	44	43	51	2	72	6	10	3	9	7	.56	8	.258	.359	.301
1990	Shreveport	AA	131	456	121	22	11	17	--	--	216	81	72	74	5	76	7	4	2	17	8	.68	8	.265	.375	.474
1991	Phoenix	AAA	137	512	159	38	6	11	--	--	242	90	109	86	4	96	4	0	10	12	7	.63	13	.311	.407	.473
1992	Phoenix	AAA	110	418	127	24	7	7	--	--	186	70	63	48	4	74	4	2	5	9	8	.53	5	.304	.377	.445
1991	San Francisco	NL	10	25	3	0	0	0	(0	0)	3	0	1	2	0	11	0	1	0	0	0	.00	0	.120	.185	.120
1992	San Francisco	NL	24	58	12	2	0	1	(0	1)	17	5	3	6	0	15	1	2	0	0	0	.00	4	.207	.292	.293
	2 ML YEARS		34	83	15	2	0	1	(0	1)	20	5	4	8	0	26	1	3	0	0	0	.00	4	.181	.261	.241

Kerry Woodson

Pitches: Right **Bats:** Right **Pos:** RP **Ht:** 6' 2" **Wt:** 190 **Born:** 05/18/69 **Age:** 24

			HOW MUCH HE PITCHED						WHAT HE GAVE UP										THE RESULTS					
Year	Team	Lg	G	GS	CG	GF	IP	BFP	H	R	ER	HR	SH	SF	HB	TBB	IBB	SO	WP	Bk	W	L	Pct.	ShO	Sv	ERA
1989	Bellingham	A	12	12	0	0	60.2	272	63	42	32	2	1	2	2	27	1	53	3	8	3	4	.429	0	0	4.75
1990	San Berndno	A	27	23	1	1	136.2	598	111	62	46	2	3	3	12	83	1	131	8	2	8	6	.571	1	0	3.03
1991	San Berndno	A	5	5	0	0	27.2	128	33	13	6	3	1	0	0	16	0	14	1	1	2	0	1.000	0	0	1.95
	Jacksnville	AA	13	13	2	0	79.1	338	73	35	27	3	1	0	5	39	0	50	8	1	4	6	.400	0	0	3.06
1992	Jacksnville	AA	11	11	0	0	68	300	74	31	27	4	2	0	5	36	0	55	11	2	5	4	.556	0	0	3.57
	Calgary	AAA	10	0	0	5	21	94	20	15	8	1	1	1	0	12	1	9	1	2	1	4	.200	0	2	3.43
1992	Seattle	AL	8	1	0	0	13.2	62	12	7	5	0	0	0	2	11	0	6	1	0	0	1	.000	0	0	3.29

Tracy Woodson

Bats: Right **Throws:** Right **Pos:** 3B **Ht:** 6' 3" **Wt:** 215 **Born:** 10/05/62 **Age:** 30

								BATTING												BASERUNNING				PERCENTAGES		
Year	Team	Lg	G	AB	H	2B	3B	HR	(Hm	Rd)	TB	R	RBI	TBB	IBB	SO	HBP	SH	SF	SB	CS	SB%	GDP	Avg	OBP	SLG
1987	Los Angeles	NL	53	136	31	8	1	1	(1	0)	44	14	11	9	2	21	2	0	1	1	1	.50	2	.228	.284	.324
1988	Los Angeles	NL	65	173	43	4	1	3	(2	1)	58	15	15	7	1	32	1	0	2	1	2	.33	4	.249	.279	.335
1989	Los Angeles	NL	4	6	0	0	0	0	(0	0)	0	0	0	0	0	1	0	0	0	0	0	.00	0	.000	.000	.000
1992	St. Louis	NL	31	114	35	8	0	1	(0	1)	46	9	22	2	0	10	1	1	0	0	0	.00	1	.307	.331	.404
	4 ML YEARS		153	429	109	20	2	5	(3	2)	148	38	48	19	3	64	4	1	3	2	3	.40	9	.254	.290	.345

Todd Worrell

Pitches: Right **Bats:** Right **Pos:** RP **Ht:** 6' 5" **Wt:** 222 **Born:** 09/28/59 **Age:** 33

			HOW MUCH HE PITCHED						WHAT HE GAVE UP										THE RESULTS					
Year	Team	Lg	G	GS	CG	GF	IP	BFP	H	R	ER	HR	SH	SF	HB	TBB	IBB	SO	WP	Bk	W	L	Pct.	ShO	Sv	ERA
1985	St. Louis	NL	17	0	0	11	21.2	88	17	7	7	2	0	2	0	7	2	17	2	0	3	0	1.000	0	5	2.91
1986	St. Louis	NL	74	0	0	60	103.2	430	86	29	24	9	7	6	1	41	16	73	1	0	9	10	.474	0	36	2.08
1987	St. Louis	NL	75	0	0	54	94.2	395	86	29	28	8	4	2	0	34	11	92	1	0	8	6	.571	0	33	2.66
1988	St. Louis	NL	68	0	0	54	90	366	69	32	30	7	3	5	1	34	14	78	6	2	5	9	.357	0	32	3.00
1989	St. Louis	NL	47	0	0	39	51.2	219	42	21	17	4	3	1	0	26	13	41	3	3	3	5	.375	0	20	2.96
1992	St. Louis	NL	67	0	0	14	64	256	45	15	15	4	3	0	1	25	5	64	1	1	5	3	.625	0	3	2.11
	6 ML YEARS		348	0	0	232	425.2	1754	345	133	121	34	20	16	3	167	61	365	14	6	33	33	.500	0	129	2.56

Craig Worthington

Bats: Right **Throws:** Right **Pos:** 3B **Ht:** 6' 0" **Wt:** 200 **Born:** 04/17/65 **Age:** 28

								BATTING												BASERUNNING				PERCENTAGES		
Year	Team	Lg	G	AB	H	2B	3B	HR	(Hm	Rd)	TB	R	RBI	TBB	IBB	SO	HBP	SH	SF	SB	CS	SB%	GDP	Avg	OBP	SLG
1988	Baltimore	AL	26	81	15	2	0	2	(0	2)	23	5	4	9	0	24	0	0	0	1	0	1.00	2	.185	.267	.284
1989	Baltimore	AL	145	497	123	23	0	15	(12	3)	191	57	70	61	2	114	4	3	1	1	2	.33	10	.247	.334	.384
1990	Baltimore	AL	133	425	96	17	0	8	(3	5)	137	46	44	63	2	96	3	7	3	1	2	.33	13	.226	.328	.322
1991	Baltimore	AL	31	102	23	3	0	4	(1	3)	38	11	12	12	0	14	1	1	0	0	1	.00	3	.225	.313	.373
1992	Cleveland	AL	9	24	4	0	0	0	(0	0)	4	0	2	2	0	4	0	0	0	0	1	.00	0	.167	.231	.167
	5 ML YEARS		344	1129	261	45	0	29	(16	13)	393	119	132	147	4	252	8	11	4	3	6	.33	28	.231	.323	.348

Rick Wrona

Bats: Right **Throws:** Right **Pos:** C **Ht:** 6' 0" **Wt:** 180 **Born:** 12/10/63 **Age:** 29

								BATTING												BASERUNNING				PERCENTAGES		
Year	Team	Lg	G	AB	H	2B	3B	HR	(Hm	Rd)	TB	R	RBI	TBB	IBB	SO	HBP	SH	SF	SB	CS	SB%	GDP	Avg	OBP	SLG
1988	Chicago	NL	4	6	0	0	0	0	(0	0)	0	0	0	0	0	1	0	0	0	0	0	.00	0	.000	.000	.000
1989	Chicago	NL	38	92	26	2	1	2	(0	2)	36	11	14	2	1	21	1	0	2	0	0	.00	1	.283	.299	.391
1990	Chicago	NL	16	29	5	0	0	0	(0	0)	5	3	0	2	1	11	0	1	0	1	0	1.00	0	.172	.226	.172
1992	Cincinnati	NL	11	23	4	0	0	0	(0	0)	4	0	0	0	0	3	0	0	0	0	0	.00	2	.174	.174	.174
	4 ML YEARS		69	150	35	2	1	2	(0	2)	45	14	14	4	2	36	1	1	2	1	0	1.00	3	.233	.255	.300

Eric Yelding

Bats: Right **Throws:** Right **Pos:** SS **Ht:** 5'11" **Wt:** 165 **Born:** 02/22/65 **Age:** 28

Year Team	Lg	G	AB	H	2B	3B	HR	(Hm	Rd)	TB	R	RBI	TBB	IBB	SO	HBP	SH	SF	SB	CS	SB%	GDP	Avg	OBP	SLG
1989 Houston	NL	70	90	21	2	0	0	(0	0)	23	19	9	7	0	19	1	2	2	11	5	.69	2	.233	.290	.256
1990 Houston	NL	142	511	130	9	5	1	(0	1)	152	69	28	39	1	87	0	4	5	64	25	.72	11	.254	.305	.297
1991 Houston	NL	78	276	67	11	1	1	(0	0)	83	19	20	13	3	46	0	3	1	11	9	.55	4	.243	.276	.301
1992 Houston	NL	9	8	2	0	0	0	(0	0)	2	1	0	0	0	3	0	0	0	0	0	.00	0	.250	.250	.250
4 ML YEARS		299	885	220	22	6	2	(0	2)	260	108	57	59	4	155	1	9	8	86	39	.69	17	.249	.294	.294

Anthony Young

Pitches: Right **Bats:** Right **Pos:** RP/SP **Ht:** 6'2" **Wt:** 200 **Born:** 01/19/66 **Age:** 27

Year Team	Lg	G	GS	CG	GF	IP	BFP	H	R	ER	HR	SH	SF	HB	TBB	IBB	SO	WP	Bk	W	L	Pct.	ShO	Sv	ERA
1987 Little Fls	A	14	9	0	0	53.2	247	58	37	27	6	2	2	1	25	1	48	4	0	3	4	.429	0	0	4.53
1988 Little Fls	A	15	10	4	2	73.2	304	51	33	18	1	1	3	0	34	0	75	9	1	3	5	.375	0	0	2.20
1989 Columbia	A	21	17	8	2	129	548	115	60	50	5	1	3	4	55	1	127	7	3	9	6	.600	1	0	3.49
1990 Jackson	AA	23	23	3	0	158	633	116	38	29	3	6	1	3	52	5	95	7	1	15	3	.833	1	0	1.65
1991 Tidewater	AAA	25	25	3	0	164	702	172	74	68	13	9	5	1	67	2	93	6	1	7	9	.438	1	0	3.73
1991 New York	NL	10	8	0	2	49.1	202	48	20	17	4	1	1	1	12	1	20	1	0	2	5	.286	0	0	3.10
1992 New York	NL	52	13	1	26	121	517	134	66	56	8	11	4	1	31	5	64	3	1	2	14	.125	0	15	4.17
2 ML YEARS		62	21	1	28	170.1	719	182	86	73	12	12	5	2	43	6	84	4	1	4	19	.174	0	15	3.86

Curt Young

Pitches: Left **Bats:** Right **Pos:** RP/SP **Ht:** 6'1" **Wt:** 180 **Born:** 04/16/60 **Age:** 33

Year Team	Lg	G	GS	CG	GF	IP	BFP	H	R	ER	HR	SH	SF	HB	TBB	IBB	SO	WP	Bk	W	L	Pct.	ShO	Sv	ERA
1983 Oakland	AL	8	2	0	0	9	50	17	17	16	1	0	0	1	5	0	5	1	0	0	1	.000	0	0	16.00
1984 Oakland	AL	20	17	2	0	108.2	475	118	53	49	9	1	4	8	31	0	41	3	0	9	4	.692	1	0	4.06
1985 Oakland	AL	19	7	0	5	46	214	57	38	37	15	0	1	1	22	0	19	1	0	0	4	.000	0	0	7.24
1986 Oakland	AL	29	27	5	0	198	826	176	88	76	19	8	9	7	57	1	116	7	2	13	9	.591	2	0	3.45
1987 Oakland	AL	31	31	6	0	203	828	194	102	92	38	6	4	3	44	0	124	2	1	13	7	.650	0	0	4.08
1988 Oakland	AL	26	26	1	0	156.1	651	162	77	72	23	3	5	4	50	3	69	3	6	11	8	.579	0	0	4.14
1989 Oakland	AL	25	20	1	2	111	495	117	56	46	10	1	0	3	47	2	55	4	4	5	9	.357	0	0	3.73
1990 Oakland	AL	26	21	0	0	124.1	527	124	70	67	17	4	2	2	53	1	56	3	0	9	6	.600	0	0	4.85
1991 Oakland	AL	41	1	0	6	68.1	306	74	38	38	8	3	1	2	34	2	27	2	1	4	2	.667	0	0	5.00
1992 2 ML Teams		23	7	0	5	67.2	295	80	35	30	2	3	3	2	17	2	20	0	0	4	2	.667	0	0	3.99
1992 Kansas City	AL	10	2	0	2	24.1	107	29	14	14	1	0	1	0	7	1	7	0	0	1	2	.333	0	0	5.18
New York	AL	13	5	0	3	43.1	188	51	21	16	1	3	2	2	10	1	13	0	0	3	0	1.000	0	0	3.32
10 ML YEARS		248	159	15	18	1092.1	4667	1119	574	523	142	29	29	33	360	11	532	26	14	68	52	.567	3	0	4.31

Eric Young

Bats: Right **Throws:** Right **Pos:** 2B **Ht:** 5'9" **Wt:** 180 **Born:** 11/26/66 **Age:** 26

Year Team	Lg	G	AB	H	2B	3B	HR	(Hm	Rd)	TB	R	RBI	TBB	IBB	SO	HBP	SH	SF	SB	CS	SB%	GDP	Avg	OBP	SLG
1989 Dodgers	R	56	197	65	11	5	2	--	--	92	53	22	33	1	16	3	1	1	41	10	.80	1	.330	.432	.467
1990 Vero Beach	A	127	460	132	23	7	2	--	--	175	101	50	69	1	35	6	5	4	76	16	.83	4	.287	.384	.380
1991 San Antonio	AA	127	461	129	17	4	3	--	--	163	82	35	67	0	36	2	8	1	71	26	.73	13	.280	.373	.354
Albuquerque	AAA	1	5	2	0	0	0	--	--	2	0	0	0	0	0	0	0	0	0	0	.00	0	.400	.400	.400
1992 Albuquerque	AAA	94	350	118	16	5	3	--	--	153	61	49	33	0	18	4	13	7	28	11	.72	10	.337	.393	.437
1992 Los Angeles	NL	49	132	34	1	0	1	(0	1)	38	9	11	8	0	9	0	4	0	6	1	.86	3	.258	.300	.288

Gerald Young

Bats: Both **Throws:** Right **Pos:** RF/CF **Ht:** 6'2" **Wt:** 185 **Born:** 10/22/64 **Age:** 28

Year Team	Lg	G	AB	H	2B	3B	HR	(Hm	Rd)	TB	R	RBI	TBB	IBB	SO	HBP	SH	SF	SB	CS	SB%	GDP	Avg	OBP	SLG
1987 Houston	NL	71	274	88	9	2	1	(0	1)	104	44	15	26	0	27	1	0	2	26	9	.74	1	.321	.380	.380
1988 Houston	NL	149	576	148	21	9	0	(0	0)	187	79	37	66	1	66	3	5	5	65	27	.71	10	.257	.334	.325
1989 Houston	NL	146	533	124	17	3	0	(0	0)	147	71	38	74	4	60	2	6	5	34	25	.58	7	.233	.326	.276
1990 Houston	NL	57	154	27	4	1	1	(1	0)	36	15	4	20	0	23	0	4	1	6	3	.67	3	.175	.269	.234
1991 Houston	NL	108	142	31	3	1	1	(0	1)	39	26	11	24	0	17	0	1	2	16	5	.76	3	.218	.327	.275
1992 Houston	NL	74	76	14	1	1	0	(0	0)	17	14	4	10	0	11	0	4	0	6	2	.75	2	.184	.279	.224
6 ML YEARS		605	1755	432	55	17	3	(1	2)	530	249	109	220	5	204	6	20	15	153	71	.68	26	.246	.330	.302

Kevin Young

Bats: Right **Throws:** Right **Pos:** 3B **Ht:** 6' 3" **Wt:** 210 **Born:** 06/16/69 **Age:** 24

								BATTING											BASERUNNING				PERCENTAGES		
Year	Team	Lg	G	AB	H	2B	3B	HR	(Hm	Rd)	TB	R	RBI	TBB	IBB	SO	HBP	SH	SF	SB	CS	SB%	GDP	Avg	OBP	SLG
1990	Welland	A	72	238	58	16	2	5	--	--	93	46	30	31	2	39	7	0	5	10	2	.83	4	.244	.342	.391
1991	Salem	A	56	201	63	11	4	6	--	--	100	38	28	20	0	34	7	0	3	3	2	.60	5	.313	.390	.498
	Carolina	AA	75	263	90	19	6	3	--	--	130	36	33	15	1	38	8	0	1	9	3	.75	7	.342	.394	.494
	Buffalo	AAA	4	9	2	1	0	0	--	--	3	1	2	0	0	0	1	0	1	1	0	1.00	0	.222	.273	.333
1992	Buffalo	AAA	137	490	154	29	6	8	--	--	219	91	65	67	0	67	11	8	3	18	12	.60	11	.314	.406	.447
1992	Pittsburgh	NL	10	7	4	0	0	0	(0	0)	4	2	4	2	0	0	0	0	0	1	0	1.00	0	.571	.667	.571

Matt Young

Pitches: Left **Bats:** Left **Pos:** RP/SP **Ht:** 6' 3" **Wt:** 210 **Born:** 08/09/58 **Age:** 34

			HOW MUCH HE PITCHED						WHAT HE GAVE UP										THE RESULTS					
Year	Team	Lg	G	GS	CG	GF	IP	BFP	H	R	ER	HR	SH	SF	HB	TBB	IBB	SO	WP	Bk	W	L	Pct.	ShO	Sv	ERA
1983	Seattle	AL	33	32	5	0	203.2	851	178	86	74	17	4	8	7	79	2	130	4	2	11	15	.423	2	0	3.27
1984	Seattle	AL	22	22	1	0	113.1	524	141	81	72	11	1	5	1	57	3	73	3	1	6	8	.429	0	0	5.72
1985	Seattle	AL	37	35	5	2	218.1	951	242	135	119	23	7	3	7	76	3	136	6	2	12	19	.387	2	1	4.91
1986	Seattle	AL	65	5	1	32	103.2	458	108	50	44	9	4	3	8	46	2	82	7	1	8	6	.571	0	13	3.82
1987	Los Angeles	NL	47	0	0	31	54.1	234	62	30	27	3	1	1	0	17	5	42	3	0	5	8	.385	0	11	4.47
1989	Oakland	AL	26	4	0	1	37.1	183	42	31	28	2	4	1	0	31	2	27	5	0	1	4	.200	0	0	6.75
1990	Seattle	AL	34	33	7	0	225.1	963	198	106	88	15	7	7	6	107	7	176	16	0	8	18	.308	1	0	3.51
1991	Boston	AL	19	16	0	1	88.2	404	92	55	51	4	1	2	2	53	2	69	5	0	3	7	.300	0	0	5.18
1992	Boston	AL	28	8	1	4	70.2	321	69	42	36	7	4	3	3	42	2	57	2	0	0	4	.000	0	0	4.58
	9 ML YEARS		311	155	20	71	1115.1	4889	1132	616	539	91	33	33	34	508	28	792	51	6	54	89	.378	5	25	4.35

Pete Young

Pitches: Right **Bats:** Right **Pos:** RP **Ht:** 6' 0" **Wt:** 225 **Born:** 03/19/68 **Age:** 25

			HOW MUCH HE PITCHED						WHAT HE GAVE UP										THE RESULTS					
Year	Team	Lg	G	GS	CG	GF	IP	BFP	H	R	ER	HR	SH	SF	HB	TBB	IBB	SO	WP	Bk	W	L	Pct.	ShO	Sv	ERA
1989	Jamestown	A	18	10	0	8	65	269	63	18	14	2	0	1	5	14	0	62	6	0	5	2	.714	0	4	1.94
1990	Wst Plm Bch	A	39	12	0	25	109.1	453	106	36	30	3	3	2	2	27	1	62	6	0	8	3	.727	0	19	2.47
1991	Sumter	A	1	0	0	0	1	5	1	1	1	0	0	0	0	1	0	2	0	0	0	0	.000	0	0	9.00
	Harrisburg	AA	54	0	0	29	90	368	82	28	26	9	4	1	2	24	4	74	1	0	7	5	.583	0	13	2.60
1992	Indianaplis	AAA	36	0	0	20	48.2	216	53	19	19	5	4	3	1	21	3	34	0	0	6	2	.750	0	7	3.51
1992	Montreal	NL	13	0	0	6	20.1	85	18	9	9	0	0	2	1	9	2	11	1	0	0	0	.000	0	0	3.98

Robin Yount

Bats: Right **Throws:** Right **Pos:** CF/DH **Ht:** 6' 0" **Wt:** 180 **Born:** 09/16/55 **Age:** 37

								BATTING											BASERUNNING				PERCENTAGES		
Year	Team	Lg	G	AB	H	2B	3B	HR	(Hm	Rd)	TB	R	RBI	TBB	IBB	SO	HBP	SH	SF	SB	CS	SB%	GDP	Avg	OBP	SLG
1974	Milwaukee	AL	107	344	86	14	5	3	(3	0)	119	48	26	12	0	46	1	5	2	7	7	.50	4	.250	.276	.346
1975	Milwaukee	AL	147	558	149	28	2	8	(4	4)	205	67	52	33	3	69	1	10	5	12	4	.75	8	.267	.307	.367
1976	Milwaukee	AL	161	638	161	19	3	2	(1	1)	192	59	54	38	3	69	0	8	6	16	11	.59	13	.252	.292	.301
1977	Milwaukee	AL	154	605	174	34	4	4	(2	2)	228	66	49	41	1	80	2	11	4	16	7	.70	11	.288	.333	.377
1978	Milwaukee	AL	127	502	147	23	9	9	(5	4)	215	66	71	24	1	43	1	13	5	16	5	.76	5	.293	.323	.428
1979	Milwaukee	AL	149	577	154	26	5	8	(4	4)	214	72	51	35	3	52	1	10	3	11	8	.58	15	.267	.308	.371
1980	Milwaukee	AL	143	611	179	49	10	23	(13	10)	317	121	87	26	1	67	1	6	3	20	5	.80	8	.293	.321	.519
1981	Milwaukee	AL	96	377	103	15	5	10	(1	9)	158	50	49	22	1	37	2	4	6	4	1	.80	4	.273	.312	.419
1982	Milwaukee	AL	156	635	210	46	12	29	(9	20)	367	129	114	54	2	63	1	4	10	14	3	.82	19	.331	.379	.578
1983	Milwaukee	AL	149	578	178	42	10	17	(6	11)	291	102	80	72	6	58	3	1	8	12	5	.71	11	.308	.383	.503
1984	Milwaukee	AL	160	624	186	27	7	16	(8	8)	275	105	80	67	7	67	1	1	9	14	4	.78	22	.298	.362	.441
1985	Milwaukee	AL	122	466	129	26	3	15	(11	4)	206	76	68	49	3	56	2	1	9	10	4	.71	8	.277	.342	.442
1986	Milwaukee	AL	140	522	163	31	7	9	(4	5)	235	82	46	62	7	73	4	5	2	14	5	.74	9	.312	.388	.450
1987	Milwaukee	AL	158	635	198	25	9	21	(12	9)	304	99	103	76	10	94	1	6	5	19	9	.68	9	.312	.384	.479
1988	Milwaukee	AL	162	621	190	38	11	13	(7	6)	289	92	91	63	10	63	3	2	7	22	4	.85	21	.306	.369	.465
1989	Milwaukee	AL	160	614	195	38	9	21	(14	7)	314	101	103	63	9	71	6	3	4	19	3	.86	9	.318	.384	.511
1990	Milwaukee	AL	158	587	145	17	5	17	(8	9)	223	98	77	78	6	89	6	4	8	15	8	.65	7	.247	.337	.380
1991	Milwaukee	AL	130	503	131	20	4	10	(8	2)	189	66	77	54	4	89	4	1	9	6	4	.60	13	.260	.332	.376
1992	Milwaukee	AL	150	557	147	40	3	8	(3	5)	217	71	77	53	9	81	3	4	12	15	6	.71	9	.264	.325	.390
	19 ML YEARS		2729	10554	3025	558	123	243	(123	120)	4558	1570	1355	922	90	1257	43	99	117	262	103	.72	205	.287	.343	.432

Todd Zeile

Bats: Right **Throws:** Right **Pos:** 3B   **Ht:** 6' 1" **Wt:** 190 **Born:** 09/09/65 **Age:** 27

Year Team	Lg	G	AB	H	2B	3B	HR	(Hm	Rd)	TB	R	RBI	TBB	IBB	SO	HBP	SH	SF	SB	CS	SB%	GDP	Avg	OBP	SLG
1989 St. Louis	NL	28	82	21	3	1	1	(0	1)	29	7	8	9	1	14	0	1	1	0	0	.00	1	.256	.326	.354
1990 St. Louis	NL	144	495	121	25	2	15	(8	7)	197	62	57	67	3	77	2	0	6	2	4	.33	11	.244	.333	.398
1991 St. Louis	NL	155	565	158	36	3	11	(7	4)	233	76	81	62	3	94	5	0	6	17	11	.61	15	.280	.353	.412
1992 St. Louis	NL	126	439	113	18	4	7	(4	3)	160	51	48	68	4	70	0	0	7	7	10	.41	11	.257	.352	.364
4 ML YEARS		453	1581	413	82	11	34	(19	15)	619	196	194	206	11	255	7	1	20	26	25	.51	38	.261	.345	.392

Eddie Zosky

Bats: Right **Throws:** Right **Pos:** SS   **Ht:** 6' 0" **Wt:** 175 **Born:** 02/10/68 **Age:** 25

Year Team	Lg	G	AB	H	2B	3B	HR	(Hm	Rd)	TB	R	RBI	TBB	IBB	SO	HBP	SH	SF	SB	CS	SB%	GDP	Avg	OBP	SLG
1989 Knoxville	AA	56	208	46	5	3	2	--	--	63	21	14	10	0	32	0	2	1	1	1	.50	4	.221	.256	.303
1990 Knoxville	AA	115	450	122	20	7	3	--	--	165	53	45	26	1	73	5	6	3	3	13	.19	7	.271	.316	.367
1991 Syracuse	AAA	119	511	135	18	4	6	--	--	179	69	39	35	1	82	5	7	5	9	4	.69	11	.264	.315	.350
1992 Syracuse	AAA	96	342	79	11	6	4	--	--	114	31	38	19	0	53	1	7	4	3	4	.43	10	.231	.270	.333
1991 Toronto	AL	18	27	4	1	1	0	(0	0)	7	2	2	0	0	8	0	1	0	0	0	.00	1	.148	.148	.259
1992 Toronto	AL	8	7	2	0	1	0	(0	0)	4	1	1	0	0	2	0	0	1	0	0	.00	0	.286	.250	.571
2 ML YEARS		26	34	6	1	2	0	(0	0)	11	3	3	0	0	10	0	1	1	0	0	.00	1	.176	.171	.324

Bob Zupcic

Bats: Right **Throws:** Right **Pos:** CF/LF/RF   **Ht:** 6' 4" **Wt:** 220 **Born:** 08/18/66 **Age:** 26

Year Team	Lg	G	AB	H	2B	3B	HR	(Hm	Rd)	TB	R	RBI	TBB	IBB	SO	HBP	SH	SF	SB	CS	SB%	GDP	Avg	OBP	SLG
1987 Elmira	A	66	238	72	12	2	7	--	--	109	39	37	17	0	35	2	3	2	5	4	.56	5	.303	.351	.458
1988 Lynchburg	A	135	482	143	33	5	13	--	--	225	69	97	60	4	64	8	7	8	10	6	.63	6	.297	.378	.467
1989 Pawtucket	AAA	27	94	24	7	1	1	--	--	36	8	11	3	0	15	0	0	2	1	3	.25	2	.255	.273	.383
New Britain	AA	94	346	75	12	2	2	--	--	97	37	28	19	0	55	1	7	2	15	1	.94	7	.217	.258	.280
1990 New Britain	AA	132	461	98	26	1	2	--	--	132	45	41	36	2	63	6	6	7	10	8	.56	7	.213	.275	.286
1991 Pawtucket	AAA	129	429	103	27	1	18	--	--	186	70	70	55	2	58	1	12	8	10	6	.63	5	.240	.323	.434
1992 Pawtucket	AAA	9	25	8	1	0	2	--	--	15	3	5	8	0	6	0	0	0	0	1	.00	0	.320	.471	.600
1991 Boston	AL	18	25	4	0	0	1	(1	0)	7	3	3	1	0	6	0	1	0	0	0	.00	0	.160	.192	.280
1992 Boston	AL	124	392	108	19	1	3	(3	0)	138	46	43	25	1	60	4	7	4	2	2	.50	6	.276	.322	.352
2 ML YEARS		142	417	112	19	1	4	(4	0)	145	49	46	26	1	66	4	8	4	2	2	.50	6	.269	.315	.348

1992 Team Statistics

American League Batting

Team	G	AB	H	2B	3B	HR	(Hm	Rd)	TB	R	RBI	TBB	IBB	SO	HBP	SH	SF	SB	CS	SB%	GDP	Avg	OBP	SLG
Detroit	162	5515	1411	256	16	182	(91	91)	2245	791	746	675	42	1055	24	43	53	66	45	.59	124	.256	.337	.407
Toronto	162	5536	1458	265	40	163	(79	84)	2292	780	737	561	41	933	47	26	54	129	39	.77	123	.263	.333	.414
Minnesota	162	5582	1544	275	27	104	(56	48)	2185	747	701	527	53	834	53	46	59	123	74	.62	130	.277	.341	.391
Oakland	162	5387	1389	219	24	142	(76	66)	2082	745	693	707	46	831	49	72	59	143	59	.71	139	.258	.346	.386
Milwaukee	162	5504	1477	272	35	82	(35	47)	2065	740	683	511	45	779	33	61	72	256	115	.69	102	.268	.330	.375
Chicago	162	5498	1434	269	36	110	(54	56)	2105	738	686	622	48	784	31	47	69	160	57	.74	134	.261	.336	.383
New York	162	5593	1462	281	18	163	(88	75)	2268	733	703	536	51	903	42	26	55	78	37	.68	138	.261	.328	.406
Baltimore	162	5485	1423	243	36	148	(75	73)	2182	705	680	647	55	827	51	50	59	89	48	.65	139	.259	.340	.398
Texas	162	5537	1387	266	23	159	(71	88)	2176	682	646	550	36	1036	50	56	45	81	44	.65	115	.250	.321	.393
Seattle	162	5564	1466	278	24	149	(78	71)	2239	679	638	474	47	841	38	52	51	100	55	.65	148	.263	.323	.402
Cleveland	162	5620	1495	227	24	127	(62	65)	2151	674	637	448	46	885	45	42	44	144	67	.68	140	.266	.323	.383
Kansas City	162	5501	1411	284	42	75	(24	51)	2004	610	568	439	30	741	51	45	46	131	71	.65	121	.256	.315	.364
Boston	162	5461	1343	259	21	84	(45	39)	1896	599	567	591	46	865	31	60	43	44	48	.48	118	.246	.321	.347
California	162	5364	1306	202	20	88	(44	44)	1812	579	537	416	40	882	40	56	40	160	101	.61	137	.243	.301	.338
American	1134	77147	20006	3596	386	1776	(878	898)	29702	9802	9222	7704	626	12196	585	682	749	1704	860	.66	1808	.259	.328	.385

American League Pitching

Team	G	GS	CG	GF	IP	BFP	H	R	ER	HR	SH	SF	HB	TBB	IBB	SO	WP	Bk	W	L	Pct.	ShO	Sv	ERA
Milwaukee	162	162	19	143	1457	6040	1344	604	556	127	47	42	47	435	33	793	37	8	92	70	.568	14	39	3.43
Minnesota	162	162	16	146	1453	6086	1391	653	598	121	50	49	36	479	30	923	52	5	90	72	.556	13	50	3.70
Baltimore	162	162	20	142	1464	6193	1419	656	616	124	59	47	36	518	38	846	45	6	89	73	.549	16	48	3.79
Kansas City	162	162	9	153	1447.1	6171	1426	667	613	106	50	67	39	512	50	834	42	10	72	90	.444	12	44	3.81
Boston	162	162	22	140	1448.2	6173	1403	669	577	107	51	49	41	535	56	943	50	6	73	89	.451	13	39	3.58
California	162	162	26	136	1446	6154	1449	671	617	130	47	50	39	532	40	888	42	5	72	90	.444	13	42	3.84
Oakland	162	162	8	154	1447	6204	1396	672	599	129	56	56	41	601	46	843	67	4	96	66	.593	9	58	3.73
Toronto	162	162	18	144	1440.2	6108	1346	682	626	124	32	55	45	541	37	954	66	6	96	66	.593	14	49	3.91
Chicago	162	162	21	141	1461.2	6244	1400	690	621	123	43	45	55	550	48	810	35	6	86	76	.531	5	52	3.82
Cleveland	162	162	13	149	1470	6330	1507	746	671	159	56	56	34	566	31	890	53	12	76	86	.469	7	46	4.11
New York	162	162	20	142	1452.2	6256	1453	746	679	129	39	53	35	612	49	851	52	7	76	86	.469	9	44	4.21
Texas	162	162	19	143	1460.1	6325	1471	753	663	113	44	64	48	598	30	1034	72	6	77	85	.475	3	42	4.09
Detroit	162	162	10	152	1435.2	6254	1534	794	733	155	52	63	29	564	88	693	57	3	75	87	.463	4	36	4.60
Seattle	162	162	21	141	1445	6349	1467	799	730	129	56	53	60	661	50	894	61	6	64	98	.395	9	30	4.55
American	1134	1134	242	892	20329	86887	20006	9802	8899	1776	682	749	585	7704	626	12196	731	90	1134	1134	.500	141	619	3.94

National League Batting

Team	G	AB	H	2B	3B	HR	(Hm	Rd)	TB	R	RBI	TBB	IBB	SO	HBP	SH	SF	SB	CS	SB%	GDP	Avg	OBP	SLG
Pittsburgh	162	5527	1409	272	54	106	(51	55)	2107	693	656	569	88	872	25	89	56	110	53	.67	102	.255	.324	.381
Philadelphia	162	5500	1392	255	36	118	(67	51)	2073	686	638	509	45	1059	52	64	46	127	31	.80	111	.253	.320	.377
Atlanta	162	5480	1391	223	48	138	(72	66)	2124	682	641	493	58	924	26	93	50	126	60	.68	82	.254	.316	.388
Cincinnati	162	5460	1418	281	44	99	(60	39)	2084	660	606	563	83	888	21	66	52	125	65	.66	123	.260	.328	.382
Montreal	162	5477	1381	263	37	102	(50	52)	2024	648	601	463	43	976	43	82	55	196	63	.76	104	.252	.313	.370
St. Louis	162	5594	1464	262	44	94	(55	39)	2096	631	599	495	49	996	32	68	41	208	118	.64	96	.262	.323	.375
San Diego	162	5476	1396	255	30	135	(87	48)	2116	617	576	453	67	864	26	78	41	69	52	.57	126	.255	.313	.386
Houston	162	5480	1350	255	38	96	(49	47)	1969	608	582	506	65	1025	48	88	40	139	54	.72	97	.246	.313	.359
New York	162	5340	1254	259	17	93	(42	51)	1826	599	564	572	53	956	28	74	45	129	52	.71	117	.235	.310	.342
Chicago	162	5590	1420	221	41	104	(59	45)	2035	593	566	417	49	816	31	78	40	77	51	.60	121	.254	.307	.364
San Francisco	162	5456	1330	220	36	105	(57	48)	1937	574	532	435	53	1067	39	101	39	112	64	.64	111	.244	.302	.355
Los Angeles	162	5368	1333	201	34	72	(26	46)	1818	548	499	503	36	899	24	102	40	142	78	.65	111	.248	.313	.339
National	972	65748	16538	2967	459	1262	(675	587)	24209	7539	7060	5978	689	11342	395	983	545	1560	741	.68	1301	.252	.315	.368

National League Pitching

Team	G	GS	CG	GF	IP	BFP	H	R	ER	HR	SH	SF	HB	TBB	IBB	SO	WP	Bk	W	L	Pct.	ShO	Sv	ERA
Atlanta	162	162	26	136	1460	6072	1321	569	510	89	53	37	26	489	55	948	58	10	98	64	.605	24	41	3.14
Montreal	162	162	11	151	1468	6139	1296	581	530	92	77	35	50	525	41	1014	48	11	87	75	.537	14	49	3.25
Pittsburgh	162	162	20	142	1479.2	6162	1410	595	551	101	80	48	30	455	61	844	52	9	96	66	.593	20	43	3.35
St. Louis	162	162	10	152	1480	6140	1405	604	556	118	77	46	32	400	46	842	41	3	83	79	.512	9	47	3.38
Cincinnati	162	162	9	153	1449.2	6042	1362	609	558	109	78	47	28	470	51	1060	54	6	90	72	.556	11	55	3.46
Chicago	162	162	16	146	1469	6201	1337	624	554	107	88	52	44	575	75	901	68	11	78	84	.481	11	37	3.39
Los Angeles	162	162	18	144	1438	6192	1401	636	545	82	109	44	28	553	95	981	64	10	63	99	.389	13	29	3.41
San Diego	162	162	9	153	1461.1	6132	1444	636	578	111	93	43	21	439	53	971	25	15	82	80	.506	11	46	3.56
San Francisco	162	162	9	153	1461	6134	1385	647	586	128	88	42	35	502	61	927	34	22	72	90	.444	12	30	3.61
New York	162	162	17	145	1446.2	6118	1404	653	588	98	72	52	36	482	54	1025	34	9	72	90	.444	13	34	3.66
Houston	162	162	5	157	1459.1	6213	1386	668	603	114	87	46	38	539	60	978	45	14	81	81	.500	12	45	3.72
Philadelphia	162	162	27	135	1428	6113	1387	717	652	113	81	53	27	549	37	851	43	9	70	92	.432	7	34	4.11
National	972	972	177	795	17500.2	73658	16538	7539	6811	1262	983	545	395	5978	689	11342	566	129	972	972	.500	157	490	3.50

1992 Fielding Stats

After getting a ton of responses and suggestions following the initial run of fielding stats in the 1991 book, we made substantial revisions for 1992. With the new changes, the ton dropped down to a trickle. The only requests we received were to bring back the pitcher fielding stats (believe it or not!); we're adding them to the new section with special pitching stats. The only meaningful fielding stats you don't get here are the zone ratings (the ratio of balls turned into outs compared to balls hit in each fielder's "zone" — a number that only STATS can provide). You used to have to wait for those until The Scoreboard in February, but now you can get them in our new Player Profiles book in November!

The catchers sections stayed the same this year also. Is it our imagination or is there more talk than ever before about how Joe Pitcher does with Joe Catcher as compared with Fred Catcher? Hmmm. (There really is a guy in the Minor League Handbook named Scott Pitcher — no kidding, and yes he is!)

Here's the standard lowdown on these fielding stats for our new Handbook owners: The Regulars are in descending order by Range Factor. The Rest are in alphabetical order. Catchers in the special section are ranked by CERA, discussed at the beginning of this paragraph. (Don't forget to consider the pitching staff and team ERA's when comparing catchers from different teams.) PCS stands for Pitcher Caught Stealings and allows you to make an alternate calculation of Caught Stealing Percentage for catchers by subtracting these from total CS. And, finally, these fielding statistics are unofficial. We'd have to wait until December for official numbers and we don't think you'd like to trade getting this book in November for a few fielding stat differences. Ties in Range or Percentage are, in the vast majority of cases, not ties at all, just numbers that don't show enough digits to be unique.

First Basemen - Regulars

Player	Tm	G	Inn	PO	A	E	DP	Pct.	Rng
Morris,Hal	Cin	109	908.2	840	84	1	66	.999	---
Grace,Mark	ChN	157	1414.0	1578	141	4	120	.998	---
Hrbek,Kent	Min	104	903.1	954	67	3	76	.997	---
Mattingly,Don	NYA	143	1223.2	1212	115	4	133	.997	---
O'Brien,Pete	Sea	81	625.1	623	54	3	73	.996	---
Bagwell,Jeff	Hou	159	1401.1	1334	130	7	110	.995	---
Stevens,Lee	Cal	91	738.0	764	49	4	87	.995	---
Palmeiro,Rafael	Tex	156	1382.2	1251	142	7	130	.995	---
McGwire,Mark	Oak	139	1181.2	1119	70	6	119	.995	---
Merced,Orlando	Pit	114	834.1	882	73	5	73	.995	---
Martinez,Tino	Sea	78	663.2	678	58	4	63	.995	---
Olerud,John	Tor	133	1095.2	1057	81	7	73	.994	---
Milligan,Randy	Bal	129	1061.0	1009	75	7	109	.994	---
Karros,Eric	LA	143	1201.1	1209	126	9	98	.993	---
Kruk,John	Phi	121	958.0	980	58	7	78	.993	---
Clark,Will	SF	141	1229.2	1277	103	10	130	.993	---
Joyner,Wally	KC	145	1262.1	1239	134	10	139	.993	---
Sorrento,Paul	Cle	121	1016.2	997	75	8	109	.993	---
Thomas,Frank	ChA	158	1406.0	1428	90	13	113	.992	---
Murray,Eddie	NYN	154	1308.1	1278	94	12	111	.991	---
McGriff,Fred	SD	151	1334.2	1219	104	12	95	.991	---
Galarraga,Andres	StL	90	754.1	778	62	8	72	.991	---
Fielder,Cecil	Det	114	954.1	957	89	10	98	.991	---
Bream,Sid	Atl	120	907.1	855	72	10	70	.989	---
Vaughn,Mo	Bos	85	720.1	740	54	15	75	.981	---
Average	---	125	1059.1	1050	88	7	96	.994	---

First Basemen - The Rest

Player	Tm	G	Inn	PO	A	E	DP	Pct.	Rng
Amaral,Rich	Sea	2	2.0	0	0	0	0	.000	---
Barnes,Skeeter	Det	17	59.0	82	6	1	7	.989	---
Benzinger,Todd	LA	42	174.0	177	17	0	17	1.000	---
Bergman,Dave	Det	55	338.0	338	21	5	28	.986	---
Blankenship,Lance	Oak	7	41.0	37	2	1	4	.975	---
Blowers,Mike	Sea	3	12.0	9	2	0	0	1.000	---
Bonilla,Bobby	NYN	6	34.1	39	2	2	2	.953	---
Brett,George	KC	15	133.0	137	12	2	9	.987	---
Brewer,Rod	StL	27	206.2	214	18	0	16	1.000	---
Brogna,Rico	Det	8	58.0	48	5	1	8	.981	---
Brooks,Hubie	Cal	6	57.0	64	4	1	4	.986	---
Brosius,Scott	Oak	3	26.2	39	0	0	2	1.000	---
Brunansky,Tom	Bos	28	164.2	184	10	2	20	.990	---
Bush,Randy	Min	8	22.0	16	1	0	3	1.000	---
Carter,Gary	Mon	5	21.0	26	1	0	2	1.000	---
Carter,Joe	Tor	4	35.0	27	3	1	1	.968	---
Cianfrocco,Archi	Mon	56	386.2	373	40	3	25	.993	---
Clark,Jack	Bos	13	97.0	111	8	1	7	.992	---
Clark,Jerald	SD	11	50.0	59	0	0	1	1.000	---
Cochrane,Dave	Sea	3	26.0	20	0	0	1	1.000	---
Colbrunn,Greg	Mon	47	372.0	363	29	3	23	.992	---
Coles,Darnell	Cin	21	134.0	146	7	0	7	1.000	---
Conine,Jeff	KC	4	34.0	36	2	0	1	1.000	---
Cooper,Scott	Bos	62	420.1	446	33	5	43	.990	---
Costo,Tim	Cin	12	94.1	84	7	0	13	1.000	---
Cron,Chris	ChA	5	15.0	10	2	1	1	.923	---
Daniels,Kal	LA	8	58.0	60	5	1	5	.985	---

First Basemen - The Rest

Player	Tm	G	Inn	PO	A	E	DP	Pct.	Rng
Daugherty,Jack	Tex	8	50.2	40	5	0	2	1.000	---
Davis,Alvin	Cal	22	171.0	191	11	1	21	.995	---
Davis,Chili	Min	1	1.0	1	0	0	0	1.000	---
Davis,Glenn	Bal	2	18.0	19	1	0	1	1.000	---
Distefano,Benny	Hou	6	23.0	23	2	0	4	1.000	---
Doran,Billy	Cin	25	149.0	136	8	0	5	1.000	---
Fariss,Monty	Tex	1	3.0	2	0	0	0	1.000	---
Fermin,Felix	Cle	2	2.0	1	0	0	0	1.000	---
Fitzgerald,Mike	Cal	2	2.0	1	0	0	0	1.000	---
Foley,Tom	Mon	12	31.2	24	2	1	4	.963	---
Gaetti,Gary	Cal	44	368.2	371	32	5	36	.988	---
Gantner,Jim	Mil	2	2.0	2	0	0	0	1.000	---
Gonzales,Rene	Cal	13	63.0	75	9	0	8	1.000	---
Grotewold,Jeff	Phi	1	2.0	2	0	0	0	1.000	---
Guerrero,Pedro	StL	28	241.1	243	6	3	17	.988	---
Hare,Shawn	Det	4	17.1	21	2	0	2	1.000	---
Hayes,Charlie	NYA	4	27.0	31	0	0	3	1.000	---
Hayes,Von	Cal	4	24.0	21	2	0	2	1.000	---
Hollins,Dave	Phi	1	0.1	0	0	0	0	.000	---
Howitt,Dann	Oak	4	4.0	3	1	0	0	1.000	---
Hudler,Rex	StL	8	12.1	9	0	0	0	1.000	---
Hunter,Brian	Atl	92	532.1	528	48	2	36	.997	---
Jacoby,Brook	Cle	10	51.0	45	2	0	7	1.000	---
Jaha,John	Mil	38	290.1	286	22	0	22	1.000	---
Jefferson,Reggie	Cle	15	136.1	129	13	1	9	.993	---
Jordan,Ricky	Phi	54	438.0	415	27	2	33	.995	---
Jorgensen,Terry	Min	13	95.0	98	7	0	11	1.000	---
Kent,Jeff	Tor	3	8.0	5	1	0	0	1.000	---
King,Jeff	Pit	32	266.1	270	21	2	27	.993	---
Klesko,Ryan	Atl	5	20.0	25	0	0	2	1.000	---
Lansford,Carney	Oak	18	126.0	112	5	2	13	.983	---
Larkin,Gene	Min	55	431.2	456	29	4	50	.992	---
Lennon,Patrick	Sea	1	3.0	5	0	0	1	1.000	---
Leyritz,Jim	NYA	2	3.0	4	1	0	1	1.000	---
Litton,Greg	SF	8	35.0	26	6	0	5	1.000	---
Lyons,Steve	Mon	1	8.0	6	2	0	2	1.000	---
Lyons,Steve	Bos	8	46.0	45	5	0	3	1.000	---
Maas,Kevin	NYA	22	140.2	142	4	2	10	.986	---
Magadan,Dave	NYN	2	10.0	13	1	0	1	1.000	---
Maksudian,Mike	Tor	1	1.0	0	0	0	0	.000	---
Martinez,Carlos	Cle	37	264.0	263	20	1	40	.996	---
Martinez,Dave	Cin	21	161.1	156	11	4	22	.977	---
Martinez,Domingo	Tor	7	19.0	12	0	0	2	1.000	---
Martinez,Edgar	Sea	2	18.0	16	1	0	1	1.000	---
Maurer,Rob	Tex	3	11.0	9	1	0	0	1.000	---
McClendon,Lloyd	Pit	18	55.0	56	9	0	3	1.000	---
McGinnis,Russ	Tex	2	13.0	4	0	0	1	1.000	---
McIntosh,Tim	Mil	7	50.0	56	5	0	6	1.000	---
McKnight,Jeff	NYN	9	56.1	63	2	1	2	.985	---
Melvin,Bob	KC	3	18.0	22	2	1	3	.960	---
Molitor,Paul	Mil	48	425.2	461	26	2	45	.996	---
Neel,Troy	Oak	2	7.0	6	0	1	0	.857	---
Nilsson,Dave	Mil	3	9.0	7	0	0	1	1.000	---
Oberkfell,Ken	Cal	2	12.0	9	0	0	0	1.000	---
Oliver,Joe	Cin	1	1.0	1	0	0	0	1.000	---
Parrish,Lance	Sea	16	95.0	92	4	2	9	.980	---
Pasqua,Dan	ChA	5	32.2	32	3	0	4	1.000	---
Pecota,Bill	NYN	1	1.0	2	0	0	1	1.000	---

227

First Basemen - The Rest

Player	Tm	G	Inn	PO	A	E	DP	Pct.	Rng
Perry,Gerald	StL	29	214.1	221	11	3	23	.987	---
Quirk,Jamie	Oak	9	31.0	29	2	0	2	1.000	---
Ready,Randy	Oak	4	12.0	7	0	3	2	.700	---
Redus,Gary	Pit	36	247.1	280	16	0	16	1.000	---
Riles,Ernest	Hou	4	32.0	24	1	1	0	.962	---
Rodriguez,Henry	LA	1	4.2	3	1	0	0	1.000	---
Rose,Bobby	Cal	2	10.1	10	0	0	0	1.000	---
Rowland,Rich	Det	1	4.0	6	0	0	0	1.000	---
Royer,Stan	StL	4	27.0	33	3	2	7	.947	---
Salazar,Luis	ChN	5	32.0	34	1	0	3	1.000	---
Sasser,Mackey	NYN	12	36.2	39	0	0	4	1.000	---
Segui,David	Bal	95	385.0	374	34	1	42	.998	---
Seitzer,Kevin	Mil	1	1.0	1	0	0	0	1.000	---
Simms,Mike	Hou	1	3.0	4	0	0	0	1.000	---
Snow,J.T.	NYA	6	39.0	43	2	0	8	1.000	---
Snyder,Cory	SF	27	196.0	170	18	2	14	.989	---
Sprague,Ed	Tor	4	16.0	18	2	0	1	1.000	---
Stanley,Mike	NYA	4	19.0	21	1	0	2	1.000	---
Steinbach,Terry	Oak	5	17.0	19	3	0	4	1.000	---
Stephenson,Phil	SD	7	29.0	31	3	1	2	.971	---
Stubbs,Franklin	Mil	68	550.0	525	63	8	44	.987	---
Surhoff,B.J.	Mil	17	129.0	143	13	0	18	1.000	---
Sveum,Dale	Phi	4	29.2	21	4	0	1	1.000	---
Sveum,Dale	ChA	2	3.0	3	1	0	0	1.000	---
Tabler,Pat	Tor	34	265.1	281	20	0	22	1.000	---
Tettleton,Mickey	Det	3	5.0	3	0	0	1	1.000	---
Teufel,Tim	SD	5	32.1	29	4	0	3	1.000	---
VanderWal,John	Mon	7	28.1	23	4	0	3	1.000	---
Velasquez,Guillermo	SD	3	15.0	13	1	1	1	.933	---
Ventura,Robin	ChA	2	5.0	0	3	0	0	1.000	---
Villanueva,Hector	ChN	6	23.0	26	4	0	3	1.000	---
Wallach,Tim	Mon	71	594.2	630	61	6	42	.991	---
Wehner,John	Pit	13	74.2	81	5	1	9	.989	---
Willard,Jerry	Mon	5	25.0	18	2	1	0	.952	---
Woodson,Tracy	StL	3	24.0	26	3	0	0	1.000	---
Wrona,Rick	Cin	1	1.0	2	0	0	0	1.000	---
Young,Kevin	Pit	1	2.0	1	0	0	0	1.000	---

Second Basemen - Regulars

Player	Tm	G	Inn	PO	A	E	DP	Pct.	Rng
Sax,Steve	ChA	141	1251.1	305	391	20	73	.972	5.01
Stillwell,Kurt	SD	111	938.1	251	265	16	63	.970	4.95
Knoblauch,Chuck	Min	154	1339.2	308	416	6	104	.992	4.86
Biggio,Craig	Hou	161	1407.2	343	412	12	81	.984	4.83
Randolph,Willie	NYN	79	651.2	151	194	8	53	.977	4.76
Lemke,Mark	Atl	145	1065.0	236	324	9	57	.984	4.73
Doran,Billy	Cin	104	792.0	170	242	5	55	.988	4.68
Alomar,Roberto	Tor	150	1276.0	286	377	5	67	.993	4.68
DeShields,Delino	Mon	134	1183.1	253	360	15	71	.976	4.66
Average	---	120	1015.1	247	337	9	74	.984	5.19

Second Basemen - The Rest

Player	Tm	G	Inn	PO	A	E	DP	Pct.	Rng
Amaral,Rich	Sea	1	1.0	1	0	0	0	1.000	9.00
Backman,Wally	Phi	10	36.0	10	20	1	4	.968	7.50
Barberie,Bret	Mon	26	167.0	29	59	1	6	.989	4.74
Barnes,Skeeter	Det	7	20.0	2	3	0	1	1.000	2.25
Barrett,Tom	Bos	2	16.0	3	4	0	0	1.000	3.94
Belliard,Rafael	Atl	1	3.0	1	2	0	1	1.000	9.00
Benavides,Freddie	Cin	37	200.0	48	61	0	9	1.000	4.91
Blauser,Jeff	Atl	21	136.0	32	42	5	8	.937	4.90
Boone,Bret	Sea	32	277.2	71	93	6	22	.965	5.32
Branson,Jeff	Cin	33	179.2	45	61	6	20	.946	5.31
Briley,Greg	Sea	4	30.0	7	8	0	3	1.000	4.50
Browne,Jerry	Oak	19	78.0	14	18	0	3	1.000	3.69
Buechele,Steve	ChN	2	4.1	1	1	0	0	1.000	4.15
Candaele,Casey	Hou	9	38.2	13	9	0	1	1.000	5.12
Cochrane,Dave	Sea	1	1.0	0	0	0	0	.000	.00
Colbert,Craig	SF	2	6.2	1	1	0	0	1.000	2.70
Cooper,Scott	Bos	1	1.0	0	0	0	0	.000	.00
Cora,Joey	ChA	28	210.1	51	71	2	19	.984	5.22
Cordero,Wil	Mon	9	61.0	11	21	2	1	.941	4.72
Diaz,Mario	Tex	3	3.0	0	2	0	0	1.000	6.00
Donnels,Chris	NYN	12	84.0	19	28	1	4	.979	5.04
Downing,Brian	Tex	1	1.0	0	0	0	0	.000	.00
Duncan,Mariano	Phi	52	420.2	94	126	7	27	.969	4.71
Faries,Paul	SD	4	13.0	4	4	0	1	1.000	5.54
Fariss,Monty	Tex	17	49.0	14	13	0	5	1.000	4.96
Felder,Mike	SF	3	9.0	0	1	0	0	1.000	1.00
Fermin,Felix	Cle	7	27.0	4	8	0	3	1.000	4.00
Figueroa,Bien	StL	3	4.0	0	3	0	0	1.000	6.75
Fitzgerald,Mike	Cal	1	3.0	0	0	0	0	.000	.00
Foley,Tom	Mon	13	37.2	13	13	0	2	1.000	6.21
Franco,Julio	Tex	10	70.0	12	17	3	2	.906	3.73
Frye,Jeff	Tex	67	555.2	120	196	7	43	.978	5.12
Gallego,Mike	NYA	40	330.1	85	111	2	31	.990	5.34
Gantner,Jim	Mil	68	511.1	136	179	2	42	.994	5.54
Garcia,Carlos	Pit	14	72.1	19	24	1	8	.977	5.35
Gardner,Jeff	SD	11	45.0	11	20	0	3	1.000	6.20
Gonzales,Rene	Cal	42	322.1	78	91	1	28	.994	4.72
Griffin,Alfredo	Tor	16	68.0	16	28	4	4	.917	5.82
Guerrero,Juan	Hou	2	5.0	0	3	0	0	1.000	5.40
Haney,Todd	Mon	5	19.0	2	6	0	1	1.000	3.79
Harris,Lenny	LA	81	541.0	161	205	14	40	.963	6.09
Hill,Donnie	Min	7	36.2	10	9	1	1	.950	4.66
Hudler,Rex	StL	16	107.1	28	39	3	6	.957	5.62

Second Basemen - The Rest

Player	Tm	G	Inn	PO	A	E	DP	Pct.	Rng
Hulett,Tim	Bal	10	35.0	7	18	0	2	1.000	6.43
Huson,Jeff	Tex	47	313.2	69	83	0	22	1.000	4.36
Jefferies,Gregg	KC	1	1.0	0	0	0	0	.000	.00
Jones,Tim	StL	28	151.0	35	47	1	14	.988	4.89
Kent,Jeff	Tor	17	96.0	24	37	1	1	.984	5.72
Kent,Jeff	NYN	34	265.0	61	84	3	18	.980	4.92
King,Jeff	Pit	32	201.2	49	68	0	16	1.000	5.22
Kunkel,Jeff	ChN	3	16.0	5	4	1	1	.900	5.06
Leyritz,Jim	NYA	1	2.0	0	0	0	0	.000	.00
Listach,Pat	Mil	1	3.0	0	0	0	0	.000	.00
Litton,Greg	SF	31	217.2	52	69	1	18	.992	5.00
Lyons,Steve	Atl	2	3.0	0	1	0	0	1.000	3.00
Lyons,Steve	Bos	1	1.0	0	1	0	0	1.000	9.00
McKnight,Jeff	NYN	14	82.0	18	31	1	5	.980	5.38
McLemore,Mark	Bal	70	519.1	127	186	7	46	.978	5.42
Millette,Joe	Phi	1	8.0	1	3	0	1	1.000	4.50
Naehring,Tim	Bos	23	170.1	54	66	1	11	.992	6.34
Newman,Al	Tex	72	465.0	118	168	5	31	.983	5.54
Noboa,Junior	NYN	16	63.0	15	29	1	6	.978	6.29
Oberkfell,Ken	Cal	21	147.2	34	34	1	5	.986	4.14
Oquendo,Jose	StL	9	54.0	14	22	0	5	1.000	6.00
Patterson,John	SF	22	166.0	42	53	4	15	.960	5.15
Pecota,Bill	NYN	38	230.2	46	95	4	16	.972	5.50
Pena,Geronimo	StL	57	470.0	126	185	5	40	.984	5.96
Perezchica,Tony	Cle	4	9.0	3	0	0	0	1.000	3.00
Petralli,Geno	Tex	2	4.0	1	0	1	0	.500	2.25
Phillips,Tony	Det	57	437.1	110	167	4	40	.986	5.70
Puckett,Kirby	Min	2	0.2	0	0	0	0	.000	.00
Ready,Randy	Oak	4	21.0	8	8	1	1	.941	6.86
Reboulet,Jeff	Min	13	76.0	21	34	1	8	.982	6.51
Riles,Ernest	Hou	2	8.0	3	5	0	1	1.000	9.00
Rivera,Luis	Bos	1	4.0	1	0	0	0	1.000	2.25
Roberts,Bip	Cin	42	277.2	51	83	1	7	.993	4.34
Rose,Bobby	Cal	28	212.0	49	94	7	18	.953	6.07
Rossy,Rico	KC	3	25.0	4	6	0	1	1.000	3.60
Samuel,Juan	LA	38	254.1	75	77	4	13	.974	5.38
Samuel,Juan	KC	10	79.1	19	27	3	9	.939	5.22
Sanchez,Rey	ChN	4	15.1	5	4	0	0	1.000	5.28
Scarsone,Steve	Phi	3	19.0	3	3	0	1	1.000	2.84
Scarsone,Steve	Bal	5	16.0	5	3	1	3	.889	4.50
Schaefer,Jeff	Sea	7	28.0	6	15	0	3	1.000	6.75
Seitzer,Kevin	Mil	2	11.0	2	4	0	0	1.000	4.91
Sharperson,Mike	LA	63	331.2	104	134	5	26	.979	6.46
Shipley,Craig	SD	11	74.1	18	23	0	5	1.000	4.96
Shumpert,Terry	KC	33	260.0	50	76	4	16	.969	4.36
Snyder,Cory	SF	4	10.1	2	4	0	0	1.000	5.23
Spiers,Bill	Mil	4	21.0	5	5	0	1	1.000	4.29
Springer,Steve	Tex	0	0.0	0	0	0	0	.000	.00
Springer,Steve	NYN	1	8.0	3	1	0	1	1.000	4.50
Stankiewicz,Andy	NYA	34	238.0	52	89	1	20	.993	5.33
Strange,Doug	ChN	12	38.1	6	15	0	2	1.000	4.93
Suero,William	Mil	15	47.1	11	22	1	5	.971	6.27
Teufel,Tim	SD	52	390.1	95	125	3	20	.987	5.07
Treadway,Jeff	Atl	45	252.2	54	83	1	24	.993	4.88
Valentin,Jose	Mil	1	8.0	1	1	1	0	.667	2.25
Velarde,Randy	NYA	3	18.0	3	8	1	1	.917	5.50
Vizcaino,Jose	ChN	5	10.0	2	1	0	0	1.000	2.70
Walker,Chico	ChN	2	5.2	2	2	0	0	1.000	6.35

Second Basemen - The Rest

Player	Tm	G	Inn	PO	A	E	DP	Pct.	Rng
Walker,Chico	NYN	16	62.1	9	24	4	4	.892	4.76
Wehner,John	Pit	5	15.0	0	1	0	0	1.000	0.60
Wilkerson,Curt	KC	39	295.2	70	106	2	29	.989	5.36
Wilson,Craig	StL	11	58.0	14	24	2	6	.950	5.90
Young,Eric	LA	43	311.0	85	114	9	20	.957	5.76

Third Basemen - Regulars

Player	Tm	G	Inn	PO	A	E	DP	Pct.	Rng
Ventura,Robin	ChA	157	1395.1	141	371	23	27	.957	3.30
Wallach,Tim	Mon	85	700.2	56	184	9	17	.964	3.08
Pendleton,Terry	Atl	158	1389.0	133	322	19	28	.960	2.95
Martinez,Edgar	Sea	103	869.2	72	208	17	23	.943	2.90
Sheffield,Gary	SD	144	1247.2	99	299	16	25	.961	2.87
Williams,Matt D.	SF	144	1247.2	104	287	23	32	.944	2.82
Buechele,Steve	TOT	143	1240.1	102	285	17	16	.958	2.81
Gruber,Kelly	Tor	120	1021.2	104	214	17	11	.949	2.80
Jefferies,Gregg	KC	146	1288.1	96	302	26	23	.939	2.78
Leius,Scott	Min	125	1025.1	58	257	15	12	.955	2.76
Livingstone,Scott	Det	112	841.1	67	189	10	15	.962	2.74
Jacoby,Brook	Cle	111	731.1	46	175	10	17	.957	2.72
Boggs,Wade	Bos	117	993.2	70	230	15	22	.952	2.72
Palmer,Dean	Tex	150	1272.0	124	253	22	24	.945	2.67
Hansen,Dave	LA	108	832.1	61	183	8	14	.968	2.64
Zeile,Todd	StL	124	1079.0	81	235	13	19	.960	2.64
Seitzer,Kevin	Mil	146	1265.0	99	271	12	18	.969	2.63
Gomez,Leo	Bal	137	1221.2	106	244	18	19	.951	2.58
Hayes,Charlie	NYA	139	1211.2	95	251	13	31	.964	2.57
Sabo,Chris	Cin	94	790.0	60	158	9	12	.960	2.48
Hollins,Dave	Phi	156	1367.2	120	253	18	22	.954	2.45
Caminiti,Ken	Hou	129	1140.2	103	208	11	19	.966	2.45
Lansford,Carney	Oak	119	963.1	86	159	9	8	.965	2.29
Magadan,Dave	NYN	93	755.0	41	135	11	10	.941	2.10
Average	---	127	1078.2	88	236	15	19	.956	2.71

Third Basemen - The Rest

Player	Tm	G	Inn	PO	A	E	DP	Pct.	Rng
Amaral,Rich	Sea	17	116.1	10	32	2	3	.955	3.25
Anderson,Dave	LA	26	143.1	13	24	1	3	.974	2.32
Backman,Wally	Phi	2	1.1	0	0	0	0	.000	.00
Barberie,Bret	Mon	63	508.2	37	126	12	10	.931	2.88
Barnes,Skeeter	Det	39	266.1	34	68	9	7	.919	3.45
Benavides,Freddie	Cin	1	2.0	0	0	0	0	.000	.00
Benjamin,Mike	SF	2	2.0	0	0	0	0	.000	.00
Berry,Sean	Mon	20	124.0	10	18	4	1	.875	2.03
Blauser,Jeff	Atl	1	5.0	0	1	0	0	1.000	1.80
Blowers,Mike	Sea	29	193.1	19	41	1	8	.984	2.79
Boone,Bret	Sea	6	15.2	1	3	0	0	1.000	2.30
Branson,Jeff	Cin	8	20.1	1	2	1	0	.750	1.33
Brett,George	KC	3	26.0	2	5	1	1	.875	2.42
Briley,Greg	Sea	4	28.0	0	4	2	0	.667	1.29
Brosius,Scott	Oak	12	75.0	8	14	1	0	.957	2.64
Browne,Jerry	Oak	58	370.0	40	70	4	7	.965	2.68
Buechele,Steve	Pit	80	693.0	52	167	10	10	.956	2.84
Buechele,Steve	ChN	63	547.1	50	118	7	6	.960	2.76

Third Basemen - The Rest

Player	Tm	G	Inn	PO	A	E	DP	Pct.	Rng
Candaele,Casey	Hou	29	218.1	24	52	4	3	.950	3.13
Castilla,Vinny	Atl	4	30.0	2	5	1	0	.875	2.10
Cianfrocco,Archi	Mon	19	128.2	7	27	5	1	.872	2.38
Clayton,Royce	SF	1	1.0	1	0	0	0	1.000	9.00
Cochrane,Dave	Sea	10	61.0	1	19	2	2	.909	2.95
Colbert,Craig	SF	9	59.0	6	10	0	1	1.000	2.44
Coles,Darnell	Cin	23	147.0	8	34	0	1	1.000	2.57
Cooper,Scott	Bos	47	375.0	26	102	4	5	.970	3.07
Cora,Joey	ChA	5	27.1	0	8	1	0	.889	2.63
Diaz,Mario	Tex	1	6.0	1	0	0	0	1.000	1.50
Donnels,Chris	NYN	29	203.2	15	50	4	3	.942	2.87
Duncan,Mariano	Phi	4	26.0	2	3	1	0	.833	1.73
Easley,Damion	Cal	45	373.1	28	99	4	13	.969	3.06
Faries,Paul	SD	2	5.0	0	0	0	0	.000	.00
Fermin,Felix	Cle	17	105.1	10	24	2	2	.944	2.91
Fitzgerald,Mike	Cal	3	3.0	0	1	0	0	1.000	3.00
Fletcher,Scott	Mil	1	1.0	0	0	0	0	.000	.00
Foley,Tom	Mon	4	6.0	0	0	0	0	.000	.00
Fryman,Travis	Det	27	220.0	15	46	2	4	.968	2.50
Gaetti,Gary	Cal	67	563.1	51	163	17	16	.926	3.42
Gantner,Jim	Mil	31	150.0	17	28	1	3	.978	2.70
Gonzales,Rene	Cal	53	445.0	32	112	7	9	.954	2.91
Grebeck,Craig	ChA	7	34.0	2	6	0	0	1.000	2.12
Green,Gary	Cin	1	2.0	0	2	0	0	1.000	9.00
Greene,Willie	Cin	25	216.1	16	40	3	5	.949	2.33
Guerrero,Juan	Hou	12	62.2	3	12	1	0	.938	2.15
Harris,Lenny	LA	33	127.1	12	26	5	5	.884	2.69
Hemond,Scott	Oak	2	3.0	0	0	0	0	.000	.00
Hemond,Scott	ChA	1	1.0	0	0	0	0	.000	.00
Hill,Donnie	Min	5	18.0	2	4	0	0	1.000	3.00
Hulett,Tim	Bal	27	219.1	16	69	6	7	.934	3.49
Huson,Jeff	Tex	1	0.0	0	0	0	0	.000	.00
Jones,Tim	StL	2	5.0	0	1	0	0	1.000	1.80
Jorgensen,Terry	Min	9	51.0	4	15	1	3	.950	3.35
Kent,Jeff	Tor	49	372.1	33	74	10	3	.915	2.59
Kent,Jeff	NYN	1	6.0	1	6	0	1	1.000	10.50
King,Jeff	Pit	73	565.1	44	140	9	14	.953	2.93
LaValliere,Mike	Pit	1	1.0	0	1	0	0	1.000	9.00
Lemke,Mark	Atl	13	32.2	0	10	0	0	1.000	2.76
Lewis,Mark	Cle	1	8.0	0	3	1	0	.750	3.38
Leyritz,Jim	NYA	2	9.0	1	2	0	0	1.000	3.00
Litton,Greg	SF	10	39.0	1	6	1	1	.875	1.62
Martinez,Carlos	Cle	28	213.1	13	37	3	6	.943	2.11
Mayne,Brent	KC	8	45.0	4	10	0	1	1.000	2.80
McGinnis,Russ	Tex	2	10.0	1	1	0	0	1.000	1.80
McKnight,Jeff	NYN	3	10.0	0	4	1	0	.800	3.60
Meulens,Hensley	NYA	2	12.0	0	3	0	2	1.000	2.25
Millette,Joe	Phi	3	12.0	0	1	0	0	1.000	0.75
Naehring,Tim	Bos	10	76.2	4	18	1	1	.957	2.58
Newman,Al	Tex	28	167.1	12	28	1	8	.976	2.15
Noboa,Junior	NYN	3	3.0	0	0	1	0	.000	.00
Pagliarulo,Mike	Min	37	232.0	11	65	3	3	.962	2.95
Pecota,Bill	NYN	48	228.1	12	51	5	6	.926	2.48
Perezchica,Tony	Cle	9	20.0	1	6	1	0	.875	3.15
Petralli,Geno	Tex	4	5.0	0	1	0	0	1.000	1.80
Phillips,Tony	Det	20	104.0	11	24	1	4	.972	3.03
Prince,Tom	Pit	1	1.0	0	0	0	0	.000	.00
Puckett,Kirby	Min	2	2.1	0	0	0	0	.000	.00

Third Basemen - The Rest

Player	Tm	G	Inn	PO	A	E	DP	Pct.	Rng
Quinlan,Tom	Tor	13	41.0	4	6	1	0	.909	2.20
Quinones,Luis	Min	1	7.0	3	2	2	0	.714	6.43
Quirk,Jamie	Oak	2	2.0	0	0	0	0	.000	.00
Ramirez,Rafael	Hou	1	1.2	0	1	0	0	1.000	5.40
Ready,Randy	Oak	7	33.0	4	10	1	2	.933	3.82
Reboulet,Jeff	Min	22	117.1	11	32	0	3	1.000	3.30
Riles,Ernest	Hou	5	36.0	1	6	0	0	1.000	1.75
Rivera,Luis	Bos	1	3.0	2	1	0	1	1.000	9.00
Roberts,Bip	Cin	36	271.2	20	68	5	6	.946	2.92
Rohde,Dave	Cle	5	20.0	4	6	1	1	.909	4.50
Rossy,Rico	KC	9	56.0	9	15	2	1	.923	3.86
Rowland,Rich	Det	1	4.0	0	1	0	0	1.000	2.25
Royer,Stan	StL	5	29.1	1	8	1	2	.900	2.76
Salazar,Luis	ChN	40	260.1	19	68	6	6	.935	3.01
Scarsone,Steve	Bal	2	22.0	0	5	1	1	.833	2.05
Schaefer,Jeff	Sea	21	40.0	2	9	1	0	.917	2.47
Scott,Gary	ChN	30	237.0	17	42	5	3	.922	2.24
Sharperson,Mike	LA	60	335.0	15	85	8	5	.926	2.69
Shipley,Craig	SD	8	46.1	5	10	0	1	1.000	2.91
Snyder,Cory	SF	14	112.0	7	22	2	2	.935	2.33
Sojo,Luis	Cal	9	61.1	5	19	1	0	.960	3.52
Spiers,Bill	Mil	1	2.0	0	0	0	0	.000	.00
Sprague,Ed	Tor	1	2.0	0	0	0	0	.000	.00
Springer,Steve	NYN	1	1.0	0	0	0	0	.000	.00
Strange,Doug	ChN	33	186.0	19	34	6	2	.898	2.56
Surhoff,B.J.	Mil	3	15.0	1	2	0	0	1.000	1.80
Sveum,Dale	Phi	5	21.0	2	4	0	1	1.000	2.57
Sveum,Dale	ChA	2	4.0	1	0	0	0	1.000	2.25
Tabler,Pat	Tor	1	3.0	0	1	0	0	1.000	3.00
Tackett,Jeff	Bal	1	1.0	0	0	0	0	.000	.00
Tatum,Jimmy	Mil	5	24.0	6	2	0	0	1.000	3.00
Teufel,Tim	SD	26	162.0	13	34	4	1	.922	2.61
Thome,Jim	Cle	40	308.0	21	61	11	3	.882	2.40
Treadway,Jeff	Atl	1	3.0	0	2	0	1	1.000	6.00
Turner,Shane	Sea	18	121.0	8	29	5	5	.881	2.75
Velarde,Randy	NYA	26	219.2	14	35	5	7	.907	2.01
Vizcaino,Jose	ChN	29	226.2	18	51	2	6	.972	2.74
Walker,Chico	ChN	2	11.2	0	4	1	0	.800	3.09
Walker,Chico	NYN	36	239.2	14	54	2	2	.971	2.55
Wehner,John	Pit	34	199.1	15	58	3	8	.961	3.30
Wilkerson,Curt	KC	5	32.0	4	8	1	1	.923	3.38
Wilson,Craig	StL	18	140.2	9	23	1	2	.970	2.05
Woodson,Tracy	StL	26	226.0	17	35	3	4	.945	2.07
Worthington,Craig	Cle	9	64.0	6	18	4	1	.857	3.38
Young,Kevin	Pit	7	20.0	2	1	1	0	.750	1.35

Shortstops - Regulars

Player	Tm	G	Inn	PO	A	E	DP	Pct.	Rng
Bell,Jay	Pit	159	1411.1	268	527	22	94	.973	5.07
Gagne,Greg	Min	141	1146.1	207	438	18	82	.973	5.06
Velarde,Randy	NYA	75	606.1	129	212	9	42	.974	5.06
Smith,Ozzie	StL	132	1156.1	231	418	10	82	.985	5.05
Stankiewicz,Andy	NYA	81	696.0	132	252	11	54	.972	4.97
Rivera,Luis	Bos	93	732.0	118	285	14	56	.966	4.95
Vizquel,Omar	Sea	136	1152.0	224	403	7	93	.989	4.90
Fryman,Travis	Det	137	1202.2	205	443	20	88	.970	4.85

Shortstops - Regulars

Player	Tm	G	Inn	PO	A	E	DP	Pct.	Rng
Listach,Pat	Mil	148	1279.0	238	451	24	89	.966	4.85
DiSarcina,Gary	Cal	157	1376.1	250	485	25	110	.967	4.81
Howard,Dave	KC	74	616.0	124	203	8	52	.976	4.78
Grebeck,Craig	ChA	85	728.2	110	276	8	45	.980	4.77
Larkin,Barry	Cin	140	1207.2	232	405	11	69	.983	4.75
Schofield,Dick	TOT	142	1153.2	207	391	7	79	.988	4.67
Ripken,Cal	Bal	162	1440.0	287	445	12	117	.984	4.57
Lewis,Mark	Cle	121	1017.1	184	333	25	72	.954	4.57
Belliard,Rafael	Atl	139	860.1	150	287	14	48	.969	4.57
Clayton,Royce	SF	94	787.2	142	256	11	52	.973	4.55
Thon,Dickie	Tex	87	678.2	117	225	15	38	.958	4.54
Owen,Spike	Mon	116	972.0	188	300	9	45	.982	4.52
Weiss,Walt	Oak	103	859.2	144	269	19	56	.956	4.32
Lee,Manuel	Tor	128	1079.1	186	330	7	68	.987	4.30
Fernandez,Tony	SD	155	1348.1	241	403	11	65	.983	4.30
Offerman,Jose	LA	149	1290.0	208	398	42	75	.935	4.23
Average	---	123	1033.0	188	351	14	69	.973	4.70

Shortstops - The Rest

Player	Tm	G	Inn	PO	A	E	DP	Pct.	Rng
Alexander,Manny	Bal	3	13.0	3	3	0	1	1.000	4.15
Alicea,Luis	StL	4	27.0	6	6	3	2	.800	4.00
Amaral,Rich	Sea	17	108.0	17	37	1	8	.982	4.50
Anderson,Dave	LA	7	48.1	8	17	3	4	.893	4.66
Arias,Alex	ChN	30	244.0	44	74	4	7	.967	4.35
Baez,Kevin	NYN	5	34.0	5	11	2	2	.889	4.24
Barberie,Bret	Mon	1	3.0	0	2	0	1	1.000	6.00
Batiste,Kim	Phi	41	336.2	69	85	13	17	.922	4.12
Bell,Juan	Phi	46	390.1	82	129	6	22	.972	4.87
Beltre,Esteban	ChA	43	307.1	53	91	12	13	.923	4.22
Benavides,Freddie	Cin	34	213.0	33	68	6	18	.944	4.27
Benjamin,Mike	SF	33	211.2	34	71	1	12	.991	4.46
Blauser,Jeff	Atl	106	587.2	87	182	9	28	.968	4.12
Bordick,Mike	Oak	70	577.2	108	185	10	50	.967	4.56
Bournigal,Rafael	LA	9	58.0	11	17	1	6	.966	4.34
Branson,Jeff	Cin	1	1.0	0	0	0	0	.000	.00
Brosius,Scott	Oak	1	2.0	1	0	0	0	1.000	4.50
Browne,Jerry	Oak	1	1.0	1	0	0	0	1.000	9.00
Candaele,Casey	Hou	65	391.1	79	137	7	30	.969	4.97
Castilla,Vinny	Atl	4	11.2	0	7	0	1	1.000	5.40
Cedeno,Andujar	Hou	70	563.0	83	175	11	27	.959	4.12
Cochrane,Dave	Sea	3	8.0	2	1	0	0	1.000	3.38
Colon,Cris	Tex	14	102.0	17	36	3	5	.946	4.68
Cooper,Scott	Bos	1	1.0	0	0	0	0	.000	.00
Cora,Joey	ChA	6	26.0	9	5	0	3	1.000	4.85
Cordero,Wil	Mon	35	255.1	40	71	6	11	.949	3.91
Diaz,Mario	Tex	16	85.0	15	24	1	2	.975	4.13
Duncan,Mariano	Phi	42	231.0	37	80	5	15	.959	4.56
Dunston,Shawon	ChN	18	143.2	28	42	1	9	.986	4.39
Easley,Damion	Cal	3	6.1	2	2	1	0	.800	5.68
Elster,Kevin	NYN	5	40.0	8	10	0	3	1.000	4.05
Faries,Paul	SD	1	4.0	0	0	0	0	.000	.00
Fermin,Felix	Cle	55	420.2	64	134	6	36	.971	4.24
Figueroa,Bien	StL	9	30.1	7	8	1	0	.938	4.45
Fletcher,Scott	Mil	22	159.0	29	64	5	14	.949	5.26
Foley,Tom	Mon	33	237.2	37	81	4	14	.967	4.47

Shortstops - The Rest

Player	Tm	G	Inn	PO	A	E	DP	Pct.	Rng
Gallego,Mike	NYA	14	119.0	26	41	4	11	.944	5.07
Garcia,Carlos	Pit	8	33.0	6	11	1	3	.944	4.64
Gonzales,Rene	Cal	8	32.1	6	14	1	4	.952	5.57
Green,Gary	Cin	6	27.2	1	3	0	0	1.000	1.30
Griffin,Alfredo	Tor	48	335.2	45	108	3	13	.981	4.10
Guerrero,Juan	Hou	19	133.1	15	35	1	5	.980	3.38
Guillen,Ozzie	ChA	12	107.1	20	38	0	7	1.000	4.86
Harris,Lenny	LA	10	37.2	6	16	6	4	.786	5.26
Hemond,Scott	Oak	3	5.0	1	0	1	0	.500	1.80
Hernandez,Jose	Cle	3	8.0	3	3	1	0	.857	6.75
Hill,Donnie	Min	10	59.2	9	24	2	4	.943	4.98
Hulett,Tim	Bal	5	9.0	2	4	1	2	.857	6.00
Huson,Jeff	Tex	82	507.0	109	167	9	45	.968	4.90
Jones,Tim	StL	34	237.1	40	66	3	16	.972	4.02
Jorgensen,Terry	Min	2	2.0	1	2	0	0	1.000	13.50
Kent,Jeff	NYN	1	9.0	1	3	0	0	1.000	4.00
King,Jeff	Pit	6	35.1	4	6	1	1	.909	2.55
Knoblauch,Chuck	Min	1	0.1	0	0	0	0	.000	.00
Kunkel,Jeff	ChN	6	18.0	4	10	0	1	1.000	7.00
Lansford,Carney	Oak	1	1.0	1	0	0	0	1.000	9.00
Leius,Scott	Min	10	21.2	5	4	0	1	1.000	3.74
Litton,Greg	SF	3	12.0	2	3	2	2	.714	3.75
McKnight,Jeff	NYN	3	7.0	1	3	0	1	1.000	5.14
Millette,Joe	Phi	26	205.2	32	82	3	14	.974	4.99
Morandini,Mickey	Phi	3	11.2	3	3	1	1	.857	4.63
Naehring,Tim	Bos	30	224.0	36	86	1	18	.992	4.90
Newman,Al	Tex	20	87.2	19	27	2	8	.958	4.72
Noboa,Junior	NYN	2	10.0	4	2	1	1	.857	5.40
Oquendo,Jose	StL	5	29.0	4	8	1	2	.923	3.72
Pecota,Bill	NYN	39	202.0	34	71	3	11	.972	4.68
Perezchica,Tony	Cle	4	24.0	4	5	1	0	.900	3.38
Phillips,Tony	Det	1	4.0	0	1	0	0	1.000	2.25
Puckett,Kirby	Min	1	0.0	0	0	0	0	.000	.00
Quinones,Luis	Min	1	1.0	0	0	0	0	.000	.00
Ramirez,Rafael	Hou	57	357.0	60	113	7	17	.961	4.36
Reboulet,Jeff	Min	36	222.0	37	97	4	22	.971	5.43
Riles,Ernest	Hou	6	11.2	1	3	0	1	1.000	3.09
Rossy,Rico	KC	51	381.0	60	135	8	37	.961	4.61
Salazar,Luis	ChN	12	81.1	14	27	0	5	1.000	4.54
Sanchez,Rey	ChN	68	593.1	143	198	9	52	.974	5.17
Scarsone,Steve	Bal	1	2.0	1	0	0	0	1.000	4.50
Schaefer,Jeff	Sea	33	177.0	28	67	8	7	.922	4.83
Schofield,Dick	Cal	1	9.0	3	1	0	0	1.000	4.00
Schofield,Dick	NYN	141	1144.2	204	390	7	79	.988	4.67
Scott,Gary	ChN	2	2.0	1	1	0	0	1.000	9.00
Sharperson,Mike	LA	2	4.0	1	0	0	0	1.000	2.25
Shipley,Craig	SD	23	108.2	29	41	1	11	.986	5.80
Shumpert,Terry	KC	1	1.0	0	0	0	0	.000	.00
Silvestri,Dave	NYA	6	31.0	3	12	2	4	.882	4.35
Snyder,Cory	SF	3	5.0	1	0	1	0	.500	1.80
Sojo,Luis	Cal	5	22.0	4	7	1	1	.917	4.50
Spiers,Bill	Mil	5	16.0	1	1	0	1	1.000	1.13
Suero,William	Mil	1	1.0	0	0	0	0	.000	.00
Sveum,Dale	Phi	34	252.2	56	91	8	18	.948	5.24
Sveum,Dale	ChA	37	292.1	39	97	8	19	.944	4.19
Trammell,Alan	Det	28	229.0	46	80	3	16	.977	4.95
Uribe,Jose	SF	62	444.1	75	157	7	37	.971	4.70
Valentin,John	Bos	58	491.1	78	181	10	44	.963	4.74

Shortstops - The Rest

Player	Tm	G	Inn	PO	A	E	DP	Pct.	Rng
Valentin,Jose	Mil	1	2.0	0	0	0	0	.000	.00
Vizcaino,Jose	ChN	50	386.2	73	143	7	29	.969	5.03
Wilkerson,Curt	KC	69	449.1	73	143	7	27	.969	4.33
Yelding,Eric	Hou	2	3.0	0	0	0	0	.000	.00
Zosky,Eddie	Tor	8	25.0	2	10	1	2	.923	4.32

Left Fielders - Regulars

Player	Tm	G	Inn	PO	A	E	DP	Pct.	Rng
Gonzalez,Luis	Hou	111	859.1	259	5	2	1	.992	2.76
Raines,Tim	ChA	129	1118.1	312	12	2	0	.994	2.61
Gladden,Dan	Det	95	754.2	202	9	3	2	.986	2.52
Anderson,Brady	Bal	148	1330.0	359	10	7	4	.981	2.50
Gilkey,Bernard	StL	110	814.0	216	8	5	3	.978	2.48
Henderson,Rickey	Oak	108	883.1	229	8	4	1	.983	2.41
Hall,Mel	NYA	99	860.0	218	9	2	1	.991	2.38
Clark,Jerald	SD	115	958.0	241	9	3	2	.988	2.35
Vaughn,Greg	Mil	131	1147.0	288	6	3	0	.990	2.31
Bonds,Barry	Pit	139	1240.2	310	4	3	0	.991	2.28
Mack,Shane	Min	150	1265.0	306	7	4	1	.987	2.23
Reimer,Kevin	Tex	110	840.2	197	7	11	1	.949	2.18
Maldonado,Candy	Tor	129	1123.0	257	13	6	2	.978	2.16
Polonia,Luis	Cal	99	841.0	191	8	4	2	.980	2.13
McReynolds,Kevin	KC	94	818.0	184	4	2	0	.989	2.07
Bass,Kevin	TOT	84	603.2	137	1	2	0	.986	2.06
Gant,Ron	Atl	138	1096.2	236	3	4	0	.984	1.96
Hatcher,Billy	TOT	86	701.2	145	5	5	0	.968	1.92
May,Derrick	ChN	98	667.2	134	3	5	0	.965	1.85
Average	---	114	943.0	232	6	4	1	.983	2.29

Left Fielders - The Rest

Player	Tm	G	Inn	PO	A	E	DP	Pct.	Rng
Abner,Shawn	ChA	12	71.2	17	0	0	0	1.000	2.13
Alou,Moises	Mon	79	578.0	118	4	2	0	.984	1.90
Amaral,Rich	Sea	3	20.0	5	0	0	0	1.000	2.25
Amaro,Ruben	Phi	27	188.0	66	1	0	0	1.000	3.21
Anthony,Eric	Hou	1	1.0	1	0	0	0	1.000	9.00
Ashley,Billy	LA	1	8.0	1	1	1	0	.667	2.25
Azocar,Oscar	SD	31	206.2	55	1	4	0	.933	2.44
Baines,Harold	Oak	6	40.0	8	0	0	0	1.000	1.80
Barnes,Skeeter	Det	4	7.0	0	0	1	0	.000	.00
Bass,Kevin	SF	56	396.0	81	1	1	0	.988	1.86
Bass,Kevin	NYN	28	207.2	56	0	1	0	.982	2.43
Bell,Derek	Tor	24	208.0	49	2	0	0	1.000	2.21
Bell,George	ChA	15	124.0	27	0	1	0	.964	1.96
Belle,Albert	Cle	52	423.2	94	1	3	0	.969	2.02
Benzinger,Todd	LA	18	137.2	40	0	1	0	.976	2.62
Bergman,Dave	Det	1	1.0	0	0	0	0	.000	.00
Berroa,Geronimo	Cin	3	18.0	2	1	0	0	1.000	1.50
Blankenship,Lance	Oak	22	114.2	32	0	0	0	1.000	2.51
Boston,Daryl	NYN	66	472.2	95	5	1	1	.990	1.90
Braggs,Glenn	Cin	56	401.2	65	5	1	0	.985	1.50
Brewer,Rod	StL	4	31.0	6	1	0	1	1.000	2.03
Briley,Greg	Sea	27	133.0	32	0	0	0	1.000	2.17
Brito,Bernardo	Min	3	15.0	3	0	1	0	.750	1.80
Brosius,Scott	Oak	4	12.0	2	0	0	0	1.000	1.50
Brown,Jarvis	Min	4	17.0	3	0	1	0	.750	1.59
Browne,Jerry	Oak	17	108.0	36	0	1	0	.973	3.00
Bruett,J.T.	Min	5	34.0	8	0	0	0	1.000	2.12
Brumfield,Jacob	Cin	7	14.0	3	1	0	0	1.000	2.57
Bush,Randy	Min	3	17.0	8	0	0	0	1.000	4.24
Calderon,Ivan	Mon	46	371.1	79	2	1	0	.988	1.96
Candaele,Casey	Hou	20	71.0	13	0	0	0	1.000	1.65
Cangelosi,John	Tex	36	90.1	30	1	3	0	.912	3.09
Canseco,Ozzie	StL	7	58.0	5	0	1	0	.833	0.78
Carr,Chuck	StL	5	39.0	7	1	0	0	1.000	1.85
Carreon,Mark	Det	64	527.0	136	5	2	1	.986	2.41
Carter,Joe	Tor	6	53.0	10	0	0	0	1.000	1.70
Castillo,Braulio	Phi	2	2.0	0	0	1	0	.000	.00
Chamberlain,Wes	Phi	28	202.2	48	2	3	1	.943	2.22
Cianfrocco,Archi	Mon	5	24.1	5	0	0	0	1.000	1.85
Clark,Dave	Pit	1	3.0	1	0	0	0	1.000	3.00
Clark,Phil	Det	4	21.0	6	0	1	0	.857	2.57
Cochrane,Dave	Sea	16	83.0	17	0	1	0	.944	1.84
Cole,Alex	Cle	18	130.1	29	1	1	0	.968	2.07
Coleman,Vince	NYN	42	314.2	54	2	1	2	.982	1.60
Coles,Darnell	Cin	3	14.0	4	0	0	0	1.000	2.57
Conine,Jeff	KC	22	178.2	39	1	0	0	1.000	2.01
Cotto,Henry	Sea	63	402.1	114	2	0	0	1.000	2.59
Cron,Chris	ChA	1	1.0	0	0	0	0	.000	.00
Curtis,Chad	Cal	48	352.0	71	2	3	0	.961	1.87
Daniels,Kal	LA	21	162.0	26	1	1	0	.964	1.50
Daniels,Kal	ChN	28	195.1	33	3	0	0	1.000	1.66
Dascenzo,Doug	ChN	25	99.1	28	1	2	0	.935	2.63
Daugherty,Jack	Tex	16	76.0	12	1	1	0	.929	1.54
Davis,Chili	Min	1	1.0	1	0	0	0	1.000	9.00
Davis,Eric	LA	69	573.0	108	0	4	1	.964	1.70
Diaz,Alex	Mil	2	8.0	2	0	0	0	1.000	2.25
Distefano,Benny	Hou	7	27.2	13	0	0	0	1.000	4.23
Dozier,D.J.	NYN	17	120.2	33	0	1	0	.971	2.46
Ducey,Rob	Tor	3	19.0	3	0	0	0	1.000	1.42
Ducey,Rob	Cal	17	134.0	28	2	2	1	.938	2.01
Duncan,Mariano	Phi	65	514.0	123	1	3	0	.976	2.17
Eisenreich,Jim	KC	24	195.0	48	0	0	0	1.000	2.22
Espy,Cecil	Pit	11	64.0	13	0	2	0	.867	1.83
Fariss,Monty	Tex	28	182.2	34	0	0	0	1.000	1.68
Felder,Mike	SF	53	214.2	49	1	0	0	1.000	2.10
Fitzgerald,Mike	Cal	5	26.0	5	0	0	0	1.000	1.73
Foley,Tom	Mon	1	1.0	0	0	0	0	.000	.00
Fox,Eric	Oak	20	79.2	24	1	0	1	1.000	2.82
Franco,Julio	Tex	4	16.0	9	0	0	0	1.000	5.06
Gallagher,Dave	NYN	22	123.2	30	2	2	1	.941	2.33
Gonzalez,Jose	Cal	11	73.0	19	1	0	1	1.000	2.47
Gonzalez,Juan	Tex	31	229.0	68	3	2	0	.973	2.79
Goodwin,Tom	LA	35	145.2	34	0	0	0	1.000	2.10
Grebeck,Craig	ChA	1	0.2	0	0	0	0	.000	.00
Greenwell,Mike	Bos	41	360.0	85	1	0	0	1.000	2.15
Gregg,Tommy	Atl	2	4.0	2	0	0	0	1.000	4.50
Grotewold,Jeff	Phi	2	8.0	1	0	0	0	1.000	1.13
Guerrero,Juan	Hou	3	9.2	1	0	0	0	1.000	0.93
Guerrero,Pedro	StL	10	69.0	17	0	1	0	.944	2.22
Gwynn,Chris	KC	5	35.0	12	0	0	0	1.000	3.09
Hamilton,Darryl	Mil	30	231.0	49	2	0	0	1.000	1.99

Left Fielders - The Rest

Left Fielders - The Rest

Player	Tm	G	Inn	PO	A	E	DP	Pct.	Rng
Hare,Shawn	Det	3	7.0	2	0	0	0	1.000	2.57
Harris,Donald	Tex	5	13.2	9	0	0	0	1.000	5.93
Harris,Lenny	LA	7	30.2	7	1	1	0	.889	2.35
Haselman,Bill	Sea	2	14.0	3	0	0	0	1.000	1.93
Hatcher,Billy	Cin	23	156.0	29	0	1	0	.967	1.67
Hatcher,Billy	Bos	63	545.2	116	5	4	0	.968	2.00
Hemond,Scott	Oak	1	8.0	2	0	0	0	1.000	2.25
Hemond,Scott	ChA	2	11.0	2	1	0	0	1.000	2.45
Hernandez,Cesar	Cin	12	47.2	11	0	0	0	1.000	2.08
Hill,Glenallen	Cle	50	460.0	108	5	6	2	.950	2.21
Howard,Thomas	Cle	68	453.0	115	3	2	0	.983	2.34
Howitt,Dann	Oak	4	25.0	7	0	1	0	.875	2.52
Howitt,Dann	Sea	10	87.1	22	1	0	0	1.000	2.37
Hudler,Rex	StL	5	10.1	2	0	0	0	1.000	1.74
Huff,Mike	ChA	10	39.0	9	0	0	0	1.000	2.08
Humphreys,Mike	NYA	2	15.0	7	1	0	0	1.000	4.80
Hunter,Brian	Atl	1	3.0	0	0	0	0	.000	.00
Incaviglia,Pete	Hou	57	401.0	115	3	3	1	.975	2.65
Jackson,Darrin	SD	5	15.0	8	0	0	0	1.000	4.80
Jaha,John	Mil	1	2.0	0	0	0	0	.000	.00
James,Chris	SF	60	430.0	106	2	3	1	.973	2.26
James,Dion	NYA	8	47.0	6	0	0	0	1.000	1.15
Javier,Stan	LA	15	64.1	14	0	0	0	1.000	1.96
Javier,Stan	Phi	27	208.1	64	2	0	0	1.000	2.85
Jeter,Shawn	ChA	1	2.0	1	0	0	0	1.000	4.50
Johnson,Howard	NYN	16	124.0	25	1	1	0	.963	1.89
Jones,Chris	Hou	17	72.0	12	0	2	0	.857	1.50
Jordan,Brian	StL	27	206.1	42	3	1	0	.978	1.96
Jordan,Ricky	Phi	11	74.1	12	0	0	0	1.000	1.45
Kelly,Roberto	NYA	47	391.1	103	2	2	0	.981	2.41
Kingery,Mike	Oak	2	10.0	0	0	0	0	.000	.00
Kirby,Wayne	Cle	1	3.0	1	0	0	0	1.000	3.00
Koslofski,Kevin	KC	15	70.2	18	1	0	0	1.000	2.42
Kruk,John	Phi	6	41.1	11	0	0	0	1.000	2.40
Kunkel,Jeff	ChN	3	20.0	9	0	0	0	1.000	4.05
Lampkin,Tom	SD	1	4.0	0	0	0	0	.000	.00
Leonard,Mark	SF	33	244.0	56	2	1	2	.983	2.14
Lindeman,Jim	Phi	4	6.1	0	0	0	0	.000	.00
Litton,Greg	SF	1	1.0	0	0	0	0	.000	.00
Lyons,Steve	Atl	2	3.0	0	0	0	0	.000	.00
Lyons,Steve	Mon	7	18.2	4	0	0	0	1.000	1.93
Marsh,Tom	Phi	25	183.0	44	0	1	0	.978	2.16
Martin,Al	Pit	7	21.0	6	0	0	0	1.000	2.57
Martinez,Dave	Cin	3	26.0	8	1	0	0	1.000	3.12
McClendon,Lloyd	Pit	10	49.0	10	0	1	0	.909	1.84
McCray,Rodney	NYN	1	1.0	2	0	0	0	1.000	18.00
McIntosh,Tim	Mil	9	40.1	9	0	0	0	1.000	2.01
Mercedes,Luis	Bal	1	9.0	3	0	0	0	1.000	3.00
Miller,Keith	KC	16	117.0	41	0	2	0	.953	3.15
Mitchell,Kevin	Sea	69	570.2	130	4	0	0	1.000	2.11
Morris,John	Cal	5	20.0	6	0	0	0	1.000	2.70
Moses,John	Sea	17	81.0	18	0	0	0	1.000	2.00
Munoz,Pedro	Min	7	42.0	6	0	0	0	1.000	1.29
Murphy,Dale	Phi	1	0.0	0	0	0	0	.000	.00
Naehring,Tim	Bos	1	1.2	1	0	0	0	1.000	5.40
Neel,Troy	Oak	9	41.0	10	1	2	0	.846	2.41
Newman,Al	Tex	1	2.0	0	0	0	0	.000	.00
Newson,Warren	ChA	17	94.0	19	3	0	2	1.000	2.11

Player	Tm	G	Inn	PO	A	E	DP	Pct.	Rng
Nieves,Melvin	Atl	3	13.0	4	0	1	0	.800	2.77
Nixon,Otis	Atl	2	11.0	3	0	0	0	1.000	2.45
Orsulak,Joe	Bal	14	105.0	25	1	1	0	.963	2.23
Peltier,Dan	Tex	1	8.0	1	0	1	0	.500	1.13
Pennyfeather,William	Pit	1	2.0	0	0	0	0	.000	.00
Phillips,Tony	Det	14	111.0	42	0	2	0	.955	3.41
Plantier,Phil	Bos	13	95.0	18	0	2	0	.900	1.71
Pulliam,Harvey	KC	1	4.0	3	0	0	0	1.000	6.75
Ready,Randy	Oak	22	124.2	33	1	0	0	1.000	2.45
Reboulet,Jeff	Min	1	1.0	2	0	0	0	1.000	18.00
Redus,Gary	Pit	2	17.0	4	0	0	0	1.000	2.12
Reed,Darren	Mon	8	39.0	6	0	0	0	1.000	1.38
Reed,Darren	Min	10	61.0	10	1	0	0	1.000	1.62
Reynolds,Harold	Sea	1	0.2	0	0	0	0	.000	.00
Rhodes,Karl	Hou	1	0.2	0	0	0	0	.000	.00
Rivera,Luis	Bos	1	1.0	0	0	0	0	.000	.00
Roberts,Bip	Cin	69	496.1	115	1	1	0	.991	2.10
Rodriguez,Henry	LA	17	104.0	26	6	2	2	.941	2.77
Russell,John	Tex	1	2.0	0	0	1	0	.000	.00
Salazar,Luis	ChN	33	206.1	46	2	0	0	1.000	2.09
Sanders,Deion	Atl	12	87.2	25	0	0	0	1.000	2.57
Sanders,Reggie	Cin	53	275.2	57	3	0	1	1.000	1.96
Sasser,Mackey	NYN	7	35.2	7	0	0	0	1.000	1.77
Segui,David	Bal	3	20.0	4	0	0	0	1.000	1.80
Smith,Dwight	ChN	20	116.2	24	1	1	0	.962	1.93
Smith,Lonnie	Atl	35	241.1	61	2	3	0	.955	2.35
Snyder,Cory	SF	22	134.0	33	0	0	0	1.000	2.22
Stairs,Matt	Mon	10	65.0	14	0	1	0	.933	1.94
Stephenson,Phil	SD	10	63.0	11	0	0	0	1.000	1.57
Strawberry,Darryl	LA	2	14.0	4	0	0	0	1.000	2.57
Surhoff,B.J.	Mil	5	28.2	9	0	0	0	1.000	2.83
Tabler,Pat	Tor	5	19.0	3	0	0	0	1.000	1.42
Tartabull,Danny	NYA	1	9.0	8	0	0	0	1.000	8.00
Tettleton,Mickey	Det	1	7.0	2	0	0	0	1.000	2.57
Thompson,Milt	StL	35	252.1	61	1	1	1	.984	2.21
Thurman,Gary	KC	7	29.0	9	0	0	0	1.000	2.79
Turner,Shane	Sea	15	53.0	12	0	0	0	1.000	2.04
VanderWal,John	Mon	55	370.2	97	2	2	0	.980	2.40
Varsho,Gary	Pit	14	83.0	18	1	0	0	1.000	2.06
Velarde,Randy	NYA	14	93.0	22	1	0	0	1.000	2.23
Velasquez,Guillermo	SD	2	11.0	2	0	0	0	1.000	1.64
Walker,Chico	ChN	6	19.0	10	0	0	0	1.000	4.74
Walker,Chico	NYN	9	46.2	8	1	1	0	.900	1.74
Walton,Jerome	ChN	22	144.2	34	0	2	0	.944	2.12
Ward,Kevin	SD	36	203.1	45	2	1	0	.979	2.08
Ward,Turner	Tor	2	18.0	2	0	0	0	1.000	1.00
Webster,Mitch	LA	36	198.2	46	0	0	0	1.000	2.08
Williams,Bernie	NYA	4	37.0	8	1	0	0	1.000	2.19
Winningham,Herm	Bos	36	228.2	61	4	1	1	.985	2.56
Wood,Ted	SF	6	41.0	13	0	0	0	1.000	2.85
Yelding,Eric	Hou	2	2.0	1	0	0	0	1.000	4.50
Young,Gerald	Hou	6	15.0	4	0	0	0	1.000	2.40
Zupcic,Bob	Bos	32	216.1	39	4	1	1	.977	1.79

Center Fielders - Regulars

Player	Tm	G	Inn	PO	A	E	DP	Pct.	Rng
Wilson,Willie	Oak	118	903.0	351	2	7	1	.981	3.52
Nixon,Otis	Atl	102	826.0	291	6	2	2	.993	3.24
Sanders,Reggie	Cin	77	600.2	205	8	6	3	.973	3.19
White,Devon	Tor	152	1307.0	443	8	7	2	.985	3.11
Lofton,Kenny	Cle	143	1256.1	419	14	8	4	.982	3.10
Dykstra,Lenny	Phi	85	750.2	252	6	3	4	.989	3.09
McRae,Brian	KC	148	1283.1	421	8	3	2	.993	3.01
Kelly,Roberto	NYA	99	877.1	286	6	5	3	.983	3.00
Jackson,Darrin	SD	152	1338.1	425	18	2	7	.996	2.98
Johnson,Lance	ChA	157	1364.0	433	11	6	4	.987	2.93
Lankford,Ray	StL	153	1369.0	439	5	2	1	.996	2.92
Cuyler,Milt	Det	88	733.2	233	4	4	1	.983	2.91
Felix,Junior	Cal	125	1076.2	334	9	6	3	.983	2.87
Puckett,Kirby	Min	149	1274.2	394	9	3	3	.993	2.85
Yount,Robin	Mil	139	1196.0	371	6	2	0	.995	2.84
Lewis,Darren	SF	94	720.1	224	3	0	2	1.000	2.84
Van Slyke,Andy	Pit	154	1373.2	421	11	5	3	.989	2.83
Finley,Steve	Hou	160	1352.1	417	8	3	3	.993	2.83
Devereaux,Mike	Bal	155	1396.0	431	5	5	3	.989	2.81
Griffey Jr,Ken	Sea	137	1187.0	358	8	1	4	.997	2.78
Gonzalez,Juan	Tex	123	1023.1	309	6	8	1	.975	2.77
Martinez,Dave	Cin	105	718.2	212	5	2	1	.991	2.72
Grissom,Marquis	Mon	157	1402.1	402	7	7	2	.983	2.62
Dascenzo,Doug	ChN	80	634.2	177	1	3	0	.983	2.52
Butler,Brett	LA	155	1318.1	354	9	2	2	.995	2.48
Johnson,Howard	NYN	84	713.0	181	3	3	0	.984	2.32
Average	---	126	1076.2	337	7	4	2	.988	2.88

Center Fielders - The Rest

Player	Tm	G	Inn	PO	A	E	DP	Pct.	Rng
Abner,Shawn	ChA	14	92.0	45	0	0	0	1.000	4.40
Alou,Moises	Mon	13	62.2	23	2	0	1	1.000	3.59
Amaral,Rich	Sea	1	0.2	0	0	0	0	.000	.00
Amaro,Ruben	Phi	27	203.1	60	1	1	0	.984	2.70
Anderson,Brady	Bal	7	64.0	17	0	1	0	.944	2.39
Anthony,Eric	Hou	2	2.0	0	0	0	0	.000	.00
Barnes,Skeeter	Det	6	14.0	6	1	0	1	1.000	4.50
Bell,Derek	Tor	18	105.0	38	1	0	0	1.000	3.34
Bichette,Dante	Mil	1	8.0	2	0	0	0	1.000	2.25
Blankenship,Lance	Oak	16	108.2	29	0	1	0	.967	2.40
Boston,Daryl	NYN	16	92.1	23	0	0	0	1.000	2.24
Briley,Greg	Sea	13	89.0	23	0	2	0	.920	2.33
Brown,Jarvis	Min	9	22.0	8	0	0	0	1.000	3.27
Browne,Jerry	Oak	23	161.1	48	0	0	0	1.000	2.68
Bruett,J.T.	Min	20	96.0	27	1	0	0	1.000	2.63
Brumfield,Jacob	Cin	8	35.2	10	0	0	0	1.000	2.52
Buhner,Jay	Sea	2	3.0	1	0	0	0	1.000	3.00
Burks,Ellis	Bos	63	535.2	122	3	2	0	.984	2.10
Candaele,Casey	Hou	1	2.0	1	0	0	0	1.000	4.50
Cangelosi,John	Tex	24	121.0	35	2	0	1	1.000	2.75
Carr,Chuck	StL	9	52.0	19	0	0	0	1.000	3.29
Carreon,Mark	Det	1	8.0	2	0	1	0	.667	2.25
Castillo,Braulio	Phi	6	49.0	8	0	0	0	1.000	1.47
Clark,Jerald	SD	1	10.0	4	0	0	0	1.000	3.60
Cole,Alex	Cle	5	27.0	3	0	0	0	1.000	1.00
Cole,Alex	Pit	1	2.0	1	0	0	0	1.000	4.50

Center Fielders - The Rest

Player	Tm	G	Inn	PO	A	E	DP	Pct.	Rng
Coleman,Vince	NYN	21	174.1	58	0	0	0	1.000	2.99
Cotto,Henry	Sea	30	162.1	50	0	0	0	1.000	2.77
Curtis,Chad	Cal	35	278.1	78	3	2	0	.976	2.62
Daugherty,Jack	Tex	1	2.0	2	0	0	0	1.000	9.00
Davis,Eric	LA	5	26.0	7	0	0	0	1.000	2.42
Diaz,Alex	Mil	10	22.0	8	0	0	0	1.000	3.27
Ducey,Rob	Tor	2	6.0	1	0	0	0	1.000	1.50
Ducey,Rob	Cal	1	2.0	0	0	0	0	.000	.00
Eisenreich,Jim	KC	1	10.0	7	0	0	0	1.000	6.30
Espy,Cecil	Pit	18	81.0	25	0	0	0	1.000	2.78
Fariss,Monty	Tex	10	45.0	7	0	0	0	1.000	1.40
Felder,Mike	SF	58	376.1	106	1	1	0	.991	2.56
Fox,Eric	Oak	19	132.1	45	1	1	0	.979	3.13
Gallagher,Dave	NYN	13	76.0	19	1	0	1	1.000	2.37
Gant,Ron	Atl	23	141.1	40	2	0	1	1.000	2.67
Gladden,Dan	Det	17	121.2	24	0	0	0	1.000	1.78
Gonzalez,Jose	Cal	5	14.0	5	0	0	0	1.000	3.21
Goodwin,Tom	LA	9	43.2	9	0	0	0	1.000	1.85
Gregg,Tommy	Atl	4	15.0	7	0	0	0	1.000	4.20
Hamilton,Darryl	Mil	32	226.0	79	0	0	0	1.000	3.15
Harris,Donald	Tex	15	72.0	25	1	1	1	.963	3.25
Hatcher,Billy	Bos	13	106.1	29	0	1	0	.967	2.45
Henderson,Dave	Oak	9	66.0	14	0	1	0	.933	1.91
Hernandez,Cesar	Cin	6	24.0	5	1	1	0	.857	2.25
Hill,Glenallen	Cle	1	9.0	1	0	0	0	1.000	1.00
Howard,Dave	KC	2	2.0	0	0	0	0	.000	.00
Howard,Thomas	Cle	22	177.2	44	1	0	0	1.000	2.28
Howell,Pat	NYN	28	176.2	66	0	0	0	1.000	3.36
Howitt,Dann	Oak	5	29.0	14	0	1	0	.933	4.34
Hudler,Rex	StL	1	2.0	1	0	0	0	1.000	4.50
Huff,Mike	ChA	3	3.0	2	0	0	0	1.000	6.00
Hulse,David	Tex	29	194.0	58	0	1	0	.983	2.69
Huson,Jeff	Tex	2	3.0	0	0	0	0	.000	.00
James,Dion	NYA	12	88.2	16	0	0	0	1.000	1.62
Javier,Stan	LA	2	3.0	1	0	0	0	1.000	3.00
Javier,Stan	Phi	49	395.0	147	5	3	1	.981	3.46
Jeter,Shawn	ChA	1	2.0	1	0	0	0	1.000	4.50
Jones,Chris	Hou	5	19.1	4	0	0	0	1.000	1.86
Jones,Tim	StL	1	0.0	0	0	0	0	.000	.00
Jordan,Brian	StL	9	53.0	23	0	0	0	1.000	3.91
Kingery,Mike	Oak	6	46.0	14	0	0	0	1.000	2.74
Koslofski,Kevin	KC	18	136.0	53	1	1	0	.982	3.57
Listach,Pat	Mil	1	1.0	0	0	0	0	.000	.00
Lyons,Steve	Mon	1	3.0	0	0	0	0	.000	.00
Lyons,Steve	Bos	2	3.2	2	0	0	0	1.000	4.91
Mack,Shane	Min	9	58.1	13	2	0	1	1.000	2.31
McCray,Rodney	NYN	1	2.0	2	0	0	0	1.000	9.00
McGee,Willie	SF	31	248.1	66	2	0	1	1.000	2.46
Mercedes,Luis	Bal	2	4.0	3	0	0	0	1.000	6.75
Moses,John	Sea	1	3.0	1	0	0	0	1.000	3.00
Patterson,John	SF	5	42.0	23	0	0	0	1.000	4.93
Peguero,Julio	Phi	9	30.0	10	0	0	0	1.000	3.00
Pennyfeather,William	Pit	6	14.0	5	0	0	0	1.000	3.21
Pettis,Gary	SD	13	44.0	16	0	1	0	.941	3.27
Pettis,Gary	Det	46	389.1	144	2	1	0	.993	3.38
Phillips,Tony	Det	24	169.0	48	1	0	0	1.000	2.61
Raines,Tim	ChA	1	0.2	1	0	0	0	1.000	13.50
Ramsey,Fernando	ChN	15	61.0	17	0	0	0	1.000	2.51

Center Fielders - The Rest

Player	Tm	G	Inn	PO	A	E	DP	Pct.	Rng
Reboulet,Jeff	Min	1	2.0	0	0	0	0	.000	.00
Redus,Gary	Pit	1	5.0	2	0	0	0	1.000	3.60
Roberts,Bip	Cin	16	70.1	23	0	0	0	1.000	2.94
Sanders,Deion	Atl	60	477.1	137	2	2	0	.986	2.62
Smith,Dwight	ChN	27	198.0	51	1	1	0	.981	2.36
Snyder,Cory	SF	13	73.2	21	1	0	0	1.000	2.69
Sosa,Sammy	ChN	67	573.1	145	4	6	1	.961	2.34
Surhoff,B.J.	Mil	1	4.0	0	0	0	0	.000	.00
Thompson,Milt	StL	1	3.0	1	0	0	0	1.000	3.00
Thompson,Ryan	NYN	26	185.0	62	1	1	0	.984	3.06
Thurman,Gary	KC	2	16.0	7	0	0	0	1.000	3.94
Varsho,Gary	Pit	2	4.0	1	0	0	0	1.000	2.25
Vatcher,Jim	SD	1	8.0	4	0	0	0	1.000	4.50
Velarde,Randy	NYA	2	1.0	0	0	0	0	.000	.00
Walker,Chico	NYN	4	27.1	8	0	0	0	1.000	2.63
Walton,Jerome	ChN	1	2.0	0	0	0	0	.000	.00
Ward,Kevin	SD	9	60.2	14	0	1	0	.933	2.08
Ward,Turner	Tor	4	22.0	9	1	0	0	1.000	4.09
Webster,Mitch	LA	8	47.0	18	0	1	0	.947	3.45
Williams,Bernie	NYA	55	485.1	169	3	1	0	.994	3.19
Williams,Reggie	Cal	12	75.0	26	0	0	0	1.000	3.12
Winningham,Herm	Bos	32	227.1	51	3	2	0	.964	2.14
Yelding,Eric	Hou	1	1.0	0	0	0	0	.000	.00
Young,Gerald	Hou	14	82.2	31	0	2	0	.939	3.38
Zupcic,Bob	Bos	68	575.1	172	6	5	1	.973	2.78

Right Fielders - Regulars

Player	Tm	G	Inn	PO	A	E	DP	Pct.	Rng
Justice,Dave	Atl	140	1198.0	313	9	8	3	.976	2.42
Whiten,Mark	Cle	144	1278.1	321	14	7	2	.980	2.36
Canseco,Jose	TOT	90	766.2	195	5	3	3	.985	2.35
Orsulak,Joe	Bal	98	812.1	203	8	3	1	.986	2.34
Deer,Rob	Det	106	919.0	229	8	4	1	.983	2.32
Jose,Felix	StL	127	1117.1	271	11	6	1	.979	2.27
Pasqua,Dan	ChA	81	622.0	152	4	6	0	.963	2.26
O'Neill,Paul	Cin	143	1209.2	291	12	1	2	.997	2.25
Hayes,Von	Cal	85	681.2	169	1	3	0	.983	2.24
Brunansky,Tom	Bos	92	784.1	189	6	4	2	.980	2.24
Bonilla,Bobby	NYN	121	988.0	238	7	2	1	.992	2.23
Gwynn,Tony	SD	127	1127.2	270	9	5	3	.982	2.23
Buhner,Jay	Sea	150	1325.1	312	14	2	4	.994	2.21
Carter,Joe	Tor	123	1043.2	246	10	8	2	.970	2.21
Munoz,Pedro	Min	117	920.1	214	8	3	3	.987	2.17
McGee,Willie	SF	90	721.0	164	9	6	1	.966	2.16
Walker,Larry	Mon	139	1216.2	269	16	2	2	.993	2.11
Sierra,Ruben	TOT	144	1269.1	284	6	7	0	.976	2.06
Bichette,Dante	Mil	101	846.0	186	6	2	3	.990	2.04
Anthony,Eric	Hou	113	900.1	172	6	5	0	.973	1.78
Dawson,Andre	ChN	139	1182.1	222	11	2	4	.991	1.77
Average	---	117	996.2	233	8	4	1	.983	2.19

Right Fielders - The Rest

Player	Tm	G	Inn	PO	A	E	DP	Pct.	Rng
Abner,Shawn	ChA	75	351.0	93	2	0	0	1.000	2.44
Alou,Moises	Mon	15	107.2	28	0	2	0	.933	2.34
Amaral,Rich	Sea	1	1.0	0	0	0	0	.000	.00
Amaro,Ruben	Phi	68	451.1	106	3	1	1	.991	2.17
Anderson,Brady	Bal	3	22.0	6	0	0	0	1.000	2.45
Ashley,Billy	LA	26	206.0	33	1	5	0	.872	1.49
Azocar,Oscar	SD	6	44.0	9	0	0	0	1.000	1.84
Baines,Harold	Oak	17	100.0	19	0	1	0	.950	1.71
Barfield,Jesse	NYA	30	236.0	53	3	2	0	.966	2.14
Barnes,Skeeter	Det	5	7.0	3	0	0	0	1.000	3.86
Bass,Kevin	SF	21	144.2	36	0	1	0	.973	2.24
Bass,Kevin	NYN	13	83.0	19	1	0	0	1.000	2.17
Bell,Derek	Tor	15	82.0	18	1	0	1	1.000	2.09
Benzinger,Todd	LA	33	257.1	47	1	0	0	1.000	1.68
Blankenship,Lance	Oak	20	101.0	29	1	1	0	.968	2.67
Boston,Daryl	NYN	14	65.1	15	0	0	0	1.000	2.07
Braggs,Glenn	Cin	29	191.2	37	1	5	0	.884	1.78
Briley,Greg	Sea	4	25.0	3	1	0	0	1.000	1.44
Brosius,Scott	Oak	19	99.0	18	1	0	0	1.000	1.73
Brown,Jarvis	Min	18	33.1	9	0	0	0	1.000	2.43
Browne,Jerry	Oak	6	32.2	11	0	0	0	1.000	3.03
Bruett,J.T.	Min	22	47.0	11	0	1	0	.917	2.11
Brumfield,Jacob	Cin	1	8.0	7	0	0	0	1.000	7.88
Bush,Randy	Min	21	114.1	26	0	0	0	1.000	2.05
Candaele,Casey	Hou	1	2.0	0	0	0	0	.000	.00
Cangelosi,John	Tex	10	60.0	11	1	0	0	1.000	1.80
Canseco,Jose	Oak	77	655.2	163	5	2	3	.988	2.31
Canseco,Jose	Tex	13	111.0	32	0	1	0	.970	2.59
Canseco,Ozzie	StL	1	10.0	3	0	0	0	1.000	2.70
Carr,Chuck	StL	6	54.0	13	0	0	0	1.000	2.17
Carreon,Mark	Det	19	138.0	39	0	1	0	.975	2.54
Castillo,Braulio	Phi	16	117.0	35	0	1	0	.972	2.69
Chamberlain,Wes	Phi	48	388.0	84	1	1	0	.988	1.97
Clark,Dave	Pit	7	55.0	9	0	0	0	1.000	1.47
Clark,Jerald	SD	22	167.0	40	1	0	1	1.000	2.21
Clark,Phil	Det	9	57.0	21	0	1	0	.955	3.32
Cochrane,Dave	Sea	9	49.0	9	3	3	1	.800	2.20
Cole,Alex	Cle	2	4.0	1	0	0	0	1.000	2.25
Cole,Alex	Pit	52	398.1	84	4	1	0	.989	1.99
Coles,Darnell	Cin	2	6.2	3	0	0	0	1.000	4.05
Conine,Jeff	KC	1	1.0	0	0	0	0	.000	.00
Cotto,Henry	Sea	6	34.0	7	0	0	0	1.000	1.85
Curtis,Chad	Cal	62	448.2	101	11	1	3	.991	2.25
Cuyler,Milt	Det	1	8.0	0	0	0	0	.000	.00
Dascenzo,Doug	ChN	28	89.0	16	0	0	0	1.000	1.62
Daugherty,Jack	Tex	11	59.0	16	0	1	0	.941	2.44
Davis,Chili	Min	3	15.0	4	0	0	0	1.000	2.40
Davis,Eric	LA	4	25.2	8	0	1	0	.889	2.81
Distefano,Benny	Hou	5	21.1	3	1	0	0	1.000	1.69
Ducey,Rob	Tor	8	27.0	7	0	0	0	1.000	2.33
Ducey,Rob	Cal	2	11.0	4	0	0	0	1.000	3.27
Eisenreich,Jim	KC	66	499.0	125	1	1	1	.992	2.27
Espy,Cecil	Pit	56	210.2	45	1	2	0	.958	1.97
Fariss,Monty	Tex	12	90.0	16	0	0	0	1.000	1.60
Felder,Mike	SF	11	22.0	4	0	0	0	1.000	1.64
Felix,Junior	Cal	4	14.0	5	0	0	0	1.000	3.21
Fitzgerald,Mike	Cal	6	21.0	0	0	0	0	.000	.00
Fox,Eric	Oak	16	109.0	22	1	0	0	1.000	1.90

235

Right Fielders - The Rest

Player	Tm	G	Inn	PO	A	E	DP	Pct.	Rng
Franco,Julio	Tex	1	7.0	0	0	0	0	.000	.00
Gallagher,Dave	NYN	48	207.1	55	1	0	1	1.000	2.43
Gibson,Kirk	Pit	13	112.0	25	1	0	1	1.000	2.09
Gilkey,Bernard	StL	1	8.0	1	1	0	0	1.000	2.25
Gonzalez,Jose	Cal	8	42.0	6	0	0	0	1.000	1.29
Gonzalez,Juan	Tex	1	2.0	2	0	0	0	1.000	9.00
Goodwin,Tom	LA	2	2.0	0	0	0	0	.000	.00
Grebeck,Craig	ChA	1	1.2	0	0	0	0	.000	.00
Gregg,Tommy	Atl	4	11.0	6	0	0	0	1.000	4.91
Gwynn,Chris	KC	14	115.1	21	0	0	0	1.000	1.64
Hall,Mel	NYA	37	302.0	63	1	1	1	.985	1.91
Hamilton,Darryl	Mil	74	599.0	151	8	0	0	1.000	2.39
Hare,Shawn	Det	7	39.0	10	0	0	0	1.000	2.31
Harris,Donald	Tex	5	15.0	2	0	0	0	1.000	1.20
Harris,Lenny	LA	8	48.0	13	0	1	0	.929	2.44
Hemond,Scott	Oak	1	8.0	0	0	0	0	.000	.00
Henderson,Dave	Oak	3	21.0	5	0	0	0	1.000	2.14
Hernandez,Cesar	Cin	1	7.1	2	1	0	1	1.000	3.68
Hill,Donnie	Min	1	1.0	0	0	0	0	.000	.00
Hill,Glenallen	Cle	8	78.2	17	0	0	0	1.000	1.94
Hosey,Steve	SF	18	128.0	24	0	1	0	.960	1.69
Howard,Thomas	Cle	13	106.0	26	1	0	0	1.000	2.29
Howitt,Dann	Oak	12	73.0	14	3	0	3	1.000	2.10
Howitt,Dann	Sea	1	9.0	3	0	0	0	1.000	3.00
Hudler,Rex	StL	7	25.0	4	0	0	0	1.000	1.44
Huff,Mike	ChA	45	236.1	57	2	0	0	1.000	2.25
Hulse,David	Tex	2	18.0	3	0	0	0	1.000	1.50
Hunter,Brian	Atl	5	34.0	14	1	2	0	.882	3.97
Incaviglia,Pete	Hou	48	351.0	74	5	3	0	.963	2.03
Jackson,Darrin	SD	2	4.0	1	0	0	0	1.000	2.25
James,Chris	SF	2	11.0	6	0	0	0	1.000	4.91
James,Dion	NYA	27	166.0	40	1	0	0	1.000	2.22
Javier,Stan	LA	11	22.1	2	0	0	0	1.000	0.81
Javier,Stan	Phi	1	1.0	1	0	0	0	1.000	9.00
Jeter,Shawn	ChA	6	31.1	8	0	1	0	.889	2.30
Johnson,Howard	NYN	1	4.0	0	0	0	0	.000	.00
Jones,Chris	Hou	25	56.0	11	0	0	0	1.000	1.77
Jordan,Brian	StL	21	178.2	36	1	0	0	1.000	1.86
Karkovice,Ron	ChA	1	2.0	3	0	0	0	1.000	13.50
King,Jeff	Pit	1	6.0	1	0	0	0	1.000	1.50
Kingery,Mike	Oak	2	3.0	0	0	0	0	.000	.00
Kirby,Wayne	Cle	1	3.0	2	0	0	0	1.000	6.00
Koslofski,Kevin	KC	23	149.0	35	3	0	0	1.000	2.30
Kruk,John	Phi	29	225.2	47	0	1	0	.979	1.87
Larkin,Gene	Min	43	286.0	53	5	1	1	.983	1.83
Leonard,Mark	SF	4	22.2	4	0	0	0	1.000	1.59
Leyritz,Jim	NYA	2	16.0	2	0	0	0	1.000	1.13
Lindeman,Jim	Phi	7	30.0	6	0	0	0	1.000	1.80
Lyons,Steve	Atl	4	17.1	4	0	0	0	1.000	2.08
Lyons,Steve	Bos	3	13.0	4	0	0	0	1.000	2.77
Mack,Shane	Min	4	18.0	3	0	0	0	1.000	1.50
Maldonado,Candy	Tor	4	28.0	3	0	0	0	1.000	0.96
Marsh,Tom	Phi	12	90.0	22	0	1	0	.957	2.20
Martinez,Chito	Bal	52	426.0	104	4	3	1	.973	2.28
Martinez,Dave	Cin	6	26.0	6	1	0	1	1.000	2.42
May,Derrick	ChN	14	112.0	19	0	0	0	1.000	1.53
McClendon,Lloyd	Pit	50	343.1	70	0	2	0	.972	1.83
McCray,Rodney	NYN	11	14.1	2	0	0	0	1.000	1.26

Right Fielders - The Rest

Player	Tm	G	Inn	PO	A	E	DP	Pct.	Rng
McIntosh,Tim	Mil	1	8.0	4	0	0	0	1.000	4.50
McKnight,Jeff	NYN	1	1.0	0	0	0	0	.000	.00
McReynolds,Kevin	KC	12	109.2	19	0	1	0	.950	1.56
Merced,Orlando	Pit	17	112.2	23	3	0	1	1.000	2.08
Mercedes,Luis	Bal	13	100.2	34	2	2	0	.947	3.22
Morris,John	Cal	9	38.1	7	0	0	0	1.000	1.64
Moses,John	Sea	1	1.0	0	0	0	0	.000	.00
Murphy,Dale	Phi	16	121.0	19	0	1	0	.950	1.41
Newson,Warren	ChA	33	217.1	48	2	0	0	1.000	2.07
Nieves,Melvin	Atl	3	22.0	4	0	2	0	.667	1.64
Nixon,Otis	Atl	16	125.0	38	0	1	0	.974	2.74
Peguero,Julio	Phi	5	4.0	0	0	0	0	.000	.00
Peltier,Dan	Tex	9	41.0	5	0	0	0	1.000	1.10
Pennyfeather,William	Pit	5	8.2	3	0	0	0	1.000	3.12
Pettis,Gary	SD	1	9.0	4	0	0	0	1.000	4.00
Phillips,Tony	Det	35	259.2	90	2	4	0	.958	3.19
Plantier,Phil	Bos	63	529.2	128	6	2	1	.985	2.28
Ready,Randy	Oak	2	8.0	1	0	0	0	1.000	1.13
Reboulet,Jeff	Min	5	5.0	0	0	0	0	.000	.00
Redus,Gary	Pit	12	68.1	15	0	1	0	.938	1.98
Reed,Darren	Mon	21	132.2	31	1	0	0	1.000	2.17
Reed,Darren	Min	4	13.0	4	0	0	0	1.000	2.77
Rhodes,Karl	Hou	1	0.1	0	0	0	0	.000	.00
Rodriguez,Henry	LA	31	242.2	39	1	1	0	.976	1.48
Russell,John	Tex	1	2.0	0	0	0	0	.000	.00
Salazar,Luis	ChN	1	1.0	1	1	0	1	1.000	18.00
Salmon,Tim	Cal	21	189.1	40	1	2	1	.953	1.95
Samuel,Juan	LA	1	3.0	1	0	1	0	.500	3.00
Samuel,Juan	KC	18	137.0	26	2	3	0	.903	1.84
Sanders,Deion	Atl	9	52.1	12	2	1	0	.933	2.41
Sasser,Mackey	NYN	2	12.0	1	0	0	0	1.000	0.75
Segui,David	Bal	15	103.0	27	1	0	0	1.000	2.45
Sierra,Ruben	Tex	119	1055.1	225	6	7	0	.971	1.97
Sierra,Ruben	Oak	25	214.0	59	0	0	0	1.000	2.48
Simms,Mike	Hou	9	46.0	6	2	0	0	1.000	1.57
Smith,Dwight	ChN	22	82.2	18	0	0	0	1.000	1.96
Snyder,Cory	SF	48	332.1	67	6	1	1	.986	1.98
Stephenson,Phil	SD	6	31.0	6	0	0	0	1.000	1.74
Strawberry,Darryl	LA	40	330.1	63	2	1	0	.985	1.77
Stubbs,Franklin	Mil	1	3.0	0	0	0	0	.000	.00
Surhoff,B.J.	Mil	1	1.0	0	0	0	0	.000	.00
Tabler,Pat	Tor	3	15.0	4	0	0	0	1.000	2.40
Tartabull,Danny	NYA	68	599.1	135	3	3	1	.979	2.07
Tettleton,Mickey	Det	1	8.0	1	0	0	0	1.000	1.13
Thompson,Milt	StL	11	83.0	12	0	1	0	.923	1.30
Thompson,Ryan	NYN	10	54.2	15	1	0	0	1.000	2.63
Thurman,Gary	KC	59	436.1	122	5	2	0	.984	2.62
Turner,Shane	Sea	1	0.2	1	0	0	0	1.000	13.50
VanderWal,John	Mon	4	11.0	2	0	0	0	1.000	1.64
Varsho,Gary	Pit	28	164.2	43	0	1	0	.977	2.35
Vatcher,Jim	SD	12	49.1	9	1	0	0	1.000	1.82
Vaughn,Greg	Mil	1	0.0	0	0	0	0	.000	.00
Velarde,Randy	NYA	7	38.0	11	0	0	0	1.000	2.61
Walker,Chico	ChN	1	1.0	0	0	0	0	.000	.00
Walker,Chico	NYN	2	17.0	3	0	0	0	1.000	1.59
Walton,Jerome	ChN	1	1.0	0	0	0	0	.000	.00
Ward,Kevin	SD	8	29.0	9	0	2	0	.818	2.79
Ward,Turner	Tor	6	27.0	7	0	0	0	1.000	2.33

Right Fielders - The Rest

Player	Tm	G	Inn	PO	A	E	DP	Pct.	Rng
Webster, Mitch	LA	56	300.2	65	0	2	0	.970	1.95
Williams, Bernie	NYA	4	29.0	10	1	0	1	1.000	3.41
Williams, Gerald	NYA	12	66.0	20	1	2	0	.913	2.86
Wilson, Craig	StL	3	4.0	1	0	0	0	1.000	2.25
Wilson, Willie	Oak	3	22.0	5	0	0	0	1.000	2.05
Winfield, Dave	Tor	26	217.1	52	1	0	0	1.000	2.19
Wood, Ted	SF	10	79.0	22	0	1	0	.957	2.51
Young, Gerald	Hou	43	82.1	18	0	0	0	1.000	1.97
Zupcic, Bob	Bos	22	121.1	29	1	0	1	1.000	2.23

Catchers - Regulars

Player	Tm	G	Inn	PO	A	E	DP	PB	Pct.
Pagnozzi,Tom	StL	138	1189.0	688	53	1	10	6	.999
Olson,Greg	Atl	94	754.2	522	43	1	9	4	.998
Berryhill,Damon	Atl	84	661.0	427	30	1	6	9	.998
Tettleton,Mickey	Det	113	943.0	475	47	2	10	4	.996
Alomar Jr,Sandy	Cle	88	729.2	477	39	2	5	3	.996
Hundley,Todd	NYN	121	892.1	701	47	3	2	6	.996
Hoiles,Chris	Bal	95	817.1	500	32	3	7	4	.994
LaValliere,Mike	Pit	92	767.0	421	62	3	7	4	.994
Manwaring,Kirt	SF	108	874.0	563	68	4	12	8	.994
Nokes,Matt	NYA	111	903.0	552	47	4	6	7	.993
Macfarlane,Mike	KC	104	845.0	527	43	4	7	9	.993
Pena,Tony	Bos	132	1084.0	786	55	6	11	7	.993
Taubensee,Eddie	Hou	103	804.1	557	66	5	6	9	.992
Oliver,Joe	Cin	141	1199.2	924	63	8	10	6	.992
Borders,Pat	Tor	137	1160.2	784	88	8	7	11	.991
Girardi,Joe	ChN	86	651.1	370	52	4	6	8	.991
Surhoff,B.J.	Mil	109	926.0	546	59	6	7	5	.990
Karkovice,Ron	ChA	119	915.0	533	53	6	9	6	.990
Valle,Dave	Sea	122	972.1	608	61	7	10	4	.990
Carter,Gary	Mon	85	665.0	482	50	6	3	1	.989
Ortiz,Junior	Cle	86	652.2	402	39	5	2	5	.989
Scioscia,Mike	LA	108	864.2	642	74	9	9	14	.988
Daulton,Darren	Phi	141	1200.2	760	69	11	8	12	.987
Steinbach,Terry	Oak	124	998.2	579	70	10	6	7	.985
Harper,Brian	Min	133	1114.0	744	58	13	8	12	.984
Rodriguez,Ivan	Tex	116	982.2	764	84	15	10	10	.983
Santiago,Benito	SD	103	885.1	584	53	12	6	0	.982
Average	---	110	905.2	589	55	5	7	6	.991

Catchers - The Rest

Player	Tm	G	Inn	PO	A	E	DP	PB	Pct.
Afenir,Troy	Cin	15	92.2	57	2	0	1	1	1.000
Allanson,Andy	Mil	9	66.0	30	3	2	0	0	.943
Bailey,Mark	SF	7	52.1	33	2	0	0	1	1.000
Bilardello,Dann	SD	14	94.0	73	9	0	3	0	1.000
Bradley,Scott	Sea	1	1.0	1	2	0	0	0	1.000
Bradley,Scott	Cin	2	4.0	2	0	0	0	0	1.000
Cabrera,Francisco	Atl	1	1.0	0	0	0	0	0	.000
Cerone,Rick	Mon	28	143.2	106	7	0	0	1	1.000
Cochrane,Dave	Sea	21	87.0	58	5	0	1	1	1.000
Colbert,Craig	SF	35	217.0	140	13	1	4	6	.994
Davis,Doug	Tex	1	1.0	0	0	0	0	0	.000
Decker,Steve	SF	15	118.2	94	4	0	1	1	1.000
Dempsey,Rick	Bal	8	30.0	13	1	0	0	1	1.000
Fisk,Carlton	ChA	54	429.2	252	26	2	2	4	.993
Fitzgerald,Mike	Cal	74	468.0	291	20	3	4	3	.990
Flaherty,John	Bos	34	195.1	102	7	2	2	0	.982
Fletcher,Darrin	Mon	69	518.0	360	32	2	3	3	.995
Gedman,Rich	StL	40	291.0	227	12	3	2	2	.988
Grotewold,Jeff	Phi	2	4.0	3	0	0	0	0	1.000
Haselman,Bill	Sea	5	33.0	16	2	0	0	0	1.000
Heffernan,Bert	Sea	5	26.0	19	1	0	0	1	1.000
Hemond,Scott	Oak	8	47.0	29	5	0	0	0	1.000
Hemond,Scott	ChA	1	1.0	0	0	0	0	0	.000
Hernandez,Carlos	LA	63	434.0	295	37	7	4	5	.979
Knorr,Randy	Tor	8	47.0	33	3	0	0	1	1.000

Catchers - The Rest

Player	Tm	G	Inn	PO	A	E	DP	PB	Pct.
Kreuter,Chad	Det	62	475.2	271	23	5	6	4	.983
Lake,Steve	Phi	17	125.2	71	8	2	1	0	.975
Laker,Tim	Mon	28	127.1	102	8	1	1	4	.991
Lampkin,Tom	SD	7	49.2	30	3	0	0	0	1.000
Levis,Jesse	Cle	21	87.2	59	5	1	0	1	.985
Leyritz,Jim	NYA	18	121.2	88	13	1	2	2	.990
Lopez,Javier	Atl	9	41.0	28	2	0	0	0	1.000
Marzano,John	Bos	18	134.0	81	8	3	0	0	.967
Mayne,Brent	KC	62	458.1	277	23	3	1	3	.990
McGinnis,Russ	Tex	10	62.0	40	3	0	2	6	1.000
McIntosh,Tim	Mil	14	77.0	53	5	1	0	0	.983
McNamara,Jim	SF	30	198.2	131	8	1	1	1	.993
Melvin,Bob	KC	21	144.0	77	7	0	2	2	1.000
Mercedes,Henry	Oak	9	16.0	7	0	1	0	0	.875
Merullo,Matt	ChA	16	107.0	64	3	2	0	3	.971
Myers,Greg	Tor	18	145.1	92	12	1	1	2	.990
Myers,Greg	Cal	8	44.0	33	3	0	0	0	1.000
Natal,Bob	Mon	4	14.0	10	0	1	0	0	.909
Nilsson,Dave	Mil	46	388.0	224	16	2	1	0	.992
O'Brien,Charlie	NYN	64	427.1	288	43	7	4	1	.979
Orton,John	Cal	43	344.1	238	22	5	3	1	.981
Parent,Mark	Bal	16	100.0	73	7	1	1	1	.988
Parks,Derek	Min	7	24.0	18	1	0	0	0	1.000
Parrish,Lance	Cal	22	177.0	107	8	3	2	1	.975
Parrish,Lance	Sea	34	239.0	183	12	1	4	3	.995
Pedre,Jorge	ChN	4	6.2	3	0	0	0	0	1.000
Petralli,Geno	Tex	54	367.2	263	22	3	6	3	.990
Piazza,Mike	LA	16	139.1	94	7	1	1	1	.990
Pratt,Todd	Phi	11	97.2	65	4	2	1	1	.972
Prince,Tom	Pit	19	114.0	76	8	2	0	1	.977
Quirk,Jamie	Oak	59	384.2	258	24	8	3	1	.972
Reed,Jeff	Cin	6	38.0	29	2	0	0	0	1.000
Rowland,Rich	Det	3	17.0	6	0	0	1	0	1.000
Russell,John	Tex	4	19.0	14	2	0	0	0	1.000
Santovenia,Nelson	ChA	2	9.0	3	0	0	0	0	1.000
Sasser,Mackey	NYN	27	127.0	84	5	1	0	3	.989
Servais,Scott	Hou	73	524.0	386	27	2	5	3	.995
Sinatro,Matt	Sea	18	86.2	43	4	0	1	0	1.000
Slaught,Don	Pit	79	598.2	365	32	5	3	6	.988
Sprague,Ed	Tor	15	87.0	64	3	1	0	1	.985
Stanley,Mike	NYA	55	427.2	266	27	6	2	7	.980
Stephens,Ray	Tex	6	28.0	12	2	0	0	0	1.000
Tackett,Jeff	Bal	64	516.2	311	32	1	4	9	.997
Tingley,Ron	Cal	69	412.2	270	35	4	3	0	.987
Tucker,Scooter	Hou	19	131.0	75	6	2	0	1	.976
Villanueva,Hector	ChN	28	222.0	155	20	4	1	3	.978
Walters,Dan	SD	55	432.0	328	25	3	5	2	.992
Webster,Lenny	Min	49	315.0	190	11	1	4	2	.995
Wedge,Eric	Bos	5	35.0	19	2	0	1	1	1.000
Wilkins,Rick	ChN	73	589.0	408	47	3	5	3	.993
Willard,Jerry	Atl	1	2.0	2	0	0	0	0	1.000
Wilson,Dan	Cin	9	57.0	42	4	0	0	0	1.000
Wrona,Rick	Cin	10	58.0	50	5	2	0	1	.965

Catchers - Regulars - Special

Player	Tm	G	Inn	SBA	CS	PCS	CS%	ER	CERA
Berryhill,Damon	Atl	84	661.0	91	20	5	.22	210	2.86
LaValliere,Mike	Pit	92	767.0	115	44	9	.38	253	2.97
Carter,Gary	Mon	85	665.0	136	38	3	.28	232	3.14
Scioscia,Mike	LA	108	864.2	130	43	11	.33	302	3.14
Surhoff,B.J.	Mil	109	926.0	96	39	4	.41	325	3.16
Hundley,Todd	NYN	121	892.1	122	33	7	.27	328	3.31
Pagnozzi,Tom	StL	138	1189.0	123	36	3	.29	444	3.36
Oliver,Joe	Cin	141	1199.2	134	47	10	.35	456	3.42
Olson,Greg	Atl	94	754.2	115	45	20	.39	288	3.43
Pena,Tony	Bos	132	1084.0	119	39	7	.33	420	3.49
Steinbach,Terry	Oak	124	998.2	121	53	3	.44	388	3.50
Girardi,Joe	ChN	86	651.1	78	32	4	.41	261	3.61
Manwaring,Kirt	SF	108	874.0	93	47	11	.51	354	3.65
Santiago,Benito	SD	103	885.1	115	42	15	.37	367	3.73
Karkovice,Ron	ChA	119	915.0	102	33	4	.32	383	3.77
Rodriguez,Ivan	Tex	116	982.2	110	57	6	.52	416	3.81
Alomar Jr,Sandy	Cle	88	729.2	78	35	5	.45	309	3.81
Borders,Pat	Tor	137	1160.2	167	51	3	.31	493	3.82
Hoiles,Chris	Bal	95	817.1	109	22	6	.20	348	3.83
Harper,Brian	Min	133	1114.0	170	52	16	.31	477	3.85
Macfarlane,Mike	KC	104	845.0	95	28	5	.29	369	3.93
Taubensee,Eddie	Hou	103	804.1	102	35	2	.34	357	3.99
Daulton,Darren	Phi	141	1200.2	137	49	10	.36	556	4.17
Nokes,Matt	NYA	111	903.0	141	33	8	.23	425	4.24
Ortiz,Junior	Cle	86	652.2	86	27	2	.31	322	4.44
Tettleton,Mickey	Det	113	943.0	113	39	10	.35	474	4.52
Valle,Dave	Sea	122	972.1	124	40	13	.32	506	4.68
Average	---	110	905.2	115	39	7	.34	372	3.70

Catchers - The Rest - Special

Player	Tm	G	Inn	SBA	CS	PCS	CS%	ER	CERA
Afenir,Troy	Cin	15	92.2	6	1	0	.17	28	2.72
Allanson,Andy	Mil	9	66.0	7	0	0	0	48	6.55
Bailey,Mark	SF	7	52.1	1	1	0	1.00	15	2.58
Bilardello,Dann	SD	14	94.0	24	7	1	.29	25	2.39
Bradley,Scott	Sea	1	1.0	0	0	0	0	0	0.00
Bradley,Scott	Cin	2	4.0	1	0	0	0	2	4.50
Cabrera,Francisco	Atl	1	1.0	0	0	0	0	0	0.00
Cerone,Rick	Mon	28	143.2	19	4	1	.21	72	4.51
Cochrane,Dave	Sea	21	87.0	13	3	1	.23	51	5.28
Colbert,Craig	SF	35	217.0	25	9	1	.36	96	3.98
Davis,Doug	Tex	1	1.0	0	0	0	0	0	0.00
Decker,Steve	SF	15	118.2	4	2	2	.50	51	3.87
Dempsey,Rick	Bal	8	30.0	4	0	0	0	7	2.10
Fisk,Carlton	ChA	54	429.2	61	20	4	.33	190	3.98
Fitzgerald,Mike	Cal	74	468.0	59	18	8	.31	194	3.73
Flaherty,John	Bos	34	195.1	23	7	3	.30	91	4.19
Fletcher,Darrin	Mon	69	518.0	94	24	9	.26	171	2.97
Gedman,Rich	StL	40	291.0	40	3	0	.08	112	3.46
Grotewold,Jeff	Phi	2	4.0	0	0	0	0	0	0.00
Haselman,Bill	Sea	5	33.0	3	2	0	.67	5	1.36
Heffernan,Bert	Sea	5	26.0	5	1	0	.20	21	7.27
Hemond,Scott	Oak	8	47.0	9	3	0	.33	22	4.21
Hemond,Scott	ChA	1	1.0	0	0	0	0	0	0.00
Hernandez,Carlos	LA	63	434.0	59	15	0	.25	186	3.86
Knorr,Randy	Tor	8	47.0	4	3	1	.75	27	5.17

Catchers - The Rest - Special

Player	Tm	G	Inn	SBA	CS	PCS	CS%	ER	CERA
Kreuter,Chad	Det	62	475.2	48	22	5	.46	251	4.75
Lake,Steve	Phi	17	125.2	18	4	0	.22	61	4.37
Laker,Tim	Mon	28	127.1	15	2	0	.13	45	3.18
Lampkin,Tom	SD	7	49.2	6	2	0	.33	21	3.81
Levis,Jesse	Cle	21	87.2	9	2	0	.22	41	4.21
Leyritz,Jim	NYA	18	121.2	25	10	1	.40	61	4.51
Lopez,Javier	Atl	9	41.0	9	1	0	.11	12	2.63
Marzano,John	Bos	18	134.0	20	5	0	.25	57	3.83
Mayne,Brent	KC	62	458.1	44	18	6	.41	168	3.30
McGinnis,Russ	Tex	10	62.0	9	2	0	.22	36	5.23
McIntosh,Tim	Mil	14	77.0	12	2	0	.17	28	3.27
McNamara,Jim	SF	30	198.2	16	5	0	.31	70	3.17
Melvin,Bob	KC	21	144.0	20	6	1	.30	76	4.75
Mercedes,Henry	Oak	9	16.0	3	0	0	0	6	3.38
Merullo,Matt	ChA	16	107.0	13	3	2	.23	39	3.28
Myers,Greg	Tor	18	145.1	27	7	1	.26	85	5.26
Myers,Greg	Cal	8	44.0	8	1	1	.13	30	6.14
Natal,Bob	Mon	4	14.0	3	0	0	0	10	6.43
Nilsson,Dave	Mil	46	388.0	33	12	0	.36	155	3.80
O'Brien,Charlie	NYN	64	427.1	66	30	5	.45	197	4.15
Orton,John	Cal	43	344.1	40	18	6	.45	145	3.79
Parent,Mark	Bal	16	100.0	11	4	0	.36	48	4.32
Parks,Derek	Min	7	24.0	6	1	0	.17	7	2.63
Parrish,Lance	Cal	22	177.0	32	10	3	.31	91	4.63
Parrish,Lance	Sea	34	239.0	50	13	2	.26	93	3.50
Pedre,Jorge	ChN	4	6.2	0	0	0	0	4	5.40
Petralli,Geno	Tex	54	367.2	42	20	1	.48	189	4.63
Piazza,Mike	LA	16	139.1	14	4	0	.29	57	3.68
Pratt,Todd	Phi	11	97.2	9	0	0	0	38	3.50
Prince,Tom	Pit	19	114.0	12	4	1	.33	46	3.63
Quirk,Jamie	Oak	59	384.2	61	20	1	.33	183	4.28
Reed,Jeff	Cin	6	38.0	5	1	1	.20	26	6.16
Rowland,Rich	Det	3	17.0	2	0	0	0	11	5.82
Russell,John	Tex	4	19.0	5	2	0	.40	7	3.32
Santovenia,Nelson	ChA	2	9.0	1	1	0	1.00	11	11.00
Sasser,Mackey	NYN	27	127.0	27	4	0	.15	66	4.68
Servais,Scott	Hou	73	524.0	63	15	3	.24	197	3.38
Sinatro,Matt	Sea	18	86.2	7	3	2	.43	54	5.61
Slaught,Don	Pit	79	598.2	70	25	6	.36	252	3.79
Sprague,Ed	Tor	15	87.0	8	1	0	.13	22	2.28
Stanley,Mike	NYA	55	427.2	60	19	2	.32	195	4.10
Stephens,Ray	Tex	6	28.0	5	3	1	.60	17	5.46
Tackett,Jeff	Bal	64	516.2	51	18	1	.35	214	3.73
Tingley,Ron	Cal	69	412.2	51	23	4	.45	157	3.42
Tucker,Scooter	Hou	19	131.0	18	4	1	.22	52	3.57
Villanueva,Hector	ChN	28	222.0	32	11	1	.34	66	2.68
Walters,Dan	SD	55	432.0	65	18	2	.28	168	3.50
Webster,Lenny	Min	49	315.0	38	9	3	.24	116	3.31
Wedge,Eric	Bos	5	35.0	4	0	0	0	17	4.37
Wilkins,Rick	ChN	73	589.0	78	29	3	.37	223	3.41
Willard,Jerry	Atl	1	2.0	0	0	0	0	0	0.00
Wilson,Dan	Cin	9	57.0	7	3	0	.43	18	2.84
Wrona,Rick	Cin	10	58.0	4	2	0	.50	28	4.34

Special Pitcher Stats

With the exception of requests for Pitcher Projections, our most frequent Major League Handbook suggestions have always been for yearly pitcher hitting and fielding totals. You asked for it, so here it is. And as you can always expect from STATS, we're giving you more than you asked for. We decided to throw in career hitting, as well as 1992 data on holding runners. Fans of the number zero will love this new section! Because American League pitchers don't hit there are enough goose eggs running loose in here to make even old Fay Vincent consider the DH (not that it matters **what** Fay thinks anymore). You will find plenty of numerical action in Matt Young's portion of the fielding section, though. His six errors in 16 chances last year is a new low, even for him. (Maybe Matt's kids can buy Dad a Pitchback for Christmas.)

The only technicality to explain is that the Caught Stealing Percentages in this section **do** include the Pitcher Caught Stealings, unlike in the Special Catchers section.

Pitchers Hitting, Fielding and Holding Runners

Pitcher	1992 Hitting						Career Hitting										1992 Fielding and Holding Runners										
	Avg	AB	H	HR	RBI	SH	Avg	AB	H	2B	3B	HR	RBI	BB	SO	SH	G	Inn	PO	A	E	DP	Pct.	SBA	CS	PCS	CS%
Abbott, Jim	.000	0	0	0	0	0	.000	0	0	0	0	0	0	0	0	0	29	211.0	11	34	0	1	1.000	27	4	9	.48
Abbott, Kyle	.069	29	2	0	2	6	.069	29	2	1	0	0	2	1	18	6	31	133.1	3	16	0	0	1.000	16	5	2	.44
Abbott, Paul	.000	0	0	0	0	0	.000	0	0	0	0	0	0	0	0	0	6	11.0	2	3	0	1	1.000	2	0	0	.00
Acker, Jim	.000	0	0	0	0	0	.167	54	9	1	0	0	1	2	32	0	17	30.2	0	5	0	0	1.000	2	1	0	.50
Agosto, Juan	.000	4	0	0	0	0	.100	20	2	0	0	0	0	1	7	1	39	50.0	1	15	0	1	1.000	6	0	0	.00
Aguilera, Rick	.000	0	0	0	0	0	.203	138	28	3	0	3	11	6	37	16	64	66.2	2	5	0	0	1.000	5	0	0	.00
Aldred, Scott	.000	0	0	0	0	0	.000	0	0	0	0	0	0	0	0	0	16	65.0	5	10	0	1	1.000	11	2	2	.36
Alexander, Gerald	.000	0	0	0	0	0	.000	0	0	0	0	0	0	0	0	0	3	1.2	1	0	0	0	1.000	0	0	0	.00
Alvarez, Wilson	.000	0	0	0	0	0	.000	0	0	0	0	0	0	0	0	0	34	100.1	4	14	2	1	.900	17	3	5	.47
Andersen, Larry	.000	1	0	0	0	0	.108	37	4	0	0	0	0	2	15	4	34	35.0	4	5	1	0	.900	8	1	0	.13
Appier, Kevin	.000	0	0	0	0	0	.000	0	0	0	0	0	0	0	0	0	30	208.1	19	21	1	4	.976	27	9	0	.33
Aquino, Luis	.000	0	0	0	0	0	.000	0	0	0	0	0	0	0	0	0	15	67.2	4	16	0	1	1.000	4	2	1	.75
Armstrong, Jack	.000	0	0	0	0	0	.092	119	11	1	0	0	5	2	54	22	35	166.2	13	25	4	2	.905	24	9	0	.38
Arnsberg, Brad	.000	0	0	0	0	0	.000	0	0	0	0	0	0	0	0	0	8	10.2	2	0	0	0	1.000	0	0	0	.00
Ashby, Andy	.091	11	1	0	1	2	.067	23	2	0	0	0	1	0	16	3	10	37.0	1	6	0	0	1.000	6	2	0	.33
Assenmacher, Paul	.000	4	0	0	0	0	.059	34	2	1	0	0	0	5	12	7	70	68.0	3	6	0	1	1.000	11	1	1	.18
Astacio, Pedro	.125	24	3	0	1	5	.125	24	3	0	0	0	1	0	14	5	11	82.0	4	13	2	1	.895	8	3	0	.38
Austin, Jim	.000	0	0	0	0	0	.000	0	0	0	0	0	0	0	0	0	47	58.1	2	2	0	0	1.000	6	4	0	.67
Avery, Steve	.171	76	13	0	4	9	.184	185	34	3	2	0	6	7	60	16	35	233.2	16	34	3	1	.943	56	8	6	.25
Ayala, Bobby	.000	9	0	0	0	1	.000	9	0	0	0	0	0	0	6	1	5	29.0	3	8	0	2	1.000	5	3	0	.60
Ayrault, Bob	.000	0	0	0	0	0	.000	0	0	0	0	0	0	0	0	0	30	43.1	1	8	0	0	1.000	3	0	0	.00
Bailes, Scott	.000	0	0	0	0	0	.000	0	0	0	0	0	0	0	0	0	32	38.2	1	4	0	1	1.000	5	1	0	.20
Baller, Jay	.000	0	0	0	0	0	.071	14	1	0	0	0	0	0	7	2	8	11.0	1	1	0	0	1.000	5	2	0	.40
Bankhead, Scott	.222	9	2	0	0	2	.222	9	2	0	0	0	0	0	7	2	54	70.2	5	2	2	0	.778	5	0	0	.00
Banks, Willie	.000	0	0	0	0	0	.000	0	0	0	0	0	0	0	0	0	16	71.0	9	5	0	0	1.000	12	4	0	.33
Bannister, Floyd	.000	0	0	0	0	0	.175	80	14	1	0	0	1	2	26	11	36	37.0	4	5	0	0	1.000	4	0	1	.25
Barnes, Brian	.276	29	8	0	1	6	.138	87	12	0	0	0	2	9	41	9	20	100.0	6	17	0	2	1.000	21	3	4	.33
Barton, Shawn	.000	0	0	0	0	0	.000	0	0	0	0	0	0	0	0	0	14	12.1	2	3	1	0	.833	3	1	2	1.00
Batista, Miguel	.000	0	0	0	0	0	.000	0	0	0	0	0	0	0	0	0	1	2.0	0	0	0	0	.000	0	0	0	.00
Beck, Rod	.500	2	1	0	0	2	.500	2	1	0	0	0	0	0	1	2	65	92.0	2	13	1	0	.938	6	4	0	.67
Belcher, Tim	.105	76	8	1	4	7	.112	322	36	7	0	2	18	2	127	38	35	227.2	23	27	1	3	.980	17	11	0	.65
Belinda, Stan	.667	3	2	0	2	0	.133	15	2	1	0	0	3	2	8	3	59	71.1	4	4	0	1	1.000	14	2	0	.14
Bell, Eric	.000	0	0	0	0	0	.000	0	0	0	0	0	0	0	0	0	7	15.1	0	5	0	0	1.000	5	1	0	.20
Benes, Andy	.149	67	10	1	5	5	.113	213	24	3	0	3	10	13	95	18	34	231.1	14	34	1	1	.980	31	11	0	.35
Berenguer, Juan	.000	2	0	0	0	0	.083	24	2	0	0	0	0	2	9	4	47	78.0	4	9	1	2	.929	10	1	1	.20
Bielecki, Mike	.125	24	3	0	0	4	.079	267	21	0	0	0	12	11	135	34	19	80.2	5	14	0	1	1.000	10	2	0	.20
Birkbeck, Mike	.000	2	0	0	0	0	.000	2	0	0	0	0	0	0	0	0	1	7.0	3	1	1	1	.800	1	0	0	.00
Black, Bud	.056	54	3	0	2	10	.128	125	16	4	0	0	8	2	36	19	28	177.0	5	36	0	4	1.000	21	8	6	.67
Blair, Willie	.059	17	1	0	0	1	.059	17	1	0	0	0	0	1	14	1	29	78.2	4	7	2	0	.846	10	4	0	.40
Blyleven, Bert	.000	0	0	0	0	0	.131	451	59	7	0	0	25	5	193	56	25	133.0	5	13	0	1	1.000	14	4	0	.29
Boddicker, Mike	.000	0	0	0	0	0	.000	0	0	0	0	0	0	0	0	0	29	86.2	12	13	1	1	.962	15	2	0	.13
Boever, Joe	.000	7	0	0	0	0	.125	16	2	0	0	0	0	0	3	0	81	111.1	4	19	2	2	.920	12	5	0	.42
Bohanon, Brian	.000	0	0	0	0	0	.000	0	0	0	0	0	0	0	0	0	18	45.2	5	3	1	0	.889	3	2	1	1.00
Bolton, Tom	.000	14	0	0	0	1	.000	14	0	0	0	0	0	0	5	1	37	75.1	3	14	1	1	.944	6	1	0	.17
Bones, Ricky	.000	0	0	0	0	0	.077	13	1	0	0	0	1	2	5	4	31	163.1	17	13	2	2	.938	15	2	0	.13
Borbon, Pedro	.000	0	0	0	0	0	.000	0	0	0	0	0	0	0	0	0	2	1.1	0	0	0	0	.000	0	0	0	.00
Bosio, Chris	.000	0	0	0	0	0	.000	0	0	0	0	0	0	0	0	0	33	231.1	20	26	0	5	1.000	19	7	0	.37
Boskie, Shawn	.185	27	5	0	1	3	.192	104	20	4	1	1	6	5	32	8	23	91.2	8	21	1	2	.967	3	1	0	.33
Bottenfield, Kent	.375	8	3	0	0	1	.375	8	3	0	0	0	0	0	3	1	10	32.1	2	2	0	0	1.000	3	0	0	.00
Boucher, Denis	.000	0	0	0	0	0	.000	0	0	0	0	0	0	0	0	0	8	41.0	3	3	0	0	1.000	1	1	0	1.00
Bowen, Ryan	.111	9	1	0	0	0	.161	31	5	1	0	0	0	3	14	1	11	33.2	0	3	0	0	1.000	8	3	0	.38
Brantley, Cliff	.214	14	3	0	1	7	.136	22	3	0	0	0	1	1	8	9	28	76.1	6	14	3	1	.870	15	5	0	.33
Brantley, Jeff	.111	9	1	0	0	0	.152	33	5	1	0	0	2	1	12	8	56	91.2	4	9	0	0	1.000	5	1	0	.20
Brink, Brad	.083	12	1	0	0	1	.083	12	1	0	0	0	0	0	5	1	8	41.1	0	2	1	0	.667	5	2	0	.40
Briscoe, John	.000	0	0	0	0	0	.000	0	0	0	0	0	0	0	0	0	2	7.0	0	1	1	0	.500	1	1	0	1.00
Brocail, Doug	.200	5	1	0	0	0	.200	5	1	0	0	0	0	0	0	0	3	14.0	1	1	1	0	.667	0	0	0	.00
Brown, Keith	.000	2	0	0	0	1	.000	2	0	0	0	0	0	0	4	2	8	2.0	0	1	1	0	.500	0	0	0	.00
Brown, Kevin	.000	0	0	0	0	0	.000	1	0	0	0	0	0	0	0	0	35	265.2	36	36	8	4	.900	19	11	1	.63
Brown, Kevin D.	.000	0	0	0	0	0	.000	0	0	0	0	0	0	0	0	0	2	3.0	0	1	0	0	1.000	0	0	0	.00
Browning, Tom	.226	31	7	0	2	2	.149	570	85	12	1	1	28	23	168	66	16	87.0	6	14	1	3	.952	12	1	0	.08
Bullinger, Jim	.250	20	5	1	2	1	.250	20	5	1	0	0	2	1	7	1	39	85.0	17	17	0	2	1.000	10	2	0	.20
Burba, Dave	.067	15	1	0	1	3	.067	15	1	0	0	0	1	1	8	3	23	70.2	3	8	0	1	1.000	5	1	0	.20
Burke, Tim	.000	0	0	0	0	0	.045	44	2	0	0	0	1	4	24	3	38	43.1	3	12	1	0	.938	6	1	0	.17
Burkett, John	.018	55	1	0	2	8	.052	174	9	2	0	0	6	12	86	25	32	189.2	11	18	1	0	.967	24	6	1	.29
Burns, Todd	.000	0	0	0	0	0	.000	0	0	0	0	0	0	0	0	0	35	103.0	5	8	1	1	.929	8	7	0	.88
Butcher, Mike	.000	0	0	0	0	0	.000	0	0	0	0	0	0	0	0	0	19	27.2	0	3	0	0	1.000	3	0	0	.00
Cadaret, Greg	.000	0	0	0	0	0	.000	0	0	0	0	0	0	0	0	0	46	103.2	5	17	0	2	1.000	26	2	5	.27
Campbell, Kevin	.000	0	0	0	0	0	.000	0	0	0	0	0	0	0	0	0	32	65.0	1	6	0	0	1.000	7	4	1	.71
Campbell, Mike	.000	0	0	0	0	0	.000	0	0	0	0	0	0	0	0	0	3	3.2	0	0	0	0	.000	1	0	0	.00
Candelaria, John	.000	0	0	0	0	0	.174	596	104	20	3	1	48	44	162	43	50	25.1	0	5	0	0	1.000	2	0	0	.00
Candiotti, Tom	.107	56	6	0	1	12	.107	56	6	1	0	0	1	1	9	12	32	203.2	16	32	1	3	.980	35	5	0	.14
Carman, Don	.000	0	0	0	0	0	.057	209	12	0	0	0	5	2	75	28	2	2.1	0	0	0	0	.000	0	0	0	.00

	1992 Hitting						Career Hitting										1992 Fielding and Holding Runners										
Pitcher	Avg	AB	H	HR	RBI	SH	Avg	AB	H	2B	3B	HR	RBI	BB	SO	SH	G	Inn	PO	A	E	DP	Pct.	SBA	CS	PCS	CS%
Carpenter, Cris	.333	3	1	0	2	1	.267	30	8	0	0	0	5	0	6	6	73	88.0	7	10	0	1	1.000	14	3	0	.21
Carter, Larry	.200	10	2	0	0	1	.200	10	2	0	0	0	0	0	5	1	6	33.0	4	1	0	0	1.000	2	1	0	.50
Casian, Larry	.000	0	0	0	0	0	.000	0	0	0	0	0	0	0	0	0	6	6.2	1	1	0	0	1.000	0	0	0	.00
Castillo, Frank	.092	65	6	0	1	5	.110	100	11	0	0	0	2	5	34	11	33	205.1	10	28	1	2	.974	27	9	0	.33
Chapin, Darrin	.000	0	0	0	0	0	.000	0	0	0	0	0	0	0	0	0	1	2.0	0	0	0	0	.000	0	0	0	.00
Chiamparino, Scott	.000	0	0	0	0	0	.000	0	0	0	0	0	0	0	0	0	4	25.1	1	2	2	0	.600	2	1	0	.50
Christopher, Mike	.000	0	0	0	0	0	.000	0	0	0	0	0	0	0	0	0	10	18.0	1	2	0	0	1.000	4	2	0	.50
Clark, Mark	.139	36	5	0	1	4	.116	43	5	0	0	0	1	0	20	5	20	113.1	2	13	1	0	.938	19	2	0	.11
Clemens, Roger	.000	0	0	0	0	0	.000	0	0	0	0	0	0	0	0	0	32	246.2	19	25	1	0	.978	36	11	1	.33
Clements, Pat	.000	1	0	0	0	0	.059	17	1	0	0	0	0	0	10	1	49	48.1	3	14	0	2	1.000	6	1	0	.17
Cole, Victor	.000	4	0	0	0	1	.000	4	0	0	0	0	0	0	0	1	8	23.0	3	3	0	0	1.000	3	1	0	.33
Combs, Pat	.125	8	1	0	2	1	.147	95	14	4	0	0	4	6	36	8	4	18.2	0	6	0	0	1.000	5	0	1	.20
Cone, David	.092	65	6	0	4	7	.154	395	61	8	0	0	20	16	86	36	35	249.2	18	22	2	1	.952	59	10	0	.17
Cook, Dennis	.000	0	0	0	0	0	.250	96	24	2	1	7	3	12	8	32	158.0	3	15	1	2	.947	18	6	4	.56
Cooke, Steve	.333	3	1	0	1	2	.333	3	1	0	0	0	1	0	0	2	11	23.0	0	3	0	0	1.000	0	0	0	.00
Cormier, Rheal	.102	59	6	0	2	10	.138	80	11	0	2	0	3	0	18	11	31	186.0	9	34	0	2	1.000	15	3	1	.27
Corsi, Jim	.000	0	0	0	0	0	.000	1	0	0	0	0	0	0	1	0	32	44.0	5	10	0	0	1.000	10	5	0	.50
Cox, Danny	.071	14	1	0	1	0	.109	359	39	3	1	0	12	13	152	41	25	62.2	7	8	2	1	.882	6	1	0	.17
Crews, Tim	.286	7	2	0	0	0	.136	22	3	0	0	0	1	1	12	1	49	78.0	5	10	1	0	.938	18	6	0	.33
Crim, Chuck	.000	0	0	0	0	0	.000	0	0	0	0	0	0	0	0	0	57	87.0	7	12	1	0	.950	12	4	1	.42
Darling, Ron	.000	0	0	0	0	0	.145	525	76	21	2	2	21	15	175	65	34	206.1	11	26	4	2	.902	23	11	2	.57
Darwin, Danny	.000	0	0	0	0	0	.124	193	24	5	2	1	16	5	103	8	51	161.1	9	13	1	2	.957	20	6	0	.30
Davis, Mark	.000	1	0	0	0	0	.153	163	25	3	4	1	9	8	53	23	72	113.1	5	2	6	1	.889	9	1	0	.11
Davis, Storm	.000	0	0	0	0	0	.063	16	1	0	0	0	0	0	10	1	48	89.1	3	14	0	3	1.000	11	2	0	.18
DeLeon, Jose	.115	26	3	0	1	5	.092	413	38	1	1	0	9	15	166	50	32	117.1	7	10	0	1	1.000	17	5	0	.29
DeLucia, Rich	.000	0	0	0	0	0	.000	0	0	0	0	0	0	0	0	0	30	83.2	8	6	1	0	.933	7	2	0	.29
Deshaies, Jim	.207	29	6	0	0	5	.090	367	33	0	0	0	12	23	182	43	15	96.0	2	21	0	0	1.000	16	5	5	.63
Dewey, Mark	.000	1	0	0	0	0	.000	2	0	0	0	0	0	1	2	0	20	33.1	3	5	0	0	1.000	4	3	0	.75
Dibble, Rob	.400	5	2	0	1	0	.083	24	2	0	0	0	0	0	5	0	63	70.1	5	3	1	1	.889	10	2	0	.20
DiPino, Frank	1.000	1	1	0	0	0	.125	72	9	2	0	0	2	1	34	1	9	11.0	1	3	0	0	1.000	0	0	0	.00
Doherty, John	.000	0	0	0	0	0	.000	0	0	0	0	0	0	0	0	0	47	116.0	10	19	1	4	.967	8	4	0	.50
Dopson, John	.000	0	0	0	0	0	.055	55	3	1	0	0	1	3	34	4	25	141.1	19	18	1	1	.974	24	7	0	.29
Downs, Kelly	.000	14	0	0	0	2	.123	211	26	3	1	0	11	7	76	21	37	144.1	9	11	0	0	.952	25	8	0	.32
Drabek, Doug	.157	89	14	0	6	8	.160	469	75	11	2	1	26	13	144	37	34	256.2	29	36	3	5	.956	32	14	0	.44
Drahman, Brian	.000	0	0	0	0	0	.000	0	0	0	0	0	0	0	0	0	5	7.0	1	0	1	0	.500	1	0	0	.00
Dunne, Mike	.000	0	0	0	0	0	.101	109	11	0	0	0	6	9	34	14	4	12.2	1	2	0	1	1.000	3	0	0	.00
Eckersley, Dennis	.000	0	0	0	0	0	.133	180	24	3	0	3	12	9	84	5	69	80.0	3	10	0	1	1.000	10	1	0	.10
Edens, Tom	.000	0	0	0	0	0	.000	0	0	0	0	0	0	0	3	0	52	76.1	8	4	0	0	1.000	20	3	2	.25
Eichhorn, Mark	.000	0	0	0	0	0	.000	2	0	0	0	0	0	0	0	0	64	86.2	5	19	1	0	.960	8	2	0	.23
Eiland, Dave	.111	9	1	1	2	1	.111	9	1	0	0	1	2	0	4	1	7	27.0	1	5	0	0	1.000	4	0	0	.00
Eldred, Cal	.000	0	0	0	0	0	.000	0	0	0	0	0	0	0	0	0	14	100.1	4	12	1	0	.941	12	4	0	.33
Embree, Alan	.000	0	0	0	0	0	.000	0	0	0	0	0	0	0	0	0	4	18.0	1	0	1	0	.500	3	0	0	.00
Erickson, Scott	.000	0	0	0	0	0	.000	0	0	0	0	0	0	0	0	0	32	212.0	18	34	1	3	.981	30	7	0	.23
Farr, Steve	.000	0	0	0	0	0	.000	0	0	0	0	0	0	0	0	0	50	52.0	2	4	2	1	.750	7	0	0	.00
Fassero, Jeff	.143	7	1	0	0	1	.100	10	1	0	0	0	0	1	5	3	70	85.2	1	15	0	0	1.000	14	2	0	.14
Fernandez, Alex	.000	0	0	0	0	0	.000	0	0	0	0	0	0	0	0	0	29	187.2	10	33	2	4	.956	19	4	0	.21
Fernandez, Sid	.203	74	15	0	0	7	.198	464	92	14	2	1	29	10	170	56	32	214.2	4	21	1	1	.962	26	6	3	.35
Fetters, Mike	.000	0	0	0	0	0	.000	0	0	0	0	0	0	0	0	0	50	62.2	3	11	0	1	1.000	7	3	0	.43
Filer, Tom	.000	3	0	0	0	0	.067	15	1	1	0	0	0	0	8	1	9	22.0	3	4	1	0	.875	4	1	0	.25
Finley, Chuck	.000	0	0	0	0	0	.000	0	0	0	0	0	0	0	0	0	31	204.1	3	17	3	3	.870	39	15	3	.46
Fireovid, Steve	.000	0	0	0	0	0	.143	7	1	0	0	0	0	0	4	0	3	6.2	1	2	0	2	1.000	2	2	0	1.00
Fisher, Brian	.000	0	0	0	0	0	.124	105	13	2	0	2	10	8	54	7	22	91.1	5	13	1	0	.947	9	3	0	.33
Flanagan, Mike	.000	0	0	0	0	0	.000	0	0	0	0	0	0	0	0	0	42	34.2	6	5	1	2	.923	2	0	0	.00
Fleming, Dave	.000	0	0	0	0	0	.000	0	0	0	0	0	0	0	0	0	33	228.1	4	33	1	4	.974	32	9	5	.44
Fortugno, Tim	.000	0	0	0	0	0	.000	0	0	0	0	0	0	0	0	0	14	41.2	0	4	0	0	1.000	7	1	1	.29
Fossas, Tony	.000	0	0	0	0	0	.000	0	0	0	0	0	0	0	0	0	60	29.2	2	6	0	0	1.000	6	1	1	.33
Foster, Steve	.200	5	1	0	0	0	.200	5	1	0	0	0	0	0	1	0	31	50.0	5	11	0	1	1.000	2	1	0	.50
Franco, John	.000	1	0	0	0	0	.115	26	3	0	0	0	0	1	0	8	3	31	33.0	2	11	0	2	1.000	5	1	2	.60
Freeman, Marvin	.500	4	2	0	0	0	.125	40	5	0	0	0	0	0	25	4	58	64.1	4	5	2	0	.818	12	5	0	.42
Frey, Steve	.000	0	0	0	0	0	.000	3	0	0	0	0	0	1	2	0	51	45.1	4	5	0	1	1.000	6	1	2	.50
Frohwirth, Todd	.000	0	0	0	0	0	.000	2	0	0	0	0	0	0	2	2	65	106.0	8	24	1	4	.970	13	2	0	.15
Gardner, Mike	.000	0	0	0	0	0	.000	0	0	0	0	0	0	0	0	0	28	130.2	13	15	1	1	.966	5	1	1	.40
Gardner, Mark	.140	50	7	0	2	8	.116	155	18	1	2	0	7	4	63	21	33	179.2	14	22	2	0	.947	40	11	0	.28
Gibson, Paul	.000	6	0	0	0	1	.000	6	0	0	0	0	0	1	3	1	43	62.0	2	6	0	1	1.000	10	2	1	.30
Glavine, Tom	.247	77	19	0	7	9	.185	356	66	5	2	0	27	26	92	43	33	225.0	18	32	0	2	1.000	23	6	4	.43
Gleaton, Jerry Don	.000	2	0	0	0	0	.000	2	0	0	0	0	0	0	1	1	23	31.2	0	6	0	0	1.000	6	2	1	.50
Gooden, Dwight	.264	72	19	1	9	4	.198	648	128	13	3	5	54	13	119	75	30	206.0	9	38	6	1	.887	33	10	1	.33
Gordon, Tom	.000	0	0	0	0	0	.000	0	0	0	0	0	0	0	0	0	40	117.2	11	14	1	1	.962	12	6	1	.58
Gossage, Goose	.000	0	0	0	0	0	.106	85	9	1	0	0	2	4	37	4	29	38.0	2	4	0	0	1.000	6	2	0	.33
Gott, Jim	.500	2	1	0	0	0	.183	71	13	2	0	4	5	1	39	5	68	88.0	11	15	0	0	1.000	11	5	0	.45
Gozzo, Mauro	.000	0	0	0	0	0	.000	0	0	0	0	0	0	0	0	0	2	1.2	0	0	0	0	.000	0	0	0	.00
Grahe, Joe	.000	0	0	0	0	0	.000	0	0	0	0	0	0	0	0	0	46	94.2	12	13	3	1	.893	12	5	0	.42
Grant, Mark	.000	0	0	0	0	0	.067	104	7	0	0	0	2	10	46	14	23	81.0	6	7	3	0	.813	6	2	0	.33
Greene, Tommy	.125	24	3	0	0	0	.214	117	25	3	0	2	7	4	31	6	13	64.1	3	7	3	0	.769	14	1	0	.07

242

	1992 Hitting					Career Hitting										1992 Fielding and Holding Runners										
Pitcher	Avg	AB	H	HR	RBI	SH	Avg	AB	H	2B	3B	HR	RBI	BB	SO	SH	G	Inn	PO	A	E	DP	Pct.	SBA	CS	PCS	CS%
Groom, Buddy	.000	0	0	0	0	0	.000	0	0	0	0	0	0	0	0	0	12	38.2	0	6	0	0	1.000	2	1	1	1.00
Gross, Kevin	.095	63	6	0	0	3	.157	548	86	17	1	4	26	23	226	54	34	204.2	11	25	1	1	.973	27	8	1	.33
Gross, Kip	1.000	2	2	0	1	1	.167	24	4	0	0	0	2	0	6	4	16	23.2	1	7	0	0	1.000	3	1	0	.33
Gubicza, Mark	.000	0	0	0	0	0	.000	0	0	0	0	0	0	0	0	0	18	111.1	10	12	0	2	1.000	8	3	1	.50
Guetterman, Lee	.000	2	0	0	0	0	.000	2	0	0	0	0	0	0	2	0	58	66.0	4	8	0	1	1.000	6	1	0	.17
Gullickson, Bill	.000	0	0	0	0	0	.141	576	81	16	0	3	27	20	152	63	34	221.2	21	26	1	3	.979	28	8	0	.29
Gunderson, Eric	.000	0	0	0	0	0	.000	6	0	0	0	0	0	0	4	0	9	9.1	1	1	0	0	1.000	4	2	1	.75
Guthrie, Mark	.000	0	0	0	0	0	.000	0	0	0	0	0	0	0	0	0	54	75.0	4	6	1	0	.909	8	0	2	.25
Guzman, Johnny	.000	0	0	0	0	0	.000	0	0	0	0	0	0	0	0	0	2	3.0	0	0	0	0	.000	0	0	0	.00
Guzman, Jose	.000	0	0	0	0	0	.000	0	0	0	0	0	0	0	0	0	33	224.0	16	22	1	3	.974	31	15	0	.48
Guzman, Juan	.000	0	0	0	0	0	.000	0	0	0	0	0	0	0	0	0	28	180.2	13	11	0	1	1.000	35	8	0	.23
Haas, Dave	.000	0	0	0	0	0	.000	0	0	0	0	0	0	0	0	0	12	61.2	3	8	0	0	1.000	2	1	0	.50
Habyan, John	.000	0	0	0	0	0	.000	0	0	0	0	0	0	0	0	0	56	72.2	3	15	0	1	1.000	5	0	0	.00
Hammond, Chris	.136	44	6	1	4	3	.222	81	18	4	0	1	5	8	31	4	28	147.1	9	22	2	1	.939	11	3	1	.36
Haney, Chris	.222	9	2	0	3	1	.114	35	4	0	0	0	4	0	4	4	16	80.0	2	6	0	0	1.000	13	3	1	.31
Hanson, Erik	.000	0	0	0	0	0	.000	0	0	0	0	0	0	0	0	0	31	186.2	14	23	1	2	.974	19	3	1	.21
Harkey, Mike	.267	15	4	0	0	0	.241	87	21	4	0	0	4	2	24	10	7	38.0	1	6	0	1	1.000	6	3	0	.50
Harnisch, Pete	.164	67	11	0	8	5	.132	129	17	6	0	0	12	6	33	12	34	206.2	16	15	2	1	.939	33	6	0	.18
Harris, Gene	.333	3	1	0	0	0	.250	4	1	0	0	0	0	0	2	1	22	30.1	1	4	3	0	.625	4	0	0	.00
Harris, Greg	.000	0	0	0	0	0	.215	65	14	2	2	0	4	1	28	2	70	107.2	3	16	2	0	.905	9	5	1	.67
Harris, Greg W.	.129	31	4	0	1	5	.086	105	9	1	1	0	3	8	48	17	20	118.0	10	21	5	0	.861	23	4	1	.22
Hartley, Mike	.000	4	0	0	0	0	.043	23	1	0	0	0	0	0	10	3	46	55.0	2	6	1	0	.889	10	2	0	.20
Hartsock, Jeff	.000	2	0	0	0	0	.000	2	0	0	0	0	0	0	0	0	4	9.1	0	2	0	0	1.000	3	2	0	.67
Harvey, Bryan	.000	0	0	0	0	0	.000	0	0	0	0	0	0	0	0	0	25	28.2	0	1	0	0	1.000	2	0	0	.00
Hathaway, Hilly	.000	0	0	0	0	0	.000	0	0	0	0	0	0	0	0	0	2	5.2	0	0	0	0	.000	0	0	0	.00
Heaton, Neal	.000	0	0	0	0	0	.171	187	32	3	0	0	12	6	51	15	32	42.0	5	2	1	0	.875	9	0	0	.00
Henke, Tom	.000	0	0	0	0	0	.000	0	0	0	0	0	0	0	0	0	56	54.2	2	2	0	0	1.000	3	1	0	.33
Henneman, Mike	.000	0	0	0	0	0	.000	1	0	0	0	0	0	0	1	0	60	77.1	9	9	1	1	.947	3	1	0	.33
Henry, Butch	.148	54	8	1	7	5	.148	54	8	0	0	1	7	1	10	5	28	165.2	13	30	3	2	.935	17	3	4	.41
Henry, Doug	.000	0	0	0	0	0	.000	0	0	0	0	0	0	0	0	0	68	65.0	11	4	0	2	1.000	7	3	0	.43
Henry, Dwayne	.250	4	1	0	0	0	.200	5	1	0	0	0	0	0	4	0	60	83.2	5	13	2	0	.900	8	2	0	.25
Hentgen, Pat	.000	0	0	0	0	0	.000	0	0	0	0	0	0	0	0	0	28	50.1	0	4	0	1	1.000	5	0	0	.00
Heredia, Gil	.111	9	1	0	0	1	.250	16	4	0	0	0	0	1	2	1	20	44.2	0	5	0	0	1.000	8	3	0	.38
Hernandez, Jeremy	.000	2	0	0	0	0	.000	4	0	0	0	0	0	0	1	0	26	36.2	2	6	0	1	1.000	4	1	0	.25
Hernandez, Roberto	.000	0	0	0	0	0	.000	0	0	0	0	0	0	0	0	0	43	71.0	7	4	1	2	.917	8	4	0	.50
Hernandez, Xavier	.000	9	0	0	0	0	.045	22	1	0	0	0	0	2	13	1	77	111.0	9	7	1	0	.941	14	4	0	.29
Hershiser, Orel	.221	68	15	0	5	6	.196	555	109	22	2	0	36	19	130	78	33	210.2	28	42	3	2	.959	20	6	1	.35
Hesketh, Joe	.000	0	0	0	0	0	.070	86	6	0	0	0	2	10	58	9	30	148.2	6	22	4	1	.875	21	1	3	.19
Hibbard, Greg	.000	0	0	0	0	0	.000	0	0	0	0	0	0	0	0	0	31	176.0	6	36	3	4	.933	15	5	1	.40
Hickerson, Bryan	.000	4	0	0	0	0	.000	16	0	0	0	0	0	0	9	1	61	87.1	1	5	0	0	1.000	7	4	2	.86
Hill, Ken	.177	62	11	1	4	10	.150	193	29	4	1	1	11	15	51	30	33	218.0	21	36	4	3	.934	38	7	1	.21
Hill, Milt	.000	0	0	0	0	0	.000	1	0	0	0	0	0	0	1	0	14	20.0	3	2	0	0	1.000	1	0	0	.00
Hillegas, Shawn	.000	0	0	0	0	0	.069	29	2	0	0	0	0	3	16	3	26	86.0	7	5	3	0	.800	22	6	0	.27
Hillman, Eric	.077	13	1	0	0	5	.077	13	1	0	0	0	0	0	7	5	11	52.1	1	7	0	0	1.000	9	3	2	.56
Hitchcock, Sterling	.000	0	0	0	0	0	.000	0	0	0	0	0	0	0	0	0	3	13.0	0	2	0	0	1.000	2	0	1	.50
Hollins, Jessie	.000	0	0	0	0	0	.000	0	0	0	0	0	0	0	0	0	4	4.2	1	0	0	0	1.000	0	0	0	.00
Holmes, Darren	.000	0	0	0	0	0	.000	0	0	0	0	0	0	0	0	0	41	42.1	5	4	1	1	.900	5	1	0	.20
Honeycutt, Rick	.000	0	0	0	0	0	.133	181	24	3	0	0	8	16	43	28	54	39.0	3	3	1	0	.857	5	1	0	.20
Horsman, Vince	.000	0	0	0	0	0	.000	0	0	0	0	0	0	0	0	0	58	43.1	1	5	0	0	1.000	2	2	0	1.00
Hough, Charlie	.000	0	0	0	0	0	.208	130	27	4	0	1	12	2	24	10	27	176.1	7	21	0	1	1.000	20	2	1	.15
Howe, Steve	.000	0	0	0	0	0	.074	27	2	0	0	0	0	2	10	1	20	22.0	2	7	1	0	.900	8	1	0	.13
Howell, Jay	.000	0	0	0	0	0	.000	9	0	0	0	0	0	1	1	2	41	46.2	6	7	0	0	1.000	8	1	0	.13
Hoy, Peter	.000	0	0	0	0	0	.000	0	0	0	0	0	0	0	0	0	5	3.2	0	1	0	0	1.000	2	0	0	.00
Hurst, Bruce	.159	69	11	0	1	9	.114	273	31	5	0	0	8	20	140	36	32	217.1	10	32	1	0	.977	28	8	2	.36
Hurst, Jon	.000	4	0	0	0	2	.000	4	0	0	0	0	0	0	2	2	3	16.1	2	2	0	0	1.000	4	2	1	.75
Innis, Jeff	.000	2	0	0	0	0	.000	9	0	0	0	0	0	0	2	1	76	88.0	13	21	0	1	1.000	13	4	1	.38
Irvine, Daryl	.000	0	0	0	0	0	.000	0	0	0	0	0	0	0	0	0	21	28.0	3	5	0	0	1.000	1	1	0	1.00
Jackson, Danny	.083	60	5	0	2	9	.122	246	30	4	1	0	13	3	133	27	34	201.1	9	33	8	3	.840	34	7	6	.38
Jackson, Mike	.000	2	0	0	0	0	.105	19	2	0	0	0	0	0	3	3	67	82.0	6	9	1	0	.938	9	3	0	.33
Jeffcoat, Mike	.000	0	0	0	0	0	.500	2	1	1	0	0	1	1	0	0	6	19.2	1	3	0	1	1.000	1	1	0	1.00
Johnson, Jeff	.000	0	0	0	0	0	.000	0	0	0	0	0	0	0	0	0	13	52.2	1	7	0	0	1.000	6	1	1	.33
Johnson, Randy	.000	0	0	0	0	0	.125	16	2	0	0	0	0	0	9	2	31	210.1	5	20	3	2	.893	58	8	8	.28
Johnston, Joel	.000	0	0	0	0	0	.000	0	0	0	0	0	0	0	0	0	5	2.2	0	0	0	0	.000	0	0	0	.00
Jones, Barry	.000	2	0	0	0	0	.063	16	1	0	0	0	0	1	5	2	60	69.2	4	13	0	2	1.000	6	1	0	.17
Jones, Calvin	.000	0	0	0	0	0	.000	0	0	0	0	0	0	0	0	0	38	61.2	3	7	3	1	.769	9	3	0	.33
Jones, Doug	.000	4	0	0	0	0	.000	4	0	0	0	0	0	0	2	0	80	111.2	5	12	2	0	.895	9	4	0	.44
Jones, Jimmy	.167	36	6	0	4	9	.168	184	31	2	0	2	11	15	58	28	25	139.1	9	17	0	1	1.000	25	5	0	.20
Kamieniecki, Scott	.000	0	0	0	0	0	.000	0	0	0	0	0	0	0	0	0	28	188.0	15	20	0	3	1.000	23	6	3	.17
Key, Jimmy	.000	0	0	0	0	0	.000	0	0	0	0	0	0	0	0	0	33	216.2	18	27	1	2	.978	23	6	3	.39
Kiely, John	.000	0	0	0	0	0	.000	0	0	0	0	0	0	0	0	0	39	55.0	8	15	0	3	1.000	3	1	0	.33
Kile, Darryl	.156	32	5	0	2	5	.071	70	5	0	0	0	3	6	38	9	22	125.1	2	12	5	0	.737	13	3	0	.33
King, Eric	.000	0	0	0	0	0	.000	0	0	0	0	0	0	0	0	0	17	79.1	6	5	1	0	.917	11	3	0	.27
Kipper, Bob	.000	0	0	0	0	0	.137	95	13	2	0	0	2	2	30	11	25	38.2	0	6	0	1	1.000	3	0	2	.67
Knudsen, Kurt	.000	0	0	0	0	0	.000	0	0	0	0	0	0	0	0	0	47	70.2	6	7	0	2	1.000	11	4	1	.45

	1992 Hitting					Career Hitting										1992 Fielding and Holding Runners										
Pitcher	Avg	AB	H	HR	RBI	SH	Avg	AB	H	2B	3B	HR	RBI	BB	SO	SH	G	Inn	PO	A	E	DP	Pct	SBA	CS	PCS	CS%
Kramer, Randy	.000	0	0	0	0	0	.122	41	5	1	0	0	2	0	15	3	4	16.1	1	0	0	0	1.000	3	0	0	.00
Krueger, Bill	.000	3	0	0	0	1	.000	3	0	0	0	0	0	0	2	1	36	178.2	4	11	0	0	1.000	26	1	3	.15
Lamp, Dennis	.000	1	0	0	0	0	.164	201	33	3	0	0	7	6	37	17	21	28.0	4	4	0	0	1.000	4	2	0	.50
Lancaster, Les	.000	0	0	0	0	0	.102	128	13	4	0	0	5	4	62	11	41	86.2	3	9	1	3	.923	6	3	0	.50
Landrum, Bill	.000	0	0	0	0	0	.080	25	2	0	0	0	0	0	9	2	18	20.0	2	2	0	0	1.000	5	1	0	.20
Langston, Mark	.000	2	0	0	0	0	.157	66	11	2	0	0	3	0	28	1	33	229.0	6	41	2	3	.959	31	4	6	.32
Leach, Terry	.000	0	0	0	0	0	.097	72	7	2	0	0	3	5	39	6	51	73.2	9	13	1	1	.957	10	3	0	.30
Leary, Tim	.000	0	0	0	0	0	.221	163	36	6	0	1	19	5	57	28	26	141.0	10	18	0	3	1.000	32	5	0	.16
Lefferts, Craig	.077	52	4	0	0	9	.121	132	16	2	0	1	3	1	64	14	32	196.1	8	27	2	0	.946	30	6	4	.33
Leibrandt, Charlie	.121	58	7	0	4	8	.120	267	32	3	2	0	14	13	72	33	32	193.0	20	41	3	2	.953	44	3	13	.36
Leiter, Al	.000	0	0	0	0	0	.000	0	0	0	0	0	0	0	0	0	1	1.0	0	0	0	0	.000	0	0	0	.00
Leiter, Mark	.000	0	0	0	0	0	.000	0	0	0	0	0	0	0	0	0	35	112.0	8	15	1	1	.958	16	7	2	.56
Leon, Danilo	.000	0	0	0	0	0	.000	0	0	0	0	0	0	0	0	0	14	18.1	3	1	0	0	1.000	2	1	0	.50
Lewis, Richie	.000	0	0	0	0	0	.000	0	0	0	0	0	0	0	0	0	2	6.2	1	1	0	0	1.000	3	0	0	.00
Lewis, Scott	.000	0	0	0	0	0	.000	0	0	0	0	0	0	0	0	0	21	38.1	3	8	0	2	1.000	5	3	0	.60
Lilliquist, Derek	.000	0	0	0	0	0	.213	108	23	1	0	2	8	1	20	5	71	61.2	3	9	0	0	1.000	6	2	0	.33
Linton, Doug	.000	0	0	0	0	0	.000	0	0	0	0	0	0	0	0	0	8	24.0	1	2	0	1	1.000	2	2	0	1.00
MacDonald, Bob	.000	0	0	0	0	0	.000	0	0	0	0	0	0	0	0	0	27	47.1	2	2	0	0	1.000	4	0	0	.00
Maddux, Greg	.170	88	15	1	8	13	.184	490	90	10	0	2	29	6	127	45	35	268.0	30	64	3	1	.969	39	13	0	.33
Maddux, Mike	.111	9	1	0	0	3	.073	82	6	1	0	0	4	6	25	14	50	79.2	9	17	1	1	.963	18	1	2	.17
Magnante, Mike	.000	0	0	0	0	0	.000	0	0	0	0	0	0	0	0	0	44	89.1	8	20	0	3	1.000	12	3	0	.25
Magrane, Joe	.200	10	2	1	2	1	.143	245	35	8	0	4	12	12	79	32	5	31.1	1	5	0	0	1.000	3	1	0	.33
Mahomes, Pat	.000	0	0	0	0	0	.000	0	0	0	0	0	0	0	0	0	14	69.2	5	3	0	0	1.000	17	7	1	.47
Mallicoat, Rob	.000	1	0	0	0	0	.000	2	0	0	0	0	0	0	0	0	21	23.2	0	3	0	0	1.000	4	1	0	.25
Manuel, Barry	.000	0	0	0	0	0	.000	0	0	0	0	0	0	0	0	0	3	5.2	0	0	0	0	.000	2	0	0	.00
Martinez, Dennis	.189	74	14	0	2	10	.141	440	62	9	0	0	26	12	144	55	32	226.1	21	44	4	3	.942	39	17	0	.44
Martinez, Pedro	.000	2	0	0	0	0	.000	2	0	0	0	0	0	0	0	0	2	8.0	0	0	0	0	.000	0	0	0	.00
Martinez, Ramon	.120	50	6	0	2	5	.124	251	31	2	0	1	20	3	88	25	25	150.2	11	18	2	1	.935	26	7	0	.27
Mason, Roger	.000	10	0	0	0	0	.060	50	3	0	0	0	0	3	26	2	65	86.0	6	7	1	0	.929	9	5	0	.36
Mathews, Greg	.000	14	0	0	0	2	.136	162	22	2	0	0	5	6	60	18	14	52.1	1	6	0	0	1.000	6	2	1	.50
Mathews, Terry	.000	0	0	0	0	0	.000	0	0	0	0	0	0	0	0	0	40	42.1	5	4	0	1	1.000	4	4	0	1.00
Maysey, Matt	.000	0	0	0	0	0	.000	0	0	0	0	0	0	0	0	0	2	2.1	0	0	0	0	.000	1	1	0	1.00
McCaskill, Kirk	.000	0	0	0	0	0	.000	0	0	0	0	0	0	0	0	0	34	209.0	24	31	2	0	.965	21	9	0	.43
McClure, Bob	.000	0	0	0	0	0	.222	9	2	0	0	0	0	0	1	0	71	54.0	2	8	0	1	1.000	3	1	1	.67
McCullers, Lance	.000	0	0	0	0	0	.104	48	5	0	0	0	4	5	23	6	5	5.0	1	2	0	1	1.000	1	0	0	.00
McDonald, Ben	.000	0	0	0	0	0	.000	0	0	0	0	0	0	0	0	0	34	227.0	20	27	0	3	1.000	28	7	1	.29
McDowell, Jack	.000	0	0	0	0	0	.000	0	0	0	0	0	0	0	0	0	34	260.2	16	26	2	3	.955	45	13	3	.36
McDowell, Roger	.000	3	0	0	0	1	.217	69	15	0	0	0	6	5	26	5	65	83.2	8	21	3	2	.906	5	2	0	.40
McElroy, Chuck	.667	6	4	0	1	0	.438	16	7	3	1	0	3	0	3	0	72	83.2	3	8	1	2	.917	7	3	0	.43
Meacham, Rusty	.000	0	0	0	0	0	.000	0	0	0	0	0	0	0	0	0	64	101.2	13	18	1	1	.969	1	1	0	1.00
Melendez, Jose	.000	5	0	0	0	1	.080	25	2	1	0	0	0	1	18	1	56	89.1	2	8	1	1	.909	7	4	0	.57
Menendez, Tony	.000	0	0	0	0	0	.000	0	0	0	0	0	0	0	0	0	3	4.2	0	0	0	0	.000	0	0	0	.00
Mercker, Kent	.000	5	0	0	0	0	.053	19	1	0	0	0	2	1	14	0	53	68.1	1	2	0	0	1.000	14	2	0	.14
Mesa, Jose	.000	0	0	0	0	0	.000	0	0	0	0	0	0	0	0	0	28	160.2	12	20	2	0	.941	22	7	1	.36
Milacki, Bob	.000	0	0	0	0	0	.000	0	0	0	0	0	0	0	0	0	23	115.2	14	10	0	0	1.000	12	1	0	.08
Militello, Sam	.000	0	0	0	0	0	.000	0	0	0	0	0	0	0	0	0	9	60.0	2	4	2	0	.750	7	0	0	.00
Miller, Paul	.000	3	0	0	0	0	.000	6	0	0	0	0	0	0	3	0	6	11.1	0	1	0	0	1.000	1	1	0	1.00
Mills, Alan	.000	0	0	0	0	0	.000	0	0	0	0	0	0	0	0	0	35	103.1	9	17	0	2	1.000	16	4	0	.25
Minor, Blas	.000	0	0	0	0	0	.000	0	0	0	0	0	0	0	0	0	1	2.0	0	1	1	1	.500	0	0	0	.00
Mlicki, Dave	.000	0	0	0	0	0	.000	0	0	0	0	0	0	0	0	0	4	21.2	6	3	0	1	1.000	8	1	0	.13
Moeller, Dennis	.000	0	0	0	0	0	.000	0	0	0	0	0	0	0	0	0	5	18.0	0	5	0	0	1.000	2	0	0	.00
Monteleone, Rich	.000	0	0	0	0	0	.000	0	0	0	0	0	0	0	0	0	47	92.2	6	7	0	1	1.000	8	5	0	.63
Montgomery, Jeff	.000	0	0	0	0	0	.000	2	0	0	0	0	0	0	1	0	65	82.2	12	13	1	2	.962	7	2	0	.29
Moore, Mike	.000	0	0	0	0	0	.000	0	0	0	0	0	0	0	0	0	36	223.0	17	22	3	5	.929	32	13	0	.41
Morgan, Mike	.108	74	8	0	5	11	.101	257	26	0	0	0	11	6	64	27	33	233.0	19	45	3	3	.955	15	9	0	.60
Morris, Jack	.000	0	0	0	0	0	.000	1	0	0	0	0	0	0	0	0	33	234.2	20	26	1	1	.979	38	16	0	.42
Mulholland, Terry	.096	83	8	0	3	6	.082	294	24	3	0	0	6	7	131	19	31	229.0	5	46	3	2	.944	7	4	1	.71
Munoz, Mike	.000	0	0	0	0	0	.000	1	0	0	0	0	0	0	1	0	65	48.0	8	12	0	0	1.000	4	1	0	.25
Murphy, Rob	.000	1	0	0	0	1	.111	9	1	0	0	0	0	0	3	2	58	55.2	2	12	0	0	1.000	5	1	0	.20
Mussina, Mike	.000	0	0	0	0	0	.000	0	0	0	0	0	0	0	0	0	32	241.0	13	31	1	0	.978	18	9	0	.50
Mutis, Jeff	.000	0	0	0	0	0	.000	0	0	0	0	0	0	0	0	0	3	11.1	0	2	0	0	1.000	0	0	0	.00
Myers, Randy	.143	7	1	0	0	1	.179	56	10	2	0	0	4	1	31	4	66	79.2	2	12	0	0	1.000	5	2	1	.29
Nabholz, Chris	.123	65	8	0	2	7	.101	138	14	3	0	0	3	5	35	12	32	195.0	14	40	2	3	.964	29	1	5	.21
Nagy, Charles	.000	0	0	0	0	0	.000	0	0	0	0	0	0	0	0	0	33	252.0	22	43	1	4	.985	27	13	2	.56
Navarro, Jaime	.000	0	0	0	0	0	.000	0	0	0	0	0	0	0	0	0	34	246.0	17	18	4	1	.897	28	11	0	.39
Neagle, Denny	.000	11	0	0	0	2	.000	11	0	0	0	0	0	0	2	2	55	86.1	2	11	0	0	1.000	17	1	2	.18
Nelson, Gene	.000	0	0	0	0	0	.000	1	0	0	0	0	0	0	0	0	28	51.2	3	4	0	0	1.000	7	3	0	.43
Nelson, Jeff	.000	0	0	0	0	0	.000	0	0	0	0	0	0	0	0	0	66	81.0	3	12	2	2	.882	7	3	0	.43
Nichols, Rod	.000	0	0	0	0	0	.000	0	0	0	0	0	0	0	0	0	30	105.1	4	14	0	0	1.000	8	2	0	.25
Nied, Dave	.286	7	2	0	0	0	.286	7	2	0	0	0	0	0	2	0	6	23.0	0	2	0	0	1.000	2	0	0	.00
Nielsen, Jerry	.000	0	0	0	0	0	.000	0	0	0	0	0	0	0	0	0	19	18.2	1	4	0	0	1.000	4	0	2	.50
Nunez, Edwin	.000	0	0	0	0	0	.000	0	0	0	0	0	0	0	0	0	49	59.1	3	4	1	1	.875	3	2	0	.67
Ojeda, Bobby	.102	49	5	0	3	5	.127	347	44	2	1	1	9	11	102	30	29	166.1	5	37	2	1	.955	35	7	8	.43
Olin, Steve	.000	0	0	0	0	0	.000	0	0	0	0	0	0	0	0	0	72	88.1	4	16	0	1	1.000	6	4	0	.67

	1992 Hitting					Career Hitting										1992 Fielding and Holding Runners										
Pitcher	Avg	AB	H	HR	RBI	SH	Avg	AB	H	2B	3B	HR	RBI	BB	SO	SH	G	Inn	PO	A	E	DP	Pct.	SBA	CS	PCS	CS%
Olivares, Omar	.235	68	16	1	4	3	.225	138	31	5	0	2	14	3	39	7	32	197.0	14	40	0	4	1.000	24	12	1	.54
Oliveras, Francisco	.143	7	1	0	0	0	.136	22	3	0	0	0	0	1	10	0	16	44.2	0	9	1	0	.900	3	3	0	1.00
Olson, Gregg	.000	0	0	0	0	0	.000	0	0	0	0	0	0	0	0	0	60	61.1	5	9	0	2	1.000	10	0	0	.00
Orosco, Jesse	.000	0	0	0	0	0	.172	58	10	0	0	0	4	6	24	7	59	39.0	2	3	0	0	1.000	7	2	2	.57
Osborne, Donovan	.121	58	7	0	0	2	.121	58	7	0	1	0	0	0	21	2	34	179.0	6	18	2	2	.923	18	3	0	.17
Osuna, Al	.000	0	0	0	0	0	.000	2	0	0	0	0	0	1	0	1	66	61.2	2	11	0	0	1.000	5	0	1	.20
Otto, Dave	.000	0	0	0	0	0	.000	0	0	0	0	0	0	0	0	0	18	80.1	3	14	1	1	.944	13	1	1	.15
Palacios, Vince	.071	14	1	0	0	2	.061	49	3	0	0	0	0	2	24	7	20	53.0	5	7	1	1	.923	6	4	0	.67
Pall, Donn	.000	0	0	0	0	0	.000	0	0	0	0	0	0	0	0	0	39	73.0	5	6	1	2	.917	11	1	0	.09
Parker, Clay	.000	0	0	0	0	0	.000	0	0	0	0	0	0	0	0	0	8	33.1	1	4	1	0	.833	4	1	0	.25
Parrett, Jeff	.000	0	0	0	0	0	.087	23	2	0	0	0	1	2	10	2	66	98.1	5	7	1	2	.923	18	4	0	.22
Patterson, Bob	.333	6	2	0	4	0	.115	52	6	1	0	0	4	2	22	6	60	64.2	3	7	0	1	1.000	4	2	1	.75
Patterson, Ken	.000	1	0	0	0	1	.000	1	0	0	0	0	0	0	1	1	32	41.2	4	6	1	0	.909	5	2	1	.60
Pavlik, Roger	.000	0	0	0	0	0	.000	0	0	0	0	0	0	0	0	0	13	62.0	6	3	1	0	.900	11	7	1	.73
Pena, Alejandro	.000	2	0	0	0	0	.112	179	20	3	0	1	7	3	71	9	41	42.0	2	1	0	0	1.000	6	1	0	.17
Pena, Jim	.200	5	1	0	0	3	.200	5	1	0	0	0	0	0	2	3	25	44.0	1	11	3	1	.800	1	0	0	.00
Perez, Melido	.000	0	0	0	0	0	.000	0	0	0	0	0	0	0	0	0	33	247.2	15	28	10	2	.811	36	18	0	.50
Perez, Mike	.000	4	0	0	0	2	.000	5	0	0	0	0	0	0	2	2	76	93.0	9	15	0	3	1.000	7	2	0	.29
Pichardo, Hipolito	.000	0	0	0	0	0	.000	0	0	0	0	0	0	0	0	0	31	143.2	19	16	2	2	.946	14	3	0	.21
Pierce, Eddie	.000	0	0	0	0	0	.000	0	0	0	0	0	0	0	0	0	2	5.1	0	1	0	0	1.000	1	0	1	1.00
Plesac, Dan	.000	0	0	0	0	0	.000	0	0	0	0	0	0	0	0	0	44	79.0	1	8	0	1	1.000	5	1	2	.60
Plunk, Eric	.000	0	0	0	0	0	.000	0	0	0	0	0	0	0	0	0	58	71.2	7	7	1	0	.933	5	2	0	.40
Poole, Jim	.000	0	0	0	0	0	.000	0	0	0	0	0	0	0	0	0	6	3.1	0	2	0	0	1.000	3	0	1	.33
Portugal, Mark	.107	28	3	0	0	6	.161	174	28	4	0	1	10	6	30	20	18	101.1	16	13	3	1	.906	13	6	0	.46
Powell, Dennis	.000	0	0	0	0	0	.176	17	3	3	0	0	0	0	8	2	49	57.0	3	5	0	1	1.000	6	3	0	.50
Power, Ted	.000	0	0	0	0	0	.089	157	14	3	0	1	7	10	93	20	54	99.1	4	13	0	1	1.000	11	3	0	.27
Pugh, Tim	.077	13	1	0	0	1	.077	13	1	0	0	0	0	1	4	1	7	45.1	2	6	0	0	1.000	2	1	0	.50
Quantrill, Paul	.000	0	0	0	0	0	.000	0	0	0	0	0	0	0	0	0	27	49.1	4	6	2	0	.833	5	2	0	.40
Raczka, Mike	.000	0	0	0	0	0	.000	0	0	0	0	0	0	0	0	0	8	6.1	0	0	0	0	.000	0	0	0	.00
Radinsky, Scott	.000	0	0	0	0	0	.000	0	0	0	0	0	0	0	0	0	68	59.1	2	9	0	1	1.000	4	3	0	.75
Rapp, Pat	.000	2	0	0	0	1	.000	2	0	0	0	0	0	0	2	1	3	10.0	2	2	0	0	1.000	5	1	0	.20
Rasmussen, Dennis	.000	0	0	0	0	1	.193	259	50	8	0	0	14	13	82	19	8	42.2	1	13	0	0	1.000	9	0	7	.78
Reardon, Jeff	.000	0	0	0	0	0	.091	55	5	1	0	0	2	1	36	6	60	58.0	2	4	0	1	1.000	4	0	0	.00
Reed, Rick	.000	0	0	0	0	0	.171	35	6	1	0	0	3	3	12	0	19	100.1	6	17	1	1	.958	9	3	0	.33
Reed, Steve	.000	0	0	0	0	0	.000	0	0	0	0	0	0	0	0	0	18	15.2	3	4	0	0	1.000	1	0	0	.00
Revenig, Todd	.000	0	0	0	0	0	.000	0	0	0	0	0	0	0	0	0	2	2.0	0	0	0	0	.000	0	0	0	.00
Reynolds, Shane	.500	4	2	0	0	2	.500	4	2	1	0	0	0	0	2	2	8	25.1	0	7	1	0	.875	7	0	1	.14
Reynoso, Armando	.000	2	0	0	0	0	.000	9	0	0	0	0	0	1	6	1	3	7.2	0	2	0	1	1.000	1	1	0	1.00
Rhodes, Arthur	.000	0	0	0	0	0	.000	0	0	0	0	0	0	0	0	0	15	94.1	1	12	0	2	1.000	8	3	1	.50
Righetti, Dave	.143	7	1	0	0	4	.100	10	1	0	0	0	0	0	6	5	54	78.1	3	6	1	1	.900	11	3	1	.36
Rijo, Jose	.194	72	14	0	6	6	.174	276	48	4	0	1	15	5	66	31	33	211.0	19	31	2	2	.962	29	12	0	.41
Risley, Bill	.000	2	0	0	0	0	.000	2	0	0	0	0	0	0	0	0	1	5.0	0	1	0	0	1.000	2	0	0	.00
Ritchie, Wally	.000	1	0	0	0	0	.125	8	1	0	0	0	0	1	4	0	40	39.0	1	5	0	0	1.000	3	0	0	.00
Ritz, Kevin	.000	0	0	0	0	0	.000	0	0	0	0	0	0	0	0	0	23	80.1	4	10	0	1	1.000	16	5	0	.31
Rivera, Ben	.091	33	3	0	2	2	.091	33	3	0	0	0	2	2	11	2	28	117.1	3	19	0	1	1.000	19	3	1	.21
Robinson, Don	.389	18	7	0	1	0	.231	631	146	23	0	13	69	16	168	15	11	60.0	2	3	0	0	1.000	11	0	0	.00
Robinson, Jeff	.000	12	0	0	0	0	.137	161	22	0	0	2	10	3	60	15	48	77.0	7	13	0	1	1.000	17	8	0	.47
Robinson, Jeff M.	.091	11	1	0	1	2	.091	11	1	0	0	0	0	0	8	2	24	82.0	8	9	0	2	1.000	12	4	1	.42
Robinson, Ron	.000	0	0	0	0	0	.153	144	22	2	0	0	6	1	58	15	8	35.1	5	2	1	0	.875	4	1	0	.25
Rodriguez, Rich	.000	6	0	0	0	2	.000	14	0	0	0	0	0	2	3	2	61	91.0	4	17	1	4	.955	11	3	2	.45
Rogers, Kenny	.000	0	0	0	0	0	.000	0	0	0	0	0	0	0	0	0	81	78.2	4	17	2	0	.913	5	1	2	.60
Rogers, Kevin	.222	9	2	0	0	3	.222	9	2	0	0	0	0	0	6	3	6	34.0	1	3	0	0	1.000	3	0	2	.67
Rojas, Mel	.067	15	1	0	0	0	.045	22	1	0	0	0	0	0	14	4	67	99.2	9	12	2	1	.913	14	3	0	.21
Rosenthal, Wayne	.000	0	0	0	0	0	.000	0	0	0	0	0	0	0	0	0	6	4.2	0	1	0	0	1.000	1	0	0	.00
Ruffin, Bruce	.000	0	0	0	0	0	.080	263	21	3	0	0	6	18	128	20	25	58.0	4	5	0	0	1.000	8	3	0	.38
Ruskin, Scott	.000	3	0	0	0	2	.154	13	2	1	1	0	1	1	9	2	57	53.2	2	8	0	0	1.000	8	1	2	.38
Russell, Jeff	.000	0	0	0	0	0	.139	79	11	3	0	1	10	5	33	7	59	66.1	7	8	0	0	1.000	4	3	0	.75
Ryan, Ken	.000	0	0	0	0	0	.000	0	0	0	0	0	0	0	0	0	7	7.0	1	2	0	0	1.000	0	0	0	.00
Ryan, Nolan	.000	0	0	0	0	0	.110	852	94	10	2	2	36	38	371	65	27	157.1	2	15	3	1	.850	38	11	1	.32
Saberhagen, Bret	.107	28	3	0	0	3	.107	28	3	0	0	0	0	1	9	3	16	97.2	7	24	0	2	1.000	11	5	0	.45
Sampen, Bill	.000	6	0	0	0	1	.111	27	3	0	0	0	0	1	5	5	52	83.0	10	15	0	1	1.000	17	2	0	.12
Sanderson, Scott	.000	0	0	0	0	0	.100	460	46	13	0	2	26	25	213	65	32	190.2	4	16	2	1	.909	25	7	1	.32
Sauveur, Rich	.000	0	0	0	0	0	.333	3	1	0	0	0	0	0	1	1	18	14.1	0	1	0	0	1.000	0	0	0	.00
Scanlan, Bob	.000	4	0	0	0	0	.036	28	1	0	0	0	1	1	11	2	69	87.1	5	22	2	0	.931	9	3	0	.33
Scheid, Rich	.000	1	0	0	0	0	.000	1	0	0	0	0	0	0	1	0	7	12.0	1	1	0	0	1.000	2	0	0	.00
Schilling, Curt	.156	64	10	0	3	8	.164	67	11	1	0	0	4	1	22	8	42	226.1	14	21	3	1	.921	14	7	0	.50
Schmidt, Dave	.000	0	0	0	0	0	.000	3	0	0	0	0	0	0	0	0	3	3.1	0	0	0	0	.000	0	0	0	.00
Schooler, Mike	.000	0	0	0	0	0	.000	0	0	0	0	0	0	0	0	0	53	51.2	1	10	0	1	1.000	9	1	0	.11
Schourek, Pete	.048	42	2	0	1	2	.078	64	5	1	0	0	4	2	22	2	22	136.0	7	13	0	2	1.000	20	3	2	.25
Scott, Tim	.000	0	0	0	0	0	.000	0	0	0	0	0	0	0	0	0	33	37.2	0	4	0	0	1.000	7	1	0	.14
Scudder, Scott	.000	0	0	0	0	0	.113	71	8	0	0	1	3	6	30	7	23	109.0	13	12	0	0	1.000	21	7	0	.33
Searcy, Steve	.000	0	0	0	0	0	.000	4	0	0	0	0	0	0	3	0	10	10.1	0	2	0	0	1.000	1	1	0	1.00
Seminara, Frank	.118	34	4	0	0	2	.118	34	4	0	0	0	0	1	9	2	19	100.1	9	23	2	1	.941	16	5	1	.38
Service, Scott	.000	2	0	0	0	0	.000	2	0	0	0	0	0	0	2	0	5	7.0	0	0	0	0	.000	0	0	0	.00

	1992 Hitting					Career Hitting										1992 Fielding and Holding Runners										
Pitcher	Avg	AB	H	HR	RBI	SH	Avg	AB	H	2B	3B	HR	RBI	BB	SO	SH	G	Inn	PO	A	E	DP	Pct.	SBA	CS	PCS	CS%
Shaw, Jeff	.000	0	0	0	0	0	.000	0	0	0	0	0	0	0	0	0	2	7.2	0	2	1	0	.667	1	0	0	.00
Shepherd, Keith	.000	0	0	0	0	0	.000	0	0	0	0	0	0	0	0	0	12	22.0	0	5	0	0	1.000	6	2	1	.50
Shifflett, Steve	.000	0	0	0	0	0	.000	0	0	0	0	0	0	0	0	0	34	52.0	5	6	1	0	.917	4	0	1	.25
Simons, Doug	.000	0	0	0	0	0	.000	3	0	0	0	0	0	0	0	1	7	5.1	0	1	1	0	.500	0	0	0	.00
Slocumb, Heathcliff	.000	4	0	0	0	0	.000	5	0	0	0	0	0	0	3	0	30	36.0	3	4	2	0	.778	8	4	0	.50
Slusarski, Joe	.000	0	0	0	0	0	.000	0	0	0	0	0	0	0	0	0	15	76.0	2	6	0	0	1.000	10	4	0	.40
Smiley, John	.000	0	0	0	0	0	.110	254	28	6	0	0	15	12	89	23	34	241.0	4	35	0	4	1.000	41	6	10	.39
Smith, Bryn	.000	3	0	0	0	1	.155	490	76	12	0	3	37	28	139	77	13	21.1	3	3	0	0	1.000	4	0	0	.00
Smith, Dan	.000	0	0	0	0	0	.000	0	0	0	0	0	0	0	0	0	4	14.1	1	1	0	0	1.000	3	1	1	.67
Smith, Dave	.000	0	0	0	0	0	.068	44	3	0	0	0	1	4	21	5	11	14.1	0	2	0	0	1.000	2	0	0	.00
Smith, Lee	.000	0	0	0	0	0	.048	62	3	0	0	0	1	2	3	41	4	70	75.0	1	7	1	1	.889	13	1	0	.08
Smith, Pete	.038	26	1	0	2	3	.096	166	16	1	0	0	5	9	38	22	12	79.0	3	13	1	2	.941	10	2	0	.20
Smith, Zane	.122	49	6	0	3	3	.156	443	69	11	2	0	27	13	85	64	23	141.0	6	29	0	2	1.000	13	3	1	.31
Smoltz, John	.160	75	12	1	4	10	.137	293	40	7	1	2	17	24	123	34	35	246.2	23	26	1	5	.980	18	7	0	.39
Springer, Russ	.000	0	0	0	0	0	.000	0	0	0	0	0	0	0	0	0	14	16.0	0	1	0	0	1.000	3	0	0	.00
St. Claire, Randy	.000	0	0	0	0	0	.267	15	4	0	0	0	0	2	6	4	10	15.1	0	4	0	0	1.000	0	0	0	.00
Stanton, Mike	.500	2	1	0	0	0	.500	8	4	1	0	0	1	1	1	0	65	63.2	3	10	0	2	1.000	3	1	1	.67
Stewart, Dave	.000	0	0	0	0	0	.196	51	10	1	1	0	4	3	17	6	31	199.1	8	13	3	2	.875	25	10	0	.40
Stieb, Dave	.000	0	0	0	0	0	.000	1	0	0	0	0	0	0	0	0	21	96.1	7	21	0	1	1.000	9	6	0	.67
Stottlemyre, Todd	.000	0	0	0	0	0	.000	0	0	0	0	0	0	0	0	0	28	174.0	15	17	1	2	.970	20	3	0	.15
Sutcliffe, Rick	.000	0	0	0	0	0	.184	539	99	21	1	4	54	34	137	51	36	237.1	11	24	3	2	.921	27	2	3	.19
Swan, Russ	.000	0	0	0	0	0	.000	3	0	0	0	0	0	0	0	0	55	104.1	7	23	1	0	.968	7	1	1	.29
Swift, Bill	.157	51	8	0	3	5	.157	51	8	0	0	0	3	1	18	5	30	164.2	18	33	1	3	.981	9	4	0	.44
Swindell, Greg	.125	80	10	0	4	5	.125	80	10	2	0	0	4	1	15	5	31	213.2	6	32	1	3	.974	26	3	6	.35
Tanana, Frank	.000	0	0	0	0	0	.000	0	0	0	0	0	0	0	1	0	32	186.2	6	27	2	1	.943	32	2	9	.34
Tapani, Kevin	.000	0	0	0	0	0	.000	2	0	0	0	0	0	0	1	0	34	220.0	17	26	2	0	.956	37	11	0	.30
Taylor, Scott	.000	0	0	0	0	0	.000	0	0	0	0	0	0	0	0	0	4	14.2	0	3	0	0	1.000	1	0	1	1.00
Terrell, Walt	.000	0	0	0	0	0	.120	192	23	5	0	3	10	6	87	7	36	136.2	13	22	1	0	.972	10	3	0	.30
Tewksbury, Bob	.086	70	6	0	3	6	.124	185	23	3	0	0	8	12	72	22	33	233.0	14	42	1	2	.982	11	4	0	.36
Thigpen, Bobby	.000	0	0	0	0	0	.000	0	0	0	0	0	0	0	0	0	55	55.0	7	6	0	2	1.000	3	0	0	.00
Timlin, Mike	.000	0	0	0	0	0	.000	0	0	0	0	0	0	0	0	0	26	43.2	2	5	0	1	1.000	7	3	0	.43
Tomlin, Randy	.138	65	9	0	1	7	.141	142	20	2	0	0	3	6	40	22	35	208.2	13	52	1	3	.985	29	1	7	.28
Trlicek, Ricky	.000	0	0	0	0	0	.000	0	0	0	0	0	0	0	0	0	2	1.2	0	0	0	0	.000	0	0	0	.00
Trombley, Mike	.000	0	0	0	0	0	.000	0	0	0	0	0	0	0	0	0	10	46.1	1	6	0	1	1.000	5	3	0	.60
Valdez, Sergio	.000	3	0	0	0	0	.167	12	2	0	0	0	0	0	5	0	27	37.1	8	4	0	0	1.000	10	1	0	.10
Valera, Julio	.000	0	0	0	0	0	.200	5	1	0	0	0	2	0	1	0	30	188.0	10	13	1	0	.958	18	4	0	.22
Viola, Frank	.000	0	0	0	0	0	.140	179	25	2	0	0	6	3	40	22	35	238.0	6	47	2	6	.964	17	4	1	.29
Vitko, Joe	.000	0	0	0	0	0	.000	0	0	0	0	0	0	0	0	0	3	4.2	1	0	2	0	.333	1	1	0	1.00
Wagner, Paul	.333	3	1	0	0	0	.333	3	1	0	0	0	0	0	1	0	6	13.0	2	2	0	0	1.000	1	1	0	1.00
Wakefield, Tim	.071	28	2	0	0	4	.071	28	2	0	0	0	0	3	9	4	13	92.0	6	19	0	1	1.000	13	8	1	.69
Walk, Bob	.093	43	4	0	2	1	.148	452	67	10	2	1	46	16	152	43	36	135.0	10	28	1	2	.974	24	4	1	.21
Walker, Mike	.000	0	0	0	0	0	.000	0	0	0	0	0	0	0	0	0	5	14.2	1	3	2	0	.667	3	0	0	.00
Walton, Bruce	.000	0	0	0	0	0	.000	0	0	0	0	0	0	0	0	0	7	10.0	0	1	0	0	1.000	0	0	0	.00
Ward, Duane	.000	0	0	0	0	0	.000	1	0	0	0	0	0	0	0	0	79	101.1	4	11	1	0	.938	18	4	0	.22
Wayne, Gary	.000	0	0	0	0	0	.000	0	0	0	0	0	0	0	0	0	41	48.0	1	13	0	0	1.000	5	0	0	.00
Weathers, Dave	.000	0	0	0	0	0	.000	0	0	0	0	0	0	0	0	0	2	3.1	0	0	0	0	.000	0	0	0	.00
Wegman, Bill	.000	0	0	0	0	0	.000	0	0	0	0	0	0	0	0	0	35	261.2	35	43	2	3	.975	24	6	0	.25
Welch, Bob	.000	0	0	0	0	0	.151	581	88	7	1	2	30	22	171	59	20	123.2	4	13	1	0	.944	13	4	1	.38
Wells, David	.000	0	0	0	0	0	.000	0	0	0	0	0	0	0	0	0	41	120.0	9	14	1	3	.958	20	4	2	.30
West, David	.000	0	0	0	0	0	.429	7	3	1	0	0	0	0	2	0	9	28.1	0	5	2	0	.714	2	0	0	.00
Weston, Mickey	.000	2	0	0	0	0	.000	2	0	0	0	0	0	0	2	0	1	3.2	0	0	0	0	.000	1	0	0	.00
Wetteland, John	.200	5	1	0	0	1	.152	33	5	1	0	1	6	0	15	7	66	82.0	7	6	1	0	.929	17	3	0	.18
Whitehurst, Wally	.182	22	4	0	3	1	.188	64	12	2	0	0	3	4	12	8	44	97.0	6	17	1	1	.958	12	3	0	.25
Whiteside, Matt	.000	0	0	0	0	0	.000	0	0	0	0	0	0	0	0	0	20	28.0	3	2	1	0	.833	1	0	0	.00
Wickander, Kevin	.000	0	0	0	0	0	.000	0	0	0	0	0	0	0	0	0	44	41.0	0	5	0	1	1.000	3	0	0	.00
Wickman, Bob	.000	0	0	0	0	0	.000	0	0	0	0	0	0	0	0	0	8	50.1	4	6	0	4	1.000	9	1	0	.11
Williams, Brian	.133	30	4	0	4	5	.121	33	4	1	0	0	4	0	13	7	16	96.1	8	14	2	0	.917	10	3	0	.30
Williams, Mike	.400	10	4	0	2	1	.400	10	4	0	0	0	0	0	4	1	5	28.2	0	5	0	0	1.000	2	0	1	.50
Williams, Mitch	.250	4	1	0	0	0	.133	15	2	0	0	0	3	1	4	0	66	81.0	1	11	3	0	.800	15	3	3	.33
Williamson, Mark	.000	0	0	0	0	0	.000	0	0	0	0	0	0	0	0	0	12	18.2	1	0	0	0	1.000	3	1	0	.33
Willis, Carl	.000	0	0	0	0	0	.250	4	1	0	0	0	0	0	0	0	59	79.1	6	6	1	1	.923	3	1	0	.33
Wilson, Steve	.333	3	1	0	0	0	.138	58	8	1	0	0	3	4	17	0	60	66.2	2	9	1	1	.917	5	0	1	.00
Wilson, Trevor	.077	39	3	0	3	7	.172	134	23	2	0	1	9	10	49	21	26	154.0	7	30	2	2	.949	13	5	2	.54
Witt, Bobby	.000	0	0	0	0	0	.000	1	0	0	0	0	0	0	1	0	31	193.0	14	20	1	2	.971	32	10	0	.31
Wohlers, Mark	.000	0	0	0	0	0	.000	0	0	0	0	0	0	0	0	0	32	35.1	2	7	0	0	1.000	4	1	0	.20
Woodson, Kerry	.000	2	0	0	0	0	.000	0	0	0	0	0	0	0	0	0	8	13.2	3	2	0	1	1.000	4	0	0	.00
Worrell, Todd	.000	0	0	0	0	0	.080	25	2	0	1	0	0	1	18	2	67	64.0	2	2	0	0	1.000	13	0	0	.00
Young, Anthony	.111	27	3	0	0	2	.122	41	5	1	0	0	0	1	17	3	52	121.0	13	15	2	1	.933	16	6	0	.38
Young, Curt	.000	0	0	0	0	0	.000	1	0	0	0	0	0	0	0	0	23	67.2	4	10	1	1	.933	7	1	1	.29
Young, Matt	.000	0	0	0	0	0	.000	3	0	0	0	0	0	0	2	0	28	70.2	2	8	6	0	.625	13	2	1	.23
Young, Pete	.000	0	0	0	0	0	.000	0	0	0	0	0	0	0	0	0	13	20.1	3	1	0	0	1.000	3	1	0	.33

Park Data

We are more than pleased with the way this section turned out. For the uninitiated, the purpose of analyzing park data is to determine which parks favor hitters and which parks favor pitchers. There are very dominant tendencies from park to park. The data we present here allows us to analyze trends from year to year and see the effects of new parks, pulled-in fences, etc.

In the charts that follow, the first block of columns shows how much the featured team totalled at home, how much opponents totalled against the featured team at home and the grand totals of both. The second block of columns shows how much the featured team totalled in away games, how much opponents totalled in away games and the grand totals of both. By combining both the featured team's and opponent totals, most team variance is negated and only the park variance is left. For example, if the featured team has a big home run hitter who hit 20 homers at home and 20 on the road, his numbers won't affect the park factor for homers one iota. However, if this guy hit 39 dingers at home and only one on the road, the park factor will be affected tremendously, and rightly so.

Now for the Index (probably the only thing you wondered about in the first place). In a nutshell, the Index tells you whether the park favors the stat you happen to be looking at. For example, how much of an advantage has Cecil Fielder (a right-handed power hitter) had hitting in Tiger Stadium since 1990, his first big home run year? To determine the Index, you need to determine the frequency of the stat — in this case home runs — at Home vs. the frequency of the stat on the Road. Since 1990, right-handed batters have hit 350 home runs in 16,396 at-bats at Tiger Stadium, a frequency of 47 AB per HR; in Tigers' road games, the frequency is 52 at-bats per HR (16,696/323). Dividing the Road frequncy by the Home Frequency (52/47) gives us a figure of 1.11. This number is multiplied by 100 to make it more recognizable: 111. What does an Index of 111 mean? In this case it means it's 11% easier for righties to hit home runs in Tiger Stadium than it is in other American League parks.

The greater the Index is over 100, the more favorable the park is for that statistic, the lower the Index is under 100, the less favorable the park is for that statistic. A park that was neutral in a category will have an Index of 100. The only question left to answer is, what is **E-Infield**? This is infield **fielding** errors. Obviously, a ballpark itself doesn't have any effect on throwing errors, although there can be some official scoring bias that can affect the number of throwing errors charged. One amazing thing we've learned is that Royals Stadium induces more errors than other American League parks, on average — the only artificial turf park with such a characteristic.

For those of you who can stand even further technicalities: The index for the following categories are determined on a per at-bat basis: 2B, 3B, HR, SO, LHB-HR and RHB-HR. The index for AB, R, H, E and E-Infield are determined using per game ratios. All the other indices are based on the raw figures shown in the chart.

Finally, for most parks you'll notice that we include 1992 data as well as three-year totals (1990-1992). However, for parks where there have been changes over the last three years, we never combine data. For example, for Comiskey Park, we show you 1992 data as well as 1991-1992 combined. On the other hand, for Seattle where they moved the fences back between the 1991 and 1992 seasons, we show you 1991 and 1992 separately. (The reason we don't combine 1990 and 1991 for Seattle is that they also moved the fences prior to the 1991 season.)

Atlanta Braves

| | 1992 Season | | | | | | | 1990-1992 | | | | | | |
| | Home Games | | | Away Games | | | Index | Home Games | | | Away Games | | | Index |
	Braves	Opp	Total	Braves	Opp	Total		Braves	Opp	Total	Braves	Opp	Total	
G	81	81	162	81	81	162	---	243	243	486	243	243	486	---
Avg	.258	.246	.252	.250	.237	.244	103	.264	.260	.262	.244	.244	.244	107
AB	2636	2780	5416	2844	2687	5531	98	8084	8455	16539	8356	7991	16347	101
R	343	290	633	339	279	618	102	1113	1085	2198	1000	949	1949	113
H	681	684	1365	710	637	1347	101	2137	2200	4337	2037	1952	3989	109
2B	106	118	224	117	118	235	97	370	377	747	371	360	731	101
3B	19	9	28	29	21	50	57	40	40	80	64	61	125	63
HR	72	45	117	66	44	110	109	240	188	428	201	147	348	122
SO	434	470	904	490	478	968	95	1337	1429	2766	1503	1426	2929	93
E	61	69	130	48	68	116	112	228	227	455	177	188	365	125
E-Infield	47	56	103	36	62	98	105	189	190	379	132	163	295	128
LHB-Avg	.257	.268	.261	.255	.246	.251	104	.266	.279	.272	.250	.248	.249	109
LHB-HR	36	18	54	29	20	49	116	106	65	171	78	50	128	135
RHB-Avg	.260	.235	.245	.244	.231	.238	103	.263	.249	.256	.239	.242	.240	106
RHB-HR	36	27	63	37	24	61	103	134	123	257	123	97	220	114

ATLANTA

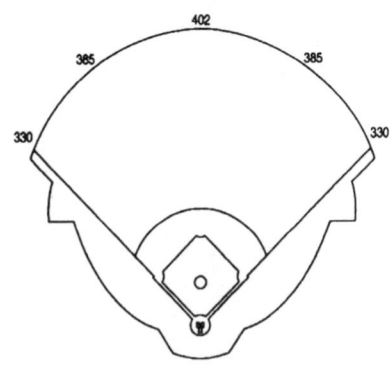

BALTIMORE

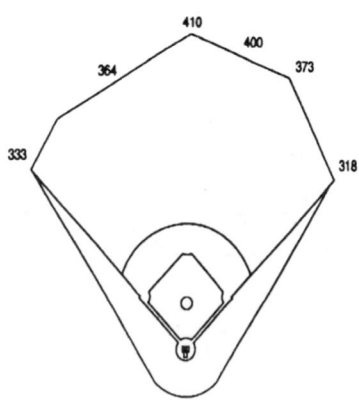

Baltimore Orioles

| | 1992 Season | | | | | | | 1990-1991 | | | | | | |
| | Home Games | | | Away Games | | | Index | Home Games | | | Away Games | | | Index |
	Orioles	Opp	Total	Orioles	Opp	Total		Orioles	Opp	Total	Orioles	Opp	Total	
G	81	81	162	81	81	162	---	161	161	322	162	162	324	---
Avg	.254	.248	.251	.264	.265	.265	95	.240	.262	.251	.259	.275	.267	94
AB	2679	2829	5508	2806	2702	5508	100	5311	5659	10970	5703	5446	11149	99
R	339	333	672	366	323	689	98	649	724	1373	706	770	1476	94
H	681	702	1383	742	717	1459	95	1272	1481	2753	1477	1498	2975	93
2B	108	119	227	135	131	266	85	234	271	505	256	307	563	91
3B	19	15	34	17	16	33	103	24	10	34	27	30	57	61
HR	75	69	144	73	55	128	113	154	154	308	148	154	302	104
SO	392	422	814	435	424	859	95	958	893	1851	978	751	1729	109
E	40	40	80	53	51	104	77	92	128	220	92	112	204	109
E-Infield	31	33	64	40	38	78	82	75	114	189	75	94	169	113
LHB-Avg	.265	.236	.248	.268	.261	.263	94	.239	.262	.253	.247	.273	.263	96
LHB-HR	22	26	48	14	18	32	151	50	68	118	38	56	94	124
RHB-Avg	.249	.257	.253	.263	.269	.266	95	.240	.261	.250	.264	.277	.269	93
RHB-HR	53	43	96	59	37	96	99	104	86	190	110	98	208	94

249

Boston Red Sox

	1992 Season							1990-1992						
	Home Games			Away Games			Index	Home Games			Away Games			Index
	Red Sox	Opp	Total	Red Sox	Opp	Total		Red Sox	Opp	Total	Red Sox	Opp	Total	
G	81	81	162	81	81	162	---	243	243	486	243	243	486	---
Avg	.259	.266	.263	.233	.244	.238	110	.276	.264	.270	.249	.250	.250	108
AB	2684	2860	5544	2777	2636	5413	102	8156	8550	16706	8351	7940	16291	103
R	328	341	669	271	328	599	112	1100	1033	2133	929	1012	1941	110
H	696	761	1457	647	642	1289	113	2252	2261	4513	2079	1986	4065	111
2B	149	143	292	110	117	227	126	506	431	937	356	384	740	123
3B	11	13	24	10	15	25	94	38	39	77	39	52	91	83
HR	45	46	91	39	61	100	89	175	166	341	141	180	321	104
SO	402	487	889	463	456	919	94	1188	1524	2712	1292	1415	2707	98
E	79	53	132	60	57	117	113	202	193	395	176	162	338	117
E-Infield	65	46	111	50	44	94	118	177	152	329	146	126	272	121
LHB-Avg	.257	.265	.261	.241	.236	.239	109	.292	.270	.280	.257	.239	.247	113
LHB-HR	20	9	29	15	18	33	80	51	45	96	42	54	96	96
RHB-Avg	.261	.267	.264	.229	.247	.238	111	.269	.261	.265	.245	.257	.251	106
RHB-HR	25	37	62	24	43	67	94	124	121	245	99	126	225	107

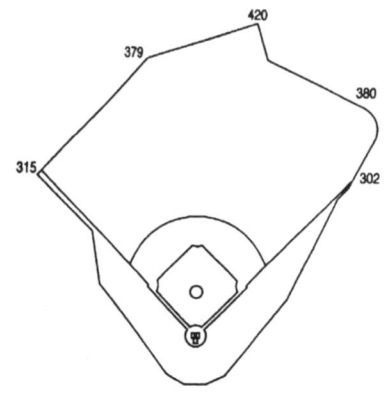

BOSTON

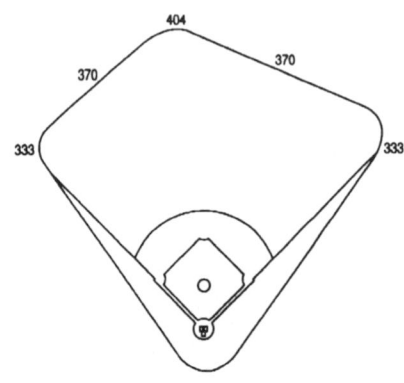

CALIFORNIA

California Angels

	1992 Season							1990-1992						
	Home Games			Away Games			Index	Home Games			Away Games			Index
	Angels	Opp	Total	Angels	Opp	Total		Angels	Opp	Total	Angels	Opp	Total	
G	81	81	162	81	81	162	---	243	243	486	243	243	486	---
Avg	.250	.266	.258	.238	.262	.250	103	.253	.258	.255	.253	.264	.258	99
AB	2637	2830	5467	2727	2654	5381	102	8005	8433	16438	8399	7998	16397	100
R	311	340	651	268	331	599	109	962	997	1959	960	1029	1989	98
H	658	753	1411	648	696	1344	105	2025	2172	4197	2125	2110	4235	99
2B	100	104	204	102	117	219	92	302	341	643	382	365	747	86
3B	10	7	17	10	10	20	84	34	27	61	42	45	87	70
HR	44	60	104	44	70	114	90	192	189	381	158	188	346	110
SO	415	447	862	467	441	908	93	1319	1443	2762	1491	1379	2870	96
E	69	83	152	64	60	124	123	197	198	395	180	195	375	105
E-Infield	60	74	134	50	56	106	126	164	161	325	149	170	319	102
LHB-Avg	.242	.264	.252	.253	.278	.265	95	.254	.259	.256	.265	.286	.274	94
LHB-HR	6	12	18	12	15	27	67	60	45	105	53	57	110	99
RHB-Avg	.254	.267	.261	.229	.255	.243	108	.252	.257	.255	.245	.253	.249	102
RHB-HR	38	48	86	32	55	87	97	132	144	276	105	131	236	114

Chicago Cubs

| | 1992 Season | | | | | | | 1990-1992 | | | | | | |
| | Home Games | | | Away Games | | | | Home Games | | | Away Games | | | |
	Cubs	Opp	Total	Cubs	Opp	Total	Index	Cubs	Opp	Total	Cubs	Opp	Total	Index
G	81	81	162	81	81	162	---	245	245	490	239	239	478	---
Avg	.257	.237	.247	.251	.255	.253	98	.266	.263	.264	.248	.253	.250	106
AB	2768	2817	5585	2822	2623	5445	103	8393	8655	17048	8319	7852	16171	103
R	315	297	612	278	327	605	101	1073	1130	2203	905	1002	1907	113
H	711	669	1380	709	668	1377	100	2230	2274	4504	2059	1988	4047	109
2B	120	122	242	101	139	240	98	371	394	765	322	383	705	103
3B	25	22	47	16	13	29	158	55	70	125	48	62	110	108
HR	59	49	108	45	58	103	102	227	197	424	172	148	320	126
SO	411	479	890	405	422	827	105	1253	1421	2674	1311	1284	2595	98
E	59	65	124	55	67	122	102	191	221	412	160	192	352	114
E-Infield	46	56	102	46	55	101	101	160	188	348	127	170	297	114
LHB-Avg	.273	.253	.262	.270	.251	.259	101	.266	.278	.274	.256	.255	.256	107
LHB-HR	16	27	43	18	31	49	82	44	99	143	42	74	116	114
RHB-Avg	.247	.222	.236	.241	.258	.248	95	.265	.247	.257	.243	.251	.246	104
RHB-HR	43	22	65	27	27	54	121	183	98	281	130	74	204	133

CHICAGO CUBS   WHITE SOX

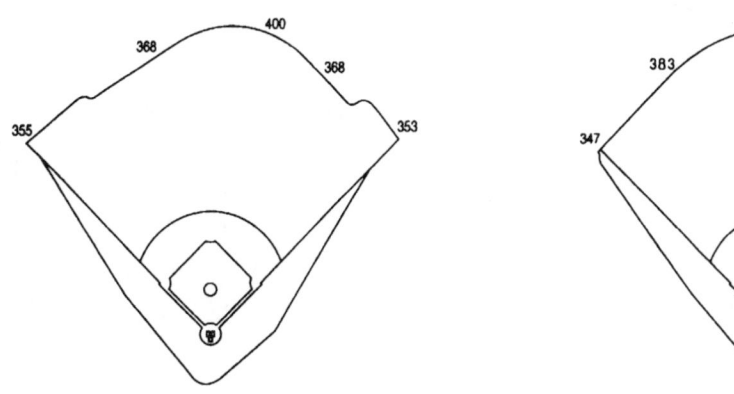

Chicago White Sox

| | 1992 Season | | | | | | | 1991-1992 | | | | | | |
| | Home Games | | | Away Games | | | | Home Games | | | Away Games | | | |
	White Sox	Opp	Total	White Sox	Opp	Total	Index	White Sox	Opp	Total	White Sox	Opp	Total	Index
G	82	82	164	80	80	160	---	163	163	326	161	161	322	---
Avg	.258	.243	.250	.264	.262	.263	95	.264	.242	.253	.258	.249	.254	100
AB	2694	2848	5542	2804	2703	5507	98	5407	5615	11022	5685	5384	11069	98
R	368	314	682	370	376	746	89	746	651	1397	750	720	1470	94
H	695	691	1386	739	709	1448	93	1430	1359	2789	1468	1343	2811	98
2B	129	87	216	140	137	277	77	237	200	437	258	239	497	88
3B	19	12	31	17	22	39	79	39	26	65	36	38	74	88
HR	54	62	116	56	61	117	99	128	141	269	121	136	257	105
SO	348	432	780	436	378	814	95	774	884	1658	906	849	1755	95
E	59	57	116	70	58	128	88	121	109	230	124	129	253	90
E-Infield	52	42	94	61	45	106	87	104	85	189	109	104	213	88
LHB-Avg	.262	.249	.256	.266	.258	.263	97	.270	.246	.259	.263	.241	.254	102
LHB-HR	17	24	41	18	18	36	117	47	51	98	44	42	86	112
RHB-Avg	.255	.238	.246	.261	.265	.263	94	.260	.239	.249	.254	.254	.254	98
RHB-HR	37	38	75	38	43	81	90	81	90	171	77	94	171	102

Cincinnati Reds

	1992 Season							1990-1992						
	Home Games			Away Games				Home Games			Away Games			
	Reds	Opp	Total	Reds	Opp	Total	Index	Reds	Opp	Total	Reds	Opp	Total	Index
G	81	81	162	81	81	162	--	243	243	486	243	243	486	--
Avg	.262	.242	.252	.258	.261	.259	97	.265	.247	.256	.257	.254	.255	100
AB	2625	2753	5378	2835	2666	5501	98	7979	8279	16258	8507	8009	16516	98
R	355	289	644	305	320	625	103	1062	977	2039	980	920	1900	107
H	687	666	1353	731	696	1427	95	2115	2041	4156	2188	2031	4219	99
2B	146	120	266	135	129	264	103	427	351	778	388	369	757	104
3B	18	23	41	26	25	51	82	47	54	101	64	60	124	83
HR	60	60	120	39	49	88	139	234	210	444	154	150	304	148
SO	422	565	987	466	495	961	105	1318	1563	2881	1489	1523	3012	97
E	40	63	103	56	63	119	87	137	167	304	186	194	380	80
E-Infield	32	51	83	46	57	103	81	116	138	254	159	170	329	77
LHB-Avg	.279	.261	.270	.254	.258	.256	105	.273	.252	.262	.254	.254	.254	103
LHB-HR	20	17	37	13	22	35	109	76	73	149	46	64	110	138
RHB-Avg	.249	.230	.239	.260	.263	.262	91	.260	.243	.252	.259	.253	.256	98
RHB-HR	40	43	83	26	27	53	159	158	137	295	108	86	194	154

CINCINNATI

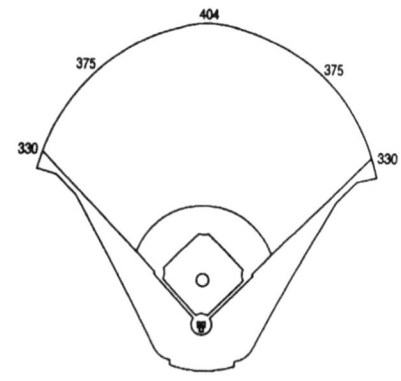

CLEVELAND

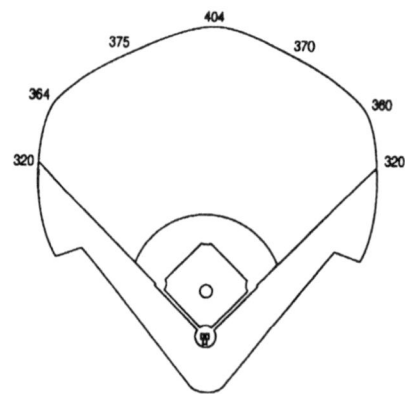

Cleveland Indians

	1992 Season							1991 Season						
	Home Games			Away Games				Home Games			Away Games			
	Indians	Opp	Total	Indians	Opp	Total	Index	Indians	Opp	Total	Indians	Opp	Total	Index
G	81	81	162	81	81	162	--	82	82	164	80	80	160	--
Avg	.283	.272	.277	.250	.265	.257	108	.262	.272	.267	.247	.280	.263	101
AB	2781	2920	5701	2839	2695	5534	103	2693	2900	5593	2777	2723	5500	99
R	366	397	763	308	349	657	116	271	377	648	305	382	687	92
H	786	794	1580	709	713	1422	111	705	788	1493	685	763	1448	101
2B	117	135	252	110	110	220	111	122	128	250	114	151	265	93
3B	15	10	25	9	17	26	93	15	22	37	11	16	27	135
HR	62	94	156	65	65	130	116	22	41	63	57	69	126	49
SO	429	475	904	456	415	871	101	393	447	840	495	415	910	91
E	85	58	143	56	47	103	139	75	52	127	73	59	132	94
E-Infield	68	47	115	46	36	82	140	59	41	100	57	53	110	89
LHB-Avg	.279	.272	.276	.259	.272	.265	104	.256	.279	.268	.253	.302	.279	96
LHB-HR	28	24	52	21	22	43	113	4	11	15	19	21	40	38
RHB-Avg	.286	.272	.278	.242	.260	.251	111	.265	.267	.266	.243	.265	.253	105
RHB-HR	34	70	104	44	43	87	119	18	30	48	38	48	86	54

Detroit Tigers

| | 1992 Season | | | | | | | 1990-1992 | | | | | | |
| | Home Games | | | Away Games | | | Index | Home Games | | | Away Games | | | Index |
	Tigers	Opp	Total	Tigers	Opp	Total		Tigers	Opp	Total	Tigers	Opp	Total	
G	80	80	160	82	82	164	---	242	242	484	244	244	488	---
Avg	.254	.278	.266	.257	.275	.266	100	.254	.268	.262	.254	.276	.265	99
AB	2640	2850	5490	2875	2696	5571	101	7948	8448	16396	8593	8103	16696	99
R	389	399	788	402	395	797	101	1198	1200	2398	1160	1142	2302	105
H	671	792	1463	740	742	1482	101	2020	2268	4288	2181	2237	4418	98
2B	126	130	256	130	124	254	102	345	387	732	411	399	810	92
3B	8	11	19	8	15	23	84	37	38	75	37	55	92	83
HR	91	90	181	91	65	156	118	292	254	546	271	203	474	117
SO	523	363	886	532	330	862	104	1550	1213	2763	1642	1075	2717	104
E	53	53	106	63	73	136	80	168	186	354	183	189	372	96
E-Infield	42	46	88	49	62	111	81	130	158	288	147	160	307	95
LHB-Avg	.260	.278	.269	.248	.275	.260	103	.253	.276	.264	.252	.272	.261	101
LHB-HR	33	30	63	24	20	44	141	110	86	196	84	67	151	132
RHB-Avg	.250	.278	.265	.264	.276	.270	98	.255	.264	.260	.255	.278	.267	98
RHB-HR	58	60	118	67	45	112	109	182	168	350	187	136	323	111

DETROIT

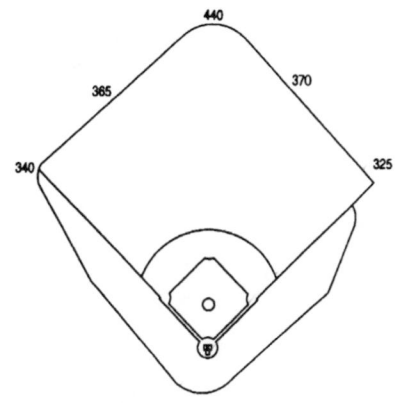

440
365 370
340 325

HOUSTON

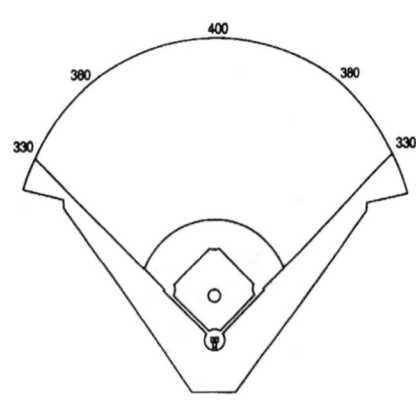

400
380 380
330 330

Houston Astros

| | 1992 Season | | | | | | | 1990-1991 | | | | | | |
| | Home Games | | | Away Games | | | Index | Home Games | | | Away Games | | | Index |
	Astros	Opp	Total	Astros	Opp	Total		Astros	Opp	Total	Astros	Opp	Total	
G	81	81	162	81	81	162	---	162	162	324	162	162	324	---
Avg	.251	.237	.244	.242	.268	.255	96	.251	.236	.243	.236	.267	.251	97
AB	2733	2843	5576	2747	2659	5406	103	5362	5552	10914	5521	5383	10904	100
R	302	293	595	306	375	681	87	600	601	1201	578	772	1350	89
H	685	673	1358	665	713	1378	99	1344	1308	2652	1302	1435	2737	97
2B	145	106	251	110	149	259	94	245	238	483	204	247	451	107
3B	22	20	42	16	29	45	90	52	36	88	23	30	53	166
HR	49	41	90	47	73	120	73	62	91	153	111	168	279	55
SO	540	539	1079	485	439	924	113	995	1033	2028	1029	854	1883	108
E	50	47	97	64	52	116	84	138	105	243	154	106	260	93
E-Infield	41	37	78	53	48	101	77	115	91	206	124	93	217	95
LHB-Avg	.248	.243	.245	.248	.278	.264	93	.243	.246	.245	.223	.280	.254	96
LHB-HR	23	18	41	24	31	55	75	28	41	69	46	72	118	57
RHB-Avg	.253	.231	.242	.237	.257	.247	98	.256	.225	.242	.244	.254	.249	97
RHB-HR	26	23	49	23	42	65	71	34	50	84	65	96	161	53

253

Kansas City Royals

	1992 Season							1990-1992						
	Home Games			Away Games				Home Games			Away Games			
	Royals	Opp	Total	Royals	Opp	Total	Index	Royals	Opp	Total	Royals	Opp	Total	Index
G	81	81	162	81	81	162	---	243	243	486	242	242	484	---
Avg	.258	.259	.258	.256	.259	.257	101	.267	.258	.262	.259	.265	.262	100
AB	2656	2845	5501	2845	2657	5502	100	8130	8618	16748	8443	8016	16459	101
R	314	336	650	296	331	627	104	1028	1056	2084	1016	1042	2058	101
H	684	738	1422	727	688	1415	100	2168	2221	4389	2183	2127	4310	101
2B	134	148	282	150	117	267	106	445	436	881	445	353	798	108
3B	25	17	42	17	11	28	150	84	62	146	43	42	85	169
HR	24	41	65	51	65	116	56	113	127	240	179	200	379	62
SO	327	416	743	414	418	832	89	1164	1450	2614	1425	1394	2819	91
E	66	64	130	56	47	103	126	197	191	388	172	165	337	115
E-Infield	58	50	108	49	43	92	117	166	155	321	145	141	286	112
LHB-Avg	.261	.249	.256	.264	.249	.258	99	.270	.262	.266	.263	.272	.267	100
LHB-HR	8	10	18	24	31	55	32	36	47	83	74	92	166	48
RHB-Avg	.253	.267	.261	.246	.266	.257	102	.263	.254	.258	.254	.260	.257	101
RHB-HR	16	31	47	27	34	61	79	77	80	157	105	108	213	74

KANSAS CITY

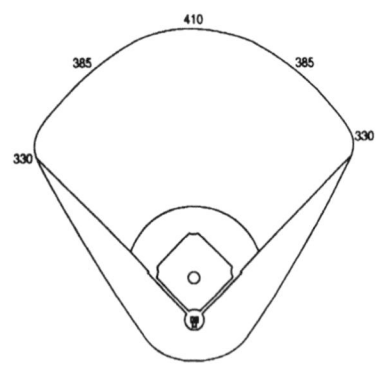

LOS ANGELES

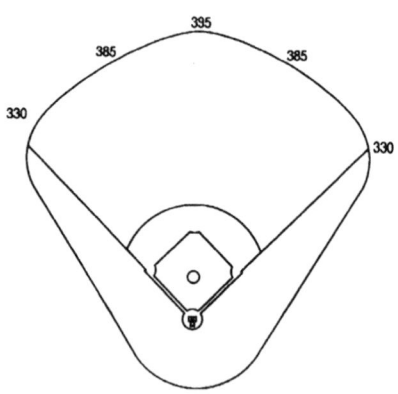

Los Angeles Dodgers

	1992 Season							1990-1992						
	Home Games			Away Games				Home Games			Away Games			
	Dodgers	Opp	Total	Dodgers	Opp	Total	Index	Dodgers	Opp	Total	Dodgers	Opp	Total	Index
G	81	81	162	81	81	162	---	243	243	486	243	243	486	---
Avg	.253	.253	.253	.244	.261	.252	100	.256	.244	.250	.252	.254	.253	99
AB	2627	2777	5404	2741	2680	5421	100	7947	8380	16327	8320	8002	16322	100
R	277	281	558	271	355	626	89	970	884	1854	971	1002	1973	94
H	664	702	1366	669	699	1368	100	2038	2048	4086	2097	2029	4126	99
2B	96	105	201	105	121	226	89	274	292	566	340	369	709	80
3B	19	15	34	15	18	33	103	41	35	76	49	56	105	72
HR	26	33	59	46	49	95	62	137	152	289	172	163	335	86
SO	404	508	912	495	473	968	95	1320	1615	2935	1488	1415	2903	101
E	85	84	169	89	55	144	117	212	244	456	215	158	373	122
E-Infield	74	66	140	75	43	118	119	191	205	396	183	122	305	130
LHB-Avg	.251	.257	.254	.239	.282	.259	98	.263	.251	.257	.256	.266	.261	99
LHB-HR	11	23	34	18	24	42	75	84	71	155	101	72	173	89
RHB-Avg	.255	.249	.251	.249	.242	.246	102	.248	.238	.242	.247	.242	.244	99
RHB-HR	15	10	25	28	25	53	51	53	81	134	71	91	162	84

Milwaukee Brewers

| | 1992 Season | | | | | | | 1990-1992 | | | | | | |
| | Home Games | | | Away Games | | | Index | Home Games | | | Away Games | | | Index |
	Brewers	Opp	Total	Brewers	Opp	Total		Brewers	Opp	Total	Brewers	Opp	Total	
G	81	81	162	81	81	162	---	242	242	484	244	244	488	---
Avg	.260	.234	.247	.276	.257	.267	93	.260	.256	.258	.270	.269	.270	96
AB	2580	2747	5327	2924	2721	5645	94	7935	8486	16421	8683	8268	16951	98
R	339	254	593	401	350	751	79	1093	1026	2119	1178	1082	2260	95
H	671	644	1315	806	700	1506	87	2063	2172	4235	2345	2228	4573	93
2B	111	112	223	161	138	299	79	366	362	728	400	408	808	93
3B	17	8	25	18	18	36	74	61	30	91	63	54	117	80
HR	35	51	86	47	76	123	74	157	183	340	169	212	381	92
SO	361	382	743	418	411	829	95	1152	1251	2403	1250	1172	2422	102
E	47	77	124	42	69	111	112	184	190	374	172	203	375	101
E-Infield	42	61	103	40	63	103	100	157	153	310	150	170	320	98
LHB-Avg	.254	.225	.238	.266	.262	.264	90	.267	.249	.258	.267	.268	.267	96
LHB-HR	9	13	22	14	30	44	54	44	63	107	49	81	130	86
RHB-Avg	.263	.242	.253	.282	.254	.269	94	.255	.261	.258	.273	.271	.272	95
RHB-HR	26	38	64	33	46	79	85	113	120	233	120	131	251	95

MILWAUKEE

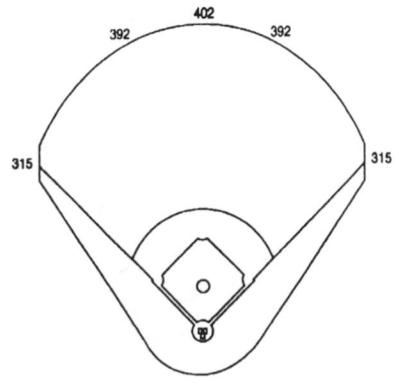

MINNESOTA

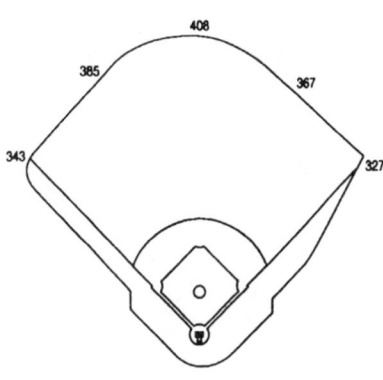

Minnesota Twins

| | 1992 Season | | | | | | | 1990-1992 | | | | | | |
| | Home Games | | | Away Games | | | Index | Home Games | | | Away Games | | | Index |
	Twins	Opp	Total	Twins	Opp	Total		Twins	Opp	Total	Twins	Opp	Total	
G	81	81	162	81	81	162	---	243	243	486	243	243	486	---
Avg	.282	.256	.269	.271	.252	.262	103	.289	.263	.276	.260	.259	.259	106
AB	2723	2826	5549	2859	2646	5505	101	8179	8487	16666	8458	8007	16465	101
R	375	326	701	372	327	699	100	1152	1048	2200	1037	986	2023	109
H	769	724	1493	775	667	1442	104	2363	2229	4592	2196	2073	4269	108
2B	132	157	289	143	115	258	111	430	460	890	396	365	761	116
3B	18	21	39	9	12	21	184	72	61	133	36	37	73	180
HR	56	56	112	48	65	113	98	164	200	364	180	194	374	96
SO	408	515	923	426	408	834	110	1106	1445	2551	1224	1226	2450	103
E	39	51	90	56	71	127	71	127	182	309	164	196	360	86
E-Infield	32	43	75	49	60	109	69	102	146	248	139	162	301	82
LHB-Avg	.262	.264	.263	.246	.257	.252	104	.270	.270	.270	.251	.269	.261	104
LHB-HR	19	18	37	12	21	33	111	65	60	125	61	58	119	102
RHB-Avg	.289	.252	.272	.280	.249	.266	102	.297	.258	.278	.263	.253	.258	108
RHB-HR	37	38	75	36	44	80	93	99	140	239	119	136	255	93

Montreal Expos

	1992 Season							1991-1992						
	Home Games			Away Games				Home Games			Away Games			
	Expos	Opp	Total	Expos	Opp	Total	Index	Expos	Opp	Total	Expos	Opp	Total	Index
G	81	81	162	81	81	162	--	149	149	298	174	174	348	--
Avg	.256	.241	.249	.248	.234	.241	103	.250	.235	.242	.248	.246	.247	98
AB	2624	2758	5382	2853	2694	5547	97	4841	5076	9917	6048	5721	11769	98
R	331	334	665	317	247	564	118	547	567	1114	680	669	1349	96
H	673	665	1338	708	631	1339	100	1209	1195	2404	1501	1405	2906	97
2B	136	136	272	127	95	222	126	231	242	473	268	243	511	110
3B	17	22	39	20	12	32	126	30	42	72	49	31	80	107
HR	50	48	98	52	44	96	105	85	81	166	112	122	234	84
SO	438	521	959	538	493	1031	96	874	946	1820	1158	977	2135	101
E	57	64	121	67	51	118	103	114	117	231	143	129	272	99
E-Infield	51	56	107	56	42	98	109	99	103	202	119	114	233	101
LHB-Avg	.257	.251	.254	.264	.233	.248	102	.251	.250	.250	.258	.242	.250	100
LHB-HR	17	27	44	23	17	40	115	30	38	68	49	50	99	83
RHB-Avg	.256	.233	.245	.237	.235	.236	104	.249	.224	.236	.241	.249	.245	97
RHB-HR	33	21	54	29	27	56	98	55	43	98	63	72	135	85

MONTREAL

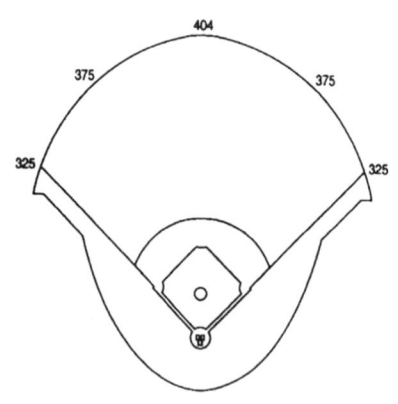

NEW YORK METS

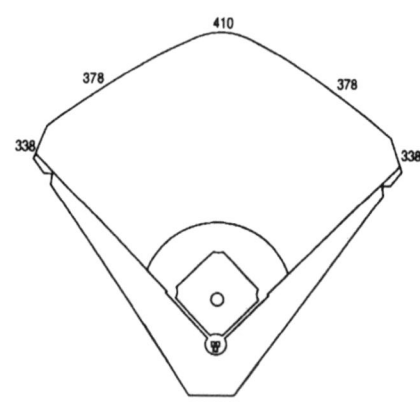

New York Mets

	1992 Season							1990-1992						
	Home Games			Away Games				Home Games			Away Games			
	Mets	Opp	Total	Mets	Opp	Total	Index	Mets	Opp	Total	Mets	Opp	Total	Index
G	81	81	162	81	81	162	--	244	244	488	241	241	482	--
Avg	.232	.251	.242	.238	.263	.250	97	.243	.250	.246	.247	.257	.252	98
AB	2585	2820	5405	2755	2654	5409	100	7900	8460	16360	8303	7923	16226	100
R	288	305	593	311	348	659	90	1017	933	1950	997	979	1976	97
H	599	707	1306	655	697	1352	97	1918	2111	4029	2051	2035	4086	97
2B	123	137	260	136	130	266	98	370	364	734	417	343	760	96
3B	10	26	36	7	30	37	97	31	71	102	31	68	99	102
HR	42	49	91	51	49	100	91	185	156	341	197	169	366	92
SO	465	528	993	491	497	988	101	1246	1715	2961	1350	1555	2905	101
E	52	58	110	64	48	112	98	186	202	388	205	155	360	106
E-Infield	43	47	90	59	38	97	93	162	167	329	183	122	305	107
LHB-Avg	.235	.259	.247	.247	.269	.257	96	.246	.252	.249	.257	.257	.257	97
LHB-HR	24	24	48	35	16	51	96	102	59	161	98	58	156	103
RHB-Avg	.228	.245	.237	.229	.258	.243	98	.239	.248	.244	.237	.257	.247	99
RHB-HR	18	25	43	16	33	49	86	83	97	180	99	111	210	85

New York Yankees

| | 1992 Season | | | | | | | 1990-1992 | | | | | | |
| | Home Games | | | Away Games | | | | Home Games | | | Away Games | | | |
	Yankees	Opp	Total	Yankees	Opp	Total	Index	Yankees	Opp	Total	Yankees	Opp	Total	Index
G	81	81	162	81	81	162	---	243	243	486	243	243	486	---
Avg	.262	.265	.263	.261	.262	.261	101	.255	.261	.258	.251	.270	.260	99
AB	2735	2863	5598	2858	2654	5512	102	8130	8521	16651	8487	8045	16532	101
R	385	387	772	348	359	707	109	1037	1128	2165	973	1144	2117	102
H	717	758	1475	745	695	1440	102	2075	2223	4298	2127	2170	4297	100
2B	135	137	272	146	133	279	96	386	394	780	352	439	791	98
3B	8	15	23	10	18	28	81	26	44	70	30	75	105	66
HR	88	70	158	75	59	134	116	234	232	466	223	193	416	111
SO	422	436	858	481	415	896	94	1302	1384	2686	1489	1312	2801	95
E	50	58	108	64	57	121	89	179	160	339	193	162	355	95
E-Infield	44	52	96	52	46	98	98	153	138	291	162	136	298	98
LHB-Avg	.274	.274	.274	.259	.272	.266	103	.262	.269	.266	.249	.272	.260	102
LHB-HR	42	31	73	27	18	45	175	112	93	205	91	64	155	139
RHB-Avg	.255	.259	.257	.262	.254	.258	100	.251	.256	.253	.252	.268	.260	98
RHB-HR	46	39	85	48	41	89	89	122	139	261	132	129	261	96

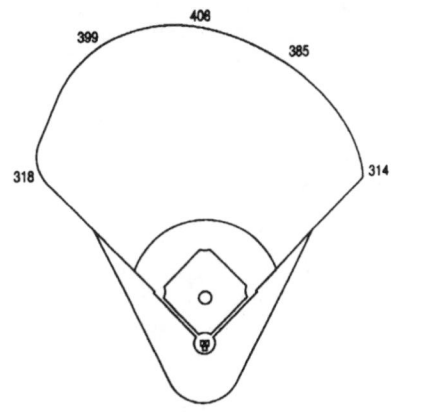

NY YANKEES

408
399
385
318
314

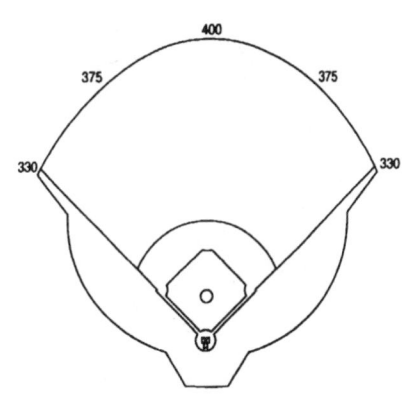

OAKLAND

400
375
375
330
330

Oakland Athletics

| | 1992 Season | | | | | | | 1990-1992 | | | | | | |
| | Home Games | | | Away Games | | | | Home Games | | | Away Games | | | |
	Athletics	Opp	Total	Athletics	Opp	Total	Index	Athletics	Opp	Total	Athletics	Opp	Total	Index
G	81	81	162	81	81	162	---	243	243	486	243	243	486	---
Avg	.251	.247	.249	.264	.266	.265	94	.246	.238	.242	.260	.265	.262	92
AB	2574	2764	5338	2813	2682	5495	97	7813	8259	16072	8417	8077	16494	97
R	365	326	691	380	346	726	95	1043	921	1964	1195	1097	2292	86
H	645	682	1327	744	714	1458	91	1924	1965	3889	2186	2143	4329	90
2B	97	101	198	122	134	256	80	300	328	628	374	398	772	83
3B	14	11	25	10	20	30	86	28	44	72	37	57	94	79
HR	76	73	149	66	56	122	126	221	192	413	244	215	459	92
SO	398	462	860	433	381	814	109	1354	1363	2717	1450	1203	2653	105
E	62	65	127	63	58	121	105	159	193	352	160	189	349	101
E-Infield	50	53	103	52	48	100	103	128	157	285	126	154	280	102
LHB-Avg	.262	.262	.262	.246	.277	.264	99	.241	.244	.243	.256	.267	.263	92
LHB-HR	15	24	39	14	24	38	106	41	62	103	38	91	129	79
RHB-Avg	.245	.234	.240	.274	.257	.266	90	.248	.232	.241	.261	.264	.262	92
RHB-HR	61	49	110	52	32	84	134	180	130	310	206	124	330	98

Philadelphia Phillies

| | 1992 Season | | | | | | | 1990-1992 | | | | | | |
| | Home Games | | | Away Games | | | | Home Games | | | Away Games | | | |
	Phillies	Opp	Total	Phillies	Opp	Total	Index	Phillies	Opp	Total	Phillies	Opp	Total	Index
G	81	81	162	81	81	162	---	245	245	490	241	241	482	---
Avg	.256	.249	.253	.250	.265	.257	98	.254	.247	.250	.246	.257	.251	100
AB	2685	2752	5437	2815	2649	5464	100	8158	8424	16582	8398	7908	16306	100
R	369	331	700	317	386	703	100	1021	1032	2053	940	1094	2034	99
H	688	685	1373	704	702	1406	98	2070	2079	4149	2064	2035	4099	100
2B	133	120	253	122	143	265	96	376	421	797	364	379	743	105
3B	19	26	45	17	16	33	137	47	61	108	49	50	99	107
HR	67	49	116	51	64	115	101	175	169	344	157	179	336	101
SO	526	474	1000	533	377	910	110	1486	1450	2936	1514	1229	2743	105
E	65	57	122	66	64	130	94	165	158	323	202	197	399	80
E-Infield	54	50	104	56	54	110	95	138	135	273	173	167	340	79
LHB-Avg	.270	.258	.265	.259	.274	.266	100	.266	.250	.258	.259	.264	.261	99
LHB-HR	41	20	61	26	20	46	138	95	74	169	69	59	128	134
RHB-Avg	.242	.243	.242	.241	.258	.250	97	.243	.245	.244	.233	.253	.244	100
RHB-HR	26	29	55	25	44	69	78	80	95	175	88	120	208	81

PHILADELPHIA

PITTSBURGH

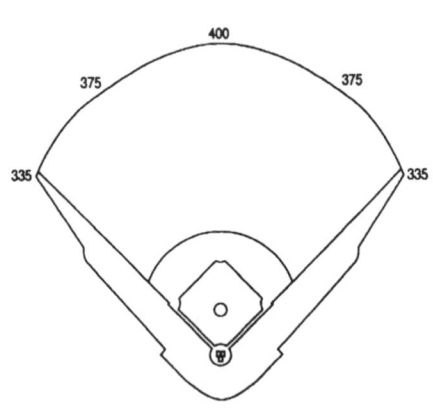

Pittsburgh Pirates

| | 1992 Season | | | | | | | 1990-1992 | | | | | | |
| | Home Games | | | Away Games | | | | Home Games | | | Away Games | | | |
	Pirates	Opp	Total	Pirates	Opp	Total	Index	Pirates	Opp	Total	Pirates	Opp	Total	Index
G	81	81	162	81	81	162	---	246	246	492	240	240	480	---
Avg	.264	.256	.260	.246	.252	.249	104	.259	.251	.255	.259	.256	.258	99
AB	2676	2834	5510	2851	2715	5566	99	7963	8441	16404	8401	8078	16479	97
R	363	277	640	330	318	648	99	1096	890	1986	1098	956	2054	94
H	707	726	1433	702	684	1386	103	2059	2121	4180	2178	2067	4245	96
2B	141	143	284	131	121	252	114	417	389	806	402	348	750	108
3B	30	16	46	24	18	42	111	76	54	130	70	44	114	115
HR	51	37	88	55	64	119	75	171	155	326	199	198	397	82
SO	413	459	872	459	385	844	104	1284	1417	2701	1403	1194	2597	104
E	50	60	110	51	48	99	111	164	162	326	191	160	351	91
E-Infield	44	54	98	39	37	76	129	140	134	274	152	125	277	97
LHB-Avg	.292	.257	.274	.261	.246	.254	108	.269	.255	.263	.272	.254	.264	99
LHB-HR	31	12	43	33	28	61	74	102	50	152	116	78	194	80
RHB-Avg	.243	.256	.250	.234	.256	.245	102	.249	.249	.249	.247	.257	.252	99
RHB-HR	20	25	45	22	36	58	76	69	105	174	83	120	203	85

San Diego Padres

	1992 Season							1990-1992						
	Home Games			Away Games			Index	Home Games			Away Games			Index
	Padres	Opp	Total	Padres	Opp	Total		Padres	Opp	Total	Padres	Opp	Total	
G	81	81	162	81	81	162	---	243	243	486	243	243	486	---
Avg	.271	.264	.267	.239	.258	.248	108	.257	.255	.256	.247	.259	.253	101
AB	2689	2833	5522	2787	2702	5489	101	8056	8484	16540	8382	8116	16498	100
R	339	334	673	278	302	580	116	996	1002	1998	930	953	1883	106
H	730	747	1477	666	697	1363	108	2073	2166	4239	2073	2100	4173	102
2B	126	102	228	129	118	247	92	329	314	643	373	336	709	90
3B	14	11	25	16	16	32	78	49	44	93	52	45	97	96
HR	87	64	151	48	47	95	158	215	214	429	164	183	347	123
SO	394	497	891	470	474	944	94	1350	1515	2865	1485	1305	2790	102
E	57	51	108	58	52	110	98	191	183	374	178	197	375	100
E-Infield	49	41	90	47	41	88	102	165	140	305	154	164	318	96
LHB-Avg	.255	.272	.264	.259	.273	.266	99	.264	.258	.261	.263	.267	.265	99
LHB-HR	28	29	57	18	25	43	134	71	89	160	59	80	139	116
RHB-Avg	.282	.258	.270	.224	.248	.236	114	.252	.253	.253	.234	.253	.244	104
RHB-HR	59	35	94	30	22	52	178	144	125	269	105	103	208	128

SAN DIEGO

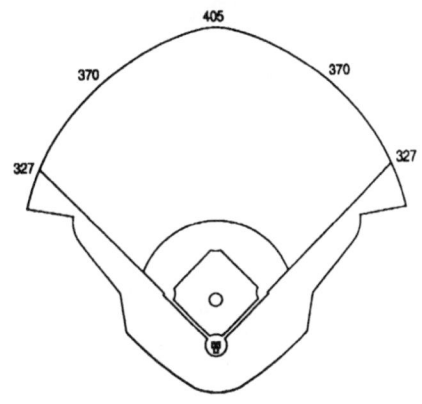

SAN FRANCISCO

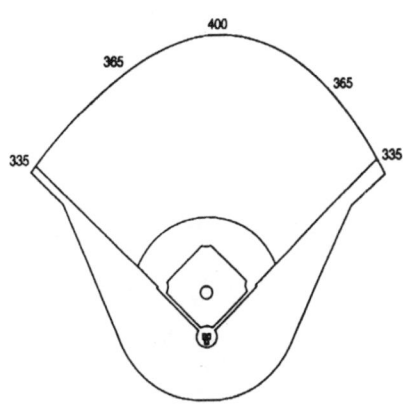

San Francisco Giants

	1992 Season							1990-1992						
	Home Games			Away Games			Index	Home Games			Away Games			Index
	Giants	Opp	Total	Giants	Opp	Total		Giants	Opp	Total	Giants	Opp	Total	
G	81	81	162	81	81	162	---	243	243	486	243	243	486	---
Avg	.252	.240	.246	.236	.267	.251	98	.256	.247	.251	.246	.271	.258	97
AB	2687	2783	5470	2769	2684	5453	100	8072	8381	16453	8420	8062	16482	100
R	307	294	601	267	353	620	97	993	939	1932	949	1115	2064	94
H	677	668	1345	653	717	1370	98	2064	2072	4136	2070	2187	4257	97
2B	130	103	233	90	140	230	101	354	334	688	302	394	696	99
3B	21	15	36	15	22	37	97	60	41	101	59	56	115	88
HR	57	60	117	48	68	116	101	207	192	399	191	210	401	100
SO	467	466	933	600	461	1061	88	1392	1377	2769	1621	1243	2864	97
E	60	49	109	53	69	122	89	168	189	357	161	192	353	101
E-Infield	51	43	94	46	54	100	94	132	163	295	136	161	297	99
LHB-Avg	.273	.246	.258	.248	.275	.264	98	.268	.257	.262	.261	.278	.270	97
LHB-HR	19	22	41	10	27	37	106	65	74	139	47	94	141	98
RHB-Avg	.240	.235	.238	.230	.260	.243	98	.248	.239	.244	.236	.266	.250	97
RHB-HR	38	38	76	38	41	79	99	142	118	260	144	116	260	101

Seattle Mariners

	1992 Season							1991 Season						
	Home Games			Away Games				Home Games			Away Games			
	Mariners	Opp	Total	Mariners	Opp	Total	Index	Mariners	Opp	Total	Mariners	Opp	Total	Index
G	81	81	162	81	81	162	---	81	81	162	81	81	162	---
Avg	.268	.271	.270	.259	.261	.260	104	.259	.246	.252	.251	.260	.255	99
AB	2742	2863	5605	2822	2656	5478	102	2706	2833	5539	2788	2653	5441	102
R	355	398	753	324	401	725	104	374	319	693	328	355	683	101
H	736	775	1511	730	692	1422	106	701	697	1398	699	690	1389	101
2B	173	165	338	105	138	243	136	137	130	267	131	128	259	101
3B	13	11	24	11	14	25	94	19	16	35	10	16	26	132
HR	78	63	141	71	66	137	101	69	69	138	57	67	124	109
SO	417	485	902	424	409	833	106	411	534	945	400	469	869	107
E	55	60	115	57	48	105	110	51	40	91	59	63	122	75
E-Infield	53	49	102	50	43	93	110	41	31	72	49	58	107	67
LHB-Avg	.275	.287	.280	.263	.259	.262	107	.272	.250	.263	.237	.264	.247	106
LHB-HR	36	17	53	31	18	49	108	43	20	63	20	22	42	146
RHB-Avg	.263	.262	.263	.254	.261	.258	102	.241	.244	.243	.270	.258	.263	92
RHB-HR	42	46	88	40	48	88	97	26	49	75	37	45	82	91

SEATTLE

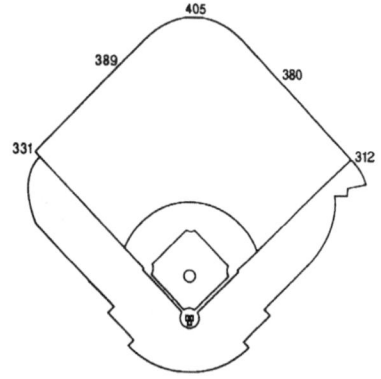

St. LOUIS

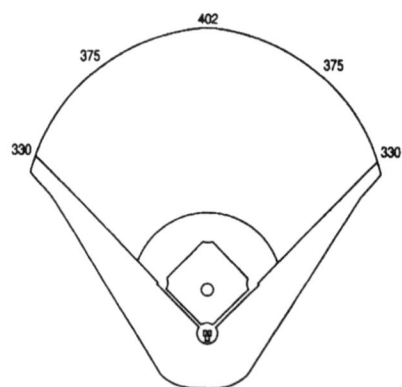

St. Louis Cardinals

	1992 Season							1990-1991						
	Home Games			Away Games				Home Games			Away Games			
	Cardinals	Opp	Total	Cardinals	Opp	Total	Index	Cardinals	Opp	Total	Cardinals	Opp	Total	Index
G	81	81	162	81	81	162	---	165	165	330	159	159	318	---
Avg	.268	.243	.255	.256	.261	.258	99	.254	.254	.254	.257	.262	.259	98
AB	2786	2877	5663	2808	2708	5516	103	5401	5699	11100	5423	5157	10580	101
R	328	297	625	303	307	610	102	664	659	1323	586	687	1273	100
H	746	698	1444	718	707	1425	101	1372	1449	2821	1392	1350	2742	99
2B	119	134	253	143	118	261	94	241	294	535	253	237	490	104
3B	26	14	40	18	20	38	103	56	55	111	38	28	66	160
HR	55	52	107	39	66	105	99	75	88	163	66	124	190	82
SO	489	433	922	507	409	916	98	789	830	1619	912	825	1737	89
E	51	47	98	43	50	93	105	118	114	232	119	128	247	91
E-Infield	39	39	78	37	40	77	101	89	92	181	97	104	201	87
LHB-Avg	.273	.241	.256	.255	.266	.261	98	.253	.259	.256	.263	.270	.266	96
LHB-HR	27	23	50	13	32	45	104	23	32	55	25	53	78	64
RHB-Avg	.264	.244	.254	.256	.257	.256	99	.255	.250	.252	.252	.255	.253	100
RHB-HR	28	29	57	26	34	60	95	52	56	108	41	71	112	96

Texas Rangers

	1992 Season							1990-1992						
	Home Games			Away Games			Index	Home Games			Away Games			Index
	Rangers	Opp	Total	Rangers	Opp	Total		Rangers	Opp	Total	Rangers	Opp	Total	
G	81	81	162	81	81	162	---	244	244	488	242	242	484	---
Avg	.253	.256	.255	.248	.272	.260	98	.263	.255	.259	.257	.262	.259	100
AB	2727	2844	5571	2810	2724	5534	101	8167	8515	16682	8542	8141	16683	99
R	317	376	693	365	377	742	93	1075	1124	2199	1112	1139	2251	97
H	689	729	1418	698	742	1440	98	2145	2170	4315	2197	2130	4327	99
2B	131	143	274	135	144	279	98	409	389	798	402	422	824	97
3B	15	10	25	8	19	27	92	51	51	102	30	47	77	132
HR	71	63	134	88	50	138	96	214	199	413	232	178	410	101
SO	541	564	1105	495	470	965	114	1581	1665	3246	1548	1388	2936	111
E	82	44	126	72	63	135	93	227	154	381	194	162	356	106
E-Infield	62	38	100	54	50	104	96	174	125	299	156	121	277	107
LHB-Avg	.247	.253	.250	.252	.269	.260	96	.260	.244	.252	.268	.256	.262	96
LHB-HR	25	23	48	29	19	48	104	89	70	159	86	54	140	114
RHB-Avg	.257	.259	.258	.245	.275	.260	99	.265	.263	.264	.248	.266	.257	103
RHB-HR	46	40	86	59	31	90	91	125	129	254	146	124	270	94

TEXAS

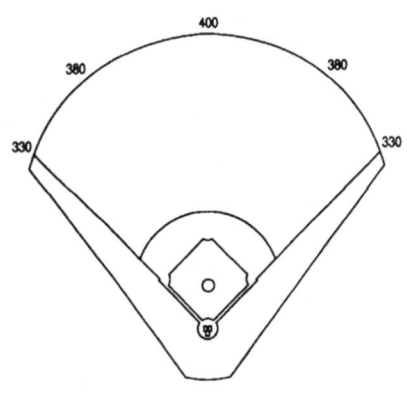

TORONTO

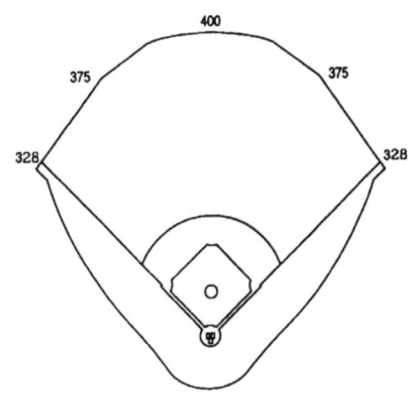

Toronto Blue Jays

	1992 Season							1990-1992						
	Home Games			Away Games			Index	Home Games			Away Games			Index
	Blue Jays	Opp	Total	Blue Jays	Opp	Total		Blue Jays	Opp	Total	Blue Jays	Opp	Total	
G	81	81	162	81	81	162	---	243	243	486	243	243	486	---
Avg	.261	.245	.252	.266	.251	.259	98	.264	.253	.258	.259	.244	.252	103
AB	2641	2765	5406	2895	2667	5562	97	8076	8466	16542	8538	7960	16498	100
R	390	334	724	390	348	738	98	1134	1019	2153	1097	946	2043	105
H	688	677	1365	770	669	1439	95	2136	2140	4276	2213	1941	4154	103
2B	129	144	273	136	116	252	111	421	389	810	402	347	749	108
3B	24	9	33	16	9	25	136	80	35	115	55	43	98	117
HR	79	60	139	84	64	148	97	247	214	461	216	174	390	118
SO	439	488	927	494	466	960	99	1412	1447	2859	1534	1370	2904	98
E	41	65	106	52	68	120	88	146	165	311	160	190	350	89
E-Infield	33	47	80	39	58	97	82	124	140	264	123	157	280	94
LHB-Avg	.275	.245	.258	.275	.248	.261	99	.277	.254	.266	.264	.247	.257	104
LHB-HR	12	18	30	24	20	44	65	68	60	128	80	62	142	87
RHB-Avg	.253	.244	.249	.262	.253	.258	97	.255	.252	.253	.255	.242	.248	102
RHB-HR	67	42	109	60	44	104	112	179	154	333	136	112	248	137

1992 Lefty-Righty Stats

. . . or The Strat-O-Matic Bible. Juan Gonzalez vs. righties .
. . Oooooh. Mark McGwire vs. lefties . . . Aaaaah. Henry
Mercedes . . . AAAAAHHHHH!!! (Henry Mercedes? Sorry,
we got carried away. He won't even get a card.) For those of
you who don't immediately tear this section out and laminate
it, there's league averages added this year — yet another
reader suggestion realized.

Batters vs. Left-Handed and Right-Handed Pitchers

Batter	vs	Avg	AB	H	2B	3B	HR	BI	BB	SO	OBP	SLG	Batter	vs	Avg	AB	H	2B	3B	HR	BI	BB	SO	OBP	SLG
Abner,Shawn	L	.254	122	31	6	0	1	9	8	20	.304	.328	Barrett,Tom	L	.000	0	0	0	0	0	0	0	0	.000	.000
Bats Right	R	.314	86	27	4	1	0	7	4	15	.352	.384	Bats Both	R	.000	3	0	0	0	0	0	2	0	.400	.000
Afenir,Troy	L	.150	20	3	0	1	0	3	3	4	.261	.250	Bass,Kevin	L	.222	144	32	13	1	4	17	3	22	.236	.410
Bats Right	R	.214	14	3	1	1	0	1	2	8	.313	.429	Bats Both	R	.295	258	76	10	4	5	22	20	48	.345	.422
Alexander,M	L	.000	0	0	0	0	0	0	0	0	.000	.000	Batiste,Kim	L	.205	73	15	2	0	0	4	2	10	.224	.233
Bats Right	R	.200	5	1	0	0	0	0	0	3	.200	.200	Bats Right	R	.206	63	13	2	0	1	6	2	8	.224	.286
Alicea,Luis	L	.294	85	25	4	3	0	12	5	10	.340	.412	Bell,Derek	L	.255	47	12	3	1	2	6	3	9	.333	.489
Bats Both	R	.222	180	40	5	8	2	20	22	30	.311	.372	Bats Right	R	.237	114	27	3	2	0	9	12	25	.320	.298
Allanson,Andy	L	.143	7	1	0	0	0	0	0	1	.143	.143	Bell,George	L	.310	142	44	8	0	7	28	10	17	.355	.514
Bats Right	R	.389	18	7	1	0	0	0	1	1	.421	.444	Bats Right	R	.239	485	116	19	0	18	84	21	80	.276	.390
Alomar,R	L	.308	156	48	5	0	5	23	25	17	.414	.436	Bell,Jay	L	.324	238	77	19	4	1	20	26	42	.396	.450
Bats Both	R	.311	415	129	22	8	3	53	62	35	.401	.424	Bats Right	R	.228	394	90	17	2	8	35	29	61	.282	.343
Alomar Jr,S	L	.190	58	11	4	0	0	3	5	6	.277	.259	Bell,Juan	L	.194	62	12	2	0	0	3	7	13	.286	.226
Bats Right	R	.266	241	64	12	0	2	23	8	26	.298	.340	Bats Both	R	.212	85	18	1	1	1	5	11	16	.296	.282
Alou,Moises	L	.294	136	40	11	0	2	14	7	13	.329	.419	Belle,Albert	L	.254	138	35	10	0	8	27	12	33	.307	.500
Bats Right	R	.273	205	56	17	2	7	42	18	33	.327	.478	Bats Right	R	.262	447	117	13	1	26	85	40	95	.325	.470
Amaral,Rich	L	.216	37	8	1	0	1	4	2	3	.256	.324	Belliard,R	L	.197	61	12	0	0	0	3	1	13	.210	.197
Bats Right	R	.254	63	16	2	0	0	3	3	13	.288	.286	Bats Right	R	.214	224	48	6	1	0	11	13	30	.267	.250
Amaro,Ruben	L	.253	154	39	8	3	2	17	18	14	.343	.383	Beltre,E	L	.235	51	12	1	0	1	5	1	7	.245	.314
Bats Both	R	.195	220	43	7	3	5	17	19	40	.275	.323	Bats Right	R	.153	59	9	1	0	0	5	2	11	.180	.169
Anderson,B	L	.226	190	43	8	2	5	26	31	35	.345	.368	Benavides,F	L	.256	90	23	7	0	1	15	8	15	.323	.367
Bats Left	R	.291	433	126	20	8	16	54	67	63	.386	.485	Bats Right	R	.205	83	17	3	1	0	2	2	19	.224	.265
Anderson,Dave	L	.250	64	16	4	0	2	7	4	7	.286	.406	Benjamin,Mike	L	.250	36	9	1	1	1	3	3	4	.308	.417
Bats Right	R	.400	20	8	0	0	1	1	0	4	.400	.550	Bats Right	R	.103	39	4	1	0	0	0	1	11	.125	.128
Anthony,Eric	L	.212	156	33	6	0	5	28	12	44	.269	.346	Benzinger,T	L	.270	126	34	5	1	1	16	3	12	.282	.349
Bats Left	R	.254	284	72	9	1	14	52	26	54	.314	.440	Bats Both	R	.216	167	36	11	1	3	15	12	42	.264	.347
Arias,Alex	L	.317	41	13	4	0	0	2	4	3	.378	.415	Bergman,Dave	L	.143	14	2	1	0	0	0	2	5	.250	.214
Bats Right	R	.276	58	16	2	0	0	5	7	10	.373	.310	Bats Left	R	.240	167	40	2	0	1	10	18	14	.310	.269
Ashley,Billy	L	.333	30	10	2	0	2	4	1	6	.355	.600	Berroa,G	L	.286	14	4	1	0	0	0	2	1	.412	.357
Bats Right	R	.169	65	11	3	0	0	2	4	28	.217	.215	Bats Right	R	.000	1	0	0	0	0	0	0	0	.000	.000
Azocar,Oscar	L	.400	5	2	1	0	0	0	0	0	.400	.600	Berry,Sean	L	.667	3	2	0	0	0	0	0	0	.667	.667
Bats Left	R	.184	163	30	5	0	0	8	9	12	.225	.215	Bats Right	R	.315	54	17	1	0	0	4	1	11	.327	.389
Backman,Wally	L	.000	1	0	0	0	0	0	0	1	.000	.000	Berryhill,D	L	.233	73	17	3	0	1	11	4	10	.269	.315
Bats Left	R	.277	47	13	1	0	0	6	6	8	.358	.298	Bats Both	R	.226	234	53	13	1	9	32	13	57	.268	.406
Baerga,Carlos	L	.375	168	63	9	0	4	35	3	19	.387	.500	Bichette,D	L	.286	119	34	8	2	2	23	9	27	.336	.437
Bats Both	R	.290	489	142	23	1	16	70	32	57	.343	.440	Bats Right	R	.287	268	77	19	0	3	18	7	47	.309	.392
Baez,Kevin	L	.000	6	0	0	0	0	0	0	0	.000	.000	Biggio,Craig	L	.275	218	60	10	1	3	14	50	22	.410	.372
Bats Right	R	.286	7	2	0	0	0	0	0	0	.286	.286	Bats Right	R	.278	395	110	22	2	3	25	44	73	.359	.367
Bagwell,Jeff	L	.290	210	61	13	3	10	34	38	31	.394	.524	Bilardello,D	L	.200	5	1	1	0	0	1	1	0	.333	.400
Bats Right	R	.263	376	99	21	3	8	62	46	66	.354	.399	Bats Right	R	.107	28	3	0	0	0	0	3	8	.194	.107
Bailey,Mark	L	.000	3	0	0	0	0	0	0	1	.000	.000	Blankenship,L	L	.247	89	22	9	0	0	5	30	11	.455	.348
Bats Both	R	.174	23	4	1	0	0	1	3	6	.269	.217	Bats Right	R	.238	260	62	15	1	3	29	52	46	.368	.338
Baines,Harold	L	.245	53	13	0	0	1	8	5	16	.310	.302	Blauser,Jeff	L	.303	142	43	11	1	9	24	25	30	.402	.585
Bats Left	R	.254	425	108	18	0	15	68	54	45	.334	.402	Bats Right	R	.234	201	47	8	2	5	22	21	52	.317	.368
Barberie,Bret	L	.164	67	11	3	0	0	7	9	18	.288	.209	Blowers,Mike	L	.130	23	3	1	0	0	0	2	6	.200	.174
Bats Both	R	.252	218	55	8	0	1	17	38	44	.374	.303	Bats Right	R	.220	50	11	2	0	1	2	4	14	.278	.320
Barfield,J	L	.152	33	5	0	0	1	2	6	7	.282	.242	Boggs,Wade	L	.272	158	43	10	1	1	21	12	13	.326	.367
Bats Right	R	.129	62	8	2	0	1	5	3	20	.167	.210	Bats Left	R	.253	356	90	12	3	6	29	62	18	.364	.354
Barnes,S	L	.254	118	30	5	1	3	19	6	15	.294	.390	Bonds,Barry	L	.311	222	69	19	3	13	44	55	35	.445	.599
Bats Right	R	.319	47	15	3	0	0	6	4	3	.377	.383	Bats Left	R	.311	251	78	17	2	21	59	72	34	.465	.645

Batters vs. Left-Handed and Right-Handed Pitchers

Batter	vs	Avg	AB	H	2B	3B	HR	BI	BB	SO	OBP	SLG	Batter	vs	Avg	AB	H	2B	3B	HR	BI	BB	SO	OBP	SLG
Bonilla,Bobby	L	.240	175	42	7	0	4	21	17	15	.307	.349	Bullock,Eric	L	.000	0	0	0	0	0	0	0	0	.000	.000
Bats Both	R	.255	263	67	16	0	15	49	49	58	.373	.487	Bats Left	R	.000	5	0	0	0	0	0	0	1	.000	.000
Boone,Bret	L	.150	40	6	1	0	0	1	2	12	.190	.175	Burks,Ellis	L	.197	66	13	2	1	3	8	10	8	.299	.394
Bats Right	R	.213	89	19	3	0	4	14	2	22	.239	.382	Bats Right	R	.278	169	47	6	2	5	22	15	40	.339	.426
Borders,Pat	L	.233	120	28	8	0	0	9	18	14	.333	.300	Bush,Randy	L	.000	8	0	0	0	0	0	0	4	.000	.000
Bats Right	R	.244	360	88	18	2	13	44	15	61	.274	.414	Bats Left	R	.224	174	39	8	1	2	22	11	33	.274	.316
Bordick,Mike	L	.336	131	44	5	2	1	15	12	12	.393	.427	Butler,Brett	L	.296	223	66	2	3	1	17	39	31	.402	.345
Bats Right	R	.287	373	107	14	2	2	33	28	47	.346	.351	Bats Left	R	.318	330	105	12	8	2	22	56	36	.420	.421
Boston,Daryl	L	.319	47	15	3	0	1	4	5	9	.407	.447	Cabrera,F	L	.222	9	2	0	0	2	3	1	1	.300	.889
Bats Left	R	.236	242	57	11	2	10	31	33	51	.325	.421	Bats Right	R	1.000	1	1	0	0	0	0	0	0	1.000	1.000
Bournigal,R	L	.125	8	1	0	0	0	0	1	2	.222	.125	Calderon,Ivan	L	.333	51	17	7	1	0	3	6	5	.414	.510
Bats Right	R	.167	12	2	1	0	0	0	0	0	.231	.250	Bats Right	R	.235	119	28	7	1	3	21	8	17	.281	.387
Bradley,Scott	L	.000	0	0	0	0	0	0	0	0	.000	.000	Caminiti,Ken	L	.303	208	63	13	1	7	35	18	29	.357	.476
Bats Left	R	.333	6	2	0	0	0	1	2	1	.500	.333	Bats Both	R	.289	298	86	18	1	6	27	26	39	.345	.416
Braggs,Glenn	L	.248	145	36	7	2	5	24	21	24	.343	.428	Candaele,C	L	.266	128	34	7	0	1	9	12	11	.331	.344
Bats Right	R	.223	121	27	9	1	3	14	15	24	.314	.388	Bats Both	R	.177	192	34	5	1	0	9	12	25	.226	.214
Branson,Jeff	L	.125	8	1	0	0	0	0	0	3	.125	.125	Cangelosi,J	L	.158	19	3	1	0	1	3	7	3	.385	.368
Bats Left	R	.308	107	33	7	1	0	15	5	13	.336	.393	Bats Both	R	.197	66	13	1	0	0	3	11	13	.312	.212
Bream,Sid	L	.242	33	8	4	0	1	7	1	5	.265	.455	Canseco,Jose	L	.255	94	24	3	0	7	16	16	33	.372	.511
Bats Left	R	.263	339	89	21	1	9	54	45	46	.347	.410	Bats Right	R	.241	345	83	12	0	19	71	47	95	.336	.441
Brett,George	L	.277	184	51	11	1	0	20	7	24	.320	.348	Canseco,Ozzie	L	.375	8	3	2	0	0	1	3	0	.545	.625
Bats Left	R	.289	408	118	24	4	7	41	28	45	.334	.419	Bats Right	R	.238	21	5	3	0	0	2	4	4	.360	.381
Brewer,Rod	L	.292	24	7	2	0	0	2	0	3	.292	.375	Carr,Chuck	L	.250	24	6	1	0	0	0	1	3	.280	.292
Bats Left	R	.304	79	24	4	0	0	8	8	9	.371	.354	Bats Both	R	.200	40	8	2	0	0	3	8	3	.333	.250
Briley,Greg	L	.000	5	0	0	0	0	0	0	0	.000	.000	Carreon,Mark	L	.198	111	22	1	0	2	8	5	13	.235	.261
Bats Left	R	.282	195	55	10	0	5	12	4	31	.297	.410	Bats Right	R	.249	225	56	10	1	8	33	17	44	.299	.409
Brito,B	L	.286	7	2	1	0	0	2	0	2	.250	.429	Carter,Gary	L	.230	139	32	13	0	2	14	15	15	.301	.367
Bats Right	R	.000	7	0	0	0	0	0	0	2	.000	.000	Bats Right	R	.205	146	30	5	1	3	15	18	22	.298	.315
Brogna,Rico	L	.500	2	1	0	0	0	0	0	0	.500	.500	Carter,Joe	L	.312	157	49	14	0	7	20	11	22	.355	.535
Bats Left	R	.167	24	4	1	0	1	3	3	5	.259	.333	Bats Right	R	.247	465	115	16	7	27	99	25	87	.294	.486
Brooks,Hubie	L	.220	82	18	2	0	1	8	4	10	.256	.280	Castilla,V	L	.167	6	1	0	0	0	0	0	1	.167	.167
Bats Right	R	.214	224	48	11	0	7	28	8	36	.244	.357	Bats Right	R	.300	10	3	1	0	0	1	1	3	.417	.400
Brosius,Scott	L	.292	24	7	0	0	3	7	2	5	.346	.667	Castillo,B	L	.182	33	6	0	1	1	4	0	5	.182	.333
Bats Right	R	.190	63	12	2	0	1	6	1	8	.224	.270	Bats Right	R	.209	43	9	3	0	1	3	4	10	.277	.349
Brown,Jarvis	L	.000	3	0	0	0	0	0	1	1	.250	.000	Cedeno,A	L	.203	64	13	5	2	0	4	7	18	.282	.344
Bats Right	R	.083	12	1	0	0	0	0	1	3	.214	.083	Bats Right	R	.160	156	25	8	0	2	9	7	53	.211	.250
Browne,Jerry	L	.184	49	9	1	0	0	5	3	6	.226	.204	Cerone,Rick	L	.276	29	8	1	0	1	2	2	0	.323	.414
Bats Both	R	.305	275	84	11	2	3	35	37	34	.389	.393	Bats Right	R	.265	34	9	3	0	0	5	1	5	.306	.353
Bruett,J.T.	L	.167	6	1	0	0	0	1	1	0	.286	.167	Chamberlain,W	L	.260	104	27	8	0	3	15	5	15	.291	.423
Bats Left	R	.257	70	18	4	0	0	1	5	12	.316	.314	Bats Right	R	.257	171	44	10	0	6	26	5	40	.281	.421
Brumfield,J	L	.100	20	2	0	0	0	2	1	3	.182	.100	Cianfrocco,A	L	.247	97	24	2	4	4	17	6	25	.286	.433
Bats Right	R	.200	10	2	0	0	0	0	1	1	.273	.200	Bats Right	R	.237	135	32	3	0	2	13	5	41	.270	.304
Brumley,Mike	L	.000	0	0	0	0	0	0	0	0	.000	.000	Clark,Dave	L	.000	1	0	0	0	0	0	0	1	.000	.000
Bats Both	R	.000	1	0	0	0	0	0	0	0	.000	.000	Bats Left	R	.219	32	7	0	0	2	7	6	7	.333	.406
Brunansky,Tom	L	.227	132	30	10	0	6	20	26	20	.354	.439	Clark,Jack	L	.295	95	28	6	0	2	14	30	27	.460	.421
Bats Right	R	.282	326	92	21	3	9	54	40	76	.354	.448	Bats Right	R	.160	162	26	5	0	3	19	26	60	.278	.247
Buechele,S	L	.304	207	63	17	1	5	26	21	33	.372	.469	Clark,Jerald	L	.276	152	42	9	2	6	20	6	26	.306	.480
Bats Right	R	.233	317	74	6	3	4	38	31	72	.310	.309	Bats Right	R	.227	344	78	13	4	6	38	16	71	.266	.340
Buhner,Jay	L	.230	148	34	4	0	10	25	21	38	.327	.459	Clark,Phil	L	.487	39	19	4	0	1	5	4	6	.535	.667
Bats Right	R	.248	395	98	12	3	15	54	50	108	.335	.408	Bats Right	R	.200	15	3	0	0	0	0	2	3	.294	.200

Batters vs. Left-Handed and Right-Handed Pitchers

Batter	vs	Avg	AB	H	2B	3B	HR	BI	BB	SO	OBP	SLG	Batter	vs	Avg	AB	H	2B	3B	HR	BI	BB	SO	OBP	SLG
Clark,Will	L	.307	205	63	12	0	2	30	21	31	.366	.395	Davis,Eric	L	.236	89	21	4	0	4	11	23	19	.393	.416
Bats Left	R	.295	308	91	28	1	14	43	52	51	.396	.529	Bats Right	R	.225	178	40	4	1	1	21	13	52	.286	.275
Clayton,Royce	L	.250	96	24	4	2	0	4	11	21	.327	.333	Davis,Glenn	L	.252	107	27	3	1	4	18	6	22	.287	.411
Bats Right	R	.213	225	48	3	2	4	20	15	42	.260	.298	Bats Right	R	.285	291	83	12	1	9	30	31	43	.356	.426
Cochrane,Dave	L	.276	58	16	2	0	1	3	5	15	.333	.362	Dawson,Andre	L	.287	195	56	12	1	7	35	10	24	.321	.467
Bats Both	R	.234	94	22	3	0	1	9	7	19	.294	.298	Bats Right	R	.271	347	94	15	1	15	55	20	46	.314	.450
Colbert,Craig	L	.232	56	13	2	1	1	10	3	3	.267	.357	Decker,Steve	L	.077	13	1	0	0	0	0	1	3	.143	.077
Bats Right	R	.229	70	16	3	1	0	6	6	19	.286	.300	Bats Right	R	.200	30	6	1	0	0	1	5	4	.333	.233
Colbrunn,Greg	L	.222	72	16	2	0	1	9	2	14	.237	.292	Deer,Rob	L	.293	99	29	3	0	14	21	12	30	.369	.747
Bats Right	R	.302	96	29	6	0	1	9	4	20	.337	.396	Bats Right	R	.231	294	68	17	1	18	43	39	101	.326	.480
Cole,Alex	L	.286	49	14	0	2	0	3	6	14	.368	.367	Dempsey,Rick	L	.000	3	0	0	0	0	0	1	1	.250	.000
Bats Left	R	.249	253	63	4	5	0	12	22	53	.308	.304	Bats Right	R	.167	6	1	0	0	0	0	1	0	.286	.167
Coleman,Vince	L	.283	60	17	4	1	1	9	7	11	.358	.433	DeShields,D	L	.314	185	58	6	2	2	21	22	33	.389	.400
Bats Both	R	.272	169	46	7	0	1	12	20	30	.354	.331	Bats Left	R	.281	345	97	13	6	5	35	32	75	.343	.397
Coles,Darnell	L	.320	97	31	11	1	1	12	2	9	.330	.485	Devereaux,M	L	.351	168	59	9	2	9	29	10	24	.383	.589
Bats Right	R	.295	44	13	0	1	2	6	1	6	.304	.477	Bats Right	R	.249	485	121	20	9	15	78	34	70	.300	.421
Colon,Cris	L	.200	15	3	0	0	0	1	1	3	.250	.200	Diaz,Alex	L	.000	1	0	0	0	0	0	0	0	.000	.000
Bats Both	R	.143	21	3	0	0	0	0	0	5	.143	.143	Bats Both	R	.125	8	1	0	0	0	1	0	0	.125	.125
Conine,Jeff	L	.304	23	7	1	0	0	3	5	5	.429	.348	Diaz,Mario	L	.222	18	4	0	0	0	1	0	1	.222	.222
Bats Right	R	.235	68	16	4	2	0	6	3	18	.268	.353	Bats Right	R	.231	13	3	1	0	0	0	1	1	.286	.308
Cooper,Scott	L	.268	41	11	3	0	1	5	7	6	.375	.415	DiSarcina,G	L	.228	114	26	4	0	0	4	5	12	.264	.263
Bats Left	R	.277	296	82	18	0	4	28	30	27	.341	.378	Bats Right	R	.252	404	102	15	0	3	38	15	38	.288	.312
Cora,Joey	L	.222	27	6	2	0	0	3	5	4	.353	.296	Distefano,B	L	.000	2	0	0	0	0	0	0	1	.000	.000
Bats Both	R	.253	95	24	5	1	0	6	17	9	.376	.326	Bats Left	R	.241	58	14	0	2	0	7	5	13	.313	.310
Cordero,Wil	L	.471	34	16	1	0	0	2	3	4	.514	.500	Donnels,Chris	L	.167	24	4	1	0	0	1	2	8	.231	.208
Bats Right	R	.239	92	22	3	1	2	6	6	27	.293	.359	Bats Left	R	.175	97	17	3	0	0	5	15	17	.286	.206
Costo,Tim	L	.214	14	3	1	0	0	1	2	2	.294	.286	Doran,Billy	L	.200	125	25	5	0	2	11	30	13	.353	.288
Bats Right	R	.227	22	5	1	0	0	1	3	4	.320	.273	Bats Both	R	.252	262	66	11	2	6	36	34	27	.337	.378
Cotto,Henry	L	.321	168	54	9	0	4	21	14	25	.375	.446	Downing,Brian	L	.281	121	34	8	0	3	14	30	30	.429	.421
Bats Right	R	.175	126	22	2	1	1	6	0	24	.175	.230	Bats Right	R	.276	199	55	10	0	7	25	32	28	.392	.432
Cron,Chris	L	.000	6	0	0	0	0	0	0	3	.000	.000	Dozier,D.J.	L	.167	30	5	0	0	0	2	4	11	.278	.167
Bats Right	R	.000	4	0	0	0	0	0	0	1	.000	.000	Bats Right	R	.235	17	4	2	0	0	0	0	8	.235	.353
Curtis,Chad	L	.270	122	33	6	1	6	22	26	18	.393	.484	Ducey,Rob	L	.111	9	1	1	0	0	0	1	5	.200	.222
Bats Right	R	.254	319	81	10	1	4	24	25	53	.318	.329	Bats Left	R	.197	71	14	3	0	0	2	4	17	.237	.239
Cuyler,Milt	L	.291	86	25	2	0	2	8	3	11	.337	.384	Duncan,M	L	.286	231	66	14	1	4	19	6	42	.308	.407
Bats Both	R	.220	205	45	9	1	1	20	7	51	.249	.288	Bats Right	R	.254	343	87	26	2	4	31	11	66	.281	.376
Daniels,Kal	L	.231	65	15	4	0	1	9	4	19	.296	.338	Dunston,S	L	.417	24	10	0	0	0	0	0	4	.417	.417
Bats Left	R	.245	147	36	7	0	5	16	18	35	.323	.395	Bats Right	R	.265	49	13	3	1	0	2	3	9	.308	.367
Dascenzo,Doug	L	.243	169	41	7	1	0	10	8	7	.275	.296	Dykstra,Lenny	L	.322	146	47	7	0	4	23	16	15	.389	.452
Bats Both	R	.266	207	55	6	3	0	10	19	25	.326	.324	Bats Left	R	.286	199	57	11	0	2	16	24	17	.364	.372
Daugherty,J	L	.167	30	5	1	0	0	1	2	6	.212	.200	Easley,Damion	L	.278	36	10	1	0	0	3	2	6	.316	.306
Bats Both	R	.216	97	21	8	0	0	8	14	15	.319	.299	Bats Right	R	.252	115	29	4	0	1	9	6	20	.304	.313
Daulton,D	L	.257	202	52	16	0	11	40	30	45	.363	.500	Eisenreich,J	L	.240	75	18	4	1	0	7	5	15	.284	.320
Bats Left	R	.279	283	79	16	5	16	69	58	58	.399	.541	Bats Left	R	.277	278	77	9	2	2	21	19	21	.321	.345
Davis,Alvin	L	.167	12	2	0	0	0	1	1	1	.231	.167	Elster,Kevin	L	.167	6	1	0	0	0	0	0	0	.167	.167
Bats Left	R	.261	92	24	8	0	0	15	12	8	.343	.348	Bats Right	R	.250	12	3	0	0	0	0	0	0	.250	.250
Davis,Chili	L	.256	121	31	5	0	4	22	13	25	.321	.397	Espy,Cecil	L	.210	62	13	2	0	1	4	7	6	.290	.290
Bats Both	R	.300	323	97	22	2	8	44	60	51	.408	.455	Bats Both	R	.280	132	37	5	3	0	16	8	34	.319	.364
Davis,Doug	L	.000	0	0	0	0	0	0	0	0	.000	.000	Faries,Paul	L	.500	6	3	1	0	0	1	0	1	.500	.667
Bats Right	R	1.000	1	1	0	0	0	0	0	0	1.000	1.000	Bats Right	R	.400	5	2	0	0	0	0	1	1	.500	.400

Batters vs. Left-Handed and Right-Handed Pitchers

Batter	vs	Avg	AB	H	2B	3B	HR	BI	BB	SO	OBP	SLG	Batter	vs	Avg	AB	H	2B	3B	HR	BI	BB	SO	OBP	SLG
Fariss,Monty	L	.187	75	14	1	0	2	11	8	30	.274	.280	Garcia,Carlos	L	.000	8	0	0	0	0	1	0	1	.000	.000
Bats Right	R	.242	91	22	6	1	1	10	9	21	.317	.363	Bats Right	R	.258	31	8	1	0	0	3	0	8	.250	.290
Felder,Mike	L	.307	88	27	5	0	1	6	5	7	.340	.398	Gardner,Jeff	L	.000	2	0	0	0	0	0	0	1	.000	.000
Bats Both	R	.278	234	65	8	3	3	17	16	22	.327	.376	Bats Left	R	.118	17	2	0	0	0	0	1	7	.167	.118
Felix,Junior	L	.271	118	32	7	1	3	18	3	30	.285	.424	Gedman,Rich	L	.000	11	0	0	0	0	0	1	4	.083	.000
Bats Both	R	.238	391	93	15	4	6	54	30	98	.291	.343	Bats Left	R	.245	94	23	4	0	1	8	10	18	.314	.319
Fermin,Felix	L	.333	42	14	1	0	0	4	8	3	.440	.357	Gibson,Kirk	L	.000	7	0	0	0	0	0	0	2	.000	.000
Bats Right	R	.254	173	44	6	2	0	9	10	7	.296	.312	Bats Left	R	.224	49	11	0	0	2	5	3	10	.269	.347
Fernandez,T	L	.280	207	58	9	0	1	18	22	12	.349	.338	Gilkey,B	L	.352	176	62	7	2	2	20	16	18	.402	.449
Bats Both	R	.272	415	113	23	4	3	19	34	50	.331	.369	Bats Right	R	.260	208	54	12	2	5	23	23	34	.333	.409
Fielder,Cecil	L	.231	134	31	5	0	9	31	24	45	.352	.470	Girardi,Joe	L	.299	137	41	2	1	0	5	9	16	.342	.328
Bats Both	R	.248	460	114	17	0	26	93	49	106	.317	.454	Bats Right	R	.241	133	32	1	0	1	7	10	22	.297	.271
Figueroa,Bien	L	.000	1	0	0	0	0	0	0	0	.000	.000	Gladden,Dan	L	.282	124	35	8	1	4	18	12	17	.341	.460
Bats Right	R	.200	10	2	1	0	0	4	1	2	.273	.300	Bats Right	R	.242	293	71	12	0	3	24	18	47	.288	.314
Finley,Steve	L	.279	226	63	8	5	1	19	17	31	.336	.372	Goff,Jerry	L	.000	0	0	0	0	0	0	0	0	.000	.000
Bats Left	R	.299	381	114	21	8	4	36	41	32	.366	.428	Bats Left	R	.000	3	0	0	0	0	0	0	3	.000	.000
Fisk,Carlton	L	.204	49	10	0	0	0	0	9	10	.328	.204	Gomez,Leo	L	.250	104	26	7	0	4	17	23	17	.391	.433
Bats Right	R	.237	139	33	4	1	3	21	14	28	.308	.345	Bats Right	R	.269	364	98	17	0	13	47	40	61	.345	.423
Fitzgerald,M	L	.304	69	21	2	0	3	12	10	13	.392	.464	Gonzales,Rene	L	.268	71	19	3	0	3	11	10	11	.369	.437
Bats Right	R	.158	120	19	0	0	3	5	12	21	.235	.233	Bats Right	R	.279	258	72	14	1	4	27	31	35	.361	.388
Flaherty,John	L	.200	20	4	1	0	0	0	1	0	.238	.250	Gonzalez,Jose	L	.196	46	9	2	0	0	1	6	14	.288	.239
Bats Right	R	.196	46	9	1	0	0	2	2	7	.224	.217	Bats Right	R	.111	9	1	0	0	0	1	1	6	.182	.111
Fletcher,D	L	.286	14	4	1	0	0	1	3	3	.412	.357	Gonzalez,Juan	L	.253	158	40	6	0	8	28	12	43	.302	.443
Bats Left	R	.240	208	50	9	2	2	25	11	25	.280	.332	Bats Right	R	.263	426	112	18	2	35	81	23	100	.304	.561
Fletcher,S	L	.308	104	32	5	1	0	13	7	10	.360	.375	Gonzalez,Luis	L	.350	80	28	6	2	1	13	7	11	.404	.513
Bats Right	R	.262	282	74	13	2	3	38	23	23	.326	.355	Bats Left	R	.215	307	66	13	1	9	42	17	41	.258	.352
Foley,Tom	L	.158	19	3	0	0	0	1	1	5	.190	.158	Goodwin,Tom	L	.250	8	2	0	0	0	0	0	1	.250	.250
Bats Left	R	.177	96	17	3	1	0	4	7	16	.238	.229	Bats Left	R	.231	65	15	1	1	0	3	6	9	.296	.277
Fox,Eric	L	.227	22	5	1	0	0	1	2	6	.292	.273	Grace,Mark	L	.280	225	63	11	1	3	29	17	19	.329	.378
Bats Both	R	.240	121	29	4	2	3	12	11	23	.301	.380	Bats Left	R	.323	378	122	26	4	6	50	55	17	.409	.460
Franco,Julio	L	.333	39	13	3	0	1	3	5	8	.409	.487	Grebeck,Craig	L	.291	86	25	8	0	0	9	6	8	.344	.384
Bats Right	R	.176	68	12	4	0	1	5	10	9	.282	.279	Bats Right	R	.259	201	52	13	2	3	26	24	26	.339	.388
Frye,Jeff	L	.309	68	21	5	0	1	6	5	10	.356	.426	Green,Gary	L	.333	6	2	0	0	0	0	0	0	.333	.333
Bats Right	R	.229	131	30	4	1	0	6	11	17	.301	.275	Bats Right	R	.333	6	2	1	0	0	0	0	2	.333	.500
Fryman,Travis	L	.285	158	45	7	1	7	31	12	30	.337	.475	Greene,Willie	L	.250	28	7	0	1	0	4	2	7	.290	.321
Bats Right	R	.259	501	130	24	3	13	65	33	114	.309	.397	Bats Left	R	.277	65	18	5	1	2	9	8	16	.356	.477
Gaetti,Gary	L	.250	124	31	6	0	5	15	8	13	.299	.419	Greenwell,M	L	.224	58	13	1	0	0	5	6	8	.308	.241
Bats Right	R	.217	332	72	7	2	7	33	13	66	.256	.313	Bats Left	R	.238	122	29	1	0	2	13	12	11	.307	.295
Gagne,Greg	L	.181	105	19	4	0	1	6	6	20	.225	.248	Gregg,Tommy	L	.000	4	0	0	0	0	0	0	3	.000	.000
Bats Right	R	.266	334	89	19	0	6	33	13	63	.297	.377	Bats Left	R	.333	15	5	0	0	1	1	1	4	.375	.533
Galarraga,A	L	.320	125	40	7	1	6	19	5	23	.348	.536	Griffey Jr,K	L	.358	173	62	10	0	12	35	11	23	.413	.624
Bats Right	R	.195	200	39	7	1	4	20	6	46	.242	.300	Bats Left	R	.286	392	112	29	4	15	68	33	44	.339	.495
Gallagher,D	L	.262	103	27	5	1	0	13	13	8	.333	.330	Griffin,A	L	.310	29	9	1	0	0	2	4	3	.394	.345
Bats Right	R	.208	72	15	6	0	1	8	6	8	.268	.333	Bats Both	R	.215	121	26	6	0	0	8	5	16	.242	.264
Gallego,Mike	L	.237	38	9	2	1	0	4	10	3	.396	.342	Grissom,M	L	.269	212	57	14	4	6	24	17	26	.325	.458
Bats Right	R	.259	135	35	5	0	3	10	10	19	.327	.363	Bats Right	R	.279	441	123	25	2	8	42	25	55	.321	.399
Gant,Ron	L	.254	177	45	7	3	5	32	17	32	.322	.412	Grotewold,J	L	.200	10	2	0	0	1	1	2	4	.333	.500
Bats Right	R	.262	367	96	15	3	12	48	28	69	.320	.417	Bats Left	R	.200	55	11	2	0	2	4	7	12	.302	.345
Gantner,Jim	L	.206	34	7	1	0	0	5	5	0	.300	.235	Gruber,Kelly	L	.243	107	26	5	1	3	10	7	20	.291	.393
Bats Left	R	.252	222	56	11	1	1	13	7	17	.274	.324	Bats Right	R	.224	339	76	11	2	8	33	19	52	.270	.339

266

Batters vs. Left-Handed and Right-Handed Pitchers

Batter	vs	Avg	AB	H	2B	3B	HR	BI	BB	SO	OBP	SLG	Batter	vs	Avg	AB	H	2B	3B	HR	BI	BB	SO	OBP	SLG
Guerrero,Juan	L	.197	61	12	3	0	0	8	8	14	.286	.246	Hill,G	L	.267	105	28	7	0	7	18	7	14	.319	.533
Bats Right	R	.203	64	13	1	2	1	6	2	18	.235	.328	Bats Right	R	.231	264	61	9	1	11	31	13	59	.274	.398
Guerrero,P	L	.211	38	8	1	0	1	2	4	6	.286	.316	Hoiles,Chris	L	.288	80	23	0	0	4	5	16	7	.406	.438
Bats Right	R	.222	108	24	5	1	0	14	7	19	.265	.287	Bats Right	R	.270	230	62	10	1	16	35	39	53	.376	.530
Guillen,Ozzie	L	.158	19	3	3	0	0	1	0	3	.158	.316	Hollins,Dave	L	.322	245	79	16	3	17	45	23	44	.391	.620
Bats Left	R	.238	21	5	1	0	0	6	1	2	.261	.286	Bats Both	R	.232	341	79	12	1	10	48	53	66	.355	.361
Gwynn,Chris	L	.250	8	2	0	1	1	2	0	2	.250	.875	Horn,Sam	L	.000	2	0	0	0	0	0	1	1	.500	.000
Bats Left	R	.289	76	22	3	1	0	5	3	8	.309	.355	Bats Left	R	.238	160	38	10	1	5	19	20	59	.320	.406
Gwynn,Tony	L	.327	205	67	8	1	3	16	14	5	.368	.420	Hosey,Steve	L	.276	29	8	0	0	1	3	0	8	.267	.379
Bats Left	R	.311	315	98	19	2	3	25	32	11	.372	.413	Bats Right	R	.222	27	6	1	0	0	3	0	7	.214	.259
Hall,Mel	L	.257	179	46	8	1	2	18	8	23	.284	.346	Howard,Dave	L	.208	72	15	2	1	0	2	2	15	.230	.264
Bats Left	R	.290	404	117	28	2	13	63	21	30	.322	.465	Bats Both	R	.231	147	34	4	1	1	16	13	28	.290	.293
Hamilton,D	L	.247	89	22	3	1	0	13	10	9	.323	.303	Howard,Thomas	L	.288	104	30	3	0	2	11	6	21	.327	.375
Bats Left	R	.310	381	118	16	6	5	49	35	33	.363	.423	Bats Both	R	.272	257	70	12	2	0	21	11	39	.300	.323
Haney,Todd	L	.286	7	2	0	0	0	1	0	0	.286	.286	Howell,Pat	L	.219	32	7	1	0	0	1	1	9	.242	.250
Bats Right	R	.333	3	1	1	0	0	0	0	0	.333	.667	Bats Both	R	.163	43	7	0	0	0	0	1	6	.200	.163
Hansen,Dave	L	.196	46	9	2	0	0	1	4	8	.255	.239	Howitt,Dann	L	.000	7	0	0	0	0	0	1	2	.125	.000
Bats Left	R	.217	295	64	9	0	6	21	30	41	.291	.308	Bats Left	R	.205	78	16	4	1	2	10	7	7	.261	.359
Hare,Shawn	L	.000	1	0	0	0	0	0	0	1	.000	.000	Hrbek,Kent	L	.265	83	22	5	0	1	9	7	14	.319	.361
Bats Left	R	.120	25	3	1	0	0	5	2	3	.179	.160	Bats Left	R	.238	311	74	15	0	14	49	64	42	.366	.421
Harper,Brian	L	.275	109	30	6	0	1	13	13	6	.339	.358	Hudler,Rex	L	.346	52	18	4	0	2	3	1	10	.358	.538
Bats Right	R	.316	393	124	19	0	8	60	13	16	.344	.425	Bats Right	R	.130	46	6	0	0	1	2	1	13	.163	.196
Harris,Donald	L	.278	18	5	1	0	0	1	0	10	.278	.333	Huff,Mike	L	.213	89	19	5	0	0	8	9	16	.280	.270
Bats Right	R	.067	15	1	0	0	0	0	0	5	.067	.067	Bats Right	R	.192	26	5	0	0	0	0	1	8	.250	.192
Harris,Lenny	L	.139	36	5	0	0	0	0	3	6	.205	.139	Hulett,Tim	L	.294	68	20	4	0	2	9	5	13	.342	.441
Bats Left	R	.286	311	89	11	0	0	30	21	18	.331	.322	Bats Right	R	.284	74	21	3	2	0	12	5	18	.338	.378
Haselman,Bill	L	.429	7	3	0	0	0	0	0	0	.429	.429	Hulse,David	L	.286	21	6	1	0	0	1	1	5	.318	.333
Bats Right	R	.167	12	2	0	0	0	0	0	7	.167	.167	Bats Left	R	.310	71	22	3	0	0	1	2	13	.329	.352
Hatcher,Billy	L	.241	141	34	6	1	2	7	7	15	.275	.340	Humphreys,M	L	.000	6	0	0	0	0	0	0	0	.000	.000
Bats Right	R	.254	268	68	13	1	1	26	15	37	.298	.321	Bats Right	R	.250	4	1	0	0	0	0	0	0	.250	.250
Hayes,Charlie	L	.213	150	32	3	0	6	18	9	23	.262	.353	Hundley,Todd	L	.177	113	20	3	0	4	10	4	32	.217	.310
Bats Right	R	.276	359	99	16	2	12	48	19	77	.312	.432	Bats Both	R	.224	245	55	14	0	3	22	15	44	.274	.318
Hayes,Von	L	.119	42	5	1	0	0	4	5	11	.208	.143	Hunter,Brian	L	.271	155	42	10	1	12	32	16	23	.326	.581
Bats Left	R	.242	265	64	16	1	4	25	32	43	.321	.355	Bats Right	R	.181	83	15	3	1	2	9	5	27	.225	.313
Heffernan,B	L	.000	0	0	0	0	0	0	0	0	.000	.000	Huson,Jeff	L	.281	32	9	2	0	1	3	4	10	.361	.438
Bats Left	R	.091	11	1	1	0	0	1	0	1	.091	.182	Bats Left	R	.259	286	74	12	3	3	21	37	33	.339	.353
Hemond,Scott	L	.200	20	4	1	0	0	2	2	7	.261	.250	Incaviglia,P	L	.282	170	48	13	1	7	27	16	50	.344	.494
Bats Right	R	.250	20	5	1	0	0	0	2	6	.318	.300	Bats Right	R	.251	179	45	9	0	4	17	9	49	.295	.369
Henderson,D	L	.208	24	5	1	0	0	2	0	8	.208	.250	Jackson,D	L	.202	188	38	6	4	7	19	9	33	.242	.388
Bats Right	R	.103	39	4	0	0	0	2	8	.146	.103	Bats Right	R	.271	399	108	17	1	10	51	17	73	.302	.393
Henderson,R	L	.267	105	28	5	1	5	13	24	17	.403	.476	Jacoby,Brook	L	.258	97	25	3	0	2	11	8	17	.311	.351
Bats Right	R	.289	291	84	13	2	10	33	71	39	.434	.450	Bats Right	R	.263	194	51	4	0	2	25	20	37	.330	.314
Hernandez,C	L	.287	108	31	3	0	3	9	7	9	.336	.398	Jaha,John	L	.174	46	8	1	0	1	5	6	10	.268	.261
Bats Right	R	.215	65	14	1	0	0	8	4	12	.284	.231	Bats Right	R	.253	87	22	2	1	1	5	6	20	.305	.333
Hernandez,C	L	.342	38	13	4	0	0	2	0	6	.342	.447	James,Chris	L	.302	116	35	7	1	2	13	5	18	.333	.431
Bats Right	R	.077	13	1	0	0	0	2	0	4	.077	.077	Bats Right	R	.189	132	25	3	3	3	19	9	27	.243	.326
Hernandez,J	L	.000	0	0	0	0	0	0	0	0	.000	.000	James,Dion	L	.214	14	3	0	0	1	4	4	2	.421	.429
Bats Right	R	.000	4	0	0	0	0	0	0	2	.000	.000	Bats Left	R	.267	131	35	8	0	2	13	18	13	.351	.374
Hill,Donnie	L	.000	2	0	0	0	0	0	0	1	.000	.000	Javier,Stan	L	.219	146	32	8	1	0	5	12	22	.283	.288
Bats Both	R	.306	49	15	3	0	0	2	5	5	.382	.367	Bats Both	R	.271	188	51	9	0	1	24	25	32	.359	.335

Batters vs. Left-Handed and Right-Handed Pitchers

Batter	vs	Avg	AB	H	2B	3B	HR	BI	BB	SO	OBP	SLG	Batter	vs	Avg	AB	H	2B	3B	HR	BI	BB	SO	OBP	SLG
Jefferies,G	L	.257	179	46	10	0	3	12	7	11	.282	.363	Kreuter,Chad	L	.182	66	12	4	0	1	7	10	12	.289	.288
Bats Both	R	.296	425	126	26	3	7	63	36	18	.348	.421	Bats Both	R	.290	124	36	5	0	1	9	10	26	.338	.355
Jefferson,R	L	.263	19	5	1	1	1	3	1	7	.300	.579	Kruk,John	L	.314	210	66	9	1	1	18	37	42	.414	.381
Bats Both	R	.357	70	25	5	1	0	3	0	10	.366	.457	Bats Left	R	.330	297	98	21	3	9	52	55	46	.430	.512
Jeter,Shawn	L	.000	4	0	0	0	0	0	0	1	.000	.000	Kunkel,Jeff	L	.045	22	1	1	0	0	0	0	7	.045	.091
Bats Left	R	.143	14	2	0	0	0	0	0	6	.143	.143	Bats Right	R	.429	7	3	1	0	0	1	0	1	.429	.571
Johnson,H	L	.227	132	30	8	0	4	21	23	30	.340	.379	Lake,Steve	L	.303	33	10	1	0	1	2	1	2	.314	.424
Bats Both	R	.220	218	48	11	0	3	22	32	49	.323	.312	Bats Right	R	.150	20	3	1	0	0	0	0	6	.150	.200
Johnson,Lance	L	.266	158	42	3	2	0	14	8	15	.302	.310	Laker,Tim	L	.235	17	4	1	0	0	1	1	4	.278	.294
Bats Left	R	.284	409	116	12	10	3	33	26	18	.324	.384	Bats Right	R	.207	29	6	2	0	0	3	1	10	.233	.276
Jones,Chris	L	.174	46	8	1	0	0	2	4	14	.240	.196	Lampkin,Tom	L	.000	2	0	0	0	0	0	0	0	.000	.000
Bats Right	R	.235	17	4	1	1	1	2	3	7	.350	.588	Bats Left	R	.267	15	4	0	0	0	0	6	1	.500	.267
Jones,Tim	L	.229	35	8	2	0	0	1	2	7	.270	.286	Lankford,Ray	L	.255	216	55	11	2	4	32	27	61	.345	.380
Bats Left	R	.191	110	21	2	0	0	2	9	22	.252	.209	Bats Left	R	.314	382	120	29	4	16	54	45	86	.385	.537
Jordan,Brian	L	.219	64	14	2	0	4	10	6	14	.286	.438	Lansford,C	L	.280	132	37	12	0	1	17	11	8	.342	.394
Bats Right	R	.202	129	26	7	4	1	12	4	34	.231	.341	Bats Left	R	.255	364	93	18	1	6	58	32	31	.319	.360
Jordan,Ricky	L	.371	132	49	11	0	3	21	2	18	.372	.523	Larkin,Barry	L	.355	200	71	20	4	6	29	33	18	.443	.585
Bats Right	R	.243	144	35	8	0	1	13	3	26	.259	.319	Bats Right	R	.273	333	91	12	2	6	49	30	40	.336	.375
Jorgensen,T	L	.296	27	8	1	0	0	2	1	4	.333	.333	Larkin,Gene	L	.218	55	12	6	0	0	5	6	8	.295	.327
Bats Right	R	.323	31	10	0	0	0	3	2	7	.364	.323	Bats Both	R	.252	282	71	12	1	6	37	22	35	.311	.365
Jose,Felix	L	.374	182	68	11	2	6	31	15	33	.419	.555	LaValliere,M	L	.161	31	5	0	1	0	5	5	5	.297	.226
Bats Both	R	.251	327	82	11	1	8	44	25	67	.306	.364	Bats Left	R	.267	262	70	13	0	2	24	39	16	.356	.340
Joyner,Wally	L	.240	192	46	13	0	2	20	15	24	.307	.339	Lee,Manuel	L	.212	118	25	4	0	0	12	15	17	.299	.246
Bats Left	R	.284	380	108	23	2	7	46	40	26	.352	.411	Bats Both	R	.284	278	79	6	1	3	27	35	56	.362	.345
Justice,Dave	L	.283	159	45	9	1	5	17	16	28	.352	.447	Leius,Scott	L	.314	118	37	5	0	0	10	11	13	.372	.356
Bats Left	R	.243	325	79	10	4	16	55	63	57	.362	.446	Bats Right	R	.223	291	65	13	2	2	25	23	48	.283	.302
Karkovice,Ron	L	.224	107	24	5	1	4	15	13	30	.314	.402	Lemke,Mark	L	.228	145	33	1	1	5	14	13	11	.289	.352
Bats Right	R	.243	235	57	7	0	9	35	17	59	.297	.387	Bats Both	R	.227	282	64	6	3	1	12	37	28	.316	.280
Karros,Eric	L	.277	213	59	10	0	8	32	16	26	.325	.437	Lennon,P	L	.000	0	0	0	0	0	0	0	0	.000	.000
Bats Right	R	.244	332	81	20	1	12	56	21	77	.291	.419	Bats Right	R	.000	2	0	0	0	0	0	0	0	.000	.000
Kelly,Pat	L	.228	114	26	5	1	3	7	9	25	.288	.368	Leonard,Mark	L	.158	19	3	0	0	0	0	2	6	.238	.158
Bats Right	R	.225	204	46	17	1	4	20	16	47	.307	.377	Bats Left	R	.248	109	27	7	0	4	16	14	25	.346	.422
Kelly,Roberto	L	.277	184	51	9	0	4	21	20	28	.344	.391	Levis,Jesse	L	1.000	2	2	1	0	0	1	0	0	1.000	1.500
Bats Right	R	.270	396	107	22	2	6	45	21	68	.310	.381	Bats Left	R	.244	41	10	3	0	1	2	0	5	.244	.390
Kent,Jeff	L	.217	92	20	5	0	3	14	10	20	.291	.370	Lewis,Darren	L	.216	125	27	3	0	1	5	12	16	.285	.264
Bats Right	R	.249	213	53	16	2	8	36	17	56	.321	.455	Bats Right	R	.241	195	47	5	1	0	13	17	30	.302	.277
King,Jeff	L	.236	216	51	12	2	6	32	13	18	.277	.394	Lewis,Mark	L	.289	97	28	10	0	2	10	8	13	.343	.454
Bats Right	R	.227	264	60	9	0	8	33	14	38	.269	.352	Bats Right	R	.256	316	81	11	0	3	20	17	56	.297	.320
Kingery,Mike	L	.000	1	0	0	0	0	0	0	0	.000	.000	Leyritz,Jim	L	.245	102	25	5	0	5	20	10	14	.339	.441
Bats Left	R	.111	27	3	0	0	0	1	1	3	.143	.111	Bats Right	R	.286	42	12	1	0	2	6	4	8	.347	.452
Kirby,Wayne	L	.000	2	0	0	0	0	0	0	1	.000	.000	Lind,Jose	L	.237	177	42	6	1	0	14	11	16	.277	.282
Bats Left	R	.188	16	3	1	0	1	1	3	1	.316	.438	Bats Right	R	.234	291	68	8	0	0	25	15	13	.273	.261
Klesko,Ryan	L	.000	1	0	0	0	0	0	0	1	.000	.000	Lindeman,Jim	L	.167	24	4	1	0	1	2	2	6	.231	.333
Bats Left	R	.000	13	0	0	0	0	1	0	4	.071	.000	Bats Right	R	.400	15	6	0	0	0	4	1	5	.438	.400
Knoblauch,C	L	.315	124	39	6	2	1	9	17	11	.401	.419	Listach,Pat	L	.345	148	51	7	3	1	18	8	25	.382	.453
Bats Right	R	.292	476	139	13	4	1	47	71	49	.380	.342	Bats Both	R	.271	431	117	12	3	0	29	47	99	.342	.313
Knorr,Randy	L	.429	7	3	0	0	1	2	1	0	.500	.857	Litton,Greg	L	.255	47	12	2	0	3	12	3	8	.300	.489
Bats Right	R	.167	12	2	0	0	0	0	0	5	.167	.167	Bats Right	R	.215	93	20	3	0	1	3	8	25	.277	.280
Koslofski,K	L	.429	14	6	0	0	0	1	4	3	.556	.429	Livingstone,S	L	.289	45	13	2	0	1	7	4	8	.340	.400
Bats Left	R	.227	119	27	0	2	3	12	8	20	.279	.336	Bats Left	R	.282	309	87	19	0	3	39	17	28	.316	.372

Batters vs. Left-Handed and Right-Handed Pitchers

Batter	vs	Avg	AB	H	2B	3B	HR	BI	BB	SO	OBP	SLG	Batter	vs	Avg	AB	H	2B	3B	HR	BI	BB	SO	OBP	SLG
Lofton,Kenny	L	.369	122	45	6	1	0	12	21	15	.466	.434	McGee,Willie	L	.283	159	45	6	2	1	12	4	36	.305	.365
Bats Left	R	.262	454	119	9	7	5	30	47	39	.331	.346	Bats Both	R	.305	315	96	14	0	0	24	25	52	.355	.349
Lopez,Javier	L	.333	6	2	1	0	0	0	0	0	.333	.500	McGinnis,Russ	L	.240	25	6	2	0	0	2	2	5	.296	.320
Bats Right	R	.400	10	4	1	0	0	2	0	1	.400	.500	Bats Right	R	.250	8	2	2	0	0	2	1	2	.333	.500
Lyons,Steve	L	.333	6	2	0	0	0	1	0	1	.333	.333	McGriff,Fred	L	.283	205	58	10	3	13	50	28	49	.369	.551
Bats Left	R	.184	49	9	0	2	0	3	3	7	.231	.265	Bats Left	R	.288	326	94	20	1	22	54	68	59	.409	.558
Maas,Kevin	L	.185	54	10	0	0	1	4	2	19	.214	.241	McGwire,Mark	L	.330	97	32	4	0	14	27	22	14	.447	.804
Bats Left	R	.263	232	61	12	0	10	31	23	44	.324	.444	Bats Right	R	.251	370	93	18	0	28	77	68	91	.368	.527
Macfarlane,M	L	.261	138	36	10	1	7	18	10	28	.331	.500	McIntosh,Tim	L	.161	31	5	1	0	0	4	2	2	.229	.194
Bats Right	R	.220	264	58	18	2	10	30	20	61	.298	.417	Bats Right	R	.196	46	9	2	0	0	2	1	7	.229	.239
Mack,Shane	L	.297	128	38	10	3	4	24	11	21	.357	.516	McKnight,Jeff	L	.385	26	10	1	0	0	5	1	1	.407	.423
Bats Right	R	.320	472	151	21	3	12	51	53	85	.403	.453	Bats Both	R	.220	59	13	2	1	2	8	1	7	.233	.390
Magadan,Dave	L	.308	120	37	3	0	0	7	16	22	.390	.333	McLemore,Mark	L	.276	58	16	2	0	0	10	5	9	.333	.310
Bats Left	R	.269	201	54	6	1	3	21	40	22	.390	.353	Bats Both	R	.235	170	40	5	2	0	17	16	17	.299	.288
Maksudian,M	L	.000	0	0	0	0	0	0	0	0	.000	.000	McNamara,Jim	L	.167	6	1	0	0	0	0	0	2	.167	.167
Bats Left	R	.000	3	0	0	0	0	0	0	0	.000	.000	Bats Left	R	.221	68	15	1	0	1	9	6	23	.284	.279
Maldonado,C	L	.291	117	34	4	1	4	16	22	26	.400	.444	McRae,Brian	L	.233	163	38	8	2	3	20	10	27	.282	.362
Bats Right	R	.266	372	99	21	3	16	50	37	86	.342	.468	Bats Both	R	.219	370	81	15	3	1	32	32	61	.287	.284
Manwaring,K	L	.305	131	40	4	3	0	6	10	12	.355	.382	McReynolds,K	L	.345	113	39	11	0	5	22	26	13	.461	.575
Bats Right	R	.206	218	45	6	2	4	20	19	30	.285	.307	Bats Right	R	.204	260	53	14	0	8	27	41	35	.309	.350
Marsh,Tom	L	.182	66	12	1	1	1	6	1	14	.203	.273	Melvin,Bob	L	.360	50	18	4	0	0	5	5	7	.411	.440
Bats Right	R	.220	59	13	2	1	1	10	1	9	.230	.339	Bats Right	R	.200	20	4	1	0	0	1	0	6	.190	.250
Martin,Al	L	.000	2	0	0	0	0	0	0	1	.000	.000	Merced,O	L	.190	84	16	3	0	0	7	14	11	.306	.226
Bats Left	R	.200	10	2	0	1	0	2	0	4	.182	.400	Bats Both	R	.262	321	84	25	5	6	53	38	52	.339	.427
Martinez,C	L	.260	96	25	5	1	1	14	4	9	.287	.365	Mercedes,H	L	1.000	2	2	0	0	0	0	0	0	1.000	1.000
Bats Right	R	.265	132	35	4	0	4	21	3	12	.281	.386	Bats Right	R	.667	3	2	0	1	0	1	0	1	.667	1.333
Martinez,C	L	.308	39	12	2	0	2	9	3	13	.364	.513	Mercedes,Luis	L	.167	36	6	2	0	0	4	5	4	.279	.222
Bats Left	R	.258	159	41	8	1	3	16	28	34	.366	.377	Bats Right	R	.071	14	1	0	0	0	0	3	5	.235	.071
Martinez,Dave	L	.271	59	16	5	0	0	8	7	15	.348	.356	Merullo,Matt	L	.333	3	1	0	0	0	0	0	0	.333	.333
Bats Left	R	.251	334	84	15	5	3	23	35	39	.319	.353	Bats Left	R	.170	47	8	1	1	0	3	1	8	.200	.234
Martinez,D	L	.667	6	4	0	0	1	3	0	0	.667	1.167	Meulens,H	L	.000	0	0	0	0	0	0	0	0	.000	.000
Bats Right	R	.500	2	1	0	0	0	0	0	1	.500	.500	Bats Right	R	.600	5	3	0	0	1	1	1	0	.667	1.200
Martinez,E	L	.376	141	53	16	0	4	17	18	14	.444	.574	Miller,Keith	L	.267	120	32	9	2	0	10	12	15	.333	.375
Bats Right	R	.331	387	128	30	3	14	56	36	47	.390	.532	Bats Right	R	.291	296	86	15	2	4	28	19	31	.360	.395
Martinez,Tino	L	.228	101	23	4	0	3	19	5	23	.261	.356	Millette,Joe	L	.120	25	3	0	0	0	1	2	2	.185	.120
Bats Left	R	.265	359	95	15	2	13	47	37	54	.332	.426	Bats Right	R	.245	53	13	0	0	0	1	3	8	.310	.245
Marzano,John	L	.100	10	1	1	0	0	0	0	2	.100	.200	Milligan,R	L	.280	107	30	6	0	3	14	35	22	.462	.421
Bats Right	R	.075	40	3	1	1	0	1	2	10	.140	.150	Bats Right	R	.228	355	81	15	1	8	39	71	59	.356	.344
Mattingly,Don	L	.284	204	58	17	0	2	32	10	18	.318	.397	Mitchell,K	L	.380	92	35	5	0	5	27	11	11	.438	.598
Bats Left	R	.289	436	126	23	0	12	54	29	25	.330	.424	Bats Right	R	.254	268	68	19	0	4	40	24	35	.320	.369
Maurer,Rob	L	.000	1	0	0	0	0	0	0	0	.000	.000	Molitor,Paul	L	.424	132	56	11	1	6	32	14	11	.464	.659
Bats Left	R	.250	8	2	0	0	0	1	1	2	.333	.250	Bats Right	R	.291	477	139	25	6	6	57	59	55	.369	.407
May,Derrick	L	.250	76	19	2	0	2	9	3	13	.288	.355	Morandini,M	L	.198	121	24	1	1	1	8	7	19	.240	.248
Bats Left	R	.280	275	77	9	0	6	36	11	27	.311	.378	Bats Left	R	.292	301	88	7	7	2	22	18	45	.331	.382
Mayne,Brent	L	.136	22	3	0	0	0	1	2	3	.208	.136	Morris,Hal	L	.252	139	35	5	0	1	11	13	30	.325	.309
Bats Left	R	.236	191	45	10	0	0	17	9	23	.266	.288	Bats Left	R	.281	256	72	16	3	5	42	32	23	.359	.426
McClendon,L	L	.259	166	43	8	1	2	17	24	18	.351	.355	Morris,John	L	.250	4	1	0	0	0	0	0	0	.250	.250
Bats Right	R	.208	24	5	0	0	1	3	4	6	.345	.333	Bats Left	R	.189	53	10	1	0	1	3	4	11	.259	.264
McCray,Rodney	L	.000	0	0	0	0	0	0	0	0	.000	.000	Moses,John	L	.000	3	0	0	0	0	0	0	0	.000	.000
Bats Both	R	1.000	1	1	0	0	0	1	0	0	1.000	1.000	Bats Both	R	.158	19	3	1	0	0	1	5	4	.333	.211

Batters vs. Left-Handed and Right-Handed Pitchers

Batter	vs	Avg	AB	H	2B	3B	HR	BI	BB	SO	OBP	SLG
Mulliniks,R	L	1.000	1	1	0	0	0	0	0	0	1.000	1.000
Bats Left	R	.000	1	0	0	0	0	0	1	0	.500	.000
Munoz,Pedro	L	.295	122	36	6	1	3	21	6	23	.326	.434
Bats Right	R	.260	296	77	10	2	9	50	11	67	.287	.399
Murphy,Dale	L	.194	31	6	1	0	1	3	1	7	.219	.323
Bats Right	R	.129	31	4	0	0	1	4	0	6	.129	.226
Murray,Eddie	L	.238	202	48	16	1	3	35	16	16	.286	.371
Bats Both	R	.275	349	96	21	1	13	58	50	58	.364	.453
Myers,Greg	L	.000	5	0	0	0	0	0	0	1	.000	.000
Bats Left	R	.247	73	18	7	0	1	13	5	10	.288	.384
Naehring,Tim	L	.235	68	16	3	0	2	9	3	12	.284	.368
Bats Right	R	.229	118	27	5	0	1	5	15	19	.321	.297
Natal,Bob	L	.000	4	0	0	0	0	0	1	1	.200	.000
Bats Right	R	.000	2	0	0	0	0	0	0	0	.000	.000
Neel,Troy	L	.400	5	2	0	0	1	2	0	1	.400	1.000
Bats Left	R	.250	48	12	3	0	2	7	5	14	.333	.438
Newman,Al	L	.268	56	15	1	0	0	3	14	9	.423	.286
Bats Both	R	.205	190	39	4	0	0	9	20	17	.281	.226
Newson,Warren	L	.250	4	1	0	0	0	0	3	2	.571	.250
Bats Left	R	.220	132	29	3	0	1	11	34	36	.380	.265
Nieves,Melvin	L	.200	5	1	0	0	0	0	1	3	.333	.200
Bats Both	R	.214	14	3	1	0	0	1	1	4	.267	.286
Nilsson,Dave	L	.222	27	6	2	0	0	7	2	3	.276	.296
Bats Left	R	.234	137	32	6	0	4	18	15	15	.309	.365
Nixon,Otis	L	.343	178	61	8	1	2	16	11	15	.379	.433
Bats Both	R	.263	278	73	6	1	0	6	28	39	.329	.291
Noboa,Junior	L	.240	25	6	0	0	0	3	2	4	.310	.240
Bats Right	R	.045	22	1	0	0	0	0	1	4	.087	.045
Nokes,Matt	L	.197	71	14	4	0	5	15	8	18	.275	.465
Bats Left	R	.230	313	72	5	1	17	44	29	44	.297	.415
O'Brien,C	L	.247	89	22	6	0	1	6	9	9	.316	.348
Bats Right	R	.164	67	11	6	0	1	7	7	9	.253	.299
O'Brien,Pete	L	.214	56	12	2	1	1	8	7	6	.288	.339
Bats Left	R	.224	340	76	13	0	13	44	33	21	.289	.376
O'Neill,Paul	L	.225	173	39	6	0	2	26	14	46	.279	.295
Bats Left	R	.257	323	83	13	1	12	40	63	39	.379	.415
Oberkfell,Ken	L	.083	12	1	0	0	0	0	0	0	.083	.083
Bats Left	R	.291	79	23	1	0	0	10	8	5	.348	.304
Offerman,Jose	L	.269	201	54	8	1	1	7	20	27	.332	.333
Bats Both	R	.255	333	85	12	7	0	23	37	71	.330	.333
Olerud,John	L	.258	97	25	4	0	3	15	22	16	.393	.392
Bats Left	R	.291	361	105	24	0	13	51	48	45	.370	.465
Oliver,Joe	L	.307	176	54	11	0	4	24	16	22	.359	.438
Bats Right	R	.249	309	77	14	1	6	33	19	53	.291	.359
Olson,Greg	L	.256	117	30	5	2	1	10	6	7	.288	.359
Bats Right	R	.227	185	42	9	0	2	17	28	24	.332	.308
Oquendo,Jose	L	.167	12	2	1	0	0	1	3	2	.333	.250
Bats Both	R	.304	23	7	2	1	0	2	2	1	.360	.478
Orsulak,Joe	L	.250	80	20	5	1	0	11	4	10	.307	.338
Bats Left	R	.299	311	93	13	2	4	28	24	24	.351	.392

Batter	vs	Avg	AB	H	2B	3B	HR	BI	BB	SO	OBP	SLG
Ortiz,Junior	L	.277	65	18	2	0	0	6	6	3	.338	.308
Bats Right	R	.240	179	43	5	0	0	18	6	20	.280	.268
Orton,John	L	.120	25	3	1	0	1	5	2	11	.241	.280
Bats Right	R	.247	89	22	2	0	1	7	5	21	.287	.303
Owen,Spike	L	.286	161	46	10	2	4	23	16	11	.346	.447
Bats Both	R	.258	225	58	6	1	3	17	34	19	.350	.333
Pagliarulo,M	L	.167	6	1	0	0	0	0	0	2	.167	.167
Bats Left	R	.202	99	20	4	0	0	9	1	15	.216	.242
Pagnozzi,Tom	L	.244	176	43	9	1	5	15	11	28	.287	.392
Bats Right	R	.252	309	78	17	2	2	29	17	36	.292	.340
Palmeiro,R	L	.281	178	50	7	3	5	27	20	27	.365	.438
Bats Left	R	.263	430	113	20	1	17	58	52	56	.347	.433
Palmer,Dean	L	.252	143	36	7	0	8	20	18	41	.333	.469
Bats Right	R	.221	398	88	18	0	18	52	44	113	.303	.402
Parent,Mark	L	.111	9	1	0	0	1	1	2	2	.273	.444
Bats Right	R	.280	25	7	1	0	1	3	1	5	.333	.440
Parks,Derek	L	.400	5	2	0	0	0	0	1	0	.500	.400
Bats Right	R	.000	1	0	0	0	0	0	0	1	.500	.000
Parrish,Lance	L	.232	95	22	7	0	4	10	12	18	.315	.432
Bats Right	R	.233	180	42	6	1	8	22	12	52	.282	.411
Pasqua,Dan	L	.111	18	2	0	0	0	2	2	4	.200	.111
Bats Left	R	.219	247	54	16	1	6	31	34	53	.312	.364
Patterson,J	L	.240	25	6	1	0	0	1	1	6	.269	.280
Bats Both	R	.167	78	13	1	0	0	3	4	18	.217	.192
Pecota,Bill	L	.234	107	25	6	0	2	13	9	12	.291	.346
Bats Right	R	.222	162	36	7	0	0	13	16	28	.294	.265
Pedre,Jorge	L	.000	1	0	0	0	0	0	0	0	.000	.000
Bats Right	R	.000	3	0	0	0	0	0	0	1	.000	.000
Peguero,Julio	L	.143	7	1	0	0	0	0	0	2	.143	.143
Bats Both	R	.500	2	1	0	0	0	0	3	1	.800	.500
Peltier,Dan	L	.000	1	0	0	0	0	0	0	1	.000	.000
Bats Left	R	.174	23	4	0	0	0	2	0	2	.174	.174
Pena,Geronimo	L	.328	67	22	3	0	3	10	9	10	.425	.507
Bats Both	R	.294	136	40	9	1	4	21	15	27	.365	.463
Pena,Tony	L	.252	111	28	6	0	1	11	2	14	.270	.333
Bats Right	R	.237	299	71	15	1	0	27	22	47	.289	.294
Pendleton,T	L	.357	207	74	11	0	8	41	13	13	.390	.527
Bats Both	R	.289	433	125	28	1	13	64	24	54	.323	.448
Pennyfeather,W	L	.000	4	0	0	0	0	0	0	0	.000	.000
Bats Right	R	.400	5	2	0	0	0	0	0	0	.400	.400
Perezchica,T	L	.083	12	1	1	0	0	1	1	4	.154	.167
Bats Right	R	.125	8	1	0	0	0	0	1	2	.222	.125
Perry,Gerald	L	.200	25	5	0	0	0	2	4	2	.310	.200
Bats Left	R	.246	118	29	8	0	1	16	11	21	.311	.339
Petralli,Geno	L	.136	22	3	0	0	0	0	0	8	.136	.136
Bats Left	R	.206	170	35	12	0	1	18	20	26	.289	.294
Pettis,Gary	L	.302	43	13	3	3	0	6	10	12	.434	.512
Bats Both	R	.164	116	19	2	0	1	6	19	33	.279	.207
Phillips,Tony	L	.270	174	47	9	1	5	23	37	21	.401	.420
Bats Both	R	.278	432	120	23	2	5	41	77	72	.382	.375

Batters vs. Left-Handed and Right-Handed Pitchers

Batter	vs	Avg	AB	H	2B	3B	HR	BI	BB	SO	OBP	SLG	Batter	vs	Avg	AB	H	2B	3B	HR	BI	BB	SO	OBP	SLG
Piazza,Mike	L	.267	30	8	2	0	0	4	2	5	.313	.333	Ripken,Cal	L	.230	165	38	6	1	2	13	14	8	.297	.315
Bats Right	R	.205	39	8	1	0	1	3	2	7	.262	.308	Bats Right	R	.258	472	122	23	0	12	59	50	42	.332	.383
Plantier,Phil	L	.155	71	11	1	0	0	1	7	22	.238	.169	Rivera,Luis	L	.179	78	14	3	0	0	7	10	16	.273	.218
Bats Left	R	.270	278	75	18	0	7	29	37	61	.356	.410	Bats Right	R	.229	210	48	8	1	0	22	16	40	.293	.276
Polonia,Luis	L	.227	132	30	3	0	0	5	9	25	.280	.250	Roberts,Bip	L	.292	185	54	7	0	3	15	17	20	.350	.378
Bats Left	R	.303	445	135	14	4	0	30	36	39	.353	.353	Bats Both	R	.340	347	118	27	6	1	30	45	34	.416	.461
Pratt,Todd	L	.303	33	10	1	0	1	8	3	7	.361	.424	Rodriguez,H	L	.400	15	6	0	0	0	1	1	5	.438	.400
Bats Right	R	.231	13	3	0	0	1	2	1	5	.286	.462	Bats Left	R	.198	131	26	7	0	3	13	7	25	.237	.321
Prince,Tom	L	.095	21	2	1	0	0	2	5	5	.259	.143	Rodriguez,I	L	.276	105	29	4	0	2	9	7	14	.319	.371
Bats Right	R	.087	23	2	1	0	0	3	1	4	.120	.130	Bats Right	R	.254	315	80	12	1	6	28	17	59	.293	.356
Puckett,Kirby	L	.328	125	41	7	0	3	22	12	23	.381	.456	Rohde,Dave	L	.000	3	0	0	0	0	0	0	3	.000	.000
Bats Right	R	.329	514	169	31	4	16	88	32	74	.372	.498	Bats Both	R	.000	4	0	0	0	0	0	2	0	.333	.000
Pulliam,H	L	.250	4	1	1	0	0	0	1	2	.400	.500	Rose,Bobby	L	.167	24	4	0	0	1	2	4	2	.286	.292
Bats Right	R	.000	1	0	0	0	0	0	0	1	.000	.000	Bats Right	R	.233	60	14	5	0	1	8	4	7	.299	.367
Quinlan,Tom	L	.000	4	0	0	0	0	0	2	3	.333	.000	Rossy,Rico	L	.200	50	10	5	0	0	6	9	5	.317	.300
Bats Right	R	.091	11	1	1	0	0	2	0	6	.091	.182	Bats Right	R	.222	99	22	3	1	1	6	11	15	.306	.303
Quinones,Luis	L	.000	0	0	0	0	0	0	0	0	.000	.000	Rowland,Rich	L	.250	8	2	0	0	0	0	2	1	.400	.250
Bats Both	R	.200	5	1	0	0	0	1	0	0	.167	.200	Bats Right	R	.167	6	1	0	0	0	0	1	2	.286	.167
Quirk,Jamie	L	.238	21	5	1	0	0	1	0	5	.238	.286	Royer,Stan	L	.500	8	4	1	0	0	3	0	1	.444	.625
Bats Left	R	.218	156	34	6	1	2	10	16	23	.301	.308	Bats Right	R	.261	23	6	1	0	2	6	1	3	.292	.565
Raines,Tim	L	.252	135	34	3	2	0	11	25	10	.369	.304	Russell,John	L	.200	5	1	0	0	0	1	0	1	.333	.200
Bats Both	R	.308	416	128	19	7	7	43	56	38	.383	.438	Bats Right	R	.000	5	0	0	0	0	1	1	3	.143	.000
Ramirez,R	L	.329	82	27	5	0	1	6	3	14	.353	.427	Sabo,Chris	L	.247	146	36	8	1	6	21	14	23	.311	.438
Bats Right	R	.181	94	17	1	0	0	7	4	10	.222	.191	Bats Right	R	.242	198	48	11	2	6	22	16	31	.295	.409
Ramsey,F	L	.063	16	1	0	0	0	2	0	5	.063	.063	Salazar,Luis	L	.250	156	39	6	2	4	18	6	16	.273	.391
Bats Right	R	.222	9	2	0	0	0	0	0	1	.222	.222	Bats Right	R	.141	99	14	1	0	1	7	5	18	.181	.182
Randolph,W	L	.276	105	29	2	1	2	8	21	5	.397	.371	Salmon,Tim	L	.231	13	3	0	0	1	2	3	4	.375	.462
Bats Right	R	.238	181	43	9	0	0	7	19	29	.324	.287	Bats Right	R	.167	66	11	1	0	1	4	8	19	.263	.227
Ready,Randy	L	.271	59	16	0	0	3	13	11	12	.375	.424	Samuel,Juan	L	.288	104	30	5	2	0	9	8	19	.345	.375
Bats Right	R	.136	66	9	2	0	0	4	14	11	.288	.167	Bats Right	R	.258	120	31	4	0	0	14	6	30	.295	.317
Reboulet,Jeff	L	.222	27	6	1	0	0	2	5	6	.364	.259	Sanchez,Rey	L	.283	106	30	8	2	0	8	7	4	.327	.396
Bats Right	R	.182	110	20	6	1	1	14	18	20	.297	.282	Bats Right	R	.228	149	34	6	1	1	11	3	13	.255	.302
Redus,Gary	L	.258	151	39	5	3	2	10	16	22	.329	.371	Sandberg,Ryne	L	.340	206	70	13	4	4	24	23	19	.403	.500
Bats Right	R	.240	25	6	2	0	1	2	1	3	.269	.440	Bats Right	R	.286	406	116	19	4	22	63	45	54	.355	.515
Reed,Darren	L	.167	66	11	3	0	3	6	4	21	.208	.348	Sanders,Deion	L	.271	48	13	1	4	2	5	2	12	.300	.583
Bats Right	R	.188	48	9	1	0	2	8	4	13	.264	.333	Bats Left	R	.310	255	79	5	10	6	23	16	40	.354	.478
Reed,Jeff	L	.000	4	0	0	0	0	0	0	0	.000	.000	Sanders,R	L	.314	175	55	15	4	7	18	19	30	.391	.566
Bats Left	R	.190	21	4	0	0	0	2	1	4	.227	.190	Bats Right	R	.233	210	49	11	2	5	18	29	68	.328	.376
Reed,Jody	L	.260	154	40	12	1	1	7	21	14	.345	.370	Santiago,B	L	.292	130	38	7	0	7	17	7	17	.326	.508
Bats Right	R	.242	396	96	15	0	2	33	41	30	.312	.295	Bats Right	R	.230	256	59	14	0	3	25	14	35	.267	.320
Reimer,Kevin	L	.247	89	22	4	0	2	8	12	29	.356	.360	Santovenia,N	L	.000	0	0	0	0	0	0	0	0	.000	.000
Bats Left	R	.272	405	110	28	2	14	50	30	74	.332	.454	Bats Right	R	.333	3	1	0	0	1	2	0	0	.333	1.333
Reynolds,H	L	.250	116	29	6	0	0	12	17	4	.348	.302	Sasser,Mackey	L	.222	18	4	0	0	0	2	0	1	.211	.222
Bats Both	R	.246	342	84	17	3	3	21	28	37	.304	.339	Bats Left	R	.244	123	30	6	0	2	16	3	9	.254	.341
Rhodes,Karl	L	.000	0	0	0	0	0	0	0	0	.000	.000	Sax,Steve	L	.229	157	36	8	0	1	7	11	7	.278	.299
Bats Left	R	.000	4	0	0	0	0	0	0	2	.000	.000	Bats Right	R	.239	410	98	18	4	3	40	32	35	.294	.324
Riles,Ernest	L	.000	6	0	0	0	0	0	0	1	.000	.000	Scarsone,S	L	.125	16	2	0	0	0	0	0	9	.125	.125
Bats Left	R	.291	55	16	1	0	1	4	2	10	.310	.364	Bats Right	R	.214	14	3	0	0	0	0	2	3	.313	.214
Ripken,Billy	L	.229	109	25	7	0	0	9	7	5	.280	.294	Schaefer,Jeff	L	.154	26	4	1	0	0	0	1	5	.185	.192
Bats Right	R	.231	221	51	8	0	4	27	11	21	.272	.321	Bats Right	R	.091	44	4	1	0	1	3	1	5	.111	.182

271

Batters vs. Left-Handed and Right-Handed Pitchers

Batter	vs	Avg	AB	H	2B	3B	HR	BI	BB	SO	OBP	SLG	Batter	vs	Avg	AB	H	2B	3B	HR	BI	BB	SO	OBP	SLG
Schofield,D	L	.200	145	29	6	2	2	17	23	28	.316	.310	Sprague,Ed	L	.400	10	4	1	0	0	3	1	0	.455	.500
Bats Right	R	.209	278	58	12	0	2	19	38	54	.308	.273	Bats Right	R	.189	37	7	1	0	1	4	2	7	.231	.297
Scioscia,Mike	L	.235	81	19	1	2	1	10	8	6	.297	.333	Springer,S	L	.400	5	2	1	0	0	0	0	1	.400	.600
Bats Left	R	.217	267	58	5	1	2	14	24	25	.283	.266	Bats Right	R	.000	0	0	0	0	0	0	0	0	.000	.000
Scott,Gary	L	.167	30	5	2	0	1	6	1	4	.194	.333	Stairs,Matt	L	.000	2	0	0	0	0	0	2	0	.500	.000
Bats Right	R	.152	66	10	0	0	1	5	4	10	.200	.197	Bats Left	R	.179	28	5	2	0	0	5	5	7	.294	.250
Segui,David	L	.205	78	16	3	0	0	9	7	14	.271	.244	Stankiewicz,A	L	.272	136	37	5	1	0	10	10	11	.336	.324
Bats Both	R	.252	111	28	6	0	1	8	13	9	.331	.333	Bats Right	R	.265	264	70	17	1	2	15	28	31	.339	.360
Seitzer,Kevin	L	.313	128	40	10	1	2	17	21	9	.404	.453	Stanley,Mike	L	.241	112	27	4	0	5	16	22	26	.366	.411
Bats Right	R	.257	412	106	25	0	3	54	36	35	.315	.340	Bats Right	R	.262	61	16	3	0	3	11	11	19	.384	.459
Servais,Scott	L	.248	145	36	8	0	0	15	8	14	.297	.303	Steinbach,T	L	.300	110	33	5	0	5	18	11	15	.361	.482
Bats Right	R	.217	60	13	1	0	0	0	3	11	.288	.233	Bats Right	R	.271	328	89	15	1	7	35	34	43	.340	.387
Sharperson,M	L	.312	199	62	13	0	3	22	27	15	.390	.422	Stephens,Ray	L	.182	11	2	0	0	0	0	0	5	.182	.182
Bats Right	R	.280	118	33	8	0	0	14	20	18	.381	.347	Bats Right	R	.000	2	0	0	0	0	0	0	0	.000	.000
Sheffield,G	L	.365	189	69	9	2	13	38	18	13	.420	.640	Stephenson,P	L	.400	5	2	0	0	0	0	0	2	.400	.400
Bats Right	R	.313	368	115	25	1	20	62	30	27	.367	.549	Bats Left	R	.136	66	9	2	1	0	8	10	9	.250	.197
Shields,Tommy	L	.000	0	0	0	0	0	0	0	0	.000	.000	Stevens,Lee	L	.159	44	7	2	0	0	5	4	9	.245	.205
Bats Right	R	.000	0	0	0	0	0	0	0	0	.000	.000	Bats Left	R	.231	268	62	17	0	7	32	25	55	.295	.373
Shipley,Craig	L	.294	34	10	1	0	0	0	1	6	.314	.324	Stillwell,K	L	.250	112	28	1	2	1	8	7	19	.289	.321
Bats Right	R	.225	71	16	5	0	0	7	1	15	.236	.296	Bats Both	R	.217	267	58	14	1	1	16	19	39	.268	.288
Shumpert,T	L	.207	29	6	3	0	1	6	1	4	.233	.414	Strange,Doug	L	.158	19	3	0	0	0	1	4	4	.304	.158
Bats Right	R	.123	65	8	2	1	0	5	2	13	.149	.185	Bats Both	R	.160	75	12	1	0	1	4	6	11	.222	.213
Sierra,Ruben	L	.339	171	58	10	3	5	33	14	13	.385	.520	Strawberry,D	L	.242	66	16	1	0	2	10	7	15	.324	.348
Bats Both	R	.253	430	109	24	4	12	54	31	55	.299	.412	Bats Left	R	.233	90	21	7	0	3	15	12	19	.320	.411
Silvestri,D	L	.286	7	2	0	1	0	1	0	1	.286	.571	Stubbs,F	L	.256	43	11	1	1	1	10	0	12	.256	.395
Bats Right	R	.333	6	2	0	1	0	0	0	2	.333	.667	Bats Left	R	.224	245	55	10	0	8	32	27	56	.303	.363
Simms,Mike	L	.286	14	4	1	0	1	2	1	4	.375	.571	Suero,William	L	.273	11	3	1	0	0	0	2	1	.385	.364
Bats Right	R	.200	10	2	0	0	0	1	1	5	.273	.200	Bats Right	R	.000	5	0	0	0	0	0	0	0	.167	.000
Sinatro,Matt	L	.286	7	2	0	0	0	0	0	0	.286	.286	Surhoff,B.J.	L	.270	126	34	3	1	2	20	11	17	.329	.357
Bats Right	R	.048	21	1	0	0	0	0	0	5	.048	.048	Bats Left	R	.246	354	87	16	0	2	42	35	24	.309	.308
Slaught,Don	L	.322	174	56	9	1	3	21	11	13	.362	.437	Sveum,Dale	L	.203	69	14	5	0	0	5	15	24	.345	.275
Bats Right	R	.395	81	32	8	2	1	16	6	10	.429	.580	Bats Both	R	.194	180	35	8	0	4	23	13	44	.242	.306
Smith,Dwight	L	.200	20	4	0	0	1	4	0	5	.200	.350	Tabler,Pat	L	.284	67	19	2	0	0	12	8	4	.355	.313
Bats Left	R	.284	197	56	10	3	2	20	13	35	.329	.396	Bats Right	R	.221	68	15	3	0	0	4	3	10	.254	.265
Smith,Lonnie	L	.277	65	18	4	1	3	14	7	13	.347	.508	Tackett,Jeff	L	.288	52	15	1	0	4	7	6	5	.373	.538
Bats Right	R	.226	93	21	4	1	3	19	10	24	.308	.387	Bats Right	R	.220	127	28	7	1	1	17	11	23	.280	.315
Smith,Ozzie	L	.272	202	55	10	1	0	13	21	14	.339	.332	Tartabull,D	L	.286	119	34	6	0	11	35	50	29	.494	.613
Bats Both	R	.310	316	98	10	1	0	18	38	20	.384	.348	Bats Right	R	.258	302	78	13	0	14	50	53	86	.368	.440
Snow,J.T.	L	.000	3	0	0	0	0	0	0	1	.000	.000	Tatum,Jimmy	L	.250	4	1	0	0	0	0	0	1	.250	.250
Bats Both	R	.182	11	2	1	0	0	2	5	4	.438	.273	Bats Right	R	.000	4	0	0	0	0	0	1	1	.200	.000
Snyder,Cory	L	.294	170	50	12	0	6	20	9	31	.331	.471	Taubensee,E	L	.234	47	11	3	0	2	5	6	12	.333	.426
Bats Right	R	.250	220	55	10	2	8	37	14	65	.295	.423	Bats Left	R	.220	250	55	12	0	3	23	25	66	.292	.304
Sojo,Luis	L	.221	95	21	2	0	0	6	5	10	.260	.242	Tettleton,M	L	.274	135	37	8	0	8	23	22	28	.373	.511
Bats Right	R	.289	273	79	10	3	7	37	9	14	.313	.425	Bats Both	R	.226	390	88	17	0	24	60	100	109	.381	.454
Sorrento,Paul	L	.156	45	7	1	0	0	4	6	16	.250	.178	Teufel,Tim	L	.239	92	22	6	0	4	14	12	13	.333	.435
Bats Left	R	.281	413	116	23	1	18	56	45	73	.351	.472	Bats Right	R	.214	154	33	4	0	2	11	19	32	.299	.279
Sosa,Sammy	L	.280	75	21	3	0	5	0	8	19	.353	.320	Thomas,Frank	L	.357	140	50	15	1	8	26	28	20	.456	.650
Bats Right	R	.251	187	47	4	2	8	20	11	44	.302	.422	Bats Right	R	.312	433	135	31	1	16	89	94	68	.433	.499
Spiers,Bill	L	.000	3	0	0	0	0	1	0	1	.000	.000	Thome,Jim	L	.214	14	3	0	0	0	0	0	8	.214	.214
Bats Left	R	.385	13	5	2	0	0	1	1	3	.429	.538	Bats Left	R	.204	103	21	3	1	2	12	10	26	.282	.311

Batters vs. Left-Handed and Right-Handed Pitchers

Batter	vs	Avg	AB	H	2B	3B	HR	BI	BB	SO	OBP	SLG	Batter	vs	Avg	AB	H	2B	3B	HR	BI	BB	SO	OBP	SLG
Thompson,Milt	L	.318	22	7	3	0	0	0	2	5	.375	.455	Vizquel,Omar	L	.229	105	24	4	0	0	5	8	4	.283	.267
Bats Left	R	.290	186	54	6	1	4	17	14	34	.347	.398	Bats Both	R	.312	378	118	16	4	0	16	24	34	.356	.376
Thompson,R	L	.280	164	46	14	1	1	11	20	22	.357	.396	Voigt,Jack	L	.000	0	0	0	0	0	0	0	0	.000	.000
Bats Right	R	.247	279	69	11	0	13	38	23	53	.319	.427	Bats Right	R	.000	0	0	0	0	0	0	0	0	.000	.000
Thompson,Ryan	L	.216	37	8	4	0	0	0	6	4	.326	.324	Walker,Chico	L	.322	90	29	4	0	0	13	4	13	.340	.367
Bats Right	R	.225	71	16	3	1	3	10	2	20	.243	.423	Bats Both	R	.270	163	44	8	1	4	25	23	37	.356	.405
Thon,Dickie	L	.293	99	29	7	2	3	17	11	13	.360	.495	Walker,Larry	L	.316	209	66	8	2	10	42	10	38	.354	.517
Bats Right	R	.222	176	39	8	1	1	20	9	27	.254	.295	Bats Left	R	.292	319	93	23	2	13	51	31	59	.353	.498
Thurman,Gary	L	.244	123	30	5	3	0	15	5	19	.273	.333	Wallach,Tim	L	.263	198	52	11	1	7	29	17	25	.329	.434
Bats Right	R	.247	77	19	1	0	0	5	4	15	.293	.260	Bats Right	R	.201	339	68	18	0	2	30	33	65	.276	.271
Tingley,Ron	L	.200	35	7	1	0	1	1	2	12	.263	.314	Walling,Denny	L	.000	0	0	0	0	0	0	0	0	.000	.000
Bats Right	R	.196	92	18	1	1	2	7	11	23	.288	.293	Bats Left	R	.333	3	1	0	0	0	0	0	0	.333	.333
Trammell,Alan	L	.357	28	10	4	0	0	6	3	0	.406	.500	Walters,Dan	L	.262	61	16	4	0	1	8	1	9	.270	.377
Bats Right	R	.243	74	18	3	1	1	5	12	4	.356	.351	Bats Right	R	.246	118	29	7	1	3	14	9	19	.308	.398
Treadway,Jeff	L	.100	10	1	0	0	0	0	2	2	.250	.100	Walton,Jerome	L	.149	47	7	0	1	0	1	7	10	.273	.191
Bats Left	R	.233	116	27	6	1	0	5	7	14	.276	.302	Bats Right	R	.000	8	0	0	0	0	0	2	3	.273	.000
Tucker,S	L	.105	19	2	0	0	0	2	2	5	.227	.105	Ward,Kevin	L	.253	87	22	2	0	3	9	9	27	.320	.379
Bats Right	R	.129	31	4	1	0	0	1	1	8	.182	.161	Bats Right	R	.117	60	7	3	0	0	3	5	11	.209	.167
Turner,Shane	L	.000	0	0	0	0	0	0	0	0	.000	.000	Ward,Turner	L	.625	8	5	2	0	0	2	1	0	.667	.875
Bats Left	R	.270	74	20	5	0	0	5	9	15	.341	.338	Bats Both	R	.238	21	5	1	0	1	1	3	4	.333	.429
Uribe,Jose	L	.302	53	16	4	1	1	6	3	9	.333	.472	Webster,Lenny	L	.321	28	9	4	0	1	7	4	4	.406	.571
Bats Both	R	.211	109	23	5	0	1	7	11	16	.283	.284	Bats Right	R	.267	90	24	6	1	0	6	5	7	.305	.356
Valentin,John	L	.212	33	7	3	0	1	3	8	2	.381	.394	Webster,Mitch	L	.292	130	38	8	1	3	17	15	18	.361	.438
Bats Right	R	.289	152	44	10	0	4	22	12	15	.343	.434	Bats Both	R	.242	132	32	4	3	3	18	12	31	.309	.402
Valentin,Jose	L	.000	0	0	0	0	0	0	0	0	.000	.000	Wedge,Eric	L	.306	36	11	1	0	4	8	5	8	.390	.667
Bats Both	R	.000	3	0	0	0	0	0	1	0	.000	.000	Bats Right	R	.188	32	6	1	0	1	3	8	10	.350	.313
Valle,Dave	L	.283	120	34	4	0	4	11	11	16	.348	.417	Wehner,John	L	.179	56	10	3	0	0	3	5	9	.246	.232
Bats Right	R	.219	247	54	12	1	5	19	16	42	.284	.336	Bats Right	R	.179	67	12	3	0	0	1	7	13	.257	.224
Van Slyke,A	L	.297	269	80	22	4	4	41	18	46	.341	.454	Weiss,Walt	L	.135	74	10	0	1	0	2	5	3	.190	.162
Bats Left	R	.345	345	119	23	8	10	48	40	53	.411	.545	Bats Both	R	.236	242	57	5	1	0	19	38	36	.337	.264
VanderWal,J	L	.241	29	7	0	0	0	1	2	6	.290	.241	Whitaker,Lou	L	.355	62	22	6	0	2	15	15	11	.481	.548
Bats Left	R	.239	184	44	8	2	4	19	22	30	.320	.370	Bats Left	R	.266	391	104	20	0	17	56	66	35	.370	.448
Varsho,Gary	L	.231	13	3	1	0	1	3	0	3	.231	.538	White,Devon	L	.212	179	38	5	0	5	19	13	41	.272	.324
Bats Left	R	.221	149	33	5	3	3	19	10	29	.269	.356	Bats Both	R	.262	462	121	21	7	12	41	34	92	.315	.416
Vatcher,Jim	L	.000	2	0	0	0	0	0	1	1	.333	.000	Whiten,Mark	L	.283	127	36	7	0	3	8	23	21	.401	.409
Bats Right	R	.286	14	4	1	0	0	2	2	5	.375	.357	Bats Both	R	.244	381	93	12	4	6	35	49	81	.328	.344
Vaughn,Greg	L	.248	105	26	4	1	6	23	21	19	.370	.476	Wilkerson,C	L	.294	68	20	2	0	1	7	6	10	.351	.368
Bats Right	R	.222	396	88	14	1	17	55	39	104	.297	.391	Bats Both	R	.237	228	54	8	1	1	22	12	37	.273	.294
Vaughn,Mo	L	.190	79	15	3	0	5	14	10	17	.281	.418	Wilkins,Rick	L	.280	50	14	3	0	0	1	5	10	.345	.340
Bats Left	R	.246	276	68	13	2	8	43	37	50	.339	.395	Bats Left	R	.268	194	52	6	1	8	21	23	43	.344	.433
Velarde,Randy	L	.307	140	43	10	0	4	22	15	23	.376	.464	Willard,Jerry	L	.000	0	0	0	0	0	0	0	0	.000	.000
Bats Right	R	.254	272	69	14	1	3	24	23	55	.310	.346	Bats Left	R	.229	48	11	1	0	2	8	2	10	.260	.375
Velasquez,G	L	.167	6	1	0	0	0	0	0	1	.167	.167	Williams,B	L	.298	84	25	6	1	1	9	10	11	.379	.429
Bats Left	R	.353	17	6	0	0	1	5	1	6	.389	.529	Bats Both	R	.271	177	48	8	1	4	17	19	25	.342	.395
Ventura,Robin	L	.258	182	47	12	1	2	28	26	34	.348	.368	Williams,G	L	.357	14	5	1	0	2	4	0	2	.357	.857
Bats Left	R	.293	410	120	26	0	14	65	67	37	.387	.459	Bats Right	R	.231	13	3	1	0	1	2	0	1	.231	.538
Villanueva,H	L	.152	46	7	2	0	0	5	5	11	.235	.196	Williams,M	L	.226	164	37	2	2	10	21	13	30	.279	.445
Bats Right	R	.152	66	10	4	0	2	8	6	13	.222	.303	Bats Right	R	.227	365	83	11	3	10	45	26	79	.290	.356
Vizcaino,Jose	L	.216	88	19	3	3	0	5	3	7	.242	.318	Williams,R	L	.250	8	2	1	0	0	2	1	3	.333	.375
Bats Both	R	.228	197	45	7	1	1	12	11	28	.268	.289	Bats Both	R	.222	18	4	0	1	0	0	0	7	.222	.333

Batters vs. Left-Handed and Right-Handed Pitchers

Batter	vs	Avg	AB	H	2B	3B	HR	BI	BB	SO	OBP	SLG
Wilson,Craig	L	.288	52	15	2	0	0	6	6	10	.356	.327
Bats Right	R	.333	54	18	4	0	0	7	4	8	.379	.407
Wilson,Dan	L	.417	12	5	1	0	0	3	0	4	.417	.500
Bats Right	R	.308	13	4	0	0	0	0	3	4	.438	.308
Wilson,Willie	L	.248	121	30	7	0	0	14	13	30	.316	.306
Bats Both	R	.280	275	77	8	5	0	23	22	35	.334	.345
Winfield,Dave	L	.301	146	44	7	1	8	28	24	21	.395	.527
Bats Right	R	.286	437	125	26	2	18	80	58	68	.370	.478
Winningham,H	L	.143	21	3	1	0	0	1	0	7	.143	.190
Bats Left	R	.244	213	52	7	1	1	13	10	46	.278	.300
Wood,Ted	L	.385	13	5	0	0	0	0	0	2	.429	.385
Bats Left	R	.156	45	7	2	0	1	3	6	13	.255	.267
Woodson,Tracy	L	.372	43	16	4	0	1	11	1	4	.386	.535
Bats Right	R	.268	71	19	4	0	0	11	2	6	.297	.324
Worthington,C	L	.188	16	3	0	0	0	2	1	2	.235	.188
Bats Right	R	.125	8	1	0	0	0	0	1	2	.222	.125
Wrona,Rick	L	.000	6	0	0	0	0	0	0	2	.000	.000
Bats Right	R	.235	17	4	0	0	0	0	0	1	.235	.235
Yelding,Eric	L	.250	4	1	0	0	0	0	0	1	.250	.250
Bats Right	R	.250	4	1	0	0	0	0	0	2	.250	.250
Young,Eric	L	.273	66	18	0	0	1	6	3	4	.304	.318
Bats Right	R	.242	66	16	1	0	0	5	5	5	.296	.258
Young,Gerald	L	.171	35	6	0	0	0	4	6	5	.293	.171
Bats Both	R	.195	41	8	1	1	0	0	4	6	.267	.268
Young,Kevin	L	.000	1	0	0	0	0	0	1	0	.500	.000
Bats Right	R	.667	6	4	0	0	0	4	1	0	.714	.667
Yount,Robin	L	.280	125	35	10	1	2	18	16	24	.359	.424
Bats Right	R	.259	432	112	30	2	6	59	37	57	.315	.380
Zeile,Todd	L	.278	133	37	5	1	1	15	26	16	.394	.353
Bats Right	R	.248	306	76	13	3	6	33	42	54	.333	.369
Zosky,Eddie	L	.500	2	1	0	0	0	1	0	1	.333	.500
Bats Right	R	.200	5	1	0	1	0	0	0	1	.200	.600
Zupcic,Bob	L	.293	133	39	8	1	0	15	13	14	.356	.368
Bats Right	R	.266	259	69	11	0	3	28	12	46	.304	.344
AL	L	.265	--	--	--	--	--	--	--	--	.339	.397
	R	.257	--	--	--	--	--	--	--	--	.325	.381
NL	L	.262	--	--	--	--	--	--	--	--	.323	.386
	R	.245	--	--	--	--	--	--	--	--	.311	.358
MLB	L	.263	--	--	--	--	--	--	--	--	.330	.391
	R	.252	--	--	--	--	--	--	--	--	.319	.371

Pitchers vs. Left-Handed and Right-Handed Batters

Pitcher	vs	Avg	AB	H	2B	3B	HR	BI	BB	SO	OBP	SLG	Pitcher	vs	Avg	AB	H	2B	3B	HR	BI	BB	SO	OBP	SLG
Abbott,Jim	L	.273	128	35	9	1	0	9	13	17	.343	.359	Bannister,F	L	.174	46	8	4	0	2	9	8	12	.288	.391
Throws Left	R	.261	662	173	19	1	12	57	55	113	.320	.347	Throws Left	R	.333	93	31	7	0	1	20	13	18	.414	.441
Abbott,Kyle	L	.326	129	42	2	1	3	17	8	28	.370	.426	Barnes,Brian	L	.233	60	14	3	0	2	7	9	14	.347	.383
Throws Left	R	.269	391	105	14	7	17	55	37	60	.328	.471	Throws Left	R	.209	302	63	12	0	7	22	37	51	.297	.318
Abbott,Paul	L	.200	25	5	1	0	0	0	4	10	.310	.240	Barton,Shawn	L	.389	18	7	2	1	0	4	1	1	.421	.611
Throws Right	R	.389	18	7	1	1	1	7	1	3	.429	.722	Throws Left	R	.125	24	3	0	0	1	2	6	3	.300	.250
Acker,Jim	L	.407	59	24	6	0	2	6	3	1	.435	.610	Batista,M	L	.500	6	3	0	0	1	2	3	1	.667	1.000
Throws Right	R	.284	74	21	5	0	2	18	9	10	.353	.432	Throws Right	R	.250	4	1	0	0	0	0	0	0	.250	.250
Agosto,Juan	L	.349	63	22	8	0	0	17	5	10	.414	.476	Beck,Rod	L	.178	180	32	6	1	2	13	6	47	.212	.256
Throws Left	R	.314	140	44	5	1	2	25	7	15	.342	.407	Throws Right	R	.204	147	30	2	0	2	12	9	40	.248	.259
Aguilera,Rick	L	.248	129	32	1	0	3	17	11	29	.310	.326	Belcher,Tim	L	.277	512	142	29	6	9	51	59	78	.350	.410
Throws Right	R	.228	123	28	7	0	4	15	6	23	.262	.382	Throws Right	R	.178	331	59	13	2	8	39	21	71	.228	.302
Aldred,Scott	L	.280	50	14	2	0	2	11	2	6	.308	.440	Belinda,Stan	L	.193	135	26	6	0	4	15	17	21	.277	.326
Throws Left	R	.313	211	66	15	1	10	33	31	28	.403	.536	Throws Right	R	.256	125	32	7	2	4	26	12	36	.314	.440
Alexander,G	L	.250	4	1	1	0	0	1	0	1	.200	.500	Bell,Eric	L	.133	15	2	0	0	0	1	3	1	.316	.133
Throws Right	R	.667	6	4	0	0	1	4	1	0	.714	1.167	Throws Left	R	.417	48	20	5	0	1	13	6	9	.473	.583
Alvarez,W	L	.225	89	20	6	0	0	11	19	19	.355	.292	Benes,Andy	L	.276	533	147	23	5	10	63	45	94	.333	.394
Throws Left	R	.286	290	83	7	0	12	47	46	47	.389	.434	Throws Right	R	.246	337	83	16	1	4	21	16	75	.283	.335
Andersen,L	L	.203	69	14	2	0	1	9	8	17	.295	.275	Berenguer,J	L	.341	135	46	9	3	8	39	22	14	.430	.630
Throws Right	R	.200	60	12	0	0	1	8	0	18	.197	.250	Throws Right	R	.188	165	31	9	0	2	13	14	31	.257	.279
Appier,Kevin	L	.205	370	76	15	4	7	29	41	67	.283	.324	Bielecki,Mike	L	.271	177	48	8	3	0	13	17	29	.335	.350
Throws Right	R	.227	401	91	22	2	3	24	27	83	.278	.314	Throws Right	R	.230	126	29	8	2	2	10	10	33	.288	.373
Aquino,Luis	L	.314	118	37	7	0	2	12	8	3	.354	.424	Birkbeck,Mike	L	.407	27	11	3	0	3	6	0	2	.407	.852
Throws Right	R	.295	149	44	7	0	3	17	12	8	.348	.403	Throws Right	R	.250	4	1	0	0	0	0	1	0	.400	.250
Armstrong,J	L	.274	277	76	10	2	10	42	39	39	.366	.433	Black,Bud	L	.229	140	32	5	1	4	10	10	20	.281	.364
Throws Right	R	.265	377	100	18	2	13	50	28	75	.315	.427	Throws Left	R	.272	537	146	22	5	19	57	49	62	.332	.438
Arnsberg,Brad	L	.429	14	6	0	0	3	5	3	2	.529	1.071	Blair,Willie	L	.250	156	39	8	1	1	17	16	25	.322	.333
Throws Right	R	.259	27	7	1	0	3	7	8	3	.459	.630	Throws Right	R	.248	141	35	8	2	4	29	9	23	.294	.418
Ashby,Andy	L	.318	85	27	4	0	4	15	13	9	.406	.506	Blyleven,Bert	L	.261	253	66	10	2	6	26	17	38	.305	.387
Throws Right	R	.250	60	15	3	2	2	11	8	15	.338	.467	Throws Right	R	.308	273	84	14	1	11	45	12	32	.345	.487
Assenmacher,P	L	.220	91	20	5	0	3	11	9	28	.294	.374	Boddicker,M	L	.292	168	49	6	2	2	25	16	16	.355	.387
Throws Left	R	.297	175	52	13	1	3	28	17	39	.364	.434	Throws Right	R	.249	173	43	16	0	3	28	21	31	.350	.393
Astacio,Pedro	L	.244	180	44	3	2	1	7	18	17	.315	.300	Boever,Joe	L	.242	186	45	7	2	1	20	28	30	.346	.317
Throws Right	R	.269	134	36	5	0	0	11	2	26	.283	.306	Throws Right	R	.252	230	58	6	0	2	21	17	37	.306	.304
Austin,Jim	L	.220	82	18	5	0	0	5	11	8	.316	.280	Bohanon,Brian	L	.235	34	8	0	0	1	11	5	5	.325	.324
Throws Right	R	.171	117	20	4	0	2	11	21	22	.302	.256	Throws Left	R	.310	158	49	7	2	6	27	20	24	.389	.494
Avery,Steve	L	.258	155	40	5	0	3	18	20	38	.341	.348	Bolton,Tom	L	.256	82	21	2	2	1	8	10	21	.344	.366
Throws Left	R	.243	723	176	26	6	11	61	51	91	.291	.342	Throws Left	R	.295	220	65	10	0	8	24	27	29	.378	.450
Ayala,Bobby	L	.286	63	18	6	0	0	7	8	14	.366	.381	Bones,Ricky	L	.268	302	81	13	3	9	22	21	22	.321	.421
Throws Right	R	.313	48	15	4	0	1	5	5	9	.389	.458	Throws Right	R	.260	339	88	14	2	18	52	27	43	.322	.472
Ayrault,Bob	L	.253	79	20	4	1	0	10	7	13	.310	.329	Borbon,Pedro	L	.250	4	1	1	0	0	0	0	1	.250	.500
Throws Right	R	.162	74	12	5	1	0	10	10	14	.264	.257	Throws Left	R	.500	2	1	0	0	0	1	1	0	.667	.500
Bailes,Scott	L	.360	50	18	3	0	0	10	6	7	.431	.420	Bosio,Chris	L	.273	421	115	19	2	10	39	24	40	.310	.399
Throws Left	R	.347	118	41	4	0	7	31	22	18	.447	.559	Throws Right	R	.236	457	108	19	1	11	49	20	80	.273	.354
Baller,Jay	L	.238	21	5	1	0	2	6	6	4	.407	.571	Boskie,Shawn	L	.303	195	59	16	0	10	34	31	27	.392	.538
Throws Right	R	.263	19	5	0	0	3	5	4	5	.375	.737	Throws Right	R	.259	143	37	9	0	4	16	5	12	.296	.406
Bankhead,S	L	.227	128	29	7	2	3	10	19	21	.327	.383	Bottenfield,K	L	.194	62	12	2	1	1	7	7	6	.271	.306
Throws Right	R	.211	133	28	3	2	1	13	10	32	.275	.286	Throws Right	R	.241	58	14	3	0	0	2	4	8	.297	.293
Banks,Willie	L	.293	140	41	7	1	3	17	16	22	.363	.421	Boucher,Denis	L	.346	26	9	3	0	1	3	6	2	.469	.577
Throws Right	R	.283	138	39	8	2	3	25	21	15	.377	.435	Throws Left	R	.293	133	39	2	1	8	25	14	15	.358	.504

Pitchers vs. Left-Handed and Right-Handed Batters

Pitcher	vs	Avg	AB	H	2B	3B	HR	BI	BB	SO	OBP	SLG
Bowen,Ryan	L	.395	76	30	5	1	2	19	16	6	.511	.566
Throws Right	R	.265	68	18	4	0	6	16	14	16	.390	.588
Brantley,C	L	.301	153	46	5	1	3	25	32	13	.420	.405
Throws Right	R	.192	130	25	4	0	3	12	26	19	.338	.292
Brantley,Jeff	L	.181	193	35	7	0	4	16	32	58	.300	.280
Throws Right	R	.246	130	32	5	0	4	24	13	28	.320	.377
Brink,Brad	L	.284	102	29	3	1	2	13	7	6	.330	.392
Throws Right	R	.343	70	24	5	1	0	10	6	10	.403	.443
Briscoe,John	L	.389	18	7	0	0	0	3	5	3	.522	.389
Throws Right	R	.417	12	5	2	0	0	2	4	1	.563	.583
Brocail,Doug	L	.306	36	11	3	0	1	4	3	9	.359	.472
Throws Right	R	.286	21	6	2	0	1	4	2	6	.348	.524
Brown,Keith	L	.421	19	8	2	0	2	5	3	3	.500	.842
Throws Right	R	.154	13	2	1	0	0	0	2	2	.267	.231
Brown,Kevin	L	.268	488	131	26	0	7	46	51	75	.339	.365
Throws Right	R	.252	519	131	14	1	4	58	25	98	.294	.306
Brown,K	L	.500	4	2	1	0	0	2	0	0	.500	.750
Throws Left	R	.250	8	2	0	1	1	2	3	2	.455	.875
Browning,Tom	L	.325	83	27	7	1	1	20	8	8	.385	.470
Throws Left	R	.307	264	81	21	6	5	25	20	25	.355	.489
Bullinger,Jim	L	.212	170	36	4	5	6	27	33	17	.343	.400
Throws Right	R	.259	139	36	5	0	3	17	21	19	.360	.360
Burba,Dave	L	.318	151	48	11	1	1	18	12	18	.370	.424
Throws Right	R	.250	128	32	4	1	3	26	19	29	.344	.367
Burke,Tim	L	.218	78	17	3	1	0	2	6	8	.274	.282
Throws Right	R	.365	96	35	11	0	3	25	12	7	.436	.573
Burkett,John	L	.296	466	138	26	6	11	58	27	56	.334	.448
Throws Right	R	.208	269	56	8	1	2	25	18	51	.265	.268
Burns,Todd	L	.235	166	39	8	1	2	9	15	20	.308	.331
Throws Right	R	.259	224	58	18	1	6	30	17	35	.310	.429
Butcher,Mike	L	.290	31	9	0	0	1	7	6	9	.421	.387
Throws Right	R	.253	79	20	2	0	2	8	7	15	.322	.354
Cadaret,Greg	L	.227	88	20	3	1	3	10	13	13	.340	.386
Throws Left	R	.279	301	84	14	1	9	46	61	60	.397	.422
Campbell,K	L	.259	108	28	5	0	2	11	25	20	.396	.361
Throws Right	R	.273	139	38	7	1	2	18	20	18	.363	.381
Campbell,Mike	L	.286	7	2	1	0	1	3	1	1	.375	.857
Throws Right	R	.167	6	1	0	0	0	1	1	1	.286	.167
Candelaria,J	L	.269	52	14	1	1	1	12	5	19	.328	.385
Throws Left	R	.154	39	6	1	0	0	4	8	4	.292	.179
Candiotti,Tom	L	.246	407	100	16	3	6	32	47	75	.322	.344
Throws Right	R	.227	339	77	19	1	7	38	16	77	.266	.351
Carman,Don	L	.333	3	1	0	0	0	0	0	0	.333	.333
Throws Left	R	.375	8	3	0	0	0	1	0	2	.375	.375
Carpenter,C	L	.222	162	36	8	1	6	27	15	23	.287	.395
Throws Right	R	.219	151	33	5	1	4	18	12	23	.290	.344
Carter,Larry	L	.266	79	21	4	3	5	13	8	11	.330	.582
Throws Right	R	.277	47	13	5	0	1	3	10	10	.404	.447
Casian,Larry	L	.083	12	1	0	0	0	0	0	2	.083	.083
Throws Left	R	.400	15	6	1	0	0	0	1	0	.438	.467

Pitcher	vs	Avg	AB	H	2B	3B	HR	BI	BB	SO	OBP	SLG
Castillo,F	L	.228	451	103	21	1	11	43	49	74	.303	.353
Throws Right	R	.238	319	76	21	3	8	26	14	61	.280	.398
Chapin,Darrin	L	.000	4	0	0	0	0	0	0	1	.000	.000
Throws Right	R	.500	4	2	1	0	1	2	0	0	.500	1.500
Charlton,Norm	L	.296	71	21	4	1	2	10	6	11	.359	.465
Throws Left	R	.251	231	58	14	0	5	31	20	79	.313	.377
Chiamparino,S	L	.310	42	13	2	1	1	3	4	6	.370	.476
Throws Right	R	.222	54	12	3	0	1	6	1	7	.232	.333
Christopher,M	L	.278	18	5	1	1	0	2	5	3	.435	.444
Throws Right	R	.245	49	12	3	1	2	7	5	10	.309	.469
Clark,Mark	L	.266	263	70	12	2	6	29	25	25	.326	.395
Throws Right	R	.264	178	47	6	2	6	17	11	19	.305	.421
Clemens,Roger	L	.226	447	101	15	1	6	27	30	98	.277	.304
Throws Right	R	.222	460	102	24	1	5	43	32	110	.280	.311
Clements,Pat	L	.234	77	18	3	0	0	8	5	15	.298	.273
Throws Left	R	.297	101	30	4	0	0	16	18	5	.410	.337
Cole,Victor	L	.250	48	12	3	0	1	3	11	7	.390	.375
Throws Right	R	.275	40	11	3	0	0	7	3	5	.318	.350
Combs,Pat	L	.250	12	3	0	1	0	1	3	2	.400	.417
Throws Left	R	.283	60	17	5	0	0	9	9	9	.371	.367
Cone,David	L	.230	505	116	17	4	10	48	72	123	.331	.339
Throws Right	R	.207	411	85	13	5	5	33	39	138	.281	.299
Cook,Dennis	L	.235	98	23	3	1	4	12	3	10	.257	.408
Throws Left	R	.259	513	133	31	2	25	64	47	86	.322	.474
Cooke,Steve	L	.217	23	5	1	0	0	1	0	3	.217	.261
Throws Left	R	.266	64	17	5	0	2	6	4	7	.309	.438
Cormier,Rheal	L	.288	132	38	10	1	1	12	5	25	.324	.402
Throws Left	R	.265	588	156	24	2	14	58	28	92	.301	.384
Corsi,Jim	L	.357	70	25	3	0	1	8	6	8	.408	.443
Throws Right	R	.211	90	19	1	1	1	10	12	11	.298	.278
Cox,Danny	L	.287	129	37	6	1	3	22	20	20	.377	.419
Throws Right	R	.254	114	29	6	0	2	19	7	28	.295	.360
Crews,Tim	L	.331	151	50	7	3	3	25	14	16	.383	.477
Throws Right	R	.290	155	45	3	0	3	24	6	27	.319	.368
Crim,Chuck	L	.241	137	33	5	0	2	21	9	8	.286	.321
Throws Right	R	.328	204	67	10	1	9	44	20	22	.399	.520
Darling,Ron	L	.270	371	100	25	3	6	37	45	40	.348	.402
Throws Right	R	.238	412	98	19	2	9	46	27	59	.290	.359
Darwin,Danny	L	.281	274	77	18	4	1	31	28	47	.345	.387
Throws Right	R	.238	344	82	13	2	10	39	25	77	.297	.375
Davis,Mark	L	.305	59	18	3	0	1	9	6	8	.368	.407
Throws Left	R	.299	154	46	12	1	8	36	35	26	.422	.545
Davis,Storm	L	.241	137	33	2	0	2	15	21	28	.338	.299
Throws Right	R	.246	187	46	6	1	3	23	15	25	.306	.337
DeLeon,Jose	L	.282	245	69	12	4	5	33	26	38	.351	.424
Throws Right	R	.211	199	42	14	0	2	20	22	41	.286	.312
Delucia,Rich	L	.316	152	48	12	0	4	19	17	20	.385	.474
Throws Right	R	.275	189	52	14	1	9	35	18	46	.341	.503
Deshaies,Jim	L	.356	59	21	3	0	1	4	11	10	.451	.458
Throws Left	R	.239	297	71	13	1	5	24	22	36	.293	.340

Pitchers vs. Left-Handed and Right-Handed Batters

Pitcher	vs	Avg	AB	H	2B	3B	HR	BI	BB	SO	OBP	SLG
Dewey,Mark	L	.254	67	17	1	0	0	2	5	6	.306	.269
Throws Right	R	.308	65	20	4	0	2	15	5	18	.357	.462
Dibble,Rob	L	.180	128	23	2	1	2	17	22	64	.298	.258
Throws Right	R	.207	121	25	3	1	1	17	9	46	.271	.273
DiPino,Frank	L	.188	16	3	1	0	0	3	1	5	.235	.250
Throws Left	R	.240	25	6	1	0	0	1	2	3	.296	.280
Doherty,John	L	.240	200	48	6	0	1	26	8	17	.287	.285
Throws Right	R	.323	257	83	7	1	3	25	17	20	.374	.393
Dopson,John	L	.276	257	71	12	1	5	23	18	17	.324	.389
Throws Right	R	.296	297	88	18	0	12	39	20	38	.343	.478
Downs,Kelly	L	.274	263	72	12	2	1	24	36	25	.359	.346
Throws Right	R	.235	277	65	11	0	7	30	34	46	.329	.350
Drabek,Doug	L	.261	548	143	21	3	11	47	42	90	.314	.370
Throws Right	R	.189	397	75	14	1	6	28	12	87	.217	.275
Drahman,Brian	L	.083	12	1	1	0	0	2	0	0	.083	.167
Throws Right	R	.333	15	5	0	0	0	1	2	1	.412	.333
Dunne,Mike	L	.222	27	6	0	0	0	2	1	3	.250	.222
Throws Right	R	.300	20	6	1	0	0	4	5	3	.462	.350
Eckersley,D	L	.262	149	39	7	0	3	11	8	33	.299	.369
Throws Right	R	.159	145	23	4	1	2	7	3	60	.181	.241
Edens,Tom	L	.248	109	27	1	2	0	12	7	29	.299	.294
Throws Right	R	.229	166	38	7	1	1	14	29	28	.347	.301
Eichhorn,Mark	L	.341	129	44	4	2	2	20	14	25	.400	.450
Throws Right	R	.202	208	42	7	2	1	23	11	36	.246	.269
Eiland,Dave	L	.364	66	24	6	2	1	12	2	4	.382	.561
Throws Right	R	.184	49	9	2	0	0	5	3	6	.231	.224
Eldred,Cal	L	.188	154	29	2	0	2	4	11	21	.251	.240
Throws Right	R	.221	213	47	8	3	2	10	12	41	.262	.315
Embree,Alan	L	.100	10	1	0	0	0	0	2	2	.308	.100
Throws Left	R	.300	60	18	5	0	3	11	6	10	.353	.533
Erickson,S	L	.241	410	99	10	4	7	39	41	41	.311	.337
Throws Right	R	.264	371	98	19	1	11	39	42	60	.345	.410
Farr,Steve	L	.217	83	18	0	0	1	6	15	14	.347	.253
Throws Right	R	.160	100	16	4	0	1	10	4	23	.190	.230
Fassero,Jeff	L	.269	93	25	2	1	1	12	6	24	.320	.344
Throws Left	R	.241	232	56	10	4	0	20	28	39	.323	.319
Fernandez,A	L	.251	351	88	16	2	9	49	19	45	.295	.385
Throws Right	R	.288	385	111	14	1	12	38	31	50	.346	.423
Fernandez,Sid	L	.188	149	28	6	5	0	12	16	45	.272	.295
Throws Left	R	.215	622	134	31	4	12	48	51	148	.273	.336
Fetters,Mike	L	.225	71	16	3	0	1	8	15	9	.360	.310
Throws Right	R	.164	134	22	5	0	2	18	9	34	.250	.246
Filer,Tom	L	.150	40	6	0	1	1	2	3	3	.209	.275
Throws Right	R	.293	41	12	3	0	1	3	3	6	.341	.439
Finley,Chuck	L	.402	87	35	5	1	1	9	6	9	.441	.517
Throws Left	R	.262	675	177	29	2	23	79	92	115	.349	.413
Fireovid,S	L	.300	10	3	1	0	0	1	3	0	.462	.400
Throws Right	R	.412	17	7	0	1	0	5	1	0	.444	.529
Fisher,Brian	L	.234	167	39	7	0	2	13	32	9	.351	.311
Throws Right	R	.234	175	41	13	0	7	26	15	17	.298	.429
Flanagan,Mike	L	.274	62	17	0	0	0	6	10	11	.378	.274
Throws Left	R	.384	86	33	6	1	3	30	13	6	.481	.581
Fleming,Dave	L	.248	141	35	8	1	2	12	11	24	.307	.362
Throws Left	R	.258	736	190	45	3	11	69	49	88	.306	.372
Fortugno,Tim	L	.286	28	8	0	0	1	6	4	6	.364	.393
Throws Left	R	.225	129	29	4	0	4	16	15	25	.306	.349
Fossas,Tony	L	.214	56	12	6	0	0	9	3	16	.254	.321
Throws Left	R	.345	55	19	4	1	1	15	11	3	.463	.509
Foster,Steve	L	.300	90	27	3	2	2	9	5	10	.333	.444
Throws Right	R	.253	99	25	5	1	2	10	8	24	.306	.384
Franco,John	L	.250	28	7	1	0	0	3	7	6	.389	.286
Throws Left	R	.195	87	17	5	1	1	7	4	14	.228	.310
Freeman,M	L	.246	114	28	1	0	5	17	16	13	.336	.386
Throws Right	R	.256	129	33	8	1	2	24	13	28	.329	.380
Frey,Steve	L	.189	53	10	0	0	5	8	5	9	.271	.472
Throws Left	R	.261	111	29	4	0	1	9	17	15	.356	.324
Frohwirth,T	L	.246	142	35	3	0	1	15	19	15	.341	.289
Throws Right	R	.248	250	62	12	0	3	37	22	43	.311	.332
Gardiner,Mike	L	.258	221	57	8	5	3	23	23	38	.327	.380
Throws Right	R	.249	277	69	7	1	9	41	35	41	.333	.379
Gardner,Mark	L	.272	397	108	23	3	7	49	31	62	.330	.398
Throws Right	R	.242	293	71	13	0	8	30	29	70	.316	.369
Gibson,Paul	L	.338	71	24	4	2	3	10	10	12	.420	.577
Throws Left	R	.266	173	46	13	1	4	30	15	37	.323	.422
Glavine,Tom	L	.273	176	48	7	1	1	17	23	32	.353	.341
Throws Left	R	.225	663	149	30	3	5	53	47	97	.277	.302
Gleaton,J	L	.286	42	12	2	0	1	3	7	7	.388	.405
Throws Left	R	.282	78	22	4	0	3	10	12	11	.374	.449
Gooden,Dwight	L	.267	450	120	22	1	9	45	48	63	.337	.380
Throws Right	R	.238	323	77	21	6	2	41	22	82	.288	.359
Gordon,Tom	L	.287	202	58	10	1	3	27	22	45	.352	.391
Throws Right	R	.235	247	58	13	1	6	36	33	53	.331	.368
Gossage,Goose	L	.286	56	16	1	0	1	2	7	8	.365	.357
Throws Right	R	.193	83	16	1	0	4	12	12	18	.303	.349
Gott,Jim	L	.264	148	39	4	1	3	17	28	39	.382	.365
Throws Right	R	.192	172	33	2	0	1	9	13	36	.249	.221
Gozzo,Mauro	L	.667	6	4	1	0	1	3	0	0	.667	1.333
Throws Right	R	.500	6	3	1	0	1	3	0	1	.500	1.167
Grahe,Joe	L	.287	157	45	5	0	1	14	16	16	.365	.338
Throws Right	R	.212	189	40	7	0	4	23	23	23	.300	.312
Grant,Mark	L	.336	149	50	9	0	3	13	11	17	.385	.456
Throws Right	R	.289	173	50	13	1	3	18	11	25	.333	.428
Greene,Tommy	L	.370	127	47	8	2	2	15	21	16	.459	.512
Throws Right	R	.214	131	28	6	0	3	16	13	23	.281	.328
Groom,Buddy	L	.355	31	11	0	1	0	5	5	5	.432	.419
Throws Left	R	.311	119	37	10	1	4	19	17	10	.394	.513
Gross,Kevin	L	.276	409	113	23	4	5	48	52	75	.356	.389
Throws Right	R	.199	347	69	7	1	6	23	25	83	.255	.277
Gross,Kip	L	.326	46	15	3	1	0	5	7	8	.415	.435
Throws Right	R	.321	53	17	2	0	1	6	3	6	.357	.415

Pitchers vs. Left-Handed and Right-Handed Batters

Pitcher	vs	Avg	AB	H	2B	3B	HR	BI	BB	SO	OBP	SLG	Pitcher	vs	Avg	AB	H	2B	3B	HR	BI	BB	SO	OBP	SLG
Gubicza,Mark	L	.228	215	49	10	2	5	22	18	39	.285	.363	Henry,Butch	L	.298	141	42	10	0	2	13	12	14	.351	.411
Throws Right	R	.290	210	61	9	1	3	22	18	42	.348	.386	Throws Left	R	.281	508	143	28	5	14	56	29	82	.318	.439
Guetterman,L	L	.278	90	25	4	0	1	9	10	6	.353	.356	Henry,Doug	L	.208	106	22	4	0	1	12	16	17	.306	.274
Throws Left	R	.362	185	67	12	2	9	45	17	14	.408	.595	Throws Right	R	.292	144	42	10	2	5	28	8	35	.329	.493
Gullickson,B	L	.280	414	116	18	4	18	52	28	21	.322	.473	Henry,Dwayne	L	.208	130	27	9	3	3	15	24	29	.335	.392
Throws Right	R	.255	439	112	20	1	17	46	22	43	.288	.421	Throws Right	R	.192	167	32	5	1	1	17	20	43	.274	.251
Gunderson,E	L	.385	13	5	1	0	0	2	0	1	.357	.462	Hentgen,Pat	L	.253	87	22	5	1	1	6	19	13	.383	.368
Throws Left	R	.292	24	7	2	0	1	9	5	1	.419	.500	Throws Right	R	.255	106	27	6	0	6	17	13	26	.333	.481
Guthrie,Mark	L	.205	88	18	3	1	0	6	5	22	.242	.261	Heredia,Gil	L	.310	87	27	4	0	1	18	11	13	.384	.391
Throws Left	R	.220	186	41	3	0	7	17	18	54	.289	.349	Throws Right	R	.224	76	17	4	0	3	7	9	9	.314	.395
Guzman,Johnny	L	.400	5	2	0	0	0	1	0	0	.400	.400	Hernandez,J	L	.294	68	20	1	0	3	10	8	13	.350	.441
Throws Left	R	.500	12	6	2	0	0	3	0	0	.538	.667	Throws Right	R	.288	66	19	2	1	1	5	3	12	.324	.394
Guzman,Jose	L	.278	399	111	32	1	6	44	29	65	.323	.409	Hernandez,R	L	.187	107	20	7	0	1	13	11	36	.264	.280
Throws Right	R	.260	454	118	20	3	11	42	44	114	.330	.390	Throws Right	R	.175	143	25	4	0	3	11	9	32	.237	.266
Guzman,Juan	L	.214	323	69	7	0	1	16	34	58	.288	.245	Hernandez,X	L	.211	209	44	7	2	2	13	29	51	.310	.292
Throws Right	R	.201	329	66	17	1	5	32	38	107	.284	.304	Throws Right	R	.190	195	37	4	0	3	22	13	45	.245	.256
Haas,Dave	L	.284	116	33	4	0	3	9	9	12	.336	.397	Hershiser,O	L	.286	455	130	21	3	11	45	56	60	.366	.418
Throws Right	R	.269	130	35	5	1	5	20	7	17	.312	.438	Throws Right	R	.221	357	79	21	0	4	34	13	70	.257	.314
Habyan,John	L	.339	118	40	7	0	2	15	10	10	.388	.449	Hesketh,Joe	L	.255	98	25	5	0	2	13	4	20	.288	.367
Throws Right	R	.263	167	44	6	2	4	27	11	34	.313	.395	Throws Left	R	.280	490	137	34	2	13	56	54	84	.349	.437
Hammond,Chris	L	.291	117	34	4	3	5	17	12	20	.356	.504	Hibbard,Greg	L	.224	85	19	1	0	1	7	6	15	.302	.271
Throws Left	R	.259	444	115	16	5	8	45	43	59	.327	.372	Throws Left	R	.285	590	168	24	5	16	75	51	54	.342	.424
Haney,Chris	L	.258	66	17	5	2	2	12	1	16	.290	.485	Hickerson,B	L	.235	102	24	5	1	1	8	6	15	.273	.333
Throws Left	R	.245	237	58	16	1	9	30	25	38	.315	.435	Throws Left	R	.236	212	50	14	0	6	27	15	53	.286	.387
Hanson,Erik	L	.241	365	88	11	3	5	45	26	56	.291	.329	Hill,Ken	L	.222	469	104	19	4	6	32	50	80	.298	.318
Throws Right	R	.333	363	121	23	1	9	54	31	56	.390	.477	Throws Right	R	.242	343	83	17	1	7	35	25	70	.295	.359
Harkey,Mike	L	.233	86	20	2	3	3	8	9	12	.302	.430	Hill,Milt	L	.040	25	1	0	0	0	1	5	4	.200	.040
Throws Right	R	.259	54	14	4	0	1	5	6	9	.339	.389	Throws Right	R	.304	46	14	3	1	1	7	0	6	.313	.478
Harnisch,Pete	L	.234	466	109	17	7	10	52	41	78	.300	.365	Hillegas,S	L	.358	165	59	8	3	4	23	21	21	.428	.515
Throws Right	R	.233	313	73	20	1	8	33	23	86	.285	.380	Throws Right	R	.253	178	45	11	1	9	29	16	28	.311	.478
Harris,Gene	L	.135	52	7	2	0	0	3	7	10	.250	.173	Hillman,Eric	L	.297	37	11	2	0	0	2	2	6	.350	.351
Throws Right	R	.271	59	16	1	0	3	8	8	15	.358	.441	Throws Left	R	.322	174	56	8	1	9	29	8	10	.353	.534
Harris,Greg	L	.211	142	30	5	1	2	14	25	27	.335	.303	Hitchcock,S	L	.333	6	2	2	0	0	1	1	1	.500	.667
Throws Right	R	.217	240	52	6	3	4	26	35	46	.317	.317	Throws Left	R	.382	55	21	3	0	2	11	5	5	.433	.545
Harris,G	L	.279	287	80	10	1	11	40	23	34	.330	.436	Hollins,J	L	.333	9	3	0	0	0	1	2	0	.455	.333
Throws Right	R	.205	161	33	8	0	2	15	12	32	.267	.292	Throws Right	R	.455	11	5	1	0	1	7	3	0	.500	.818
Hartley,Mike	L	.252	107	27	6	0	0	9	13	23	.331	.308	Holmes,Darren	L	.224	67	15	4	0	0	5	5	11	.278	.284
Throws Right	R	.257	105	27	6	2	5	17	10	30	.333	.495	Throws Right	R	.225	89	20	2	2	1	6	6	20	.289	.326
Hartsock,Jeff	L	.348	23	8	1	0	0	5	4	4	.429	.391	Honeycutt,R	L	.258	62	16	2	0	1	9	3	13	.313	.339
Throws Right	R	.412	17	7	0	0	2	7	0	2	.412	.765	Throws Left	R	.281	89	25	3	2	1	17	7	19	.337	.393
Harvey,Bryan	L	.172	58	10	1	0	2	7	4	18	.222	.293	Horsman,Vince	L	.203	74	15	0	0	1	11	11	9	.302	.243
Throws Right	R	.250	48	12	1	0	2	5	7	16	.333	.396	Throws Left	R	.296	81	24	4	0	2	6	10	9	.374	.420
Hathaway,H	L	.500	4	2	0	0	1	1	1	0	.600	1.250	Hough,Charlie	L	.236	267	63	10	0	7	22	26	25	.304	.352
Throws Left	R	.300	20	6	1	0	0	4	2	1	.348	.350	Throws Right	R	.241	403	97	15	4	12	52	40	51	.316	.387
Heaton,Neal	L	.222	54	12	1	0	1	5	7	11	.313	.296	Howe,Steve	L	.200	20	4	0	0	0	2	0	0	.200	.200
Throws Left	R	.292	106	31	5	0	4	16	16	20	.382	.453	Throws Left	R	.093	54	5	0	0	1	5	3	12	.138	.148
Henke,Tom	L	.190	105	20	4	0	2	13	14	23	.279	.286	Howell,Jay	L	.242	91	22	2	0	2	7	8	19	.310	.330
Throws Right	R	.204	98	20	5	0	3	6	8	23	.264	.347	Throws Right	R	.218	87	19	1	0	0	7	10	17	.296	.230
Henneman,Mike	L	.278	144	40	8	1	2	18	9	22	.314	.389	Hoy,Peter	L	.600	5	3	2	0	0	3	2	0	.714	1.000
Throws Right	R	.235	149	35	3	1	4	17	11	36	.284	.349	Throws Right	R	.417	12	5	0	0	0	2	0	2	.417	.417

Pitchers vs. Left-Handed and Right-Handed Batters

Pitcher	vs	Avg	AB	H	2B	3B	HR	BI	BB	SO	OBP	SLG
Hurst,Bruce	L	.305	151	46	3	1	8	22	10	26	.348	.497
Throws Left	R	.259	684	177	28	2	14	63	41	105	.299	.367
Hurst,Jon	L	.325	40	13	2	1	1	6	5	2	.400	.500
Throws Right	R	.208	24	5	1	0	0	1	2	2	.296	.250
Innis,Jeff	L	.289	159	46	8	1	2	23	28	16	.399	.390
Throws Right	R	.244	160	39	3	2	2	12	8	23	.291	.325
Irvine,Daryl	L	.244	45	11	2	1	0	3	8	2	.370	.333
Throws Right	R	.317	63	20	2	0	1	12	6	8	.370	.397
Jackson,Danny	L	.246	118	29	2	0	2	14	16	20	.333	.314
Throws Left	R	.277	657	182	37	6	4	66	61	77	.338	.370
Jackson,Mike	L	.265	162	43	11	1	3	14	24	33	.363	.401
Throws Right	R	.236	140	33	3	2	4	20	9	47	.291	.371
Jeffcoat,Mike	L	.350	20	7	0	0	0	2	1	2	.364	.350
Throws Left	R	.350	60	21	6	2	2	13	4	4	.385	.617
Johnson,Jeff	L	.308	39	12	3	1	1	8	3	4	.364	.513
Throws Left	R	.333	177	59	14	1	3	31	20	10	.402	.475
Johnson,Randy	L	.187	75	14	1	0	1	9	12	19	.303	.240
Throws Left	R	.208	674	140	32	2	12	81	132	222	.348	.315
Johnston,Joel	L	.000	4	0	0	0	0	0	0	0	.000	.000
Throws Right	R	.429	7	3	0	0	2	3	2	0	.556	1.286
Jones,Barry	L	.338	136	46	10	0	0	18	19	8	.418	.412
Throws Right	R	.279	140	39	9	2	3	32	16	22	.354	.436
Jones,Calvin	L	.250	84	21	7	0	2	12	26	16	.420	.405
Throws Right	R	.212	137	29	2	1	6	18	21	33	.321	.372
Jones,Doug	L	.253	217	55	11	1	3	20	12	41	.296	.355
Throws Right	R	.214	192	41	3	2	2	17	5	52	.249	.281
Jones,Jimmy	L	.283	300	85	16	4	9	32	27	33	.343	.453
Throws Right	R	.223	224	50	11	1	4	20	12	36	.272	.335
Kamieniecki,S	L	.279	337	94	17	1	5	35	35	43	.345	.380
Throws Right	R	.261	380	99	21	0	8	46	39	45	.335	.379
Key,Jimmy	L	.176	131	23	4	0	2	8	6	19	.216	.252
Throws Left	R	.261	697	182	41	1	22	73	53	98	.314	.418
Kiely,John	L	.179	84	15	2	0	0	7	13	7	.286	.202
Throws Right	R	.259	112	29	8	0	2	16	15	11	.341	.384
Kile,Darryl	L	.255	271	69	14	4	5	32	46	45	.361	.391
Throws Right	R	.268	205	55	12	2	3	17	17	45	.329	.390
King,Eric	L	.291	141	41	6	0	7	23	15	16	.357	.482
Throws Right	R	.280	175	49	6	2	5	22	13	29	.332	.423
Kipper,Bob	L	.250	44	11	2	0	3	8	2	6	.313	.500
Throws Left	R	.276	105	29	3	0	5	12	12	16	.356	.448
Knudsen,Kurt	L	.266	109	29	5	0	4	17	16	7	.357	.422
Throws Right	R	.263	156	41	8	1	5	26	25	44	.366	.423
Kramer,Randy	L	.341	44	15	4	0	1	5	4	3	.396	.500
Throws Right	R	.484	31	15	2	0	1	7	3	3	.543	.645
Krueger,Bill	L	.308	104	32	9	1	1	11	4	13	.345	.442
Throws Left	R	.262	599	157	28	1	17	63	49	86	.320	.397
Lamp,Dennis	L	.280	50	14	1	0	2	7	7	4	.379	.420
Throws Right	R	.302	63	19	2	1	1	7	2	11	.333	.413
Lancaster,Les	L	.358	120	43	10	0	2	20	32	14	.490	.492
Throws Right	R	.259	224	58	11	0	9	59	19	21	.321	.429
Landrum,Bill	L	.341	44	15	3	0	3	8	3	5	.396	.614
Throws Right	R	.308	39	12	1	1	0	4	6	2	.413	.385
Langston,Mark	L	.173	110	19	4	1	2	12	9	21	.252	.282
Throws Left	R	.252	742	187	34	2	12	71	65	153	.313	.352
Leach,Terry	L	.263	99	26	3	1	0	6	11	3	.333	.313
Throws Right	R	.187	166	31	6	2	2	17	9	19	.246	.283
Leary,Tim	L	.234	244	57	14	2	7	35	39	24	.336	.393
Throws Right	R	.277	267	74	12	0	5	36	48	22	.395	.378
Lefferts,C	L	.244	123	30	5	1	2	13	3	25	.258	.350
Throws Left	R	.289	636	184	28	3	17	67	38	79	.327	.423
Leibrandt,C	L	.228	171	39	2	1	1	13	9	23	.276	.269
Throws Left	R	.267	570	152	32	3	8	53	33	81	.308	.375
Leiter,Al	L	.000	0	0	0	0	0	0	1	0	1.000	.000
Throws Left	R	.200	5	1	0	0	0	1	1	0	.333	.200
Leiter,Mark	L	.312	189	59	9	5	4	26	25	24	.384	.476
Throws Right	R	.248	230	57	10	1	5	21	18	51	.307	.365
Leon,Danilo	L	.280	25	7	1	0	1	5	3	5	.379	.440
Throws Right	R	.239	46	11	1	1	4	8	7	10	.364	.565
Lewis,Richie	L	.385	13	5	1	0	0	3	3	0	.500	.462
Throws Right	R	.421	19	8	2	0	1	5	4	4	.500	.684
Lewis,Scott	L	.211	57	12	1	0	0	1	10	5	.328	.228
Throws Right	R	.286	84	24	1	0	3	8	4	13	.323	.405
Lilliquist,D	L	.200	90	18	4	0	1	7	5	24	.245	.278
Throws Left	R	.176	119	21	6	0	4	11	13	23	.259	.328
Linton,Doug	L	.324	37	12	1	0	2	6	9	5	.447	.514
Throws Right	R	.322	59	19	4	0	3	13	8	11	.397	.542
MacDonald,Bob	L	.143	63	9	2	0	0	4	1	14	.156	.175
Throws Left	R	.336	122	41	10	2	4	19	15	12	.410	.549
Maddux,Greg	L	.233	566	132	23	4	6	41	51	118	.304	.320
Throws Right	R	.176	393	69	13	1	1	23	19	81	.226	.221
Maddux,Mike	L	.235	162	38	4	1	1	12	15	31	.294	.290
Throws Right	R	.237	139	33	3	1	1	14	9	29	.284	.295
Magnante,Mike	L	.375	72	27	2	1	1	9	8	7	.438	.472
Throws Left	R	.312	282	88	15	1	4	42	27	24	.368	.415
Magrane,Joe	L	.133	15	2	0	0	0	2	3	3	.278	.133
Throws Left	R	.299	107	32	3	2	2	10	12	17	.377	.421
Mahomes,Pat	L	.281	135	38	8	2	3	20	17	17	.355	.437
Throws Right	R	.276	127	35	11	2	2	19	20	27	.374	.441
Mallicoat,Rob	L	.353	34	12	3	1	1	11	4	9	.436	.588
Throws Left	R	.241	58	14	3	1	1	11	15	11	.423	.379
Manuel,Barry	L	.167	6	1	0	0	0	0	0	2	.167	.167
Throws Right	R	.294	17	5	1	0	2	6	1	7	.368	.706
Martinez,D	L	.211	503	106	15	0	8	39	34	94	.261	.288
Throws Right	R	.212	311	66	11	0	4	25	26	53	.288	.286
Martinez,P	L	.200	15	3	2	0	0	2	1	2	.250	.333
Throws Right	R	.200	15	3	1	0	0	0	0	6	.200	.267
Martinez,R	L	.256	316	81	19	2	9	40	54	47	.367	.415
Throws Right	R	.232	259	60	11	0	2	28	15	54	.282	.297
Mason,Roger	L	.216	162	35	9	2	2	10	22	26	.306	.333
Throws Right	R	.276	163	45	5	1	9	31	11	30	.333	.485

Pitchers vs. Left-Handed and Right-Handed Batters

Pitcher	vs	Avg	AB	H	2B	3B	HR	BI	BB	SO	OBP	SLG	Pitcher	vs	Avg	AB	H	2B	3B	HR	BI	BB	SO	OBP	SLG
Mathews,Greg	L	.313	48	15	4	0	2	9	6	9	.400	.521	Morgan,Mike	L	.248	491	122	22	3	8	35	57	57	.328	.354
Throws Left	R	.257	152	39	9	0	5	16	18	18	.333	.414	Throws Right	R	.215	377	81	17	0	6	35	22	66	.257	.308
Mathews,Terry	L	.328	61	20	3	0	2	10	9	9	.414	.475	Morris,Jack	L	.263	460	121	22	3	10	57	42	61	.322	.389
Throws Right	R	.275	102	28	10	0	2	18	22	17	.398	.431	Throws Right	R	.229	442	101	19	0	8	50	38	71	.302	.326
Maysey,Matt	L	.429	7	3	0	0	0	1	0	0	.429	.429	Mulholland,T	L	.211	161	34	7	1	4	18	11	25	.263	.342
Throws Right	R	.250	4	1	0	0	1	1	0	1	.400	1.000	Throws Left	R	.272	710	193	36	2	10	73	35	100	.306	.370
McCaskill,K	L	.280	379	106	16	4	6	50	47	43	.358	.391	Munoz,Mike	L	.192	73	14	2	0	0	4	7	10	.259	.219
Throws Right	R	.209	417	87	15	4	5	49	48	66	.295	.300	Throws Left	R	.283	106	30	4	1	3	14	18	13	.384	.425
McClure,Bob	L	.198	91	18	7	0	4	13	10	18	.272	.407	Murphy,Rob	L	.256	86	22	2	0	0	12	11	17	.337	.279
Throws Left	R	.315	108	34	6	0	2	16	15	6	.405	.426	Throws Left	R	.264	129	34	6	3	2	22	10	25	.312	.403
McCullers,L	L	.125	8	1	0	0	0	0	2	0	.300	.125	Mussina,Mike	L	.220	422	93	18	2	1	17	29	64	.269	.280
Throws Right	R	.000	7	0	0	0	0	2	6	3	.462	.000	Throws Right	R	.255	466	119	21	3	15	48	19	66	.286	.410
McDonald,Ben	L	.235	405	95	20	2	14	41	44	74	.311	.398	Mutis,Jeff	L	.500	12	6	1	1	1	3	0	1	.500	1.000
Throws Right	R	.258	458	118	24	3	18	59	30	84	.311	.441	Throws Left	R	.409	44	18	2	1	3	9	6	7	.462	.705
McDowell,Jack	L	.263	486	128	20	6	13	46	44	85	.328	.409	Myers,Randy	L	.270	63	17	6	0	0	9	13	20	.390	.365
Throws Right	R	.239	497	119	25	3	8	44	31	93	.287	.350	Throws Left	R	.282	238	67	10	0	7	44	21	46	.337	.412
McDowell,R	L	.318	154	49	5	1	3	29	30	20	.428	.422	Nabholz,Chris	L	.267	131	35	2	1	3	14	12	33	.336	.366
Throws Right	R	.295	183	54	5	1	0	16	12	30	.337	.333	Throws Left	R	.239	591	141	27	6	8	49	62	97	.313	.345
McElroy,Chuck	L	.275	102	28	7	1	2	16	12	30	.345	.422	Nagy,Charles	L	.250	424	106	15	2	5	38	27	68	.292	.330
Throws Left	R	.218	206	45	12	2	3	26	39	53	.339	.340	Throws Right	R	.267	520	139	26	2	6	41	30	101	.308	.360
Meacham,Rusty	L	.188	144	27	3	1	1	15	12	23	.247	.243	Navarro,Jaime	L	.257	435	112	25	3	6	41	32	46	.304	.370
Throws Right	R	.261	234	61	12	2	4	32	9	41	.283	.380	Throws Right	R	.235	477	112	17	3	8	38	32	54	.288	.333
Melendez,Jose	L	.281	160	45	4	0	6	22	15	34	.341	.419	Neagle,Denny	L	.228	92	21	5	0	2	13	15	27	.343	.348
Throws Right	R	.219	169	37	5	0	3	20	5	48	.249	.302	Throws Left	R	.254	236	60	12	1	7	26	28	50	.332	.403
Menendez,Tony	L	.000	4	0	0	0	0	0	0	1	.000	.000	Nelson,Gene	L	.333	93	31	3	3	0	14	15	10	.411	.430
Throws Right	R	.091	11	1	0	0	1	1	0	4	.091	.364	Throws Right	R	.336	110	37	5	0	5	26	7	13	.373	.518
Mercker,Kent	L	.260	73	19	4	0	1	11	9	18	.337	.356	Nelson,Jeff	L	.287	108	31	4	1	2	10	25	18	.418	.398
Throws Left	R	.185	173	32	6	0	3	21	26	31	.302	.272	Throws Right	R	.220	182	40	6	2	5	30	19	28	.311	.357
Mesa,Jose	L	.305	328	100	19	0	8	33	29	23	.363	.436	Nichols,Rod	L	.292	171	50	8	3	7	29	12	21	.335	.497
Throws Right	R	.237	291	69	14	1	6	36	41	39	.332	.354	Throws Right	R	.260	246	64	8	2	6	29	19	35	.315	.382
Milacki,Bob	L	.261	211	55	14	2	6	24	22	25	.329	.431	Nied,Dave	L	.190	42	8	4	0	0	3	4	5	.261	.286
Throws Right	R	.326	261	85	17	2	10	47	22	26	.380	.521	Throws Right	R	.057	35	2	1	0	0	0	1	14	.083	.086
Militello,Sam	L	.262	107	28	7	0	5	13	15	12	.352	.467	Nielsen,Jerry	L	.273	22	6	1	0	1	3	6	4	.414	.455
Throws Right	R	.132	114	15	6	0	1	7	17	30	.256	.211	Throws Left	R	.229	48	11	1	1	0	3	12	8	.383	.292
Miller,Paul	L	.300	20	6	2	0	0	2	0	2	.300	.400	Nunez,Edwin	L	.230	87	20	6	2	3	17	10	20	.303	.448
Throws Right	R	.217	23	5	3	0	0	4	1	3	.240	.348	Throws Right	R	.291	148	43	7	1	3	23	12	29	.348	.412
Mills,Alan	L	.244	168	41	10	1	2	17	24	15	.337	.351	Ojeda,Bobby	L	.216	116	25	4	0	1	12	13	27	.290	.276
Throws Right	R	.191	194	37	6	1	3	20	30	45	.297	.278	Throws Left	R	.280	515	144	25	6	7	64	68	67	.362	.392
Minor,Blas	L	.500	2	1	0	0	0	0	0	0	.500	.500	Olin,Steve	L	.324	145	47	6	1	1	12	13	19	.385	.400
Throws Right	R	.286	7	2	1	1	0	0	0	0	.286	.714	Throws Right	R	.188	176	33	2	0	7	20	14	28	.254	.318
Mlicki,Dave	L	.304	46	14	2	1	1	4	8	8	.418	.457	Olivares,Omar	L	.285	428	122	28	2	13	47	40	65	.345	.451
Throws Right	R	.250	36	9	1	0	2	4	8	8	.386	.444	Throws Right	R	.218	308	67	7	1	7	27	23	59	.275	.315
Moeller,D	L	.500	6	3	0	0	1	4	1	0	.500	1.000	Oliveras,F	L	.255	94	24	7	0	7	14	7	9	.307	.553
Throws Left	R	.318	66	21	4	0	4	11	10	6	.397	.561	Throws Right	R	.243	70	17	3	0	4	7	3	8	.276	.457
Monteleone,R	L	.226	146	33	8	2	1	11	10	17	.276	.329	Olson,Gregg	L	.195	113	22	4	0	0	8	9	30	.252	.230
Throws Right	R	.241	203	49	5	2	6	30	17	45	.299	.374	Throws Right	R	.229	105	24	0	1	3	9	15	28	.322	.333
Montgomery,J	L	.205	146	30	4	0	2	11	16	36	.293	.274	Orosco,Jesse	L	.273	55	15	2	0	2	10	5	16	.328	.418
Throws Right	R	.205	151	31	3	0	3	18	11	33	.261	.285	Throws Left	R	.207	87	18	2	0	3	14	8	24	.278	.333
Moore,Mike	L	.261	445	116	20	1	8	51	41	48	.326	.364	Osborne,D	L	.318	151	48	13	0	3	23	8	23	.348	.464
Throws Right	R	.278	407	113	23	3	12	51	62	69	.373	.437	Throws Left	R	.263	552	145	26	5	11	53	30	81	.302	.388

Pitchers vs. Left-Handed and Right-Handed Batters

Pitcher	vs	Avg	AB	H	2B	3B	HR	BI	BB	SO	OBP	SLG	Pitcher	vs	Avg	AB	H	2B	3B	HR	BI	BB	SO	OBP	SLG
Osuna,Al	L	.247	73	18	4	0	2	8	12	16	.349	.384	Rapp,Pat	L	.316	19	6	1	1	0	5	4	2	.435	.474
Throws Left	R	.231	147	34	3	0	6	18	26	21	.341	.374	Throws Right	R	.133	15	2	2	0	0	2	2	1	.278	.267
Otto,Dave	L	.352	54	19	4	0	1	7	5	3	.407	.481	Rasmussen,D	L	.200	20	4	0	0	0	0	1	1	.273	.200
Throws Left	R	.330	276	91	13	0	11	50	28	29	.392	.496	Throws Left	R	.220	127	28	6	0	2	9	7	11	.259	.315
Palacios,V	L	.328	122	40	6	1	0	10	16	14	.406	.393	Reardon,Jeff	L	.306	108	33	5	1	5	15	5	12	.342	.509
Throws Right	R	.205	78	16	4	0	1	13	11	19	.300	.295	Throws Right	R	.279	122	34	6	0	1	22	4	27	.302	.352
Pall,Donn	L	.291	103	30	2	0	2	13	13	12	.373	.369	Reed,Rick	L	.201	169	34	11	1	5	18	9	27	.236	.367
Throws Right	R	.262	187	49	11	0	7	30	14	15	.314	.433	Throws Right	R	.326	218	71	10	1	5	20	11	22	.370	.450
Parker,Clay	L	.279	68	19	6	0	2	11	4	9	.311	.456	Reed,Steve	L	.273	22	6	3	0	0	5	1	3	.304	.409
Throws Right	R	.394	71	28	6	0	4	15	7	11	.463	.648	Throws Right	R	.189	37	7	1	0	2	7	2	8	.250	.378
Parrett,Jeff	L	.278	144	40	6	1	2	24	23	29	.376	.375	Revenig,Todd	L	.333	3	1	1	0	0	0	0	1	.333	.667
Throws Right	R	.192	214	41	11	1	5	23	19	49	.258	.322	Throws Right	R	.250	4	1	0	0	0	0	0	0	.250	.250
Patterson,Bob	L	.256	78	20	3	1	1	10	9	15	.330	.359	Reynolds,S	L	.413	63	26	8	2	1	13	5	6	.449	.651
Throws Left	R	.241	162	39	9	1	6	20	14	28	.299	.420	Throws Right	R	.348	46	16	3	1	1	6	1	4	.362	.522
Patterson,Ken	L	.266	64	17	3	1	0	4	9	11	.365	.344	Reynoso,A	L	.615	13	8	3	0	2	3	1	0	.667	1.308
Throws Left	R	.270	89	24	6	1	7	21	18	12	.378	.596	Throws Right	R	.200	15	3	1	0	0	3	1	2	.250	.267
Pavlik,Roger	L	.271	133	36	4	2	1	16	18	26	.353	.353	Rhodes,Arthur	L	.250	40	10	0	0	0	2	6	9	.348	.250
Throws Right	R	.291	103	30	3	2	2	7	16	19	.402	.417	Throws Left	R	.250	308	77	20	4	6	28	32	68	.322	.399
Pena,A	L	.205	78	16	3	0	5	11	6	19	.262	.436	Righetti,Dave	L	.236	89	21	5	2	0	9	13	17	.330	.337
Throws Right	R	.304	79	24	2	0	2	10	7	15	.356	.405	Throws Left	R	.283	205	58	8	1	4	22	23	30	.351	.390
Pena,Jim	L	.296	54	16	2	0	2	8	5	12	.356	.444	Rijo,Jose	L	.266	429	114	20	3	6	33	32	89	.317	.368
Throws Left	R	.275	120	33	11	1	2	11	15	20	.358	.433	Throws Right	R	.205	347	71	6	1	9	28	12	82	.234	.305
Perez,Melido	L	.247	430	106	16	1	8	37	50	99	.324	.344	Risley,Bill	L	.214	14	3	0	0	0	1	1	1	.267	.214
Throws Right	R	.225	471	106	17	2	8	51	43	119	.293	.321	Throws Right	R	.333	3	1	1	0	0	0	0	1	.333	.667
Perez,Mike	L	.244	156	38	3	0	2	17	20	20	.328	.301	Ritchie,Wally	L	.220	59	13	2	1	1	12	4	11	.270	.339
Throws Right	R	.181	177	32	3	2	2	9	12	26	.232	.254	Throws Left	R	.330	94	31	8	1	2	14	13	8	.411	.500
Pichardo,H	L	.287	244	70	18	1	3	25	23	21	.346	.406	Ritz,Kevin	L	.295	129	38	8	0	2	20	23	30	.404	.403
Throws Right	R	.252	310	78	13	1	6	30	26	38	.313	.358	Throws Right	R	.267	187	50	6	0	2	22	21	27	.341	.332
Pierce,Eddie	L	.250	4	1	0	0	0	0	0	1	.250	.250	Rivera,Ben	L	.236	250	59	12	3	4	24	27	32	.317	.356
Throws Left	R	.471	17	8	0	0	1	2	4	2	.545	.647	Throws Right	R	.221	181	40	6	2	5	18	18	45	.294	.359
Plesac,Dan	L	.254	67	17	4	0	2	11	8	18	.342	.403	Robinson,Don	L	.313	128	40	6	1	2	19	1	11	.311	.422
Throws Left	R	.221	213	47	13	0	3	27	27	36	.309	.324	Throws Right	R	.264	106	28	7	0	5	15	6	15	.302	.472
Plunk,Eric	L	.237	118	28	6	0	1	9	10	18	.297	.314	Robinson,Jeff	L	.290	155	45	8	1	2	16	14	25	.351	.394
Throws Right	R	.223	148	33	3	0	4	22	28	32	.343	.324	Throws Right	R	.231	134	31	7	2	3	14	26	21	.358	.381
Poole,Jim	L	.286	7	2	0	0	0	2	0	2	.286	.286	Robinson,J	L	.258	151	39	3	1	5	20	18	11	.335	.391
Throws Left	R	.167	6	1	0	0	0	2	1	1	.286	.167	Throws Right	R	.272	162	44	12	0	3	22	18	21	.342	.401
Portugal,Mark	L	.244	205	50	10	3	5	19	26	40	.328	.395	Robinson,Ron	L	.347	75	26	8	1	2	11	9	5	.417	.560
Throws Right	R	.171	152	26	3	1	2	8	15	22	.250	.243	Throws Right	R	.316	79	25	4	0	1	13	5	7	.368	.405
Powell,Dennis	L	.250	68	17	4	0	2	13	6	14	.311	.397	Rodriguez,R	L	.233	103	24	4	0	2	12	11	21	.304	.330
Throws Left	R	.232	138	32	9	0	3	12	23	21	.354	.362	Throws Left	R	.227	233	53	10	1	2	21	18	43	.282	.305
Power,Ted	L	.226	133	30	7	0	1	9	13	25	.302	.301	Rogers,Kenny	L	.261	92	24	5	0	1	12	3	21	.284	.348
Throws Right	R	.261	222	58	7	0	6	42	22	26	.324	.374	Throws Left	R	.262	214	56	12	1	6	38	23	49	.332	.411
Pugh,Tim	L	.279	86	24	5	2	0	3	12	8	.367	.384	Rogers,Kevin	L	.280	25	7	0	0	0	3	0	4	.280	.280
Throws Right	R	.274	84	23	6	0	2	9	1	10	.287	.417	Throws Right	R	.280	107	30	2	0	4	11	13	22	.364	.411
Quantrill,P	L	.260	73	19	3	1	0	5	7	11	.333	.329	Rojas,Mel	L	.196	199	39	7	0	1	11	20	40	.268	.246
Throws Right	R	.305	118	36	3	0	1	8	8	13	.344	.356	Throws Right	R	.203	158	32	8	2	1	11	14	30	.274	.297
Raczka,Mike	L	.273	11	3	1	0	0	4	1	1	.438	.364	Rosenthal,W	L	.286	7	2	0	0	0	0	0	0	.286	.286
Throws Left	R	.333	15	5	1	1	0	5	1	1	.353	.533	Throws Right	R	.357	14	5	1	0	1	1	2	1	.438	.643
Radinsky,S	L	.182	66	12	1	1	2	8	8	24	.280	.318	Ruffin,Bruce	L	.221	68	15	2	0	1	11	14	12	.354	.294
Throws Left	R	.269	156	42	10	1	1	26	26	24	.375	.365	Throws Left	R	.325	157	51	9	2	6	33	27	33	.417	.522

Pitchers vs. Left-Handed and Right-Handed Batters

Pitcher	vs	Avg	AB	H	2B	3B	HR	BI	BB	SO	OBP	SLG	Pitcher	vs	Avg	AB	H	2B	3B	HR	BI	BB	SO	OBP	SLG
Ruskin,Scott	L	.250	68	17	4	0	1	14	9	23	.333	.353	Smiley,John	L	.259	139	36	8	2	1	12	12	16	.316	.367
Throws Left	R	.287	136	39	6	0	5	22	11	20	.342	.441	Throws Left	R	.226	747	169	43	2	16	72	53	147	.280	.353
Russell,Jeff	L	.245	110	27	7	1	1	8	14	17	.339	.355	Smith,Bryn	L	.270	37	10	2	0	0	2	3	3	.341	.324
Throws Right	R	.206	136	28	3	0	2	14	11	31	.264	.272	Throws Right	R	.227	44	10	0	0	3	8	2	6	.292	.432
Ryan,Ken	L	.000	7	0	0	0	0	0	2	2	.222	.000	Smith,Dan	L	.143	7	1	1	0	0	0	0	2	.143	.286
Throws Right	R	.250	16	4	0	0	2	5	3	3	.350	.625	Throws Left	R	.347	49	17	6	0	1	8	8	3	.431	.531
Ryan,Nolan	L	.245	294	72	14	3	5	30	43	69	.339	.364	Smith,Dave	L	.333	27	9	1	1	0	5	3	1	.400	.444
Throws Right	R	.231	286	66	13	0	4	30	26	88	.316	.318	Throws Right	R	.214	28	6	0	0	0	1	1	2	.233	.214
Saberhagen,B	L	.226	212	48	10	3	3	22	20	48	.292	.344	Smith,Lee	L	.220	164	36	5	4	2	19	20	38	.303	.335
Throws Right	R	.243	148	36	4	1	3	14	7	33	.291	.345	Throws Right	R	.222	117	26	3	0	2	12	6	22	.260	.299
Sampen,Bill	L	.305	141	43	6	1	3	22	23	13	.401	.426	Smith,Pete	L	.253	178	45	9	2	1	10	22	21	.333	.343
Throws Right	R	.247	162	40	4	1	1	20	9	24	.297	.302	Throws Right	R	.161	112	18	2	0	2	6	6	22	.203	.232
Sanderson,S	L	.300	367	110	14	4	13	50	38	40	.362	.466	Smith,Zane	L	.215	93	20	1	1	2	9	2	17	.232	.312
Throws Right	R	.274	402	110	21	5	15	54	26	64	.319	.463	Throws Left	R	.271	436	118	22	3	6	41	17	39	.298	.376
Sauveur,Rich	L	.200	15	3	0	0	0	3	1	3	.333	.200	Smoltz,John	L	.246	544	134	17	3	9	38	49	103	.309	.338
Throws Left	R	.300	40	12	1	0	1	2	7	4	.404	.400	Throws Right	R	.191	377	72	22	2	8	34	31	112	.254	.324
Scanlan,Bob	L	.231	160	37	7	1	3	22	20	20	.319	.344	Springer,Russ	L	.320	25	8	0	1	0	5	4	7	.433	.400
Throws Right	R	.239	163	39	6	0	1	11	10	22	.282	.294	Throws Right	R	.256	39	10	4	0	0	8	6	5	.356	.359
Scheid,Rich	L	.200	10	2	0	0	0	0	2	2	.333	.200	St. Claire,R	L	.231	26	6	2	0	0	2	5	4	.355	.308
Throws Left	R	.300	40	12	3	0	2	7	4	6	.364	.525	Throws Left	R	.324	34	11	3	0	1	7	3	3	.378	.500
Schilling,C	L	.197	456	90	15	3	7	30	39	77	.259	.289	Stanton,Mike	L	.237	76	18	3	0	4	9	12	24	.344	.434
Throws Right	R	.207	363	75	15	1	4	31	20	70	.247	.287	Throws Left	R	.252	163	41	8	0	2	18	8	20	.289	.337
Schmidt,Dave	L	.333	6	2	1	0	1	5	1	0	.429	1.000	Stewart,Dave	L	.262	340	89	17	1	11	39	47	51	.351	.415
Throws Right	R	.500	10	5	0	0	0	2	2	1	.583	.500	Throws Right	R	.217	397	86	11	5	14	44	32	79	.282	.375
Schooler,Mike	L	.278	79	22	4	1	3	19	15	10	.394	.468	Stieb,Dave	L	.279	172	48	12	0	4	34	20	20	.354	.419
Throws Right	R	.273	121	33	2	0	4	26	9	23	.321	.388	Throws Right	R	.270	185	50	9	2	5	24	23	25	.355	.422
Schourek,Pete	L	.258	120	31	4	1	2	8	16	14	.341	.358	Stottlemyre,T	L	.282	284	80	14	0	6	34	32	21	.355	.394
Throws Left	R	.262	404	106	24	4	7	44	28	46	.312	.394	Throws Right	R	.247	385	95	17	0	14	54	31	77	.310	.400
Scott,Tim	L	.270	63	17	2	2	3	12	17	16	.420	.508	Sutcliffe,R	L	.265	431	114	19	4	13	49	37	44	.320	.418
Throws Right	R	.265	83	22	3	1	1	8	4	14	.307	.361	Throws Right	R	.280	489	137	18	3	7	50	37	65	.335	.372
Scudder,Scott	L	.299	251	75	11	1	5	36	31	30	.376	.410	Swan,Russ	L	.198	81	16	2	0	0	6	8	15	.275	.222
Throws Right	R	.309	191	59	12	1	5	21	24	36	.384	.461	Throws Left	R	.278	316	88	20	4	8	53	37	30	.354	.443
Searcy,Steve	L	.231	13	3	0	1	0	3	1	2	.286	.385	Swift,Bill	L	.264	383	101	16	3	5	31	38	36	.332	.360
Throws Left	R	.370	27	10	2	0	0	7	7	3	.486	.444	Throws Right	R	.196	219	43	3	1	1	9	5	41	.218	.233
Seminara,F	L	.294	204	60	7	2	4	25	32	24	.390	.407	Swindell,Greg	L	.242	165	40	9	1	2	11	9	29	.284	.345
Throws Right	R	.216	176	38	5	1	1	13	14	37	.282	.273	Throws Right	R	.264	643	170	28	2	12	52	32	109	.298	.370
Service,Scott	L	.467	15	7	0	1	0	4	3	2	.556	.600	Tanana,Frank	L	.225	102	23	5	0	2	10	8	15	.282	.333
Throws Right	R	.381	21	8	1	0	1	7	2	9	.435	.571	Throws Left	R	.274	602	165	29	2	20	78	82	76	.362	.429
Shaw,Jeff	L	.364	11	4	0	0	1	5	2	0	.462	.636	Tapani,Kevin	L	.279	434	121	31	4	12	56	24	78	.313	.452
Throws Right	R	.188	16	3	0	0	1	2	2	3	.278	.375	Throws Right	R	.259	405	105	22	1	5	38	24	60	.304	.356
Shepherd,K	L	.261	46	12	3	0	0	7	4	4	.308	.326	Taylor,Scott	L	.286	14	4	0	1	1	3	1	2	.333	.643
Throws Right	R	.226	31	7	3	0	0	4	2	6	.265	.323	Throws Left	R	.231	39	9	2	1	3	9	3	5	.286	.564
Shifflett,S	L	.272	81	22	3	0	5	12	8	9	.337	.494	Terrell,Walt	L	.285	235	67	15	0	3	29	20	20	.342	.387
Throws Right	R	.284	116	33	5	1	1	9	9	16	.344	.371	Throws Right	R	.308	312	96	12	2	11	55	28	41	.362	.465
Simons,Doug	L	.444	9	4	0	0	1	3	1	3	.545	.778	Tewksbury,Bob	L	.242	517	125	19	2	10	36	7	57	.250	.344
Throws Left	R	.524	21	11	3	0	2	8	1	3	.522	.952	Throws Right	R	.256	359	92	20	2	5	22	13	34	.286	.365
Slocumb,H	L	.413	75	31	0	0	3	17	13	14	.506	.533	Thigpen,Bobby	L	.338	80	27	2	0	1	12	15	10	.429	.400
Throws Right	R	.288	73	21	3	0	0	12	8	13	.349	.329	Throws Right	R	.237	131	31	7	0	3	23	18	35	.340	.359
Slusarski,Joe	L	.269	134	36	8	3	6	18	12	18	.324	.507	Timlin,Mike	L	.311	74	23	5	0	0	17	12	11	.407	.378
Throws Right	R	.297	165	49	9	0	9	22	15	20	.370	.515	Throws Right	R	.239	92	22	1	0	0	12	8	24	.304	.250

Pitchers vs. Left-Handed and Right-Handed Batters

Pitcher	vs	Avg	AB	H	2B	3B	HR	BI	BB	SO	OBP	SLG
Tomlin,Randy	L	.250	148	37	5	0	2	9	11	26	.304	.324
Throws Left	R	.289	653	189	40	7	9	66	31	64	.324	.413
Trlicek,Ricky	L	.000	2	0	0	0	0	0	1	1	.333	.000
Throws Right	R	.400	5	2	0	0	0	2	1	0	.500	.400
Trombley,Mike	L	.278	79	22	7	0	2	10	10	17	.360	.443
Throws Right	R	.221	95	21	5	0	3	8	7	21	.282	.368
Valdez,Sergio	L	.225	71	16	1	1	1	8	8	14	.304	.310
Throws Right	R	.141	64	9	4	0	1	7	4	18	.191	.250
Valera,Julio	L	.292	336	98	18	1	4	26	27	33	.343	.387
Throws Right	R	.236	382	90	20	2	11	43	37	80	.306	.385
Viola,Frank	L	.211	109	23	6	0	1	11	10	9	.281	.294
Throws Left	R	.246	777	191	34	0	12	77	79	112	.317	.336
Vitko,Joe	L	.500	12	6	1	0	0	6	1	2	.500	.583
Throws Right	R	.400	15	6	1	0	1	3	0	4	.400	.667
Wagner,Paul	L	.263	19	5	1	0	0	1	4	2	.391	.316
Throws Right	R	.143	28	4	2	0	0	0	1	3	.172	.214
Wakefield,Tim	L	.213	202	43	6	1	1	12	25	35	.297	.267
Throws Right	R	.264	125	33	6	1	2	13	10	16	.319	.376
Walk,Bob	L	.289	287	83	17	2	6	33	30	21	.359	.425
Throws Right	R	.218	225	49	9	1	4	17	13	39	.273	.320
Walker,Mike	L	.308	26	8	1	0	0	3	5	2	.419	.346
Throws Right	R	.351	37	13	3	0	4	11	4	3	.405	.757
Walton,Bruce	L	.375	16	6	1	0	0	2	1	1	.412	.438
Throws Right	R	.379	29	11	3	0	1	8	2	6	.406	.586
Ward,Duane	L	.197	183	36	6	1	5	20	25	61	.289	.322
Throws Right	R	.217	184	40	4	1	0	12	14	42	.275	.250
Wayne,Gary	L	.250	48	12	4	0	1	8	3	13	.302	.396
Throws Left	R	.264	129	34	7	3	1	15	16	16	.349	.388
Weathers,Dave	L	.500	6	3	0	0	0	1	0	2	.500	.500
Throws Right	R	.286	7	2	0	0	1	2	2	1	.444	.714
Wegman,Bill	L	.209	469	98	20	0	7	30	25	30	.247	.296
Throws Right	R	.286	535	153	30	2	21	63	30	97	.334	.467
Welch,Bob	L	.266	241	64	6	1	6	18	22	20	.325	.373
Throws Right	R	.227	220	50	5	0	7	22	21	27	.299	.345
Wells,David	L	.293	92	27	5	0	3	16	4	13	.363	.446
Throws Left	R	.288	386	111	30	2	13	60	32	49	.342	.477
West,David	L	.238	21	5	1	0	0	2	4	4	.360	.286
Throws Left	R	.284	95	27	4	0	3	18	16	15	.386	.421
Weston,Mickey	L	.444	9	4	1	0	0	2	0	0	.444	.556
Throws Right	R	.375	8	3	1	0	1	3	1	0	.500	.875
Wetteland,J	L	.200	175	35	5	1	3	17	21	66	.288	.291
Throws Right	R	.230	126	29	3	0	3	14	15	33	.326	.325
Whitehurst,W	L	.260	204	53	14	1	3	28	18	41	.323	.382
Throws Right	R	.269	171	46	11	3	1	22	15	29	.333	.386
Whiteside,M	L	.294	51	15	3	0	1	6	5	2	.357	.412
Throws Right	R	.200	55	11	3	0	0	4	6	11	.274	.255
Wickander,K	L	.278	54	15	1	1	0	6	15	19	.431	.333
Throws Left	R	.250	96	24	4	0	1	8	13	19	.357	.323
Wickman,Bob	L	.281	89	25	4	3	1	13	10	8	.347	.427
Throws Right	R	.265	98	26	5	0	1	10	10	13	.342	.347
Williams,B	L	.269	223	60	8	2	5	26	27	29	.345	.390
Throws Right	R	.232	138	32	8	0	5	16	15	25	.305	.399
Williams,Mike	L	.247	73	18	7	1	2	13	5	3	.291	.452
Throws Right	R	.282	39	11	2	0	1	3	2	2	.317	.410
Williams,M	L	.265	49	13	1	0	0	7	8	9	.379	.286
Throws Left	R	.235	238	56	15	3	4	31	56	65	.387	.374
Williamson,M	L	.188	32	6	0	0	0	5	3	7	.257	.188
Throws Right	R	.286	35	10	1	1	1	8	7	7	.405	.457
Willis,Carl	L	.231	108	25	1	2	2	10	5	15	.265	.333
Throws Right	R	.254	189	48	11	1	2	27	6	30	.273	.354
Wilson,Steve	L	.255	98	25	2	2	2	15	10	25	.318	.378
Throws Left	R	.299	164	49	11	1	4	24	19	29	.371	.451
Wilson,Trevor	L	.261	134	35	4	0	3	16	15	30	.351	.358
Throws Left	R	.266	440	117	21	4	15	56	49	58	.339	.434
Witt,Bobby	L	.243	292	71	11	3	4	38	63	52	.373	.342
Throws Right	R	.265	423	112	17	0	12	41	51	73	.342	.390
Wohlers,Mark	L	.231	65	15	1	0	0	2	11	12	.342	.246
Throws Right	R	.241	54	13	2	0	0	6	3	5	.288	.278
Woodson,Kerry	L	.368	19	7	1	0	0	5	5	2	.500	.421
Throws Right	R	.167	30	5	1	0	0	4	6	4	.342	.200
Worrell,Todd	L	.174	121	21	2	0	3	8	12	38	.254	.264
Throws Right	R	.226	106	24	5	0	1	4	13	26	.311	.302
Young,Anthony	L	.324	259	84	13	7	3	34	18	31	.366	.463
Throws Right	R	.237	211	50	10	2	5	24	13	33	.282	.374
Young,Curt	L	.392	51	20	4	0	0	13	1	7	.396	.471
Throws Left	R	.274	219	60	16	1	2	18	16	13	.326	.384
Young,Matt	L	.269	52	14	3	0	1	10	11	15	.409	.385
Throws Left	R	.253	217	55	9	0	6	33	31	42	.347	.378
Young,Pete	L	.343	35	12	3	2	0	11	8	5	.444	.543
Throws Right	R	.158	38	6	2	0	0	3	1	6	.200	.211
AL	L	.260	--	--	--	--	--	--	--	--	.330	.375
	R	.259	--	--	--	--	--	--	--	--	.327	.392
NL	L	.259	--	--	--	--	--	--	--	--	.331	.377
	R	.246	--	--	--	--	--	--	--	--	.303	.361
MLB	L	.260	--	--	--	--	--	--	--	--	.330	.376
	R	.253	--	--	--	--	--	--	--	--	.317	.378

Leader Boards

This is the fourth installment of the Leader Boards Section of the Handbook. Once again, we are more than happy to pen a few words about the lists that take up the next fourteen pages of this book.

The first point to be made is that these Leader Boards have reached such a state of perfection as to have been the only section of this book not requiring any changes at all. No small feat, considering the STATS' staff pores over every section of the Handbook trying to find ways to make it better. Point #2: while the format has not changed, the numbers have. These Leader Boards are brand new: no retreads from 1991, no surprise lists from the bottom of the 1988 file. Just 100% 1992 information.

Here's a sampling of the tidbits you'll come across:

Which batters received the most Intentional Walks? Which pitchers allowed the lowest Opposition Batting Average? The answers are in the first group, comprising the "regular" 1992 AL and NL Batting and Pitching Leaders.

Who was the best batter with runners in scoring position? Which relievers allowed the fewest of their inherited runners to score? There are four pages of Special Batting and Pitching Leader boards.

In the Active Career Batting and Pitching Leaders section, you'll be able to find out how far up the list of Career Slugging Percentages Barry Bonds propelled himself in 1992 by slugging .624. Or how far down the list of Career Winning Percentages Dwight Gooden careened after suffering the first losing season (10-13, .435) of his career.

The last section of the Leader Boards covers Offensive Winning Percentage, Runs Created, Secondary Average, Cheap Wins, and Slow Hooks, among others. For those unfamiliar with this last group — staples of the Bill James Leader Boards — or any of the other lists contained herein, there are definitions located in the Glossary at the end of the Handbook.

Enjoy!

1992 American League Batting Leaders

Batting Average

Player, Team	AB	H	AVG
E MARTINEZ, Sea	528	181	.343
K Puckett, Min	639	210	.329
F Thomas, ChA	573	185	.323
P Molitor, Mil	609	195	.320
S Mack, Min	600	189	.315
C Baerga, Cle	657	205	.312
R Alomar, Tor	571	177	.310
K Griffey Jr, Sea	565	174	.308
B Harper, Min	502	154	.307
M Bordick, Oak	504	151	.300

On-Base Percentage

Player, Team	PA	OB	OBP
F THOMAS, ChA	711	312	.439
D Tartabull, NYA	526	215	.409
R Alomar, Tor	665	269	.405
E Martinez, Sea	591	239	.404
S Mack, Min	681	268	.394
P Molitor, Mil	696	271	.389
T Phillips, Det	728	282	.387
L Whitaker, Det	539	208	.386
C Davis, Min	529	204	.386
M McGwire, Oak	571	220	.385

Slugging Percentage

Player, Team	AB	TB	SLG
M McGWIRE, Oak	467	273	.585
E Martinez, Sea	528	287	.544
F Thomas, ChA	573	307	.536
K Griffey Jr, Sea	565	302	.535
J Gonzalez, Tex	584	309	.529
J Carter, Tor	622	310	.498
D Winfield, Tor	583	286	.491
K Puckett, Min	639	313	.490
D Tartabull, NYA	421	206	.489
A Belle, Cle	585	279	.477

Games

C RIPKEN, Bal	162
T Fryman, Det	161
C Baerga, Cle	161
K Puckett, Min	160
F Thomas, ChA	160

Plate Appearances

B ANDERSON, Bal	749
T Phillips, Det	733
T Fryman, Det	721
C Baerga, Cle	716
C Ripken, Bal	715

At Bats

T FRYMAN, Det	659
C Baerga, Cle	657
M Devereaux, Bal	653
D White, Tor	641
D Mattingly, NYA	640

Hits

K PUCKETT, Min	210
C Baerga, Cle	205
P Molitor, Mil	195
S Mack, Min	189
F Thomas, ChA	185

Singles

C BAERGA, Cle	152
C Knoblauch, Min	151
K Puckett, Min	149
L Polonia, Cal	144
P Listach, Mil	142

Doubles

E MARTINEZ, Sea	46
F THOMAS, ChA	46
D Mattingly, NYA	40
R Yount, Mil	40
K Griffey Jr, Sea	39

Triples

L JOHNSON, ChA	12
M Devereaux, Bal	11
B Anderson, Bal	10
T Raines, ChA	9
R Alomar, Tor	8
K Lofton, Cle	8

Home Runs

J GONZALEZ, Tex	43
M McGwire, Oak	42
C Fielder, Det	35
J Carter, Tor	34
A Belle, Cle	34

Total Bases

K PUCKETT, Min	313
J Carter, Tor	310
J Gonzalez, Tex	309
F Thomas, ChA	307
M Devereaux, Bal	303

Runs Scored

T PHILLIPS, Det	114
F Thomas, ChA	108
R Alomar, Tor	105
K Puckett, Min	104
C Knoblauch, Min	104

Runs Batted In

C FIELDER, Det	124
J Carter, Tor	119
F Thomas, ChA	115
A Belle, Cle	112
G Bell, ChA	112

Ground Double Play

G BELL, ChA	29
T Martinez, Sea	24
G Jefferies, KC	24
T Steinbach, Oak	20
L Johnson, ChA	20

Sacrifice Hits

J BROWNE, Oak	16
M Bordick, Oak	14
T Pena, Bos	13
S Sax, ChA	12
P Listach, Mil	12
G Gagne, Min	12

Sacrifice Flies

J CARTER, Tor	13
C Knoblauch, Min	12
R Yount, Mil	12
P Molitor, Mil	11
F Thomas, ChA	11

Stolen Bases

K LOFTON, Cle	66
P Listach, Mil	54
B Anderson, Bal	53
L Polonia, Cal	51
R Alomar, Tor	49

Caught Stealing

L POLONIA, Cal	21
C Curtis, Cal	18
P Listach, Mil	18
B Anderson, Bal	16
G Vaughn, Mil	15

Walks

F THOMAS, ChA	122
M TETTLETON, Det	122
T Phillips, Det	114
R Milligan, Bal	106
D Tartabull, NYA	103

Intentional Walks

W BOGGS, Bos	19
M Tettleton, Det	18
K Griffey Jr, Sea	15
B Anderson, Bal	14
C Ripken, Bal	14
D Tartabull, NYA	14

Hit by Pitch

S MACK, Min	15
M MACFARLANE, KC	15
K Miller, KC	14
C Baerga, Cle	13
J Carter, Tor	11

Strikeouts

D PALMER, Tex	154
C Fielder, Det	151
J Buhner, Sea	146
T Fryman, Det	144
J Gonzalez, Tex	143

1992 National League Batting Leaders

Batting Average

Player, Team	AB	H	AVG
G SHEFFIELD, SD	557	184	.330
A Van Slyke, Pit	614	199	.324
J Kruk, Phi	507	164	.324
B Roberts, Cin	532	172	.323
T Gwynn, SD	520	165	.317
T Pendleton, Atl	640	199	.311
B Bonds, Pit	473	147	.311
B Butler, LA	553	171	.309
M Grace, ChN	603	185	.307
R Sandberg, ChN	612	186	.304

On-Base Percentage

Player, Team	PA	OB	OBP
B BONDS, Pit	612	279	.456
J Kruk, Phi	607	257	.423
B Butler, LA	652	269	.413
F McGriff, SD	632	249	.394
B Roberts, Cin	600	236	.393
G Sheffield, SD	618	238	.385
D Daulton, Phi	585	225	.385
W Clark, SF	601	231	.384
A Van Slyke, Pit	685	261	.381
M Grace, ChN	687	261	.380

Slugging Percentage

Player, Team	AB	TB	SLG
B BONDS, Pit	473	295	.624
G Sheffield, SD	557	323	.580
F McGriff, SD	531	295	.556
D Daulton, Phi	485	254	.524
R Sandberg, ChN	612	312	.510
L Walker, Mon	528	267	.506
A Van Slyke, Pit	614	310	.505
R Lankford, StL	598	287	.480
W Clark, SF	513	244	.476
T Pendleton, Atl	640	303	.473

Games

S FINLEY, Hou	162
J BAGWELL, Hou	162
C BIGGIO, Hou	162
T Pendleton, Atl	160
2 Players with	159

Plate Appearances

C BIGGIO, Hou	721
J Bell, Pit	712
M Grissom, Mon	707
J Bagwell, Hou	697
T Fernandez, SD	694

At Bats

M GRISSOM, Mon	653
T Pendleton, Atl	640
J Bell, Pit	632
T Fernandez, SD	622
A Van Slyke, Pit	614

Hits

A VAN SLYKE, Pit	199
T PENDLETON, Atl	199
R Sandberg, ChN	186
M Grace, ChN	185
G Sheffield, SD	184

Singles

B BUTLER, LA	143
T Pendleton, Atl	138
M Grace, ChN	134
O Smith, StL	131
T Fernandez, SD	131

Doubles

A VAN SLYKE, Pit	45
W Clark, SF	40
R Lankford, StL	40
M Duncan, Phi	40
M Grissom, Mon	39
T Pendleton, Atl	39

Triples

D SANDERS, Atl	14
S Finley, Hou	13
A Van Slyke, Pit	12
B Butler, LA	11
L Alicea, StL	11

Home Runs

F McGRIFF, SD	35
B Bonds, Pit	34
G Sheffield, SD	33
D Hollins, Phi	27
D Daulton, Phi	27

Total Bases

G SHEFFIELD, SD	323
R Sandberg, ChN	312
A Van Slyke, Pit	310
T Pendleton, Atl	303
F McGriff, SD	295
B Bonds, Pit	295

Runs Scored

B BONDS, Pit	109
D Hollins, Phi	104
A Van Slyke, Pit	103
R Sandberg, ChN	100
M Grissom, Mon	99

Runs Batted In

D DAULTON, Phi	109
T Pendleton, Atl	105
F McGriff, SD	104
B Bonds, Pit	103
G Sheffield, SD	100

Ground Double Play

D JACKSON, SD	21
G Sheffield, SD	19
J Bagwell, Hou	17
T Pendleton, Atl	16
4 Players with	15

Sacrifice Hits

B BUTLER, LA	24
J Bell, Pit	19
S Finley, Hou	16
R Belliard, Atl	13
G Maddux, ChN	13

Sacrifice Flies

J BAGWELL, Hou	13
W Clark, SF	11
A Van Slyke, Pit	9
4 Players with	8

Stolen Bases

M GRISSOM, Mon	78
D DeShields, Mon	46
S Finley, Hou	44
B Roberts, Cin	44
O Smith, StL	43

Caught Stealing

R LANKFORD, StL	24
B Butler, LA	21
T Fernandez, SD	20
O Nixon, Atl	18
2 Players with	16

Walks

B BONDS, Pit	127
F McGriff, SD	96
B Butler, LA	95
C Biggio, Hou	94
J Kruk, Phi	92

Intentional Walks

B BONDS, Pit	32
F McGriff, SD	23
W Clark, SF	23
J Oliver, Cin	19
P O'Neill, Cin	15

Hit by Pitch

D HOLLINS, Phi	19
J Bagwell, Hou	12
R Amaro, Phi	9
4 Players with	8

Strikeouts

R LANKFORD, StL	147
D Hollins, Phi	110
M Williams, SF	109
F McGriff, SD	108
M Duncan, Phi	108
D DeShields, Mon	108

1992 American League Pitching Leaders

Earned Run Average

Pitcher, Team	IP	ER	ERA
R CLEMENS, Bos	**246.2**	**66**	**2.41**
K Appier, KC	208.1	57	2.46
M Mussina, Bal	241.0	68	2.54
J Guzman, Tor	180.2	53	2.64
J Abbott, Cal	211.0	65	2.77
M Perez, NYA	247.2	79	2.87
C Nagy, Cle	252.0	83	2.96
J McDowell, ChA	260.2	92	3.18
B Wegman, Mil	261.2	93	3.20
J Smiley, Min	241.0	86	3.21

Won-Lost Percentage

Pitcher, Team	W	L	WL%
M MUSSINA, Bal	**18**	**5**	**.783**
J Morris, Tor	21	6	.778
J Guzman, Tor	16	5	.762
C Bosio, Mil	16	6	.727
J McDowell, ChA	20	10	.667
K Brown, Tex	21	11	.656
K Appier, KC	15	8	.652
J Smiley, Min	16	9	.640
C Nagy, Cle	17	10	.630
D Fleming, Sea	17	10	.630

Opposition Average

Pitcher, Team	AB	H	AVG
R JOHNSON, Sea	**749**	**154**	**.206**
J Guzman, Tor	652	135	.207
K Appier, KC	771	167	.217
R Clemens, Bos	907	203	.224
J Smiley, Min	886	205	.231
M Perez, NYA	901	212	.235
D Stewart, Oak	737	175	.237
M Mussina, Bal	888	212	.239
C Hough, ChA	670	160	.239
F Viola, Bos	886	214	.242

Games

K ROGERS, Tex	**81**
D Ward, Tor	79
S Olin, Cle	72
D Lilliquist, Cle	71
G Harris, Bos	70

Games Started

M MOORE, Oak	**36**
R SUTCLIFFE, Bal	**36**
F Viola, Bos	35
B Wegman, Mil	35
B McDonald, Bal	35
K Brown, Tex	35

Complete Games

J McDOWELL, ChA	**13**
R Clemens, Bos	11
K Brown, Tex	11
C Nagy, Cle	10
M Perez, NYA	10

Games Finished

D ECKERSLEY, Oak	**65**
S Olin, Cle	62
J Montgomery, KC	62
R Aguilera, Min	61
G Olson, Bal	56
D Henry, Mil	56

Wins

K BROWN, Tex	**21**
J MORRIS, Tor	**21**
J McDowell, ChA	20
R Clemens, Bos	18
M Mussina, Bal	18

Losses

E HANSON, Sea	**17**
M Perez, NYA	16
J Abbott, Cal	15
J Armstrong, Cle	15
R Sutcliffe, Bal	15

Saves

D ECKERSLEY, Oak	**51**
R Aguilera, Min	41
J Montgomery, KC	39
G Olson, Bal	36
T Henke, Tor	34

Shutouts

R CLEMENS, Bos	**5**
M Mussina, Bal	4
D Fleming, Sea	4
4 Players with	3

Hits Allowed

K BROWN, Tex	**262**
B Wegman, Mil	251
R Sutcliffe, Bal	251
J McDowell, ChA	247
C Nagy, Cle	245

Doubles Allowed

K TAPANI, Min	**53**
D FLEMING, Sea	**53**
J Guzman, Tex	52
J Smiley, Min	51
B Wegman, Mil	50

Triples Allowed

J McDOWELL, ChA	**9**
S SANDERSON, NYA	**9**
K McCaskill, ChA	8
R Sutcliffe, Bal	7
6 Players with	6

Home Runs Allowed

B GULLICKSON, Det	**35**
B McDonald, Bal	32
D Cook, Cle	29
B Wegman, Mil	28
S Sanderson, NYA	28

Batters Faced

K BROWN, Tex	**1108**
J McDowell, ChA	1079
B Wegman, Mil	1079
C Nagy, Cle	1018
R Sutcliffe, Bal	1018

Innings Pitched

K BROWN, Tex	**265.2**
B Wegman, Mil	261.2
J McDowell, ChA	260.2
C Nagy, Cle	252.0
M Perez, NYA	247.2

Runs Allowed

R SUTCLIFFE, Bal	**123**
K Brown, Tex	117
S Sanderson, NYA	116
K McCaskill, ChA	116
J Morris, Tor	114

Strikeouts

R JOHNSON, Sea	**241**
M Perez, NYA	218
R Clemens, Bos	208
J Guzman, Tex	179
J McDowell, ChA	178

Walks Allowed

R JOHNSON, Sea	**144**
B Witt, Oak	114
M Moore, Oak	103
C Finley, Cal	98
K McCaskill, ChA	95

Hit Batters

R JOHNSON, Sea	**18**
N Ryan, Tex	12
J Morris, Tor	10
K Brown, Tex	10
T Stottlemyre, Tor	10

Wild Pitches

M MOORE, Oak	**22**
J Guzman, Tor	14
R Johnson, Sea	13
M Perez, NYA	13
R Darling, Oak	13
J Parrett, Oak	13

Balks

D COOK, Cle	**5**
J Armstrong, Cle	3
J Dopson, Bos	3
R Monteleone, NYA	3
13 Players with	2

1992 National League Pitching Leaders

Earned Run Average

Pitcher, Team	IP	ER	ERA
B SWIFT, SF	**164.2**	**38**	**2.08**
B Tewksbury, StL	233.0	56	2.16
G Maddux, ChN	268.0	65	2.18
C Schilling, Phi	226.1	59	2.35
D Martinez, Mon	226.1	62	2.47
M Morgan, ChN	240.0	68	2.55
J Rijo, Cin	211.0	60	2.56
K Hill, Mon	218.0	65	2.68
G Swindell, Cin	213.2	64	2.70
S Fernandez, NYN	214.2	65	2.73

Won-Lost Percentage

Pitcher, Team	W	L	WL%
B TEWKSBURY, StL	**16**	**5**	**.762**
T Glavine, Atl	20	8	.714
C Leibrandt, Atl	15	7	.682
M Morgan, ChN	16	8	.667
D Cone, NYN	13	7	.650
G Maddux, ChN	20	11	.645
K Hill, Mon	16	9	.640
J Jones, Hou	10	6	.625
B Walk, Pit	10	6	.625
J Rijo, Cin	15	10	.600

Opposition Average

Pitcher, Team	AB	H	AVG
C SCHILLING, Phi	**819**	**165**	**.201**
G Maddux, ChN	959	201	.210
S Fernandez, NYN	771	162	.210
D Martinez, Mon	814	172	.211
D Cone, NYN	728	162	.222
J Smoltz, Atl	921	206	.224
K Hill, Mon	812	187	.230
D Drabek, Pit	945	218	.231
F Castillo, ChN	770	179	.233
P Harnisch, Hou	779	182	.234

Games

J BOEVER, Hou	**81**
D Jones, Hou	80
M Perez, StL	77
X Hernandez, Hou	77
J Innis, NYN	76

Games Started

S AVERY, Atl	**35**
J SMOLTZ, Atl	**35**
G MADDUX, ChN	**35**
6 Players with	34

Complete Games

T MULHOLL'D, Phi	**12**
D Drabek, Pit	10
C Schilling, Phi	10
J Smoltz, Atl	9
G Maddux, ChN	9

Games Finished

D JONES, Hou	**70**
J Wetteland, Mon	58
R Myers, SD	57
M Williams, Phi	56
L Smith, StL	55

Wins

G MADDUX, ChN	**20**
T GLAVINE, Atl	**20**
B Tewksbury, StL	16
K Hill, Mon	16
M Morgan, ChN	16
D Martinez, Mon	16

Losses

O HERSHISER, LA	**15**
T CANDIOTTI, LA	**15**
K Abbott, Phi	14
A Young, NYN	14
A Benes, SD	14
T Belcher, Cin	14
T Wilson, SF	14

Saves

L SMITH, StL	**43**
R Myers, SD	38
J Wetteland, Mon	37
D Jones, Hou	36
M Williams, Phi	29

Shutouts

T GLAVINE, Atl	**5**
D CONE, NYN	**5**
5 Players with	4

Hits Allowed

A BENES, SD	**230**
T Mulholland, Phi	227
R Tomlin, Pit	226
B Hurst, SD	223
D Drabek, Pit	218

Doubles Allowed

R TOMLIN, Pit	**45**
D Gooden, NYN	43
T Mulholland, Phi	43
3 Players with	42

Triples Allowed

S FERNANDEZ, NYN	**9**
A YOUNG, NYN	**9**
4 Players with	8

Home Runs Allowed

B BLACK, SF	**23**
B Hurst, SD	22
O Olivares, StL	20
K Abbott, Phi	20
F Castillo, ChN	19

Batters Faced

G MADDUX, ChN	**1061**
D Drabek, Pit	1021
J Smoltz, Atl	1021
S Avery, Atl	969
M Morgan, ChN	966

Innings Pitched

G MADDUX, ChN	**268.0**
D Drabek, Pit	256.2
J Smoltz, Atl	246.2
M Morgan, ChN	240.0
S Avery, Atl	233.2

Runs Allowed

T BELCHER, Cin	**104**
O Hershiser, LA	101
T Mulholland, Phi	101
D Jackson, Pit	99
J Burkett, SF	96
B Hurst, SD	96

Strikeouts

J SMOLTZ, Atl	**215**
D Cone, NYN	214
G Maddux, ChN	199
S Fernandez, NYN	193
D Drabek, Pit	177

Walks Allowed

D CONE, NYN	**82**
B Ojeda, LA	81
J Smoltz, Atl	80
T Belcher, Cin	80
M Morgan, ChN	79

Hit Batters

G MADDUX, ChN	**14**
D Cone, NYN	9
M Gardner, Mon	9
D Martinez, Mon	9
O Hershiser, LA	8

Wild Pitches

J SMOLTZ, Atl	**17**
D Henry, Cin	12
K Hill, Mon	11
M Morgan, ChN	11
F Castillo, ChN	11
D Drabek, Pit	11

Balks

T WILSON, SF	**7**
B BLACK, SF	**7**
K Hill, Mon	4
B Scanlan, ChN	4
D Kile, Hou	4

1992 American League Special Batting Leaders

Scoring Position

Player, Team	AB	H	AVG
L WHITAKER, Det	**111**	**41**	**.369**
T Raines, ChA	108	39	.361
L Sojo, Cal	90	32	.356
R Alomar, Tor	147	52	.354
K Puckett, Min	188	65	.346
K Miller, KC	88	30	.341
T Steinbach, Oak	97	33	.340
S Fletcher, Mil	107	36	.336
K Griffey Jr, Sea	150	50	.333
M Lee, Tor	94	31	.330

Leadoff On-Base%

Player, Team	PA	OB	OBP
R HENDERSON, Oak	**495**	**211**	**.426**
B Downing, Tex	244	101	.414
P Molitor, Mil	154	59	.383
C Knoblauch, Min	305	115	.377
T Phillips, Det	650	245	.377
G Jefferies, KC	162	61	.377
B Anderson, Bal	738	276	.374
S Mack, Min	406	150	.370
O Vizquel, Sea	284	104	.366
K Miller, KC	318	115	.362

Cleanup Slugging%

Player, Team	AB	TB	SLG
M McGWIRE, Oak	**225**	**133**	**.591**
J Gonzalez, Tex	218	119	.546
D Tartabull, NYA	224	110	.491
D Winfield, Tor	583	286	.491
A Belle, Cle	585	279	.477
F Thomas, ChA	171	81	.474
R Sierra, Oak	394	186	.472
W Joyner, KC	144	66	.458
C Fielder, Det	590	268	.454
T Brunansky, Bos	351	156	.444

Vs LHP

P MOLITOR, Mil	**.424**
E Martinez, Sea	.376
C Baerga, Cle	.375
K Lofton, Cle	.369
K Griffey Jr, Sea	.358

Vs RHP

E MARTINEZ, Sea	**.331**
K Puckett, Min	.329
S Mack, Min	.320
B Harper, Min	.315
O Vizquel, Sea	.312

Late & Close

J BROWNE, Oak	**.465**
R Alomar, Tor	.430
E Martinez, Sea	.390
D Hamilton, Mil	.362
J Olerud, Tor	.361

Bases Loaded

M HALL, NYA	**.667**
C Davis, Min	.625
B Harper, Min	.571
J Browne, Oak	.556
M McGwire, Oak	.556

OBP vs LHP

D TARTAB'L, NYA	**.494**
K Lofton, Cle	.466
P Molitor, Mil	.464
R Milligan, Bal	.462
K McReynolds, KC	.461

OBP vs RHP

F THOMAS, ChA	**.433**
C Davis, Min	.408
S Mack, Min	.403
R Alomar, Tor	.401
E Martinez, Sea	.390

BA at Home

R ALOMAR, Tor	**.354**
C Baerga, Cle	.353
K Puckett, Min	.348
B Harper, Min	.324
T Brunansky, Bos	.323

BA on the Road

E MARTINEZ, Sea	**.373**
F Thomas, ChA	.342
P Molitor, Mil	.334
T Steinbach, Oak	.326
S Mack, Min	.325

SLG vs LHP

P MOLITOR, Mil	**.659**
F Thomas, ChA	.650
K Griffey Jr, Sea	.624
D Tartabull, NYA	.613
M Devereaux, Bal	.589

SLG vs RHP

J GONZALEZ, Tex	**.561**
E Martinez, Sea	.532
M McGwire, Oak	.527
F Thomas, ChA	.499
K Puckett, Min	.498

SB Success %

H COTTO, Sea	**92.0**
D White, Tor	90.2
T Raines, ChA	88.2
R Kelly, NYA	84.9
K Lofton, Cle	84.6

Times on Base

F THOMAS, ChA	**312**
T Phillips, Det	282
B Anderson, Bal	276
C Knoblauch, Min	271
P Molitor, Mil	271

AB per HR

M McGWIRE, Oak	**11.1**
J Gonzalez, Tex	13.6
M Tettleton, Det	16.4
D Tartabull, NYA	16.8
J Canseco, Tex	16.9

Ground/Fly Ratio

S SAX, ChA	**2.64**
L Polonia, Cal	2.51
L Johnson, ChA	2.29
S Mack, Min	2.29
P Listach, Mil	2.12

GDP/GDP Opp

K MAAS, NYA	**1.9**
K MILLER, KC	1.9
B Anderson, Bal	1.9
P Listach, Mil	3.0
J Orsulak, Bal	3.2

% CS by Catchers

I RODRIGUEZ, Tex	**51.8**
S Alomar Jr, Cle	44.9
T Steinbach, Oak	43.8
B Surhoff, Mil	40.6
M Tettleton, Det	34.5

Pitches Seen

B ANDERSON, Bal	**2976**
T Phillips, Det	2898
F Thomas, ChA	2840
M Devereaux, Bal	2782
M Tettleton, Det	2761

Pitches per PA

M TETTLETON, Det	**4.22**
J Canseco, Tex	4.19
D Tartabull, NYA	4.14
R Milligan, Bal	4.07
D Palmer, Tex	4.04

% Pitches Taken

L BL'NK'NSH'P, Oak	**69.3**
R Henderson, Oak	69.1
B Downing, Tex	65.8
J Reed, Bos	64.9
M Tettleton, Det	64.9

Steals of Third

R ALOMAR, Tor	**12**
L POLONIA, Cal	**12**
R Henderson, Oak	9
P Listach, Mil	9
L Johnson, ChA	9

1992 National League Special Batting Leaders

Scoring Position

Player, Team	AB	H	AVG
T PENDLETON, Atl	161	63	.391
B Larkin, Cin	144	49	.340
G Sheffield, SD	127	43	.339
A Van Slyke, Pit	145	49	.338
B Roberts, Cin	98	33	.337
W McGee, SF	101	34	.337
J Bell, Pit	120	40	.333
W Clark, SF	112	37	.330
R Lankford, StL	162	53	.327
M Grace, ChN	138	45	.326

Leadoff On-Base%

Player, Team	PA	OB	OBP
B ROBERTS, Cin	571	226	.396
C Biggio, Hou	704	266	.378
R Lankford, StL	269	101	.375
L Dykstra, Phi	392	147	.375
B Butler, LA	380	142	.374
D DeShields, Mon	374	137	.366
V Coleman, NYN	253	90	.356
O Nixon, Atl	485	167	.344
M Grissom, Mon	344	118	.343
A Cole, Pit	208	71	.341

Cleanup Slugging%

Player, Team	AB	TB	SLG
B BONDS, Pit	339	232	.684
F McGriff, SD	530	295	.557
L Walker, Mon	512	261	.510
J Bagwell, Hou	264	126	.477
J Kruk, Phi	370	174	.470
D Daulton, Phi	130	61	.469
D Justice, Atl	387	177	.457
A Dawson, ChN	446	202	.453
C Snyder, SF	221	100	.452
E Anthony, Hou	190	84	.442

Vs LHP

F JOSE, StL	.374
R Jordan, Phi	.371
G Sheffield, SD	.365
T Pendleton, Atl	.357
B Larkin, Cin	.355

Vs RHP

A VAN SLYKE, Pit	.345
B Roberts, Cin	.340
M Grace, ChN	.323
B Butler, LA	.318
R Lankford, StL	.314

Late & Close

L DYKSTRA, Phi	.414
G Sheffield, SD	.410
G Braggs, Cin	.388
S Owen, Mon	.368
T Gwynn, SD	.360

Bases Loaded

E MURRAY, NYN	.667
E Karros, LA	.625
C Walker, NYN	.600
D Hollins, Phi	.500
S Bream, Atl	.500

OBP vs LHP

B BONDS, Pit	.445
B Larkin, Cin	.443
G Sheffield, SD	.420
F Jose, StL	.419
J Kruk, Phi	.414

OBP vs RHP

B BUTLER, LA	.420
B Roberts, Cin	.416
A Van Slyke, Pit	.411
F McGriff, SD	.409
M Grace, ChN	.409

BA at Home

G SHEFFIELD, SD	.365
B Roberts, Cin	.353
B Bonds, Pit	.338
W Clark, SF	.337
O Smith, StL	.335

BA on the Road

J KRUK, Phi	.340
M Grace, ChN	.330
A Van Slyke, Pit	.328
T Gwynn, SD	.326
L Walker, Mon	.317

SLG vs LHP

G SHEFFIELD, SD	.640
D Hollins, Phi	.620
B Bonds, Pit	.599
B Larkin, Cin	.585
J Blauser, Atl	.585

SLG vs RHP

F McGRIFF, SD	.558
G Sheffield, SD	.549
A Van Slyke, Pit	.545
R Lankford, StL	.537
R Sandberg, ChN	.515

SB Success %

E DAVIS, LA	95.0
M Duncan, Phi	88.5
M Grissom, Mon	85.7
L Dykstra, Phi	85.7
S Javier, Phi	85.7

Times on Base

B BONDS, Pit	279
C Biggio, Hou	271
B Butler, LA	269
A Van Slyke, Pit	261
M Grace, ChN	261

AB per HR

B BONDS, Pit	13.9
F McGriff, SD	15.2
G Sheffield, SD	16.9
D Daulton, Phi	18.0
D Hollins, Phi	21.7

Ground/Fly Ratio

W McGEE, SF	3.61
O Nixon, Atl	2.99
O Smith, StL	2.50
J Kruk, Phi	2.43
B Butler, LA	2.35

GDP/GDP Opp

D JUSTICE, Atl	0.9
M Webster, LA	1.8
D Daulton, Phi	2.4
J Blauser, Atl	3.0
S Bream, Atl	4.1

% CS by Catchers

K MANWARING, SF	50.5
J Girardi, ChN	41.0
G Olson, Atl	39.1
M LaValliere, Pit	38.3
R Wilkins, ChN	37.2

Pitches Seen

C BIGGIO, Hou	2758
B Butler, LA	2743
R Lankford, StL	2697
J Bagwell, Hou	2665
A Van Slyke, Pit	2662

Pitches per PA

B BUTLER, LA	4.06
T Zeile, StL	3.98
D DeShields, Mon	3.96
R Lankford, StL	3.95
J Kruk, Phi	3.92

% Pitches Taken

D MAGADAN, NYN	63.5
B Bonds, Pit	63.3
S Owen, Mon	62.7
T Zeile, StL	61.8
B Butler, LA	61.0

Steals of Third

M GRISSOM, Mon	24
C Biggio, Hou	12
B Butler, LA	8
J Offerman, LA	8
B Bonds, Pit	7

1992 American League Special Pitching Leaders

Baserunners Per 9 IP

Player, Team	IP	BR	BR/9
M MUSSINA, Bal	241.0	262	9.78
R Clemens, Bos	246.2	274	10.00
K Appier, KC	208.1	237	10.24
J Smiley, Min	241.0	276	10.31
J Guzman, Tor	180.2	208	10.36
C Bosio, Mil	231.1	271	10.54
J Navarro, Mil	246.0	294	10.76
B Wegman, Mil	261.2	315	10.83
C Nagy, Cle	252.0	304	10.86
J Key, Tor	216.2	268	11.13

Run Support Per 9 IP

Player, Team	IP	R	R/9
S SANDER'N,NYA	193.1	134	6.24
K Tapani, Min	220.0	148	6.05
J Morris, Tor	240.2	160	5.98
T Stottlemyre, Tor	174.0	114	5.90
J Guzman, Tex	224.0	136	5.46
J McDowell, ChA	260.2	158	5.46
J Key, Tor	216.2	129	5.36
B Gullickson, Det	221.2	131	5.32
C Bosio, Mil	231.1	134	5.21
M Moore, Oak	223.0	123	4.96

Save Percentage

Player, Team	OP	SV	SV%
D ECKERSLEY, Oak	54	51	.944
T Henke, Tor	37	34	.919
D Henry, Mil	33	29	.879
J Grahe, Cal	24	21	.875
M Henneman, Det	28	24	.857
R Aguilera, Min	48	41	.854
J Montgomery, KC	46	39	.848
S Farr, NYA	36	30	.833
G Olson, Bal	44	36	.818
S Olin, Cle	36	29	.806

Hits per 9 IP

R JOHNSON, Sea	6.59
J Guzman, Tor	6.72
K Appier, KC	7.21
R Clemens, Bos	7.41
J Smiley, Min	7.66

Home Runs per 9 IP

J GUZMAN, Tor	0.30
K Brown, Tex	0.37
C Nagy, Cle	0.39
R Clemens, Bos	0.40
K Appier, KC	0.43

Strikeouts per 9 IP

R JOHNSON, Sea	10.3
J Guzman, Tor	8.2
M Perez, NYA	7.9
R Clemens, Bos	7.6
J Guzman, Tex	7.2

GDP per 9 IP

S ERICKSON, Min	1.3
C Finley, Cal	1.2
C Nagy, Cle	1.2
E Hanson, Sea	1.2
F Viola, Bos	1.1

Vs LHB

J KEY, Tor	.176
R Meacham, KC	.188
C Eldred, Mil	.188
D Ward, Tor	.197
R Reed, KC	.201

Vs RHB

R JOHNSON, Sea	.208
K McCaskill, ChA	.209
D Stewart, Oak	.217
R Clemens, Bos	.222
M Perez, NYA	.225

OBP Leadoff Inning

J KEY, Tor	.225
C Hough, ChA	.246
B Wegman, Mil	.262
J Guzman, Tor	.267
B Krueger, Min	.271

BA Allowed ScPos

K APPIER, KC	.167
M Mussina, Bal	.175
G Harris, Bos	.193
R Johnson, Sea	.193
J Guzman, Tor	.199

SLG Allowed

J GUZMAN, Tor	.275
R Johnson, Sea	.307
R Clemens, Bos	.308
K Appier, KC	.319
F Viola, Bos	.331

OBP Allowed

M MUSSINA, Bal	.278
R Clemens, Bos	.279
K Appier, KC	.281
J Smiley, Min	.286
J Guzman, Tor	.286

PkOf Throw/Runner

K McCASKILL, ChA	2.07
M Langston, Cal	1.54
J Abbott, Cal	1.50
C Hough, ChA	1.50
J Armstrong, Cle	1.46

SB% Allowed

K BROWN, Tex	36.8
R Darling, Oak	43.5
C Nagy, Cle	44.4
M Perez, NYA	50.0
M Mussina, Bal	50.0

Pitches per Batter

B GULLICKSON, Det	3.29
G Hibbard, ChA	3.33
C Bosio, Mil	3.33
K Brown, Tex	3.41
J Navarro, Mil	3.46

Grd/Fly Ratio Off

G HIBBARD, ChA	2.47
S Erickson, Min	2.46
C Nagy, Cle	2.43
K Brown, Tex	2.41
E Hanson, Sea	2.19

K/BB Ratio

R CLEMENS, Bos	3.35
C Nagy, Cle	2.96
K Tapani, Min	2.88
C Bosio, Mil	2.73
M Mussina, Bal	2.71

Wins in Relief

R MEACHAM, KC	10
J Parrett, Oak	9
A Mills, Bal	9
E Plunk, Cle	9
S Olin, Cle	8

Holds

D WARD, Tor	25
G Harris, Bos	19
M Guthrie, Min	19
J Parrett, Oak	19
R Honeycutt, Oak	18

Blown Saves

J RUSSELL, Oak	9
G Olson, Bal	8
J Nelson, Sea	8
J Reardon, Atl	8
S Radinsky, ChA	8

% Inherited Scored

D ECKERSLEY, Oak	6.5
S Frey, Cal	10.0
D Powell, Sea	12.0
M Guthrie, Min	15.8
G Olson, Bal	16.1

1st Batter

D POWELL, Sea	.100
J Austin, Mil	.135
J Montgomery, KC	.143
J Parrett, Oak	.145
T Leach, ChA	.170

1992 National League Special Pitching Leaders

Baserunners Per 9 IP

Player, Team	IP	BR	BR/9
C SCHILLING,Phi	226.1	225	8.95
B Tewksbury, StL	233.0	240	9.27
G Maddux, ChN	268.0	285	9.57
D Martinez, Mon	226.1	241	9.58
D Drabek, Pit	256.2	278	9.75
S Fernandez, NYN	214.2	233	9.77
J Rijo, Cin	211.0	232	9.90
B Swift, SF	164.2	190	10.38
J Smoltz, Atl	246.2	291	10.62
G Swindell, Cin	213.2	253	10.66

Run Support Per 9 IP

Player, Team	IP	R	R/9
T GLAVINE, Atl	225.0	133	5.32
T Mulholland, Phi	229.0	127	4.99
G Swindell, Cin	213.2	117	4.93
C Lefferts, Bal	163.1	87	4.79
J Burkett, SF	189.2	99	4.70
D Cone, NYN	196.2	100	4.58
K Hill, Mon	218.0	109	4.50
T Belcher, Cin	227.2	113	4.47
S Fernandez, NYN	214.2	105	4.40
M Gardner, Mon	179.2	87	4.36

Save Percentage

Player, Team	OP	SV	SV%
D JONES, Hou	42	36	.857
L Smith, StL	51	43	.843
R Dibble, Cin	30	25	.833
R Myers, SD	46	38	.826
M Williams, Phi	36	29	.806
J Wetteland, Mon	46	37	.804
N Charlton, Cin	34	26	.765
S Belinda, Pit	24	18	.750
A Young, NYN	20	15	.750
R Beck, SF	23	17	.739

Hits per 9 IP

C SCHILLING, Phi	6.56
G Maddux, ChN	6.75
S Fernandez, NYN	6.79
D Martinez, Mon	6.84
D Cone, NYN	7.41

Home Runs per 9 IP

G MADDUX, ChN	0.24
T Glavine, Atl	0.24
D Jackson, Pit	0.27
B Swift, SF	0.33
C Leibrandt, Atl	0.42

Strikeouts per 9 IP

D CONE, NYN	9.8
S Fernandez, NYN	8.1
J Smoltz, Atl	7.8
J Rijo, Cin	7.3
P Harnisch, Hou	7.1

GDP per 9 IP

B SWIFT, SF	1.4
R Tomlin, Pit	1.2
M Morgan, ChN	1.1
C Nabholz, Mon	1.0
B Tewksbury, StL	1.0

Vs LHB

T WORRELL, StL	.174
R Beck, SF	.178
R Dibble, Cin	.180
J Brantley, SF	.181
S Fernandez, NYN	.188

Vs RHB

G MADDUX, ChN	.176
D Drabek, Pit	.189
J Smoltz, Atl	.191
K Gross, LA	.199
C Schilling, Phi	.207

OBP Leadoff Inning

B TEWKSBURY, StL	.226
C Schilling, Phi	.236
S Fernandez, NYN	.253
D Drabek, Pit	.259
G Maddux, ChN	.262

BA Allowed ScPos

C SCHILLING, Phi	.176
D Drabek, Pit	.177
D Cone, NYN	.180
J Smoltz, Atl	.191
S Fernandez, NYN	.192

SLG Allowed

G MADDUX, ChN	.280
D Martinez, Mon	.287
C Schilling, Phi	.288
T Glavine, Atl	.310
B Swift, SF	.314

OBP Allowed

C SCHILLING, Phi	.254
B Tewksbury, StL	.265
D Martinez, Mon	.271
G Maddux, ChN	.273
S Fernandez, NYN	.273

PkOf Throw/Runner

C NABHOLZ, Mon	1.72
C Leibrandt, Atl	1.57
D Cone, NYN	1.52
K Hill, Mon	1.50
T Glavine, Atl	1.44

SB% Allowed

T MULHOLL'D,Phi	28.6
B Black, SF	33.3
T Belcher, Cin	35.3
M Morgan, ChN	40.0
O Olivares, StL	45.8

Pitches per Batter

B TEWKSBURY, StL	3.14
C Lefferts, SD	3.29
O Hershiser, LA	3.33
R Cormier, StL	3.35
D Jackson, Pit	3.40

Grd/Fly Ratio Off

B SWIFT, SF	2.62
G Maddux, ChN	2.61
M Morgan, ChN	2.47
J Rijo, Cin	2.00
C Nabholz, Mon	1.92

K/BB Ratio

B TEWKSBURY, StL	4.55
J Rijo, Cin	3.89
R Cormier, StL	3.55
G Swindell, Cin	3.37
D Drabek, Pit	3.28

Wins in Relief

D JONES, Hou	11
S Bankhead, Cin	10
X Hernandez, Hou	9
M Perez, StL	9
J Fassero, Mon	8

Holds

T WORRELL, StL	25
P Assenmacher, ChN	20
M Freeman, Atl	16
J Innis, NYN	16
M Stanton, Atl	15

Blown Saves

J WETTELAND, Mon	9
R Myers, SD	8
L Smith, StL	8
R McDowell, LA	8
N Charlton, Cin	8

% Inherited Scored

A OSUNA, Hou	15.0
J Boever, Hou	16.4
M Rojas, Mon	17.2
R Mason, Pit	20.5
P Assenmacher, ChN	21.0

1st Batter

B HICKERSON, SF	.113
D Neagle, Pit	.133
P Assenmacher, ChN	.143
K Mercker, Atl	.152
R Mason, Pit	.153

1992 American League Active Career Batting Leaders

Batting Average

Player, Team	AB	H	AVG
W BOGGS	**6213**	**2098**	**.338**
T Gwynn	5701	1864	.327
F Thomas	1323	426	.322
K Puckett	5645	1812	.321
D Mattingly	5643	1754	.311
E Martinez	1805	561	.311
G Brett	9789	3005	.307
M Greenwell	2980	912	.306
H Morris	1220	371	.304
P Molitor	7520	2281	.303
W Clark	3778	1139	.301
K Griffey Jr	2165	652	.301
J Franco	5416	1630	.301
S Mack	1712	514	.300
P Guerrero	5392	1618	.300
B Roberts	2091	626	.299
M Grace	2807	840	.299
L Polonia	2740	818	.299
W McGee	5669	1689	.298
T Raines	6465	1923	.297
J Kruk	2948	875	.297
R Palmeiro	3270	968	.296
B Larkin	3122	924	.296
B Harper	2363	697	.295
C Baerga	1562	457	.293

On-Base Percentage

Player, Team	PA	OB	OBP
F THOMAS	**1651**	**738**	**.447**
W Boggs	7300	3124	.428
R Henderson	8256	3336	.404
E Martinez	2077	817	.393
F McGriff	3594	1406	.391
D Magadan	2467	964	.391
J Kruk	3451	1347	.390
R Milligan	2153	835	.388
T Raines	7483	2892	.386
K Daniels	2735	1045	.382
T Gwynn	6253	2382	.381
B Bonds	4252	1615	.380
A Davis	5008	1902	.380
J Clark	8216	3112	.379
J Bagwell	1344	507	.377
D Tartabull	3879	1462	.377
B Butler	7091	2663	.376
W Clark	4299	1608	.374
M Greenwell	3345	1251	.374
M Grace	3190	1193	.374
W Randolph	9363	3491	.373
K Seitzer	3758	1401	.373
G Brett	10986	4092	.372
B Downing	9249	3425	.370
P Guerrero	6106	2259	.370

Slugging Percentage

Player, Team	AB	TB	SLG
F THOMAS	**1323**	**717**	**.542**
F McGriff	3003	1586	.528
D Strawberry	4564	2336	.512
D Tartabull	3340	1706	.511
J Canseco	3655	1866	.511
C Fielder	2297	1170	.509
W Clark	3778	1917	.507
K Mitchell	3109	1574	.506
B Bonds	3584	1804	.503
M McGwire	3123	1570	.503
J Gonzalez	1279	632	.494
K Griffey Jr	2165	1069	.494
E Davis	3124	1539	.493
G Brett	9789	4801	.490
D Justice	1370	668	.488
A Dawson	8890	4333	.487
K Hrbek	5526	2678	.485
E Murray	9124	4414	.484
D Mattingly	5643	2723	.483
A Belle	1287	621	.483
P Guerrero	5392	2588	.480
D Winfield	10047	4821	.480
K Daniels	2338	1119	.479
G Bell	5713	2724	.477
J Clark	6847	3256	.476

Games

R YOUNT	**2729**
D Winfield	2707
G Brett	2562
C Fisk	2474
E Murray	2444
B Downing	2344
A Dawson	2310
G Carter	2296
O Smith	2208
W Randolph	2202
D Murphy	2154
L Whitaker	2095
W Wilson	2032
J Clark	1994
A Trammell	1965

Runs Scored

R YOUNT	**1570**
D Winfield	1551
G Brett	1514
R Henderson	1472
E Murray	1343
P Molitor	1275
C Fisk	1274
A Dawson	1259
W Randolph	1239
L Whitaker	1211
D Murphy	1196
B Downing	1188
T Raines	1138
W Wilson	1136
J Clark	1118

Runs Batted In

D WINFIELD	**1710**
E Murray	1562
G Brett	1520
A Dawson	1425
R Yount	1355
C Fisk	1326
D Murphy	1259
G Carter	1225
J Clark	1180
B Downing	1073
H Baines	1066
L Parrish	1030
C Ripken	1014
K Hrbek	950
G Bell	938

Stolen Bases

R HENDERSON	**1042**
T Raines	730
W Wilson	660
V Coleman	610
O Smith	542
B Butler	437
S Sax	437
P Molitor	412
L Smith	360
G Pettis	354
J Samuel	349
G Redus	318
R Sandberg	314
A Dawson	310
W McGee	307

Hits

R YOUNT	3025
G Brett	3005
D Winfield	2866
E Murray	2646
A Dawson	2504
C Fisk	2346
P Molitor	2281
W Randolph	2210
W Wilson	2145
O Smith	2108
D Murphy	2105
B Downing	2099
W Boggs	2098
G Carter	2092
L Whitaker	2088

Home Runs

D WINFIELD	432
E Murray	414
A Dawson	399
D Murphy	398
C Fisk	375
J Clark	340
G Carter	324
L Parrish	316
G Brett	298
D Strawberry	285
B Downing	275
C Ripken	273
K Hrbek	258
T Brunansky	255
G Bell	252

Strikeouts

D MURPHY	1733
D Winfield	1503
L Parrish	1442
J Clark	1441
C Fisk	1375
A Dawson	1349
R Yount	1257
J Barfield	1234
E Murray	1224
R Deer	1210
J Samuel	1208
B Downing	1127
D Strawberry	1119
W Wilson	1098
C Davis	1087

AB per HR

M McGWIRE	14.2
C Fielder	14.3
J Canseco	15.6
F McGriff	15.7
D Strawberry	16.0
R Deer	16.4
J Gonzalez	17.1
E Davis	17.2
K Mitchell	18.2
A Belle	18.4
D Tartabull	18.9
K Maas	18.9
G Davis	19.1
D Justice	19.3
J Buhner	19.7

Doubles

G BRETT	634
R Yount	558
D Winfield	493
E Murray	462
A Dawson	444
W Boggs	422
C Fisk	421
P Molitor	405
G Carter	371
C Ripken	369
D Mattingly	363
B Downing	360
T Wallach	360
A Trammell	356
L Whitaker	353

Walks

R HENDERSON	1286
J Clark	1262
W Randolph	1243
B Downing	1197
E Murray	1147
D Winfield	1126
G Brett	1057
L Whitaker	1047
W Boggs	1004
D Murphy	981
O Smith	949
T Raines	939
R Yount	922
B Butler	857
G Carter	848

K/BB Ratio

W BOGGS	0.47
M Scioscia	0.54
W Randolph	0.54
O Smith	0.55
T Gwynn	0.58
K Oberkfell	0.65
M Grace	0.67
C Knoblauch	0.68
M LaValliere	0.69
J Reed	0.71
D Magadan	0.71
R Henderson	0.72
T Raines	0.72
M Greenwell	0.74
B Butler	0.79

GDP/GDP Opp

D VALLE	26.3
A Belle	27.4
R Milligan	27.9
J Franco	27.9
B Harper	28.1
R Gonzales	28.1
T Pena	28.3
F Fermin	29.2
T Steinbach	29.9
F Thomas	30.1
G Petralli	30.5
C Martinez	30.6
P Borders	31.5
S Bradley	31.7
R Jordan	32.6

Triples

W WILSON	142
G Brett	134
R Yount	123
B Butler	99
T Raines	96
A Dawson	94
P Molitor	86
J Samuel	85
D Winfield	83
W McGee	83
A Van Slyke	82
A Griffin	78
T Gwynn	75
T Fernandez	70
R Sandberg	67

Intentional Walks

G BRETT	220
E Murray	201
D Winfield	163
D Murphy	158
W Boggs	150
A Dawson	135
T Raines	131
T Gwynn	128
J Clark	127
H Baines	127
C Davis	118
D Strawberry	116
P Guerrero	115
D Mattingly	113
B Bonds	113

SB Success %

E DAVIS	87.5
T Raines	85.2
M Grissom	84.7
H Cotto	84.4
W Wilson	83.3
B Larkin	81.8
V Coleman	81.6
L Dykstra	81.5
R Henderson	81.3
O Smith	80.8
G Redus	80.1
K Gibson	79.8
M Felder	79.4
A Van Slyke	79.4
R Alomar	79.3

AB per RBI

C FIELDER	4.9
J Canseco	5.0
M McGwire	5.1
F Thomas	5.2
A Belle	5.2
D Strawberry	5.3
D Tartabull	5.4
E Davis	5.5
J Gonzalez	5.6
K Mitchell	5.7
D Justice	5.7
J Clark	5.8
K Hrbek	5.8
F McGriff	5.8
E Murray	5.8

1992 American League Active Career Pitching Leaders

Wins

N RYAN	319
B Blyleven	287
J Morris	237
F Tanana	233
C Hough	202
B Welch	199
D Martinez	193
D Eckersley	181
J Candelaria	177
D Stieb	174
M Flanagan	167
F Viola	163
R Sutcliffe	155
R Clemens	152
D Stewart	146

Losses

N RYAN	287
B Blyleven	250
F Tanana	219
C Hough	191
J Morris	168
D Martinez	156
D Eckersley	145
F Bannister	143
M Flanagan	143
M Moore	142
F Viola	137
R Honeycutt	135
D Stieb	132
B Welch	129
R Sutcliffe	125

Saves

J REARDON	357
L Smith	355
G Gossage	308
D Righetti	251
D Eckersley	239
J Franco	226
T Henke	220
D Smith	216
B Thigpen	200
D Jones	164
J Howell	153
R McDowell	149
M Williams	143
D Plesac	133
R Myers	131
G Olson	131

Shutouts

N RYAN	61
B Blyleven	60
F Tanana	34
R Clemens	34
D Stieb	30
B Welch	28
J Morris	27
O Hershiser	23
B Hurst	23
D Martinez	23
D Gooden	21
D Eckersley	20
M Flanagan	19
C Leibrandt	18
R Sutcliffe	18

Games

G GOSSAGE	927
J Reardon	811
C Hough	803
N Ryan	794
L Smith	787
D Eckersley	740
B Blyleven	692
B McClure	684
J Orosco	657
D Lamp	639
D Righetti	637
C Lefferts	614
D Smith	609
L Andersen	606
F Tanana	606

Games Started

N RYAN	760
B Blyleven	685
F Tanana	584
J Morris	477
D Martinez	442
B Welch	426
D Stieb	405
M Flanagan	404
C Hough	385
F Viola	376
F Bannister	363
D Eckersley	361
J Candelaria	356
M Moore	354
S Sanderson	353

CG Freq

J MORRIS	0.36
B Blyleven	0.35
R Clemens	0.33
N Ryan	0.29
D Eckersley	0.28
C Hough	0.28
B Saberhagen	0.27
D Stieb	0.25
M Flanagan	0.25
J McDowell	0.25
F Tanana	0.24
D Martinez	0.24
B Hurst	0.24
T Candiotti	0.24
T Mulholland	0.24

Innings Pitched

N RYAN	5320.1
B Blyleven	4969.1
F Tanana	3984.0
J Morris	3530.2
C Hough	3482.1
D Martinez	3159.2
D Eckersley	2971.1
B Welch	2856.0
D Stieb	2823.0
M Flanagan	2770.0
F Viola	2577.0
J Candelaria	2506.2
R Sutcliffe	2464.1
F Bannister	2387.2
B Hurst	2366.2

Batters Faced

N RYAN	22284
B Blyleven	20491
F Tanana	16769
J Morris	14782
C Hough	14779
D Martinez	13190
D Eckersley	12213
B Welch	11885
D Stieb	11737
M Flanagan	11684
F Viola	10796
R Sutcliffe	10466
J Candelaria	10274
F Bannister	10187
B Hurst	9968

Home Runs Allowed

B BLYLEVEN	430
F Tanana	420
J Morris	357
C Hough	346
N Ryan	316
D Eckersley	307
F Bannister	291
D Martinez	286
F Viola	271
M Flanagan	251
B Hurst	249
J Candelaria	243
S Sanderson	239
B Welch	232
B Gullickson	230

Walks Allowed

N RYAN	2755
C Hough	1542
B Blyleven	1322
J Morris	1258
F Tanana	1200
D Stieb	1003
R Sutcliffe	975
M Langston	942
B Welch	935
D Martinez	926
M Moore	910
M Flanagan	890
D Stewart	861
F Bannister	846
B Witt	796

Strikeouts

N RYAN	5668
B Blyleven	3701
F Tanana	2657
J Morris	2275
C Hough	2171
D Eckersley	2118
R Clemens	1873
B Welch	1862
M Langston	1805
F Bannister	1723
F Viola	1722
D Martinez	1693
D Gooden	1686
B Hurst	1656
J Candelaria	1656

Earned Run Average

Player, Team	IP	ER	ERA
D SMITH	809.2	240	2.67
R Clemens	2031.0	631	2.80
J Orosco	875.2	276	2.84
L Smith	1067.1	339	2.86
O Hershiser	1805.0	576	2.87
G Gossage	1714.1	559	2.93
A Pena	969.1	318	2.95
D Gooden	1919.2	638	2.99
J Reardon	1061.0	360	3.05
D Cone	1267.0	437	3.10
J Magrane	805.0	278	3.11
D Drabek	1494.1	517	3.11
L Andersen	901.2	312	3.11
R McDowell	796.1	278	3.14
S Fernandez	1471.0	518	3.17

Winning Percentage

Player, Team	W	L	W%
D GOODEN	142	66	.683
R Clemens	152	72	.679
D Cone	84	51	.622
B Welch	199	129	.607
J Smiley	76	51	.598
J Candelaria	177	119	.598
J Key	116	81	.589
O Hershiser	116	82	.586
D Drabek	99	70	.586
T Browning	113	80	.585
J Morris	237	168	.585
D Stewart	146	106	.579
B Walk	92	67	.579
B Saberhagen	113	83	.577
D Stieb	174	132	.569
J Franco	58	44	.569

Opposition Batting

Player, Team	AB	H	AVG
N RYAN	19025	3869	.203
S Fernandez	5318	1092	.205
R Johnson	2958	649	.219
J Orosco	3201	718	.224
J DeLeon	6217	1397	.225
R Clemens	7537	1703	.226
D Cone	4685	1059	.226
G Gossage	6195	1404	.227
C Hough	12871	2963	.230
T Belcher	3820	881	.231
J Berenguer	4460	1034	.232
J Reardon	3955	917	.232
L Smith	3942	919	.233
D Gooden	7137	1664	.233
J Smoltz	3644	852	.234

Hits Per 9 Innings

Player, Team	IP	H	H/9
N RYAN	5320.1	3869	6.54
S Fernandez	1471.0	1092	6.68
R Johnson	818.0	649	7.14
G Gossage	1714.1	1404	7.37
J Orosco	875.2	718	7.38
J DeLeon	1697.0	1397	7.41
D Cone	1267.0	1059	7.52
R Clemens	2031.0	1703	7.55
C Hough	3482.1	2963	7.66
T Belcher	1033.2	881	7.67
J Berenguer	1205.2	1034	7.72
L Smith	1067.1	919	7.75
J Reardon	1061.0	917	7.78
D Smith	809.2	700	7.78
D Gooden	1919.2	1664	7.80

Homeruns Per 9 Innings

Player, Team	IP	HR	HR/9
J MAGRANE	805.0	32	0.36
R McDowell	796.1	33	0.37
D Smith	809.2	34	0.38
B Swift	923.2	43	0.42
D Gooden	1919.2	98	0.46
O Hershiser	1805.0	94	0.47
D Righetti	1286.0	73	0.51
D Jackson	1478.1	84	0.51
G Maddux	1442.0	82	0.51
Z Smith	1485.1	85	0.52
L Andersen	901.2	52	0.52
M Gubicza	1651.2	97	0.53
L Smith	1067.1	63	0.53
N Ryan	5320.1	316	0.53
K Brown	875.2	53	0.54

Baserunners Per 9 Innings

Player, Team	IP	BR	BR/9
R CLEMENS	2031.0	2308	10.23
S Fernandez	1471.0	1693	10.36
B Saberhagen	1758.0	2024	10.36
D Eckersley	2971.1	3489	10.57
D Drabek	1494.1	1764	10.62
D Gooden	1919.2	2270	10.64
J Smiley	1095.0	1304	10.72
J Candelaria	2506.2	2993	10.75
T Belcher	1033.2	1238	10.78
O Hershiser	1805.0	2171	10.82
J Key	1695.2	2052	10.89
J Reardon	1061.0	1284	10.89
C Lefferts	1027.2	1248	10.93
B Smith	1761.2	2144	10.95
D Cone	1267.0	1551	11.02

Strikeouts per 9 Innings

Player, Team	IP	K	K/9
N RYAN	5320.1	5668	9.59
R Johnson	818.0	818	9.00
L Smith	1067.1	1050	8.85
D Cone	1267.0	1227	8.72
S Fernandez	1471.0	1377	8.42
R Clemens	2031.0	1873	8.30
B Witt	1173.0	1076	8.26
D Gooden	1919.2	1686	7.90
M Langston	2072.2	1805	7.84
M Davis	1042.2	908	7.84
J Orosco	875.2	759	7.80
J Rijo	1287.1	1096	7.66
J DeLeon	1697.0	1422	7.54
G Gossage	1714.1	1433	7.52
M Perez	971.0	791	7.33

Walks per 9 Innings

Player, Team	IP	BB	BB/9
B TEWKSBURY	784.1	136	1.56
B Saberhagen	1758.0	358	1.83
G Swindell	1256.2	267	1.91
D Eckersley	2971.1	679	2.06
B Wegman	1175.2	271	2.07
J Candelaria	2506.2	583	2.09
J Key	1695.2	404	2.14
B Smith	1761.2	421	2.15
B Gullickson	2285.0	553	2.18
C Bosio	1190.0	289	2.19
T Mulholland	857.2	215	2.26
S Sanderson	2227.2	571	2.31
D Drabek	1494.1	387	2.33
D Schmidt	902.1	237	2.36
B Blyleven	4969.1	1322	2.39

Strikeout to Walk Ratio

Player, Team	K	BB	K/BB
R CLEMENS	1873	552	3.39
G Swindell	894	267	3.35
B Saberhagen	1174	358	3.28
D Eckersley	2118	679	3.12
D Gooden	1686	575	2.93
J Candelaria	1656	583	2.84
B Blyleven	3701	1322	2.80
D Cone	1227	460	2.67
L Smith	1050	402	2.61
C Bosio	749	289	2.59
E Hanson	577	225	2.56
S Sanderson	1443	571	2.53
A Pena	743	301	2.47
J Reardon	838	345	2.43
S Fernandez	1377	567	2.43

1992 American League Bill James Leaders

Top Game Scores of the Year

Pitcher	Date	Opp	IP	H	R	ER	BB	K	SC
Johnson R, Sea	9/16	Cal	9.0	1	1	0	1	15	97
Mussina, Bal	7/17	Tex	9.0	1	0	0	1	10	94
Tapani, Min	6/24	Cal	9.0	2	0	0	0	10	93
Clemens, Bos	4/12	Cle	9.0	2	0	0	3	12	92
McDonald, Bal	4/9	Cle	9.0	2	0	0	1	9	91

Top Game Scores of the Year

Pitcher	Date	Opp	IP	H	R	ER	BB	K	SC
Fernandez A, Ch	5/4	Mil	9.0	1	0	0	1	7	91
Appier, KC	7/23	Cle	10.0	2	0	0	1	4	91
Darwin, Bos	8/30	Cal	9.0	1	1	0	1	9	91
Nagy, Cle	8/8	Bal	9.0	1	0	0	2	7	90

Offensive Winning %

F THOMAS, ChA	.815
E Martinez, Sea	.791
M McGwire, Oak	.781
D Tartabull, NYA	.757
R Alomar, Tor	.733
P Molitor, Mil	.724
D Winfield, Tor	.717
K Griffey Jr, Sea	.716
S Mack, Min	.715
K Puckett, Min	.704

Power/Speed Number

B ANDERSON, Bal	30.1
D White, Tor	23.3
R Henderson, Oak	22.9
S Mack, Min	19.8
G Vaughn, Mil	18.2
K Puckett, Min	17.9
J Carter, Tor	17.7
P Molitor, Mil	17.3
C Curtis, Cal	16.2
E Martinez, Sea	15.8

Tough Losses

M PEREZ	13
J Abbott	9
M Langston	7
J McDowell	7
E Hanson	7
R Clemens	6
B Wegman	6
K Tapani	6
7 Pitchers with	5

Runs Created

F THOMAS, ChA	141
B Anderson, Bal	117
P Molitor, Mil	115
E Martinez, Sea	115
S Mack, Min	113
K Puckett, Min	113
R Alomar, Tor	111
D Winfield, Tor	109
M McGwire, Oak	109
C Baerga, Cle	105

Secondary Average

M McGWIRE, Oak	.507
D Tartabull, NYA	.468
M Tettleton, Det	.451
F Thomas, ChA	.431
B Anderson, Bal	.395
L Whitaker, Det	.366
J Canseco, Tex	.353
R Milligan, Bal	.349
R Alomar, Tor	.340
D Winfield, Tor	.340

Slow Hooks

Indians	22
Blue Jays	20
Brewers	19
Angels	18
Mariners	15
Orioles	13
Yankees	13
Red Sox	12
White Sox	10
Tigers	10
Rangers	9
Royals	8
Athletics	7
Twins	3

Isolated Power

M McGWIRE, Oak	.317
J Gonzalez, Tex	.269
J Carter, Tor	.235
M Tettleton, Det	.230
K Griffey Jr, Sea	.227
D Tartabull, NYA	.223
A Belle, Cle	.217
C Fielder, Det	.214
F Thomas, ChA	.213
J Canseco, Tex	.212

Cheap Wins

T LEARY	6
J MORRIS	6
M Moore	4
K McCaskill	4
J McDowell	4
K Tapani	4
B Gullickson	3
C Hough	3
R Darling	3
K Brown	3
M Perez	3
J Doherty	3

Quick Hooks

Royals	45
Athletics	29
Tigers	22
Red Sox	21
Angels	18
Mariners	18
Orioles	16
Indians	16
Brewers	16
Twins	14
Rangers	11
Blue Jays	10
Yankees	9
White Sox	8

1992 National League Bill James Leaders

Top Game Scores of the Year

Pitcher	Date	Opp	IP	H	R	ER	BB	K	SC
Gross K, LA	5/12	Mon	9.0	3	0	0	0	13	94
Bielecki, Atl	4/16	LA	9.0	2	0	0	1	9	91
Smoltz, Atl	6/24	SF	9.0	2	0	0	2	10	91
Gross K, LA	8/17	SF	9.0	0	0	0	2	6	91
Glavine, Atl	4/7	Hou	9.0	2	0	0	2	9	90

Top Game Scores of the Year

Pitcher	Date	Opp	IP	H	R	ER	BB	K	SC
Cone, NYN	4/28	Hou	9.0	2	0	0	4	11	90
Hurst, SD	5/18	NYN	9.0	1	0	0	2	7	90
Drabek, Pit	6/30	StL	9.0	3	0	0	0	9	90
Fernandez S, NY	7/24	SD	9.0	3	0	0	0	9	90
Saberhagen, NY	4/29	Hou	9.0	3	0	0	1	9	89

Offensive Winning %

B BONDS, Pit	.896
D Daulton, Phi	.806
G Sheffield, SD	.804
F McGriff, SD	.801
J Kruk, Phi	.793
A Van Slyke, Pit	.791
R Sandberg, ChN	.765
W Clark, SF	.762
B Roberts, Cin	.748
L Walker, Mon	.740

Power/Speed Number

B BONDS, Pit	36.3
R Lankford, StL	27.1
M Grissom, Mon	23.7
R Gant, Atl	22.2
R Sandberg, ChN	20.6
L Walker, Mon	20.2
F Jose, StL	18.7
D Daulton, Phi	15.6
D Jackson, SD	15.4
R Sanders, Cin	13.7
W Clark, SF	13.7

Tough Losses

K GROSS	8
G MADDUX	8
S Fernandez	7
T Candiotti	7
D Drabek	7
D Gooden	6
J Rijo	6
F Castillo	6
9 Pitchers with	5

Runs Created

B BONDS, Pit	147
A Van Slyke, Pit	121
R Sandberg, ChN	117
G Sheffield, SD	117
F McGriff, SD	116
R Lankford, StL	107
D Hollins, Phi	106
D Daulton, Phi	106
J Kruk, Phi	102
M Grace, ChN	101
T Pendleton, Atl	101

Secondary Average

B BONDS, Pit	.647
F McGriff, SD	.454
D Daulton, Phi	.454
D Justice, Atl	.349
R Lankford, StL	.338
B Bonilla, NYN	.336
R Sandberg, ChN	.335
D Hollins, Phi	.335
G Sheffield, SD	.334
W Clark, SF	.327

Slow Hooks

Dodgers	8
Mets	8
Padres	8
Braves	6
Giants	6
Reds	5
Astros	5
Pirates	5
Phillies	4
Cardinals	4
Cubs	3
Expos	3

Isolated Power

B BONDS, Pit	.313
F McGriff, SD	.269
D Daulton, Phi	.254
G Sheffield, SD	.250
R Sandberg, ChN	.206
L Walker, Mon	.205
D Hollins, Phi	.200
D Justice, Atl	.190
R Lankford, StL	.187
B Bonilla, NYN	.183

Cheap Wins

T BROWNING	3
T BELCHER	3
K HILL	3
P HARNISCH	3
P SCHOUREK	3
D OSBORNE	3
12 Pitchers with	2

Quick Hooks

Giants	34
Astros	31
Expos	30
Pirates	28
Cubs	21
Phillies	21
Reds	20
Mets	20
Braves	18
Padres	18
Cardinals	17
Dodgers	12

Player Profiles

For those of you who enjoyed our Player Profiles section in last year's Handbook, we have some good news and some bad news. First, the bad news. Last year we spent 26 pages profiling six players. This season, we are spending just four pages on three players.

The good news, is that, in return, we have put out an entire book of player profiles! If you like what you see here, then you will absolutely love the 500+ pages of *STATS 1993 Player Profiles*, which has stat splits like the ones here for every player who appeared in the majors in 1992. To order a copy, just head to the order form in the back of this book.

But enough shameless promotion. Here we have featured a hitter, a starter and a reliever who are each undeniably among the very best in baseball. Barry Bonds will likely pick up both his second MVP award in three years and his third straight Gold Glove. Roger Clemens just turned 30 and already has won as many Cy Young Awards as Bob Gibson and Don Drysdale combined, and Gregg Olson has saved 131 games in his first four full seasons in the bigs.

For Bonds, #Pit does not refer to his Pittsburgh uniform number, but rather to the number of pitches he saw last year, and #P/PA is the average number of pitches he saw per plate appearance. GB is the number of groundballs he hit last season (outs and hits alike) and FB is the number of flies. For the two hurlers, Sup refers to run support per nine innings pitched (the number of runs scored while the pitcher was in the game, per nine innings).

Again, this is just a sampling of what is in the 1993 Player Profiles book. If you want to order a copy, well, you know what to do.

Barry Bonds — Pirates

Bats Left (flyball hitter)

	Avg	G	AB	R	H	2B	3B	HR	RBI	BB	SO	HBP	GDP	SB	CS	OBP	SLG	IBB	SH	SF	#Pit	#P/PA	GB	FB	G/F
1992 Season	.311	140	473	109	147	36	5	34	103	127	69	5	9	39	8	.456	.624	32	0	7	2352	3.84	139	189	0.74
Last Five Years	.285	747	2620	501	748	160	24	135	449	492	400	15	36	183	55	.397	.519	106	1	32	11856	3.75	830	950	0.86

1992 Season

	Avg	AB	H	2B	3B	HR	RBI	BB	SO	OBP	SLG
vs. Left	.311	222	69	19	3	13	44	55	35	.445	.599
vs. Right	.311	251	78	17	2	21	59	72	34	.465	.645
Groundball	.317	142	45	13	1	8	22	40	15	.467	.592
Flyball	.303	109	33	10	1	10	26	35	24	.480	.688
Home	.338	210	71	21	2	15	44	69	35	.498	.671
Away	.289	263	76	15	3	19	59	58	34	.418	.586
Day	.305	131	40	7	2	10	32	40	21	.469	.618
Night	.313	342	107	29	3	24	71	87	48	.451	.626
Grass	.279	147	41	8	1	9	26	28	15	.393	.531
Turf	.325	326	106	28	4	25	77	99	54	.482	.666
First Pitch	.394	66	26	8	0	4	15	25	0	.553	.697
Ahead on Count	.333	120	40	11	2	12	30	60	0	.558	.758
Behind on Count	.240	129	31	6	1	5	17	0	29	.252	.419
Two Strikes	.271	199	54	12	2	15	45	44	69	.403	.578

	Avg	AB	H	2B	3B	HR	RBI	BB	SO	OBP	SLG
Scoring Posn	.314	118	37	5	3	13	71	52	16	.508	.737
Close & Late	.253	91	23	4	2	3	10	34	17	.452	.440
None on/out	.318	129	41	13	1	6	6	25	21	.432	.574
Batting #4	.327	339	111	26	4	29	85	92	52	.468	.684
Batting #5	.273	132	36	10	1	5	18	35	15	.430	.477
Other	.000	2	0	0	0	0	0	0	0	.000	.000
April	.317	63	20	2	0	7	17	11	9	.434	.683
May	.297	101	30	9	0	6	23	20	9	.423	.564
June	.244	41	10	1	1	2	3	16	8	.456	.463
July	.313	83	26	9	3	5	19	19	14	.433	.675
August	.253	83	21	5	0	3	14	28	14	.431	.422
September/October	.392	102	40	10	1	7	33		15	.537	.833
Pre-All Star	.303	238	72	17	3	15	49	52	32	.434	.588
Post-All Star	.319	235	75	19	2	19	54	75	37	.476	.660

1992 By Position

Position	Avg	AB	H	2B	3B	HR	RBI	BB	SO	OBP	SLG	G	GS	Innings	PO	A	E	DP	Fld Pct	Rng Fctr	In Zone	Outs	Zone Rtg	MLB Zone
As lf	.312	471	147	36	5	34	103	127	67	.457	.626	139	138	1240.2	310	4	3	0	.991	2.28	351	294	.838	.809

Last Five Years

	Avg	AB	H	2B	3B	HR	RBI	BB	SO	OBP	SLG
vs. Left	.294	1003	295	70	10	50	188	170	167	.397	.533
vs. Right	.280	1617	453	90	14	85	261	322	233	.398	.511
Groundball	.294	948	279	58	8	35	129	153	139	.392	.483
Flyball	.243	580	141	28	3	39	114	120	107	.371	.503
Home	.271	1246	338	65	10	62	202	246	201	.391	.489
Away	.296	1374	410	95	14	73	247	246	199	.403	.547
Day	.277	741	205	40	6	38	117	147	123	.393	.501
Night	.289	1879	543	120	18	97	332	345	277	.399	.527
Grass	.281	723	203	45	6	31	112	110	109	.372	.486
Turf	.287	1897	545	115	18	104	337	382	291	.406	.531
First Pitch	.317	378	120	30	3	25	81	59	0	.407	.611
Ahead on Count	.333	723	241	44	9	58	159	243	0	.497	.660
Behind on Count	.250	748	187	36	4	29	113	7	196	.260	.425
Two Strikes	.214	1077	231	59	6	33	140	171	399	.323	.372

	Avg	AB	H	2B	3B	HR	RBI	BB	SO	OBP	SLG
Scoring Posn	.313	594	186	35	7	35	306	194	86	.466	.572
Close & Late	.263	457	120	26	4	12	53	102	84	.394	.416
None on/out	.288	826	238	58	9	38	36	117	120	.380	.518
Batting #1	.269	1005	270	53	12	39	107	151	155	.364	.462
Batting #5	.294	1224	360	79	8	64	251	240	183	.408	.529
Other	.302	391	118	28	4	32	91	101	62	.443	.639
April	.264	375	99	27	4	21	55	34	68	.327	.525
May	.283	466	132	23	5	26	86	82	69	.396	.521
June	.297	401	119	30	4	15	53	88	55	.422	.504
July	.322	428	138	27	7	24	96	87	61	.431	.586
August	.261	479	125	23	0	24	79	102	72	.388	.459
September/October	.287	471	135	30	4	25	80	99	75	.407	.527
Pre-All Star	.284	1380	392	90	16	67	222	226	210	.385	.518
Post-All Star	.287	1240	356	70	8	68	227	266	190	.410	.521

Batter vs. Pitcher (career)

Hits Best Against	Avg	AB	H	2B	3B	HR	RBI	BB	SO	OBP	SLG
Marvin Freeman	.571	7	4	2	0	0	0	4	0	.727	.857
Tommy Greene	.538	13	7	1	0	3	9	4	3	.611	1.308
Bill Gullickson	.467	15	7	3	1	1	4	2	0	.529	1.000
Bill Sampen	.429	7	3	0	0	2	4	4	1	.636	1.286
Andy Benes	.385	13	5	0	0	3	12	4	0	.524	1.077

Hits Worst Against	Avg	AB	H	2B	3B	HR	RBI	BB	SO	OBP	SLG
Jeff Brantley	.000	13	0	0	0	0	0	1	5	.071	.000
Ben Rivera	.000	7	0	0	0	0	1	2	0	.364	.000
Chuck McElroy	.071	14	1	1	0	0	1	1	3	.125	.143
Kent Mercker	.091	11	1	0	0	0	0	0	4	.091	.091
Charlie Leibrandt	.133	15	2	1	0	0	0	0	5	.133	.133

Roger Clemens — Red Sox

	ERA	W	L	Sv	G	GS	IP	BB	SO	Avg	H	2B	3B	HR	RBI	OBP	SLG	CG	ShO	Sup	QS	#P/S	SB	CS	GB	FB	G/F
1992 Season	2.41	18	11	0	32	32	246.2	62	208	.224	203	39	2	11	70	.279	.308	11	5	4.23	23	119	24	12	364	187	1.95
Last Five Years	2.62	92	50	0	168	168	1263.2	336	1179	.225	1047	187	25	70	364	.280	.320	53	24	4.51	124	117	100	68	1617	1120	1.44

1992 Season

	ERA	W	L	Sv	G	GS	IP	H	HR	BB	SO
Home	2.88	8	6	0	17	17	128.1	117	5	36	115
Away	1.90	10	5	0	15	15	118.1	86	6	26	93
Day	2.16	5	4	0	10	10	79.1	62	2	16	62
Night	2.53	13	7	0	22	22	167.1	143	9	46	146
Grass	2.55	14	10	0	27	27	204.1	175	7	56	181
Turf	1.70	4	1	0	5	5	42.1	28	4	6	27
April	1.38	3	2	0	5	5	39.0	25	0	9	45
May	1.76	5	1	0	6	6	51.0	33	2	8	35
June	2.43	1	2	0	5	5	37.0	35	3	14	32
July	4.00	2	2	0	5	5	36.0	31	2	12	26
August	1.90	5	1	0	6	6	47.1	40	4	8	40
September/October	3.47	2	3	0	5	5	36.1	39	0	11	30
Starter	2.41	18	11	0	32	32	246.2	203	11	62	208
Reliever	0.00	0	0	0	0	0	0.0	0	0	0	0
0-3 Days Rest	0.00	0	0	0	0	0	0.0	0	0	0	0
4 Days Rest	2.47	14	7	0	22	22	164.0	138	10	46	145
5+ Days Rest	2.29	4	4	0	10	10	82.2	65	1	16	63
Pre-All Star	2.31	9	6	0	18	18	140.0	109	5	37	120
Post-All Star	2.53	9	5	0	14	14	106.2	94	6	25	88

	Avg	AB	H	2B	3B	HR	RBI	BB	SO	OBP	SLG
vs. Left	.226	447	101	15	1	6	27	30	98	.277	.304
vs. Right	.222	460	102	24	1	5	43	32	110	.280	.311
Inning 1-6	.221	688	152	30	2	7	52	48	163	.276	.301
Inning 7+	.233	219	51	9	0	4	18	14	45	.288	.329
None on	.224	553	124	18	1	8	8	25	133	.268	.304
Runners on	.223	354	79	21	1	3	62	37	75	.295	.314
Scoring Posn	.201	209	42	12	0	0	52	26	49	.286	.258
Close & Late	.214	98	21	3	0	0	5	5	19	.274	.245
None on/out	.240	242	58	7	1	3	3	11	50	.281	.314
vs. 1st Batr (relief)	.000	0	0	0	0	0	0	0	0	.000	.000
First Inning Pitched	.252	119	30	6	1	0	10	11	29	.318	.319
First 75 Pitches	.228	545	124	22	1	5	35	36	129	.280	.299
Pitch 76-90	.190	126	24	5	1	0	5	6	26	.239	.246
Pitch 91-105	.226	106	24	8	0	2	10	7	24	.278	.358
Pitch 106+	.238	130	31	4	0	4	20	13	29	.313	.362
First Pitch	.272	114	31	6	0	3	15	4	0	.317	.404
Ahead on Count	.161	416	67	14	0	2	22	0	170	.167	.209
Behind on Count	.319	182	58	12	1	4	19	21	0	.385	.462
Two Strikes	.142	451	64	14	0	2	19	37	208	.207	.186

Last Five Years

	ERA	W	L	Sv	G	GS	IP	H	HR	BB	SO
Home	2.77	42	24	0	82	82	610.1	537	35	165	590
Away	2.46	50	26	0	86	86	653.1	510	35	171	589
Day	1.96	32	12	0	55	55	423.2	322	14	98	385
Night	2.95	60	38	0	113	113	840.0	725	56	238	794
Grass	2.77	77	45	0	144	144	1071.2	906	61	293	1036
Turf	1.76	15	5	0	24	24	192.0	141	9	43	143
April	1.73	18	4	0	26	26	203.1	134	8	44	213
May	2.70	18	9	0	30	30	237.0	168	13	57	210
June	2.86	13	11	0	27	27	195.1	197	12	55	181
July	2.61	13	8	0	29	29	217.0	182	13	66	208
August	2.91	17	8	0	30	30	216.1	192	14	62	198
September/October	2.91	13	10	0	26	26	194.2	174	10	52	169
Starter	2.62	92	50	0	168	168	1263.2	1047	70	336	1179
Reliever	0.00	0	0	0	0	0	0.0	0	0	0	0
0-3 Days Rest	3.72	2	1	0	4	4	29.0	27	2	9	30
4 Days Rest	2.73	68	37	0	124	124	926.1	789	58	259	877
5+ Days Rest	2.19	22	12	0	40	40	308.1	231	10	68	272
Pre-All Star	2.52	53	26	0	93	93	707.2	567	40	177	674
Post-All Star	2.75	39	24	0	75	75	556.0	480	30	159	505

	Avg	AB	H	2B	3B	HR	RBI	BB	SO	OBP	SLG
vs. Left	.236	2462	582	107	13	31	186	197	558	.295	.328
vs. Right	.211	2200	465	80	12	39	178	139	621	.263	.312
Inning 1-6	.226	3607	816	150	20	55	307	254	907	.281	.325
Inning 7+	.219	1055	231	37	5	15	57	82	272	.278	.306
None on	.224	2877	645	105	12	45	45	178	742	.274	.316
Runners on	.225	1785	402	82	13	25	319	158	437	.290	.328
Scoring Posn	.210	975	205	37	9	11	271	105	253	.285	.301
Close & Late	.195	560	109	22	3	5	30	52	151	.269	.271
None on/out	.225	1234	278	46	4	16	16	75	308	.274	.308
vs. 1st Batr (relief)	.000	0	0	0	0	0	0	0	0	.000	.000
First Inning Pitched	.252	635	160	29	6	8	61	53	157	.312	.354
First 75 Pitches	.230	2861	657	123	17	41	231	197	730	.284	.328
Pitch 76-90	.195	606	118	20	3	10	41	42	138	.248	.287
Pitch 91-105	.229	547	125	22	1	8	37	36	136	.279	.316
Pitch 106+	.227	648	147	22	4	11	55	61	175	.296	.324
First Pitch	.307	587	180	32	5	17	72	21	0	.337	.465
Ahead on Count	.173	2308	399	74	7	23	138	0	967	.180	.241
Behind on Count	.295	823	243	45	8	16	94	155	0	.403	.428
Two Strikes	.158	2463	389	76	7	19	126	159	1179	.212	.218

Pitcher vs. Batter (career)

Pitches Best Vs.	Avg	AB	H	2B	3B	HR	RBI	BB	SO	OBP	SLG
Ron Tingley	.000	11	0	0	0	0	0	0	5	.000	.000
Tim Teufel	.000	10	0	0	0	0	1	1	3	.083	.000
Greg Vaughn	.056	18	1	0	0	0	0	0	10	.056	.056
Mike Devereaux	.071	14	1	0	0	0	1	0	3	.071	.071
Cory Snyder	.087	23	2	0	0	0	0	0	12	.087	.087

Pitches Worst Vs.	Avg	AB	H	2B	3B	HR	RBI	BB	SO	OBP	SLG
Gary Sheffield	.533	15	8	1	0	0	2	1	1	.563	.600
Alfredo Griffin	.474	19	9	3	0	0	2	1	3	.500	.632
Ken Griffey Jr	.407	27	11	5	0	1	5	5	3	.500	.704
Bill Spiers	.357	14	5	1	1	1	1	0	4	.357	.786
Eddie Murray	.346	26	9	2	0	2	3	4	2	.433	.654

	ERA	W	L	Sv	G	GS	IP	BB	SO	Avg	H	2B	3B	HR	RBI	OBP	SLG	GF	IR	IRS	Hld	SvOp	SB	CS	GB	FB	G/F
1992 Season	2.05	1	5	36	60	0	61.1	24	58	.211	46	4	1	3	17	.287	.280	56	31	5	0	44	10	0	84	43	1.95
Career (1988-1992)	2.36	17	19	131	270	0	305.1	140	303	.219	244	33	3	9	103	.308	.279	176	148	38	3	159	52	4	370	273	1.36

1992 Season

	ERA	W	L	Sv	G	GS	IP	H	HR	BB	SO		Avg	AB	H	2B	3B	HR	RBI	BB	SO	OBP	SLG
Home	1.38	1	1	17	31	0	32.2	20	2	12	28	vs. Left	.195	113	22	4	0	0	8	9	30	.252	.230
Away	2.83	0	4	19	29	0	28.2	26	1	12	30	vs. Right	.229	105	24	0	1	3	9	15	28	.322	.333
Day	2.86	0	3	10	21	0	22.0	23	1	9	26	Inning 1-6	.000	0	0	0	0	0	0	0	0	.000	.000
Night	1.60	1	2	26	39	0	39.1	23	2	15	32	Inning 7+	.211	218	46	4	1	3	17	24	58	.287	.280
Grass	1.33	1	2	31	50	0	54.0	32	2	21	51	None on	.232	112	26	3	1	2	13	29	.312	.330	
Turf	7.36	0	3	5	10	0	7.1	14	1	3	7	Runners on	.189	106	20	1	0	1	15	11	29	.261	.226
April	2.35	0	1	3	7	0	7.2	8	1	4	9	Scoring Posn	.175	63	11	1	0	0	13	7	18	.250	.190
May	1.15	0	1	9	13	0	15.2	14	1	5	13	Close & Late	.228	162	37	4	1	3	17	19	41	.306	.321
June	1.86	1	0	8	9	0	9.2	3	1	4	11	None on/out	.222	45	10	2	1	0	0	6	10	.314	.311
July	6.75	0	2	4	8	0	5.1	8	0	4	5	vs. 1st Batr (relief)	.245	53	13	2	1	1	3	6	15	.322	.377
August	2.19	0	1	7	13	0	12.1	10	0	2	9	First Inning Pitched	.225	191	43	4	1	2	16	22	46	.302	.288
September/October	0.84	0	0	5	10	0	10.2	3	0	5	11	First 15 Pitches	.222	167	37	3	1	2	12	19	40	.298	.287
Starter	0.00	0	0	0	0	0	0.0	0	0	0	0	Pitch 16-30	.167	48	8	1	0	1	5	5	16	.245	.250
Reliever	2.05	1	5	36	60	0	61.1	46	3	24	58	Pitch 31-45	.333	3	1	0	0	0	0	0	2	.333	.333
0 Days rest	1.35	0	1	11	14	0	13.1	11	0	7	13	Pitch 46+	.000	0	0	0	0	0	0	0	0	.000	.000
1 or 2 Days rest	2.96	1	3	14	26	0	27.1	19	2	9	27	First Pitch	.333	30	10	0	0	0	1	0	0	.333	.333
3+ Days rest	1.31	0	1	11	20	0	20.2	16	1	8	18	Ahead on Count	.108	102	11	2	0	0	4	0	51	.108	.127
Pre-All Star	2.06	1	3	21	33	0	35.0	30	3	15	36	Behind on Count	.349	43	15	1	1	2	8	11	0	.473	.558
Post-All Star	2.05	0	2	15	27	0	26.1	16	0	9	22	Two Strikes	.106	104	11	1	0	1	4	13	58	.205	.144

Career (1988-1992)

	ERA	W	L	Sv	G	GS	IP	H	HR	BB	SO		Avg	AB	H	2B	3B	HR	RBI	BB	SO	OBP	SLG
Home	1.94	12	2	55	135	0	148.2	102	5	74	145	vs. Left	.187	556	104	12	0	2	42	71	146	.262	.219
Away	2.76	5	17	76	135	0	156.2	142	4	66	145	vs. Right	.251	557	140	21	3	7	61	69	157	.334	.338
Day	3.83	1	10	38	73	0	84.2	82	6	35	78	Inning 1-6	.313	16	5	2	0	0	4	2	2	.389	.438
Night	1.79	16	9	93	197	0	220.2	162	3	105	225	Inning 7+	.218	1097	239	31	3	9	99	138	301	.307	.276
Grass	1.94	14	10	113	222	0	250.0	172	7	113	252	None on	.230	544	125	21	2	6	6	52	146	.301	.309
Turf	4.23	3	9	18	48	0	55.1	72	2	27	51	Runners on	.209	569	119	12	1	3	97	88	157	.314	.250
April	1.87	3	1	11	31	0	43.1	33	2	17	33	Scoring Posn	.198	363	72	7	1	1	92	69	109	.323	.231
May	1.40	2	2	22	45	0	57.2	39	2	26	64	Close & Late	.230	673	155	18	3	7	78	94	183	.325	.297
June	2.77	4	4	29	45	0	48.2	34	2	18	54	None on/out	.194	232	45	5	2	4	4	24	57	.275	.284
July	3.19	1	6	24	46	0	48.0	49	0	29	53	vs. 1st Batr (relief)	.210	243	51	6	1	3	21	23	59	.281	.280
August	3.11	2	2	22	46	0	46.1	42	2	21	37	First Inning Pitched	.232	896	208	25	2	6	90	103	239	.313	.285
September/October	2.05	5	4	23	57	0	61.1	47	1	29	62	First 15 Pitches	.237	769	182	24	2	6	65	75	202	.306	.296
Starter	0.00	0	0	0	0	0	0.0	0	0	0	0	Pitch 16-30	.174	270	47	7	0	2	30	49	81	.303	.222
Reliever	2.36	17	19	131	270	0	305.1	244	9	140	303	Pitch 31-45	.212	66	14	2	1	1	7	13	19	.342	.318
0 Days rest	2.57	4	5	40	62	0	66.2	60	1	27	64	Pitch 45+	.125	8	1	0	0	0	1	3	1	.333	.125
1 or 2 Days rest	2.30	9	9	62	127	0	140.2	107	6	74	140	First Pitch	.271	140	38	2	0	1	16	13	0	.335	.307
3+ Days rest	2.30	4	5	29	81	0	98.0	77	2	39	99	Ahead on Count	.152	538	82	14	2	3	32	1	261	.160	.203
Pre-All Star	2.10	9	9	69	135	0	162.2	121	6	69	166	Behind on Count	.324	225	73	12	1	3	28	60	0	.462	.427
Post-All Star	2.65	8	10	62	135	0	142.2	123	3	71	137	Two Strikes	.146	575	84	12	2	4	40	64	303	.235	.195

Pitcher vs. Batter (career)

Pitches Best Vs.	Avg	AB	H	2B	3B	HR	RBI	BB	SO	OBP	SLG	Pitches Worst Vs.	Avg	AB	H	2B	3B	HR	RBI	BB	SO	OBP	SLG
Ruben Sierra	.000	10	0	0	0	0	0	1	3	.091	.000	Mark McGwire	.444	9	4	0	0	1	4	3	3	.583	.778
Ellis Burks	.000	10	0	0	0	0	0	1	3	.091	.000	Danny Tartabull	.417	12	5	0	0	0	4	2	4	.500	.417
Pete O'Brien	.071	14	1	0	0	0	1	0	3	.071	.071												
Don Mattingly	.091	11	1	0	0	0	0	2	1	.231	.091												
Steve Sax	.154	13	2	0	0	0	0	0	0	.154	.154												

1993 Player Projections

Hello, and welcome to the fourth annual player projections.

John Dewan and I started the player projections after the 1989 season, projecting what players might do in 1990. Our initial operating position was we were just doing this for the heck of it, without making any claims to accuracy. After doing this for three years, we're in a very different position: we know perfectly well that we're going to be completely wrong most of the time.

No, actually, we were initially surprised by how often we were able to project a player's stats with stunning accuracy, and this is still true. I could show you literally a hundred cases from last year's book where we projected the player's 1992 performance with uncanny precision. We would also like to report that, having modified the system in a few ways, it is more accurate now than it was then.

We would like to report this, but unfortunately it isn't true; our overall accuracy last year was almost exactly what it was in the first year, and there is no reason at all to think it will be any better. In fact, statistically it will be worse next year, but that's another story. Before I complain about the problems we're going to have next year, I get to brag about last year. It's in my contract.

We had 43 projections last year with similarity scores of 950 or better, up from 41 such projections in 1991, and 174 projections with similarity scores above 900, up from 165 in 1991. A score of 950 or more means that there is a very high degree of similarity between what we had projected the player to do, and what he actually did. This one scores at 950 exactly, Mark Grace:

	G	AB	R	H	2B	3B	HR	RBI	BB	SO	SB	Avg
Projected	155	578	79	170	30	3	11	75	74	50	11	.294
Actual	158	603	72	185	37	5	9	79	72	36	6	.307

We missed his batting average by 13 points and his home run total by two, but basically, Grace did what we said he would do. There were 43 projections which met or surpassed that standard. In fact, I'll challenge you to sort some of those out. The chart below represents either what these players actually did in 1992, or what we had projected they would do. Which is it? You're a baseball fan; is this live, or is it Memorex?

	G	AB	R	H	2B	3B	HR	RBI	BB	SO	SB	Avg
Leo Gomez	147	487	69	124	23	2	19	74	72	100	2	.255
Tony Gwynn	144	567	74	180	27	5	5	63	45	24	22	.317
B Hatcher	115	389	46	99	19	2	4	32	25	43	18	.254

Those are projections; the chart below compares them to what the players actually did:

Leo Gomez

	G	AB	R	H	2B	3B	HR	RBI	BB	SO	SB	Avg
Projected	147	487	69	124	23	2	19	74	72	100	2	.255
Actual	137	468	62	124	24	0	17	64	63	78	2	.265

Tony Gwynn

	G	AB	R	H	2B	3B	HR	RBI	BB	SO	SB	Avg
Projected	144	567	74	180	27	5	5	63	45	24	22	.317
Actual	128	520	77	165	27	3	6	41	46	16	3	.317

Billy Hatcher

	G	AB	R	H	2B	3B	HR	RBI	BB	SO	SB	Avg
Projected	115	389	46	99	19	2	4	32	25	43	18	.254
Actual	118	409	47	102	19	2	3	33	22	52	4	.249

We are especially proud of the projection for Leo Gomez, because Gomez had not played regularly before, and had hit only .233 in 391 at bats in 1991. By diagnosing his minor league statistics, we were able to project his 1992 performance accurately.

This happened in other cases, including some for players who had almost no playing time prior to 1992. A few cases of first-year players who were projected accurately:

Carlos Hernandez

	G	AB	R	H	2B	3B	HR	RBI	BB	SO	SB	Avg
Projected	60	140	13	38	7	0	2	13	5	18	1	.271
Actual	69	173	11	45	4	0	3	17	11	21	0	.260

Hernandez had only 34 major league at bats before last year, with a .206 average, so this projection was based almost entirely on his minor league performance.

Todd Hundley

	G	AB	R	H	2B	3B	HR	RBI	BB	SO	SB	Avg
Projected	115	382	40	92	17	2	6	42	36	75	2	.239
Actual	123	358	32	75	17	0	7	32	19	76	3	.209

Hundley's accuracy score actually is only 923, not 950+, but it looks pretty good to me.

Jose Offerman

	G	AB	R	H	2B	3B	HR	RBI	BB	SO	SB	Avg
Projected	143	485	70	125	9	3	2	38	60	93	38	.258
Actual	149	534	67	139	20	8	1	30	57	98	23	.260

Although Offerman had hit only .181 in 81 games prior to last year, we were able to project his performance accurately by factoring in what he had done at Albuquerque. We missed his doubles, but we were extremely close on all of the most important elements — batting average, home runs, RBI, runs scored, walks, strikeouts. The similarity in this case scores at 937.

Dean Palmer

	G	AB	R	H	2B	3B	HR	RBI	BB	SO	SB	Avg
Projected	145	490	64	113	24	4	25	74	36	172	5	.231
Actual	152	541	74	124	25	0	26	72	62	154	10	.229

Palmer also had hit .181 in 97 games prior to last year. Again, by factoring in minor league performance, we were able to peg his triple crown statistics almost perfectly, although his strikeout/walk ratio was quite a bit better than we had anticipated, so the overall similarity again fell short of the 950 standard.

Reggie Sanders

	G	AB	R	H	2B	3B	HR	RBI	BB	SO	SB	Avg
Projected	140	470	63	128	19	6	11	57	40	112	16	.272
Actual	116	385	62	104	26	6	12	36	48	98	16	.270

That one actually scores at only 914, but I think it would be hard to describe it as a failure. I'll deal with the failures in a moment, I promise.

Scott Servais

	G	AB	R	H	2B	3B	HR	RBI	BB	SO	SB	Avg
Projected	70	170	15	37	8	1	1	16	8	31	1	.218
Actual	77	205	12	49	9	0	0	15	11	25	0	.239

Scott Cooper

	G	AB	R	H	2B	3B	HR	RBI	BB	SO	SB	Avg
Projected	115	275	30	73	20	1	6	30	24	44	1	.265
Actual	123	337	34	93	21	0	5	33	37	33	1	.276

All of these players were projected accurately without having significant major league experience to go on. We also had some notable success in projecting the 1992 seasons of at least a few players whose seasons were considered surprising by their teams or the public at large. Royce Clayton, who was considered a washout by the Giants, actually wasn't a long way away from our projection:

Royce Clayton

	G	AB	R	H	2B	3B	HR	RBI	BB	SO	SB	Avg
Projected	130	430	58	104	18	4	3	48	36	101	20	.242
Actual	98	321	31	72	7	4	4	24	26	63	8	.224

While Paul Sorrento, who was a pleasant surprise to the Indians, was no surprise to us:

Paul Sorrento

	G	AB	R	H	2B	3B	HR	RBI	BB	SO	SB	Avg
Projected	135	418	56	116	31	1	19	75	58	83	1	.278
Actual	140	458	52	123	24	1	18	60	51	89	0	.269

In the case of Sorrento, we would have been even more accurate if we had known that he was going to play in Cleveland. We had him projected to play in Minnesota.

Going the other way, Andres Galarraga was a major disappointment to St. Louis — but did essentially what we had said he would do:

Andres Galarraga

	G	AB	R	H	2B	3B	HR	RBI	BB	SO	SB	Avg
Projected	101	361	42	91	20	1	12	50	27	98	6	.252
Actual	95	325	38	79	14	2	10	39	11	69	5	.243

Jerry Browne may have been a shock to the A.L. West, but what he did was no surprise to us:

Jerry Browne

	G	AB	R	H	2B	3B	HR	RBI	BB	SO	SB	Avg
Projected	100	275	42	76	14	3	2	27	34	26	6	.276
Actual	111	324	43	93	12	2	3	40	40	40	3	.287

While Devon White may not have hit as well as Toronto expected following an MVP-candidate season in '91 — but we had pegged his relapse, in all modestly, almost perfectly:

Devon White

	G	AB	R	H	2B	3B	HR	RBI	BB	SO	SB	Avg
Projected	159	588	85	146	26	6	14	55	47	130	34	.248
Actual	153	641	98	159	26	7	17	60	47	133	37	.248

God, aren't we smart. Well, there is another side to the story, but as I say, I'll get to that. The easiest projections are for veteran players who do exactly what they normally do, like Tony Gwynn, which we ran before; we're always on target for Tony because he always hits .317. A few veteran players who had good projections in '92 include:

Greg Gagne

	G	AB	R	H	2B	3B	HR	RBI	BB	SO	SB	Avg
Projected	145	424	52	106	23	5	8	44	24	77	11	.250
Actual	146	439	53	108	23	0	7	39	19	83	6	.246

Sid Bream

	G	AB	R	H	2B	3B	HR	RBI	BB	SO	SB	Avg
Projected	110	350	36	88	20	1	11	55	44	54	5	.251
Actual	125	372	30	97	25	1	10	61	46	51	6	.261

Henry Cotto

	G	AB	R	H	2B	3B	HR	RBI	BB	SO	SB	Avg
Projected	111	304	41	79	12	1	6	31	17	45	16	.260
Actual	108	294	42	76	11	1	5	27	14	49	23	.259

Andre Dawson

	G	AB	R	H	2B	3B	HR	RBI	BB	SO	SB	Avg
Projected	145	525	64	140	27	4	21	89	35	79	9	.267
Actual	143	542	60	150	27	2	22	90	30	70	6	.277

Barry Larkin

	G	AB	R	H	2B	3B	HR	RBI	BB	SO	SB	Avg
Projected	142	521	80	156	24	4	12	63	48	50	23	.299
Actual	140	533	76	162	32	6	12	78	63	58	15	.304

Mark Lewis

	G	AB	R	H	2B	3B	HR	RBI	BB	SO	SB	Avg
Projected	129	417	49	110	22	2	4	52	21	50	5	.264
Actual	122	413	44	109	21	0	5	30	25	69	4	.264

Fred McGriff

	G	AB	R	H	2B	3B	HR	RBI	BB	SO	SB	Avg
Projected	155	550	94	156	26	2	35	97	112	126	5	.284
Actual	152	531	79	152	30	4	35	104	96	108	8	.286

Tom Pagnozzi

	G	AB	R	H	2B	3B	HR	RBI	BB	SO	SB	Avg
Projected	140	460	38	121	22	2	6	54	36	66	8	.263
Actual	139	485	33	121	26	3	7	44	28	64	2	.249

Danny Tartabull

	G	AB	R	H	2B	3B	HR	RBI	BB	SO	SB	Avg
Projected	129	447	63	125	27	2	22	78	64	122	4	.280
Actual	123	421	72	112	19	0	25	85	103	115	2	.266

Other players who had projections of similar accuracy to these shown above include Roberto

Alomar, Jay Bell, Albert Belle, Rafael Belliard, Mike Benjamin, Damon Berryhill, Craig Biggio, Daryl Boston, Glenn Braggs, Jay Buhner, Alex Cole, Joey Cora, Billy Doran, Cecil Espy, Tony Fernandez, Mike Fitzgerald, Darrin Fletcher, Travis Fryman, Dave Gallagher, Jim Gantner, Dan Gladden, Tom Goodwin, Ken Griffey Jr., Alfredo Griffin, Mel Hall, Brian Harper, Thomas Howard, Rex Hudler, Pete Incaviglia, Chris James, Stan Javier, Gregg Jefferies, Lance Johnson, Chuck Knoblauch, Gene Larkin, Mike LaValliere, Manuel Lee, Greg Litton, Carlos Martinez, Lloyd McClendon, Willie McGee, Orlando Merced, Mickey Morandini, Pedro Munoz, Eddie Murray, Al Newman, John Olerud, Greg Olson, Joe Orsulak, John Orton, Gary Pettis, Tony Phillips, Jamie Quirk, Tim Raines, Rafael Ramirez, Willie Randolph, Gary Redus, Kevin Reimer, Harold Reynolds, Billy Ripken, Ivan Rodriguez, Dick Schofield, Dwight Smith, Sammy Sosa, Terry Steinbach, Franklin Stubbs, Robby Thompson, Ron Tingley, Dave Valle, Gary Varsho, Robin Ventura and Robin Yount.

The one most accurate projection of the year, you ask? You've read these articles before. The one most accurate projection of the year, according to the similarity score, was for David Howard:

David Howard

	G	AB	R	H	2B	3B	HR	RBI	BB	SO	SB	Avg
Projected	65	178	15	40	4	1	1	16	14	33	3	.225
Actual	74	219	19	49	6	2	1	18	15	43	3	.224

Obviously it's an accurate projection, although why it scores as the most accurate projection (981), I couldn't tell you. Sometimes the similarity scores method seems a little arbitrary.

Normally, at this point, there are a couple of players who have exactly nailed their extra-base hit totals, or their triple crown stats — in other words, a guy that we projected to hit .274 with 19 homers, 66 RBI who actually did, or a guy we projected to hit 33 doubles, 9 triples, 8 home runs who actually did exactly that. I don't find one of those this year, so I'll turn my attention to the big blunders.

Well, out of time, got to go. No, I wouldn't do that. The spectacular errors of the season are always in one of two categories: those we projected to play well who didn't, and those who played well when we didn't expect it. In the latter category, you have to start with Gary Sheffield:

Gary Sheffield

	G	AB	R	H	2B	3B	HR	RBI	BB	SO	SB	Avg
Projected	125	490	62	132	25	2	13	62	44	38	20	.269
Actual	146	557	87	184	34	3	33	100	48	40	5	.330

Actually, we had projected Sheffield to play fairly well; he just played a lot better than fairly well. Then there's Darren Daulton:

Darren Daulton

	G	AB	R	H	2B	3B	HR	RBI	BB	SO	SB	Avg
Projected	121	366	41	81	15	1	10	44	56	64	4	.221
Actual	145	485	80	131	32	5	27	109	88	103	11	.270

While Brady Anderson, whom we might have expected to play well a few years ago, like the Carter administration, finally did:

Brady Anderson

	G	AB	R	H	2B	3B	HR	RBI	BB	SO	SB	Avg
Projected	159	623	100	169	28	10	21	80	98	98	53	.271
Actual	85	179	28	42	8	2	2	18	28	32	10	.235

This is always more impressive when you miss on the playing time, too, as we did for Brady. In the case of Eric Anthony, it looks bad because we under-projected his playing time, but actually we had projected his performance level fairly accurately:

Eric Anthony

	G	AB	R	H	2B	3B	HR	RBI	BB	SO	SB	Avg
Projected	60	188	23	46	9	0	6	25	15	53	4	.245
Actual	137	440	45	105	15	1	19	80	38	98	5	.239

If we had given him 135 games instead of 60, it would have been a great projection. Eric Karros, incidentally, hit much less than we had projected for him (.288 to .257), but will win the Rookie of the Year Award anyway because he got full-time play. Mike Bordick, we missed on about as badly as we could have missed:

Mike Bordick

	G	AB	R	H	2B	3B	HR	RBI	BB	SO	SB	Avg
Projected	81	224	23	48	7	0	1	18	22	29	2	.214
Actual	154	504	62	151	19	4	3	48	40	59	12	.300

Then there are the guys who were supposed to be good, but weren't, like Kalvoski:

Kal Daniels

	G	AB	R	H	2B	3B	HR	RBI	BB	SO	SB	Avg
Projected	142	473	77	130	25	2	21	81	80	111	8	.275
Actual	83	212	21	51	11	0	6	25	22	54	0	.241

and Kalvoski's American League cousin, Mike Greenwell:

Mike Greenwell

	G	AB	R	H	2B	3B	HR	RBI	BB	SO	SB	Avg
Projected	154	589	83	181	33	5	16	90	59	42	12	.307
Actual	49	180	16	42	2	0	2	18	18	19	2	.233

Greenwell's projection, as bad as it is, isn't the worst for a Boston outfielder. That distinction belongs to the unique, the fabulous, the just-be-glad-he-wasn't-on-YOUR-team, Phil Plantier:

Phil Plantier

	G	AB	R	H	2B	3B	HR	RBI	BB	SO	SB	Avg
Projected	143	545	92	153	27	2	32	91	81	155	4	.281
Actual	108	349	46	86	19	0	7	30	44	83	2	.246

And then of course all of the big-injury guys, like Darryl Strawberry and the Chicago shortstops (Dunston and Guillen), all of whom failed to do what we had projected for them because they weren't playing. Fortunately, we are spared the opportunity to do an ugly contest, because the way the system works is, if a guy is projected to play but doesn't play at all, that gets a zero, so our projections for guys like Joel Skinner and Beau Allred, even though we didn't really expect much from them, are technically our worst projections, scoring at zero.

When I write this article I always wind up writing about last year's projections and how they turned out, when I suppose what you are most interested in is next year's projections and how they are going to turn out. That's a hard thing to write about at this point, but we are dealing with a special problem this year: expansion. Two special problems, if Bud Selig gets his way and gets to have a big monster strike.

Anyway, expansion is a real riddle for us, and will no doubt cause a number of erroneous projections for 1993. What a player hits is colored to a very significant extent by where he plays, what park he is in. A guy who hits .290 in one park might hit .260 in another. The differences can be greater than that.

So we can project Brian Hunter in Atlanta, but he could wind up playing every day in Miami, where (it is assumed) the ball will not travel, so rather than hitting twenty home runs he might hit eight. Or Brent Mayne; we project him to hit five home runs, playing in Kansas City, but if he winds up in Denver he might hit 15.

Then you throw into the mix the Giants, who don't know where they are going to be playing; that's another curve ball. We're always in a position of projecting some players into unknown parks, and many of these projections will work out fine anyway, as they did last year for Danny Tartabull, Alex Cole, Andres Galarraga, Jerry Browne, Pete Incaviglia and Dick Schofield, all of whom did what we said they would under conditions that we couldn't possibly have guessed. It's a question of chances; when a player changes teams, like Gary Sheffield a year ago or Terry Pendleton two years ago, the chance increases substantially that his numbers will jump or dump. We've got more of that to deal with than normal..

Also, as a rule, if we get a player's playing time projected accurately, everything else will fall into place. Well, that's tough enough normally — but this time it's impossible. We're doing this in October; we don't know who is going to go where in the expansion draft, and can't guess at what the teams will do to compensate for their losses. There are any number of players (Francisco Cabrera) about whom one might say that he could bat 575 times next year — or 15.

So we're not looking to improve our average similarity score next year. One improvement that we are trying to make involves pitchers; John Dewan is trying to develop a method to project the future performance of pitchers. At this point, that is completely his baby, and I'll let him explain it, but after we get some initial results I will work with him to try to move it along to the next stage.

Well, that about does it; I could cite another hundred players that we were completely wrong about, but I don't imagine you'd be interested. Our original caveat still applies, in a somewhat tempered form: let the Rotisserie Player beware. We don't really claim to know what anybody is going to do next year. We're just havin' fun with it.

— *Bill James*

310

Introduction to the 1993 Pitcher Projections

First of all, let me start by saying what I have been saying for the last several years: **it's impossible to project pitching statistics.**

The reason for this is that pitchers are ridiculously inconsistent. Just when you think you've found a consistent pitcher . . . boom! . . . he throws in a year totally out of proportion to everything else he's ever done. Dave Stewart is an example here. He won 20 games for four straight years. I doubled the size of my list of consistently good starting pitchers after that year from one (Roger Clemens) to two. Then Stewart goes 11 and 11 with a 5.18 ERA in 1991. So my list went back to a one-man list. This year I'm going to go out on the limb and double the size again. I'm adding Greg Maddux.

There are examples the other way too. Sometimes a superlative pitching year comes completely out of the blue. How did Curt Schilling suddenly learn how to pitch this year? Kevin Brown came from virtually nowhere. Bill Wegman's 1991?

We're setting out to do the impossible. The way I look at it is that there must be **some** predictability here. Let's look at the extremes. Roger Clemens is predictable. He's simply awesome year after year. Scott Bailes is predictable. He's simply awful year after year. Frank Tanana is predictable. He's mediocre year after year. There's also a limit as to how long a pitcher can be effective. We all get old, and so do pitchers; at some point they can't throw anymore. Age is an obvious limiting factor. Relief pitchers as a whole are much more predictable. You can count on most closers getting a good number of saves year after year.

What we've done here is to start with the things that we do know about pitchers. We've taken all these factors and tried to formulize them. Here are some of the factors we've considered (in no special order): age, career and recent trends in hits allowed, home runs allowed, walks allowed, team run support based on batter projections, managerial usage tendencies (especially involving the use of relief pitchers), expected team wins, and subjective pitcher evaluations.

The most surprising thing that we discovered in our analysis is that age is a **much** less important factor for pitchers than it is for hitters. Batting performance for major league players tends to rise, in general, for a player in his early and mid-twenties. It then peaks at age 26 and 27. Following that there's a gradual decline, followed by a sharp decline as the player gets toward the mid-thirties. Pitchers have no such pattern.

How well did we do? We looked at how well we would have done in previous years and we were pleasantly surprised. We think we can do a lot better with a lot more work, but we felt good enough about them to let you have a look. Tell us what you think!

Our experimental, first-year stab at pitcher projections follows the batter projections. Our initial attempt only includes those pitchers with at least 500 innings or 150 games in their career. We intentionally limited our analysis in this way mainly because we didn't have the time to properly analyze the minor league performance of young pitchers. That's the next project for Bill and me.

— John Dewan

Projections for 1993 Batters

Batter	Age	Avg	G	AB	R	H	2B	3B	HR	RBI	BB	SO	SB	CS	OBP	SLG
Abner,Shawn	27	.235	94	204	23	48	11	1	2	17	12	35	2	2	.278	.328
Alexander,Manny	22	.238	42	126	16	30	5	1	1	11	4	17	7	4	.262	.317
Alicea,Luis	27	.253	97	261	29	66	13	4	3	24	28	33	3	4	.325	.368
Alomar,Roberto	25	.301	157	611	94	184	30	6	10	72	69	69	45	11	.372	.419
Alomar Jr,Sandy	27	.265	115	392	39	104	20	2	6	45	21	42	3	3	.303	.372
Alou,Moises	26	.263	127	388	51	102	19	3	7	48	30	55	15	6	.316	.381
Amaral,Rich	31	.265	78	234	33	62	13	1	1	16	29	39	13	5	.346	.342
Amaro,Ruben	28	.257	85	280	35	72	16	2	2	24	27	34	12	6	.322	.350
Anderson,Brady	29	.252	161	611	86	154	18	5	12	64	97	103	46	16	.355	.357
Anthony,Eric	25	.244	142	487	56	119	20	1	18	71	44	124	10	5	.307	.400
Arias,Alex	25	.255	74	204	24	52	11	0	2	17	16	19	4	2	.309	.338
Azocar,Oscar	28	.237	59	152	14	36	7	1	2	14	4	12	2	1	.256	.336
Backman,Wally	33	.260	108	131	22	34	13	1	1	13	19	23	2	1	.353	.397
Baerga,Carlos	24	.293	161	629	89	184	31	1	16	89	42	80	5	3	.337	.421
Bagwell,Jeff	25	.298	161	567	80	169	32	5	18	90	78	89	8	6	.383	.467
Baines,Harold	34	.269	135	420	56	113	24	2	14	70	61	66	1	1	.362	.436
Barberie,Bret	25	.266	122	353	44	94	16	2	5	42	57	63	10	5	.368	.365
Barfield,Jesse	33	.226	122	421	55	95	18	2	18	62	63	131	3	2	.326	.406
Barnes,Skeeter	36	.263	84	224	33	59	11	0	4	27	18	29	11	5	.318	.366
Bass,Kevin	34	.248	98	290	31	72	15	2	7	32	21	46	6	4	.299	.386
Batiste,Kim	25	.239	82	272	25	65	11	2	2	21	6	42	8	5	.255	.316
Bell,Derek	24	.267	110	420	58	112	15	4	10	53	35	72	18	8	.323	.393
Bell,George	33	.264	151	599	69	158	29	2	23	98	33	85	4	3	.302	.434
Bell,Jay	27	.262	159	611	92	160	30	5	12	59	61	104	10	6	.329	.386
Bell,Juan	25	.237	98	291	37	69	10	2	3	24	23	67	6	5	.293	.316
Belle,Albert	26	.279	156	559	75	156	27	2	32	107	40	108	6	4	.327	.506
Belliard,Rafael	31	.217	97	184	16	40	4	1	0	12	11	32	1	1	.262	.250
Beltre,Esteban	25	.218	46	101	10	22	3	0	0	8	6	18	2	1	.262	.248
Benavides,Freddie	27	.220	70	205	17	45	7	0	1	16	9	33	2	2	.252	.268
Benzinger,Todd	30	.249	93	265	24	66	14	2	4	32	16	46	3	3	.292	.362
Bergman,Dave	40	.235	60	115	11	27	4	0	2	12	18	16	1	1	.338	.322
Berry,Sean	27	.248	138	483	56	120	21	3	11	57	36	97	10	8	.301	.373
Berryhill,Damon	29	.226	107	314	28	71	16	0	9	38	20	69	2	2	.272	.363
Bichette,Dante	29	.240	130	429	45	103	22	2	11	51	21	94	13	7	.276	.378
Biggio,Craig	27	.280	159	590	80	165	27	3	7	48	72	84	29	12	.358	.371
Blankenship,Lance	29	.226	125	301	49	68	15	1	3	29	55	59	16	6	.346	.312
Blauser,Jeff	27	.265	144	437	64	116	24	3	13	56	57	85	6	6	.350	.423
Boggs,Wade	35	.315	137	517	77	163	35	3	7	53	79	42	1	1	.406	.435
Bonds,Barry	28	.285	149	502	102	143	33	5	28	103	115	75	46	13	.418	.538
Bonilla,Bobby	30	.273	144	528	87	144	31	5	20	87	68	78	4	3	.356	.464
Boone,Bret	24	.251	137	502	62	126	21	1	16	66	51	120	10	10	.320	.392
Borders,Pat	30	.252	136	409	38	103	22	2	11	49	24	65	1	1	.293	.396
Bordick,Mike	27	.240	155	550	60	132	14	1	3	46	51	72	8	6	.304	.285
Boston,Daryl	30	.249	126	301	45	75	16	3	8	33	33	50	15	8	.323	.402
Bournigal,Rafael	27	.241	40	112	9	27	2	0	0	8	4	7	1	1	.267	.259
Braggs,Glenn	30	.254	105	299	41	76	15	2	9	41	37	57	8	4	.336	.408
Branson,Jeff	26	.245	77	216	19	53	9	1	2	20	13	37	3	3	.288	.324
Bream,Sid	32	.254	126	350	33	89	23	1	10	56	41	50	5	3	.332	.411
Brett,George	40	.270	109	411	47	111	24	3	8	48	38	56	4	2	.332	.401
Brewer,Rod	27	.232	50	151	14	35	7	0	3	19	13	21	0	0	.293	.338

312

Projections for 1993 Batters

Batter	Age	Avg	G	AB	R	H	2B	3B	HR	RBI	BB	SO	SB	CS	OBP	SLG
Briley,Greg	28	.262	111	286	32	75	18	2	5	26	22	40	14	6	.315	.392
Brito,Bernardo	29	.244	62	119	15	29	10	2	5	19	6	30	0	0	.280	.487
Brooks,Hubie	36	.245	79	265	31	65	13	1	7	37	19	50	2	2	.296	.381
Brosius,Scott	26	.245	49	147	19	36	8	0	4	18	13	22	3	2	.306	.381
Browne,Jerry	27	.269	123	383	57	103	17	3	4	42	50	39	6	5	.353	.360
Brunansky,Tom	32	.235	143	477	52	112	25	2	16	68	61	94	4	5	.322	.396
Buechele,Steve	31	.238	143	517	57	123	19	2	15	66	51	105	2	2	.306	.369
Buhner,Jay	28	.245	151	550	74	135	22	2	27	88	73	156	2	3	.334	.440
Burks,Ellis	28	.275	122	407	59	112	27	4	14	57	37	66	7	7	.336	.464
Bush,Randy	34	.240	97	171	17	41	12	1	4	21	19	30	1	1	.316	.392
Butler,Brett	36	.275	149	556	86	153	19	6	3	35	93	70	37	20	.379	.347
Cabrera,Francisco	26	.263	129	380	38	100	19	1	15	57	18	64	1	1	.296	.437
Calderon,Ivan	31	.278	107	381	52	106	24	2	12	53	37	50	20	11	.342	.446
Caminiti,Ken	30	.259	146	536	60	139	25	2	9	61	48	83	8	5	.320	.364
Candaele,Casey	32	.236	122	301	25	71	14	2	2	24	28	36	6	3	.301	.316
Canseco,Jose	28	.259	139	509	94	132	24	1	33	101	76	149	18	9	.356	.505
Canseco,Ozzie	28	.238	87	143	20	34	9	0	7	20	18	44	0	0	.323	.448
Carreon,Mark	29	.248	90	234	25	58	9	0	7	27	15	34	2	1	.293	.376
Carter,Joe	33	.251	155	606	81	152	30	3	26	103	43	105	17	7	.300	.439
Castillo,Braulio	25	.241	85	174	25	42	15	1	4	21	13	43	4	2	.294	.408
Cedeno,Andujar	23	.236	81	271	25	64	13	3	6	32	13	69	4	4	.271	.373
Chamberlain,Wes	27	.251	104	355	38	89	19	1	9	46	22	59	10	7	.294	.386
Cianfrocco,Archi	26	.259	54	158	18	41	6	1	3	21	8	40	2	1	.295	.367
Clark,Jack	37	.216	77	227	32	49	12	1	9	34	55	72	1	1	.369	.396
Clark,Jerald	29	.238	121	374	34	89	18	2	11	45	21	83	2	1	.278	.385
Clark,Phil	25	.255	57	102	11	26	8	1	2	13	6	14	1	1	.296	.412
Clark,Will	29	.301	150	561	84	169	33	5	23	97	65	90	8	4	.374	.501
Clayton,Royce	23	.234	112	367	44	86	13	4	4	35	29	68	15	8	.290	.324
Cochrane,Dave	30	.247	89	255	24	63	13	1	5	28	14	56	1	1	.286	.365
Colbrunn,Greg	23	.266	118	436	41	116	28	0	11	62	13	90	4	2	.287	.406
Cole,Alex	27	.260	105	334	48	87	7	3	1	20	40	58	28	13	.340	.308
Coleman,Vince	31	.258	98	356	51	92	12	4	3	25	37	62	48	15	.328	.340
Coles,Darnell	31	.238	68	151	18	36	10	1	4	17	9	23	1	1	.281	.397
Colon,Cris	24	.256	88	246	26	63	11	2	2	31	6	49	3	3	.274	.341
Conine,Jeff	27	.282	107	341	50	96	23	4	8	49	44	64	5	4	.364	.443
Cooper,Scott	25	.267	125	419	41	112	21	1	8	43	37	58	1	1	.327	.379
Cora,Joey	28	.255	100	231	37	59	10	2	1	18	25	21	13	7	.328	.329
Cordero,Wil	21	.262	151	516	61	135	20	2	9	50	40	135	8	6	.315	.360
Costo,Tim	24	.252	55	147	17	37	9	1	5	18	11	36	2	2	.304	.429
Cotto,Henry	32	.260	91	235	31	61	9	1	4	22	13	36	16	3	.298	.357
Curtis,Chad	24	.262	154	543	71	142	22	2	11	57	55	77	45	22	.329	.370
Cuyler,Milt	24	.251	127	426	67	107	12	5	5	39	43	81	32	13	.320	.338
Daniels,Kal	29	.265	82	249	36	66	14	1	10	42	36	61	2	1	.358	.450
Dascenzo,Doug	29	.246	123	281	34	69	13	2	2	23	25	25	11	7	.307	.327
Daulton,Darren	31	.235	142	473	62	111	21	1	17	70	78	92	8	2	.343	.391
Davis,Chili	33	.254	136	464	63	118	23	2	15	65	78	98	4	4	.362	.409
Davis,Eric	31	.252	90	294	42	74	12	1	13	47	43	77	15	3	.347	.432
Davis,Glenn	32	.250	95	328	41	82	16	1	14	49	35	54	4	2	.322	.433
Dawson,Andre	38	.269	131	484	53	130	23	3	18	78	28	69	7	3	.309	.440
Decker,Steve	27	.242	86	240	21	58	11	0	5	30	17	39	1	1	.292	.350

313

Projections for 1993 Batters

Batter	Age	Avg	G	AB	R	H	2B	3B	HR	RBI	BB	SO	SB	CS	OBP	SLG
Deer,Rob	32	.214	131	439	62	94	17	1	25	64	71	155	3	3	.324	.428
DeShields,Delino	24	.276	146	557	84	154	21	6	8	56	79	121	54	24	.366	.379
Devereaux,Mike	30	.257	156	614	76	158	25	5	18	76	47	96	16	12	.310	.402
DiSarcina,Gary	25	.247	142	478	47	118	15	1	3	39	22	52	8	6	.280	.301
Donnels,Chris	27	.249	69	201	22	50	9	0	3	22	35	37	3	2	.360	.338
Doran,Billy	35	.255	123	376	49	96	18	2	6	36	63	47	11	6	.362	.362
Duncan,Mariano	30	.259	123	444	56	115	18	4	9	44	18	77	14	6	.288	.378
Dunston,Shawon	30	.261	148	522	65	136	25	5	12	56	20	77	22	8	.288	.397
Dykstra,Lenny	30	.291	99	385	65	112	20	3	6	36	57	33	28	6	.382	.405
Easley,Damion	23	.226	72	287	28	65	9	0	2	23	17	39	10	6	.270	.279
Eisenreich,Jim	34	.273	106	322	35	88	18	2	3	32	23	33	7	6	.322	.370
Elster,Kevin	28	.224	88	210	22	47	12	1	5	24	23	34	1	1	.300	.362
Espy,Cecil	30	.244	87	176	22	43	9	3	1	17	15	37	8	4	.304	.347
Fariss,Monty	25	.258	72	221	29	57	12	3	4	28	30	68	2	3	.347	.394
Felder,Mike	30	.257	136	331	47	85	9	4	3	26	28	28	20	8	.315	.335
Felix,Junior	25	.264	119	425	60	112	18	5	9	56	33	97	11	8	.317	.393
Fermin,Felix	29	.252	112	326	31	82	9	1	1	26	23	18	3	2	.301	.294
Fernandez,Tony	31	.268	153	600	80	161	29	6	5	46	61	68	23	15	.336	.362
Fielder,Cecil	29	.255	159	596	94	152	21	1	41	121	84	161	0	0	.347	.500
Finley,Steve	28	.276	161	580	73	160	23	7	6	51	48	63	37	14	.331	.371
Fisk,Carlton	45	.236	69	208	20	49	10	1	6	27	22	41	2	1	.309	.380
Fitzgerald,Mike	32	.225	78	178	19	40	8	1	4	22	27	32	3	2	.327	.348
Flaherty,John	25	.219	62	183	16	40	8	0	2	13	13	20	0	0	.270	.295
Fletcher,Darrin	26	.231	87	251	20	58	10	0	3	27	15	30	0	1	.274	.307
Fletcher,Scott	34	.247	124	384	40	95	17	2	3	46	32	43	6	5	.305	.326
Fox,Eric	29	.223	53	139	19	31	5	1	1	12	13	26	4	3	.289	.295
Franco,Julio	31	.289	120	470	76	136	21	2	8	52	61	65	24	8	.371	.394
Frye,Jeff	26	.283	140	508	82	144	30	6	4	42	58	67	11	10	.357	.390
Fryman,Travis	24	.265	158	603	76	160	35	2	23	93	42	135	9	7	.313	.444
Gaetti,Gary	34	.237	113	409	41	97	19	1	12	52	23	75	3	2	.278	.377
Gagne,Greg	31	.245	138	400	45	98	22	3	7	39	23	75	9	8	.286	.368
Galarraga,Andres	32	.250	87	292	32	73	16	1	9	38	17	74	4	3	.291	.404
Gallagher,Dave	32	.267	56	101	11	27	7	0	1	11	9	13	2	2	.327	.366
Gallego,Mike	32	.229	110	314	36	72	10	1	5	27	37	47	4	4	.311	.315
Gant,Ron	28	.264	156	568	94	150	29	5	26	87	59	98	35	15	.333	.470
Garcia,Carlos	25	.258	141	461	56	119	20	5	8	50	24	78	17	8	.295	.375
Gardner,Jeff	29	.247	114	373	40	92	12	1	0	28	49	40	3	2	.334	.284
Gedman,Rich	33	.218	40	101	7	22	6	0	2	11	11	22	0	0	.295	.337
Gilkey,Bernard	26	.264	126	413	55	109	19	4	6	37	52	48	25	13	.346	.373
Girardi,Joe	28	.260	91	265	21	69	11	1	2	23	16	32	3	2	.302	.332
Gladden,Dan	35	.257	96	346	44	89	15	2	4	32	23	49	11	5	.304	.347
Gomez,Leo	26	.254	151	548	76	139	23	2	22	77	79	104	2	2	.348	.423
Gonzales,Rene	31	.235	99	293	37	69	7	0	4	26	35	40	5	3	.317	.300
Gonzalez,Juan	23	.263	154	578	80	152	32	3	33	104	37	135	2	2	.307	.500
Gonzalez,Luis	25	.255	121	396	49	101	23	5	12	58	32	72	12	7	.311	.429
Goodwin,Tom	24	.237	96	198	25	47	8	1	1	13	15	32	14	7	.291	.303
Grace,Mark	29	.291	160	608	78	177	32	3	10	74	71	48	8	4	.365	.403
Grebeck,Craig	28	.257	136	389	43	100	21	2	6	44	49	61	2	3	.340	.368
Greene,Willie	21	.261	147	518	57	135	26	4	20	80	53	139	6	13	.329	.442
Greenwell,Mike	29	.298	146	543	71	162	30	4	13	77	54	39	10	7	.362	.440

314

Projections for 1993 Batters

Batter	Age	Avg	G	AB	R	H	2B	3B	HR	RBI	BB	SO	SB	CS	OBP	SLG
Griffey Jr,Ken	23	.314	157	567	85	178	36	3	26	96	62	74	15	8	.382	.526
Griffin,Alfredo	36	.217	64	175	16	38	7	2	1	14	11	26	2	1	.263	.297
Grissom,Marquis	26	.272	157	581	84	158	28	6	10	55	41	80	71	15	.320	.392
Grotewold,Jeff	27	.240	87	121	14	29	11	1	3	16	12	26	0	0	.308	.421
Gruber,Kelly	31	.249	110	410	50	102	17	2	15	59	30	66	10	5	.300	.410
Guerrero,Juan	26	.261	67	184	22	48	11	1	5	24	12	38	3	3	.306	.413
Guerrero,Pedro	37	.286	86	231	21	66	14	1	6	40	20	33	1	1	.343	.433
Guillen,Ozzie	29	.267	150	501	54	134	20	5	2	53	19	37	17	15	.294	.339
Gwynn,Chris	28	.261	82	207	26	54	7	2	4	26	12	32	1	0	.301	.372
Gwynn,Tony	33	.315	136	542	72	171	25	5	5	57	42	20	10	8	.365	.408
Hall,Mel	32	.275	137	480	56	132	25	2	15	67	21	46	1	1	.305	.429
Hamilton,Darryl	28	.287	145	487	72	140	18	4	3	59	43	43	32	12	.345	.359
Hansen,Dave	24	.247	135	381	41	94	14	1	5	39	45	53	3	3	.326	.328
Harper,Brian	33	.292	134	476	53	139	24	1	9	61	20	25	2	1	.321	.403
Harris,Lenny	28	.278	142	407	49	113	16	1	2	34	32	29	15	7	.330	.337
Hatcher,Billy	32	.255	96	314	35	80	16	2	3	22	19	35	10	6	.297	.347
Hayes,Charlie	28	.251	147	514	49	129	23	1	13	60	25	89	4	4	.286	.375
Hayes,Von	34	.243	76	247	35	60	13	1	5	30	37	43	8	4	.342	.364
Henderson,Dave	34	.246	105	325	42	80	19	1	11	41	30	73	3	2	.310	.412
Henderson,Rickey	34	.273	130	451	94	123	22	2	14	48	99	65	56	14	.404	.424
Hernandez,Carlos	26	.270	79	204	18	55	8	0	3	19	10	26	2	2	.304	.353
Hill,Glenallen	28	.254	95	303	42	77	14	2	12	39	23	68	9	5	.307	.432
Hoiles,Chris	28	.254	129	418	57	106	19	1	17	51	56	81	2	2	.342	.426
Hollins,Dave	27	.260	157	574	87	149	23	3	21	79	76	102	7	4	.346	.420
Horn,Sam	29	.236	86	233	28	55	11	0	13	37	32	69	0	0	.328	.451
Hosey,Steve	24	.254	40	118	15	30	6	1	3	14	8	25	4	3	.302	.398
Howard,Dave	26	.218	116	344	29	75	8	2	2	29	25	62	6	4	.271	.270
Howard,Thomas	28	.264	110	326	37	86	18	2	3	30	24	63	14	9	.314	.359
Hrbek,Kent	33	.276	127	435	60	120	23	1	18	74	68	50	4	3	.374	.457
Hudler,Rex	32	.245	55	102	13	25	5	1	2	8	5	16	6	5	.280	.373
Huff,Mike	29	.265	56	136	22	36	7	2	2	16	19	24	5	3	.355	.390
Hulett,Tim	33	.247	69	162	18	40	9	1	3	16	14	40	1	1	.307	.370
Hulse,David	25	.258	109	337	40	87	12	1	1	16	13	91	12	9	.286	.309
Hundley,Todd	24	.231	119	347	35	80	17	1	6	36	28	68	2	1	.288	.337
Hunter,Brian	25	.235	136	442	53	104	18	1	20	65	36	85	3	3	.293	.416
Huson,Jeff	28	.239	132	331	49	79	14	2	2	28	44	44	13	5	.328	.311
Incaviglia,Pete	29	.250	97	300	34	75	16	1	13	44	27	83	2	2	.312	.440
Jackson,Darrin	29	.244	153	508	61	124	17	2	18	58	29	96	10	4	.285	.392
Jacoby,Brook	33	.267	118	367	40	98	18	1	8	48	35	50	1	2	.331	.387
Jaha,John	27	.284	130	497	84	141	25	1	20	85	57	107	13	7	.357	.459
James,Chris	30	.258	72	213	21	55	11	2	5	25	12	31	2	2	.298	.399
Javier,Stan	29	.246	131	284	42	70	12	3	2	24	34	49	13	5	.327	.331
Jefferies,Gregg	25	.284	151	577	77	164	33	3	14	73	49	35	19	7	.340	.425
Jefferson,Reggie	24	.273	117	374	50	102	20	2	11	50	26	79	1	1	.320	.425
Johnson,Howard	32	.244	133	483	75	118	23	1	21	76	66	96	30	11	.335	.427
Johnson,Lance	29	.274	159	576	72	158	16	8	2	50	33	46	36	17	.314	.340
Jones,Tim	30	.218	53	119	9	26	5	0	1	9	11	21	4	2	.285	.286
Jordan,Brian	26	.233	39	116	13	27	4	1	2	11	6	21	4	2	.270	.336
Jordan,Ricky	28	.271	112	354	39	96	22	1	7	48	13	53	2	1	.297	.398
Jorgensen,Terry	26	.267	115	345	40	92	24	2	6	38	32	45	1	1	.329	.400

Projections for 1993 Batters

Batter	Age	Avg	G	AB	R	H	2B	3B	HR	RBI	BB	SO	SB	CS	OBP	SLG
Jose,Felix	28	.276	145	526	63	145	27	2	13	71	42	102	21	11	.329	.409
Joyner,Wally	31	.276	159	601	73	166	33	1	18	84	63	63	6	3	.345	.424
Justice,Dave	27	.265	140	483	79	128	25	2	23	80	79	94	8	7	.368	.468
Karkovice,Ron	29	.239	121	309	42	74	15	1	10	39	29	74	5	3	.305	.392
Karros,Eric	25	.276	151	551	68	152	31	1	18	78	42	95	4	6	.327	.434
Kelly,Pat	25	.251	112	347	47	87	18	3	6	34	23	63	15	6	.297	.372
Kelly,Roberto	28	.278	158	580	80	161	27	2	15	67	42	109	37	12	.326	.409
Kent,Jeff	25	.244	126	431	64	105	27	1	12	58	51	100	13	7	.324	.394
King,Jeff	28	.237	142	511	63	121	20	2	16	67	36	64	6	5	.287	.378
Kirby,Wayne	29	.262	41	103	14	27	4	1	1	9	6	10	6	3	.303	.350
Knoblauch,Chuck	24	.293	156	584	94	171	26	7	3	59	75	44	29	10	.373	.377
Koslofski,Kevin	26	.263	107	323	38	85	11	4	4	34	30	64	7	7	.326	.359
Kreuter,Chad	28	.214	75	196	26	42	9	1	3	19	32	45	1	1	.325	.316
Kruk,John	32	.293	146	492	69	144	22	3	12	70	77	85	7	4	.388	.423
Laker,Tim	23	.221	57	154	18	34	7	1	3	19	10	34	1	1	.268	.338
Lankford,Ray	26	.268	155	567	76	152	31	9	16	77	62	116	40	19	.340	.439
Larkin,Barry	29	.292	141	538	81	157	26	5	12	68	59	57	23	6	.362	.426
Larkin,Gene	30	.261	94	272	32	71	16	1	4	29	29	33	4	2	.332	.371
LaValliere,Mike	32	.264	112	329	26	87	14	1	3	36	45	25	2	2	.353	.340
Lee,Manuel	28	.248	139	444	49	110	13	3	4	40	38	97	6	3	.307	.318
Leius,Scott	27	.257	118	319	41	82	16	2	3	29	32	48	5	4	.325	.348
Lemke,Mark	27	.241	149	439	48	106	18	2	6	39	49	41	2	2	.318	.333
Leonard,Mark	28	.260	121	438	52	114	16	1	13	55	54	91	2	2	.341	.390
Levis,Jesse	25	.284	110	275	23	78	17	1	5	31	23	26	2	2	.339	.407
Lewis,Darren	25	.254	79	256	34	65	7	2	1	19	24	30	16	7	.318	.309
Lewis,Mark	23	.266	123	436	47	116	22	1	6	47	24	58	5	5	.304	.362
Leyritz,Jim	29	.244	77	221	27	54	11	0	5	26	27	39	1	2	.327	.362
Lind,Jose	29	.251	124	418	39	105	18	3	2	40	27	39	5	2	.297	.323
Listach,Pat	25	.266	157	567	90	151	16	5	2	48	59	127	46	17	.335	.323
Litton,Greg	28	.233	88	193	19	45	12	1	4	25	15	40	1	1	.288	.368
Livingstone,Scott	27	.272	110	345	44	94	16	0	6	43	27	44	2	2	.325	.371
Lofton,Kenny	26	.280	159	586	87	164	16	9	4	45	57	79	49	14	.344	.358
Lopez,Javier	22	.306	118	310	39	95	19	1	10	36	11	35	3	1	.330	.471
Maas,Kevin	28	.241	111	352	51	85	16	1	17	46	54	90	3	2	.342	.438
Macfarlane,Mike	29	.244	146	475	52	116	29	3	18	67	34	93	2	2	.295	.432
Mack,Shane	29	.299	154	588	93	176	21	4	17	76	58	110	24	13	.362	.435
Magadan,Dave	30	.284	121	387	53	110	19	2	4	47	73	49	1	1	.398	.375
Maldonado,Candy	32	.244	131	468	55	114	22	1	15	63	50	110	3	2	.317	.391
Manwaring,Kirt	27	.227	112	331	23	75	11	2	3	27	24	41	2	1	.279	.299
Martin,Al	25	.245	81	212	30	52	10	3	5	24	14	50	8	4	.292	.392
Martinez,Carlos	27	.279	63	197	20	55	10	1	4	28	8	29	2	2	.307	.401
Martinez,Chito	27	.252	127	432	59	109	15	2	24	62	50	134	4	4	.330	.463
Martinez,Dave	28	.277	121	393	51	109	14	5	7	39	30	52	15	10	.329	.392
Martinez,Domingo	25	.254	43	130	13	33	6	0	4	16	9	28	1	1	.302	.392
Martinez,Edgar	30	.309	146	527	89	163	33	2	14	58	75	66	5	4	.395	.459
Martinez,Tino	25	.259	156	560	69	145	28	2	17	73	65	73	3	3	.336	.407
Mattingly,Don	32	.291	136	532	67	155	34	1	14	73	38	34	1	1	.339	.438
Maurer,Rob	26	.284	148	483	68	137	36	2	18	78	69	151	2	2	.373	.478
May,Derrick	24	.275	131	418	44	115	22	1	8	54	18	48	5	5	.305	.390
Mayne,Brent	25	.250	105	324	31	81	12	1	2	37	29	43	3	3	.312	.312

Projections for 1993 Batters

Batter	Age	Avg	G	AB	R	H	2B	3B	HR	RBI	BB	SO	SB	CS	OBP	SLG
McClendon,Lloyd	34	.244	70	135	17	33	6	0	3	16	16	20	1	1	.325	.356
McGee,Willie	34	.282	130	478	62	135	22	5	4	44	34	83	17	7	.330	.374
McGriff,Fred	29	.284	155	550	88	156	26	2	34	100	105	119	6	4	.398	.524
McGwire,Mark	29	.239	149	486	80	116	21	1	32	92	101	111	1	1	.370	.484
McIntosh,Tim	28	.254	83	197	26	50	12	1	6	28	11	26	2	2	.293	.416
McLemore,Mark	28	.222	87	239	33	53	8	1	1	22	24	37	8	5	.293	.276
McRae,Brian	25	.247	135	518	67	128	22	7	6	55	32	80	17	8	.291	.351
McReynolds,Kevin	33	.257	135	474	60	122	25	2	17	68	64	54	7	4	.346	.426
Merced,Orlando	26	.254	127	398	59	101	19	4	7	50	52	71	8	5	.340	.374
Mercedes,Luis	25	.291	110	423	61	123	12	2	3	33	43	66	24	11	.356	.350
Meulens,Hensley	26	.248	136	516	73	128	17	1	18	72	51	162	8	5	.316	.390
Miller,Keith	30	.265	128	471	67	125	20	2	4	38	41	69	24	9	.324	.342
Milligan,Randy	31	.253	126	419	60	106	20	2	13	57	91	82	3	3	.386	.403
Mitchell,Kevin	31	.275	126	443	65	122	22	2	23	79	49	67	3	4	.348	.490
Molitor,Paul	36	.290	149	601	90	174	32	4	12	66	68	69	22	7	.362	.416
Morandini,Mickey	27	.257	129	432	54	111	17	5	3	31	37	67	12	4	.316	.340
Morris,Hal	28	.294	145	489	64	144	27	2	11	58	48	62	11	6	.358	.425
Munoz,Pedro	24	.288	138	458	54	132	24	3	14	69	28	85	12	7	.329	.445
Murphy,Dale	37	.248	119	371	40	92	19	1	14	55	36	82	3	1	.314	.418
Murray,Eddie	37	.271	151	520	66	141	28	1	18	85	64	71	6	3	.351	.433
Myers,Greg	27	.250	121	384	37	96	20	0	9	44	30	49	0	0	.304	.372
Naehring,Tim	26	.240	108	317	32	76	17	0	8	35	33	57	0	0	.311	.369
Natal,Bob	27	.235	59	162	17	38	8	0	4	19	13	34	0	0	.291	.358
Neel,Troy	27	.266	96	252	34	67	16	0	8	38	35	53	2	2	.355	.425
Newman,Al	33	.220	103	227	24	50	8	1	0	17	24	22	6	4	.295	.264
Newson,Warren	28	.272	66	162	24	44	7	1	4	20	33	43	4	3	.395	.401
Nieves,Melvin	21	.264	52	106	15	28	6	1	5	19	10	32	1	1	.328	.481
Nilsson,Dave	23	.285	96	323	40	92	22	2	5	46	29	28	5	4	.344	.412
Nixon,Otis	34	.273	124	366	63	100	7	1	1	21	39	44	52	18	.343	.306
Nokes,Matt	29	.251	135	406	44	102	15	1	19	60	31	54	2	2	.304	.433
O'Brien,Charlie	32	.198	54	111	10	22	6	0	1	11	11	15	0	0	.270	.279
O'Brien,Pete	35	.247	93	295	30	73	15	1	8	39	29	28	1	0	.315	.386
O'Neill,Paul	30	.250	151	517	63	129	28	1	18	75	72	100	11	7	.341	.412
Offerman,Jose	24	.258	155	550	74	142	13	4	2	40	67	105	36	19	.339	.307
Olerud,John	24	.277	149	531	75	147	29	1	21	78	86	84	1	1	.378	.454
Oliver,Joe	27	.248	136	420	36	104	21	0	11	54	35	76	2	1	.305	.376
Olson,Greg	32	.238	119	357	37	85	16	1	6	36	39	46	1	1	.313	.339
Oquendo,Jose	29	.258	98	271	26	70	9	2	1	22	47	29	1	1	.368	.317
Orsulak,Joe	31	.269	133	442	50	119	19	3	6	46	36	43	6	5	.324	.367
Ortiz,Junior	33	.254	75	169	14	43	6	0	1	16	12	16	1	2	.304	.308
Orton,John	27	.200	53	140	15	28	6	0	2	13	12	40	1	2	.263	.286
Owen,Spike	32	.233	139	424	45	99	19	4	4	31	56	51	7	5	.323	.325
Pagliarulo,Mike	33	.241	106	299	26	72	16	1	8	30	21	49	1	1	.291	.381
Pagnozzi,Tom	30	.255	145	483	36	123	22	2	5	49	34	68	6	8	.304	.340
Palmeiro,Rafael	28	.295	160	621	90	183	36	4	20	86	64	72	3	3	.361	.462
Palmer,Dean	24	.231	155	550	75	127	26	3	29	81	54	181	6	5	.300	.447
Parrish,Lance	37	.219	94	342	32	75	14	1	12	40	32	96	1	1	.286	.371
Pasqua,Dan	31	.248	94	262	34	65	13	1	10	39	36	55	1	1	.339	.420
Patterson,John	26	.252	42	139	17	35	7	2	1	12	7	19	7	3	.288	.353
Pecota,Bill	33	.244	89	238	32	58	10	1	3	22	26	35	9	4	.318	.332

317

Projections for 1993 Batters

Batter	Age	Avg	G	AB	R	H	2B	3B	HR	RBI	BB	SO	SB	CS	OBP	SLG
Pena,Geronimo	26	.258	129	496	75	128	20	5	11	50	63	116	30	14	.342	.385
Pena,Tony	36	.245	121	387	40	95	18	1	5	42	30	57	5	3	.300	.336
Pendleton,Terry	32	.279	155	595	76	166	28	3	13	78	40	69	7	4	.324	.402
Perry,Gerald	32	.246	54	114	13	28	7	0	2	15	10	15	5	3	.306	.360
Petralli,Geno	33	.247	73	146	12	36	7	1	1	13	19	23	1	0	.333	.329
Pettis,Gary	35	.215	58	121	18	26	5	1	1	8	20	37	11	5	.326	.298
Phillips,Tony	34	.254	147	559	88	142	21	3	9	55	96	91	13	8	.363	.351
Piazza,Mike	24	.280	140	415	42	116	22	2	12	51	28	76	0	2	.325	.429
Plantier,Phil	24	.276	108	337	54	93	19	1	16	51	48	88	2	2	.366	.481
Polonia,Luis	28	.299	140	528	76	158	18	7	3	43	43	60	41	21	.352	.377
Pratt,Todd	26	.254	49	118	12	30	7	0	3	16	14	25	0	0	.333	.390
Puckett,Kirby	32	.307	150	590	87	181	33	4	15	88	44	81	11	6	.355	.453
Pulliam,Harvey	25	.250	85	208	27	52	13	2	5	28	18	36	2	1	.310	.404
Quirk,Jamie	38	.224	82	183	14	41	7	0	2	19	17	36	0	0	.290	.295
Raines,Tim	33	.282	142	532	90	150	26	5	8	57	79	54	46	13	.375	.395
Ramirez,Rafael	34	.243	87	226	21	55	12	1	2	19	12	30	3	2	.282	.332
Ramsey,Fernando	27	.250	61	132	15	33	5	1	1	10	5	22	6	3	.277	.326
Randolph,Willie	38	.254	79	252	29	64	10	1	1	21	37	26	2	1	.349	.313
Ready,Randy	33	.241	53	116	17	28	7	1	2	15	22	18	1	1	.362	.371
Reboulet,Jeff	29	.225	77	200	22	45	11	1	1	19	31	27	3	2	.329	.305
Redus,Gary	36	.242	64	132	20	32	9	2	3	12	16	22	7	3	.324	.409
Reed,Darren	27	.170	70	188	19	32	8	0	8	23	13	55	0	0	.224	.340
Reed,Jody	30	.271	144	561	71	152	36	1	5	51	66	51	6	5	.348	.365
Reimer,Kevin	29	.262	155	550	58	144	31	4	18	76	48	116	3	3	.321	.431
Reynolds,Harold	32	.250	142	529	73	132	24	4	3	43	62	48	24	12	.328	.327
Ripken,Billy	28	.248	106	310	32	77	15	1	2	27	19	30	2	2	.292	.323
Ripken,Cal	32	.272	162	610	79	166	33	2	23	86	66	52	4	2	.343	.446
Rivera,Luis	29	.228	83	259	29	59	13	1	3	27	22	49	3	2	.288	.320
Roberts,Bip	29	.296	155	550	93	163	25	5	6	46	59	69	44	16	.365	.393
Rodriguez,Henry	25	.242	92	231	25	56	12	2	6	31	14	35	1	2	.286	.390
Rodriguez,Ivan	21	.268	139	474	43	127	21	1	13	58	19	73	1	1	.296	.399
Rose,Bobby	26	.249	74	269	30	67	10	2	5	31	18	44	2	1	.296	.357
Rossy,Rico	29	.228	36	114	14	26	4	0	1	9	16	13	1	2	.323	.289
Rowland,Rich	26	.249	97	261	38	65	15	0	11	41	32	55	3	2	.331	.433
Sabo,Chris	31	.265	135	502	73	133	33	2	18	64	46	64	16	8	.327	.446
Salazar,Luis	37	.244	73	209	19	51	8	1	5	22	10	31	1	1	.279	.364
Salmon,Tim	24	.258	143	538	78	139	24	1	20	74	67	175	7	8	.340	.418
Samuel,Juan	32	.250	129	448	54	112	24	6	9	47	40	105	22	10	.311	.391
Sanchez,Rey	25	.252	81	250	24	63	8	1	1	19	14	15	4	3	.292	.304
Sandberg,Ryne	33	.280	152	583	94	163	28	4	22	81	67	82	20	8	.354	.455
Sanders,Deion	25	.257	103	272	48	70	8	6	6	27	25	46	23	8	.320	.397
Sanders,Reggie	25	.284	139	521	81	148	27	7	16	62	60	117	21	10	.358	.455
Santiago,Benito	28	.265	132	475	52	126	21	2	14	66	27	79	6	7	.305	.406
Sasser,Mackey	30	.279	102	219	19	61	13	1	4	31	10	15	0	0	.310	.402
Sax,Steve	33	.270	142	560	68	151	22	3	5	43	41	40	33	11	.319	.346
Scarsone,Steve	27	.240	50	129	14	31	6	1	2	13	7	28	2	2	.279	.349
Schofield,Dick	30	.219	137	420	51	92	14	3	4	34	62	77	8	5	.320	.295
Scioscia,Mike	34	.245	61	163	14	40	8	0	3	18	20	14	2	1	.328	.350
Scott,Gary	24	.223	57	112	12	25	9	0	2	13	8	17	1	1	.275	.357
Segui,David	26	.272	96	250	28	68	13	0	2	29	26	23	2	2	.341	.348

318

Projections for 1993 Batters

Batter	Age	Avg	G	AB	R	H	2B	3B	HR	RBI	BB	SO	SB	CS	OBP	SLG
Seitzer,Kevin	31	.281	154	544	75	153	27	3	6	54	61	51	10	7	.354	.375
Servais,Scott	26	.231	73	212	17	49	8	0	1	18	10	32	1	1	.266	.283
Sharperson,Mike	31	.281	128	310	37	87	14	1	2	30	42	33	6	4	.366	.352
Sheffield,Gary	24	.294	157	568	83	167	31	2	22	86	54	43	17	11	.355	.472
Shipley,Craig	30	.234	64	154	10	36	5	0	2	13	4	23	1	1	.253	.305
Shumpert,Terry	26	.218	67	142	17	31	11	2	1	14	9	24	5	3	.265	.345
Sierra,Ruben	27	.289	156	620	89	179	35	6	23	102	52	81	13	4	.344	.476
Silvestri,Dave	25	.253	72	158	28	40	13	2	4	24	19	40	4	3	.333	.437
Slaught,Don	34	.282	97	262	24	74	18	2	4	32	25	32	1	1	.345	.412
Smith,Dwight	29	.262	117	244	30	64	16	2	4	29	20	43	8	6	.318	.393
Smith,Lonnie	37	.265	83	219	31	58	14	2	4	25	29	42	5	3	.351	.402
Smith,Ozzie	38	.268	134	492	63	132	19	2	1	37	64	35	30	8	.353	.321
Snow,J.T.	25	.273	96	264	38	72	18	1	7	37	31	40	2	1	.349	.428
Snyder,Cory	30	.235	120	374	41	88	19	1	14	49	20	103	2	2	.274	.404
Sojo,Luis	27	.255	115	381	40	97	14	1	5	33	15	27	6	6	.283	.336
Sorrento,Paul	27	.268	142	474	56	127	29	1	19	70	59	103	1	1	.349	.454
Sosa,Sammy	24	.241	138	503	70	121	20	4	14	58	33	136	30	14	.287	.380
Spiers,Bill	27	.272	135	419	63	114	14	4	6	49	28	50	15	9	.318	.368
Sprague,Ed	25	.244	79	213	23	52	11	1	7	26	16	43	1	1	.297	.404
Stairs,Matt	24	.263	73	240	28	63	14	2	4	29	21	31	6	4	.322	.388
Stankiewicz,Andy	28	.237	99	304	38	72	13	1	1	26	31	40	12	6	.307	.296
Stanley,Mike	30	.249	98	193	25	48	9	1	4	23	36	41	0	0	.367	.368
Steinbach,Terry	31	.264	131	443	43	117	20	1	10	60	31	67	2	2	.312	.381
Stevens,Lee	25	.241	128	449	46	108	23	1	13	58	38	101	3	3	.300	.383
Stillwell,Kurt	28	.250	99	328	37	82	16	3	4	34	27	45	2	2	.307	.354
Strawberry,Darryl	31	.262	83	282	46	74	14	1	16	54	39	63	6	4	.352	.489
Stubbs,Franklin	32	.228	65	193	24	44	7	1	7	25	20	44	8	4	.300	.383
Surhoff,B.J.	28	.270	146	508	61	137	22	3	6	65	41	39	13	8	.324	.360
Sveum,Dale	29	.229	74	179	21	41	11	1	3	23	19	48	1	1	.303	.352
Tackett,Jeff	27	.206	75	209	23	43	6	0	3	19	23	30	2	2	.284	.278
Tartabull,Danny	30	.277	135	476	74	132	27	2	25	88	84	129	4	3	.386	.500
Tatum,Jimmy	25	.266	113	289	37	77	22	1	7	47	20	50	3	4	.314	.422
Taubensee,Eddie	24	.245	99	278	27	68	15	1	5	28	25	65	1	1	.307	.360
Tettleton,Mickey	32	.233	147	484	74	113	19	1	22	67	111	141	3	4	.376	.413
Teufel,Tim	34	.228	99	241	30	55	17	1	6	29	31	51	3	2	.316	.382
Thomas,Frank	25	.331	160	562	116	186	38	3	30	112	139	102	5	4	.464	.569
Thome,Jim	22	.288	110	337	39	97	20	3	5	44	33	73	4	2	.351	.409
Thompson,Milt	34	.269	124	320	43	86	15	3	4	27	30	53	20	8	.331	.372
Thompson,Robby	31	.256	142	485	64	124	25	3	13	50	48	90	12	7	.323	.400
Thompson,Ryan	25	.237	122	380	46	90	17	3	8	35	24	91	9	7	.282	.361
Thon,Dickie	35	.248	80	274	25	68	11	2	4	25	17	42	7	3	.292	.347
Thurman,Gary	28	.267	68	180	22	48	6	2	1	14	11	35	12	5	.309	.339
Tingley,Ron	34	.205	68	132	14	27	5	0	2	12	11	33	1	1	.266	.288
Trammell,Alan	35	.269	105	390	49	105	18	2	8	54	46	38	9	6	.346	.387
Treadway,Jeff	30	.277	80	235	26	65	12	1	4	25	16	20	2	2	.323	.387
Uribe,Jose	34	.236	82	208	21	49	7	2	1	12	16	28	3	3	.290	.303
Valentin,John	26	.239	100	335	33	80	20	1	6	33	36	46	0	0	.313	.358
Valentin,Jose	23	.217	59	129	17	28	7	1	2	13	11	29	2	1	.279	.333
Valle,Dave	32	.219	93	310	35	68	11	1	7	29	34	48	1	1	.297	.329
Van Slyke,Andy	32	.274	143	532	78	146	26	6	15	75	66	91	12	4	.355	.430

Projections for 1993 Batters

Batter	Age	Avg	G	AB	R	H	2B	3B	HR	RBI	BB	SO	SB	CS	OBP	SLG
VanderWal,John	27	.248	84	234	28	58	14	2	4	25	25	54	2	1	.320	.376
Varsho,Gary	32	.238	100	151	19	36	9	1	2	17	12	27	6	3	.294	.351
Vaughn,Greg	27	.238	147	512	77	122	25	2	24	84	58	122	10	8	.316	.436
Vaughn,Mo	25	.266	128	410	47	109	22	1	14	62	53	81	2	2	.350	.427
Velarde,Randy	30	.247	121	332	40	82	20	2	6	35	32	70	4	3	.313	.373
Ventura,Robin	25	.276	158	576	78	159	28	1	14	82	82	63	3	4	.366	.401
Villanueva,Hector	28	.238	101	298	29	71	14	1	11	42	25	63	0	0	.297	.403
Vizcaino,Jose	25	.248	97	234	21	58	7	2	1	19	14	27	4	3	.290	.308
Vizquel,Omar	26	.261	144	460	42	120	15	3	2	33	38	37	10	7	.317	.320
Walker,Chico	34	.237	77	177	21	42	7	1	3	18	19	36	6	2	.311	.339
Walker,Larry	26	.281	146	506	72	142	26	3	20	72	49	106	20	9	.344	.462
Wallach,Tim	35	.244	120	443	45	108	24	1	11	58	37	71	3	3	.302	.377
Walters,Dan	26	.250	122	404	31	101	17	0	7	44	22	49	0	0	.289	.344
Walton,Jerome	27	.256	66	160	28	41	10	1	2	12	18	31	5	3	.331	.369
Webster,Lenny	28	.250	72	220	27	55	13	0	3	25	22	24	1	1	.318	.350
Webster,Mitch	34	.245	126	249	32	61	16	4	5	31	19	49	9	4	.299	.402
Wedge,Eric	25	.239	96	226	24	54	14	0	6	29	28	40	0	0	.323	.381
Wehner,John	26	.259	55	170	21	44	8	0	2	16	14	21	6	3	.315	.341
Weiss,Walt	29	.240	86	263	31	63	9	1	1	22	31	31	6	3	.320	.293
Whitaker,Lou	36	.257	131	451	73	116	21	2	13	60	81	57	6	3	.370	.399
White,Devon	30	.246	156	618	91	152	27	6	15	58	55	138	33	9	.308	.382
Whiten,Mark	26	.271	143	516	69	140	18	5	13	52	53	100	12	8	.339	.401
Wilkerson,Curt	32	.229	99	231	23	53	8	2	1	22	14	42	8	4	.273	.294
Wilkins,Rick	26	.244	104	303	28	74	12	1	11	36	27	66	2	2	.306	.399
Williams,Bernie	24	.263	153	632	95	166	29	5	13	67	86	112	26	14	.351	.386
Williams,Gerald	26	.251	83	235	33	59	15	1	6	33	16	44	11	7	.299	.400
Williams,Matt D.	27	.251	142	530	66	133	22	3	27	85	34	115	6	5	.296	.457
Wilson,Craig	28	.245	86	188	19	46	11	1	1	19	16	20	2	2	.304	.330
Wilson,Dan	24	.235	41	102	8	24	6	0	1	10	7	15	1	1	.284	.324
Wilson,Willie	37	.259	109	290	35	75	14	5	1	32	25	52	18	6	.317	.352
Winfield,Dave	41	.252	145	544	69	137	24	3	18	78	65	102	3	2	.332	.406
Winningham,Herm	31	.233	70	116	13	27	5	1	1	7	7	26	3	3	.276	.319
Wood,Ted	26	.252	32	103	13	26	4	1	2	12	11	20	2	2	.325	.369
Woodson,Tracy	30	.245	55	184	18	45	8	1	3	21	11	22	1	1	.287	.348
Worthington,Craig	28	.239	50	138	15	33	7	0	3	16	16	29	0	0	.318	.355
Young,Eric	26	.258	98	314	37	81	9	1	2	25	25	21	24	10	.313	.312
Young,Kevin	24	.291	75	230	34	67	14	3	3	29	21	32	6	5	.351	.417
Yount,Robin	37	.252	135	504	69	127	27	4	9	70	58	83	10	6	.329	.375
Zeile,Todd	27	.261	142	498	64	130	27	2	13	63	68	80	9	8	.350	.402
Zosky,Eddie	25	.239	36	109	11	26	4	1	1	9	5	18	1	2	.272	.321
Zupcic,Bob	26	.248	107	335	36	83	18	0	5	35	26	50	4	4	.302	.346

320

These Guys Can Play Too and
Might Get An Even Better Shot Than Usual in 1993

Batter	Age	Avg	G	AB	R	H	2B	3B	HR	RBI	BB	SO	SB	CS	OBP	SLG
Allred,Beau	28	.250	135	412	51	103	19	5	11	49	37	78	0	1	.312	.400
Barbara,Don	24	.240	115	225	25	54	11	0	1	23	28	50	2	2	.324	.302
Berroa,Geronimo	28	.291	119	447	56	130	27	2	15	66	25	80	3	5	.328	.461
Blosser,Greg	22	.235	130	430	50	101	24	2	18	60	46	133	0	1	.309	.426
Bolick,Frank	27	.246	141	476	50	117	23	4	21	71	57	99	2	6	.326	.443
Casillas,Adam	27	.287	90	143	15	41	6	1	0	11	13	6	1	2	.346	.343
Delarosa,Juan	24	.317	136	499	61	158	30	9	11	47	11	100	12	12	.331	.479
Dorsett,Brian	32	.255	131	470	53	120	31	0	15	79	29	72	0	0	.299	.417
Hale,Chip	29	.268	132	463	61	124	23	7	0	42	59	44	2	2	.351	.348
Jennings,Doug	28	.244	78	119	17	29	6	1	4	18	16	26	2	1	.333	.412
Jones,Chipper	21	.287	67	258	31	74	13	4	8	31	7	36	8	0	.306	.450
Klesko,Ryan	22	.235	123	409	50	96	19	1	15	47	31	74	2	4	.289	.396
Knorr,Randy	24	.242	61	219	20	53	11	0	8	20	12	39	0	0	.281	.402
Maksudian,Mike	27	.252	101	326	28	82	14	0	10	43	23	66	2	1	.301	.387
Manto,Jeff	28	.273	127	439	52	120	21	0	11	54	43	65	0	1	.338	.396
McCarty,Dave	23	.272	137	475	70	129	17	2	15	75	45	92	4	5	.335	.411
Mondesi,Raul	22	.241	53	191	19	46	3	2	3	18	5	63	3	5	.260	.325
Nieves,Mel	21	.268	100	343	50	92	21	2	18	63	33	103	3	3	.332	.499
O'Leary,Troy	23	.282	122	422	55	119	20	4	3	47	30	84	16	5	.330	.363
Oliva,Jose	22	.260	124	439	53	114	26	5	14	69	31	167	2	0	.309	.437
Ortiz,Ray	25	.272	120	393	48	107	27	0	11	58	20	62	0	0	.308	.425
Pirkl,Greg	22	.243	138	490	41	119	27	1	12	46	15	118	2	2	.265	.376
Robbins,Doug	26	.279	93	276	37	77	13	0	2	30	43	51	4	4	.376	.348
Roberson,Kevin	25	.271	51	188	17	51	12	2	5	24	3	48	0	0	.283	.436
Russo,Paul	23	.244	126	414	55	101	13	2	18	65	36	124	0	0	.304	.415
Shave,Jon	25	.276	118	446	53	123	21	4	1	33	28	72	4	7	.319	.348
Sherman,Darrell	25	.253	135	454	68	115	13	0	6	29	47	69	30	12	.323	.322
Spehr,Tim	26	.226	71	203	24	46	13	0	6	21	31	58	1	1	.329	.379
Twardoski,Mike	28	.271	70	118	13	32	7	1	3	11	21	19	0	1	.381	.424
Walbeck,Matt	23	.285	105	376	39	107	20	0	7	34	21	59	0	5	.322	.394
Wilson,Nigel	23	.265	137	514	76	136	32	5	25	61	25	146	9	8	.299	.492

Projections for 1993 Pitchers

Pitcher	Age	ERA	W	L	Sv	G	GS	IP	H	HR	BB	SO	BR/9
Abbott,Jim	25	3.36	13	12	0	31	31	222	220	14	71	141	11.8
Acker,Jim	34	3.78	3	2	0	29	1	50	49	5	18	26	12.1
Agosto,Juan	35	3.77	4	3	0	50	1	62	68	3	24	30	13.4
Aguilera,Rick	31	2.69	6	3	41	64	0	67	56	4	22	58	10.5
Andersen,Larry	40	2.34	2	1	3	40	0	50	41	1	13	46	9.7
Appier,Kevin	25	3.29	13	10	0	31	30	208	195	13	68	154	11.4
Armstrong,Jack	28	4.33	8	10	0	32	23	158	161	19	63	107	12.8
Assenmacher,Paul	32	3.26	5	4	14	72	0	80	73	7	27	81	11.3
Avery,Steve	23	3.46	15	12	0	35	35	226	219	17	69	135	11.5
Bailes,Scott	30	4.81	2	3	0	35	0	43	47	5	24	28	14.9
Bankhead,Scott	29	3.63	4	3	0	42	3	67	64	6	27	42	12.2
Belcher,Tim	31	3.20	16	10	0	34	34	222	191	17	78	155	10.9
Belinda,Stan	26	3.04	5	3	21	59	0	74	57	7	33	65	10.9
Benes,Andy	25	3.18	16	11	0	34	34	229	209	20	60	169	10.6
Berenguer,Juan	38	3.21	4	3	1	48	1	73	62	8	29	50	11.2
Bielecki,Mike	33	3.58	5	5	0	32	10	98	96	8	33	53	11.8
Black,Bud	36	3.71	11	11	0	30	30	189	177	21	63	90	11.4
Blyleven,Bert	42	4.25	5	6	0	17	16	89	100	11	19	47	12.0
Boddicker,Mike	35	3.51	5	4	0	29	15	118	120	8	39	64	12.0
Boever,Joe	32	3.53	6	5	4	77	0	107	98	7	54	83	12.8
Bosio,Chris	30	3.12	15	10	0	33	33	222	212	19	42	121	10.3
Brantley,Jeff	29	3.39	5	4	2	60	3	93	81	7	44	77	12.1
Brown,Kevin	28	3.35	16	11	0	34	34	247	244	15	71	140	11.5
Browning,Tom	33	4.13	8	8	0	23	23	135	140	16	43	63	12.2
Burke,Tim	34	3.14	4	3	0	49	0	63	59	5	19	35	11.1
Burkett,John	28	3.55	12	11	0	33	33	195	201	16	46	117	11.4
Burns,Todd	29	3.00	5	3	14	38	7	87	75	6	32	45	11.1
Cadaret,Greg	31	4.09	5	5	4	53	9	110	109	8	63	82	14.1
Candiotti,Tom	35	3.22	14	10	0	33	31	215	196	16	67	155	11.0
Carpenter,Cris	28	3.00	6	4	0	68	0	81	69	8	24	49	10.3
Charlton,Norm	30	2.80	6	3	5	56	4	90	76	6	34	75	11.0
Clemens,Roger	30	2.54	20	8	0	33	33	255	212	14	64	221	9.7
Clements,Pat	31	3.89	2	2	0	37	0	37	39	2	19	17	14.1
Cone,David	30	3.36	16	12	0	35	34	244	204	18	108	254	11.5
Cox,Danny	33	4.03	3	3	1	24	10	76	76	9	30	43	12.6
Crews,Tim	32	3.51	4	4	0	53	1	77	81	7	19	51	11.7
Crim,Chuck	31	3.89	4	5	2	60	0	88	96	8	26	36	12.5
Darling,Ron	32	3.88	12	12	0	33	33	202	199	21	71	115	12.0
Darwin,Danny	37	3.74	5	5	0	38	14	130	131	15	39	94	11.8
Davis,Mark	32	4.50	2	3	0	28	6	56	52	6	40	47	14.8
Davis,Storm	31	4.13	4	5	0	49	4	98	108	9	36	52	13.2
DeLeon,Jose	32	3.27	9	7	0	31	21	132	112	10	54	93	11.3
Deshaies,Jim	33	3.36	8	6	0	19	19	118	104	10	40	66	11.0
Dibble,Rob	29	1.95	7	2	39	64	0	74	51	3	27	110	9.5
Dopson,John	29	3.79	6	6	0	17	17	95	98	9	25	37	11.7
Downs,Kelly	32	3.79	7	7	0	40	17	133	124	10	65	69	12.8
Drabek,Doug	30	2.86	18	10	0	34	34	249	224	18	52	162	10.0
Eckersley,Dennis	38	2.28	7	2	47	68	0	79	62	8	10	91	8.2
Eichhorn,Mark	32	2.83	6	3	2	67	0	86	85	3	21	61	11.1
Erickson,Scott	25	3.57	13	11	0	32	32	209	195	16	82	105	11.9

322

Projections for 1993 Pitchers

Pitcher	Age	ERA	W	L	Sv	G	GS	IP	H	HR	BB	SO	BR/9
Farr,Steve	36	2.33	5	2	36	53	0	58	44	3	20	44	9.9
Fernandez,Sid	30	2.63	16	7	0	30	30	202	149	17	63	175	9.4
Finley,Chuck	30	3.91	11	13	0	32	32	212	195	19	102	145	12.6
Fisher,Brian	31	4.57	3	4	0	15	9	61	61	6	31	17	13.6
Flanagan,Mike	41	3.86	2	3	0	49	0	56	58	4	22	30	12.9
Fossas,Tony	35	4.15	3	3	1	61	0	39	42	3	17	24	13.6
Franco,John	32	3.06	4	2	30	50	0	53	51	2	17	41	11.5
Frey,Steve	29	3.98	2	3	2	44	0	43	41	5	23	23	13.4
Frohwirth,Todd	30	2.53	7	3	2	60	0	103	85	4	38	69	10.7
Gardner,Mark	31	3.38	12	9	0	31	29	176	158	16	59	121	11.1
Gibson,Paul	33	4.19	3	4	0	51	1	73	78	7	34	45	13.8
Glavine,Tom	27	3.22	16	11	0	33	33	232	214	16	72	158	11.1
Gleaton,Jerry Don	35	3.33	3	2	0	31	0	46	41	4	20	29	11.9
Gooden,Dwight	28	3.27	13	10	0	30	30	201	189	11	68	149	11.5
Gordon,Tom	25	3.50	5	5	0	42	12	131	116	11	67	122	12.6
Gossage,Goose	41	3.46	3	2	0	35	0	39	32	4	17	27	11.3
Gott,Jim	33	3.21	5	4	1	64	0	84	72	5	40	71	12.0
Grant,Mark	29	4.00	2	2	0	15	7	54	59	5	18	35	12.8
Gross,Kevin	32	3.65	10	9	0	38	23	175	170	13	66	138	12.1
Gubicza,Mark	30	3.71	7	7	0	21	21	119	126	7	38	82	12.4
Guetterman,Lee	34	3.58	4	4	2	60	0	73	75	6	23	30	12.1
Gullickson,Bill	34	4.12	12	14	0	34	34	223	245	27	50	77	11.9
Guzman,Jose	30	3.45	14	10	0	30	30	206	199	14	67	159	11.6
Habyan,John	29	2.88	6	3	4	59	0	78	76	4	20	54	11.1
Hanson,Erik	28	3.49	12	9	0	30	29	183	180	13	56	129	11.6
Harnisch,Pete	26	3.21	15	10	0	34	34	210	187	17	65	167	10.8
Harris,Greg	37	3.14	7	5	2	64	8	129	110	9	59	92	11.8
Harris,Greg W.	29	3.00	9	6	0	20	20	123	104	11	36	79	10.2
Harvey,Bryan	30	2.31	6	3	39	63	0	74	50	7	27	94	9.4
Heaton,Neal	33	3.53	3	2	0	35	0	51	48	5	16	26	11.3
Henke,Tom	35	2.33	5	2	36	54	0	54	39	5	16	52	9.2
Henneman,Mike	31	3.04	5	3	26	60	0	80	76	4	27	53	11.6
Henry,Dwayne	31	3.35	5	3	0	57	0	78	63	6	45	65	12.5
Hernandez,Xavier	27	3.32	6	4	12	62	2	95	85	8	39	70	11.7
Hershiser,Orel	34	3.19	14	10	0	31	31	203	192	9	66	128	11.4
Hesketh,Joe	34	4.32	8	9	1	33	22	150	156	17	59	103	12.9
Hibbard,Greg	28	3.71	11	10	0	31	28	182	184	14	59	69	12.0
Hill,Ken	27	3.15	14	10	0	32	32	206	183	13	71	140	11.1
Hillegas,Shawn	28	4.24	3	4	0	34	7	85	87	9	41	57	13.6
Honeycutt,Rick	39	3.69	3	3	1	50	0	39	40	3	15	30	12.7
Hough,Charlie	45	3.52	12	9	0	28	28	184	160	20	69	90	11.2
Howell,Jay	37	2.44	4	2	17	42	0	48	39	2	14	37	9.9
Hurst,Bruce	35	3.16	15	10	0	32	32	219	202	20	51	136	10.4
Innis,Jeff	30	2.79	7	3	0	74	0	87	76	4	30	43	11.0
Jackson,Danny	31	4.04	9	10	0	28	27	158	169	11	60	74	13.0
Jackson,Mike	28	3.11	6	4	2	69	0	84	69	7	38	76	11.5
Jeffcoat,Mike	33	4.05	2	2	0	27	2	40	46	3	11	20	12.8
Johnson,Randy	29	3.96	12	12	0	32	32	207	164	18	142	236	13.3
Jones,Barry	30	3.32	5	4	0	66	0	76	71	4	33	40	12.3
Jones,Doug	36	2.91	6	4	31	65	1	96	92	6	21	72	10.6

Projections for 1993 Pitchers

Pitcher	Age	ERA	W	L	Sv	G	GS	IP	H	HR	BB	SO	BR/9
Jones,Jimmy	29	4.04	8	9	0	25	23	138	150	14	39	79	12.3
Key,Jimmy	32	3.70	13	12	0	33	33	214	217	20	58	122	11.6
King,Eric	29	3.67	7	6	0	20	17	103	102	8	36	47	12.1
Kipper,Bob	28	3.33	3	2	0	34	0	46	38	5	18	27	11.0
Krueger,Bill	35	3.97	10	11	0	36	28	177	191	16	53	95	12.4
Lancaster,Les	31	3.85	5	5	0	49	4	110	112	10	44	63	12.8
Landrum,Bill	34	3.00	3	2	0	32	0	39	36	2	11	21	10.8
Langston,Mark	32	3.06	15	11	0	33	33	235	200	18	76	176	10.6
Leach,Terry	39	2.88	5	3	0	51	0	72	71	3	17	27	11.0
Leary,Tim	34	4.84	6	9	0	27	21	134	136	13	83	66	14.7
Lefferts,Craig	35	3.62	9	8	0	39	21	154	159	15	32	88	11.2
Leibrandt,Charlie	36	3.07	15	9	0	33	33	205	199	13	45	113	10.7
Maddux,Greg	27	2.77	19	10	0	36	36	266	237	13	70	199	10.4
Maddux,Mike	31	2.83	6	3	3	55	1	86	80	4	24	55	10.9
Martinez,Dennis	38	2.40	18	7	0	32	32	225	180	11	60	135	9.6
Martinez,Ramon	25	3.57	11	10	0	28	28	174	148	15	80	118	11.8
Mathews,Greg	31	4.37	1	1	0	9	5	35	36	3	18	15	13.9
McCaskill,Kirk	32	3.89	12	12	0	33	33	199	192	14	90	92	12.8
McClure,Bob	40	4.21	3	4	0	62	0	47	48	5	21	24	13.2
McDowell,Jack	27	3.21	17	11	0	34	34	258	233	22	74	185	10.7
McDowell,Roger	32	3.60	5	5	12	67	0	90	92	3	41	46	13.3
McElroy,Chuck	25	3.50	5	5	2	72	0	90	78	6	53	86	13.1
Milacki,Bob	28	4.17	8	9	0	26	22	138	141	15	52	73	12.6
Montgomery,Jeff	31	2.54	6	3	44	66	0	85	69	5	28	76	10.3
Moore,Mike	33	3.66	14	12	0	35	35	219	201	15	101	136	12.4
Morgan,Mike	33	3.09	16	11	0	34	34	239	212	14	79	132	11.0
Morris,Jack	38	3.63	15	13	0	34	34	243	231	18	83	147	11.6
Mulholland,Terry	30	3.25	15	11	0	33	33	230	233	16	46	133	10.9
Murphy,Rob	33	4.25	3	4	0	58	0	53	57	5	24	43	13.8
Myers,Randy	30	3.25	6	4	41	63	4	97	81	6	49	89	12.1
Nagy,Charles	26	3.40	15	12	0	33	33	238	249	15	54	143	11.5
Navarro,Jaime	26	3.46	15	12	0	34	34	242	248	16	63	108	11.6
Nelson,Gene	32	3.53	3	2	0	33	1	51	48	5	18	24	11.6
Nunez,Edwin	30	3.75	3	3	2	40	0	48	45	5	21	40	12.4
Ojeda,Bobby	35	4.09	10	11	0	30	30	174	174	12	85	105	13.4
Olin,Steve	27	3.23	5	4	33	64	0	78	77	4	25	49	11.8
Olson,Gregg	26	2.35	6	2	41	64	0	65	52	2	26	63	10.8
Orosco,Jesse	36	3.95	3	3	1	55	0	41	39	5	18	36	12.5
Pall,Donn	31	3.56	3	2	1	43	0	43	41	4	14	21	11.5
Parrett,Jeff	31	3.70	4	4	0	50	0	73	70	6	35	57	12.9
Patterson,Bob	34	3.32	4	3	5	58	0	65	61	7	17	49	10.8
Patterson,Ken	28	4.04	2	3	0	36	1	49	44	6	27	27	13.0
Pena,Alejandro	34	2.95	4	2	10	47	0	55	49	5	16	47	10.6
Perez,Melido	27	3.49	15	12	0	33	33	232	209	21	87	209	11.5
Plesac,Dan	31	3.47	4	3	2	44	6	83	74	8	36	62	11.9
Plunk,Eric	29	4.02	4	4	5	53	3	85	78	9	47	73	13.2
Portugal,Mark	30	3.63	8	7	0	23	20	124	111	12	50	83	11.7
Powell,Dennis	29	4.50	2	2	0	33	0	38	43	3	19	22	14.7
Power,Ted	38	3.22	6	4	5	65	0	95	89	7	34	52	11.7
Radinsky,Scott	25	3.00	5	3	22	68	0	63	53	3	32	49	12.1

324

Projections for 1993 Pitchers

Pitcher	Age	ERA	W	L	Sv	G	GS	IP	H	HR	BB	SO	BR/9
Rasmussen,Dennis	34	3.74	5	4	0	13	12	77	82	8	15	36	11.3
Reardon,Jeff	37	3.72	4	3	20	59	0	58	60	7	12	41	11.2
Righetti,Dave	34	3.55	4	4	2	56	3	76	74	5	34	53	12.8
Rijo,Jose	28	2.41	18	7	0	32	32	209	174	11	44	172	9.4
Robinson,Don	36	3.60	5	4	0	19	13	80	86	9	9	46	10.7
Robinson,Jeff	32	4.18	3	4	0	46	3	71	73	7	33	46	13.4
Robinson,Jeff M.	31	4.55	3	4	0	23	14	89	92	12	47	47	14.1
Rodriguez,Rich	30	3.10	6	4	0	62	1	87	78	6	36	50	11.8
Rogers,Kenny	28	3.74	5	5	19	75	3	89	88	7	40	68	12.9
Ruffin,Bruce	29	4.38	3	3	0	27	9	78	90	6	34	50	14.3
Ruskin,Scott	30	3.63	4	3	0	59	0	57	56	4	26	43	12.9
Russell,Jeff	31	2.79	5	3	7	62	0	71	57	6	28	48	10.8
Ryan,Nolan	46	2.76	13	6	0	27	27	163	118	10	71	177	10.4
Saberhagen,Bret	29	2.83	14	8	0	28	28	191	167	11	53	141	10.4
Sampen,Bill	30	3.98	4	4	0	49	4	86	88	8	36	51	13.0
Sanderson,Scott	36	4.23	11	13	0	33	33	198	204	25	66	116	12.3
Schooler,Mike	30	3.33	3	2	20	47	0	46	44	3	16	35	11.7
Smiley,John	28	3.25	16	10	0	34	33	230	210	20	62	150	10.6
Smith,Bryn	37	3.09	6	4	0	30	20	140	132	12	32	66	10.5
Smith,Lee	35	2.68	6	3	40	69	0	74	65	4	22	69	10.6
Smith,Pete	27	3.72	7	6	0	26	18	116	111	11	41	66	11.8
Smith,Zane	32	2.81	13	7	0	27	26	170	165	10	23	81	10.0
Smoltz,John	26	3.02	17	10	0	35	35	241	205	18	78	184	10.6
Stanton,Mike	26	2.91	5	3	12	68	0	68	61	5	21	48	10.9
Stewart,Dave	36	3.76	13	12	0	32	32	208	194	20	83	134	12.0
Stieb,Dave	35	3.54	5	4	0	17	12	84	76	6	38	40	12.2
Stottlemyre,Todd	28	3.90	11	11	0	30	29	189	188	18	68	103	12.2
Sutcliffe,Rick	37	4.03	11	12	0	30	30	190	200	15	60	92	12.3
Swift,Bill	31	2.98	13	8	20	37	30	169	162	7	44	83	11.0
Swindell,Greg	28	3.45	14	11	0	32	31	222	226	20	43	151	10.9
Tanana,Frank	39	4.52	10	13	0	32	32	197	197	23	95	96	13.3
Tapani,Kevin	29	3.32	15	11	0	34	34	228	225	19	50	134	10.9
Terrell,Walt	35	4.43	4	5	0	32	10	122	144	12	44	49	13.9
Tewksbury,Bob	32	2.79	16	9	0	32	31	219	219	14	19	86	9.8
Thigpen,Bobby	29	3.45	4	3	27	59	0	60	50	6	29	46	11.9
Viola,Frank	33	3.66	14	13	0	35	35	236	228	18	88	127	12.1
Walk,Bob	36	3.73	8	7	0	32	19	128	126	13	41	65	11.7
Ward,Duane	29	2.36	8	3	7	80	0	103	80	5	35	106	10.0
Wegman,Bill	30	3.50	15	12	0	33	33	239	238	25	50	113	10.8
Welch,Bob	36	3.75	10	9	0	25	25	156	147	17	54	67	11.6
Wells,David	30	3.21	6	4	0	41	19	146	137	15	37	82	10.7
Williams,Mitch	28	3.69	5	4	30	67	0	83	67	5	62	75	14.0
Williamson,Mark	33	3.46	2	2	1	30	0	39	37	3	15	27	12.0
Willis,Carl	32	2.39	6	2	1	53	0	83	73	4	15	48	9.5
Wilson,Steve	28	3.71	3	3	0	46	0	51	51	5	18	37	12.2
Wilson,Trevor	27	3.51	12	10	0	34	29	190	165	17	79	121	11.6
Witt,Bobby	29	4.04	9	10	0	26	26	158	146	10	93	116	13.6
Worrell,Todd	33	2.51	4	2	5	45	0	43	32	3	17	43	13.1
Young,Curt	33	4.10	3	3	0	29	5	68	72	7	27	27	13.1
Young,Matt	34	3.74	3	3	0	25	11	77	73	5	40	60	13.2

About STATS, Inc.

It all starts with the system. The STATS scoring method, which includes pitch-by-pitch information and the direction, distance, and velocity of each ball hit into play, yields an immense amount of information. Sure, we have all the statistics you're used to seeing, but where other statistical sources stop, STATS is just getting started.

Then, there's the network. Our information is timely because our game reporters send their information by computer as soon as the game is over. Statistics are checked, rechecked, updated, and are available daily.

Analysis comes next. STATS constantly searches for new ways to use this wealth of information to open windows into the workings of baseball. Accurate numbers, intelligent computer programming, and a large dose of imagination all help coax the most valuable information from its elusive cover.

Finally, distribution!

For 13 years now, STATS has served over a dozen Major League teams. The box scores that STATS provides to *The Associated Press* and *USA Today* have revolutionized what baseball fans expect from a box score. *Baseball Weekly* is chock full of STATS handiwork, while ESPN's nightly baseball coverage is supported by a full-time STATS statistician. We provide statistics for *Earl Weaver Baseball, Tony LaRussa Baseball, Rotisserie Baseball* and many other baseball games and fantasy leagues all over the country.

For the baseball fan, STATS publishes monthly and year-end reports on each Major League team. We offer a host of year-end statistical breakdowns on paper or disk that cover hitting, pitching, catching, baserunning, fielding, and more. STATS even produces custom reports on request.

Computer users with modems can access the STATS computer for information with STATS On-Line. If you own a computer with a modem, there is no other source with the scope of baseball information that STATS can offer.

STATS and Bill James enjoy an on-going affiliation that has produced the book you are now holding. We also administer Bill James Fantasy Baseball (BJFB), the ultimate baseball game, designed by Bill James himself, which allows you to manage your own team and compete with other team owners around the country. Whether you play BJFB or another fantasy game, our new STATSfax report can show you what your players did the previous night as soon as you can get to the fax machine in the morning. STATS also offers a head-to-head fantasy football game STATS Fantasy Football. BJFB The Winter Game is a brand new, totally unique, historically based fantasy baseball game for those who can't wait for spring.

Always innovative, STATS has other exciting future projects underway for sports fans nationwide. It is the purpose of STATS to make the best possible sports information available to all interests: fans, player, teams, and media. For more information write to:

STATS, Inc.
7366 North Lincoln Ave.
Lincolnwood, IL 60646-1708

. . . or call us at 1-708-676-3322. We can send you a STATS brochure, a free information kit on Bill James Fantasy Baseball, the BJFB Winter Game or STATS Fantasy Football, and/or information on STATS On-Line or STATSfax.

To maintain our information, STATS hires people around the country to cover games using the STATS scoring method. If you are interested in applying for a part-time reporter's position, please write or call STATS.

For the story behind the numbers, check out STATS' other publications: The STATS 1993 Baseball Scoreboard: The first edition of this book in 1990 took the nation's baseball fans by storm. This all new 1993 edition, available in book stores or directly from STATS, is back with the same great writing, great graphics and stats you won't find anywhere else. The Major Leauge Handbook's brother, the STATS 1993 Minor League Handbook, will add to your 1993 reference library, especially important for the coming expansion. STATS continues a tradition with The Scouting Report:1993, available in book stores in the Spring of 1993. You'll find scouting reports on over 700 players, including team prospect reports, backed by statistical findings you can only get from STATS, Inc. Last, but certainly not least, the new addition to the STATS Publishing family, the STATS 1993 Player Profiles Book, is full of breakdowns and situational stats for every Major League player, identical to the few we offer in this book.

Turn to the last pages in this book to find a handy order form and additional information about the fine products from STATS.

Glossary

% Inherited Scored
A Relief Pitching statistic indicating the percentage of runners on base at the time a relief pitcher enters a game that he allows to score.

1st Batter OBP
The On-Base Percentage allowed by a relief pitcher to the first batter he faces in a game.

Active Career Batting Leaders
Minimum of 1,000 At Bats required for Batting Average, On-Base Percentage, Slugging Percentage, At Bats Per HR, At Bats Per GDP, At Bats Per RBI, and K/BB Ratio. One hundred (100) Stolen Base Attempts required for Stolen Base Success %. Any player who appeared in 1992 is eligible for inclusion provided he meets the category's minimum requirements.

Active Career Pitching Leaders
Minimum of 750 Innings Pitched required for Earned Run Average, Opponent Batting Average, all of the "Per 9 Innings" categories, and Strikeout to Walk Ratio. Two hundred fifty (250) Games Started required for Complete Game Frequency. One hundred (100) decisions required for Win-Loss Percentage. Any player who appeared in 1992 is eligible for inclusion provided he meets the category's minimum requirements.

BA ScPos Allowed
Batting Average Allowed with Runners in Scoring Position.

Batting Average
Hits divided by At Bats.

Catcher's ERA
The Earned Run Average of a catcher. To figure this for a catcher, multiply the Earned Runs Allowed by the pitchers while he was catching times nine and divide that by his number of Innings Caught.

Cheap Wins/Tough Losses/Top Game Scores
First determine the starting pitcher's Game Score as follows: (1)Start with 50. (2)Add 1 point for each out recorded by the starting pitcher. (3)Add 2 points for each inning the pitcher completes after the fourth inning. (4)Add 1 point for each strikeout. (5)Subtract 2 points for each hit allowed. (6)Subtract 4 points for each earned run allowed. (7)Subtract 2 points for an unearned run. (8)Subtract 1 point for each walk.

If the starting pitcher scores over 50 and loses, it's a Tough Loss. If he wins with a game score under 50, it's a Cheap Win. All Game Scores of 90 or above are listed.

Cleanup Slugging%
The Slugging Percentage of a player when batting fourth in the batting order.

Complete Game Frequency
Complete Games divided by Games Started.

Earned Run Average
(Earned Runs times 9) divided by Innings Pitched.

Fielding Percentage
(Putouts plus Assists) divided by (Putouts plus Assists plus Errors).

Hold

A Hold is credited anytime a relief pitcher enters a game in a Save Situation (see definition below), records at least one out, and leaves the game never having relinquished the lead. Note: a pitcher cannot finish the game and receive credit for a Hold.

Isolated Power

Slugging Percentage minus Batting Average.

K/BB Ratio

Strikeouts divided by Walks.

Late & Close

A Late & Close situation meets the following requirements: (1)the game is in the seventh inning or later, and (2)the batting team is either leading by one run, tied, or has the potential tying run on base, at bat, or on deck. Note: this situation is very similar to the characteristics of a Save Situation.

Leadoff On Base%

The On-Base Percentage of a player when batting first in the batting order.

Offensive Winning Percentage

The Winning Percentage a team of nine Will Clarks (or anybody) would compile against average pitching and defense. The formula: (Runs Created per 27 outs) divided by the League average of runs scored per game. Square the result and divide it by (1+itself).

On Base Percentage

(Hits plus Walks plus Hit by Pitcher) divided by (At Bats plus Walks plus Hit by Pitcher plus Sacrifice Flies).

Opponent Batting Average

Hits Allowed divided by (Batters Faced minus Walks minus Hit Batsmen minus Sacrifice Hits minus Sacrifice Flies minus Catcher's Interference).

PA*

The divisor for On Base Percentage: At Bats plus Walks plus Hit By Pitcher plus Sacrifice Flies; or Plate Appearances minus Sacrifice Hits and Times Reached Base on Defensive Interference.

PCS (Pitchers' Caught Stealing)

The number of runners officially counted as Caught Stealing where the initiator of the fielding play was the pitcher, not the catcher. Note: such plays are often referred to as "pickoffs", but appear in official records as Caught Stealings. The most common "pitcher caught stealing scenario" is a 1-3-6 fielding play, where the runner is officially charged a Caught Stealing because he broke for second base. "Pickoff" (fielding play 1-3 being the most common) is not an official statistical category.

PkOf Throw/Runner

The number of pickoff throws made by a pitcher divided by the number of runners on first base.

Plate Appearances

At Bats plus Total Walks plus Hit By Pitcher plus Sacrifice Hits plus Sacrifice Flies plus Times Reached on Defensive Interference.

Power/Speed Number

A way to look at power and speed in one number. A player must score high in both areas to earn a high Power/Speed Number. The formula: (HR x SB x 2) divided by (HR + SB).

Quick Hooks and Slow Hooks

A Quick Hook is the removal of a pitcher who has pitched less than 6 innings and given up 3 runs or less. A Slow Hook goes to a pitcher who pitches more than 9 innings, or allows 7 or more runs, or whose combined innings pitched and runs allowed totals 13 or more.

Range Factor

The number of Chances (Putouts plus Assists) times nine divided by the number of Defensive Innings Played. The average for a Regular Player at each position in 1991:

Second Base: 5.19   Left Field: 2.29
Third Base: 2.71   Center Field: 2.88
Shortstop: 4.70   Right Field: 2.19

Run Support Per 9 IP

The number of runs scored by a pitcher's team while he was still in the game times nine divided by his Innings Pitched.

Runs Created

A way to combine a batter's total offensive contributions into one number. The formula:
(H + BB + HBP - CS - GIDP) times (Total Bases + .26(TBB - IBB + HBP) + .52(SH + SF + SB)) divided by (AB + TBB + HBP +SH + SF).

Save Percentage

Saves (SV) divided by Save Opportunities (OP).

Save Situation

A Relief Pitcher is in a Save Situation when:

upon entering the game with his club leading, he has the opportunity to be the finishing pitcher (and is not the winning pitcher of record at the time), and meets any one of the three following conditions:

(1) he has a lead of no more than three runs and has the opportunity to pitch for at least one inning, or;

(2) he enters the game, regardless of the count, with the potential tieing run either on base, at bat, or on deck; or

(3) has the opportunity to pitch three or more innings and not be the winning pitcher.

SB Success%

Stolen Bases divided by (Stolen Bases plus Caught Stealing).

Secondary Average

A way to look at a player's extra bases gained, independent of Batting Average. The formula: (Total Bases - Hits + TBB + SB) divided by At Bats.

Slugging Percentage

Total Bases divided by At Bats.

Total Bases

Hits plus Doubles plus (2 times Triples) plus (3 times Homeruns).

Win-Loss Percentage or Winning Percentage

Wins divided by (Wins plus Losses).

Two More Hits from
Bill James and STATS, Inc.

Bill James/STATS 1993 Minor League Handbook
Available November 1, 1992!

- Bill James' Major League Equivalencies for every AAA and AA player.

- Official career year-by-year statistical data for all 1992 AAA and AA players.

- 1992 stats for all A and Rookie League players.

- Minor League Leader Boards, Team Stats and more

"STATS has been very helpful over the years in assisting me to evaluate players and in making trades."
Larry Himes, Chicago Cubs, executive vice president, baseball operations

STATS 1993 Player Profiles
All New for 1993! **Available November 1, 1992!**

- Player breakdowns are great for fantasy, rotisserie and tabletop game players!

- Pitcher Breakdowns Include: Ahead/Behind in Count, First Batter Faced, Days Rest, Pitch Counts

- Batter Breakdowns Include: By Batting Position, Home/Road, Grass/Turf, Clutch Situations, Two Strikes

- Plus Much More

"There's not a stat that STATS, Inc. doesn't have or can't provide. They don't hit or pitch, but they're like a 26th player."
Sandy Alderson, Oakland Athletics, vice president, baseball operations

To order, use the STATS order form on the last page of this book.

Bill James
FANTASY
BASEBALL

If You Like Fantasy Baseball, You'll Love Bill James Fantasy Baseball...

"Hi, This is Bill James. A few years ago I designed a set of rules for a new fantasy baseball league, which has been updated with the benefits of experience and the input of a few thousand owners.

The idea of a fantasy league, of course, is that it forges a link between you and your ballplayers; YOU win or lose based on how the players that you picked have performed. My goal was to develop a fantasy league based on the simplest and yet most realistic principles possible — a league in which the values are as nearly as possible what they ought to be, without being distorted by artificial category values or rankings, but which at the same time are so simple that you can keep track of how you've done just by checking the boxscores. There are a lot of different rules around for fantasy leagues, but none of them before this provided exactly what I was looking for. Here's what we want:

1)We want it to be realistic. We don't want the rules to make Randy Johnson the MVP because of his strikeouts. We don't want Kenny Lofton to be worth more than Dave Hollins because he steals lots of bases. We want good ballplayers to be good ballplayers.

2) We prefer it simple. We want you to be able to look up your players in the morning paper, and know how you've done.

3) We want you to have to develop a real team. We don't want somebody to win by stacking up starting pitchers and leadoff men. We don't want somebody to corner the market on home run hitters.

I made up the rules and I'll be playing the game with you. STATS, Inc. is running the leagues. They'll run the draft, man the computers, keep the rosters straight and provide you with weekly updates. Of course you can make trades, pick up free agents and move players on and off the inactive list; that's not my department, but there are rules for that, too. It all starts with a draft..."

• Draft Your Own Team and Play vs. Other Owners! Play by Mail or With a Computer On-Line!

• Manage Your Roster All Season With Daily Transactions! Live Fantasy Phone Lines Every Day of the Baseball Season!

• Realistic Team and Individual Player Totals That Even Take Fielding Into Account!

• The Best Weekly Reports in the Business!

• Play Against Bill James' Own Drafted Teams!

• Get Discounted Prices by Forming Your Own Private League of 11 or 12 Owners! (Call or write for more information)

• Money-Back Guarantee! Play one month, and if not satisfied, we'll return your franchise fee!

All This, All Summer Long — For Less Than An Average of $5 per week.

Reserve your BJFB team now! Sign up with the STATS Order Form on the next page, or send for additional Free Information.

STATS Order Form

Product (date available)	Quantity	Your Price	Total
Bill James Fantasy Baseball Franchise		$25 deposit	
Bill James/STATS 1993 Major League Handbook (11/92)		$17.95	
Bill James/STATS 1993 Minor League Handbook (11/92)		17.95	
STATS 1993 Player Profiles (11/92)		17.95	
STATS 1993 Baseball Scoreboard (2/93)		15.00	
The Scouting Report: 1993 (2/93)		16.00	
Discounts on previous editions while supplies last:			
Bill James/STATS 1992 Major League Handbook		9.95	
Bill James/STATS 1991 Major League Handbook		9.95	
Bill James/STATS 1990 Major League Handbook		9.95	
Bill James/STATS 1992 Minor League Handbook		9.95	
STATS 1992 Baseball Scoreboard		9.95	
STATS 1991 Baseball Scoreboard		9.95	
The STATS Baseball Scoreboard (1990)		7.95	
The Scouting Report: 1992		9.95	
U.S. – For First Class Mailing – add $2.50 per book		2.50	
Canada – all orders – add $3.50 per book		3.50	
Order 2 or more books – subtract $1 per book		–1.00	–
Subtotal			
Illinois Residents Include 7% Sales Tax			
Total			

☐ Yes, I can't wait! Sign me up to play Bill James Fantasy Baseball in 1993. Enclosed is my deposit of $25.00 on the franchise fee of $89.00. A processing fee of $1.00 per player is charged during the season for roster moves.

Team Nickname:_____ _____ (example: San Francisco Crab)

Would you like to play in a league with a team drafted by Bill James? Yes No (circle one)

Would you like to receive information on playing BJFB on-line by computer? Yes No (circle one)

Please Rush Me These Free Informational Brochures: ☐ STATS On-Line Brochure

☐ **Bill James Fantasy Baseball Info Kit**   ☐ STATS Fantasy Football Info Kit

☐ **STATS Year-End Reports Brochure**   ☐ STATS Reporter Brochure

☐ **STATSfax Brochure (sent via fax)**   ☐ STATS Pro-Line Brochure

Please Print:

Name_____Phone_____

Address_____Fax_____

City_____State_____Zip_____

Method of Payment (U.S. Funds only):

☐ Check (no Canadian checks)   ☐ Money Order   ☐ Visa   ☐ MasterCard

Credit Card Information:

Cardholder Name_____

Visa/MC #_____Exp. Date_____

Signature_____

Return this form (don't tear your book; copy this page) to:

**STATS, Inc.
7366 N. Lincoln Ave.
Lincolnwood, IL
60646-1708**

For faster credit card service: call 1-800-63-STATS to place your order, or fax this page to 1-708-676-0821.

hb93